GE Capital

Charles K. McKay
Senior Vice President
Commercial Finance
General Electric Capital Corporation
201 High Ridge Road, Stamford, CT 06927
*203 316-7595, Dial Comm: 8*228-7595*
*Fx: 203 316-7976, 8*228-7976*
A GE Capital Services Company

The Logistics Handbook

The Logistics Handbook

Editors-in-Chief

James F. Robeson

Former Dean
Richard T. Farmer School of Business
Miami University

William C. Copacino

Partner
Andersen Consulting

Associate Editor

R. Edwin Howe

THE FREE PRESS
A Division of Macmillan, Inc.
NEW YORK

Maxwell Macmillan Canada
TORONTO

Maxwell Macmillan International
NEW YORK OXFORD SINGAPORE SYDNEY

The Free Press
A Division of Macmillan, Inc.
866 Third Avenue, New York, N. Y. 10022

Maxwell Macmillan Canada, Inc.
1200 Eglinton Avenue East
Suite 200
Don Mills, Ontario M3C 3N1

Macmillan, Inc. is part of the Maxwell Communication Group of Companies.

Printed in the United States of America

printing number
1 2 3 4 5 6 7 8 9 10

Library of Congress Cataloging-in-Publication Data

The logistics handbook / editors-in-chief James F. Robeson, William C. Copacino; associate editor R. Edwin Howe.
p. cm.
Includes index.
ISBN 0–02–926595–9
1. Business logistics. 2. Materials management. 3. Physical distribution of goods—Management. I. Robeson, James F. II. Copacino, William C. III. Howe, R. Edwin.
HD38.5.L615 1994
658.5—dc20 93–48859
CIP

Credits

Chapter 5: This material is from Douglas M. Lambert and James R. Stock, *Logistics Management*, 3d ed. (Homewood, Ill.: Irwin, 1993). No part of this material may be reproduced in any form without the written permission of the publisher, Richard D. Irwin.

Chapter 6: This chapter is based in its entirety on excerpts from Louis W. Stern and Adel I. El-Ansary, *Marketing Channels*, 4th ed., © 1992, pp. 203–266. Reprinted by permission of Prentice-Hall, Englewood Cliffs, N. J.

Chapter 9: Portions of this chapter have been adapted from C. John Langley, Jr., and Mary C. Holcomb, "Achieving Customer Value Through Logistics Management," in Michael J. Stahl and Gregory M. Bounds, eds., *Competing Globally Through Customer Value* (New York: Quorum Books, 1991); C. John Langley, Jr., and Mary Holcomb, "Creating Logistics Customer Value," *Journal of Business Logistics* 13, no. 2 (1992); and John J. Coyle, Edward J. Bardi, and C. John Langley, Jr., "Logistics Quality" (chap. 13), in *The Management of Business Logistics*, 5th ed. (St. Paul: West, 1992).

Chapter 12: Portions of this chapter are from Douglas M. Lambert and James R. Stock, *Strategic Logistics Management*, 3d ed. (Homewood, Ill.: Irwin, 1993). No part of this material may be reproduced in any form without the written permission of the publisher, Richard D. Irwin.

Chapter 14: Some sections of this chapter are adapted from J. F. Magee, W. C. Copacino, and D. B. Rosenfield, *Modern Logistics Management* (New York: Wiley, 1985).

Chapter 23: This chapter is based on the research report *Purchasing's Involvement in Transportation Decision Making*, by Julie J. Gentry (Tempe, Ariz.: Center for Advanced Purchasing Studies/National Association of Purchasing Management, Inc., 1991).

To Teddi, Bradley, and Christopher—Thanks for your patience, love, and support.
—JFR

To Jan, Michael, and Steven—Thanks for your support, consideration, and love.
—WCC

To my family—Thank you for your love and encouragement.
—REH

Contents

Preface

Organization and Structure

The Logistics Handbook was developed to meet the needs of those interested in finding solutions to logistics problems. It was designed to serve as a single source to which those interested in logistics could turn for complete, authoritative information.

The experienced logistics executive will feel comfortable with the organization of the book. It is logical. As a reference book, it offers readers a conceptual explanation for almost any logistics or logistics-related topic, followed by practical, "how-to" information, often in the form of checklists. An extensive bibliography is also included where appropriate to direct readers to more in-depth treatment.

The book should also prove useful to students of logistics, especially when they want to trace how a particular thread, or functional activity, is woven into the total fabric of logistics.

While most of the contents are applicable at all levels of the channel of distribution—producer, wholesaler, and retailer—most of the material is treated from either the total-channel or producer's perspective.

Contributors

The Logistics Handbook is the product of the efforts of many people. What distinguishes it from other books in the field of logistics is the number and qualifications of those who developed, wrote, and edited it. The authors and editors are, by any standards, among the finest educators, practitioners, and consultants in logistics.

The overall structure, design, and content of the book were developed by the two editors. They then recruited section editors for each of the ten sections. Each section editor was responsible for recommending individuals to write one or more chapters in the section. Once approved, the section editors recruited the authors, offered guidance regarding content, and made editorial suggestions. Final, comprehensive editing to eliminate redundancy, ensure appropriate topical coverage, and provide cross-referencing was completed by the associate editor and the two editors.

Contents

Section I. Perspectives on Logistics Management, Bernard J. LaLonde, Editor. The practice of logistics as a formal business management discipline is only a few decades old. Yet, even in this short time the discipline has matured, and this maturing process promises to continue and perhaps accelerate into the twenty-first century. This section reviews the evolution of the process and speculates about likely changes in the twenty-first century.

Section II. Strategic Logistics Planning, Kevin A. O'Laughlin, Editor. Change. It can be a thorny management challenge or an important competitive strategy. One thing is certain—as firms search for new ways to succeed in the ever more competitive global economy, change will be the order of the day. For logistics practitioners, change comes in many forms: faster order cycle times; increasingly differentiated products and services; and ever more sophisticated technologies to help manage all this complexity. One consequence of change is the need for more dynamic, responsive logistics systems that can readily adapt and respond to new and different requirements. Logistics is a boundary-spanning, holistic, process-oriented activity that integrates traditional, functionally oriented activities with the total-cost concept to focus companies on customer service. Developing the capabilities and competencies necessary to be truly flexible in this integrated logistics framework is the key to mastering change as a competitive weapon.

This section explores the building blocks of effective logistics strategies and presents frameworks, methodologies, and tools essential for the design and implementation of responsive, change-based, and time-sensitive logistics strategies and capabilities.

Section III. Logistics Quality and Productivity, Douglas M. Lambert, Editor. Corporate success in the 1990s will depend upon a company's ability to focus on the customer and be a value-added supplier as well as to become a low-cost producer. Logistics quality processes and productivity measurement will be key factors in achieving these ends. This section contains materials that will help readers increase the competitiveness of their corporation in an increasingly competitive global marketplace.

Section IV. Materials Management, Joseph L. Cavinato, Editor. Raw materials, supplies, and finished goods are the physical essence of virtually all logistics systems. Hence, thoughtful management of these materials is crucial to the success of most logistics operations. This section addresses topics related to effective materials management including forecasting, determining inventory investment, managing suppliers, planning, maintaining control, manufacturing, and packaging. As technology has improved in both computing and materials handling, managers have access to increasingly sophisticated tools and concepts that were previously unavailable or too exotic for everyday use. These tools and concepts allow managers to dramatically improve materials management decisions. But to do so effectively, managers must understand the fundamental issues of both traditional and progressive materials management approaches. Each chapter provides insightful discussion for managers seeking to understand materials management and improve the efficiency and effectiveness of their investments in materials and associated operations.

Section V. Transportation Management, C. John Langley, Jr., Editor. Innovation and creativity are words that characterize the current and future state of the transportation industry in the 1990s. They represent notable and refreshing contrasts to the turbulent and traumatic changes faced by both shippers and carriers in the preceding decade. Correspondingly, this section provides perspectives on several topics that are central to the types of changes that have been experienced, as well as those that lie ahead.

Section VI. Distribution Facilities Management, Thomas W. Speh, Editor. An effective distribution center has a major impact on the organization's overall logistics mission. To maximize the opportunity to positively affect the logistics mission, the facility must be located at the optimal site, employ handling systems appropriate for the product, utilize proper handling equipment, and be supported by an effective information system. This section examines these important aspects of facility management.

Section VII. International Logistics Management, David L. Anderson, Editor. It's the new world order. Countries are banding together into regional trading blocs, redefining the concept of global competition, and creating new opportunities to sell products wordwide. Innovations in transportation and streamlined regulations are accelerating product flows. Madonna's compact disc released this Friday in Los Angeles is available by next Friday in Tokyo, Moscow, and Cairo.

The message is becoming clear—we are on the verge of a global trade revolution. Are we truly on the way to developing a global economy or will international logistics managers see "more of the same" (e.g., nontariff barriers, inefficient modal hand-offs, complex paperwork) in the 1990s? No longer may companies focus entirely on their home markets or in selected markets worldwide. Global competitors, using scale production economies, superior logistics, and detailed, real-time consumer preference data will negate brand and location advantages. Survival will depend increasingly on the flexibility and responsiveness of a company's products and global logistics network. Will your company be a global winner in the 1990s? Logistics will be crucial, if not paramount, to its success.

Section VIII. Logistics Information Systems, Donald J. Bowersox, Editor. One of the oldest elements of business operations is logistics. No commercial activity is possible without logistical support. Despite its fundamental, historical foundations, logistics is undergoing dramatic change. Many observers feel that logistical management is experiencing a renaissance—more change has occurred during the past decade than during all decades combined since the Industrial Revolution. Information technology is at the core of this change and is the enabler of the integrated logistics concept. The availability of timely, accurate, inexpensive information is opening the door for unprecedented quality and productivity improvements in the logistics process. Armed with expanded information capabilities, managers are reengineering traditional processes to better meet customer and operating requirements. The four chapters that constitute perspectives on Logistics Information Systems view varied impacts of information technology on logistics best practice.

Section IX. Logistics Organizations and Human Resources Management, Jonathan L. S. Byrnes, Editor. The focus of Logistics has shifted in a subtle but crucial way. Both executives and educators speak increasingly of "logistics management" rather than simply "logistics" when they describe their most important issues and achievements. Because logistics is rooted in product flow, and product flow crosses both functional department and company boundaries, the insightful management of organizational relations and human resources has become the key ingredient for success.

Section X. Contemporary Issues in Logistics, R. William Gardner, Editor. The focus of this section is on the late 1990s and the early 2000s and the issues logistics managers are or will soon be facing. The overall effort of the authors of this section is one of documenting current trends, identifying areas of opportunity and awakening the reader to the many possibilities for improvement of practices which yield significant cost savings and margin improvement opportunities.

The appendix entitled *Publications and Other Sources of Information* contains suggestions for additional reading that should prove helpful to the reader with a specialized interest or problem. The appendix also identifies organizations that may be of interest to logistics professionals.

Acknowledgments

The editors and associate editor are indebted to many people who were instrumental in completing this manuscript. We would like to acknowledge their contributions.

Donna Stevens of Miami University, Veronica Laino and Fran Capillo of Andersen Consulting, New York, and Mona Kim Altschuler of Andersen Consulting, Boston, were heavily involved in the day-to-day administrative aspects of manuscript preparation. Keith Worthington of Andersen Consulting, Chicago, Theresa Mercado of Andersen Consulting, New York, and Julie Grinnell were also quite helpful.

Tod Roberts of Roberts Communication, Cleveland, provided significant assistance with the editing. Mary Angert of Andersen Consulting, Chicago, was also quite helpful.

Kristi Loar and Debbie Manning were very helpful in manuscript preparation. June Edwards and Marianne Hart of Arthur Andersen, New York, were heavily involved in the preparation of the artwork. Eric Steiner and the members of the SSP Mac Lab staff at Andersen Consulting, New York, provided technical assistance.

George Gecowets, Executive Vice President of the Council of Logistics Management, gave the Council's support and encouragement and was very helpful in making CLM material available for the benefit of our readers.

Bob Wallace, Iris Cohen, Eileen DeWald, Bob Harrington, Elena Vega, and Lisa Cuff of The Free Press were supportive, helpful, and, above all, patient.

To all of those who contributed, a sincere thank you.

James F. Robeson
William C. Copacino

The Logistics Handbook

SECTION I

Perspectives on Logistics Management

Bernard J. La Londe
Section Editor

The practice of logistics as a formal business management discipline is only a few decades old. Yet, even in this short time there has been a maturing process in the discipline, and this maturing process promises to continue and perhaps accelerate into the twenty-first century. This section reviews the evolution of this process and speculates about the changes that are likely in the twenty-first century.

In Chapter 1, Bernard J. La Londe broadly traces the evolution of the logistics concept. Starting with the concept of "physical distribution" and identifying some of the key change factors, he traces the evolution through to the "logistics" concept and beyond.

In Chapter 2, James M. Masters and Terrance L. Pohlen identify the transformation processes that led to a new management profession, the logistics professional. The logistics profession is divided into three broad phases in this chapter: (1) functional management of physical distributions (1960s–1970s), (2) internal integration of logistics functions (1980s), and (3) external integration of logistics between firms (1990s).

In Chapter 3, Martha C. Cooper identifies those trends and issues that will affect logistics management in the 1990s and beyond. The impact of these factors on the practice of logistics is evaluated and a potential range of management response from new organizational formats to technology integration is considered. The chapter provides a perspective on change and the impact of change on the logistics profession.

CHAPTER 1

Evolution of the Integrated Logistics Concept

Bernard J. La Londe

One of the challenges in writing on the subject of "evolution of the integrated logistics concept" is trying to decide where to begin. To be sure, logistics was an integral part of warfare dating from the dawn of recorded history. The ability to move people, machines, arms, and supplies was an important determinant of the winner and loser in early conflicts and remains so today. In a book on the Gulf War, it is noted on the first page that U.S. forces planned, moved, and served 122 million meals during the brief engagement—a task comparable to feeding all the residents of Wyoming and Vermont three meals a day for forty days.[1] There is a long and illustrious history of logistics as an element of both ancient and modern warfare. One view of the derivation of *logistics* is that it comes from *logistique,* the title given to an officer in Napoleon's army responsible for quartering the troops and finding forage for the horses and other animals.

The importance of transporting products from their point of production to their point of consumption is also well documented in historical files. Applied logistics probably began when early cultures found that, because of a refined expertise, one community produced excess quantities of certain goods such as arrowheads and another community downstream could make better goods of another sort, such as pottery, because of access to better materials. Thus, applied logistics began with the inception of trade. In a more contemporary context, the industrial revolution and the advent of the mass production and mass consumption economy heralded the beginning of mass distribution in the industrialized countries of the world. As early as 1915, the two functions of marketing were identified as demand creation and physical supply.[2] With urbanization and scale economies in the factory, the buyer and the seller grew further apart and it was necessary to bring the goods to the buyer. Specialized middlemen and transportation services emerged to serve this growing need. The task of the seller was not only to make and sell the product but also to deliver it to the buyer. In the early days of the United States, this often meant serving a buyer at a great distance without the benefit of roads or regular delivery services or agents.

The purpose of this introduction is to present a view of the "evolution of the logistics concept." As noted in the earlier discussion, distribution—or logistics—was recognized as a vital business process from an early time.[3] However, during the past three decades, logistics has evolved considerably. This introductory chapter traces that evolution by addressing three questions:

- What is integrated logistics management?
- Why did the issue of integrated logistics (distribution) become important?
- How has integrated logistics evolved over the past three decades?

Executives and managers should be familiar with the history of integrated logistics management, for the history is enlightening and useful in today's business environment. Integrated logistics management did not develop by accident; the fundamental reasons for its evolution are as valid today as they were at its outset and can provide lessons and frameworks for tackling new challenges.

Integrated Logistics Management

The very definition of *integrated logistics management* is difficult and complicated by the fact that there has been a broad-based shift in business terminology during the past decade. When management first became interested in the potential of material flow to reduce cost or increase service, the term commonly used was *physical distribution.*[4] The use of this terminology began in the 1920s and was adopted by post–World War II business management. In 1948, the American Marketing Association defined physical distribution management as "The movement and handling of goods from the point of production to the point of consumption or use."[5]

Figure 1-1 identifies the distinction between various approaches to integration in the materials flow process.[6] These distinctions were presented early in the development of physical distribution management theory to show the three basic approaches. The first approach, *physical distribution,* focuses on the flow of outbound finished goods. The second approach, *materials management,* is best described by Dean Ammer:

> That aspect of the industrial management concerned with the activities involved in the acquisition and use of all materials employed in the production of the finished product. These

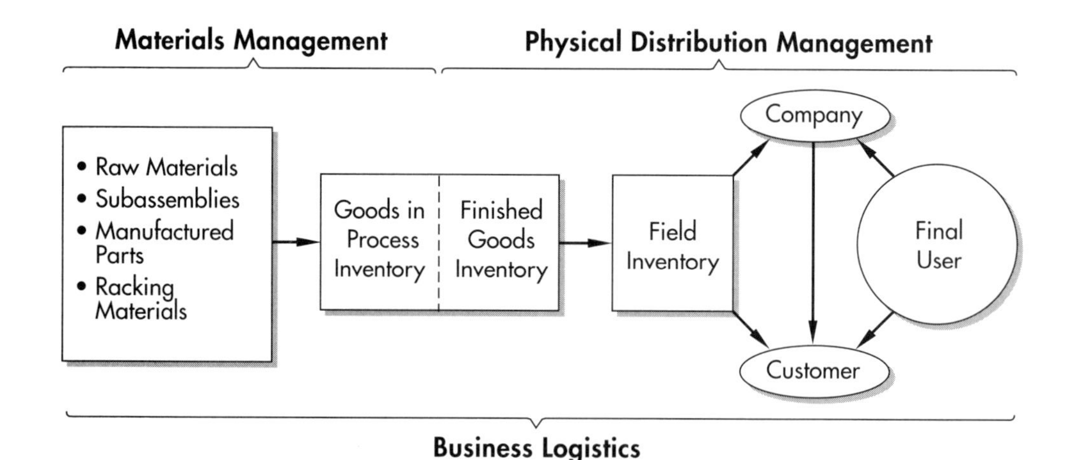

Figure 1-1
Alternative Approaches to Integrated Logistics Management

Source: Prof. Bernard J. La Londe, The Ohio State University. Adapted from Bernard J. La Londe, "Integrated Distribution Management—The American Perspective," *Journal of the Society for Long Range Planning* (London), no. 1 (December 1969): 61–71. © 1969 Bernard J. La Londe. Revision © 1993 by Bernard J. La Londe.

> activities may include production and inventory control, purchasing, traffic, materials handling and receiving.[7]

The third approach, *business logistics,* encompasses the total material flow process from raw material through finished goods inventory. Here is an early definition of this approach:

> A total approach to the management of all activities involved in physically acquiring, moving and storing raw materials, in-process inventory, and finished goods inventory from point of origin to the point of use or consumption.[8]

In the relatively few short years since the logistics concept was accepted by major firms, department names for the function have quickly changed.[9] Each year The Ohio State University conducts a study on logistics career patterns. The study indicates, as shown in Figure 1-2, that the commonly accepted distribution or marketing titles are giving way to reflect the new emphasis on logistics, which now accounts for almost one-third of logistics-related department names.

Over the past two decades there has been a broadening of executive responsibility for total material flow. Executive scope has been expanded to control functions that had previously been fragmented among separate departments, with little operational integration and even less attention from senior executives. Now, some firms regard logistics as a strategic function on a par with other major departments such as production, finance, product development, and marketing. Figure 1-3 shows the level of logistics responsibility by functional activity. The broadening of scope is demonstrated well by the changes in functional responsibility for international distribution. In the first Career Patterns study in 1972, international distribution management re-

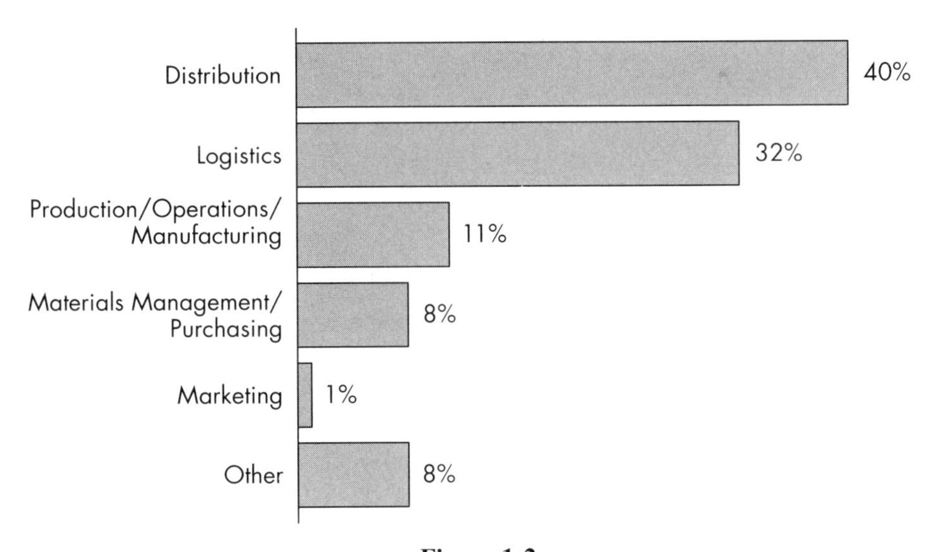

Figure 1-2
Department Names for
Logistics-Related Functions

Source: Adapted from the annual *Ohio State University Survey of Career Patterns in Logistics* studies by permission of the Council of Logistics Management. 1992 study.

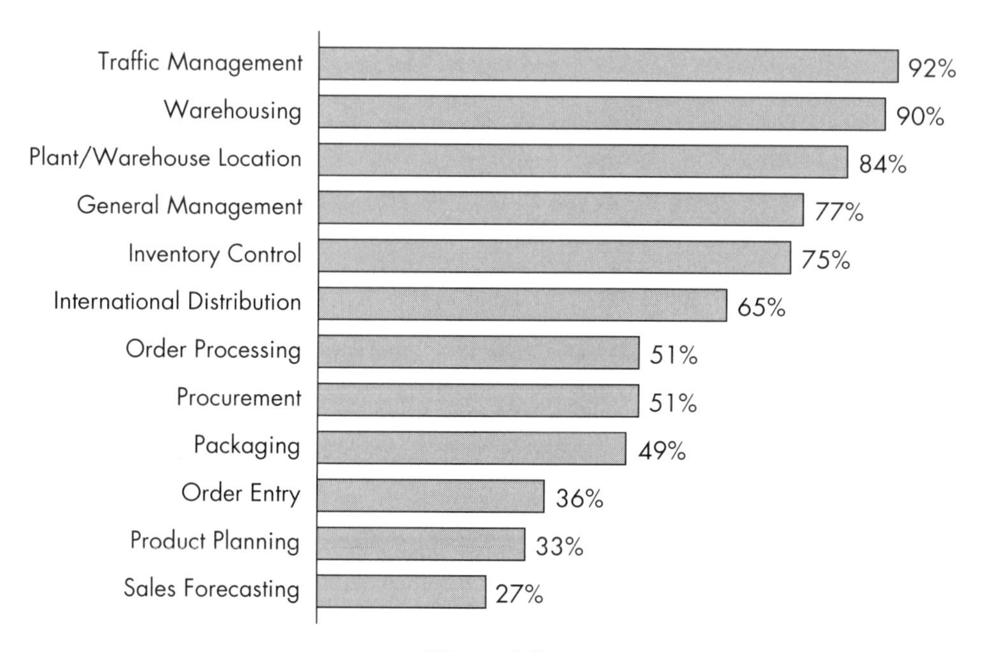

Figure 1-3
Logistics Department Responsibility for Material Flow Activities

Source: Adapted from the annual *Ohio State University Survey of Career Patterns in Logistics* studies by permission of the Council of Logistics Management. 1992 study.

ceived a 9% response, whereas in the 1992 survey, 65% of logistics-related departments had international responsibility.

Thus, structural changes in business organization and a new focus on bringing value to the customer have created a range of adaptive behavior on the part of business firms. For forward-looking companies, integrated logistics management as a dominant material flow strategy emerged during the last half of the 1980s and the first half of the 1990s. Neither a single prototype organization nor a single set of performance metrics characterizes firms that have adopted integrated material flow solutions. Rather, in the early stages of change, the firms that have adopted integrated logistics management choose continuous innovation and improvement as their path to change.

Development of Integrated Distribution

Integrated distribution systems developed during the 1950s and 1960s. Four primary factors shaped the development of distribution thinking during this period: scientific management, data processing technology, a customer focus, and profit leverage.[10]

Scientific Management

By the end of World War II, large gains had been made in production technology that, in turn, renewed interest in scientific management of the business enterprise. In the post–World War II period, particularly during the late 1950s and the 1960s, there was increasing emphasis on the marketing function. During this period, the amount spent on advertising in the American economy quadrupled and the number of new products launched increased almost geometrically. Thus, by the mid-1950s, businesspeople were in a situation where production technology was well advanced and marketing costs were steadily increasing. To reduce costs and remain competitive in the increasingly crowded marketplace, it was necessary to look to one of the few areas that was relatively untouched, the distribution costs of the firm.

In most firms, the cost of distribution represents from 10% to 30% of total costs. These costs, however, are diffused throughout the company. Some of the costs are incurred in inventory, some in materials handling, some in transportation, others in warehousing and storage, and so on. It is logical that this focus on efficiency in distribution was an outgrowth of the American business environment, for distribution was one of the last remaining frontiers for significant operational cost savings. The principal method of securing such cost reduction opportunity was to view distribution as an integrated task rather than as the many traditional fragmented tasks taking place in many parts of the firm.

Data Processing Technology

Another major precipitator of the "distribution revolution" was the advent of new technology in data processing. As computer technology became increasingly powerful, less costly, and more accessible, the possibility of automated inventory control procedures was realized. Distribution data generally require high-input, low-calculation, and high-output processing—the type of processing that both management and workers prefer to automate, as it is time-intensive and tedious. The new technology contributed to the technical capability of handling large amounts of order and shipment data in a rapid and efficient manner. Computers allowed data to be entered once and reused for various purposes including order tracking, production scheduling, shipping, invoicing, and analysis. Data processing technologies reduced repetitive, error-prone manual data recording and manipulation work.

A side effect of the computer was its impact on total integration of management within the firm. Data processing caused some breakdown in the traditional departmentalization within firms and paved the way for integrated distribution management, which, of course, cuts across departmental lines just as data do. Undoubtedly, increasing levels of computer technology will continue to contribute to expanding information system applications in logistics problem-solving and operations.

Customer Focus

The 1950s and 1960s brought increased management attention to logistics, for logistics was recognized as important in providing customer satisfaction. Management finally began to realize that selling a product is really only half the job. Getting the product to the customer at the right time in the right quantity and with the right logistical support (parts and service) is the other equally important half. There was increased recognition that marketing management could not have a successful sales and marketing program unless the logistics system provided adequate support.

Customer satisfaction and logistical support of sales were of particular importance for those companies selling relatively homogeneous products like chemicals, paper, and dairy foods. Such companies often competed on the basis of efficiency in logistics, and their profits, in large measure, were determined by their success in effecting a sound logistics system. Of course, companies selling differentiated products like automobiles, pharmaceuticals, and clothing also found customer satisfaction and logistical support to be important, especially those in premium niches requiring great attention to detail.

Profit Leverage

Management also realized that there was significant profit leverage available from reduced logistics costs. As markets constantly expanded during the 1950s and 1960s, emphasis was on increased sales. As the tempo of domestic and international competition increased, a "profit squeeze" was reflected in the financial statements of many American firms. This prompted many firms to look for cost reduction opportunities along with market expansion opportunities in the previously untouched logistics area.

Evolution of Integrated Logistics Management

There are many factors that impact how a firm uses its resources to focus on strategic opportunities in the marketplace. Among them are external issues such as technology, globalization, and competition. There are also internal factors, which include management style, culture, human resources, and facilities. A firm must place its available resources against the more uncertain external resources in effecting strategy. Strategy, in turn, must leverage certain advantages that the firm has or feels it can achieve in the marketplace. Many firms have chosen to allocate resources to logistics as a strategy to gain advantage.

Those firms choosing to be in the forefront of the logistics concept development did not simply stumble upon "logistics" or distribution as a strategy. Rather, they reviewed alternative ways of bringing value to their customers and then decided that logistics offered more opportunity to impact value at the customer level than other business processes. Companies have pursued three general stages in their evolution into integrated logistics management: physical distribution focus, internal linkages, and external linkages.[11]

Many firms do not even get to the first stage; or even if they do, they can be stalled for many years, depending on the combination of internal and external factors that play on decision-making processes of the firm. Thus, an explanation of evolution must not be viewed as a "biological" phenomenon that companies will naturally and automatically pass through, but rather as a characterization of change in the thinking of leading companies over the past three decades.

Underlying the stages of evolution philosophy is the concept that all manufacturing firms typically have three internal material flow loops. Figure 1-4 shows the internal loops as procurement, operations, and physical distribution. Procurement is the material flow loop that extends from the point of vendor location to the point of first manufacture (or perhaps reprocessing or simply repackaging). Operations is the material flow loop that extends from the point of first manufacture to a completed finished good. Accountants refer to material in this loop as work-in-process (WIP). Physical distribution is the material flow loop that extends from finished goods to the ultimate consumer.

Evolution of integrated logistics management is best framed in terms of inventory, because inventory represents 35% to 50% of current assets for an average company. This level of investment demands the attention of a firm's most senior executives and advisers. In a typical company, 30% of total inventory is in the procurement loop, 30% is in the operations loop, and 40% is in the physical distribution loop. Inventory was used as a buffer between the three internal

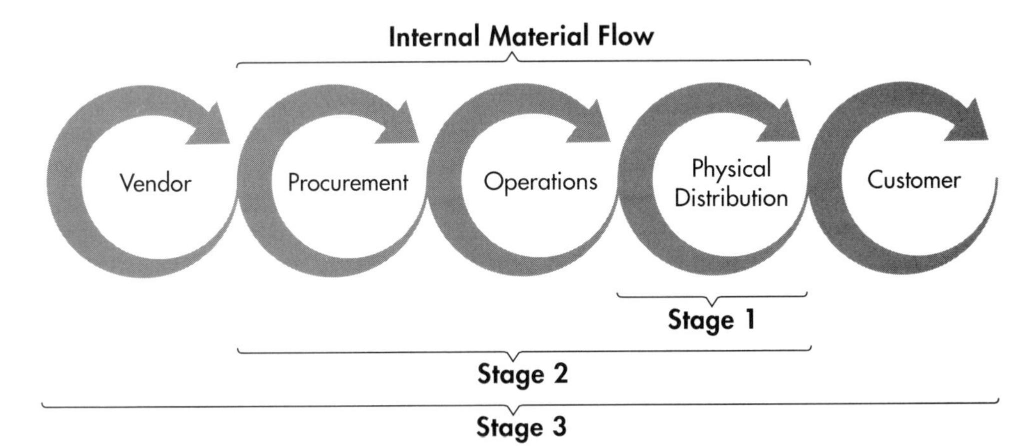

Figure 1-4
Evolution of the Integrated Logistics Concept

material flow loops and indeed was used as a buffer between the internal operations and the two flanking external material flow loops—between the vendor and procurement on the inbound side and between physical distribution and the customer on the outbound side. The net result of this multiple inventory buffering was inventory turns (total unit flow ÷ average unit level) far below what could have been achieved if common inventory theory had been used.

Stage 1: Physical Distribution

Not surprisingly, the first stage, physical distribution, occurring in the 1950s and 1960s, focused on the 40% of inventory investment in finished goods. In this stage firms attempted to integrate finished goods transportation, warehousing, inventory management, customer service, and other functions directly related to delivering product to the customer. The focus of physical distribution management was to manage finished goods distribution in a way that met customer expectations at the lowest possible cost. So the firm's basic approach was to find the appropriate balance between costs and service (optimize the cost-service trade-off curve) with respect to customer requirements and the firm's resources. At that time, the National Council of Physical Distribution Management was active and carried both the title and focus that characterized this approach.

There were three reasons why the integration process started with finished goods. These reasons are still valid today for firms seeking to begin a logistics evolution. First, finished goods is the largest single segment of inventory to be managed. Second, because of its proximity, visibility, and frequent contact with customers, finished goods distribution most directly impacts customer service expectations and performance. Third, management of finished goods allows intervention in an important process without venturing into production processes or other powerful cost centers of the firm. That is, altering physical distribution management is a low-risk, high-gain endeavor relative to altering other functions.

The disadvantage of the physical distribution stage is identical to its primary advantage; it soon became obvious that managing finished goods dealt with only 40% of the total inventory commitment. Even if finished goods are efficiently managed, all the good work can be financially counterbalanced by poor management of either WIP or raw materials.

Although today's logistics concepts and practices are advanced beyond those of the physical distribution stage, managers must remain cognizant of the fundamentals that brought about the stage: focus on high-impact finished goods distribution inventories and operations, and careful monitoring and control of the cost-service trade-off.

Stage 2: Internal Linkages

The focus of the concepts in stage two, internal linkages, was an attempt to join two or all three of the internal material flow loops so that 60% to 100% of the firm's total inventory could be better managed. Logistics did not necessarily reflect an organizational change within the firm, but rather a change in the way the firm thought about value linkages across the three internal material flow loops. Developing internal linkages frequently entailed the elimination of buffer inventories between loops. The concept of inventory velocity was developed and embraced by practitioners of this business process. Thus, inventory flow was thought to be a process that involved horizontal movement of inventory and measurement of inventory from the time the raw material was delivered until an accounts receivable was recorded by the firm (a sale made and the product shipped). Prior to this time, most inventory thinking really involved *level* rather than *flow* of inventory. Pure economic-order-quantity (EOQ) thinking was supplemented by inventory velocity philosophies for many firms. At about the time this movement toward integrated logistics management began, around 1985, the National Council of Physical Distribution Management changed its name to Council of Logistics Management to reflect logistics rather than physical distribution thinking on the part of members. Most similar professional associations around the world did the same.

Stage 3: External Linkages

External linkages, stage three of the evolution, shifted the logistics concept to include externally focused change. Firms began to think "out of the box" and searched for efficiencies in relationships with vendors, customers, and third parties. In many cases, external relationships began with one link, such as supplier-customer, and migrated to multiple links, such as vendor-supplier-customer. The extended view of enterprise offered firms an opportunity to think in new ways about bringing value to the customer. It also allowed firms to use new and/or improving technologies to manage the relational interface between themselves, vendors, third-party logistics support agencies, and customers.

The development of Electronic Data Interchange (EDI), Just-in-Time processes (JIT), Distribution Requirements Planning (DRP), and other elements of the logistics parlance appeared. Today, aggressive firms are able to reduce inventory and improve value by expanding their concept of logistics efficiency and effectiveness to include elements outside the firm. For example, reducing inventory held at the inbound external linkage reduces a firm's costs because vendors reduce extra holding and handling expenses that ultimately get built into the price of raw materials.

Future Directions

There is ample evidence of two current trends that will significantly impact the practice of logistics management. The first trend is cycle-time-to-market and the second is supply chain management. Both will change the focus of what is now termed "logistics management" and increase corporate management's expectations of the logistics function.

Cycle-Time-to-Market

Cycle-time-to-market is variously interpreted in different industries and in different channels by different acronyms and titles. For example, it is becoming increasingly common to see considerations of JIT, Quick Response (QR), process reengineering, and other initiatives, some of which are even copyrighted such as "JIT II."[12] Although these different words usually have different meanings as they are applied in the marketplace, a thread of commonality runs through all: the removal of time as a competitive factor. For example, time might be removed by reducing the design-build-ship cycle. The major difference in the terms for time reduction initiatives usually has to do with the segment of the total order cycle that is covered. For example, some approaches to cycle-time reductions involve virtually all processes and linkages including the vendor, the design process, the manufacturing process, and the distribution process. However, other approaches simply focus on a single element such as transit time from the end of the production line to the customer or vendor lead times.

Organizational structures among leading-edge firms are being redefined to focus on cycle-time reductions and process step eliminations. Many business firms are attempting to promote cycle-time approaches to developing competitive advantages and bring new values to customers. These firms must integrate and manage this extended process, both internally and between themselves and their customers. To capitalize on these opportunities the logistics manager must stand ready to build a boundary spanning consensus across the traditional functional "stovepipe" alignments of the firm. The elements required for success are new skill sets, new organizations, new information systems, and new sets of corporate performance measurement metrics within the firms and at the firms' interfaces with suppliers, third parties, and customers.

Supply Chain Management

The second and related trend will also impact the practice of logistics management during the last half of the 1990s and on into the twenty-first century. A growing number of companies are using the term *supply chain* to describe a process whereby both internal and external units are forged together to bring low-cost and high-value performance to the consumer. The supply chain concept is related to the cycle-time concept in that the firms that develop a continuous flow inventory system frequently do so with a limited number of primary accounts, often using third-party logistics support agencies.

Thus, implementation of a cycle-time-to-market strategy may result in a focused implementation of a supply chain management strategy. The movement toward more responsive inventory systems, especially for primary accounts, will lead many firms to reorganize according to supply chain management. An increasing number of *Fortune* 500 firms have managers with "supply chain" in their official title. Usually, these managers design, develop, and maintain a set of relationships both within and outside the firm (between the firm and vendors, third parties, and customers) capable of executing the overall corporate strategy. As organizational restructuring continues, traditional logistics organizations will evolve into organizations that design and manage internal and external supply chains.

Supply chain management presents a whole new range of career options for individuals who select logistics as the foundation of their management careers. The ability to manage *between* functions will become as important as the ability to manage *within* a function. The ability to develop a consensus across function groups will become more important than the traditional functional management skills. Also, the ability to manage across national borders may become more important than the ability to manage in the home country.

Whatever the future holds, it is certain that logistics managers will not blindly follow past patterns and restrict themselves to past practices. Rather, firms, executives, and managers who have an understanding of the past can adapt successful strategies to new situations and avoid previous errors. The future will undoubtedly present a range of opportunities, both domestic and global, that will challenge the energy and creativity of even the most progressive firms and the most intrepid logistics executives.

Notes

1. Lt. General William G. Pagonis (with Jeffrey Curikshank), *Moving Mountains, Lessons in Leadership and Logistics from the Gulf War* (Cambridge, Mass.: Harvard Business School Press, 1992).
2. Arch W. Shaw, *Some Problems in Market Distribution* (Cambridge, Mass.: Harvard University Press, 1915).
3. Bernard J. La Londe and Leslie M. Dawson, "Early Development of Physical Distribution Thought," *Readings in Physical Distribution Management, The Logistics of Marketing,* chap 2 (Editors: Bowersox, La Londe, and Smykay) (London: Macmillan 1969).
4. Peter F. Drucker, "Physical Distribution: The Frontier of Modern Management." Speech given at the Annual Meeting of the National Council of Physical Distribution (now the Council of Logistics Management), April 1965.
5. "1948 Report of the Definitions Committee of the American Marketing Association," *Journal of Marketing,* 13 (October 1948): 212.
6. Bernard J. La Londe, "Integrated Distribution Management—The American Perspective," *Journal of the Society for Long Range Planning* (London), 2, no. 1 (December 1969): 61–71.
7. Dean S. Ammer, "Materials Management as a Profit Center," *Harvard Business Review* 47, no. 1 (January–February 1969): 39–47.
8. Bernard J. La Londe, John R. Grabner, and James F. Robeson, "Integrated Distribution Management: A Management Perspective," *International Journal of Physical Distribution* 1, no. 1 (October 1970): 44.
9. The Ohio State University Annual Survey of Logistics Executives for 1992. Each year the chief logistics executives of member firms of the Council of Logistics Management are surveyed; the findings are based on approximately two hundred executive responses. The results are presented at each annual CLM conference and published in the proceedings.
10. La Londe, et al., "Integrated Distribution Management": 44.
11. See Chapter 2. Also see *Measuring and Improving Productivity in Physical Distribution.* National Council of Physical Distribution Management [NCPDM], Oak Brook, Ill., 1984, p. 17, a study prepared by A. T. Kearney, Inc., under contract to NCPDM, now the Council of Logistics Management.
12. Lance Dixon, "JIT II: A New Approach to Supply Management," *Center for Quality Management Journal* 1, no. 1 (Autumn 1992): 15–18. JIT II was developed by Bose and involves placing vendor representatives in Bose facilities and giving them unprecedented authority usually reserved for internal departments.

CHAPTER 2

Evolution of the Logistics Profession

James M. Masters
Terrance L. Pohlen

The organization of the business logistics function has undergone several transformations since American firms began to embrace the logistics concept following World War II. These transformations resulted from a growing recognition and understanding of how logistics processes affect the firm's costs, performance, and competitiveness. Each evolving level of understanding has in turn driven major changes in the organization of logistics functions. The role of the logistics executive has undergone similar changes. The scope of the logistician's responsibilities has expanded beyond narrowly defined functional roles, such as shipping department supervisor, and has broadened to encompass the management and control of the full spectrum of the firm's logistical processes, as signified by a title like vice president of corporate logistics. This chapter describes the evolution of the logistics organization and the evolving role of the logistics executive. The discussion traces the development of logistics practice from the fragmentary management of logistics functions that occurred during the late 1950s and includes a description of how leading-edge firms have begun positioning their logistics organizations for the 1990s. The chapter also demonstrates how the growth of the logistics executive's role in the organization has paralleled the growth in the importance of business logistics. It closes with a statistical profile of the contemporary logistician developed through surveys of American corporate logistics executives.

The evolution of the logistics organization has been clearly documented in the many logistics books and articles published over the last four decades. A careful review of this literature provides a foundation for tracing the evolution of the logistics organization and the changing role of the logistics executive. The literature includes many professional journal articles specifically addressing issues confronting logistics managers during these periods. Organizations like the Council of Logistics Management, the American Society of Transportation and Logistics, and various consulting firms have periodically surveyed logistics professionals, and this discussion incorporates selected results from these studies to demonstrate how firms have reorganized and realigned responsibilities of logistics executives in attempts to address changing workplace, marketplace, and environmental forces. The evolution of business logistics can be divided into three phases:

- Functional management (1960s–1970s)
- Internal integration (1980s)
- External integration (1990s)

Functional Management (1960s–1970s)

During the 1960s and 1970s, most firms made a gradual transition from the fragmentary management of individual processes like traffic, purchasing, and warehousing to the integrated management of related functions under the two common headings materials management and physical distribution. The term *materials management* came to mean the "single-manager organization concept embracing the planning, organizing, motivating, and controlling of all those activities and personnel principally concerned with the flow of materials into an organization."[1] Materials management included functions like purchasing, raw materials, work-in-process inventory control, inbound transportation, surplus material, and production scheduling. Physical distribution was envisioned as "the broad range of activities concerned with efficient movement of finished products from the end of the production line to the consumers."[2] Physical distribution thus included functions like freight, warehousing, materials handling, protective packaging, order processing, demand forecasting, inventory control, and customer service.[3]

Management of these processes prior to 1960 was typically practiced on a narrow, functional basis and often suffered from neglect. Senior management tended to view distribution activities as largely "unskilled" and unworthy of attention, and the high costs of distribution disappeared in general catchalls such as "indirect labor" or "overhead."[4] Because businesses usually spread distribution responsibilities across their organizational structure and into different cost centers, it was difficult to understand the true extent of distribution costs and to manage them effectively.

Materials management and physical distribution management began to replace the fragmented management approach during the early 1960s. Several forces contributed to this transformation in organization and management. A 1956 Harvard Business School study of air freight introduced total cost analysis to distribution management. This study demonstrated how a firm could use the high speed of air freight, despite its high costs, to offset inventory and thus to reduce the sum of its total inventory, warehousing, and transportation costs.[5] In addition, advances in computerized modeling provided new capability to address questions about the design and operation of the distribution function, such as the number and location of warehouses, the assignment of customers to warehouses, and how best to organize the distribution process.[6] Analyses could now be conducted in an integrated fashion so that cost trade-offs between functions like transportation and inventory could be deliberately explored and exploited. Finally, the economic climate of the late 1950s and 1960s encouraged many firms to reduce production costs to improve profits. Distribution functions now provided a previously undiscovered opportunity for cost reduction.[7] The organization of materials management and physical distribution functions that emerged during this period often resulted in distribution executives who were several organizational layers distant from senior management The senior materials manager and the physical distribution manager often reported to different vice presidents.

Major Forces in the 1960s and 1970s

Each phase in the evolution of business logistics had notable changes in the basic operating environment. The first phase had changes that were so dramatic that they are still taking place in organizations today.

Application of Computers

The application of computers to materials management and physical distribution problems led to a tremendous increase in the number and sophistication of tools available to the manager. Computers enabled managers to manipulate large databases and perform complex calculations in short periods of time. The application of computers to distribution problems made many traditional management approaches obsolete. Materials requirements planning (MRP) was a case in point. MRP introduced an alternative to the traditional approaches of managing manufacturing inventory. MRP exploited the dependent demand relationship between the end item produced and all the component parts required for its manufacture.[8] The ability to synchronize the inbound flow of materials with the production requirement yielded inventory reductions and overcame the demand forecasting problems that had plagued the traditional order point models. The MRP approach was simple and intuitive, but a successful implementation in a large-scale manufacturing system was feasible only on a computer because of the many detailed calculations required. Once sufficiently powerful and economical computer hardware became available, MRP software became a popular approach to materials management.

Firms quickly applied the computer to solving other problems as well. A National Council of Physical Distribution Management (NCPDM) survey found that:

> Over 90 percent of the companies indicated that they used the computer in some capacity to handle inventory control. The next most frequently mentioned activities utilizing the computer were order processing, planning and forecasting, and production planning. Over 75 percent of the companies indicated that the computer was utilized in transportation and warehousing. Over 40 percent indicated they used the computer in warehouse selection and customer service.[9]

Computers also provided the means to address one of the most compelling reasons for integrating materials and distribution functions—the dollars involved. The computer made it practical to extract costs frequently buried in manufacturing or selling overhead and thus to determine true distribution costs.[10]

Customer Service and Productivity

Efforts to reduce transportation and distribution costs often had adverse effects on customer service. Firms attempted to reduce costs by decreasing the number of stocking locations, drawing down inventory, and reducing the breadth of stockage in the distribution system, thus reducing the level of customer service provided.[11] However, managers were experiencing pressure to improve customer service while decreasing the costs of distribution operations. Distribution costs accounted for nearly 50% of the cost of many consumer products, yet few firms understood the extent of these costs, how to reduce them, or the impact of the marketing program on distribution costs.[12] Intensive management of distribution functions emerged as a corporate strategy to achieve the goal of increasing customer service while simultaneously decreasing operating costs.

A landmark study in 1976 provided insight into how business defined the concept of "customer service" and measured the level of customer service provided. The study found no consistent definition of customer service among firms. Instead, firms viewed customer service either as an activity, a performance level, or a management philosophy.[13] The study offered the following definition:

> A customer oriented corporate philosophy which integrates and manages all of the elements of the customer interface within a predetermined optimum cost-service mix.[14]

Many firms had no comprehensive or consistent customer service objectives or standards in place. Firms with customer service standards generally used inappropriate measures or did not include the customer's point of view, which led in turn to increased inventory, transportation, and warehousing costs.[15] The growing attention to customer service issues changed management practice. Firms began to explore the linkages between customer service objectives and their effect on distribution costs. Cost/revenue trade-off models became an accepted approach for establishing appropriate service levels. ABC analysis also provided a useful tool for categorizing customers by profit contribution and for determining the appropriate level of service.

Management also suffered from a lack of productivity standards and measurement. In 1978, an NCPDM-sponsored study identified $40 billion of potential productivity gains in the physical distribution of goods.[16] Only 50% of the surveyed companies had begun programs to improve distribution productivity, and only 20% had reached a meaningful level of measurement to support productivity improvement. Implementation of productivity improvement programs in distribution was expected to produce a 10% improvement in the average firm's productivity.[17]

These customer service and productivity studies clearly demonstrated the benefits of integrated distribution activities that many innovative firms were beginning to achieve. Corporations could achieve improved levels of customer service at lower cost by recognizing available trade-offs. Firms could further improve their profit margins by improving the productivity of their distribution activities. The ability to capture these savings required a manager with sufficient authority to direct the necessary changes.

Formation of MM and PD Organizations

The integration of materials management and physical distribution functions did not proceed without debate. Consolidation of functions located in manufacturing, marketing, and finance generated controversy and "turf battles." The debate became more intense as more firms began to explore the materials management/physical distribution concept. By 1962, 45% of U.S. manufacturing firms had adopted some kind of physical distribution organization, and half again as many had plans to do so.[18] However, a 1971 NCPDM survey found that most corporations had not placed the fully integrated distribution organization into action. Most companies had not yet organized to do a total distribution job.[19]

Practitioners strongly advocated integrating existing functions within materials management and physical distribution organizations. The basic theme of their approach was "to establish a costing system which would identify all physical distribution costs and enable decision-making which would permit operation of the system at lowest total cost consistent with predetermined standards of customer service."[20] They further argued that these functions accounted for a high proportion of total operating costs, and that centralized management of these functions provided the most effective means for controlling these costs.[21] Opposition to functional integration arose primarily in departments that stood to lose functions to the materials management and physical distribution organizations. Executives argued that they would lose control of essential functions, and that coordination within the existing organizational structure could achieve the same results. Some viewed integration efforts as "empire building" within the traffic or distribution functions. However, history indicates that the proponents of integration overcame these arguments because of the problems associated with fragmented management.

Role of the Materials Management/Physical Distribution Executive

Integration led to the executive managing a broader range of activities. This increased scope required more highly and broadly educated managers. Executives also began to report to different senior executives at higher organizational levels.

Scope of Management Responsibility. Integration expanded the role of the executive by increasing the scope of responsibility. Fragmented management spread responsibilities across the organization and limited the scope of responsibility to specific areas like transportation, raw materials warehousing, returned goods, or import/export.[22] This limited scope prevented the manager from achieving cost reductions across internal organizational boundaries.[23] Many firms saw integration as a means to correct this deficiency. Purchasing's role expanded to include the management of the inbound flow of material.[24] A typical materials manager had responsibility for related functions such as purchasing, production control, inbound traffic, warehousing, MIS control, inventory planning and control, and salvage and scrap disposal.[25] Physical distribution managers experienced a comparable growth in their responsibilities. The single distribution manager had responsibility for the efficient, cost-effective flow of outbound material. An integrated distribution operation might include subordinate units like transportation, distribution facilities, inventory and planning control, and sales-order service.[26]

Education Requirements. The broadened range of responsibility increased educational requirements for materials and physical distribution managers. The restructuring of these functions prompted the distribution executive to learn more about the areas of finance, data processing, and planning skills.[27] A 1972 *Traffic Management* survey found that over 65% of distribution executives holding director or vice presidential positions had undergraduate degrees. However, most executives did not have specific college course work or an academic major field in distribution.[28] As a result, many entrants into distribution management positions desired follow-on education and professional development in distribution management. As one reaction to this need:

> The National Council of Physical Distribution Management was formed in 1963 to develop the theory and understanding of the process, promote the art and science of managing systems and to foster professional dialogue and development in the field operating exclusively without profit and in cooperation with other organizations and institutions.[29]

Organizational Level. The stature of the distribution executive improved as firms began to recognize the importance and contribution of the distribution function. The perception of distribution activity shifted from "donkey work" to that of a key decision maker within the firm at the vice presidential level.[30] Surveys revealed upward mobility for distribution executives.[31,32] A 1972 *Traffic Management* survey found that 45% of its respondents held titles that had not existed in 1962. The report also found a 69% increase in the number of vice presidents and directors within physical distribution organizations.

Impetus for Change

External and internal forces continued to generate change in business organizations and in the role of the distribution executive. Notable forces driving change were the increased cost of performing distribution processes and the deregulation of the transportation industry.

High Cost of Performing Distribution Functions. The cost of operations skyrocketed during the 1970s. Inflation continued at unprecedented rates, and interest rates reached double-digit figures by 1980.[33] As a result, labor, facilities, and capital costs all drove cost increases in distribution. Additionally, fuel costs escalated owing to the OPEC oil embargo.[34] These increasing operating costs compelled managers to examine further integration of distribution functions.

Deregulation of the Transportation Industry. Deregulation enabled managers to pursue a new set of options to reduce costs and increase performance.

> Deregulation allowed (or perhaps encouraged) a new relationship between the buyer, the seller, and carrier. While part of this relationship came from the new electronic linkages between buyer, seller, and carrier, part of it emerged from the way shippers wanted to do business. There was a fundamental shift away from a day-to-day, transaction-to-transaction relationship to a longer term, contractual relationship. There was the emergence of some form of an interdependence between shipper and carrier over some fixed time horizon. This relationship involved a closer and more frequent interchange on a wide range of topics such as productivity, quality, and technology, to name only a few. It typically involved a wide range of contracts between personnel in the shipper organization and personnel in the carrier organization to solve problems or to initiate changes that were mutually advantageous to all parties in the process.[35]

By the end of the 1970s, many managers had come to view the materials management and physical distribution activities as an organic whole, and the term *logistics* became the common way to describe the entire activity.

Internal Integration (1980s)

Logistics organizations had experienced a decided shift in the positioning of distribution and materials management functions by the early 1980s. The Ohio State University Survey of Career Patterns in Logistics detected substantial changes occurring during the last half of the 1970s, with these trends stabilizing by 1981.[36] The findings suggested a linkage between the distribution function and pre-production activities (i.e., purchasing, production planning, etc.) and the emergence of a total material flow organization.[37] "Integrated logistics" emerged as the term coined to describe this linkage or internal boundary spanning and integration of logistics functions.

Integrated logistics is the "total range of activities concerned with the movement of materials, including information and control systems; logistics constitutes a strand running through all the traditional functional responsibilities—from raw materials procurement to product delivery."[38] It encompasses the traditional responsibilities of physical distribution and materials management, as well as several functions previously performed by marketing and manufacturing (i.e., production planning, sales forecasting, raw materials/work in process, and customer service).

Several studies during the 1980s traced the development of the integrated logistics organizational structure. A 1981 A.T. Kearney study found distribution (logistics) departments transitioned through three stages:

> Stage One: Management views its mission as controlling finished goods transportation and warehousing. Management has an operational orientation.

Stage Two: Management's mission is to integrate finished goods distribution and control inbound transportation. The orientation here is managerial, where individual activities are planned and controlled as parts of a total physical distribution process. The manager seeks out opportunities to improve by balancing trade-offs.

Stage Three: Management's mission is to integrate the total logistics process as part of the total corporate endeavor. Management's orientation turns to strategic issues like evaluating basic changes in the company's logistics/operations strategy and pursuing opportunities presented by changes to the external environment.[39]

The study found a steady expansion in the range of functions managed by logistics organizations during the period from 1973 to 1981, with the trend accelerating in the 1980s.[40] Firms reporting stage one responsibilities rose from 55% to 70%, stage two increased from 43% to 47%, and stage three increased from no responsibility to 16%.

The movement towards a stage three, or the "integrated logistics" firm, continued throughout the 1980s. Subsequent studies performed by A.T. Kearney in 1983, 1985, and 1987 demonstrated a continuing trend. Companies exhibiting only stage one characteristics leveled off near 47%.[41] Companies exhibiting only stage two characteristics decreased as many "graduated" to stage three, while this category accounted for approximately 35% by 1987.[42,43]

The integrated logistics organizational structure provided several benefits to implementing firms. A comparison using stage one as a baseline found stage two companies incurred only 84.7% of the logistics costs of stage one companies, and stage three companies incurred only 80.7% of the costs.[44] Other benefits include a competitive advantage through lower costs and higher profits, enhanced relationships with suppliers and customers, and additional value to the supply chain.[45]

Internal integration of logistical activities became widespread during the mid-1980s. The National Council of Physical Distribution Management encouraged this trend by changing its name to the Council of Logistics Management in 1985. The change enabled the organization to encompass the full range of logistical issues and serve a wider range of logistics professionals. The council's definition of logistics reflected its broadened scope:

> Logistics is the process of planning, implementing, and controlling the efficient, cost effective flow and storage of raw materials, in-process inventory, finished goods, and related information from point of origin to point of consumption for the purpose of conforming to customer requirements.[46]

Major Forces Shaping Business Logistics

The pace of change quickened for logistics executives during the 1980s. The postderegulation era expanded the range and combination of services available in the marketplace. Third-party logistics providers exploited the service emphasis and emerged as a major player in providing a full range of logistics services. Communications and information processing applications accelerated, with numerous firms employing electronic data interchange, barcoding, and personal computers. Customer service increased in importance as firms attempted to use logistics to achieve a competitive advantage in the marketplace.

Postderegulation Expansion of Services. Deregulation influenced the logistics organization by changing the relationship between carriers and shippers. The shipping organizations focused their efforts on achieving rate reductions and transportation cost savings. Shippers decreased their carrier base and concentrated their shipments, with fewer carriers to obtain increased negotiating leverage.[47] As a result, a smaller number of shippers would account for a larger proportion of a carrier's total business. Carriers had to position themselves to be in the smaller set of carriers selected by specific shippers. Successful carriers accomplished this through superior customer service, value-added services, and reasonable prices.[48] A wide variety of innovative practices emerged as carriers and shippers attempted to reduce costs and improve services, including automated freight billing and audit, and the use of electronic data interchange to assist in paperless billing, shipment tracing, rate lookup, claims tracking, and freight payment. Many shippers and carriers implemented programs such as guaranteed backhauls, uniform rate and contract formats, or cost-based discounts.[49] "Logistics companies" emerged as transportation firms expanded their operations to include the full range of logistics services—other modes of transportation, freight consolidation and forwarding, warehousing, and packaging, to name a few. These firms gained acceptance as shippers attempted to limit their investment in "noncore" businesses or acquired needed logistics expertise in areas like carrier selection, rate negotiation, or freight payment.[50]

Third-Party Logistics Firms. Third-party or contract logistics firms represent the outgrowth of the movement toward "logistics companies." Third-party logistics involves the use of external companies to perform logistics functions previously performed within the organization. The functions can encompass the entire logistics process or a selected subset of those activities.[51] A combination of economic and regulatory forces contributed to their growth and acceptance during the 1980s. Sheffi identified several of these forces, including increased competition from foreign companies, a more demanding marketplace in the form of stockless retailers and just-in-time production lines, the high service levels yet long supply lines experienced in globalized operations, and the restructuring of corporate America to eliminate debt by cutting costs, reducing the asset base, and trimming the labor force.[52] Many firms found the use of third parties attractive because it allowed them to concentrate on their core competencies, to obtain a streamlined logistics system, to exploit the third party's economies of scale, to achieve a higher level of specialization, and to reduce financial risk.[53]

Communications and Information Technology. Logistics organizations developed an insatiable appetite during the 1980s for the ability to rapidly communicate, trace shipments, and exchange data. Information, as indicated in the CLM definition of logistics, had become a key component in providing logistics services and acted as a catalyst for further integrating logistical activities. Firms used information technology to further integrate their logistics functions, compress time, and eliminate cost from the supply chain. Integration resulted from the interconnection of hundreds of steps in the management and control process made possible by the rapid exchange of information.[54] Compression of the supply chain permitted firms to "trade information for inventory." Near real-time access to retailer inventory and sales data enabled manufacturers and wholesalers to more accurately project future requirements and to therefore reduce or eliminate safety stocks used as buffers against uncertainty.

Electronic data interchange (EDI) provided a medium to interconnect internal as well as external logistics functions. EDI is "the interorganization exchange of business data in standard, machine-processable form."[55] It eliminated the rekeying of data and provided a quick and accurate means for electronically exchanging data. EDI proved especially important in supporting the informational requirements for implementing distribution requirements planning or just-in-time inventories and production.

Distribution Resource Planning (DRP). DRP became a popular inventory planning and deployment tool based on exploiting the information and connectivity of integrated systems. The development of DRP enabled managers to effectively plan and efficiently deploy their finished goods inventories throughout the complex, multilevel distribution networks that most large manufacturers have established to move product from plants to customers. A DRP system operates by applying the basic logic of MRP to the control of finished goods distribution inventories. Deploying a DRP system required obtaining field-level sales forecasts from the distribution system for input into the production system's master production schedule. The integration of demand forecasts into production scheduling resulted in several benefits including reduced inventory investment, reduced transportation costs, increased inventory turnover, and increased inventory availability.[56] Implementation of DRP had the potential to significantly impact the organization of logistics functions. Traditional marketing and manufacturing activities such as forecasting and production scheduling would become more highly integrated and would most likely merge with distribution. The relatively small number of stage three firms indicates the difficulty of achieving the integration and level of coordination necessary for successful DRP implementation.

Just-in-Time (JIT). JIT production scheduling also achieved greater acceptance owing to the increased organizational integration and new information technology that became available during the 1980s. JIT is an organizational philosophy that strives for excellence and has the aim of eliminating all waste and consistently improving quality.[57] A JIT approach to purchasing in a manufacturing environment requires the supplier to produce for and deliver to the manufacturer precisely the necessary units in the necessary quantities, at the necessary time, as determined by the manufacturer's production schedule, with the requirement that products produced by the supplier conform to performance specifications every time.[58] In comparison with other forms of exchange relationships, JIT exchanges have a longer-term orientation and require closer coordination to achieve specific value-added service.[59] The establishment of JIT relationships imposes new requirements on logistical organizations. The supplier and manufacturer must jointly perform long-term planning, work together to achieve continuous improvement in key processes and products, interface at multiple points on a continuous basis, and operate in a potentially high-risk, sole-source environment. JIT extends the integration of logistical activities beyond an individual firm's boundaries to achieve even greater efficiencies and process improvements. JIT takes the firms beyond stage three integration and into supply or value-added chain management.

Customer Service. Customer service continued as a dominating force in the shaping of the logistics organization throughout the 1980s. Logistics executives consistently ranked customer service as one of the major forces influencing the growth and development of the corporate logistics function.[60,61,62] Repeated surveys of logistics executives indicated that most considered customer service the second-most important force, while only cost reduction, deregulation, or computer applications received higher rankings. The Council of Logistics Management commissioned a follow-on to the 1976 La Londe and Zinszer study to examine how customer service had evolved over the subsequent ten years. The study redefined customer service to reflect the internal and external integration occurring in logistics organizations:

> Customer service is a process for providing significant value-added benefits to the supply chain in a cost effective way.[63]

The study's findings also identified specific areas where customer service had shaped the evolution of the logistics organization. Customer service had become an important way of strategically differentiating the product or service for many firms. Firms relied heavily on the processing and release of timely information to achieve efficient, effective customer service. The customer had begun to play an active role in determining the types of services provided by the seller. For example, many buyers required their vendors to install an EDI capability. Contractual relationships had become the dominant mode of customer service relationships. The scope of customer service extended beyond the domestic market to address the issues faced in a global supply chain. Strong pressure had been placed on firms to maintain consistently high levels of customer service, and this trend was expected to continue and intensify over the visible horizon.[64] During the 1980s, firms truly recognized the capability of logistics to provide a strategic advantage in the marketplace, and the logistics executive's stature within the organization reflected this recognition.

Role of the Logistics Executive

Logistics executives directly benefited from the emphasis on using logistics as a competitive weapon. The number of senior executive appointments grew significantly, and their management scope had expanded beyond materials management or physical distribution to encompass the entire spectrum of logistics activities. However, the increased responsibilities placed new demands on the logistics executive and changed the skill set and competencies required for success in the discipline.

Scope of Management Responsibility. Integration of materials management, production planning, and physical distribution into one logistics organization greatly increased the logistics executive's responsibilities. The 1987 A.T. Kearney study demonstrated a 15% increase in the number of stage three, or fully integrated, logistics firms, and the range of logistics responsibilities had widened across virtually all industries.[65] The study also found a growing population of logistics organizations, with approximately 22% of the survey companies having established a logistics department within the last three years. Globalization also played a major role in expanding the logistics executive's responsibilities. Logistics executives reporting international responsibilities increased to over 65% by 1987, from 30.5% in 1980 and only 9.5% in 1974.[66,67]

Organizational Level. The Ohio State Survey of Career Patterns in Logistics found significant growth in the number of senior logistics executives.[68] The number of senior-level positions increased at a rate of about 6% per year during the 1980s. Some 56% of the firms established a senior-level logistics position during the 1980s, compared with a total of 25% prior to 1980. Only 19% of the surveyed companies had not yet established a senior position. The increased number of senior executives suggests an even greater logistics input into corporate decision making and planning. A 1992 CLM-sponsored study of strategic planning found an increasing number of logistics personnel participating in the corporate planning process and developing strategic logistics plans during the latter half of the 1980s.[69]

Educational Requirements. The wider range of activities managed demanded a more comprehensive background for most logistics executives. They could no longer rely on a baseline of transportation or purchasing expertise to move into senior positions. Instead, they required a broader background in logistics (e.g., inventory, warehousing, production planning, etc.) and in the firm's other major departments (e.g., manufacturing, marketing, and particularly finance). The senior logistics executive cultivated an extensive background in logistics and has grown into a position of authority; however, the senior executive also acquired the necessary education to function at a higher corporate level. By 1989, 89% of the surveyed executives had baccalaureate degrees, and 45% had graduate degrees. Some 62% of the baccalaureate degrees and 88% of the graduate degrees were in business. And 12% of the graduate and 8% of the baccalaureate degrees were in logistics.[70] When questioned regarding which topics the senior executive would specifically choose for future study, the most frequent responses included corporate finance and information technology.

The logistics executive's broadened scope of responsibilities has also affected the educational requirements sought in new career entrants. *Traffic Management*'s 1989 survey of 20 top logistics executives found a definite preference for applicants with a logistics-related degree; however, the applicants also must have possessed a familiarity with computer applications and basic business concepts.[71]

Impetus for Change

Events occurring toward the end of the 1980s signaled a new direction for the logistics organization and executive. Leveraged buyouts and corporate restructuring forced many firms to downsize their operations. American firms recognized the full potential of international markets as a means to expand existing markets and to source materials. The marketplace also placed increasing demands on firms to expand competitiveness beyond cost to include time and quality. These forces intensified the pressure on logistics to maintain high customer service standards while simultaneously improving productivity and decreasing costs.

Corporate Restructuring. Many firms restructured during the 1980s to gain a competitive advantage and to avoid hostile takeovers. Corporate management restructured to dispose of unsuccessful businesses, de-layer management, match cost generation with debt service, and "lean-out" the organization.[72] Restructuring sometimes drastically altered the logistics organization. Many logistics departments faced the prospect of consolidation within another firm's logistics organization or the formation of a new enterprise that needed to create an entire management infrastructure with a logistics function of its own.[73]

International Markets. American firms increasingly expanded their international sourcing of raw materials, subassemblies, and other materials to obtain a cost advantage.[74] The success of this strategy in one firm would cause the practice to spread to the firm's competitors. International markets presented a growth opportunity for many companies with mature domestic markets. The development of major trading blocks such as the European Community and the opening of eastern Europe provided opportunities for expansion. However, the international market placed new requirements on the logistics department to contain costs while expanding operations in more distant markets.

Time and Quality. A new pattern for obtaining competitive advantage emerged by providing the most value for the lowest cost in the least amount of time. By decreasing "time to market," firms increased productivity, decreased costs without penalty, reduced their risk, and increased market share.[75] The incorporation of quality into the logistics process meant improved customer service, order fulfillment, and logistics processes. These quality gains provided key advantages that the competition often could not easily duplicate: improved on-time delivery, order completeness, invoice accuracy, order-cycle-time reduction, and overall logistics productivity improvements.[76]

The combination of these factors forced senior management to search for even more innovative techniques for improving logistics performance and gaining competitive footholds. However, the costs of technology, global expansion, and labor frequently prohibited action by individual firms. Instead, many companies in the 1980s explored the potential of external integration to achieve their objectives without substantially increasing costs or risk.

External Integration (1990s)

The organizational structure emerging for logistics activities in the 1990s follows the pattern of external integration. The integration of internal functions during the 1970s and 1980s focused on avoiding suboptimization of specific functions and optimizing results for the entire firm. "Supply chain management extends this concept of functional integration beyond the firm to all firms in the supply chain, bringing the concept of integration into the 1990s."[77] The focus has shifted to viewing the firm within the context of an overall chain of value-creating activities of which the firm itself is only one part.[78] This drive toward external integration has resulted from a channel member's desire to gain competitive advantage through improving overall channel efficiency by reducing costs, reducing risk, and effectively leveraging the corporate resources of specific channel members.

Costs. Adopting a supply chain framework for strategically relevant activities permits an understanding of the behavior of costs and the sources of differentiation. "Suppliers and distribution channels have profit margins that are important to identify in understanding a firm's cost or differentiation positioning, because end-use customers ultimately pay for all the profit margins throughout the value chain."[79] Tyndall recommends using a comprehensive costing methodology for assigning costs at each level within the chain similar to the approach used in direct product pricing. The approach enables supply chain members to understand each individual member's costs and identifies areas where costs should be reduced or productivity improved. The information also permits an assessment of alternative channel structures.[80]

Risk Reduction. Integration across the supply chain reduces an individual firm's risk by spreading the investment, leveraging information against inventory, and pooling expertise. Multiple firms in the supply chain will share the investment in product distribution. The investment can take the form of manufacturing capability, product transportation, inventory levels, marketing of the product, and handling. Collective planning among channel members may also identify opportunities to eliminate asset-specific investments. Product and packaging design would permit the use of common handling, storage, and transportation equipment. The channel members leverage information existing within the channel to reduce risk. Adopting a DRP or JIT system would eliminate redundant inventories or buffer stocks. Manufacturing could produce to demand or rely on more accurate and timely forecasts of consumer demand. Channel members could also pool their expertise to identify areas driving costs and improve overall productivity. Specific actions could include techniques to eliminate unnecessary material handling, improve vertical warehousing, increase storability, or eliminate duplicate processing of information.

Leveraging Resources. The supply chain can leverage individual channel members' resources to gain a competitive advantage. The channel could select retailers with access to new markets, share process innovations to streamline operations and reduce flow times, exchange demand and production information to eliminate inventories, ship material on other channel members' backhaul routes, share technology, and allow each channel member to concentrate on its specific core competencies.

Major Forces Shaping Business Logistics

Three major factors have shaped the business logistics environment during the early 1990s. These factors include globalization of national economies, demographic and lifestyle changes, and the revolution in information and communications technology.[81] These factors will influence all aspects of business, including logistics.

Globalization. The growing trend toward internationalization has become a way of doing business in the 1990s. Sustained economic growth in developing countries has generated new product markets and skilled labor pools. American firms have increasingly turned overseas to reduce manufacturing costs and expand market size. However, foreign firms have also continued to increase their market share in numerous sectors of the American economy. This competitive pressure will induce American firms to reduce production and distribution costs through improved quality, productivity, and delivery systems.

The growth in international trade has driven further changes in the logistics organization. Many firms have expanded logistics to include an international branch responsible for all international movements of goods. Other firms have established freestanding international divisions with a specialized international logistics branch, frequently with overseas offices. Third parties have also attempted to fill the gap by offering specialized services (e.g., customs clearance, bonded warehousing, etc.), or in some instances, all-encompassing international logistics service.

Demographic Forces. Demographic shifts occurring during the past several decades have changed the nature of the American marketplace. The maturing of the baby-boom generation will reshape the economy in unknown ways; however, changes will most likely occur in housing and health care. Declining birthrates of the 1960s have shrunken the entry-level labor pool. Concern has focused on the quality of American education and its ability to provide the technologically sophisticated labor force needed in the modern workplace. The growth in two-income families has driven consumer demand and expectations regarding product quality, variety, and acceptable levels of customer service.

Logistics organizations have confronted these problems by leveraging other resources in place of human labor. Firms have attempted to substitute technology for labor. Automated warehouses, computerized order processing, and EDI are examples of logistics practices that reduce labor requirements. The quality movement and process improvements have reduced or eliminated inspection requirements, materials handling, and returns of defective items. Other firms have increased third-party use to avoid increased labor costs and to take advantage of their specialized work force and greater economies of scale.

Information and Communications. The explosive development of information and communications technology has had a pervasive effect on all aspects of modern life. The falling costs and increasing capabilities of these technologies have particularly benefited what have been traditionally information-intensive logistics processes. Logistics managers have been able to substitute inexpensive information investments for expensive logistics assets like inventory and transportation.

Profile of the Logistics Executive

A statistical portrait of the contemporary American logistics executive can be compiled from a series of detailed mail surveys conducted over the last 20 years. This research project, the Ohio State University Survey of Career Patterns in Logistics, has sampled the membership of the Council of Logistics Management. Respondents each year included executives at the organizational level of manager, director, or vice president in manufacturing and merchandising firms. All surveys were conducted anonymously to insure confidentiality and encourage candor in the responses.

Respondents were presented with a list of basic functions and asked whether each was considered part of the logistics organization's responsibility in their firm. Summary results are shown in Figure 2-1, which contrasts the findings of the 1985 and 1991 surveys.

As Figure 2-1 shows, most firms have integrated their warehousing, traffic, and inventory control functions into the logistics organization, and more recently most firms have included full responsibility for international distribution as well. On the other hand, a considerably smaller percentage of firms have integrated the purchasing function, and responsibility for such tasks as packaging, product planning, and demand forecasting remain outside the scope of the logistics organization in most firms. Note also, however, that the movement from 1985 to 1991 in each of these areas is toward broadening the scope of logistics to include these activities.

Although American firms use many different structural designs to operate their logistics organizations, most can be categorized as one of four basic types. One common form is a "centralized" design, where a logistics staff at corporate headquarters manages the logistics operation for the entire firm. Other firms operate with a "divisional" structure, where each division of the firm has its own logistics organization that operates independently of the logistics operations in the other divisions. A third common organizational type is the "combination," in which some logistics processes are managed centrally, while other functions are decentralized at the division level. Finally, logistics is organized in some firms as a "separate division" that provides logistics services to the product divisions of the firm and operates on a profit-and-loss basis on an equal footing with the other divisions.

Figure 2-2 portrays the percentage of firms that have reported using each of these four basic organizational types over the period from 1975 through 1991. In each case there is a certain amount of random sampling variation from year to year, and so a trend line is fitted to the annual data to reveal the long-term trend. The predominant organizational type is the combination, with about 40% of the firms using this form, and this percentage is relatively stable over time. The divisional form is also reasonably stable, with about 20% of all firms using this structure. The separate division organization is becoming more rare. While about 20% of firms used this type in the late 1970s, only around 10% show this organization over the last few years. On the other hand, the centralized form is clearly gaining in favor, with recent surveys showing 25% to 30% of all firms choosing this form.

Some specific demographic characteristics of the logistics executive are also worth noting. As can be seen in Figure 2-3, most of these executives are between 39 and 50 years of age, and the median age is 42. Although the vice presidents tend on average to be older and the managers tend to be younger, these differences are quite small.

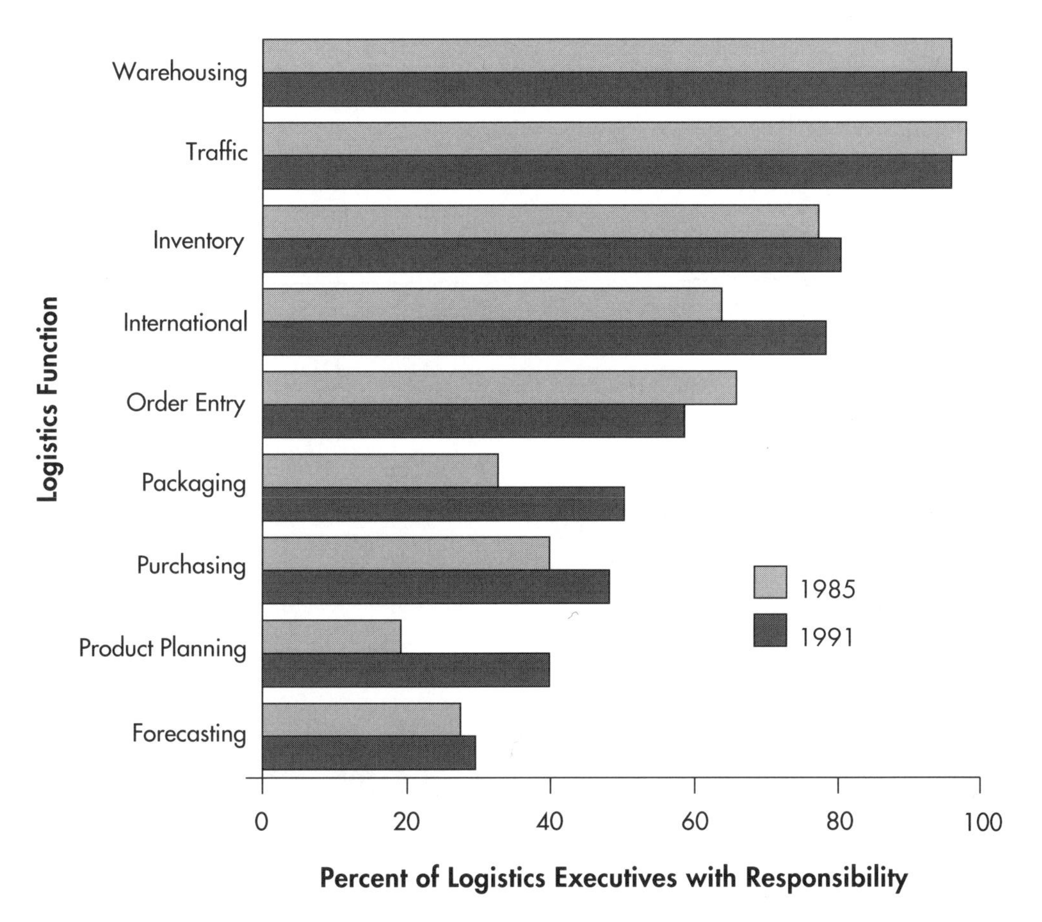

Figure 2-1
Scope of the Logistics Organization

Source: Adapted from the annual *Ohio State University Survey of Career Patterns in Logistics* studies with the permission of the Council of Logistics Management.

Logistics executives show a high level of formal education (see Figure 2-4). About 92% hold a bachelor's degree, while 41% have completed a graduate degree and 22% hold formal certification in the discipline. Some 52% of the bachelor's degrees are in business or management (see Figure 2-5), while 73% of the advanced degrees are in business (virtually all are MBAs).

A history of executive compensation is shown in Figure 2-6, where average annual salaries for managers, directors, and vice presidents are reported at five-year intervals from 1975 through 1990. In addition, the figures are adjusted for inflation by using the Consumer Price Index to express each salary in 1990 dollars. Manager compensation in real terms has been level over this period, in the range of $60,000 to $64,000. Director salaries show slight growth in the range of $80,000 to $84,000. Salaries for vice presidents have moved up and now average about $125,000.

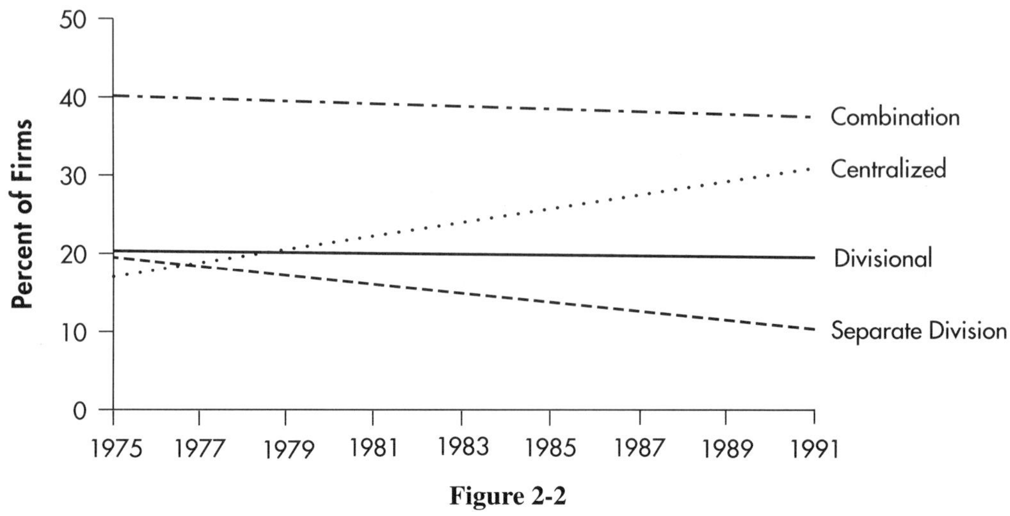

Figure 2-2
Trends in Organizational Types

Source: Adapted from the annual *Ohio State University Survey of Career Patterns in Logistics* studies with the permission of the Council of Logistics Management.

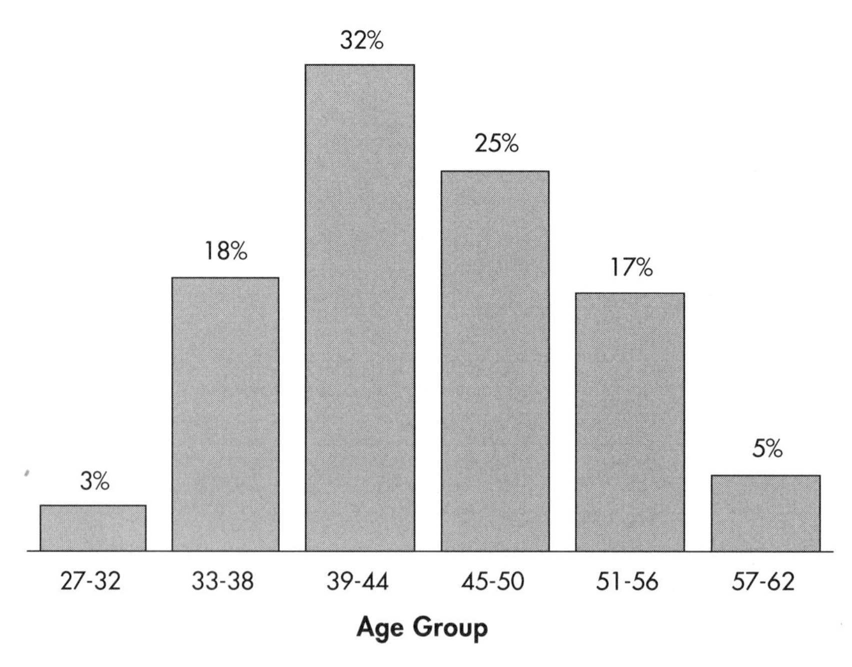

Figure 2-3
Age of Logistics Executives
(1991)

Source: Adapted from the annual *Ohio State University Survey of Career Patterns in Logistics* studies with the permission of the Council of Logistics Management.

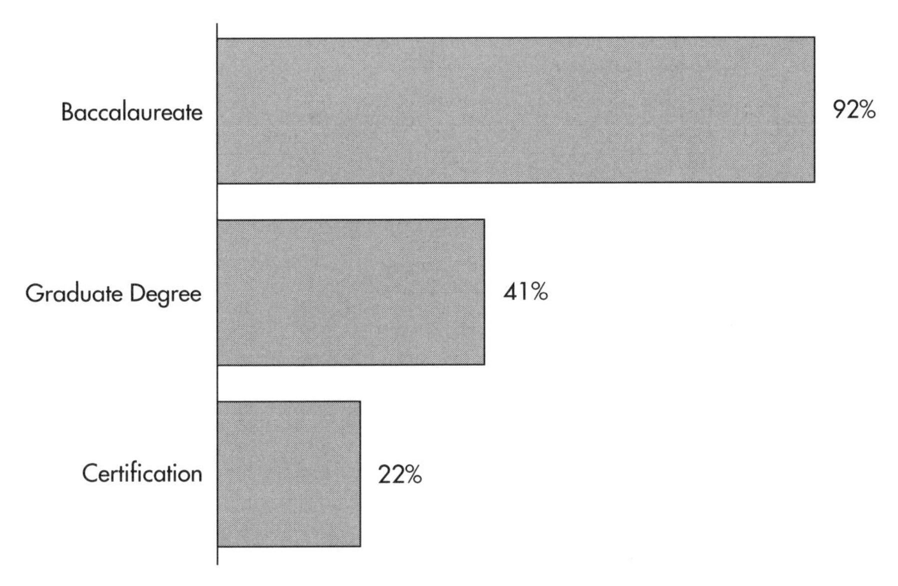

Figure 2-4
Formal Education of Logistics Executives
(1991)

Source: Adapted from the annual *Ohio State University Survey of Career Patterns in Logistics* studies with the permission of the Council of Logistics Management.

Change in the 1990s and Beyond

The integration of the logistics process during the past three decades has transformed the logistics organization from the "mob in the shipping room" supervised by "incompetents," as discussed by Peter Drucker in 1962, to a sophisticated management organization led by a senior executive at the vice presidential level.[82] The transformation has resulted from a variety of factors, but the principal driver has continually evolved around the notion of achieving a competitive advantage through logistics. The competitive advantage could take many forms, from lower costs and increased profitability to improved and differentiated customer service.

The logistics organization will undoubtedly continue to evolve and change. Forecasting the future remains difficult at best, especially in an area as dynamic and diverse as logistics. However, the evolution of logistics suggests that the pace of change will continue to accelerate during the 1990s, and that the changes will have a global impact. The ability of the logistics organization to adapt, to incorporate new technology, and to improve bottom-line performance ensures that it will remain in the forefront of business practice during the 1990s and beyond.

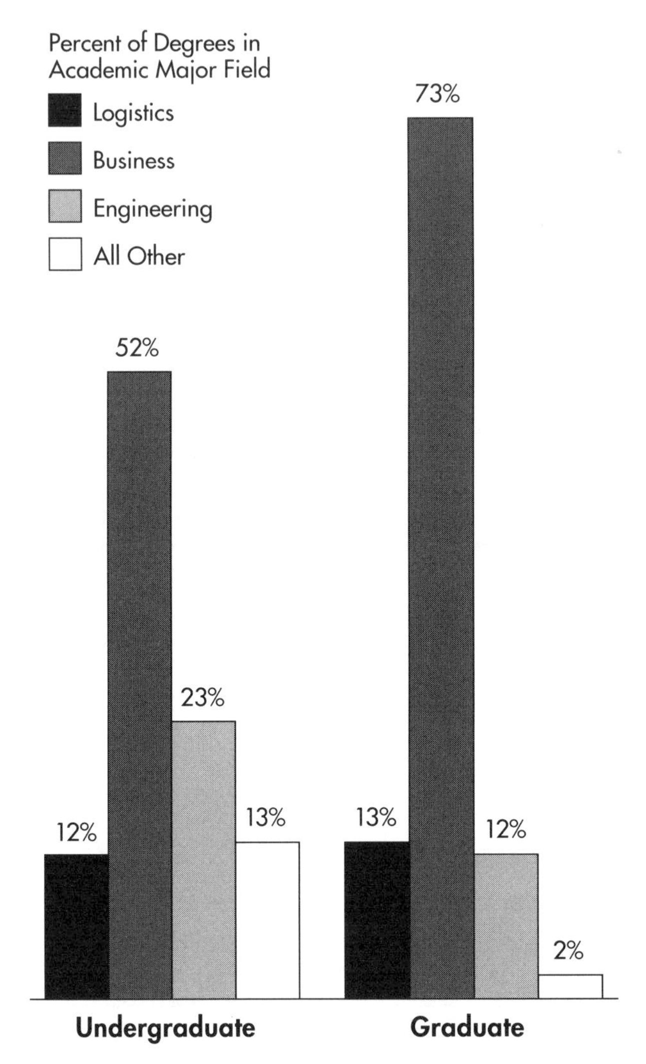

Figure 2-5
Education of the Logistics Executive
(1991)

Source: Adapted from the annual *Ohio State University Survey of Career Patterns in Logistics* studies with the permission of the Council of Logistics Management.

Figure 2-6
Average Annual Compensation for Logistics Executives

Source: Adapted from the annual *Ohio State University Survey of Career Patterns in Logistics Studies* with the permission of the Council of Logistics Management.

Notes

1. Harold E. Fearon, "Materials Management: A Synthesis and Current View," *Journal of Purchasing* 9, no. 1 (February 1973): 33.
2. H. J., Bullen, "The Growing Importance of Physical Distribution Management," *Management Review* (July 1965): 31.
3. "Marketing and Physical Distribution," *Marketing Forum* (October 1966): 16–20.
4. Peter F. Drucker, "The Economy's Dark Continent," *Fortune* (April 1962): 266.
5. Howard T. Lewis, James W Culliton, and Jack D. Steele, *The Role of Air Freight in Physical Distribution* (Boston: Harvard Business School, 1956).
6. Harvey N. Shycon and Richard B. Maffei, "Simulation—Tool for Better Distribution," *Harvard Business Review,* 38 (November–December 1960): 65–75.
7. Donald J. Bowersox, David J. Closs, and Omar K. Helferich, *Logistical Management* 3d ed., (New York: MacMillan Publishing Company, 1986): p. 6.

8. Joseph Orlicky, *Material Requirements Planning* (New York: McGraw-Hill, 1973): p. 21.
9. William D. Kirchner, "Physical Distribution: More Talk Than Action," *Handling and Shipping* (October 1971): 57.
10. Herbert W. Davis, "Organization and Management of the Logistics Function in Industry," *Logistics Spectrum* (Fall 1972): 11.
11. Bernard J. La Londe and Paul H. Zinszer, *Customer Service: Meaning and Measurement* (Chicago: National Council of Physical Distribution Management, 1976): 1.
12. Drucker, "The Economy's Dark Continent": p. 103.
13. La Londe: pp. 157–59.
14. La Londe: p. 159.
15. La Londe: p. 164.
16. A.T. Kearney, Inc., *Measuring Productivity in Physical Distribution* (Chicago: National Council of Physical Distribution Management, 1978): p. 28.
17. Ibid., p. 27.
18. Robert C. Montgomery, "Marketing and the Physical Distribution Concept: When Top Management Recognizes 'Frustration from Fragmentation,' It Is in Line for Effective Cost Control and Profit Improvement," *Physical Distribution,* Report No. 4, New York: Drake Sheahan/Stewart Dougall, 1969.
19. William D. Kirchner, "Physical Distribution: More Talk Than Action," *Handling and Shipping* (October 1971): 54–57.
20. Montgomery, "Marketing and the Physical Distribution Concept," p. 3.
21. J. D. Steel, "PDM—A Management Concept Not a Function," *Freight Management* (November 1972): 47–49.
22. George E. Evans, "The Distribution Manager and His Place in the Organization," *AMA Management Report #49,* American Management Association, 1960, p. 30.
23. Robert M. Sutton, "Upgrading the Isolated Man," *DS/SD Reports* (New York: Drake Sheahan/Stewart Dougall, June 1972): p. 1.
24. Michael R. Leenders, Harold E. Fearon, and Wilbur B. England, *Purchasing and Materials Management,* 7th ed. (Homewood, Ill.: Irwin, 1980): pp. 1–3.
25. James R. Stock and Douglas M. Lambert, *Strategic Logistics Management,* 2d ed. (Homewood: Irwin, 1987): p. 440.
26. H. G. Becker, "Physical Distribution Management: A View From the Top," *Handling & Shipping* (August 1967): 41.
27. Bernard J. La Londe, Douglas M. Lambert, and James R. Stock, "The PD Executive—An Emerging Professional," Draft Copy, May 1979, quoted in Robert C. Camp, Robert E. Bowles, Thys J. Van Hout, and Dale T. Wachner, *Educational Needs in Physical Distribution Management* (Oak Brook, Ill.: National Council of Physical Distribution Management, October 1979), p. 23.
28. E. J. Marien, *College and University Courses in Physical Distribution Management* (Oakwood, Ill.: National Council of Physical Distribution Management, 1978), quoted in Camp, et al., "The PD Executive," p. 20.
29. Stock and Lambert, *Strategic Logistics Management,* pp. 20–21.
30. Drucker, "The Economy's Dark Continent," p. 266.
31. "Who are Today's Decision-Makers in Physical Distribution?" *Handling & Shipping* (September 1964): 57.
32. Linda Lufkin, "Developments and Trends in the Traffic–Physical Distribution Profession," *Traffic Management* (January 1972): p. 51.

33. Bowersox, Closs, and Helferich, p. 11.
34. John J. Coyle, Edward J. Bardi, and Joseph L. Cavinato, *Transportation,* 3d ed. (St. Paul, Minn.: West Publishing Co., 1986), p. 128.
35. Bernard J. La Londe, James M. Masters, Arnold B. Maltz, and Lisa R. Williams, *The Evolution, Status, and Future of the Corporate Transportation Function,* American Society of Transportation and Logistics, 1991, p. 2.
36. Bernard J. La Londe and Martha Cooper, "Distribution Careers—1981," *Distribution* (November 1981): 61.
37. Bernard J. La Londe and Martha Cooper, "Career Patterns in Distribution: Profile 1981, *Proceedings of the Nineteenth Annual Conference of the National Council of Physical Distribution Management,* 1981, p. 17.
38. Graham Sharman, "The Rediscovery of Logistics," *Harvard Business Review* (September–October 1984): 72.
39. "Organizing Physical Distribution to Improve Bottom Line Results," *Proceedings of the Nineteenth Annual Conference of the National Council of Physical Distribution Management,* 1981, pp. 4–5. Also see *Measuring and Improving Productivity in Physical Distribution,* prepared by A.T. Kearney for the National Council of Physical Distribution Management (now the Council of Logistics Management), NCPDM, Oak Brook, Ill., 1984, p. 17.
40. Jack W. Farrell, "Distribution Departments Gain Ground," *Transportation* (September 1981): 45.
41. Figure does not include stage two and stage three firms.
42. Jack W. Farrell, "New Clout for Logistics," *Traffic Management* (September 1985): 37–43.
43. Jack W. Farrell, "Logistics: The Evolution Continues," *Traffic Management* (September 1987): 88–101.
44. Ronald E. Seger and William J. Best, "Integrated Logistics Management: The Trend Continues," A.T. Kearney Research Report, February 1986.
45. Lisa H. Harrington, "Integrated Logistics Management," *Traffic Management* (November 1987): 34.
46. *What It's All About* (Oak Brook, Ill.: Council of Logistics Management): pp. 3–4.
47. La Londe, et al., *Evolution, Status,* p. 22.
48. Bernard J. La Londe and Martha C. Cooper, *Partnerships in Providing Customer Service: A Third-Party Perspective* (Oak Brook, Ill.: Council of Logistics Management, 1989): p. 13.
49. La Londe, et al., *Evolution, Status,* pp. 20–21.
50. Ibid., pp. 22–23.
51. Robert C. Lieb, *The Use of Third Party Logistics Services by Large American Manufacturers,* Unpublished Report, Northeastern University, November 26, 1991, p. 1.
52. Yosef Sheffi, "Third Party Logistics: Present and Future Prospects," *Journal of Business Logistics* 2, no. 2 (1990): 28–29.
53. La Londe and Cooper, *Partnerships in Providing Customer Service,* pp. 110–13.
54. John F. Rockart and James E. Short, "IT in the 1990s: Managing Organizational Interdependence," *Sloan Management Review* (Winter 1989): 7–10.
55. Margaret A. Emmelhainz, "Electronic Data Interchange: A Tutorial," *Proceedings of the Council of Logistics Management* 2 (1989): 115.
56. James M. Masters, Greg M. Allenby, Bernard J. La Londe, and Arnold Maltz, "On the Adoption of DRP,"*Journal of Business Logistics* 13, no. 1 (1992): 47.
57. Richard J. Tersine, *Principles of Inventory and Materials Management* (New York: North Holland, 1988): p. 409.

58. Gary L. Frazier, Robert E. Spekman, and Charles R. O'Neal, "Just-in-Time Exchange Relationships in Industrial Markets," *Journal of Marketing* 52 (October 1988): p. 53.
59. Ibid., p. 54.
60. Bernard J. La Londe, "Distribution Careers: 1984," *Proceedings of the National Council of Physical Distribution Management* 1984, p. 6.
61. Bernard J. La Londe and Mary Margaret Weber, "Career Patterns in Logistics: Profile 1987," *Council of Logistics Management Annual Conference Proceedings,* 1987, p. 363.
62. James M. Masters and Bernard J. La Londe, "The 1989 Ohio State University Study of Career Patterns in Logistics," *Council of Logistics Management Annual Conference Proceedings,* 1989, p. 43.
63. Bernard J. La Londe, Martha C. Cooper, and Thomas G. Noordewier, *Customer Service: A Management Perspective* (Oak Brook, Ill.: Council of Logistics Management, 1988): p. 5.
64. Ibid., pp. 5–7.
65. Jack W. Farrell, "Logistics: the Evolution Continues," p. 88.
66. Bernard J. La Londe and Martha Cooper, "Career Patterns in Distribution: 1980," *Proceedings of the National Council of Physical Distribution Management,* 1980, p. 15.
67. La Londe and Weber, "Career Patterns," p. 357.
68. Masters and La Londe, "The 1989 Ohio State Study," pp. 15–47.
69. Martha C. Cooper, Daniel E. Innis, and Peter R. Dickson, *Strategic Planning for Logistics* (Oak Brook, Ill.: Council of Logistics Management, 1992): p. C22.
70. Masters and La Londe, "The 1989 Ohio State Study," p. 21.
71. Francis J. Quinn, "What It Takes to Get Ahead," *Traffic Management* (September 1989): 69.
72. George Stalk, Jr, and Thomas M. Hout, *Competing Against Time: How Time-Based Competition is Shaping Global Markets* (New York: Free Press, 1990): p. 27.
73. Jack W. Farrell, "Organization Trends—What Managers Foresee," *Traffic Management* (May 1981): 78–79.
74. C. John Langley, "The Evolution of the Logistics Concept," *Journal of Business Logistics* 7, no. 2 (1986): 9.
75. George Stalk, Jr., and Thomas M. Hout, *Competing Against Time: How Time-Based Competition is Shaping Global Markets* (New York: The Free Press, 1990), p. 31.
76. Patrick M. Byrne and William J. Markham, *Improving Quality and Productivity in the Logistics Process* (Oak Brook, Ill.: Council of Logistics Management, 1991): p. 8.
77. Lisa M. Ellram and Martha C. Cooper, "Supply Chain Management, Partnerships, and Shipper-Third Party Relationship," *International Journal of Logistics Management* 1, no. 2 (1990): 1.
78. John K. Shank and Vijay Govindarajan, "Strategic Cost Management and the Value Chain," *Journal of Cost Management* 5, no. 2 (Winter 1992): 5.
79. Ibid., p. 6.
80. Gene R. Tyndall, "Analyzing the Costs and Value of the Product Distribution Chain," *Journal of Cost Management* 2, no. 1 (Spring 1988): 45–51.
81. Bernard J. La Londe and James M. Masters, "Logistics: Perspectives for the 1990s," *International Journal of Logistics Management* 1, no. 1 (1990): 1–6.
82. Drucker, "The Economy's Dark Continent," p. 265.

CHAPTER 3

Logistics in the Decade of the 1990s

Martha C. Cooper

To help their companies survive and succeed in the twenty-first century, logistics managers need to continually analyze trends and their effects on their industries and companies.[1] This chapter looks to the future while examining the following questions:

- What are the key trends and issues for logistics in the 1990s?
- How should companies prepare for and take advantage of these changes?

Several trends and issues both external and internal to the firm are identified that affect logistics management in the 1990s. Although not exhaustive, this framework highlights trends and issues that logistics managers must address:

External

- globalization—economic and political change
- "Workforce 2000"—the changing nature of the work force
- technology
- environmental concerns

Internal

- a focus on customer service and quality
- the current state and future of logistics performance
- third-party networks
- supply chain management
- changes in management and organization style

There is the immediate need for logistics managers to anticipate, prepare for, and take advantage of the opportunities and threats posed by these changes. As a conclusion to the chapter, some propositions and suggestions are offered to assist the logistics manager in taking an active role in meeting these challenges.

Trends and Issues to Consider in the 1990s

The continuing changes in the world order are the harbingers of considerable change in logistics and corporate practice. The age, gender, culture, education, and values of the work force are changing both at home and abroad. Technological advances are exploding in communications, data processing, and data analysis that can improve the management capabilities of logistics managers. Public, government, and company concern for the environment affect logistics in both packaging and transportation of regular and hazardous goods.

In addition to factors outside the firm, several changes inside are also affecting logistics managers. Companies are discovering what logistics managers have always known—the focus of the firm must be on the customer, both current and potential. There are rising expectations for customer service from both customers and logistics managers. Firms have determined what activities they can shift outside because they have had to strip down to fight leveraged buyouts and takeover bids, as well as just compete in the marketplace. This contracting out, or outsourcing, has already had a major impact on many firms. Others will continue to review whether outsourcing is a viable alternative to such logistics activities as private fleets and warehousing. A matter that is both external and internal is supply chain management with the goal of creating a competitive supply chain in a world marketplace. Finally, as managements come and go, their individual styles and organizational preferences may affect how logistics is practiced within the firm.

External Trends and Issues

Many factors external to the firm are affecting logistics practice. The trends and issues discussed here are grouped under economic and political issues, the changing nature of the work force, technological advances, and environmental concerns.

GLOBALIZATION—ECONOMIC AND POLITICAL CHANGE

Although we speak many different languages, we are working ever more closely together, regardless of a product's origin, destination, or manufacturing location. Even if your firm focuses on the domestic market, failing to consider international competitors is no longer viable. Logistics managers are increasingly getting involved in nondomestic purchases and sales.

Regional Changes. There is growing regional, or multicountry, coordination of trade beyond traditional trade agreements. Regions preparing for closer cooperation include Canada-United States-Mexico, the Pacific Rim, and Europe. For example, as European market integration approached, more European countries wanted a share of the pie. In October 1991, the European Free Trade Agreement (EFTA) countries signed an agreement with the European Community (EC), bringing the EFTA countries closer to EC membership. This enlarges the already potential 350 million market of the EC and indicates at least the possibility of the eventual economic union of western Europe. Add to this the unification of former East and West Germany and the changes in former Soviet-bloc countries and this constitutes major political and economic changes by the year 2000, if not sooner.

What does this mean for logistics managers? First, if firms are not in Europe doing business by now, the market may be a tougher one to enter. Major U.S. firms, such as General Electric, Ford, 3M, and Procter and Gamble, have been operating in Europe for decades, and some, such as NCR, for a century. Many of these established firms have already reconfigured their production and logistics networks to take advantage of present and expected relaxation in border-crossing requirements and more consistent regulations. Mearsk has already begun transcontinental railroad operation between Italy and Denmark with high-speed container trains.

Logistics managers should identify regional changes so that impacts on the business can be evaluated and strategies or tactics planned. For the EC, an evaluation framework might start with a simple overview of selected changes:

EC Integration Benefits

- Faster service across borders
- Production economies of scale
- Lower cost to distribute across borders
- Reduced price differentials among countries
- More common standards for vehicles

EC Integration Concerns

- Shakeup in the marketplace
- Potential protectionism of some products
- Barriers to entry for outside firms[2]

Continental and Hemispheric Economies. How will the globalization process occur? Will we go straight from national economies to a global economy? Of course, this depends on how a global economy is defined. In terms of basic goods movement, we may already be there. In terms of more closely related economies, then perhaps a growth pattern will occur moving from regional to continental to hemispheric, and, finally, global economic integration.

The EC is one bold start, now connected with EFTA, and soon probably some of the former Soviet-bloc eastern European countries. The EC's recent vote for adopting the common monetary standard, the ECU, moves Europe toward a more common economy. The U.S.-Canada trade agreement, to be followed by a Mexico-U.S.-Canada trade agreement, moves North America toward a more common economy too. Of course, the process may not always take place through formal, political agreements.

The Pacific Rim economies continue to grow as Hong Kong, Japan, Korea, and Singapore are leading traders, with others rapidly developing. Many Asian countries view their transportation systems as based on water. The Asian hemispheric economy will most probably be connected by water. Japan will reportedly test a 50-knot container ship shortly that, when introduced, will speed water transportation within regions or between continents.

> Many see an intra-Asia (all the way through Russia) market and economic system. This is similar to the expected Canada-U.S.-Mexico trading area. There will be hemisphere economies before there are global ones.[3]

Global Competition. Global competition can no longer be ignored. Firms and countries are spending large amounts of capital to be in the global competitive arena. Those making the investment are in for the long term and have a higher probability of survival. For example, Hong Kong is updating three ports at a cost of billions of dollars. Large logistics services companies, such as Sealand, Mitsui, Maersk, and TNT, are all making moves to connect the world.

Those concentrating on domestic or even small-niche markets, by product line or geography, cannot ignore global competition. Their raw materials may come from international trade. Their next competitor may be from a different hemisphere. The niche marketer must carefully construct a marketing strategy that continues to serve customers very well at the best possible cost, or someone else will.

> Even niche marketers have to take an international perspective to survive.[4]
>
> The Global economy only works if there is an infrastructure of good operating logistics systems. Many firms who believe this are spending billions of dollars on the future, assuming a global economy.[5]

Communications and Regulations. Another factor facilitating globalization is the efforts to agree on common standards for information transmission, and to reduce conflicting regulations. Adoption of the harmonized code has already been useful in transportation. Whereas once there were many different coding systems for goods movement, now a single four- or six-digit code can carry much information and is useful across carriers, freight forwarders, shippers, and consignees. A common electronic data interchange standard seems much further away, but the United Nations code is an attempt to move in that direction. Common means of communication will facilitate better logistics service and management.

The agreements among EC members to eliminate conflicting regulations is particularly helpful to logistics managers in charge of goods movement. Examples include working toward common standards for vehicle manufacturing, single forms for border crossings, and changes in cabotage regulations for goods pickup in a nonorigin or nondestination country. Similar moves among other trading partners will help move toward a global economy.

Global Market-Driven Economies. As barriers to trade are reduced within and among countries, customer satisfaction becomes paramount. Constraints will not be caused as much by production, raw materials, or distance as by what the customer wants. Some suggest that the next "era" in business will be true global marketing, which we have not seen except for the isolated examples of certain multinational firms and the Japanese approach.

Marketing programs need good logistics programs to support them. A customer orientation requires effective transportation, inventory, and information management to be responsive to customer needs.

> We are going to go back to where we thought we were in the 1960s, to a market-driven society. We have global banking, finance, and manufacturing, but not global marketing.[6]

"Workforce 2000"

A major responsibility of logistics managers is the supervision and motivation of their personnel in warehouse, transportation, and customer service roles. These pools of people are becoming more diverse and have different needs. Reasons for taking particular jobs are often not strictly economic. The U.S. work force is estimated to be 44% white male. The traditional majority is dwindling with the increasing entrance of diverse minorities. Being able to work with a wide range of people is an important skill for logistics managers.

Diversity. The working population differs on several dimensions, including age, gender, culture, education, and values.[7] These same issues are addressed in other parts of the world that experience expatriates or commonwealth members shifting among countries to find work. Although diversity is a challenge, it can also provide opportunities for part-time employees to balance work loads from a pool that includes college students, spouses, and older, possibly retired persons, whose expertise can benefit the company.

Individual Needs. Two-income families bring special needs and relocation constraints. Companies are moving to spousal relocation programs and consideration of a spouse in relocation decisions. Singles may prefer different benefit packages than married couples. Matching the company's and the individual's values is becoming a more common technique to retain productive employees.

Downsizing. Downsizing is nearly a worldwide phenomenon, according to a survey of 12,000 managers around the world.[8] As firms downsize, the dislocation of people will be substantial and wages may decline. For example, an auto manufacturer may permanently eliminate a $30-per-hour job and the affected employee might take a $15-per-hour newly created position in the service industry. There will be a wealth of experience on the market. In Europe the problem may not be so much the cost of firing, because of union agreements, but rather inflexibility in reallocating human resources. Former communist countries are experiencing similar problems as they move from full-employment guarantees to market-economy competition. One concern of logistics managers has been the lack of skilled employees for logistics tasks. The reductions in work forces for some firms may help alleviate the shortages for others.

Technology

Technology has been a boon to the information-intensive aspects of logistics, such as materials management, electronic data interchange, barcoding, and decision support. Handling-intensive aspects have also been helped by technology. Transactions occur faster with fewer mistakes as technology helps support minimum inventory systems like JIT and Quick Response. The importance of technology in logistics will probably continue to increase in the 1990s.

Communications. Electronic data interchange (EDI), teleconferencing, and voice mail systems reduce the cycle time in communication. Simple things like eliminating time spent on "telephone tag" can boost productivity; the ability to leave detailed messages in one's own voice, any time day or night, facilitates communication while traveling, in different time zones, or after hours. The ability to track shipments around the world and to divert those in transit is possible only through linked communication systems.

Figure 3-1 indicates substantial increases in the use of EDI. Respondents were asked in 1990 to think back to 1988 and indicate how much change had already occurred, then project future usage. On average, the amount of customer orders received via EDI had tripled in two years, from 5% to 15%. Another tripling of usage was projected over the next five years, so that we can expect nearly half of all orders to be received via EDI. A similar pattern occurs for purchase orders placed with vendors, but the trends and projections are lower.

Physical Handling. Barcoding and materials handling technologies are being used for more efficient distribution center and inventory management. Automatic guided vehicles, stacker cranes, and information-driven conveyor systems continue to improve and to be more highly integrated. As shown in Figure 3-2, the number of firms not using barcoding decreased by almost one-third between 1988 and 1990, and only about one-fifth of responding firms did not expect to be using barcoding by 1995.[9]

The upper tenth percentile of responses was examined for additional understanding. Those

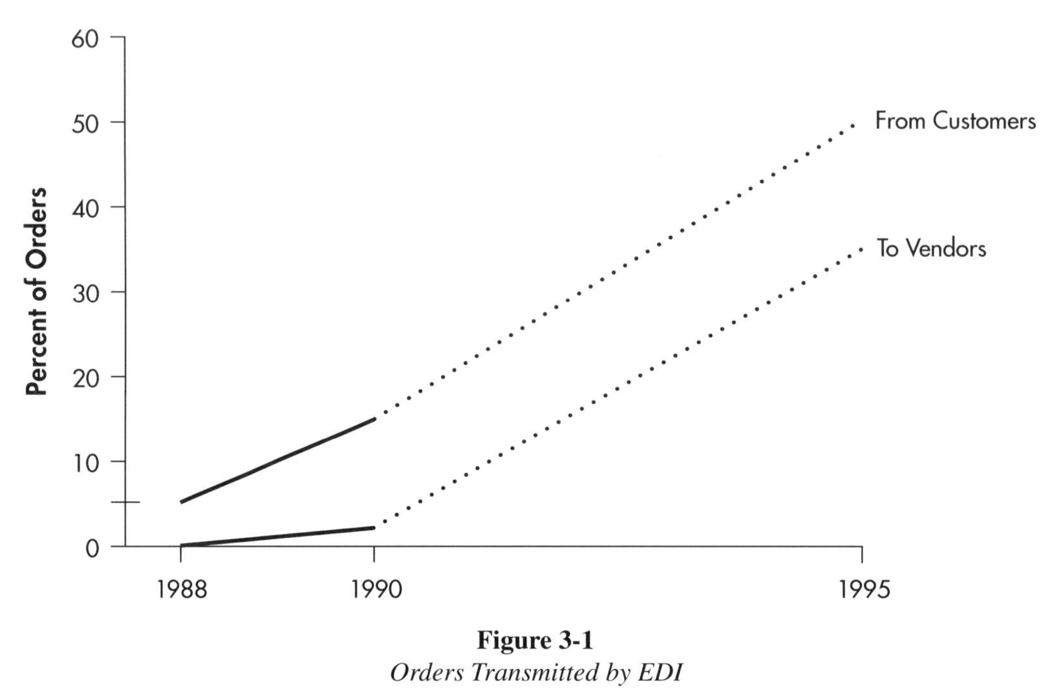

Figure 3-1
Orders Transmitted by EDI

Source: Adapted from Martha C. Cooper, Daniel E. Innis, and Peter R. Dickson, *Strategic Planning for Logistics* (Oak Brook, Ill.: Council of Logistics Management, 1992).

firms using barcoding are doing so in a significant way. Figure 3-3 contains the median and upper tenth (ninetieth) percentile responses for inbound merchandise that is barcoded in a format that the company can use. The barcoding practices of foreign and domestic vendors were questioned separately. The median, or middle, response was zero in both 1988 and 1990 for foreign vendors. Domestic barcoding was 10% in 1990 and expected to rise to 50% by 1995. However, the ninetieth percentile responses were at or close to the 100% mark for both 1990 and 1995. Those companies that have embraced barcoding are doing so for almost all the merchandise passing through their systems. Upward trends were also observed for outbound barcoding and warehouse automation.

Substituting Information for Inventory. The cost of information has been declining relative to other expenses, such as land, labor, and capital. Thus, it is more efficient to use information, wherever possible, in lieu of more expensive assets.[10] Finished goods inventory is not produced or deployed with large safety stock quantities if the information system is comprehensive and responsive. Cutting the order lead time allows greater transit time that, in turn, permits stocking items further away while maintaining customer service delivery time targets. The number of transshipments is reduced with better decisions on stocking locations and quantities.

Combining Technologies. The real payoff of technology in the future will result from combining technologies. Companies are already integrating barcoding, EDI, scanner data, and advanced materials handling equipment to make their systems more effective. Software continues to be developed for interfacing warehouses to carriers, in addition to customers and shippers. It is possible to transfer store-level scanner sales data to suppliers for inventory forecasting and

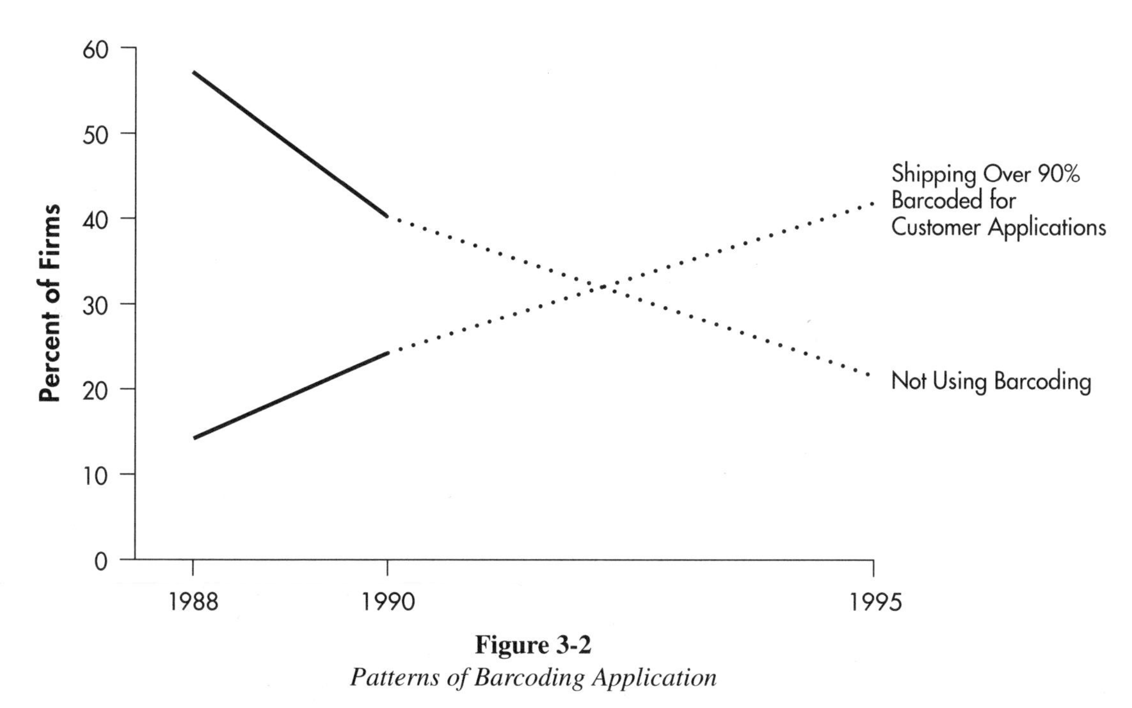

Figure 3-2
Patterns of Barcoding Application

Source: Adapted from Martha C. Cooper, Daniel E. Innis, and Peter R. Dickson, *Strategic Planning for Logistics* (Oak Brook, Ill.: Council of Logistics Management, 1992).

automated, demand-driven ordering for store shelf restocking. With barcoded stock in the warehouse and information systems containing stock locations and product date codes, products can be quickly picked, packed, and shipped. The information systems for ordering, distribution center operations, accounting, and transportation can be linked together. Partners up and down the supply chain can also be connected. A totally integrated system is still on the horizon for most companies because pockets of unconnected information systems remain.

Environmental Concerns

Logistics activities are in the middle of many environmental issues. Transportation of hazardous goods is an obvious concern. Packaging is another. The concern about products being "green" from cradle to grave also involves logistics. Recycling has, to some extent, already been generally adopted. For example, recycling has been implemented particularly well in the soft drink bottling industry, as recently developed routing algorithms consider both pickups and deliveries allowing the collection of empty containers for reuse.

Green Packaging and Products. The European Community and Canada have been particularly active in legislation in response to public concern for the environment. Germany and Japan, among others are taking steps in recycling, emissions control, and environmental concerns affecting logistics.

The environmental impact of a company's actions is becoming more important. Some companies are requiring a section in the strategic plan of each function to state how the function plans to respond to environmental issues relevant to its operations.

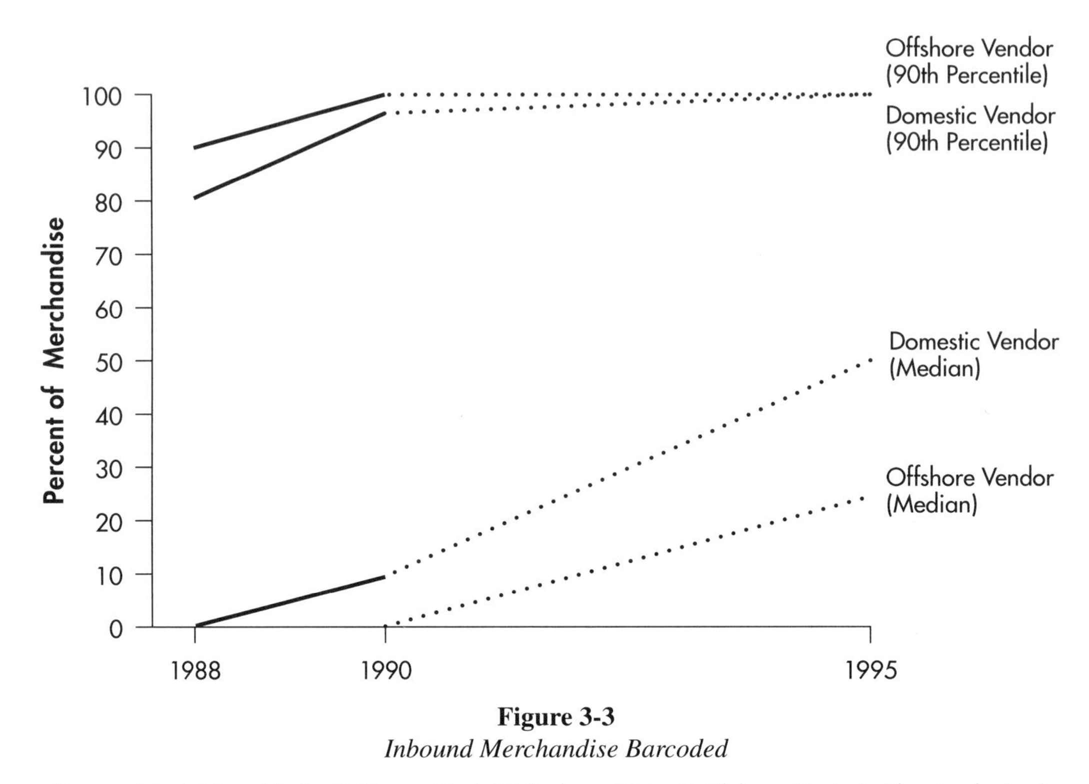

Figure 3-3
Inbound Merchandise Barcoded

Source: Adapted from Martha C. Cooper, Daniel E. Innis, and Peter R. Dickson, *Strategic Planning for Logistics* (Oak Brook, Ill.: Council of Logistics Management, 1992).

Hazardous Waste Movement and Disposal. A vast and intricate web of regulations and restrictions is being woven by federal, state, and local governments. Companies are seeking ways to ensure awareness of and compliance with increasing and changing regulations across many divisions and locations. One chemical company devotes an expert to studying what is occurring so that its employees have a reliable and current source of information. The company's many dispatchers and others involved in goods movement do not have the time or resources to follow the changes in regulations. Additionally, this company is taking a lead in bringing government and industry together to reconcile inconsistent laws and to improve the environment.

Internal Trends and Issues

Internal trends and issues include the firm's relationships with customers, suppliers, and the broader supply chain, as well as the effects of organization and management styles.

Customer Service/Quality Focus

The buzzword of the late 1980s was "customer service." As products become standardized, customer service achieves greater importance as a competitive, differentiating marketing tool as well as an expected product attribute. As cultural and national barriers break down, requirements for customer service become more consistent and more stringent.

Increasing Performance Expectations. Hardly anyone in recent surveys has expected any slackening of customer service performance standards. Virtually all the case study firms in The Ohio State University surveys expect customer service requirements to tighten. Indeed, as the Walmarts of the world become more knowledgeable about logistics, the standards tighten considerably. These enterprises would like suppliers to manage inventory to the individual store shelf level in many cases. In these cases, the burden of monitoring inventory and replenishment shifts to the supplier. Some customers share the burden of inventory with suppliers, such as sharing costs of component parts rather than finished goods. These strategies are being used not only by Walmart and its discount retail competitors like K-Mart and Target but also by other next-to-final-consumer firms like drug stores, grocery stores, convenience marts, department stores, and specialty retailers, to name a few.

Companies are putting tighter constraints on themselves by defining customer service factors more specifically, such as defining fill rate as orders shipped complete rather than simply shipped, albeit partially. Combining customer service measures also makes reaching target service levels more difficult. Reaching high levels of order completeness and on-time delivery as separate measures is easier than reaching the same level on a combined measure of fill rate and delivery.

Figures 3-4 and 3-5 reinforce the perceived tightening of customer service windows. Inventory turnover at corporate and public warehouses had increased by about one turn from 1988 to 1990 for survey respondents. These turn rates, along with contract warehouse turn rates, are expected to increase dramatically by 1995. Cycle time had decreased by one-fifth (one day) from 1988 to 1990 and is expected to decrease another day by 1995, to three days. A day of transit time is expected to be wrung out of the system over the same period.

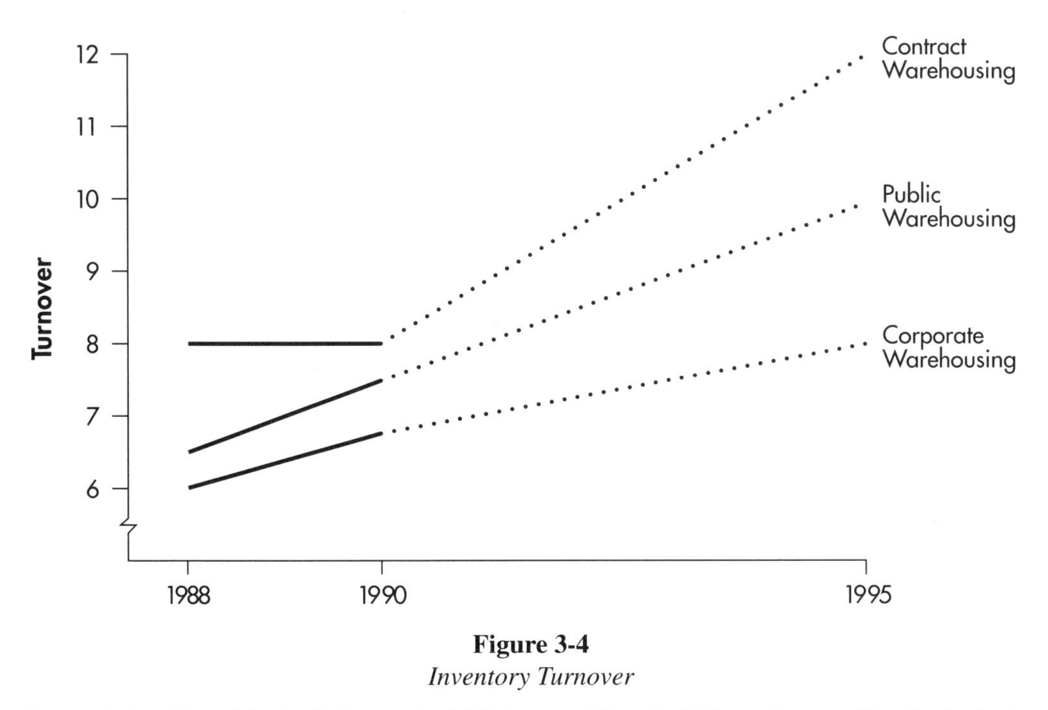

Figure 3-4
Inventory Turnover

Source: Adapted from Martha C. Cooper, Daniel E. Innis, and Peter R. Dickson, *Strategic Planning for Logistics* (Oak Brook, Ill.: Council of Logistics Management, 1992).

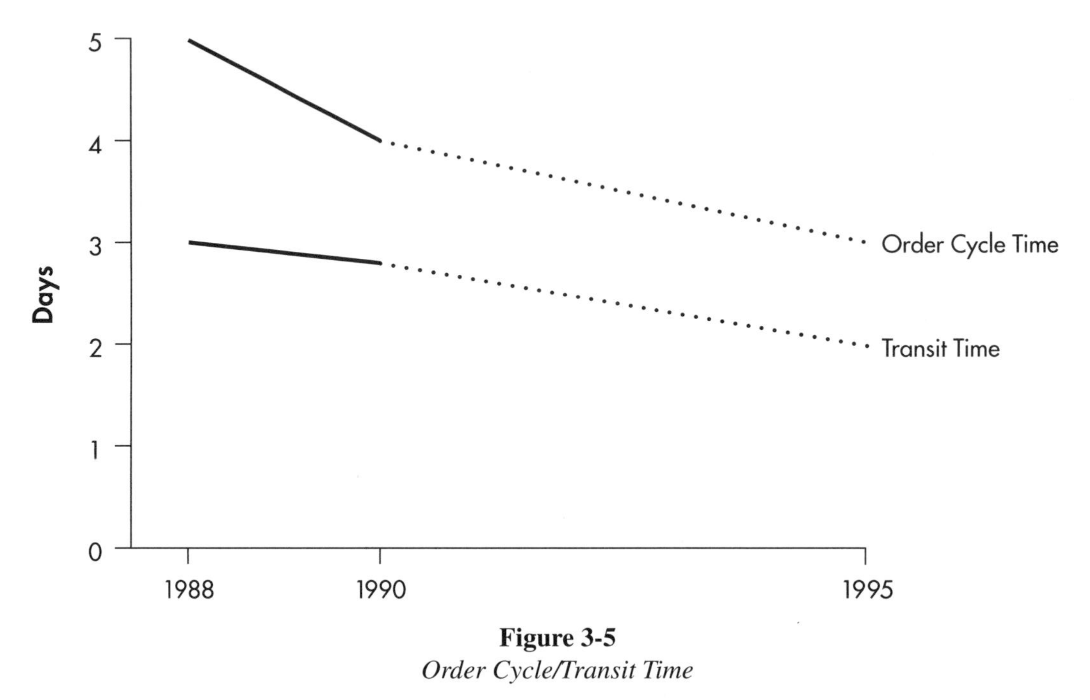

Figure 3-5
Order Cycle/Transit Time

Source: Adapted from Martha C. Cooper, Daniel E. Innis, and Peter R. Dickson, *Strategic Planning for Logistics* (Oak Brook, Ill.: Council of Logistics Management, 1992).

The transit time of an overseas shipment is no longer an acceptable excuse for missing service targets. Global competition allows firms to find suppliers closer as well as overseas. Faster transportation or strategic placement of inventories may be required to meet target service levels, regardless of the goods' origin. Methods to shorten order cycle time are needed to remain competitive. Breakdowns of regional barriers facilitate faster movement, but again, remove excuses for poor performance. For example, EXEL Logistics provides one week ground delivery from London to Moscow for Pizza Hut.

ISO-9000 and Other Worldwide Standards. The International Standards Organization (ISO) is applying the concept of quality to business processes in the same manner as it has been applied to products. The ISO is working in Europe to establish certification standards for company efforts to improve their business processes. Consistent standards for business practices is consistent with efforts within the EC to level the playing field by specifying standards by product and service. Some suggest that this certification may become a requirement for doing business with many firms in the EC.

Official and unofficial quality standards and process initiatives are becoming more common. The criteria for evaluating firms for the Malcolm Baldridge National Quality Award in the United States and a similar award in Japan are not only needed to win the honor but also are being used privately to improve internal operations and sometimes mandated by customers to qualify as a vendor. Delivering a product on time and according to customer specifications is fast becoming "merely adequate"; the way in which that process occurs is becoming subject to specifications and standards.

Total Quality Management (TQM). Many believe that the terms *quality* and *customer service* cannot be separated. That is, high customer service levels imply high quality in service delivery. Several case study firms indicated that the team approach and total quality management programs had helped integrate the functions of their firms and solved complex, interdisciplinary problems.

TQM is being applied to logistics as firms try to determine the cost of nonperformance on customer service. Some are finding that the cost of even a few out-of-stock situations is not only lost sales but potentially a lost channel customer.

Customer Service Segmentation. As customer service becomes more of a competitive weapon, companies are offering differentiated service packages for various markets. And because of the different offerings, customer service requirements themselves have become a basis for industrial market segmentation. For example, different levels of sensitivity to delivery service prompted the overnight package business. Different service factors, such as speed and consistency of service, may be important to different groups.[11] In the United States, offerings must be varied within the constraints of the Robinson-Pattman Act. However, differences in cost and price justify offers of different service options and packages to separate market segments.

Time-Based Competition. As time-based competition increases, the need to meet ever-tighter service requirements also increases. Figure 3-6 suggests that companies are shipping and receiving more goods on a just-in-time basis. The percentage of tonnage received just in time doubled from 1988 to 1990. This trend is expected to continue almost linearly through 1995, when one-quarter of goods are expected to be received just in time. The importance of time-based competition is confirmed by a similar pattern for product shipped to customers just in time.

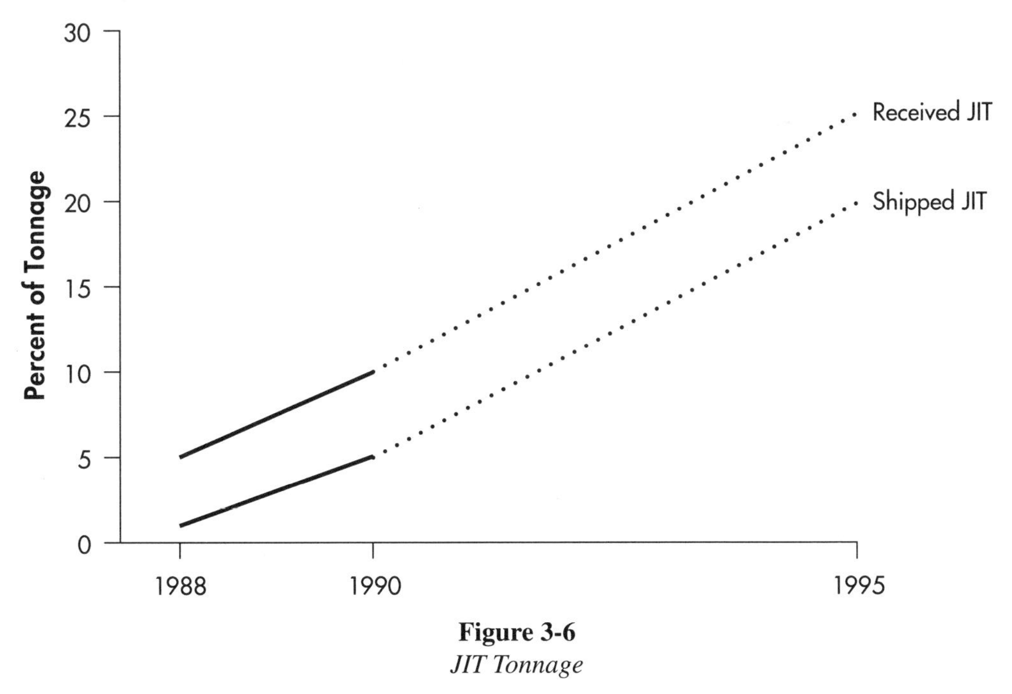

Figure 3-6
JIT Tonnage

Source: Adapted from Martha C. Cooper, Daniel E. Innis, and Peter R. Dickson, *Strategic Planning for Logistics* (Oak Brook, Ill.: Council of Logistics Management, 1992).

Managing Across Organizations

The need to manage global sourcing, production, and distribution networks and to deliver high-quality customer service suggests possible changes to relationships within the distribution channel. Supply chain management involves close coordination. Functions may be outsourced or internally "spun off" to compete under the same requirements of other vendors (and sometimes even seek external customers to augment revenues and justify existence). Many relationships are developing into partnerships.

Supply Chain Management. Supply chain management is a concept sometimes shrouded in complex jargon, but it is very much what the individual words imply: supervising all the steps of a product's movement, regardless of corporate, political, or geographic boundaries, from raw material supply through final delivery to ultimate user to satisfy a particular customer group. It is an integrative philosophy to manage the total flow of distribution.[12] Supply chain management suggests a channel focus across channel members rather than a traditional, endemic, individual company focus.

Originally, supply chain management was discussed in a logistics context of inventory management throughout the channel. The intent was to manage the inventories as efficiently and effectively as possible. This implied that each channel member should not necessarily hold redundant inventories, and that less inventory could be spread over the channel with emergency situations considered, such as regional deployment rather than individual wholesaler or retailer deployment of some products.

This original concept now has broadened into the general integration of functions throughout the supply chain. This involves more than just inventory deployment and the information systems to connect chain members. This means managing the whole chain almost as if it were one entity. Decisions regarding various functions, like production, distribution, and marketing may be viewed across the entire chain rather than from each individual member's perspective. There are joint task forces across companies to address specific concerns, such as order cycle time and new product development.[13]

Outsourcing to Third Parties. Third-party logistics service companies have probably existed as long as there has been trade but perhaps less prolifically and under less glamorous labels. With high interest rates and intense efforts to reduce inventories during the 1970s and 1980s, a significant shift toward third-party logistics service providers occurred. Businesses deciding to concentrate on their core competencies or capacities continued to fuel this trend. Among others, general management guru Peter Drucker sees this trend continuing.[14] Basic services provided by third parties include transportation, warehousing, and light manufacturing, as well as specialized services, such as freight forwarding.

Depending on economies of scale and management preferences, logistics services have been provided in-house or outsourced. Some companies compare outsourcing costs with private carriage or warehouse costs as one means of measuring the efficiency of in-house operations. In one case study firm, every function was benchmarked against the cost of outsourcing as a measure of efficiency and what costs could or should be. If companies pursue such a practice, care should be taken to include not only all the relevant, direct, discrete, and identifiable costs but also less tangible costs that apply to the functions that a firm may otherwise relinquish, such as convenience and control. There are both advantages and disadvantages to outsourcing.[15]

Strategic Alliances and Partnerships. The number of suppliers and third-party providers with which a firm interacts is generally decreasing, by factors of five or more for some firms. This permits more attention to each relationship to work on mutual efficiencies. The kinds of relationships with suppliers and third-party providers can be viewed on a continuum from a one-time, or transactional, approach to viewing the relationship from a long-term perspective. Most logistics executives interviewed were moving toward the long-term perspective, consolidating to a group of key suppliers and third-party providers.

The basic concept behind partnerships is that working together will bring greater efficiencies and benefits for each party, on balance. A sports team practices together for better performance; constantly switching the lineup prevents team members from developing familiarity, resulting in poor overall team performance. Partnerships replace the focus on image and the transactional sales process with a focus on substance and the true, ultimate task at hand.

The literature about strategic alliances, partnerships, and transaction cost analyses suggests several different dimensions to these relationships. In a logistics context these have been grouped together along the following dimensions:

- *Extendedness.* The investment necessary in time, personnel, and equipment to establish an interface among channel members cannot be returned over a short period in most cases. Thus, members usually enter into contracts or have an understanding of a long-term relationship if they are involved in a partnership relationship.
- *Operational Information Exchange.* Information systems must be connected, which means having compatible equipment and software.
- *Operating Controls.* Channel members want to monitor other members' information systems to be aware of product flows and any potential supply problems.
- *Sharing of Benefits and Burdens.* There is an expectation that both benefits and burdens will be shared by channel members. If only the channel captain, or the strongest one in the channel, reaps the rewards, the other members will be constantly looking for alternative relationships. Certainly, the relationships should be reviewed periodically against other alternatives, but without sharing of benefits and burdens, the ties will be particularly tenuous and uncomfortable.
- *Planning.* Considerable planning is needed to integrate the members of the supply chain, or two partners.
- *Compatible Corporate Cultures (Trust).* Finally, there is a chemistry between partners and/or among supply chain members. Corporate cultures should be compatible among the parties involved for the partnership to work.[16]

A partnership arrangement may include some joint ventures, perhaps with ownership in each other or in a third enterprise. The U.S. government discourages close ties between the government and business. However, there are advantages to be gained by joint ventures with governments, and such partnerships are common in Asia, involving governments and banks, as well as partnerships among companies.

Organization Structure

Discussions with logistics executives indicate that the position logistics occupies within a firm relates to the organizational structure in place, the management style of top officers, and the efforts of individual logistics champions. The structure of logistics activities may change with increased outsourcing and as top management reassesses how best to manage the supply chain.

Size. A probable future influence on logistics is the relative size of firms. During the late 1960s and early 1970s companies were intent on expansion through merger and acquisition, sometimes regardless of the kind of business involved. The term *conglomerate* became fashionable. Economic theory suggests that when functions can be performed more efficiently in-house, firms will enlarge and perform those functions themselves.

The emphasis during the 1980s and 1990s is to concentrate on core business functions, hence outsourcing. Core focus has also been applied to companies reviewing their constituent parts and streamlining the number of businesses in which they participate. One of the more notable examples was Kinder Kare's divesting itself of its oil drilling business.

Restructuring of companies has been pervasive in the past few years.[17] The trend has been to streamline middle management, a prediction made in the 1960s by information systems specialists who felt that better computing power and information exchange would reduce the need for middle managers who accumulated and analyzed information. A reduction in the number of middle-management layers should also be expected.[18] What is left of middle management will use technology and models to manage what required many employees until only recently. To the extent that logistics activities are outsourced, the logistics function that remains may be one of analysis and management of relationships with other internal functions and with the third parties.

> Companies in business in ten years will be part of international federations of companies. They will buy, produce, and sell worldwide either by themselves or in partnership with others.[19]

The size of logistics services providers is coming to be known. Concentration in the market is evidenced by the presence of mega-carriers and services providers who intend to compete on a worldwide, full-service basis. They are acquiring smaller warehouse companies and carriers. There will still be room for the niche players providing specialized services, but these smaller firms may also connect to the larger providers, as feeder airlines have done in the travel industry. Huge logistics companies with local feeders are likely.[20]

Centralized Logistics Staff. There appear to be cycles in the organizational structure of firms and in management style. The case study firms for a strategic planning study were both centralized and decentralized in their management approaches, and these had changed over time. If we judge by these firms, we note there appears to be a trend toward having a corporate-level logistics staff, as there are corporate marketing and manufacturing staffs.

An opinion occasionally expressed is that logistics is really a marketing function. Although some specialization may exist, where should it be located? As one case study participant stated, "Logistics is a marketing function and its performance should be in that direction."

However, centralization puts logistics in a position to have input into the strategic planning process, and not all warehousing, materials management, and transportation activities are obviously marketing-oriented. The operational aspects of logistics activities tend to be located away from corporate headquarters at plants or customer service centers for the case study companies. "Out of sight, out of mind" has traditionally applied to logistics. But with the performance of logistics functions becoming critical to success, this isolation and relegation to a lower status may require rethinking the organizational structure.

With the moves toward process management and a concentration on the team approach and task forces to address particular problems, the walls between functions are crumbling. Specialized activities involved in manufacturing, marketing, and logistics must still be performed, and thus the walls may never come down completely. Others suggest that many of these activities will be mechanized and computerized, and there will be less need for managers in the old functional areas. Instead, management will concentrate on specific problems facing the firm that need further study.

> The functional concept doesn't make sense. Everyone has a telephone and a PC. This implies a different type of organization which is not paper-based. The span of control theory is no longer as viable since each manager can control much more, better.[21]
>
> There will still be logistics people in firms to either do or buy logistics services.[22]

Success in the 1990s and Survival Beyond

The manner in which logistics managers address the current and forthcoming changes will help determine the success of their companies in the 1990s and the prospects for survival into the next century. Ignoring the changes will, of course, lead to disaster. Embracing continual change as an ever-present fact is critical. At the very least, logistics managers must be able to recognize and react to these changes; better still, logistics managers should anticipate the changes with proactive responses.

Implications of the Issues and Trends

The issues and trends reviewed indicate some of the potential responses by companies and their logistics functions to the anticipated changes for business. The results of a stream of research suggest that flexibility and organizational change are keys not only to success but also to survival.

FLEXIBILITY

One executive refers to strategic planning as managing change. Of course, a rapidly changing world and marketplace requires the flexibility to take advantage of new opportunities.

More Challenges. Survey results indicate that logistics executives feel competition will be stronger, requiring more consistent and faster service—in short, working close to the customer to meet or exceed the customer's requirements. After earlier surveys, it was thought that perhaps some logistics managers were unnecessarily bringing the tighter constraints on themselves by expecting tighter service standards to occur. Conversations with many logistics executives suggest that indeed the customer is driving the process in many industries and that logistics must constantly and actively explore ways of improving customer service.

The make or buy issue of logistics services will continue. As managers contemplate core competencies versus the cost and control considerations of having supporting operations in-house, outsourcing will fall in and out of favor as a strategic alternative.

Some Relief. The pressure on logistics functions is tremendous. However, the ability to shorten order cycles and to provide the customer with information about orders and shipments is receiving help from such catalysts as common standards and improved technology. The efforts to achieve common standards on even a regional basis, such as those the Economic Community is pursuing, will assist logistics. Combining technology advances in materials handling and information permit faster, more accurate service delivery systems.

Organizational Change

A tough but necessary task is to anticipate the kinds of logistics networks and company relationships that will exist at the end of the 1990s. Closer relationships with fewer suppliers of goods and logistics services has been a recurring theme throughout recent studies. This suggests fewer, larger organizations or fewer systems consisting of central organizations with subsidiaries or affiliates.

Global Networks. Many companies are moving into the competitive arena of the global marketplace, where logistics managers must think globally. While one strategy is to treat all markets the same, the more common strategy is to adapt to local customs in terms of logistics services as well as products. For example, even a common mail system, regular or overnight, may require some adaptations in different parts of the world, including mode of transportation and use of subcontractors.

Specialized Networks. The approach taken by many companies and third-party providers is to concentrate on specific industries and to develop specialized networks to meet the needs of those targeted customers. The opportunities for niche markets in this sense will probably still be great by the end of this century. The opportunities for the truly small, localized niche marketers may be fewer as the world comes closer together. The need for personalized service may be the major factor keeping the niche marketer viable.

Human Resources. A crucial aspect of providing customer service is the capabilities and professionalism of the people planning and delivering the services. This suggests a concern for and good management of this key resource. Continuing education combined with varied benefit packages are some elements necessary to attract and retain the best people and ensure their productivity.

Survival of the Fittest

The 1970s and 1980s accelerated the rate of change. The 1990s will continue this acceleration. Organizations must analyze how best to survive in the kaleidoscope of change by adapting to different competitive arenas. Different internal organizational structures may be needed, such as process management, participatory management, and simply doing more with less.

Propositions and Logistics Management Actions

Logistics managers will play key roles within and across organizations to meet the challenges of the 1990s. In fact, logistics managers must take on the key role of being champions if changes are to be made in the following strategic areas: logistics performance, logistics system structure, and technology integration. For each proposition within these areas, some selected management actions are noted.

Logistics Performance

Proposition 1: The level of logistics performance expectations will continue to increase through the 1990s, narrowing the range of acceptable performance.

- Help segment markets to better serve customers.
- Ensure customer service in terms valuable to the customer.
- Combine customer service measures for more realistic service levels as viewed by the customer.

Proposition 2: Asset productivity will be a key logistics performance measure for the 1990s.

- Examine wide options for human resource productivity consistent with a diverse workforce.
- Assess other kinds of assets for improved productivity.

Proposition 3: Logistics performance in the 1990s will be more service-driven than cost-driven.

- Assess just-in-time and quick response needs.
- Cost is still important.

Logistics System Structure

Proposition 4: Increasing numbers of shippers will choose to build a closer relationship with a limited number of vendors, customers, and third parties to more effectively manage the supply chain.

- Help develop the selection and evaluation processes for third parties.
- If you are a third party provider, help develop specific competencies to provide a competitive edge.

Proposition 5: Functions within and across organizations will work more closely together.

- Take a leadership role because logistics is uniquely qualified to facilitate integration as a boundary spanning function.
- Develop participative management within the logistics function.
- Look at processes rather than functions to achieve improved productivity.

Technology Integration

Proposition 6: The trade-off of information for inventory will accelerate through the 1990s.

- Help top management to understand the ramifications of this proposition for operations, costs, and customer service.
- Set up logistics systems that can exploit this opportunity.

Proposition 7: The pattern of technology convergence among buyers, sellers, and third parties will increase through the 1990s.

- Build information systems that connect functions and organizations.
- Combine information and materials handling systems for increased efficiency and effectiveness.
- Integrate technology to help integrate functions and organizations.

Notes

1. Much of the information in this chapter is based on the results of various surveys conducted by The Ohio State University. Unless otherwise specified, all tables and figures are from a 1990 strategic planning study (Martha C. Cooper, Daniel E. Innis, and Peter R. Dickson, *Strategic Planning for Logistics* [Oak Brook, Ill.: Council of Logistics Management, 1992]). Survey results are based on 149 responses to a mailed questionnaire, case studies of ten companies, and an executive logistics seminar on strategic planning. The results of the survey are intended to serve only as general trend indicators.
2. Martha C. Cooper, Rosemary Kalapurakal, and Peter Bolt, "Europe 1992: Benefits and Challenges for International Transportation," *Transportation Journal* (Summer 1990): 33–41.
3. C. Lee Johnson, President, Limited Distribution Services, interview in the spring of 1992 by M. C. Cooper, Columbus, Ohio.
4. Paul S. Bender, Bender Management Consultants, interview in spring 1992 by M. C. Cooper, Columbus, Ohio.
5. C. Lee Johnson, interview.
6. C. Lee Johnson, interview.
7. David Jamieson, and Julie O'Mara, *Workforce 2000* (San Francisco: Jossey-Bass, 1991).
8. Rosabeth Moss Kanter, "Transcending Business Boundaries: 12,000 World Managers View Change," *Harvard Business Review* (May–June 1991): 151–64.
9. Because of the considerable diversity among respondents on the usage of barcoding, the median values are reported.
10. La Londe's concept of substituting information for inventory.
11. For examples of service segmentation, see Martha C. Cooper and Randall Rose, "The Segment Competition Matrix: A Strategic Management Tool for the Transportation Industry," *Transportation Journal* 25, no. 1 (Fall 1985): pp. 25–37; and Arun Sharma and Douglas M. Lambert, "Segmentation of Markets Based on Customer Service," *International Journal of Physical Distribution and Logistics Management* 20, no. 7 (1990): 19–27.
12. Lisa M. Ellram, and Martha C. Cooper, "Supply Chain Management, Partnerships, and the Shipper–Third Party Relationship," *International Journal of Logistics Management* 1, no. 2 (1990): 1–10.
13. For more discussion of supply chain management, see John B. Houlihan, "International Supply Chain Management," *International Journal of Physical Distribution and Materials Management* 15, no. 1 (1985): 22–38; Ellram and Cooper, "Supply Chain Management"; Hau L. Lee and Corey Billington, "Managing Supply Chain Inventory: Pitfalls and Opportunities," *Sloan Management Review* 33, no. 3 (Spring 1992): 65–73; Charles Scott and Roy Westbrook, "New Strategic Tools for Supply Chain Management, *International Journal of Physical Distribution and Logistics Management* 21, no. 1 (1991): 23–33.
14. Peter F. Drucker, *Managing for the Future* (New York: Truman Talley Books/Dutton, 1992).
15. Bernard J. La Londe, Martha C. Cooper, and Thomas G. Noordewier, *Customer Service: A Management Perspective* (Oak Brook, Ill.: Council of Logistics Management, 1988).
16. John Gardner and Martha Cooper, "Elements of Strategic Partnership," *Partnerships: A Natural Evolution in Logistics,* J. E. McKeon ed. (Cleveland: Logistics Resource, April 1988), pp. 15–32.
17. Kanter, "Transcending Business Boundaries."
18. Drucker, *Managing for the Future.*
19. Bender, interview.

20. Johnson, interview.
21. Bender, interview.
22. Johnson, interview.

Bibliography

Bender, Paul S. *Resource Management: An Alternative View of Management.* New York: Wiley, 1983.

Cooper, Martha C. "Managerial Considerations for Integrating Information Technology." *RPS News* (October, 1990): 3,7.

Cooper, Martha C., Daniel E. Innis, and Peter R. Dickson. *Strategic Planning for Logistics* Oak Brook, Ill.: Council of Logistics Management, 1992.

Cooper, Martha C., Richard H. Goodspeed, and Charles B. Lounsbury. "Logistics as an Element of Marketing Strategy, Both Inside and Outside the Firm." *Proceedings of the Council of Logistics Management Conference.* Boston (October, 1988): 51–71.

Cooper, Martha C., Rosemary Kalapurakal, and Peter Bolt. "Europe 1992: Benefits and Challenges for International Transportation," *Transportation Journal* (Summer, 1990): 33–41.

Drucker, Peter F. *Managing for the Future.* New York: Truman Talley Books/Dutton, division of Penguin Books, 1992.

Ellram, Lisa M. "Supply Chain Management: The Industrial Organization Perspective." *International Journal of Physical Distribution and Logistics Management* 21, no. 1 (1991): 13–22.

Ellram, Lisa M., and Martha C. Cooper. "Supply Chain Management, Partnerships, and the Shipper-Third Party Relationship." *International Journal of Logistics Management* 1, no. 2 (1990): 1–10.

Gardner, John, and Martha Cooper. "Elements of Strategic Partnership." *Partnerships: A Natural Evolution in Logistics,* J. E. McKeon ed. Cleveland: Logistics Resource, April, 1988, pp. 15–32.

Houlihan, John B. "International Supply Chain Management." *International Journal of Physical Distribution and Materials Management* 15, no. 1 (1985): 22–38.

Jamieson, David, and Julie O'Mara. *Workforce 2000.* San Francisco: Jossey-Bass 1991.

Kanter, Rosabeth Moss. "Transcending Business Boundaries: 12,000 World Managers View Change." Harvard Business Review (May–June 1991): 151–164.

La Londe, Bernard J., Martha C. Cooper, and Thomas G. Noordewier. *Customer Service: A Management Perspective.* Oak Brook, Ill.: Council of Logistics Management, 1988.

La Londe, Bernard J., and Martha C. Cooper. *Partnerships in Providing Customer Service: A Third Party Perspective.* Oak Brook, Ill.: Council of Logistics Management, 1989.

Lee, Hau L., and Corey Billington, "Managing Supply Chain Inventory: Pitfalls and Opportunities." *Sloan Management Review* 33, no. 3 (Spring 1992): 65–73.

Sewell, Carl, and Paul B. Brown. *Customers for Life.* New York: Doubleday-Currency, 1991.

Scott, Charles, and Roy Westbrook. "New Strategic Tools for Supply Chain Management." *International Journal of Physical Distribution and Logistics Management* 21, no. 1 (1991): 23–33.

Sharma, Arun, and Douglas M. Lambert, "Segmentation of Markets Based on Customer Service." *International Journal of Physical Distribution and Logistics Management* 20, no. 7 (1990): 19–27.

SECTION II

Strategic Logistics Planning

Kevin A. O'Laughlin
Section Editor

Change. It can be a thorny management challenge, or an important competitive strategy. One thing is certain—as firms search for new ways to succeed in the ever more competitive global economy, change will be the order of the day. For logistics practitioners, change comes in many forms: faster order cycle times, increasingly differentiated products and services, and ever more sophisticated technologies to help manage all of this complexity. One consequence of this is the need for more dynamic and responsive logistics systems which can readily adapt and respond to changing needs and requirements. Developing the capabilities and competencies necessary to be truly flexible is the key to mastering change as a competitive weapon.

In this section, we explore the building blocks of effective logistics strategies and present frameworks, methodologies, and tools essential for the design and implementation of responsive, change based, and time sensitive logistics systems.

In Chapter 4, Kevin A. O'Laughlin and William C. Copacino present a holistic framework for integrating logistics activities within a broader marketing and manufacturing context. They propose an approach for addressing the key questions in logistics strategy development and logistics planning that will determine how the building blocks should fit to achieve the desired service outcome.

A logistics system is a competitive advantage only to the extent it provides customers with products and services they need, when they need them. In Chapter 5, Douglas M. Lambert describes a methodology for developing tailored customer service strategies and designing performance measurement systems necessary for tracking and monitoring results.

Once customer services strategies are identified, marketing and distribution channels must be designed to perform to the required standards. In Chapter 6, Louis W. Stern and Adel I. El-Ansary discuss the key issues to consider in designing effective marketing channels, and the management systems needed to keep channels operating efficiently and smoothly.

In Chapter 7, Paul T. Chapman describes how analytical tools can be used to optimally allocate and deploy financial and human resources to achieve desired levels of service in a logistics network. He decomposes logistics decisions into four core activities and describes models and other devices which can be successfully used to help manage each. He makes the important point that new information intensive approaches to logistics management are essential for a fully integrating the total supply chain.

In Chapter 8, Allen D. Rose describes the management issues and challenges surrounding implementation of new, enhanced, or modified logistics systems. He makes the crucial point that preparing the organization for doing work differently may be the most important step in successfully implementing new logistics strategies. That—and managing a variety of risks—are paramount in implementing new logistics strategies that position change as a strategic capability.

CHAPTER 4

Logistics Strategy

Kevin A. O'Laughlin
William C. Copacino

In the 1970s, few executives realized that the function of logistics could play a strategic role in their company's success. In fact, the business meaning of the word *logistics* was not widely used or accepted. This function was normally referred to in terms of physical distribution, procurement and receipt of raw materials, transformation of those materials into products, storage of finished goods in warehouses and distribution centers, and shipment of goods to customers. This view of individual and discreet activities mirrored the way firms planned and managed these operations.

Today, business logistics has gained respectability and importance for companies in almost all industries and markets. In fact, the growing awareness of supply chain management's critical impact on a company's competitiveness and profitability has made logistics a truly strategic issue.

Much of the credit for this enlightened understanding of logistics belongs to progressive managers with the vision needed to transcend traditional ideas about buying, making, moving, and selling products. Their willingness to challenge time-tested business practices—plus dramatic progress in the development and application of advanced information systems—have brought logistics to the center stage of corporate strategy.

Defining Logistics as a Strategic Function

In a recent *Harvard Business Review* article focusing on "capabilities-based competition," authors George Stalk, Philip Evans, and Lawrence E. Shulman analyze the phenomenal success of Wal-Mart, a fast-growing firm that has in effect redefined the mass merchandising industry.[1] In explaining Wal-Mart's devotion to building customer loyalty through everyday low pricing and ready availability of merchandise, the authors assert that the key to achieving Wal-Mart's goals of consistently superior service to customers was "to make the way the company replenished inventory the centerpiece of its competitive strategy." This strategic vision "reached its fullest expression in a largely invisible logistic technique known as 'cross-docking.' "

How did a logistics tactic—which in itself appeared to be so mundane—become the centerpiece of a retailer's entire competitive strategy? First, it is important to recognize that effective corporate strategy inevitably requires a dynamic balance between small details and

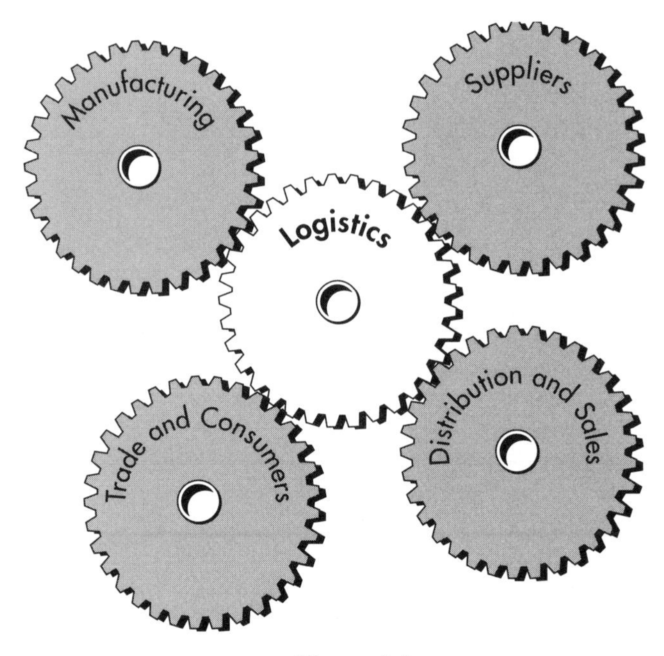

Figure 4-1
The Central Role of Logistics

the big picture. Because it spans all key corporate functions, logistics by nature plays a strategic role in maintaining that balance. If the specific technique of cross-docking is a key to Wal-Mart's success, it is because the company's senior managers see it—and logistics generally—in the larger context of corporate strategy. This relationship is shown graphically in Figure 4-1.

Second, the essence of good strategy is in finding, implementing, and maintaining a differentiated—and not easily imitated—position in the marketplace. Excelling at seemingly mundane but hard-to-implement processes and activities like cross-docking affords powerful advantages in terms of cost reduction and sales gains from superior merchandising support. More important, such capabilities are so difficult to duplicate that even disclosing them as "trade secrets" does nothing to undermine their strategic value.

A senior logistics manager at a large consumer products manufacturer once alluded to the importance—and challenge—of logistics by describing it in terms of his own career. When asked why he found logistics management so appealing, he replied, "Because it is so complicated. In many other businesses and functions the key to mega-success is in doing one big thing very well. In logistics, I have to coordinate the delivery of hundreds and sometimes thousands of orders and shipments every day. If any one of those things goes wrong, I know I'll hear about it, and my company may even lose a customer. It's the complexity I find so challenging—and the desire to master it instead of letting it master me."

When the hundreds of its individual components are integrated into a complete, well-managed whole—and when those activities are executed with creativity, precision, and discipline—logistics can take on strategic importance in any firm's core capabilities and competencies.

Leveraging Logistics for Strategic Advantage

Wal-Mart is certainly not alone in its use of logistics as a strategic lever. Many other firms have successfully viewed logistics as a core capability and have been able to achieve strategic value through their logistics operations. Two additional examples are discussed below.

Baxter Healthcare

Baxter Healthcare is a major medical supplies manufacturer with operations in the United States, Europe, and around the world. In the United States, Baxter held a significant share in the medical supplies market, which comprises mainly hospitals, clinics and laboratories, and doctors' offices. In the early 1980s, Baxter, like all medical supplies manufacturers, was being pressured by its distributors and customers to cut prices in response to government reimbursement programs that were capping prices on supplies and increasingly stringent service requirements placed by hospitals on distributors and manufacturers. Baxter feared that eventually it would be left in a position where prices would be dictated by these external forces, and that it would lose its ability to differentiate itself on service as distributors grew more powerful in their dealings with the hospitals.

As part of its strategic response to this environment, Baxter acquired American Hospital Supply Corporation, one of the largest hospital supplies manufacturers in the United States. The logic behind the acquisition was elegant and simple. By maintaining a distribution company with direct access to its customers, Baxter would be offering its own products *and* those of competitors. Not only could it track and influence sales of products to its customer accounts, it could also devise and deliver value-added services—such as just-in-time delivery programs—to its customers. And the extra volume of complementary product lines of other manufacturers would contribute to the overall efficiency of the operation. Moreover, the distribution organization, by keeping Baxter in close contact with customers, would help the company improve its position with key accounts. Baxter has introduced several generations of logistics services since its acquisition. Leveraging investments in its electronic order entry system, ASAP, Baxter offers tiers of scenarios, from its enhanced logistics services programs to full-fledged just-in-time and stockless programs (Valuelink).

Implementing the strategy has proved challenging at times. Some have wondered why Baxter chose to buy into a distribution business whose profit margins are small in comparison with the manufacturing enterprises that made up the core of the premerger company. These are without question important concerns. But the value Baxter has gained from its ability to work more closely with its customers, while difficult to quantify, is exceptionally important. And there is little doubt that its distribution business has permitted Baxter to become the largest and among the most effective hospital supplies companies in the United States today.

Benetton

Benetton, the Italian sportswear manufacturer, has made logistics the focal point of its marketing success.[2] This well-known company distributes 50 million pieces of clothing worldwide through a highly efficient Quick Response linkage among manufacturing, warehousing, sales, and the retailers they serve. When, for example, a popular style of winter-weight slacks is about to sell out early in the fall, a retailer reorders the product through direct links with Benetton's mainframe computer in Italy. The order is downloaded to an automated machine that makes the slacks in the necessary range of sizes and colors. Workers pack the order in a bar-coded carton addressed to the retail store, and then send the box to Benetton's single warehouse—a highly automated $30 million facility shipping 230,000 pieces of clothing a day to 5,000 stores in 60 countries. Including manufacturing time, Benetton can ship the completed order in only four weeks—several weeks sooner than most of its competitors.

As highlighted in Chapter 29, Benetton owes much of its success to its early and effective commitment to the principles and practices of world-class logistics. Logistics professionals marvel at the globally integrated production and distribution processes Benetton has successfully implemented. As a world leader in the retailing industry, Benetton represents the vanguard of what some observers call "advanced logistics"—a level of operational performance that will increasingly become the norm rather than the exception.

These examples point up how companies, whether operating domestically or globally, can realize significant benefits by giving logistics a central role in their business strategies.

Realizing the Strategic Potential of Logistics

Once a firm recognizes the strategic potential of logistics, it then faces the challenge of actually realizing that potential. This is, of course, not an easy exercise. While many firms claim they view logistics strategically, only a few have been able to achieve the same level of success as Wal-Mart, Baxter, or Benetton.

The first step in harnessing the power of logistics lies in understanding how the components of a logistics system work in harmony to create buyer value for the customer and strategic value for the firm. As shown in Figure 4-2, there are ten key components of a logistics strategy, organized on four key levels, which must be fully coordinated and integrated to achieve world-class logistics performance.

The building blocks pictured in the figure apply whether one is designing an inbound or outbound logistics strategy. Customer requirements, the top block in the pyramid, include requirements of *internal* customers, such as manufacturing centers, if one is building a strategy for inbound logistics systems (for example, the coordination of component and subassembly flows into assembly plants) or *external* customers, such as retailers, hospitals, OEMs (original equipment manufactures, or service businesses), and the like, if one is designing an outbound finished goods logistics system. Each level and component of the logistics strategy pyramid are discussed in greater detail below.

Level 1—Setting Strategic Direction Through Customer Service

Customer service requirements drive the structure of the entire supply chain, including manufacturing, marketing, and logistics. For this reason, it is essential to start with a clear understanding of what customers demand and to develop a customer service strategy that can meet those expectations. Customer service strategies can be simple or complex, depending on a firm's products, markets, and customer service goals.

For example, several Japanese auto manufacturers are purportedly developing new production and distribution systems that will allow them to guarantee delivery of a vehicle—customized to an individual buyer's specifications—within three days of placing the order. While simple in concept, this customer service strategy (often referred to as a "buy-one/make-one" strategy) will require a complete revamping of these automakers' manufacturing and distribution operations and will redefine the role of the retail dealer in serving the customer.

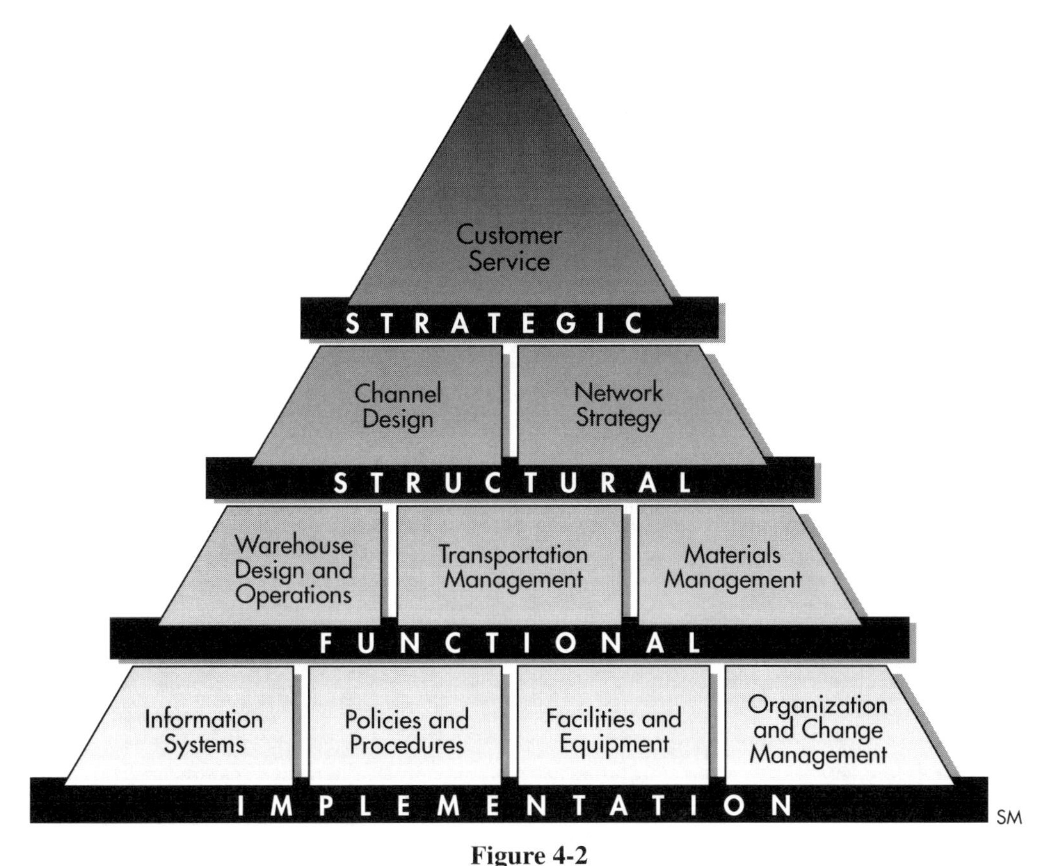

Figure 4-2
Key Components of Logistics Strategy

Source: Service Mark by Andersen Consulting.

Other firms may seek to implement more complex strategies that differentiate service programs offered to customers on the basis of how profitable—or strategically important—the customer is to the business. For example, consumer-packaged-goods manufacturers typically sell to several classes of trade—wholesalers, mass merchandisers, drug store chains, grocery chains, and independents. As the industry has matured and as each class of trade has broadened its product offerings, these "class of trade" distinctions are less useful for segmenting customers and understanding their needs and behavior.

A more useful customer segmentation framework is by "operating sophistication" and "merchandising orientation," as shown in Figure 4-3. This framework allows a different, more insightful, and more valuable segmentation of customers.

- *Traditional chains and wholesalers* have the least stringent customer service requirements. However, these retailers are rapidly migrating to other segments.
- *Pipeline optimizers* (e.g., Wal-Mart) are imposing stringent conditions on their vendors, demanding error-free fill rates and 100% delivery reliability as they try to smooth the flow in their supply chains.

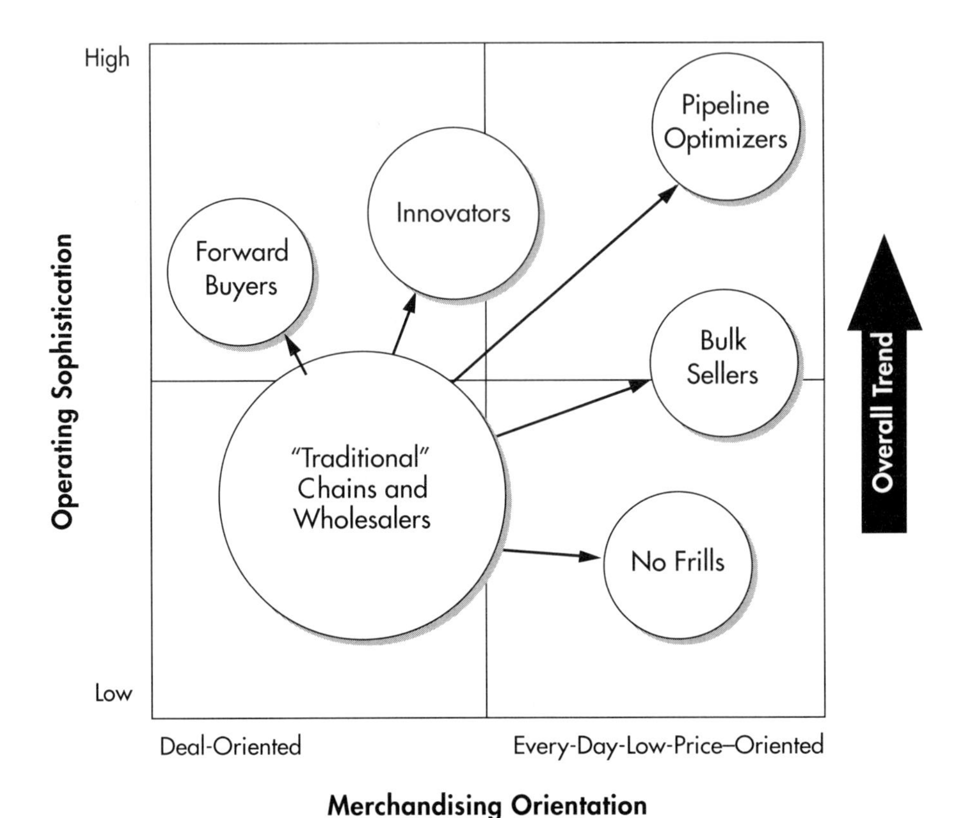

Figure 4-3
Packaged Goods Retailer Segmentation Framework

- *Bulk sellers* (e.g., Price Club and other warehouse club stores) are demanding special product offerings (e.g., large variety packs), short delivery times, and direct-store-delivery.
- *Innovators* are developing innovative merchandising programs for their consumers and want their suppliers to be flexible and create customized merchandising programs to support these store-level merchandising initiatives.
- *No-frills* retailers (e.g., Food Lion) want to operate at the lowest possible cost and want their suppliers to work closely with them to enhance channel efficiency.
- *Forward buyers* are implementing forward-buying programs—trading off the cost of holding inventory with the savings reaped by buying in bulk during manufacturers' promotional programs.

By segmenting customers in this nontraditional way, and by understanding the buyer values and customer service requirements of each segment, a manufacturer selling to the retail trade can provide the basic customer service requirements and those value-added services that will meet the needs of each segment. Creative segmentation is an essential task for all firms seeking to win a differentiated position in their marketplaces.

It is extremely important that a company understand service requirements in terms of *what* customers want, *not how* they expect to have their requirements met. Customers often explain their service requirements by describing how they want their supplier to operate. "I want my vendor to have a warehouse within two hours of my warehouse" needs to be understood in the context of the actual performance the customer expects. "I expect delivery of all of my orders with 24 hours of placement" is a more useful and accurate depiction of the customer's need, and gives the supplier greater flexibility in designing a logistics system that meets that need in the most cost-effective way. Chapter 5 expands on the issues related to customer service and presents approaches for customer service assessment and management.

When thinking about how logistics operations can create value for their companies, logistics managers should ask two key questions:

- What base capabilities do we need to meet competitor performance and customer needs?
- Can we distinguish our company through superior logistics capabilities in one of five areas of logistics differentiation?

In developing their logistics strategy and plan, most companies address the first question. Few address the second question, although it can be a valuable question to consider, as Wal-Mart, Baxter, and Benetton have shown.

Traditionally, most logistics functions have not been deeply involved in the development of their company's strategic plan. In developing its strategy, a company can benefit by explicitly considering how to create competitive advantage from its logistics capabilities. Managers can use logistics in five ways to significantly improve their company's competitive advantage.[3] Specifically, they can offer:

- *Low cost.* Through superior efficiency, logistics can contribute to a cost advantage that can be leveraged to increase market share or enhance profitability. Low-cost logistics is particularly important in logistics-intensive industries where there is little differentiation among commoditylike products (such as certain segments of the chemical or paper industries). In these industries, logistics costs can exceed 15% of the goods sold.
- *Superior customer service.* The most notable measures for customer service include short-order lead times and in-stock availability. Such measures also may include order and invoice accuracy, access to information on order status, ability to respond to customer inquiries, and so forth. Most customers are willing to pay a premium for superior customer service, and logistics can play an important role in service differentiation.
- *Value-added services.* This involves providing services that enhance customers' ability to compete and includes activities like pricing and ticketing of merchandise, assembling mixed pallets, making drop shipments direct to stores, arranging for quick replenishment or continuous replenishment, and providing training or software to the customer.
- *Flexibility.* A logistics system can create an advantage by being flexible enough to customize its service and cost offerings to meet the needs of distinct customer segments or of individual accounts. The flexibility to meet diverse customer needs in a cost-effective way can distinguish a company and allow it to serve a broader customer base.
- *Regeneration.* Genuine value and competitive advantage can be provided by a logistics system with the capability to reinvent itself. This means it has the capability to innovate or develop new ways to serve a market. For example, because manufacturers of generic pharmaceuticals have begun to serve the channel directly, wholesalers of those pharmaceuticals have had to reinvent themselves to focus on high-service niches. Regeneration requires an organization to take several important steps: it must implement the means to

constantly take the pulse of its existing and emerging customer markets; develop the capability to change rapidly; develop flexible information systems that can adapt to new ways of doing business; develop the vision to recognize the need for and the direction of change; and develop the leadership to drive that change.

Logistics capabilities do not necessarily have to be superior in all five areas. Generally, they must stand out in one or two of the five categories and be adequate in the remaining ones. This basic framework for assessing customer service requirements and the strategic requirements from logistics not only provide a structure for managers to examine how the logistics function is adding value and how it is aligned with their company's goals, but also represent a way to clarify and communicate their goals within their company.

Level 2—The Structural Components of Logistics Systems

Once a company understands its customers' service requirements and how it will use logistics to compete, it must then decide how to meet them. The next two components of the strategy—the channel structure and the facility network structure—lay the foundation for meeting those requirements.

Channel Design

Channel design involves determining what activities and functions need to be performed for a desired level of service and which player(s) in the channel will perform them. Decisions about whether to serve customers directly—or to have distributors handle some or all of the marketing, selling, product delivery, or billing functions—are critical at this stage.

Several factors influence the channel strategy, including customer demands, channel economics, channel power, and channel players' roles. Although it is important to understand how each of these factors works today, a company must also consider how it will change in the future. Market share and size often dictate the economics behind direct versus indirect distribution decisions. For example, in the hospital supplies market, firms like Baxter Healthcare have the necessary size and scale to implement direct distribution systems and have done so for important strategic reasons. Other firms, such as Becton Dickinson and Kendall, serve their accounts by sharing the customer support functions with hospital supply distributors. The best channel structure ultimately depends on both economics and strategy.

The design of channel structure requires careful analysis and vision because the structure, once implemented, often cannot be easily or quickly changed. Nevertheless, as customer requirements change and as competitors reposition themselves, channel strategy must be reevaluated to protect or extend market position. Chapter 6 explains the channel strategy design issues in greater detail and describes an approach for developing channel strategies in the context of an overall business strategy.

Physical Network Strategy

The second major component at this level is the physical facility network. The network strategy should provide answers to such questions as:

- How many facilities are needed, where should they be located, and what should be the mission of each (for example, full-stocking facility, cross-dock operation, or surge inventory facility)?
- Which customers and/or product lines should be served from each facility?
- How much inventory should be maintained in each facility to satisfy specified service levels?
- What transportation services should be used to meet customer service expectations?
- How should return flows (for example, equipment returned for repair or packaging material returned for disposal) be managed in the system?
- Should all or any part of the operation be managed by a third-party logistics service provider?

The network strategy must be integrated with the channel strategy in a way that maximizes value to the customer. For example, it makes little sense for a manufacturer's and a distributor's warehouses several miles away to be holding large quantities of the same inventory (a common occurrence). The coordination and integration of channel participants plays an increasingly important role in overall logistics system performance.

Similarly, the logistics network strategy must be fully integrated with the production and inbound logistics strategy of the firm. The "buy-one/make-one" strategy being pursued in the automotive industry requires an integrated plan for inbound logistics (manufacturing and assembly) and outbound logistics (shipment of finished products to customers) to achieve the anticipated performance targets. The need to coordinate and analyze production *and* distribution systems simultaneously complicates the analysis of cost/service trade-offs. Because of the complexity involved in integrated production and distribution planning, many companies separate these decisions. This is a mistake. Today's planning and control approaches allow for integrated production and distribution planning, and can considerably enhance a company's cost position and investment performance.

A given level of customer service can be achieved through various logistics approaches. The challenge is to design and implement one that supports service requirements without ignoring such important factors as *costs* (including operating costs and one-time implementation expenses); *risk* (such as that posed by disruption of service); and *flexibility* (for example, the ability to expand or modify distribution quickly if necessary). This complex process typically involves many steps, all of which must be managed with an understanding of the big picture—first, identifying potential logistics system solutions; then understanding the cost, service, benefits, risks, and flexibility of each; and finally, identifying additional alternatives to consider. Clearly, computer-based modeling tools are invaluable in coping with the immense range and complexity of these variables. One way to understand this trade-off is through a cost/service curve, as shown in Figure 4-4.

The curve confirms an obvious truth—it costs more to provide higher levels of service. However, considerable subtlety is required to understand the precise balance among costs and service levels. For that reason, it is important to apply an iterative process of identifying and evaluating alternative physical networks. Customer service criteria can then be mapped against the curve to establish what set of choices are the most attractive from a cost and service standpoint. At that point, qualitative criteria like risk and flexibility can be assessed to determine the preferred network choice.

Advanced modeling tools are invaluable for exploring alternative facility network choices, not only in terms of a specific company's costs but also in terms of *total* channel costs. Chapter

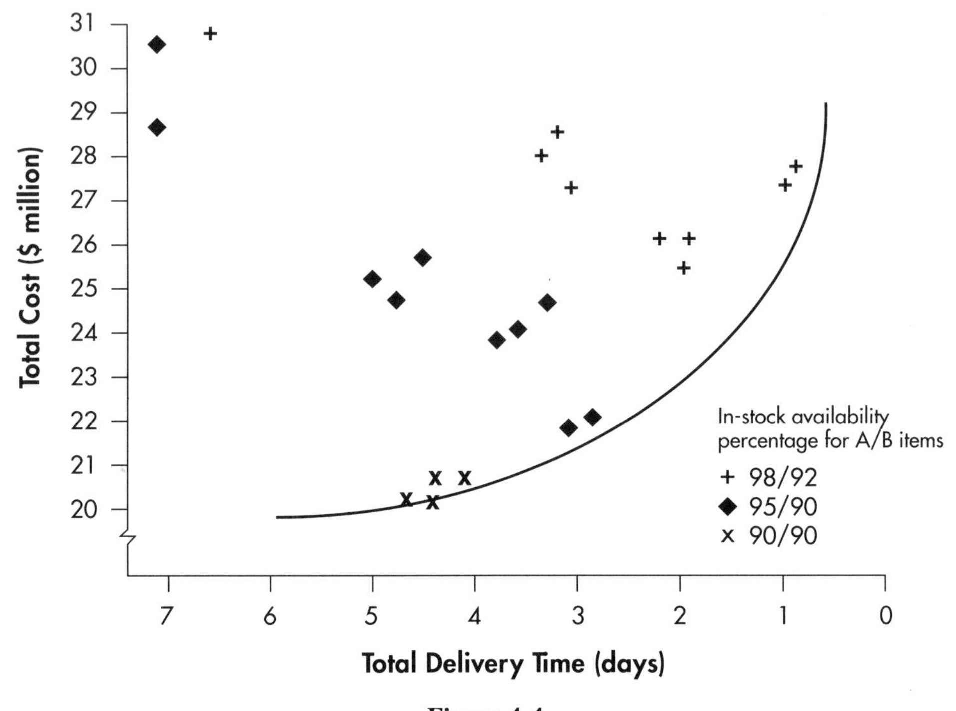

Figure 4-4
The Cost/Service Trade-off Curve

7 describes how firms are using the latest generation of modeling tools to analyze and manage the added complexity of total channel systems.

A common mistake in developing a physical network strategy is to limit alternatives to the "tried and true." Although a current logistics system may turn out to be the best choice, it is wise to challenge existing warehousing practices, inventory deployment policies, transportation management practices, management procedures, staff organization, and systems. Every alternative must withstand the scrutiny of certain basic questions—Does the proposed system make our customer service easier to manage? cheaper? faster? more responsive? more competitive?

No analytical models or methodologies can guarantee logistics breakthroughs because developing the best approach is by nature a challenging process that requires creativity, solid analytical skills, experience, and the intestinal fortitude to challenge the status quo. However, experienced logistics strategists, with an effective modeling tool, can create considerable value for their company.

Level 3—Functional Components of a Logistics Strategy

The third level in the logistics strategy pyramid involves a thorough analysis of the functional components of the logistics strategy, specifically, transportation, warehousing, and materials management. As used here, materials management involves the full replenishment process including forecasting, inventory planning, production planning, manufacturing scheduling, and purchasing. The analysis here should involve both strategic and tactical considerations. Strategic considerations of the functional components address issues such as:

- Should our company outsource more of its logistics activities?
- Should we consider third-party services for warehousing or transportation?
- Should we own, lease, or contract our warehousing services?

These questions often force companies to carefully determine the critical success factors for their business and their core competence. These are difficult but important considerations. Wal-Mart, for example, opted to excel at warehousing and transportation management. With the expanding quality of third-party warehousing and with transportation companies offering high-quality services and unique capabilities (such as load consolidation planning, repackaging services, etc.), many companies are opting for third-party logistics service providers. Chapter 24 provides perspectives on how to evaluate this strategic decision.

On the tactical level, companies must assess how they can enhance functional excellence. In transportation, this analysis may include considerations like carrier selection, carrier rationalization, shipment consolidation, load planning, routing and scheduling, fleet management, or carrier performance measurement. Similarly, warehousing considerations may include facility layout, materials handling technology selection, productivity, safety, regulatory compliance, among other considerations. In materials management, the analysis may focus on best practices or improvements in forecasting, inventory management, production scheduling, and/or purchasing.

In assessing these tactical considerations, companies have taken a variety of approaches. Outside experts are sometimes used to review functional performance. In addition, benchmarking is often a useful technique to understand the opportunities for potential improvement of functional performance and/or to understand the approaches or best practices to follow to enhance performance.

There are two cautions to consider in using benchmarking information: First, everyone's logistics system is different. Sourcing constraints, market patterns, and service requirements can differ by company and can result in cost and service differences. Second, a company must carefully consider the performance of the whole process or system, not just the functional performance. For example, one can lower transportation costs by using an alternative, slower mode of transportation or by shipping less frequently, but this tactic may increase inventory levels and cost, and reduce customer service performance. Alternatively, a better approach might involve the use of shipment planning analytic software to increase shipment consolidations. This focus on process or system excellence must not be sacrificed in search of lower individual functional costs.

Many logistics operations can enhance their functional performance. Markets, sourcing patterns, and customer service requirements change over time, and logistics operations must be modified to meet the new requirements. For example, as shipment frequencies increase and shipment sizes decrease, both warehouse and transportation operations must be modified to achieve optimal performance. Warehouse operations must consider new picking disciplines or new technologies (see Chapters 25 and 26) as shipment sizes change from full pallets to cases to split-cases. Similarly, transportation must consider the use of pool distribution, consolidated shipments with stop-offs, or other techniques as shipment sizes decrease.

Level 4—Implementation Level

The final level of the strategic logistics pyramid involves implementation and includes information systems to support logistics, policies and procedures to guide day-to-day logistics operations, installation and maintenance of facilities and equipment, and organization and people issues. Information systems and organization issues are particularly vital to effective logistics performance and are discussed below.

Logistics Information Systems

Information systems are the enabler of the integrated logistics concept. Companies cannot effectively manage costs, provide superior customer service, and be leaders in logistics performance without leading-edge information systems. These capabilities are a requirement for the 1990s. Advanced logistics information systems involve four aspects, as outlined in Figure 4-5.

First, timely and accurate information is essential. This requires source data capture (input of each transaction at the time and place of occurrence) and real-time information processing capabilities. For example, a warehouse worker should not have to send pick documents to an office for keypunching and batch processing, but should scan or keypunch each transaction as it occurs.

Second, logistics processes must be carefully designed to assure superior logistics performance. Often, a "reengineering" or rethinking of the key logistics processes from "a clean sheet of paper approach" can yield impressive benefits. Specifically, careful attention should be given to the *order management process* and the *replenishment process.*

As shown in Figure 4-6, these processes have important linkages. Inventory management is the key activity that links these two critical processes. Careful attention must be given to how these processes are designed and managed, and how the organization's structure, roles, measures, and information systems support the process approach.

More important, it is critical to think of each process as a complete effort. For example, the order management process involves order entry and order processing activities through inventory management and allocation through shipment planning, picking, and shipping through invoicing, collection, and deduction reconciliation. Viewing this full set of activities as a process, rather than separate activities or functions, can lead to nontraditional solutions and quantum performance improvements. For example, one company redesigned its order management process by organizing "cells" or complete processing units based on the technology used to transmit the order. One cell focused on traditional paper, fax, and phone orders; a second cell handled electronic data inter-

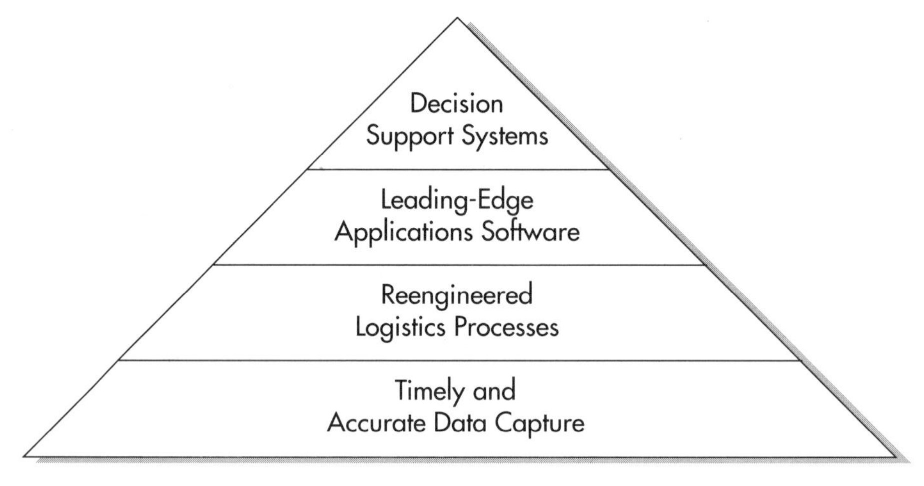

Figure 4-5
Hierarchy of Logistics Information Systems Needs

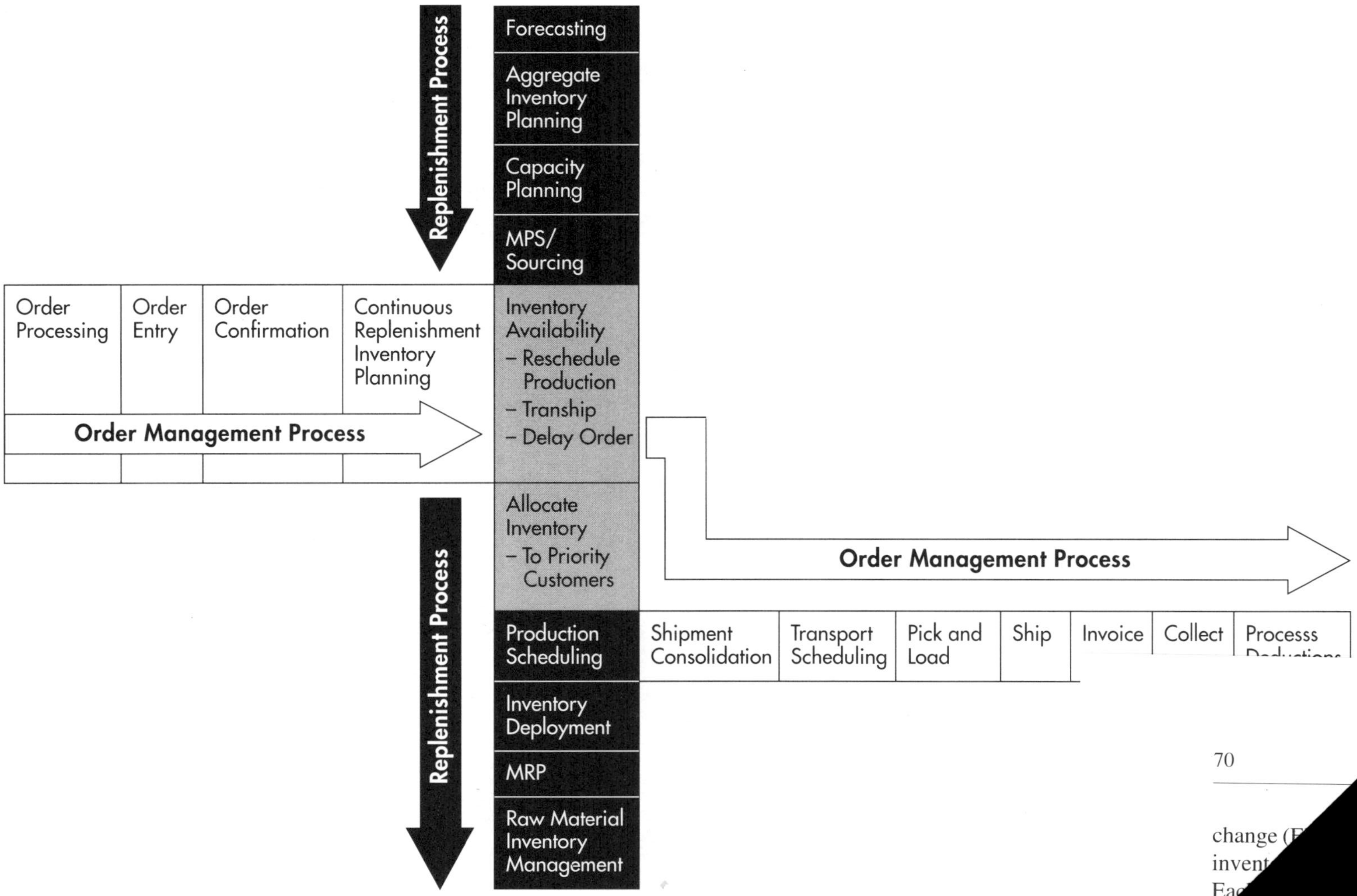

Replenishment Process

Forecasting

Aggregate Inventory Planning

Capacity Planning

MPS/ Sourcing

Order Processing

Order Entry

Order Confirmation

Continuous Replenishment Inventory Planning

Order Management Process

Inventory Availability
- Reschedule Production
- Tranship
- Delay Order

Allocate Inventory
- To Priority Customers

Order Management Process

Replenishment Process

Production Scheduling

Shipment Consolidation

Transport Scheduling

Pick and Load

Ship

Invoice

Collect

Processs Deductions

Inventory Deployment

MRP

Raw Material Inventory Management

Figure 4-6

Linkage of Order Management and Replenishment Processes

DI) orders; a third cell handled continuous replenishment orders (i.e., vendor-managed ory where the supplier managed and replenished the inventory at its customer's warehouses). h cell managed the full set of activities—from order entry through collection and deduction reconciliation. The orders did not flow from one department to another, but each cell conducted all processing functions. This arrangement shortened the average order cycle times from 12 to 5 days, reduced administrative costs by 30%, and reduced errors and invoice deductions by 50%.

Third, integrated application software with full functionality is a key part of an effective logistics information system. Full functionality will differ for each company but may include capabilities like the ability to allocate inventory to a specific customer or lot traceability.

Fourth, advanced decision support is an important part of a logistics information system. Capabilities in this area include logistics network planning models that allow a what-if simulation of the cost and customer service impacts of alternative logistics network structures and policies; analytic tools to optimize production planning and manufacturing scheduling; routing and scheduling analytic programs that can be used to reduce transportation costs; order consolidation programs that can design the best shipment planning strategies; and analytic software to evaluate alternative inventory deployment and management strategies.

ORGANIZATION

An integrated and high-performing organization is key to successful logistics performance. Integrated logistics management does not necessarily mean centralization of the logistics activities into a single organizational unit. However, integrated logistics management requires careful design of three key elements, as indicated in Figure 4-7.

- *Structure.* No single organizational structure is the best for all companies. The assignment of the responsibility for operational activities (purchasing, inbound transportation, forecasting, inventory planning, inventory control, order entry, customer service, outbound transportation, warehousing, and manufacturing planning) to the marketing, manufacturing, finance, or a logistics or distribution function must be determined considering the key competitive factors, customer needs, culture, and philosophy of each individual company.
- *Roles and responsibilities.* The structuring of logistics activities is often less important than how they work together. In designing organizational relationships, we generally follow an important rule. In a stable environment, design for functional efficiency; let each function manage more independently, with the goal of achieving functional excellence and the greatest functional efficiency.

  In an uncertain or dynamic environment, design for functional integration; develop an organization that has close working relationships among functions and operates in an integrated way. Tactics to achieve this goal include teaming by product (for example, Procter and Gamble has created a "supply manager" position that manages the full supply chain

Figure 4-7
Building an Effective Logistics Organization

activities for each product family) and the sales and operations planning meeting (SOPM), where all key functions meet weekly to carefully monitor and manage the production and distribution plans in light of changing market conditions.

Over the past decade, most companies have faced a more uncertain and complex operating environment. Therefore, the need for and benefits of effective, functional integration have increased and will continue to increase for most companies.

- *Performance measures.* To have an effective, integrated logistics system, a company must align performance measures with desired results. It is foolish to ask a purchasing manager to work to lower the total cost of a purchased item (purchase price, transportation, inventory, quality, returns, administrative costs) if the manager is evaluated solely on purchase price. Similarly, a transportation manager will not set up the most effective and efficient logistics system if a company pays bonuses based on transportation cost reduction targets alone. Performance measures are the most overlooked area of logistics and offer considerable opportunity in most companies.

Strategic Logistics Planning Process

With the strategic logistics pyramid as the centerpiece, the specific process for logistics strategy development and planning should involve four steps, as outlined in Figure 4-8.[4]

Step 1—Visioning

As outlined in Figure 4-8, the first step in logistics strategic planning (LSP) is visioning. We define visioning to include the systematic development of an organizational consensus regarding the key inputs to the logistics planning process, as well as the identification of potential, alternative logistics approaches. Significant value is added through the visioning process. Achieving an organizational consensus on the key inputs to the logistics planning process both unites the company and grounds it in a common way of thinking. Subsequently, visioning potential logistics alternatives and scoping the planning effort expands the perspectives of all the players and opens new horizons for the company.

As noted earlier, visioning sessions are an effective way to extract, enhance, and/or build consensus on these three key inputs to the logistics strategic planning process:

1. Clarify the strategic direction of the company and the implications for logistics, and articulate a concise vision of logistics requirements.
2. Understand the service requirements of different segments of customers.
3. Explore external factors and directions such as transportation services and rates, environmental and regulatory restrictions, social legislation, competitive factors, and other external events that would impact logistics. Moreover, visioning sessions are essential for defining strategic alternatives or new logistics possibilities and defining the scope of the planning effort, as outlined in Figure 4-9.

The logistics visioning activity normally involves two to five working sessions. These sessions have several purposes. First, they must define or confirm the customer service requirements, key external forces, and the mission and goals for the logistics function. Second, they

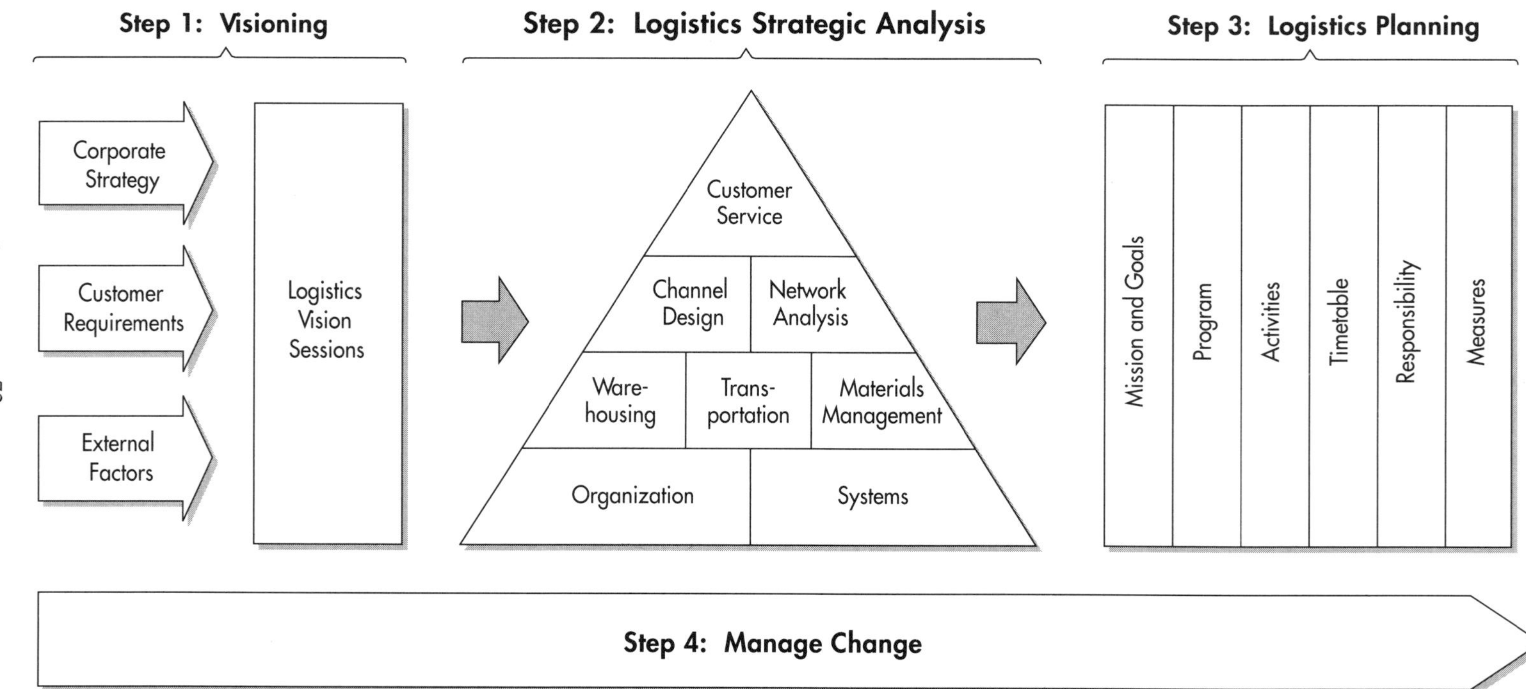

Figure 4-8
Framework for Logistics Strategic Planning

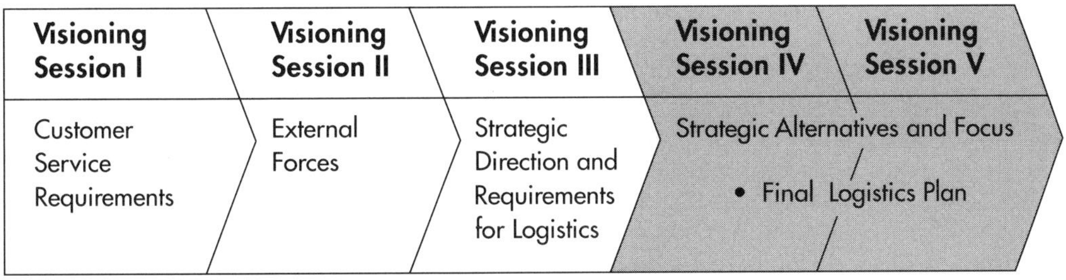

Visioning Session I	Visioning Session II	Visioning Session III	Visioning Session IV	Visioning Session V
Customer Service Requirements	External Forces	Strategic Direction and Requirements for Logistics	Strategic Alternatives and Focus • Final Logistics Plan	

Figure 4-9
Overview of Visioning Process

must scope the logistics strategy planning activities for the next two years. Third, the sessions must explore alternatives for each analytic activity planned for the coming year. Fourth, the sessions must review and confirm the detailed logistics plan that will be completed in step three.

Effective strategy development requires the capability to think beyond the current way of operating. All assumptions, existing constraints, conventional wisdom, and traditional ways of operating must be challenged. The visioning sessions provide a framework for companies to think "outside of the box" and contemplate fundamentally new logistics strategies.

Step 2—Logistics Strategic Analysis

The second major step in the logistics planning process is to conduct the analysis required for making thoughtful choices among potential logistics alternatives. The logistics strategy pyramid, shown in Figure 4-2, depicts the essential components of a logistics strategy. The specific components to be reviewed during the strategic analysis step are identified during the visioning process. The scope may range from broad rethinking of entire ways of operating, to assessing how the productivity or the effectiveness of any single activity might be improved.

Step 3—Logistics Planning

As the logistics strategic analysis is completed, the logistics plan is then assembled. The logistics plan is a road map that outlines the *mission* and *goals* for the logistics function and the *programs* and *activities* to achieve these goals. The goals should include targets for customer service and cost performance, as well as the major analyses or projects targeted for completion during the current year. In addition, the plan should include identification of the specific performance *measures* for logistics.

Logistics strategy development (steps one and two) and logistics planning (step three) are iterative and overlapping processes. That means some of the tasks or activities of the logistics strategy development process (e.g., customer service survey, warehouse network configuration analysis, transportation functional analysis, etc.) may be incorporated as specific projects in the logistics plan. The logistics strategy development activity then is a true process, which never ends and continues to be refined and enhanced over time. The logistics planning activity is more of a discrete event that establishes annual goals and the analyses or activities to be completed during the current year.

Step 4—Managing Change

The final step in the logistics planning process involves managing change; that is, coaching the organization to effectively implement enhanced ways of conducting business. Several factors are key to effective change management:

- *Visible Plan.* The mission, goals, direction, and specific objectives for the logistics activities need to be clear. A formalized process for logistics strategy development and logistics planning is an important activity to achieve buy-in across the company concerning the objectives for customer service and logistics. Moreover, the development of a specific plan, summarizing these goals and key initiatives, is an important communication vehicle. Beyond this activity, the logistics leadership group needs to periodically (both formally and informally) reinforce the key directions and goals for the logistics function to the logistics team and the organization at large.
- *A champion in the management ranks.* Successful change is more likely with a leader who will represent logistics to other functions in the company and to customers and other external parties, and who can coalesce and unite the logistics group. Moreover, each logistics project in the logistics plan requires an owner with responsibility and accountability for that activity.
- *Training and coaching.* It is important that the logistics leadership group understand that change is often difficult, and that training and coaching are required for success. Training focuses on developing the needed content knowledge and process skills to operate in the new environment. These capabilities and skills are often best attained through formal courses, seminars and/or conferences.

  In addition, effective coaching is also important. Successful logistics executives have developed a team of high performers by counseling their managers on how to be most effective, by providing a broad perspective for the managers that extends beyond their individual jobs, and by reinforcing the vision, goals, and imperatives the organization must achieve to be successful.

Summary

Logistics is a challenging and important activity because it serves as an integrating or boundary-spanning function. It links suppliers with customers, and it integrates functional entities across a company. It is critical that logistics be aligned with the company's strategy. Moreover, beyond alignment, companies should actively explore how logistics can contribute as a source of competitive advantage (in a way that Wal-Mart, Benetton, and Baxter have achieved).

The logistics strategy pyramid frames the issues that need to be assessed in developing a logistics strategy. The pyramid frames issues on four levels: (1) strategy and customer service imperatives; (2) structural issues, specifically channel strategy and network configuration; (3) function excellence; and (4) effective implementation.

Finally, the four-step process for logistics strategy development and planning provides a useful approach when developing a logistics strategy. Step one involves visioning and includes an understanding or assessment of the company's strategic direction, the opportunity to use logistics as a differentiator, the customer service requirements by customer segment, and the external factors that would particularly impact logistics. Most important, the visioning process provides clarity on the role and requirements of the logistics function and establishes specific goals for logistics and customer service performance. Step two involves the strategic logistics analysis on all four levels of the logistics strategy pyramid. Step three involves the development of the annual logistics plan. And step four involves the continuous process of managing change.

The remaining chapters drive deeper into each component of the logistics strategy pyramid and provide insight into specific approaches, methodologies, and tactics that can be used to enhance logistics performance.

Notes

1. George Stalk, Philip Evans, and Lawrence E. Schulman, "Competing on Capabilities: The New Rules of Corporate Strategy," *Harvard Business Review* (March–April 1992): 57.
2. The following text is derived from the Fall 1991 *Logistics Perspectives* and from Chapter 29, "International Logistics Environment," by David L. Anderson and Dennis Colard. William C. Copacino, Kenneth R. Ernst, and Bruce S. Richmond, "Quick Response: Is It Right for Your Company?" *Logistics Perspectives* issue 4 (Chicago, Ill.: Andersen Consulting, Fall 1991), p. 1.
3. William C. Copacino, "Real Advantages from Logistics," *Traffic Management* 31, no. 11 (November 1992): 63.
4. Material in this section is adapted from *Reconfiguring European Logistics Systems;* prepared for the Council of Logistics Management by Andersen Consulting and the Cranfield School of Management. Kevin A. O'Laughlin, James Cooper, Eric Cabocel, *Reconfiguring European Logistics Systems* (Oak Brook, Ill.: CLM, January 1993).

CHAPTER 5

Customer Service Strategy and Management

Douglas M. Lambert

A world-class organization must provide high levels of logistics service to customers.[1] Knowledge of customer expectations and an understanding of the firm's performance on logistics service attributes relative to competitors are vital to achieving service excellence.[2] As the levels of domestic and international competition and customer demand increase, management must use logistics as a weapon to create a sustainable competitive advantage in the marketplace.

As stated in *Business Week:*

> It seems so simple. Businesses exist to serve customers and should bend over backward to satisfy their needs. But too many companies still don't get it. And in the 1990s, more customers are likely to take the opportunity to reward the ones that do.[3]

Customer service represents the output of the logistics system and the "place" component of the firm's marketing mix. It is a measure of the effectiveness of the logistics system in creating time and place utility for a product. The level of customer service determines not only whether existing clients will remain customers but how many potential customers will become actual ones. Thus a firm's customer service level has a direct impact on its market share, its total logistics costs, and ultimately, its profitability.[4] For this reason, it is imperative that customer service be an integral part of the design and operation of any logistics system.

Logistics and the Marketing Function

The importance of a marketing orientation for business success has been well documented.[5] How management allocates scarce resources to the components of the marketing mix—product, price, promotion, and place—will determine a company's market share and profitability.[6] Management can improve a firm's competitive position by spending more dollars on the marketing mix, by allocating resources more effectively and efficiently to the individual components of the marketing mix, and/or by making changes within a component that will increase effectiveness and/or efficiency.[7] Figure 5-1 summarizes the cost trade-offs that management must make. The objec-

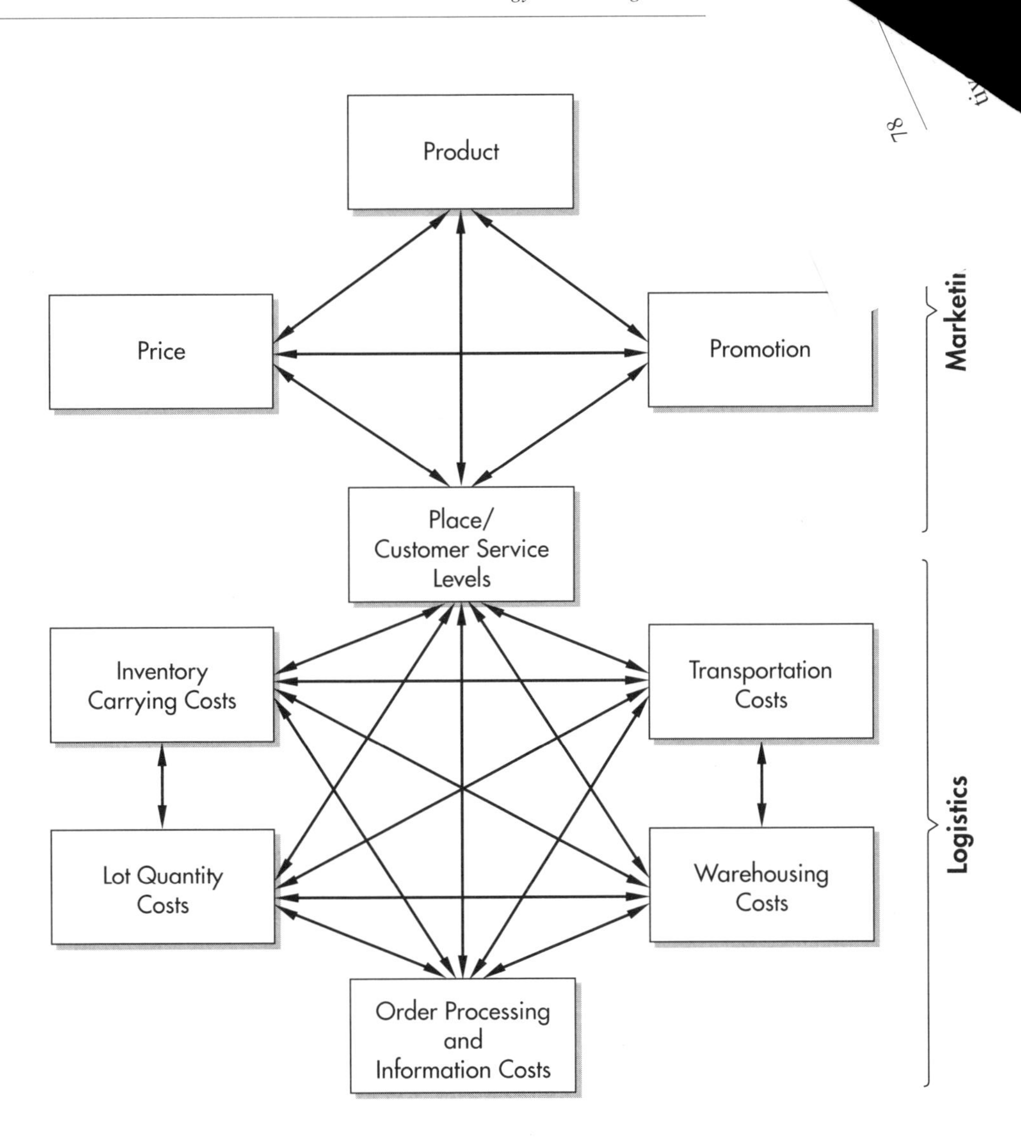

Marketing Objective
Allocate resources to the marketing mix to maximize the long-run profitability of the firm.

Logistics Objective
Minimize total costs, given the customer service objective where:
Total costs = Transportation costs + Warehousing costs + Order processing and information costs + Lot quantity costs + Inventory carrying costs.

Figure 5-1
Cost Trade-Offs Required in a Logistics System

Source: Adapted from Douglas M. Lambert, The Development of an Inventory Costing Methodology: A Study of the Costs Associated with Holding Inventory (Chicago: National Council of Physical Distribution Management, 1976), p. 7.

...e is to allocate resources to the product, price, promotion, and place components of the marketing mix in a manner that will lead to the greatest long-run profits.

Product

Product is the bundle of attributes the customer receives from the purchase. Management may allocate resources to product development to bring new products to market or improve the quality of existing products. The quality of the product influences demand in the marketplace and the price the company can charge. Reducing quality lowers manufacturing costs and increases short-run profits but may erode long-run profitability. In the global marketplace, all major competitors will be required to have high-quality products. To quote a senior vice president of a *Fortune* 500 firm: "A high-quality product is simply the price of admission; the Japanese competitors all have high-quality innovative products. It is very difficult if not impossible to differentiate the firm based on the product."

In some industries, success depends on spending substantial sums on research and development to bring a continuous stream of new products to the marketplace. However, many "new" products are nothing more than product line extensions that do little to increase total market size but do increase the cost of doing business. In these situations, the market is simply carved up into smaller and less profitable pieces. Management must carefully consider the profit impact of changes in the product offering.

Price

Price is the payment the manufacturer receives for its product. Management must determine how changes in price will affect the purchase behavior of intermediaries and ultimate consumers. Price changes are not limited to changes in a product's list price. When a manufacturer demands faster payment of accounts receivable, provides a discount for early payment, offers inventory on consignment, or otherwise changes the financial terms of sale, it is changing the price of its products, and such changes may affect demand. The price that the manufacturer receives for its products varies, depending on the channel of distribution.

Management may attempt to increase sales and profitability by reducing prices. However, in mature industries this is a questionable strategy. For example, if a firm's net profit after taxes is 4% of sales, a 2% price reduction will lower net profit after taxes from 4% to 3% in the absence of an increase in sales. A substantial sales increase is required just to break even and maintain the 4% profit. Achieving the necessary sales increase in a mature market is very difficult. Typically, competitors will match price reductions, and every firm will then make less profit because industry sales increase very little or not at all.

Promotion

Promotion includes both advertising and personal selling. Increasing expenditures for advertising will increase sales, but at some point additional advertising expenditures will not increase sales enough to justify the expenditure.

The amount of sales support required depends on the channel of distribution. For example, manufacturers that use direct sales have to spend more on salespeople. The size of the sales force influences the size of the potential market and the manufacturer's market share. To justify the additional expense, however, increased expenditures for promotion must lead to an equal or greater increase in contribution as a result of increased sales.[8] In many industries there is an opportunity to use personal selling more effectively by training salespeople to sell the value added provided by excellent logistics.

Place/Customer Service

The place component represents the manufacturer's expenditure for customer service, which can be thought of as the output of the logistics system.[9] Customer service is the interface of logistics with marketing. Although customer service is the output of the logistics system, customer satisfaction results when the company performs well on all components of the marketing mix. Product availability and order cycle time can be used to differentiate the product and may influence the market price if customers are willing to pay more for better service. In addition, manufacturers add logistics costs to product costs, so logistics costs may affect the market price set by the company.

For many firms customer service may be the best method of gaining a competitive advantage.[10] The firm may be able to improve its market share and profitability significantly by spending more than competitors on customer service/logistics. By systematically adjusting the customer service package, however, the firm may improve service and reduce the total costs of logistics. When evaluating alternative customer service strategies, management should try to maximize the firm's long-run profitability.

Increases in expenditures for the various components of the marketing mix require sales increases just to recover the additional costs. Most companies have limited resources and therefore must allocate them in a manner to increase market share and profitability. Shifting marketing mix dollars to customer service from areas in which the money is not achieving sufficient sales may result in cost savings as well as improved customer service. The advantage of this measure is that the contribution margin on resulting sales increases goes directly to the bottom line of the profit-and-loss statement. The impact on net profit is substantial because cost reductions in other components of the marketing mix offset the increased cost of customer service, and it is not necessary to deduct the incremental service costs from the incremental contribution generated. Also, customer service improvements are not as easily duplicated by competitors as are changes in product, price, and promotion.

Figure 5-1 illustrates the cost trade-offs necessary to implement the integrated logistics management concept successfully. Total cost analysis is the key to managing the logistics function. Management should strive to minimize the total cost of logistics rather than the cost of each activity. Attempts to reduce the cost of individual activities may lead to increased total costs. For example, consolidating finished goods inventory in a small number of distribution centers will reduce inventory carrying costs and warehousing costs but may lead to a substantial increase in freight expense or a lower sales volume as a result of reduced levels of customer service. Similarly, savings associated with large-volume purchases may be less than the associated increase in inventory carrying costs.

Management must consider the *total* of all the logistics costs described in Figure 5-1. Reductions in one cost invariably lead to cost increases of other components. Effective management and real cost savings can be accomplished only by viewing logistics as an *integrated system* and minimizing its total cost, given the firm's customer service objectives. It is impossible to design an efficient and effective logistics system without first establishing the firm's customer service objectives.

What Is Customer Service?

Customer service can be defined as:

> a process which takes place between buyer, seller, and third party. The process results in a value-added to the product or service exchanged. This value added in the exchange process might be short term as in a single transaction or longer term as in a contractual relationship. The value-added is also shared, in that each of the parties to the transaction or contract is better off at the completion of the transaction than they were before the transaction took place. Thus, in a process view: Customer service is a process for significant value-added benefits to the supply chain in a cost-effective way.[11]

Successful implementation of the marketing concept requires both obtaining customers and keeping them, while satisfying the firm's objectives for long-range profit and return on investment. Creating demand—obtaining customers—is often thought of solely in terms of promotion (selling and advertising), product, and price. However, customer service can have a significant impact on demand. In addition, customer service determines whether customers will *remain* customers.

Bernard J. La Londe and Paul Zinszer categorized the elements of customer service into three groups—"pretransaction, transaction, and posttransaction." Figure 5-2 summarizes the customer service elements identified by La Londe and Zinszer.[12]

Pretransaction Elements

The pretransaction elements of customer service tend to be nonroutine and policy-related, and they require management input. These activities, although not specifically involved with logistics, have a significant impact on product sales. The specific elements of pretransaction customer service include the following:

1. *A written statement of customer service policy.* The customer service policy statement would reflect customer needs, define service standards, determine who reports the performance measurements to whom and with what frequency, and would be operational.
2. *A written statement of service policy for customers.* It makes little sense to provide a level of service designed to improve market penetration and then fail to inform the customer of what is being provided. A written statement reduces the likelihood that the customer will have unrealistic expectations of performance. It also informs the customer how to communicate with the firm if specified performance levels are not attained.
3. *Organization structure.* Although there is no one organization structure best suited to successful implementation of a customer service policy, the structure selected should facilitate communication and cooperation between and among those functions involved in implementing the customer service policy. In addition, the firm should provide customers with the name and phone number of a specific individual who can satisfy their information needs. The individuals who manage the customer service components must have the appropriate responsibility and authority, and must be rewarded in a manner that encourages them to interface with other corporate functions.
4. *System flexibility.* Flexibility is required for the system to respond effectively to unplanned events, such as snowstorms, shortages of raw materials or energy, and strikes.

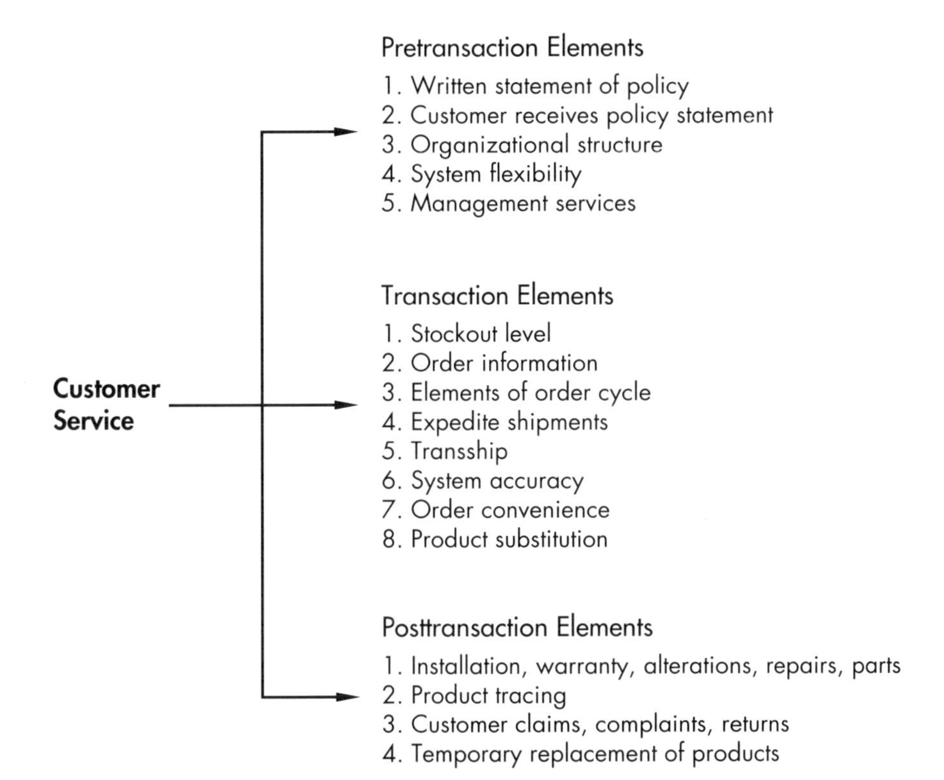

Figure 5-2
Elements of Customer Service

Source: Bernard J. La Londe and Paul H. Zinszer, *Customer Service: Meaning and Measurement* (Chicago: National Council of Physical Distribution Management, 1976), p. 281.

5. *Management services.* Training manuals and seminars designed to help the customer improve inventory management, ordering, or merchandising are elements of customer service.

All of these pretransaction elements of customer service are essential components of a successful marketing strategy.

Transaction Elements

Transaction elements are the activities normally associated with customer service, including the following:

1. *Stockout level.* The stockout level is a measure of product availability. Stockouts should be recorded by product and by customer to determine where problems exist. When stockouts occur, customer goodwill can be maintained by arranging for suitable product substitution and/or expediting the shipment when the product is replenished.
2. *Order information.* Order information is the ability to provide the customer fast and accurate information about the status of inventory, orders, expected shipping and delivery

dates, and back orders. A back-order capability allows orders that require immediate attention to be identified and expedited. The number of back orders and their associated order cycle times can be used to measure system performance. The ability to back order is important because the alternative may be to force a stockout. The number of back orders should be recorded by customer and by product category to identify and correct poor system performance.

3. *Elements of the order cycle.* The order cycle is the total elapsed time from initiation of the order by the customer until delivery to the customer. Individual components of the order cycle include order communication, order entry, order processing, order picking and packing, and delivery. Because customers are mainly concerned with total order cycle time, it is important to monitor and manage each of the components of the order cycle to determine the cause of variations.
4. *Expedite shipments.* Expedited shipments are those that receive special handling to reduce the normal order cycle times. Although expediting costs considerably more than standard handling, the cost of a lost customer may be even higher. It is important for management to determine which customers qualify for expedited shipments and which do not. Presumably, such a policy would be based on how much individual customers contribute to the manufacturer's profitability.
5. *Transshipments.* Transshipments are the transporting of product between field locations to avoid stockouts. They are often made in anticipation of customer demand.
6. *System accuracy.* Mistakes in system accuracy—the accuracy of quantities ordered, products ordered, and billing—are costly to both manufacturer and customer. Errors should be recorded and reported as a percentage of the number of orders handled by the system.
7. *Order convenience.* Order convenience refers to the degree of difficulty that a customer experiences when placing an order. Problems may result from confusing order forms or using nonstandard terminology; either can lead to errors and poor customer relations. An appropriate performance measurement is number of errors as a percentage of number of orders. These problems can be identified and reduced or eliminated by conducting field interviews with customers.
8. *Product substitution.* Substitution occurs when the product ordered is replaced by the same item in a different size or by another product that will perform as well or better. For example, a customer may order a case of shampoo for normal hair in 15-ounce bottles. If the customer is willing to accept 8-ounce or 20-ounce bottles during a stockout, the manufacturer can increase the customer service level as measured by product availability within some specified period. Two product substitutions allow the manufacturer to increase the customer service level from 70% to 97% with no change in inventory (see Figure 5-3). If the firm attained a 97% customer service level without product substitution, two product substitutions would enable it to maintain the same service level with a 28% reduction in inventory.

To develop an appropriate product substitution policy, the manufacturer should work closely with customers to inform them or gain their consent. It should also keep product substitution records to monitor performance. A successful product substitution program requires good communication between the manufacturer and customers.

The transaction elements of customer service are the most visible because of their direct impact on sales.

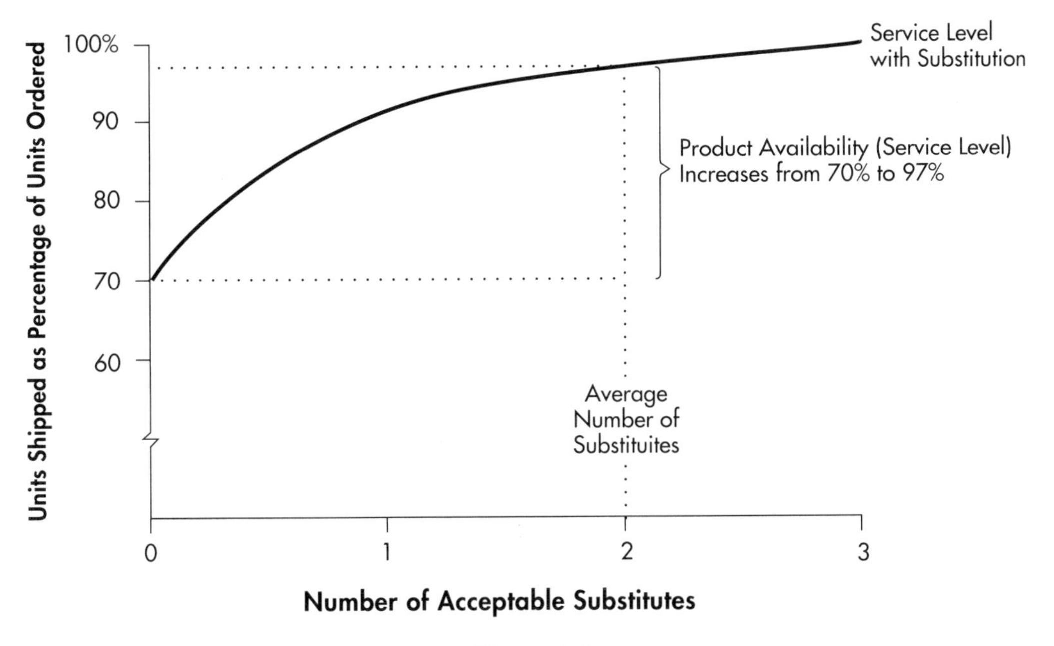

Figure 5-3
Impact of Substitution on Service Level

Posttransaction Elements

The posttransaction elements of customer service support the product after it has been sold. The specific posttransaction elements include:

1. *Installation warranty, alterations, repairs, parts.* These elements of customer service can be a significant factor in the decision to purchase; they should be evaluated in a manner similar to that for transaction elements. To perform these functions, the following are necessary: (1) assistance in seeing that the product is functioning as expected when the consumer begins using it; (2) availability of parts and/or repair workers; (3) documentation support for the field force to assist in performing their jobs, as well as accessibility to a supply of parts; and (4) an administrative function that validates warranties.[13]
2. *Product tracing.* Product tracing is another necessary component of customer service. To avoid litigation, manufacturers must be able to recall potentially dangerous products from the marketplace.
3. *Customer claims, complaints, and returns.* Usually, logistics systems are designed to move products in one direction—toward the customer. Nevertheless, almost every manufacturer has some goods returned, and nonroutine handling of these items is expensive. A corporate policy should specify how to handle claims, complaints, and returns. The company should maintain data on claims, complaints, and returns to provide valuable consumer information to product development, marketing, logistics, and other corporate functions.
4. *Product replacement.* Temporary placement of product with customers waiting for receipt of a purchased item or waiting for a previously purchased product to be repaired is an element of customer service.

Establishing a Customer Service Strategy

A firm's entire marketing effort can be rendered ineffective by poorly conceived customer service policies. Yet customer service is often a forgotten component of the marketing mix, and the level of customer service is often based on industry norms, management judgment, or past practices—not on what the customer wants, or what would maximize corporate profitability. What is the advantage of having a well-researched and needed product, priced to sell and well promoted, if customers cannot find it on the retailer's shelf? However, too much customer service will needlessly reduce corporate profits. It is essential that a firm adopt a customer service policy that is based on actual customer needs, is consistent with overall marketing strategy, and advances the corporation's long-range profit objectives.

The customer service audit evaluates the level of service a company is providing and is a benchmark for appraising the impact of changes in customer service policy. The audit is designed to identify the important elements of customer service, the manner in which performance is controlled, and the internal communication system. Audit procedures should have four distinct stages: an external customer service audit, an internal customer service audit, the identification of potential solutions, and the establishment of customer service levels.[14]

The External Customer Service Audit

The starting point in any thorough study of customer service is the external audit. The key objectives of an external audit are (1) to identify the elements of customer service that customers believe to be important when making the decision to buy, and (2) to determine how customers perceive the service being offered by each of the major vendors in the market.

The first step of an external audit is the identification of the customer service variables relevant to the firm's customers. For a consumer-packaged-goods firm, the relevant customer service variables might include some or all of the following: average order cycle time, order cycle variability, orders shipped complete, in-stock variability, accuracy in filling orders, order status information, action on complaints, returns policy, remote order transmission (computer-to-computer order entry), ability to expedite emergency orders, billing procedure, palletized and unitized loads for handling efficiency, speed and accuracy in billing, handling of claims, availability of inventory status, freight at the manufacturers' warehouses, backhaul policy, and ability to select the carrier.

It is important to develop the list of variables based on interviews with the firm's customers. A list like the one above, or one created by management, might be a useful starting point in discussions with customers. If marketing executives are involved, the list could be expanded to include other marketing mix components, such as product quality, price, terms of sale, quantity discount structure, number of sales calls, and cooperative advertising support for the product.

There are three advantages to including the marketing function. First, marketing involvement facilitates the balancing of trade-offs within the marketing mix. Second, marketing often has considerable expertise in questionnaire design, which is the next step in the process. Third, marketing's involvement adds credibility to the research findings, which increases acceptance and facilitates successful implementation.

Alternatives to using the corporate market research department include an outside market research firm; a local university where the research might be conducted by an MBA class, a doctoral student and/or a professor; or a consulting firm or vendor with specific expertise. The advantages of these alternatives are that the sponsoring company does not have to be identified, and assistance is available for developing the questionnaires. Identifying the sponsoring firm may bias responses, and the length and clarity of the questionnaire will influence the response rate.

The variables used in the external audit must be specifically tailored to the industry under study. Using variables from past research instruments as survey questions leads to misinterpretation and nonresponse when applied to different industries and channel structures.[15] In addition, the quantity and type of variables used to select and evaluate vendors is complex and not subject to simple replication of previous research endeavors.

For example, in a comprehensive study of the plastics industry, the 110 variables used were categorized by marketing mix components as follows: product (21), price (14), promotion (29), and customer service (46). Similar research in the office systems industry was conducted prior to the plastics industry research. However, only 34 variables were the same as those used in the office systems industry, 12 were revised from variables in the office systems research, and 64 were specific to the plastics industry. While almost one-half of the price, promotion, and customer service variables were similar to those used in the office systems industry, 17 of the 21 product variables were different.[16]

When the relevant customer service elements have been determined, the second step in the external audit procedure is to design a questionnaire to gain feedback from a statistically valid sample of customers. Appendix 5-A contains an example of a questionnaire format designed to determine the importance customers attach to marketing variables. On a scale of 1 to 7, customers were asked to circle the number that best expressed the importance they attached to each variable. The survey defined an important variable as possessing significant weight in the evaluation of suppliers, whereas an unimportant variable did not.[17] Respondents were asked to make a check mark if the variable was not used.

An important consideration in the external audit is determining competitive performance ratings for major vendors. This can be accomplished by asking respondents to evaluate major vendors' performance on each of the variables (see Part A of Appendix 5-A). Responses to these questions help the firm compare customers' perceptions of vendor performance. Obviously vendors want to score high on variables that are highest in importance to customers.

The questionnaire should include questions that require respondents to rate their overall satisfaction with each vendor and indicate the percentage of business they allocate to each vendor (see Part B of the questionnaire). Part C of the questionnaire also seeks to obtain specific levels of expected performance for such key variables as type of account (wholesaler, retailer, etc.), market served (national versus regional), specific geographic location, sales volume, sales growth, profit as a percent of sales, and sales volume of each vendor's products.

Before mailing the questionnaire, it should be pretested with a small group of customers to ensure that the questions are understandable and that important variables have not been ignored. The mailing list can be developed from an accounts receivable list; a sales/marketing department list of prospects; or lists of contracts, projects, bids lost, or inactive accounts. The accounts receivable list enables stratification of the sample to achieve an adequate number of large, medium, and small customers. If management wants an analysis of inactive accounts, it can send color-coded questionnaires to identify these accounts.

The results of the customer service survey used in the external audit enable management to identify problems and opportunities. Table 5-1 illustrates the type of information that can be provided. This survey evaluated both customer service and other marketing mix variables. The two columns on the left side of Table 5-1 show that the ranking of variables was not influenced by the order of the questions on the questionnaire.

In this example, 7 of the 12 variables with the highest mean customer importance scores were

TABLE 5-1
Overall Importance Compared with Selected Performance of Major Manufacturers as Evaluated by Dealers

			Overall Importance—All Dealers		Dealer Evaluations of Manufacturers									
					Mfr. 1		Mfr. 2		Mfr. 3		Mfr. 4		Mfr. 5	
Rank		Variable Description	Mean	Std. Dev.	Mean	Std. Dev.	Mean	Std. Dev.	Mean	Std. Dev.	Mean	Std. Dev.	Mean	Std. Dev.
1	9	Ability of manufacturer to meet promised delivery date (on-time shipments)	6.4	.8	5.9	1.0	4.1	1.6	4.7	1.6	6.6	.6	3.3	1.6
2	39	Accuracy in filling orders (correct product is shipped)	6.4	.8	5.6	1.1	4.7	1.4	5.0	1.3	5.8	1.1	4.4	1.5
3	90	*Competitiveness* of price	6.3	1.0	5.1	1.2	4.9	1.4	4.5	1.5	5.4	1.3	3.6	1.8
4	40	Advance notice on shipping delays	6.1	.9	4.6	1.9	3.0	1.6	3.7	1.7	5.1	1.7	3.1	1.7
5	94	Special pricing discounts available on contract/project quotes	6.1	1.1	5.4	1.3	4.0	1.7	4.1	1.6	6.0	1.2	4.5	1.8
6	3	Overall manufacturing and design *quality* of product relative to the price range involved	6.0	.9	6.0	1.0	5.3	1.3	5.1	1.2	6.5	.8	4.8	1.5
7	16	Updated and current price data, specifications, and promotion materials provided by manufacturer	6.0	.9	5.7	1.3	4.1	1.5	4.8	1.4	6.3	.9	4.3	1.9
8	47	*Timely* response to requests for assistance from manufacturer's sales representative	6.0	.9	5.2	1.7	4.6	1.6	4.4	1.6	5.4	1.6	4.3	1.7

Rank		Variable Description	Overall Importance—All Dealers		Dealer Evaluations of Manufacturers									
					Mfr. 1		Mfr. 2		Mfr. 3		Mfr. 4		Mfr. 5	
			Mean	Std. Dev.	Mean	Std. Dev.	Mean	Std. Dev.	Mean	Std. Dev.	Mean	Std. Dev.	Mean	Std. Dev.
9	14	Order cycle consistency (small variability in promised vs. actual delivery, i.e., vendor consistently meets expected date)	6.0	.9	5.8	1.0	4.1	1.5	4.8	1.4	6.3	.9	4.4	1.7
10	4b	Length of promised order cycle (lead) times (from order submission to delivery) for base line/in-stock (quick ship) product	6.0	1.0	6.1	1.1	4.5	1.4	4.9	1.5	6.2	1.1	3.7	2.0
11	54	Accuracy of manufacturer in forecasting and committing to estimated shipping dates on contract/project orders	6.0	1.0	5.5	1.2	4.0	1.6	4.3	1.4	6.3	1.1	3.5	1.6
12	49a	Completeness of order (% of line items eventually shipped complete)—made to order product (contract orders)	6.0	1.0	5.5	1.2	4.3	1.2	4.7	1.3	6.0	1.1	4.0	1.6
⋮														
50	33a	Price *range* of product line offering (e.g., low, medium, high price levels) for major vendor	5.0	1.3	4.4	1.5	4.6	1.6	5.1	1.5	5.2	1.4	3.9	1.6
⋮														
101	77	Store layout planning assistance from manufacturer	2.9	1.6	4.2	1.7	3.0	1.5	3.4	1.6	4.7	1.6	3.4	1.2

Note: Mean (average score) based on a scale of 1 (not important) through 7 (very important).

Source: Douglas M. Lambert and Jay U. Sterling, "Developing Customer Service Strategy," unpublished manuscript, University of South Florida, March 1986.

: variables. This result highlights the importance of customer service within the
g mix. A small standard deviation in customer importance ratings means there
ion in the respondents' individual evaluations of a variable's importance. For
a large standard deviation, however, it is important to use the demographic information (see Part D of the questionnaire) to determine which customers want which services. The same argument holds for the last variable, "Store layout planning assistance from manufacturer." For example, do large-volume, high-growth customers rate this higher in importance than small customers?

The previously described study in the plastics industry revealed similar results regarding the importance of customer service. The 18 variables rated as most important by the respondents (those with a mean score of 6.0 or more on a scale of 1 to 7) were as follows:

Nine Logistics/Customer Service Variables

1. Accuracy in filling orders
2. Consistent lead times
3. Ability to expedite emergency orders in a fast, responsive manner
4. Information provided when order is placed—projected shipping date
5. Advance notice of shipping delays
6. Information provided when order is placed—projected delivery date
7. Action on complaints
8. Length of promised lead times
9. Information provided when order is placed—inventory availability

Five Product Quality Variables

1. Supplier's resins are of consistent quality
2. Processability of the resin
3. Supplier's resins are of consistent color
4. Supplier's resins are of consistent melt flow
5. Overall quality of resin relative to price

Two Price Variables

1. Competitiveness of price
2. Adequate advance notice of price changes

Two Promotion-related Variables

1. Quality of the sales force—honesty
2. Quality of the sales force—prompt follow-up[18]

The honesty of the sales force variable was to a large extent a logistics variable. The in-depth interviews revealed that the honesty variable was related to the degree of accurate information about product availability and delivery provided by the sales force. Because inventory records were not on-line and real-time, customers would be told that inventory was available when in fact it had been sold, and the batch process system had not updated the inventory levels. Customers did not realize there was a problem until their order failed to arrive.

Although the mix of most important attributes is somewhat different for the two industries, a review of Table 5-1 reveals that the following variables were the same: ability to meet promised delivery date, accuracy in filling orders, advance notice of shipping delays, consistent lead times (order cycle consistency), shipping date information, length of lead time, overall product quality relative to price, competitiveness of price, and prompt follow-up from the sales force. These variables have also been identified as the most important attributes in other industries.

Most customer service studies emphasize the importance ratings of the variables being researched, reflecting an assumption that the variables rated the highest determine the share of business given to each vendor. But this may not be true, for one or more of the following reasons:

- All of an industry's major suppliers may be performing at "threshold" levels, or at approximately equal levels, which makes it difficult to distinguish among suppliers.
- Variables for which there are significant variances in vendor performance may be better predictors of market share than the variables described above.
- Customers may rate a variable as extremely important, but few or many suppliers may be providing satisfactory levels of service for that variable. Such variables offer opportunities to provide differential service in the marketplace.
- A variable may be rated low in importance with a low variance in response. In addition, no single supplier may be providing adequate service levels. Therefore, customers do not recognize the advantages of superior service for that variable. If one vendor improved performance, it could lead to gains in market share.[19]

To determine what variables represent the best opportunity for increasing market share and/or profitability, both importance and performance measures are necessary. For this reason, Table 5-1 contains customer evaluations of perceived performance for the firm being researched and its four major competitors. This gives management some insight into the relative competitive position of each vendor, as viewed by the firm's customers. It is important for management to determine what the top-rated vendor is doing to create this perception. Management also must consider what actions it can take to improve customers' perceptions of its service.

The company must compare customer perceptions of service with internal measures of performance. This may show that the customer is not aware of the service being provided or that management is measuring service performance incorrectly.

The Internal Customer Service Audit

The internal audit requires a review of the firm's current practices.[20] This provides a benchmark for appraising the impact of changes in customer service strategy. The internal customer service audit should provide answers to the following questions:

- How is customer service currently measured within the firm?
- What are the units of measurement?
- What are the performance standards or objectives?
- What is the current level of attainment (results versus objectives)?
- How are these measures derived from corporate information flows and the order processing system?
- What is the internal customer service reporting system?
- How does each of the functional areas of the business (e.g., logistics, marketing, etc.) perceive customer service?
- What is the relation among these functional areas in terms of communications and control?[21]

The overall purpose of the internal audit is to identify inconsistencies between the firm's practices and its customers' expectations. It is also important to verify customer perceptions, because customers may perceive service performance to be worse than it really is. In such a situation, the firm should change customer perceptions rather than the level of service provided.

The communications system largely determines the sophistication and control of customer service within a company. As La Londe and Zinszer stated, "Without good control of information flow within the firm and between the firm and its customers, the customer service function is usually relegated to reporting performance-level statistics and reacting to special problems."[22] That is why an internal audit must evaluate the communications flow from customers to the company and the communications flow within the company, and must review the customer service measurement and reporting system. The internal audit should give top management a clear understanding of the firm's communications with customers.

Most communications between customer and firm can be grouped into the following eight categories relating to the ordering/shipping/billing cycle: (1) order entry, (2) post–order-entry inquiries/changes, (3) delivery, (4) postdelivery reports of damages, shortages, or overages, (5) billing, (6) postbilling dispute, (7) payment delay, and (8) payment.[23] The extent to which these communications are organized and managed can significantly affect both market share and profitability. The audit will help assess the effectiveness and cost of these communications.

Management interviews are another way to gather data. Interviews should be conducted with managers responsible for order processing, inventory management, warehousing, transportation, customer service, accounting/finance, production, materials management, and sales/marketing. Such interviews help determine how managers of each of these functions perceive customer service, communicate with customers, and interface with other functional areas. Specifically, the interviews address the following:

- Definition of responsibilities
- Size and organizational structure
- Decision-making authority and processes
- Performance measurements and results
- Definition of customer service
- Management's perception of how customers define customer service
- Plans to alter or improve customer service
- Intrafunctional communications
- Interfunctional communications
- Communications with key contacts like consumers, customers, common carriers, and suppliers

Management must also evaluate the customer service measurement and reporting system to determine how customer service is measured, the units of measurement, performance standards employed, current results, the corporate function controlling each activity, sources of data, reporting formats and compilation methods, reporting frequency, distribution of reports, and transmission methods. It is equally important to understand how customers obtain information from the company. Thus, the internal audit should determine the types of information available to customers, the person in the company who provides each type of information, the way in which customers reach these departments, the average time taken to respond to customer inquiries, and the availability of information needed by the person(s) responsible for answering the inquiry.

At the end of the chapter an example of the questions that can be asked during an internal customer service audit is provided (Appendix 5-B).

Identifying Potential Solutions

The external audit enables management to identify problems with the firm's customer service and marketing strategies. Used in combination with the internal audit, it may help management adjust these strategies and vary them by segment to increase profitability. But if management wants to use such information to develop customer service and marketing strategies for optimal profitability, it must use these data to benchmark against its competitors.

The most meaningful competitive benchmarking occurs when customer evaluations of competitors' performance are compared with one another and to customers' evaluations of the importance of vendor attributes.[24] Once management has used this type of analysis to determine opportunities for gaining a competitive advantage, every effort should be made to identify "best practices"—that is, the most cost-effective use of technology and systems, regardless of the industry in which it has been successfully implemented. For obvious reasons, noncompetitors are much more likely to share their knowledge; such an approach may reveal key opportunities for significant competitive advantage over industry rivals.

A methodology for competitive benchmarking is presented with data collected from a segment of the chemical industry. The analysis involves a comparison of the performance of two major vendors in the industry. The products marketed by these firms were considered to be commodities. In this example, only two firms are analyzed, but the analysis can be expanded to more than one competitor or more than one segment.

The first step is to generate a table with importance evaluations for each of the variables as well as the performance evaluations of the firm and its major competitor (see Table 5-2). To simplify the data for this example, only customer service attributes are considered and only ten of them are included. Attributes were sorted by mean importance rating (to customers), and a systematic random sample of ten measures was selected. Those selected ensured that the analysis and discussion were based on a set of attributes that were representative of the full range of importance to customers.

The next step is to prepare a competitive position matrix with two dimensions: importance and relative performance. The performance is determined by calculating the difference in the evaluation of the sponsor's company less the evaluation of the major competitor. The nine cells in the matrix can be grouped into three broad categories:

1. *Competitive advantage*
   a. Major strength (high importance, high relative performance)
   b. Minor strength (low importance, high relative performance)
2. *Competitive parity*
3. *Competitive disadvantage*
   a. Major weakness (high importance, low relative performance)
   b. Minor weakness (low importance, low relative performance)

The first and most important cell represents the major strengths of the company. The attributes in this cell need to be emphasized in communications with customers. The second-most important cell represents the major weaknesses of the company. These need to be improved, or customers need to be convinced that these attributes are not important. The minor strengths cell represents those things that the firm does well but that customers believe are not important. Customers need to be convinced that these attributes are important to them, or expenditures need to be reduced.

The competitive position matrix can be created in various ways, depending on management's objectives. For example, the company can be compared with the average of all competitors for the entire industry. This matrix represents the company's competitive position in the entire market. A second option is to compare the company to the average of all competitors for each segment. This matrix represents the company's competitive position in each segment and suggests segment-specific strategies. A third option is to compare the company with the average of all competitors for any major account. This matrix represents the company's competitive position for a single account and suggests account-specific strategies.

These analyses can be extended to study the firm's competitive position relative to specific competitors in the industry or within market segments. Performing the analysis using specific competitors will allow management to target the primary customers of those competitors when the firm is the second or third source of supply. It also provides information that can be used to design strategies to protect the firm's primary customers from competitive threats.

The relative performance of Company A compared with that of Company B is presented in

TABLE 5-2
Importance and Performance Evaluations for Selected Customer Service Attributes

			Performance Evaluation		
No.	**Attribute**	**Importance**	**Company A**	**Company B**	**Relative Performance**
1	Accuracy in filing orders	6.42	5.54	5.65	–0.11
2	Ability to expedite emergency orders in a fast, responsive manner	6.25	4.98	5.23	–0.25
3	Action on complaints (e.g., order servicing, shipping, product, etc.)	6.07	4.82	5.18	–0.36†
4	Accuracy of supplier in forecasting and committing to shipping date for custom-made products	5.92	4.53	4.73	–0.20
5	Completeness rate (percentage of order eventually shipped)	5.69	5.29	5.27	+0.02
6	Rapid adjustment of billing and shipping errors	5.34	4.64	4.90	–0.24
7	Availability of blanket orders	4.55	5.03	4.15	+0.88*
8	Frequency of deliveries (supplier consolidates multiple/split shipments into one larger, less frequent shipment)	4.29	5.07	5.03	+0.04
9	Order processing personnel located in your market area	3.58	5.33	5.21	+0.12
10	Computer-to-computer order entry	2.30	4.07	3.53	+0.54*

* Performance evaluations of A and B are significantly different at $\rho \leq 0.01$.
† Performance evaluations of A and B are significantly different at $\rho \leq 0.05$.

Source: Douglas M. Lambert and Arun Sharma, "A Customer-Based Competitive Analysis for Logistics Decisions," *International Journal of Physical Distribution and Logistics Management* 20, No. 1 (1990): 18.

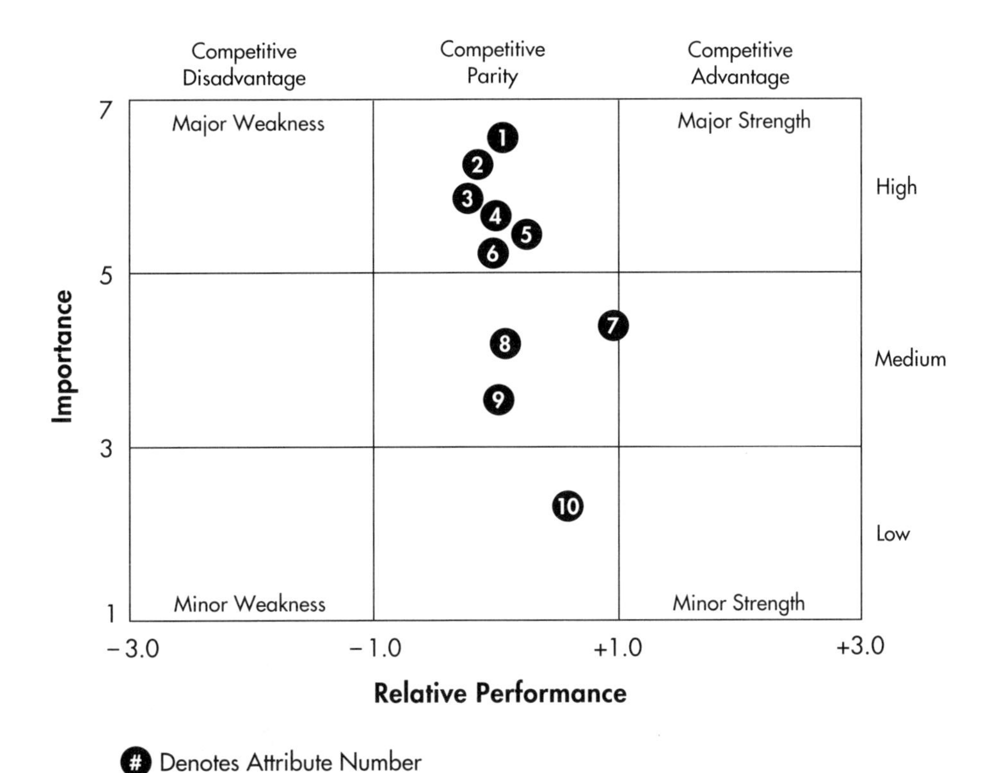

Figure 5-4
Competitive Position Matrix

Source: Lambert and Sharma, "A Customer-Based Competitive Analysis for Logistics Decisions," p. 21.

Table 5-2. Firms A and B are very similar in performance evaluations, the maximum and minimum differences being 0.88 and 0.02, respectively, on a 7-point scale. The evaluations are statistically different for three of the attributes.

The competitive position matrix presented in Figure 5-4 shows that the performance of the major competitors was viewed as virtually identical by customers. In addition, no managerially useful differences in performance evaluations could be found based on geography, customer type, or sales volume.

The top cell in the competitive parity column suggests that performance improvements should be made on attributes 1, 2, 3, 4, 5, and 6 as long as the incremental costs associated with achieving these improvements are not greater than the incremental revenues earned by doing so. For example, implementation of a service quality program in the distribution center may result in a significant improvement in the accuracy in filling orders, and this achievement may be at a relatively low cost or no net cost to the firm. On the other hand, accuracy in forecasting and committing to shipping date for custom-made products may require a new forecasting package and/or production planning model. Also, improving the order completeness rate may require new computer systems or significant increases in inventory. In summary, two variables can be manipulated.

First, the preference can be improved by actually performing better by changing buyers' perceptions regarding the firm's performance, if their perceptions can be shown to be incorrect using the firm's internal performance data. Second, the importance of each attribute can be changed by proving to the customer why it should be more or less important than the customer perceives it to be.

As will be shown, there is a risk in using the competitive position matrix by itself to identify strategic opportunities for gaining a competitive advantage. A performance evaluation matrix must be used in conjunction with the competitive position matrix. The performance evaluation matrix is obtained by creating a three-by-three matrix with the importance of each attribute and evaluation of the performance of the company as to dimensions. The matrix is divided into nine cells as follows:

1. Maintain/improve service (high importance, high performance)
2. Improve service (high importance, medium performance)
3. Definitely improve service (high importance, low performance)
4. Improve service (medium importance, low performance)
5. Maintain service (medium importance, medium performance)
6. Maintain service (low importance, low performance)
7. Reduce/maintain service (medium importance, high performance)
8. Reduce/maintain service (low importance, medium performance)
9. Reduce/maintain service (low importance, high performance)

The performance evaluation matrix presented in Figure 5-5 shows that company A was not meeting customer expectations on four of the six variables rated highest in importance by customers, and was exceeding expectations on the two least important variables (those evaluated as 2.30 and 3.58 in importance). Similar results were found for the other vendors evaluated by the respondents: No vendor was performing up to customer expectations on all of the variables rated high in importance by customers, and all were performing above expectations on the variables rated lowest in importance. A cautionary note is in order: High standard deviations in importance or performance evaluations make it necessary to determine whether market segments exist. If segments do exist, this analysis must be performed by market segment.

Figure 5-5 implies that if marketing resources were being allocated in the most efficient and effective manner, all the numbers should fall on the diagonal. That is, one would want to perform at a level of five or more on those variables that customers evaluated as high in importance, between three and five for those variables rated as medium in importance, and so on. However, as will be shown in step four, this may not be the ideal strategy when the information contained in Figure 5-4 is also considered.

The two matrices (Figures 5-4 and 5-5) must be used together because the competitive position matrix by itself also may result in incorrect conclusions about areas of improvement. For example, the competitive position matrix implies that management should increase expenditures on attributes 1, 2, 3, 4, 5, and 6 to make them major strengths. In fact, all six attributes appear to offer comparable opportunities. However, the performance evaluation matrix suggests that attributes 2, 3, 4, and 6 offer the greatest opportunities for building a competitive advantage.

The evaluation shows the competitors to be very similar on all the attributes. Consequently, the performance evaluation matrix needs to be studied to identify what areas offer the greatest opportunity for improvement. In some cases, the entire industry may be performing badly on an attribute, and improving the firm's performance may represent a substantial opportunity to gain a competitive advantage. As an example, customers felt that accuracy in filling orders (attribute 1) was one of the most important attributes of customer service (6.4 on a 7-point scale). How-

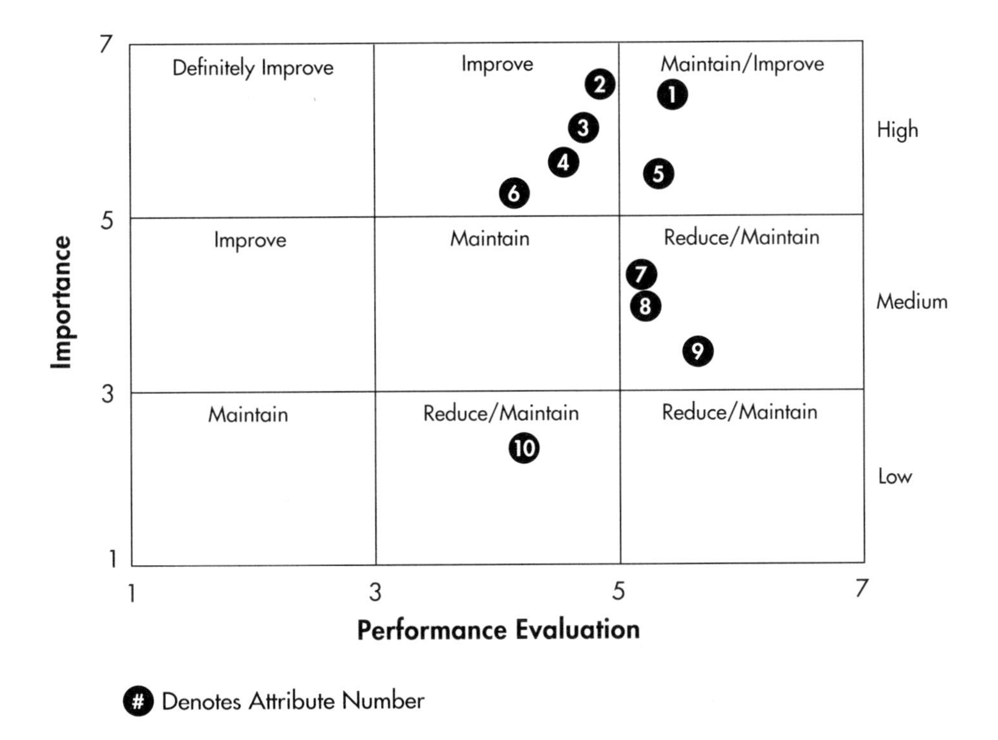

Figure 5-5
Performance Evaluation Matrix

Source: Lambert and Sharma, "A Customer-Based Competitive Analysis for Logistics Decisions," p. 21.

ever, the company and its major competitor were rated at virtually the same level of performance on this attribute (5.5 and 5.7, respectively). Thus, there is a definite opportunity for improvement.

When Figures 5-4 and 5-5 are considered simultaneously, attribute 5 does not represent the same potential for improvement as attributes 1, 2, 3, 4, and 6. This is because company A is performing close to customer expectations on attribute 5. While Figure 5-5 suggests that the firm can reduce its expenditures on attributes 7, 8, 9, and 10, Figure 5-4 suggests that caution be exercised with attributes 8, 9, and 10 because reductions in expenditures may result in relative competitive weaknesses. Clearly, the data must be interpreted carefully with respect to some attributes. For example, "computer-to-computer order entry" received a low overall importance score. However, this attribute may be of vital importance to a small number of large customers. Failure to implement computer-to-computer ordering systems might result in losing these customers. On the other hand, small molders and extruders might view this technology as "star wars." For these customers, simply having someone at the vendor location to answer the telephone and input the order through a computer terminal with on-line capability is all that is necessary. More in-depth study would be required to determine whether expenditures can be reduced without significantly affecting the purchase decision.

Figure 5-6 provides the greatest insight in terms of where expenditures can be changed to achieve a competitive advantage, because it illustrates the strategic opportunities for gaining a competitive advantage based on the importance of the attributes to customers and the firm's performance relative to its major competitor.

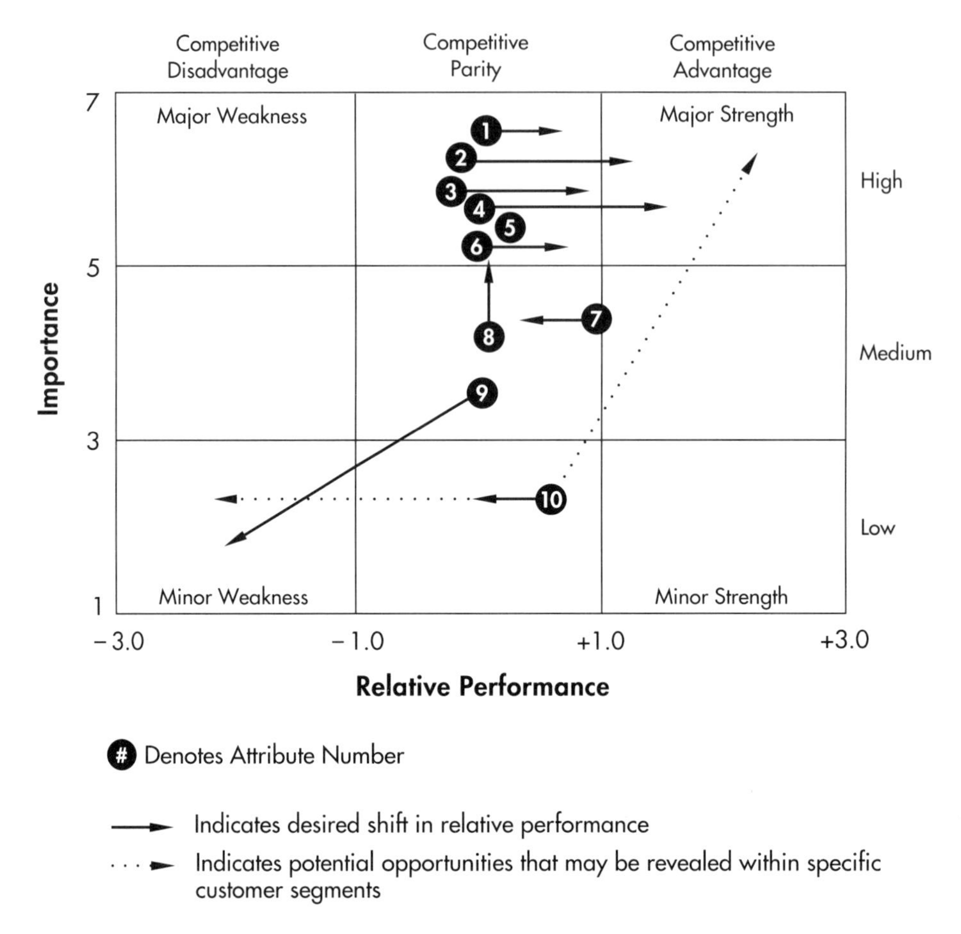

Figure 5-6
Strategic Opportunities for a Competitive Advantage

Source: Lambert and Sharma, "A Customer-Based Competitive Analysis for Logistics Decisions," p. 23.

Figure 5-6 shows that attributes 1, 2, 3, 4, or 6 can become relative competitive strengths and that attributes 2 and 4 have the potential to become major strengths and a source of competitive advantage. To make attributes 1, 3, 5, and 6 into major strengths, customers would have to be convinced that these attributes are more important to them. Otherwise, a relative competitive performance of more than +1.0 would require that company A's performance exceed customer expectations. Emphasis on attribute 7 should be reduced for all customers unless a segment of profitable customers views this attribute to be high in importance. If such a segment exists, attribute 7 should be stressed for it.

Customers should be shown why frequency of deliveries (attribute 8) is more important to them than they currently believe. Typically, when multiple/split shipments are consolidated into a larger, less frequent delivery, customers prefer the service because of the consistency, which increases their ability to plan. Also, customers should be convinced that it is not necessary to have order processing personnel located in local markets (attribute 9), and expenditures for local order entry should be reduced. High levels of performance with centralized order processing personnel would change customer perceptions about the need for a local presence. Analysis of segments may reveal that attribute 10 should be moved to the major strength category for large, profitable customers, and that expenditures should be reduced for small molders and extruders who rate computer-to-computer capability as low in importance.

The performance evaluation matrix and the competitive position matrix can be used together to guide the development of logistics strategy for competitive advantage. A company's logistics strategy needs to be designed with full consideration of the company's basic strategy and also the costs required to change that strategy. Within the customer service package, it may be possible to lengthen lead times for certain customers and use the additional planning time to provide them with higher levels of in-stock availability and more consistent delivery. This may improve service without increasing costs and may thereby improve profitability. If the improvement in service leads to increased sales, profits will increase further.

When customers prefer lower levels of marketing service in exchange for higher levels of customer service, the firm's marketing mix should be adjusted. Of course, the management of the firm has a major impact on whether this is possible.

Establishing Customer Service Levels

The final steps in the audit procedure are the actual establishment of service performance standards and the ongoing measurement of performance. Management must set target service levels for segments such as type of customer, geographic area, channel of distribution, and product line. Management must inform all employees responsible for implementing the customer service levels and develop compensation schemes that encourage attainment of the customer service objectives. Formal reports that document performance are a necessity. Finally, management must repeat the entire procedure periodically to ensure that the customer service package reflects current customer needs. In fact, it is the collection of customer information over time that is most useful in guiding corporate strategy.

Developing and Reporting Customer Service Standards

Once management has determined which elements of customer service are the most important, it must develop standards of performance. Designated employees should regularly report results to the appropriate levels of management. William Hutchinson and John Stolle offer the following four steps for measuring and controlling customer service performance:

1. Establish quantitative standards of performance for each service element.
2. Measure actual performance for each service element.
3. Analyze variance between actual services provided and the standard.
4. Take corrective action as needed to bring actual performance into line.[25]

Customer cooperation is essential for the company to obtain information about speed, dependability, and condition of the delivered product. To be effective, the service measurement/monitoring must convince customers that it will help improve future service. Figure 5-7 shows several possible measures of service performance.

The emphasis any manufacturer places on individual elements must be based on what that manufacturer's customers believe to be important. Such service elements as inventory avail-

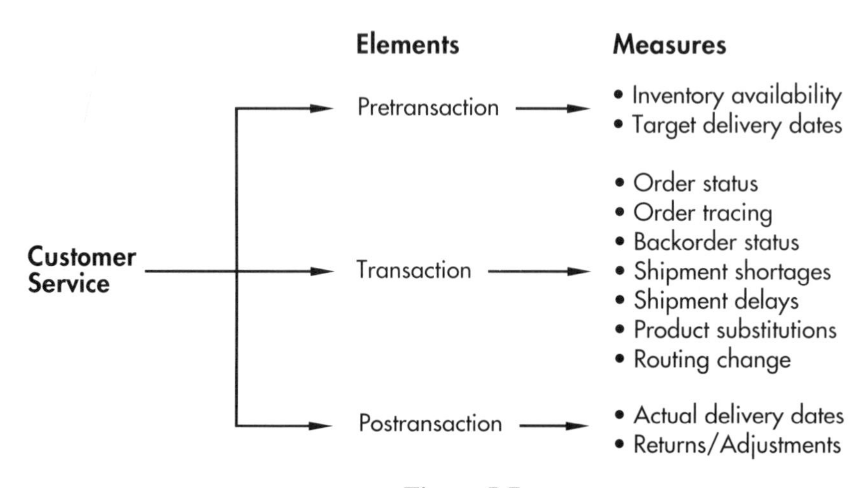

Figure 5-7
Possible Measures of Customer Service Performance

ability delivery dates, order status, order tracing, and back-order status require good communications between manufacturer and customer. Because many companies have not kept pace with technology in order processing, this area offers significant potential for improving customer service. Consider the possibilities for improved communications if customers can either phone their orders to customer service representatives who have computer terminals or input orders on their own terminals. Immediate information on inventory availability can be provided and product substitution can be arranged in a stockout. Customers also can be given the target delivery dates. Figure 5-8 provides examples of customer service standards.

The standards chosen should best reflect what customers need rather than what management *thinks* customers need. Designated employees should measure and compare performance with the standard and report this information to the appropriate levels of management on a regular and timely basis.

The firm's order processing and accounting information systems can provide much of the information necessary for developing a customer-product contribution matrix and meaningful customer service management reports.

Impediments to an Effective Customer Service Strategy

Many companies have no effective customer service strategy. Even the best-managed firms may be guilty of one of the following "Hidden Eleven Cost of Customer Service":

1. Misdefining customer service
2. Overlooking customer profitability
3. Using unrealistic customer service policies
4. Failing to research
5. Burying customer service costs
6. Misusing customer service as a sales incentive

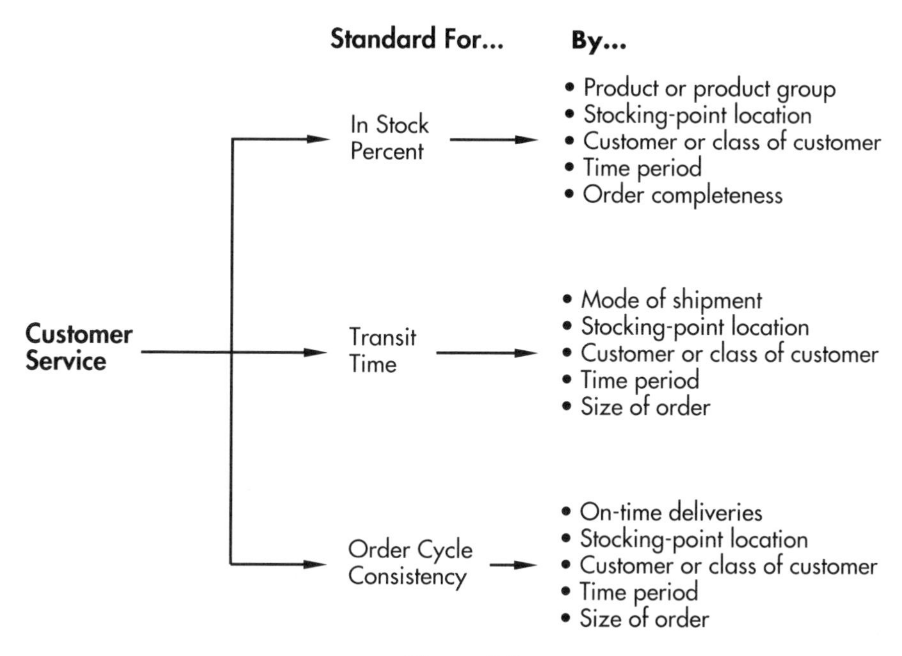

Figure 5-8
Examples of Customer Service Standards

7. Blurring lines of authority
8. Equating the number of warehouses with customer service
9. Adding bodies rather than systems
10. Employing undertrained, undercompensated personnel
11. Misreading the seller's market[26]

Failing to segment markets in terms of the service offered may be a costly mistake. Management often hesitates to offer different levels of service for fear of violating the Robinson-Patman Act. The act requires firms to cost-justify such policies. However, most firms do not have the necessary cost information.[27] Nevertheless, management can segment markets based on customers' evaluations of the importance of marketing services, and can obtain the necessary financial data using sampling techniques.

Salespeople can misuse customer service by promising faster delivery to obtain an order. But most customers value reliability and consistency in filling orders over speed of delivery. Consequently, attempting to decrease the order cycle on an ad hoc basis increases transportation costs for the expedited shipments; order assembly costs also rise because of the disruption of normal work flow. In addition, neither the customer nor the company has much to gain. When salespeople override customer service policies on shipping dates, lead times, shipping points, modes of transportation, and units of sale, they disrupt other customers' orders and increase logistics costs. In other situations, salespeople have been known not to "sell" the services being provided by the company.[28]

A firm's customer service standards and performance expectations are affected substantially by the competitive environment and what is perceived to be traditional industry practices. Consequently, management must understand industry norms, expectations, and the costs of providing high levels of customer service. Evidence suggests that:

> Many firms do not measure the cost effectiveness of service levels and have no effective way of determining competitive service levels. Information is fed back into the company through a sales organization that is often times concerned with raising service levels or through industry anecdotes and/or outraged customers. The net result of this information feedback is that firms may overreact to imprecise cues from the marketplace, or even from within their own organizations.[29]

Considering the vast sums of money firms spend on research and development and advertising, it makes little sense for a company not to adequately research the levels of customer service necessary for profitable long-range business development.

Improving Customer Service Performance

A firm can improve its customer service by the following actions:

1. Thoroughly research customers' needs.
2. Set service levels that make realistic trade-offs between revenues and expenses.
3. Use the latest technology in order processing systems.
4. Measure and evaluate the performance of individual logistics activities.

An effective customer service strategy must be based on an understanding of how customers define service. The customer service audit and surveys of customers are imperative.

Many customer service surveys show that customers define service differently than suppliers and prefer a lower but more reliable service level than that currently offered. Under these circumstances, there is no reason why a firm can't improve service as their customers perceive it and at the same time cut costs. To improve service as measured by this objective standard is often less costly than to improve service as measured by arbitrary in-house standards.[30]

Once it has determined its customers' view of service, management must select a customer service strategy that advances the firm's objectives for long-range profit and return on investment. The optimum level of customer service retains the "right" or "desired" customers. As Sabath has said:

> It should be clear that the optimum service level is not always the lowest cost level. The optimum level is one that retains customers at the lowest possible costs—and meets the company's growth needs. Defined this way, an optimum service level may be achieved by trading off some [logistics] cost savings for more valuable marketing advantages or manufacturing efficiencies. The point is that with objective, customer-defined service levels and a good handle on costs, everyone knows exactly what is being traded and what is received in return.[31]

Many firms have antiquated order processing systems. For them, automation of order processing is a significant opportunity for improving customer service. The primary benefit is the reduction in order cycle time. Given that most customers prefer a consistent delivery cycle to a shorter one, it usually is unnecessary—or unwise—to reduce their order cycle time. But by using the additional time internally for planning, the company can achieve savings in transportation, warehousing, inventory carrying costs, production planning, and purchasing. Automation improves customer service by providing the following benefits: better product availability, more accurate invoices, the ability to lower safety-stock levels and the associated carrying costs, and improved access to information on order status. In short, automated order processing systems enhance the firm's ability to perform all the transaction and posttransaction elements of customer service.

Finally, the development of an effective customer service program requires the establishment of customer service standards that:

- Reflect the customer's point of view
- Provide an operational and objective measure of service performance
- Provide management with cues for corrective action[32]

Management should also measure and evaluate the impact of individual logistics activities—transportation, warehousing, inventory management, production planning/purchasing, and order processing—on customer service. Designated employees should report achievement regularly to the appropriate levels of management. Management should compare actual performance to standards and take corrective action when performance is inadequate. For management to be successful and efficient, a firm needs timely information. It is also necessary to hold individuals accountable for their performance, because information alone does not guarantee improved decision making.

World-Class Customer Service

In 1987, the Malcolm Baldrige National Quality Award was established by Public Law 100–107, to promote quality awareness, recognize quality achievements of U.S. companies, and to publicize successful quality strategies.[33] Seven major categories, 28 subcategories, and 89 individual measures of quality are examined in the award process. According to an article in *Business America:* "The criteria for the Award are substantive, comprehensive, well-defined, and widely accepted. They amount to a practical definition of world-class quality."[34]

Thirty percent of the 1,000 points used to evaluate firms for the Baldrige Award are in the "customer focus and satisfaction" category and include the following six items: (1) customer relationship management, (2) commitment to customers, (3) customer satisfaction determination, (4) customer satisfaction results, (5) customer satisfaction comparison, and (6) future requirements and expectations of customers. It is in this area of "customer focus and satisfaction" that logistics can have its greatest impact on service quality. Logistics can also have a positive influence on sales/revenues and profits as a result of high service quality, thereby helping to create a world-class business organization.

If management expects the firm to compete successfully for the Malcolm Baldrige National Quality Award, the customer service audit described earlier is critical. Also, the customer service audit enables management to develop a customer service strategy consistent with marketing and corporate strategies. The customer service audit is a method of determining the existing service levels, determining how performance is measured and reported, and appraising the impact of changes in customer service policy. Questionnaires are a means of finding out what management and customers view as important aspects of customer service.

Although customer service may represent the best opportunity for a firm to achieve a sustainable competitive advantage, many firms implement customer service strategies that simply duplicate those implemented by their major competitors. The customer service audit can be used by management to collect and analyze customer and competitive information that fuels strategies to beat, not meet, competitors. World-class performance requires focus:

> The first step in becoming a "world class" organization is to develop strategies for improving the firm's performance on those logistics service attributes that are deemed to be most important to customers. The excellent firm will be the one that provides a quality product accompanied by superior customer service at a competitive price. To be a "world class" competitor requires a commitment to excellence and a recognition that the firm can not do all things well, but must do a few things exceedingly well.[35]

It is important to measure the various components of customer service as well as the firm's performance on those attributes. It is impossible to manage that which is not measured. Measuring customer expectations and knowing how the firm compares with competitors on customer service performance are critical for success. A firm that implements changes in systems, programs, and employee training must be able to measure the results of its actions. An initial measurement of customer expectations on customer service attributes as well as the performance of the firm and its major competitors provides only a static view—that is, at a single point in time. A longitudinal view is necessary to provide the firm with information on how its actions are being perceived by the marketplace. Therefore, ongoing surveys of customers and competitive benchmarking (i.e., a comparison of a firm's performance with that of its competitors on those attributes considered the most important to customers) must occur. In that way, the firm can respond with various strategies to create world-class customer service.[36]

APPENDIX 5-A

Survey of Marketing and Distribution Practices in the Blood Banking Reagent Industry

Source: Department of Management, Marketing and Logistics, University of North Florida, Jacksonville, Fl.

PART A: IMPORTANCE OF FACTORS CONSIDERED WHEN SELECTING AND EVALUATING SUPPLIERS OF BLOOD BANKING REAGENTS

INSTRUCTIONS

Listed on the following pages are various factors often provided by **suppliers** of reagents to their customers. **This Section involves two tasks.** Each task will be explained separately.

The first task involves your evaluation of the various factors that you might consider when you select a new reagent supplier, or when you evaluate the performance of one of your current suppliers. Please circle on a scale of 1 to 7, the number which best expresses the *importance* of each of these factors. If a factor is not used or possesses very little weight in your evaluation of suppliers, please circle number 1 (not important). A rating of 7 (very important) should be reserved for those factors that would cause you to *reevaluate* the amount of business done with a supplier, or cause you to drop the supplier in the event of inadequate performance.

The second task is to *evaluate the current performance of three major suppliers.* Please list below in the spaces labeled "Supplier A", "Supplier B" and "Supplier C" three major suppliers of reagents. If you use fewer than three suppliers, please evaluate only those that you use. Next, using the scale labeled PERCEIVED PERFORMANCE, please insert the number between 1 and 7 which best expresses your perception of the supplier's current performance under the appropriate supplier heading. If you perceive that a supplier's performance is poor, insert a 1. Reserve a rating of 7 for excellent performance. If a service is not available from a supplier, please write NA, NOT AVAILABLE, in the appropriate space.

Please identify your major suppliers below:

SUPPLIER A (**the largest amount** of your reagent purchases are from this supplier): ____________

SUPPLIER B (**second largest amount** of your reagent purchases are from this supplier): ____________

SUPPLIER C (**third largest amount** of your reagent purchases are from this supplier): ____________

EXAMPLE

FACTORS CONSIDERED	1 Not Important	2	3	4	5	6	7 Very Important	A	B	C
	IMPORTANCE							PERCEIVED PERFORMANCE SUPPLIERS (Scale of 1 to 7)		
• Product Quality	1	2	3	4	5	6	7	___	___	___
• Average Lead Time	1	2	3	4	5	6	7	___	___	___

FACTORS CONSIDERED	1 Not Important	2	3	4	5	6	7 Very Important	A	B	C
	IMPORTANCE							PERCEIVED PERFORMANCE SUPPLIERS (Scale of 1 to 7)		
1. Accurate and timely billing (invoicing)	1	2	3	4	5	6	7	___	___	___
2. Lowest Price	1	2	3	4	5	6	7	___	___	___
3. Computer-to-computer order entry	1	2	3	4	5	6	7	___	___	___
4. Consistent lead times (supplier consistently meets promised delivery date)	1	2	3	4	5	6	7	___	___	___
5 Cash discounts for early payment or prepayment	1	2	3	4	5	6	7	___	___	___
6. Ability of supplier to meet specific service and delivery needs	1	2	3	4	5	6	7	___	___	___
7. Order processing personnel are located in:										
• your city	1	2	3	4	5	6	7	___	___	___
• your state	1	2	3	4	5	6	7	___	___	___
• one centralized U.S. location	1	2	3	4	5	6	7	___	___	___
8. Rapid adjustment of billing errors (due to pricing errors)	1	2	3	4	5	6	7	___	___	___
9. Supplier absorbs cost of expedited freight and handling when the supplier experiences a stockout	1	2	3	4	5	6	7	___	___	___

FACTORS CONSIDERED	IMPORTANCE: Not Important 1	2	3	4	5	6	Very Important 7	PERCEIVED PERFORMANCE SUPPLIERS (Scale of 1 to 7) A	B	C
10. Adequate identification/ labeling of shipping carton	1	2	3	4	5	6	7	___	___	___
11. Participation of vendor in conventions	1	2	3	4	5	6	7	___	___	___
12 Adequate advance notice of price changes provided	1	2	3	4	5	6	7	___	___	___
13. Supplier adequately tests new products before delivering to market	1	2	3	4	5	6	7	___	___	___
14. Availability of status information on orders	1	2	3	4	5	6	7	___	___	___
15. Number of tests per 10ml. bottle	1	2	3	4	5	6	7	___	___	___
16. Long term (longer than 1 year) contractual relationship available with supplier	1	2	3	4	5	6	7	___	___	___
17. Supplier holds dedicated inventory in return for a commitment to buy	1	2	3	4	5	6	7	___	___	___
18. Adequate availability (supplier's ability to deliver) of new products at time of introduction	1	2	3	4	5	6	7	___	___	___
19. Supplier's adherence to special shipping instructions	1	2	3	4	5	6	7	___	___	___
20. Availability of educational material from supplier	1	2	3	4	5	6	7	___	___	___
21. Bar code location:										
• outer carton	1	2	3	4	5	6	7	___	___	___
• on the product itself	1	2	3	4	5	6	7	___	___	___
22. Supplier offers monoclonal reagents	1	2	3	4	5	6	7	___	___	___
23. Supplier combines purchases of different products in order to compute volume discount	1	2	3	4	5	6	7	___	___	___
24. Product stability (shelf life)										
• Red cells	1	2	3	4	5	6	7	___	___	___
• Antiserum	1	2	3	4	5	6	7	___	___	___
25. Free WATS line (800 number) provided										
• for entering orders	1	2	3	4	5	6	7	___	___	___
• for technical or repair service	1	2	3	4	5	6	7	___	___	___
26. Quality/cleanliness of packaging materials	1	2	3	4	5	6	7	___	___	___
27. Supplier sponsored technical seminars:										
• at user's location	1	2	3	4	5	6	7	___	___	___
• at supplier's location	1	2	3	4	5	6	7	___	___	___
28. Supplier gives you an adequate period of price protection after a price increase is announced	1	2	3	4	5	6	7	___	___	___
29. Supplier's warehousing facility is located in your immediate area	1	2	3	4	5	6	7	___	___	___
30. Coded products (type of code used):										
• bar coding	1	2	3	4	5	6	7	___	___	___
• color coding	1	2	3	4	5	6	7	___	___	___
31. Availability of published price schedule	1	2	3	4	5	6	7	___	___	___
32. Sales rep has authority to negotiate special prices	1	2	3	4	5	6	7	___	___	___
33. Availability of blanket purchase orders	1	2	3	4	5	6	7	___	___	___
34. Damage-free shipments	1	2	3	4	5	6	7	___	___	___

FACTORS CONSIDERED	Not Important 1	2	IMPORTANCE 3	4	5	Very Important 6	7	PERCEIVED PERFORMANCE SUPPLIERS (Scale of 1 to 7) A	B	C
35. Supplier replaces entire allotment when there is evidence of defective product	1	2	3	4	5	6	7	___	___	___
36. National trade journal advertising by supplier	1	2	3	4	5	6	7	___	___	___
37. Sales representative characteristics:										
• accessibility	1	2	3	4	5	6	7	___	___	___
• honesty	1	2	3	4	5	6	7	___	___	___
• product knowledge	1	2	3	4	5	6	7	___	___	___
• industry knowledge	1	2	3	4	5	6	7	___	___	___
• technical knowledge	1	2	3	4	5	6	7	___	___	___
• concern/empathy	1	2	3	4	5	6	7	___	___	___
38. Development of new products by supplier	1	2	3	4	5	6	7	___	___	___
39. Prompt handling of claims due to overages, shortages or shipping errors	1	2	3	4	5	6	7	___	___	___
40. Extended dating programs (supplier allows more than 60 days for payment)	1	2	3	4	5	6	7	___	___	___
41. Order processing personnel can provide information on:										
• product characteristics	1	2	3	4	5	6	7	___	___	___
• technical questions	1	2	3	4	5	6	7	___	___	___
• inventory availability	1	2	3	4	5	6	7	___	___	___
• projected shipping date	1	2	3	4	5	6	7	___	___	___
• projected delivery date	1	2	3	4	5	6	7	___	___	___
• availability of substitute products	1	2	3	4	5	6	7	___	___	___
42. Availability of technical materials from supplier	1	2	3	4	5	6	7	___	___	___
43. Quantity discount structure based on total annual purchases	1	2	3	4	5	6	7	___	___	___
44. Length of promised lead times (from order submission to delivery):										
• Normal orders	1	2	3	4	5	6	7	___	___	___
• Emergency orders	1	2	3	4	5	6	7	___	___	___
45. Supplier absorbs cost of freight and handling on returns due to damage or product shipped in error	1	2	3	4	5	6	7	___	___	___
46. Action on complaints related to order servicing and shipping	1	2	3	4	5	6	7	___	___	___
47. Dealing directly with the supplier (vs. distributor)	1	2	3	4	5	6	7	___	___	___
48. Contact with supplier's top management	1	2	3	4	5	6	7	___	___	___
49. Assistance/counselling provided by supplier on:										
• credit	1	2	3	4	5	6	7	___	___	___
• inventory management	1	2	3	4	5	6	7	___	___	___
• technical assistance	1	2	3	4	5	6	7	___	___	___
• data management	1	2	3	4	5	6	7	___	___	___
• work flow improvement	1	2	3	4	5	6	7	___	___	___
50. Consistency of supplier's delivered product after initial evaluation of samples by my facility	1	2	3	4	5	6	7	___	___	___
51. Supplier reacts quickly to competitive price reductions	1	2	3	4	5	6	7	___	___	___
52. Advance information (literature, specs, prices, etc.) on new product introductions	1	2	3	4	5	6	7	___	___	___
53. Supplier sponsored entertainment	1	2	3	4	5	6	7	___	___	___
54. Product reliability (consistent performance from shipment to shipment)	1	2	3	4	5	6	7	___	___	___

FACTORS CONSIDERED	IMPORTANCE: Not Important 1	2	3	4	5	6	Very Important 7	PERCEIVED PERFORMANCE SUPPLIERS (Scale of 1 to 7) A	B	C
55. Environmental considerations	1	2	3	4	5	6	7	___	___	___
56. Technical service personnel characteristics:										
• accessibility	1	2	3	4	5	6	7	___	___	___
• responsiveness	1	2	3	4	5	6	7	___	___	___
• problem-solving capability	1	2	3	4	5	6	7	___	___	___
• product knowledge	1	2	3	4	5	6	7	___	___	___
• follow up	1	2	3	4	5	6	7	___	___	___
• new techniques/ methods	1	2	3	4	5	6	7	___	___	___
57. Quality/durability of reagent packaging (protects integrity of reagent during shipping)	1	2	3	4	5	6	7	___	___	___
58. Accuracy in filling orders (correct reagent is shipped)	1	2	3	4	5	6	7	___	___	___
59. Frequency of deliveries (supplier consolidates multiple and/or split shipments into one larger, less frequent shipment)	1	2	3	4	5	6	7	___	___	___
60. Service support if salesperson is not available	1	2	3	4	5	6	7	___	___	___
61. Assistance from supplier in handling carrier loss and damage claims	1	2	3	4	5	6	7	___	___	___
62. Sensitivity (specifity) of reagent	1	2	3	4	5	6	7	___	___	___
63. Advance notice of shipping delays	1	2	3	4	5	6	7	___	___	___
64. Supplier provides promotional gifts (calendars, mugs, etc.)	1	2	3	4	5	6	7	___	___	___
65. Availability of quality control information from supplier	1	2	3	4	5	6	7	___	___	___
66. Supplier sponsored training	1	2	3	4	5	6	7	___	___	___
67. Supplier has complete assortment of reagents	1	2	3	4	5	6	7	___	___	___
68. Ability of supplier to respond to changes in requested delivery dates	1	2	3	4	5	6	7	___	___	___
69. Prompt and comprehensive response to competitive bid quotations	1	2	3	4	5	6	7	___	___	___
70. Competitiveness of price	1	2	3	4	5	6	7	___	___	___
71. Supplier expedites emergency orders in a fast, responsive manner	1	2	3	4	5	6	7	___	___	___
72. Timely response to requests for assistance from supplier's sales representative	1	2	3	4	5	6	7	___	___	___
73. Prompt notification of technical analysis results	1	2	3	4	5	6	7	___	___	___
74. Supplier's ability to work with you to improve your processes (work flow)	1	2	3	4	5	6	7	___	___	___
75. Supplier provides references for consultation service	1	2	3	4	5	6	7	___	___	___
76. Quantity discount structure based on size of individual order	1	2	3	4	5	6	7	___	___	___
77. Number of sales calls you personally receive per year from supplier's sales representatives	1	2	3	4	5	6	7	___	___	___
78. Supplier provides timely notification of product problems	1	2	3	4	5	6	7	___	___	___
79. Freight paid by supplier	1	2	3	4	5	6	7	___	___	___
80. Supplier does not raise prices more than once per year	1	2	3	4	5	6	7	___	___	___

PART B: MEASUREMENT OF OVERALL PERFORMANCE

1. Please indicate the percent that each supplier currently represents of your annual requirements, as well as the percent that you would *prefer* to give each supplier under ideal conditions in the future (Your totals should add to 100%).

	Current %	Ideal (Preferred) %
SUPPLIER A (the **largest amount** of your REAGENT purchases are from this supplier):	______%	______%
SUPPLIER B (**second largest amount** of your REAGENT purchases are from this supplier):	______%	______%
SUPPLIER C (**third largest amount** of your REAGENT purchases are from this supplier):	______%	______%
Other Suppliers	______%	______%
	100 %	100 %

2. Please mark a point anywhere on the lines below that best expresses your *level of satisfaction* with the above suppliers. If you are extremely dissatisfied with a supplier's performance, a mark should be placed very near the left end of the line (labeled Poor). If you are exceptionally pleased with the Supplier's performance, a mark should be placed very near the right end of the line (labeled Excellent). A midpoint has been placed on the line to correspond with a "Satisfactory" performance level.

OVERALL SUPPLIER PERFORMANCE

	Poor	Satisfactory	Excellent
SUPPLIER A	I________________	.	________________I
SUPPLIER B	I________________	.	________________I
SUPPLIER C	I________________	.	________________I

	SUPPLIER A	SUPPLIER B	SUPPLIER C
3. Would you recommend this supplier to another laboratory?	___ Yes ___ No	___ Yes ___ No	___ Yes ___ No
4. Have you ever reported a problem to this supplier over the service you received?	___ Yes ___ No	___ Yes ___ No	___ Yes ___ No
5. Did this supplier respond adequately to the problem you reported?	___ Yes ___ No	___ Yes ___ No	___ Yes ___ No
6. What percentage of your shipments are received on-time from your major suppliers during a typical month?	______%	______%	______%

7. If your major supplier is a DISTRIBUTOR (rather than a manufacturer), what is the **primary** reason you buy from them? (Check *only one* item)

_____ faster delivery	_____ price	_____ only available source of preferred reagents
_____ small quantities	_____ local service	_____ other (Specify) ____________________

8. For the three suppliers that you have evaluated, please give the lowest price supplier a score of 0 %. For the others, indicate the percentage premium that you pay for their services. If two or more suppliers offer the same price, give them the same score. (EXAMPLE: If Supplier B was the lowest price supplier, they would be assigned a 0; if Supplier A's price was 2 % higher than Supplier B's, they would be assigned a 2 %; if Supplier C charged the same price as Supplier A they would also be assigned a 2 %; if Supplier C's price was 3% higher than Supplier B's, it would be assigned a 3%).

SUPPLIER A ______ % **SUPPLIER B** ______ % **SUPPLIER C** ______ %

PART C: EXPECTED PERFORMANCE LEVELS

Please provide the following information with respect to the levels of customer service that you need from your suppliers of blood banking reagents. ***Supplier A** is identified as the supplier from whom you make your largest amount of* **reagent** *purchases.*

1. How many sales contacts do you receive from **SUPPLIER A** during a typical year?
   a. face-to-face calls : _____ per year b. telephone calls : _____ per year

2. How many sales contacts would you **prefer** to receive from **SUPPLIER A** during a typical year?
   a. face-to-face calls : _____ per year b. telephone calls : _____ per year

3. What response time do you expect and currently receive from **SUPPLIER A** 's sales representative?

	Expect	Currently Receive
a. Response time in Emergency situations	______ hours	______ hours
b. Response time in Non - emergency situations	______ hours	______ hours

4. How much advance notice do you *need* from **SUPPLIER A** on price changes?
   _____days _____weeks _____months

5. How much advance notice do you *currently receive* from **SUPPLIER A** on price changes?
   _____days _____weeks _____months

6. Under **normal conditions**, how frequently do you submit orders to **SUPPLIER A**? (Check one)
   a. Several times a day _____ b. Once a day _____ c. Several times a week _____
   d. Once a week _____ e. Several times a month _____ f. Once a month _____
   g. Other (please specify) _______________

7. Under **normal conditions,** what is the total average lead time (from time order is placed to day received) in calendar days :
   a. that you *need* from **SUPPLIER A**? _____ days
   b. that you *actually receive* from **SUPPLIER A**? _____ days

8. How many orders do you place with **SUPPLIER A** in a typical month? _____ orders.

9. What is the maximum number of days beyond the promised delivery date that you consider to be an acceptable delay? _____ days

10. Once you have placed an order, how long does it take to receive notification from **SUPPLIER A** as to the expected (promised) delivery date? *(Please specify the number of minutes, hours or days. If none is provided, answer "N")*
    _____ minutes _____hours _____days

11. Please indicate the percentage of your reagent orders that are initially transmitted to **SUPPLIER A** by each of the following:
    a. U.S. Mail .... _____ %
    b. TWX, FAX machine and/or other communication terminal........... _____ %
    c. Toll-free telephone line (paid by supplier)............................ _____ %
    d. Other telephone communication (paid by you).......................... _____ %
    e. Hand delivered to manufacturer's sales rep............................. _____ %
    f. Other (Specify) _______________ _____ %
    TOTAL 100 %

12. What percentage of your orders are "emergency" orders that require expedited service? _____ %

13. For products that are available from more than one supplier, identify the percentage of times that the following alternatives are used in the event that your order cannot be filled by the committed and/or requested delivery date?
    a. Backorder (hold until all product is available and ship complete) .. _____%
    b. Cancel unavailable items and ship balance by committed date..... _____%
    c. Split ship (ship quantities as they become available)................ _____%
    d. Cancel order and go to another supplier .... _____%
    e. Purchase unavailable items from another supplier..................... _____%
    f. Other (Specify)_______________ _____%
    TOTAL 100%

14. What terms of payment (e.g. 2/10, net 30) are *offered* by your major suppliers for *early payment*?

	Discount %	Number of days	Net No. of days
a. **SUPPLIER A**	_____%	_____	_____
b. **SUPPLIER B**	_____%	_____	_____
c. **SUPPLIER C**	_____%	_____	_____

15. What payment terms do you *actually receive* from **SUPPLIER A** : number of days _____ % discount for early payment _____

16. What percentage premium for handling and freight **should** a supplier charge you for an emergency, expedited order? _____ %

18. What is the typical **dollar value** of your average order of reagents from **SUPPLIER A**? $ _____________.00

19. What is the **minimum dollar value** order **SUPPLIER A** will ship? $ _____________.00

20. What percentage of the product is delivered by **SUPPLIER A**'s promised delivery date? _________ %

21. What percentage of **SUPPLIER A's** products arrive damage free? _________ %

22. Do you evaluate suppliers using: *(check one)* a. Formal process/system ____ b. Informal process/system ____
    c. No evaluation process/system ____ d. Don't know/uncertain____

23. How frequently do you evaluate supplier performance: (check *one*)
    a. constantly ___ b. weekly ___ c. monthly ___ d. quarterly ___ e. annually ___ f. never ___

24. What proportion of your orders do you realistically need to have within:

same day	_______ %
1 day	_______ %
3 days	_______ %
5 days	_______ %
7 days	_______ %
10 days or more	_______ %
TOTAL	100%

25. In your evaluation of supplier performance, which of the following factors do you consider? (Please check all that apply)
a. Fill rate on first shipment ____ b. Lead time ____ c. Lead time variability ____ d. Accuracy in invoicing ____
e. Quality of products shipped ____ f. Damage ____ g. Others (Please List)________________

PART E: DEMOGRAPHIC DATA

This information is required in order to identify major market segments and to provide more meaningful analyses of the previous sections. Please use approximate figures in the event that exact data are not readily available.

1. What has been the average rate of growth in your purchases of reagents for the company over the last 5 years? *(indicate decline in purchases with a negative sign)* ________ %

2. What is your approximate annual budget for reagents ? $ ________.00

3. How much reagent inventory (average number of days of supply of product) do you carry ? ______ days

4. How many supply sources of reagent products have you added and deleted during the last 12 months, 2 years and 5 years?

	Last 12 Months	Last 2 Years	Last 5 Years
Suppliers added	________	________	________
Suppliers deleted (dropped)	________	________	________

5. What percentage of your operating cost is represented by your purchases of reagents ? ________ %

6. Please indicate your overall evaluation of each of the following reagent suppliers.

SUPPLIER	Insufficient Information To Evaluate	Very Unfavorable 1	2	3	4	5	6	Very Favorable 7
Baxter Dade	____	1	2	3	4	5	6	7
Gamma Diagnostics	____	1	2	3	4	5	6	7
Immucor	____	1	2	3	4	5	6	7
Organon Teknika (BCA)	____	1	2	3	4	5	6	7
Ortho Diagnostic Systems	____	1	2	3	4	5	6	7
Other ________________	____	1	2	3	4	5	6	7

7. Please indicate the major specialty(s) of your hospital (you may check more than one):
___ Trauma Center ___ Cancer Research/ Treatment ___ Open-Heart Surgery ___ Neonatal Intensive Care
___ Burn Center ___ Organ/ Tissue Transplants ___ Obstetrics ___ Medical Technical Facility/ Affiliation
___ Other ________________ ___ Other ________________

	Yes	No	Uncertain
8. Do you have the authority to select (or specify) a specific (preferred) supplier of reagents?	___	___	___
9. Do you have the authority to **reject** a specific supplier of reagents?	___	___	___
10. Does your instituition belong to a **buying group** or **organization** which makes volume purchases from laboratory suppliers?	___	___	___

If yes, to which buying group do you belong? ________________

11. How do you order reagents from suppliers? ____ personally order reagents directly from suppliers
____ place orders through instituition's purchasing department

12. What is your position or title? ________________
How long have you held this position? ________ years

13. What is you highest education level? High School Diploma ____ Community College Degree ____
Undergraduate (bachelors) degree ____ Graduate degree ____

14. Please indicate the percentage of your time devoted to: a. administrative duties ______ %
b. laboratory (i.e. "bench") work ______ %
100 %

15. What are the first three numbers of your zip code? ________

Thank you for yourparticipation and cooperation in completing this survey. Your time and effort are sincerely appreciated. Please return the questionnaire in the envelope provided or mail to:

DOUGLAS M. LAMBERT, Ph.D and RONALD ADAMS, Ph.D
Department of Management, Marketing and Logistics • College of Business Administration
University of North Florida • Jacksonville, Florida 32216 • Phone : (904) 646-2780

APPENDIX 5-B

The Internal Customer Service Audit

1. Do you have a written customer service policy?
2. Do customers receive a copy of this policy?
3. Can you provide us with a definition of customer service as viewed by your company?
4. Do you provide different levels of customer service by product or customer?
5. Do your customer service standards change?
6. If your company designates particular area as customer service (or customer relations, distribution services, etc.):
   a. How many people are assigned to the area?
   b. Describe the major responsibilities of these individuals.
   c. To what department does this area report?
   d. If possible, please provide us with all job descriptions which include customer service/customer relations in the title.
7. Relative to your company's order cycle time, how frequently do you monitor the order cycle?
8. Indicate (by circling the appropriate letters from the choices below) which of the following dates are part of your measurement:
   a. Order prepared by customer.
   b. Order received by you.
   c. Order processed and released by customer service.
   d. Order received at D/C.
   e. Order picked and/or packed.
   f. Order shipped by D/C.
   g. Order received by customer.
9. Is order processing centralized in one location or decentralized?
10. On average, how many orders do you process each day, week, month?
11. What is the dollar value of a typical order? Number of line items?
12. What percentage of customer orders are placed by company field salespeole?
13. What percentage of total customer orders are placed by inside salespeople/order clerks who call the customer to get the order?
14. What percentage of total customer orders are placed by customers unaided by either company field or inside salespeople?

Source: Adapted from Jay U. Sterling and Douglas M. Lambert, "A Methodology for Assessing Logistics Operating Systems," *International Journal of Physical Distribution and Materials Management 15,* no. 6 (1985): 29–44.

	Field Salespeople		Customers		Inside Sales Order Clerks	
Order Entry Methods	**Total Company**	**This Location**	**Total Company**	**This Location**	**Total Company**	**This Location**
Mail	%	%	%	%	%	%
Telephone (paid by customer						
Free inward WATS telephone						
TWX and/or other communication terminal						
Hand-delivered to field sales rep/office						
Other (specify)						
Total	100%	100%	100%	100%	100%	100%

15. In terms of methods of order entry:
    How does each customer group above enter orders? If they use multiple methods, please indicate the percentage of their total entered via each method.
16. How many order entry locations exist in the company?
17. Once received by the firm, does the order taker:
    ______ Fill out a preprinted order form? If yes, ask for a copy.
    ______ Enter the order into the computer via a data terminal off-line?
    ______ Enter the order into the computer via a data terminal on-line?
18. Does the order taker:
    ______ Verify credit?
    ______ Verify inventory availability?
    ______ Assign inventory to the order?
    ______ Make product substitutions?
    ______ Price the order?
    ______ Confirm delivery date?
    ______ Attempt to increase order size to achieve an efficient quantity?
19. Are the following reference files manual or computerized?

File	*Manual*	*Computerized*
Customer		
Product model dictionary		
Prices (standard data)		
Prices (special quotes/projects data)		
Promotions		
Inventory balances		
Ship schedules		
Order history		

Bills of lading
Freight payment data
Production schedules
Credit
Other (please specify)

20. How are orders processed?
    ______ Batch processed
    ______ Individually processed (on-line, real-time environment)
21. How does the order taker transmit order information to:
    a. *Transportaion,* for determining route, loading sequence, and ship date?
    b. *Warehouse,* for picking and packing?
22. Do salespeople or customers receive an order acknowledgement?
    ______ Sales When? ______ How Transmitted? ______
    ______ Customers When? ______ How Transmitted? ______
    ______ Both When? ______ How Transmitted? ______
    ______ Neither
23. Do you have a *single* point of contact for customers or do certain departments handle different types of inquiries/complaints?
24. Do you provide customers with a telephone number? If so, how do you make them aware of it?
25. Do your competitors have an established method of communication for their customers who want to contact them about some aspect of their order after the order has been entered?
26. Do you have a precalculated cost for cutting a customer order?
27. Do you compute a standard cost for a stockout? (cost of lost sales?)
28. Do you use a standard cost for a back order?
29. Describe exact procedures in assigning transportation route.
30. How do you determine that you will comply with a customer's request to change to a nonstandard carrier on prepaid shipments?
31. Who determines if an expedite charge will be assessed?
32. What percentage of orders phoned in require expedited service?
33. What are criteria used to process following types of orders/order adjustments?
    a. Request for premium and/or special, nonstandard transport mode.
    b. Revisions/adjustments to production schedules.
    c. Split shipments.
34. Do you attempt to differentiate service to different customers (prioritize)?
35. Has marketing told customer service the service standards it expects for various customers—specific and/or distinct groups of customers?
36. What is the distinguishing feature between "cooperative" and "non cooperative" customer accounts
37. How do you view your interface with production planning and scheduling?
38. What type of data do you provide production planning?
39. What effort is made to encourage a scheduled delivery program with customers—particularly for those operating under "LTL" policies?
40. How are orders physically transmitted to the distribution center(s)?
41. Please describe the exact procedures followed in sorting/preparing (picking lists) for submission to the distribution center(s).

Notes

1. This material is from Douglas M. Lambert and James R. Stock, *Strategic Logistics Management,* 3d ed. (Homewood, Ill.: Irwin, 1993). No part of this material may be reproduced in any form without the written permission of the publisher. For expanded treatment of these and other logistics-related issues, please refer to *Strategic Logistics Management.*
2. James R. Stock and Douglas M. Lambert, "Becoming a 'World Class' Company with Logistics Service Quality," *International Journal of Logistics Management* 3, no. 1 (1992): 73.
3. S. Phillips, A. Dunkin, J. B. Treece, and N. H. Hammonds, "King Customer," *Business Week* (March 12,1990): 88. Also see Patricia Sellers, "What Customers Really Want," *Fortune* 121, no. 13 (June 4, 1990): 58–68.
4. The relationship between customer service and market share has been documented in Jay U. Sterling, "Integrating Customer Service and Marketing Strategies in a Channel of Distribution: An Empirical Study," Ph.D. diss., Michigan State University, 1985.
5. See, for example, Thomas J. Peters and Robert H. Waterman, Jr., *In Search of Excellence* (New York: Harper & Row, 1982).
6. This material is taken from Douglas M. Lambert, "Improving Profitability by Managing Marketing Costs," a paper presented at the American Marketing Association Accounting/Marketing Conference, 1981; and Douglas M. Lambert and Douglas E. Zemke, "The Customer Service Component of the Marketing Mix," *Proceedings of the 20th Annual Conference of the National Council of Physical Distribution Management* (NCPDM; now Council of Logistics Management [CLM]), 1982, pp. 1–24.
7. See Jay U. Sterling and Douglas M. Lambert, "Establishing Customer Service Strategies Within the Marketing Mix," *Journal of Business Logistics* 8, no. 1 (1987): 1–30.
8. Contribution is equal to the selling price minus the variable costs of production, marketing, and logistics.
9. The place component also considers the firm's channels of distribution. The channels used affect the level of customer service required as well as total logistics costs. Consequently, logistics system costs will influence channel design.
10. Sterling and Lambert, "Establishing Customer Service Strategies," pp. 1–20.
11. Bernard J. La Londe, Martha C. Cooper, and Thomas G. Noordewier, *Customer Service: A Management Perspective* (Chicago: Council of Logistics Management, 1988), p. 5.
12. Bernard J. La Londe and Paul H. Zinszer, *Customer Service: Meaning and Measurement* (Chicago: National Council of Physical Distribution Management, 1976), pp. 156–59.
13. Ibid., p. 278.
14. The following material is adapted from Douglas M. Lambert and Douglas E. Zemke, "The Customer Service Component of the Marketing Mix," *Proceedings of the 20th Annual Conference of the National Council of Physical Distribution Management,* 1982, pp. 1–24.
15. Sterling and Lambert, "Establishing Customer Service Strategies," pp. 1–30.
16. Douglas M. Lambert and Thomas C. Harrington, "Establishing Customer Service Strategies Within the Marketing Mix: More Empirical Evidence," *Journal of Business Logistics* 10, no. 2 (1989).
17. Although a considerable body of research in service quality in service industries uses expectations sales with "strongly agree" and "strongly disagree" as the anchor points, research has shown that results obtained are the same as those obtained using importance scales. See Douglas M. Lambert and M. Christine Lewis, "A Comparison of Attribute Importance and Expectation Scales for Measuring Service Quality," in *Enhancing Knowledge Development*

in Marketing, ed. William Bearden et al. (Chicago: American Marketing Association, 1990), p. 291.
18. Lambert and Harrington, "Establishing Customer Service Strategies," p. 50.
19. Sterling and Douglas, "Establishing Customer Service Strategies," pp. 1–30.
20. This section is adapted from Douglas M. Lambert and M. Christine Lewis, "Managing Customer Service to Build Market Share and Increase Profit," *Business Quarterly* 48, no. 3 (Autumn 1983): 50–57.
21. Ibid., p. 52.
22. La Londe and Zinszer, *Customer Service,* p. 168.
23. Lambert and Lewis, "Managing Customer Service," p. 53.
24. The material in this section is from Douglas M. Lambert and Arun Sharma, "A Customer-Based Competitive Analysis for Logistics Decisions," *International Journal of Physical Distribution and Logistics Management* 20, no. 1 (1990): 17–24.
25. William H. Hutchinson, Jr., and John F. Stolle, "How to Manage Customer Service," *Harvard Business Review* 46, no. 6 (November–December 1968): 85–96.
26. Warren Blanding, "The Hidden Eleven Costs of Customer Service," *Transportation and Distribution Management* 14, no. 4 (July–August 1974): 6–10.
27. See Douglas M. Lambert, *The Distribution Channels Decision* (New York: National Association of Accountants, and Hamilton, Ontario: Society of Management Accountants of Canada, 1978); Douglas M. Lambert and John T. Mentzer, "Is Integrated Physical Distribution Management a Reality?" *Journal of Business Logistics* 2, no. 1(1980): 18–27; and Douglas M. Lambert and Howard M. Armitage, "Distribution Costs: The Challenge," *Management Accounting* (May 1979): 33–37, 45.
28. Douglas M. Lambert, James R. Stock, and Jay U. Sterling, "A Gap Analysis of Buyer and Seller Perceptions of the Importance of Marketing Mix Attributes," in *Enhancing Knowledge Development in Marketing,* ed. William Bearden et al. (Chicago: American Marketing Association, 1990), p. 208.
29. La Londe, Copper, and Noordewier, *Customer Service,* p. 29.
30. Robert E. Sabath, "How Much Service Do Customers Really Want?" *Business Horizons* (April 1978): 26.
31. Ibid., p. 26.
32. La Londe and Zinszer, *Customer Service,* p. 180.
33. *1992 Award Criteria,* Malcolm Baldrige National Quality Award, Washington, DC: U.S. Department of Commerce, 1992.
34. M. Katherine Glover, "Xerox and Milliken get Baldrige Award," *Business America* 110, no. 23 (November 20, 1989): 3.
35. James R. Stock and Douglas M. Lambert, "Becoming a 'World Class' Company with Logistics Service Quality," *International Journal of Logistics Management* 3, no. 1 (1992): 79.
36. Ibid., p. 79.

CHAPTER 6

Marketing Channels

Strategy, Design, and Management

Louis W. Stern
Adel I. El-Ansary

Individual consumers and corporate/organizational buyers are aware that literally thousands of goods and services are available through a large number of diverse channel outlets. What they may not be as well aware of is that the channel structure—or the set of institutions, agencies, and establishments through which the product must move to get to them—can be amazingly complex.[1]

Rudiments of Marketing Channel Structure

Usually, combinations of institutions specializing in manufacturing, wholesaling, retailing, and many other areas join forces in marketing channel arrangements to make possible the delivery of goods to industrial users or customers and to final consumers. The same is true for the marketing of services. For example, in the case of health care delivery, hospitals, ambulance services, physicians, laboratories, insurance companies, and drugstores combine efforts in an organized channel arrangement to ensure the delivery of a critical service. All these institutions depend on one another to cater effectively to consumer demand. Therefore, marketing channels can be viewed as sets of interdependent organizations involved in the process of making a product or service available for use or consumption.

From the outset, it should be recognized that not only do marketing channels satisfy demand by supplying goods and services at the right place, quantity, quality, and price but they also stimulate demand through the promotional activities of the units (e.g., retailers, manufacturers' representatives, sales offices, and wholesalers) they comprise. Therefore, the channel should be viewed as an orchestrated network that creates value for the user or consumer through the utilities of form, possession, time, and place.

The major focus of marketing channel management is on *delivery.* It is only through distribution that public and private goods can be made available for consumption. Producers of such goods (including manufacturers of industrial and consumer goods, legislators passing laws, educational administrators conceiving new means for achieving quality education, and insurance companies developing unique health insurance coverage, among many others) are individually capable of generating only form or structural utility for their "products." They can organize their production capabilities in such a way that the products they have developed can, in fact, be seen, analyzed, debated, and, perhaps by a select few, digested. But the actual large-scale delivery of the products to the consuming public demands different types of efforts that create time, place, and possession utilities. In other words, consumers cannot obtain a finished product unless the product is transported to where they can gain possession of it. In fact, the four types of utility (form, time, place, and possession) are inseparable; there can be no "finished" product without incorporating all four into any given object, idea, or service.

In every marketing channel, the members that do business together have some kind of working relationship. At the extreme ends of the continuum of these relationships are purely *transactional* relationships on one side and purely *collaborative* ones on the other. Transactional relationships occur when the customer and supplier focus on the timely exchange of basic products for highly competitive prices. Collaborative relationships, or *partnerships,* occur through partnering—a process whereby customer and supplier form strong and extensive social, economic, service, and technical ties *over time.* The intent in a strategic partnership/alliance is to lower total costs and/or increase value for the channel, thereby achieving mutual benefit. A strategic alliance can also denote horizontal partnerships that develop between two organizations at the same marketing level. Partnerships capitalize on the notion that marketing channels are *vertical value-adding chains that create competitive advantage.*

An outgrowth of partnerships is the *seamless channel,* an extension of the concept of the seamless organization, which has all departments working together to serve their customer, thereby blurring the organizational lines that separate departments within the organization. The seamless channel blends the borders of channel members by having multiple levels in each organization to deliver quality service to the customer. Partnerships contribute to the seamless channel by giving channel members a sense of being on the same *team.* The adversarial relationship that is so prevalent is replaced by one built on trust and cooperation.

Viewing channels as competitive units is significant for all companies, including those that market their products through several different channels and those that develop assortments of goods and services by purchasing from various suppliers. The way individual manufacturers coordinate their activities with their various intermediaries and vice versa determines the viability of one type of channel alignment over others made up of different institutions and agencies handling similar or substitutable merchandise.

Channel Planning

Creative, well-executed marketing channel strategies provide some of the more potent means by which companies can enhance their ability to compete domestically and internationally. For example, Baxter Hospital Supply Division (formerly American Hospital Supply Corporation) has combined elements of vertical integration of supply, outsourcing, and sophisticated electronic linkages with its customers to dominate its markets. Caterpillar (Cat) has built such a formidable dealer system for heavy construction equipment that it represents Cat's primary advantage over its archrival, Komatsu. Steelcase has set such a high standard for distribution performance in delivering complex office furniture installations complete and on time that its competitors have had to struggle simply to stay in sight. And Federal Express set the small-package delivery industry on its ear with radically new, efficient, and customer-oriented approaches.

The approach of this chapter, if followed step-by-step, answers the following questions:

1. What *kinds of services* must be provided by marketing channels to end users to ensure their satisfaction, regardless of the specific channels employed?
2. What kinds of *marketing and/or logistical activities* or functions must be performed to generate those services, and how much will those activities cost?
3. Which *types of institutions or agencies* are in the best position to perform the activities, from the standpoint of their effectiveness and their efficiency at doing so? Is it possible for potential channel members (e.g., manufacturers, wholesalers, and retailers) to divide distribution among themselves, or is vertical integration more appropriate in certain circumstances?

The approach focuses on the design of what have been called "customer-driven distribution systems."[2] The examples (although disguised) and insights provided throughout this chapter in illustrating the approach have been drawn from a decade of studies of major corporations in highly diverse industries.[3]

A Blueprint for Designing Marketing Channels

The implementer of the process suggested here should be forewarned—the ten steps discussed in detail below are not simple or quick. Furthermore, none of them should be skipped in the interest of expediency, even though the process may be accelerated by performing some of them concurrently rather than sequentially. Being complete is mandatory, because of all the marketing decisions a corporation can make, distribution decisions are the most long-term in nature. A company can change its prices, its advertising, hire or fire a market research agency, revamp its sales promotion program, and modify its product line in the short run. Once management sets up its distribution channels, however, considerable evidence suggests there is great reluctance to modify them.

On the other hand, change, while frequently difficult and frustrating, is indeed possible. IBM violated all its cultural norms by marketing its personal computers through retailers like Sears and Computerland and through its own IBM Product Centers. (It later sold its Product Centers to NYNEX in yet another shift in channel strategy.) The J. I. Case Division of Tenneco moved swiftly following its acquisition of International Harvester's farm equipment business and reduced the number of dealers in the combined enterprise by nearly 800. But such pruning can be very painful and can stimulate costly lawsuits. In other words, channel change should be approached slowly and carefully.

Step 1: Examine What is Being Sold for Value

The first axiom of distribution design is that all the hard work required to structure channels will go to waste unless the product or service being marketed has real value. If the end users do not perceive it as useful or meaningful, distribution—no matter how well thought through—will not save it. Salespeople, distribution centers, retailers, distributors, manufacture's representatives, brokers, and all the other organizations and individuals who assume roles in marketing channels know when products and services are inferior. Contrary to some beliefs, distribution cannot make a weak product strong, even though marketing efforts may hype sales in the short run.

The remainder of this discussion is based on the assumption that the product or service for which the distribution system is being designed has some inherent value for at least some niche or segment. If that assumption cannot be supported, the channel design process will probably be a waste of time, effort, and capital.

Step 2: End-User Segment Analysis: A Zero-Based Approach

A fresh approach to channel strategy requires that a firm forget it already has a distribution system in place. The best way to design a system is to start from scratch, leaving history behind. Management must suspend conventional wisdom for the time being and not bind its imagination by adhering to the existing model.

In addition, questions about direct vs. indirect channels must be ignored during this step. The first task is to learn what end users want in the way of *service outputs,* regardless of the outlets from which they are to obtain the firm's products or services. And because there is no such thing as a truly homogeneous market where all end users want exactly the same service outputs, attention must focus on what limited, though substantial, segments desire or on how the market might be broken into segments desiring common service outputs.

Therefore, step 2 in the channel design process calls for thorough research, as discussed in Chapter 5, to find out (1) what end users want from the buying process, beyond a first-rate product, and (2) how these preferences can be used to group end users into discrete segments. For a personal computer, service outputs could be such things as product demonstration; provision of long-term warranties; accurate delivery; flexible financing; user training; repair, installation, and burn-in services; availability of "loaners" during repair; and technical advice. Four generic types of service outputs are (1) *lot size* (does an end user want to buy in units of one or in multiple units?), (2) *market decentralization* (does an end user value around-the-corner convenience, information, and technical assistance, or is he willing to deal across great distances, say, via a toll-free phone call?), (3) *delivery or waiting time* (does the end user want immediate delivery or is she more concerned about delivery assurance?), and (4) *product variety* (does the end user value one-stop shopping for associated products?).[4]

Once it is known what end users seem to value, examination of the segmentation issue can proceed in two different ways. Either the sample group of respondents can be divided into a priori segments (such as those often employed in product or advertising decisions) and then analyzed to see whether those segments share desired purchasing patterns. Or, as mentioned above, the data can be allowed to speak for themselves and define segments that seem best to match end users with purchasing patterns.

From a purely theoretical perspective, it is much better to follow the latter path, because how end users prefer to shop for products and services does not necessarily correlate highly with their preferences for product features, their media habits, their lifestyles, or whatever other common segmentation schemes management usually employs. For example, in marketing industrial goods, firms generally use what might be called (generously) a "convenient" segmentation scheme: they divide their markets into small (say, 1 to 50 employees), medium (50 to 500 employees), and large (over 500 employees) companies. It is sometimes difficult to understand why products developed with large companies in mind might not also appeal to small companies; be that as it may, it is even more difficult to understand why the service outputs desired by one segment should necessarily differ from those desired by another. It would be far better to let the data determine the answer rather than to impose an arbitrary segmentation scheme or one based on convenience or conventional wisdom.

In either case, one must identify the linkage between purchasing patterns and relevant segments. This matching keeps the focus where it belongs—on segments rather than on markets made up of potential or existing buyers with heterogeneous needs. For example, if one is selling office equipment to the small-business market, self-employed accountants are likely to make up an important segment, one no doubt having much different needs than a segment made up of, say, start-up scientific research firms.

It is not enough, however, to generate a laundry list of shopping attributes desired by specific segments, because the list is likely to contain items that are either too grandiose or too trivial for consideration. Given "free choice," individuals will always opt for everything. Respondents must be motivated to make trade-offs among attributes (e.g., locational convenience vs. low price vs. extensive product variety vs. expert sales assistance) so that, eventually, it will be possible to weight the attributes relative to one another. Several marketing research techniques are available to aid in this step of the process, including conjoint analysis, hybrid modeling, and constant-sum scales.[5]

Several examples of this type of analysis, using constant-sum scales, illustrate this approach. In each case, focus groups were first conducted of existing and potential buyers to determine all the possible service outputs that end users might desire. The long lists of service outputs generated by these focus groups were then screened for trivial (e.g., availability of ash trays) and clearly redundant (but differently worded) shopping preferences. The remaining service outputs were then submitted to a sample of respondents who were asked, via a structured survey, whether the service outputs could be related, in any way, to existing distribution systems and, if yes, how well they related.

Data from this sample were then factor analyzed; the resulting clusters, once labeled, provided the final list of service outputs desired by all possible segments (however defined) in the market targeted for attack. Then, a much larger sample of respondents (usually stratified, so as to include potentially important groups of end users) was questioned, again using a structured survey instrument, about their preferences. In one part of the survey, respondents were asked to allocate 100 points (a constant-sum) among the service outputs, indicating by their allocation how much they preferred one output over another.

Table 6-1 shows the disguised results of the allocation relative to office equipment and ser-

TABLE 6-1
Service Output Segments for Corporate Office Equipment and Services
(Relative importance on 100-scale by service output)

	Segments				
Service Outputs	**Brand Variety/ Demonstration**	**Support-Intensive**	**Relationship**	**Price-Sensitive**	**Product Variety/ Advice**
Ongoing relationship/personal calls	13	8	30	6	11
Wide range of products/advice	13	9	12	7	29
Support/maintenance/reliability	23	58	29	33	32
Brand variety	14	8	8	7	6
Low price	20	9	10	37	12
Product demonstration	17	9	10	9	10
TOTAL	100	100	100	100	100
Portion of revenue in this cluster	21%	26%	25%	15%	13%

Source: Gemini Consulting and Louis W. Stern. © 1986 by Lewis W. Stern. Data have been disguised.

vices being sold to the business (as opposed to residential) marketplace. The service outputs (ongoing relationship/personal calls, wide range of products/service, etc.) are listed on the left side of the table. The resulting segments (brand variety/demonstration, support-intensive, etc.) are listed over each column.

The names assigned to the segments were derived from the strength of the preferences for specific service outputs. For example, the support-intensive segment assigned 58 out of 100 points to the service output support/maintenance/reliability. Finally, the percent of revenue accounted for by each segment is given at the bottom of each column, indicating that each segment represents a substantial amount of money in this multibillion dollar marketplace.

Several interesting insights can be derived from Table 6-1. First, marketing channels serving the various segments must be able to deliver more of some service outputs than others. It is unlikely that any one channel will be able to satisfy the needs of all segments. Second, every segment values support highly; therefore, support capability must be designed into every channel, and/or any channel selected to market office equipment and services had better be able to provide support to its customers. Third, because of the importance attached to support, separate attention was required, highlighting its delivery from the kinds of outputs that are normally generated by sales channels.

Once segments are isolated, demographic profiles can be developed for each to determine whether the end users comprising them come from the same industry, are approximately the same size, are located in particular regions of the country, and so on. If there are commonalities, then marketing to the segments will be much easier than if the segments represent a random cross section of the population. For example, the support-intensive segment was heavily (but not completely) represented by large firms selling financial services.

Table 6-2 is an analysis similar to that of Table 6-1, only here the focal product is printing supplies, and the market targeted is small business.

Any type of goods or services can be analyzed with this approach. For instance, financial services are as susceptible to (and ripe for) this kind of analysis as telecommunications equipment and services, printing supplies, or automobiles. According to the MAC Group:

> When customers select a financial services provider, they look for knowledgeable advice or convenient hours. Customers do not pay for tellers, ATMs [automated teller machines], brokers, or career agents. They pay for the value of service, convenience, and advice each of these options delivers.[6]

It is important to note that step 2 is not a snapshot in time of existing customer needs. It focuses on service outputs or benefits rather than on specific channel mechanisms that presently exist. For example, the research involved asks end users about "convenient access to money without waiting in line" rather than about ATMs per se. This fact lengthens the half-life of this kind of research and also allows for more creative design of ideal channels in later steps.

Step 3: Distribution Outlet Design for End Users

Step 3 focuses on the clusters of shopping attributes or service outputs that define a segment. Suppose, for example, that the following attributes cluster together relative to the purchase of a consumer durable (e.g., television set, dishwasher, refrigerator, or automobile): very low price, self-service, somewhat broad assortments of merchandise, limited after-sale service, relatively spartan atmosphere, multiple brands available. Clearly, the set of consumers attracted to such

TABLE 6-2
Service Output Segments for Office Supplies
(Relative importance on a 100-point scale by service outputs)

	Selected Segment Examples*		
Service Outputs	**Segment A**	**Segment B**	**Segment C**
Advice/Relationship	9	42	10
Variety	5	8	6
See/Touch	3	4	2
Returns	8	9	9
Quality	12	10	9
Well-known	2	3	2
Price	48	11	18
Sales calls	2	5	4
Service	11	8	40
TOTAL	100	100	100
Portion of Sample	11%	20%	13%

* Not all segments are shown.

Source: Gemini Consulting and Louis W. Stern. © 1986 by Louis W. Stern. Data have been disguised.

an outlet is willing to trade off the amenities of upscale service and close-in convenience for very low prices. Indeed, those characteristics seem more to typify a discount store operation than an upscale department store. For industrial goods, such as maintenance, operating, and repair items, one cluster of shopping characteristics might contain moderate (reasonable, but not lowest) price, emergency delivery service, extended credit terms, availability of multiple brands and very broad assortments, locally maintained inventories, ordering simplicity (e.g., via computer terminal), and occasional advice on new items and uses. This set seems more to typify an industrial/full-function distributor than a manufacturer's distribution center. Here, customers appear to want lots of service and availability and are willing to sacrifice some price benefits to get them.

Each cluster of service outputs should, if possible, be labeled with the names of existing institutional types to provide an anchor point for step 4. For example, the retailing concepts relative to the sale of new cars are shown as follows:

Retail Concept Definitions for New Car Sales

- *Department Store.* Many brands, all models merchandised by product category, upscale decor, inventory on site, many services, reasonably convenient.
- *General merchandise store.* Single brand, all models, extensive inventory on site, limited services, nonfocal product merchandise available, reasonably convenient.
- *High-priced specialty store.* Most major luxury brands of the focal product, upscale decor, separate service facility, no inventory—special orders only, reasonably convenient.

- *Supermarket.* Most major brands, fast-selling models, purchase from inventory, limited services, separate service facility, reasonably convenient, low prices.
- *Convenience store.* Selected fast-selling brands and models, purchase from inventory, very limited services, no after-sales support, very convenient, high prices.
- *Warehouse store.* Most major brands, fast-selling models, bare decor, purchase from inventory, limited services, no after-sale support, not convenient, very low prices.
- *Catalog showroom.* Most major brands, fast-selling models, special orders only, limited services, no after-sale support, reasonably convenient, low prices.
- *Discount house.* Most major brands, inexpensive economy models, purchase from inventory, bare decor, very limited services, no after-sale support, reasonably convenient, low prices.
- *Existing retailer.* Single brand, all models, inventory on site, many services, convenient.
- *Emerging retailer.* Many brands, all models, inventory on site, many services, not convenient.

It is important, however, to keep one's eyes open for hybrids and to note carefully the deviations in the clusters from any institution or agency presently available in distribution. And as in the preceding list, labeling should not be hamstrung by industry experience. For instance, if the chemical industry has no analogy to a discount store or a rack jobber but that is what the service outputs desired by a significant segment of end users describe, then the appropriate label should be affixed to the clusters, regardless of industry history. It helps the creative channel design process to think across industries as well as across consumer and industrial channel types. There is no reason to assume that consumer channel types could not be adapted to business-to-business marketing and vice versa—for example, CompUSA Superstores selling computers and software, Staples Superstores selling office supplies.

Because this process is more social science than rocket science, there is no need to adhere to it rigidly. Even approximations provide useful insights. For example, in another proprietary study for a company marketing a consumer electronics durable, three major consumer segments were isolated: price shoppers, price and training/repair buyers, and support/relationship seekers. Based on analysis of the service output data for these segments, the "ideal" outlets shown later, on the bottom row of Table 6-3, were isolated.

Of all the steps in the process, step 3 is the most creative. In looking at the clusters that come out of step 2, the ability to visualize an outlet is critical. As mentioned above, labeling the clusters is important, because the labels are reference points, anchoring the outlets to existing institutional types but not necessarily describing them in any exact way. If it is possible to "hook" the outlets to real-world analogs, it will be possible to learn from experience (rather than reinventing the wheel) by eventually questioning experts familiar with setting up similar systems and obtaining their advice. For clusters that do not fit well-known categories, new names may have to be coined that permit positioning them along the extremely wide continuum of industrial or consumer goods intermediaries.

In collecting data in step 2, it is also extremely important to admit as many service outputs as possible to the analysis, because if end users are not given the opportunity to assess the value of an attribute, that attribute will not appear later in the analysis. In other words, for a shopping characteristic to influence the labeling of a cluster of characteristics in step 3, it must have the opportunity to show up in step 3. Myopia during steps 2 and 3 of this process could undermine the whole exercise.

Step 4: Designing the "Ideal" Distribution System

Up to this point, the entire focus has been on clustering market-driven service outputs and imagining these as outlet types that satisfy end users. No other constraints have been imposed on the process. The customer is king, emperor, baron, and potentate wrapped into one. In step 4, it is still important to hold onto this perspective. However, now the process will be subjected to the first of many reality checks, as shown in Table 6-3.

At this juncture, it is essential to assess whether it is feasible to combine the statistically derived attributes into outlets, as done in step 3. As suggested above, this often requires collecting opinions of individuals intimately familiar with outlets similar to those isolated. In this feasibility check, negative reactions should not be taken as final judgments. A presumption should be made, however, against any outlet that experts believe combines attributes in ways that would be impossible to realize or foolhardy to attempt.

Next, it is necessary to enumerate the kinds of effort required to assure that the service outputs can be delivered to relevant segments by the set of feasible outlets. Outlets do not work in isolation; they are the endpoints of distribution systems. The entire distribution system works to assure that the desired output is achieved. And if the effort is likely to be endless, no matter what kind of help is recruited, it is better to give up on that system during this step in the process.

The energy sources fueling the service outputs are distribution activities called marketing

TABLE 6-3
"Ideal Outlets" for Service Output Segments
for a Consumer Electronics Durable

	Segments		
	Price Shoppers	**Price and Training/Repair Buyers**	**Support/Relationship Seekers**
Portion of respondents	33%	28%	39%
Key channel characteristics	• Low price • Low support	• Low price • Training • Rapid repair • Brand variety	• Advice/relationship • Product information • Rapid repair • Training
Channel missions/ requirements	• Provide low-priced purchase fulfillment to self-reliant buyers • Other services, if offered, priced separately	• Provide lowest generally available price in market • Describe product features, as necessary, to potential buyers • Close "push" sales of most profitable items • Provide access to training and repair	• Provide product information and advice • Provide full range after-sale training and support • Form personal relationships with buyers/engage in consultative selling • Offer broad range of products and brands
"Ideal outlet"	• Inbound telemarketing • Discount outlet	• Low-price retailer backed up with strong training/ repair	• High support, relationship-oriented retailer

Source: Gemini Consulting and Louis W. Stern. © 1986 by Louis W. Stern. Data have been disguised.

TABLE 6-4
Marketing Flow Costs

Marketing Flow	Costs Represented
Physical possession	Storage and delivery
Ownership	Inventory carrying costs
Promotion	Personal selling, advertising, sales promotion, publicity, public relations costs
Negotiation	Time and legal costs
Risking	Price guarantees, warranties, insurance, installation, repair and after-sale service costs
Financing	Credit terms, terms and conditions of sale
Ordering	Order processing costs
Payment	Collections, bad debt cost

flows or functions. Although the list can be changed to fit the circumstances of any given industry, as shown later, eight generic marketing flows are listed in Table 6-4. Each flow has associated costs that must be incurred if the service outputs desired by end users are ever to see the light of day.

Suppose, for example, that a segment of end users requires rapid delivery. That is, people in this segment desire instant ("off-the-shelf") possession of their purchase. In terms of the marketing flows, this means that the "ideal" distribution system (made up of an "ideal" outlet and backup support) must somehow provide for local storage; otherwise, the product will not be available fast enough. Saying this, however, implies nothing about the flow of ownership, because title does not have to transfer instantaneously, only physical possession. Therefore, merchandise can often be consigned to local stocks (as in the case of Hanes's L'Eggs Hosiery or Continental's Wonder Bread) to make certain that enough of it is on hand to satisfy consumer needs for immediate delivery .

The critical task of step 4, therefore, is to determine what it will take, in the way of marketing flows or activities (and their associated costs), to deliver the service outputs. This is, of course, a difficult task. By and large, such cost allocations are mainly an art form, demanding a great amount of inventive thinking and the ability to concentrate on direct and traceable costs.

At this point in the process, it should be reasonably clear to the analyst what it will take, in terms of energy, effort, and money, to satisfy the shopping requirements of end users, segment by segment. It is here that questions about make or buy are raised for the first time. Make (doing it all oneself via vertical integration) should basically be treated as a default, or fall-back, position because companies should almost always want to divide labor with others rather than incurring themselves the full costs of distribution.

Indeed, it is very difficult to find *any* company that is fully vertically integrated with regard to each of the eight flows listed above. Furthermore, most companies would prefer to invest in research and development or new concepts that permit them to bring forth the new generation of their product. Investing in distribution via vertical integration often yields only low returns. To a large extent, this is why Chrysler has handed over the European distribution of replacement parts to Caterpillar Logistics Services, a subsidiary of the earth-moving equipment company, and Supermarket General Corp., Cullum Companies, and Kodak have handed over their data processing functions to IBM's Integrated Systems Solutions unit.[7]

While there are certainly exceptions to these bold assertions, the rule of thumb suggested here is that companies should be asked to prove why they insist on spending their money to own the entire marketing channel or even selected parts of it rather than outsourcing. (Vertical integra-

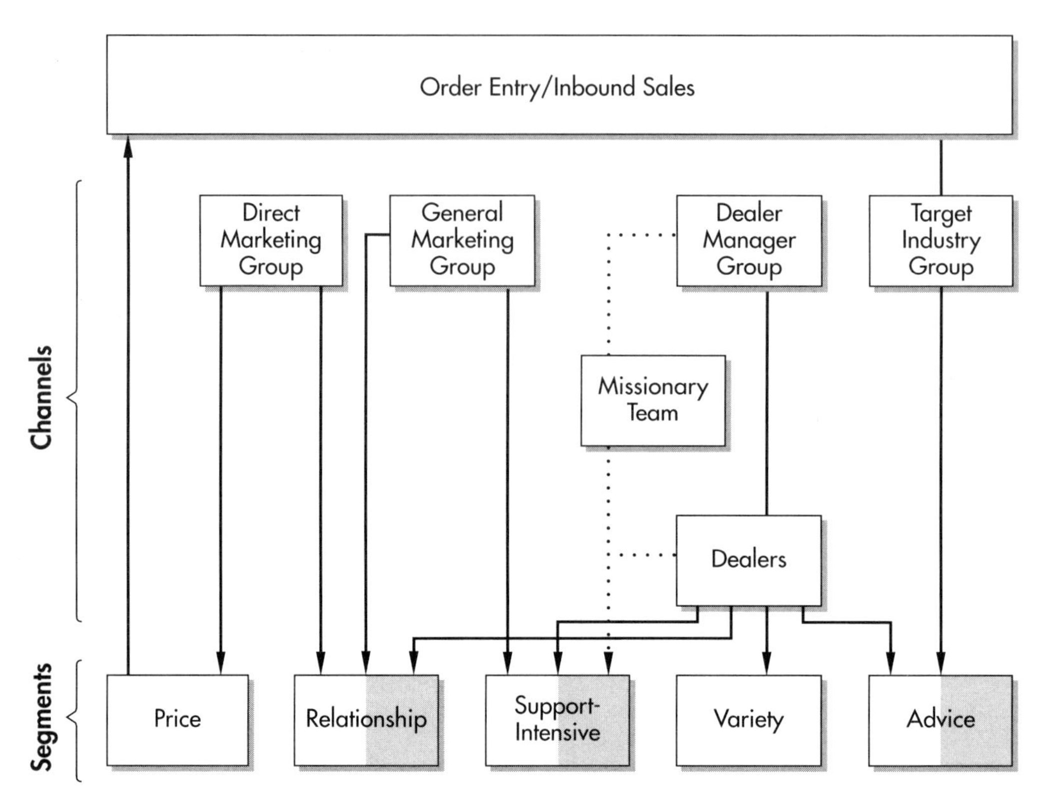

Figure 6-1
"Ideal" Channel System for Corporate Office Equipment and Services

Source: Gemini Consulting and Louis W. Stern. © 1986 by Louis W. Stern. Data have been disguised.

tion, when carefully assessed, is often driven more by a psychological need to control than by economies.)

There is a simple, straightforward answer to why companies might want to break the rule right here, during step 4. (The answer gets much more complicated later on.) It revolves around service outputs and end user satisfaction. That is, if it is immediately apparent that there is next to no chance that the service outputs can be delivered to end users by relying on third parties or outsiders, then it is time to integrate vertically. (But before breaking the rule, it might be useful to read the remainder of this text, because there are ways to accomplish things in distribution without always making rather than buying.)

Whatever is decided at this stage—to make or to buy—the marketing channels that result from this step of the process are supposedly "ideal" from end users' perspectives. They are truly customer-driven distribution systems. Figure 6-1 provides a snapshot of how the "ideal" sales channels might look for office equipment and services. The unshaded areas of certain segments represent small end users whose needs are the same as large-user members of the same segment. The complexity of Figure 6-1 indicates once again that, when faced with a heterogeneous marketplace, companies will be required to use multiple channels to serve the needs of multiple segments.

It is also possible to combine different channels to obtain a mutually supportive yet highly efficient approach to the market. For example, Dell Computer constructed a modular channel that merged internal and external resources for a cost-efficient solution. It used advertising, direct mail, and telemarketing to identify buyers; mail order and a toll-free number to handle orders; public warehouses and United Parcel Service (UPS) to handle delivery; and Xerox field service and a toll-free number to provide postsale and technical support. Hybrid, or modular, channels are becoming increasingly popular means for the division of distribution labor.[8]

Step 5: Analysis of the Existing System

After step 2 has been completed, a thorough analysis can be made of the distribution system presently being used by a company, *concurrent* with the search for the ideal distribution system. An examination (and assessment) of existing marketing channels requires isolating:

- The company's operative paths to the marketplace
- The logistic and sales functions being performed within each path
- The way in which labor (i.e., the marketing flows) is divided between the company and external organizations
- The economics of the system (costs, discounts, and the like), and, most important
- The effectiveness of the existing system in meeting the service output requirements of customers

It also involves an analysis of the existing channels used by competitors and by the industry at large.

An example of how to analyze the performance of existing channels in providing service outputs is available from the study of the market for office equipment and services referred to previously. Three of the numerous existing channels employed by this industry involve the use of equipment company representatives, service company representatives, and retail stores. A sample of existing and potential users was asked how well each of the channel providers do with regard to delivering desired service outputs. The disguised results are shown in Table 6-5.

Several facts jump out from the data in this table. First, the channels differ significantly in the value they provide to end users. Equipment company reps are best at establishing ongoing relationships and retail stores are worst, while retail stores are best at offering products/services from different companies and service company reps are worst. Second, the highest possible rating is 9 and the highest actual rating is a 6.3 (earned by equipment company reps for their ability to provide after-sale support and maintenance). Most of the scores are below 5. This means (to put it mildly) there is a major opportunity to serve end users better in this industry.

Another example, less bleak but highly informative, comes from the study of printing supplies. Again, the data have been disguised. From the results in Table 6-6, it is clear that existing outlets in the form of local dealers or office supply stores do a better job at providing many of the service outputs required by end users. They are not perceived to be as strong as other existing channels in the pricing, sales call, and general reputation/recognition areas, however.

It is important to note that both Table 6-5 and 6-6 deal with aggregate end user data. Also an

TABLE 6-5
Evaluating Three Existing Channels for
Corporate Office Equipment and Services

How well do each of these characteristics describe the following procedures (on a scale of 1 through 9, where 1 means "does not describe at all," and 9 means "describes perfectly")?

Characteristics	Equipment Company Representative	Service Company Representative	Retail Store
Establish ongoing relationship; call on me in person	4.0	5.1	2.7
Provide after-sale support, maintenance; provide reliable products/services	6.3	5.5	3.7
Offer products/services from different companies	2.0	3.1	5.0
Offer lowest price level available	3.2	4.6	4.9
Provide demonstrations of product/services in use	4.1	2.8	5.0
Standard Errors	0.1	0.1	0.1

Source: Gemini Consulting and Louis W. Stern. © 1986 by Louis W. Stern. Data have been disguised.

TABLE 6-6
Evaluating Five Existing Channels for Printing Supplies

	Direct Mail Catalogs	Representatives of a Manufacturer	Warehouse Wholesaler	Local Dealer	Salespeople Who Contact You Over the Phone
Has knowledgeable sales people	3.4	5.2	2.8	7.3	3.6
Offers a wide variety of products	6.5	2.6	5.1	7.0	3.6
Lets you see and touch the products you buy	1.7	3.9	4.6	7.3	1.9
Accepts product returns without hassle	5.0	4.6	4.4	7.8	3.3
Carries high-quality products	6.2	6.6	5.2	7.8	4.1
Is part of a well-known, recognized company	6.3	6.7	4.6	5.7	3.4
Has generally low price levels	6.5	4.1	6.0	5.6	3.9
Will make personal sales calls at your office	1.6	6.1	1.8	5.4	3.0
Offers a full range of services	6.4	5.8	3.1	71	4.2

Source: Gemini Consulting and Louis W. Stern. © 1986 by Louis W. Stern. Data have been disguised.

essential part of step 5 is the breaking down of the data by relevant end user segments. For example, in the printing supply study, once the appropriate segmentation scheme was overlaid on the data, it became obvious that the price-sensitive segment (which represents a significant number of end users) was not altogether enamored of local dealers.

An additional part of the analysis that should be carried out in step 5 relates to a point made above—understanding the division of labor within the existing channel system. One issue concerns redundancies and overlaps, because these can frequently elevate distribution costs as well as breed contention in the system. An example of a relatively complex system for a specialty food manufacturer is shown in Figure 6-2. Surprisingly, the overlaps and redundancies are minor, considering all the different actors involved in marketing the product. Another example, in Figure 6-3, shows how a comparison of distribution activities and costs can identify mismatches in compensation.

Step 6: Investigating External and Internal Constraints and Opportunities

Eventually, when this long, tortuous ten-step process is finished, management will be called upon to decide on the firm's marketing channels. Up to this point, however, relatively few realities have been faced. Some appear in step 4 when the ideal marketing channel is designed. A number of others show up in step 5, when the existing system is analyzed and assessed.

But it is in step 6 where in-depth perspectives are required of the environmental factors surrounding the channel decision. It is also here where accounting is made for management's biases, objectives, and constraints. Because these two parts of the analysis are so important to the channel design process and because they focus on different issues, they are isolated as steps 6a and 6b.

STEP 6A: ASSESSING ENVIRONMENTAL/EXTERNAL DRIVERS

Much research has been conducted over the past decade on how environmental factors affect the structure of marketing channels.[9] Basically, this research indicates that the more variable, diverse, turbulent, and uncertain a channel's environment is, the more control is required over the behavior of channel members to cope with all the contingencies facing the channel. But flexibility is also needed in adapting to the rapidly changing marketplace, and this need is at odds with the need for control. Therefore, there is a constant strain in channels faced with complex, dynamic environments.

To assess how external conditions might inhibit the decision space of firms, it is necessary to examine each of the following factors:

- Industry concentration
- Macroeconomic indicators
- Present and projected state of technology
- Extent of regulation/deregulation and trends
- Entry barriers
- Competitors' behavior
- Strength of end-user loyalties
- Geographical dispersion of end users
- Stage in the product life cycle

	Broker Chain/ Coop Warehouse	Broker Grocery Distributor Chain/ Independent Refrigerated Section		Broker Grocery Disributor Chain/ Independent Specialty Section		Health Food Distributor	
		Broker	Grocery Distributor	Broker	Grocery Distributor	Chain/ Independent Specialty	Health Food Store
Headquarters Activities							
New Product Authorization	Broker	●	–	◓	●	●	●
Promotion Authorization	Broker	●	–	○	◓	●	●
Cooperative Advertising	Broker	●	–	●	○	◓	○
Planogram Design	Broker	●	–	○	●	●	○
Receivables Carrying	Mfg Broker	–	●	–	●	●	●
Order Placement	Mfg Broker	●	○	○	●	●	●
Order Processing	Mfg Broker	○	●	–	●	●	●
Planogram Reset Authorization	Mfg Broker	●	○	○	●	●	○
Store Level Activities							
Planogram Resets	Mfg Broker	●	◓	○	●	●	○
Promotional Displays	Mfg Broker	◓	◓	◓	◓	●	●
Shelf Monitoring & Maintenance	Mfg Broker	◓	◓	◓	●	●	◓
Movement Analysis	Mfg Broker	●	○	◓	◓	●	◓
Store Delivery	Mfg Broker	–	●	–	●	●	●
Pricing	Chain/Coop	–	●	–	●	●	○

Key to Activity: ● = Heavy ◓ = Moderate ○ = Light

Figure 6-2

Analysis of Possible Redundancies and Overlaps in a Specialty Food Manufacturer's Channel System

Source: Gemini Consulting and Louis W. Stern. © 1986 by Louis W. Stern.

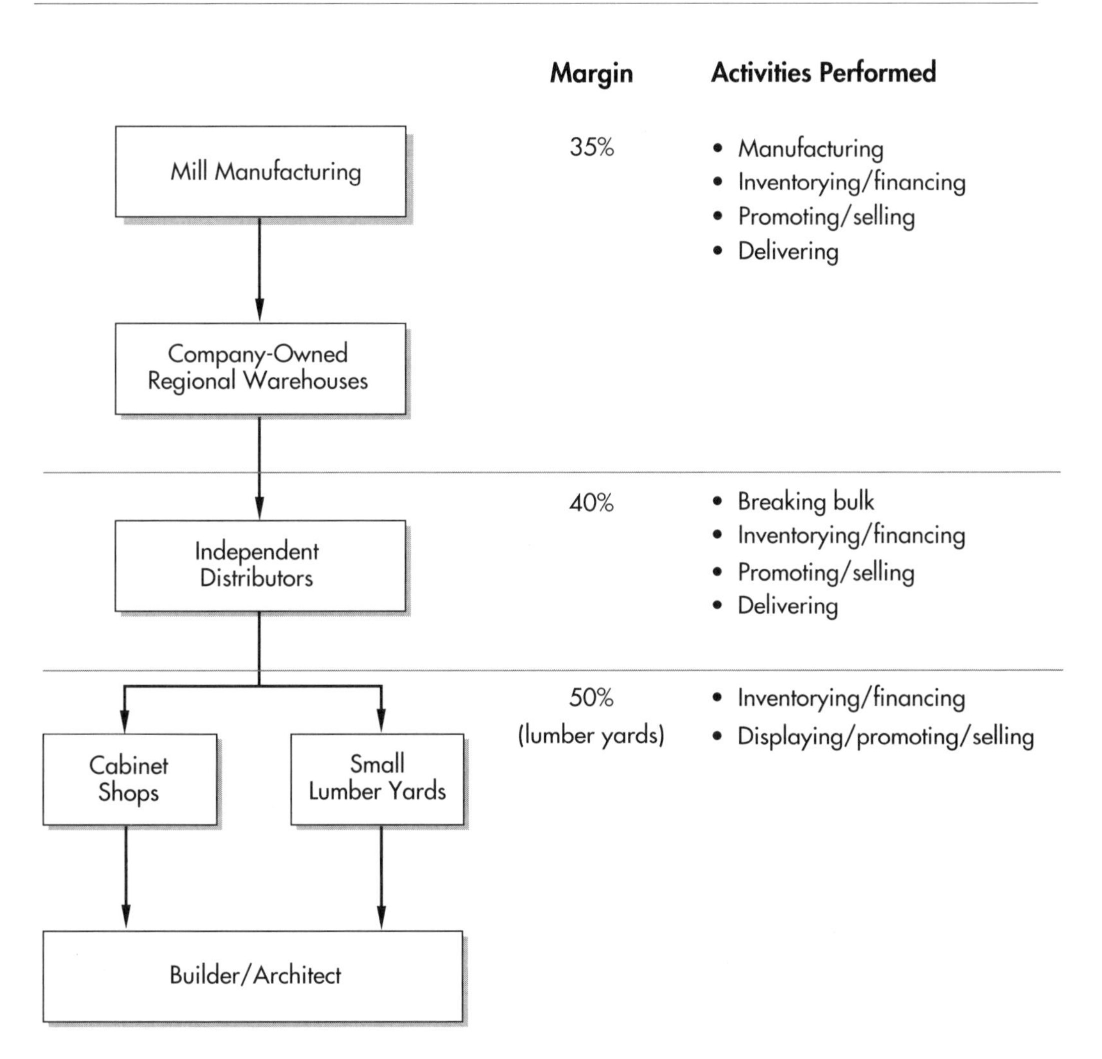

Figure 6-3
Compensation Mismatches in Existing Channels

Source: Gemini Consulting and Louis W. Stern. Adapted with permission by Louis W. Stern.

The industry that sells paper to printers and publishers, for example, has significantly consolidated key end-user markets and has experienced increased power of indirect marketing channels (i.e., paper merchants), industry capacity additions, heavy investment in fixed costs, rising costs of raw materials, growth of geographically dispersed end-user segments, and arrival at the maturity stage of the product life cycle for most of its products.

All these factors constrain a company's channels. With regard to the product life cycle, for instance, Lele argues that the best channels for a product change over time.[10] In the introductory stage, the most appropriate channels are those that add substantial value. In the growth stage, channels must be able to handle greater sales volume, but they won't have to provide all the services offered by the channels in the introductory stage. In the maturity stage, channels do not emphasize value-added service, because end users focus on low price. And in the decline stage, channels like direct mail that add even less value become dominant.[11] It should be noted, however, that Lele's suggestions are meaningful in the aggregate. Different end-user segments focus on different things, regardless of stage in the product life cycle. This is another reason why analyzing end-user needs is so important.

Environmental factors for paper and other supplies sold to offices are different than for paper sold to printers and publishers. For office consumables, important issues are:

- *Macroeconomic* (growth in the number of small firms and the shift to a service economy)
- *End-user behavior* (increased use of office technology; increased trading off of service for price by small users)
- *Technology* (development of new, demanding paper applications for laser printers, color copiers, etc.)
- *Channel change* (emergence of new channel types such as telemarketing, warehouse clubs, and office supply superstores)

The state of the environment facing a channel can be characterized along seven different dimensions:

1. *Diversity:* the degree of similarity or differentiation among the elements of the population dealt with, including organizations, individuals, and any social forces affecting resources
2. *Dynamism:* the frequency of change and turnover in the markets in which channel members compete
3. *Concentration:* the extent to which markets are controlled by, or condensed in, a few or many organizations
4. *Capacity:* the favorableness of economic and demand conditions
5. *Interconnectedness:* the number and pattern of linkages or connections among relevant organizations
6. *Conflict:* the level of abnormal competitive stress (due to opponent rather than goal-directed behavior) in the markets in which channel members compete
7. *Interdependence:* the mutual reactivity and sensitivity to actions taken in the markets in which channel members compete[12]

The most significant of these dimensions—those that seem to cause the greatest uncertainty for firms—have been found to be environmental diversity, dynamism, concentration, and capacity.[13] All these factors are threatening and cause management to consider changing channels.

Step 6b: Company Analysis

The risk profile of the focal company's management must be assessed. Are they risk-takers or risk-avoiders? Also, internal politics, organization structure (e.g., which group "owns" channels within the firm—sales, marketing, or operations?), and culture are important. They must be well understood and appreciated if the eventual results and recommendations are going to be endorsed and implemented. For example, just how strong are the forces of conventional wisdom and inertia? Can the power of evidence and logic really win out? Does anyone in the company, including the chief executive officer, have the power and/or authority to institute channel change?

Surprisingly, and unfortunately, there appear to be enormous barriers to action in this area of management strategy.

Another part of step 6b actually permits management to "bound" the ideal distribution channel. Despite the speeches and the pep talks, management is *not* generally customer-oriented. "Market-driven" is seldom more than a slogan. By scrupulously ignoring management's prejudices until step 6b, the company gets its best chance of finding out, perhaps for the first time, what it would really take to please its end users.

Step 6b provides the opportunity for management to impose questions about efficiency (e.g., expense-to-revenue issues), effectiveness (e.g., market share and return-on-investment issues), and adaptability (e.g., issues related to the fluidity of capital invested, the ability to market new products, and the ability to adjust to new technologies in sales and marketing). A cross section of the company's marketing and sales executives is asked to declare what the specific present and future objectives are or should be with regard to any distribution channel the company might select. Managers should be encouraged to include their pet peeves about what distribution is or is not doing; the survey should be open-ended, and no limits should be imposed on answers.

At the same time, executives should be asked about the constraints they would impose on channel system design. Are there any sacred cows? Most industries have historical rigidities, and some of them get translated into laws. For example, in the automobile industry, the dealer system has existed, basically unaltered, for over 60 years, in part because of peculiarities in the legal structure of automobile distribution (e.g., franchise laws, dealer-day-in-court laws) and in part because industry folklore and values have sanctified the dealer system. Other rigidities come from deep-seated prejudices. In the high-tech medical equipment industry, for instance, executives in one major company might suffer emotional trauma if anyone even suggested they sell their equipment through distributors or dealers.

In step 6b, all rational and irrational objectives and constraints should be made explicit. Once generated, the list of objectives and constraints should be developed into a structured survey instrument and sent to all executives within the company having a stake in distribution. The executives should be forced into a trade-off analysis similar to that performed for outlet design so that, when the data are analyzed, the objectives and constraints can be weighted.

Eventually, in step 9, management is asked to support its beliefs and set aside its prejudices. These objectives and constraints are critical in determining the distribution system to be implemented. However, at this stage of the process, these prejudices remain unchallenged. They will serve to "bound" the possible "solution set" by dictating, for example, that the company remain loyal to certain types of middlemen, earn a hurdle rate of return, or limit legal exposure. Clearly, then, these factors can force a reconfiguration of the theoretically ideal system, making it over into a system that reflects not consumer demands but management's biases.

Step 7: Delineating the Options Using Gap Analysis

At the end of step 6, potentially three *different* distribution systems have been isolated: (1) an ideal (customer-driven) system, (2) the existing system, and (3) a management-bounded system (i.e., the ideal system reconfigured by management's objectives and constraints). In step 7, the three systems are compared, and a gap analysis is performed. As an illustration, Figure 6-4 depicts three possible outcomes that could emerge from the comparison.

In the first situation (fit), the existing, management-bounded, and ideal systems closely re-

Situation A: Fit

Management-Bounded Distribution System

Existing Distribution System

Ideal Distribution System

Interpretation:
Any distribution-related problems result from poor execution of the system, not poor design of the system.

Necessary Actions:
Sharpen performance; maintain existing systems.

Situation B: Partial Fit

Management-Bounded

Existing Distribution System ← GAP → Ideal Distribution System

Interpretation:
Management has designed a system that reflects its needs but has given inadequate attention to customer needs.

Necessary Actions:
Investigate validity of management constraints and objectives, and analyze customer requirements and expectations.

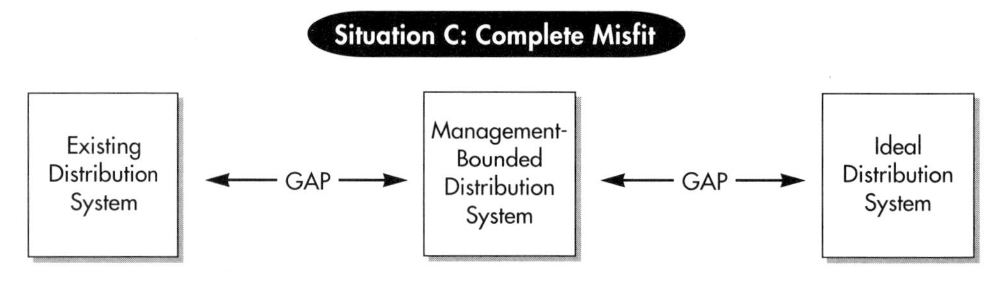

Interpretation:
End-user satisfaction can be improved without relaxing management criteria.

Preferred Actions: Examine certain management criteria to assess the possibility of bringing the existing system even closer to the ideal distribution system.

Figure 6-4
Results of a Gap Analysis

Source: Gemini Consulting and Louis W. Stern. © 1986 by Louis W. Stern.

semble one another. If this is the case, then management knows that the existing system is "on the mark" from a design perspective; that is, it has the potential to deliver what end users want. If, however, end users often complain about the existing system, management knows that the system's problems lie not with its structure but with the way it has been managed. Execution is the culprit, not basic design.

For example, many automobile buyers would undoubtedly like to shop for cars in a specialty store environment where they could examine lots of different models; receive sales and, if needed, financial assistance; drive relatively short distances to get to an outlet; obtain after-sales service; and obtain new cars at reasonable prices, in line with the service outputs they desire. Basically, what has just been described are the attributes (on paper, at least) of most new car dealerships. If this is the case, then why do so many consumers of new cars leave dealers' showrooms or service areas dissatisfied? The answer is simple—it's not the *design* of the system that may be at fault; it's the *management* of it.

In the second situation (partial fit), the existing and management-bounded systems are similar to each other but substantially different from the ideal. This outcome would suggest that the objectives/constraints adopted by management are causing the gap. Such a finding calls for a careful investigation of the validity of the objectives/constraints, which is the purpose of step 8.

In the third situation (complete misfit), all three systems are substantially different. Assuming that the management-bounded system is positioned *between* the existing and the ideal, some improvements in creating end-user satisfaction should be possible without relaxing the objectives or constraints. However, relaxation of certain management constraints would likely provide even greater end user benefits.

It should be clear at this point that the ideal system acts as a stake in the ground. It is a system or set of systems that, if actually constructed and properly managed, would satisfy end users. It is synonymous with total quality management. Therefore, if the management-bounded system is not similar to the ideal, the message is unyielding: management is willing to sacrifice end-user satisfaction (quality) to further other objectives or abide by specific constraints. Although such a deviation may be warranted, management should permit such a compromise only with full understanding of the risk. The possible consequence of this decision is that, if some alternative system is developed by a competitor that does, in fact, mirror the "ideal," the company's market stature could suffer significantly.

Step 8: External Analysis of Objectives/Constraints

This step represents a check on the validity of management's prejudices. Here, the objectives and constraints must be presented to individuals outside the company and to selected individuals within it to assess management's preferences and perceptions. For example, a common method of protecting the status quo is to claim, as a constraint, that laws restrict behavior and that change would fly in the face of the law. (The Robinson-Patman Act is probably the foremost excuse heard in corporate corridors for not making needed changes in discount structures.) This tendency is one of the reasons why the automobile industry has clung steadfastly to the dealer franchise system. Porsche's fiasco in implementing a new approach to distribution in the early 1980s only served to convince many industry executives that wholesale change is really impossible without tremendous turmoil.[14] The purpose of step 8 is to investigate such claims (e.g., to estimate how many lawsuits could be expected and what their cost might be, measured against the benefits of changing the system).

While step 3 is the most creative part of the design process, step 8 is the riskiest and the most formidable. Who is to say that management doesn't really know what it is talking about? Who can predict the future with certainty? Who can tell what course a lawsuit would take or what future laws Congress and state legislatures will pass? The fact is, no one can really say that management's objectives and constraints are dead wrong. But in the distribution area, there is such inertia that one would not be surprised to find widely differing opinions. And because most management decisions are based on judgment anyway, why shouldn't management's frame of reference be called into question if external analysis is, subjectively or objectively, skeptical of management's beliefs? A systematic assessment of the practicality of the ideal system will either generate ideas to make it attainable or lead to its modification.

Step 9: Confronting the Constraints/Objectives

Step 9 requires management to confront the gap between its position and the ideal position. It is the climax of the entire process in two senses: First, all the affected senior managers are brought on stage together; second, participants are forced to engage in self-reflection and sometimes profound change in their points of view.

To underline the significance of this event in the channel design process, an off-site session should be planned. At this meeting, descriptions of the "ideal" distribution system should be presented and the results of steps 6 and 7 shared. (In reality, senior management should be exposed to the mounting logic at key steps along the way. Otherwise, the chances of buy-in are virtually nil if management enters this step of the process with negative attitudes.) Top management should review the objectives and constraints used to bound the ideal and then be shown the effect of these factors on the ideal (that is, how the objectives and constraints resulted in "answers" different from what end users really desire). Next, data challenging the validity of these factors (the output of step 8) should be made available.

All this information will serve as background for what should prove to be a very provocative discussion. The ability of the group to experiment with possibilities can be greatly enhanced by the availability of computers programmed to readjust weights and display results instantaneously. Suppose that in step 6b, when management was permitted to bound the ideal, customer satisfaction was given a weight of 10%. Changing the weight in real-time to, say, 20%, and reweighting the other objectives/constraints enables management to see the consequences of heightened emphasis on customer satisfaction and to imagine what that will mean for structuring the distribution system.

Management may find that the achievement of the ideal requires a major restructuring of its system. Such was the case for a personal care products company. The achievement of the ideal called for the elimination of one level in its existing distribution system—its brokers. It was a big step even to contemplate, considering that the brokers had played a key role in providing access to the retail trade when the company's brand lacked visibility or strong consumer demand. Over the years, however, the brand had emerged as the best-seller in its category and had established a strong consumer franchise. The brokers' function, which had been so important in the early years, no longer added value to the distribution process. Brokers had become superfluous and expensive. Yet management still felt a strong sense of loyalty and indebtedness to them. A growing price sensitivity on the part of consumers, coupled with the inefficiencies of the broker system, placed the manufacturer in a vulnerable position. Management had to face the trade-off between its loyalty to brokers and the expectations of end users.

Step 10: Reaching the Optimal Distribution System—Preparing for Implementation

The final step in the process is to pass the ideal distribution system (from step 4) by the set of objectives/constraints still retained by management at the completion of step 9. (Executives will always hold on to some of their strongly held beliefs.) The resulting distribution system should be the subject of intensive implementation planning, because what comes out at this juncture represents the "optimal" marketing channel for the firm, taking into account everything that has been learned via the process. The optimal system may not be ideal, but it will meet, to the best of its ability, management's standards for quality (i.e., delivering end-user satisfaction), efficiency, effectiveness, and adaptability. If it is not congruent with the ideal, the optimal system will still leave the company vulnerable to competitors who actually design a customer-driven distribution system. Chances are high, however, that the optimal will be much more market-driven than the existing system.

This entire ten-step approach to designing marketing channels is pictured in Figure 6-5. The exhibit is somewhat similar to a critical path diagram because it indicates which analyses may be performed concurrently and which should be performed sequentially.

Managing Marketing Channels

Once channels have been designed, there is no guarantee they will operate successfully. Realistic, cost-effective implementation and first-rate execution are accomplished by management techniques and mechanisms. Without purposeful coordination, motivation, and direction, channels are doomed to failure regardless of their structure.

Understanding what it takes to manage marketing channels demands a clear perception of what channels really are. Strange as it may seem, channels can be viewed, conceptually at least, as *superorganizations* comprising interdependent institutions and agencies involved in the task of making products and services available for consumption by end users. The notion of channels as superorganizations may seem odd because many channels are made up of companies that pride themselves on their independence. It is highly unlikely they would admit that they are part of a larger whole—an interorganizational collective or network. But they are integral parts of something larger than themselves, and that's why the term "superorganization" has validity for channel management.

To comprehend this concept, one must first realize that organizations are the primary entities for assembling resources in such a way that the output is greater than the sum of the individual parts. Organizations are generally characterized by a series of attributes, for example:

1. Differentiation of function among their membership
2. Interdependency with respect to task performance
3. Communication and criteria for evaluating the communication
4. Structural complexity
5. Cooperation in achieving collective goals
6. Clearly defined superior-subordinate relationship or authority system

If the relationship between General Mills (a manufacturer) and Kroger (a retailer) were dissected and analyzed, it is very likely that attributes 1 through 4 would be readily discernible. Attribute 5 might be less clear, because the collective goals might not be immediately obvious. Attribute 6, however, might produce a fist fight, because neither party is likely to admit to being subordinate in the alliance.

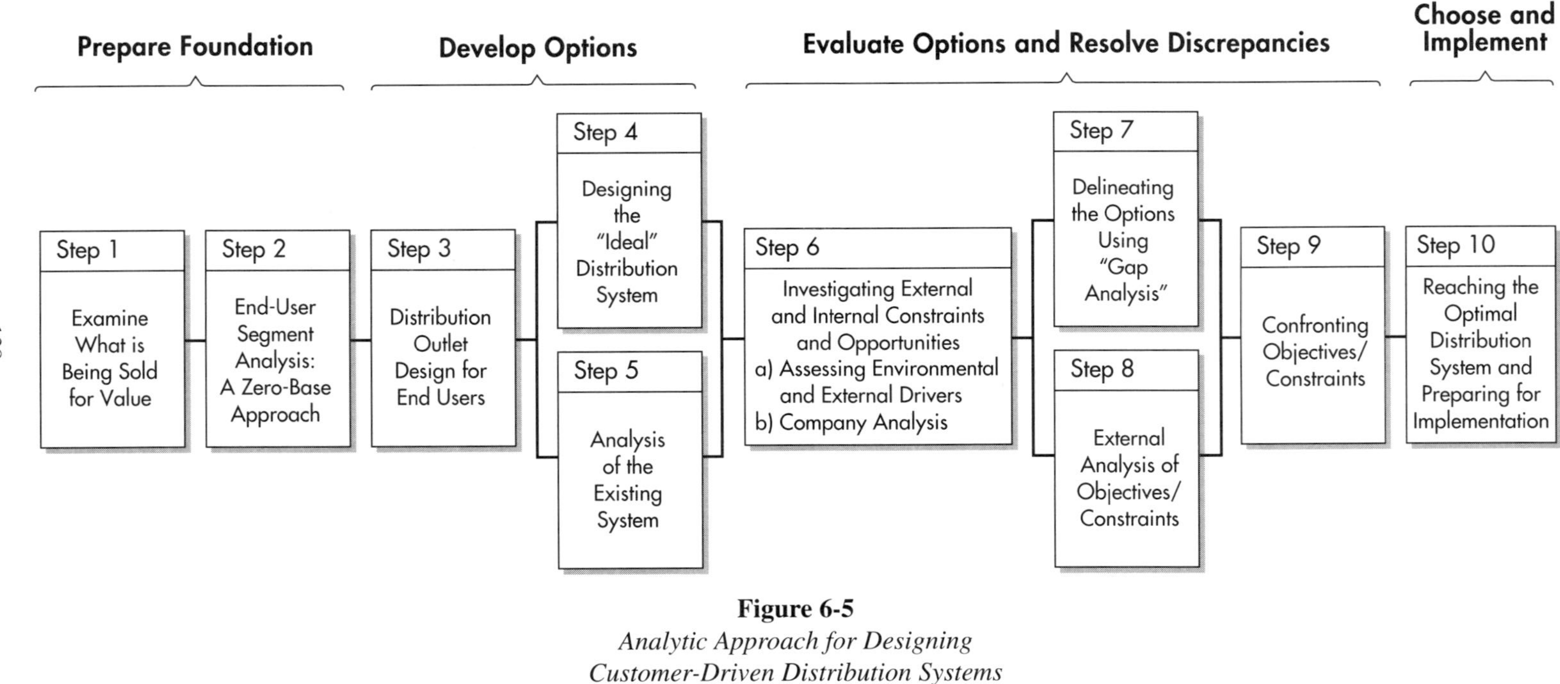

Figure 6-5
Analytic Approach for Designing Customer-Driven Distribution Systems

The truth is that the relationships between General Mills and Kroger or between General Motors and its dealers or between Republic Steel and Jorgenson (a steel service center) or between Milwaukee Tool and W.W. Grainger (an industrial distributor) have been systematically cultivated over time. They resemble the relationships that exist *within* complex organizations; that is why they reflect attributes 1 through 5. But if marketing channels are to function to the best of their ability to deliver service outputs desired by end users, they must allocate resources and direct their use. This is where the notion of superorganization is the most significant. Achieving superorganization status requires leadership, unity of purpose, and agreement on division of the "spoils."

Therefore, channel management involves two very difficult tasks. First, it is concerned with achieving both *intra-* and *inter*organizational coordination and cooperation. Second, it must deal with conflicts that arise, especially in those channels made up of independently owned and operated institutions and agencies.

The objective of channel management is the institution of cost-effective coordination mechanisms that enhance the opportunity for all channel members to achieve their respective organizational goals. Past studies point out four main streams of research-based models relating to channel coordination:

1. *Environmental models* linking channel environment to channel structure and coordination mechanisms that induce channel member tolerance and compliance.
2. *Behavioral models* focusing on the issues that may either promote or disrupt channel coordination and the effectiveness of various institutional arrangements among channel members.
3. *Institutional economics models* mainly concerned with the analysis of bipolar governance structures as coordination mechanisms. The transaction cost paradigm focuses on the efficiency, or cost-benefit analysis, of these alternative channel structures via consideration of environmental and human factors.
4. *Managerial models* dealing with linkages between strategic and operative coordination issues and channel coordination mechanisms.[15]

The extent to which the channel of distribution is managed by a leader(s) who can stipulate marketing policies to other channel members and therefore control their marketing decisions hinges on a number of interrelated factors, as shown in Figure 6-6 and explained in Table 6-7.[16] A discussion of these factors, their interrelationships, and related research findings follows.

The central theme of this section is that a high degree of interorganizational coordination is required within a marketing channel if that channel is to have a long-run impact on the markets it serves.[17] Power generally must be used in a marketing channel to specify appropriate roles, assure role congruence, gain cooperation, and induce satisfactory role performance.[18] Power is the ability of one channel member to persuade another channel member to do what it would not otherwise have done. Power is the inverse of dependence: the more dependent one channel member is on another, the more power the latter has relative to the former.

Channel members may use several power bases to evoke change or gain continued cooperation; these include rewards, coercion, expertness, reference, and legitimacy. These bases are almost invariably used in combination. However, a cost associated with their use must be an integral part of the analysis in the development of interorganization management programs.

There is a strong likelihood that role performance will deviate, at least occasionally, from prescription because of situational factors, different objectives, communication problems, and dif-

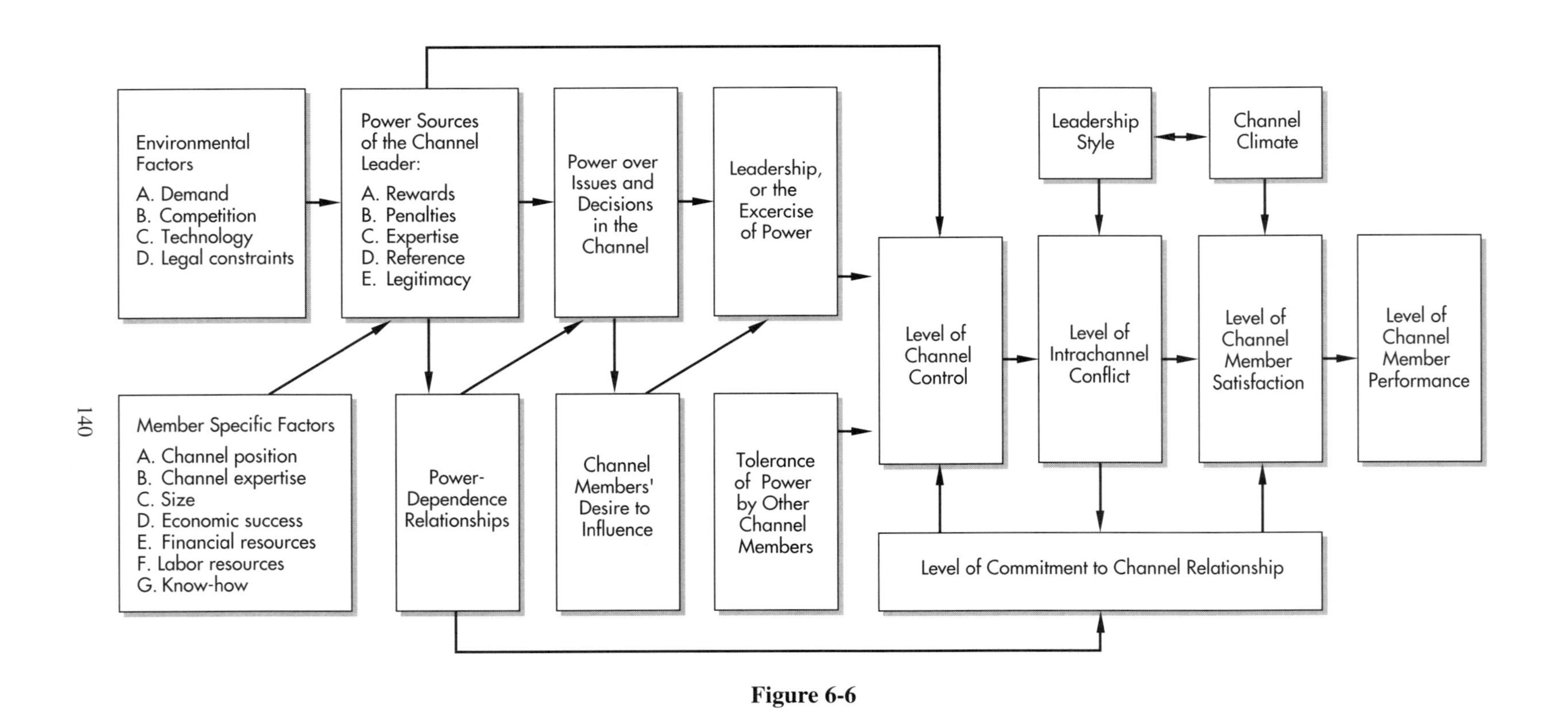

Figure 6-6

A Framework for Channel Leadership and Control

Source: Adel I. El-Ansary, Research Program in Wholesaling, University of North Florida, 1991. © 1991 by Adel I. El-Ansary.

TABLE 6-7
Framework Explanation

- Power sources accrue to channel members as a result of environmental factors and/or the specific characteristics of the channel member.
- Power is issue-oriented. Power over issues and decisions is a function of sources of power accumulated by a channel member and the power-dependence relationships vis-à-vis other channel members.
- Leadership, or the exercise of power, can materialize only when a channel member has power over issue(s) and desires to exercise that power.
- Commitment, a channel governance mode, enables channel members to achieve the benefits of cooperation without the inefficiencies of a bureaucratic organization structure. A channel member's perceptions of the other party's commitment increases:
  a. when the other party is perceived to have made idiosyncratic investments
  b. when the other party is perceived to be dealing exclusively with the channel member
  c. when the perceived level of conflict is low
- The level and effectiveness of channel control achieved is a function of the quality of leadership, nature, and magnitude of power resources deployed, and the tolerance of power by other channel members.
- Effectiveness of channel control can be judged in terms of desirable channel control outcomes, including the following sequence:
  a. reduction of dysfunctional intrachannel conflict and increase in channel member coordination and cooperation
  b. increase in the level of commitment of channel members to the channel relationship
  c. increase in channel member satisfaction
  d. improvement of channel member performance.
- Leadership style (e.g., participative, supportive, or directive) affects the level of intrachannel conflict.

Source: Adel I. El-Ansary, Research Program in Wholesaling, University of North Florida, © 1991 by Adel I. El-Ansary.

ferent expectations among channel members. More generally, conflict is brought about because of the operational interdependence of channel members. The need to cooperate is juxtaposed with the desire to retain autonomy, and thus channels can be characterized as systems encompassing mixed motives. Channel conflict occurs when one channel member perceives another channel member to be engaged in behavior that is impeding or preventing it from achieving its goals. Conflict is caused by goal incompatibility, domain dissensus, and differences in perceptions of reality, as well as by the level of interdependence in the system. It results when there is an imbalance between the rewards a member receives from and the contribution it makes to the channel. Although conflict is a positive social force that breeds adaptation and innovation, it must be managed because it can prevent a system from providing service outputs effectively and efficiently.

Perhaps one of the most significant functions of channel management is the generation of conflict management strategies, given that conflict is inherent in interorganizational systems. Therefore, channel diplomacy, joint membership in trade associations, exchange-of-persons programs, co-optation, mediation, arbitration, and establishment of superordinate goals should prove highly beneficial. The implementation of these strategies is likely to bring forth more rational and functional collective decision making within the channel.

Channel leadership will likely be a prerequisite to effective interorganization management. It is even possible that control will need to be exercised within the system. The only means remaining for achieving control in certain situations will be vertical integration. Several interorganizational programs such as franchising and programmed merchandising can be enacted, however, before actually acquiring a variety of channel institutions and agencies.

Organizational Patterns in Marketing Channels

The organization of marketing channels depends greatly on all the design and managerial factors discussed in earlier sections. The ultimate organizational configuration of any channel rests largely on such variables as the amount of power available to individual channel members, their efforts to maintain healthy rather than dysfunctional levels of conflict, and their willingness to assume leadership roles to assure that the service outputs desired by end users are delivered satisfactorily.

Conventional marketing channels made up of independently owned institutions and agencies frequently suffer from several weaknesses, the foremost being the absence of a systemwide orientation and inclusive goals. If a locus of power is also absent, role specification and conflict management in conventional channels are likely to be difficult, at best. Even when a locus of power is present (as in the marketing channel for motion pictures), there is no guarantee that channel performance will be any better than when power is diffused.

Vertical marketing systems have emerged as significant forms of channel organization. They represent, for the most part, sophisticated attempts by management to overcome the inherent weaknesses of conventional channels. Administered vertical marketing systems are those in which marketing activities are coordinated through the use of programs developed by one or a limited number of firms. Administrative strategies, combined with the exercise of power, are used to obtain systemic economies.

Contractual vertical marketing systems are those in which independent firms at different channel levels integrate their programs on a contractual basis to achieve systemic economies and increased market impact. They include, among other forms of organization, wholesaler-sponsored voluntary groups, retailer-sponsored cooperative groups, and franchise systems. By virtue of the use of legitimate power in their formulation, contractual systems tend to be more tightly knit than administered systems.

Corporate vertical marketing systems are those in which channel members assume responsibility for one or more of the marketing flows over at least two separate levels of distribution (e.g., manufacturing and wholesaling). In fact, such systems are synonymous with both forward and backward vertical integration. The key trade-offs in instituting any corporate vertical marketing system are the investment required plus the flexibility lost, versus the control secured over marketing activities of channel members plus the operating economies gained.

From a managerial perspective, vertical marketing systems appear to offer a series of advantages over conventional channels. The former employ a systemic approach and are committed to scientific decision making while engendering channel member loyalty and network stability. Tasks are routinized, and economies of standardization are likely. Because a locus of power is available and utilized in a positive manner, it is possible to gain at least some control over the cost and quality of the functions performed by various channel members. Furthermore, inherent within systems management is the notion that the channel itself is the relevant unit of competition.

To a large extent, channels should be organized by answering "make vs. buy" questions. Under what conditions is vertical integration (making the channel via internal growth or acquisition) a sensible strategy and under what conditions does relying on independently owned and operated institutions and agencies (buying the services of third parties) make more sense?

Anderson and Weitz suggest that vertical integration is a logical strategy to pursue when:

- Few outsiders are available to perform specific activities satisfactorily.
- It would take a long time and be very costly to switch to new channel partners if the existing channel partners fail to perform.

- A company's terms, procedures, and products are unique, and lots of training would be required to bring an outsider up to speed.
- The buying decision is complex and highly involved.
- Close coordination is essential for the performance of a marketing activity.
- Buyers form strong loyalties with salespeople, not companies.
- Economies of scale are present in the performance of marketing activities or flows.
- The environment is highly uncertain.
- It is extremely difficult to monitor outsider performance.
- It is easy for channel members to "free ride" on the efforts of others.
- Transactions are sizable *and* frequent.[19]

Anderson and Coughlan have extended this list by proposing that vertical integration should also be pursued when (1) a product is in the early stages of its life cycle, (2) service levels required by buyers are high, and (3) a product is closely related to the company's core business.[20]

A great deal of the reasoning underlying many of the points mentioned above has been derived from the theory of transaction cost analysis (TCA), developed by the economist Oliver E. Williamson.[21] The theory addresses the case when the costs of transacting business across a market (with outsiders or third parties or independently owned institutions and agencies) are too high relative to those of bringing the transaction in-house via vertical integration. Profit-maximizing firms will choose to undertake only those activities that are cheaper to administer internally than to purchase in the market.

Thus, according to TCA, markets fail when the costs of completing transactions become excessive. Markets are at this level when transactions are surrounded by a high degree of uncertainty because of environmental factors *and* when channel members do not trust one another because generally deceptive behavior has become commonplace among them. Also, if channel members make credible commitments by investing in transaction-specific assets, they increase their vulnerability. Under these conditions, exchange occurs between channel members only with the protection of ironclad contracts, lengthy specifications of obligations accounting for all possible contingencies in an uncertain future, and extensive auditing of performance. When this happens, vertical integration tends to be preferred to the relatively greater costs of market transactions. For example, Dwyer and Welsh have shown that vertical integration is the likely response of a marketing channel facing intense competition, resource scarcity, and variable demand.[22] Considerable empirical support has been generated for parts or all of the tenets of TCA in marketing channel contexts.[23]

Many items on the lists developed by Anderson and her colleagues Weitz and Coughlan relate to economies-of-scale issues. In fact, companies often desire control over their marketing channels to ensure the delivery of service outputs and/or to expropriate profits. This leads them to prefer vertical integration, but such arrangements are not feasible unless associated fixed costs can be spread over a large volume of business. Furthermore, as the volume of business increases, firms are able to specialize in the performance of marketing-distribution functions and reap the benefits of scalar economies.[24] The make vs. buy distribution decision is extremely complex, however, and several benefits and costs are associated with each alternative. It should be recalled from the discussion of channel design, that vertical integration ought to be considered a "default" condition. In other words, managers should make rather than buy only after they have convinced themselves, through rigorous analysis, that ownership is necessary. This attitude may deter unnecessary investments in distribution.[25] Contrast, for example, the Western versus the Japanese view of this issue:

> Whereas the classic western concept of industrial integration depends on ownership, in Japan integration works by association and minimal ownership. The typical characteristics of soft integration are: many companies providing the supply and distribution network for the "mother" company; a high level of self-sufficiency (particularly in design) in the tasks suppliers perform; and strong links among the firms, particularly in terms of personnel exchange. These inter-firm relationships are not contractual. Soft integration is also critical in distribution. Distributors and retailers in Japan tend to push the products of one company, and there is an extensive sharing of information.[26]

Legal Constraints on the Interorganization Management of Marketing Channels

Instituting effective interorganization management requires the use of power. However, significant legal constraints affect how power may be employed in the marketing channel. Prior to developing and implementing interorganizational strategies and programs, marketing managers at all levels of distribution must comprehend the intention and scope of these constraints so that any strategy or program that is promulgated will not run afoul of the various antitrust enforcement agencies.[27]

The focus here is on federal legislation, even though myriad international, state, and local laws directly affect distribution practices. In addition, attention is given only to legislation directly affecting relations among commercial channel members. Excluded from the discussion is consumer-oriented legislation, even though such legislation obviously tempers certain activities among commercial channel members.[28]

Although all legislation affects the legitimate power of channel members, the legal constraints listed here basically concern the use of power in channel management. Additional laws inhibit or prevent the means by which vertical integration can be employed to achieve the goals of a given distribution system. Therefore, the following comments center on legal limitations to the use of coercive power, reward power, *and* vertical integration.

Suppliers can implement several marketing policies to control or create incentives for their distribution systems. Numerous antitrust precedents deal with these policies, because some of them represent blatant restraints of trade. A critical issue that has evolved in antitrust cases, especially in the late 1970s in the *Sylvania* decision, is whether certain of these policies, while severely restricting *intrabrand* competition, are actually promoting, or at least not substantially lessening, *interbrand* competition.

Intrabrand competition is defined as competition among wholesalers or retailers of the same brand (e.g., Coca-Cola, Chevrolet, or Apple). Interbrand competition is defined as competition among all the suppliers of different brands of the same generic product (e.g., soft drinks, automobiles, or personal computers). By restricting intrabrand competition via stipulations regarding resellers' activities, a supplier can supposedly motivate its wholesalers and retailers to give appropriate attention to the supplier's brand. This "appropriate attention," in turn, generates interbrand competition as the resellers of brand X attempt to win out over the resellers of brand Y in the sales and servicing of product Z.

As appealing as this argument must sound to marketing strategists who would like to implement a variety of distribution policies, the issues are frequently more complex than this. Control over distribution is sought for many reasons, some of which are highly opportunistic and self-serving. Furthermore, not all distribution policies deal with intrabrand competition; several involve restricting interbrand competition directly by foreclosing competitors from resellers' outlets. Therefore, despite the increasingly sophisticated rationale employed to defend vertical restrictions in distribution, there are scores of reasons why marketing executives should remain alert to potential antitrust problems. While control over distribution practices may make abundant sense from a marketing perspective in a variety of different situations, no mandate from the Congress, the courts, or the enforcement agencies allows executives freedom to exert such control without considerable scrutiny.

When executives set marketing channel policy, they can run afoul of the antitrust laws in a host of ways. However, because of the *Sylvania* decision, many of these potential offenses will be analyzed by the courts under a rule-of-reason approach rather than viewed as illegal per se.[29] And even where decisions have tended toward a per se approach, a firm still has opportunities to show that it does not meet the standards set for illegality. In other words, with the exception of vertical price fixing, no policy area in distribution can be called an outright per se illegal offense. And there are even ways in which the vertical price-fixing prohibition is being circumvented. For example, manufacturers are permitted, under a 1982 ruling by the Federal Trade Commission involving U.S. Pioneer Electronics Corporation,[30] to set "minimum standards" for dealers, a de facto means for instituting resale restrictions and for cutting off supplies to discounters.[31]

This does not mean that marketing executives can now relax about the law. On the contrary, almost every aspect of their vertical relationships is covered, in one form or another, by the antitrust umbrella.

- *Exclusive dealing.* The requirement by a seller or lessor that its customer sell or lease only its products or at least no products in direct competition with the seller's products. Such a policy is illegal if the requirement may substantially lessen competition and is circumscribed by all three of the major antitrust acts—Sherman, Clayton, and FTC. The dominant statute here is, however, Section 3 of the Clayton Act.
- *Tying contracts.* The requirement by a seller or lessor that its customers take other products to obtain a product that they desire. Such a requirement seems to be per se illegal, although there are notable exceptions.
- *Territorial restrictions* (particularly the granting of exclusive territories). The granting by a seller of a geographical monopoly to a buyer for the resale of its product or brand. Such a policy is circumscribed by the Sherman Act and the FTC Act. The major emphasis in the analysis of such cases is on the potential effect of intrabrand restrictions on interbrand competition.
- *Resale or customer restrictions.* The requirement by a seller that its customers resell its products only to specified clientele. (The seller may agree not to compete for those clientele reserved for the customers.) This policy area is treated similarly to territorial restrictions under the antitrust laws.
- *Resale price maintenance.* The requirement by a seller that its customers resell its products only above or below a specified price or at a stipulated price. Price maintenance (fair trade) laws were nullified by the repeal of the Miller-Tydings and McGuire acts. Price maintenance is per se illegal and is mainly circumscribed by the Sherman Act.
- *Refusals to deal.* The right of the seller to choose its own customers or to stop serving a given customer. This threat obviously underlies the commercial enforcement of the policies just mentioned. Although its use is permitted under Section 2(a) of the Robinson-

Patman Act, it is forbidden if it fosters restraint of trade or substantially lessens competition.

- *Price discrimination by sellers.* The offering of different prices by a seller to two competing resellers on merchandise of like grade and quality. Such a policy is illegal when it substantially lessens competition but is legal when it can be justified on the basis of cost differentials or as being adopted in good faith to meet competition. It is directly circumscribed by the Robinson-Patman Act.
- *Price discrimination forced by buyers.* The requirement by a buyer that a seller offer it a price lower than that offered or available to its competitors. Such a policy is covered under the Robinson-Patman Act if it substantially lessens competition and under the FTC Act as an unfair method of competition.
- *Functional discounts.* The granting by a seller of price reductions to resellers on the basis of their positions in the marketing channel and the nature and scope of their marketing functions. Although no law directly deals with such discounts, they are circumscribed by the Robinson-Patman Act if they substantially lessen competition and are prohibited under the FTC Act as unfair methods of competition.
- *Promotional allowances and services.* The granting by a seller of payments to resellers for services rendered in connection with processing, handling, selling, or offering for sale any of its products sold by them. To be legal, such payments must be offered on proportionately equal terms to all resellers and must be used for the purpose for which they were intended (e.g., advertising allowances must be used for advertising). Again, the Robinson-Patmnan Act directly limits the way in which such allowances may be employed.

Vertical integration via internal expansion seems to be positively sanctioned by the antitrust enforcement agencies so long as it does not lead to monopolization in restraint of trade, a Sherman Act offense. On the other hand, vertical integration by merger is more heavily scrutinized. In the case of such mergers, Section 7 (the Celler-Kefauver Amendment) of the Clayton Act can be brought into play if the agencies believe there may be a tendency for the consummated merger to substantially lessen competition. Thus, the agencies can challenge such mergers in their incipiency.

The policy of vertical integration often leads to dual distribution conflicts in which sellers become competitors of some of their independently owned resellers. Although there are no additional laws beyond those mentioned earlier circumscribing dual distribution, this practice has undergone considerable scrutiny in Congress.

It should be noted once again that the above discussion focuses only on federal law. The states have become much more active in the antitrust arena, and thus marketing executives would make a serious mistake to ignore the vast outpouring of legislation regulating distribution practices in each of the states in which the products of their companies are sold.

Practical and Implementational Considerations

Channel strategy, design, and management are critical elements of marketing strategy. The proposed ten-step blueprint forces individuals involved in the design process to keep their eyes on the most important people in the entire channel system—end users. The blueprint is time-consuming, costly, and frustrating. At several points, it forces a doubling back over ground already covered. It is confrontational and demanding. Given all these attributes, why is it necessary?

The process is necessary because distribution still remains the dark side of marketing. It is necessary because rarely do firms invest as much in learning how end users like to obtain goods and services as they do in learning what the goods and services ought to look like. And aside from offering a quality, highly valued product, it is necessary because no other element of marketing is as important to a firm in achieving a differential advantage.

The magnitude and complexity of the task involved in following the blueprint depend largely on the extent of the modifications needed in the existing system and the nature of the required changes. It is wrong to assume that the process will always identify large gaps. For example, in one case, the existing system looked hopelessly complex when sketched on a piece of paper, but it met all the criteria of an ideal system. The recommendation: Don't mess with it! Leave it alone! Don't touch a thing!

There are problems and pitfalls in undertaking such a process, including the following:

- End users are often blinded by their own experience (which means that elements of creativity must be built into the entire exercise).
- Costing out new distribution systems demands informed guesswork.
- Management can display a pit bull hold on established distribution systems.
- The economic, political, and social impediments to channel change often make strong individuals weak in the knees.

Once channels have been designed, there is no guarantee that they will operate successfully. Realistic, cost-effective implementation and first-rate execution are accomplished by management techniques and mechanisms. Without purposive coordination, motivation, and direction, channels are doomed to failure, regardless of how they have been structured. Channel management involves two difficult tasks. First, it is concerned with achieving both *intra-* and *inter*organizational coordination and cooperation. Second, it must deal with conflicts that arise, especially in those channels that comprise independently owned and operated institutions and agencies.

The way in which marketing channels are organized is highly dependent on all the design and managerial factors discussed throughout this chapter. The ultimate organizational configuration of any channel rests largely on such variables as the amount of power available to individual channel members, their efforts to maintain healthy rather than dysfunctional levels of conflict, and their willingness to assume leadership roles in assuring that the service outputs desired by end users are delivered satisfactorily.

To a large extent, the manner in which channels should be organized is resolved by answering make vs. buy questions. Under what conditions is vertical integration (making the channel via internal growth or acquisition) a sensible strategy and under what conditions does relying on independently owned and operated institutions and agencies (buying the services of third parties) make more sense?

The make vs. buy decision in distribution is extremely complex, however, and many benefits and costs are associated with each alternative. It should be recalled from the discussion of channel design that vertical integration ought to be considered a "default" condition. In other words, managers should make rather than buy only after they have convinced themselves, through rigorous analysis, that ownership is necessary. This attitude may deter unnecessary investments in distribution.

Instituting effective interorganization management requires the use of power. There are, however, significant legal constraints on how power may be employed in the marketing channel. Before developing and implementing interorganizational strategies and programs, marketing managers at all levels of distribution must comprehend the intention and scope of these constraints so that any strategy or program that is promulgated will not run afoul of the various antitrust enforcement agencies. Although all legislation may be said to affect the legitimate power of channel members, the legal constraints examined in this chapter basically confine the use of coercive and reward power in channel management.

Notes

1. This chapter is based in its entirety on excerpts from Louis W. Stern and Adel I. El-Ansary, *Marketing Channels,* 4th ed. (Englewood Cliffs, N.J.: Prentice-Hall, 1992).
2. The approach was first outlined in Louis W. Stern and Frederick D. Sturdivant, "Customer-Driven Distribution Systems," *Harvard Business Review* 65 (July–August 1987): 34–41.
3. Special thanks for assisting in the development, improvement, and implementation of this framework are due the following officers of Gemini Consulting: Frederick D. Sturdivant, Gary A. Getz, Gail J. Breslow, Pierre Loewe, and Mark D. Johnson.
4. Louis P. Bucklin, *Productivity in Marketing* (Chicago: American Marketing Association, 1978), pp. 90–94. Also see Louis P. Bucklin, *A Theory of Distribution Channel Structure* (Berkeley, Calif.: IBER Publications, 1966).
5. See Paul E. Green, "Hybrid Models for Conjoint Analysis: An Expository Review," *Journal of Marketing Research* 21 (May 1984): 155–69. See also Gilbert A. Churchill, Jr., *Marketing Research,* 4th ed. (Chicago: Dryden Press, 1987), pp. 364–76.
6. The MAC Group, Inc., Gemini Consulting, *Distribution: A Competitive Weapon* (Cambridge, Mass.: MAC Group, 1985), p. 10.
7. Andrew Baxter, "Chrysler in Deal with CLS over Distribution in Europe," *Financial Times,* April 10,1991, p. 18; Andrew Baxter, "Caterpillar Finds Uses for Distribution Skills," *Financial Times,* June 5,1991, p. 14; "Integrated Systems Division, Supermarkets Reach Pact," *Wall Street Journal,* August 7,1991, p. B5.
8. See Rowland T. Moriarty and Ursula Moran, "Managing Hybrid Marketing Systems," *Harvard Business Review* (November–December 1990): 146–55, and Sue Heintz, "The Build-It-Yourself Phenomenon: A Modular Approach to Channel Design," *Frank Lynn & Associates, Inc. Client Communique* 3 (January 1991): 2, 3.
9. See, for example, Ravi S. Achrol, Torger Reve, and Louis W. Stern, "The Environment of Marketing Channel Dyads: A Framework for Comparative Analysis," *Journal of Marketing* 47 (Fall 1983): 55–67; Ravi S. Achrol and Louis W. Stern, "Environmental Determinants of Decision-Making Uncertainty in Marketing Channels," *Journal of Marketing Research* 25 (February 1988): 36–50; Michael Etgar, "Channel Environment and Channel Leadership," *Journal of Marketing Research* 15 (February 1977): 69–76; F. Robert Dwyer and Sejo Oh, "Output Sector Munificence Effects on the Internal Political Economy of Marketing Channels," *Journal of Marketing Research* 24 (November 1987): 347–58; and F. Robert Dwyer and M. Ann Welsh, "Environmental Relationships of the Internal Political Economy of Marketing Channels," *Journal of Marketing Research* 22 (November 1985): 397–414.
10. Milind Lele, "Matching Your Channels to Your Product's Life Cycle," *Business Marketing* (December 1986): 61–69.
11. Ibid., p. 64
12. Adapted from Achrol and Stern, "Environmental Determinants," p. 37.

13. Ibid., p. 47.
14. See David B. Tinnin, "Porsche's Civil War with Its Dealers," *Fortune,* April 16,1984, pp. 63–68.
15. Nurur Rahman, "Channel Coordination: A Managerial Perspective," in Louis M. Capella et al., eds., *Progress in Marketing Thought,* Proceedings of the Annual Meetings of the Southern Marketing Association, 1990, pp. 218–23.
16. The source for the following figure and table is Adel I. El-Ansary, Research Program in Wholesaling, University of North Florida, 1991. His work is based on the research findings of others as follows: Michael Etgar, "Channel Environment and Channel Leadership," *Journal of Marketing Research* 14 (February 1977): 70; James R. Brown, Robert F. Lusch, and Darrel D. Muehling, "Conflict and Power-Dependence Relations in Retail-Supplier Channels," *Journal of Retailing* 59 (Winter 1983): 53–80; Gary L. Frazier, "Interorganizational Exchange Behavior in Marketing Channels: A Broadened Perspective," *Journal of Marketing* 46 (Fall 1983): 68–78; John F. Gaski, "The Theory of Power and Conflict in Channels of Distribution," *Journal of Marketing* 47 (Summer 1984): 9–29; James C. Anderson and James A. Narus, "A Model of the Distributor's Perspective of Distributor–Manufacturer Working Relationships," *Journal of Marketing* 47 (Fall 1984): 62–74; John F. Gaski and John R. Nevin, "The Differential Effects of Exercised and Unexercised Power Sources in a Marketing Channel," *Journal of Marketing Research* 22 (May 1985): 130–34; Patrick L. Schul, William M. Pride, and Taylor E. Little, "The Impact of Channel Leadership Behavior on Intrachannel Conflict," *Journal of Marketing* 46 (Summer 1983): 21–34; Patrick L. Schul, Taylor E. Little, Jr., and William M. Pride, "Channel Climate: Its Impact on Channel Members' Satisfaction," *Journal of Retailing* 61 (Summer 1985): 9–37; and Erin Anderson and Barton Weitz, "The Use of Pledges to Build and Sustain Commitment in Distribution Channels," Working Paper No. 90–037, The Wharton School of the University of Pennsylvania, December 1990.
17. For an application of the concepts introduced in this chapter to a specific industrial setting (property and casualty insurance) by an industry executive, see F. Dean Hildebrandt, Jr., "The American Agency System: It's More Than a Partnership," *Best's Review* 81 (December 1980): 12ff.
18. For empirical results showing the connection between role performance and power, see Gary L. Frazier, "On the Measurement of Interfirm Power in Channels of Distribution," *Journal of Marketing Research* 20 (May 1983): 158–66.
19. Erin Anderson and Barton A. Weitz, "Make-or-Buy Decisions: Vertical Integration and Marketing Productivity," *Sloan Management Review* (Spring 1986): 3–19.
20. Erin Anderson and Anne T. Coughlan, "International Market Entry and Expansion via Independent or Integrated Channels of Distribution," *Journal of Marketing* 51 (January 1987): 74.
21. Oliver E. Williamson, *The Economic Institutions of Capitalism* (New York: Free Press, 1985); Oliver E. Williamson, "Transaction-Cost Economics: The Governance of Contractual Relations," *Journal of Law and Economics* 22 (October 1979): 233–62; and Oliver E. Williamson, *Markets and Hierarchies: Analysis and Antitrust Implications* (New York: Free Press, 1975).
22. F. Robert Dwyer and M. Ann Welsh, "Environmental Relationships in the Internal Political Economy of Marketing Channels," *Journal of Marketing Research* 22 (November 1985): 397–414.
23. See, for example, Saul Klein, Gary L. Frazier, and Victor J. Roth, "A Transaction Cost Analysis Model of Channel Integration in International Markets," *Journal of Marketing Research* 27 (May 1990): 196–208; George John and Barton A. Weitz, "Forward Integration

into Distribution: An Empirical Test of Transaction Cost Analysis," *Journal of Law, Economics, and Organization* 4 (Fall 1988): 337–55; Erin Anderson, "The Salesperson as Outside Agent or Employee: A Transaction Cost Analysis," *Marketing Science* 4 (Summer 1985): 234–54; George John, "An Empirical Investigation of Some Antecedents of Opportunism in a Marketing Channel," *Journal of Marketing Research* 21 (August 1984): 278–89; and Lynn W. Phillips, "Explaining Control Losses in Corporate Marketing Channels: An Organization Analysis," *Journal of Marketing Research* 19 (November 1982): 525–49.

24. See Klein, Frazier, and Roth, "Transaction Cost Analysis Model," p. 204.
25. Increasing numbers of firms are adopting this perspective. For example, see "There Are No Products—Only Services," *Fortune,* January 14,1991, p. 32, and "Contracted Business Services," *Financial Times,* Section IV, March 11, 1990.
26. Simon Holberton, "In Topsy-Turvy Fashion," *Financial Times,* October 26,1990, p. 11.
27. Some of the material here comes directly from Louis W. Stern and Thomas L. Eovaldi, *Legal Aspects of Marketing Strategy: Antitrust and Consumer Protection Issues* (Englewood Cliffs, N.J.: Prentice-Hall, 1984). For elaboration of many of the topics covered in this chapter, the reader is encouraged to refer to that book.
28. The Federal Trade Commission has attacked thousands of devious schemes in distribution that directly affect the consumer. The largest categories have been fictitious pricing, wherein goods are falsely advertised as bargains; "bait and switch" advertising, by which customers, lured into a store by a spectacular bargain not intended to be sold, are "switched" to other, more expensive purchases; exaggerated claims for the efficacy of drugs and cosmetics; the selling of used products as new; failure to disclose the limitations of guarantees; and misrepresentations of the quality of products. In addition, the FTC polices the labeling of furs and textiles, so that a buyer can be sure the product is made of the material claimed on the label; the Flammable Fabrics Act, to protect consumers from dangerously flammable clothing; the Fair Packaging and Labeling Act, to inform the consumer of the net contents of a package; the Truth in Lending Act, which enables consumers to shop for credit by comparing the finance charges and the annual percentage rates of creditors; the Fair Credit Reporting Act, which seeks to protect consumers from the reporting of erroneous personal information by credit bureaus; and the Consumer Product Safety Act, which attempts to minimize the number of physical injuries to consumers caused by dangerous or defective products. Major federal consumer legislation is reviewed in Stern and Eovaldi, *Legal Aspects.*
29. *Continental T.V., Inc. v. GTE Sylvania, Inc.,* 433 U.S. 36 (1977).
30. *In the Matter of U.S. Pioneer Electronics Corp.,* Federal Trade Commission docket No. C-2755, November 5, 1982.
31. See Claudia Ricci, "Discounters, Alleging Price-Fixing, are Fighting Cuts in Their Supplies," *Wall Street Journal,* June 21, 1983, p. 35.

CHAPTER 7

Logistics Network Modeling

Paul T. Chapman

For many companies, managing logistics implies managing a complex network of facilities and flows of materials and finished goods among those facilities. Viewed comprehensively, as in Figure 7-1, the logistics network is the overall physical channel by which materials are transformed into finished products and placed in the hands of customers.

There are three fundamental reasons why logistics networks are challenging to manage:

1. *Logistics networks are frequently large and complex.* Many companies execute the movement of hundreds (or thousands) of items through a number of plants and warehouses. In addition, managing different product groups within a logistics network often creates a variety of specialized storage, handling, and transportation requirements.
2. *Logistics networks must effectively meet market needs.* In a customer-driven world, effective management of product flow through the logistics network is critical to responding to customer requirements.
3. *Logistics networks must be cost-efficient.* Generally, the cost of operations (manufacturing, transportation, handling, and storage costs) is a significant percentage of company revenues. Therefore, network management must not only be effective in meeting customer needs but it must also be as efficient as possible from a cost perspective.

Logistics network models are computer-based analytical tools that facilitate better design and management of logistics networks. They provide management with concise information and insight into the best alternatives for meeting emerging logistics network needs. In essence, logistics network models provide clarity and understanding to critical management issues—namely, logistics network design and management—that are inherently complex.

The proven practical value of network models has led to their widespread adoption by the logistics profession for addressing a number of logistical problems, ranging from strategic issues like facility location (where to place warehouses and plants within a logistics network) to detailed deployment of stock (how to deploy available supplies to meet immediate demands). The value of network models lies in their analytical power, which is made possible through advancements in computer technology and decision sciences.

Logistics consulting firms currently employ various computer-based modeling tools to help companies address logistics network design issues. Moreover, sophisticated modeling capabilities, inexpensive computer power, and increased user friendliness in modeling software have led many companies to install analytical support tools on-site for use by their own staff. Recognizing a growing market, both consulting firms and software vendors now offer a wide choice

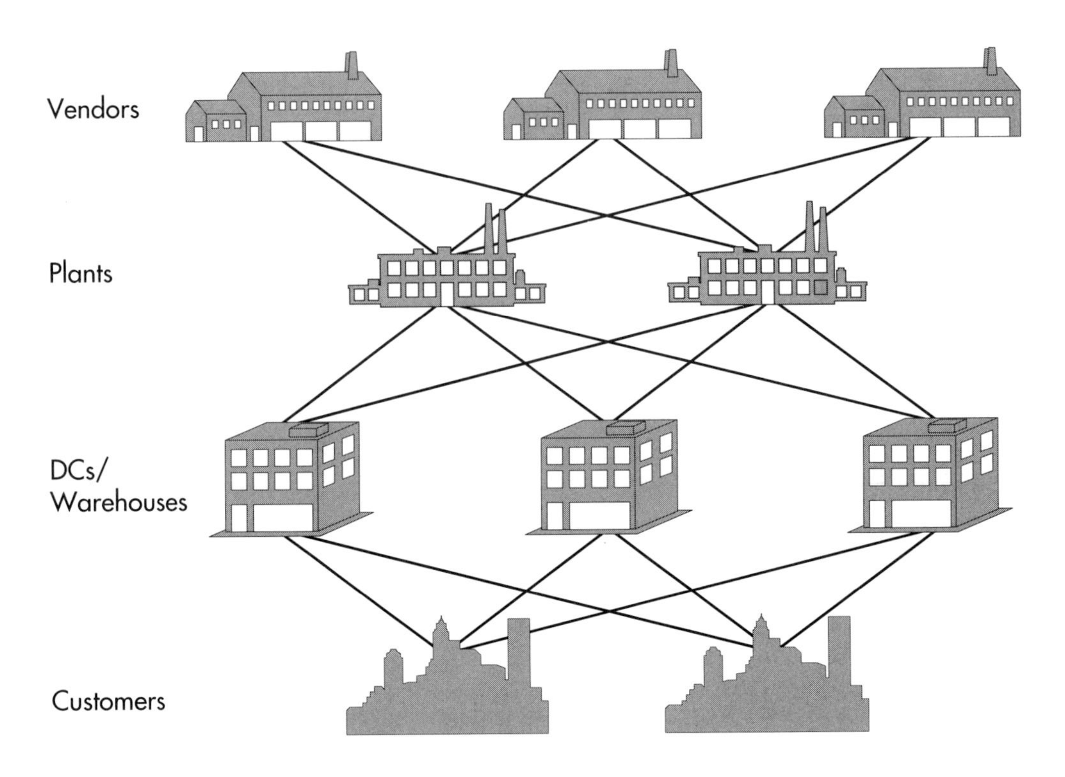

Figure 7-1
A Logistics Network:
Facilities and Material Flows

of logistics modeling software. Consequently, logistics professionals armed with powerful but easy-to-use tools now have immediate access to sophisticated decision support.

This chapter provides a guide to the practical use of logistics network modeling. With this goal in mind, the chapter will:

- Provide a practitioner-oriented guide to network modeling
- Describe how network modeling has been successfully applied to several logistics network problems
- Describe practical approaches to incorporating network modeling into a company's logistics decision-making process

Supporting a Variety of Management Decisions

In recent years, the logistics profession has made substantial progress in improving customer service, attaining better utilization of assets (e.g., inventory management), and reducing operating costs. Compared with earlier times, companies today are generally much more proficient in their ability to meet customer service demands, contain logistics costs, and manage inventories effectively.

Emerging Logistics Challenges

Despite this process, logistics challenges are increasing because the overall business climate is becoming more dynamic and competitive. These pressures call for even better performance along the traditional measures of logistics performance: order fill rates, inventory turns, and operating costs. Moreover, logistics critical success factors are expanding:

- Beyond traditional performance measures, there is an increasing emphasis on flexibility, responsiveness, and speed.
- Logistics must respond to "mass customization": the fracturing of previously stable commodity markets into a variety of specialty markets, each with individual, stringent service requirements.
- Cost-cutting pressures call for streamlined organizations and greater white-collar productivity. In the logistics function, there is a need for increased productivity from a core group of "empowered" logistics professionals. Logistics professionals' job content must continue to evolve from detailed labor-intensive clerical activities toward more sophisticated planning and management activities. This requires automating as many detailed, clerical tasks as possible and enhancing the effectiveness of logistics professionals through the innovative application of information technology.
- Companies are increasingly compelled to take a total supply chain approach to operations, where sourcing, manufacturing, and distribution are viewed as interrelated steps in the value-added supply chain. Companies in the 1980s learned how to make improvements in isolated functional areas of logistics—such as exploiting the opportunities of transportation deregulation and improving finished goods inventory management. But many companies have not fully adopted an integrated, cross-functional approach to operations network design and management, and the additional cost and service improvements that companies seek can be obtained only from such an integrated approach.

A Spectrum of Decision Support

As highlighted in Figure 7-2, network modeling is regularly used to support logistical decision making in several areas, including:

- *Network structure.* How do we position assets (plants, distribution centers, warehouses) and construct customer service regions to achieve best systemwide performance?
- *Tactical planning.* How do we best utilize manufacturing and distribution assets over the next several months to meet anticipated needs?
- *Distribution scheduling.* How do we provide accurate, detailed information on distribution requirements over the next several weeks to those who are responsible for providing distribution with product (i.e., the company's manufacturing or purchasing decision makers)?
- *Deployment.* How do we deploy available supplies over the short term to satisfy immediate requirements?

As can be seen in Figure 7-2, the operational scope and time frames differ significantly among these four activities. Network structure, for instance, must encompass the total supply chain, including production for manufacturing companies, to fully exploit the opportunities of integrated operations.

Whereas the structure of a logistics network is normally considered every few years, the is-

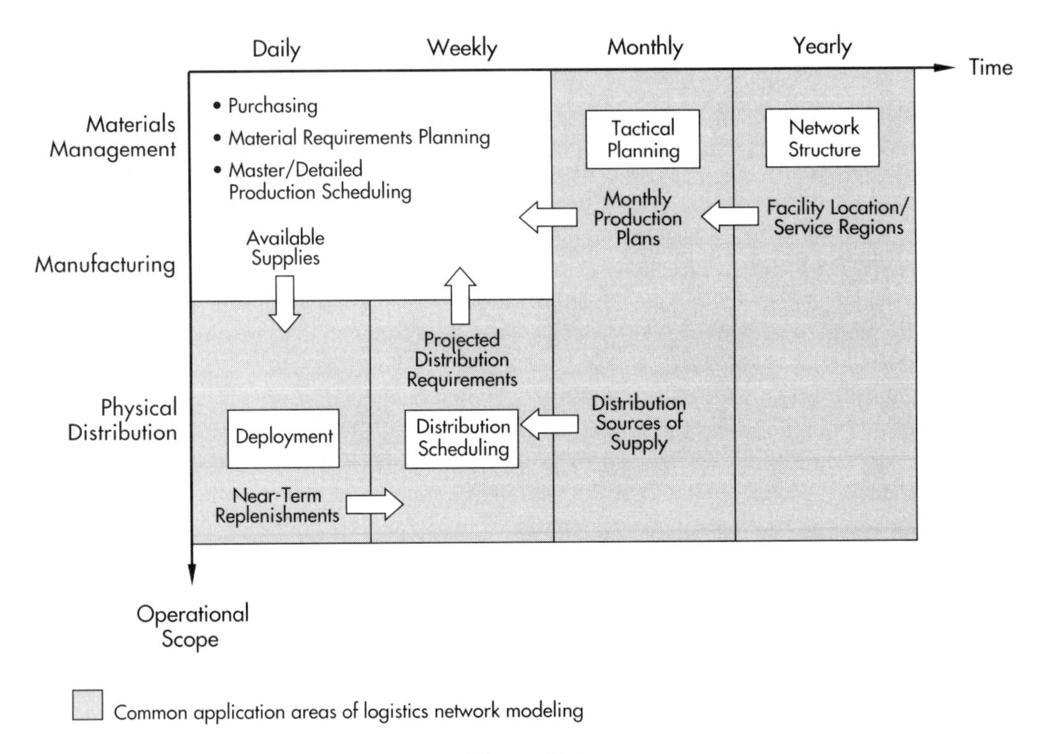

Figure 7-2
Areas of Logistical Decision Making Supported by Network Modeling

sues in tactical planning are more focused and imminent. The emphasis here is managing the current logistics network by creating production and distribution plans, several months into the future, that will effectively meet projected needs. For instance, good production plans ensure that a company in a highly seasonal business is properly stocked during its peak demand period. In this regard, a plan might begin building inventory several months before the peak period, thereby avoiding a supply shortfall during the peak period. Distribution plans determine how warehouses will be sourced in the coming months, and even how these sources of supply will change from month to month.

Scheduling is more focused still. In physical distribution, scheduling evaluates the inventory positions and detailed projected demands of individual stock keeping units (SKUs) through a number of approaching weeks. Replenishment requirements (what, when, where, and how much) are then calculated and passed on to manufacturing or purchasing as inputs to their scheduling process.

Finally, at the most focused and short-term end of the spectrum is the issue of deployment. The concern is, how can we best match available finished goods supplies with immediate demands? Deployment, therefore, is detailed and operational. Given its concern with immediate execution, deployment's time frames are short—decisions are reviewed on a daily or semiweekly basis. However, despite its detailed, short-term focus, sophisticated deployment is imperative for companies that emphasize quick, flexible response to market demands.

As shown in Figure 7-2, the operational scope for network structure and tactical planning encompasses manufacturing (for manufacturing companies) in addition to logistics management's traditional focus on materials management (inbound logistics) and physical distribution (outbound logistics). This reflects a comprehensive approach to logistics where all operational components of the supply chain, including manufacturing, are considered in strategy and planning exercises.

A key commentary is that network modeling today provides substantial analytical support in each of these decision-making areas. Although the issues across these areas are diverse, modeling technology has matured to where there now exist specific tools for individually addressing each area.

Consequently, logistics network modeling is an extensive and rich field, and a single chapter cannot explore each of the application areas in detail. This chapter concentrates on the strategic issues of *network structure* and to a lesser degree on tactical planning—emphasizing the role of network modeling in supporting management decision making in these critical areas.

Warehouse Location

Network modeling is firmly established as a valuable aid in performing warehouse location studies. Typically, the goal in evaluating warehouse network structure is to determine the network configuration (i.e., the number, size, location, and service regions of warehouses) that provides a required level of customer service at minimum operating cost. In an effort to maintain superior distribution performance, companies periodically reconfigure their warehouse networks to respond to changing business requirements.

Alternatives and Trade-offs

Establishing an effective warehouse configuration often requires evaluating numerous network alternatives and working through a variety of complex, quantitative trade-offs. Figure 7-3 broadly outlines some of these trade-offs. Increasing the number of warehousing facilities in a logistics network generally improves customer service, because additional stocking locations reduces average delivery times to customers. However, more warehouses increase warehousing and inventory costs. Warehousing costs increase because there are more overhead and fixed costs to absorb. Inventory costs increase because a greater number of warehouses means more safety stock inventory must be held systemwide to provide a specified level of customer service.

In contrast, transportation costs decrease as the number of facilities is increased over some range. Rather than shipping smaller quantities direct from points of supply (e.g., plants) to customers, warehouses serve as product mixing centers that allow larger, consolidated shipments between supply points and warehouses. This transportation cost advantage becomes diminished, however, if too many warehouses are present because the shipment sizes between supply points and warehouses decrease to the point where there is little shipment consolidation advantage over direct shipments to customers.

Addressing these issues in large distribution networks—with a large number of products and possible facility configurations to consider—can be a massive task. Within the realm of facility location, modeling provides a framework for dealing with this complexity. Network models synthesize large amounts of data into concise, critical information that decision makers can understand. Models also help management evaluate a large number of network configuration

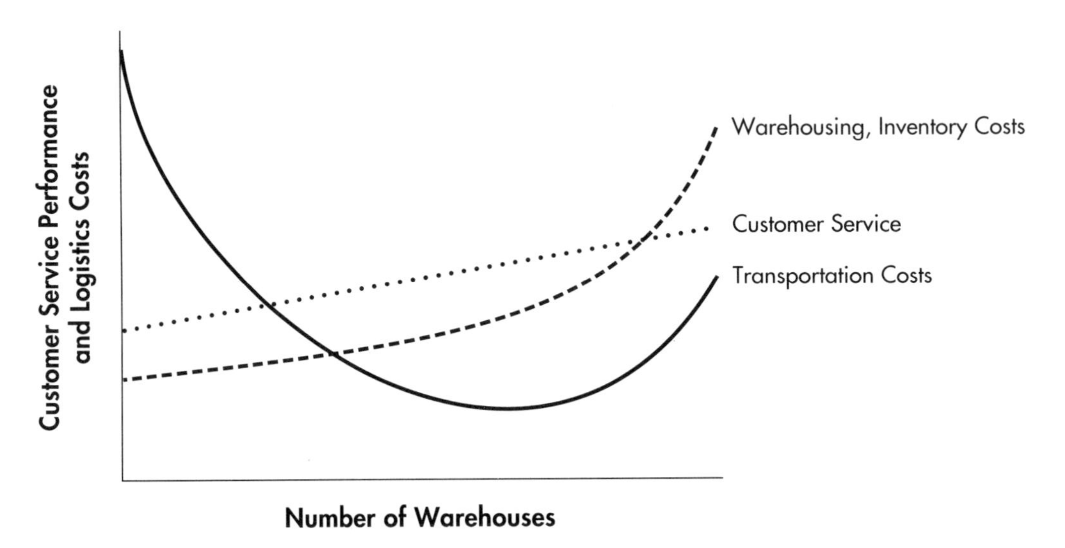

Figure 7-3
Relationship Between Service/Cost Performance and Number of Warehouse Locations

alternatives and point out best options by helping decision makers resolve an assortment of cost/service trade-offs.

A Warehouse Location Case Study

Consider, for instance, the logistics network of a North American distributor of pharmaceuticals and health and beauty aids (H&BAs). The company receives supplies from ten major vendor locations and currently distributes product to 200 major North American markets through a network of 45 distribution centers. The distributor's network is presented in a simplified format in Figure 7-4. The distribution center (DC) configuration is a single-tier, or "flat," network; all product moves from a vendor facility through a single company-controlled DC and on to customers. In other words, no company DC acts as a "master" distribution center that supplies other company stocking facilities.

The company is in the process of evaluating alternatives to its current network structure with the aid of a logistics network model, and sample logistics model assumptions concerning freight and DC operations costs are outlined in Table 7-1. Products are grouped into four major categories: fast and slow movers within the pharmaceutical and H&BA categories. These product groups have different weight and cube characteristics, dollar volume in sales, and dollar value per unit.

Table 7-2 describes seven distribution options under consideration, the first being the current network configuration. All options except 6 and 7 assume that the same 45 facilities continue to be used. In evaluating all options except the current configuration, the network model employs optimization technology to determine the overall least-cost sourcing for each market that satisfies an overall service criterion. This means that the logistics model has the ability to determine

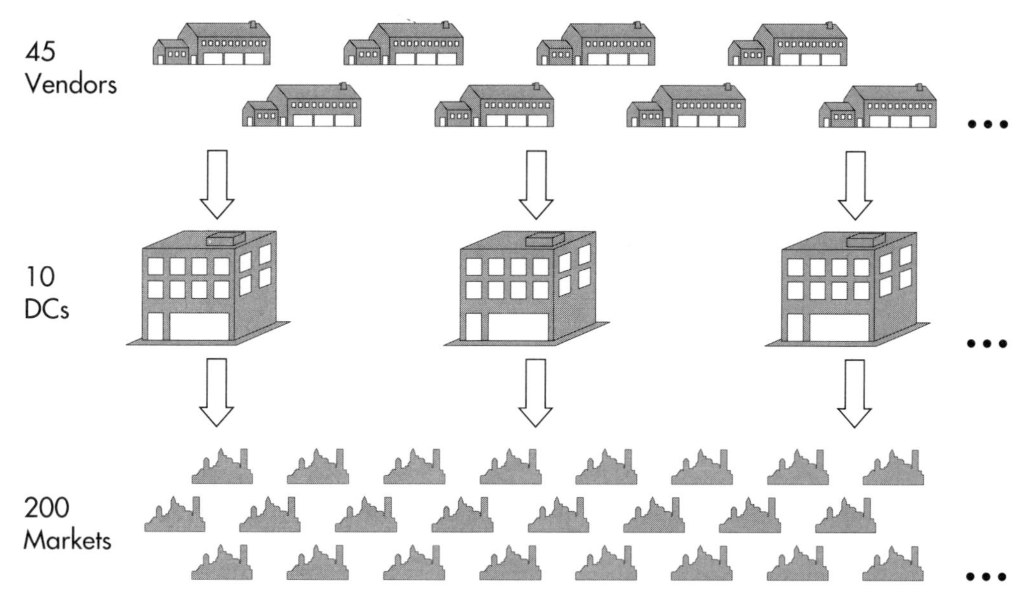

Figure 7-4
A Distributor's Logistics Network

automatically the assignment of markets to warehouses in a way that minimizes total logistics costs while meeting specified service levels.

For example, in options 2 through 5, it is specified that all markets must be served by a DC no more than 300 miles away. Within this restriction, markets should be sourced from warehouses to minimize total operational expenses. Costs include vendor purchase costs and all distribution costs (handling, moving, and storage) between vendor source points and final customer ship-to locations.

TABLE 7-1
Logistics Model Assumptions

Elements	Assumptions
Vendors	• 10 sourcing facilities • Each sources specific products with specific costs
Inbound Freight	• $0.30 per carton
DC Operations	• Currently 45 locations • $6/ft^2 fixed cost @ 125,000–250,000 ft^2 each • Product-specific handling and inventory costs
Customer Freight	• $1.65/mile for transportation
Customers	• 200 markets • 4 product groups –Fast/slow pharmaceuticals –Fast/slow H&BA

TABLE 7-2
Warehouse Network Options

Option	Name	Features
1	Base Case	• Current configuration • Customer shipments come from historical warehouses
2	Least-Cost Single Source	• Each customer receives all product from overall least-cost source • Service range = 300 miles
3	Lower-Cost Handling	• Best customer sourcing if warehouse handling costs reduced by additional 20% in newer facilities owing to additional investment • Service range = 300 miles
4	East/West Master DCs	• H&BA stocked in master DCs and cross docked (2-tier network) • Pharmaceuticals stocked regionally • Service range = 300 miles
5	East/West II	• Fast movers stocked regionally • Slow movers stocked centrally in master DCs (2-tier network) • Service range = 300 miles
6	17 New Only	• 17 newer facilities only • Newer facilities are more automated than others • Service range = 500 miles
7	17 + 1	• 17 newer facilities plus one older Midwest facility • Newer facilities are more automated than others • Service range = 500 miles

Seventeen of the 45 warehouses are more modern and efficient than the others, resulting in lower handling costs per product unit at these facilities. Moreover, the company is considering additional upgrades to the handling equipment in these newer facilities. Consequently, option 3 assumes that warehouse handling costs have been reduced 20% through investment in automation equipment in the 17 newer facilities.

Options 4 and 5 assume that the distribution network is reconfigured from a single tier of warehouses to a two-tier configuration, with two of the current facilities converted into master distribution centers. The new configuration places a master DC both east and west of the Mississippi River. Because pharmaceuticals have shorter order lead times on average than H&BA products, option 4 assumes that only pharmaceutical products are stored regionally to ensure quick order response. H&BA products are stored centrally in the two master DCs and cross-docked through the regional facilities as they are transported to customers. Option 5, however, separates all products (pharmaceuticals and H&BAs) into fast and slow movers. In contrast to option 4, all fast movers (in both the pharmaceutical and H&BA product groups) are stocked regionally, while all slow movers are inventoried at the master DCs and cross-docked through regional facilities.

In options 6 and 7, the number of DCs is substantially reduced. These options are included because the company is considering increasing the maximum distance from a warehouse to a major market from 300 to 500 miles. There is speculation that faster information processing and improved warehousing operations may allow the distributor to increase the geographical service radius of a warehouse without significantly increasing overall order response time.

It has been determined that the 17 newer facilities can service almost all major U.S. markets within a 500-mile radius. The only exception is certain regions of the northern Midwest and Pacific Northwest. Another facility is needed in this region to ensure strict adherence to the 500-mile service rule. Consequently, option 6 considers a network consisting strictly of 17 newer warehouses, while option 7 assumes that one of the older facilities is retained in the northern Midwest region to provide uniform, 500-mile coverage to all U.S. markets.

Evaluating Options

Table 7-3 summarizes the results of a logistics network modeling exercise that evaluates these seven warehouse network options. Option 2, which simply reassigns markets to the current network of warehouses, is projected to be worth $7.3 million a year in savings—approximately 3% of current logistics costs. The savings is derived from reduced customer freight and variable handling costs, which result from reassigning markets to warehouses that can service their needs more efficiently.

Reducing variable handling costs in the 17 newer warehouses (option 3) reduces overall handling costs by almost $10 million per year. In addition, better service region construction results in an additional $3.8 million savings in customer freight and inventory expenses. Notice also that the network model chose to source no material through one of the 45 facilities under option 3. This unused facility is therefore dropped from the network, reducing fixed warehousing costs by about $800,000 annually. In aggregate, the model projects an annual operational savings of $14.5 million over current costs with the capital investment in automation under consideration for the 17 newer facilities. However, $7.3 million in savings can be achieved *without* this capital investment simply by reconfiguring service regions (option 2). These figures should prove valuable to managers as they evaluate the return on investment of the automation proposal.

The modeling analysis demonstrates that centralizing H&BA inventory (option 4) can save $12 million annually in inventory-related costs. Variable handling costs are also reduced ($4.5 million), because centralized H&BA products can be efficiently stored and picked in bulk quantities in the two master DCs, and these product groups require only cross-docking (versus storing and picking) at the regional warehouses. Another $800,000 in fixed warehousing costs is saved by reducing the number of regional facilities by one. These savings are offset by a $2.6 million net increase in transportation costs, attributable to the extra transportation leg that H&BA items must travel under a two-tier distribution network.

The overall savings for option 5 are similar to those of option 4, but they are achieved differently. Compared with option 4, option 5 stores a significantly higher percentage of product volume in regional facilities. This substantially reduces the money spent on interfacility freight between master DCs and regional facilities (by $6.5 million over option 4). However, this greater regional concentration of inventory increases variable handling and inventory costs.

Somewhat surprisingly, options 6 and 7, which dramatically reduce the number of warehouses within a one-tier distribution network and increase the size of warehouse service regions, do not save as much as moving to a two-tier network with many more regional facilities. As expected, a smaller number of warehouses creates substantial reductions in fixed warehousing and inventory expenses. Relative to current costs, variable handling is reduced because the remaining facilities are the most efficient in the current distribution network. Inbound freight costs also improve, because a smaller number of inbound shipment points translates into more consolidated inbound shipments.

These savings are offset, however, by customer freight costs projected to increase about $27 million under option 7 and over $30 million under option 6. Option 7, which is created from option 6 by adding the older Northwest facility to the network consisting of the 17 newer facilities, is clearly the better of the two options. The additional facilities not only improve service to

TABLE 7-3
Evaluation of Warehouse Network Options

Option	Number of Warehouses	Network Costs ($MM)						Savings
		Inbound and Interfacility Freight	Customer Freight	Fixed Warehousing	Variable Handling	Inventory	Total	
1) Base Case	45	$37.7	$47.8	$40.8	$59.2	$52.3	$237.8	—
2) Lowest-Cost Single Source	45	37.7	41.3	40.8	58.4	52.3	230.5	$7.3
3) Lower-Cost Handling	44	37.7	44.1	40.0	49.3	52.2	223.3	14.5
4) East/West Master DCs	44	47.1	41.0	40.0	54.7	40.3	223.1	14.7
5) East/West II	44	40.6	41.3	40.0	56.2	45.4	223.5	14.3
6)17 New Only	17	31.3	78.5	19.8	51.9	46.5	228.0	9.8
7) 17 + 1	18	31.3	74.6	20.6	52.3	46.7	225.5	12.3

the Northwest region but also result in overall operating costs that are $2.5 million lower than for option 6.

Case Study Highlights

This case study highlights several of the important issues in network studies and the advantages of using logistics network modeling for addressing these issues. First, the example conveys some of the complexity in determining proper network structure. Establishing an effective structure is somewhat analogous to solving a large puzzle where a number of concerns must be simultaneously addressed. Each option considered has its relative strengths and weaknesses. Moreover, improving performance along one measure (inventory costs) often degrades performance along another (transportation costs).

The case also conveys the value of a network modeling tool. Through optimization technology, the model has evaluated a large number of alternatives in determining optimal service regions for each of the seven options—and performing such an extensive analysis is not practical without modeling support. Moreover, the model's ability to consider so many alternatives led to network configurations that meet the company's service criteria with demonstrably better cost performance.

Notice how the model transforms data into useful management information. The high-level comparison of options outlined in Table 7-3 represents the aggregation of a vast quantity of data. In its disaggregated form, these data are much too detailed and voluminous to be useful in a decision-making process. The model effectively transforms these detailed data into concise information that can be readily understood by decision makers.

Perhaps most important, the model, through its analytical power, has provided valuable insight into the company's operational characteristics and how best to respond to them. For example, the modeling exercise has shown that the company can achieve a 6.2% overall reduction in operating costs by creating distinctive distribution channels for pharmaceuticals versus H&BA products (option 4). Moreover, these savings can be achieved with a relatively small amount of up-front capital investment.

High-volume pharmaceuticals require fast order response times, and the company's network of 45 warehouses provides next-day delivery for pharmaceutical orders anywhere in the 48 contiguous states. H&BA products, in contrast, do not normally require next-day service. The company, however, is currently running its logistics operations monolithically. It has structured its network to provide uniformly fast order response times for *all* its products, because a critical segment of its product lines (pharmaceuticals) requires such service.

The logistics network model has quantified the price the company currently pays for its uniformly high-order response times, and the price is relatively significant for a company whose core business is physical distribution. With this new information in hand, the company has reason to pursue a more detailed evaluation of a policy that stores H&BA products centrally and responds to H&BA orders with a longer lead time. The key observation is that such insight and clear direction is virtually impossible to achieve in complex, modern logistics networks without sophisticated, computer-based analytical support.

Integrating the Total Supply Chain

Beyond reconfiguring warehouses, significant additional cost and service improvements can be achieved through a total-supply-chain approach to network structure. In this integrated approach,

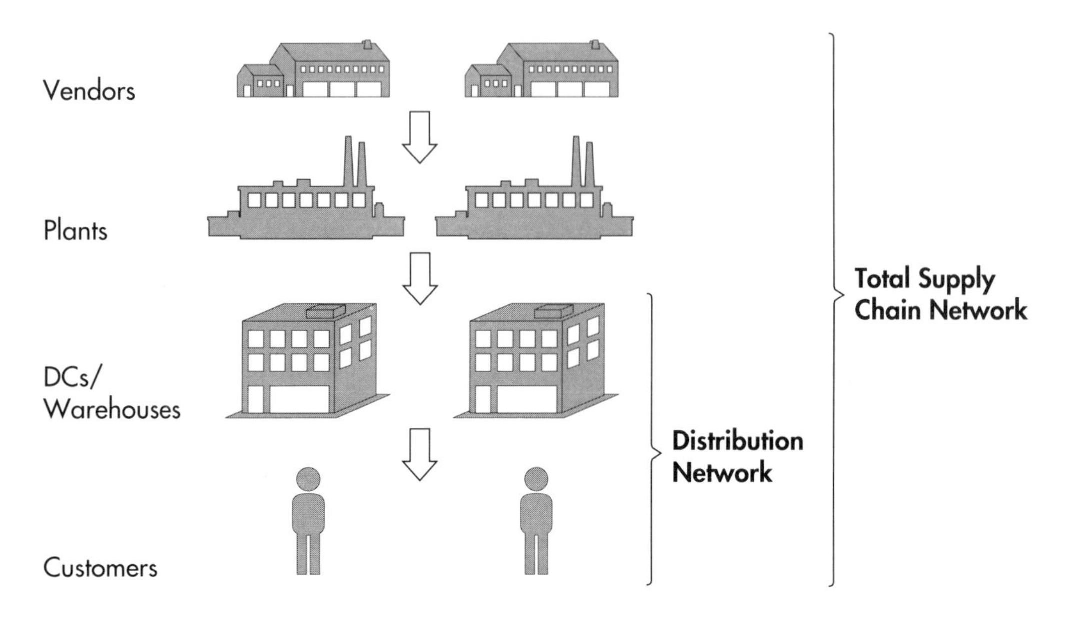

Figure 7-5
A Total-Supply-Chain Approach to Network Structure Including Manufacturing and Materials Management

sourcing, manufacturing, and distribution are viewed as interrelated activities within a comprehensive framework. Recognizing the need to further improve operational performance, companies now commonly undertake network structure studies that focus on manufacturing and plant sourcing (inbound logistics or materials management), as well as physical distribution of finished products. A total-supply-chain network is shown in Figure 7-5. The more common issues addressed include:

- *Plant location.* Which of our current plants should be retained? Should we expand our manufacturing base through building new plants or through significantly upgrading current facilities?
- *Plant loadings.* What types of manufacturing lines should we install in each plant? Which products should we make at which plant? How do we resolve make vs. buy decisions such as determining our use of copackers?
- *Sourcing.* How should plants be sourced inbound with materials?

A Strategic Exercise

Many of these issues are fundamentally strategic, with long-term consequences for a company. Altering plant locations, capacities, and capabilities often has greater capital investment consequences than reconfiguring a network of warehouses. Adjusting distribution networks to meet changing needs frequently requires less capital investment, because warehouses are generally less capital-intensive than plants. Also, a well-established public (contract) warehousing and transportation industry in North America provides a means for adding and dropping distribution capacity as required. These factors provide an element of flexibility in altering distribution net-

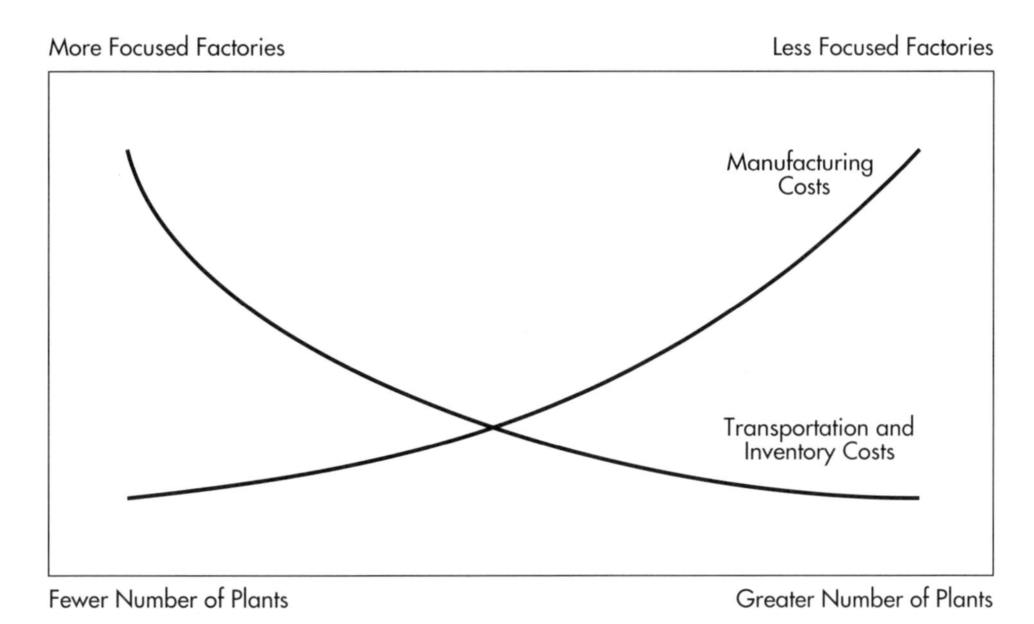

Figure 7-6
Relationship Between Cost Performance, Factory Focus, and Number of Plant Locations

works, because networks can be reconfigured without buying or selling "hard" assets like trucks and warehouses. A company has the option of leasing or renting capacity as needed.

In many businesses, however, manufacturing capacity cannot be viewed as a readily acquired and relinquished commodity. Manufacturing technology, policy, and procedures generally vary widely from industry to industry (and even from company to company within an industry). This means fewer options for contracting for capacity in an open market. Altering production capacity, therefore, tends to be more of a "bricks and mortar" issue, requiring substantial capital investment and careful planning.

Not surprisingly, including manufacturing and sourcing considerations in a network structure study can significantly complicate the analysis. Beyond the complexity already present in warehouse location, a study must deal with capabilities, costs, and capacities at additional levels of the logistics network. Consequently network modeling's strengths—its ability to synthesize data into information, evaluate various alternatives, and resolve complex trade-offs—are of considerable value in determining how to fully integrate all components of the supply chain.

Figure 7-6 outlines some of the trade-offs network modeling can address when integrating manufacturing and distribution within a comprehensive network design. Manufacturing costs frequently decrease as manufacturing is concentrated in fewer facilities—a result of economies of scale and more revenue generated per dollar spent on manufacturing infrastructure and overhead. However, more modern, flexible manufacturing technology may diminish or even eliminate the benefits of this traditional axiom in certain industries.

At the same time, fewer manufacturing facilities can place upward pressure on transportation costs, because product may have to travel farther in the pipeline between plants and warehouses. Inventory costs can also increase because more pipeline inventory is flowing among facilities in the network, and warehouses must hold additional safety stock to compensate for longer replenishment lead times from plants.

Factory focus is also an issue, also shown in Figure 7-6. Plants that focus on producing a more limited segment of a company's products to cover a larger market area may achieve greater manufacturing efficiency. But again, the trade-off may be higher transportation and inventory costs if warehouses must receive supplies from focused but regionally dispersed plants.

Individual plant costs, capabilities, and capacities must also be considered. Two plants, for instance, may be capable of producing similar products, but at significantly different production rates and unit costs. Moreover, limitations in overall plant capacity may necessitate a production shift from a more efficient but overutilized facility to a less utilized, less efficient facility.

Because evaluating manufacturing capacity is basically a strategic exercise, network models are regularly used to provide accurate estimates of return on investment (ROI) for various capital projects. For instance, a company faced with choosing between a major overhaul of an existing plant or building a new plant in a new location wants to compare the ROI estimates of the two competing proposals. Network models can be instrumental in accurately estimating the total operational savings (namely, the *return* in the ROI ratio) throughout the supply chain for each proposal.

A Total Supply Chain Case Study

To clarify the issues associated with supply chain integration, consider the following example of strategic alternatives faced by an ice cream manufacturer in rationalizing its production and distribution network. The company produces a variety of ice creams and frozen dessert specialties. Ice cream is packaged in the usual retail sizes (pints, quarts, etc.), as well as in larger bulk containers for institutional customers. Specialty items are relatively high-value items (such as sundaes, pops, and cones) that are largely sold in the frozen food sections of grocery stores and other retail outlets.

The company is a regional manufacturer and distributor, as depicted in Figure 7-7. Its products are sold in the Northeast, Mid-Atlantic, and more easterly region of the American Midwest (east of Chicago). The company currently manufactures in a Northeast and a Midwest plant. All manufactured product is stored in two company-owned cold storage warehouses that are colocated with the two plants. The Northeast plant is the older and larger. Originally it was the company's only plant. Currently, it provides ice cream to the company's two major market areas (the Northeast and Mid-Atlantic). Additionally, the Northeast plant is the sole producer of certain specialty items, which are then distributed systemwide to meet demand.

The newer Midwest plant was built later and provides ice cream to the Midwest region. In addition, it is the only manufacturer of the specialty items not produced in the Northeast plant. In other words, specialty manufacturing is focused so that each specialty product is made in just one of the two plants. In contrast to the Northeast plant, the Midwest plant is underutilized, especially in ice cream manufacturing, and usually operates at a less than desirable percentage of capacity.

The underutilization of the Midwest plant is due to a marketing expansion into the Midwest that has produced mixed results. Years ago, the company made a concerted effort to move beyond its traditional eastern markets, and the Midwest plant was built to support the westward expansion. In the interim, the company unexpectedly gained a greater share of its traditional East Coast markets, but it never attained enough Midwest market share to utilize the Midwest plant properly. So the Midwest plant is underutilized, while the Northeast plant frequently runs close

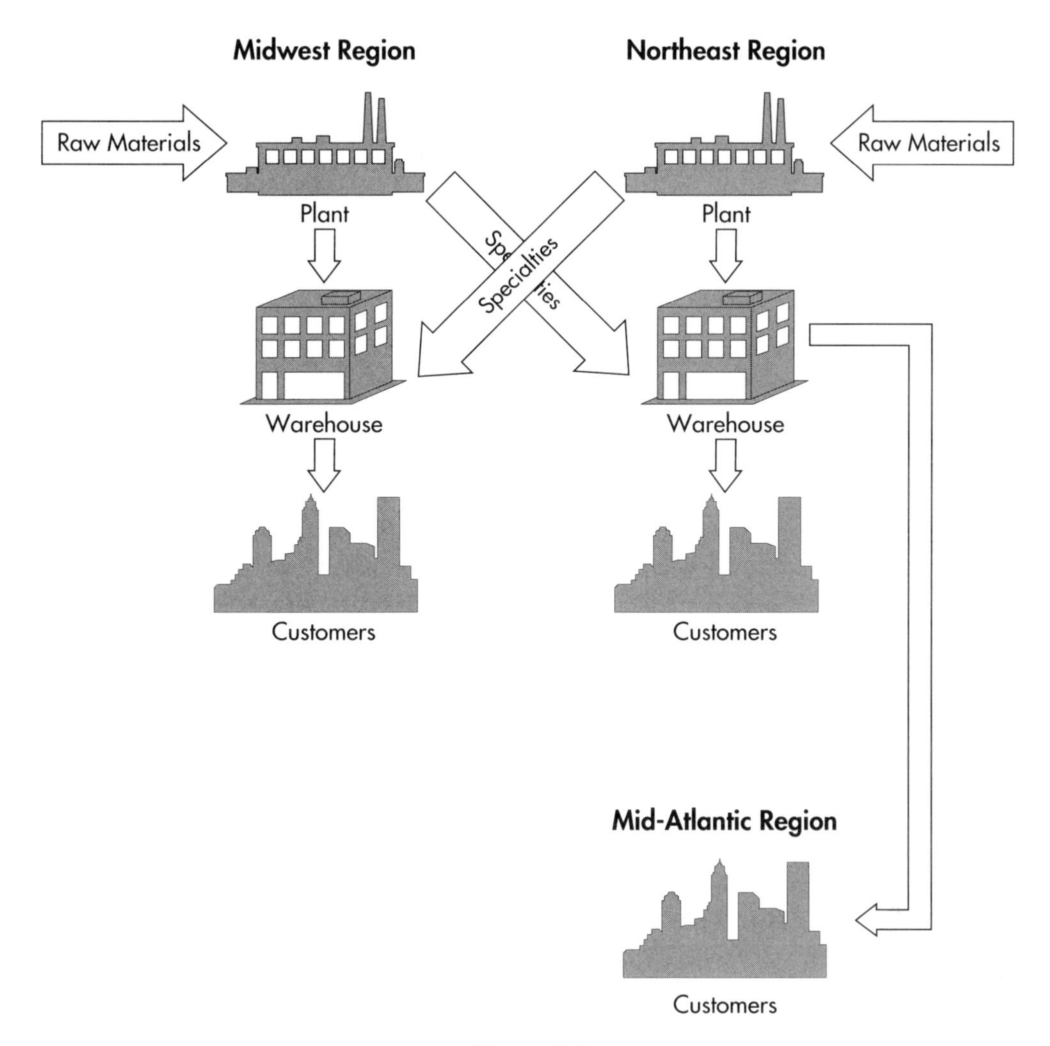

Figure 7-7
Production and Distribution Network for a Regional Ice Cream Manufacturer

to capacity. As a result, the Northeast plant cannot absorb any more manufacturing volume without some fundamental changes in infrastructure or operating procedures.

Evaluating a Plant Closing

There are several options for dealing with this manufacturing capacity imbalance. One possible option is to sell the Midwest plant (and accompanying plant warehouse) and shift its current production volume somewhere else. Consequently, the company wants to know:

- Can the company continue to meet market demands without the Midwest plant?
- What are the financial ramifications of operating without the Midwest plant?

TABLE 7-4
Implications of Closing Midwest Plant Complex
(millions of dollars)

Capital Implications		Annual Cash Flow Savings	
Gross proceeds from sales	$12.40	Reduction in bond payments	$0.70
Revenue bond payoff	(3.35)	Fixed plant expenses	1.53
Capital investment in Northeast plant for specialty products	(3.25)	Plant administration	0.75
Net capital proceeds	$5.80	Net annual cash flow savings	$2.98

Table 7-4 shows some of the financial consequences of selling the Midwest plant complex. The plant's market value is estimated at $12.4 million, of which $3.35 million would be used to pay off a revenue bond that financed the plant's construction.

It is also known that the Northeast plant must absorb the Midwest plant's specialty production if the latter plant is sold. In contrast to ice cream, whose Midwest production can potentially be outsourced to co-packers, specialty production must be retained within the company. This necessitates a $3.25 million capital investment to allow all specialty production to occur within the Northeast plant. Therefore, the net capital impact up to this point in the analysis is a $5.8 million gain from closing the Midwest plant. In addition, there is a savings of almost $3 million in annual fixed costs from closing the plant—resulting from the discontinuation of revenue bond payments plus the elimination of the plant's annual fixed expenses and administration costs.

Table 7-5 outlines three sourcing alternatives for the Midwest plant's current ice cream production. One is to engage a Midwest co-packer to manufacture the Midwest's ice cream. It is determined that a large Midwest co-packer can manufacture and sell ice cream to the company at a unit cost below the Midwest's current variable manufacturing cost per unit. The net is an annual savings of about $1.5 million. Moreover, engaging a co-packer requires no additional investment in the Northeast plant beyond the capital required to shift all specialty production to the remaining plant.

The second alternative is to expand the Northeast plant to handle companywide ice cream requirements. The Northeast plant's inability to meet companywide demand for ice cream is a warm-weather phenomenon, due to a highly seasonal demand pattern that is far greater in the

TABLE 7-5
Three Options for Producing Ice Cream
for the Midwest Region
(millions of dollars)

Option	Capital Requirements	Annual Cash Flow Savings*
1. Employ a Midwest co-packer	—	$1.47
2. Expand Northeast plant manufacturing capacity	$4.60	$1.75
3. Build inventory at Northeast plant before peak demand	$1.80	$1.13

* Annual savings in variable manufacturing costs, compared with current variable manufacturing costs in the Midwest plant.

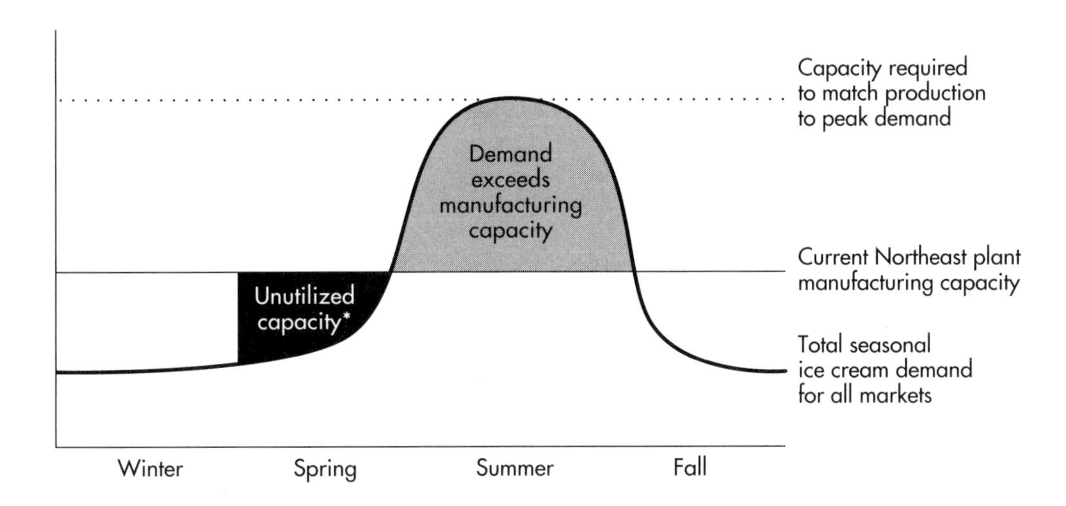

Figure 7-8
Building Inventory for Peak Summer Demands

summer than in the winter. To make this alternative viable, the company must invest in additional freezer and shipping-bay capacity to handle the large demands in the summer months. This expansion will cost $4.6 million beyond the $3.2 million required to focus all specialty manufacturing in one plant. However, the economies of scale created by shifting all ice cream production to one plant should save $1.75 million annually in variable manufacturing costs, relative to current variable manufacturing costs with two plants.

The third option of Table 7-5 represents a different approach for producing all ice cream in the Northeast plant. Ice cream can be effectively inventoried for several months before being sold. It is possible, therefore, to utilize unused manufacturing capacity in the slower spring months to build inventory for the peak summer season (see Figure 7-8).

Naturally, there are trade-offs to consider in evaluating these last two options. The second option of Table 7-5 increases manufacturing capacity, through infrastructure expansion, so that the plant can handle peak demand as the demand occurs without building inventory. The third option should not require as much additional infrastructure. However, this inventory-build option ties up more capital in inventory. Moreover, holding significant inventories usually results in other additional costs, such as handling and storing expenses. Therefore, one option generally requires more up-front capital investment, but the other option results in higher annual variable manufacturing costs.

Network Models for Tactical Planning

For the inventory-build option, the most immediate question is feasibility. For product quality reasons, the company will hold product in inventory for a maximum of two months for its higher-quality products and no more than three months for other brands. With this limitation, there may still not be enough manufacturing capacity to meet all demand from the Northeast plant.

The second consideration in evaluating this option is cost. The company would contract for outside storage capacity in the spring at a local public facility to hold the inventory build. Inventoried product would then be brought back to the company's plant warehouse as needed to be mixed with other product for shipment to customers. The extra costs incurred by this option, then, are the fixed and variable costs of contracting for outside warehousing, plus expenses associated with the extra handling and shipping that occurs as product is shuttled to the outside warehouse and back.

In fact, determining how to optimally build inventory is a complicated matter. There are several alternatives for building and depleting inventory seasonally in an outside storage facility. Evaluating this inventory-build option is an example of a *tactical planning problem.* In tactical planning, a company considers a future planning horizon and determines how it will effectively utilize assets, such as plants and warehouses, to meet projected requirements. Typically, the planning horizon is divided into periods, so that the company can evaluate its plans throughout the horizon. For instance, a common scenario is a year-long planning horizon partitioned into monthly periods.

As the ice cream manufacturing example shows, tactical planning can be a major concern for businesses with seasonal demands. Producers of candy, turkeys, or hams, for instance, must be very careful in planning for dramatic peaks in demand at holidays that fall off just as dramatically once the holiday is past. No one wants to be caught short of supply in the middle of a major season when it is too late to obtain additional supplies. Similarly, no one wants to be stuck with large inventories of unsalable product at the end of a big season.

Other businesses must engage in careful tactical planning for different reasons. Food manufacturers that process fruits and vegetables must often plan around major harvests that occur only at certain times of the year. In such cases, fluctuations in raw material supplies is a complication that must be planned for, and managers must determine the rate at which large raw material supplies should be converted into finished products.

In general, tactical planning is complicated not only by swings in supply and demand but by cost and capacity considerations. The objectives of tactical planning, therefore, are to:

- Meet demands for finished products in a timely manner
- Account for such fluctuations as in material supplies or customer demands
- Adhere to capacity limitations (e.g., manufacturing capacity, storage capacity, or material supplies)
- Minimize avoidable costs

Specialized network logistics models that employ optimization technology have proven to be very effective as aids in tactical planning. Such tools optimize planning by determining the best alternatives, through both space and time, for transforming materials into finished products and distributing them to customers. Therefore, logistics network models not only provide insight into *designing* logistics networks (e.g., facility location models); they can also provide a framework for addressing the complexities of *managing* an existing network (tactical planning models).

Tactical Modeling for Strategic Decision Making

Consider again the plant closing question facing the regional ice cream manufacturer, which is basically strategic. Can the company operate with only one manufacturing facility? In evaluat-

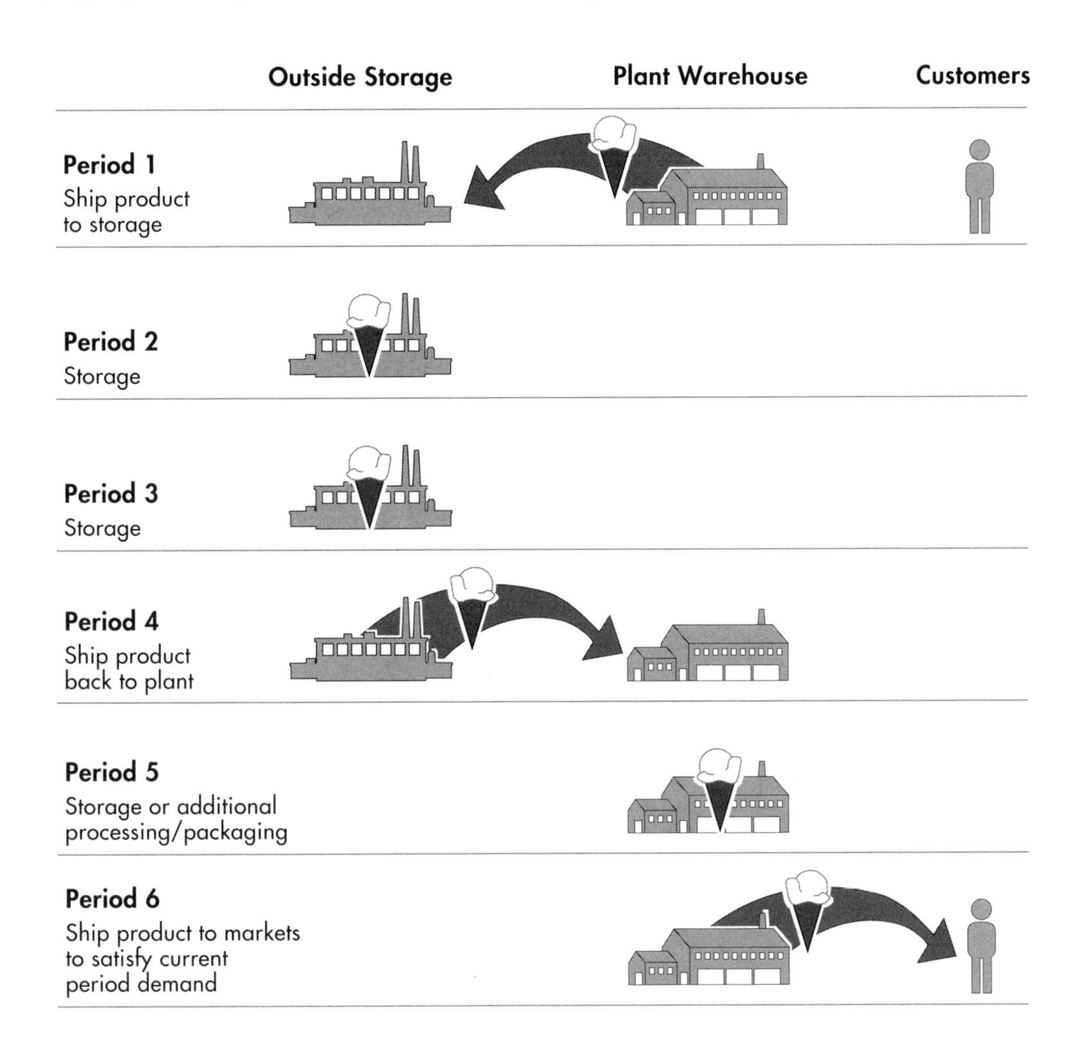

Figure 7-9
Network Modeling for Tactical Planning (Managing Product Flow Through Space and Time to Meet Peak Ice Cream Demand)

ing its options, the company has created a single-plant alternative—inventory building at the Northeast plant—whose viability depends on effective tactical planning. Consequently, to simulate the company's best possible operational performance under the inventory-build option, it employs an optimization-based tactical planning model. Whereas tactical models are normally thought of as aids for managing an existing network, this example illustrates how such tools can also be used to evaluate strategic options.

A conceptual diagram of this tactical model is given in Figure 7-9. Each column depicts the section of the physical network concerned with building and depleting inventory for the peak summer demand. Each row is associated with a planning period, and the figure illustrates inventory decisions made by the tactical model through time. Specifically, the figure illustrates the movement of product from the plant warehouse to outside storage in period 1; holding product in outside storage until period 4, at which time it is transferred back to the plant warehouse; and finally, shipping product out to markets in period 6.

Concerning the inventory-build option, the company's tactical planning exercise provides the following insights:

- The option is feasible. Despite the company's time limitations on holding ice cream in storage, the model shows that planning can meet systemwide demands through intelligent inventory builds.
- The estimated additional variable costs associated with this option are $620,000 per year. Since an optimization model was used to determine the company's best-build options, this should be the lowest possible cost for employing the build option. This cost accounts for the lower annual cash-flow savings for option 3 in Table 7-5 ($1.13 million), compared with option 2 ($1.75 million).
- The build option will require some additional freezer and shipping-bay capacity at the company's plant warehouse. The tactical planning model showed that this capacity is necessary to handle shipping and short-term storage requirements during the busy summer months. As shown in Table 7-5, the company estimates that it must spend $1.8 million to provide the required infrastructure. However, this is considerably less than the $4.6 million in capital investment required under option 2.

Distribution Considerations

Closing the Midwest plant clearly has distribution ramifications, because sources of supply will be altered and the Midwest company warehouse will no longer exist. Several distribution alternatives could be considered. Table 7-6 displays the additional annual distribution costs the company would incur for three alternatives compared with the company's current distribution costs. These comparative costs were calculated using a network logistics model.

One option is for the company to continue to make all customer deliveries using its fleet of leased trucks. With the Midwest co-packer manufacturing option, this means that the ice cream

TABLE 7-6
Distribution Options to Replace
Closed Midwest Plant
(Annual Distribution Premium,* $000)

	Manufacturing Options (from Table 7-5)	
Distribution Options for Midwest	**1 Employ a Midwest Co-Packer**	**2 and 3 Increase Northeast Capacity**
1. Company delivers all items	600	185
2. Distributor delivers all items	1,800	2,200
3. Mixed:	450	790
• Company delivers ice cream		
• Distributor delivers specialties		

* The annual distribution premium is the annual distribution "out-of-pocket" cost (cash flow) increases compared with the current systemwide distribution costs.

produced by the co-packer must be hauled back to the Northeast company warehouse to be mixed with other product in customer loads. The company has some opportunity to backhaul ice cream from the Midwest to the Northeast after completing Midwest customer shipments. Nevertheless, this option is estimated to cost the company an additional $600,000 per year for distribution over current costs. This distribution option is less expensive if all ice cream manufacturing is focused in the Northeast plant; the distribution premium with focused production is reduced to $185,000 annually.

A second distribution option is to reduce the company's fleet of leased vehicles and have a distributor handle all deliveries to the Midwest market. The premium for outsourcing Midwest distribution ranges from $1.8 million to $2.2 million a year, depending on whether Midwest ice cream is outsourced or shifted to the Northeast plant.

The third distribution option outlined in Table 7-6 is a mixed system where the company delivers ice cream to Midwest customers and a Midwest distributor handles specialty deliveries. If the co-packer is used, company trucks would haul specialties from the Northeast warehouse to the distributor's Midwest warehouse. The empty truck could then pick up ice cream at the Midwest co-packer's plant and deliver it to the customers. If the co-packer is not used, however, then two types of loads will be deployed from the Northeast warehouse to the Midwest in company trucks. One load type consists of ice cream dropped off at individual customer sites in the Midwest. The second load type contains specialty products delivered to the Midwest distributor's warehouse. With this mixed distribution system, it is estimated to be cheaper to deliver ice cream from the Midwest co-packer, because ice cream does not have to be transported from the Northeast to the Midwest. In addition, a company truck can both deliver specialties to the Midwest distributor and deliver ice cream to Midwest customers.

Summarizing the Analysis

Table 7-7 summarizes the results of the model-based plant-closing analysis. The table provides concise management information that aggregates a significant amount of data and modeling activity. The objective here is not to present an answer to the Midwest plant issue, but rather to

TABLE 7-7
Summary of Midwest
Plant Closing Analyses
(millions of dollars)

		Distribution Options—Annual Cash Flow Savings		
Manufacturing Options	**Net Capital Proceeds**	**1. Company delivers all items to Midwest**	**2. Distributor delivers all items to Midwest**	**3. Mixed delivery to Midwest (ice cream by company, specialties by distributor)**
1. Employ a Midwest co-packer	5.80	3.85	2.65	4.00
2. Expand Northeast plant manufacturing capacity	1.20	4.55	2.53	3.94
3. Build inventory at Northeast plant before peak demand	4.00	3.93	1.91	3.32

demonstrate how sophisticated quantitative analysis, supported by logistics network modeling, can provide useful information for management decision making.

Moreover, establishing corporate policy requires more than quantitative analysis; many considerations contribute to strategic decisions. For example, employing a Midwest co-packer and distributor for specialty products appears attractive from a numbers perspective in Table 7-7. Nonetheless, this alternative entails a significant shift toward outsourcing in both manufacturing and distribution. For a company that has always tightly controlled all elements of the supply chain, this would represent a radical change. Consequently, the impact of such a change must be seriously examined from several perspectives, including control, quality, employee morale, and corporate culture.

Applying Modeling Tools to Network Structure Issues

There are three principal considerations for the use of logistics network modeling tools to address network structure issues: installation and training, important model features, and market offerings.

Installation and Training

Must a company purchase modeling software, install it, and train users to attain the benefits of models when evaluating the company's network structure? If the company is hiring outside expertise to help with the evaluation, then the answer is probably no.

Organizations often turn to a logistics consulting firm for assistance when evaluating their logistics networks. The consulting firm's role is to perform a study that indicates the best network structure for meeting the company's anticipated logistics needs. A top-tier consulting firm today will most likely use a network model of some kind in performing the study, but the client need not have an intimate knowledge of how the model works to benefit from its results. Traditionally, many consulting firms would not install their analytical models or even offer clients the option of having the consulting firm's software installed. The customary role of the model has been to help create the study's "delivered product"—namely, a report or presentation indicating the client's best alternatives in future logistics network structure.

Today, however, companies increasingly want such analytical tools installed on-site. Today's more dynamic business climate means that many corporations must increase the frequency with which they address network structure issues, and they want tools readily available to help answer pertinent questions. As a result, many companies now possess relatively sophisticated tools for evaluating facility location alternatives.

Ballou and Masters recently interviewed 200 logistics executives concerning their use of logistics network modeling software.[1] Some 65% intended to review their warehouse locations within the next year. Of those who intended to review their network, 77% would perform the analysis in-house. And among those who would perform the analysis themselves, two-thirds intended to use a logistics network model. Moreover, 83% of experienced network model users claimed to be either satisfied or very satisfied with their use of models.

Advances in technology have facilitated these trends. Widespread, low-cost computer availability, combined with more sophisticated software and user-friendly interfaces that require little technical expertise, have provided the incentives for installing network modeling tools in-house.

These technical achievements have also made installation and user training less of an issue. Software installation on conventional personal computers and workstations is often relatively easy. And thankfully, advances in software sophistication have been accompanied by advances in ease of use. Quality software offerings today should provide extensive on-line or written documentation, as well as on-site user training (if required) and telephone support. Consequently, user training continues to become less of an issue.

Important Model Features

Among the experienced users surveyed by Ballou and Masters, the most important model features are user-friendliness and presentation capabilities like maps and charts. Good graphics, combined with sophisticated report generation, are excellent means for transforming detailed data into useful management information.

Mathematical sophistication and precise economic representation of the problem within the model also ranked high among model users. A major consideration for any potential user is the degree of decision support provided by the tool. Several commercially available network models offer various degrees of optimization. In practical terms, an optimization capability means that the model has the ability to automatically identify the better network options among all possible alternatives.

A tool with a high degree of optimization support can consider several logistics alternatives—plant or warehouse locations, plant loadings, and service region construction—and automatically select alternatives that are "best" according to some user-defined criteria. For instance, a highly sophisticated tool could conceivably select manufacturing and distribution facility sites automatically, determine what lines and products to produce in each plant, determine how plants should supply warehouses, and assign market zones to regional warehouses.

In contrast, network models without optimization support are sometimes called "static simulators." With such tools, a user would, for instance, preselect a configuration of facilities, plant loadings, and service regions. The simulator would then act as a sophisticated calculator that computes the service and cost performance of the selected network. Determining a superior network configuration then requires using the tool numerous times to compare and contrast various network alternatives selected by the user.

In general, optimization support is valuable because of the large number of practical alternatives many companies face when evaluating logistics network structure. Optimization-based models have repeatedly demonstrated an ability to identify best-practice options that cannot reliably be found any other way.

From a technical perspective, many network optimization problems are difficult to solve. Therefore, quality optimization software requires technical sophistication and substantial computer resources for performing a large number of calculations. In the past, these barriers limited the practical application of optimization.

Fortunately, dramatic advances in computer hardware and software mean that it is now possible to acquire a high degree of optimization support within a user-friendly computing environment that can run on conventional computers, including the most common personal computers and workstations. Within such a user-friendly environment, a logistics professional deals with the network problem at hand in familiar operational terms, not in mathematical or technical computer jargon. Therefore, today's more sophisticated network models provide optimization support without requiring the user to be technically knowledgeable about mathematical optimization or computer programming. In essence, the user obtains the substantial practical benefits of optimization without exposure to the technical challenges of performing optimization.

Market Offerings

The widespread use of network modeling for warehouse location studies means that there is an extensive choice of software tools for performing these types of studies. Many have at least some degree of optimization support. A number of them are listed in Andersen Consulting's logistics software guide.[2] In addition, 15 of the better-known systems are reviewed by Ballou and Masters.[3] The latter publication describes features, pricing, and availability of the surveyed systems.

Generally speaking, users will find less modeling software available for performing integrated network studies where manufacturing and distribution issues are considered simultaneously. In particular, many facility location systems have limited ability to model many of the manufacturing issues discussed in this chapter. This is due in part to the traditional emphasis on warehouse location problems in the logistics profession. Manufacturing and distribution location problems have traditionally been viewed as separate issues, reflecting many corporations' tendency to manage production and distribution as separate entities. In addition, modeling software that addresses the integrated network problem must generally be more sophisticated than software that is strictly oriented toward warehousing problems. The market, however, is beginning to respond to users' demands for more comprehensive network modeling tools for integrated network planning, and the logistics profession should benefit from increasingly sophisticated logistics network modeling tools in the future.

The Value of Network Modeling

An increasingly sophisticated and demanding business environment magnifies the challenges of designing and managing modern logistics networks, and many of these challenges have a significant analytical and quantitative component. Logistics network modeling provides decision support for these complex issues. Today, models provide support for a wide spectrum of logistics problems, ranging from facility location to detailed stock deployment.

The fundamental benefits of models are insight into a company's operations and clarity concerning how operations should be managed. In essence, logistics models are practical tools that complement other effective logistics management practices.

Because of their proven value, logistics network modeling is now a widely accepted practice within the logistics profession. Increasingly powerful software that is easy to use—and that runs on readily available computers—provides ready access to powerful analytical support. Users can expect this trend to continue. As the logistics profession continues to become more challenging and sophisticated, technology will keep pace, providing management with new generations of modeling software.

Notes

1. A. Ronald H. Ballou and James M. Masters, "Commercial Software for Locating Warehouses and Other Facilities," *Journal of Business Logistics,* 35, no. 2 (1993).
2. Richard C. Haverly, Douglas McW. Smith, and Lynda G. Gutman, *Logistics Software* (Oak Brook, Ill.: Andersen Consulting and The Council of Logistics Management, 1992). See also annually updated editions.
3. Ballou and Masters, Survey of Logistics Executives.

CHAPTER 8

Logistics Strategy

Integration, Implementation, and Management

Allen D. Rose

This discussion is directed primarily to logistics and operations executives. The focus is on achieving the full integration of leading-edge logistics practices in the overall drive for competitive excellence. It addresses such critical issues as achieving broad and meaningful management acceptance, organizational implications inherent in implementing an integrated logistics strategy, recognizing and managing potential risks, and a discussion of performance measurement, feedback, and adjustment mechanisms.

Competitive Excellence

Competitive excellence is not a fixed goal but an ongoing process of improvement, assessment, and adjustment over time. The firms that achieve true leadership are those that continuously improve, modify, and refine their internal capabilities through an ongoing process of analyzing their businesses, evaluating their markets, assessing their capabilities, planning their actions, efficiently executing their plans, and measuring results. Further, these firms recognize that the process is ongoing, that change is unavoidable, and that to survive this process, the full range of skills, talents, and abilities of all employees across all functional specialties must be brought to bear.

Achieving Management Acceptance

If logistics is to play a coequal role in the survival and growth of the enterprise, it is essential that logistics management fully understand the needs of the business. Senior logistics managers must be prepared to communicate the potential contribution of current logistics capability, champion the development of new capabilities, and proactively identify how those capabilities can be brought to bear to meet clearly defined business needs in terms that energize both senior management and peers.

Most companies do an outstanding job of identifying functionally defined projects, programs, and policies with time horizons of one year or less. However, these tactical issues tend to be developed outside the strategic process of the business and often are at odds, or are perceived to be, with both the basic business strategy and fundamental business and/or customer requirements.

The logistics manager of a major consumer products company devoted a significant amount of time, effort, and money to developing a strategy to reduce the number of service warehouses in his network. An implementation plan was developed and the financial returns were very attractive. When this plan was presented to the firm's management, senior sales and marketing executives strongly opposed it because several major customers required the firm to maintain a local warehousing presence.

Given the investment in this effort, the logistics manager chose to pursue the matter further and, in conversations with the management of the customer firms, discovered that the requirement for local warehousing was based on the belief that emergency response would be better with local warehousing. A review of the previous three years showed that there had been only three cases in which "emergency shipments" had been required by a customer. In two of those cases some of the product involved had been supplied from other warehouses in the network and cross-docked at the local warehouse.

Discussions with sales, marketing, and the customers involved led to establishing a commitment to meeting a 48-hour emergency response standard at no incremental cost to the customer. This was justified on the basis of available data, which showed that in the worst possible case the periodic payment of ultrapremium freight costs and extraordinary handling charges would be more than offset by the ongoing savings of reducing the number of warehouses in the network.

For every situation such as the one above that is pursued to a beneficial outcome, many that are considered less significant are either not pursued or dismissed out of hand. The key to competitive excellence, then, is to marry the technical knowledge and tactical skills that largely exist in the broad business vision with a clear understanding of true customer requirements. The challenge to the logistics executive is to become proactively involved in the broader issues of the business, to break down barriers among traditionally defined functions, and to build bridges with other executives in the firm. The key to meeting this challenge is to present logistics initiatives in terms familiar to other functional executives, to fully address their individual concerns, and to identify, where possible, benefits that they will accrue from implementation.

The Organizational Challenge

When implementing a new strategy, especially in these turbulent times, managing change is a significant challenge. The implementation of a new strategy typically requires a restructuring of tasks, if not total job responsibilities and/or organizational responsibilities and roles. The more sweeping the change, the greater the resistance at all levels of the organization.

Every business organization is a social organism subject to the forces and constraints of the prevailing myths, norms, values, and established power relationships. Further, it is composed of individuals with unique sets of values, beliefs, and expectations. Fundamental to the concept of introducing new competitive paradigms is that change will be essential, both organizationally and individually.

Change is an inherently threatening process: the rules are new, skills developed over many years lose significance, and group dynamics are disrupted. The discomfort generated by the change process contains the seeds of failure. There is a desire to retreat to the familiar, and the lure can be attractive. Most of us would like to believe that our experiences with "the bureaucracy," be it governmental or institutional, are aberrations, that these entrenched behaviors do not exist in our industry, company, or organization. Unfortunately, that is not true in the vast majority of cases.

Reaction to change takes many forms, from mild discomfort to outright resistance, from minor complaints to sabotage. In an extreme case, a highly unionized manufacturing company found that after a negotiated change in job responsibilities in its factory, employees were enclosing notes in random packages apologizing to customers for potential quality problems that resulted from changed work practices.

More typical would be the experience of a company in the service industry as it moved from traditional electric typewriters to a word processing network in the mid-eighties. Two similar departments followed essentially the same approach to implementing the change. The single difference was that the first removed all the old typewriters over the weekend before the new system was to be implemented; the other department retained several typewriters as backup in case of problems. Six months later, the second department was still using the typewriters for a significant portion of its work, and the number of system complaints was significantly higher.

From a global perspective, both examples cited above appear to be "minor and nonthreatening" changes. In the manufacturing example, jobs were protected by bargaining agreements; in the service industry example, no jobs were eliminated. The level of reaction indicates that change per se is often an issue of major significance.

Those firms who have been successful in implementing significant change fall into three categories:

1. The vast majority have been forced into that change by external forces. The imperative for them was change or die.
2. A much smaller population exists where management perceived the need for change sufficiently in advance and put in place change programs designed to evolve over generations of management.
3. And finally, an even smaller population has accepted the idea that dynamic change is the new reality and has aggressively developed the ability to execute change as a fundamental capability.

The leadership challenge consists in creating a culture in which the latter condition can be achieved. Broadly, this requires a move to true employee involvement across functional boundaries, and from the top to the bottom of the organization.

To the extent that all employees understand what is expected of them, how their contribution and success and the success of the firm are linked, and that they are truly free to contribute, the change process becomes easier.

Key to achieving the capability to change is a significant commitment to organizational learning, not merely training. Many firms will require major investments of time, money, and equipment in communications, education, and training in support of both the strategy to be implemented and the change efforts per se.

The total volume of actionable information moving through the organization will increase and will have to be communicated more rapidly and more accurately. New skills and capabilities will need to be developed. And, of key importance, employees must be made comfortable in the knowledge that as their current skills and capabilities become outmoded, the opportunity exists for them to acquire new skills.

Risk Management

If events over the last few years have done nothing else, they have taught us that significant, often wrenching change is the norm. This is not to imply that prudent managers should not consider the effect of potential events on their businesses. Rather, it suggests that firms that have developed and used effective planning and adaptive skills will prosper, while those lacking these skills will fall by the wayside.

Most disruptions of a process to implement change result from events that could and should have been addressed in the planning process. Critical to success in this area is a clear understanding of the level of control the firm can exert over a class of events. Although management may not be able to control or influence external events, it can and must control its response in a manner that is in the firm's best interest.

We can broadly define four categories of risk to which a firm is subject:

1. *Internal risks,* which are generally events over which the firm exercises some level of control. Typically these are events for which a firm carries insurance. Examples include fire, flood, product liability, business interruption, workers' compensation, labor unrest, and loss of key employees.
2. *Social risks,* which are generally events that occur in reaction to an action of the firm. These events fall largely in the area of community response and can range from bad press to threatened or actual picketing and product boycotts.
3. *Legislative risks* are the result of governmental action and typically affect more than just a single firm. These events include the actions of both legislative bodies and regulatory agencies. The firm's ability to influence these slowly evolving events is typically through lobbying (before the fact) or litigation (after the fact).
4. *Geopolitical risks,* which as a class are uncontrollable events ranging from economic downturns and currency fluctuations to civil disturbance and war. Some argue that these events can be anticipated, if not predicted. Although true in certain situations, the events in both the Middle East and the former Soviet Union in 1991 cast doubt on that idea.

For our purposes, we can assume that the first two classes of risk deal with tactical issues and have the potential to disrupt the implementation process, whereas the last two strike at broader strategic issues.

Business disruption due to technical failure is typically addressed early in the planning process. Ongoing activities will normally be protected by some level of redundant backup such as duplicating all computer software and files prior to an office move or planning a short period of parallel operation when starting up an automated warehouse or implementing new computer systems.

We have dealt with the internal human relations aspects of change in the previous section, and to a large extent the same approach is required in addressing the broader community. First accept that change will be seen as a problem. Community response to a decision to expand a plant's activity can be as strong as it is to closing a plant entirely. Community issues can range at one extreme from economic concern over loss of jobs and tax base to equally significant, and often more threatening, environmental concerns over increased traffic, changes in peak periods, noise levels, or the nature of products.

Both community leaders and the public at large should be brought into the process of change as early as possible. The intention should be both to inform and to make them part of the planning process. As with employees, this involvement must be both significant and ongoing. A level of trust and openness must be established and maintained.

Performance Measurement

The metrics that a firm uses and their relationship to its reward system drive its behavior. Many excellent strategies, supported by finely tuned implementation plans, have failed because of inadequate or inappropriate measurement systems. A classic example of this misalignment is the often-cited case of the operations executive who announced that, because his performance was evaluated and his compensation based primarily on sales per employee and accidents per employee, he was going to outsource all operations functions. Although the example is extreme (and probably apocryphal), experience has shown that all individuals, including senior managers, act in their own best interests most of the time.

The major flaw in the approach of many firms to measurement is that they view the measurement system primarily as an internal control tool. This view is the natural result of a *financial* focus on measurement. Leading-edge firms are rapidly moving toward an externally focused view of measurement as an improvement tool and are broadening their perspectives to encompass nonfinancial metrics.

The difference between these two approaches is fundamental. The traditional control view focuses on accuracy to four decimal places, establishing consistent standards and reporting results. The improvement school espouses actionable levels of accuracy, continuous improvement, changing measures as situations change, and monitoring causes.

These issues arouse strong reactions in accounting circles. Financial systems are attacked by one group as a threat to the American way of life and defended by others as an article of faith. As with most such arguments, the truth is found somewhere in the middle. Cost control is still important, but in reality cost is largely determined in the planning process. The implementation of any change is influenced by nonfinancial dimensions.

In managing change, it is essential to recognize that measurements must reflect the perspective of the individual evaluating the performance *and* the person whose performance is being evaluated. Although significant effort has been expended seeking the "magic metric" that will allow the CEO of a conglomerate to gain detailed understanding of every operation in each of the firm's businesses, such a measurement has not yet emerged.

The reality is that for any factor, the appropriate metric is contingent on both the level of the organization being measured and the behavior being encouraged. Regardless of the factor considered, the result achieved by the business is the result of the efforts of general management, functional management, departmental management, and groups and individuals. If we view this process as a hierarchy, we note there are metrics to evaluate the overall business, the contribution of general and functional management, and so on throughout the organization. An effective measurement system is designed so that logical and meaningful causal relationships exist between and among the metrics for each level of the hierarchy.

If we look at *customer satisfaction*—an area of considerable interest today—a classic example of the wrong approach would be the case of the company president who, faced with significant customer service problems, decided to measure his performance based on the number of weekly back orders. While heroic and impressive-sounding, the approach was flawed for several reasons. For one thing, his boss was not evaluating him on that basis; for another, he was not in a position to control or influence the back-order level.

More appropriate would be the following hierarchy of metrics (all are trends, not absolutes) for overall customer satisfaction. First, one should judge the *overall business* on increases in market share, operating profit, and return on capital employed. *General management* would be judged on improvement in percentage of increased sales of new products, ongoing product cycle time, and the customer service index. *Logistics management* would be measured on carrier transit time, damage levels, shipment overages/shortages, and query response time.

This approach, which focuses on measuring performance based on level of control, is designed to create a feedback and response mechanism. The lower the level in the organization in which measurement is taking place, the shorter the time frame and the more real time is the reporting.

Effective Implementation

Effective strategy implementation is not a glamorous undertaking, nor does it require exotic skills. Rather, it depends on the mundane, day-by-day way a company or business unit is managed. As part of a larger whole, with a broader mandate and mission, both the strategy and implementation plan, and associated metrics, must be accepted by superior line management and the broader organization. The firm must invest enough in the interpersonal, organizational, and community development aspects to provide a framework in which change becomes the norm, not the exception. Risk must be recognized and planned for to the extent possible. And the performance measurement and reward systems must be developed to establish appropriate targets, allow necessary feedback and control, and provide meaningful incentives for desired behavior and results.

SECTION III

Logistics Quality and Productivity

Douglas M. Lambert

Corporate success in the 1990s will depend upon a company's ability to focus on the customer and be a value-added supplier as well as become a low-cost producer. Logistics quality processes and productivity measurement will be key factors in achieving these ends. This section contains materials that will help readers increase the competitiveness of their corporation in an increasingly competitive global marketplace.

In Chapter 9, C. John Langley, Jr., and Mary C. Holcomb provide insights regarding total quality management and how the quality improvement process can be used to create customer value and enhance corporate profitability. They show logistics managers how total quality management can be used in their companies to achieve a competitive advantage through the following topics: creating customer value, formalization of quality process, the logistics quality process, improvement through quality analysis, and implementation strategies.

In Chapter 10, Jay U. Sterling describes an operational system that meets a company's marketing and logistics management information needs for both external and internal reporting requirements. This chapter develops an understanding of the functional information flows and describes an operating system that is capable of recording this information in an integrated data base. The last portion of the chapter analyzes the outputs required to successfully monitor the logistics operating system.

In Chapter 11, Martin Christopher describes the shortcomings of traditional accounting systems and proposes a method that management can use to assess costs and performance from a logistics pipeline perspective. The proposed methodology enables logistics managers to assess the impact of their decisions in terms of their impact on total costs and on sales revenue.

In Chapter 12, Douglas M. Lambert reminds us that accounting information is a requirement for successful implementation of the integrated logistics management concept because it is based on minimizing total costs for a level of customer service that meets the firm's marketing objective. The chapter examines several fundamental and advanced concepts that are useful for analyzing and managing logistics processes, including accounting for logistics, distribution cost trade-off analysis, controlling logistics activities, activity-based costing, and a distribution data base for decision making.

In Chapter 13, Robert C. Camp provides valuable insights into one of the hottest yet least understood areas, benchmarking. He begins by defining benchmarking, then describes the types of benchmarking, what to benchmark, what organizations to benchmark against, information sources, objectives, success factors, and management considerations. He finishes the chapter with a description of the L.L. Bean/Xerox benchmarking experience.

CHAPTER 9

Total Quality Management in Logistics

C. John Langley, Jr.
Mary C. Holcomb

In a continuing quest for competitive advantage, companies are calling upon logistics managers to find innovative ways to reduce cost, enhance service, and increase customer satisfaction.[1] As a result, many companies have taken significant steps toward identifying and implementing logistics quality improvement processes. While some of these processes are consistent with broader, corporatewide quality initiatives, logistics frequently assumes the leadership role in implementation of the formal quality process.

Because of the increasing popularity of formal quality processes, logistics managers need to be well versed in how the following topics manifest themselves in logistics:

- Creating customer value
- Formalization of quality processes
- Logistics quality process
- Improvement through quality analysis
- Implementation strategies

For quality initiatives to be accepted by the employees and suppliers who must implement them, the ultimate goal of these initiatives must be clearly understood and enthusiastically supported. Providing added value for customers enhances a company's ability to gain and retain profitable business relationships. Quality programs lay the foundation for this customer value, ensuring that customer needs are understood and satisfied.

Unless logistics managers have the proper orientation before embarking on a quality program, they may undertake the journey with no particular destination in mind and wander into failure. Because customer value is the goal, it is also the final destination in the quality journey (described later as the final phase in the evolution of the quality process). Thus, a discussion of the meaning of customer value must precede a discussion of quality.

Creating Customer Value

The 1980s introduced significant technological and environmental changes to logistics systems. Yet through all these changes, the focus in logistics has remained on customers and the company's need to provide the best comparative net value through effectiveness, efficiency, and differentiation of services.[2] The quest to create and improve customer value through logistics has required the quest for quality within logistics.

Just a few decades ago, most managers involved in logistics had operational responsibility for a single function like inventory, order placement, or transportation. However, as customer requirements became more complex, physical distribution and materials management were integrated, and this resulted in increased responsiveness to customer needs and requirements.

Logistics as a Value-Creating Function

The attributes of logistics management can create customer value in three general ways:

1. *Effectiveness.* Effectiveness refers to performance meeting customer requirements in key result areas (KRAs). For example, L.L. Bean has identified seven customer service KRAs[3]:
   - Product guarantee
   - In-stock availability
   - Fulfillment time (turnaround)
   - Convenience
   - Retail service
   - Innovation
   - Market standing (image)
2. *Efficiency.* Efficiency refers to an organization's ability to provide the desired product/service mix at a price acceptable to the customer. Wise resource management and leveraging expense into customer value are implicit in this concept. Activity-based cost management systems reinforce efficiency.
3. *Differentiation.* Differentiation refers to the ability to create value uniqueness and distinctiveness of service. For example, the Limited Stores Distribution Division marks and tags all merchandise prior to store delivery, creating value for the company-owned retail stores within its overall system. Also, the ability of the Frito-Lay driver/salesperson to provide product integrity at the store level is valuable to independently owned retail stores. Finally, the PartsBank® Service provided by Federal Express Business Logistics Services maintains inventories of repair and emergency parts for companies that occasionally have an immediate need for such shipments to locations throughout the world.

Evolving Strategic Role of Logistics

Traditionally, the role of logistics in creating customer value has been viewed as the trade-off between cost efficiency and competitive service levels (the cost-service curve). Customers can choose "average" service at an "average" cost, nearly "perfect" service at an extraordinarily high cost, or very low cost but poor service. Although this philosophy is customer-oriented through its integration of logistics activities and customer contact, it presupposes an optimal cost-service mix.[4]

Strategic logistics distinguishes itself from the traditional perspective through its ability to coordinate as well as integrate many interdependent activities simultaneously across major functional areas. This coordination provides additional means for logistics to create customer value. Simply put, customer value is enhanced by adopting a total channel perspective in logistics. Integration of attributes such as customization, flexibility, innovation, and responsiveness results in highly valued and expected levels of service. These levels of service become the new standards required to achieve competitive advantage.[5]

The scope and role of logistics has evolved to the extent that many companies now believe that a strategic logistics orientation is required to create customer value and to sustain a competitive advantage.[6] The proposition that logistics can create value relative to a company's product and service offerings is simple and intuitively appealing. It is a proposition that companies have increasingly come to accept. However, implementation of value-added logistics processes is challenging because it involves altering the strategic perspective. Based on the premise that value is created when customer satisfaction is achieved, quality in logistics has evolved to mean much more than simply having the "right product at the right place at the right time in the right condition for the right cost."[7]

Identifying Logistics Needs

Understanding the specific needs of customers is necessary to delivering quality and value-added service with logistics. Essential for creating value are the willingness, desire, and capability to become a better supplier. Aside from achieving a one-time understanding of customer needs and requirements, the continually changing priorities of the customer must be formally monitored. Although internal resources can be directed to such a task, the use of outside consultants or services to provide objective information on a regular basis may be justified.

Needs identification is not always straightforward. It is often complicated by issues surrounding perceived value versus real value and basic needs versus value-added expectations. Customers can be surveyed to validate their perceptions, and by ranking various aspects of the logistics services, one can discriminate between basic needs and value-added expectations. However, the process often entails considerable scrutiny and judgment.

For example, a chemical manufacturer found that it had misperceptions about customer views of product offerings. To correct these misperceptions, a corporate-level function was created to handle customer service and orders, supported by a highly sophisticated information system. The change in refocusing service on customers, rather than on plants, provided the company with the necessary information to increase control over shipments and performance. Also, it provided the necessary basis for integrating transportation and production scheduling, further improving performance.

Management focus in logistics is expanding beyond the existing company structure to involve suppliers. Historically, many companies treated customers with respect and dignity while bearing down unmercifully on vendors. Progressive companies now regard the role of suppliers as essential to achieve customer satisfaction. These companies are spending more time with suppliers, explaining not only their own but also their customers' needs. Interorganizational alliances and partnerships are evolving that enable companies to make aggressive performance commitments for customers in advance, and then meet those commitments. These new performance capabilities arise from close and positive supplier relationships; anything less is counterproductive to adding value.

Internal Value Creation

The needs of internal "customers" are equal in importance to those of external customers, for value creation involves improving effectiveness and efficiency for *all* users. The internal customer concept is rooted in the idea that the various intercompany functions both "buy" and "sell" their goods and services to one another. Internal value creation improves the total system, creating synergies that make value creation for external customers easier. The distinction between internal and external customers should make no difference in terms of the quality of service offered.

For example, the business needs of those involved in production/operations, marketing, and financial management should be recognized by those in the logistics area, and suitable initiatives should be taken to facilitate accomplishment of those needs. At companies such as Land O'Lakes, internal value creation is dealt with through the institution of interdivisional task forces that identify problems from customer service surveys, customer inquiries/complaints, and day-to-day operations. The task force is a cross-functional group that spans all relevant areas.[8] Although the task force approach has been quite successful at Land O'Lakes, experience at other firms sometimes has evidenced a number of limitations as well as advantages to this type of initiative. Also, the notion that task forcing should be a principal responsibility of managers all the time is worthy of scholarly as well as pragmatic deliberation.

Areas of Critical Importance

Adding value requires a focus not on the individual business or its functional components but on the entire supply chain to enhance efficiency, effectiveness, and differentiation throughout. There are three related areas of focus for value creation:

1. *Goals.* Objectives must be set for achieving customer satisfaction. This involves finding out exactly how customers perceive the organization as a whole, not just a single product or line.
2. *Responsibilities.* Determine and assign responsibility for systems and processes that are necessary for creating and sustaining customer value. In many instances, this responsibility spans traditional functional boundaries and may even require reengineering of some processes.
3. *Benefits.* Marketing basics must be incorporated into the process of logistics delivery, transforming these basics into benefits that yield value.

The key to successful management of the logistics function as a value-creating operation is to recognize that a company is viewed from many different perspectives. Each perspective must be taken into account if logistics is going to contribute to achieving the best comparative net value for the customer.

Formalization of Quality Processes

A popular trend has been the development of, and commitment to, a formal quality process. The quality process has enabled companies to ensure value creation for customers. The evolution of a quality process is a movement through four distinct phases with notable characteristics[9]:

1. *Quality Control (QC).* Quality control entails the basic procedural and statistical management of quality.
   - Defect-free services
   - Management-driven
2. *Quality Assurance (QA).* A greater emphasis on achieving customer satisfaction through customer-driven quality characterizes the shift from QC to QA.

- 100% satisfied customer
- Customer-driven

3. *Total Quality Management (TQM).* Management, employees, customers, and suppliers all working together toward a common goal characterizes the evolution to TQM.
   - Significant competitive advantage
   - Common goals
4. *Customer Value.* Customer value reflects the need to do things that create the best comparative net value for the customer.[10]

Impact of Quality on Profitability

It is no wonder that companies are focusing on quality. A profit impact of marketing strategy (PIMS) study found that "companies with high quality and high market share generally tend to have profit margins five times higher than companies in the opposite extreme."[11] Figure 9-1 charts companies' return on sales (ROS) and return on investment (ROI) by the relative quality percentile in which their customers perceive them. These observations are reinforced by studies published by the Council of Logistics Management.[12]

Several PIMS studies show that achieving superior quality yields two fundamental benefits:

1. The relatively low cost of quality implies lower overall cost than that of competitors.
2. Quality is frequently a key attribute when selecting suppliers.

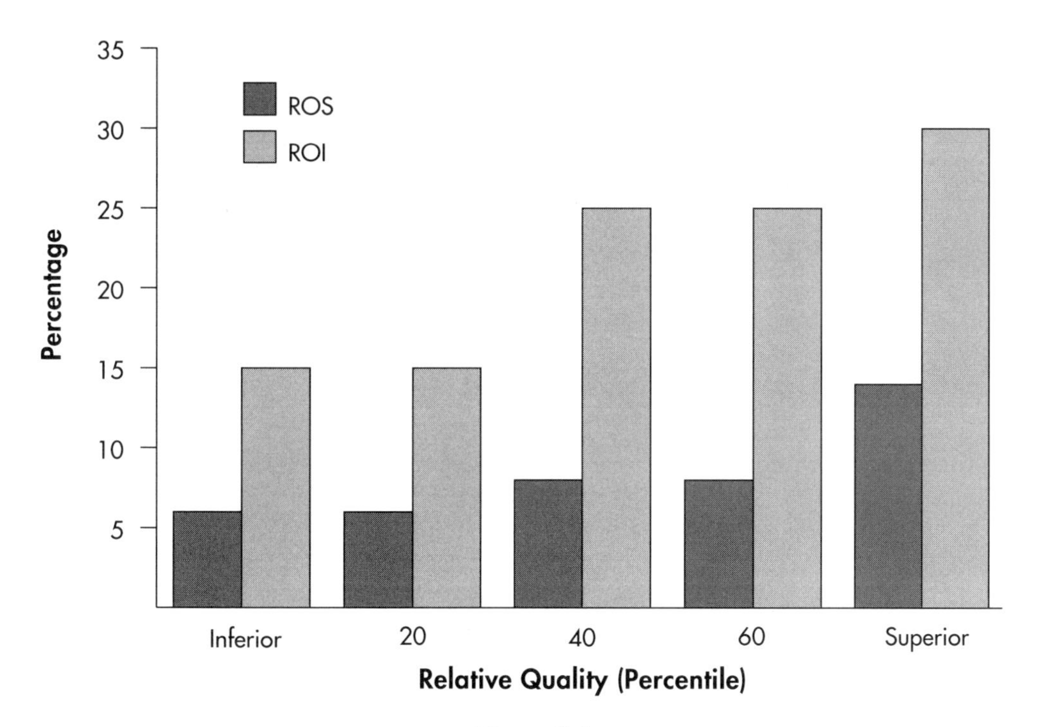

Figure 9-1
Relative Quality Boosts Rates of Return

Source: Strategic Planning Institute, *Profit Impact of Market Strategy* (PIMS) (Cambridge, Mass.: 1988).

The study also found that companies ranking in the top third for relative quality sold their products or services at prices 5% to 6% higher, on average, than their competitors in the bottom half.

Defining and Understanding Logistics Quality

Generally, logistics quality may be defined as "anticipating and exceeding customer requirements and expectations."[13] While individual companies search for variations on this theme to characterize their particular commitments to quality, most formal quality processes have several elements in common:

- Emphasis on customer requirements and expectations
- Concern for the logistics process itself
- Continuous improvement
- Elimination of waste and rework
- Measurement and concern for variability
- Total organizational commitment
- Dedication to a formal quality process[14]

Adherence to a formal quality process will be accompanied by a greater likelihood of long-term, sustainable improvement. While some companies have maintained excellent reputations for product and service quality in the eyes of customers, only formalization of the quality process will ensure those enviable customer opinions as both competition and customer expectations increase.

Several experts and visionaries, sometimes referred to as "quality gurus" because of their dedicated followers, have emerged in the field of quality. The list is impressive, including Dr. W. Edward Deming, Dr. Joseph Juran, Philip Crosby, Genichi Taguchi, Kaoru Ishikawa, and recently others.[15] There is a tendency for companies to choose an individual philosophy on which to base their quality process. Figure 9-2 shows some of the features emphasized in the more popular approaches of Deming, Juran, and Crosby.

Logistics Quality Process

The pursuit of quality must entail more than slogans, especially if a company desires to leverage quality into customer value. A recent study found that of 22 major U.S. corporations examined, 19 had a formal quality process.[16] Some of the processes were more comprehensive than others, but at least a strong commitment to quality was evident, particularly within logistics. Companies such as Hewlett-Packard, Xerox, Procter and Gamble, Dow Chemical, Campbell Soup Company, Rohm and Haas, IBM, and General Motors have taken significant quality process initiatives.[17] Inbound and outbound logistics have been key ways for companies to enhance the value provided to external customers. Similarly, the formal logistics quality process has, in general, enhanced the coordination and efficiencies of internal activities.

A formal logistics quality process is developed in six steps, as shown in Figure 9-3.[18]

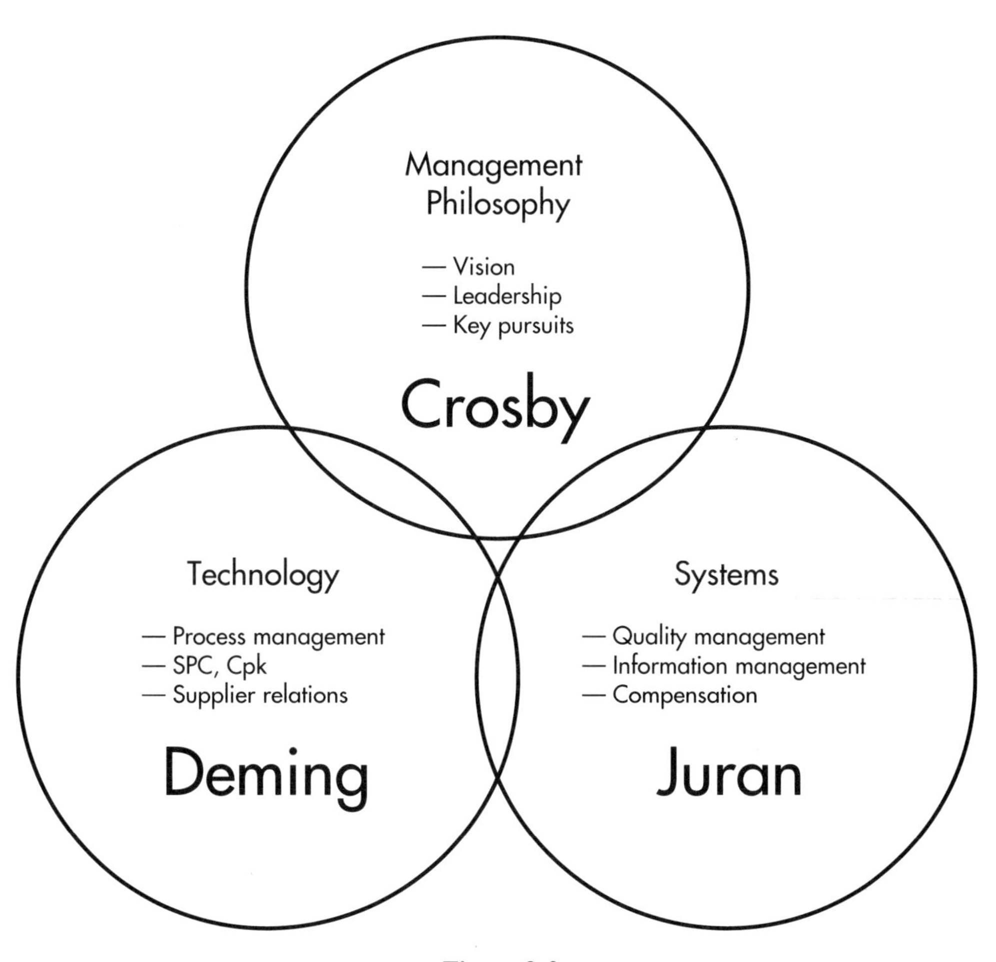

Figure 9-2
Elements of Total Quality Management

Source: C. John Langley, Jr., Mary Holcomb, Joel Baudouin, Alexander Donnan, and Paul Caruso, "Approaches to Logistics Quality," *Proceedings,* 1989 Council of Logistics Management Annual Conference (Oak Brook, Ill.: CLM, 1989), p. 85.

Step 1: Organizational Commitment

Top management must be the driving force behind quality. This commitment applies not only to corporate management but also to the vice president or director of logistics. These managers must be fully dedicated to the objectives and initiatives, for they are ultimately responsible for the success or failure. They must also provide adequate resources and continual encouragement to the people in their organizations for tangible results.

At the outset of a formal quality process, logistics should have meaningful, well-developed statements of mission, goals, and objectives; the quality process must fit within the overall framework of the business. Logistics in particular, because of its operational focus and frequent contact with both vendors and customers, has the potential to be the leader of the quality program.

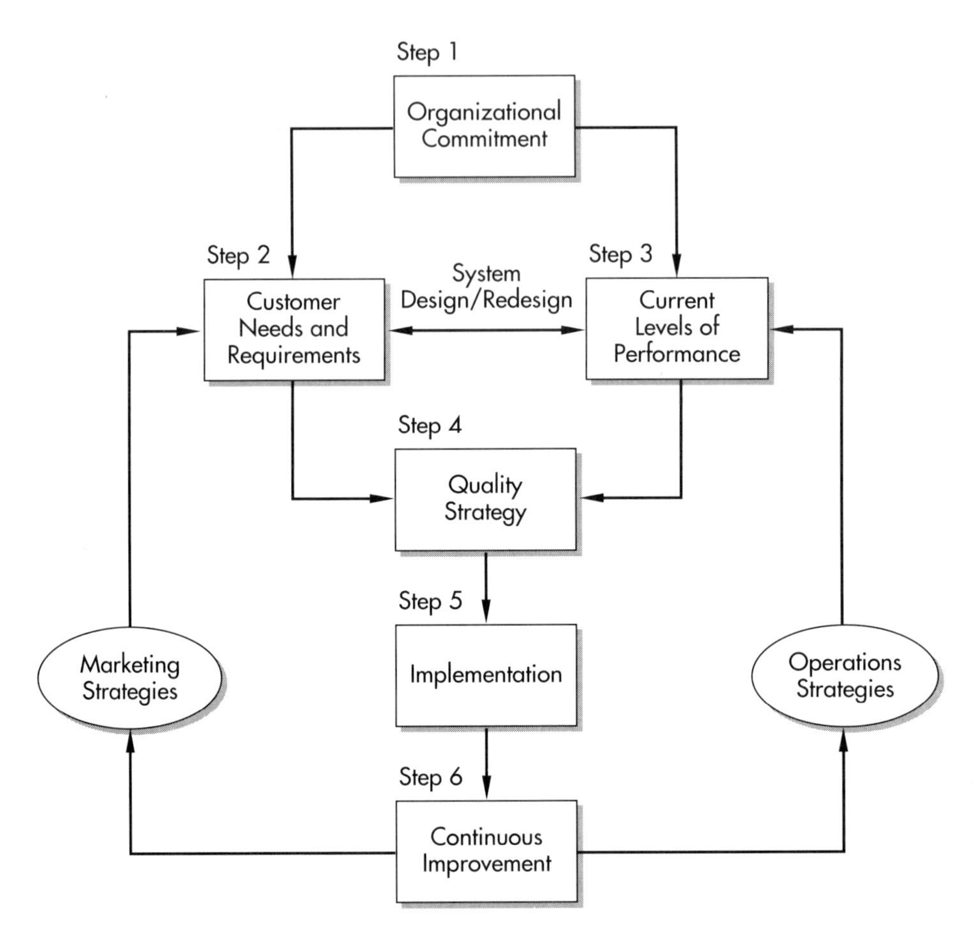

Figure 9-3
Logistics Quality Process

Source: C. John Langley, Jr., "Quality in Logistics: A Competitive Advantage," *Proceedings* of the R. Hadly Waters Logistics and Transportation Symposium (University Park, Pa.: Penn State University, The Center for Logistics Research, 1990).

Success in the logistics area yields positive external praise, which can boost the commitment in other functional areas by underscoring the relevance of quality.

Step 2: Customer Requirements

Emphasis must be placed on understanding the requirements of the logistics function's customers. While companies traditionally focus on the logistical needs of their external customers, equally important are the needs of internal customers like marketing, manufacturing, finance, and logistics co-workers.

Besides achieving a one-time understanding of customer needs and requirements, the marketplace's changing priorities should be regularly monitored. Outside consultants or services can provide objective information on a regular basis if a company chooses not to dedicate internal resources.

Companies desiring a successful quality process should begin to think of their suppliers and other channel partners as customers. The companies in a truly integrated supply chain must share significant coordination and singularity of purpose. A shortsighted company's failure to view these other entities as customers will prove counterproductive to quality.

Step 3: Current Levels of Performance

After specific requirements have been determined, the company must measure how well it is currently performing for each one. For this information to be useful, it must be accurate, meaningful, and understandable. For the information to be valid, it should be gathered scientifically; validity may be important when defending a measurement of poor performance requiring painful changes.

In addition to gathering performance-related information pertaining to key areas like transportation, inventory, warehousing, information processing, and packaging, benchmarking against other companies or industry standards is valuable for understanding relative performance. Once current levels of performance have been established, a company is likely to identify and immediately implement short-term initiatives for logistics system redesign (or reengineering), as some deficiencies are very easy to correct or too great to overlook.

Step 4: Quality Strategy

The term *quality strategy* refers to the specific initiatives selected as cornerstones for the overall quality structure. A first step is to study the philosophies of the quality gurus. Although the company should consider many approaches, its ultimate priorities should focus on the following aspects:

- Understanding customers' needs
- Continual improvement
- Performance measurement and variance monitoring
- Education and training
- Overall organizational commitment

The strategy chosen should improve performance from the current levels. Successful quality processes utilize a number of tools and techniques to measure changes in performance. Most prominent among the tools are those that are simple to create and easy to use, such as flow charts, cause-and-effect diagrams, check sheets, Pareto analyses, histograms, run charts, control charts (statistical process control [SPC]), and scatter diagrams (correlation charts).[19] Logistics departments have been using a growing number of quality comparison techniques like benchmarking,[20] quality function deployment,[21] and customer research. These tools and comparison techniques help identify and explain logistics quality issues, remove causes of quality failures, and enhance the company's prospects.

Step 5: Implementation

Smooth and effective implementation is essential for success. A company should direct considerable attention to designing an overall quality strategy that will "roll out" productively and effectively.

Implementation has significant logistics implications. The people involved in logistics operations have the greatest impact on the service levels received by the company's external and internal customers. They are in a position to make positive contributions to the overall quality process. Although management is ultimately responsible for the success of the quality process, it is the inventory control specialists, warehouse and dock workers, vehicle drivers, product packaging personnel, order entry clerks and staff, and others who ultimately perform the work and often have the most direct contact with customers.

An effective implementation plan should include a timetable as well as a comprehensive list of necessary resources. These will help ensure the success of a well-conceived logistics quality process.

Step 6: Continuous Improvement

Although there is a temptation to think of this step as the last one, the process should be continuing, and one should remember that an effective and meaningful quality process has no end as such. Continuous improvement demands more than one-time performance. Goals should not be set once, only to be achieved and maintained forever. Rather, reasonable goals should be set and *reset higher* as they are attained. Continuous improvement requires balance. Goals that are either overly ambitious or not at all challenging are counterproductive. Finally, continuous improvement calls for relevant, current information. Customer needs must constantly be monitored so that reactions to variations in performance, and the setting of new goals, can be done in a manner benefiting the customer.

A dedication to continuous improvement will result in modification and enhancement not only of the company's logistics strategy but also its marketing and operations strategies. Feedback from the logistics quality process will identify the changing needs and emerging problems customers face.

In the quest to create value for the customer, a formal commitment to quality represents another way for logistics to deliver the service essential to successful competition in today's business environment.

Improvement Through Quality Analysis

Market response can be explained through analysis of the perceptions of suppliers and their customers with respect to service levels. The perceptual process model (Figure 9-4) gives insight into sales response (customer response) to logistical customer service.[22] The perceptions studied are actual service levels offered by the supplier and comparative service levels offered by competitors. The bases for perceptions include past experience, industry standards, standards of competitors, and situational requirements. The model suggests that understanding the source of perceptions will provide greater understanding for making customer service decisions. The anticipated response by customers in terms of sales revenues is also a benefit of the model, hence sales response.[23]

There are five critical discrepancies, or gaps, that may exist and should be closed to achieve customer satisfaction and positive sales response. The magnitude of each discrepancy can be reduced using the tools and techniques of quality analysis.

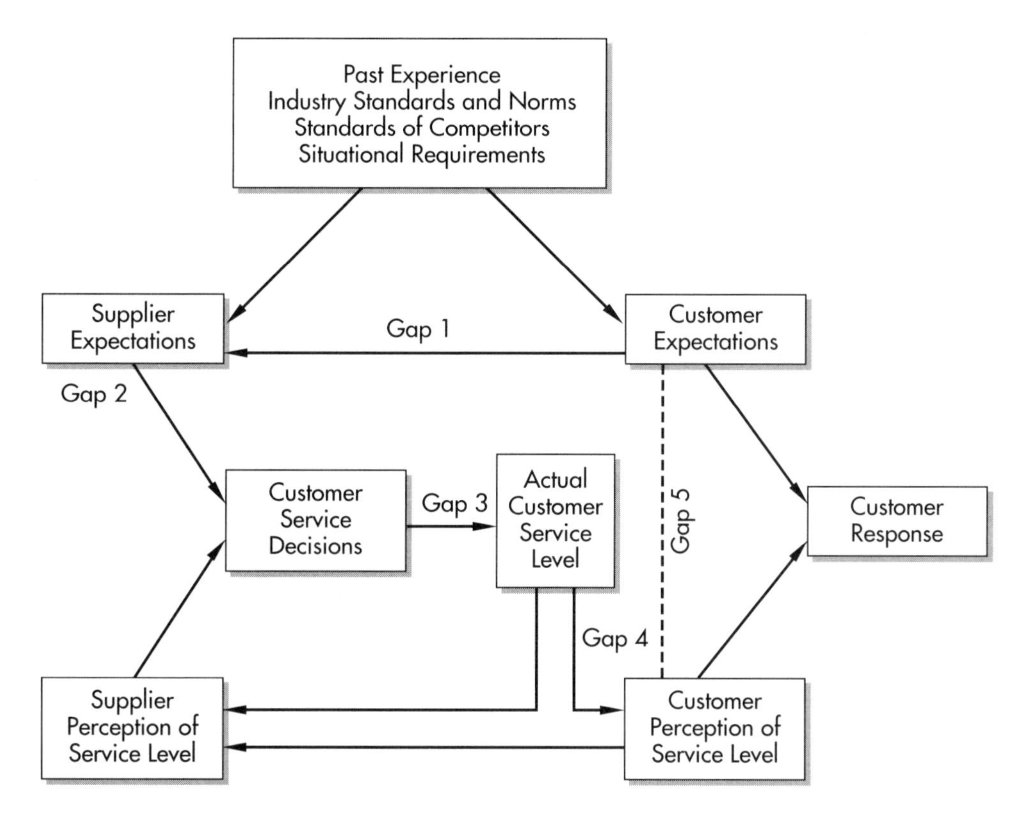

Figure 9-4
A Perceptual Process Model of Customer Service

Source: Adapted from R. Mohan Pisharodi and C. John Langley, Jr., "A Perceptual Process Model of Customer Service Based on Cybernetic/Control Theory," *Journal of Business Logistics* 11, no. 1 (1990): 35.

Gap 1: The gap between expectations held by a supplier and its customer may be closed through the use of better customer research and benchmarking. In combination, these ensure greater congruity between the two sets of expectations.

Gap 2: The gap between a supplier's expectations and the system designed to meet them may be closed through greater commitment to overall service quality, and the use of quality function deployment (QFD) to help translate these expectations into actionable customer service decisions.

Gap 3: This is the discrepancy between the customer service decisions and the actual levels of service provided. Such methods as statistical process control (SPC) are very helpful in understanding variability and bringing actual service levels into line with the levels the system was designed to provide.

Gap 4: Sometimes the customer's perception of service level may differ from what is actually provided. The customer may not have accurate measurements of actual service quality. This gap may be closed through more effective communication between supplier and customer, particularly to ensure the validity of customers' service measurements. Also, suppliers may find that providing customers with measurement data, such as SPC charts, reduces the gap.

Gap 5: The discrepancy between what customers expect and what they receive, in terms of logistics service quality, is the most important gap. In effect, the magnitude of this gap depends on the extent to which gaps 1 through 4 are seen to exist. Thus, closing gap 5 depends on meaningful application of quality analysis techniques like benchmarking, customer research, QFD, and SPC, as well as measurement accuracy and communication between supplier and customer.

Implementation Strategies

In addition to the adoption of a *formal* quality process, six implementation priorities, discussed in the suggested order of implementation, will enhance the likelihood of success:

Priority 1—Quality Audit: Conduct a quality audit to identify opportunities for quality improvement throughout the logistics area. This should be a relatively formal examination of the company's logistics processes and the extent to which a gap may exist between supplier and customer expectations.

Priority 2—Executive Education: Conduct a formal two- to three-day course for executives and managers in the logistics area on matters pertaining to quality and quality processes. The objectives should include familiarity and "buy-in" to the basic concepts relating to logistics quality.

Priority 3—Strategic Quality Plan: The elements of the quality process, including education, timing, and responsibilities, should be delineated in this step. With regard to education, the needs of executives, managers, supervisors, and workers should be given thoughtful consideration.

Priority 4—Quality Improvement Projects: Accomplishment of specific quality improvement projects will prove to be the best way to promote logistics quality. Quality improvement teams should be formed to address specific quality issues and to communicate these to others in the logistics area.

Priority 5—Employee Education: Once the executives and managers have received formal education on the topic of logistics quality and a few quality improvement projects have been completed, it is helpful to introduce quality education at the supervisory and worker levels. These educational sessions are critical to the success of the overall logistics quality process and should be designed with the intended recipients in mind.

Priority 6—Implementation and Continuous Improvement: The results of the logistics quality process will prove helpful to creating customer value through efficiency, effectiveness, and differentiation. Continuing this process will greatly benefit the company and its customers alike.

Malcolm Baldrige National Quality Award

Congress established the Malcolm Baldrige National Quality Award in 1987 to recognize specific quality achievements by U.S. companies and to promote a general awareness of quality among American businesses.[24] Named in honor of the late Malcolm Baldrige, who served as secretary of commerce from 1981 to 1987, the award is presented in three categories: manufac-

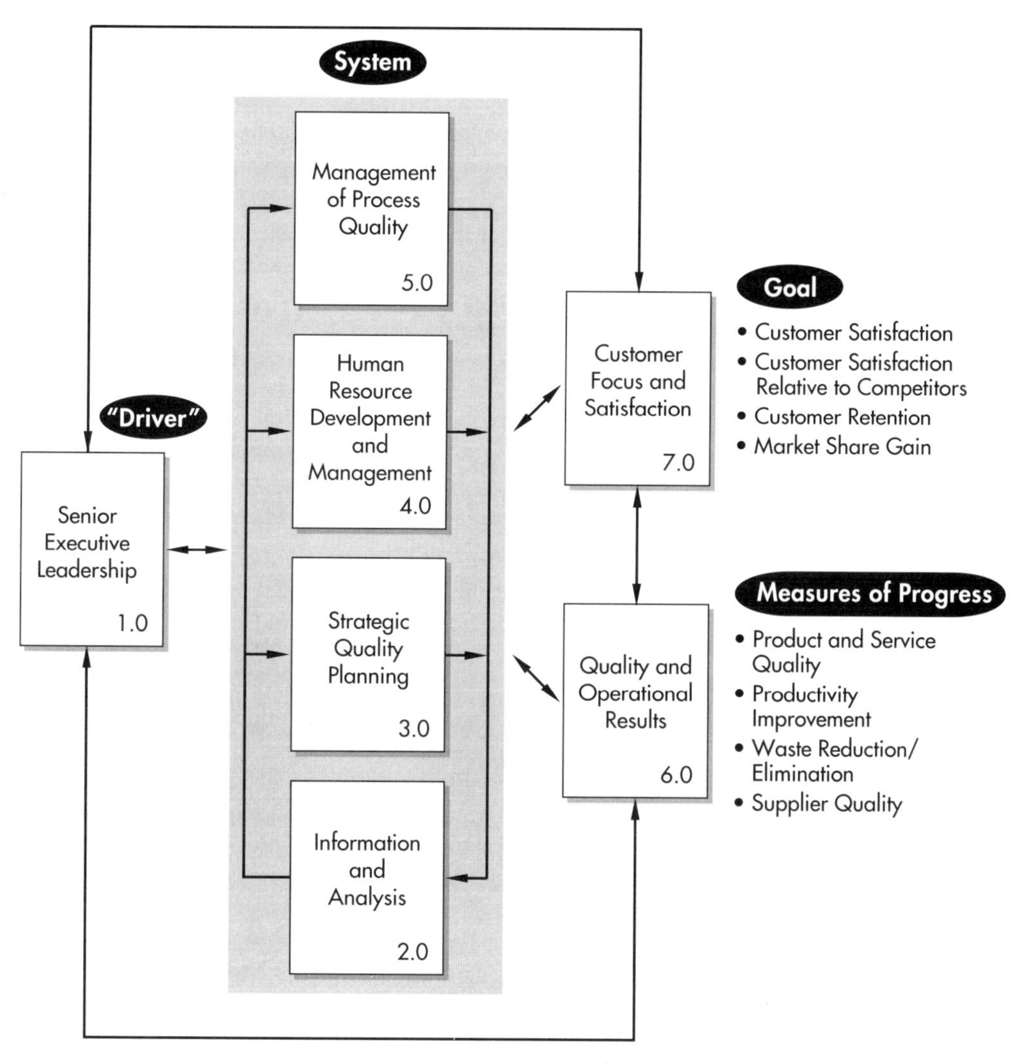

Figure 9-5
Baldrige Award Criteria Framework
Dynamic Relationships

Source: U.S. Department of Commerce, *1993 Award Criteria*—Malcolm Baldrige National Quality Award, 1993.

turing, services, and small businesses. Up to two awards can be given yearly in each category. Both privately owned and public companies incorporated and located in the United States are eligible. Winners can advertise and publicize that they have won the award.

Among the judging criteria are leadership, information and analysis, planning, human resource utilization, quality assurance, quality assurance results, and customer satisfaction (Figure 9-5). Many companies have found that pursuing the criteria required to win the award, whether actually applying for it, has helped implementation of a formal quality process. The criteria provide a convenient and widely used framework on which quality can be built.

Continued Opportunities

There are tremendous opportunities for the logistics function to create customer value through a formal quality process and the principles of total quality management. Strategies to enhance effectiveness, efficiency, and differentiation through logistics management should be considered high return and high priority in terms of their potential positive impact on both the customer base and profits.

Dedication and commitment to quality should help the logistics area establish itself within the company as key to the creation of customer value. As our collective understanding of these principles and approaches accelerates, the true power of logistics quality will become even more apparent and will continually present new opportunities.

Notes

1. Portions of this chapter have been adapted from C. John Langley, Jr., and Mary C. Holcomb, "Achieving Customer Value through Logistics Management," in Michael J. Stahl and Gregory M. Bounds, eds., *Competing Globally Through Customer Value* (New York: Quorum Books, 1991); C. John Langley, Jr., and Mary C. Holcomb, "Creating Logistics Customer Value," *Journal of Business Logistics* 13, no. 2 (1992), and John J. Coyle, Edward J. Bardi, and C. John Langley, Jr., "Logistics Quality" (chap. 13), in *The Management of Business Logistics* 5th ed. (St. Paul: West, 1992).
2. The concept of "best comparative net value" for customers is introduced and developed further in various chapters included in Stahl and Bounds, *Competing Globally.* Of particular interest would be Michael J. Stahl and Gregory M. Bounds, "Global Competition: The Need for Educational and Business Responses," pp. 3–13; G. Harlan Carothers, Jr., and Mel Adams, "Competitive Advantage through Customer Value: The Role of Value-Based Strategies," pp. 32–66; and G. Harlan Carothers and Gregory M. Bounds, "Customer Value Determination and System Improvement Cycles," pp. 98–116.
3. Bernard J. La Londe, Martha C. Cooper, and Thomas G. Noordeweier, *Customer Service: A Management Perspective* (Oak Brook, Ill.: Council of Logistics Management, 1988), pp. 117–21.
4. Bernard J. La Londe and Paul H. Zinszer, *Customer Service: Meaning and Measurement* (Chicago: Council of Logistics Management, 1976).
5. C. John Langley, Jr., Deborah Rosen, Howard S. Gochberg, Robert A. Dickinson, and Robert J. Quinn, "Logistics and the Concept of Value-Added," *Annual Conference Proceedings* (Oak Brook, Ill.: Council of Logistics Management, 1989), pp. 157–66.
6. Donald J. Bowersox and Robert E. Murray, "Logistics Strategic Planning for the 1990's," *Annual Conference Proceedings* (Oak Brook, Ill.: Council of Logistics Management, 1987), pp. 231–43.
7. These are the five "rights" of a logistics system referred to by Dr. E. Grosvenor Plowman, a distribution consultant and former vice president of traffic for the U.S. Steel Corporation (now USX Corporation). They are referred to in George A. Gecowets, "Physical Distribution Management," *Defense Transportation Journal* 35, no. 4 (August 1979): 11.
8. C. John Langley, Jr., Deborah Rosen, Howard S. Gochberg, Robert A. Dickinson, and Robert J. Quinn, "Logistics and the Concept of Value-Added," *Annual Conference Proceedings* (Oak Brook, Ill.: Council of Logistics Management, 1989), pp. 157–66.

9. John J. Coyle, Edward J. Bardi, and C. John Langley, Jr., *The Management of Business Logistics,* 5th ed. (St. Paul: West, 1992), p. 458. Adapted, with permission, from Table 13–1; © 1992 by West Publishing Company. All rights reserved.
10. The issue of customer value is treated comprehensively in Michael J. Stahl and Gregory M. Bounds, *Competing Globally Through Customer Value* (Westport, Conn.: Quorum Books, 1991). In particular, see C. John Langley, Jr., and Mary C. Holcomb, chap. 22: "Achieving Customer Value Through Logistics Management," pp. 547–65.
11. The PIMS research program represents an extensive data bank relating to business performance and various factors related to performance. The program is conducted by the Strategic Planning Institute, Cambridge, Mass.
12. Council of Logistics Management, *Improving Quality and Productivity in the Logistics Process* (Oak Brook, Ill.: Council of Logistics Management, 1991).
13. C. John Langley, Jr., "Logistics Quality: Challenge for the 1990's" speech given to the Health and Personal Care Distribution Conference—1991 Educational Program, Longboat Key, Florida, October 22, 1991.
14. See C. John Langley, Jr., "Quality in Logistics: A Competitive Advantage," *Proceedings* of the R. Hadly Waters Logistics and Transportation Symposium (University Park, Pa.: Penn State University, The Center for Logistics Research, 1990); and C. John Langley, Jr., Mary C. Holcomb, Joel Baudouin, Alexander Donnan, and Paul Caruso, "Approaches to Logistics Quality," *Annual Conference Proceedings* (Oak Brook, Ill.: Council of Logistics Management, 1989), pp. 73–78.
15. For an excellent discussion of several individuals who have distinguished themselves in the field of quality, see "The Gurus of Quality," *Traffic Management* (July 1990): 34–39.
16. Langley, "Quality in Logistics," p. 28. Based on a study performed at the University of Tennessee.
17. A growing number of companies could be cited as having made significant progress in the area of a formal logistics quality process. Those listed are representative of only the broader number of firms having made significant accomplishments of this type.
18. These steps are described in more detail in Langley, "Quality in Logistics," pp. 27–33.
19. Excellent sources on these topics include Donald J. Wheeler and David S. Chambers, *Understanding Statistical Process Control* (Knoxville, Tenn.: Statistical Process Controls, 1986), and Kaoru Ishikawa, *Guide to Quality Control* (Tokyo: Asian Productivity Organization, 1982).
20. Robert C. Camp, *Benchmarking* (Milwaukee: ASQC Quality Press, 1989).
21. Quality function deployment (QFD) is an approach popularized by the American Supplier Institute. Although applicable to a wide variety of industries, much of its experience to date in the United States has been in automobile manufacturing. For an excellent discussion of the use and potential of QFD in the logistics area, see James H. Foggin, "Closing the Gaps in Services Marketing: Designing to Satisfy Customer Expectations," in Stahl and Bounds, eds., *Competing Globally,* pp. 510–30.
22. R. Mohan Pisharodi and C. John Langley, Jr., "A Perceptual Process Model of Customer Service Based on Cybernetic/Control Theory," *Journal of Business Logistics* 11, no. 1 (1990): 26–46. The perceptual process model was developed by Rammohan Pisharodi.
23. Also of interest is a comparable model developed by Valarie A. Zeithaml, Leonard L. Berry, and A. Parasuraman, "Communication and Control Processes in the Delivery of Service Quality," *Journal of Marketing* 52 (April 1988): 35–48. In addition, the use of quality analysis techniques as a means to close the gaps was suggested by James H. Foggin, "Closing

the Gaps in Services Marketing," pp. 510–30, chap. 20 in Stahl and Bounds, *Competing Globally.*

24. See "Application Guidelines" for the Malcolm Baldrige National Quality Award, available from the National Institute of Standards and Quality, United States Department of Commerce.

CHAPTER 10

Measuring the Performance of Logistics Operations

Jay U. Sterling

An operational system that adequately meets a company's marketing and logistics management information needs must provide for both its external and internal requirements. Most traditional management information systems adequately provide for external needs like financial reports for shareholders, lenders, and tax authorities. However, it is critical that an operational system also satisfy internal needs. From a logistics perspective, there are two types of internal needs: (1) a knowledge of the relevant functional costs and performance levels as they are incurred, or shortly thereafter, and (2) the attachment of these functional costs and measurements to relevant marketing and logistics activities in order to determine each function's contribution to the overall logistics system.

This chapter develops an understanding of these functional flows and then proposes an operating system to record this information in an integrated data base that supports an integrated management information system (MIS).[1] The objective of this integrated data base is to attach any given data module to all relevant functions and/or activities. Therefore, the form of the inputs into the data base is extremely important. The last part of this chapter analyzes the outputs required to successfully monitor the logistics operating system.

Functional Costs

The normal flow of inventories in a distribution channel is shown in Figure 10-1. This process consists of the acquisition of raw materials obtained outside the company or, if it is vertically integrated, within it. These materials are transported to initial production points or stored until production occurs. Then a series of production steps transforms the raw materials and parts into the forms salable to the company's markets. Concurrently, promotional programs are used to cultivate and sustain markets. Following production, goods are moved directly to market or to storage and thence to intermediary markets (e.g., wholesalers or retailers) or to end users.

The activities in an individual manufacturer's portion of the flow are detailed in Figure 10-2. Logistics managers are concerned with controlling activities regarding (1) the two general types of inventory—raw/in-process inventory and finished goods—and (2) the two general types of stocking locations—manufacturing plants and field warehouses.

In each of the distribution channel activities described in the previous paragraphs and figures, a series of functions is performed. Each function is an activity center where costs are in-

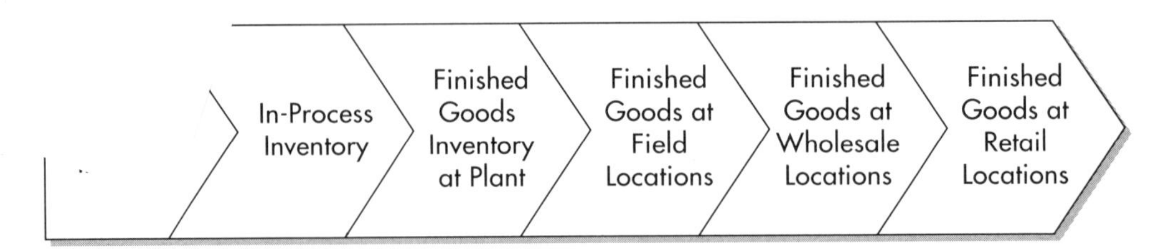

Figure 10-1
Inventory Positions in the Logistics System

curred based on the principal activity engaged in at each particular point. The planning and control of expenditures occurs mainly in these functional centers. The flow of these functional activities, and thus the structure of the distribution channel, varies with the nature of the business and the markets to be served.

Another way to describe this relationship between costs and functional activities is the value chain, as proposed by strategist Michael Porter.[2] This concept divides a company's efforts into the technologically and economically distinct activities it performs in the course of doing business, which are called "value activities." The value a company creates is measured by the amount that its customers are willing to pay for a product or service. Figure 10-3 describes this chain and illustrates that a company's support activities—human resource management, technology development (research and engineering), and procurement—can indeed add value to each primary activity that leads to satisfied customers.

A business will be profitable if the value it creates for customers exceeds the cost of performing these value-adding activities. To gain competitive advantage over its rivals, a company must either perform these activities at a lower cost or perform them in a way that leads to differentiation at a premium price (more value). Therefore, the key tasks are to (1) identify these value-adding activities (functions), (2) attach all relevant costs to each activity, (3) assign these activities and associated costs to each business unit, and (4) compile meaningful productivity measurements using the appropriate units of activity (e.g., units shipped). Table 10-1 lists the various activities that might be included across a company's entire value chain/distribution chan-

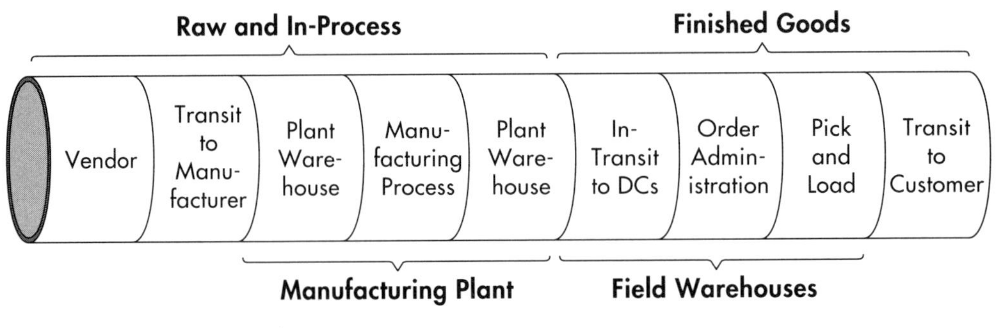

Figure 10-2
Inventory Pipeline

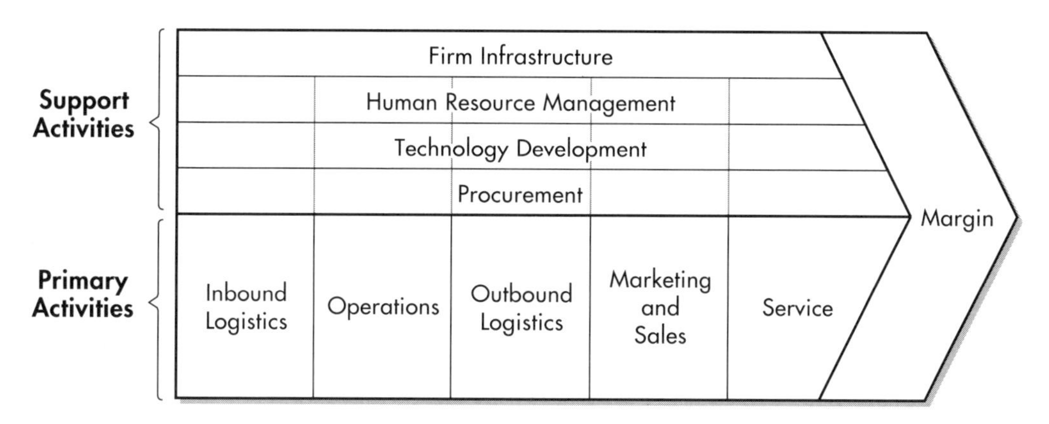

Figure 10-3
The Value Chain

Source: From *Competitive Advantage: Creating and Sustaining Superior Performance* by Michael E. Porter. Copyright © 1985 by Michael E. Porter. Reprinted by permission of The Free Press, a division of Macmillan, Inc.

nel. Productivity reports for these activities should include expenses incurred across the company's entire value-chain/distribution channel.

The basic question concerning any functional cost is whether it can be attached to the work being performed. In a sense, attachment is similar to moving through a cafeteria.[3] As individuals pass by alternative foods in a cafeteria line, they select foods and place them on their tray. For each article selected, a unit price is provided and the sum total of the unit prices of the foods selected becomes the total cost of the meal. It is exactly this way with functional costs. For example, the product or service being produced utilizes certain functions with specific unit costs. The functional costs incurred are attached to the product or customer order, and the sum of these costs is then attached to the appropriate business activity.

A company's chart of accounts and database files should be designed so that each function receives as many charges as possible on a direct basis rather than through arbitrary allocations. Therefore, work units, or "cost drivers," that cause costs to vary, both in the short and the long

TABLE 10-1
Value Chain/Distribution Channel Activities

Transportation/Distribution	Information systems
Warehousing	Receiving and inspection
Personal selling	Production setup
Advertising/promotion	Order processing
Installation	Scheduling production
After-sale service	Inventory movements, tracking, and counts
Engineering design	Shipment scheduling and processing
Engineering change orders	Quality assurance
Process improvement	Credits, returns, and allowance
Purchasing	Inventory carrying costs

run, must be identified. These units of variability depend on several considerations, such as type of function, product handled and shipped, sales territory, customer class or group, and channel of distribution. Cost drivers should be readily measurable, produce reasonably accurate results, be economical to apply, display a demonstrable relationship to the marketing or distribution activity, and be fair and equitable.[4]

All costs incurred at the functional cost level can be viewed as either fixed or variable. Fixed costs are fixed in total for a given level of functional activity and do not vary in total with a change in the level of activity, given a fixed capacity. Variable costs increase with an increase in the volume of activity in the function and are more or less constant per unit within a given level of output. Table 10-2 provides a template for the planned versus actual cost structure of a company-owned distribution center on a year-to-date (YTD) basis. It illustrates how this logistics activity contains both fixed and variable costs, as well as subfunctions.

A primary attribute of variable costs is that they can be used to develop standard costs for each logistics function or subfunction. Each standard cost, which is a reasonable estimate of the per unit cost, is based only on the variable cost of the function, because fixed costs are static with respect to output. It is this standard that is attached to the product or service as it is processed through each function or value-chain activity. As the product moves through the production functions into the market, appropriate standard costs can be attached to both marketing and logistics activities. Fixed costs should be assigned to a particular activity only if they are performed as part of it. In the hierarchy of activity costs, fixed costs from a function or activity are attached to the first activity in which the fixed costs are specifically applicable. If an attachment to a low-level activity or function is unreasonable, then the activities or functions must be aggregated until such fixed costs are attachable.[5]

Building an Integrated Database

Intelligent databases allow information to be managed to facilitate ease of storage, access, and use. This capability has evolved as a result of the integration of traditional approaches to managing databases with recent improvements in computer hardware and programming capabilities. These improvements include fourth-generation languages, expert systems, personal computer–based object-oriented programming, and local area network (LAN) systems that link desktop computers to mainframe systems. It is possible to define an overall unifying structure that combines these technologies into a blueprint for an intelligent database.

As stated, an operational database system that provides adequate managerial information must meet the internal as well as the external needs of the company. These internal needs consist of measuring the operations of functional cost centers, such as logistics, as well as managing the company's various business segments. Therefore, this internal system requires:

- Identification of relevant functional cost centers
- Establishment of standard costs within each cost center
- Collection of cost drivers and/or units of activity (e.g., units shipped) within each cost center
- Identification of relevant business segments
- Establishment of a system of cost, revenue, and performance activity flows through the functional cost centers[6]

TABLE 10-2
Distribution Center Financial Summary

Profit & Loss Statement	**Last YTD ($)**	**YTD Planned ($)**	**YTD Actual ($)**	**YTD Actual Percent of Totals (%)**
Revenues:				
Storage				
Handling				
Other				
Total Revenues				100
Expenses				
Fixed:				
Facilities				
Supervision				
Allocated general and administrative				
Variable:				
Direct labor				
Equipment operation				
Subtotal—fixed and variable				
Nonallowable items:				
Loss and damage				
Demurrage				
Repairs				
Total Expenses				100
Net Profit (Loss)				100

Performance Ratios:		**Last YTD**	**YTD Planned**	**YTD Actual**
Profit:				
Revenue excluding nonallowable	(%)			
Total net profit	(%)			
Facilities:				
Storage revenue	(%)			
Warehouse utilization	(%)			
Revenue/ft^2	($)			
Facilities cost/ft^2	($)			
Labor:				
Handling revenue	(%)			
Inventory:				
Average unit turnover	($)			
Revenue per unit	($)			
Cost per unit	($)			
Profit (loss) per unit	($)			

With advanced information systems, it is possible to access the required data in the required form on demand. Typical accounting and financial systems require aggregations, sortations, and reaggregations to the point that there are long lags in the availability of the data relative to when they are needed. Also, some accuracy is lost, owing to the allocation processes typically used.

To measure the operations of functional cost centers and business units, databases must be capable of receiving transactions in a coded form so that selected data can be retrieved quickly for management decision processes. These coding procedures create modules of information in a special logistics system file so that each module can be quickly retrieved or combined with other modules. This basic technique can be used by the smallest of businesses. In the recommended information system of special cost, revenue, and activity flows, the required information is collected on-line in a unique logistics database directly from source documents. The key to this operating and information system is the integration of various computer-generated data files that are normally available in most companies, such as:

- Customer order history
- Inventory activity that includes a summary of receipts, shipments, and month-end balances for each individual item (SKU)
- Paid freight bills
- Debit and credit adjustments processed to and from customers
- Accounts payable transactions pertaining to general ledger expense accounts, such as:
  —company-owned warehousing operating costs
  —public warehousing charges
  —property taxes paid on inventories
  —insurance paid on inventories
  —warranty and service-related costs
  —private fleet operating costs

The source documents and transactions used as a source for this integrated database are depicted in Figure 10-4. By extracting selected data from operating system files and developing standard costs from an analysis of the cost components contained in the marketing cost file, it is possible to aggregate these costs with costs from the other data files into functional cost and revenue reports, such as selling, transportation, warehousing, inventory, and order processing activities. These data can be further grouped into segment analyses by strategic business unit (SBU), product, customer, channel, geographic sales area, order type, and cost center.

Because many of the expenses related to marketing and logistics activities are variable in their behavior, they can be converted into standard costs and attached to individual items (SKUs) in the same manner as manufacturing costs (e.g., raw and in-process material, direct labor, and variable overhead). In addition, non–out-of-pocket expenses in the form of journal entry transactions can also be obtained and used to develop standard costs that, in turn, can be attached to products, channels, customers, or order-types.

To meet the needs of management fully, the information system must be able to assemble costs by well-defined functions and then attach these functional costs to the various categories relevant to analyzing logistics performance. Therefore, a basic task of any logistics database is to capture major logistics activities like transportation, warehousing, purchasing, and inventory management in reasonable detail. Unfortunately, few companies do an adequate job. The issue is *cost* and therefore *value,* because data for data's sake are worthless. It takes skillful analysis and effective links with management to provide benefits that justify the cost of collecting and categorizing detailed data, but the payback can be large.[7]

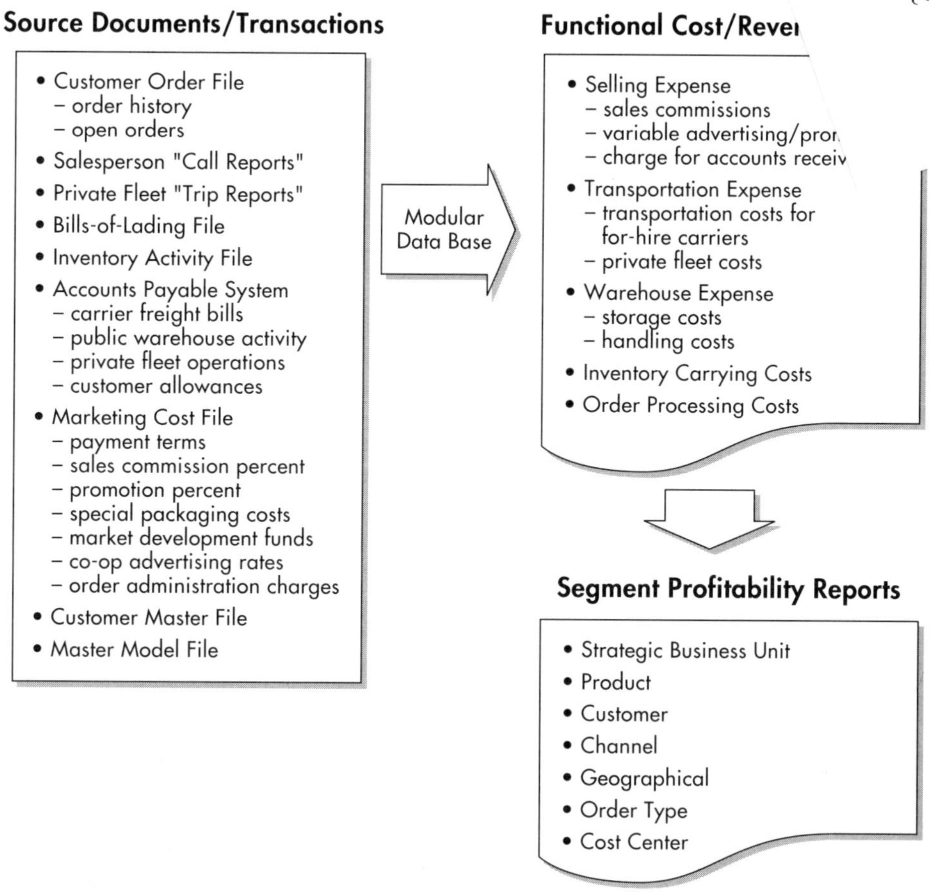

Source Documents/Transactions

- Customer Order File
  - order history
  - open orders
- Salesperson "Call Reports"
- Private Fleet "Trip Reports"
- Bills-of-Lading File
- Inventory Activity File
- Accounts Payable System
  - carrier freight bills
  - public warehouse activity
  - private fleet operations
  - customer allowances
- Marketing Cost File
  - payment terms
  - sales commission percent
  - promotion percent
  - special packaging costs
  - market development funds
  - co-op advertising rates
  - order administration charges
- Customer Master File
- Master Model File

Modular Data Base

Functional Cost/Revei

- Selling Expense
  - sales commissions
  - variable advertising/pror
  - charge for accounts receiv
- Transportation Expense
  - transportation costs for for-hire carriers
  - private fleet costs
- Warehouse Expense
  - storage costs
  - handling costs
- Inventory Carrying Costs
- Order Processing Costs

Segment Profitability Reports

- Strategic Business Unit
- Product
- Customer
- Channel
- Geographical
- Order Type
- Cost Center

Figure 10-4
Marketing Financial Information System: Source Documents and Management Reports

Another primary purpose of an integrated database is to collect, monitor, and report information to management for decision-making and control purposes. Once a database has been properly established, initial inputs into the system from source documents should be sufficient to accommodate all subsequent analyses. The benefits of an integrated database are difficult to describe in specific terms. However, some general benefits can be identified:

- Ability of managers to achieve effective and efficient decisions
- Simultaneous consideration of various managerial variables
- Facilitation of rapid revisions of information
- Improved communication within the company
- Facilitation of long-term management perspectives
- Stimulation of changes within the company
- Facilitation of effective strategic management

- Availability of more accurate and timely information to decision makers
- Faster and better decision making
- More accurate forecasting[8]

Customer orders, or cash register sales in the case of retailers, activate or affect virtually every operating system and/or source document file in manufacturing, wholesaling, and retailing companies. Customer orders are the single most important source for analyzing product, customer, and channel business segments. The sequential process involved in processing an order is described in Figure 10-5.

Once an order has been received by mail, telephone, or computer, it is entered into the company's order processing system. This process involves edits to: (1) verify data like correct item numbers and customers' names and addresses; (2) input other data like prices, weights and dimensions, and product classifications; and (3) qualify the shippable status of each order line by ascertaining the inventory availability of each item ordered.

Once the editing process has been completed and shippable quantities have been achieved, the order is transmitted to a warehouse/distribution center to be picked, packed, and shipped. Normally, a document such as a picking list is prepared to assist the warehouse in these tasks. After an order has been picked and before it is loaded onto trucks or into railcars, the line items are verified for the correctness of each item number and adjusted for any variances in quantities. Other information such as carrier, trailer number, and ship date are also entered into a warehouse information system linked to the order processing system. Then, a combined manifest/bill-of-lading/packing slip is generated and several copies are normally provided to the carrier. At this time, the warehouse notifies the corporate order processing system, usually electronically, that the order has been shipped so that an invoice can be prepared and mailed to the customer.

When the carrier delivers the shipment, the carrier sends a transportation invoice (pro bill) to the responsible party (shipper in the case of prepaid terms or consignee in the case of collect terms). If the freight bill is accompanied by a copy of the bill of lading (a practice required by many shippers), the pro bill can be linked back to the customer's order and invoice, because the bill of lading contains a reference to the applicable customer order number.

Each of the preceding activities creates unique information and data files that can all be linked to a single transaction—the customer's order. Selected data from these files can then be extracted from each file and entered into an integrated database to analyze logistics performance. To accomplish this consolidation of data into one database, common coding structures must be utilized. For instance, the first three digits of the customer's zip code can be used to aggregate orders and freight payments into common geographic areas. Company shipping (for customer shipments) and receiving (for stock transfers) facilities can be assigned a common code in freight bills, bills of lading, and order history files. Transportation modes contained in paid freight bill and bills-of-lading files can be assigned a common set of classifications. Individual products (SKUs) can be categorized into a concise, common set in the bills-of-lading, order history, and inventory activity files. These data can be used to develop and track key performance indicators for cross-functional processes such as the order management process (e.g., to measure cycle time or customer service) and the replenishment process. Finally, customers can be grouped by business segment based on fields of data typically contained in the customer name and address file.

Figure 10-6 depicts the various operating files required to develop logistics performance reports. Each primary file contains many fields of information. However, relatively few fields are required, mostly from the first three files, to develop an integrated database for analyzing most

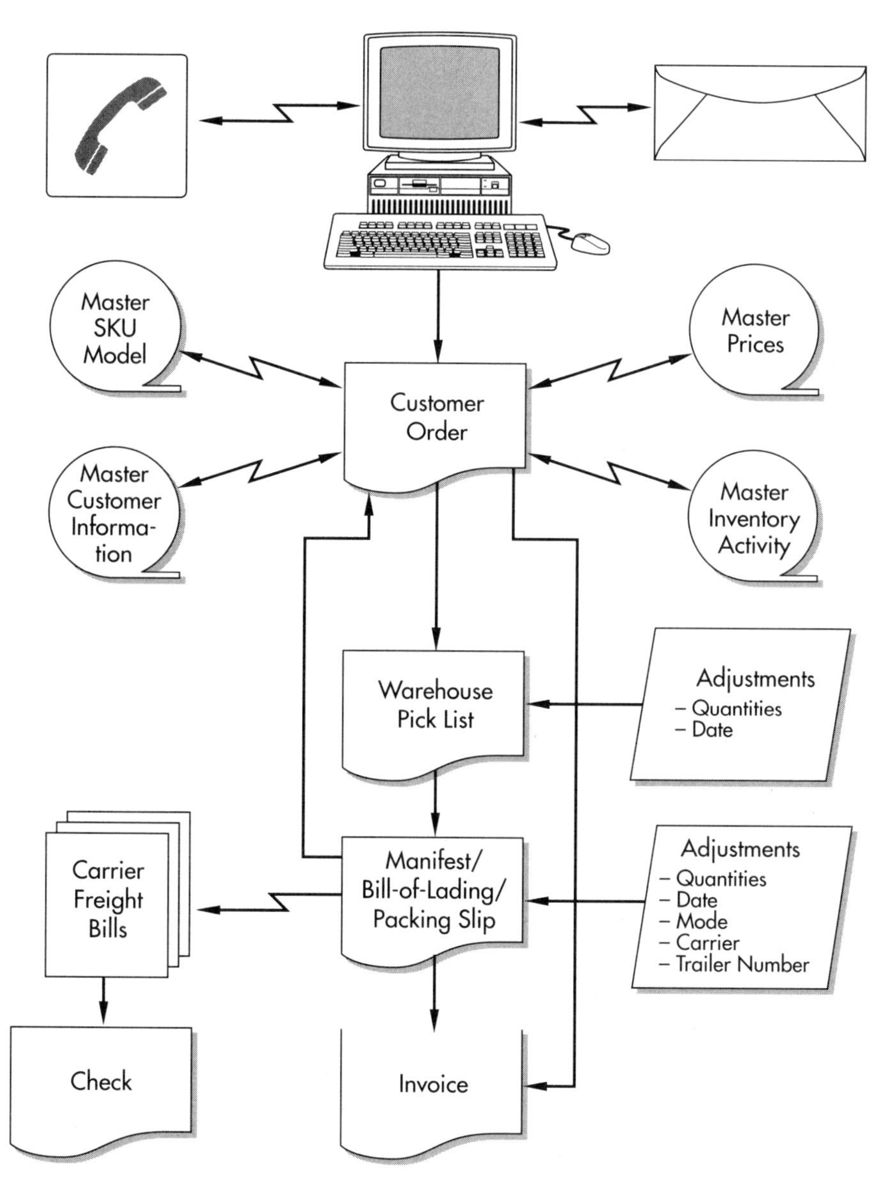

Figure 10-5
Source Document Data Files:
Order-Based Transactions

logistics activities. The general data extracted from each file are highlighted in Figure 10-6 under the first three columns, and the file structure and data requirements are described in greater detail in Table 10-3 for order history, Table 10-4 for paid freight bills, and Table 10-5 for inventory activity.

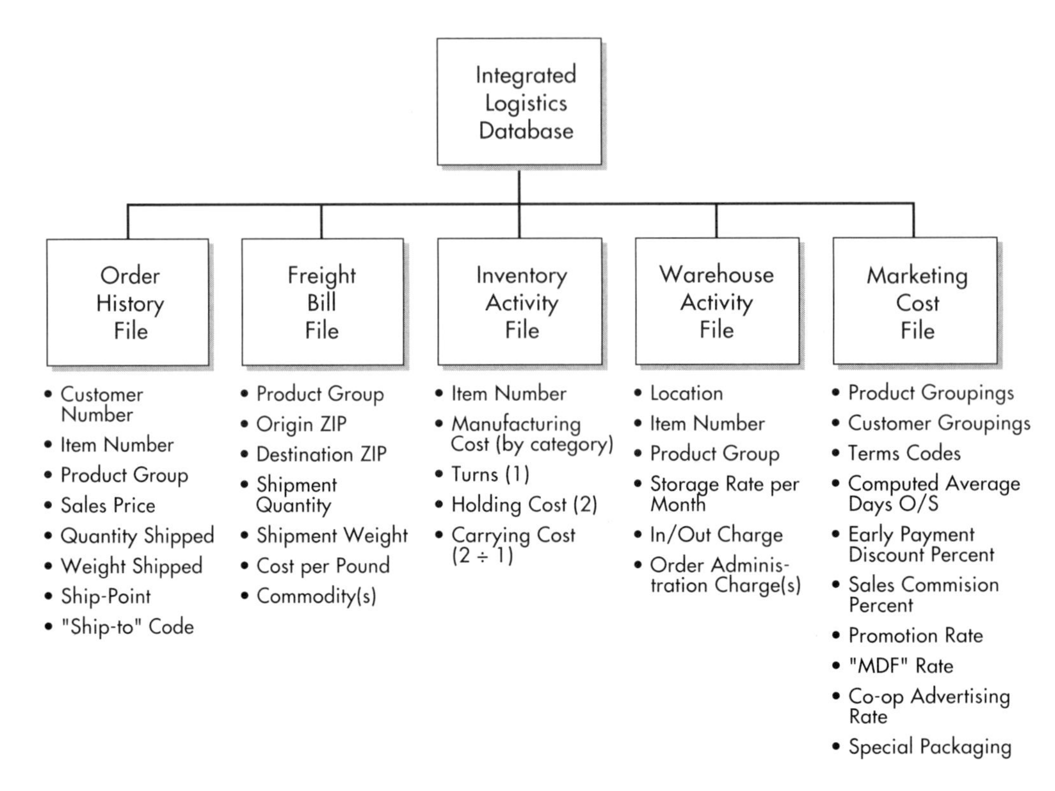

Figure 10-6
Files Required to Develop Integrated Logistics Reports

Evaluating Functional Performance

The following sections describe the major categories of activities that must be measured and evaluated on a regular basis to control operations effectively. Of course, as one measures and improves the performance of individual functions, one must be aware of the performance of the entire logistics process. Such awareness, through cross-functional evaluations, helps avoid individual functional performance optimization at the expense of total system performance. Nevertheless, the most straightforward approach to enhancing logistics performance is to initially pursue improvements within the major functional areas of warehousing, transportation, and inventory (while remaining aware of their interrelations).

Warehousing Costs

Warehouse activity data can be obtained in several ways. If a company uses public warehouses, then negotiated rates can be used to assign monthly storage charges and handling (in and out) costs to various product categories at each distribution center. If a company operates its own warehouses, the costs to operate these facilities can be aggregated and assigned to products in the same manner used by public warehouse operators. This is accomplished by assigning all *fixed* costs (e.g., office administration, building depreciation or rent, utilities, facility mainte-

TABLE 10-3
Order History File

Header (one for each order)	Detail (one record for each line)
1. Order number	1. Order number
2. Customer number	2. Line number
3. Customer classification/group code	3. Item (SKU) number
4. Ship-to ZIP code	4. Product family
5. Number of lines	5. Shipment number indicator (e.g., "A" for 1st shipment of the line, "B" for 2nd shipment, etc.)
6. Number of pieces/items/units ordered	6. Quantity data
7. Number of pieces/items/units shipped	a. original quantity ordered
8. Total weight of order	b. quantity shipped
9. Total weight of items shipped	c. quantity back ordered
10. Date information	7. Over pack quantify (items per case)
a. date of order	8. Unit price
b. customer's date wanted	9. Unit weight per piece/case
c. date received	10. "ABC" stock classification
11. Freight terms (e.g., prepaid, collect, UPS, etc.)	11. Freight class
	12. Ship-point location code
	13. Date information (where available)
	a. accumulated/reserved
	b. release to DC
	c. picked
	d. packed/loaded
	e. shipped
	14. Carrier code/reference
	15. Bill-of-lading reference (if available)

nance, supervisory labor, etc.) to "storage" activities. *Variable* costs (e.g., direct labor, materials handling equipment depreciation or rent, fuel, maintenance, etc.) are assigned to "handling" activities. Computing "storage" and "handling" rates enables a company to convert data regarding its company-owned warehouses to a "public" warehouse equivalent basis. Such a perspective enables these facilities to be operated as profit centers as well as to be compared with outside vendors (public warehouses) with respect to costs, productivity measurements (efficiency), and customer service performance levels (effectiveness). This process is described in Table 10-6.

Because individual products, cartons, containers, and so on sold by a company vary with respect to their dimensions and cube, raw warehousing costs need to be refined to recognize these variations. This is accomplished by developing equivalent unit measurements. With equivalent units, both storage and handling costs can be assigned to individual products or product classes in the same manner employed by manufacturing systems (e.g., MRP) to calculate master capacity plans and production schedules. That is, not all products consume the same cubic space

TABLE 10-4
Paid Freight Bill File

1. Company ship point/origin code
2. Destination code
   a. company facility
   b. customer ID
3. ZIP code (first three digits)
   a. origin
   b. destination
4. Amount paid
   a. for this bill
   b. total amount paid per master bill of lading
5. Weight data
   a. total weight of shipment
   b. deficit weight (if applicable)
   c. weight for each freight classification or commodity code
6. Number of pieces/cartons, etc., on shipment
7. Shipment type
   a. customer shipment
   b. stock transfer
   c. inbound material/component parts
   d. returned goods
8. Carrier name/code (SCAC, etc.)
9. Mode code
10. Prepaid/collect indicator
11. Bill-of-lading reference (outbound finished goods)
12. Master bill-of-lading reference (for consolidated shipments)
13. Order number reference

when stored or require the same amount of direct labor hours and materials handling equipment to unload and put away receipts and pick or load orders. Converting each individual product to an equivalent unit basis permits managers to compare products on an "apples-to-apples" basis with respect to both costs and productivity measurements. This concept is depicted in Figure 10-7 and the calculation is shown in Table 10-7 for a distribution center containing major home appliances.

In this example, the item shown (a particular type of home appliance in its storage packaging) requires 4.05 equivalent square feet of warehouse floor space (its "footprint") *for the purposes of comparison* with other items. The *actual* footprint for a single unit of this item is 5.92 square feet, but because of gains from stacking and losses from other space utilization needs (which is considered nonproductive space in the calculation because such space is not used directly for storage of inventory), 4.05 square feet is the equivalent unit measurement. The equiv-

TABLE 10-5
Inventory Activity File

Unit Activity (by SKU)	Cost Data
1. Item (model) number	1. Latest sales price
2. Selling organization (SBU)	2. Material cost
3. Product family/line	3. Labor cost
4. Product code (group) number	4. Fixed overhead/burden
5. "ABC" inventory classification	5. Variable overhead/burden
6. Unit weight per item and case	
7. Shipments (in pieces) last 12 months a. either accumulated, if available b. or shipments for each of the past 12 months	
8. Month-end balance (in pieces) for each of the past 12 months	

TABLE 10-6
Financial Control:
Forecasting Warehouse Rates

1. *Draft pro forma operating statement*
   a. based on current year's profit-and-loss statement
   b. adjust to reflect inflation and other increases
   c. allocate to fixed and variable categories:
      Fixed: Facilities costs
      General and administrative
      Supervision and office
      Variable: Direct labor
      Equipment operation
2. *Forecast planned inventory levels*
   a. monthly unit receipts
   b. month-end unit inventories
   c. by product categories
3. *Compute equivalent unit factors*
   a. based on stacking height, cube, and "footprint"
   b. adjust for "short stacking" provision
   c. select smallest product as base factor (1.000)
4. *Calculate annual equivalent unit volumes*
   a. storage (sum of month end balances + 60% of receipts)
   b handling (inbound receipts)
   c. multiply by equivalent unit factors
5. *Extract equivalent unit rates*
   a. storage rate per month:
      (fixed cost + profit factor) ÷ equivalent units (inventory)
   b. handling rate per month:
      (variable costs + profit factor) ÷ equivalent units (receipts)
6. *Ascertain individual product rates*
   a. equivalent unit rate (step 5) × individual equivalent unit factor (step 3)

alency measurement permits valid comparisons with other items and properly describes the item's "consumption" of the warehouse's total available floor space, because in reality these items are not stored as stand-alones but rather they are stacked in groups (up to 16 pieces together) as described.

Similar equivalency measurements can also be developed for units handled (throughput) by determining the capacity of units or cartons that can be handled by a fork truck for each major product category. Storage and warehouse handling equivalent unit values can be used to quantify and evaluate a variety of productivity-related measurements, including:

- Calculating revenue per product and per square foot
- Calculating facilities costs per square foot
- Compiling direct labor per unit by function
- Compiling handled or processed units per hour, broken down by functions such as unloading, put-away, picking, packing, and loading
- Scheduling direct labor requirements, by product class, based on projected receipts and shipments
- Comparing company-owned facilities' costs and productivity with outside, public warehouse vendors
- Determining profit contributions of company-owned facilities versus using outside public warehouses

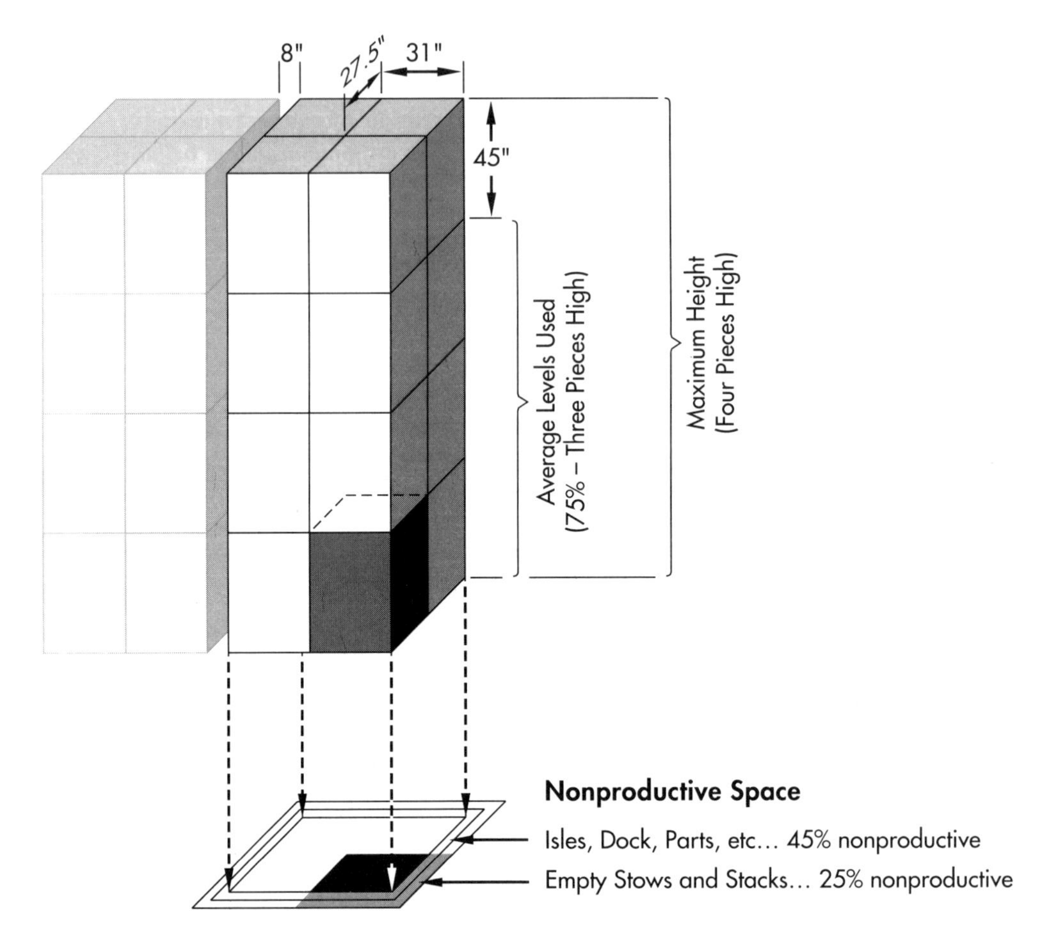

Figure 10-7
Appliance Inventory Storage Configuration

Private Fleet Operations

Private fleet operations need to be measured and evaluated as if they were outside carriers. To achieve meaningful comparisons, the costs and unit outputs (e.g., miles driven and pounds delivered) need to be converted to a basis comparable to those available for common or contract carriers. This can be accomplished by calculating the private fleet operating cost per mile for each trip and then converting to a cost per pound.

Table 10-8 recasts the operating costs of a hypothetical private fleet operation into variable and fixed expense categories. Once this task has been completed, a variable cost per mile is obtained by segregating the total variable cost by the total miles driven during the accounting period involved (e.g., six months). The source for mileage data is trip reports completed by drivers. Fixed costs can be assigned to each trip by dividing the total fixed cost by the total number of trips driven.

Table 10-9 describes how this cost per trip (in this example, $118.07) can be assigned a "cost per mile" value depending on the length of each trip. This is achieved by dividing the trips dri-

TABLE 10-7
Equivalent Unit Square Footage Space Calculation

		Per Piece Equivalent Unit Footprint Calculation:
70	in.	(31 inches width per piece × 2 pieces wide in stack) + 8 inches stack spacing
×55	in.	27.5 inches depth per piece× 2 pieces deep in stack
=3,850	in.²/stack	stack footprint
÷144	in.²/ft.²	conversion to feet
=26.74	ft.²/stack	stack footprint
÷16	pieces/stack	allocation of stack's footprint to individual pieces
=1.67	ft.²/piece	per piece equivalent unit footprint before nonstorage (nonproductive) space adjustments
÷55	%	productive isle, dock, and parts space (100% – 45% nonproductive)
=3.04	ft.²/piece	
÷75	%	productive stows and stack space (100% – 25% nonproductive)
=4.05	ft.²/piece	per piece equivalent unit footprint
		Per Piece Actual Footprint Calculation:
31.0	in.	width
×27.5	in.	depth
= 852.5	in.²/piece	actual footprint for a single item standing alone
÷144	in.²/ft.²	conversion to feet
=5.92	ft.²/piece	actual footprint for a single item standing alone

ven into range categories (e.g., 0–99, 100–299 ... 1700+ miles) and then dividing the fixed cost per trip by the average miles driven in each range category. Thus, a trip in the first mileage range (0–99 miles) averaged 48 miles. Dividing this number into the previously computed fixed cost per trip of $118.07 results in a cost per mile of $2.460, and a total cost per mile rate of $3.191. One advantage of this technique is that short-distance trips are assigned significantly higher costs per mile than long-haul trips. For example, a trip of 1,700 miles or greater results in a cost of $0.790 per mile, less than half the per mile cost of the shortest trip.

One final adjustment is required before valid analyses and comparisons can be achieved. The rates per mile for each mileage range must be adjusted to reflect empty miles driven (i.e., partial trips involving empty trailers). In other words, if a private fleet operated as a common or contract carrier, it would have to recover all its operating costs (both fixed and variable) to achieve targeted profit levels. Therefore, the costs associated with empty miles must be absorbed by paying customers or, in the case of a private fleet, the company itself. The adjustment can be accomplished by dividing the mileage rates previously developed by a fraction equal to one minus the percent of empty miles. Additionally, a similar adjustment can be made to develop customer rates (or intercompany transfer rates) by considering the target profit for the transportation function. An example of these calculations is shown in Table 10-10. Once rates have been established, a private fleet's costs can be compared with those for other modes (this is discussed in the next section, dealing with transportation measurements).

The various routes currently driven by the private fleet should be reviewed to determine any imbalances between outbound and inbound shipments, as well as the premium cost associated with these imbalances. Table 10-11 describes such an analysis with five hypothetical market ar-

TABLE 10-8
Operating Costs
(from company records for the last six months)

Variable Costs	Amount	Fixed Costs	Amount
Wages—Drivers	$79,840	Salaries	$20,770
Wages—Mechanics	25,996	Wages—billing and collection	13,461
Federal payroll tax	8,239	Payroll taxes	2,809
State payroll tax	396	Workers' compensation	2,634
Workers' compensation	8,509	Group insurance	2,184
Group insurance	6,328	Vehicle and driver insurance	59,810
Fuel and oil	52,775	Depreciation—tractors	12,159
Parts and outside repairs	29,983	Depreciation—service eqipment	2,754
Tires	35,949	Depreciation—trailers	43,512
Room and meals	13,076	Office supplies	4,151
Federal fuel tax	13,524	General supplies	2,335
Federal registration and license	19,113	Advertising and promotion	1,657
State fuel tax	17,758	Real estate tax	339
State registration	19,362	Miscellaneous taxes	75
Cargo insurance	3,308	Building insurance	822
Tractor and trailer rental	12,071	Miscellaneous insurance	320
Owner/operator costs	362,214	Utilities	2,850
Miscellaneous supplies	5,225	Communications	410
Claims	1,054	Rent—building	6,415
Communications	7,204	Rent—data processing equipment	4,448
Commissions—freight	17,579	Retirement of equipment	(2,279)
		Dock rental	(750)
		Accounting and legal	1,667
		Loading fees	326
		Interest expense	18,076
Total Variable Cost	$739,503	Total Fixed Cost	$200,955
Miles Driven	1,011,390	Number of Trips	1,702
		Average Fixed Cost per Trip	$118.07
Variable Cost per Mile	$0.731	Average Fixed Cost per Mile	$0.199

eas and the outbound versus inbound trips for each over a three-month sample period. Each trip in this example is a "full" trailer that may contain more than one shipment; "full" trailer implies a standard truckload quantity even if the trailer is not literally full. It is apparent from this analysis that several opportunities exist because of imbalances in the number of trips into and out of the various geographic zones. The total cost incurred by going out or returning empty is itemized in the last column.

If we assume this fleet is located in Detroit, by combining several of these routes into triangular trips, we can eliminate most of the empty miles. For example, 49 empty returns from the

TABLE 10-9
Cost per Mile Calculation:
Private Fleet Operations
(six-month sample)

				Cost Per Mile			
Mileage Range	**Average Miles/Trip**	**Number of Trips**	**Total Miles**	**Variable**	**Fixed**	**Total Loaded**	**Including Empty Miles**
0–99	48	49	2,352	$0.731	$2.460	$3.191	$3.989
100–299	215	329	70,735	0.731	0.549	1.280	1.600
300–499	398	421	167,558	0.731	0.297	1.028	1.285
500–699	594	390	231,660	0.731	0.199	0.930	1.163
700–899	791	223	176,395	0.731	0.149	0.880	1.100
900–1,099	1,000	113	113,000	0.731	0.118	0.849	1.061
1,100–1,299	1,175	68	79,931	0.731	0.100	0.831	1.039
1,300–1,499	1,371	46	63,066	0.731	0.086	0.817	1.021
1,500–1,699	1,490	38	56,620	0.731	0.079	0.810	1.013
1,700 and up	2,003	25	50,075	0.731	0.059	0.790	0.988
Totals	594	1,702	1,011,390	$0.731	$0.199	$0.930	$1.163

Georgia area (zone D) can be redirected to the Kentucky area (zone E). For the redirected portion of the trips, these trailers can replace tonnage currently shipped via common carrier or take on another company's freight under contract (there are savings even if the trailers are redirected and remain empty). Such a redirection eliminates the need to dispatch 49 empty trailers from Detroit to Kentucky. Figure 10-8 shows the original routing as well as a routing scheme that reduces the empty deadheads to just three (to zone E).

Three additional reports should be used routinely to review and measure the overall performance of a private fleet. The first report, shown in Table 10-12, summarizes a fleet's actual expenditures into broad fixed and variable categories and then compares these data with planned (budgeted) numbers. The table also recasts each variable expense category into a cost per mile

TABLE 10-10
Adjusting Cost per Mile to Reflect Empty Miles and Target Profit Levels
(mileage range: overall average)

Adjustment for Empty Miles:	
Cost per mile	
Fixed	$0.199
Variable	0.731
Cost per mile	$0.930
Empty miles %	20.0%
Adjusted cost per mile [cost per mile ÷ (1 – empty mile %)]	$1.163
Adjustment for Profit Factor:	
Target profit % (before income taxes)	10.0%
Rate to customers [adjusted cost per mile ÷ (1 –target profit %)]	$1.292

TABLE 10-11
Geographic Zones with Cover-Off Opportunities
Fleet Center = Detroit, Michigan
(three-month sample)

Geographic Zone			Number of Trips						
Zone Code	**State Area**	**3-digit ZIP Code**	**Inbound from Zone**	**Outbound to Zone**	**Difference**	**Average One-Way Miles**	**Potential Miles**	**Cost per Mile**	**Total Cost**
A	MA, RI,	014–061	34	20	14	950	13,300	$1.15	$15,300
	NH, ME, CT								
B	CT, NY,	064–075	20	63	(43)	780	33,540	1.20	40,250
	North-NJ	100–125							
C	West-PA,	152–166	31	4	27	440	11,880	1.40	16,625
	North-OH	440–446							
D	SC, GA,	292–314	41	90	(49)	860	42,140	1.15	48,450
	East TN	372–379							
E	Central-KY,	400–402	60	6	54	370	19,980	1.40	27,975
	South-IN	461–462							
		471–479							

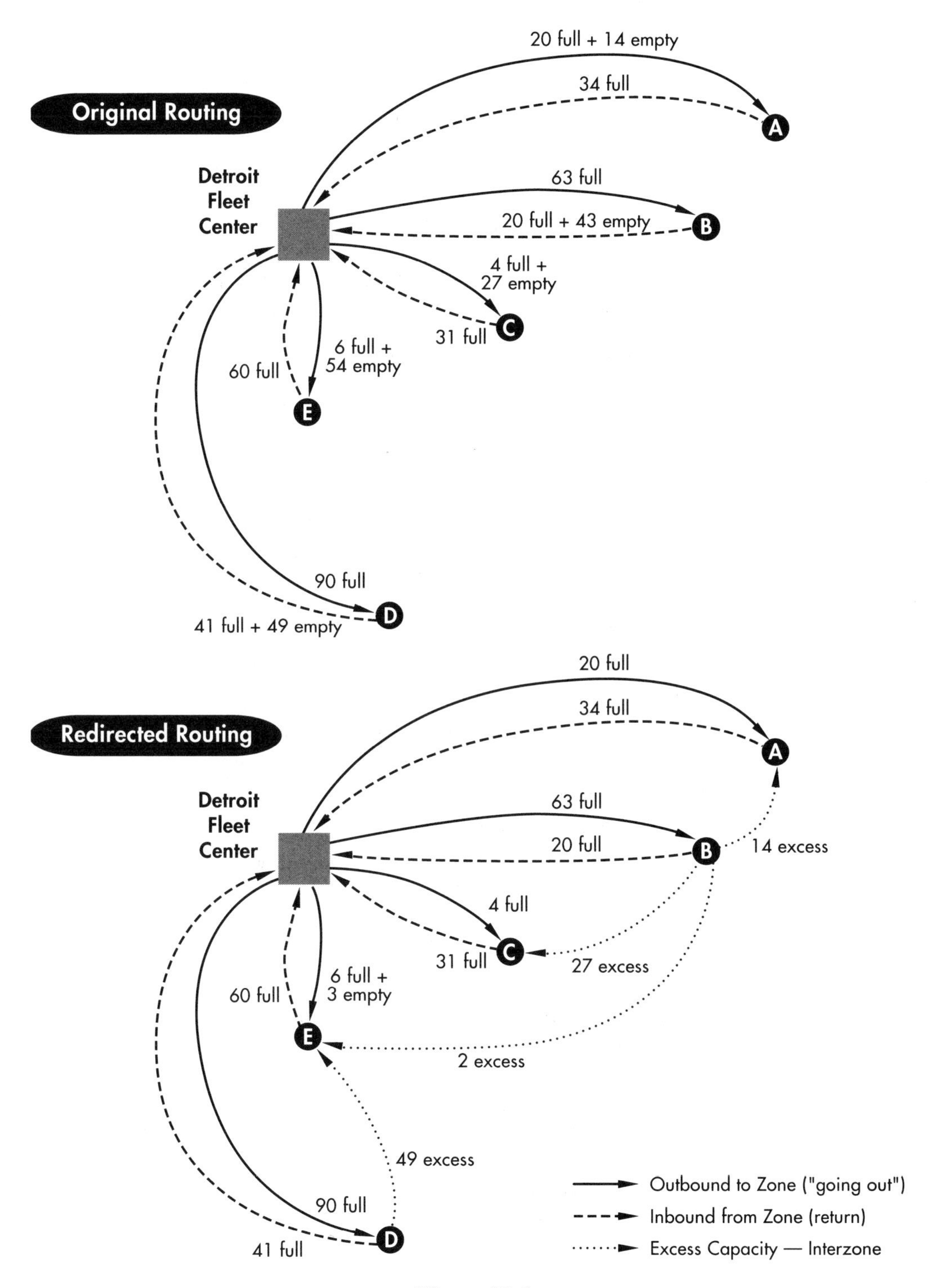

Figure 10-8
Eliminating Empty Trips with Cover-Offs

TABLE 10-12
Private Fleet Expenditures
Budget versus Actual
Total Miles Driven: Plan ______ Actual ______ Variance ______

Expense Categories		**$ Amount**		**$/Mile**		**Variance from Plan**		
		Plan	**Actual**	**Plan**	**Actual**	**$ Fixed**	**Miles**	**$/Mile**
Payroll:								
Drivers wages and benefits								
Management fee and dispatcher	(fixed)							
Layovers and petty cash								
Equipment Costs:								
Leases	(fixed)							
Rentals								
Depreciation	(fixed)							
Equipment Operations:								
Fuel								
Taxes and permits								
Maintenance								
Vehicle and driver insurance								
Administration:								
Payroll (fixed)								
Legal and consulting	(fixed)							
General insurance	(fixed)							
Miscellaneous	(fixed)							
Total								

number for similar comparisons to plan. This report should be created for each month's activity and for year-to-date activity.

The second report, Table 10-13, provides a continuing weekly comparison of key ratios, such as miles driven, gross costs, net costs (after deducting any recoveries from outside, for-hire business), trailer cube utilization percentages, and empty miles. All these measurements should be compared with planned quantities/ratios. This table also demonstrates why it is necessary to measure more than one factor when evaluating the performance of a private fleet operation. Only then can a fleet be professionally managed. Attempting to optimize only one measurement, such as cost per mile, can lead to severe operating deficiencies such as excessive empty miles, excessive driver wages, or poor utilization of trailer capacity.

The third report, shown in Table 10-14, breaks the miles driven category into its several components, such as local cartage, line-haul, outside backhauls, and satellite operations. This detail is necessary to forecast and budget fleet operations accurately, because the cost and potential backhaul revenue will be different for each of these subgroups.

Transportation Activities

Reports prepared by traffic managers frequently find their way into unused files (like wastebaskets!). Typical reports tend to be so voluminous and detailed that they offer top management little help in achieving a major objective: improving the efficiency of the total logistics system. This section describes several reports that logistics managers can use to identify both the ineffective use of transportation services and opportunities to eliminate inefficient channel flows.

TABLE 10-13
Private Fleet Operating Summary

Operational Measure	Week 1	Week 2	Week 3	Week 4
Miles Driven:				
Plan				
Actual				
Variance				
Net Cost:				
Gross:				
Plan				
Actual				
Variance				
Net of Recoveries:				
Plan				
Actual				
Variance				
Cost Per Mile:				
Gross:				
Plan				
Actual				
Variance				
Net:				
Plan				
Actual				
Variance				
Trailer Utilization:				
Planned				
Actual				
Variance				
Empty Miles:				
Planned				
Actual				
Variance				

In performing these analyses, one should provide measurements that can disclose excessive costs or inefficient product flows, such as cost per hundredweight or pound; cost per unit/carton shipped; variances by geographic market area; trailer cube utilization by mode; outbound versus inbound volumes, by origin location; costs per pound or unit by product or product class, mode, and customer or destination area; and consolidation opportunities.

To implement these types of reports, it is necessary to capture more than just freight dollars paid to carriers. Tables 10-3,10-4, and 10-5 list the key variables that should be captured when developing an integrated logistics database. These key data include the weight, number of units/containers (quantity), origin ZIP code or company facility code, destination ZIP code, customer or customer class code, transportation mode and/or carrier, weight of each product/product class involved, customer order number, and type of shipment involved (e.g., customer shipment or stock transfer). All these data fields can be obtained if the carrier's freight bill is matched to the applicable bill of lading. Therefore, when developing a logistics management information system, one of the first tasks is to automate the manifest/bill-of-lading/packing slip documentation and process. This file provides the missing link between customer orders and carrier freight bills. Automating this file permits logistics managers to match and assign transportation charges to customers' orders as well as to individual products, product classes, and geographic market areas. Unless automation is achieved, it is almost impossible to manage the

TABLE 10-14
Private Fleet Miles

Mileage Components	January	February	March	1st Quarter (YTD)
Current Year:				
Local Cartage:				
Plan				
Actual				
Variance				
Line Haul:				
Plan				
Actual				
Variance				
Outside Backhauls:				
Plan				
Actual				
Variance				
Satellite Operations:				
Plan				
Actual				
Variance				
Total Current Year:				
Plan				
Actual				
Variance				
Total Last Year:				
Actual				
Annual Actual Change				

transportation function so that it can maximize its contribution to corporate profitability and efficient channel flows.

In addition to linking freight bills to individual customer orders, several other tasks are required:

- Determining the difference in costs per pound of different size shipments
- Differentiating between "customer" shipments and "stock transfers"
- Deleting obvious errors in paid freight bill files (e.g., excessive cost and weight)
- Creating geographic market areas and/or freight consolidation territories with 3-digit ZIP codes.
- Disaggregating costs into matrixlike combinations of:
  —Shipment type (customers vs. transfers)
  —Company origins
  —Destination areas
  —Shipment size
  —Mode
  —Product/freight class

Once these tasks have been completed, it is possible to prepare a few basic reports that will graphically identify improvement opportunities. The first analysis, shown in Table 10-15, consists of assigning transportation cost data to the various modes. This analysis provides a broad

TABLE 10-15
Customer Freight by Mode

	Mode					
	TL	**LTL**	**TOFC**	**Parcel**	**Air**	**Total**
Current Month's Sales:						$4,450,000
Number of shipments	245	987	1	1,203	3	2,439
Shipped weight (lbs)	5,525,310	1,441,188	22,500	47,714	42	7,036,754
$ Cost	178,256	256,874	555	111,043	67	546,795
Average $/cwt	3.23	17.82	2.47	232.73	159.52	7.77
Average $/shipment	727.58	260.26	555.00	92.31	22.33	224.19
Mode's weight as % of total	78.52	20.48	0.32	0.68	<0.01	100.00
Mode's cost as % of sales	4.01	5.77	0.01	2.50	<0.01	12.29
Year-to-Date Sales:						$49,950,000
Number of shipments	1,197	7,236	5	1,611	43	10,092
Shipped weight (lbs)	19,519,860	6,211,263	122,850	34,399	702	25,889,079
$ cost	1,498,500	2,263,365	3,891	37,137	759	3,803,652
Average $/cwt	7.68	36.44	3.17	107.96	108.12	14.69
Average $/shipment	1,251.88	312.79	778.20	23.05	17.65	376.90
Mode's weight as % of total	75.40	23.99	0.47	0.13	<0.01	100.00
Mode's cost as % of sales	3.00	4.53	0.01	0.07	<0.01	7.61

overview of the percentage that each mode represents of the total tonnage shipped, as well as a comparison of costs per hundred pounds (also known as "hundred weight"—cwt; C = Roman numeral 100 and WT = abbreviation for *weight*) and dollars paid. This information is useful when developing annual budgets and identifying excessive occurrences of premium-priced modes like air freight or underutilization of inexpensive modes like trailer-on-flat-car (TOFC) rail service.

Shipments can also be broken down according to their size (in pounds). Table 10-16 demonstrates how the cost per hundredweight varies by the weight of the shipment and in fact increases exponentially as the weight declines to the very small categories (e.g., 1,000 pounds and less). The table also provides basic insight into consolidation opportunities and the potential savings of increasing LTL volumes from small-size categories to those larger than 10,000 pounds.

A more detailed analysis compares the costs per hundredweight and total weight shipped in various weight categories for each major transportation mode. This report, shown in Table 10-17, compares the costs per hundredweight of common carriers to a private fleet by shipment size. This table clearly reflects the premium cost associated with using private carriage for less-than-truckload shipments: $28.25/cwt versus $17.41/cwt for the smallest shipment size category (0–2,000 lbs). The private fleet disadvantage for the smallest category occurs because the cost to ship product via private carriage is a function of the distance traveled, not the weight of the shipment. This table also identifies that 66% of the weight shipped by common carriers are in shipments of 10,000 pounds or less while the private fleet performs more consolidation, shipping only 10% of its total weight in small loads. Such an analysis is another example of how these types of reports can be used to identify freight consolidation opportunities, especially when the analyses are further detailed by geographical market area.

TABLE 10-16
Average Outbound Shipment by Size
one month of sample data (4.3 weeks)

Shipment Size Category (lbs)	Category Weight (lbs)	Average Weight (lbs)	Total Cost ($)	$/cwt	Number of Shipments	Pounds per Week	Shipments per Week
0–100	13,778	68	7,045	51.13	203	3,204	47
101–500	105,980	268	18,477	17.43	396	24,647	92
501–1,000	140,334	743	14,976	10.67	189	32,636	44
1,001–2,000	246,231	1,558	18,767	7.62	158	57,263	37
2,001–3,000	336,640	2,494	18,453	5.48	135	78,288	31
3,001–4,000	290,830	3,462	14,599	5.02	84	67,635	20
4,001–5,000	351,770	4,690	17,590	5.00	75	81,807	17
Subtotal	1,485,563	1,198	109,907	7.40	1,240	345,480	288
5,001–7,500	592,830	6,049	25,511	4.30	98	137,867	23
7,501–10,000	619,213	9,106	26,317	4.25	68	144,003	16
Subtotal	1,212,043	7,301	51,828	4.28	166	281,870	389
10,001–12,000	515,782	11,213	19,501	3.78	46	119,949	11
12,001–15,000	643,380	13,987	27,220	4.23	46	149,623	11
15,001–20,000	790,577	16,821	29,232	3.70	47	183,855	11
20,001–30,000	1,393,026	24,018	55,068	3.95	58	323,960	13
30,000+	1,909,600	39,783	68,746	3.60	48	444,093	11
Subtotal	5,252,365	21,438	197,767	3.77	245	1,221,480	57
Total	7,949,971	4,815	359,502	4.52	1,651	1,848,830	384

Table 10-18 summarizes the average trailer cube of shipments for the same company. These data were obtained by a manually compiled sample of both inbound and outbound trailers over a six-week period. This analysis is valuable because it collects data normally not available from freight bills. Cube utilization data are vitally important if the products shipped will normally cube out a trailer before the maximum weight, roughly 40,000 pounds, is reached. Table 10-18 confirms what is implied in Table 10-17; that is, a large percentage of shipments either arrive or leave the company's facility in small bundles, failing to utilize capacity available from both carriers and the private fleet. In fact, on average only one-half of this company's total available trailer capacity is used (both private and outside carriers), and 35 percent of the trailers are virtually empty with only one-eighth of the space used.

The final analysis of transportation consists of a validation of the "Rule of 5." This rule of thumb states that when a company employs a decentralized network of regional warehouses and branch facilities to ship its product to customers, five things typically occur (all undesirable!): (1) local volume inflation, (2) local stockouts, (3) increased transshipments, (4) artificial demand shift, and (5) shipment size emphasis shift.

1. *Local Volume Inflation.* First, regional DCs and branch locations will ship large orders (half truckloads or more) to local customers rather than request that the central DC ship truckload quantities to the customer directly. Local truckload shipments inflate volume and justify the existence of possibly unnecessary stocking locations. Table 10-19 shows

TABLE 10-17
Freight Paid
Common Carrier and Private Fleet
three-month sample

Shipment Size Categories by Weight (lbs)	**0–2,000**	**2,001–4,000**	**4,001–6,000**	**6,001–10,000**	**10,001–15,000**	**15,001–20,000**	**20,001–30,000**	**30,001–40,000**	**Total**
Common Carriers:									
Number of shipments	7,816	507	206	158	99	40	54	11	8,891
Category weight (lbs)	3,068,622	1,415,536	996,796	1,236,283	1,246,567	619,200	1,304,132	352,865	10,240,001
% of total weight	30%	14%	10%	12%	12%	6%	13%	3%	100%
Category cost ($)	534,268	153,068	94,044	102,781	105,324	33,233	51,257	10,359	1,084,334
% of total cost	49%	14%	9%	9%	10%	3%	5%	1%	100%
$/cwt	17.41	10.81	9.43	8.31	8.45	5.37	3.93	2.94	10.59
Private Fleet:									
Number of shipments	11	19	16	28	35	37	79	12	237
Category weight (lbs)	9,618	56,269	81,808	218,176	425,023	647,091	1,996,883	387,191	3,822,059
% of total weight	<1%	1%	2%	6%	11%	17%	52%	10%	100%
Category cost ($)	2,717	6,108	9,795	18,709	25,761	27,430	68,437	10,360	169,317
% of total cost	2%	4%	6%	11%	15%	16%	40%	6%	100%
$/cwt	28.25	10.86	11.97	8.58	6.06	4.24	3.43	2.68	4.43

TABLE 10-18
Trailer Cube Utilization
(six-week sample)

	Number of Trailers	Average Cube Utilization (%)	% Fully Loaded	% 1/8 Full
Private Fleet:				
Inbound	1,971	72	56	18
Outbound	1,753	71	58	19
Total Private Fleet	3,724	71	57	18
Outside Carriers:				
Inbound	1,760	33	17	60
Outbound	1,514	39	20	46
Total Outside Carriers	3,274	36	18	54
Total:				
Inbound	3,731	53	38	38
Outbound	3,267	56	40	32
Grand Total	6,998	55	39	35

three regional warehouses making shipments that should be handled directly from the primary stocking location (central DC).

2. *Local Stockouts.* Consequently, stockouts will increase because inventory intended for short lead time, small orders (such as emergency orders or JIT continuous replenishments) has been used unwisely to serve volume orders.
3. *Increased Transshipments.* As a result, transshipment between DCs and branches or between DCs and distant, nonassigned customers will increase to alarming levels. As shown in Table 10-20, when nonassigned customers are served, the negotiated transportation rates from assigned DCs are not utilized and excessive transportation expenditures occur.
4. *Artificial Demand Shift.* Next, demand will be incorrectly logged against the wrong shipping location. This artificial demand shift creates errors in both forecasting regional demand and in DRP replenishment calculations.

TABLE 10-19
Truckload Shipments from Regional Warehouses
(three-month sample)

	Truckload Weight Categories (lbs)						
Regional Warehouses:	10,001–12,500	12,501–15,000	5,001–20,000	20,001–30,000	Sub–Total	% of Total As Truckload	Total of All Shipments
Warehouse A:							
weight (lbs)	146,254	25,360	20,000	0	191,614	36.7%	521,531
# of shipments	14	2	1	0	17	9.4%	180
Warehouse B:							
weight (lbs)	56,482	92,696	80,021	80,280	309,479	52.8%	586,177
# of shipments	7	5	5	3	20	15.5%	129
Warehouse C:							
weight (lbs)	139,084	74,223	254,705	163,192	631,204	50.7%	1,245,740
# of shipments	12	5	15	7	39	17.7%	220

TABLE 10-20
Shipment Data by Origin
Volumes to Nonassigned Market Areas
three-month sample

3-digit ZIP Codes: From 456 Elkhatt, IN to Destination . . .	**Number of Shipments**	**Average Weight (lbs)**	**Realized Rate ($/cwt)**	**Average Actual Cost Paid ($)**	**Assigned DC's Rate ($/cwt)**	**Average Normal Expense ($)**	**Realized Excess Expense ($)**
020 Boston, MA	1	590	18.14	107	9.87	58	49
086 Trenton, NJ	16	795	16.98	135	7.38	59	1,216
148 Elmira, NY	9	45	108.89	49	23.80	11	342
172 Chambersburg, PA	2	80	62,50	50	21.59	17	66
175 Lancaster, PA	11	834	38.73	323	11.69	97	2486
197 Wilmington, DE	4	28	185.71	52	61.71	17	140
327 Orlando, FL	20	300	25.67	77	6.85	21	1,120
350 Cullman, AL	30	28	132.14	37	17.43	5	960
Total	93						6,379

5. *Shipment Size Emphasis Shift.* Finally, factories or central mixing warehouses will shift their emphasis from volume and truckload shipments (stock transfers to branches and direct shipments to large customers) to small, emergency, and LTL shipments to both regional DCs and branches or distant customers. As shown in Table 10-21, a manufacturing plant has shifted its emphasis so that while LTL shipments account for only 25% of the plant's total product weight shipped, they account for 85% of the number of shipments. One might expect a manufacturing plant to ship virtually all its product weight in truckload quantities (assuming that it is not co-located with a warehouse/distribution center)

TABLE 10-21
Shipment Summary
Manufacturing Plant A
three-month sample

Weight Category (lbs)	**Number of Shipments**		**Weight (lbs)**	
0–100	22	10%	1,172	<1%
101–500	78	34	21,029	2
501–1,000	22	10	16,273	1
1,001–2,000	21	9	30,510	2
2,001–3,000	15	7	37,950	3
3,001–4,000	3	1	11,368	1
4,001–5,000	7	3	29,908	2
5,001–7,500	23	10	133,823	11
7,501–10,000	3	1	27,851	2
LTL Subtotal	194	85	309,884	25
TL Subtotal (10,001 +)	35	15	924,480	75
Total	229	100%	1,234,364	100%

and have almost no LTL shipments. The behavior of this plant is more similar to that expected of a local or regional warehouse.

Therefore, managers operating in a decentralized environment must guard against the Rule of 5 phenomenon by diligently monitoring truckload shipments from remote facilities, shipments of all kinds to nonassigned, distant customers, and LTL shipments from manufacturing or central mixing locations.

Inventory Costs

Evaluating inventory should be viewed as one of the most opportunistic, if not the most rewarding, activities available to managers. If one is looking for an immediate payback or profit improvement, inventories should be the first logistics-related activity considered. Unfortunately, too many executives (especially top management) approach this task as if edicts will produce desired results. They believe they can will reductions by issuing broad, sweeping commands, like "cut inventories 10%," "double inventory turns," "split-ship available product and worry about the rest of the order later," or "ship the product from someplace—I don't care, but just ship it."

This type of management does little to solve underlying problems, like inaccurate forecasts, haphazard placement of product in field locations, excessive quantities of obsolete or inactive inventories, and failure to recognize the difference between fast-moving product (class-A items) and slow movers (class-C items). To control and manage inventories, one needs to recognize the following basic rules:

- Inventory turns should be calculated for each SKU, using month-end inventory balances and annual shipment volumes based on units rather than dollars. Using dollars to calculate turns can distort these data because of changes in sales mix dollars, manufacturing and purchasing costs, and markdowns or write-offs that routinely occur during the year.
- Understand the need to use variable versus full manufactured costs and opportunity cost of capital when calculating inventory carrying costs (see Chapter 12).
- Include all variable marketing and logistics costs when calculating the profit contribution of each item or product class (see Chapters 11 and 12.)
- Differentiate fast movers (high volume) from slow movers (low volume) in the analyses.
- Recognize and quantify the impact of inventory turns on inventory carrying costs and profit contribution.

There are a few basic processes that a manager should use to identify inventory-related opportunities. The first is "ABC" analysis, perhaps the single most important technique available for managing inventories. (One should be aware that "ABC" is also used as an acronym for Activity Based Costing, which is *not* the topic being discussed here.)

ABC analysis is attributed to Vilfredo Pareto, a nineteenth-century Renaissance man. Pareto, educated as an engineer and renowned as an economist, sociologist, and political scientist, noted that many situations were dominated by a relatively few vital elements, and that the relative characteristics of members of a population were *not* uniform. He surmised that controlling the relatively few elements would go a long way toward controlling the overall situation. Another way of stating this principle is that a small percentage of a group accounts for the largest fraction of its impact or value. The principle is also known as the "80–20 rule," which generally states that 80% of a population's characteristic is displayed by only 20% of its members. For example, 80%

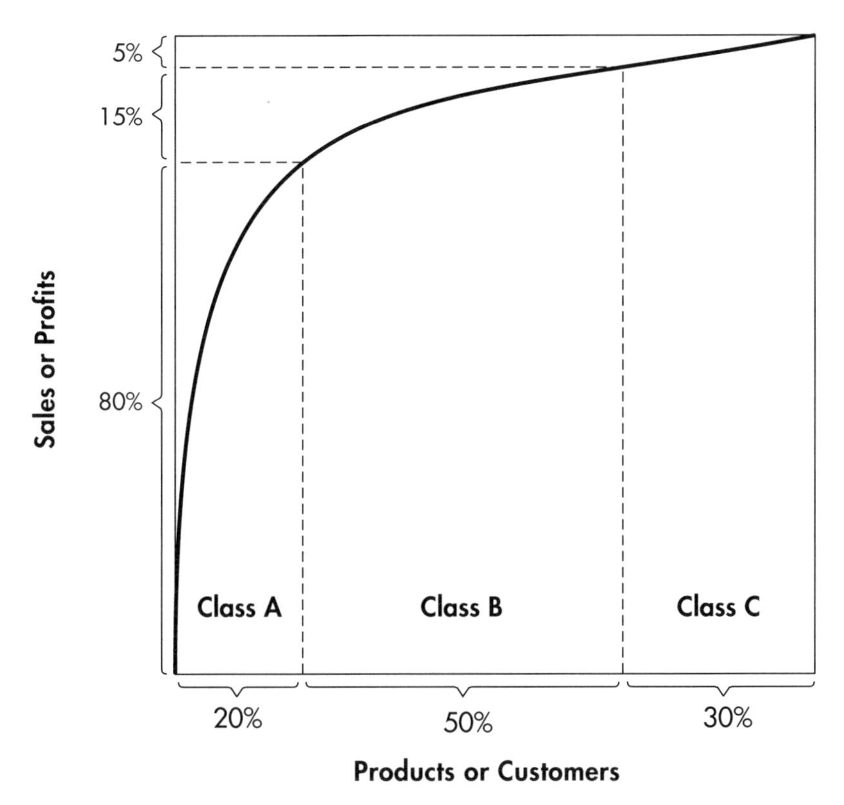

Figure 10-9
The "Pareto Principle" or "80–20 Rule"

of a company's sales revenue is typically derived from only 20% of its customer base. Figure 10-9 shows this relationship graphically.

ABC classification is the stratification of items in decreasing order of annual dollar volume or other criteria (e.g., dollar value of inventory, total unit sales, dollar sales of products/product lines, dollar sales to customers/customer groups). This array is then normally split into three classes, called A, B, and C, to which managers apply different levels of control and attentiveness. Identification of both extremes concerning the vital few and the trivial many is typically achieved by categorizing groups as follows:

- A—Top 80% of the sample's total value
- B— Next 15% of total value
- C— Bottom 5% of total value

Class A contains the items with the highest annual dollar volume, which should receive the most attention, such as (1) frequent forecast review and evaluation, (2) frequent cycle counting with tight accuracy tolerances, (3) on-line updates of balances, (4) frequent review of reorder quantities and safety stock calculations, and (5) close follow-up and expediting of replenishments to reduce or minimize lead times. The next grouping, class B, receives controls similar to

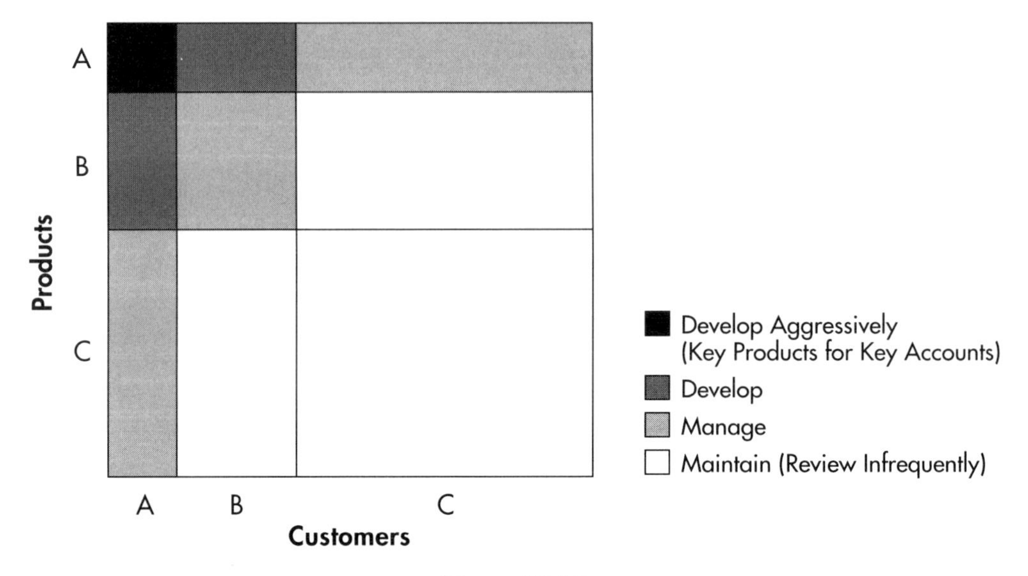

Figure 10-10
Customer Service and the 80–20 Rule

those for class A but with less stringent and less frequent attention. Class C, which contains the low dollar volume items, is controlled routinely or sporadically. Class C is sometimes identified as simply the second half of the declining annual dollar volume (or other criteria) list. The basic rule for class-C items is simply to have them available. Thus, order quantities will be larger and less frequent. Simple rules of thumb such as two-bin systems or maintain 60 days of stock can be used, because the demand for class-C items is relatively small and infrequent. The underlying principle is that effort saved through relaxed controls on low-value items can be applied to improved control of high-value items (see Chapter 16, which explains in more detail how to perform ABC classification.) Customers can also be stratified with ABC classification to facilitate marketing activities like targeting an increase of purchases of medium-volume buyers (class-B customers) or enhancing the loyalty of high-volume buyers (class-A customers). Differential service based on both product class and customer class is visually described in Figure 10-10.

Another technique that can be used to reduce inventories without adversely affecting customer service levels consists of computing the profitability of individual SKUs and product lines. This can be accomplished by using contribution analysis. When contribution analyses are combined with ABC analyses, managers can show dramatic results to top management by quantifying the impact of slow-moving, obsolete, and inactive products on profitability.

The next three tables chart the effect of turnovers on overall inventory investment and profitability. Table 10-22 shows that the company involved in this analysis could reduce inventories by $2.9 million and associated inventory carrying costs by $700,000 if it could increase turns one time, to 5.5. Doubling turns to 8.5 from the current 4.4 would cut inventories in half, to $7.5 million, and reduce carrying costs by $1.7 million a year. On the other hand, if turns actually decrease one time to 3.5, inventory investment would increase by $4.4 million and carrying costs by $900,000. This table demonstrates that the effect of increasing turns is exponential; that is,

TABLE 10–22
Potential Inventory Savings

Scenarios	Annual Unit Volume	Inventory Turns	Average Units of Inventory	Inventory Value at Variable Manufacturing Cost	25% Carrying Cost	Variance from Current	
						Inventory Investment	Carrying Cost
Current	501,044	4.4	114,626	$14,011,400	$3,502,800		
What-if:							
+1 Turn	501,044	5.5	91,099	11,135,500	2,783,900	$2,875,900	$718,900
+2 Turns	501,044	6.5	77,084	9,422,400	2,355,600	4,589,000	1,147,200
+3 Turns	501,044	7.5	66,806	8,166,100	2,041,500	5,845,300	1,461,300
+4 Turns	501,044	8.5	58,946	7,205,400	1,801,300	6,806,000	1,701,500
+5 Turns	501,044	9.5	52,741	6,446,900	1,611,700	7,564,500	1,891,100
−1 Turn	501,044	3.5	143,155	17,498,700	4,374,700	(3,487,300)	(871,900)

inventory levels go down as turns go up, but at a declining rate, and begin to flatten out around 8 to 10 turns.

Table 10-23 classifies inventories and associated contribution by ABC inventory category. It clearly reflects a decline in both inventory turns and profitability percentages as one moves from A to B to C categories.

The final analysis, Table 10-24, examines two product groups and distinguishes slow-moving (class-C items) from the total product line. The table shows that slow movers in product group Z are negative contributors. Both product groups show a dramatic drop in the net contribution percentages for slow movers as compared with all items. Finally, the table confirms that slow movers represent a disproportionately large percentage of inventory investment, especially considering their volume, sales, and contribution percentages.

Once these relationships are understood, managers can use these analyses to identify the specific SKUs causing subpar profitability as well as to identify and track inactive and obsolete inventories.

A few basic definitions enable one to track slow or excess inventories. For example, Table 10-25 contains a sample of products for a manufacturer of heating and cooling products. In this case, "excess inventories" were defined as balances in excess of the next six months' marketing forecast (a compromise criterion that satisfied both financial and marketing personnel). This report not only identifies investments in excess inventories and associated carrying costs but also quantifies the warehouse square footage used by these excess balances (i.e., underutilized space).

The report in Table 10-26 can be used to identify obsolete inventory. In this example, "obsolete" refers to those products where production has been discontinued for at least six months while sales levels have significantly declined. The table tracks inventory balances, inventory turns, and monthly carrying costs (monthly obsolescence costs). Although not shown on the table, an item's monthly obsolescence cost should be accumulated over time.

Once the various analyses described in this section have been implemented, managers can intelligently develop specific strategies to improve profitability, increase turnover, and reduce inventory investment. The various alternatives are depicted in Figure 10-11. The earns-turns matrix is a method of assigning items, categories, or whole departments to one of four quadrants in a profitability matrix. Plotting individual SKUs on this matrix graphically separates the strong

TABLE 10-23
Inventory Contribution
Overview by ABC

	Class-A Items	Class-B Items	Class-C Items
Overall Activity:			
Number of SKUs	204	178	765
Annual units shipped	410,447	67,127	23,124
Average units of inventory	68,778	24,086	21,695
Average inventory value	$16,318,268	$5,991,874	$4,524,926
Inventory turns	5.97	2.79	1.07
Manufacturing Contribution ($/unit):			
Average sales price	$415.57	$420.63	$343.77
Variable manufacturing cost	237.26	248.77	208.57
Manufacturing contribution	$178.31	$171.86	$135.20
Variable Marketing and Distribution Cost ($/unit):			
Sales commission	2.28	2.72	3.17
Transportation	26.12	25.73	21.97
Inventory carrying cost	9.72	22.29	30.86
Net Contribution ($/unit)	$140.19	$121.12	$79.20
Performance Ratios:			
Manufacturing contribution : sales	43%	41%	39%
Net contribution : sales	34%	29%	23%

Note: Average inventory value based on variable manufacturing cost.

items from the weak. The matrix also assists managers in developing specific options based on these two parameters. For example, the weakest category (losers—low turns and low profitability) can be outsourced, eliminated, marked down for clearance, centralized into one location, or made to order.

Customer Service

Once all relevant logistics inputs (costs) have been compiled, reported, and analyzed, the output of the logistics operating system (customer service) can be measured using an integrated database as described in the first section of this chapter. This process is necessary to accurately evaluate the trade-offs involved in setting service levels to customers, such as order cycle times (lead times) or higher fill rates (in-stock availability).

It is imperative that the costs or savings associated with any revisions in service levels, such as transportation, warehousing and inventory carrying costs, be identified and attached to these potential changes. Remember, the primary task of logistics planners must always be to conceptualize and construct a distribution system that will minimize costs, *given* the customer service package that meets customer expectations/standards and/or achieves a differential, competitive advantage in key areas. Customers typically consider six logistics-oriented attributes when evaluating service levels from vendors/suppliers:

TABLE 10-24
Product Profitability
class-C items compared with all items

Comparative Data:	Product Group X			Product Group Z		
	Class C (≤4 turns)		**All Items**	**Class C (≤1 turn)**		**All Items**
Number of items	135	40%	340	64	36%	180
Annual volume (units)	7,422	5%	148,527	2,214	19%	11,810
Average inventory (units)	12,370	33%	37,132	5,032	51%	9,842
Inventory turns	0.6		4.0	0.4		1.2
Average inventory value ($000)	3,134	30%	10,325	1,716	43%	3,997
Annual sales ($000)	3,021	4%	68,315	1,165	15%	7,859
Annual net contribution ($000)	149	1%	19,947	(90)	(5%)	1,705
Annual net contribution as percent of annual sales	5%		29%	(8%)		22%
Per Unit Detail:						
Sales price ($/unit)	406.98		459.95	526.28		665.49
Variable manufacturing cost ($/unit)	253.35		278.05	341.02		406.07
Manufacturing contribution ($/unit)	153.63		181.90	185.26		259.42
Net contribution ($/unit)	20.14		134.30	(40.52)		144.37

Note: Average inventory value based on variable manufacturing cost.

1. Ability to meet promised delivery dates
2. Consistent, on-time delivery
3. Length of the promised order cycle (lead time)
4. Variability in actual order cycle times
5. Percentage of an order delivered on time
6. Order completeness (percent of the order eventually delivered)

The consideration of these six attributes involves three basic calculations: (1) order cycle/lead times, (2) fill-rate percentages, and (3) early/late deliveries. These measurements should also be further delineated whenever possible, as shown in Table 10-27.

The source for all these calculations is the order history data downloaded from the order processing system into the integrated logistics database. The collection and accumulation of the data, described previously in Figure 10-6, are extremely important because these data are the primary source of information for several key decisions: computing customer service levels; assigning transportation costs to products, customers, channels of distribution, and business units; and compiling customer profitability (contribution) reports.

It is important, therefore, to perform certain key data transformations during the analytical process. Order dates (e.g., 11-20-95) need to be converted to a composite, sequential numbering system, so that order cycle times can be efficiently calculated. "Current" orders (those that contain no requested ship date, or whose requested ship dates are equal to or less than the company's standard cycle time) should be separated from advance, or future, orders (those whose requested ship dates exceed the company's stated standard). All measurements should be based on the quantity (units, cartons, containers, etc.) ordered per individual order line. Calculations

TABLE 10-25
Slow/Excess Inventory

Item Code	Ending Inventory (units)	Demand Forecast (units)	Excess Inventory (units)	Variable Manufacturing Cost ($/unit)	Handling Cost ($/unit)	Excess Cost per Month	Warehouse Space Utilization		Months of Supply
							Current Square Footage	Excess Square Footage	
A	528	325	203	$269	$5.60	$1,137	137	53	9.7
B	1,525	225	1,300	300	6.25	8,125	394	336	40.7
C	502	175	327	355	7.40	2,420	282	183	17.2
D	333	175	158	450	9.38	1,482	187	89	11.4
Total	2,888	900	1,988			$13,164	1,000	661	

Notes: Ending inventory is the previous month's last on-hand balance.
Demand forecast is for the next 6 months.
Excess units = ending inventory – demand forecast.
Monthly holding cost = (variable manufacturing cost × 25%) ÷ 12 months.
Months of supply = ending inventory ÷ (demand forecast ÷ 6 months).
Months of supply is the estimated number of months to liquidate existing inventory based on current sales levels.
Inventory turnover (not shown) = 12 months ÷ months of supply.

TABLE 10-26
Obsolete Inventory and Holding Costs

Item Code	Units Shipped	Average Inventory (units)	Inventory Turnover	Ending Inventory (units)	Unit Standard Cost	Inventory Value	Unit Holding Cost	Monthly Obsolescence Cost	Months Obsolete
M	140	126	1.11	1	$257	$257	$5.35	$5.35	7
N	82	72	1.14	8	267	2,136	5.56	44.48	8
O	2	14	0.14	13	306	3,978	6.38	82.94	8
P	1	35	0.03	34	319	10,846	6.65	226.10	3
Q	21	18	1.17	1	275	275	5.73	5.73	2
Total	246			57		$17,492		364.60	

Notes: Units shipped is the shipment history for the previous 12 months.
Ending inventory is the previous month's last on-hand balance.
Average inventory is the average on-hand balance for the previous 12 months.
Inventory turns = units shipped in last 12 months ÷ average inventory.
Monthly holding cost = (unit standard cost × 25%) ÷ 12 months.
Monthly obsolescence cost = ending inventory × unit holding cost.

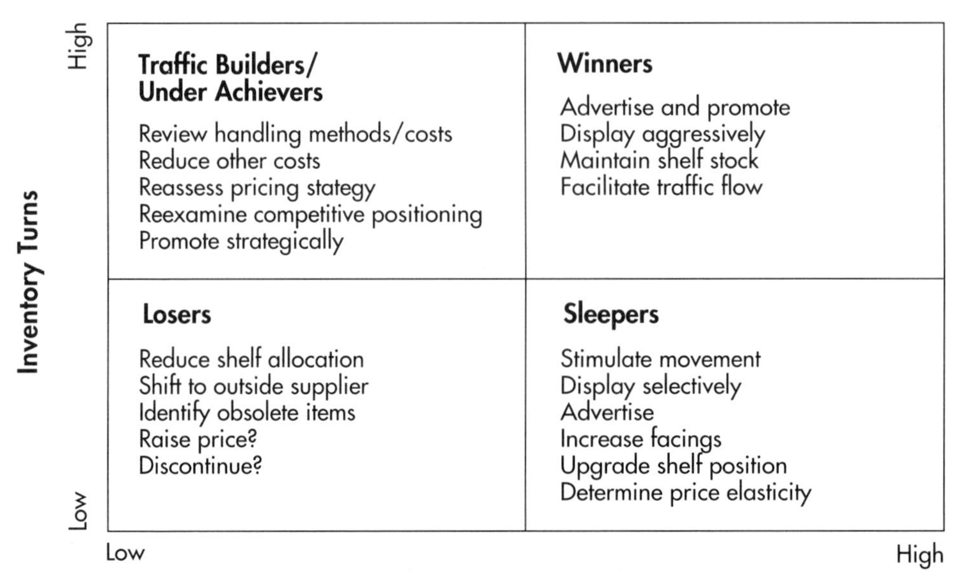

Figure 10-11
Earn-Turns Matrix Analysis
Quadrants and Alternative Strategies

Source: Adapted from Kathy Boyle, *Direct Product Profit—A Primer* (Washington, D.C.: Food Marketing Institute, 1987), p. 10. Used with permission.

of averages should be weighted by the quantity ordered, so that the performance on a small order (e.g., one carton) does not receive the same weight as the performance on a large order quantity, such as a full truckload of one item.

Finally, the median value (the middle number or average of two middle numbers in a given ascending sequence) should also be calculated when evaluating order cycle times, because the distribution of orders across the range of order cycle times tends to be skewed toward the right (in excess) of the average (mean). The mean value will always exceed the median because of the existence of a few extremely long order cycle times.

Many types and variations of reports can be used to measure customer service performance; the following five tables provide such examples. Table 10-28 is an overview of service levels for a manufacturer of electronic controls sold to distributors (trade accounts) and to original equipment manufacturers (OEM accounts). This company accepts two kinds of orders: (1) those shipped from on-hand inventories (designated as A-models), and (2) those manufactured to order (designated as B-models). The standard lead times for these two types of orders are two and four weeks, respectively. The overview in Table 10-28 clearly indicates substandard performance across both customer groups, as well as order types. Order cycle times far exceed standards, as well as the percent of product shipped on time (i.e., the initial shipment).

To discover the reasons for these poor service levels, one needs to slice the data into additional components, such as the order cycle analysis for A-models sold to trade customers described in Table 10-29. This table shows that 9 days of the average 16.5-day lead time are consumed by waiting for sufficient product even though these orders represent stock items that

TABLE 10-27
Customer Service Performance Ratios

Measurement Category/Ratio	Description
1. Order Cycle/Lead times	*Length of time between initiation and completion of an activity*
• Order cycle by component	
—Customer to receipt	
—Receipt to back order reservation	
—Reserve to DC shipping point	
—DC to pick/pack	
—Load to ship	
—Received by customer	
2. Fill-Rate Percentages	*Measures of the company's performance in supplying the products and quantities customers request*
• Stock availability	Percent of open orders covered by on-hand inventory at month end
• Dollar fill	Dollar value of orders filled as percent of total dollar value ordered
• Order completeness	Percent of items ordered versus percent of items shipped (without regard to the number of shipments required)
• Line item fill	Percent of items ordered versus shipped on:
	—1st shipment
	—2nd shipment
	—3rd shipment
	—Final shipment
3. Early/Late Deliveries	*Actual performance versus the company's standard or the customer's date requested, whichever is the greater*
• Timeliness	Days shipped early/late on:
	—lst shipment
	—2nd shipment
	—3rd shipment
	—Final shipment
• Late Deliveries	Percent of orders shipped after date customer had requested
• Early deliveries	Percent of orders shipped before date customer had requested
4. Other Measures	
• Orders above minimum : total orders	
• Orders canceled : total orders	
• Customer complaints : total orders	
• Errors : total orders	Percent of total orders with certain types of errors such as:
	—billing errors
	—shipping errors

TABLE 10-28
Customer Service Overview
five-week sample

	Promised Lead Time (days)	Actual Order Cycle (days)	Customer Request vs. Ship Date (days)	Fill Rate		Shipments	
				All Shipments	First Shipment Only	Lines on First Shipment	Average Number per Line
Trade							
A-models	14.7	16.5	+13.1	99%	71%	71%	1.7
B-models	25.2	28.7	+26.2	94%	36%	36%	2.8
OEM							
A-models	29.0	32.4	+11.1	97%	64%	65%	1.8
B-models	53.5	54.2	+11.9	81%	37%	41%	3.4

Notes: A-Models are inventoried products with a standard lead time of two weeks.
B-Models are built-to-order products with a standard lead time of four weeks.

should have been in inventory. This analysis also illustrates the effect of the excessive order cycle times of a few orders (up to 161 days) on the overall average cycle time (16.5 days). In this situation, the median value of 9.5 days is probably a better representation of what customers experience and expect.

Table 10-30 spreads the order cycle times for all four customer and order type categories across weekly increments. The table demonstrates the variation across the different customer/order type combinations, as well as both the range and extent of excessive lead times. It is particularly disturbing to see that the performance on made-to-order products (B-models) is significantly lower than that for orders of in-stock products (A-models). Such performance naturally displeases customers. If customers allow vendors longer lead times on orders to be shipped from future production, they reasonably and rightfully expect on-time delivery and high fill rates because the vendor has known about the need for the product and has had ample time to plan and produce it.

From a customer's perspective this failure to perform on time is shown clearly in Table 10-31. This analysis compares actual delivery times with promised ship dates. The table clearly identifies the extent of late deliveries, particularly on orders of A-models for both trade and OEM accounts.

Two final calculations need to be reported to logistics and marketing managers: (1) order fill rate percentages, and (2) service of supply measurements. Table 10-32 describes fill-rate per-

TABLE 10-29
Internal Order Cycle Time
A-models to trade customers
(all measurements in days)

	Average	Standard Deviation	Range	Median	Mode
Received to accumulate	9.1	19.9	1–113	1.3	1
Accumulate to release	4.0	4.9	1–42	2.5	1
Release to ship	5.5	1.6	2–9	5.9	7
Total Cycle	16.5	19.0	2–161	9.5	9

TABLE 10-30
Comparative Analysis:
Internal Order Cycle Time

	Trade Customers (%)		OEM Customers (%)	
Cycle Time (weeks)	**A-Models**	**B-Models**	**A-Models**	**B-Models**
1	27.4	9.9	14.9	5.0
2	40.6	25.2	20.1	5.5
3	8.6	10.8	12.6	3.3
4	5.2	9.9	12.1	3.6
5	4.4	13.5	9.0	6.9
6	6.5	10.8	6.9	14.9
7	0.8	5.4	2.9	11.6
8–9	0.7	4.5	4.9	13.2
10–11	0.6	0.9	4.1	11.8
12–14	1.0	1.8	4.6	14.3
15–17	0.5	0.9	2.9	3.3
18 +	3.7	6.4	5.0	6.6
Total Lines Shipped	100.0	100.0	100.0	100.0

formance for a manufacturer of heating and cooling products. It calculates the percent of orders shipped versus ordered, according to the order type and by the order size (measured as lines per order). Fill-rate percentages are provided based on both the number of orders received and their dollar value. These latter two calculations demonstrate the differences between a calculation based on order volume and one based on dollar value. For example, on advance/future orders the fill rate is 55% based on the number of orders, but it is 87% based on the dollar value of orders. This table also identifies lower performance on the dollar fill of large regular orders (11 lines per order and greater) compared with small regular orders (10 and fewer lines per order). The dollar fill measures are 79% for large orders and 90% for small orders, while the proportional value of the total regular orders placed are 47% and 53%, respectively. (These last calcu-

TABLE 10-31
Comparative Analysis:
Date Promised vs. Date Shipped

	Trade Customers (%)		OEM Customers (%)	
Cycle Time (weeks)	**A-Models**	**B-Models**	**A-Models**	**B-Models**
2 weeks plus early	6.5	10.6	11.0	19.0
0 to 2 weeks early	25.1	27.9	30.3	32.1
1 week late	45.0	31.7	33.4	26.8
2 weeks late	21.4	4.8	24.0	9.7
3 to 4 weeks late	1.9	24.0	1.0	11.2
5 weeks plus late	0.1	1.0	0.3	1.2
Total Lines Shipped	100.0	100.0	100.0	100.0

TABLE 10-32
Order-Fill Performance

		Number of Orders			Dollar Value of Orders		
Order Type	**Lines per Order**	**Placed**	**Shipped**	**Fill Rate (%)**	**Placed ($)**	**Shipped ($)**	**Fill Rate (%)**
Advance/Future	1–3	1	0	0	6,196	6,196	100
	4–10	12	3	25	424,508	329,523	78
	11–20	10	8	80	538,621	482,878	90
	21–30	5	4	80	280,790	269,434	96
	31 +	1	1	100	73,382	67,689	92
	Total	29	16	55	1,323,497	1,155,720	87
Priority	1–3	14	13	93	7,242	6,596	91
	4–10	1	1	100	271	271	100
	Total	15	14	93	7,513	6,867	91
Regular	1–3	78	65	83%	112,761	101,327	90
	4–10	14	6	43	165,707	149,625	90
	11–20	4	2	50	103,151	74,901	73
	21–30	2	2	100	107,800	83,468	77
	31 +	1	1	100	37,525	37,525	100
	Total	99	76	77	526,944	446,846	85
Grand Total		143	106	74	1,857,954	1,609,433	87

lations are not readily shown in the table; the regular orders must first be regrouped into large and small categories.)

The final measurement that is useful when evaluating customer service performance represents service of supply, shown in Table 10-33. Service of supply should be calculated at the end of each month by comparing open back orders and orders due out during the coming month to the month-end on-hand inventory balance. Table 10-33 segregates this measurement into five sub components: (1) assigned ship-from point (warehouse A); (2) business unit (residential products); (3) product family (Fl, F2, F3); (4) stock and nonstock (made-to-order) products; and (5) ABC inventory classification. Thus, the managers responsible for forecasting, production planning/scheduling, and inventory deployment can identify critical deficiencies and request the responsible parties to take corrective action.

Summary

This chapter described how to build an integrated database to measure and evaluate logistics operating systems. It also developed and described various types of management reports that can be used to analyze the costs or profit contributions of each functional component of a logistics organization—warehousing, private fleet operations, transportation administration, and inventory management. Finally, it defined the output of the logistics system—customer service—and illustrated how the various components of customer service such as order cycle time, on-time delivery, and fill rates can be measured and reported to management.

TABLE 10-33
Service of Supply
ship-from location: warehouse A
business unit: residential products

	Stock Items			Nonstock Items			All Items
Family/ Class	**Number of SKUs**	**Available SKUs**	**Availability (%)**	**Number of SKUs**	**Available SKUs**	**Availability (%)**	**Availability (%)**
F1-A	30	23	77	15	15	100	84
F1-B	25	22	88	2	1	50	85
F1-C	62	60	97	33	32	97	97
Family 1	117	105	90	50	48	96	92
F2-A	68	62	91	0	0	n/a	91
F2-B	107	75	70	0	0	n/a	70
F2-C	231	222	96	29	29	100	97
Family 2	406	359	88	29	29	100	89
F3-A	209	161	77	3	0	0	76
F3-B	1,752	1,422	81	88	88	100	82
F3-C	1,725	1,574	91	125	105	84	91
Family 3	3,686	3,157	86	216	193	89	86

When designing a performance measurement system it is extremely important to understand that:

- Different customer groups and product groups exist.
- These different customer and product groups require different service levels.
- Small shipments—*not* small orders—contribute greatly to a company's LTL transportation problems.
- Variability in order cycle time and split shipments are expensive to both vendors/suppliers and customers.
- Order cycle time is often viewed differently by manufacturers and customers.
- The 80–20 rule applies to both customers and product lines.
- Costs should be reduced only if they do *not* result in substandard service levels.
- Performance should be measured not only within but also across functions, with a cross-functional or process perspective.

Notes

1. This material is adapted from material to be used in a forthcoming text. All rights reserved by the author.
2. Michael E. Porter, *Competitive Advantage* (New York: Free Press, 1985), chap. 2.
3. Frank H. Mossman, W. J. E. Crissy, and Paul M. Fischer, *Financial Dimensions of Marketing Management* (New York: Wiley, 1978), chap. 3.

4. Robin Cooper and Robert S. Kaplan, "How Cost Accounting Distorts Product Costs," *Management Accounting* (April 1988): 20–27.
5. Ibid.
6. Mossman et al., *Financial Dimensions of Marketing Management,* chap. 3.
7. Michael A. Kole, "Controlling Costs with a Database System," *Management Accounting* (June 1988): 31–35.
8. Ibid.

CHAPTER 11

Integrating Logistics Strategy in the Corporate Financial Plan

Martin Christopher

After a century or more of reliance on traditional cost accounting procedures to provide an often unreliable insight into profitability, managers are now starting to question the relevance of these methods.[1] The accounting frameworks still used by most companies today rely on arbitrary methods for allocating shared and indirect costs and hence frequently distort the true profitability of both products and customers. Indeed, these traditional accounting methods seldom allow accurate analysis of the profitability of customers and markets because they were originally devised to measure product costs.

Because logistics management is a flow-oriented concept aimed at integrating resources across a pipeline extending from suppliers to final customers, companies need a way to assess costs and performance of that pipeline flow.

The adoption of an integrated approach to logistics and distribution management has proved difficult because firms lack appropriate cost information. The need to manage the *total* distribution activity, the combined effects of decisions among many separate cost activities, has implications for the cost accounting systems of the whole company. Typically, conventional accounting systems group costs into broad, aggregated categories that prevent the more detailed analysis necessary to identify the true costs of serving customers with particular product mixes. Without the ability to analyze aggregated cost data, it becomes impossible to identify potential cost trade-offs within the logistics system.

Generally, the effects of trade-offs are assessed in two ways: their impact on total costs and on sales revenue. For example, it may be possible to trade off costs in such a way that total costs increase, yet because of the better service now being offered, sales revenue also increases. If the difference between revenue and costs is greater than before, the trade-off may be regarded as leading to improved cost-effectiveness. However, without a logistics-oriented cost accounting system, it is extremely difficult to identify the extent to which a particular trade-off is cost-effective.

The Concept of Total Cost Analysis

Many problems at the operational level in logistics management arise because not all impacts of specific decisions, both direct and indirect, throughout the corporate system are taken into account.

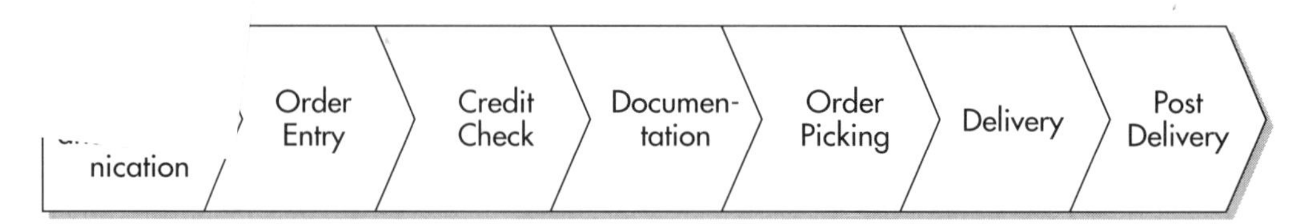

Figure 11-1
Cost Elements:
Order Processing Cycle

Too often decisions taken in one area can lead to unforeseen results in other areas. Changes in policy on minimum order value, for example, may influence customer ordering patterns and lead to additional costs. Similarly, changes in production schedules that aim to improve production efficiency may lead to fluctuations in finished stock availability and thus affect customer service.

The problems associated with identifying the total system impact of distribution policies are immense. By its very nature, logistics cuts across traditional functions and has cost impacts on most of those functions. Conventional accounting systems do not usually assist in the identification of these companywide impacts; they frequently absorb logistics-related costs in other cost elements. The cost of processing orders, for example, is an amalgam of specific costs incurred in different functional areas of the business that generally prove extremely difficult to bring together. Figure 11-1 outlines the various cost elements involved in the complete order processing cycle; each of these elements will have a fixed and variable cost component that will lead to a different total cost per order.

Accounting practice for budgeting and standard setting has tended to result in a compartmentalization of company accounts; thus budgets tend to be set on a functional basis. The trouble is that policy costs do not usually confine themselves within the same watertight boundaries. It is the nature of logistics that, like a stone thrown into a pond, the effects of policies spread beyond their immediate area of impact.

A further feature of logistics decisions that contributes to the complexity of generating appropriate cost information is that they are usually made in the context of an existing system. The purpose of total cost analysis in this context is to identify the change in costs brought about by these decisions. The cost must therefore be viewed in incremental terms—the change in total costs caused by the change to the system. Thus, the addition of an extra warehouse to the distribution network will bring about cost changes in transport, inventory investment, and communications (e.g., order processing). The *incremental cost difference* is the relevant accounting information for decision making in this case. Figure 11-2 shows how total logistics costs can be influenced by the addition, or removal, of a distribution center (DC) from the system.

It can be seen therefore that the logistics cost accounting problem is substantial and yet must be solved to realize the full potential of improved logistics management.

Principles of Logistics Costing

The problem of developing an appropriate logistics-oriented costing system is primarily one of focusing on the output of the distribution system (in essence, the provision of customer service)

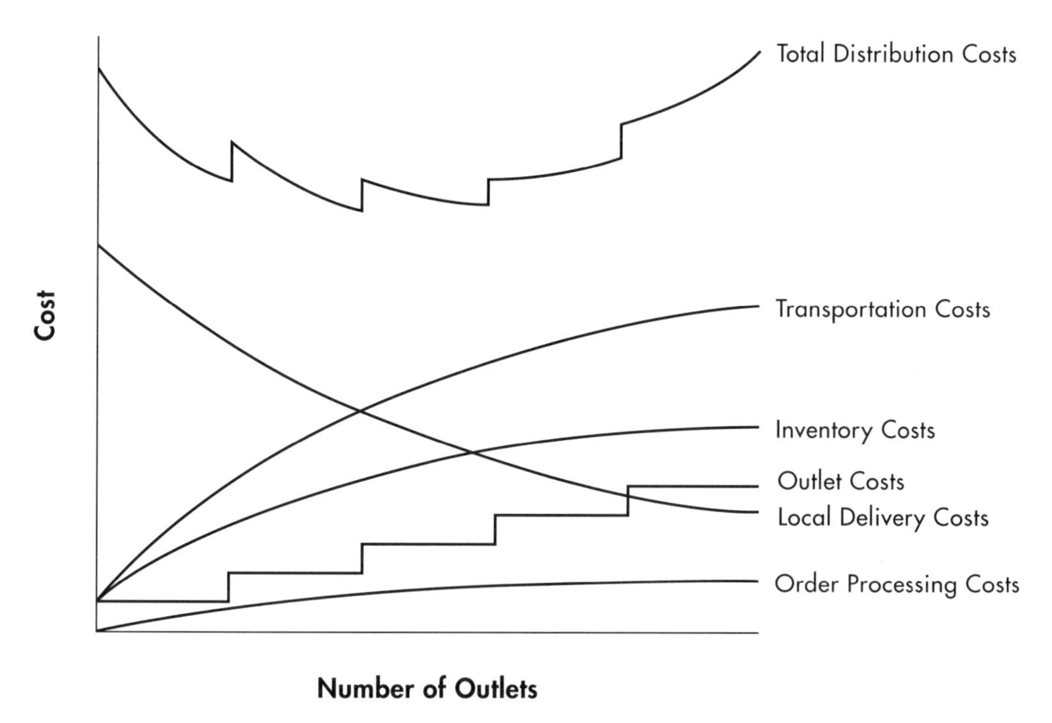

Figure 11-2
Total Costs of a Distribution Network

and identifying the unique costs associated with that output. Traditional accounting methods lack this focus, mainly because they were designed with something else in mind.

One of the basic principles of logistics costing, it has been argued, is that the system should mirror the material flow by identifying the costs that result from serving customers in the marketplace. A second principle is that it should be capable of analyzing costs and revenues by customer type and by market segment or distribution channel. This latter requirement emerges because of the dangers inherent in dealing solely with averages (e.g., the average cost per delivery), because they often conceal substantial variations on either side of the mean.

To operationalize these principles requires an output orientation to costing. In other words, we must first define the desired outputs of the logistics system and then seek to identify the costs associated with providing them. A useful concept here is the idea of mission. In the context of logistics, a mission is a set of customer service goals to be achieved by the system within a specific product/market context. Missions can be defined by type of market served, by products, and by service and cost constraints. A mission by its very nature cuts across traditional functional lines. Figure 11-3 illustrates the concept and demonstrates the difference between an output based on missions and the input orientation based on functions.

The successful achievement of defined mission goals requires inputs from a large number of functional areas and activity centers within the firm. Thus, an effective distribution costing system must seek to determine the total system costs of meeting desired distribution objectives (the output of the system) and the costs of the various inputs involved in meeting these outputs. Interest has been growing in an approach to this problem known as "mission costing."[2]

Figure 11-4 illustrates how three distribution missions may have varying impacts on activity

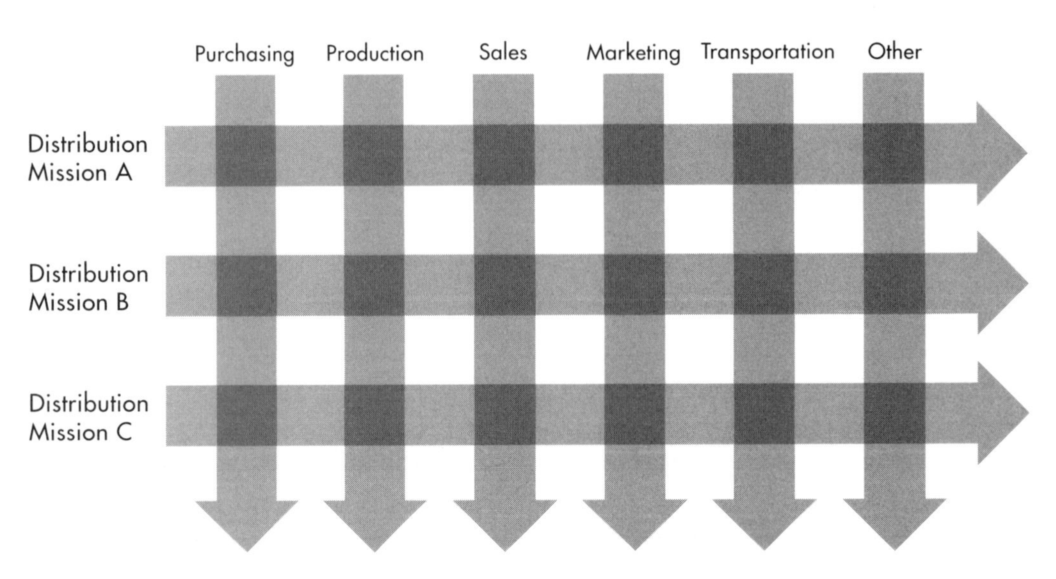

Figure 11-3
Logistics Missions That Cut Across Functional Boundaries

center/functional area costs and, in so doing, provide a logical basis for costing within the company. As a cost or budgeting method, mission costing is the reverse of traditional techniques: under this scheme a functional budget is determined now by the demands of the mission it serves. Thus, in Figure 11-4, the cost per mission is identified horizontally; the functional budgets may be determined by summing vertically.

Given that the logic of mission costing is sound, how might it be made to work in practice? The pioneering work of Barrett developed a framework for the application of mission costing.[3] This approach requires first that the activity centers associated with a particular distribution mission be identified (e.g., transport, warehousing, inventory), and second that the incremental costs for each activity center incurred as a result of undertaking that mission be isolated. Incremental costs are used because it is important not to take into account sunk costs, or costs that would still be incurred even if the mission were abandoned. Barrett makes use of the idea of attributable costs to operationalize the concept: "Attributable cost is a cost per unit that could be avoided if a product or function were discontinued entirely without changing the supporting organization structure."[4]

In determining the costs of an activity center (e.g., transport) attributable to a specific mission, the question should be asked, "What costs would we avoid if this customer/segment/channel were no longer served?" These avoidable costs are the true incremental costs of serving the customer, segment, and channel. Often they will be substantially lower than the average cost because so many distribution costs are fixed and/or shared. For example, a vehicle leaves a DC in Cleveland to make deliveries in Pittsburgh and Chicago. If customers in Pittsburgh were abandoned but those in Chicago retained, what would be the difference in the total cost of transport? The answer would be not very much. However, if the customers in Chicago were dropped, but not those in Pittsburgh, there would be a greater savings because of the reduction in miles traveled.

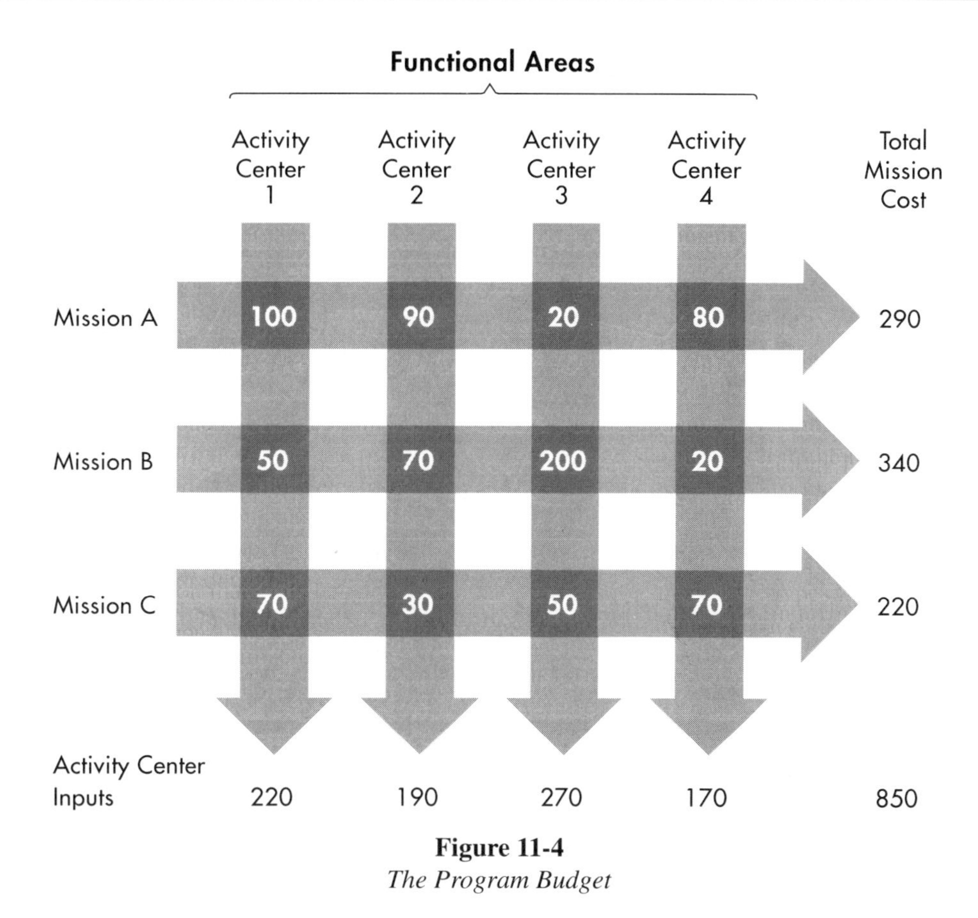

Figure 11-4
The Program Budget

This approach becomes particularly powerful when combined with a customer revenue analysis, because even customers with relatively few sales orders may still be profitable in incremental terms, if not on an average cost basis. In other words, the company would be worse off if those customers were abandoned.

Such insights as this can be gained by extending the mission costing concept to produce profitability analyses for customers, market segments, or distribution channels. The term "customer profitability accounting" describes any attempt to relate the revenue produced by a customer, market segment, or distribution channel to the costs of servicing that customer/segment/channel. The principles of customer profitability accounting are explored in detail later in this chapter.

Logistics and the Bottom Line

The turbulent business environment of the late twentieth century has made managers increasingly aware of the financial dimension of decision making. The bottom line has become the driving force that, perhaps erroneously, guides the company. In some cases this had led to a limiting, and potentially dangerous, focus on short-term results. Hence, we find that investment in brands, in R&D, and in expanded capacity may well be curtailed if there is little prospect of an immediate payback.

Just as powerful an influence on decision making and management views is cash flow. Although there is no necessary connection between cash and profits, it makes sense to include cash flow in the discussion here. Strong positive cash flow has become as much a desired goal of management as profit.

The third financial dimension affecting management decisions is resource utilization—specifically the use of fixed and working capital. The pressure in most firms is to improve the productivity of capital—"to make the assets sweat." In this regard it is common to use the concept of return on investment (ROI), the ratio between the net profit and the capital employed to produce that profit. Thus:

$$\text{ROI} = \text{Profit} \div \text{Capital Employed}$$

This ratio can be further expanded:

$$\text{ROI} = (\text{Profit} \div \text{Sales}) \times (\text{Sales} \div \text{Capital Employed})$$

It will be seen that ROI is the product of two ratios: the first, profit/sales, being commonly referred to as the *margin,* and the second, sales/capital employed, termed *capital turnover.* Thus, to improve ROI, one or the other or both of these ratios must increase. Typically many companies focus mainly on the margin in their attempt to drive up ROI, yet it can often be more effective to use the leverage of improved capital turnover to boost ROI. Many successful retailers have long since recognized that very small net margins can lead to excellent ROI if the productivity of capital is high (through, say, limited inventory, high sales per square foot, premises that are leased rather than owned, and so on).

The ways in which logistics management can impact ROI are many and varied. Figure 11-5 highlights the major elements determining ROI and the potential for improvement through more effective logistics management. Let us look at each of these "boxes" in turn.

Sales Revenue

While the direct relationship between service and sales may not be measurable, there is plentiful evidence that superior customer service leads to improved sales. Other factors being equal, service can be a powerful source of differentiation in the marketplace.

Costs

Across European and North American industry, it has been estimated that distribution costs as a percentage of sales revenue typically range between 5 and 10%, as summarized in Table 11-1.

While over recent years these costs have fallen as a percentage of sales through better logistics management, they still represent a considerable burden to any company. It must also be recognized that when expressed as a percentage of *added value,* logistics costs are actually rising for most firms. This is because added value is falling as these companies outsource more and more of their input requirements (e.g., components, packaging, services, etc.). Most companies can still improve costs through better logistics management and hence leverage profit. Figure 11-6 highlights the possibility for gearing up profitability when profit margins are low, relative to distribution costs.

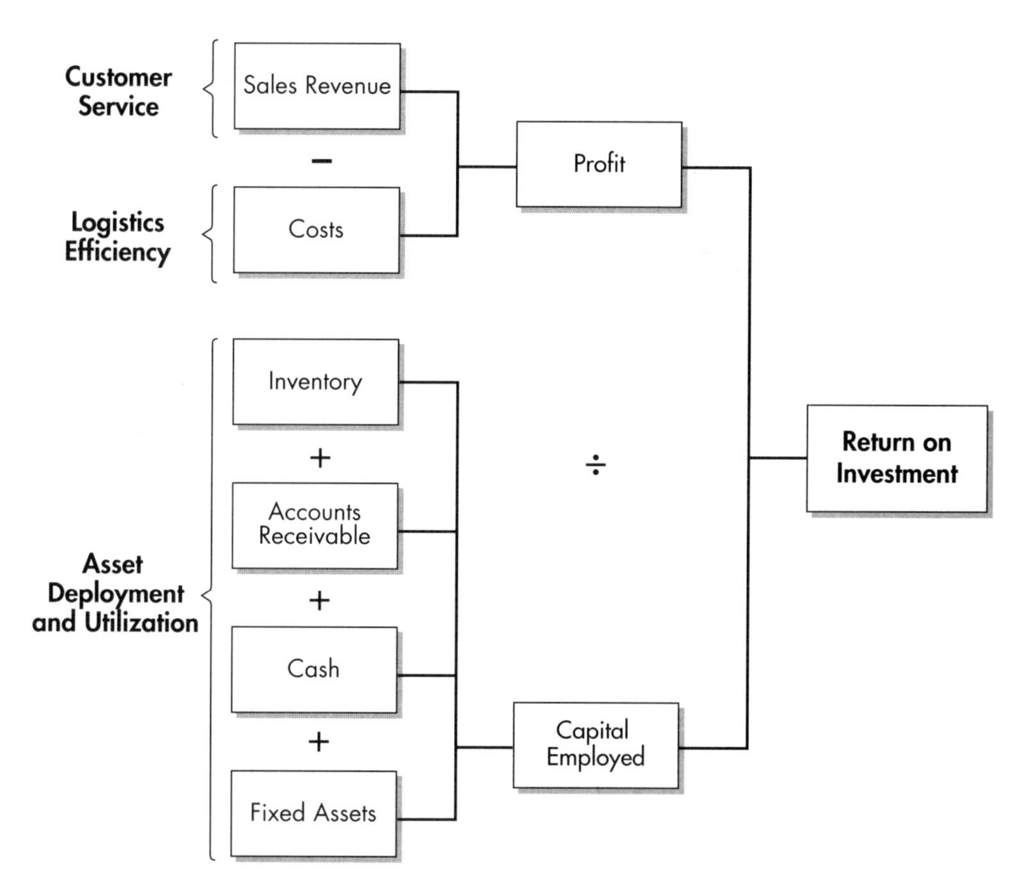

Figure 11-5
Logistics Impact on ROI

TABLE 11-1
Logistics Costs As a Percentage of Sales Revenue

Cost Element	Country				
	France	Germany	Netherlands	U.K.	U.S.A.
Transport	2.43	5.81	1.44	2.65	2.92
Warehousing	2.50	2.60	2.07	2.02	1.83
Order Entry	1.30	2.27	1.38	0.72	0.55
Administration	0.65	0.65	0.32	0.27	0.39
Inventory	1.83	0.72	1.53	2.08	1.91
Total	8.71	12.05	6.07	7.74	7.60

Source: P-E International, Egham, Surrey, U.K., 1991.

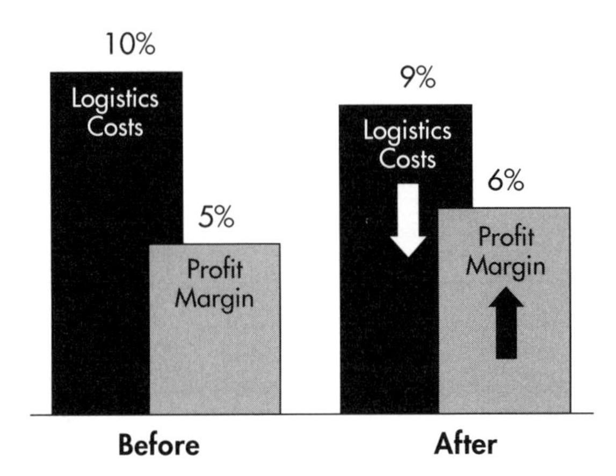

Figure 11-6
Profit Leverage and Logistics

In this case a 10% reduction in logistics costs results in a 20% improvement in profit, other factors being equal.

A hidden cost of logistics is the interest charged on inventory holding. Because this is rarely separately identified by most management accounting systems, many managers are unaware of what inventory is costing them. Of course, not just the interest charge or cost of capital has to be balanced against inventory holding; we must also take into account other costs like obsolescence and deterioration, insurance, stock losses, inventory control costs, and so on. It is estimated that it costs a minimum of 25% per annum of the book value of inventory just to hold it.

Asset Development and Utilization

The closing years of the century have been marked by record high levels of *real* interest rates—the nominal interest rate less the rate of inflation. Thus, if interest rates are 12% but inflation is 18% then the real interest rate is –6%. If, however, inflation is only 4% but interest rates are still 12%, then the real interest rate is now +8%.

High real interest rates have had a traumatic effect on business and have prompted a search for dramatic improvements in asset productivity. Better logistics management has the power to transform performance in this crucial area. Figure 11-7 summarizes the major elements of the balance sheet and links to each the relevant logistics management component. Examining each element of the balance sheet shows how logistics variables can influence its final shape.

Cash and Receivables

This component of current assets is crucial to the liquidity of the business. In recent years its importance has been recognized as more companies become squeezed for cash. It is not always recognized, however, that logistics variables have a direct impact on this part of the balance sheet. For example, the shorter the order cycle time (from order placement to goods delivery), the sooner the invoice can be issued. Likewise the order completion rate can affect the cash flow if the invoice is not issued until after the goods are dispatched. One of the less obvious logistics

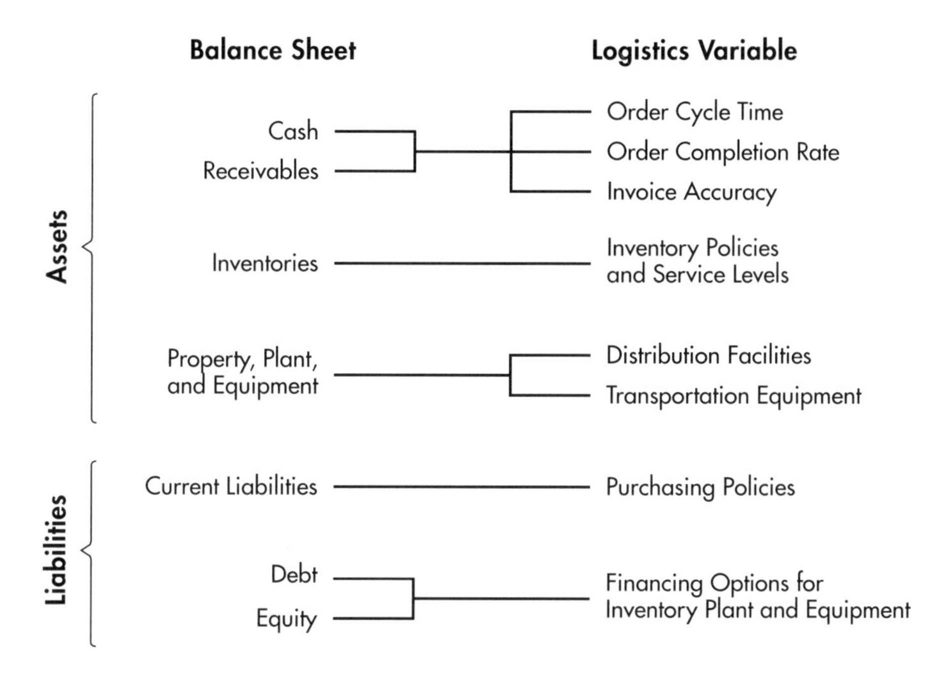

Figure 11-7
Logistics Management and the Balance Sheet

variables affecting cash and receivables is invoice accuracy. Customers who find the invoice inaccurate are likely to extend payment lead time until the problem is solved.

Inventories

Fifty percent or more of a company's current assets are often tied up in inventory. Logistics is concerned with all inventory within the business, from raw materials, subassembly, or outsourced components through work in progress to finished goods. The company's policies on inventory levels and stock locations clearly influence total inventory size. Also influential is the extent to which inventory levels are monitored and managed and the extent to which available systems and controls minimize inventory requirements.

Property, Plant, and Equipment

The logistics system of any business is usually a heavy user of fixed assets. The plant, DCs, and warehouses that form the logistics network, if valued realistically on a replacement basis, represent a substantial part of total capacity employed (assuming they are owned rather than rented or leased). Materials handling equipment, vehicles, and other equipment involved in storage and transport can also add considerably to the total sum of fixed assets. Many companies fail to recognize the true significance of logistics fixed assets because they are valued for balance sheet purposes at historical cost. Warehouses, for example, with their associated storage and handling equipment, represent a major investment. Obviously, it is important to ask, "Is this the most effective way to deploy our assets?"

Current Liabilities

The current liabilities of the business are debts that must be paid in cash within a specified period of time. From the logistics point of view, the key elements are accounts payable for bought-in materials, components, and the like. A greater integration of purchasing with operations management can yield dividends in this area. The traditional concepts of economic order quantities can often lead to excessive levels of raw materials inventory because those quantities may not reflect actual manufacturing or distribution requirements. The phasing in of supplies to match the total logistics requirements of the system can be achieved through the twin techniques of materials requirements planning (MRP) and distribution resource planning (DRP). Minimizing premature commitment of materials should lead to an improved position on current liabilities.

Debt/Equity

Whereas the balance between debt and equity has many ramifications for the financial management of the total business, it is worth reflecting on the impact of alternative logistics strategies. More companies are leasing plant facilities and equipment and thus converting a fixed asset into a continuing expense. The growing use of third-party suppliers for warehousing and transport instead of owning and managing these facilities in-house is a parallel development. These changes obviously affect the funding requirements of the business. They may also affect the means whereby the funding is achieved (i.e., through debt rather than equity). The ratio of debt to equity, usually referred to as "gearing" or "leverage," will influence the return on equity and will also affect cash flow in terms of interest payments and debt repayment.

Customer Profitability Analysis

One of the basic questions that conventional accounting procedures have difficulty answering is, "How profitable is this customer compared with another?" Usually customer profitability is calculated only at the level of gross profit—the net sales revenue generated by the customer in a period less the cost of goods sold for the actual product mix purchased. However, many other costs must also be considered before the real profitability of an individual customer can be known. The same is true when trying to identify the relative profitability of different market segments or distribution channels.

The significance of these costs that occur as a result of servicing customers can be profound in terms of how logistics strategies should be developed. First, customer profitability analysis often reveals a proportion of customers who make a negative contribution, as shown in Figure 11-8.

The reason for this is very simply that the costs of serving a customer can vary considerably—even between two customers who may make equivalent purchases. The costs of service begin with the order itself: How much time does the salesperson spend with the customer? Is there a key account manager whose time is spent wholly or in part working with that customer? What commission is paid on those sales?

Order processing is another important source of costs that differ according to the number of lines on the orders and their complexity. Others include transport costs, materials handling costs, and often inventory and warehousing costs—particularly if the products are held on a dedicated basis for customers (e.g., private-label products).

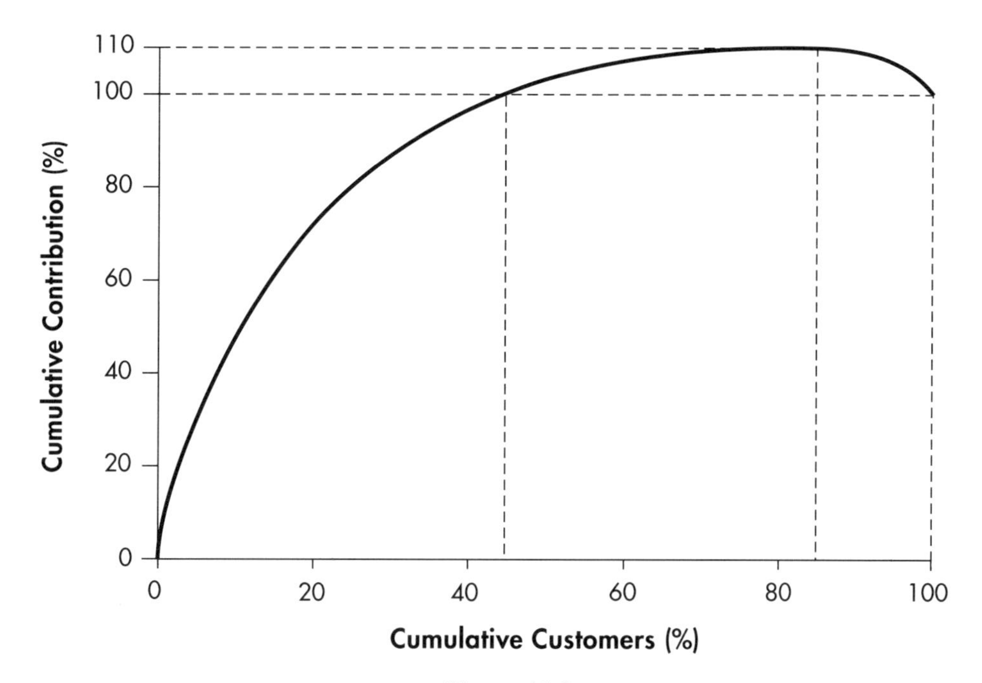

Figure 11-8
Customer Profitability Analysis

Source: G.V. Hill, *Logistics—The Battleground of the 1990s* (London: A.T. Kearney, 1989).

For many customers, the supplying company allocates specific funds for customer promotions, advertising support, additional discounts, and the like. In the case of promotions (e.g., a special pack for a particular retailer), the supplier may incur additional, hidden costs. For example, the disruption to production schedules and the additional inventory holding cost are rarely accounted for and assigned to specific customers.

The basic principle of customer profitability analysis is that the supplier should assign all costs that are specific to individual accounts. A useful test to apply when examining these costs is to ask, "What costs would I *avoid* if I ceased doing business with this customer?"

The principle of avoidability helps reveal that many costs of serving customers are actually shared among several or many customers. The warehouse is a good example. Unless the supplier could release warehousing space for other purposes, it would be incorrect to allocate a proportion of the total warehousing costs to a particular customer.

A checklist of costs to include when drawing up the profit-and-loss account for specific customers is given in Table 11-2.

Although it would not be practical for a business with many thousands of customer accounts to conduct individual profitability analyses, it would certainly be possible to select representative customers on a sample basis to reveal relative costs associated with different types of accounts or distribution channels.

What sort of costs should be taken into account in this type of analysis? Figure 11-9 presents a basic model that seeks to identify only those avoidable customer-related costs (i.e., if the customer did not exist, these costs would not be incurred).

TABLE 11-2
The Customer Profit-and-Loss Account

Revenues:
Net sales value
Less Attributable Costs:
Cost of sales (actual product mix)
Commissions
Sales calls
Key account management time
Trade bonuses and special discount
Order processing costs
Promotional costs (visible and hidden)
Merchandising costs
Nonstandard packaging/unitization
Dedicated inventory holding costs
Dedicated warehouse space
Materials handling costs
Transport costs
Documentation/communications costs
Returns/refusals
Trade credit (actual payment period)
Equals Customer Profit or Loss

The starting point is the gross sales value of the order from which is then subtracted the discounts given on that order to the customer. This leaves the net sales value from which must be subtracted the direct production costs or cost of goods sold. Indirect costs are not allocated unless they are fully attributable to that customer. The same principle applies to sales and marketing costs, as attempts to allocate indirect costs, like national advertising can be done only on an arbitrary and usually misleading basis. The attributable distribution costs can then be assigned to give customer gross contribution. Finally, any other customer-related costs, such as trade credit, returns, and so forth, are subtracted to show a net contribution to overhead and profit. Often the figure that emerges as the bottom line can be revealing, as shown in Table 11-3.

In this case a gross contribution of $70,000 becomes a net contribution of $56,400 as soon as the costs unique to this customer are taken into account. If the analysis were extended by allocating overhead (a step not to be advised because of the problems usually associated with such allocation), what might at first seem to be a profitable customer could be the opposite. However, as long as the net contribution is positive and there is no opportunity cost in serving that customer, the company would be better off with the business than without out it.

The value of this type of analysis can be substantial. The information could be used first when the next sales contract is negotiated and, second as the basis for directing effort away from less profitable types of account toward more profitable business. More important, it can point the way to alternative strategies for managing customers with high service costs. Ideally, we require all our customers to be profitable in the medium to long term; where customers currently are profitable, we should seek to expand that profitability.

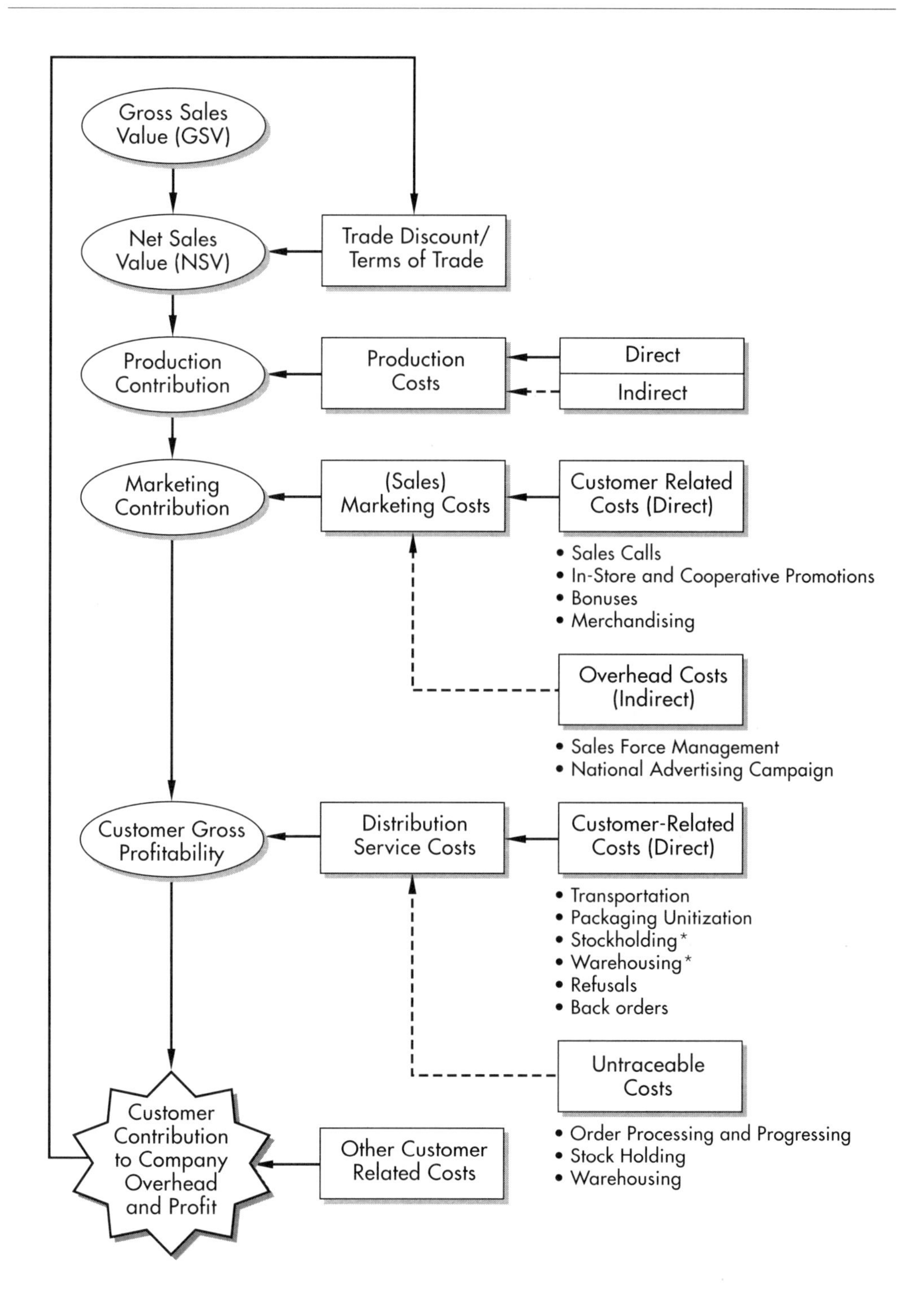

Figure 11-9
Customer Account Profitability: A Basic Model

TABLE 11-3
Analysis of Revenue for a Specific Customer

	$	$
Gross sales value		100,000
Less discount	10,000	
Net sales value		90 000
Less direct cost of goods sold	20,000	
Gross contribution		70,000
Less sales and marketing costs		
Sales calls	3,000	
Cooperative promotions	1,000	
Merchandising	3,000	
	7,000	
Less distribution costs:		
Order processing	500	
Storage and handling	600	
Inventory financing	700	
Transport	2,000	
Packaging	300	
Refusals	500	
	4,600	
Customer's Gross Contribution		58,400
Less other customer-related costs:		
Credit financing	1,500	
Returns	500	
	2,000	
Customer's Net Contribution		56,400

The customer profitability matrix shown in Figure 11-10 provides general guidance. The appropriate strategies for each quadrant of the matrix are described below.

Build. These customers are relatively cheap to serve but their net sales value is low. Can volume be increased without a proportionate increase in the costs of service? Can our sales team be directed to seek to influence these customers' purchases toward a more profitable sales mix?

Danger Zone. These customers should be looked at very carefully. Is there any medium- to long-term prospect of either improving net sales value or of reducing the costs of service? Is there a strategic reason for keeping them? Do we need them for their volume even if their profit contribution is low?

Cost-Engineer. These customers could be more profitable if the costs of serving them could be reduced. Is there any scope for increasing drop sizes? Can deliveries be consolidated? If new accounts in the same geographic area were developed, would it make delivery more economical? Is there a cheaper way of gathering orders from these customers (e.g., tele-sales)?

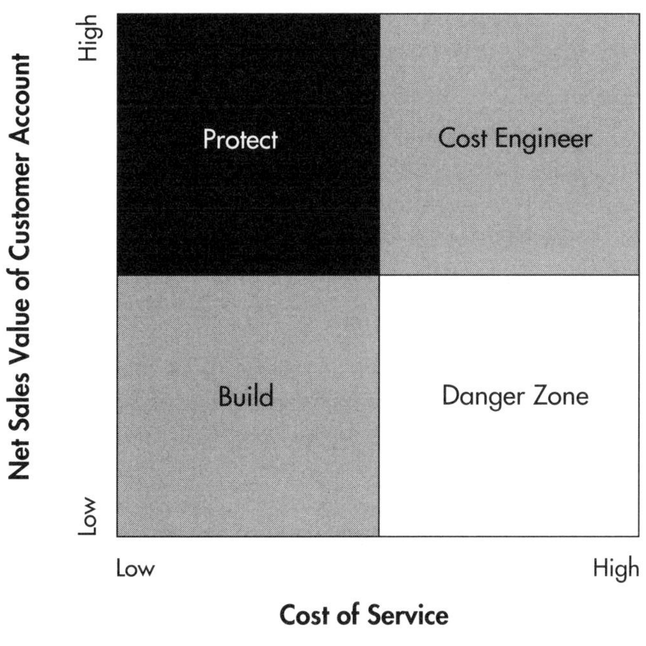

Figure 11-10
Customer Profitability Matrix

Protect. Customers with high net sales value who are relatively cheap to serve are worth their weight in gold. The strategy for these customers should be to seek relationships that make them less likely to seek alternative suppliers. At the same time we should constantly seek opportunities to develop our volume of business while keeping strict control of costs.

Ideally the firm should develop an accounting system that routinely collects and analyzes data on customer profitability. Unfortunately, most accounting systems focus on *products* rather than *customers.* Likewise, cost reporting is traditionally on a *functional* rather than *transactional* basis. For example, we know the costs of transport as a whole or the costs of making a particular product; we do not know the costs of delivering a specific mix of product to a particular customer.

There is a pressing need for companies to move toward a system of accounting for customers and marketing as well as accounting for products, because *customers, not products, make profits.*

Direct Product Profitability

An application of logistics cost analysis that has gained widespread acceptance, particularly in the retail industry, is a technique known as direct product profitability (DPP). It is somewhat analogous to customer profitability analysis in that it attempts to identify all the costs that attach to a product or an order as it moves through the distribution channel.

The idea behind DPP is that in many transactions, the customer incurs costs other than the immediate purchase price of the product. Sometimes these costs are hidden, and often they can be substantial—certainly big enough to reduce or even eliminate net profit on a particular item.

TABLE 11-4
Direct Product Profit (DPP)
The net profit contribution from the sale of a product after allowances are added and all costs that can be rationally allocated or assigned to an individual product are subtracted.

	Sales
–	Cost of Goods Sold
=	Gross Margin
+	Allowances and Discounts
=	Adjusted Gross Margin
–	Warehouse Costs
	labor (labor model—case, cube, weight)
	occupancy (space and cube)
	inventory (average inventory)
–	Transportation Costs (cube)
–	Retail Costs
	stocking labor
	front-end labor
	occupancy
	inventory
=	*Direct Product Profit*

For the supplier it is important to understand DPP because the ability to be a low-cost supplier is clearly influenced by the costs incurred as that product moves through the logistics system. Similarly, as distributors and retailers are now much more conscious of an item's DPP, it is also to the supplier's advantage to understand the cost drivers that affect DPP.

As DPP has been primarily used in the retail industry (although the principle has a much wider application), we explain the concept in the context of retail business. Direct product profit is the contribution to profit of an item that is calculated by:

- Adjusting the gross margin for each item to reflect deals, allowances, net forward buy income, prompt payment discounts, etc.
- Identifying and measuring the costs that can be directly attributed to individual products (like labor, space, inventory, and transport)

Table 11-4 describes the steps in moving from a crude gross margin measure to a more precise DPP.

Because product characteristics and the associated costs vary so much by item (e.g., cube, weight, case pack count, handling costs, space occupied, and turnover), the retailer needs to look at DPP at the item level. Similarly, because shelf space is the limiting factor for the retailer, the key measure of performance becomes DPP/square foot. Some examples of how DPP/square foot can differ dramatically from simple gross margin are shown in Table 11-5 for different products moving through a retailer's own distribution system.

The importance to the supplier of DPP comes back to the objective of customer service strategy as being "to reduce the customer's costs of ownership." Suppliers should be looking at their products and asking, "How can I favorably influence the DPP of my customers by changing either the characteristics of the products I sell or the way I distribute them?" The manufacturer or

TABLE 11-5
Direct Product Profit (DPP)
(Gross margin does not predict profit.)

	Gross Margin (%)	**DPP (%)**	**Average DPP/m² ($)**
Baby food	11	3.4	0.11
Beans and rice	11	3.9	0.24
Shortening and oil	11	7.3	0.98
Paper products	19	7.2	0.47
Cake mix	19	10.1	0.44
Jelly and jam	22	16.7	1.01
Household cleaners	24	17.3	1.05
Ice cream	23	6.2	0.99
Butter	10	4.6	1.97
Frozen vegetables	34	23.1	2.60
Frozen fruit	24	17.3	3.28
Cigarettes	12	13.2	6.56
Dentifrice	31	18.6	1.42
Facial tissues	15	—	(0.01)

supplier may be able to vary several elements to influence DPP/square foot positively (for example, changing the case size or packaging design, increasing the delivery frequency, delivering directly to stores, etc.).

Cost Drivers and Activity-Based Costing

As indicated briefly at the start of this chapter, there is a growing dissatisfaction with conventional cost accounting, particularly as it relates to logistics management. Essentially these problems can be summarized as follows:

- There is a general ignorance of the true costs of serving different customer types, channels, and market segments.
- Costs are captured at too high a level of aggregation.
- Full cost allocation still dominates.
- Conventional accounting systems focus on functions rather than outputs.
- Companies understand product costs but not customer costs.

The common theme is that managers lack an understanding of total costs throughout the logistics pipeline. In short, they need a way of identifying costs as products and orders flow toward the customer.

To overcome this problem, the basis of cost accounting must change from the notion that all expenses must be allocated (often on an arbitrary basis) to individual units (such as products). Instead, the expenses must be separated and matched to the level of activity that consumes the resources.[5] The key to activity-based costs (ABC) is to seek out the cost drivers along the logistics pipeline that cause costs because they consume resources. Thus, for example, in

TABLE 11-6
Activity-Based Costing vs. Traditional Cost Bases (000)

Traditional Cost Bases		**Activity Cost Bases . . .**		**. . . and their drivers**
Salaries	$550	Sales order processing	$300	Number of orders
Wages	580	Holding inventory	600	Value of shipment
Depreciation	250	Picking	300	Number of order lines
Rent/electricity/telephone	700	Packing/assembly of orders	100	Number of order lines
Maintenance	100	Loading	200	Weight
Fuel	200	Transportation	500	Location of customer
Total Cost	$2,580	Delivery to customer	200	Number of drops
		Solving problems	380	Number of order lines
		Total Cost	$2,580	

Source: Adapted from G. Simmons, and D. Steeple, "Overhead Recovery—It's as Easy as ABC," *Focus,* Institute of Logistics and Distribution Management 10, no. 8 (October 1991).

the past we may have assigned the costs of order picking to orders by calculating an average cost per order. An activity-based approach might suggest that it is *the number of lines on an order* that consumes the order picking resources; hence, this measurement should be seen as the cost driver.

Table 11-6 shows an example of how the ABC approach differs from the traditional method.

There are certain parallels between activity-based costing and mission costing (introduced earlier in this chapter). Essentially mission costing seeks to identify the unique costs generated as a result of specific logistics/customer service strategies aimed at targeted market segments. The aim is to establish a better matching of the service needs of the various markets that the company addresses with its inevitably limited resources. There is little point in committing incremental costs where the incremental benefits do not justify the expenditure.

The basic aim of logistics cost analysis is to provide managers with reliable information that will enable a better allocation of resources. Given that logistics management ultimately focuses on meeting customer service requirements in the most cost-effective way, it is essential that those responsible have the most accurate and meaningful data possible. An article in *Fortune* summarized the issue most succinctly:

> Few companies have seized the opportunity that awaits those that modernize their accounting practices. Consequently most firms suffer from the same insidious problem: The methods they use to allocate costs are hopelessly obsolete.
>
> Quite simply, accurate cost information can give a company a competitive advantage.[6]

Notes

1. H. T. Johnson and R. S. Kaplan. *Relevance Cost The Rise and Fall of Management Accounting* (Cambridge, Mass.: Harvard Business School Press, 1987).
2. M. G. Christopher, *Total Distribution: A Framework for Analysis, Costing and Control* (Epping, N.H.: Gower Press, 1971).

3. T. Barrett, "Mission Costing: A New Approach to Logistics Analysis," *International Journal of Physical Distribution and Materials Management* 12, no. 7 (1982).
4. G. Shillinglaw, "The Concept of Attributable Cost," *Journal of Accounting Research* 1, no. 1 (Spring 1963).
5. R. Cooper, and R. S. Kaplan, "Profit Priorities from Activity-Based Costing," *Harvard Business Review* (May–June 1991).
6. Ford S. Worthing, "Accounting Bores You? Wake Up!," *Fortune* (October 12, 1987).

CHAPTER 12

Logistics Cost, Productivity, and Performance Analysis

Douglas M. Lambert

Logistics costs are a major component of the total cost of doing business, and distribution assets represent a major portion of a firm's total assets. Clearly, managers can improve corporate profits by improving logistics productivity.[1]

Rather than attempt to minimize the costs of individual logistics components, one should select the level of expenditure for each component that leads to the greatest profit for the firm. Thus, total cost analysis is critical to the successful management of logistics. Accounting information plays a significant role in the analysis and management process, for without accurate cost data it is impossible to design or control the distribution system.

This chapter examines several fundamental and advanced concepts that are useful for analyzing and managing logistics processes:

- Accounting for logistics
- Distribution cost trade-off analysis
- Controlling logistics activities
- Activity-based costing
- A distribution database for decision making

Accounting for Logistics

The lack of adequate cost data has prevented the full implementation of integrated logistics management in many firms. Accountants have not kept pace with developments in logistics and, in fact, have shown relatively little interest in the area. Consequently, much of the necessary cost analysis is not performed.[2] Costs related to separate functional areas and their interaction must be made available to logistics decision makers. With this information they can use total cost analysis to manage logistics operations, determine selling prices, and justify price differentials.

The quality of accounting data influences the quality of the decisions made. To support quality decisions, the accounting system must be capable of providing information to continually investigate fundamental logistics issues. Figure 12-1 shows the logistics pyramid that serves as a conceptual model in which logistics decisions can be framed in an organized and strategic manner. Sample questions are listed in Table 12-1, by category, that managers might investigate when seeking to improve logistics productivity and corporate profits.

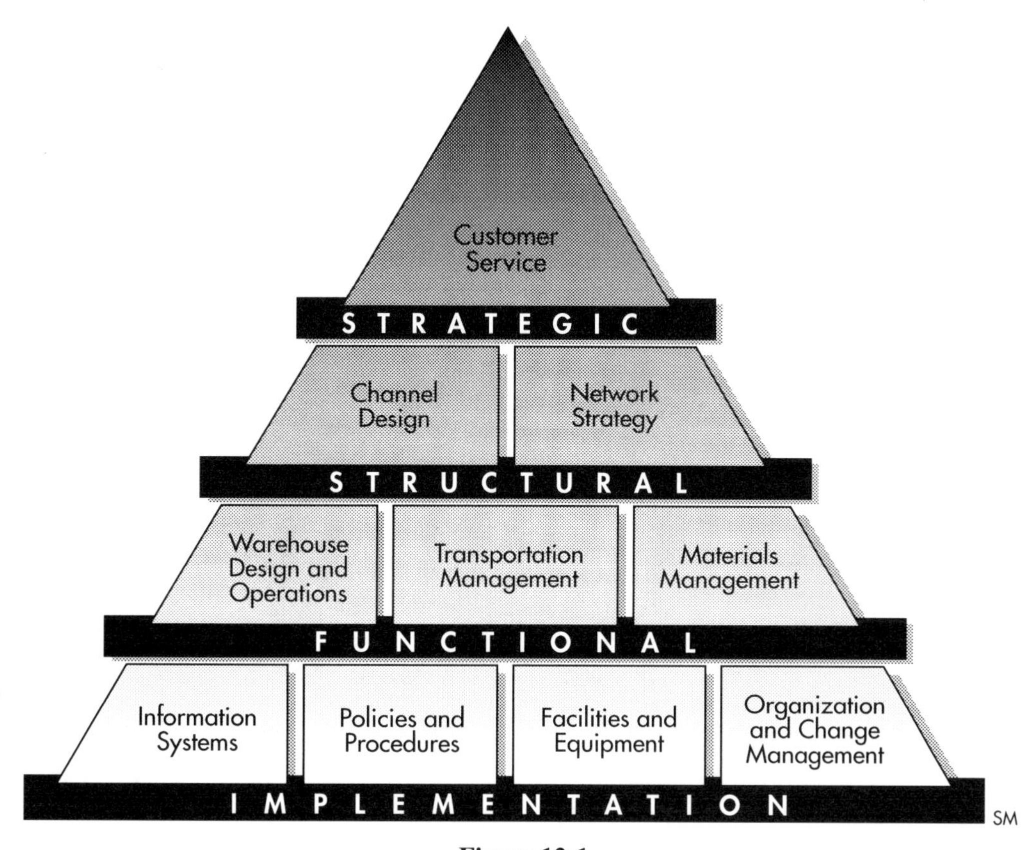

Figure 12-1
The Logistics Pyramid

Source: Andersen Consulting, Arthur Andersen & Co., S.C., Logistics Strategy Practice. Copyright © 1989 by Andersen Consulting. All Rights Reserved.

This type of decision making is severely hampered by the lack of proper accounting data or the inability to use such data when available. The best and most sophisticated models are only as good as the accuracy of the data inputs. Several studies attest to the gross inadequacies of logistics cost data.[3]

To answer these and other questions requires knowledge of the costs and revenues that will change if the logistics system changes. That is, determining a product's contribution should be based on how corporate revenues, expenses, and hence profitability would change if the product line were dropped. Any costs or revenues unaffected by this decision are irrelevant to the problem. For example, a relevant cost would be public warehouse handling charges associated with a product's sales; a nonrelevant cost would be the overhead costs associated with the firm's private trucking fleet.

Key Accounting Concepts

The accounting concepts necessary for logistics are the same as those used in manufacturing cost analysis. Functional cost analysis is a prerequisite to the identification of costs and their be-

TABLE 12-1
Sample Logistics Questions Requiring Accounting Information

Pyramid Category	Sample Questions
• Customer service	What are the costs associated with providing additional levels of customer service? What trade-offs are necessary and what are the incremental benefits or losses? What do customers and ultimate consumers expect of us?
• Channel design	Who should be involved in delivering products to customers? Should we distribute through wholesalers, directly to retailers, or directly to consumers with a catalog? What are the effects of logistics costs on contribution by product, by territory, by customer, and by salesperson? Can we exploit new markets? What are the roles of each channel member (manufacturer, wholesaler, distributor, retailer)?
• Network strategy	How many field warehouses should be used and where should they be located?
• Warehouse design and operations	How much space do we need? Can we modify existing facilities to increase our capacity and throughput?
• Transportation management	What mix of transportation modes and carriers should be used? Can we take advantage of innovative transportation systems? How do we choose between common carriers and private trucking?
• Materials management	What is the optimal amount of inventory? How sensitive is the inventory level to changes in warehousing patterns or to changes in customer service levels? How much does it cost to hold inventory? Should we increase deliveries or increase inventories? Should we make changes in packaging?
• Production planning	How many production setups are required? Which plants will produce each product? (While not an immediate element of the logistics pyramid, production planning has a major impact on all supply chain management decisions.)
• Information systems	To what extent should the order processing system be automated? What systems are needed to support new strategies (e.g., must we implement electronic data interchange or collect point-of-sale data?)
• Policies and procedures	How should we modify "standard" rules to meet changing conditions? What activities must we perform to support channel relationships?
• Facilities and equipment	Should we update buildings, systems hardware, or materials handling equipment? If so, when? Can we eliminate or reduce current capabilities without harming customer service?
• Organization and change management	Are current communications with employees adequate, or should they be improved? Who should be involved in planning our responses to changing conditions? How should the process be structured?

havior. Although logistics activities are organized along functional lines like warehousing, transportation, order processing, and inventory, many firms capture costs not on a functional basis but rather in broad, "natural" account categories like salaries, depreciation, and general and administrative expenses.

Natural accounts are used to group costs for financial reporting on the firm's income statement and balance sheet. For example, all payments for salaries might be grouped into a salaries account, whether they are for production, marketing, logistics, or finance, and the total shown on the financial statements at the end of the reporting period. Other examples of natural accounts might include rent, depreciation, selling expenses, general and administrative expenses, and interest expense. It is entirely possible that a firm with a strong financial accounting orientation may not give separate headings in the natural accounts to logistics costs such as warehousing and transportation. Instead, they are lumped into such diverse catchalls as overhead, selling, or general expense.

Further, there has been a tendency, particularly in the case of freight, to abandon the accrual accounting concept and match costs of one period with revenues of another. These conditions make it difficult to determine logistics expenditures, control costs, or perform trade-off analyses.

Each firm must analyze its own logistics activities to determine meaningful functional account categories. The next step is to code the accounting data to make identification of the costs possible. Several key accounting concepts are applicable to the logistics function, including cost categorization, costing methods, and general cost analysis.

COST CATEGORIZATION

Within functional account categories, costs can be further characterized by their nature. This subcategorization provides managers with additional details about costs that impact decisions.

Controllable vs. Noncontrollable. It is necessary to separate the more controllable costs from the less controllable or noncontrollable costs so that individual managers are held responsible only for incurring those costs over which they exercise control. Generally, costs that vary with the volume of effort expended in an activity are *controllable costs.* These costs should be related to an appropriate unit of service and separately identified to assist in cost control. Costs that are fixed or budgeted for the fiscal period should be considered when logistics effort and capacity is subject to change.

Direct vs. Indirect. In manufacturing, *direct costs* are readily traceable to products (for example, direct material and direct labor). Direct costs also include those incurred by specific functions and are distinguished from allocated or transferred costs. In logistics, the classification of costs as direct or indirect depends on the business segment. The more general the segment (sales division or sales territory), the greater the portion of costs directly traceable to it; the more specific the segment (products, customers), the greater the proportion of indirect costs. Direct costs are those that can be traced to a business segment. If that segment were eliminated, the costs no longer would be incurred. *Indirect costs,* costs such as general administrative expenses, are often allocated to segments, but this process is arbitrary at best and should be avoided.

Fixed vs. Variable. The study of cost behavior in logistics is quite similar to that in manufacturing because most of the activities are repetitive in nature. Physical measurements like labor hours, units handled, and orders processed can be used to measure the activity. Changes in cost are usually caused by changes in activity.

Understanding logistics cost behavior requires establishing relationships between costs and appropriate activity measures. *Variable costs* change proportionally with changes in volume. *Fixed costs* remain the same despite volume. An example of a variable cost is the handling charge in a public warehouse. An example of a fixed cost is the salary of the transportation manager. Figure 12-2 depicts both fixed and variable cost behaviors as well as variations.

Mixed costs contain both a fixed and a variable component. An example is warehouse labor; a basic crew of three may be required to cover the normal range of activity (fixed), but if volume exceeds the crew's capacity, overtime or part-time employees are necessary (variable).

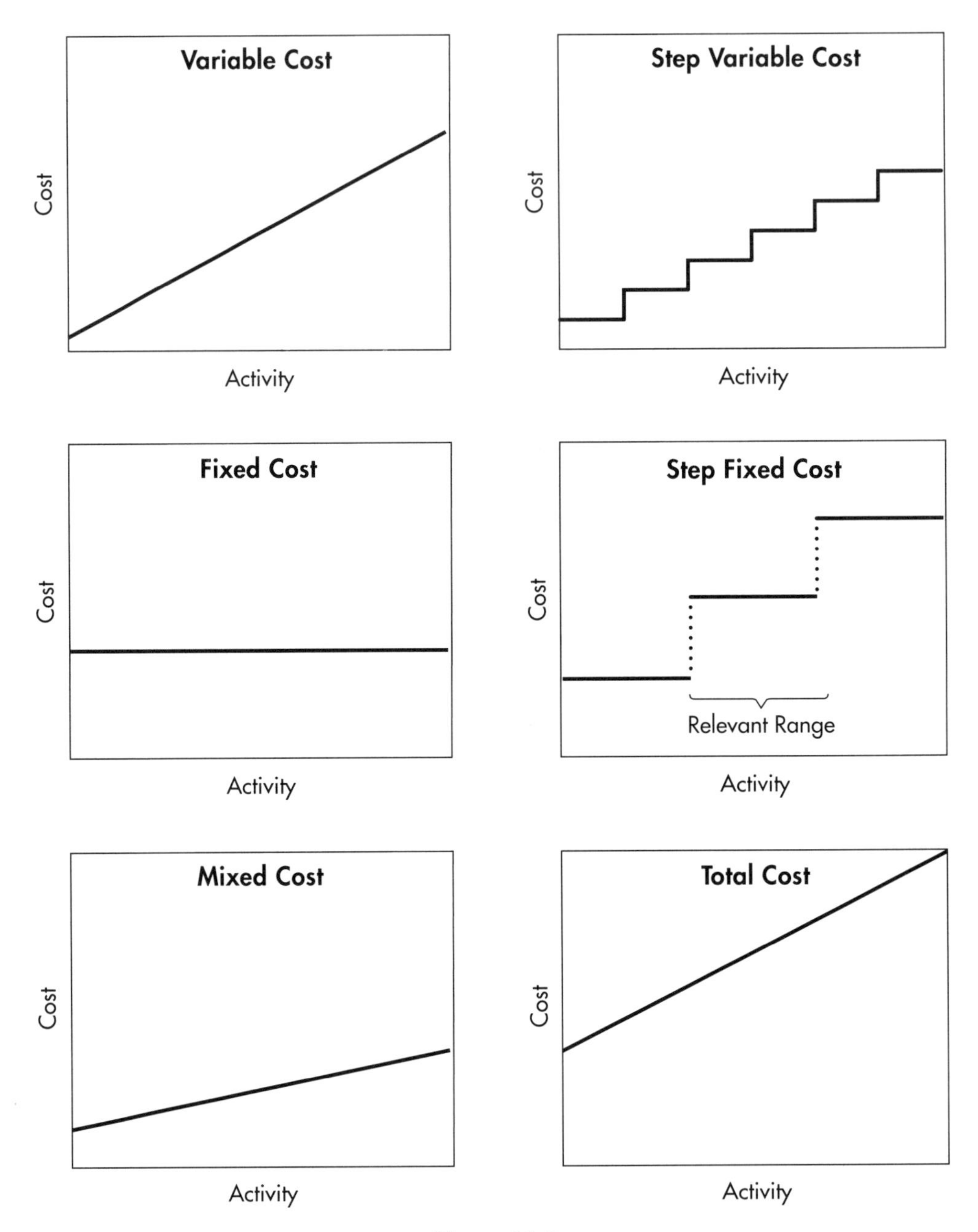

Figure 12-2
Types of Cost Behavior

Step variable costs and step fixed costs are fixed over a relevant range but may increase in steps. The major distinction between the two is the size of the steps. For example, in an order processing department of 20 people, labor might safely be considered variable because a small percentage increase in the number of orders could result in the need for more employees. However, in a department of three people the cost might be considered a step fixed cost because a large percentage increase in the number of orders processed would be required to add an employee. Other examples of step fixed costs include management salaries, depreciation, and taxes associated with each company warehouse. Effective planning and control require that the *total costs* be separated into the fixed and variable components.

Actual vs. Opportunity. The conservative nature of accounting requires the use of current actual costs or allocations of historic costs in cases such as depreciation. *Actual costs,* of course, result from transactions that actually occur. However, for management decision making, actual costs and opportunity costs must be considered. An *opportunity cost* is the sacrifice associated with the choice of a specific alternative, the value of transactions that were possible but rejected. Examples of opportunity costs include the rate of return that could be earned on money not invested in inventory and the possible income from leasing or selling a warehouse. Although opportunity costs do not appear on corporate profit-and-loss statements, these costs are real. For instance, if a company could invest $5 million less in inventories, the cash could be used for something else productive, even if it were simply invested in Treasury bills. The rate of return that would be earned on the Treasury bills is the opportunity cost.

Relevant vs. Sunk. *Relevant costs* change with a decision management is about to make. Any costs unaffected by the decision should not be included in the evaluation of alternatives. The costs that will not change are *sunk costs.* An example of a sunk cost is the price of a forklift truck after it has been purchased. When making the decision to keep or sell the forklift truck, the relevant costs are the cash flows experienced by keeping the piece of equipment, its current market value, and any income tax implications associated with the decision to sell it; the original purchase price is no longer relevant but rather it is "sunk."

Costing Methods

Categorization is not the only way to characterize costs. The cost recording methods themselves can add useful information to the data. Both methods discussed here can be used alone or in conjunction with each other.

Standards and Standard Costs. *Standard costing* records costs in two parts, the standard or expected cost plus the deviation from that standard that is actually incurred. The application of performance standards to the efficient control of manufacturing costs is widespread, but relatively few firms have developed standards for distribution activities. A decision to use standard costs requires a systematic review of logistics operations to determine the most efficient means of achieving desired output—that is, to determine the standards. Accounting, logistics, and engineering personnel must work together using time-and-motion studies, efficiency studies, and regression analysis to develop a series of flexible budgets for various operating levels in different logistics cost centers. Standards can and have been set for such warehouse operations as stock picking, loading, receiving, replenishing, storing, and packing merchandise. In addition, they have been successfully utilized in order processing, transportation, and even clerical functions.

It may not be necessary to have standards for all logistics costs. Management should be selective about the activities to which it applies standards. Standards should be used only where the costs involved and the possibilities of inefficiency suggest the need for continued attention to cost control.

Full Costing vs. Marginal Costing. *Full costing,* or *absorption costing,* is a method of product costing that charges the product with both variable and fixed manufacturing costs. *Marginal costing,* or *incremental costing* (also called direct or variable costing), is a system of product costing that associates only variable costs with products while treating fixed costs as period costs. In addition to the direct costing versus absorption costing distinction, companies may value inventories based on actual costs or standard costs. The following are four distinct costing alternatives:

1. *Actual absorption costing.* Includes actual costs for direct material and direct labor, plus predetermined variable and fixed manufacturing overhead.
2. *Standard absorption costing.* Includes predetermined costs for direct material and direct labor, plus predetermined variable and fixed overhead.
3. *Actual direct costing.* Includes actual costs for direct material and direct labor, plus predetermined variable manufacturing overhead; excludes fixed manufacturing overhead.
4. *Standard direct costing.* Includes predetermined costs for direct material and direct labor, plus predetermined variable manufacturing overhead; excludes fixed manufacturing overhead.

The distinction between full costing and direct (marginal) costing is particularly meaningful for the calculation of inventory carrying costs, because only the direct costs are converted to cash by reducing inventory levels.

General Cost Analysis

The characterization of costs by functional categorization, subcategorization, and progressive costing methods simplifies general cost analyses by providing data in readily usable form. Break-even analysis and analyses based on the cost of capital (time-value-of-money techniques) are typical decision-making tools frequently useful in logistics.

Break-Even Analysis. The break-even point is the level of sales required to cover variable costs plus fixed costs (see Figure 12-3). For example, if management wishes to determine whether customer service levels should be increased from 90% to 95%, it should know how much sales need to increase to break even. If an adequate sales increase is not realistic, perhaps the service level should not be increased.

Cost of Capital. The cost of capital, the rate paid to use funds, is a useful tool for deciding among investment alternatives. Basically, if the return is greater than the cost of capital, then the investment deserves further consideration.[4] This concept is known as "hurdle rate," the rate over which projects must "leap" to be accepted.

Defining the cost of capital is difficult because the concept continues to evolve. Three easy rate calculations deserve brief mention:

1. *Simple cost of capital.* The simplest calculation is the current market rate of debt (i.e., loans, bonds, etc.), that is, interest plus financing costs. However, this calculation ignores

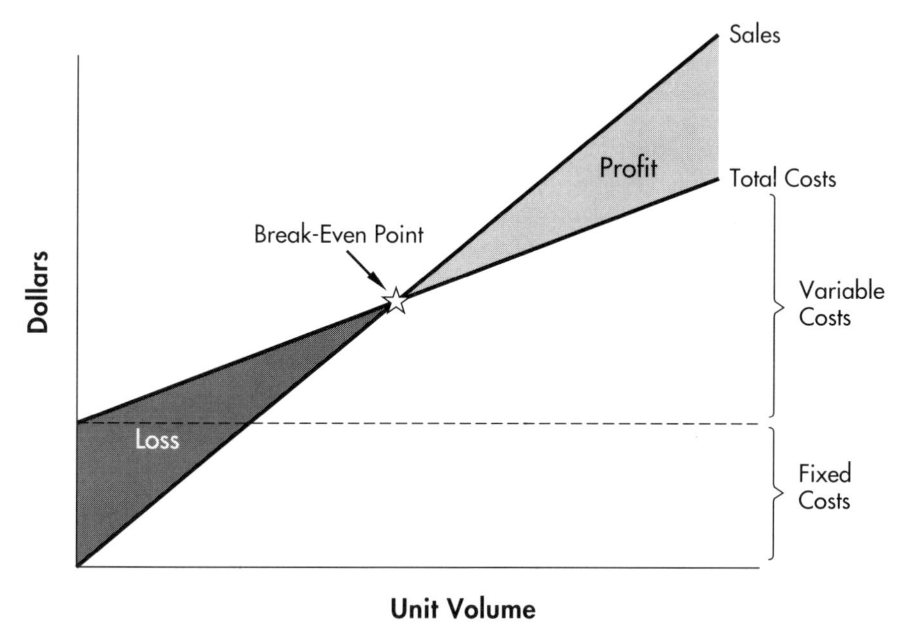

Figure 12-3
Break-Even Analysis

equity holders who may also demand some rate of return, although they may not explicitly state the rate.

2. *Weighted average cost of capital.* A "textbook" formula[5] for weighted-average cost of capital (r^*) is:

$$r^* = [r_D(1 - T_C)\ (D \div V)] + [r_E(E \div V)]$$

where:
r^* = adjusted cost of capital
r_D = firm's current borrowing rate
T_C = marginal corporate income tax rate (not effective rate)
r_E = expected rate of return on the firm's stock (which depends on the firm's business risk and its debt ratio)
D,E = market values of currently outstanding debt and equity
V = D + E = total market value of the firm

The weighted-average cost of capital is calculated for the firm as a whole, not just the capital required for the investment in question. Thus, this calculation may wrongly assume that unlimited funds will continue to be available at the historical rate and that there are no restrictions on the makeup of the capital structure.[6]

3. *Opportunity cost of capital.* Opportunity cost is the rate of return that could be realized from some other use of money than the investment being considered. "For most decision-making situations, it is the opportunity calculated cost of capital which is far more important for a given decision than an actual calculated cost of capital based upon something

which happened yesterday."[7] When a firm's capital is rationed rather than unlimited, the hurdle rate is the rate of return on marginal investments due to the principle of opportunity cost.[8] The principle of opportunity cost is best described by example:

> Consider, for example, a firm which pays 10 percent for the funds that it acquires and that, because of capital rationing, is currently turning down marginal investments promising annual returns of 15 percent. For this company the hurdle rate in investment decisions is 15 percent, although the cost of capital is only 10 percent. This means that the relevant time value of money is measured by the return on the most lucrative investments forgone by the firm, rather than by the price at which the funds were originally acquired. Of course, the 15 percent hurdle rate could also be designated as the cost of capital to the firm, if this term is interpreted generically.[9]

The return on the investment is determined by calculating the internal rate of return (IRR), which is simply the rate at which the foreseeable and reasonable cash flows must be discounted to equal the initial cash outflow.

Although some maintain that any project that yields more than the cost of money should be accepted, one should be cautious of the short-run approach:

> The principal objection to the short-run approach is the insidious effect of low-cost debt financing on projects over a series of years. To illustrate, the cost of 100 percent financing by 6 percent bonds is only 3 percent after applying a tax rate of 50 percent. If unlimited debt could be arranged in a given year, any project with an after-tax return of over 3 percent would be accepted. Next year, the debt limit for an optimum capital structure may already be reached, and equity financing may show a high cost of 20 percent after taxes. This would mean that any project that could not produce such a high return would be automatically rejected.[10]

Some companies may differentiate among projects by categorizing them according to risk and looking for rates of return that reflect the perceived level of risk. For example, management could group projects into high, medium, and low categories of risk. High-risk projects might include investments in new products, because market acceptance is difficult to predict, or new equipment for the plant, if technology is changing so rapidly that the equipment could be obsolete within a short time. The desired rate of return on high-risk projects might be 25% after taxes. Medium-risk projects, on the other hand, may be required to obtain an 18% tax return. Low-risk projects, which may include such investments as warehouses, private trucking, and inventory, might be expected to achieve an after-tax return of 10%. In the company just described, corporate aversion to risk would require that cash made available by a reduction in inventory be used for another low-risk category of investment. Consequently, the cost of money for inventory carrying costs would be 10% after taxes, which equals 20% before taxes.

Distribution Cost Trade-Off Analysis

Profitable business development requires that management allocate scarce resources to logistics and the other elements of the marketing mix—product, price, and promotion.[11] This is because the total dollars spent on marketing influence the company's market share and profitability. The more dollars a company invests in the marketing mix relative to its competitors, the larger the market share achieved, assuming that all competitors spend their dollars equally effectively. However, this is rarely the case. Significant advantage can be achieved by allocating dollars to the marketing mix more efficiently and effectively than one's competitors. The objective is to allocate resources to the price, product, promotion, and place components of the marketing mix in a manner that leads to the greatest long-term profits.

The place component represents the manufacturer's expenditure for customer service, which is the output of the logistics system. Customer service represents the logistics interface with demand creation. Logistics represents the demand supply part of marketing. Customer service not only impacts the place component of the marketing mix but also influences the price of the product. Product availability and order cycle time can be used to differentiate the product and may influence the market price if customers are willing to pay more for better service. In addition, logistics costs are added to product costs and as such may affect the market price set by the company. Figure 12-4 illustrates the cost trade-offs required to successfully implement the integrated logistics management concept; in this chapter it is used as a model for making financial decisions related to logistics.

Importance of Total Cost Analysis

Total cost analysis is the key to managing the logistics function. Management should strive to minimize the total costs of logistics rather than attempt to minimize the cost of each component. Attempts to reduce the cost of individual logistics activities in isolation may even lead to increased total costs.[12] For example, consolidating finished goods inventory in a small number of distribution centers reduces inventory carrying costs and warehousing costs but may lead to a substantial increase in freight expense or lower sales volume as a result of reduced levels of customer service. Similarly, the savings associated with large-volume purchases may be less than the increased inventory carrying costs.

It is important that management consider the total of all logistics costs. Reductions in the cost of one logistics activity invariably lead to increased costs of other cost components. Effective management and real cost savings can be accomplished only by viewing logistics as an integrated system and minimizing its total cost. The cost categories introduced in Figure 12-3 are customer service levels (the cost of lost sales), transportation costs, warehousing costs, order processing and information costs, production lot quantity costs, and inventory carrying costs. Each category is discussed in turn.

Customer Service Levels

The cost associated with customer service levels is the cost of lost sales—not only the margin lost by not meeting the current sales demand but the present value of all future contributions to profit forfeited when a customer is lost because of poor product availability. This cost is difficult, if not impossible, for most firms to measure.

For this reason, only the *measurable* costs associated with back ordering or expediting should be included in this category. The objective then becomes to minimize the total of the other logistics costs, given a level of customer service. With this information, it is possible to judge the likelihood of recovering, through increased sales, the increase in total system costs brought about by an increase in customer service levels. Another approach would be to reduce spending in some other component of the marketing mix (promotion, for example) to maintain profits with a similar sales volume. Likewise, with decreases in customer service levels, profitability can be

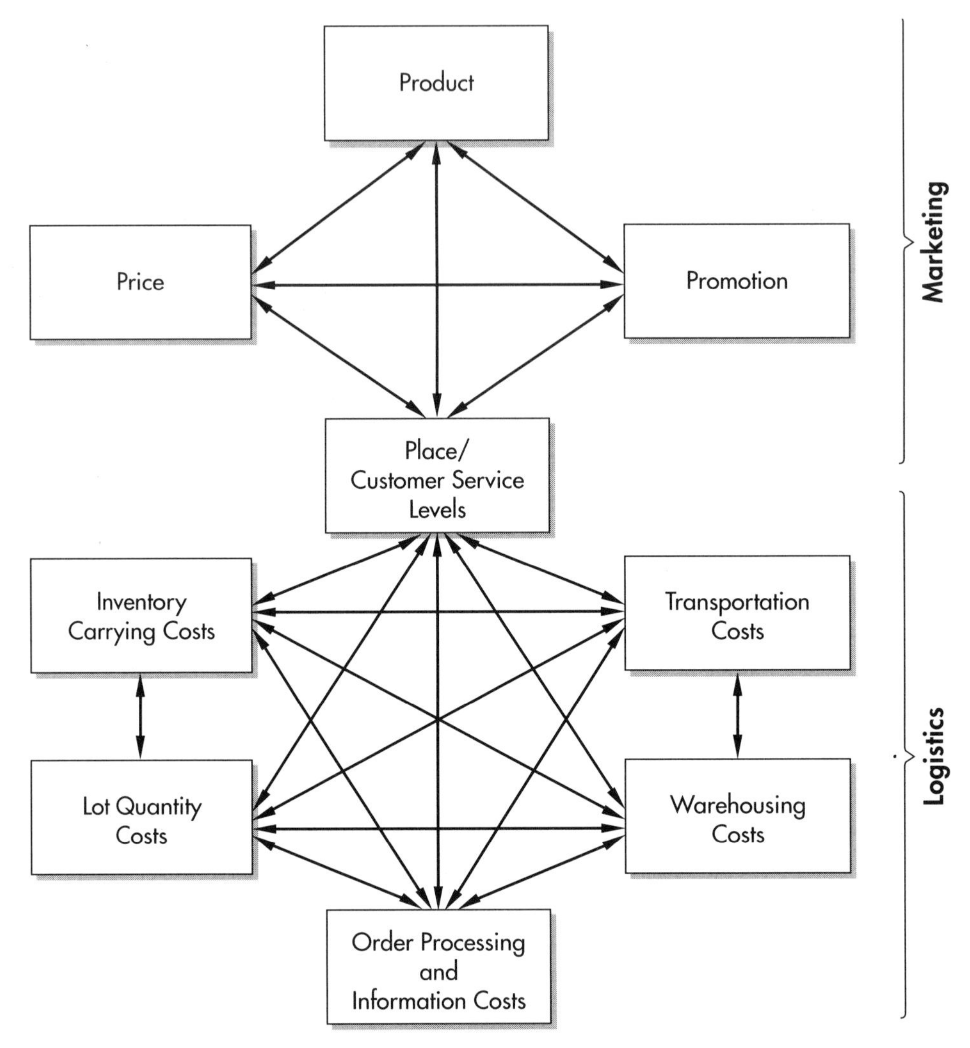

Figure 12-4

Logistics and Marketing Cost Trade-Offs

Marketing objective: Allocate resources to the marketing mix to maximize the long-term profitability of the firm.

Logistics objective: Minimize total costs, given the customer service objective.

Total costs = Transportation Costs + Warehousing Costs + Order Processing and Information Costs + Lot Quantity Costs + Inventory Carrying Costs.

Source: Adapted from Douglas M. Lambert, *The Development of an Inventory Costing Methodology: A Study of the Costs Associated with Holding Inventory* (Chicago: NCPDM, 1976), p. 7. Copyright © 1975 by Douglas M. Lambert.

improved or more can be spent on other components of the marketing mix to maintain or improve market position.

Even though the costs of lost sales may be impossible to quantify, if management determines service levels based on actual customer needs, better decisions are possible. The goal is to determine the *least total cost,* given the customer service objectives. Accurate cost data must therefore be available for the other five cost categories shown in Figure 12-4.

Transportation Costs

Transportation costs can be managed in total or on an incremental basis. If not currently available in any other form, transportation costs can be determined by a statistical audit of freight bills for common carriers or from corporate accounting records for private fleets. Also, standard costs can be established for the transportation activity. For example, a firm used a computerized system with standard charges and routes for 25,000 routes and eight different methods of transportation.[13] Up to 300,000 combinations were possible and the system was updated regularly. Clerks at any location could obtain from the computer the optimum method of shipment. A monthly computer printout listed the following information by customer:

- Destination
- Standard freight cost to customer
- Actual freight paid for shipments to customer
- Standard freight to warehouse cost
- Total freight cost
- Origin of shipment
- Sales district office
- Method of shipment
- Container used
- Weight of shipment
- Variance in excess of a given amount per hundredweight

Another monthly report listed the deviation from standard freight cost for each customer and the amount of the variance. This system obviously provided the firm with a measure of freight performance. Equally important, the standards provided the means for determining individual customer profitability and for identifying opportunities for logistics cost trade-offs. Because this firm used standards as an integral part of its management information system, it could easily determine the impact of such a system change as an improved, automated order processing system on transportation costs.

Warehousing Costs

Warehousing costs comprise all the expenses that can be eliminated or must be increased because of a change in the number of warehousing facilities. Sometimes warehousing costs are wrongfully included in inventory carrying costs. That is wrong because most warehousing costs do not change with the level of inventory stocked but rather with the number of stocking locations. In addition, the costs of leased or owned facilities are primarily fixed and would not change with a change in the amount of inventory. However, additional labor costs may be incurred if the throughput increases. Therefore, warehousing costs should be separated into two distinct categories: throughput costs and storage costs.

1. *Throughput costs.* Throughput costs are the costs associated with selling a product in a given market by moving it into and out of a warehouse in that market. Examples of throughput costs are the charges that public warehouses assess for product handling into and out of their facilities. These charges are related to how much of a product is sold in that market. Throughput costs should be included in warehousing costs so that the increments can be added or subtracted easily with changes in distribution system configuration. The difficulty experienced in isolating warehousing costs is different for public warehouses and privately owned or leased facilities.
2. *Storage costs.* Storage space costs are those that public warehousing assigns to customers according to the amount of inventory stored in the facility and should be included in inventory carrying costs, not warehousing costs.

Public Warehouses. Generally, determining public warehousing costs presents no problem. Most public warehouses charge on a per hundredweight or per case basis for both handling and storage. Consequently, these costs are totally variable. In some instances, however, a one-shot billing system is used whereby the handling charge implicitly includes a storage component. With this type of billing, it is usually necessary to guarantee a specified number of inventory turns; a penalty is charged for recurring storage if turns do not meet or exceed the standard.

Privately Owned or Leased Facilities. As discussed previously, most of the costs associated with company-owned or leased facilities are fixed and do not change over the course of the year. Those costs that are variable vary with throughput. Care must be exercised when allocating these costs to users.

For example, a multidivision corporation that manufactured and sold high-margin pharmaceuticals as well as a number of lower-margin packaged goods products maintained several field warehouse locations managed by the corporate logistics group. These climate-controlled facilities were designed for the pharmaceutical business and required security and housekeeping practices that far exceeded those necessary for packaged goods. To utilize the facilities fully, the corporation encouraged nonpharmaceutical divisions to store their products in these distribution centers. The costs of operating the warehouses were primarily fixed, although additional warehouse employees or overtime payments were necessary if the volume of product handled (throughput) increased.

The corporate policy was to allocate costs to user divisions based on the percentage of the total number of square feet used by each division in the warehouses. The high cost associated with facilities used for warehousing pharmaceuticals made the corporate allocations significantly higher than they would have been for public warehousing rates for general merchandise. The vice president of logistics in one of the divisions realized that similar services could be obtained at lower cost to his division by using public warehouses. For this reason, he withdrew the division's products from the corporate facilities and put them in public warehouses in the same cities.

Although the volume of product handled and stored in the corporate distribution centers decreased substantially, savings were minimal in terms of the total costs incurred by these facilities. This was because of the high proportion of fixed costs. Consequently, approximately the same cost was allocated to fewer users, thus encouraging other divisions to change to public warehouses to obtain lower rates.

The result was higher, not lower, total company warehousing costs. The corporate warehousing costs were primarily fixed and would not be altered significantly if the space was totally occupied or a major portion of it was left unused. When the nonpharmaceutical divisions moved to public warehouses, the company continued to incur approximately the same total expense for the corporate-owned and -operated warehouses, and also incurred additional public warehousing charges. In effect, the logistics costing system motivated the divisional logistics managers to act in a manner that harmed the company's interests and raised total costs. This example confirms the importance of understanding cost behavior.

Order Processing And Information Costs

Order processing and information costs include those for issuing and closing orders, the related handling costs, and associated communication costs. It is important to include only those costs that will change with the decision being made. Many managers make the mistake of arriving at estimates of these costs by dividing the total cost of the order processing department by the number of orders processed. This is incorrect because of the large portion of fixed costs that are included. Such a procedure overstates the savings associated with a reduction in the number of orders processed. A better estimate could be obtained by dividing the change in order processing department costs over the previous two years (adjusted for inflation) by the change in the number of orders processed. Other methods include engineering-type time-and-motion studies and regression analysis, which are discussed later in the section on inventory-related damage.

Production Lot Quantity Costs

Production lot quantity costs change as the distribution system changes; they usually include some or all of the following:

- Production preparation costs (setup time, inspection, setup scrap, inefficiency of beginning operation)
- Lost capacity due to changeover
- Materials handling, scheduling, and expediting

The production preparation costs and lost capacity costs are usually available because they are used as inputs to production planning. The other costs can be approximated by taking the incremental total costs incurred for two different levels of activity and dividing by the increment in volume. Regression analysis is another technique that can be used to isolate fixed and variable cost components. The numbers obtained can be used as an input to the design of a logistics system.

Inventory Carrying Costs

Inventory carrying costs should include only those costs that vary with the level of inventory stored. Because some of the concepts required to identify these costs are ambiguous, determining them can be difficult. Inventory carrying costs can be categorized into the following four groups: (1) capital costs, (2) inventory service costs, (3) storage space costs, and (4) inventory risk costs.

Capital Costs on Inventory Investment. Holding inventory ties up money that could be used for other types of investments. Consequently, the company's opportunity cost of capital should be used to reflect accurately the true cost involved. All inventory carrying cost components must be stated in before-tax numbers because all the other costs in the trade-off analysis, such as transportation and warehousing, are reported in before-tax dollars.

In some very special circumstances, such as the fruit-canning industry, short-term financing may be used to finance the seasonal buildup of inventories. In this case, the actual cost of borrowing is the acceptable cost of money. Once the cost of money has been established, it is necessary to determine the value of the inventory on which the inventory carrying cost is to be based. At this point it is necessary to know which of the costing alternatives is being used. For example, is the company using direct costs in determining the inventory value or is it using some form of absorption costing?

There are three common methods of accounting for inventory:

1. *FIFO (first-in, first out).* Stock acquired earliest is assumed to be sold first, leaving stock acquired more recently in inventory.
2. *LIFO (last-in, first out).* Sales are made from the most recently acquired stock, leaving items acquired in the earliest time period in inventory. This method attempts to match the most recent costs of acquiring inventory with sales. LIFO will result in lower inventory valuation and lower profits than the FIFO method in periods of rising prices. The reverse is true when prices are declining.
3. *Average cost.* This method could use either a moving average in which each new purchase is averaged with the remaining inventory to obtain a new average price, or a weighted average in which the total cost of the opening inventory, plus all purchases, is divided by the total number of units.

Neither FIFO nor LIFO isolates and measures the effects of cost fluctuations as special managerial problems. However, when standard costing is used, the currently attainable standards automatically provide a measure of cost variance, gains or losses, that can be reported separately.

For calculating inventory carrying costs, it is immaterial whether the company uses LIFO, FIFO, or average cost for inventory valuation. The value of the inventory for calculating carrying costs is determined by multiplying the number of units of each product in inventory by the standard or actual variable costs associated with manufacturing the product and moving it to the storage location. A manufacturer decreases its inventory investment by selling a unit from inventory and not producing a replacement. Similarly, inventories are increased by manufacturing more product units than are currently demanded. Consequently, in either case, it is current manufacturing costs that are relevant for decision making, because these costs will be saved if inventories are reduced and will be incurred if inventories are increased. Likewise, if products are held in field locations, the transportation cost incurred to move them there, plus the variable costs associated with moving them into storage, are inventoried just as are direct labor costs, direct material costs, and the variable manufacturing overhead.

The implicit assumption is that a reduction in finished goods inventory will lead to a corresponding reduction in inventory throughout the system (see Figure 12-5). That is, a one-time reduction in finished goods inventory results in a one-time reduction in raw materials purchases as inventory is pushed back through the system. Similarly, a planned increase in finished goods inventory results in a one-time increase in the quantity of raw materials purchased and subsequently pushed through the system. When this one-time change in inventory value, a balance sheet account, is multiplied by the opportunity cost of money, it becomes an annual cost, a profit-and-loss statement account. This is important because all other components of the inventory carrying annual cost are annual costs and affect the profit-and-loss statement, as do the other cost categories like transportation, warehousing, production lot quantity, and order processing.

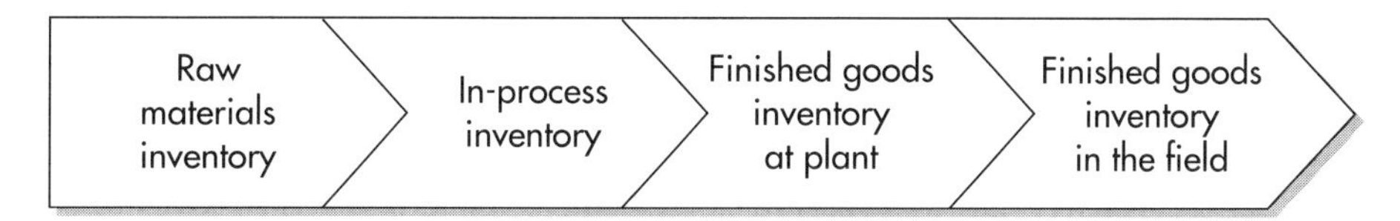

Assumption:
A one-time increase (decrease) in finished goods inventory results is a one-time increase (decrease) in raw materials purchased

Figure 12-5
Inventory Positions in the Physical Distribution System

Source: Adapted from Douglas M. Lambert, *The Development of an Inventory Costing Methodology: A Study of the Costs Associated with Holding Inventory* (Chicago: NCPDM, 1976), p. 14. Copyright © 1975 by Douglas M. Lambert.

Inventory Service Costs. Inventory service costs comprise taxes and insurance paid as a result of holding inventory. Taxes vary, depending on the state in which inventories are held; in some states, inventories are tax-exempt. In general, taxes vary directly with inventory levels. Insurance rates are not strictly proportional to inventory levels because insurance is usually purchased to cover a certain value of product for a specified time period. However, normally insurance policies are periodically revised according to expected inventory changes. In some instances, policies can be issued where premiums are based on the monthly amounts insured. Insurance rates vary, depending on the materials used in the construction of the building, its age, and considerations such as type of fire prevention equipment installed.

For both insurance and taxes, the actual dollars spent on each of these expenses during the past year can be calculated as a percentage of that year's inventory value and added to the cost of money component of the carrying cost. If budgeted figures are available for the coming year, they can be used as a percentage of the inventory value based on the inventory plan—the forecast inventory level—to provide a future-oriented carrying cost. Generally, few significant changes occur in the taxes and insurance components of the inventory carrying cost.

Storage Space Costs. In general, four types of warehouse facilities should be considered: (1) plant, (2) public, (3) rented (leased), and (4) company-owned (private).

1. *Plant Warehouses.* The costs associated with plant warehouses are primarily fixed. The few variable expenses that would change with the level of stored inventory, like the cost of taking an inventory, should be included in inventory carrying costs. Fixed charges and allocated costs are not relevant for inventory policy decisions. If the warehouse space could be rented or used for some other productive purpose when not used for storing inventory, and the associated opportunity costs are not readily available to the manager, then it makes sense to substitute the appropriate fixed or allocated costs as surrogate measures for opportunity cost.

2. *Public Warehouses.* Charges for public warehouse facilities usually are based on the amount of product handled and the amount of inventory held in storage. In some cases, the first month's storage must be paid when the products are moved into the facility. In effect, this makes the first month's storage a handling charge because it must be paid on every case of product, regardless of how long it is held in storage. Public warehouses are usually used because they offer the most economical way to provide the desired level of customer service without incurring

excessive transportation costs. For this reason, the majority of costs incurred from the use of public warehouses, the related handling charges, should be considered as throughput costs, and only charges for recurring storage that are explicitly included in the warehouse rates should be considered in inventory carrying costs. In situations where a given throughput rate is based on the number of inventory turns, it is necessary to estimate the storage cost component by considering how the throughput cost per case would change if the number of inventory turns changed. Of course, the public warehouse charges paid at the time that inventory is placed into field storage should be included when calculating the value of the inventory investment.

3. *Rented (Leased) Warehouses.* Space in rented or leased facilities is normally contracted for a specified period of time. The amount of rented space is based on the maximum storage required during the period covered by the contract. Thus, the rate of warehouse rental charges does not fluctuate from day to day with changes in the inventory level, although the rental rates can vary from month to month or year to year when a new contract is negotiated. Most costs, such as rent payment, the manager's salary, security costs, and maintenance expenses, are fixed when related to time. However, some expenses, such as warehouse labor and equipment-operating costs, vary with throughput. During the contract very few, if any, costs will vary with the amount of inventory stored. All the costs could be eliminated by not renewing the contract and are therefore a relevant input for decision making. However, operating costs that are not variable with the quantity of inventory held should not be included in the carrying costs but rather in the warehousing cost category of the cost trade-off analysis. Fixed costs and costs that are variable with throughput should not be included in inventory carrying costs. Such a practice will result in erroneous decisions.

4. *Company-Owned (Private) Warehouses.* The costs associated with company-owned warehouses are primarily fixed, although some may be variable with throughput. All operating costs that could be eliminated by closing a company-owned warehouse or the net savings resulting from a change to public warehouses should be included in the warehousing costs and not in inventory carrying costs. Only costs that are variable with the quantity of inventory belong in inventory carrying costs.

Inventory Risk Costs. Inventory risk costs vary from company to company but typically include charges for (1) obsolescence, (2) damage, (3) pilferage, and (4) relocation.

1. *Obsolescence.* The cost of obsolescence is the aggregate cost of each unit that must be disposed of at a loss because it is no longer possible to sell it at regular price. It is the difference between the original cost of the unit and its salvage value, or the original selling price and the reduced selling price, if the price has been lowered to move the product to avoid obsolescence. This figure may or may not show up on the profit-and-loss statement as a separate item. Usually, obsolescence results in an overstatement of the cost-of-goods-manufactured account or the cost-of-goods-sold account. Consequently, some difficulty may be experienced in arriving at this figure.

2. *Damage.* This cost should include only the portion of damage that is variable with the amount of inventory held. Damage incurred during shipping should be considered a throughput cost because this damage will be incurred regardless of inventory levels. Damage attributed to a public warehouse operation is usually charged to the warehouse operator if it is above some specified maximum amount. Often damage is identified as the net amount after claims. Because it is not always known just what portions of damage, shrinkage, and relocation costs are related

to the amount of inventory held, it may be necessary to determine mathematically whether a relationship does exist. Damage can be a function of such factors as throughput, general housekeeping, the quality and training of management and labor, the type of product, the protective packaging used, the materials handling system, the number of times that the product is handled, and how it is handled. To say which factor is the most important and how much damage each one accounts for is extremely difficult. Even an elaborate reporting system may not yield the desired results, because employees may try to shift the blame. The quality of inspection during the receiving function and the fact that higher inventories may hide damaged product until inventories are reduced may contribute to the level of damage reported, regardless of the cause. The portion of a cost that is variable with inventory can be determined by the use of regression analysis or plotting the data graphically.[14] Simple linear regression can be used as a tool for segregating the portion of a cost component that is related to the level of inventory held. The principal objective in simple linear regression analysis is to establish a quantitative relationship between two related variables. To establish the relationship between two variables, x and y, a number of paired observations similar to those in Table 12-2 must be obtained. Suppose we are able to obtain the total damage figure in dollars for a number of time periods but we do not know how much of this damage is directly related to the level of inventory. The first pair of observations ($y = 80$, $x = 11$) indicates that $80,000 worth of damage occurred in the period when inventory was worth $11 million.

Now the data can be plotted on graph paper with each pair of observations represented by a point on the chart (see Figure 12-6). A point is obtained by plotting the independent variable x along the horizontal axis and the dependent variable y along the vertical axis. When all the pairs of observations have been plotted, a straight line is drawn that attempts to minimize the distance of all the points from the line (the statistical technique is called least squares regression).

Once this has been done, any two points, A and B, should be selected on the estimated regression line (see Figure 12-6). The increment in the damage from A to B and the change in the inventory from A to B should be expressed as a percentage:

$$100\%(D \div I) = 100\%(\$10{,}000 \div \$2{,}000{,}000) = 0.5\%$$

The 0.5 percent can be interpreted as the percentage of the inventory investment that is damaged because product is being held in inventory. This percentage can be added to the other cost components to determine the total carrying cost percentage. If damage does in fact increase with increased levels of inventory, then the estimated regression line must move upward to the right. A line that is vertical, horizontal, or sloping upward to the left would indicate that such a relationship does not exist. The ability to fit a line through the plotted points successfully depends

TABLE 12-2
Damage and Corresponding Inventory Levels at Various Points in Time

Time Period	**1**	**2**	**3**	**4**	**5**	**6**	**7**
y, Damage ($ thousands)	80	100	70	60	50	70	100
x, Inventory ($ millions)	11	15	13	10	7	9	13

Source: Douglas M. Lambert and James R. Stock, *Strategic Logistics Management,* 3d ed. (Homewood, Ill.: Irwin, 1993), p. 376.

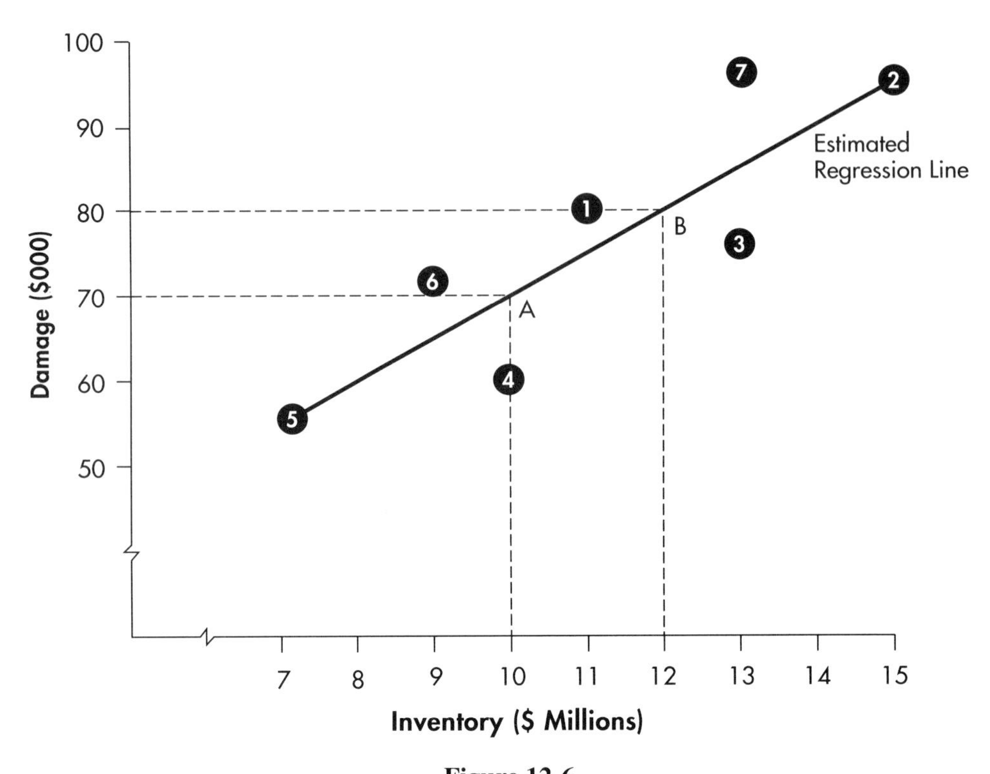

Figure 12-6

Relationship Between Damage and Inventory Level

Source: Douglas M. Lambert and James R. Stock, *Strategic Logistics Management,* 3d ed. (Homewood, Ill.: Irwin, 1993), p. 377.

on the strength of the relationship present or the degree of correlation. Figure 12-7 depicts three possibilities:

a. *No correlation.* Points are scattered, indicating no relationship.
b. *Moderate correlation.* Points are all situated relatively close to the estimated regression line, indicating a moderate relationship.
c. *Perfect correlation.* All the points fall on the line. This would be a correlation of 1.0. The closer the correlation is to 1.0, the stronger the relationship.

3. *Shrinkage.* In the opinion of many authorities, inventory theft is a more serious problem than cash embezzlement. It is far more common, involves far more employees, and is difficult to control. However, this cost may be more closely related to company security measures than to inventory levels, even though it definitely varies with the number of warehouse locations. Consequently, in many companies it may be appropriate to assign some or all of the shrinkage costs to the warehousing cost category.

4. *Relocation.* Relocation costs are incurred when inventory is transshipped from one warehouse location to another to avoid obsolescence. For example, products that are selling well in the Midwest may not be selling on the West Coast. By shipping the products to the location

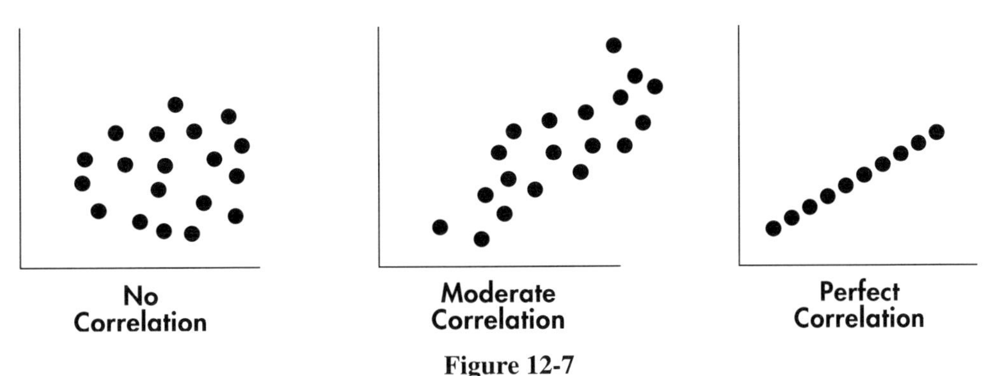

Figure 12-7

Example of Relationship Strength Between Two Variables

Source: James R. Stock and Douglas M. Lambert *Strategic Logistics Management*, 2d ed. (Homewood, Ill.: Irwin, 1987), p. 373.

where they will sell, the company avoids the obsolescence cost but incurs additional transportation costs. Often, these costs are not reported separately but are simply included in transportation costs. In such cases, a managerial estimate or a statistical audit of freight bills can be used to isolate the transshipment costs. The frequency of these shipments determines which approach is the most practical in any given situation. That is, if such shipments are rare, the percentage component of the carrying cost will be very small and a managerial estimate should suffice. In some cases, transshipment costs may be incurred as a result of inventory stocking policies. For example, if inventories are set too low in field locations, stockouts may occur and may be rectified by shipping products from the nearest warehouse that has the items in stock. Consequently, the costs are a result of decisions that involve trade-offs between or among transportation costs, warehousing costs, inventory carrying costs, and/or stockout costs. These are transportation costs and should not be classified as inventory carrying costs.

The methodology that should be used to calculate inventory carrying costs is summarized in Figure 12-8. The model shown there is referred to as normative because its use will result in a carrying cost figure that accurately reflects a firm's costs.

Controlling Logistics Activities

One of the major reasons for improving the availability of logistics cost data is to control and monitor logistics performance. Without accurate cost data, performance analysis is next to impossible. How, for example, can a firm expect to control the cost of shipping a product to a customer if it does not know what the cost should be? How can management determine whether distribution center costs are high or low in the absence of performance measurements? Are inventory levels satisfactory, too high, or too low? The list is not all-inclusive, but it serves to illustrate the need for accurate cost data.

The importance of a good measurement program for the management and control of logistics performance was addressed by the Council of Logistics Management in a 1978 study:

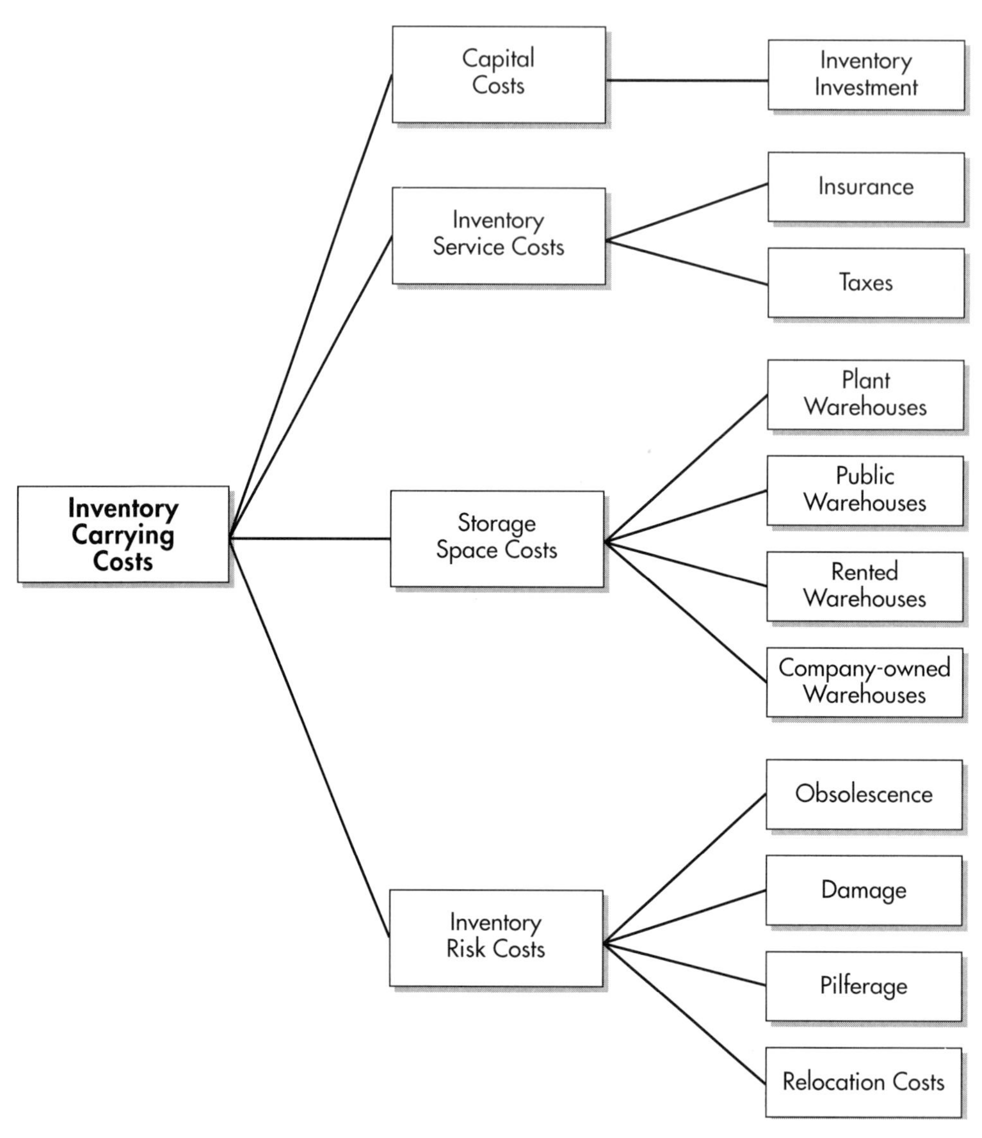

Figure 12-8

Normative Model of Inventory Carrying Cost Methodology

Source: Douglas M. Lambert, *The Development of an Inventory Costing Methodology: A Study of the Costs Associated with Holding Inventory* (Chicago: NCPDM, 1976), p. 68. Copyright © 1975 by Douglas M. Lambert.

If no measurement program exists, the "natural" forces shaping the behavior of busy managers tend to place the emphasis on the negative. Issues only attract management attention when something is "wrong." In this type of situation, there is often little reinforcement of positive results. A formal measurement program helps improve employee morale.... Once a plan has been established, actual results can be measured and compared with the plan to identify variances requiring management attention.[15]

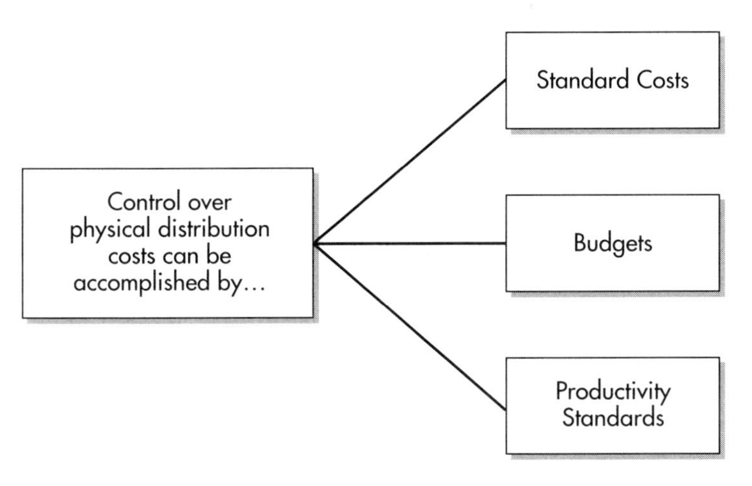

Figure 12-9
Controlling Logistics Cost

Source: James R. Stock and Douglas M. Lambert, *Strategic Logistics Management,* 2d ed. (Homewood, Ill.: Irwin, 1987), p. 576.

The challenge is not so much to create new data, because much of it already exists in one form or another, but to tailor the existing data in the accounting system to meet the needs of the logistics function.[16] By improving the availability of logistics cost data, management will be in a better position to make both operational and strategic decisions. It stands to reason that abnormal levels of costs can be detected and controlled only if normal cost ranges have been determined for various levels of activity. As shown in Figure 12-9, logistics performance can be monitored by standard costs, budgets, and productivity standards.

Standard Costs and Flexible Budgets

Control of costs through predetermined standards and flexible budgets is the most comprehensive type of control system available.[17] The use of standard costs represents a frontal assault on the logistics costing problem because it attempts to determine what the costs should be, rather than basing future cost predictions on past cost behavior.

Nevertheless, the use of standards has not been widespread. In part, this is because logistics costs are believed to be, by nature, quite different from those in other areas of the business. Although there may be some merit to this argument, logistics activities are, by nature, repetitive, and such operations lend themselves to control by standards. A more compelling reason why standard costs have not achieved widespread acceptance is that few attempts have been made to install such systems. In fact, it is only recently that the importance of logistics cost control has been recognized.

The lack of standard costs for logistics is unfortunate because management accountants and industrial engineers of most firms have developed a wealth of experience in installing standard costs in the production area, which, with some effort, could be expanded into logistics. However, developing standards for logistics may be more complex because the output measures are often more diverse than they are in production. For example, in developing a standard for the picking function, the eventual control measure could be stated as a standard cost per order, a standard cost per order line, a standard cost per unit shipped, or a standard cost per shipment. Despite these complexities, work measurement does appear to be increasing in logistics activities.

The use of standards as a management control system is illustrated in Figure 12-10, which shows how standards may result from formal investigation, from philosophy or intuition, or from both. The following explains the various steps in the system.[18]

Once standards have been set, the firm must compare actual performance with the particular standard to see if it is acceptable. If performance is acceptable, the system is deemed to be under control and that is the end of the control process. Inherent in this notion is that management operates under the principle of exception, exerting no changes in the system so long as it operates satisfactorily; and the measure of "satisfactory" is found in the standard.

It is highly unlikely that performance will exactly equal standard. Where there is a departure, the procedure is to break the variance into its components to try to ascertain its sources. For example, the standard may be a budgeted amount for transportation in a territory. If the actual exceeds the budget, management would like to see the variance analyzed into separate measures of volume and efficiency. It is impossible to know how to proceed unless the variance is analyzed into meaningful sources.

The next question is whether the observed variance is great enough to be deemed significant. It is possible to handle such a question in strictly statistical terms, setting quality control limits about the standard. This may be done in terms of standard deviations and an acceptable limit established on the downside only, or the limit may be on either side of the standard. Thus, in the latter case, if performance exceeds standard, management may decide to raise the standard or reward the performer accordingly. Probably of greater concern are those departures in which performance is below standard.

Much of logistics lends itself to measures of statistical significance in departures from standard. However, as with demand-obtaining activities, it is probably more meaningful to judge departures from standard in terms of their practical significance. A form of sensitivity analysis here raises the question of how critical is the departure in its effects on bottom-line performance (net profit).

Regardless of how the assessment is made, the variance will be termed either significant or not significant. If it is not significant, performance is judged acceptable and the control process ends. If significant, the next question is whether action is required.

The variance may be significant but, in analyzing and explaining it, we do not judge the departure from standard controllable. If so, no action may be indicated and the control process is terminated. If action is indicated, it will be one of two broad kinds. Either the standard is held to be wrong and must be changed, or the process itself is not producing the results it should and thus must be changed. The feedback goes up to the appropriate levels. If the process is changed and the standard is held, comparisons are again made. If the standard is changed and the process remains unchanged, the feedback is to the standard. It is possible they both would be changed. Thus, both feedbacks may result from the action phase, and the system will cycle through again.

A standard tells management the expected cost of performing selected activities and allows comparisons to be made to determine whether operating inefficiencies have occurred. For example, Table 12-3 shows a sample report that can be useful at the operating level. It shows why warehouse labor for the picking activity was $320 over budget for a one-week period.

Actual costs of logistics activities can be aggregated by department, division, function, or total, and then compared with their standard. The results can be included as part of a regular weekly or monthly performance report. One such level of aggregation that would be of interest to a com-

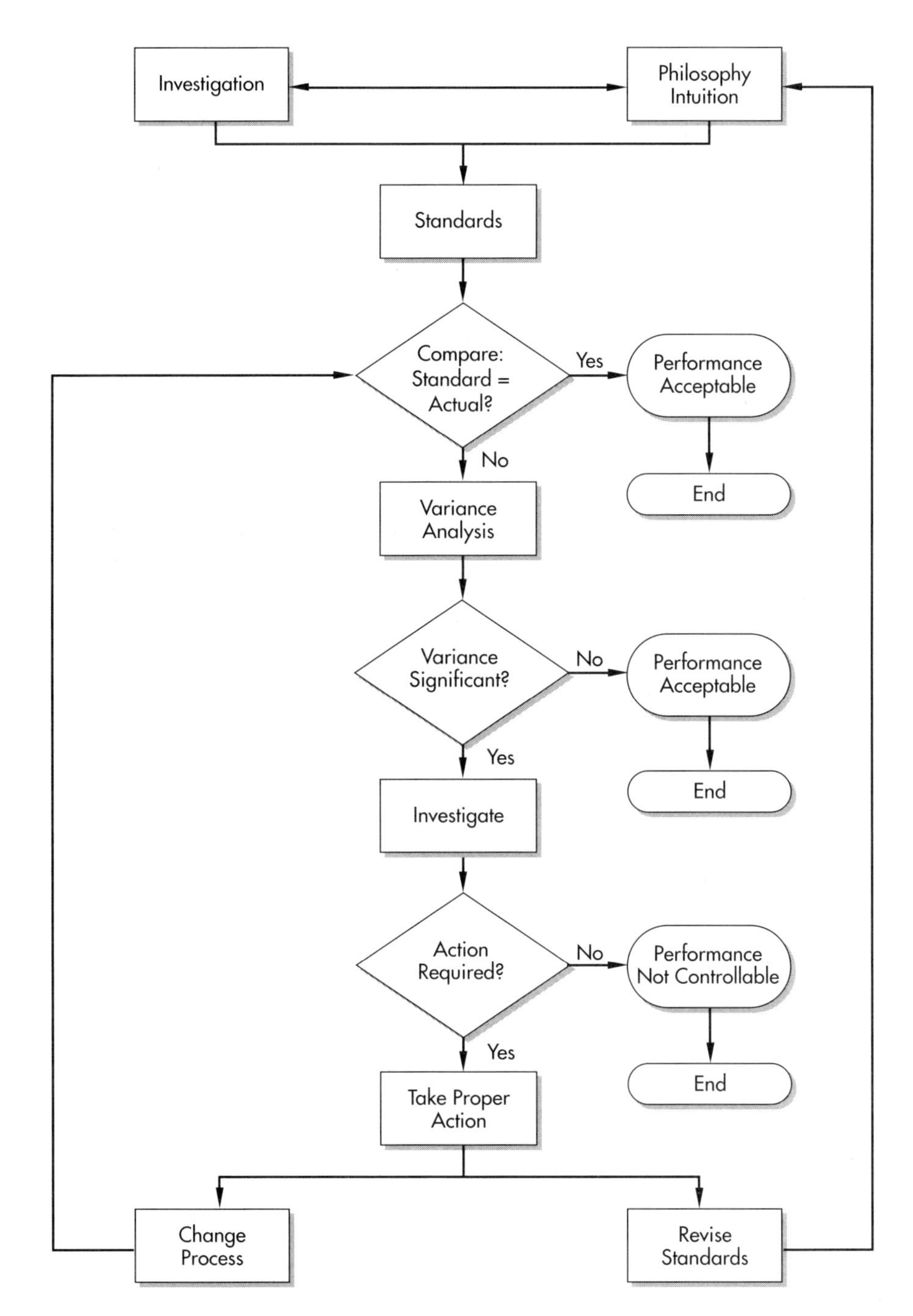

Figure 12-10

The Use of Standards as a Management Control System

Source: Richard J. Lewis and Leo G. Erickson, "Distribution System Costing: An Overview," in John R. Grabner and William S. Sargent, eds., *Distribution System Costing: Concepts and Procedures* (Columbus, Ohio: Transportation and Logistics Research Foundation, 1972), p. 17A.

TABLE 12-3
Summary of Warehouse Picking Operation
week of 12/14

Items picked during week	14,500
Standard item picks per hour	50
Standard hours allowed for picks performed	290
Actual hours accumulated on picking activities	330
Difference between standard and actual hours	(40)
Standard cost per labor hour	$8.00
Variation in cost due to inefficiency	($320.00)

Source: Douglas M. Lambert and James R. Stock, *Strategic Logistics Management,* 3d ed. (Homewood, Ill.: Irwin, 1993), p. 598.

pany president is shown in Table 12-4. This report allows the president to see why targeted net income has not been reached. On the one hand, there is a $3 million difference due to ineffectiveness, which simply indicates the net income the company has forgone because of its inability to meet its budgeted level of sales. On the other hand, there is also an inefficiency factor of $1.4 million. This factor indicates that at the level of sales actually achieved, the segment-controllable margin should have been $18 million. The difference between $18 million and the actual outcome of $16.6 million is the variation due to inefficiencies within the marketing and logistics functions.

In this example, it is assumed that actual sales revenue decreased as a result of lower volume and the average price paid per unit sold remained the same. If the average price per unit changes, then an additional variance (the marketing variance) can be computed. This analysis can be performed for segments like products, customers, geographic areas, or divisions.

The difference in income, the total variance of the segment contribution margin ($16.6 million – $21 million), is an unfavorable variance (loss) of $4.4 million, which can be explained by:

- Ineffectiveness—inability to reach target sales objective, resulting in a $3 million unfavorable variance
- Inefficiency—failure to perform to standards at the actual operating level of $80 million, resulting in a $1.4 million unfavorable variance

Standard Costs and Flexible Budgets for Warehousing

The first step in the development of standard costs and flexible budgets is to define operating characteristics and the possible units of measure such as order, case, shipment, stock keeping unit, line item, arrival, and/or overpacked carton.[19] In this example, the basic operating elements consist of receiving (unloading and clerical), shipping (clerical and order consolidation), stock put away, stock replenishment, order picking, and overpacking. A description of the process is shown in Figure 12-11.

Next, a 45-day sample was obtained and data were accumulated for the various important functions of the operation. The results of the sample are shown in Table 12-5.

The average number of occurrences observed and the standard deviation (SD) make up a mea-

TABLE 12-4
Segmental Analysis Using a Contribution Approach
($ millions)

	Budget 1	Actual Results 2	Standard Allowed for Actual Output 3	(3-1) Effectiveness Variance 4	(3-2) Efficiency Variance 5	(2-1) Total Variance 6
Net sales	90.0	80.0	80.0	(10.0)	—	(10.0)
Cost of goods sold*	40.5	36.0	36.0	(4.5)	—	(4.5)
Manufacturing contribution	49.5	44.0	44.0	(5.5)	—	(5.5)
Variable sales costs†	22.5	21.4	20.0	(2.5)	(1.4)	(1.1)
Segment contribution margin	27.0	22.6	24.0	(3.0)	(1.4)	(4.4)
Assignable nonvariable costs‡	6.0	6.0	6.0	—	—	—
Segment-controllable margin	21.0	16.6	18.0	(3.0)	(1.4)	(4.4)

* Also known as variable manufacturing cost.
† More accurately described as variable marketing and physical distribution costs. These out-of-pocket costs vary directly with sales to the segment; they might include sales commissions, transportation costs, warehouse handling costs, order processing costs, and a charge for accounts receivable.
‡ These costs are incurred specifically for the segment during the period; they might include salaries, segment-related advertising, bad debts, and inventory carrying costs. The fixed costs associated with corporate owned and operated facilities would be included if, and only if, the warehouse was solely for this segment of the business.

Source: Adapted from Douglas M. Lambert and James R. Stock, *Strategic Logistics Management,* 3d ed. (Homewood, Ill.: Irwin, 1993), p. 599.

sure of central tendency or variation around the average. The larger the standard deviation, the more variation there is in day-to-day activity. Because receiving activities tend to fluctuate more than the shipping activities, the receiving function has higher standard deviations than the shipping function.

Now that the process has been described and its operating characteristics and activity levels are known, the next step is to develop activity standards. These have been developed using empirical standards. They could have been developed based on industry standards, engineering studies, or historical data, but the empirical method of observing the operation and using judgment to develop estimates is thought to be the most appropriate in the example being described (see Table 12-6). With the daily activities, the approximate levels of activity, and knowledge of the process determined, this information is used to develop standard costs.

The information in Table 12-7, which includes the standard times and hourly wage rates, allows an incremental cost per unit of measure to be calculated. The unit of measure for each activity might be different (in fact, in this case they are different—that is, piece, SKU, line item, and freight shipment). In some cases it is possible to lump activities together as they are in the receiving function, but this is not possible in every situation. The standard cost per unit of measure is obtained by dividing the labor costs per labor hour by the estimated standard time.

If this warehousing operation were using flexible budgeting, the standard costs would be used to develop the flexible budget. An example is contained in Table 12-8. In that week 4,200 cases were received, 1,000 stockkeeping units were replenished, and so on. These activity levels, when multiplied by the standard costs per unit, gave the total standard costs for each activity. The actual costs incurred during the week also are shown, and variances—favorable or unfavorable—

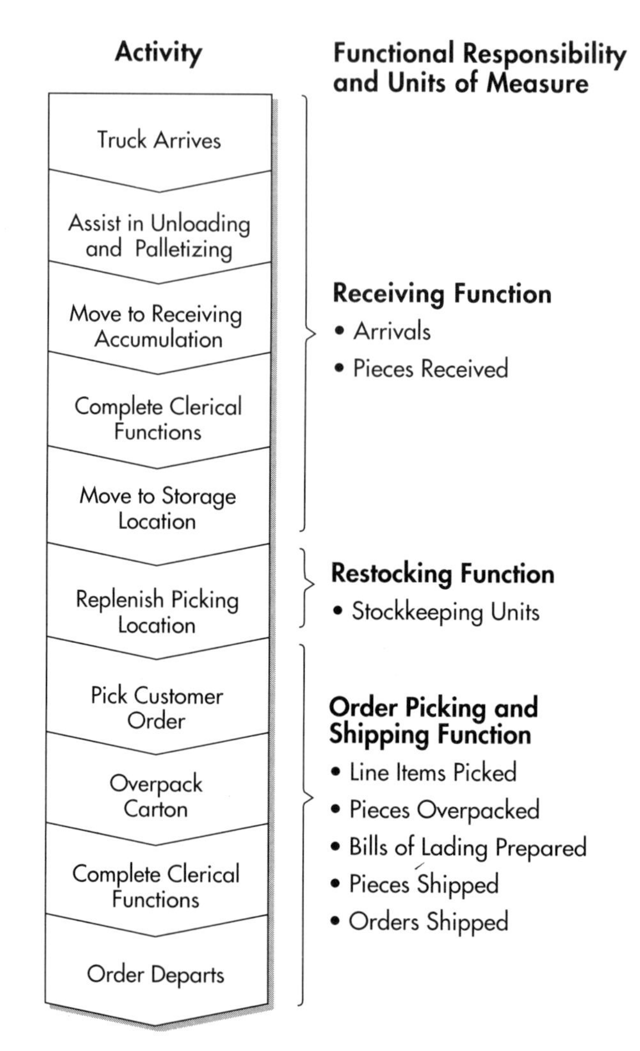

Figure 12-11
Operating Characteristics

Source: Adapted from Howard M. Armitage and James F. Dickow, "Controlling Distribution with Standard Cost and Flexible Budgets," *1979 Annual Conference Proceedings* of the National Council of Physical Distribution (Chicago: NCPDM, 1979), p. 117. Adapted by permission.

are calculated. For the activity levels achieved during the week, a net unfavorable variance of $125 was calculated. Because this activity level was significantly higher than the average level of activity, the unfavorable variance would have been larger had a fixed budget approach been used.

Developing standard costs and using them to develop a flexible budget gives management a tool to measure the performance of individuals. The minimization of unfavorable variances is a goal that, when achieved, yields increased profits.

TABLE 12-5
Activity Levels
45-day sample

Function	Unit of Measure	Average (per Day)	Standard Deviation (per Day)
Receiving Functions			
Arrivals	Arrivals	18	14
Unloaded	Pieces	735	731
Stock put away	Pieces	735	731
Replenishment Functions			
Volume	SKUs	200	0
Shipping Functions			
Order picking	Line items	279	72
Overpacking	Pieces	85	37
Orders	Orders	113	31
Freight shipments	Bill of lading	61	41
Small shipments	Pieces	83	24
Load	Pieces	863	198

Source: Adapted from Howard M. Armitage and James F. Dickow, "Controlling Distribution with Standard Cost and Flexible Budgets," *1979 Annual Conference Proceedings* of the National Council of Physical Distribution (Chicago: NCPDM, 1979), p. 117. Adapted by permission.

TABLE 12-6
Activity Standards
developed empirically

Operating Function	Unit of Measure	Time Standard
Warehouse Receiving		
Unload truck	Pieces/labor hour	250
Check receipts	Pieces/labor hour	167
Clerical function	Pieces/labor hour	500
Putaway stock	Pieces/labor hour	150
Warehouse Shipping		
Order picking	Line items/labor hour	30
Order packing	Pieces/labor hour	22.7
UPS/small shipment	Pieces/labor hour	100
Freight shipping	Bills of lading/labor hour	15
Warehouse Stockkeeping		
Bulk items	Skill/labor hour	70
QA and shelf items	Skill/labor hour	50

Source: Howard M. Armitage and James F. Dickow, "Controlling Distribution with Standard Cost and Flexible Budgets," *1979 Annual Conference Proceedings* of the National Council of Physical Distribution (Chicago: NCPDM, 1979), p. 118. Reprinted by permission.

TABLE 12-7
Standard Costs

Function	Unit of Measure (u/m)	Daily Activity	Time Standard (u/m per minute)	Hourly Rate ($ per minute)	Standard Cost (¢ per u/m)
Receiving					
Unload truck	Pieces	735	250	7.50	3.0
Check receipts	Pieces	735	167	7.50	4.5
Clerical	Pieces	735	500	7.50	1.5
Putaway stock	Pieces	735	150	7.50	5.0
					14.0
Replenishment					
Replenish	SKUs	200	50	7.50	5.0
Shipping					
Order picking	Line item	279	30	8.00	27.0
Overpacking	Pieces	86	23	7.50	33.0
Small shipping	Pieces	83	100	8.00	8.0
Freight shipping	Shipments	61	15	8.25	55.0

Source: Howard M. Armitage and James F. Dickow, "Controlling Distribution with Standard Cost and Flexible Budgets," *1979 Annual Conference Proceedings* of the National Council of Physical Distribution (Chicago: NCPDM, 1979), p. 119. Reprinted by permission.

BUDGETS

Conceptually, there is little doubt regarding the general superiority of standard costs for control. However, there will be times when the use of standards is inappropriate. This is particularly true in situations that involve essentially nonrepetitive tasks and for which work unit measurements are difficult to establish. In these situations, control still can be achieved through budgetary prac-

TABLE 12-8
Application to a Flexible Budget

			Weekly Summary			
Function	Unit of Measure (u/m)	Standard Cost ($ per u/m)	Activity (u/m)	Standard Cost ($)	Actual Cost ($)	Variance ($)
Receiving	Piece	0.14	4,200	588	800	212 U
Replenishment	SKU	0.15	1,000	150	100	50 F
Shipping						
Order picking	Line item	0.27	1,430	386	450	64 U
Order packing	Piece	0.33	350	116	100	16 F
Small shipping	Piece	0.03	500	40	25	15 F
Freight shipping	Shipments	0.55	400	220	150	70 F
				1500	1625	125 U

Source: Howard M. Armitage and James F. Dickow, "Controlling Distribution with Standard Cost and Flexible Budgets," *1979 Annual Conference Proceedings* of the National Council of Physical Distribution (Chicago: NCPDM, 1979), p. 120. Reprinted by permission.

tices. However, the extent to which the budget is successful depends on whether individual cost behavior patterns can be predicted and whether the budget can be "flexed" to reflect changes in operating conditions.

Most logistics budgets are static; that is, they are plans developed for a budgeted level of output. If actual activity happens to be the same as the budgeted level, a realistic comparison of costs can be made and control will be effective. However, this is seldom the case. Seasonality and internal factors invariably lead to different levels of activity, the efficiency of which can be determined only if the reporting system can compare the actual costs with what they should have been at the operating level actually achieved. In a warehouse, for example, the estimated or budgeted level of activity may be 1,000 line items per week. The actual level of activity, however, may be only 750.

Comparing the budgeted costs at 1,000 line items against the actual costs at 750 leads to the erroneous conclusion that the operation has been efficient since items such as overtime, temporary help, packing, postage, and order processing are less than the budgeted figures. A flexible budget, on the other hand, indicates what the costs should have been at the 750 line items level of activity, and a true dollar measure of efficiency results.

The key to successful implementation of a flexible budget lies in the analysis of cost behavior patterns. To date, little of this analysis has been carried out in the logistics function. The expertise of the management accountant and industrial engineer can be invaluable in applying tools like scatter diagram techniques and regression analysis to determine the fixed and variable components of costs. These techniques utilize previous cost data to determine a variable rate per unit of activity and a total fixed cost component. However, unlike engineered standards, the techniques are based on past cost behavior patterns that undoubtedly contain inefficiencies. The predicted measure of cost, therefore, may not be a measure of what the activity should cost but an estimate of what it will cost based on the results of previous periods. Once fixed and variable costs have been determined, flexible budget for control becomes a reality.

Productivity Ratios

Logistics costs also can be controlled by the use of productivity ratios. These ratios take the form of :

Productivity = Measure of Output ÷ Measure of Input

For example, a warehouse operation might make use of such productivity ratios as:

Number of orders shipped this period ÷ Number of orders received this period
Number of orders shipped this period ÷ Average number of orders shipped per period
Number of orders shipped this period ÷ Number of direct labor hours worked this period

Productivity ratios for transportation might include:

Ton miles transported ÷ Total actual transportation cost
Stops served ÷ Total actual transportation cost
Shipments transported to destination ÷ Total actual transportation cost

TABLE 12-9
Transportation Activity/Input Matrix

Activities	Labor	Facilities	Equipment	Energy	Financial Investment	Overall (cost)
Company-Operated Over-the-Road Trucking						
Loading	X					X
Line-haul	X			X		X
Unloading	X					X
Overall	X		X	X		X
Company-Operated Pickup/Delivery Trucking						
Pretrip	X					X
Stem driving	X			X		X
On-route driving	X			X		X
At-stop	X					X
End-of-trip	X					X
Overall	X		X	X		X
Outside Transportation —All Modes						
Loading						X
Line-haul						X
Unloading						X
Transportation/Traffic Management						
Company-operated						X
Outside transportation						X

Source: *Measuring and Improving Productivity in Physical Distribution* (Chicago: National Council of Physical Distribution Management, 1984), p. 144.

The transportation resource inputs for which productivity ratios can be generated include labor, equipment, energy, and cost. The specific relationships among these inputs and transportation activities are illustrated in Table 12-9. An X in a cell of the matrix denotes an activity/input combination that could be measured. Similar activity/input matrices are shown for warehousing (Table 12-10); purchasing, inventory management, and production management (Table 12-11); and customer service (Table 12-12).

Productivity measures of this type can and have been developed for most logistics activities. They are particularly useful in the absence of a standard costing system with flexible budgeting, because they do provide some guidelines on operating efficiencies. Furthermore, these measures are easily understood by management and employees. However, productivity measures are not without their shortcomings:

- *Units of Measure.* Productivity measures are expressed in terms of physical units; therefore, actual dollar losses due to inefficiencies and predictions of future logistics costs can-

TABLE 12-10
Warehouse Activity/Input Matrix

Activities	**Labor**	**Facilities**	**Equipment**	**Energy**	**Financial**	**Overall**
Company-Operated Warehousing						
Receiving	X	X	X			X
Put-away	X		X			X
Storage		X		X		X
Replenishment	X		X			X
Order selection	X		X			X
Checking	X		X			X
Packing and marking	X	X	X			X
Staging and order consolidation	X	X	X			X
Shipping	X	X	X			X
Clerical and administration	X		X			X
Overall	X	X	X	X	X	X
Purchased-Outside Warehousing						
Storage						X
Handling						X
Consolidation						X
Administration						X
Overall						X

Source: *Measuring and Improving Productivity in Physical Distribution* (Chicago: National Council of Physical Distribution Management, 1984), p. 195.

not be made. This makes it extremely difficult to cost-justify any system changes that will result in improved productivity.

- *Lack of Standards.* The actual productivity measure calculated is seldom compared with a productivity standard. For example, a productivity measure may compare the number of orders shipped during a period with the number of direct labor hours worked during that period, but it does not indicate what the relationship ought to be. Without work measurement or some form of cost estimation, it is impossible to know what the productivity standard should be for efficient operations.
- *Distortion.* Changes in output levels may in some cases distort measures of productivity. Distortion occurs because the fixed and variable elements are seldom delineated. Consequently, the productivity measure computes utilization, not efficiency. For example, if 100 orders shipped represents full labor utilization and 100 orders were received this period, then productivity is 100 percent, as measured by:

$$\text{Number of orders shipped this period} \div \text{Number of orders received this period} \times 100\%$$

However, if 150 orders had been received and 100 orders shipped, productivity would have been 66.67%, even though there was no real drop in either efficiency or productivity.

TABLE 12-11
Purchasing, Inventory Management, and Production Management Activity/Input Matrix

Functions/Activities	Inputs			
	Labor	**Equipment**	**Financial**	**Overall**
Purchasing				
Sourcing	X			X
Procurement	X	X		X
Cost control	X			X
Overall				X
Inventory Management				
Forecasting	X	X		X
Planning and budgeting	X	X		X
Execution and control	X	X		X
Overall			X	X
Production Management				
Production planning	X			X
Production control	X			X
Scheduling and dispatching	X	X		X
Shop floor data collection	X	X		X
Overall				X

Source: *Measuring and Improving Productivity in Physical Distribution* (Chicago: National Council of Physical Distribution Management, 1984), p. 242.

Performance Measurement

For performance measurement systems to be truly effective, the data must be captured on formal reports. As an example, reporting practices for transportation are considered. Successful administration of the traffic function requires that day-to-day performance of for-hire carriers and private carriage be measured and controlled. Operating standards in terms of speed of service, size of order shipped, on-time delivery, transit time variability, and damage must be established, and individual carrier performance must be measured. In cases where performance standards are not being met, corrective action must be taken.

Activity-Based Costing

One method of solving the problem of insufficient cost data that has been receiving increased attention is activity-based costing. Traditional accounting systems in manufacturing firms allocate factory overhead to products based on direct labor. In the past, this method of allocation may have resulted in minor distortions. However, product lines and channels have proliferated and overhead costs have increased dramatically, making traditional allocation methods prone to serious error. An activity-based system allows examination of the demands made by particular products (or customers) on indirect resources.[20] There are three useful rules to follow when making this examination[21]:

TABLE 12-12
Customer Service
(Order Processing/Customer Communication)
Activity/Input Matrix

	Inputs			
Activity	**Labor**	**Facilities/ Equipment**	**Working Capital**	**Overall**
Order Processing				
Order entry/editing	X	X	X	X
Scheduling	X			X
Order/shipping set preparation	X	X		X
Invoicing	X	X		X
Customer Communication				
Order modification	X	X		X
Order status inquiries	X	X		X
Tracing and expediting	X	X		X
Error correction	X			X
Product information requests	X			X
Credit and Collection				
Credit checking	X	X		X
Accounts receivable processing and collecting	X	X	X	X

Source: *Measuring and Improving Productivity in Physical Distribution* (Chicago: National Council of Physical Distribution Management, 1984), p. 282.

1. Focus on expensive resources.
2. Emphasize resources whose consumption varies significantly by product and product type.
3. Focus on resources whose demand(s) are uncorrelated with traditional allocation methods like direct labor or materials cost.[22]

The process of tracing costs, first from resources to activities and then from activities to specific products (or customers), cannot be done with surgical precision. However, it is better to be basically correct with activity-based costing, say, within 5 or 10% of the actual demands a product (or customer) makes on organizational resources, than to be precisely wrong (perhaps by as much as 200%) using outdated allocation techniques or including indirect, common costs.

The major shortcoming of activity-based costing is that it is simply another method of allocation, and by definition any method of allocation is arbitrary. The potential problems associated with using activity-based costing for logistics were made very clear in a 1991 article in *Management Accounting.*[23] The article described the use of activity-based costing for marketing and made the claim that physical distribution is the most effective area for application. However, the examples used were simply average costs where selling costs were reported as 5% of sales, advertising costs were 40¢ per unit sold, warehousing costs were 10¢ per pound shipped, packing and shipping costs were 20¢ per unit sold, and general office expenses were allocated at $20 per order.[24]

Clearly, activity-based costing implemented in this manner represents an average cost system that totally distorts the true profitability of business segments. For example, transportation costs need to be identified by origin and destination ZIP codes and by shipment size categories before they can be assigned to customers and/or products. The overriding rule is to *include, in segment reports, only those costs that would disappear if the revenues of the segment were lost.* With this philosophy in mind, we recommend a hybrid system that combines the detailed manufacturing cost structure provided by an activity-based system with the marketing and distribution cost components recognized in the contribution approach to measure segment profits.

Once segment contribution reports are implemented, managers can begin to accurately assess strategic options such as which product lines to drop or whether prices can be raised on inelastic products or reduced on high-volume products. Added emphasis can be placed on those segments that are most profitable. Product lines can be accurately assessed using 80–20 analyses to eliminate unprofitable items. The firms that have developed and implemented segment profitability reports have been able to identify products and customers that were either unprofitable or did not meet corporate financial objectives. Ironically, many of these products/customers were previously thought to be profitable, owing either to their sales volumes or to manufacturing margins. *It is difficult for U.S. firms to compete with foreign competitors even when the U.S. firms have accurate financial information. It is almost impossible to compete effectively with inaccurate information.*

A Distribution Database for Decision Making

One of the most promising database systems for generating logistics cost information and profit contribution performance reports is the modular database concept (see Figure 12-12).[25]

This is a central storage system where source documents like invoices, transportation bills, and other expenses and revenue items are fed in coded form into a database.

Inputs are coded at the lowest possible level of aggregation according to function, subfunction, territory, product, salesperson, channel of distribution, revenue, or expense, to name just a few categories. For example, the following information may be recorded by customer order:

- Customer number
- Customer name
- Order number
- Previous order number
- Customer order number
- Customer billing address
- Customer shipping address
- Customer order date
- Requested shipping date
- Ship date
- Date, time, and operator
- Priority code
- Salesperson number
- Territory
- Region
- Partial shipment back-order number
- Credit limit
- Credit outstanding
- Prepaid/collect freight
- Terms
- Instruction, shipping, product substitution
- Quantity, product number, price
- Packing and shipping instructions
- Carrier
- Bill of lading number

The system is capable of filing large amounts of data and allows rapid aggregation and retrieval of various modules of information for decision making or external reporting. When combined with standard costs, the modular database is capable of generating both cost reports for functions like warehousing and transportation, and segment contribution reports. The system works by charging functions, such as warehousing and transportation with actual costs that are

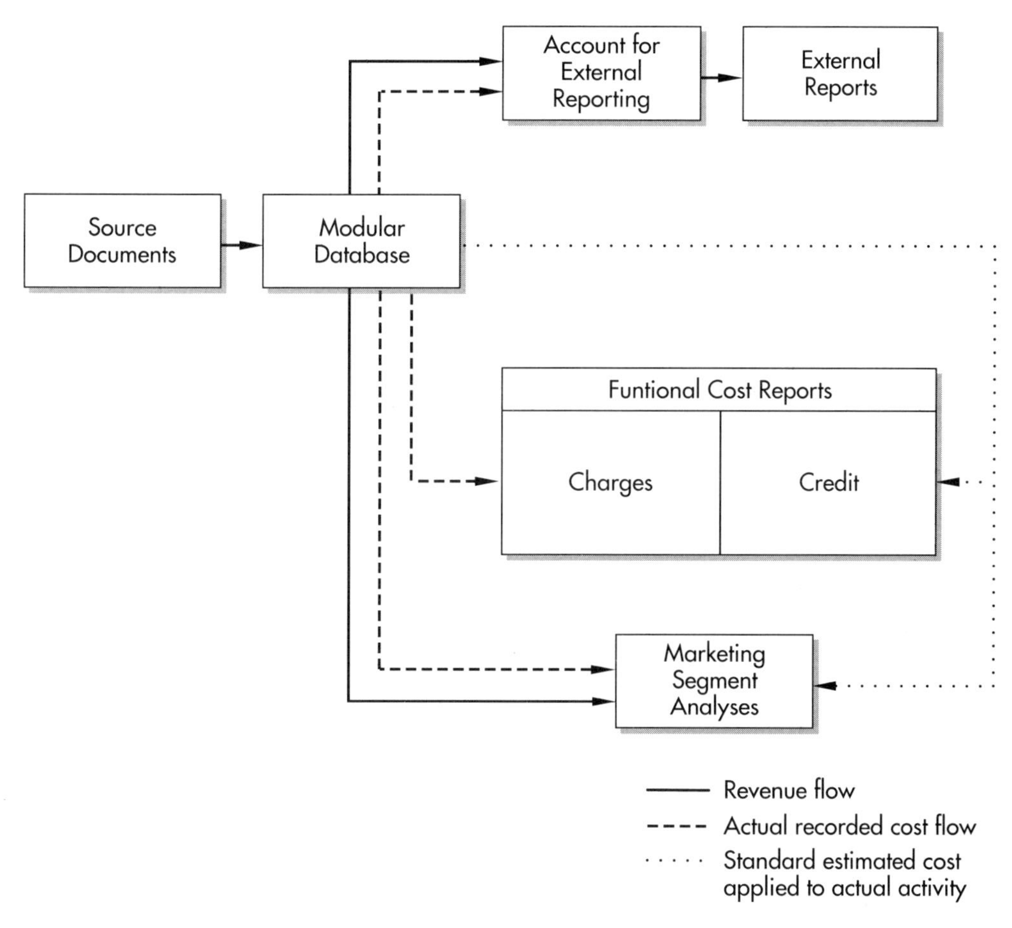

Figure 12-12

Modular Database System for Reporting Cost and Revenue Flows

Source: Frank H. Mossman, Paul M. Fischer, and W. J. E. Crissy, "New Approaches to Analyzing Marketing Profitability," *Journal of Marketing* 38 (April 1974): 45. Reproduced by permission.

then compared with predetermined standards. Individual segments like customers or products are credited with segment revenues and charged the standard cost plus controllable variances.

A channels of distribution example illustrates the modular database approach. To monitor the contribution from selling to department stores, grocery chains, drugstores, and discount stores, the accounting system must be able to provide revenue data by channel (which requires summing the revenues of all products sold per channel type) as well as the manufacturing, distribution, and marketing costs associated with the sales to each channel.

The first step is to determine the variable costs of goods manufactured. Firms using a direct costing system for internal reporting already have this information available. Firms that include all overhead costs (fixed and variable) as product costs must remove the fixed costs. The marketing and logistics costs associated with warehousing, transportation, order processing, inventory, accounts receivable, and sales commissions must be attached to each channel of distribution. Finally, assignable nonvariable costs like sales promotion, advertising, and bad debts should be iden-

TABLE 12-13
Profitability by Major Channels: A Contribution Approach
($000)

		Type of Account			
	Total Company	Department Stores	Grocery Chains	Drug-stores	Discount Stores
Sales	$42,500	$6,250	$10,500	$19,750	$6,000
Less discounts, returns, and allowances	2,500	250	500	1,750	—
Net sales	40,000	6,000	10,000	18,000	6,000
Cost of goods sold (variable manufacturing costs)	20,000	2,500	4,800	9,200	3,500
Manufacturing contribution	20,000	3,500	5,200	8,800	2,500
Variable selling and distribution costs:					
Sales commissions	800	120	200	360	120
Transportation costs	2,500	310	225	1,795	170
Warehouse handling	600	150	—	450	—
Order processing costs	400	60	35	280	25
Charge for investment in accounts receivable	700	20	50	615	15
Contribution margin	15,000	2,840	4,690	5,300	2,170
Assignable nonvariable costs (costs incurred specifically for the segment during the period):					
Sales promotion and slotting allowances	1,250	60	620	400	170
Advertising	500	—	—	500	—
Bad debts	300	—	—	300	—
Display racks	200	—	—	200	—
Inventory carrying costs	1,250	150	200	800	100
Segment controllable margin	$11,500	$2,630	$3,870	$3,100	$1,900
Segment controllable margin-to-sales ratio	27.1%	42.1%	36.9%	15.7%	31.7%

Note: This approach could be modified to include a charge for the assets employed by each of the segments, as well as a deduction for the change in market value of these assets. The results would be referred to as the net segment margin (residual income).

Source: Douglas M. Lambert and Jay U. Sterling, "Educators are Contributing to Major Deficiencies in Marketing Profitability Reports," *Journal of Marketing Education* 12, no. 3 (Fall, 1990): 43–44.

tified by the specific channel in which they were incurred. Only those assignable, nonvariable costs that would be incurred or eliminated by adding or dropping a channel should be included.

The following example illustrates the recommended approach. Traditional accounting data showed a net profit of $2.5 million before taxes on sales of $42.5 million. Although management believed this profit was not adequate, traditional accounting gave few clues with regard to the specific problem. However, a contribution approach to profitability analysis by type of account can be used to diagnose areas where performance is inadequate (see Table 12-13). In this example, sales to drugstores were the largest of the four channels used by the manufacturer, but the segment controllable margin-to-sales ratio was the lowest; it was less than one-half that of the second-most profitable segment, and only 37% of the most profitable segment. Neverthe-

TABLE 12-14
Profitability by Drugstore Subchannels:
A Contribution Approach
($000)

		Type of Account		
	Drugstore Channel	**National Drug Chains**	**Regional Drug Chains**	**Independent Pharmacies**
Sales	$19,750	$4,250	$5,500	$10,000
Less discounts, returns, and allowances	1,750	750	500	1,000
Net sales	18,000	4,000	5,000	9,000
Cost of goods sold (variable manufacturing costs)	9,200	2,100	2,600	4,500
Manufacturing contribution	8,800	1,900	2,400	4,500
Variable selling and distribution costs:				
Sales commissions	360	80	100	180
Transportation costs	1,795	120	200	1,475
Warehouse handling	450	—	100	350
Order processing costs	280	25	55	200
Charge for investment in accounts receivable	615	20	35	560
Contribution margin	$5,300	$1,655	$1,910	$1,735
Assignable nonvariable costs (costs incurred specifically for the segment during the period):				
Sales promotion and slotting allowances	400	90	110	200
Advertising	500	—	—	500
Bad debts	300	—	—	300
Display racks	200	—	—	200
Inventory carrying costs	800	80	100	620
Segment controllable margin	$3,100	$1,485	$1,700	($85)
Segment controllable margin-to-sales ratio	15.7%	34.9%	30.9%	—

Note: This approach could be modified to include a charge for the assets employed by each of the segments, as well as a deduction for the change in market value of these assets. The result would be referred to as the net segment margin (residual income).

Source: Douglas M. Lambert and Jay U. Sterling, "Educators are Contributing to Major Deficiencies in Marketing Profitability Reports," *Journal of Marketing Education* 12, no. 3 (Fall 1990): 44–45.

less, at $3.1 million the segment controllable margin is substantial, and it is doubtful that elimination of drugstores would be a wise decision.

A product-channel matrix analysis showed that product mix was not the source of the problem. Further segmentation of the drugstore channel revealed that national drugstore chains had a segment controllable margin-to-sales ratio almost as large as that of the grocery chains and somewhat better than discount stores, that regional drugstore chains were almost as profitable as discount stores, and that small, independent pharmacies were losing money (see Table 12-14). With this information, management could determine the impact on corporate profitability if the independent pharmacies were served by drug wholesalers or by field warehouses supported by telemarketing and scheduled deliveries. The alternative that would lead to the greatest improvement in long-term profitability should be selected. A framework for performing this analysis that incorporates marketing cost trade-offs is illustrated in Table 12-15.

Rather than contribution reports, most firms use a full costing system, which assigns fixed costs to individual segments.[26] However, this system provides incorrect information because costs common to multiple segments are allocated to segments according to some arbitrary measure of activity. Vital information about the controllability and behavior of segment costs is lost. For example, if a segment is found to be unprofitable under a full-costing approach and as a result is discontinued, the fixed costs will simply be reallocated to the remaining segments.

Research has identified the following shortcomings of the profitability reports used by executives in major corporations:

- Full manufactured costs (which sometimes included a profit for the plant) were used in calculating costs of goods sold.
- Operating costs like development, selling, and administration were fully allocated to products often on a percentage-of-sales basis.
- Costs such as transportation, warehousing, sales commissions, and sales promotions were not reported as separate line items.[27]
- When marketing and logistics costs were identified explicitly as expenses, they usually were allocated to products on a percentage-of sales basis.
- Inconsistencies in terminology were common. When executives referred to contribution margins, often the numbers used were actually manufacturing contribution.
- Opportunity costs like inventory carrying costs, a charge for accounts receivable, and a charge for other assets employed did not appear on profitability reports.
- Reports that covered more than one year were not adjusted for inflation.
- Reports were not adjusted to reflect replacement costs.

In summary, cost allocations can seriously distort a segment's profitability. "Seriously distorted product costs can lead managers to choose a losing competitive strategy by de-emphasizing and overpricing products that are highly profitable and by expanding commitments to complex, unprofitable lines. The company persists in the losing strategy because executives have no alternative sources of information to signal when product costs are distorted."[28]

Table 12-16 illustrates how the channel profitability analysis contained in Table 12-13 would change if it were calculated using average costs. Drugstores would show by far the largest dollar profit. The profit-to-sales ratio for drugstores would compare favorably with that of the other channels (82% of the profit-to-sales ratio for grocery chains), whereas the controllable margin-to-sales ratio of the drugstore channel was less than half (43%) of that earned by the grocery channel. The differences in the two methods of accounting would be much greater in a product profitability analysis because manufacturing, marketing, and logistics costs would vary more across products. If the costs in Table 12-15 had been allocated on a percentage of sales basis, as is the practice in most firms, the profit-to-sales ratios for the four channels would have been equal.

Poor performance by a channel does not necessarily mean the channel should be eliminated. Factors like the percentage of potential market being reached by the channel, the stage of the product life cycle of the products involved, and the stage in the life cycle of the institutions in-

TABLE 12-15
Impact Calculation
(How Manufacturers Can Determine the Impact of Using a Wholesaler)

Costs associated with manufacturer selling direct to retailers		
Costs of direct selling versus using an intermediary		$__________
Additional promotional expenses associated with direct sales		$__________
Customer service costs		
Cost of sales lost at retail level due to stockouts resulting from long and/or erratic lead time	$__________	
Return forgone on capital invested in accounts receivable	__________	
Credit losses associated with accounts receivable	__________	__________
Order filling costs		
Cost of dealing with many customers	$__________	
Cost of filling small orders	__________	
Cost of filling frequent orders	__________	__________
Inventory carrying costs		
Return forgone on capital invested in inventory	$__________	
Insurance paid on inventory	__________	
Taxes paid on inventory	__________	
Storage costs	__________	
Cost of obsolescence	__________	
Cost of damaged product	__________	
Cost of pilferage	__________	
Transshipment costs	__________	__________
Warehousing costs		
Return forgone on capital invested in field warehouses (if owned)	$__________	
Operating expenses associated with such warehouses	__________	__________
Transportation costs		
Cost of processing shipping documents (for many LTL shipments)	$__________	
Cost of processing freight claims	__________	
Excessive freight costs (associated with LTL shipments)	__________	__________
General and administrative		
Reduction in management costs associated with holding and supervising inventory		$__________
Annual cost of direct selling	Total	$__________
Less volume discounts to wholesaler		__________
Total amount saved by using a wholesaler		$__________

Source: Adapted from Douglas M. Lambert and Bernard J. La Londe, "The Economics of Using a Frozen Food Distributor," *Frozen Food Factbook and Directory* (Hershey, Pa.: National Frozen Food Association, 1975), p. 60. Reprinted with permission.

TABLE 12-16
Profitability by Major Channels:
A Full Cost Approach
($000)

		Type of Account			
	Total Company	**Department Stores**	**Grocery Chains**	**Drug-stores**	**Discount Stores**
Net sales	$40,000	$6,000	$10,000	$18,000	$6,000
Cost of goods sold (full manufacturing costs)	25,000	3,750	6,250	11,250	3,750
Manufacturing margin	15,000	2,250	3,750	6,750	2,250
Less expenses:					
Sales commissions	800	120	200	360	120
Transportation costs ($/case)	2,500	375	625	1,125	375
Warehouse handling ($/cu. ft.)	600	90	150	270	90
Order processing costs ($/order)	400	30	50	300	20
Sales promotion (% of sales)	1,250	187	312	563	188
Advertising (% of sales)	500	75	125	225	75
Bad debts (% of sales)	300	45	75	135	45
General overhead and administrative expense (% of sales)	6,150	922	1,538	2,768	922
Net profit (before taxes)	$2,500	$406	$675	$1,004	$415
Profit-to-sales ratio	6.3%	6.8%	6.8%	5.6%	6.9%

Source: Douglas M. Lambert and Jay U. Sterling, "Educators are Contributing to Major Deficiencies in Marketing Profitability Reports," *Journal of Marketing Education* 12, no. 3 (Fall 1990): p. 49.

volved also deserve consideration. In addition, elimination of an unprofitable channel may not be the only viable solution for the firm striving to improve corporate profitability. Changing the logistical system or shifting some of the business to another channel, as in the previous example, may be the most desirable solution. Also, a customer-product contribution matrix may be used within a channel to isolate customers or products as candidates for elimination or revitalization.

In addition to being able to evaluate the profitability of individual customers, product lines, territories, and channels of distribution, the database system permits the user to simulate trade-off decisions and determine the effect of proposed system changes on total cost. The report-generating capabilities of the modular database are summarized in Figure 12-13. To implement the modular database approach, it is necessary to collect the raw logistics cost data and break them down into fixed variable and direct-indirect components. In other words, the data must be sufficiently refined to permit the formulation of meaningful modules. Full implementation of the integrated logistics management concept and knowledgeable decision making in the areas of strategic and operational planning require a sophisticated management information system.

Notes

1. Portions of this chapter are from Douglas M. Lambert and James R. Stock, *Strategic Logistics Management,* 3d ed. (Homewood, Ill.: Irwin, 1993). No part of this material may be re-

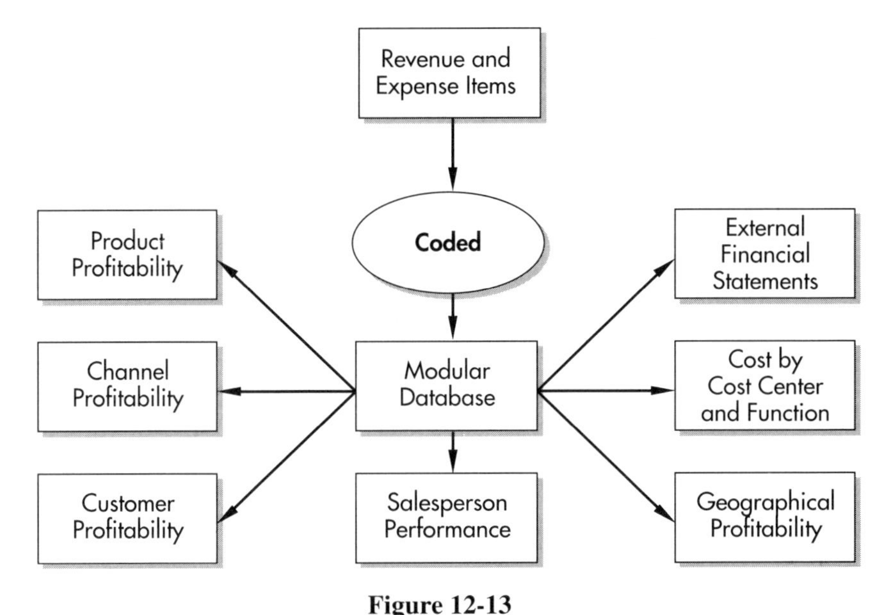

Figure 12-13

Report-Generating Capabilities of the Modular Database

Source: Douglas M. Lambert and James R. Stock, *Strategic Logistics Management,* 3d ed. (Homewood, Ill.: Irwin, 1993), p. 544.

produced in any form without the written permission of the publisher, Richard D. Irwin. For expanded treatment of these and other logistics-related issues, the interested reader is referred to *Strategic Logistics Management.*

2. Douglas M. Lambert and Howard M. Armitage, "Distribution Costs: The Challenge," *Management Accounting* (May 1979): 33, and Douglas M. Lambert and Jay U. Sterling, "What Types of Profitability Reports Do Marketing Managers Receive?" *Industrial Marketing Management* 16, no. 4 (1987): 295–303.
3. For example, David Ray, "Distribution Costing and The Current State of the Art," *International Journal of Logistics* 6, no. 2 (1975): 75–107 at p. 88; Michael Schiff, *Accounting and Control in Logistics Management* (Chicago: NCPDM, 1971), pp. 4–21; Douglas M. Lambert and John T. Mentzer, "Is Integrated Physical Distribution Management A Reality?" *Journal of Business Logistics* 2, no. 1 (1980): 18–34; Douglas M. Lambert, *The Distributions Channels Decision* (New York: National Association of Accountants, and Hamilton, Ontario: The Society of Management Accountants of Canada, 1978); Douglas M. Lambert, *The Product Abandonment Decision* (New York: National Association of Accountants, and Hamilton, Ontario: The Society of Management Accountants of Canada, 1985), p. 98, pp. 127–32; and Lambert and Sterling, "What Types of Profitability Reports," pp. 295–303.
4. Detailed discussions of cost of capital, its uses, and various calculation methods can be found in most financial management texts and handbooks, as well as in many accounting books.
5. Richard A. Brealey and Stewart C. Meyers, *Principles of Corporate Finance,* 3d ed. (New York: McGraw-Hill, 1988), p. 451
6. Charles T. Horngren and George Foster, *Cost Accounting: A Managerial Emphasis,* 7th ed. (Englewood Cliffs, N.J.: Prentice-Hall, 1991).

7. Sam R. Goodman, *Financial Manager's Manual and Guide* (Englewood Cliffs, N.J.: Prentice Hall, 1973), p. 220.
8. James C. T. Mao, *Quantitative Analysis of Financial Decisions* (Toronto: Collier Macmillan Canada, 1969), p. 373.
9. Ibid.
10. Horngren and Foster, *Cost Accounting.*
11. This section draws heavily from Douglas M. Lambert, *The Development of An Inventory Costing Methodology: A Study of the Costs Associated with Holding Inventory* (Chicago: National Council of Physical Distribution management, 1976), pp. 5–15, 59–67.
12. Marvin Flaks, "Total Cost Approach to Physical Distribution," *Business Management* 24 (August 1963): 55–61; and Raymond LeKashman and John F. Stolle, "The Total Cost Approach to Distribution," *Business Horizons* 8 (Winter 1965): 33–46.
13. Michael Schiff, *Accounting and Control in Physical Distribution Management* (Chicago: NCPDM, 1972), pp. 4-63–4-70.
14. For more information on regression analysis, refer to any basic statistics book. For example, see Terry Sincich, *A Course in Modern Business Statistics* (San Francisco: Dellen, 1991), pp. 339–456.
15. A. T. Kearney, *Measuring Productivity in Physical Distribution* (Chicago: NCPDM, 1978), pp. 18–19.
16. A system for recording accounting data in the necessary format is discussed later in this chapter.
17. The discussions of standard costs, budgets, and productivity standards are adapted from Douglas M. Lambert and Howard M. Armitage, "Managing Distribution Costs for Better Profit Performance, *Business* (September–October 1980): 50–51.
18. Richard J. Lewis and Leo G. Erickson, "Distribution System Costing: An Overview," in John R. Grabner and William S. Sargent, eds., *Distribution System Costing: Concepts and Procedures* (Columbus, Ohio: Transportation and Logistics Research Foundation, 1972), pp. 18–20.
19. This material is adapted from Howard M. Armitage and James F. Dickow, "Controlling Distribution with Standard Costs and Flexible Budgets," *1979 Annual Conference Proceedings* (Chicago: National Council of Physical Distribution Management, 1979), pp. 116–20.
20. Robin Cooper and Robert S. Kaplan, "Measure Costs Right: Make the Right Decisions," *Harvard Business Review* 66, no. 5 (September-October 1988): 96–103.
21. Ibid.
22. Ibid.
23. Ronald J. Lewis, "Activity-Based Costing for Marketing," *Management Accounting* 73, no. 5 (November 1991): 33–38.
24. Ibid.
25. See Frank H. Mossman, Paul M. Fischer, and W. J. E. Crissy, "New Approaches to Analyzing Marketing Profitability," *Journal of Marketing* 38 (April 1974): 43–48.
26. Douglas M. Lambert and Jay U. Sterling, "What Types of Profitability Reports Do Marketing Managers Receive?" *Industrial Marketing Management* 16, no. 4 (1987): 295–303.
27. Ibid.
28. Robert S. Kaplan, "One Cost System Isn't Enough," *Harvard Business Review* 66 (January-February 1988): 61–66.

CHAPTER 13

Benchmarking

The Search for Industry Best Practices That Lead to Superior Performance

Robert C. Camp

The hottest and least understood new term in the quality field is *benchmarking*. Xerox does it. Ford does it. GTE, IBM, and Motorola do it. Just what is benchmarking? Benchmarking is an ongoing investigation and learning experience ensuring that best industry practices are uncovered, adopted, and implemented. Benchmarking is a process of industrial research that enables managers to perform company-to-company comparisons of processes and practices to identify the "best of the best" and attain a level of superiority or competitive advantage. Searching out and emulating the best can fuel the motivation of everyone involved, often producing breakthrough results.

Xerox Corporation, known for pioneering a process called *competitive benchmarking,* led the way in 1979 by demonstrating the power of benchmarking in its manufacturing operations. The company compared U.S. manufacturing costs with those of foreign and domestic competitors. Its study revealed that competitors were selling products at Xerox's cost of producing them. As a result, the company quickly adopted externally set benchmark targets to drive its business plans.

The experience so dramatically turned the manufacturing operation around that Xerox adopted benchmarking as a corporatewide effort in 1981. Today the company includes benchmarking as a key component of its total quality effort and has broadened its benchmarking activities to include analysis of best practices within any industry.

The Japanese word *dantotsu* (striving to be "the best of the best") captures the essence of benchmarking. Benchmarking is a positive, proactive process to change operations in a structured fashion to achieve superior performance. The purpose of benchmarking is to increase the probability of success in gaining a competitive advantage.

Benchmarking can be both a survival and a competitive strategy. In the case of Xerox, it was clear that the company was not going to survive without improving the way it worked, so it pursued benchmarking as a survival strategy. But benchmarking was so successful at helping find and implement better practices that it became the strategy to improve performance continuously and thereby achieve a competitive advantage. To survive in today's marketplace a company cannot rest on its laurels. Companies must continuously look for a better way to do business. Benchmarking is that way.

Benchmarking and Logistics

Logistics was one of the first business functions to employ benchmarking. One of the earliest articles on benchmarking, in the *Harvard Business Review,* described how it was conducted at L. L. Bean. Since then, benchmarking has become widely accepted and practiced. An indication of this is the attention devoted to this topic by the Council of Logistics Management. Benchmarking has been a significant theme at the Council's annual conferences, and many of the special conference topics are based on benchmarking research conducted by the council. The logistics profession can be justifiably proud of its accomplishments.

Benchmarking Defined

Benchmarking is *the continuous process of measuring products, services, and practices against the company's toughest competitors or those companies renowned as the industry leaders.* In particular, functions like billing, inventory management, distribution, and manufacturing are examined. This involves determining how these identified firms achieve their performance levels and adapt their successful strategies.

Although the formal definition has never been changed (because there have been important lessons learned in the pursuit of benchmarking embedded in the wording), the formal definition is not the most straightforward description of what is wanted from teams commissioned to conduct benchmarking. Therefore, an operational definition of benchmarking has been developed. That definition is *finding and implementing best practices.* In its most elemental terms that is what benchmarking is all about. And benchmarking teams can readily understand what is expected of them from the operational definition.

Determining best practices is an iterative process, as shown in Figure 13-1.

Types of Benchmarking

Four types of benchmarking can be performed: internal, competitive, functional, and generic process benchmarking. Each has specific outcomes and benefits.

Internal Benchmarking

In large organizations multiple operations are set up to perform similar functions. Distribution centers, order entry functions, and service operations are just a few examples. Internal benchmarking appears to be a good source of better work practices.

Conducting internal benchmarking should be viewed as a starting point for benchmarking. Similarly, internal functions can provide a pilot for conducting benchmarking and may reveal some best practices that can be replicated elsewhere and place the operation on the path to continuous improvement. However, internal benchmarking has another and equally important result. To conduct effective benchmarking, it is imperative to document the internal work processes. And conducting internal benchmarking has been shown to be the most straightforward way of doing just that.

For example, Xerox marketing districts wanted to set up customer problem resolution groups to quickly and effectively handle customer problems and inquiries. The challenge was to determine what the "best practices" were on which to set up such an operation. It turned out that the Canadian affiliate had already determined the best practices by conducting benchmarking to set

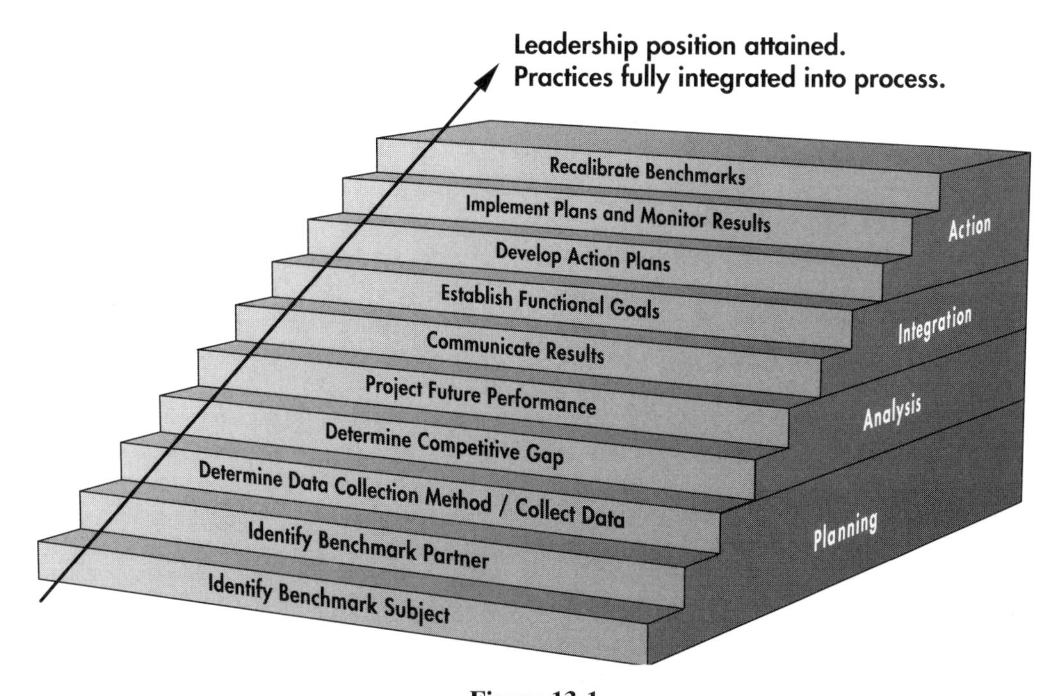

Figure 13-1
Benchmarking Process Phases

up the Xerox Canada Customer Information Centre. U.S. Operations, therefore, had only to go within the Xerox family to find the best practices. The best practices were typified by:

- Customers wanting feedback within 48 hours on the status of their inquiries, even if the problem was not resolved
- having no more than one handoff to a specialist from the first person taking the request.

Competitive Benchmarking

Competitive benchmarking is the comparison of the work process with that of the best competitor. This is a necessity to ensure that the practices of the competition are known and to find out how one compares. In addition, comparison will reveal what performance measure levels must be surpassed. At some stage, the gap between the competition and the internal operations must be known to assess the organization's strengths and weaknesses.

For example, Xerox had a four-layer process of getting parts from manufacturing to region to marketplace to the service person. Comparison with competitors revealed a two-and-one-half echelon structure for one competitor (one-half an echelon to represent the storage of emergency parts), a three-echelon structure for another, and a three-echelon structure for the U.S. dealer operations being supplied by their overseas manufacturers. This discrepancy was marked and had severe consequences. Each layer, or echelon, represented activities where material was handled and stored, so there were consequences relating to the overall cost of the operation and its effect on assets or investment. The magnitude of the competitive cost and investment discrepancy was in almost direct proportion to the number of echelons. Namely, Xerox was at a disadvantage by having costs and investment one quarter greater than two competitors and 30% greater than one competitor.

Functional Benchmarking

Functional benchmarking is comparing one's work process practices with those of the functional leader, who is often not in the same industry, and with those who are renowned as the best at what they do. Despite different business focuses, comparability can be maintained. The classic example at Xerox was the comparison of warehouse item picking operations with those of L. L. Bean. The common characteristic was that both operations were manual picking operations because the products varied widely in size, shape, and the way they had to be handled. But Bean's products were being picked three times faster. This led to a complete analysis of the picking process that permitted such a performance gap and revealed some unique practices that were adapted for use at Xerox. It was also the first time that a case had been made for finding better practices outside one's own industry (the office products industry for Xerox) but for a similar function.

For example, some rough analysis of the Bean operation from an article that appeared in a logistics-related publication indicated that Bean was picking its orders three times faster than Xerox. The functions, however, were quite comparable because both required manual picking of the products handled. Because of varying size, weight, and fragility, items could not be placed in automated dispensing devices. The investigation turned to understanding how Bean could pick so much faster for essentially the same function. The fundamental answer was that Bean sorted its orders, within specified times during the day, to place all the similar items (like red flannel shirts) together so that the picker had to make just one trip to the bin storage location. Bean consciously minimized the picker travel distance by sorting because it was the single greatest contributor to improving picking performance.

Generic Process Benchmarking

If the organization has matured to the point of pursuing a quality initiative, often referred to as total quality management, then generic process benchmarking has been shown to have the greatest return. A different approach to benchmarking has emerged in recent years, namely, the pursuit of benchmarking to improve the basic, generic business processes on which most businesses and public organizations base their operations. Most organizations have to take an order, fill it, often service the product, create an invoice, and collect payment. These functions are conducted as generic processes by all organizations. And so if the basic business processes have been identified, benchmarking to improve practices can be sourced from whichever company is the best, regardless of industry or other restrictions. This type of benchmarking activity typically shows breakthrough results.

For example, some organizations have had to give thought to how they will prioritize their benchmarking efforts to make careful use of the scarce resources available for continuous improvement, including benchmarking. What has emerged from those that have investigated this topic is that the greatest returns appear to be derived when the focus is on the basic business processes of the business. Therefore those organizations that have launched this effort have identified and classified their key business processes and are now actively documenting and improving them through benchmarking. The classification usually starts with some high-level definition of process such as customer order to collection, meaning, in this instance, everything that happens between the factory and the completion of the transaction. Following this would be a cascade or hierarchy of business processes, each of which has up to four levels of detail, until the order taking process is defined. It is at this point that benchmarking is pursued to find the best practices, wherever they may exist. Most of the business processes defined in this manner are generic in the sense that they exist in many businesses. Thus this type of benchmarking is not constrained by any particular industry and therefore is defined as generic process benchmarking.

These four different types of benchmarking are usually pursued, in the order covered, by mature benchmarking organizations.

Benchmarking Fundamentals

To embark on a benchmarking activity first requires these fundamentals:

- *Know your operation.* Assess strengths and weaknesses. This should involve documenting work process steps and practices as well as defining critical performance measurements used, including pre-, post- and in-process measures as well as overall results.
- *Know industry leaders and competitors.* You can differentiate capabilities only by knowing the strengths and weaknesses of the leaders.
- *Incorporate the best and gain superiority.* Emulate the strengths of the best and go beyond.

Benchmarking can be divided into two parts, practices and measures. In Xerox's experience benchmarking should first investigate industry best practices. The measures that quantify the effect of incorporating the practices in an operation can be analyzed or synthesized later. Generally, measures chosen should be true indicators of the process performance and may include customer satisfaction, unit cost, cycle time, and appropriate asset measurements.

It is equally important that the benchmark process and findings be understood by the organization to obtain commitment to take action to change. This requires carefully designed communications to the organization as well as concerted management support.

Experience with benchmarking has resulted in an eleven-step process, grouped into five essential phases, for conducting a benchmarking investigation, similar to those illustrated in Figure 13-1.

Planning

- *What to benchmark.* Every function has a product or output. These are priority candidates to benchmark for opportunity to improve performance.
- *What companies to benchmark.* World-class leadership companies or functions with superior work practices, wherever they exist, are the appropriate comparisons.
- *Data sources and data collection.* A wide array of sources exists, and a good starting point is a business library. An electronic search of recently published information on the area of interest can be requested.

Analysis

- *Measuring the gap.* It is important to have a full understanding of the internal business processes before comparison to external organizations as the baseline for analyzing best practices.

- *Projecting the gap.* Whether negative, positive, or parity, these provide an objective basis on which to act and to determine how to achieve a performance edge.

INTEGRATION

- *Report progress.* Progress should be reported to all employees who need to know. Based on the benchmarking findings, a vision or end-point picture of the operation can be developed.
- *Revise performance goals.*

ACTION

- *Specific actions.* Specific implementation actions, periodic measurements, and assessments of achievement should be put in place.
- *Assign responsibility.* People who actually perform the work should be responsible for implementing the benchmarking findings.
- *Continuous improvement.* The company should stay current with ongoing industry changes by continuously benchmarking and updating work practices.

MATURITY

- *Institutionalize.* Maturity is achieved when best practices are incorporated in all business processes and the benchmarking approach is institutionalized.

What to Benchmark

The first step to determine what should be benchmarked is identifying the product or output of the business function. Fundamental to this is the development of a clear mission statement detailing the reason for the organization's existence, including typical outputs expected by customers. Next, the function's broad purpose should be broken down into specific outputs to be benchmarked. Outputs should be documented to a level of detail necessary for cost analysis, analysis of key tasks, handoffs and measurement.

One good way to determine outputs most in need of benchmarking is to pose a set of questions that might reveal current issues facing the function. Questions might focus on customer care, including service, cost, or perceptions of products. A further way to identify outputs is to convert the problems, issues, and challenges faced by the function into problem statements and then to develop these into a cause-and-effect Ishikawa diagram, as shown in Figure 13-2. The causes in the diagram are candidates for benchmarking.

Another way to determine what should be benchmarked is to ask customers. Customers will readily indicate which companies they perceive to be the best. This has produced some interesting results, because these companies' practices, on investigation, may not be judged to be leading-edge. Perhaps the organization is not the best at the process being benchmarked, but maybe it is the best at communicating a perception of excellence. Such perceptual differences must be dealt with.

If the process perspective is pursued, then the process must be documented before any benchmarking can be started. The response to documenting business processes is often less than enthusiastic, and one can get mired in the details. To make it easier to understand, there are four essential elements to documenting processes: a picture of the process, a description of the process, a description of what it does, and a description of how it is done.

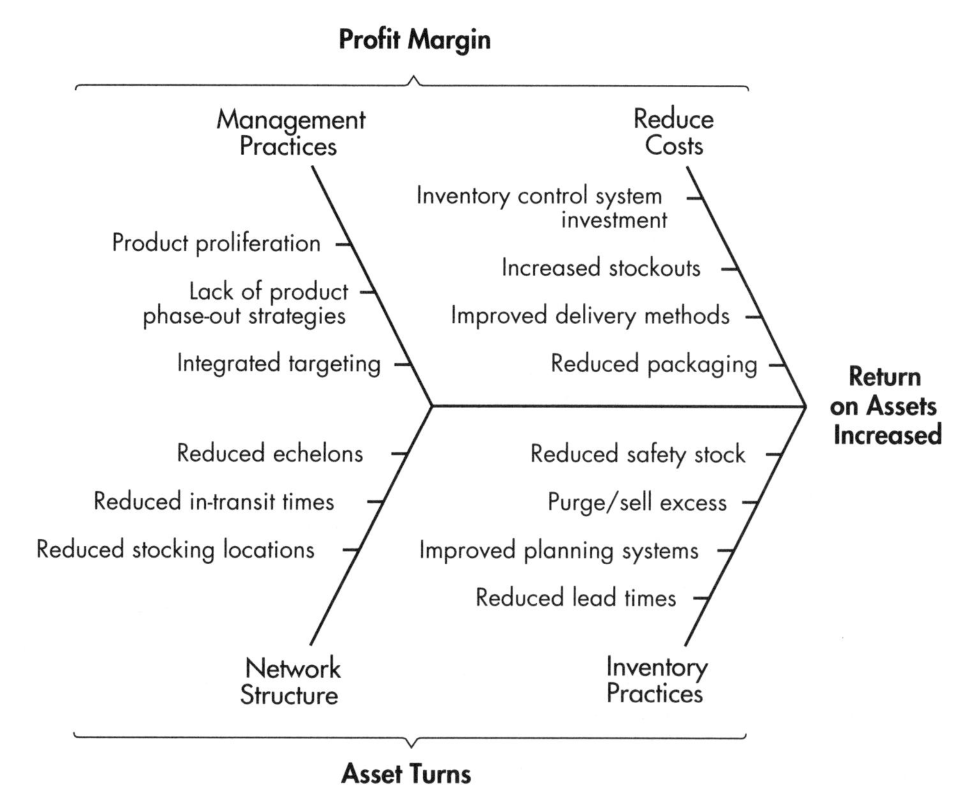

Figure 13-2
Ishikawa Cause & Effect Diagram

The organization should not be forced to document in a single, uniform way. One innovative way to document a process is to have those knowledgeable in the process individually write down the steps on Post-It® notes. Then, direct them to a blank wall as a group, and ask them to arrange the notes in proper sequence. This usually results in a spirited discussion about what individuals think the process is and the correct sequence for the notes. However, eventually the representation is decided and there is agreement on the way work is done. The notes become the picture, and once they have, it is not too difficult to develop the description of the process, what it does, and how it operates.

Regardless of how the business process is documented, successful benchmarking requires that "how you do your work" be well understood. That understanding is the prerequisite to conducting benchmarking comparisons with outside organizations, whether competitive, functional, or having generic processes. It is the only credible way to make comparisons between what you do and what other companies do. You must be able to say, "Here's how we do this work process in distinct steps. Now how does your operation do it?" See Figure 13-3.

One way to deal with benchmarking is to assemble a preliminary list of best practices, take the list to customer groups, and have customers prioritize them. This process develops a list of fundamental customer requirements. Once the customer requirements are truly known, the benchmarking can focus on companies that are the best at those practices. Those companies could be sourced through industry associations, articles on the functional areas, and discussions

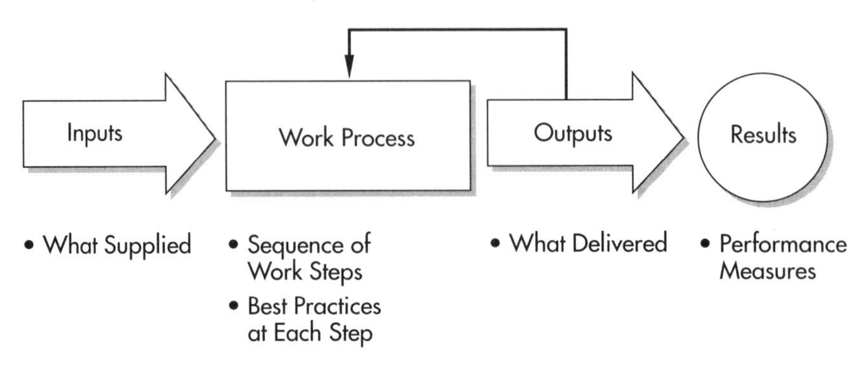

Figure 13-3
Benchmarking Processes

with vendors and suppliers. Software providers are also good resources. Find a software application that applies to a particular business process and ask the software provider which clients use the product exceptionally well.

As a result of a benchmarking visit, Xerox incorporated several of L. L. Bean's practices in a logistics program to modernize its warehouse operations. Of the 8 to 10% productivity gains subsequently realized, 3 to 5% were a direct result of benchmarking activities. Other practices benchmarked at L. L. Bean ranged from barcoding materials for stock tracking through management of inventories, and office supply product distribution to quality assurance processes.

What Organizations to Benchmark Against

Deciding on the organizations against which to benchmark is a problem of identifying those leading-edge companies or functions within companies that have best industry practices. This search starts by considering, in broad terms, who the operation competes with, and progressively relaxing constraints. Comparability is needed, but not at the expense of finding where business practice breakthroughs are likely to occur.

One approach found to be successful is to consider similar operations first. These are of two types: operations that produce the same product and processes that have the same output but not the same product. Second, expand the list to consider those in the same industry. The question will be, What is the industry? How narrowly or broadly will the industry be defined? Xerox could be classified as being in the copying industry, the office products industry, or the electronics industry. Each would provide different candidates. Next, go to those companies that are believed to have best practices. With some consideration it is possible to identify companies that are preeminent in what they do. Increasingly, periodicals are citing those they believe to be "best in class."

Over the past decade, the list of companies that Xerox has benchmarked has grown. The list includes the names of some of America's largest corporations, such as American Express (billing and collection), American Hospital Supply (automated inventory control), Ford Motor Co. (manufacturing floor layout), General Electric (robotics), L. L. Bean, Hershey Foods, and Mary Kay Cosmetics (warehousing and distribution), Westinghouse (National Quality Award application process, warehouse controls, barcoding), and Florida Power and Light (quality process).

As a multinational corporation, Xerox operates in more than 100 countries and performs benchmarking in each. Rank Xerox Limited benchmarks leading companies within the group of 24 operating companies in 80 countries in Europe and Africa where it manufactures and markets products and services. Xerox regularly benchmarks with Fuji Xerox, the company's affiliate in Japan and the 1980 winner of the Deming Award. Fuji Xerox, as a result of its own benchmarking activities, has instituted many practices aimed at meeting and exceeding the performance of other Japanese companies and companies in Asia and Australia.

Information Sources

There are three important sources of benchmarking information—internal, external, and original research. No benchmarking investigation is complete until and unless these sources are researched to ensure thoroughness of canvasing all potential data and information. They are briefly described below.

Internal Sources

Internal sources are typified by internal experts, publications, reviews, and the ability to access the more than 5,000 electronic databases of documents that exist in the public domain. It is crucial that all existing internal information be gathered as a basis for documenting what is known about practices and companies for the four types of benchmarking. It is often surprising what professionals in the logistics field already know about the industry, and it is wise to catalog this knowledge to start weaving the fabric of information that will be completed by the remaining sources.

The access to public databases, however, provides the largest single source of information to conduct benchmarking. They should allow data to be collected on at least two topics: (1) information on practices in specific functions, like the picking operation, and (2) information about named companies that may be candidates for benchmarking site visits. Using a trained information researcher to access the databases is recommended. Trained researchers can determine the key words under which articles are catalogued and access the abstracts to the documents, whether periodicals, books, or specific reports.

External Sources

External sources are extensive and are typified by professional associations, industry publications, journals, seminars, industry data firms, industry experts, and software vendors. This list is not complete but representative of the variety of available sources. These sources should be used to ensure a level of preparation such that the benchmarking visit itself can concentrate on validating what is known and filling in the remainder. Preparation should prevent the benchmarking company from being blindsided by information that may already be in the public domain and for which it is not necessary to bother the benchmarking partner.

All sources are important; assessing them should be based on the best judgment of the process manager. Two particular sources deserve comment—professional associations and software providers. Professional associations can be a rich source of information because they are committed to keeping in touch with their business function in a wide cross section of industries. They often conduct research on topics of benchmarking interest and, at a minimum, should have references regarding who would have information if they do not.

Software providers are an interesting source. Because business functions are so heavily computerized, there is a software package for practically every activity. It is often instructive to contact the software providers and ask not only about their software capabilities but also about the clients they believe use the software exceptionally well. In doing so, one is sourcing companies that might have best practices and would be desirable candidates for benchmarking.

Original Research

Finally, there is the option of conducting original research, when appropriate. This activity obviously requires resources, time, and funding and is the most difficult to conduct. It is typified by customer feedback, telephone surveys, inquiry services, networks, the use of outside consulting firms, and an eventual site visit to a benchmarking partner.

All these avenues should be considered. At some point, it is desirable to ask the customer about the importance of the best practices for the business process affected. Learning whom they perceive as the best practitioners can be revealing. Other types of research help one to make contacts before conducting in-depth research or to gather information over an extended period of time to assemble the desired picture.

Electronic networks have been helpful in coordinating visits and groups of individuals representing their organizations for the purpose of benchmarking. Using these networks has been shown to be an effective way to conduct ongoing benchmarking. Consulting firms may provide the needed resources to conduct initial benchmarking, including maintaining confidentiality where needed. They can quickly assemble a team to conduct benchmarking and will generally be able to shorten the cycle to complete a study.

Site visits should be left until last. Stated differently, all the preceding sources should be utilized before assuming that a site visit is necessary. Site visits are very important, however, because they are a final confirmation to validate known information and they allow one to see the actual process and practices firsthand.

Objectives of Benchmarking

The purpose of benchmarking is derived primarily from the need to establish more credible goals and pursue continuous improvement. It is first a direction-setting process, but more important, it is a means by which the practices needed to reach new goals are discovered and understood.

Benchmarking also legitimizes goals and direction by basing them on an external orientation. It is an alternative to the traditional way of establishing targets, namely, by extrapolation of past practices and trends. Conventional goal setting often fails because the external environment changes at a pace significantly faster than projected.

The ultimate benefit is that customer (and other end-user) requirements are more adequately met because benchmarking forces a continual focus on the external environment.

Success Factors for Benchmarking

Having those who work the process conduct their own benchmarking is fundamental to its success and is second only to documenting the work process as a prerequisite to conducting effective benchmarking. Those who work the process know it the best and are almost always the most qualified to analyze it. There are other reasons for them to conduct their own benchmarkings well, such as to ensure that those who must implement the best practices and make the changes are involved in finding and adapting them. When "process owners" conduct their own benchmarking, they develop a commitment to the process and resulting best practices. If that commitment is not obtained during the benchmarking process, there will be problems with implementation.

Successful benchmarking is not done by separate staffs. The actual benchmarking is done by process owners or process representatives with appropriate assistance, but there are individuals who should act to assure the competency of the benchmarking process.

Behavioral Benefits

Internally, benchmarking can also drive consensus. If performance levels are aligned with the best in the industry, then all energy within the organization can be turned to accomplishing results, not arguing over what should be done. True productivity follows, which is derived from workers at all levels solving real problems of the business revealed by the benchmarking findings.

There are other behavioral aspects of benchmarking. When individuals visit competing organizations to conduct competitive benchmarking, they get defensive. They come up with the 101 reasons why "that can't be done, that won't work—we tried that one year; the engineers said it wouldn't work." They also get stuck in the "we do it better" syndrome. Teams visiting competitors need to be prepared for an intensely challenging experience. They must lower their defenses, demonstrate humility, and approach the visit with open ears, eyes, and minds so that they can achieve maximum benefit.

When the same individuals analyze best practices in a completely different industry, they tend to see the possibilities readily. In nondefensive settings they start to think "that's unique, we should try that; with minor adaptations that might apply." They don't go out and just copy what they see other companies doing; rather, they have a tendency to be creative and "think out of the box." So functional and generic benchmarking, conducted under the right circumstances, can be quite creative.

Management Considerations

Management must address several considerations related to benchmarking activities. Among them is the way the concept of benchmarking is communicated, which can make a big difference. Certain words have developed less than desirable connotations; unfortunately, *productivity* is one of them. When individuals are told they must become more productive, they have a natural tendency to think their jobs are in jeopardy. *Productivity* has come to mean reduction in workforce. It is more appropriate to replace *productivity* with *continuous improvement.* When the term *continuous improvement* is used, there is not necessarily an immediate association with cutting staff. *Continuous improvement* means that all must work together to improve how things are done to be a stronger company. Benchmarking is the process undertaken to find the best practices implemented in work processes that lead to continuous improvement.

One must also recognize how to find resources to conduct benchmarking. Although some incremental resources are needed for new benchmarking, there is often another option. Somewhere in the organization are resources devoted to continuous improvement. (Nearly all organizations have devoted some resources to this effort.) Some of these resources should be devoted to conducting benchmarking. Benchmarking should be viewed as part of the ongoing effort to improve and as part of the process owner's job, not as extra work. There are an unlimited number of best practices, each offering significant potential for improvement, for increased results, and for superior performance. Process operators should be urged to find those practices.

Getting the most out of benchmarking does not involve blindly copying other companies. That won't get superior performance; creatively implementing best practices will. The implementation phase of benchmarking can be or should be the creative phase. Combining benchmarking with the creative talents of the people running the processes yields results. Creative implementation of best practices is the way an organization can establish a competitive advantage. That is what is important. To get the most benefit from benchmarking it is necessary to find, understand, and creatively adapt the best practices.

For example, Xerox is most concerned with customer satisfaction. In its benchmarking with L. L. Bean, it became patently aware of Bean's customer satisfaction policy. If a customer is unhappy with a product, Bean will take it back and return the money. Xerox believed Bean's unconditional return policy to be a best practice. But Xerox went beyond just copying the practice. It asked customers for feedback about the best practice and found some interesting results. Customers did not want their money back; they wanted the device to work. So Xerox had to adapt the best practice to work for it.

The Xerox Total Satisfaction Guarantee now says that if the customer is dissatisfied with a Xerox product within a stated time frame after purchase, Xerox will replace it, at the customer's request, until the customer is satisfied with the product. So Xerox did not just copy the L. L. Bean best practice. It went a step further to adapt that best practice to its specific customer needs.

Competitiveness

The bottom-line benefit of benchmarking is competitiveness. Benchmarking helps to develop a picture of how the operation should look after the change to attain superior competitive performance. This is a powerful way to marshal the energies of the operation to become competitive and then outdistance the competition.

The L. L. Bean/Xerox Experience—A Case Study

One way to measure the performance of your organization is to benchmark against the competition. However, there are a number of problem areas to consider before performing a competitive benchmark:

- Comparisons with competition may uncover practices that are unworthy of emulation.
- While competitive benchmarking may help you meet your competitor's performance, it is unlikely to reveal practices for surpassing them.
- Obviously, getting information about competitors is difficult.
- According to observation, people are more receptive to new ideas that come from outside their own industry.

An alternative method, noncompetitive benchmarking, focuses on the best functional practices in *any* industry. Adoption of these functional practices can help a corporation or department achieve a competitive advantage. Xerox managers have come to realize that understanding the practices, processes, and methods of an industry leader is important because these define the changes necessary to reach the benchmark.

Xerox Participants and Group

One of Xerox's most valuable benchmarking studies was conducted by its logistics and distribution (L&D) unit, which is responsible for inventory management, warehousing, and transport of machines, parts, and supplies.

Historically, L&D's productivity increases have been 3 to 5% per year. However, it was clear that this level of increase was not adequate and that further cost-effectiveness was required. Improvement was necessary to maintain profit margins in the face of industry price cuts.

Where would the L&D unit start its benchmarking activities? Furthermore, what priorities would define where initial benchmarking efforts should be directed to be the most productive? The following benchmark experience with L. L. Bean is indicative of the first steps to be taken by a firm interested in benchmarking the best functional practices in any industry.

Planning Phase

Identify Subject for Benchmarking

After benchmarking best practices with a leading expert in the field, the inventory control area installed a new planning system. Because the distribution center managers expressed rising concern about their inability to keep up with industry changes, warehousing was targeted as the next area for improvement. These managers identified the picking area as the greatest bottleneck in the receiving-through-shipping process cycle.

This led L&D to concentrate its benchmarking efforts on warehouse productivity, more specifically, to benchmark materials handling functions that were the most critical to long-term effectiveness and superior performance.

The warehouse productivity problem was divided into two major areas of investigation:

1. Streamlining the flow of materials through the warehouse—principally a matter of layout and equipment design
2. Efficiently utilizing the established design on a daily and hourly basis as orders were received to minimize the travel distance to pick, pack, and ship an order

A new technology for materials handling—automated storage and retrieval systems (AS/RS)—was the subject of hot debate. A high-rise AS/RS warehouse for raw materials and assembly parts had just been erected in Webster, New York. This AS/RS facility was in the same complex as a large finished goods distribution center.

This setup presented L&D with the ability to investigate the AS/RS innovation for applicability to handling finished goods. However, evaluations revealed that the heavy initial investment in capital equipment for AS/RS could not be justified for the variety of size, shape, and weight usually found in finished goods. A different means of improving warehousing and materials handling productivity would be needed. But what?

The benchmarking subject was defined to be an investigation of the best industry practices for:

- The picking operation
- The entire receiving-to-shipping process cycle.

It was not assumed that the best practices would be found in the same industry, nor that the best practices for each step (receiving, picking, packing, and shipping) would all be found at one firm. The investigation launched a search for best practices wherever they existed with the challenge to adopt, adapt, and combine the best of the best and thereby ensure superior performance.

Identify Best Competitor

After identifying the benchmark subject, the formal benchmarking activities started. L&D wanted to define best practices for the materials handling process, wherever they existed. Therefore, the decision was made to perform a functional benchmark of industry leaders. This decision was based on the premise that the materials handling process is generic to a wide range of products, companies, and industries. The exact product being warehoused was of less concern, providing that product characteristics were reasonably comparable.

L&D assigned one person to the project half-time for a period of six months. Because this was one of the earliest Xerox benchmarking investigations, the exact level of resources necessary to conduct the project was unknown. A part-time investigation over an extended time frame was considered a feasible approach.

The expanded time frame allowed thorough investigation of external data including:

- *Trade journals in the materials handling and logistics field.* These were reviewed for the prior three years.
- *Principal logistics and materials handling professional associations.* These were contacted to uncover any recent presentations at annual conferences that discussed efficient design of materials handling for packaged goods warehouses
- *Several materials handling consulting firms.* These were contacted for names of established materials handling designers. Most of these contacts were by telephone on a professional-to-professional basis.

The goal of the external data collection was twofold:

- To identify recent developments in the warehousing and materials handling field
- To identify companies that had implemented the best practices

As candidate companies were identified, the characteristics of their processes, systems, and products were tabulated. The researcher then compiled a list of the best companies against which to benchmark, targeting them with generic product characteristics and service levels similar to Xerox reprographic parts and supplies.

An initial report was prepared detailing the information known to date. The report revealed major differences between Xerox internal operations and external candidate benchmarking partners. In addition, the report proved that the benchmarking project warranted the assignment of a dedicated, full-time staff member. Other resources were drawn from planning and operations on an as-needed basis. This marked the formalization of benchmarking as an ongoing commitment.

At about this time, a materials handling article was published, citing L. L. Bean's warehousing operation. The article focused on several facts:

- The warehouse is still a manual operation but carefully planned and directed by computer system to minimize the labor input.
- The warehouse operation does not lend itself to automation because of the variety of sizes, shapes, and weights of items ordered by customers.
- The warehouse design relies on very basic handling techniques to streamline the materials flow and minimize the picker's travel distance.
- The design was selected with the full participation of the hourly work force, those who would eventually operate the process.

To the layperson, L. L. Bean products bear no resemblance to Xerox parts and supplies. To the distribution professional, however, the analogy was striking. Both companies had to develop warehousing and distribution systems to handle products that are diverse in size, shape, and weight. This diversity precluded the use of AS/RS.

The L&D researcher identified L. L. Bean as the best candidate for warehousing and materials handling benchmarking.

Data Collection Methodology

The L&D benchmark team decided to use personal, professional interviews as the data collection methodology. The manager in charge of benchmarking had briefly visited with Bean's vice president of Distribution in 1981; thus, he was able to contact him in 1982 to discuss the feasibility of a joint benchmark venture.

A meeting to review the operation was arranged in Freeport, Maine, in February 1982. The Xerox team consisted of the manager responsible for benchmarking, a headquarters planning manager for the products of primary interest, and a field distribution center manager. These managers represented the line operations that would ultimately be responsible for implementing any changes.

Substantial preparation was made for the one-day meeting, including development of a questionnaire and a discussion outline that became the basis for the agenda. These efforts assumed that effective use would be made of each party's time.

The visit included:

- A discussion with Bean's vice president of distribution about the article on materials handling which had cited their operations
- Discussion of current and planned practices
- A tour of the facility

During the tour, discussions were held with supervisors of the individual operations. Adequate time was scheduled for each step to ensure an effective exchange of ideas, data, and information.

At the end of the tour, the Xerox team held a debriefing session. Upon their return to Rochester, they documented findings from the trip and distributed them to interested parties, both in the field and at headquarters. Appreciation and an invitation for a possible reciprocal visit were extended to appropriate Bean personnel.

Analysis Phase

With data collection complete, the benchmark team entered the analysis process phase.

Determine Current Competitive Gap

When the team returned to Rochester, they documented the trip in a report based on their collective observations. The analysis then focused on describing how and why Bean's practices differed from internal Xerox operations.

Qualitative analysis was performed to reveal significant differences and potential opportunities. This analysis revealed a broader range of computer-directed activities at Bean than at Xerox. The analysis findings, with validation from other benchmarking visits and investigations, were developed into the statement of industry best practices shown in Table 13-1.

TABLE 13-1
Key Warehouse Industry Best Practices

Process Step	Industry Best Practices
Receiving	• On-line receiving input, reconciliation to purchase order and status through CRT located at receiving dock
Putaway	• Predetermined, random putaway location, sequenced to minimize distance traveled
	• 100% putaway verification through cross reference of rack location and item barcodes
Picking	• Interactive, on-line pick planning to minimize picker travel distance and maximize shipping container capacity utilization
Stock Relocation	• Automatic relocation of inventory items to coincide with order per day velocity
Pick Area Replenishment	• Automatic replenishment of picking locations from reserve stock based on preassigned thresholds, or on-demand, by key entry
Shipping	• Automatic pick sortation to correct carrier at shipping dock through label scanner
	• Automatic shipping document preparation from predetermined weight and label scan
Other Preparation	• Productivity and order-fill-error-rate analysis by area, team, and individual
	• Real-time, transaction-based inventory update and control of warehouse operations

The following specific activities were observed at Bean's distribution center:

- Arranging materials by velocity—that is, fast movers were stocked closest to the picking route
- Storing incoming materials randomly to maximize warehouse space utilization and minimize forklift travel distance
- Sorting and releasing incoming orders throughout the day to minimize picker travel distance (known as short-interval scheduling)
- Basing incentive bonuses on picking productivity offset by error rates
- Automating outbound carrier manifesting by calculating transportation costs ahead of time
- Planning for implementing automated data capture through bar coding

The level of computer-directed activities was significantly higher than those in the Xerox parts and supplies warehouses. The findings revealed a current competitive gap that, combined with other industry best practices, needed to be addressed.

In addition to the practices directly observed, the benchmarking visit also uncovered several areas where additional new methods are planned for installation. The planned improvement with the greatest potential was the installation of barcoded labels for automatic data capture.

Project Future Performance

After the analysis of the current competitive gap between the internal Xerox operations and the industry best practices, it was necessary to project the effect of incorporating the new practices into the Xerox operation.

It was found that performance measurement metrics were substantially higher at Bean. Laborers at Bean were able to pick almost three times as many lines per labor-day as the most efficient warehouse planned at the time. Table 13-2 compares the operational statistics for L. L. Bean and Xerox as of February 1982. The table compares the picking operation by itself and the warehouse total for productivity statistics based on:

- Orders
- Lines
- Pieces per labor day

Lines per labor-day is the statistic most indicative of travel distance, because it represents picker trips to a bin location. The number of pieces is the quantity picked. In the Xerox operation, this represents one complete pallet load of 40 cartons (or 40 pieces).

Table 13-2 reveals that the picking operation at Bean is substantially more productive than at Xerox. However, the Bean warehouse performs functions not performed by Xerox, such as a soft goods finishing operation. The latter statistic was documented to emphasize the need for a process comparison that reveals differences in truly comparable functions. It also indicates that best-of-best industry practices will not be found at one firm but must be assembled from the various sources in which they exist.

How is acceptance finally validated? There is no precise answer. However, an assessment can be conducted to gain some insight into and understanding of acceptance level and highlight areas that need attention. Such an assessment is illustrated in abbreviated fashion in Table 13-3. The objective is to obtain feedback from the implementing organization in a helping/hindering format or analysis of progress toward a known desired state. The analysis can be conducted through a brainstorming exercise and the results weighted by the participants to show the ranked degree of acceptance. Corrective action can then be taken to move toward the end point or desired state.

TABLE 13-2
Comparison of Picking Only and Total Warehouse
Operations for L.L. Bean and Xerox Distribution Centers

February 1982 Statistics	L. L. Bean	Xerox
Picking Only		
Orders/labor-day	550	117
Lines/labor-day	1,440	497
Pieces/labor-day	1,440	2,640
Total Warehouse		
Orders/labor-day	69	27
Lines/labor-day	132	129
Pieces/labor-day	132	616

TABLE 13-3
Gaining Benchmarking Acceptance Using End-Point Analysis

Present State	End Point (Desired) State
Need for benchmarking not recognized	Acknowledged need for industry best practices
No benchmarking activity or understanding about the 10-step process	Benchmarking institutionalized throughout the organization
No understanding or misunderstanding about industry best practices	Full understanding of benchmark practices
Competitive gap unknown	Understanding difference between present and benchmark practices, both what they are and how they differ
No ownership of practices	Full ownership of practices and practical steps toward implementation

Integration Process Phase

During the integration process phase, the first action of the benchmark team was to communicate the results of their analysis and project future performance.

Communicate Results of Analysis

The L. L. Bean experience was a classic example in gaining acceptance of benchmark findings. The L&D team knew that open communication throughout their study was a means to ensure the successful implementation and acceptance of any action plans. At the onset of their study, L&D adopted the following strategies to communicate the results of their analysis:

- *Involvement of line managers.* A questionnaire based on input from line managers was prepared before the Bean visit. A manager participating in the visit contributed to the trip report. This process ensured that anyone who could be affected by changes implemented as a result of the benchmark would be represented in the preparation and execution of the investigation
- *Involvement of the department vice president.* Throughout the benchmarking process, the team leader continually updated the department vice president and his staff on the progress of the report.
- *Involvement of field distribution center manager.* The article describing the Bean process was circulated to many managers, including field distribution center managers who would ultimately be responsible for implementing possible changes. The purpose was to acquaint these managers with potential new methods early in the investigations. Feedback on perceived application to Xerox operations was solicited.
- *Circulation of trip report.* The trip report, which documented the findings, was widely circulated and attracted a great deal of interest and attention within the logistics function. Included was a comparison of Bean's picking operation, as well as overall distribution center productivity rate in terms of lines picked per labor-day. Debate about the comparison and the measurement metric was indicative of the need for further understanding of the prac-

tices, methods, and processes used. Knowledge of what Bean had been able to achieve in a labor-intensive process supported by a computer system to direct the operations motivated logistics professionals to investigate how these practices could be creatively adapted to Xerox operations.

- *Reviews with upper management.* A significant contribution was obtained from reviews with upper management. Annual benchmarking reviews were made part of the business plan presentations. The L. L. Bean experience was cited in these briefings to demonstrate benchmarking's ability to uncover best industry practices, regardless of where they existed. The L. L. Bean experience was the first of these examples and was instrumental in broadening the focus of benchmarking to ensure obtaining superior performance data. The Bean experience became synonymous with functional, noncompetitor benchmarking to obtain competitive superiority.

L. L. Bean is a well-known firm widely praised for its exceptional customer satisfaction practices. Whenever a point about functional benchmarking was made, both in internal presentations/documents and in the press, the Bean experience was cited.

ESTABLISH FUNCTIONAL GOALS

The L. L. Bean experience was only one of many benchmarking investigations that, in total, resulted in a set of comprehensive goals and statements of operational best practices. The Bean study set many precedents:

- It was one of the earliest benchmarking visits and was instrumental in showing Xerox that major practice changes were necessary.
- The practices uncovered were fundamental in showing how a major operation, warehouse materials handling, should change.
- The approach to analyzing improvement in warehouse materials handling broke the problem into two logical components:

1. *Material flow simplification.* This exercise was essentially an operations layout design the objective of which was to minimize the steps in the process and the distance traveled from receiving inbound products to shipping customer orders.
2. *Operations management.* This exercise determined how the operation should be managed once the design was complete. This component, although less tangible, was important because its objective was to maximize the number of orders flowing through the facility while minimizing the use of resources, primarily labor. To some extent, the need for efficient operating practices dictated materials handling equipment design.

Both components incorporated best industry practices. The benefits from the streamlined flow itself were very worthwhile, although the methods of operating the new design were not well defined. The Bean visit confirmed that the opportunity was significant and extended beyond that of the streamlined flow phase. Further definition and benchmarking visits fully confirmed the potential.

Bean's computer-directed picking activities were incorporated in the logistics goals statement. Each named industry best practice was made a goal for achievement.

Action Process Phase

Their functional goals defined, the benchmark team began development of action plans.

Develop Action Plans

The combination of many benchmarking investigations, confirmed by the Bean visit, was crucial in handling the increased volumes projected. Action plans included:

- Establishment of a full-time project team to tackle delivery of the new operations that capitalized on the streamlined flow design.
- Addition of computer support for order processing—not originally contemplated in the flow streamlining phase.
- Incorporation of the best practices of L. L. Bean into the design of the warehouse modernization program, which was launched at the time benchmarking activities were starting. Originally, the modernization program focused primarily on achieving a streamlined material flow with the fewest steps possible, including material locations arranged by velocity to speed material flows and minimize picker travel distance.

The other practices, collectively described as "computer-directed picking," were not incorporated in the design. Benchmarked at Bean, along with other benchmarking investigations, these practices could provide additional efficiencies to the streamlined design and were the principle bases for definition and justification of this second phase of the warehouse design.

Implement Plans and Monitor Results

Because the extent and complexity of past practices was substantial, it was decided to use the program team approach for implementation:

- A comprehensive development project was organized.
- A requirements document was prepared, incorporating the best practices observed at Bean and at the other benchmarking partner firms.
- Potential hardware and software vendors were qualified. Proposals were requested from vendors to satisfy the benchmark requirements.
- A sizable, multiyear contract was negotiated for development and installation. For Xerox, this involved a commitment to a considerable development and of considerable implementation resources over a two-year period.
- Monitoring and reporting were implemented at two levels according to the benchmarking program and the specific findings at Bean.
- Based on the metrics, departmental targets were established. These targets, along with the individual productivity programs developed to install the best practices, were reviewed quarterly.
- To track progress by department or business unit for senior management, a summary monitoring chart, shown in Table 13-4, was developed to permit quick indication of overall progress in benchmarking. Although judgment must obviously be used in determining the relative position of different units, the chart is a quick reference to which departments are

TABLE 13-4
Monitoring Benchmark Progress Across Business Units

	Business			
	A	B	C	D
13. Leadership position attained				
12. Benchmarking institutionalized				
11. Management consensus gained				
10. Benchmark recalibrated				
9. Benchmark practices implemented				
8. Goals accepted				
7. Findings communicated				
6. Performance levels projected				
5. Competitive gap quantified				
4. Data collection methods confirmed				
3. Benchmarking partners selected				
2. Outputs identified				
1. Ground zero				

following the benchmarking steps the best and achieving benefits from a comprehensive benchmarking program.

Both long-range and operating budget submissions contained statements about benchmarking progress, which indicated not only the benchmark but also the date of achievement. These were typically part of the annual long-range reviews for the logistics plans presented to upper management These statements were also reviewed at communications meetings within the department.

"Computer-directed activities" was established as a stand-alone project with project management process and supporting software that allowed progress measurements. It was reviewed within the department and with affected organizations at agreed-upon intervals. The benchmark findings from the Bean visit were a significant portion of all such reviews. The findings at Bean caught individuals' imaginations and were interesting focal points for benchmarking.

The Bean experience was instrumental in starting the benchmarking activities on a very positive basis within the logistics function. It captured the attention of both management and employees because it was a firm they recognized. The experience taught an important lesson—that much can be learned from functional benchmarking, even outside one's own industry.

Once the process was understood, functional and generic benchmarking became much easier to perform. The approach has often been used in dissimilar industries and, provided that the characteristics of the process throughout activities are similar, the comparisons are valid. The results are pervasive. Table 13-5 shows some of the practices gained from benchmarking visits outside the office products industry that hold potential for adoption. The basic functional, noncompetitor approach has been copied many times to ensure that best methods that will lead to superior performance are uncovered. The example derived from the Bean experience was indicative of the company's having reached true maturity in the application of the benchmarking process.

TABLE 13-5
Best Practices Applicable to Warehouse Operations from Dissimilar Industry Firms

Type of Firm	Best Practice
Drug wholesaler	Electronic ordering between store and distribution center
Appliance	Forklift handling of up to six unpalletized units (appliances) at one time
Electrical components manufacturer	Automatic in-line weighing, bar code labeling, and scanning of packages
Photographic film manufacturer	Self-directed warehouse work teams
Catalog fulfillment service bureau	Item dimension and weight recording to permit order filling quality assurance based on calculated weight compared with actual

References

Biesada, Alexandra. "Benchmarking," *Financial World* 169, no. 9 (September 1991): 28–54.
Camp, Robert C. *Benchmarking: The Search for Industry Best Practices That Lead to Superior Performance.* Milwaukee: American Society for Quality Control, Quality Press, 1989.
Ishikawa, Kaoru. *Guide to Quality Control.* White Plains, N.Y.: Quality Resources, 1980.
Kelsch, John E. *Benchmarking: Shrewd Way to Keep Your Company Ahead of Its Competition, Boardroom Reports* (New York: Conference Board, December 1982), pp. 3–5.
Tucker, Francis G., Seymour M. Zivan, and Robert C. Camp. "How to Measure Yourself Against the Best." *Harvard Business Review* 87, no. 1 (January–February 1987): 8–10
"World Class Organizations: Xerox." *Industry Week* (March 9, 1990): 14, 16.

SECTION IV

Materials Management

Joseph L. Cavinato

Raw materials, supplies, and finished goods are the physical essence of virtually all logistics systems. Hence, thoughtful management of these materials is crucial to the success of most logistics operations. This section addresses topics related to effective materials management including forecasting, determining inventory investment, managing suppliers, planning, maintaining control, manufacturing, and packaging. Each chapter provides insightful discussion for managers seeking to understand materials management and improve the efficiency and effectiveness of their investments in materials and associated operations.

In Chapter 14, Donald B. Rosenfield identifies the types and nature of demand forecasts. Demand forecasts are important not only for determining production and stocking levels but also for making broad decisions such as those involving network configuration, suppliers, and marketing. The chapter discusses the most important demand patterns and forecasting methods and concludes with examples of effective demand forecasting.

In Chapter 15, Alan J. Stenger focuses on one of the main questions in materials management: How much inventory should I hold? The chapter discusses the delicate balance between investment and availability, describes ways to reduce inventories, and concludes with a detailed model for determining inventory quantities. Stenger's novel framework encourages managers to precede mathematics with business considerations of the purposes for inventory.

In Chapter 16, William L. Grenoble IV discusses the practicalities of maintaining control over inventory. The major clerical issues of record keeping, control systems, and counting are reviewed along with the managerial issues of analysis and performance measurement. Grenoble provides an efficient and understandable lesson in a very broad and complex subject.

In Chapter 17, Alan J. Stenger explains distribution resource planning (DRP) using a running case study to describe the concepts and processes of this continuous, comprehensive, and integrated planning tool. While simple systems work well with traditional inventory planning techniques, complex systems require greater sophistication to improve profits and provide accurate information for other functions like manufacturing.

In Chapter 18, Joseph L. Cavinato explores current and evolving practices in purchasing. As the scope of supply chain management broadens, companies are developing long-term supply relationships. Cavinato discusses these changes and shows how purchasing can move away from its traditionally isolated role as a support function toward a strategic role that provides competitive advantage.

In Chapter 19, R. John Aalbregtse and Roy L. Harmon discuss manufacturing in a just-in-time (JIT) environment, an issue that is dramatically affecting many logistics organizations. The chapter focuses on cellular manufacturing, quick changeovers, and pull scheduling. These practices allow manufacturers to improve flexibility and respond to direct customer demand, thereby reducing inventories, improving product quality, and enhancing customer service.

In Chapter 20, Diana Twede reviews the packaging required for manufacturing, shipping, handling, and storage. The chapter provides an overview of logistical packaging as well as a review of typical packaging challenges. Twede notes that most packaging in use today is archaic and that innovative approaches can reduce costs while increasing customer service by simplifying unpacking and reducing damage and waste.

CHAPTER 14

Demand Forecasting

Donald B. Rosenfield

Demand forecasting is concerned with the projection of demand in the future that is critical to successful logistics management.[1] Demand for products and services by end users, as well as by intermediate supply chain members, drives many basic strategic and operating decisions. Demand forecasting's primary goal is to have the right products in the right positions at the right time. However, its importance goes well beyond the need to target inventories, which is the application on which most practitioners focus. For example, longer-term forecasts will impact decisions on the network of manufacturing and logistics facilities, contracts with third-party suppliers, and other long-range logistics decisions. Intermediate-term forecasts will affect policies for dealing with seasonal buildups and intermediate workforce plans and contracts.

Forecasting is multifaceted. Demand is not a simple matter of a single prediction. Forecasts cover multiple time periods, multiple products or product groups, multiple geographic areas, and often multiple customer groups. They focus on predictions of demand as well as ranges and errors in demand. It is a true art to identify those dimensions that are crucial for logistics success and to develop systems to encompass the associated needs.

The purpose of this chapter is to describe the types and nature of demand forecasts and how they affect logistics operations and strategies, to discuss the most important patterns of demand, to describe methods and systems for demand forecasting, and to present examples that illustrate principles of effective demand forecasting.

Understanding and Applying Forecasts

Operating Principles for Demand Forecasting

Effective logistics practice and strategy can be based on several forecasting principles. These principles are discussed below and include the following:

- Good forecasts will still have significant errors.
- Forecasting requires monitoring and estimation of errors.
- One should expect and account for large uncertainties.
- Any forecasting system is based on either an implicit or explicit model.
- Effective forecasting is often based on aggregate forecasts broken down into product, geographical, or other components.
- Forecast errors are correlated in time and among geographical regions, and follow predictable relationships with time and aggregate forecast level.

Even "Good" Forecasts May Have Significant Errors

It is usually not possible to make demand estimates with great accuracy, for two reasons. First, certain factors having significant effects on demand are subject to great uncertainty. For example, in considering the stocking policies for air conditioners, the merchandiser of a major retailer suggests, from years of experience, that the single most important impact on aggregate demand is the weather in April. Many demand processes can be affected by factors that only marginally affect the need or quality of the good or service. A similar phenomenon is that demand at New England ski areas depends to a great deal on the snowfall in the metropolitan Boston area, despite the nature of the snow in the mountains. Such factors introduce significant uncertainty in the forecast of demand, and often at a time when it is difficult to plan appropriately.

The second reason is that the detail of forecasts, no matter how sophisticated they may be, reduces them to a level of significant natural uncertainty. Consider a major national retailer or manufacturer. Forecast detail at the product and store or customer zone level for an appropriate time period (say, a week) will reduce the forecast to possibly only a few units. This natural level of uncertainty is based on the Poisson process, which stipulates that the standard deviation of demand is equal to the square root of the expected demand. If a retail store expects to sell four bicycles during a sale week (even supposing that the store can account for factors that affect sales, such as economic conditions, recent store sales, the weather, and so forth, with great accuracy), then the standard deviation of that demand is two units. Because plus or minus two standard deviations is not unusual, demand can vary between zero and eight bicycles per week! And this is with a "perfect" forecasting system. Indeed, in the actual application, variations are typically three times greater than the natural Poisson variation. Two additional principles follow as a result of the extent of these uncertainties.

Forecasting Requires Monitoring and Estimation of Errors

For tasks like setting inventory targets and understanding trade-offs between inventory and transportation, one needs to understand how to translate ranges of errors into policies. The errors need to be tracked and converted into the language of statistics and probability. A logistics planning system consequently should be based on likelihood and probabilities, not on the "best" forecast. Because significant errors are possible, planners need to analyze the possibilities of demand. For example, inventory target points should be adjusted for the possible ranges of the distribution, which in turn requires the estimation of errors.

Expect and Account for Large Uncertainties

Stated another way, competitive leverage requires maximizing information for—and minimizing the time required in—forecasting situations. Because forecasting is so prone to error, planning and strategy require reducing the impact of this error as much as possible. Two strategies for doing this are, first, to eliminate errors (beyond those caused by the natural error of uncertainty) by accounting for as much causal information through information technology, and, second, to minimize the time horizon over which the forecast must be made. Because forecast errors increase with time, reduction of the forecast period can effectively reduce the magnitude of the forecast error. Implementation of this strategy is based on effective information technology and logistics. In simple terms, the logistics system needs to respond as quickly as possible to demand information within the value chain. Effective retailing, for example, requires flexibility in responding to demand trends in individual stores. One retailer used a strategy of holding merchandise at the central warehouse during promotions until early sales information indicated which stores were moving ahead of plan. This reduction of response time is a major competitive weapon in both logistics and manufacturing, and is essential for minimizing the effects of uncertainty.

All Forecasting Is Based on Either an Implicit or Explicit Model

Forecasting demand requires understanding and determining the underlying process that produces this demand. Like any aspect of logistics strategy, the forecasting decisions make implicit assumptions about the drivers of demand. What appears to be a simple or straightforward assumption about future demand may be unrealistic and significantly constrain the logistics system. For example, a constant forecast is precisely that, and there is no allowance for the effect of major external events or long term business patterns. Linkage of a forecast to some other process (for example, tennis court usage at a resort in relationship to projected guest stays) makes a very clear assumption about the drivers of that process.

The implication is that effective forecasting requires (1) an understanding of the drivers of demand, and (2) the development of a model for that demand. This model can be fairly simple, but it serves two important purposes: first, it reduces forecast errors as much as possible; second, it improves the forecaster's understanding about the drivers of the demand process.

The underlying models for the demand process can incorporate *statistical* features, such as trends or cycles, as well as *dependencies* on other variables, such as the dependence of automobile parts on the production of automobiles.

Breaking Aggregate Forecasts into Smaller Components

Forecasts require a great deal of detail: different geographical regions, different products, or different channels. Building up forecasts from data at these detailed levels is subject to a great deal of uncertainty. From a statistical point of view, because the coefficient of variation decreases as the total demand increases (the so-called laws of large numbers), an aggregate forecast will be more accurate on a percentage basis. From this perspective, it makes sense for an organization to develop an aggregate forecast for all products and all channels or geographic regions, and then disaggregate this forecast into its separate components according to some specific measure. This aggregate forecast can be used as the basis for effective production or logistics planning. The more effective forecasting systems use this type of disaggregation procedure.

Correlation and Predictability of Forecast Errors

Forecast errors are correlated in time and among geographical regions and follow predictable relationships with time and aggregate forecast level. There are clear relationships for forecasting in time, space (demand in geographic regions), and aggregate forecast level. If a business forecast of demand is high in a specific region of the country during a specific time period, it will likely be high for other regions of the country and in other time periods. The logistics and manufacturing systems need to account for this phenomenon.

Despite this correlation, there are clear statistical patterns in relationships of forecast errors in time and in space. For example, statistically, even incorporating correlation, forecast errors as a function of time tend to increase predictably. Forecast errors for an entire geographic region show a predictable pattern in terms of the forecast errors for subsections of that region. As an example, the error in the forecast over a year-long period will be greater than the error in the forecast over a six-month period. This can be quantified in a "power rule" (described further below).

Types of Forecasts

Forecasts can be classified according to the following dimensions:

- Time horizon
- Geographic area
- Product group
- Customer group
- Predicted average
- Predicted deviation

Each classification area is critical for logistics planning and strategy. Longer-range forecasts affect facility decisions, long-term contracts with third-party vendors, and other long-term decisions, while shorter-term forecasts affect inventory and transportation strategies. Geographic, product, and customer group forecasts affect policies for each of these subclassifications. Forecasts for average demands and errors in demand need to be considered both separately and together in developing an effective logistics system. Forecasts for average demand will affect the average flow of materials within the logistics system, whereas the predicted errors will affect inventory strategies as well as other contingency strategies.

Impacts of Forecasts

Areas affected by forecasts include the following:

Manufacturing facilities. Clearly the trends in demand for specific products and locations will have a significant impact on the appropriate facility strategies. The location of manufacturing facilities, as well as the choices of technologies, products, and markets served should all take into account the forecast for demand.

Distribution facilities. Decisions concerning distribution facilities are also affected by long-range forecasts. The size of the warehouse, the type of technology, and the locations all depend on the forecasts. Strategically, both logistics and manufacturing facilities need to be considered together. Both depend greatly on forecasts. As companies become more global, the forecasts for different regions become crucial in developing a global facilities strategy.

Transportation equipment and contracts. Forecasts of longer-term demand and the breakdown of demand into product groups and geographic regions will have significant impact on transportation equipment and contracts. Whether a business contracts its transportation needs to third parties or supplies them itself, it must determine the type of equipment and the level of need.

Supply contracts and purchasing. Purchasing ranges from short-term needs over the next week or month to long-term supply contracts for critical raw materials. Shorter-term supply needs and longer-term vendor relations are critically dependent on forecasts. In addition, the supply contract (for example, flexibility allowances) depends on these needs. The advent of more integrated supplier relationships has highlighted the need for more accurate forecasting in this domain.

Logistics technology. Logistics technologies include materials handling and warehousing within fixed facilities, the information systems for linking companies with suppliers and customers, and transportation (e.g., containerization, transfer of material, etc.). All these depend critically on intermediate and long-term forecasts.

Production planning and inventory control. Production planning and inventory control require accurate forecasts at the detailed level, incorporating both averages and predicted deviations. The design of the manufacturing and logistics system requires a certain level of flexibility and depends on the quality of the forecasting system.

Hierarchies of Forecasts

Given the various types of forecasts (aggregate versus geographic, product, or other breakdown detail, and average versus predicted error), it is important to understand how these various forecasts are related to one another. This section reviews some of these relationships and the resulting principles for managing logistics systems.

Time Horizons of Forecasts

The various time horizons of forecasts are discussed below:

Long-term forecasts, spanning from three to ten years, are used in the strategic analysis of fixed commitments and requirements for new plants or warehouse capacities or their locations, new supply contracts or vendor agreements, and commitments to materials handling or other logistics technologies.

Medium-term forecasts, generally on the order of six months to three years, are used to plan production in the face of intermediate-term and cyclical demand or supply. These types of decisions deal with floor space usage within existing facilities, modern expansion of facilities, materials handling systems, adjustments in third-party contracts (e.g., for transportation), or other intermediate-term decisions.

Short-term forecasts, from one week to several months, are used to control manufacturing levels and stock replenishment in the face of short-term demand variations. Short-term forecasts also deal with small-scale capital equipment, like materials handling equipment within the warehouse, short-term rental of transportation equipment like trailers, modifications of warehouse floor allocation, and changes in purchasing or procurement. The short-term logistics decisions generally involve scheduling of shipments and material flow through facilities.

When examining forecasts over different time horizons, one can develop statistical relationships for the forecast errors over the different time horizons.

Aggregate and Detailed Forecasts

Forecasting scope, as noted above, includes several different breakdowns of an aggregate forecast:

- By geographic region
- By product group or item

- By customer group or channel
- By shorter time period

Aggregate forecasts are important for two reasons. First, detailed forecasts are more appropriately determined in a hierarchical manner by first developing an aggregate forecast and then breaking it down. Second, the aggregate forecast is important in its own right, because important planning decisions require the aggregate forecast. The standard forecasting approach is to link the various hierarchical breakdowns in a forecasting decision to different planning decisions. Thus, an aggregate production plan for several time periods is based on an aggregate forecast. This is further broken down into the forecast by time period and for each of the plants or warehouses in the logistics and manufacturing system. It is worth discussing some of the methods for disaggregation and analysis for each of the major dimensions of forecast aggregation.

Geographic Breakdown

Markets are not distributed uniformly in space. They follow various distribution patterns that may be accurately predicted on the basis of past geographic breakdowns, or they may be based on more general types of economic activity. Broader types of activity could include buying power or, for a particular industry, selected consumer merchandise characteristics.

Certain types of industries may serve geographically concentrated markets. A forecast might be more appropriately based on past history for that industry or a related industry. Anything related to sales of European automobiles, for example, could be based on the history of sales, broken down geographically.

Product Group or Item Breakdown

Demand for items in the product line is characteristically far from uniform across the line. Generally the distribution of demand is highly skewed: most items have relatively low volume, while a few high-volume items account for the major part of the demand. Indeed, the distribution of items by their level of demand in numerous industries and businesses follows the type of pattern shown in Figure 14-1.[2]

The highly skewed distribution of demand suggests broad principles that are often cited. One often heard is the so-called 80–20 rule (also known as Pareto's Law): about 80% of the demand is accounted for by 20% of the items. Clearly the 80-20 rule is an approximation. Twenty percent of the items may account for much less than 80% or nearly all of the demand. The key point is that the demand is skewed.

Managerially, the skewed distribution has two implications for forecasting. First, when various economic or historical measures are used to break aggregate forecasts into detailed product line or item forecast, a firm may choose to use a different type of materials management or logistics system for the slower-moving items. For example, slow-moving items may be stocked centrally or transported differently. In addition, one may use a simple policy for all of the slow-moving items (e.g., the same order point and time supply for all of a class of items). In this way, forecasts for slow-moving items may be restricted to average demand only, and forecast errors might be tracked only for the faster-moving items.

The second implication of the skewed distribution is that it enables certain analytic techniques to extrapolate forecasts for all the items from a single aggregate forecast.

The probability distribution traditionally used to characterize the individual item demand dis-

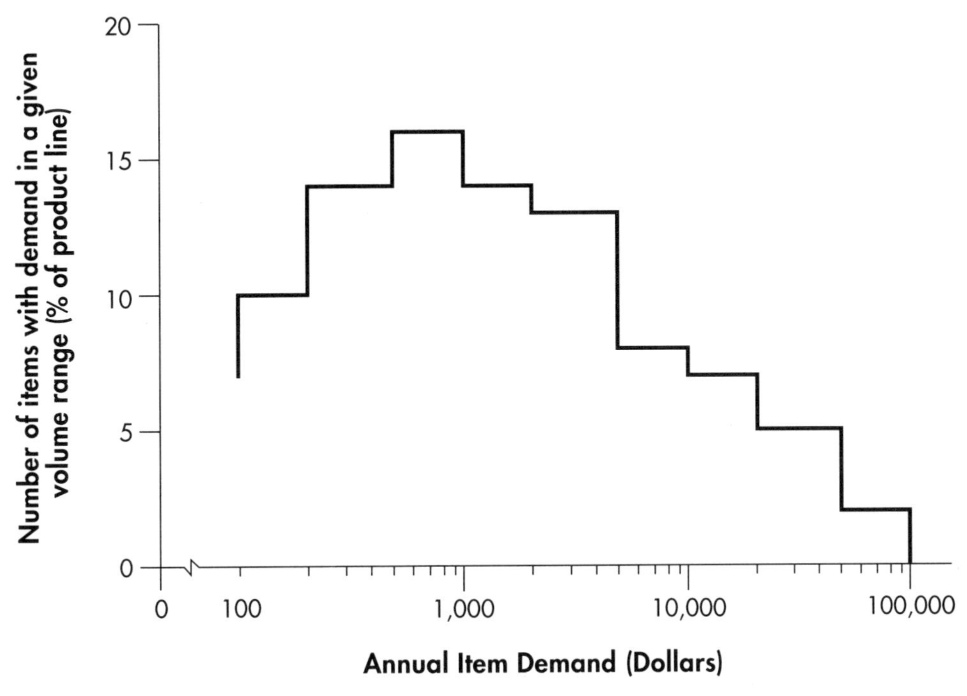

Figure 14-1

Typical Distribution of Demand By Item

Source: John F. Magee, William C. Copacino, and Donald B. Rosenfield, *Modern Logistics Management* (New York: John Wiley & Sons, Inc., 1985) p. 59. Reprinted by permission of John Wiley & Sons, Inc.

tributions is the lognormal distribution. It is given this name because the logarithms of the distributed variable—in this case, the value of item demand—fall into the familiar bell-shaped normal distribution pattern. If the cumulative distribution of demand by item is plotted on a graph in which the horizontal (demand) scale is in logarithmic units, and the vertical (cumulative distribution) scale is in standard normal probability units[3] or lognormal graph, then the distribution will follow a straight line. Figure 14-2 shows the same data as Figure 14-1, replotted, in the upper line, cumulatively on a lognormal graph.[4]

The slope of the line measures the range of item-demand rates; it can be expressed in terms of the standard ratio, the ratio of two-item demand rates that are separated by one standard deviation. The standard ratio of the distribution shown in Figures 14-1 and 14-2 is 7.5. This can be found by comparing the median item in the higher distribution, $1,400, to about the 84th percentile, $10,500. The standard ratio is $10,500 divided by $1,400, or 7.5.[5]

The lower line in Figure 14-2 is the cumulative distribution of demand as based on total demand rather than number of items. The lower line shows, for example, that the items with an annual demand equal to or less than $10,000 contributed about 13% of the total demand. The upper line shows that these items, with $10,000 or less annual demand, represent about 83% of the total items on the line. Note that the lower line, the distribution demand, follows the lognormal distribution with the same standard ratio. (The ratio of the medians is $\exp[(\ln(\text{standard ratio}))^2/2]$.)[6]

The relation between the distribution of numbers of items and of sales, illustrated by Figure

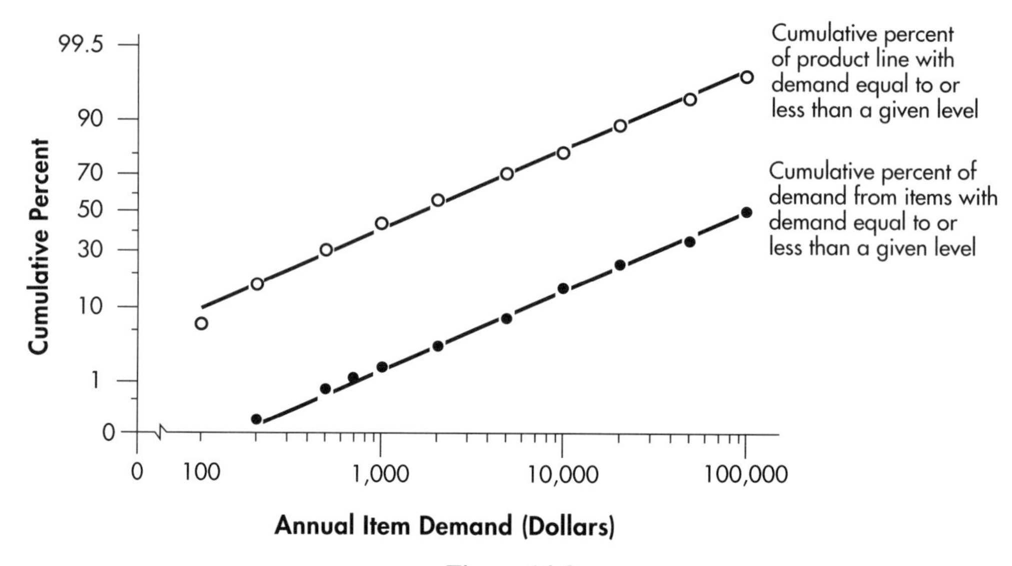

Figure 14-2
Cumulative Distribution of Items Versus Demand
The Lognormal Distribution

Source: John F. Magee, William C. Copacino, and Donald B. Rosenfield, *Modern Logistics Management* (New York: John Wiley & Sons, Inc., 1985) p. 60. Reprinted with permission of John Wiley and Sons, Inc.

14-2, is useful for estimating characteristics of warehouse activity and territory demand. For example, the lines on Figure 14-2 can be read jointly to show that the items with a total annual demand equal to or less than $1,500 make up about 52% of all items and account for 2% of total demand. The same distribution generally holds true for periods of the year or for subterritories within the total market. Therefore, by suitable changes in the horizontal scale to account for the fraction of the year or market, the distribution presents a method for calculating the demand or transaction characteristics, and hence costs, of items sold through a warehouse that serves some fraction of the total market; the movement characteristics of item demand during some short period, such as a lead time; or those of some subset of the product line.

On a more aggregate level, when forecasts are made for product groupings, one can similarly use a probability distribution to develop such aggregate measures.

Breakdowns by Customers, Orders, and Markets

Forecasts may also need to be disaggregated by market, customers, or orders. They will need to be disaggregated into markets when natural distribution channels are different for the two types of markets. Examples include overseas and domestic markets, private labels and regular markets, and markets (e.g., wholesale clubs) requiring different package sizes.

The distribution of the *value* of customer demands is also often skewed. In this case, a small number of customers may account for a large proportion of the total demand. Such a wide variation in the size and significance of customers may lead to a demand for multiple logistics channels. Larger customers may require direct shipments, but a local distribution system may be needed to serve smaller customers economically. Large retail chains usually have their own distribution systems.

Order types may also indicate certain patterns requiring disaggregation of the forecast. For example, if large orders represent a significant part of demand, the frequency of these large orders needs to be forecasted, and the logistics and inventory policies of the firm would have to be appropriately modified.

Additional patterns requiring appropriate adjustments in the logistics system include a time pattern of order arrivals that is highly batched, as well as responses to promotions, quantity discounts, and price discounts. Retailing organizations and manufacturers often need to forecast the price elasticity of demand and stock their distribution systems accordingly.

Coordination among distribution channels is especially important today. The ultimate forecast focuses on end-point demand. A manufacturer who forecasts customers' demand (i.e., the retailer) might see an unusual pattern that simply reflects policies for dealing with price promotions rather than any instabilities in the ultimate customer demand. The result of this could be significant changes in inventory in the middle of the value chain in situations when it may not be necessary.

Averages and Errors of Forecasts

One major operating principle is that forecasting systems require monitoring an estimation of both the errors and variations of forecasts in addition to the expectations of forecasts. Businesses have learned by hard experience that demand varies unpredictably around the expected level, even when adjusted for many of the exogenous factors like seasonality, trends, and other predictable factors. Because uncertainty is the norm, appropriate strategies dictate that the lead time over which a forecast is being made be as short as possible and that the uncertainty be reduced as much as possible.

The key to understanding uncertainty is that logistics systems are based on *forecast errors.* The forecast error is the difference between a demand forecast for an item over a given time period and the actual demand that is obtained. This definition (as shown in Figure 14-3) includes

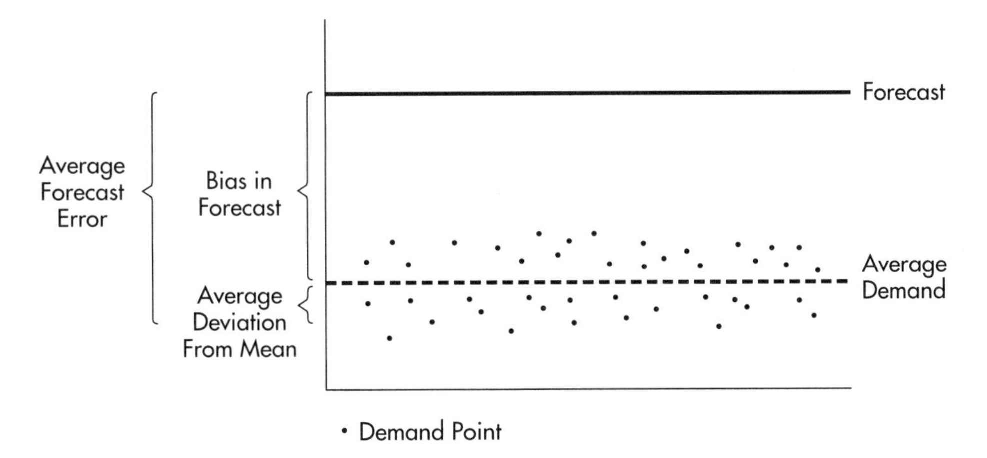

Figure 14-3
Forecast Errors

two elements of variation: the simple statistical variation of the demand time series plus any bias in the forecast.

It is thus a mistake to simply calculate the statistical variation in a demand time series. The bias can represent a significant amount of error and needs to be measured accordingly. This bias will exist because any forecast over a given period of time will be serially correlated: if the forecaster is wrong tomorrow, he or she will usually be wrong the next day.

Chance variations may be correlated in space as well as in time; that is, an unexpectedly high demand in one market may tend to be offset if the cross-correlation is negative. Both cases can be encountered in practice; the character of cross-correlation among markets depends on the forces underlying market behavior for the particular product line.

Weather, for example, influences large portions of demand for many products ranging from food items to energy and fuel. Humidity, temperature, cloud cover, and precipitation all play their part in certain product lines. Weather patterns, however, tend to dominate sizable geographic regions and to move slowly over large areas; thus, similar weather characteristics affect many markets simultaneously, or nearly so. Yet weather patterns are not uniform, and they change with time. Other influences may also be at work. Thus, the degree of correlation among markets may be positive but not high.

The degree and character of cross-correlation among markets play their part in logistics system design and operation. If the degree of cross-correlation is low or even negative, then the larger the share of the market served by a single point, such as a plant or warehouse, the more stable or relatively predictable the demand load imposed on the point. If the correlation among markets is very high and over broad areas, there is little incentive, at least on this basis, to consolidate service points to achieve a more uniform demand load.

The magnitude of the forecast error for an item can be expressed in several ways. The two most common expressions are (1) the standard deviation of the actual versus forecasted demand, and (2) the mean absolute deviation (MAD). The MAD is merely the average of the absolute values of the individual deviations observed in each period. It is a convenient measure because it is easily calculated, and it was originally developed to simplify computation. It is less useful today because computing power is no longer a real constraint.[7]

Forecasting systems can track forecast errors for every item, location, and period of time. Alternatively, the forecasting system can use aggregate patterns to estimate forecast errors from a sample or from the aggregate forecast error. To do this, one needs to estimate how forecast errors vary as a function of time and aggregate volume.

Relationships for aggregate volume can then be used to extrapolate forecast errors from one item to another or to extrapolate an aggregate national forecast to a specific region (with the appropriate share of the volume).

From a theoretical point of view, statistical rules enable one to determine how forecast errors change with respect to these two variables. If demand increments over time and space (different geographical regions) are independent, then we have the following type of relationship between an aggregate demand variation over time or space as a function of the individual demand variations.

$$\text{Var}(X_T) = \sum_{1}^{T} \text{Var } x_i = T(\text{Var } x_i) \text{ if Var } x_i = \text{Var } x_j, \text{ for } i \neq j$$

where:

x_i = Demand in time unit i or region i
T = Number of time units or regions
X_T = Aggregate demand for all regions or longer time period

Therefore the standard deviation for an aggregate demand is equal to the standard deviation of the detailed demand times the square root of the length of the time period or the number of regions. If we further assume that the different product lines behave similarly, then in comparing two time periods or two geographic regions or two product lines, this model implies that the ratio of the standard deviations is equal to the square root of the ratios of the demand. (By further extrapolating the implications of these types of relationships on inventory, one could conclude that inventory requirements vary as the square root of the average demand that they support.)

These types of relationships, known as square root laws, are powerful rules in understanding how forecast error changes with average demand. Unfortunately, there are two problems in applying such a square root law. The first is that variations in time and space are not independent of each other. There tends to be a correlation between the chance variations for one day, week, or month and the next similar time period. Usually this correlation is positive; if demand is above the expected level in one time period, it is more likely to be above the expected level in the next.

The degree of serial correlation (that is, from one time period to another) in variability of demand is very significant in logistics system design and operation. If no correlation exists, then a period with higher-than-expected demand is equally likely to be followed by a period of higher-than-normal demand or of lower-than-normal demand. The magnitude of unexplained variations in, say, a two-week period will thus be larger than in a one-week period, but not twice as large.

If the serial correlation is negative, there will be a stronger tendency for the variation in demand from one period to offset that of the previous period. The variability in a longer period, then, may be only slightly greater, about the same, or even slightly reduced. If the serial correlation is strongly positive, then the magnitude of variation in a given time period will be close to proportional to the length of the period.

The second problem in applying such a square root law is the forecast bias. If chance variations were not correlated and the forecast bias were zero, then the square root law would hold. The forecast bias implies that the correlation between forecast errors will be greater than the correlation of the actual demand itself.

The net effect of these two issues is that the actual relationship between forecast errors and aggregate demand is more appropriately characterized by what we call a generalized power rule:

$$\sigma_{T,D} = K\ T^{\alpha}D^{\beta}$$

where

$\sigma_{T,D}$ = forecast error for a given product or region as a function of the length of time period T and expected demand level D

α,β= parameters of relationship

In practice α and β are between 0.5 and 1.0. Low values correspond to little serial or spatial correlation or forecast bias, and high values correspond to the opposite. Based on a long history for scores of companies of analysis of item demands and forecast errors, the most appropriate value for both these parameters is approximately 0.7 (see Figure 14-4 for an example). In any case, it is important in a forecasting system, if these general types of relationships are to be used, to do a careful analysis of forecast and demand variations to best estimate these parameters.

The existence of these general relationships provides the capabilities for efficient aggregate planning. For example, if a national distributor wanted to expand from a single warehouse to a pair of warehouses, then the demand covered by each facility might be about one-half of the demand for the original facility. The distributor then could use the relationship between demand and demand variability to assess the increase in safety stock requirements.

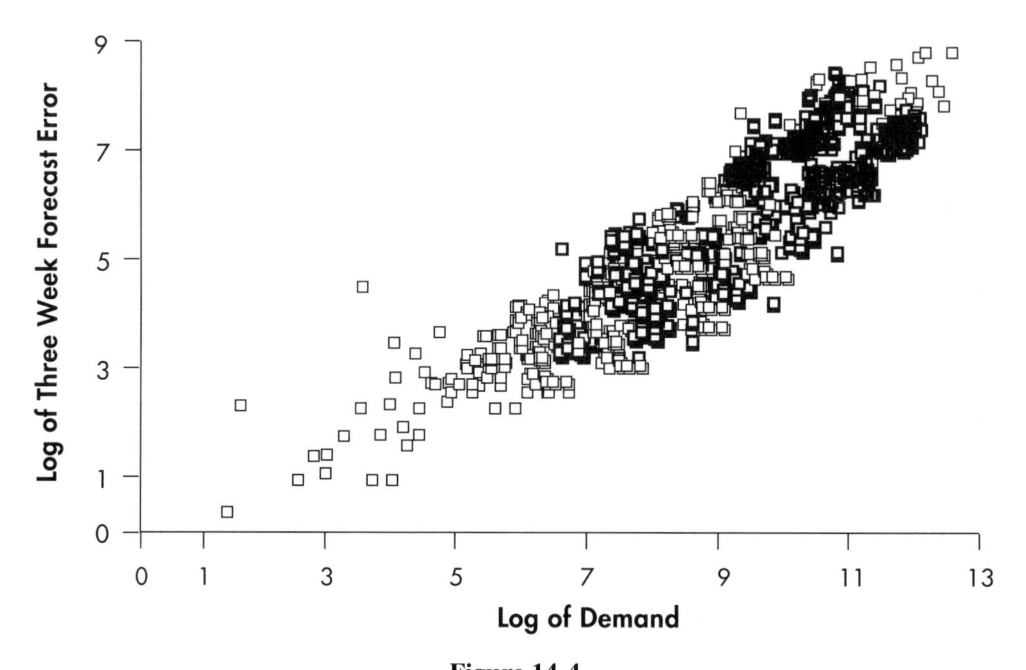

Figure 14-4
Example of Power Relationship for Consumer Goods Products

In terms of the forecasting system, these types of aggregate relationships allow general methods in tracking and monitoring forecast errors. One can track the specific errors for the high-volume, critical items, and can use an aggregate relationships to *estimate* forecast errors and develop appropriate inventory policies for the broad mass of slower-moving items.

Forecast Disaggregation and Usage

Based on these hierarchical approaches, the approach for the development of a forecasting system is as follows:

- Use a formal forecasting technique described in the subsequent sections of this chapter to develop an aggregate forecast for appropriate product lines, regions, and time intervals.
- Disaggregate this forecast into specific items or more detailed product lines, specific channels, or time periods according to appropriate historical data or economic measure. If appropriate, use a generalized distribution (e.g., lognormal or Pareto-type rule) to estimate item or group-level activities for extremely slow-moving items.
- Use an aggregate method based on the power rule to estimate forecast errors for a large number of items, or individually track forecast errors if appropriate.

The choice of aggregate techniques or detailed tracking of individual items or forecast errors depends on the business needs and the nature of the logistics system. Given modern computational methods, individual item and forecast error tracking is certainly feasible. Aggregate methods can be effective in the appropriate circumstances. Even when information systems are used to track things at a very detailed level, the aggregate methods can be effective in, for example, estimating the inventory effects of alternative logistics strategies. In any case, it is important for the logistics analyst or strategist to understand the nature of these aggregate relationships.

The Patterns and Models of Demand

To develop a system for forecasting, it is important to understand different patterns or models for demand and to emphasize that the forecasting methods depend strongly on the form of the model. As a simple example, the exponential smoothing model, which we describe in detail later in the chapter, is really based on the simple or constant model of demand. Important patterns and models are discussed below.

Simple or Horizontal Models

This model (as shown in Figure 14-5) assumes that demand varies in a random fashion around a constant *or* slowly varying level. Formally,

$$y_t = a + e_t$$

where:
y_t = demand at time t
a = average demand (constant level)
e_t = variation or noise

In mature industries this type of model is appropriate. The job of the forecasting system is to predict this constant level as accurately as possible to estimate the deviation and to detect the modest changes that may change the constant level. Simple historical forecasting approaches, like exponential smoothing or moving averages are excellent for this type of model, because any changes in the average level of demand will be estimated by the moving average or the exponentially smoothed estimate.

Trend Models

Trend models (see Figure 14-5) represent a constant growth in demand. The role of the forecasting system is to estimate the level of demand, the rate of increase in demand, and the forecast error. Forecasting systems with trend models may have separate estimation procedures for a base level and the magnitude of the trend. The formal model is:

$$y_t = a + ct + e_t$$

where *c*, the additional term, is the trend.

Seasonal and Cyclic Models

Over periodic intervals, demand may show definite and important statistical characteristics. Seasonal variation in the mean demand (see Figure 14-5) may be caused by climate-related factors or by industry practices. The general pattern may be quite predictable, although demand levels at any time and the timing of demand acceleration, peaking, or slowing down may be difficult to spot. For example, automotive antifreeze sales are almost entirely concentrated in a few autumn months. However, the actual timing of the peak demand period is closely related to the first severe cold weather and may occur at any time over several weeks. Trade practices, such as the timing of merchandise shows, can cause seasonal demand patterns of substantial magnitude.

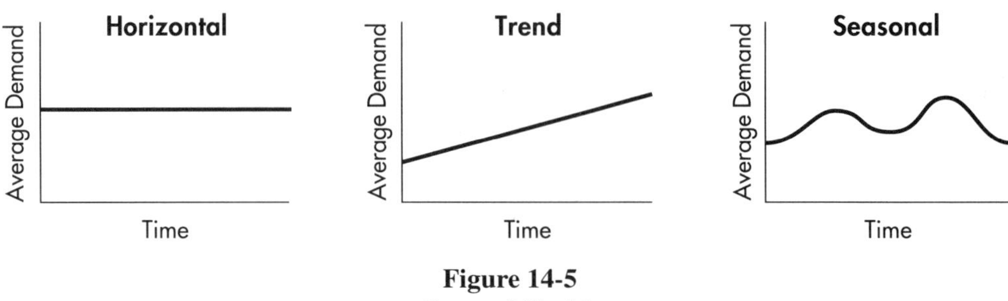

Figure 14-5
Demand Models

Most seasonal variations in demand patterns appear to be caused by traditional patterns of consumer buying, including the buying for the Christmas and Easter seasons or by climatic cycles. Demand for air conditioners, for example, is highly seasonal, as is demand for lines of clothing. Consumer buying during the Christmas holiday season creates demand surges that are passed back, stage by stage, through the logistics system of each product line, advancing in time at each stage. Other seasons are important to particular industries. Greeting card manufacturers have worked diligently to promote holidays and commemorations throughout the year to smooth out the peaks created by the Christmas season and a few special holidays like Valentine's Day.

In some cases, seasonal demand can be induced by promotional or other business policies and may simply be due to price elasticity and other promotional factors. In the automotive industry, for example, the introduction of new models in the fall induces a demand cycle. Inventory taxes may induce a timing pattern between retailers and manufacturers. In other cases, demand patterns may be affected by seasonal supply patterns, such as agricultural products whose demand is affected by harvesting and wood products whose demand varies according to seasonal ice conditions in northern climates.

Seasonal patterns are a specific example of the general case of cyclic patterns. Cyclic patterns are business cycles that take place over longer time periods than annual seasons.

In modeling seasonal factors, a forecasting system can use an additive or multiplicative approach, in which case the seasonal increase or decrease is simply added to or multiplies a base level. The seasonal factors usually have to be analyzed separately using historical data. The additive model, combining both trend and seasonality, is:

$$y_t = a + ct + s_t + e_t$$

where:

s_t = the seasonal factor for time t

The multiplicative model is:

$$y_t = s_t(a + ct) + e_t$$

Dependent or Causal Models

This type of model simply relates demand for a given item to some other exogenous variable or set of variables. Hence the forecast is a function of a set of variables, and the levels of those variables are given either exogenously or estimated based from historical data. The functional form of the model that relates demand of the item to be forecasted to these exogenous variables must also be estimated, and this estimate may be based on historical data or other means.

Promotional Models

Many companies that have promotions or occasional discounts need to forecast demand during such promotions. Like a seasonal or trend factor, the promotional effect can either add to or multiply the base forecast. The magnitude of the promotional effect may also depend on the level of the price or discount. As such, various functional forms can be assumed for price elasticity. One complexity of promotional models is how they affect base demand when the promotion is not in effect. This complicated issue calls into question the basic multiplicative or additive model.

General Approaches to Forecasting

Forecasting approaches are generally of three different methods or a combination thereof, including the following:

- Methods based on causal models
- Judgmental or expert estimates
- Historical or databased

For example, a causal model relating a demand to some other variable can be formulated, and the parameters of the model can be updated from historical data. Some of the parameters could alternatively be based on expert judgment, or the entire forecast could be modified by expert judgment.

Methods Based on Causal Models

The most general approach in forecasting is based on the causal model. In this approach the demand to be forecasted is related to some other variable or set of variables. There are several valid reasons for this type of approach. One can often develop a very accurate model relating the variable to be forecasted to the other variables, or a great deal of historical data may be available about the exogenous variable. One can also use a broader range of information and data than the simple demand process itself. Examples of this approach are described below:

- Forecasts for demand for any item related to the automobile industry are often closely related to the sale of automobiles or some other broad measure of economic activity in the automobile industry.
- In a retailing organization, sales for particular stores or particular product categories can be related to broader economic measures for that geographic area or product category.
- Demand for the use of resort facilities can be closely related to number of guests and average length of stay.

Judgmental or Expert Estimates

The second approach is judgmental or derived from expert opinion. Often a quantitative historical model or a causal model cannot take into account all the rich detail of information that may affect demand. In many cases experts familiar with the product line being forecasted can take into account a wide range of information in developing forecasts.

Although an expert system based on artificial intelligence can incorporate this other information, it is always useful to have an expert review any computed forecast. This review is usually done on a broader level, because it is simply not possible for one individual to review a great deal of detail on all products in all stores in a retail chain. The merchandiser may instead use a judgmental or expert forecast for the chain sales in that product line. The merchandiser is also capable of incorporating recent information like weather patterns and recent sales trends that may not be formally incorporated within the forecasting system. Most forecasting systems use a combination—a historically based system reviewed and potentially modified by an expert.

Historical or Databased Methods

Historical or databased methods make up the major theoretical underpinnings of demand forecasting systems. Even when causal or judgmental approaches are used, historical approaches are used in conjunction to estimate parameters in the causal approach and as an alternative or support in the judgmental case. In using historical approaches, it is important to understand the applications and uses of the various statistical methods that are part of forecasting systems.

Regression and Methods of Start-up versus Methods of Updating

Exponential smoothing, moving averages, and regression analysis are the most common methods of statistical analysis. However, they are used for very different purposes. Exponential smoothing is used mostly for updating a forecast or a parameter in a forecast, not for developing an original forecast or model of one. The moving average can be used either for updating or, for simple models, developing original estimates of parameters. Regression analysis is used primarily for developing an original forecasting model for demand. Such an original forecast needs to be updated, either by updating the parameters or by reevaluating the model at periodic intervals.

Regression is the classic method of developing an original model by relating demand to a series of other factors. The equations for the regression model are as follows:[8]

$$y_t = mx_t + b$$

where:
y_t = variable to be forecasted
x_t = level of causal variable at time t

and the estimates for m and b are:

$$\hat{m} = \frac{n(\Sigma\, x_t y_t) - (\Sigma\, x_t)(\Sigma\, y_t)}{n(\Sigma\, x_t^2) - (\Sigma\, x_t)^2}$$

$$\hat{b} = \frac{(\Sigma\, y_t) - (\Sigma(x_t^2)) - (\Sigma\, x_t)(\Sigma\, x_t y_t)}{n(\Sigma(x_t^2)) - (\Sigma\, x_t)^2}$$

for the n observations of x_t, y_t

Suppose we wish to develop a model that relates tire demand of a company to new car sales. Weekly data are as follows:

new car sales (thousands) = 165, 155, 195, 198, 260, 175, 185, 190, 220, 277, 235, 255
tire demand (thousands) = 21, 19, 22, 19, 24, 20, 19, 20, 23, 25, 25, 24

Then the estimates of the parameters from the formula above are:

$$\hat{m} = 0.052,\ \hat{b} = 10.88$$

and the forecasting model is that weekly tire demand in thousands is equal to:

$$y_t = 0.052 \text{ x (car sales}_t) + 10.88 + e_t$$

and the parameters $\hat{m}$ and $\hat{b}$ can then be updated by an appropriate updating method.

The difference between an initialization method and an updating method is illustrated by an example of forecasting individual sales for direct mailing operations. For a major catalog operation, a forecasting system was developed for the entire base of customers that had used the company's catalogs. The first two orders were used as a basis for developing an initial forecast estimate for a customer (based on purchase size and the interval between the two purchases). After that point, the forecasts were based on an updating system. Statistically, as more information is collected, one can make predictions about an individual with more precision. Thus the updating procedure can be made more precise.[9]

Moving Averages

Moving averages represent a very simple method of both forecasting and updating parameters. A moving average of demand is simply the average of the past *N* periods of demand, where *N* is the control parameter of the system. For example, using the same data for car sales, then the six-period moving averages starting from period seven are:

191.3, 194.7, 200.5, 204.7, 217.8, and 213.7

The three-period moving averages starting from period seven are:

211, 206.7,183.3,198.3, 229.0, and 244.0

Note that the larger *N* is, the more stable the forecast is, but the less sensitive the forecast is to changes in the demand process. Figure 14-6 shows the two moving averages. Figure 14-7 shows the general effect of a trend and sudden change in demand on a moving average.

These examples point out that a moving average is really appropriate only for a constant or

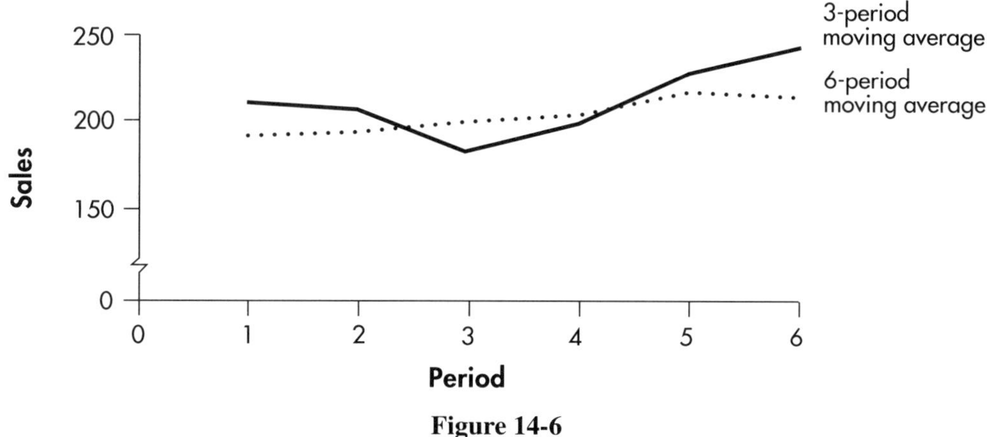

Figure 14-6
Moving Averages for Car Sales

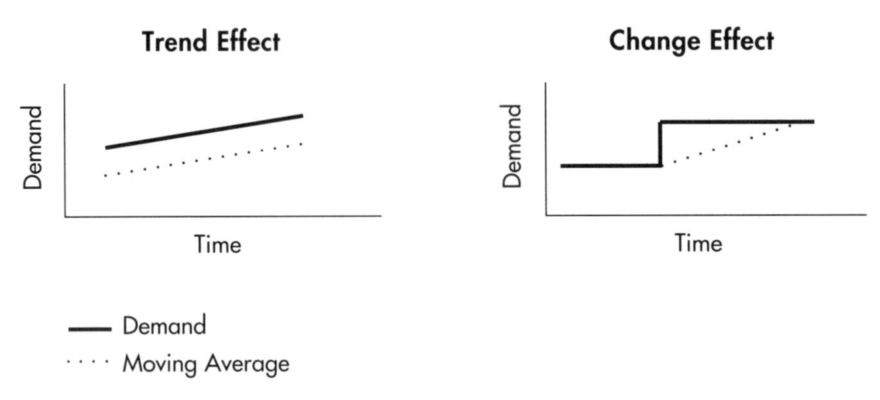

Figure 14-7
Moving Average Effects

horizontal-demand model. The method is capable of recognizing modest changes in the demand process, but major changes or trends can cause problems. A moving average can also monitor a particular parameter (e.g., a slope in a trend).

Exponential Smoothing

Exponential smoothing is probably the most widely used forecasting system. The method is most appropriate to the updating of parameters in a general model. The formal definition of the exponential model is:

$$F_t = \alpha F_{t-1} + (1 - \alpha)y_t$$

where:
F_t = Forecast after period t
y_t = Demand in period t

The parameter α is referred to as the smoothing constant. When examining the exponentially smoothed forecast over multiple periods, the previous relationship expands recursively as follows

$$F_t = \alpha^t F_0 + \alpha^{t-1} (1 - \alpha)y_1 + \cdots + (1 - \alpha)y_t$$

The name *exponential smoothing* comes from the way in which the factors relating the new forecast to previous demand decrease for demand that is further in the past.

The advantage of exponential smoothing (and the reason for its widespread acceptance) is its utter simplicity. The only data needed to update the forecast is the past forecast and the most recent demand. It is the most economical model for data collection available.

Exponential smoothing requires an alternative method for the initial estimation of a parameter. This could be done, for example, with a moving average. Like the moving-average technique, exponential smoothing can detect modest changes in demand, but it will lag behind a trend or a major change in the demand process. A higher value will be more sensitive to changes but less stable.

The necessity of a separate trend factor can be seen in an example where a demand changes from a basically horizontal process to one subject to a trend. Consider an additional six months of car sales of 260, 265, 270, 275, 280, and 285. Figure 14-8 shows the final 17 months of data

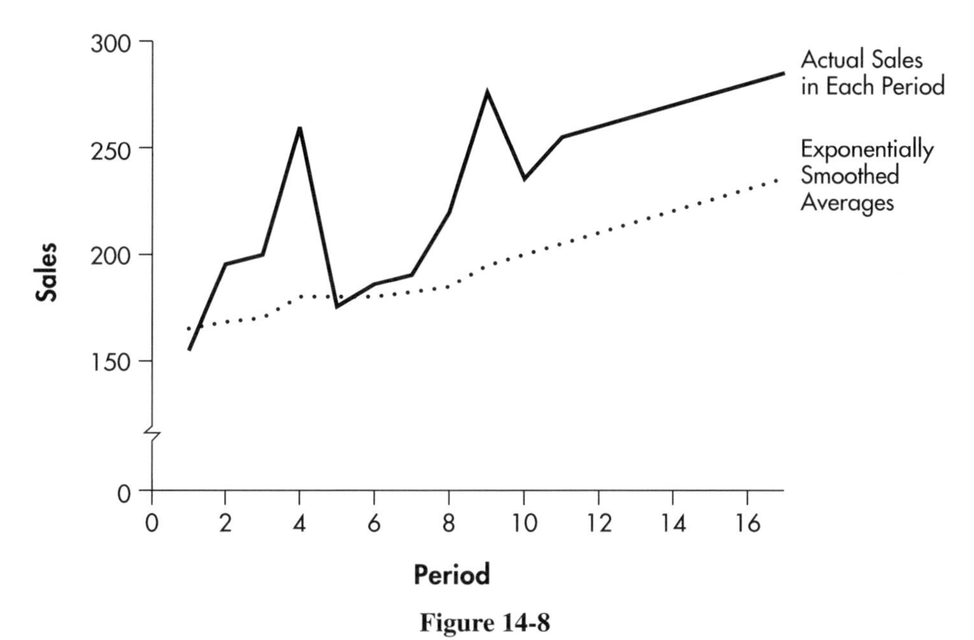

Figure 14-8

Seventeen Periods of Car Sales and Exponentially Smoothed Averages

with an exponentially smoothed average, with $a = 0.9$. (The initial forecast uses the period zero sales of 165.)

With a standard exponential smoothing model, there will be a permanent difference between the forecast and the actual demand. Hence, the extra trend term is necessary and exponential smoothing as a forecasting rather than an updating procedure is appropriate only for the horizontal model.

More Sophisticated Statistical Approaches

The quantitative methods cited are relatively simple. A more sophisticated forecasting system can involve more complex statistical methods, both in fitting and updating models. The Box-Jenkins method is an example that takes advantage of serial correlation.[10]

Developing a System for Forecasting

Because forecasting involves different types of forecasts and various tools for analyzing information, a business needs a coherent, comprehensive system for demand forecasting. Such a system should include the following four elements: (1) an underlying model; (2) data, exploratory analysis, and calibration; (3) updates to the model; and (4) measurement of forecasting errors.

The Underlying Model

The heart of the forecasting system is the *model* relating the demand to its contributing variables. A contributing variable can be something very simple, such as a constant or another variable, such as a time trend. Alternatively, it can be related to a set of exogenous variables that drive it. The development of this model can be based on a pure historical data analysis or an exploratory analysis that relates demand to a set of possible exogenous variables.

The underlying model also describes the hierarchical structure in which aggregate demand is broken down into geographic, product, or time categories. Each of these breakdowns must be modeled and, as appropriate, normalized so that the detailed forecasts add up to the aggregate forecasts.

Data, Exploratory Analysis, and Calibration

Once a model or a possible set of models has been formulated, demand forecasting requires analyzing historical data to finalize the details of the model. A model is given in terms of *structure,* which represents a general functional form and the sets of variables that the models comprise. The formulation of a trend model, for example, defines the basic structure. Further data analysis is needed to identify the specific constants that are used in the model.

Regression analysis is the standard way to develop an initial demand model. This gives the least squares formulation of a model that can be expressed in the form of a regression equation. Calibration of a model generally goes further than fitting a model to a set of data. The model must then be *tested* to another data set that comprises a period of time later than the first data set. A regression equation relating demand to a set of dependent variables might be fit using one year of data and then tested or calibrated using a second year of data.

Updating the Model

The essence of effective demand forecasting is adapting the forecast to changes. One generally assumes that the essential structure of a model is robust and remains the same over time. However, one may also assume that the constants in a model vary slowly over time. For this reason, one uses the data in every time period to update the parameters in the model. For example, each equation in a regression model might be exponentially smoothed after each time period. To illustrate, consider the following simple trend model:

$$y_t = a + ct + e_t$$

To initialize this model, we perform a regression analysis of demand over time to get the best estimates of the constant and the trend term. We then might update the model each period in the following way:

$$a_t = \alpha y_t + (1 - \alpha)(a_{t-1} + c_{t-1})$$
$$c_t = \beta(y_t - y_{t-1}) + (1 - \beta)c_t$$

where:

a_t, c_t = estimates for *a* and *c* after period t

β = smoothing constant for trend

And the new forecast is:

$$F_t = a_t + c_t$$

This method is also known as double exponential smoothing, or Holt's method.[11] A variation of this method is to update the base every period but the trend only after a set number of periods.

This same type of approach can be used for more general models. We can use exploratory analysis to fit any type of multivariable model and update the parameters with the data, using exponential smoothing each period.

Ranges and Estimating Errors

The ranges and possible errors in a forecast will have a big impact on many parts of the logistics system. As an example, forecast errors have a direct bearing on the safety stocks and inventory policies of the firm. Thus the forecasting system needs to track errors. The final part of the forecasting model is to update the forecasting error in each period, which is most appropriately measured in terms of the mean square deviation.

In addition to formally computing errors, one can use a variation of statistical process control in which important errors of the forecasts, such as for the aggregate forecast, are actually plotted, and analysts can observe whether the forecasting system is relatively stable. If the errors are becoming "out of control," one may want to consider recalibrating the model with a new set of constants or even a more general type of model.

The Process of Forecasting

Equally, if not more important, is the *process* of forecasting. By this we mean who is responsible for forecasting, who are the stakeholders of forecasting, and how are the forecasts used in the organization.

The general principle is that the stakeholders need to gain consensus on appropriate forecasts. If, for example, the marketing department of a company is responsible for forecasts and there are no incentives for marketing to hold down inventories and production, the natural tendency is to overpredict demand in any given time horizon. Unfortunately, if the other constituencies in the organization do not have faith in marketing forecasts, then they will tend to ignore the forecasts, and this can result in a great deal of game playing in the organization. "Official" forecasts, which are likely to be unsophisticated and unscientific, are generally ignored.

If the various stakeholders involved—marketing, production, and distribution—can agree on a forecast, then production and inventory plans can be linked to this forecast and the various entities of the organization will work together for competitive leverage. The operating principles are similar to those of strategic planning—the various parts of the organization need to work together.

Because consensus is so important, the process of gaining it is crucial. The organization that does the forecasting cannot work alone without reviewing these forecasts with the various parts of the organization. This underscores the importance of gaining expert judgment within the forecasting system. A good procedure to gain consensus will have a good balance between quantitative, databased methods and expert methods.

The process of forecasting also includes *monitoring* forecasts. Not only do forecast errors need to be tracked continuously, but forecasts need to be evaluated in terms of the validity of the underlying model and any new factors that influence the forecast. Monitoring can be accomplished through broad accuracy measurements, correlations with potential factors that may influence forecast and demand, and simple graphic tools like control charts of forecast errors.

The process of forecasting is important throughout the value chain among the different players involved. At any point in the value chain, a supplier, a manufacturer, or a retailer needs to understand that demand at the end of the value chain is the ultimate customer demand. Forecasts need to be coordinated, along with inventory management and logistics, to ensure the most efficient operation of the entire channel. When the different players in the value chain operate independently, sudden variations in activity at any location (caused, for example, by promotions) can distort the view observed by that player.

Forecasting Examples

The principles and methods of forecasting can best be illustrated by some examples of how manufacturers and retailers use forecasting. Three such examples are presented here.

Sunday Advertising Supplement for a Large Retailer

Large retailing organizations face extremely complex forecasting problems. These organizations have thousands of stockkeeping units and hundreds of stores. Thus there are hundreds of thousands of individual forecasts to be made. Because some of the numbers involved in these forecasts are so low, the forecasts are subject to significant variations. In addition, most retailing organizations make significant use of promotions. For one retailing organization, a large proportion of its sales were through the advertised items in the Sunday supplements of major newspapers. The retailer developed a system to forecast sales for these advertised items for every store in the chain.

The chain historically forecasted sales for these items by equating the forecast for the sale to the sales of a similar type of item at that store in a previous advertising campaign. In performing some exploratory data analysis on this type of approach, the author discovered that the classic concept of regression toward the mean underscored the problems with this type of approach. For example, if a big-ticket item like a bicycle were on sale and the store did very well previously, selling 12 units, this might indicate that the store would do better than average on the subsequent sale but would not yield the extreme result of 12. (As a comparative example, tall people tend to have tall children, but not as tall as they themselves.) The result of the analysis was the development of a new forecasting system that related promotion item share sales at a store to three separate variables:

- Sales of a similar item in a previous ad
- Sales for second similar item for a different ad
- The share of the store's sales in the total chain sales

Note that the forecast for the store was based on the *share* of the total chain sales for that item, which was forecast separately. There was still some evidence of regression toward the mean. *All* the modeling equations, therefore, had constants that were independent of the outcomes on the specific variables.

Notice that the approach embodied some of the principles and concepts outlined in this chapter. First, the equation for the share of the store sales was based on a clear model that was a function of three dependent variables. Second, the retailer developed the initial constant according to some exploratory data analysis. Third, the firm used a hierarchical approach in which the chain sales were forecast first and store sales were based on a share equation.

Forecasting the Demand for an Automobile Part

A second case study involved a forecasting system for a manufacturer who supplied the automobile companies and the automobile aftermarket with a specific type of part.

The statistical analysis of the demand resulted in an extremely accurate model for demand for these parts: the average demand was equal to a linear combination of automobile demands one month and two months in the future. There was still some uncertainty around this average, owing to the aftermarket. The resulting equation could explain a great deal of the variation in the automobile market.

The situation was a classic application of relating demand for the product to a set of exogenous variables. The problem with the approach was that forecasting automobile demand was difficult. The automobile forecasts were standard industry forecasts subject to both uncertainty and consistent bias. Indeed, in examining the forecast errors of the resulting forecast (see Figure 14-9), one sees the significant serial correlation in these errors, indicating the forecast bias. Nevertheless, the example illustrates the use of a model and the nature of forecast errors.

Forecasting Tennis Court Demand at a Resort

The Sea Pines Racquet Club was faced with forecasting how much demand for its tennis courts would grow during the growth stage of the resort during the 1970s.[12] After analyzing data on court availability during each month of the year, court usage per guest by the guests at the condominiums and hotels, and the projected guest nights at these facilities, Sea Pines developed a model to forecast tennis court usage on a monthly basis:

$$\text{courts} = \frac{\text{guest nights} \times (\text{hours per guest night})}{(\text{hours available in month}) \times \text{utilization factor}}$$

A model clearly defining drivers of tennis court usage was key to understanding the demand. By understanding how guest nights at the resort would grow and how tennis court usage per

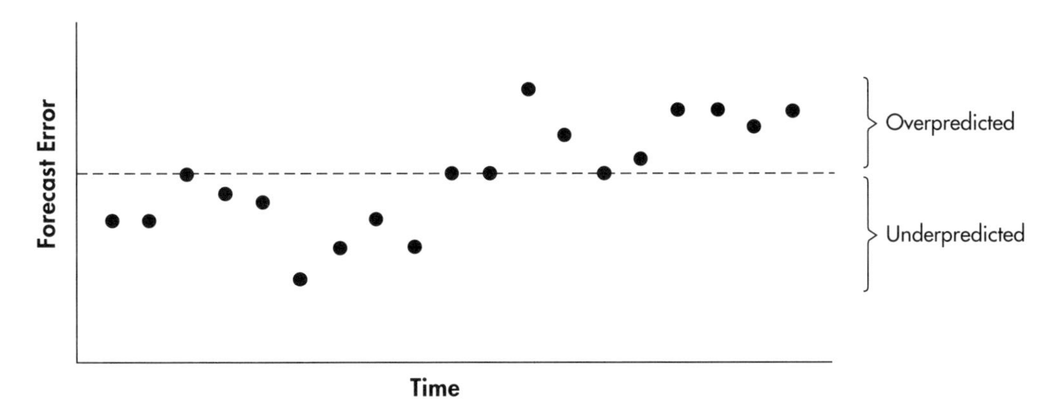

Figure 14-9
Automobile Part Demand Example of Forecast Errors
(4 months ahead)

guest night would grow (this was during the growth era of tennis playing), the company could gain a good understanding for tennis court demand.

Individual Customer Orders for Mail Order

One of the nation's major catalog sales companies has been using a computerized decision-support system for helping determine who should receive copies of its catalog. Part of the decision-support system was a forecast of the catalog purchases by every one of its customers. The forecast consisted of two parts: the first part was a probabilistic estimate of the expected purchases based on either the initial one or two orders by that customer. The second part was an exponentially smoothed estimate of the average frequency of order and the average size of the order, if the number of customer orders for that customer was three or greater.

Although we have omitted from this discussion some of the details of the assumptions of customer purchasing behavior, we note that the system had separate structures for initializing and updating the forecast for each customer.

Many examples illustrate how demand forecasting technology in conjunction with superior information systems can be used to develop competitive advantage in logistics. Superior logistics performance can be clearly linked to such effective systems.

Notes

1. Some short sections of this material are adapted from J. F. Magee, W. C. Copacino, and D. B. Rosenfield, *Modern Logistics Management* (New York: Wiley, 1985).
2. John F. Magee, William C. Copacino, Donald B. Rosenfield, *Modern Logistics Management* (New York: Wiley, 1985): p. 59. Adapted by permission of John Wiley & Sons, Inc.
3. This means that equal measures correspond to equal numbers of standard deviations. Zero-to-one standard deviation corresponds to the 50th to 83rd percentiles. One-to-two corresponds to the 83rd to 96th percentiles. On the *y*-axis, these percentile intervals are equal in size. For a more detailed discussion of the lognormal distribution, see R. G. Brown, *Statistical Forecasting for Inventory Control* (New York: McGraw-Hill, 1959), p. 1. (This note is adapted from Magee, et al., *Modern Logistics Management,* by permission of John Wiley & Sons, Inc.)
4. Magee, et al., *Modern Logistics Management,* p. 60.
5. Ibid., pp. 59–60.
6. Ibid., p. 60.
7. Ibid., pp. 62–63.
8. For further explanation, see W. L. Hays and R. L. Winkler, *Statistics Probability, Inference, and Decision* (New York: Holt, Rinehart and Winston, 1970).
9. For a theoretical treatment of this issue, see D. B. Rosenfield, "A Model for Predicting Frequencies of Random Events," *Management Science* 33, no. 8 (1987): 947–54.
10. See G.E.P. Box and G. M Jenkins, *Time Series Analysis, Forecasting, and Control* (San Francisco: Holden-Day, 1970).
11. See C. C. Holt, "Forecasting Seasonal Trends by Exponentially Weighted Moving Averages," Office of Naval Research, Memorandum No. 52 (1957).
12. Harvard Business School Case Services, "Sea Pines Racquet Club," Case 674-011, (Boston, 1980).

References

Box, G. E. P. and G. M. Jenkins. *Time Series Analysis, Forecasting, and Control.* San Francisco: Holden-Day, 1970.

Brown, R. G. *Statistical Forecasting for Inventory Control.* New York: McGraw-Hill, 1959.

Chambers, J. C., S. K. Mullick, and D. D. Smith. "How to Choose the Right Forecasting Technique." *Harvard Business Review,* 49, no. 4 (1971): 45–74.

Harvard Business School Case Services, "Sea Pines Racquet Club," Case 674-011, Boston, 1980.

Holt, C. C., "Forecasting Seasonal Trends by Exponentially Weighted Moving Averages." Office of Naval Research Memorandum No. 52,1957.

Hays, W. L. and R. L. Winkler. *Statistics: Probability, Inference, and Decision.* New York: Holt, Rinehart and Winston, 1970.

Magee, J. F., W. C. Copacino, and D. B. Rosenfield. *Modern Logistics Management.* New York: Wiley, 1985.

Nahmias, S. *Production and Operations Analysis.* Homewood, Ill.: Irwin, 1989.

Robeson, J. F. and R. House, ed. *The Distribution Handbook.* New York: Free Press, 1985.

Rosenfield, D. B. "A Model for Predicting Frequencies of Random Events." *Management Science* 33, no. 8 (1987): 947–54.

CHAPTER 15

Inventory Decision Framework

Alan J. Stenger

Many argue that inventories are undesirable and should be eliminated entirely.[1] This is more easily achieved within a manufacturing operation than in a complicated logistical supply chain. For the foreseeable future, business will continue to experience uncertainties in demand and supply, lower transportation prices for larger shipment quantities, and seasonal supply or demand for certain materials and products. In addition, transportation and other processes will continue to take a finite amount of time to accomplish. However, logistics managers should have learned from such programs as Total Quality Management, Just-in-Time, and Continuous Improvement that they must always strive:

- If not to eliminate, at least to mitigate as much as possible the factors that cause the need for inventories in the first place
- Where these factors cannot be eliminated, to carry only the minimum inventory levels necessary to respond to them

Such a goal is, of course, very challenging. Inventories do exist in most manufacturing and distributing businesses. They need to be managed as effectively as possible, and kept only as large as is absolutely necessary. Unfortunately, many inventories today not only exist but far exceed necessary levels. Some managers see little need to manage them, let alone mitigate their causes.

Before discussing inventory management, this chapter presents specific ways to eliminate the causes of inventories. Then it covers the determination of required inventory levels when the causes cannot be eliminated. The approaches discussed are based on well-developed statistical techniques that have proven valuable in many actual business situations.

The Context of Inventory Management

The Supply Chain and the Logistics Network

Most products move through a complex supply chain, or network, as various firms process and convert materials into finished products and ship them to customers. Figure 15-1 shows a typical supply chain consisting of (1) secondary vendors who supply material to primary vendors; (2) the manufacturer who buys from the primary vendors and converts the raw material into a finished product; and (3) the manufacturer's distribution center, from which the finished product is shipped to the customer's distribution point, whence it goes to the ultimate consumer.

The supply chain concept accurately represents the way one unit of a raw material might flow

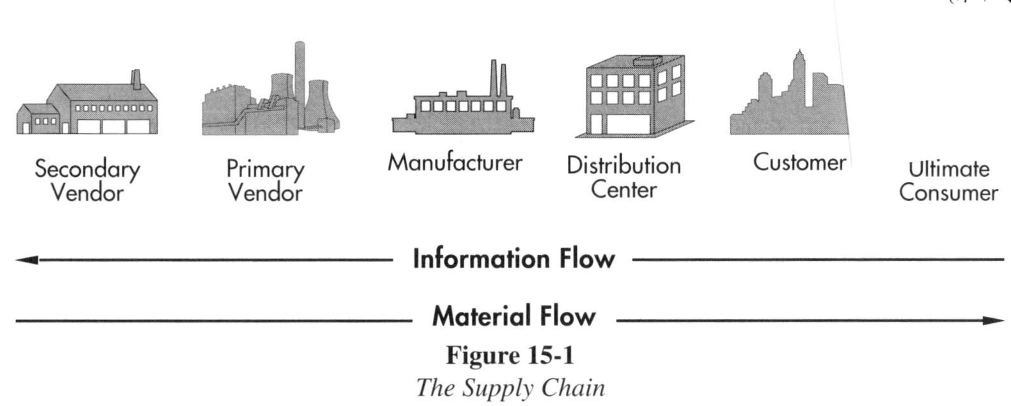

Figure 15-1
The Supply Chain

through the conversion process to become a finished item at the ultimate consumer's point of use. While in reality a firm may have multiple vendors and materials, multiple manufacturing points and distribution centers, and multiple customers involved in the supply chain, this process can be thought of in terms of a network of facilities, connected by transportation and communication operations.

Figure 15-2 shows such a network. The network is called "multi-echelon" or "multilevel" when an item moves through several steps (facilities in series) before reaching the customer. A "multilocation" network exists when there are more than one of any category of facilities (facilities in parallel, each performing the same function on the same product), as when there are multiple plants or multiple distribution centers.

Inventories usually exist throughout the network in various forms and for various reasons. At any manufacturing point, inventories may exist in the form of raw materials, work-in-process, and finished goods. They exist at the gathering and distribution warehouses; and they exist as in-transit, or pipeline, inventories on each of the paths linking the fixed facilities. All these inventories are related in the sense that:

- The downstream (toward the customer) locations create the demands on the upstream inventories.
- Demand, combined with the factors causing the need for inventories, largely determines the level of inventory required at any one point.

Furthermore, a central premise of logistics is that the lowest inventories result when the entire supply chain (or network) is managed as a total system, and that all *necessary* inventories must be coordinated throughout the chain.[2] When this is done, the results can be spectacular. For example, Xerox took over $700 million of inventory out of its operation within two years by applying supply chain management techniques.[3]

Managing the Flow of Product Through the Supply Chain

The process of managing the flow of materials, intermediates, and finished goods through the supply chain—often called "second-generation materials requirements planning" (MRPII) or the "one-number concept"—begins with forecasts of demand or demand schedules by stock keeping unit (SKU) at the points furthest downstream in the network. These points may be our

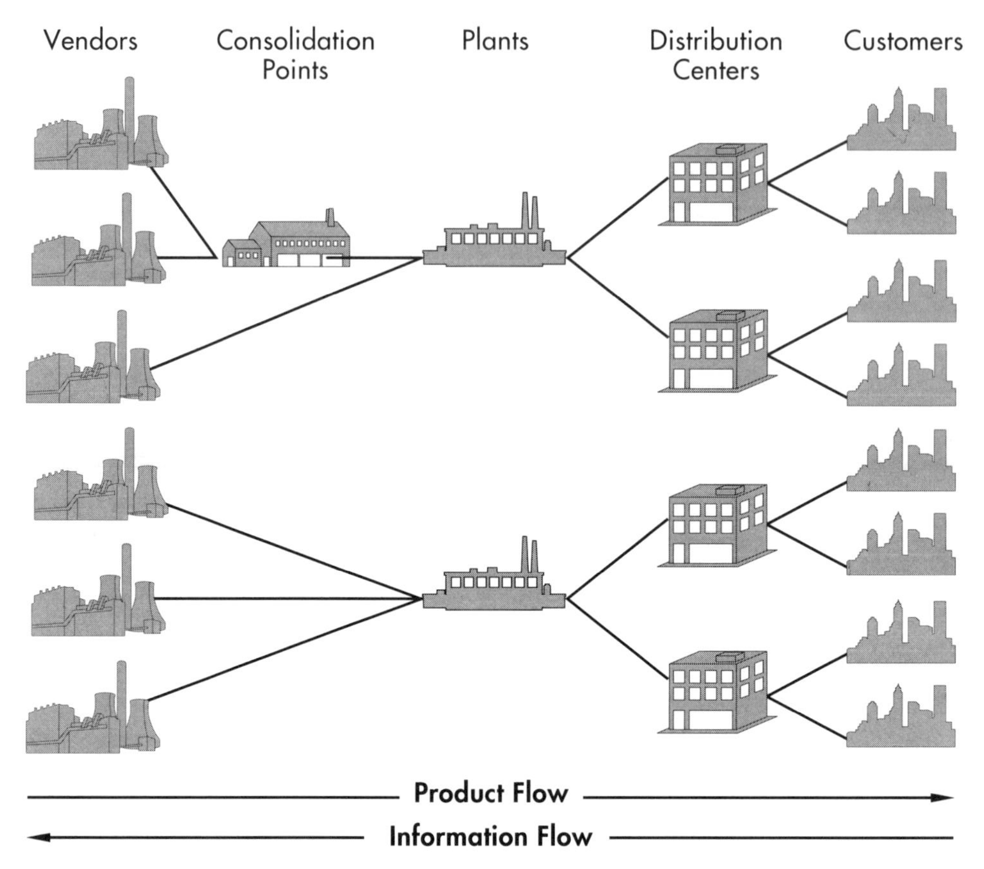

Figure 15-2
Typical Logistics Network

own plants, our own distribution centers, our customers' locations, or even our end consumers, depending on the nature of the network and the feasibility of collecting data from customers.

Decision makers use various systems to process demand data for each location at each level in the network. Results are electronically passed upstream to the inventory points that will replenish each location with the SKU in question. Those inventory points in turn further process the data and pass results to upstream suppliers.

Table 15-1 shows the typical steps in this process for a network similar to that in Figure 15-1. Forecasting and collecting customer demand plans take place at the distribution centers (DCs).

TABLE 15-1
Network Flow Planning
(Also called MRP II, or the One-Number Concept)

- Forecasts and customer demand plans
- Distribution requirements planning (DRP)
- Master production schedules (MPS)
- Materials requirement planning (MRP)

Distribution requirements planning (DRP) techniques project the need for replenishments from the supplying plant for several periods into the future ("time-phased" requirements).

The plant consolidates these projections from each DC to develop a master production schedule (MPS) for each SKU. The MPS shows when and how much of the SKU the plant will produce over the next several periods. Once the parties involved agree on the MPS, further processing combines the MPS with the bill of materials (recipe) for the SKU and develops a time-based schedule for receiving raw materials—the materials requirement plan (MRP). Based on the lead time for preparing and shipping the materials, shipping dates (for the source) can be computed easily as well. The vendor receives the appropriate MRP for the materials it supplies and then plans to meet the projected shipping dates.

Obviously this process should begin as close to the end consumer and extend as far upstream to the suppliers as is feasible from an economic, managerial, and technical perspective.[4] Electronic data transmission facilitates the communication of the information between levels in the network. In some situations, the downstream demand locations broadcast their demand requirements to several levels in the supply chain simultaneously. Given certain parameters, each location can then immediately make its own plans without waiting for data from intervening locations, but this still requires coordination throughout the chain. This may allow the work centers to operate more efficiently but will create some inventories as a price for these efficiencies.

Reasons for Holding Inventories in the Supply Chain

Inventories, when held for the right reasons, are the "lubricant" that allows the supply chain to operate smoothly and efficiently. On the other hand, when too much inventory exists in the supply chain, the operation becomes sticky and erratic. What are the "right reasons," and what inventories do they cause? There are several, as summarized in Table 15-2.

Uncertainties in demand or supply may occur throughout the supply chain. Firms hold safety stocks to protect against shortages that may occur because of these uncertainties.

Many processes in manufacturing and in transportation have economic and/or physical constraints that make it necessary to do things in *batches* or *lots*. This creates *cycle stocks* as it takes time to consume the batch. Once a batch has been depleted, a new one arrives to take its place.

The *time* required for processing or transportation gives rise to *work-in-process* or *in-transit* (also called *pipeline*) stocks.

Products and commodities often exhibit *seasonality* in supply or demand. Thus, it is often necessary to hold seasonal stocks until the item is available again, or to keep production capac-

TABLE 15-2
Forces Creating Various Types of Inventory

Creating Forces	**Type of Inventory**
Uncertainties	Safety stocks
Batching/lot size economics	Cycle stocks
Time-transportation	In-transit
Time-processing	Work-in-process
Seasonality	Seasonal stocks
Varying activity rates	Decoupling stocks
Others	Speculative stocks

ity requirements at a minimum by producing the peak-season demand over an extended period of time prior to that peak.

Varying activity rates between processes often lead to *decoupling inventories* to keep the bottleneck activity operating at full capacity.

And all manner of other initiatives taken by business managers often require the building of *speculative inventories* (e.g., marketing promotions, future price increases from suppliers, strike protection, scheduled maintenance shutdowns, and so on.)

Key Issues in Managing Supply Chain Inventories

When managing inventories in the supply chain, logistics managers face two key issues:

1. How can we eliminate, or at least mitigate, the impact of each of these causes of inventories?
2. To the extent we cannot eliminate the causes, what is the least amount of inventory required to deal with the causes that remain?

The rest of this chapter covers these two issues. To the best of this author's knowledge, no text published to date discusses the first issue comprehensively from a logistics perspective. On the other hand, many useful and valuable techniques treating the second issue do exist and have been written about extensively. Outstanding logistical operations seek not only to eliminate the causes but also to make good use of the scientific tools available to minimize those inventories that still need to exist.

The key point is that whatever the reason for the inventory, the logistics manager must always seek to eliminate the causes of that inventory and employ only as much inventory as absolutely necessary in any case.

Eliminating or Mitigating the Causes of Inventories

Leading-edge companies are making major efforts to eliminate, wherever possible, those factors that cause inventories. This section presents examples of cases where companies have been successful in doing so. Typically the opportunities lie at the interfunctional and interorganizational interfaces—at those boundaries that so many firms have previously believed to be sacrosanct. However, other opportunities exist throughout the supply chain, for all the causes listed above, and they need to be systematically addressed. This discussion takes the view of an inventory at a particular facility that faces demand for product and needs to receive periodic replenishments from a supply source.

Eliminating Uncertainties

Uncertainties exist in any supply chain, the most important of which include:

- Demand uncertainty—we do not know just exactly what demand will be in the future.
- Supply uncertainty—when we order a replenishment from the supply source, we cannot be certain it will arrive on time.

Demand Uncertainty

So-called random demand fluctuations can create large safety stock requirements throughout the supply chain. True, demand uncertainty will always exist. But the individual decisions of various firms and levels in the supply chain can exacerbate the inherent uncertainty. Developing relationships where information is shared between downstream customers and the inventory point can help reduce these demand fluctuations. The consolidation of inventory points or the consolidation of product variety can assist in this as well.

Downstream Relationships. Jay Forrester showed that the replenishment policies that downstream demand points employ can lead to wild fluctuations upstream as the effects of these policies reverberate through several levels.[5] In a case study of a combined retail/wholesale operation, this author and a colleague found that the firm could reduce wholesale safety stocks substantially by forecasting aggregate retail demand for each SKU and using distribution requirements planning techniques to develop wholesale inventory requirements. The old way consisted of forecasting wholesale demand based on the past history of warehouse shipments.[6]

Reducing demand uncertainty, then, requires close cooperation with the downstream demand points—and the further downstream, the better. Major retailers in the United States have taken the lead in this area, using their point-of-sale (POS) systems to collect demand at the lowest possible level and then communicating these data electronically to their suppliers.[7] In some cases, manufacturers like Procter and Gamble, Polaroid, and Air Products use this type of information to "push in" stock to the downstream customers.[8] In other cases, the supplying firm may just sample representative customers and use that information to resupply them.[9]

Consolidating Volume. Other means of reducing the degree of demand uncertainty focus on the fact that higher volumes of demand generally lead to relatively lower levels of variation in that demand. Figure 15-3 shows the typical relationship between the volume of demand at a point (for a given SKU) and the expected inventory level at that particular point. If the managers of the inventory use scientific techniques to set the optimum inventory levels (as discussed later in the chapter), then the inventory level should be an exponential function of the demand volume for the item:

$$\text{Inventory Level} = aV^b$$

where a is a constant specific to the situation under analysis, V is the demand volume (usually measured on an annual basis), and b is the exponent (b is usually between .5 and .8).

Figure 15-3 shows the relationship for the boundary exponentials of .5 (the lower curve) and .8 (the upper curve). The proper exponential b for a given SKU depends on the degree to which demand variations correlate across geographic areas of demand. If they are not correlated, then the relationship will be close to .5. Where they are correlated, it will be closer to 1.0.[10]

Figure 15-3 shows that, if the exponential is 0.5, then a 100% increase in demand from 4 to 8 should result in only a 41.5% increase in the inventory level:

$$(2.83 - 2.00)/2.00 = .415$$

How do we increase demand other than by getting more sales? Often companies achieve this by consolidating parallel inventory points. Using the above data, we will move from two points with demand of 4 each and inventories of 2 (for a total inventory of 4) to one point with a demand of 8 and a total inventory level of 2.83.

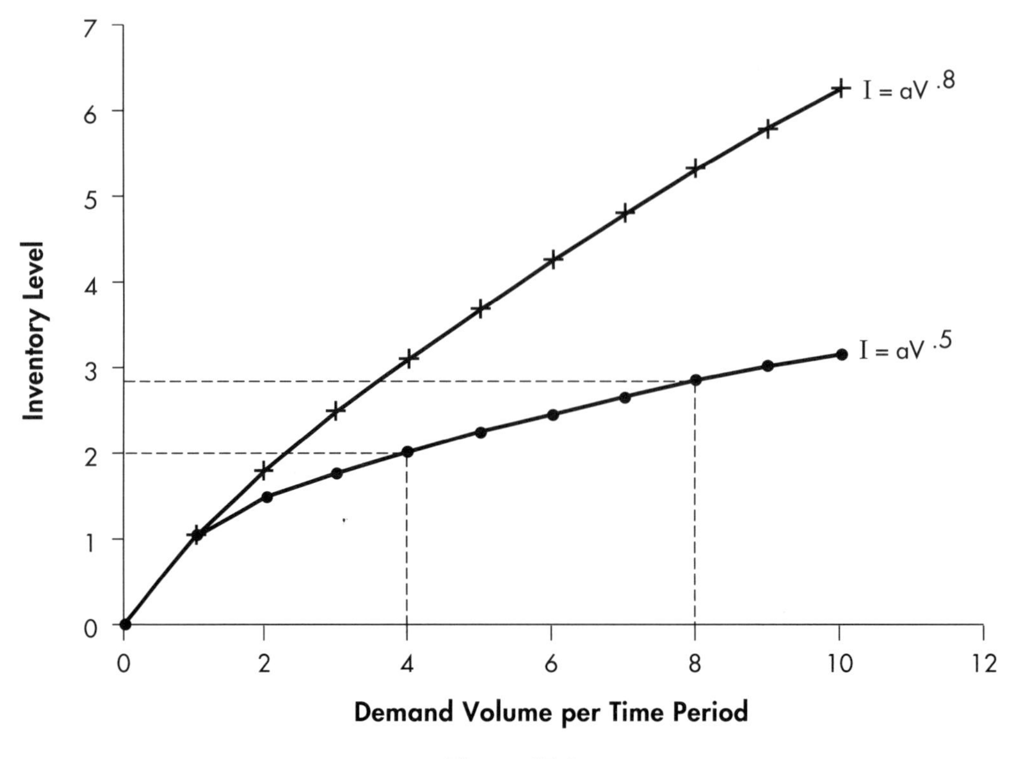

Figure 15-3
Inventory Levels vs. Demand Volume

Sharp Electronics Corporation recently put this theory into practice when it consolidated the stocking of parts for its business information systems products (copiers, fax machines, etc.) in Memphis, Tennessee. Using air freight to make up for the potential service problems associated with a single U.S. location, Sharp simultaneously has reduced inventories and improved service.[11]

Substituting one general item to serve the same purpose as several specific items also leads to consolidated volumes. While used most often on the inbound side of logistics (e.g., encouraging engineers to use common parts across several products), this technique also works on the outbound (customer) side as well. Here it is often used with the concept of *postponement.*[12] If the product can be designed so that customization takes place only *after* the customer has specifically placed an order, then the basic product can be stocked in a single, high-volume form. Thus, commitment to the final form is "postponed." Automobile companies that limit the number of options allowed or combine options into packages have long practiced this art. Such opportunities will surface even more frequently in the future as firms implement flexible manufacturing technologies.

Improving Forecasting Accuracy. Better forecasts lead to lower safety stock inventories as well. The previous chapter dealt with forecasting techniques, so they will not be discussed here at any length. However, two important issues arise at this point. First, safety stocks—when scientifically set—vary with the size of the forecast error. Thus, reducing that forecast error can reduce inventories. The absolute best way to reduce forecast errors is to maximize the use of the demand management techniques described above. Another important initiative involves working with the marketing function.

Sales incentives and promotions generally create "noise" (changes in demand patterns not driven by customers' actual needs) in the actual demand. Some companies have taken action to reduce such noise. For example, Kumar and Sharman report that at one company, "the president announced that he would personally fire anyone who took orders in the last week of the month for delivery before month's end."[13] Several consumer product manufacturers have changed their ways of promoting product to reduce the incentives customers had to buy large quantities only during price discount periods, and not to buy at times in between these promotions.[14]

But when such techniques cannot feasibly be applied or when they can be used only for a portion of the demand, then forecasts still have to be developed. Many statistical forecasting techniques exist and work well in a wide variety of situations, especially when combined with good managerial judgment. They should not be overlooked! They may help to substantially reduce the need for safety stocks.

The second way to reduce the size of errors in forecasts is to reduce the lead time needed to replenish the inventory whose demand is being forecast. The further out into the future one must forecast, the greater will be the forecast error. Many companies have achieved major gains, in many areas besides just inventories, by shortening lead times.[15]

Supply Uncertainty. Supply uncertainty arises from the nature of operations at the supply source providing the replenishment shipment, as well as from the nature of transportation operations regarding delivery from the source.

Supply Source Uncertainty. The supply source needs advance information about future requirements it will have to supply, just as does the demand source. This allows the supply source to have the material ready when it is demanded. Therefore, the demand source needs to develop the same kind of information-sharing relationships with its key supply sources (helping them with their demand management) as it has with its key customers. Requirements planning techniques help accomplish this to a great extent.

Transportation-Created Uncertainties. Freight transportation companies have in the past not provided tightly controlled service. This has been especially true in the railroad, less-than-truckload, and water carrier businesses. This uncertainty, compounded with supply point uncertainty, often leads to substantial safety stocks. Again, better information sharing on the part of the supplier, carrier, and receiver can lead to great improvements in on-time delivery and hence reductions in inventory. For example, in the food industry, the utilization of electronic data interchange and the establishment of delivery appointment windows no wider than thirty minutes have substantially reduced this problem.[16]

Eliminating Batching and Lot Size Economics

Batching economics—those factors that appear to make it more economical to perform activities on batches of material rather than on one at a time—arise frequently in logistics and production systems. Such economics occur in transportation, materials handling, and manufacturing. (The manufacturing issues are not covered here.)

Batching in Transportation

Transportation economics leading to batching pervades logistics, forced by the technology of transportation. All the modes have some basic unit of work—such as the truck, the rail carload, the airplane—which is the smallest economical unit to move. However, the negative impact of these economics on inventory levels can be mitigated, usually through some kind of consolidation—for instance, by combining replenishment orders for many items, possibly from or to several locations, into one vehicle.[17] These issues become extremely important in just-in-time supply operations.[18] Figure 15-4 shows several possible ways (direct, assembly, and milk-run) to consolidate volume to get efficient transportation while keeping inventories in line.

Consolidating Several Products from One Source to One Destination—Direct. Although transportation economics often dictates that full vehicle loads should be brought in whenever an inventory is replenished, it may not make sense to build a load containing only one item. This strategy leads to large cycle stocks. The alternative is to bring in smaller quantities and pay higher rates for less-than-vehicle-load (LVL) shipments. Another alternative is to bring in a mixed load that fills the vehicle but at the same time balances the inventories of all the items included in the load. This alternative goes by the name of "joint order" problem. Distribution resource planning (DRP) techniques provide very useful information for managing joint order situations.[19] Most good inventory software handles this problem quite effectively.[20]

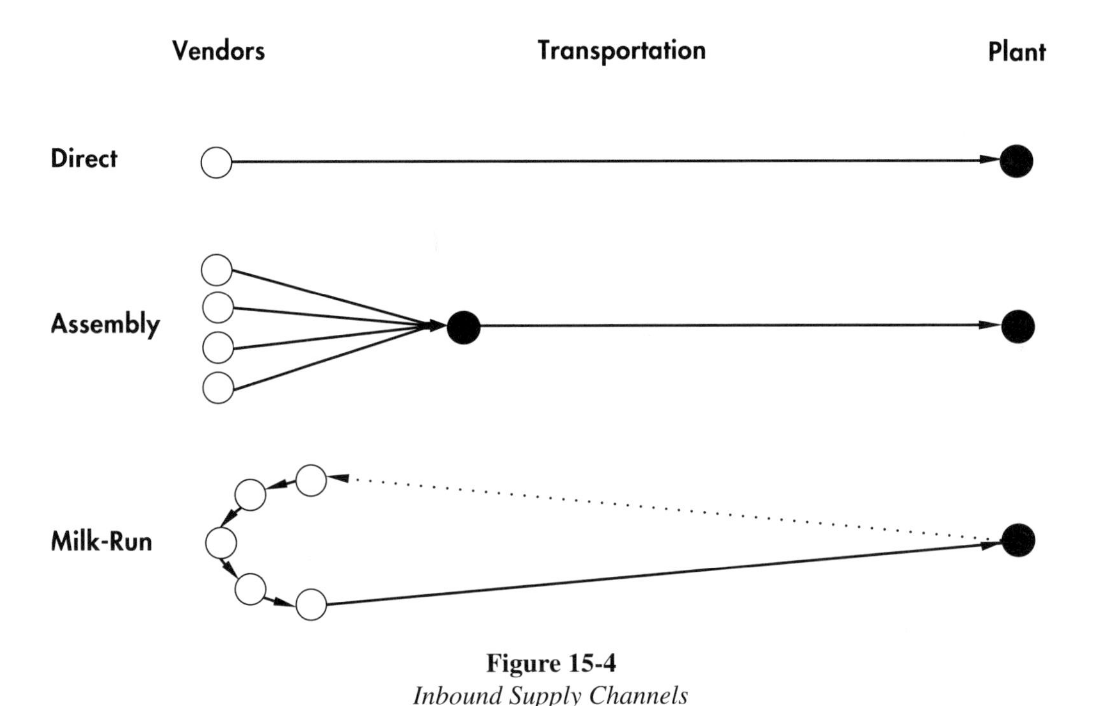

Figure 15-4
Inbound Supply Channels

Source: Reprinted with permission of the American Production and Inventory Control Society, "The Impact of the Carrier Selection Decision on Tracking and Controlling Materials Flow in JIT Supply Systems," *Just-In-Time Seminar Proceedings, 1989* (Annadale, Va.: APICS, 1989), p. 151.

Consolidating from Several Locations or to Several Locations. Often one origin or destination does not produce sufficient volume to support even mixed vehicle loads. Then we may want to consolidate the volume from (or to) several locations to collect enough for a full load. One way to do this is to employ a cross-dock assembly (or distribution) operation, where small LVL quantities are brought into the assembly point and loaded into a waiting vehicle. Another way is to send a vehicle on a "milk run" to gather material at (or distribute to) several locations. Here vehicle routing and scheduling software can be used advantageously to develop the best milk runs (the best routes and sequence of stops for each run).[21]

When deciding whether to use various consolidation techniques, it is important to thoroughly analyze the trade-offs between transportation and inventory. This is discussed later in the chapter.

Reducing the Time Required to Perform Activities

The third important creator of inventories is time—the time it takes to transport goods, or the time it takes to perform production/conversion processes. Again, only the transportation issues are discussed here.

The time it takes to move goods between locations gives rise to inventory in transit. The obvious way to reduce this time is to use faster transportation modes. But transportation experts know well that speed costs money. In-transit inventories become important as the combination of the volume moved and the value of the goods increases. The average dollar amount of inventory in-transit is expressed in the following equation:

$$(\text{annual volume in units}) \times (\text{dollar value per unit}) \times (\text{transit time in years})$$

Transit time can be critical for high-value goods like computers and pharmaceuticals, and for high-volume items like automobile parts destined for assembly plants.

Again, the trade-offs between transportation costs and the cost of carrying the inventory in-transit must be carefully balanced.

Reducing Seasonal Inventories

Both seasonal supply and seasonal demand items can create inventories. Often it is impossible to change those seasonal patterns, although one must always determine whether the seasonality is legitimate. That is, inventory managers must be sure that the inventory is not caused by the noise in the supply chain as described by Forrester.[22]

Mitigating Seasonal Supply

Many items, particularly agricultural commodities, exhibit seasonal supply characteristics. We may not be able to get rid of the seasonality in these items. The objective will be to hold them in a form that represents the lowest level of value added. For example, Heinz Food buys tomatoes only when they ripen (once a year). Tomatoes cannot be stored without some processing. Tomato processors could proceed right to ketchup production as one way to use the tomatoes. But rather than do this, they postpone producing finished product to the greatest extent possible, while minimizing the quantity and quality of space required for storage and the amount of processing cost inventoried with the material. They do this by making tomato paste, sterilizing the product and a metalized plastic bag, and sealing the paste in the bag. Then the bag needs no cold storage and only minimal protection otherwise. When finished product is required, the bags are emptied into the production process.

These kinds of options exist in many situations. Our imagination and creativity are all we need to develop such solutions.

Mitigating Seasonal Demand

Items with seasonal demand often require the building of inventories in advance of the season. The rationale for this is to better utilize productive capacity, thereby minimizing the production resources required. Today, however, some observers such as Harmon and Peterson argue that utilization should not necessarily be the driving objective. New production technology, small lot production, and drastically shorter lead times make production smoothing much less of an issue.[23]

Reducing Speculative Inventories

As with seasonal inventories, the need for speculative inventories must be verified by the logistics manager. Too often policies set by other corporate functions fail to take into consideration the impact on inventories. The potentially dysfunctional effect of sales incentives and promotions has already been noted above. Other kinds of speculations may be suspect as well. When the speculation is legitimate, then the logistics manager needs to analyze the options and risks, taking care to stock only the justified amount of inventory.

One case where the event usually justifies a speculative inventory is the forward buy—when a supplier notifies customers of a price increase and allows them to stock up in advance of that increase. Several authors have written about this problem. Formulas for the optimum quantity to buy can be found in Silver and Peterson's text.[24]

Conclusions

This section has reviewed ways to eliminate or at least mitigate the impact of those factors that create inventories. Although it is not possible to cover all possible ways of doing this, the key point should be clear: with sufficient creativity and planning, inventories can be at least partially eliminated.

Determining the Best Quantity of Inventory to Hold

When the causes of inventory cannot be totally eliminated, then we need to make a decision about how *much* inventory to hold. Many firms look at competitors for some benchmark regarding inventories. Others look at their overall turnover ratio (cost of goods sold divided by average inventories) and manage by holding that ratio at some specific level, or gradually attempting to raise it. Although these simplistic approaches have some merit (generally only when considering past performance regarding aggregate inventory levels), they do not address the key issues of the causes of inventories or the amount of inventory those causes actually require a company to hold.

Inventory decisions must move from the bottom up. Individual SKUs at each location should be examined to *scientifically determine the need for that inventory and its optimum level.* This analysis must take into account all the relevant costs associated with having the inventory in the location. Then the broader supply chain for that item must be considered.

This section first addresses the relevant costs, then the computation of the required safety, cycle, and in-transit stocks. The size of seasonal and speculative stocks is discussed briefly. Finally a methodology for evaluating inventories in the entire supply chain is presented.

There exists a variety of well-developed methods for solving the problem of setting inventory levels. Most of these have been coded into computer programs sold by software vendors. Therefore, these methods will not be repeated here. Rather, this section advises the practicing manager on what features to look for and what the important trade-offs are.[25]

Costs Relevant for Inventory Decision Making

Four categories of costs are relevant for decisions concerning inventories:

1. Holding cost—usually expressed as the cost to hold a dollar's worth of inventory for a period of time
2. *Shortage cost*—the penalty for not having inventory available when it is required
3. *Acquisition cost*—the cost to order and acquire the inventory (considered only when the cost per unit of acquisition varies as the number of units ordered changes)
4. *Control system cost*—the cost of the administrative systems needed to manage the inventory in question.

Ordinarily the objective in managing inventories is to minimize the sum of all these costs for all inventories over a period of time. Furthermore, the inventory manager should constantly try to improve performance.

Holding Costs

Douglas Lambert's treatise on inventory holding costs remains the best to date.[26] After an extensive review of all the issues, Lambert concluded that holding costs should consist of the following elements:

- *Capital costs*—firms should use the "hurdle rate" (i.e., the minimum rate of return they would expect to get on any new investment of capital); this rate is to be applied to the out-of-pocket investment necessary to acquire the average inventory.
- *Inventory service costs*—state property taxes on inventories and insurance on the inventory (for the risks of fire and loss).
- *Storage space costs*—where these costs will vary with the level of inventory held. (Remember that in many cases these costs are fixed and will not change unless inventory in the location is eliminated completely.)
- *Risk costs*—obsolescence, damage, pilferage/shrinkage, and relocation costs (when the inventory is in the wrong place), provided, of course, these risks cannot be insured against.[27]

Generally these costs are computed and then converted to a percentage. We then apply that percentage to the average, out-of-pocket value of the inventory to arrive at the total cost of holding inventories over a specific period of time. In 1975, Lambert found that the percentage figure varied from 14 to 35% in a sample of six companies.[28] This number should be computed before taxes, because most of the other costs used in inventory decision making are computed before taxes.

Companies need to compute their own numbers for this percentage, and they may have to do so for individual product lines if those lines are not homogeneous. The largest component will generally be the investment costs; the others will be smaller, making detailed calculation of them unnecessary.

In inventory decision making, the holding cost percentage is applied against the average value of the inventory to be held. That average should be the sum of the cycle stock, the safety stock, the average seasonal stock, the average speculative stock, and the average in-transit stock.

Shortage Costs

It takes more effort to calculate shortage costs because of the many different situations a firm may face. There are both long-range and short-range elements of shortage costs. In the short range, a stockout situation may result in the loss of sales for the items that are short (and the attendant loss of the gross margin on those units), or it may only mean incurring the costs to ship the shortage amount later by some premium form of transportation. There may be no penalty at all if the receiver will accept the goods when they become available. Also in the short run, a shortage may stop an entire production line until additional material arrives.

In the long run, shortages (or the accumulation of several such situations) may lead to the loss of a customer and the future sales that would have been made to that customer. Clearly the penalties of stockouts vary substantially, depending on the circumstances.

Several approaches to determining shortage costs have been proposed and tested.[29] In view of the difficulties in computing the long-term costs, most models utilize just the short-term costs. Alternatively, managers may set safety stocks to meet some targeted level of availability and ignore the costs of shortages. There are three typical ways to measure shortage costs: cost-based value of the number of units out of stock, the cost of a "shortage situation" (any shortage always resulting in a constant cost), or the cost-based value of a unit of time short multiplied by the number of time units the shortage exists. The number of units out of stock is measured by the number of units demanded while no stock was on hand. Whatever the cost employed, it is applied to the expected degree of the shortage (e.g., the cost per unit short times the expected number of units short, or the cost per day of being short times the expected number of days short, and so forth).

Acquisition Costs

The inventory decision must take acquisition costs into consideration whenever those costs will change on a unit basis as the order or replenishment quantity changes. This occurs when there are transportation and/or purchase discounts associated with bringing in large quantities at one time. For example, a purchase price may be $1.00 per unit for a shipment of up to 100 units, or $.95 per unit for purchases of over 100 units. This is known as an all units discount. In other cases, the discount may apply only to the extra units over and above a set minimum.

Another type of acquisition cost includes those that are constant per order, regardless of the order size. In production situations, these are called the setup costs—the cost to set up a machine or operation in preparation for production of a batch of the item. In logistics, this type of cost includes the ordering costs (the paperwork and communications necessary to place a replenishment order) and the transportation cost where the carrier quotes a flat rate for the vehicle (as with truckload prices quoted on a per-mile basis).

Acquisition costs are the charges that drive us to do things in batches, creating cycle stocks.

Control System Costs

Few inventory decision rules take the cost of the management control system into consideration. But many types of control systems exist. Some, such as the "two-bin" systems used for low-value items, consist only of a piece of hardware to segregate the inventory into two sections. Others require a mainframe computer, database software, terminals for real-time access, and sophisticated software for inventory planning. These might cost companies millions of dollars to acquire the technology and hundreds of thousands of dollars more in annual operating costs. The trade-offs are between the cost of operating the control system versus the penalties for having too much and/or too little inventory. Often it makes sense to use several different control systems, managing high-volume/high-value and critical items with a sophisticated system, and low-volume/low-value noncritical items with low-cost systems.[30]

The Total Cost Model for Inventory Decision Making

Figure 15-5 shows the context for inventory decision making. This microsystem embodies the basic logistics trade-offs among transportation, inventories, and service. Optimization of this will focus on the permanent inventory stocks that exist in such a system: safety stocks, cycle stocks, and in-transit stocks. Any seasonal or speculative stocks that may be needed can be added later, because they are usually transitory.

Table 15-3 shows the elements of the total cost model. It covers all the relevant costs in the microsystems. These costs are normally measured for some time period (typically a year, but any period is acceptable as long as each element covers that period). The objective is to pick the transportation option, shipment size, and service policy (inventory availability) that minimize the total costs of the microsystem. The solution methodology for this equation can be found in the references.[31] The following sections provide more detail about each of the cost elements. Table 15-4 indicates the notation used in that discussion.

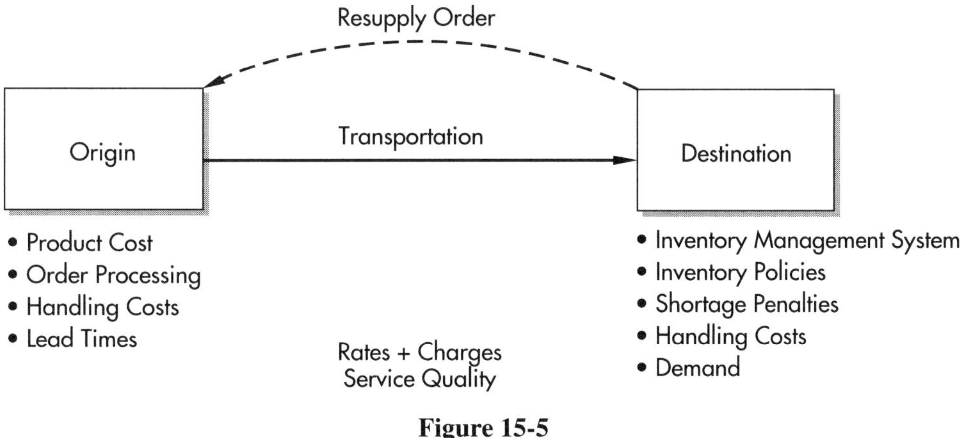

Figure 15-5
Fundamental Logistics Trade-offs

TABLE 15-3
Total Cost Model

Safety stock carrying costs
Cycle stock carrying costs
In-transit carrying costs
Acquisition costs:
Ordering
Transportation
Purchasing
Shortage costs

SAFETY STOCK COST

The safety stock carrying cost is computed as the average safety stock held in units times the value of each unit times the carrying cost factor. In the notation of Table 15-4, this is as follows:

$$k_Q s(v_Q + T_Q)r$$

where $k_Q s$ is the planned safety stock. The term in parentheses is the delivered value of the material per unit at the destination (v, the value at the origin, plus *T,* the freight rate per unit). The two cost factors and *k* have *Q* as a subscript to indicate that they may change as *Q,* the replenishment quantity, changes.

The first objective of setting safety stocks is to achieve the correct level to protect against both the supply and demand uncertainties inherent in the lead time. Well-developed techniques exist to do this.[32] To do the analysis properly, a safety stock criterion must be set first. The best approach is to set safety stocks on the basis of the cost of shortages. If computing such costs is not feasible, then a second-best choice is to pick a service standard and set safety stocks to meet some level of that standard. Typical measures of shortage costs and service standards include the following:

- Fractional charge per unit short (most appropriate when customers will not accept back orders and will cancel the order for any items not available)

TABLE 15-4
Notation Used

A	Fixed cost per order
D	Units of demand for the time period
k_Q	Safety stock multiplier
Q	Replenishment quantity
r	Cost of holding inventory (% dollar inventory)
s	Standard deviation of forecast errors in the lead time
T_Q	Transportation charges per unit
t_Q	Transit time for a carrier option
v_Q	Value of the materials at the origin

- A specified fraction of demand to be satisfied directly off the shelf (appropriate when the shortage cost cannot be determined)
- Cost per stockout occasion—a stock occasion is a replenishment cycle with any shortage. This measure is appropriate when shortages may stop a production line and any stoppage results in a major fixed cost, or when customers accept back orders
- Specified probability of no stockout in a replenishment cycle (appropriate when the shortage cost cannot be determined)
- Specified average time between stockout occasions
- Fractional charge per unit short per unit time (appropriate when machines may be idled and the idle time is equal to the duration of the shortage)

The second objective of setting safety stocks is to have a system to measure the uncertainties in the lead time. Most standard inventory software packages keep statistics (mean and standard deviation) on the magnitude of the forecast error for each SKU. Some systems also track the uncertainty of the lead time itself. These two measures can be combined to arrive at the overall standard deviation of lead time forecast errors (s in the notation of Table 15-4).[33] Safety stock in units will then be a multiple of s, $k_Q s$.

The multiplier k_Q is derived from formulas based on assumptions about the distribution of forecast errors in the lead time and the criteria for service specified. Again, most of the standard software packages do derive k_Q automatically. For example, if meeting 98% of the demand off the shelf for a given SKU is specified, then the software will determine the appropriate k_Q.

The Q is shown as a subscript to the k because generally the bigger the replenishment quantity (Q) the less frequently there will be a lead time where the possibility of a shortage exists. Thus, with less safety stock (owing to a lower k_Q), a firm can still maintain the same level of protection from stockouts.

Cycle Stock Carrying Cost

The definition of the cycle stock is simple enough—it is just one-half the replenishment quantity: $Q/2$. The cost of carrying this amount of inventory is as follows:

$$Q(v_Q + T_Q)r/2$$

In-Transit Inventory Carrying Cost

All the demand (D) in the system will have to be replenished at some time. The total cost model assumes that there will be no net change in the inventories over time, so that the input equals the output. Inventory takes time to be transported to its storage place. Thus, the average inventory in transit is based on the transit time t_Q (which is a function of the replenishment quantity when the quantity choice leads to use of a slower or faster transportation option), and the expected demand volume during the period for which we are computing the total costs. If t_Q is measured as a percentage of the total time period under consideration, then the cost of carrying the inventory transit is as follows:

$$Dt_Q vr$$

Acquisition Cost

The acquisition cost is the sum of the ordering, transportation, and purchasing costs, where D/Q is the number of replenishments (orders) for the time period:

$$AD/Q + T_Q D + v_Q D$$

Shortage Cost

Determination of the shortage cost can be more complex, depending on the measure of shortages used. Shortage cost can be calculated, but that capability does not ordinarily exist in the inventory planning software packages. Silver and Peterson provide an extensive discussion of this subject in their text.[34]

Optimizing the Total Cost Equation

Having generated the appropriate cost parameters, the standard deviation of lead time forecast errors, and the relevant service standard (or shortage cost) for the total cost model, the next step is to optimize that model—the sum of the cost measures (safety stock cost, cycle stock carrying cost, and acquisition cost), and the shortage cost if included.[35] The result of that optimization will be the appropriate transportation option and shipment size Q and the safety stock multiplier k_Q, which will provide the inventory availability required at the lowest total cost. Those numbers will be used to manage the inventory until factors change enough to justify recomputing them.

Seasonal and Speculative Stocks

Seasonal and speculative stocks have not been included in the total cost model because they do not always exist. Even if there is a need for them, it should not be permanent. Generally they have little impact on Q and K_Q with the following exception. When building these stocks in advance of their need:

- The lowest-cost transportation option (within reason) should always be used, because these stocks will have no impact on the ordinary cycle stock.
- The standard safety stock can be temporarily relaxed, because the added seasonal and speculative stock can provide the safety prior to their need. This is easier to do conceptually than in practice, because one must eventually decide when to come back in with the regular safety stock.

Considering the Full Supply Chain of Inventories

All of the considerations above focused on an inventory of a SKU at one point in the supply chain, supplied by an upstream point. However, this chapter has consistently emphasized the need to consider any such inventory in the context of that supply chain. There is no contradiction here.

The simple fact is that no tools are currently available to truly optimize the supply chain in such detail. Therefore, the goal is to determine for a set of factors the best policy for an inventory at a point and then make a simulation of the entire supply chain to see how all those policies might work together. Such a simulation allows managers to try various modifications and ask what-if questions. Thus, it provides a way to zero in on the best supply chain policy.

One way to achieve this goal is to use the what-if capabilities provided in the distribution resource planning and material resource planning software offered commercially. That tends to be cumbersome, but it can work. An alternative is to develop a simulation.[36]

Conclusion

This chapter has provided a framework within which to view inventory decisions in logistics. Several key points in the chapter deserve repeating:

- Inventory decisions must be made in the context of how they will facilitate the effective and efficient functioning of the total supply chain.
- The first step in any inventory analysis should be to seek ways to eliminate the need for the inventory entirely. If the need cannot be eliminated, management should try to reduce the intensity of the forces causing the need.
- Finally, if the inventory is still necessary, only the minimum inventory required to meet the need should be stocked. Setting the control parameters requires scientific analysis as described in the discussion of the total cost model. It requires the use of inventory management programs (probably computerized) on a regular and systematic basis.

Notes

1. See, for example, Robert Hall, *Zero Inventories* (Homewood, Ill.: Dow-Jones Irwin, 1983).
2. David J. Closs, "Inventory Management: A Comparison of Traditional vs. Systems View," *Journal of Business Logistics* 10, no. 2 (1989): 90–105; and Hau L. Lee and Corey Billington, "Managing Supply Chain Inventory: Pitfalls and Opportunities." *Sloan Management Review* 33 (Spring 1992) 3: 65–73.
3. F. Matthew Stenross and Graham J. Sweet, "Implementing an Integrated Supply Chain," in *Annual Conference Proceedings,* 1991 (Oak Brook, Ill.: Council of Logistics Management, 1992), vol. 2, pp. 341–51.
4. For further discussion of the process, see Mary Lou Fox, "Logistics Planning: The Supply Chain As an Integrated Process," *Production and Inventory Management* 11, no. 7 (July 1991): 12–15. For a manufacturing orientation, see Thomas E. Vollman, William L. Berry, and D. Clay Whybark, *Manufacturing Planning and Control Systems,* 2d ed. (Homewood, Ill.: Irwin, 1988).
5. Jay W. Forrester, "Industrial Dynamics: A Major Breakthrough for Decision Makers," *Harvard Business Review* (July-August 1958): pp. 23–52.
6. Alan J. Stenger and Joseph L. Cavinato, "Adapting MRP to the Outbound Side—Distribution Requirements Planning," *Production—Inventory Management* 20, no. 4 (4th Quarter 1979): 1–14.
7. A good example of this, discussing Wal-Mart, can be found in George Stalk, Philip Evans, and Lawrence E. Shulman, "Competing on Capabilities: New Rules of Corporate Strategy," *Harvard Business Review* (March-April 1992): 57–69.
8. Many such examples can be found in Jonathan L. S. Byrne and Roy D. Shapiro, "Intercompany Operating Ties: Unlocking the Value in Channel Restructuring," unpublished Harvard Business School Working Paper No. 92-058, 1992.

9. See Peter Drucker, "Permanent Cost Cutting," *Wall Street Journal,* January 11, 1991, p. A10.
10. See Ronald H. Ballou, "Estimating and Auditing Aggregate Inventory Levels at Multiple Stock Points," *Journal of Operations Management* 1, no. 3 (February 1981): 143–53.
11. Arthur Sherman, "Sharp and Federal Express—Partners in Success," in *Annual Conference Proceedings, 1990* (Oak Brook, Ill.: Council of Logistics Management, 1991), vol. 2, pp. 201–12.
12. Roy D. Shapiro and James L. Heskett, *Logistics Strategy: Text and Cases* (St. Paul: West, 1985), p. 52.
13. Anil Kumar and Graham Sharman, "We Love Your Product, But Where Is It?" *Sloan Management Review* (Winter 1992): 93–99.
14. Patricia Sellers, "The Dumbest Marketing Ploy," *Fortune,* October 5, 1992, pp. 88–94.
15. For some examples, see Roy L. Harmon and Leroy D. Peterson, *Reinventing the Factory* (New York: Free Press, 1990), pp. 273–387.
16. CSC Index, "Technology Helps Nabisco Foods Gain Order in a Turbulent Business," *Insights* (Spring 1991): 14–16, documents the systems Nabisco has put into place to provide its customers with predictable and on-time delivery, among other things.
17. See John Pooley and Alan J. Stenger, "Modeling and Evaluating Shipment Consolidation in a Logistics System," *Journal of Business Logistics,* 13, no. 2 (1992): 153–74.
18. A variety of alternatives used by companies is discussed in Alan J. Stenger and Bruce G. Ferrin, "The Impact of the Carrier Selection Decision on Tracking and Controlling Materials Flow in JIT Supply Systems," *Just-In-Time Seminar Proceedings, 1989* (Annandale, Va.: American Production and Inventory Control Society, 1989), pp. 148–52.
19. Edward A. Silver and Rein Peterson, *Decision Systems for Inventory Management and Production Planning,* 2d ed. (New York: Wiley, 1985), pp. 431–53
20. For example, see the documentation for software packages provided by companies such as American Software, Atlanta, Ga.; Andersen Consulting, Chicago (DCS/Logistics®); IBM (INFOREM®); Management Science America, Atlanta, Ga. (Distribution Resource Planning); Manugistics, Inc., Rockville, Md. (LOGISTICS*PLUS®), Materials Management Systems, Thetford Center, Vt. (LOGOL-II), Systems Software Associates, Chicago, IL (BPCS), and several others.
21. For a good overview of the vehicle scheduling problem, see Ronald H. Ballou, *Business Logistics Management,* 3d ed. (Englewood Cliffs, N.J.: Prentice Hall, 1992), pp. 491–504.
22. Forrester, "Industrial Dynamics," pp. 23–52.
23. See Harmon and Peterson, *Reinventing the Factory,* pp. 133, 214–20.
24. Silver and Peterson, *Decision Systems,* pp. 200–204.
25. Some excellent and comprehensive references on setting inventory levels include the following: Edward A. Silver and Rein Peterson, *Decision Systems for Inventory Management and Production Planning,* 2d ed. (New York: Wiley, 1985); Thomas E. Vollman, William L. Berry, and D. Clay Whybark, *Manufacturing Planning and Control Systems,* 3d ed. (Homewood, Ill.: Irwin, 1992); and Robert G. Brown, *Advanced Service Parts Inventory Control* (Norwich, Conn.: Materials Management Systems, 1982).
26. Douglas M. Lambert, *The Development of an Inventory Costing Methodology: A Study of the Costs Associated with Holding Inventory* (Chicago: National Council on Physical Distribution Management, 1975). (Now available from University Microfilms, Ann Arbor, Mich.).
27. Ibid, pp. 60–66, for more detail.
28. Ibid., p. 113.

29. For example, see David P. Herron, "Improving Productivity of Logistics Operations," in R. L. Schultz, ed., *Applications of Management Science* (Greenwich, Conn.: JAI Press, 1983), pp. 49–85; and M. Oral, M. Salvador, A. Reisman, and B. Dean, "On the Evaluation of Shortage Costs for Inventory Control of Finished Goods," *Management Science* 18, no. 6 B344–B351.
30. For a discussion of this subject in a manufacturing context, see Harmon and Peterson, *Reinventing Manufacturing,* chap. 8.
31. For more information on this subject, see John E. Tyworth, Kant Rao, and Alan J. Stenger, "A Logistics Cost Model for Purchasing Transportation to Replenish High-Demand Items," *Journal of the Transportation Research Forum* 32, no. 1 (1991): 146–57.
32. See Silver and Peterson, *Decision Systems,* chap. 7.
33. Ibid., pp. 296–98.
34. Ibid., chap. 7
35. See Tyworth et al, "A Logistics Cost Model," for more detail.
36. For some examples of the application of simulation techniques, see Robert M. Sloan, "Integrated Tools for Managing the Total Pipeline," in *Annual Conference Proceedings, 1989* (Oak Brook, Ill.: Council of Logistics Management, 1990), vol. 2, pp. 93–108); and Glenn Rifkin, "'What if …' Software for Manufacturers," *New York Times,* October 10, 1992, p. F–10.

CHAPTER 16

Inventory Control

William L. Grenoble IV

As shown in Figure 16-1, inventory management comprises three key components—inventory control, forecasting, and replenishment. Inventory control is the segment of inventory management that deals with the basic record-keeping foundation on which more complex and sophisticated decisions are made in the forecasting and replenishment modules. It deals with the "Where are we?" and "Where have we been?" concerns that precede the later "Where do we need to go?" and "How do we get there?" questions. Temporally, then, inventory control's focus is more on the present and past, while forecasting and replenishment are concerned more with the future.

Inventory control involves the creation of inventory records, the practices dealing with the maintenance of these records, and the counting or auditing of inventory. In its broadest sense, it also deals with many of the elements of inventory management not covered in the forecasting and replenishment segments, such as inventory administration, methods of valuing inventory, and evaluating inventory performance.

Importance of Inventory Control

As the following scenarios demonstrate, although often considered mundane, the importance of inventory control cannot be underestimated. If it is not functioning properly, the rest of the inventory system cannot operate well and results will suffer.

Scenario A: Company A is experiencing frequent stockouts in its sales to one of its most important retail customers, ShopWell Stores. District Sales Manager Ken Evans is in a heated discussion with Regional Distribution Manager Joe Stork: "Joe, I just got off the phone with the buyer at ShopWell. He told me we are down to our last chance. If we cannot start filling the shelves better in their stores, he's going to replace our line. He was irate. He had just looked at our orders from last week, and our service levels averaged about 70%. What's happening?"

"Ken, I'm not positive, but it seems to be a number of things. Often, when our order fillers go to the bin, it's empty and it's not supposed to be. At least the computer thinks there is supposed to be merchandise there. At other times, when our replenishment buyers go to place orders, the On-Hand field for an item is a negative amount. That just can't be, and so the buyer has to operate in the dark in deciding how much to order. We can fix these things—and do—but it takes time, and in the meantime we are often out of stock."

Scenario B: Two weeks after the completion of their annual physical inventory, Alice Parks, the inventory manager for Company B, is huddled with Phil Gomez, the company controller.

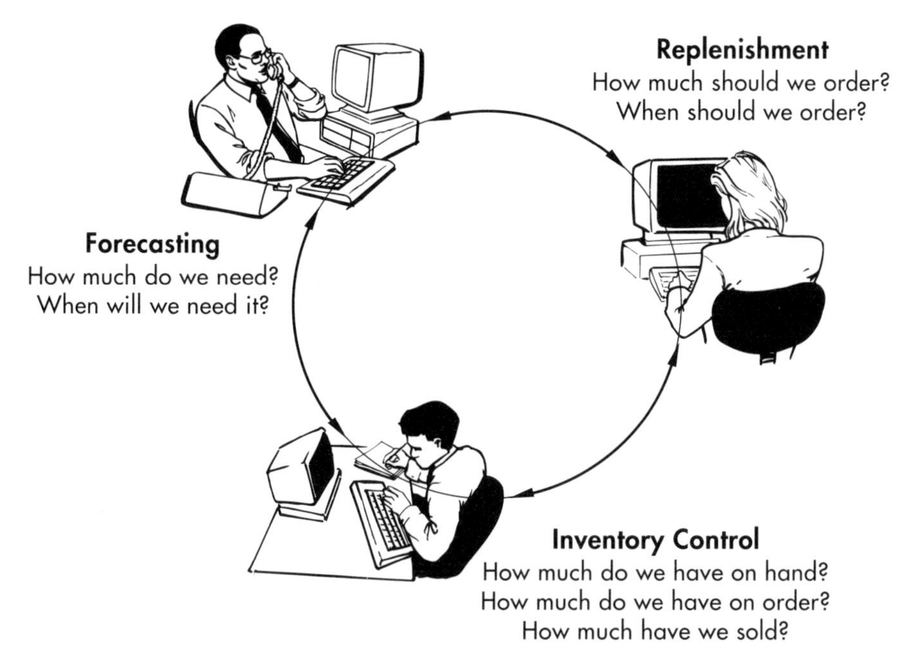

Figure 16-1
Inventory Control As the Basis of Ordering Decisions

Their conversation is not a pleasant one, because it deals with a major discrepancy in what was found to be on hand in the physical inventory and what was believed to be there. The difference amounts to a shortage of nearly $1 million.

"Alice, this is a huge problem. Actually, two huge problems. As controller, I have a lot of explaining to do as to why our perpetual inventory counts were so far out of whack with our physical inventory counts. But of equal concern is learning why our book inventory value ended up being so much higher than the valuation in the physical inventory. Top management will not be happy with the write-off we're facing."

"Phil, I'm really embarrassed about the count discrepancies. Our matchup percentages have always been higher. I'm not sure what went wrong, but I'll dig into it right away. It's a complex process, though. The source of the errors could lie in a number of areas. It might even be a theft problem. What we need to do now is audit some of the items that were so far off to see if we can find a pattern. I'll report back to you as soon as I can."

What do companies A and B have in common? It appears that both have fallen down in inventory control—particularly in keeping good records on how much merchandise is in stock. As can be seen, the compounding of relatively small mistakes in maintaining accurate inventory records can lead to serious ramifications in both service to customers and financial accountability.

Complicating Factors

Is inventory control important to companies A and B? It most certainly is. It's about to get top management attention, and bringing about improvement will soon be a high priority. But what may soon become evident is that solutions do not come easily. There are powerful complicating factors in controlling inventory.

The first is enormous *complexity.* The sheer numbers can be staggering—numbers of items to be controlled, numbers of suppliers, numbers of customers, numbers of daily transactions, and numbers of stocking locations. Large organizations dealing in spare or repair parts might have part number/location combinations in the millions. That's a lot of record keeping.

Silver and Peterson note the following concerning this complexity:

> Decision making in production planning and inventory management is therefore basically a problem of coping with large numbers and with a diversity of factors external and internal to the organization. Some decision systems for inventory management and production planning fail in practice simply because of this basic diverse nature of inventories.[1]

Another complicating factor is *organization structure.* Responsibility for maintaining good inventory records resides in many locations in the firm. Like many logistics processes, inventory control crosses several functional boundaries. In addition to people who have the word "inventory" somewhere in their title or department name, important contributions also must be made by personnel in such widespread activities as accounting, production, warehousing, transportation, order management, information systems, and even sales.

The growing need for *information immediacy*—often for customer service reasons—is also making inventory control more complicated and difficult, while at the same time increasing its importance. Consider the case of wholesale drug and hospital supply companies that are now allowing key customers on-line access to their inventory systems. These customers—with time pressures upon them—can ascertain whether an important item is in stock and if it is, then place an order that will reserve it and prevent its sale to other customers. In this environment, buffers are removed and the stakes are raised tremendously. If inventory integrity is a strength, an important competitive advantage can result. But if inventory record keeping is sloppy, some of the best customers will be driven off.

This chapter examines several aspects of inventory control, but its principal focus is on procedures and tools that help maintain the integrity of inventory record keeping. After a short discussion of the mechanics of keeping inventory records, a few considerations involved with inventory systems are introduced. Following this, several inventory control tools are reviewed, including some that embrace newer technologies. A review of techniques in auditing or counting inventory is then presented. The chapter concludes with a discussion of performance measurement in inventory management.

Inventory Record Keeping

Inventory control begins with keeping useful, accurate, and timely records of items kept in stock. This section addresses several issues related to accomplishing this task.

An Inventory Record

Inventory management normally requires that several elements of information be kept for each item carried. This information is retained in the *inventory record.* Some of the data needed are useful as background in making inventory decisions and are relatively fixed, and some of them

TABLE 16-1
Elements of an Inventory Record

Descriptive/Permanent	**Transaction/Variable**	**Miscellaneous**
Item number	Acquisition/production cost	Supplier ID
Unique company number	Average	
UPC	Current	Supplier status/rating
Supplier number		
	Landed cost	Pack size
Unit of measure		
	Selling price	Pallet quantity
Item Name		
	Gross profit	Joint order information
Item description		
Weight	Service levels	Stocking locations
Cube	Actual	
HazMat class	Targets	Warehouse locations
Shelf Life		Primary/Fixed
	Reorder point	Reserve/Random
Classifications		
ABC	Order quantity	Batch/Lot data
Fine line	ROQ	
Department	EOQ	Aging/Obsolescence code
Profitability		
	Safety stock	New item code
Assemblies/Kits/Related Items	Lead time	
Substitutes	Forecasting model	

are more dynamic and will usually change with each transaction. Table 16-1 lists these elements of an inventory record. This list is not meant to be exhaustive.

What actually is needed varies from system to system, company to company, and industry to industry. For example, a company in the chemical industry may wish to carry hazardous materials classifications. Companies interested in pursuing activity-based accounting may wish to carry size or volume characteristics to aid in cost allocations.

Maintaining Integrity

Good inventory decisions cannot be made without accurate, up-to-date information on the status of the item being considered. If a decision on how much to order is being made, and information regarding how much is on hand or how much is already on order is erroneous, then no matter how comprehensive, mathematically complex, and sophisticated the forecasting and ordering systems are, a wrong decision will result.

As noted earlier, serious consequences can occur when integrity is not maintained, but there are also less serious symptoms that should be watched to gauge the degree of accuracy being maintained. Daily order filling will sometimes result in insufficient stock on hand when the order is to be filled. The computer "thinks" the item should be in a particular location, but it is not. This is sometimes called an "in stock out" or "in stock omit." Immediate rectification is necessary, and data on the frequency of such occurrences should also be kept. The converse of this situation occurs when an inventory-on-hand record shows a negative quantity. This, too, should be investigated and corrected as soon as possible, and data also should be kept on how often this occurs. An increase in frequency of having to deal with these types of situations may prove to be a useful early warning that more serious, systemic problems are taking place.

Companies vary widely in how well inventory records are maintained. The most common difference between organizations that do it well and those that do not is usually an *attitude* pervading the organization concerning the importance of accuracy and a strong *belief* that the system is accurate and does work. In weak-performing firms, one might hear such comments as, "No, we don't go by what's in the printout. If it's important enough, we'll go out in the warehouse and check it," or "I only believe the counts at the beginning of the month because that's the only time the factory people update the work-in-process numbers." In strong-performing companies, no such uncertainty or disbelief exists. System users readily defend its integrity. As managers, the most important thing we can do is to expect and demand accuracy as the norm, not the exception.

Lessons in record-keeping reliability might be learned from certain service industries. How happy as patients or clients would we be to hear the following observations: "No, doctor, don't bother with that chart—it's never right," or "We can give you a better idea of your bank balance at the end of the month, after we get everything counted up." In hospitals and banks, the value of accurate, timely records is stressed; systems and people respond by producing accuracy. Given the importance noted above, no less should be expected in manufacturing or merchandising organizations.

Attitude tops the list of "six ingredients essential to obtain accurate inventory records" assembled by Fogarty, Blackstone, and Hoffman:

1. Having an appropriate attitude on the part of management
2. Clearly designating specific persons as responsible for maintaining the accuracy of each recording activity
3. Providing tools to minimize errors
4. Providing instruction and training
5 Establishing accuracy goals and then measuring performance
6. Auditing records and determining and correcting the underlying cause of each error[2]

Inventory Control Systems

Good record keeping is to no small degree a reflection of the inventory system in place to support it. Although the full description or specification of what should be included in an inventory system is beyond the scope of this chapter, a few basic considerations warrant attention.

Manual vs. Computerized

Although lower costs, wider availability, improved features, and increased user-friendliness have made computer systems for inventory control more accessible, many companies still rely on manual systems. Manual systems are also prevalent at lower echelons of control (e.g., stockrooms), even in companies that are otherwise computerized. Similarly, certain types of inventory, like supplies or repair parts, are sometimes relegated to manual control systems in firms in which production and finished goods are controlled by computer systems.

Also, manual systems—in the form of *kanban*—have gained popularity in manufacturing settings with the growth of just-in-time inventory systems. These systems move containers of components through production by attaching two types of order cards to the container—"conveyance *kanbans,*" which move the parts from one process to another, and "production *kanbans,*" which are used to signal when a new batch of the components has to be produced.[3] The benefits of a manual kanban system over computerized MRP systems lie in improved stability and control, but it is limited in handling various demand patterns, the type of production process employed, and adjustment to human factors.[4]

At the core of a manual system for inventory control is the stock card. This is an item record similar to that described above, but for which numerous ingenious systems for filing and control have been developed. These include strip indexing, index cards, rotary card files, visible edge indexes, hand-operated sorting systems, and microfilm.[5]

Computer systems for inventory management and control abound. They may range in complexity and cost from simple personal computer programs costing less than $100 to large, sophisticated MRP II applications supporting multiple locations that cost millions of dollars. Software programs incorporating inventory control capabilities are described in the Andersen Consulting/Council of Logistics Management annual catalog of logistics software.[6] The number of offerings in this publication that support inventory control grew from 26 in 1981 to 526 in 1990.[7]

Periodic vs. Perpetual Accounting

An inventory system must involve either continuous tracking of inventory or inventory status updated periodically (generally at the time that ordering decisions are made). A perpetual or continuous system endeavors to account for all transactions as they take place, and thus is capable of providing on-hand information at any time. A periodic system requires that someone physically count what is on hand at the time that information is needed. Thus, perpetual inventory control is closely associated with computer systems and periodic control with manual systems.

Batch vs. Real-Time Processing

Another fundamental decision in putting together an inventory system is to determine how often and when the system is updated with transaction information. Batch systems, a form of periodic accounting, accumulate transactions (sales, receipts, etc.) and then process them on a set schedule, usually daily. Real-time processing handles and incorporates changes as they occur. Real-time capability is often more expensive but may be necessary in some environments for customer service reasons.

Numbering Schemes

Inventory systems are accumulations of stock keeping units (SKUs), which are defined as items that are identical in form, fit, and function.[8] How to identify, or number, SKUs is another decision basic to establishing an inventory system. This often causes considerable confusion because multiple numbers may be associated with any one SKU, all of which have different, valid purposes. Purchasing may employ a system of vendor and item numbers, and order entry may have another totally separate series of numbers that are engineered with check digits to promote accuracy. Another system may have been implemented in inventory control that allows the alphabetization of product names on reports. Imposed on all this may also be the numbers that trading partners—suppliers and customers—use to identify the SKU. Finally, a standardized number like the Universal Product Code (UPC) may also have to be taken into account. Then, within the SKUs, batch or lot numbers may have to be recorded, and even serial numbers might need to be assigned to each product (particularly if high-value products are involved).

The good news is that computers are capable of dealing with all of this. The basic decisions a company must make in regard to numbering systems usually deal with the amount of standardization required and whether or not the company wants the numbers to be "smart" or "dumb." A smart number conveys some meaning, such as the supplier and item breakdown in a UPC code, while a dumb number is assigned at random.

Tools for Inventory Control

Fortunately, inventory controllers have several tools to aid them in dealing with the complex environment in which they operate. A few are described in this section.

ABC Classification

Managing large numbers of SKUs can be daunting. Controls, updates, checks, counts, forecasts, and ordering decisions have to be accomplished for each SKU. When the number of SKUs runs into the thousands, tens of thousands, or even hundreds of thousands, inventory management becomes a big job.

Inventory managers can take advantage of a principle called Pareto's law, discussed earlier, to aid in this task. This maxim holds that in dealing with large groups of numbers, most of the activity will be concentrated in a relatively small number of items. This is also known as the 80–20 rule, which states that 80% of the sales of a group of items will be accounted for by 20% of the items. Thus, if a company has 1,000 SKUs and $1 million in sales, 200 of these SKUs will produce $800,000 in sales.

Does this always work? Of course, it may not always be exactly 80–20, but the basic principle that a smaller number of items will be disproportionately responsible for the preponderance of activity generally does hold true.

Inventory controllers can take advantage of this principle by identifying those items at the upper end of the activity spectrum and then applying special effort to their "care and feeding"—deploying extra resources to maintain accuracy in record keeping. The more important items at the top are sometimes referred to as "A" items. A middle group is called "B" items, and the lowest group, which usually includes the largest number of items, is called "C" items. Thus, the process of categorizing and labeling inventory items according to activity level is known as ABC analysis, or ABC classification.

To accomplish ABC classifications, two things are needed—a "distribution by value (DBV) report" and a set of rules to guide the inventory manager in defining the ABC categories. The DBV report ranks all the SKUs on the basis of unit or dollar sales from the highest at the top of the report to the lowest at the bottom. It usually carries sales and inventory information about the item, as well as cumulative information. For the company in Table 16-2 (Giant Wholesale), Pareto's law applies almost exactly: 80% of sales are accounted for by 20% of the items. These items also represent 27% of inventory carried.

TABLE 16-2
The "Distribution by Value" Report

Item Count	Cumulative Percent of Items	ABC Code	Unit Sales	$ on Hand	Item Sales	Cumulative Sales	Cumulative Percent of Sales
1	2.86	A	3,656	$9,022	$274,998	$274,998	22.30
2	5.71	A	4,704	7,803	176,004	451,002	36.57
3	8.57	A	2,323	4,875	156,711	607,713	49.28
4	11.43	A	678	2,438	145,835	753,548	61.11
5	14.29	A	3,356	14,599	99,456	853,004	69.17
6	17.14	A	2,589	4,716	77,890	930,894	75.49
7	20.00	A	1,967	206	56,980	987,874	80.11
8	22.86	A	2,615	785	37,919	1,025,793	83.19
9	25.71	B	537	4,405	27,802	1,053,595	85.44
10	28.57	B	450	447	15,950	1,069,545	86.73
11	31.43	B	198	2,630	15,577	1,085,122	88.00
12	34.29	B	211	416	15,563	1,100,685	89.26
13	37.14	B	409	3,064	15,507	1,116,192	90.52
14	40.00	B	457	80	15,493	1,131,685	91.77
15	42.86	C	115	0	11,114	1,142,799	92.67
16	45.71	C	805	1,131	11,034	1,153,833	93.57
17	48.57	C	208	43	11,021	1,164,854	94.46
18	51.43	C	49	15,942	9,264	1,174,118	95.21
19	54.29	C	264	1,147	8,985	1,183,103	95.94
20	57.14	C	271	1,844	8,899	1,192,002	96.66
21	60.00	C	77	252	8,868	1,200,870	97.38
22	62.86	C	266	32	8,848	1,209,718	98.10
23	65.71	C	262	1,626	8,838	1,218,556	98.82
24	68.57	C	2	338	5,567	1,224,123	99.27
25	71.43	C	5	1,348	3,765	1,227,888	99.57
26	74.29	C	12	1,379	2,135	1,230,023	99.75
27	77.14	C	2	1,924	1,154	1,231,177	99.84
28	80.00	C	2	720	775	1,231,952	99.90
29	82.86	C	36	2,378	557	1,232,509	99.95
30	85.71	C	12	0	448	1,232,957	99.98
31	88.57	C	6	2,480	121	1,233,078	99.99
32	91.43	C	3	0	66	1,233,144	100.00
33	94.29	C	0	71	0	1,233,144	100.00
34	97.14	C	0	1,699	0	1,233,144	100.00
35	100.00	C	0	1,183	0	1,233,144	100.00
35				$91,026	$1,233,144		

The rules needed to complete ABC classifications are usually statements of what is desired in terms of the *number of items* in the A category and the *percentage of sales* that will be accounted for by items in the C category. The B items, then, are the ones that fall in between. For example, Giant Wholesale's rules may be, "We want A items to represent 10% of the items we carry, and C items to be those representing the last 5% in sales." Thus, ABC classification for Giant Wholesale is shown in Table 16-3.

As noted, the main rationale behind this technique is to allow inventory managers to put their efforts where they can do the most good. Once classification is accomplished, different levels of effort can be planned for important decisions across all areas of inventory management: inventory control, forecasting, and reordering, as shown in Table 16-4.

Classifications other than (or in addition to) dollar sales or velocity are also used to help focus on more important groupings. Criticality scales may be used, for example. A drawback to more judgmental sortings is the amount of effort that must go into the classification process. Recent research has advocated classification systems based on more than one or two criteria that may be important to a particular firm. Statistical clustering techniques may be employed to create groupings called *operations-related groups* (ORGs) based on item characteristics important to production or inventory decision making.[9] Systems for classification might also be combined with coding systems to create numbering schemes to represent the individual SKUs and their groups.[10]

Statistical Process Control

Accuracy in inventory record keeping can be measured and monitored using a group of quality management techniques known as statistical process control (SPC). Although designed in the 1920s as a tool for improving product quality in manufacturing, SPC has now been widely adapted to address service quality, in general, and logistics quality, in particular. Langley provides an excellent discussion of how SPC might be incorporated in logistics management,[11] as does a recent study by A. T. Kearney.[12]

The rationale behind SPC is to track the results of a process and measure them against goals or standards to reduce variability in the process. A basic component of SPC is the control chart, which plots results across a horizontal time axis and calculates control limits to help determine whether the process is under control.

Automatic Identification/Barcoding

Increasing transaction accuracy is one of the principal benefits for companies that have adopted barcode capabilities in order entry, production, warehousing, and transportation. The use of barcodes for order filling in warehousing, for example, will help greatly to eliminate common errors like picking the wrong item. Bar code systems also allow double checking for accuracy and even closed-loop control systems that will work to correct errors quickly, before the transaction is completed or the order is shipped. In warehouse systems, products are scanned when received, put away, moved to replenish picking locations, picked, and shipped.

The Warehousing Research Center notes:

> It would be difficult to manage a warehouse effectively without some type of information system. The warehouse information system should provide management with the ability to track inventory, locate product, measure productivity and evaluate other performance elements. In recent years, sophisticated technology has been introduced that facilitates in-

TABLE 16-3
Sample ABC Analysis

Item Count	Cumulative Percent of Items	ABC Code	Unit Sales	$ on Hand	Item Sales	Cumulative Sales	Cumulative Percent of Sales
1	2.86	A	3,656	$9,022	$274,998	$274,998	22.30
2	5.71	A	4,704	7,803	176,004	451,002	36.57
3	8.57	A	2,323	4,875	156,711	607,713	49.28
4	11.43	A	678	2,438	145,835	753,548	61.11
Total "A" Items		4		$24,139	$753,548		
5	14.29	B	3,356	14,599	99,456	853,004	69.17
6	17.14	B	2,589	4,716	77,890	930,894	75.49
7	20.00	B	1,967	206	56,980	987,874	80.11
8	22.86	B	2,615	785	37,919	1,025,793	83.19
9	25.71	B	537	4,405	27,802	1,053,595	85.44
10	28.57	B	450	447	15,950	1,069,545	86.73
11	31.43	B	198	2,630	15,577	1,085,122	88.00
12	34.29	B	211	416	15,563	1,100,685	89.26
13	37.14	B	409	3,064	15,507	1,116,192	90.52
14	40.00	B	457	80	15,493	1,131,685	91.77
15	42.86	B	115	0	11,114	1,142,799	92.67
16	45.71	B	805	1,131	11,034	1,153,833	93.57
17	48.57	B	208	43	11,021	1,164,854	94.46
Total "B" Items		13		$32,522	$411,306		
18	51.43	C	49	15,942	9,264	1,174,118	95.21
19	54.29	C	264	1,147	8,985	1,183,103	95.94
20	57.14	C	271	1,844	8,899	1,192,002	96.66
21	60.00	C	77	252	8,868	1,200,870	97.38
22	62.86	C	266	32	8,848	1,209,718	98.10
23	65.71	C	262	1,626	8,838	1,218,556	98.82
24	68.57	C	2	338	5,567	1,224,123	99.27
25	71.43	C	5	1,348	3,765	1,227,888	99.57
26	74.29	C	12	1,379	2,135	1,230,023	99.75
27	77.14	C	2	1,924	1,154	1,231,177	99.84
28	80.00	C	2	720	775	1,231,952	99.90
29	82.86	C	36	2,378	557	1,232,509	99.95
30	85.71	C	12	0	448	1,232,957	99.98
31	88.57	C	6	2,480	121	1,233,078	99.99
32	91.43	C	3	0	66	1,233,144	100.00
33	94.29	C	0	71	0	1,233,144	100.00
34	97.14	C	0	1,699	0	1,233,144	100.00
35	100.00	C	0	1,183	0	1,233,144	100.00
Total "C" Items		18		$34,364	$68,290		

TABLE 16-4
ABC Analysis As a Tool for Prioritizing Inventory Management Efforts

ABC Category	Cycle Counting	Service Level Objective (%)	Inventory Strategy	Forecast/Review Schedule
A	6 times per year	99.5	ROP/EOQ	Weekly
B	2 times per year	95.0	DRP	Monthly
C	1 time per year	90.0	Min/Max	As Needed

formation gathering. Bar codes, a type of automatic identification, are increasingly being used for this purpose. Automatic identification is a way to gather information with minimum human involvement, providing accurate collection and dissemination of data. Its primary justifications are speed and accuracy in streamlining the flow of material through the distribution facility and channel.[13]

Inventory and location system integrity can be improved significantly through the utilization of barcoding technology.

Artificial Intelligence/Expert Systems

Expert system technology—computer systems that provide decision support through the incorporation and reference to decision rules devised by company experts—shows much promise in supporting inventory management. A 1990 survey of applications in logistics showed inventory support as the largest area of usage (20 of 107 systems reported).[14] Most of these systems support inventory analysts in reviewing item-level performance and in planning corrective action.

Federal-Mogul Corporation, for example, has implemented a comprehensive inventory/MRP interface expert system called LOGIX, which provides support in such diverse activities as ordering, forecasting, packaging, order entry, and receiving prioritization.[15] Also, the U.S. Air Force has adopted expert systems called the Requirements Data Bank and the Inventory Manager's Assistant to promote accuracy in entering and maintaining voluminous inventory data.[16]

The ability of expert systems to deal with complex environments in a logical, efficient, and timely manner would indicate their future utilization in the following areas of inventory control:

- Routine maintenance and updating of stock records
- Classification guidance for new items and reclassification for all items under new rules or guidelines (for example, helping to determine levels of criticality)
- Analyzing new items and assigning identifying numbers in coding systems
- Cause-and-effect analysis for count discrepancies
- Database analysis to search for error patterns

Future advances in artificial intelligence will permit the creation of "intelligent databases" that will incorporate hypertext features, object-oriented programming, expert systems, inferencing capabilities (possibly adapted from neural network concepts), and high-level user interfaces to allow inventory managers to extract and display data relevant to the current decision in ways not believed possible. In an intelligent database, maintenance and correction of errors can be done automatically, with human intervention required only for the most difficult issues.[17]

Counting Inventory

It is necessary for both inventory control and financial audit reasons to verify the on-hand counts in inventory records with a physical inspection and count of all items. This is usually done either by counting the entire inventory at the same time, which is called a *physical inventory,* or by counting all items at varying times on a prescheduled basis, which is called *cycle counting.*

The general trend has been for companies to move from physical inventories to cycle counting. Cycle counting is generally believed to be less expensive and more conducive to promoting accuracy in inventory records. In recent years, external auditors have allowed cycle counting to replace an annual physical inventory as the basis for verifying the existence of the inventory.

Periodic Physical Inventories

"Wall-to-wall" physical inventories are expensive for at least two reasons, and possibly a third. First, the planning, preparation, and conduct incur substantial outright expense. One large manufacturing firm with a $50 million inventory recently spent 600 labor hours in preparation time and 1,200 hours to conduct the counts, while its outside audit firm spent 240 hours. Also, typical inventory auditing fees for manufacturing companies can amount to as much as 0.033% of annual sales.[18] Second, a major opportunity cost is associated with the counting, because it usually requires production and warehousing operations to be shut down. This also means that sales are discontinued and customer service might be affected. In fact, smaller firms may even pull salespeople out of their territories to assist in the inventory. Finally, there is the potential that, if the counting is not done accurately (a common occurrence), inventory integrity might be worsened, not improved.

One advantage that physical inventories have over cycle counts is that a halt in operations might improve the chances of getting a clean "cutoff" in regard to matching what is counted with all relevant paperwork. For similar reasons, firms with inventory systems that have only a "one number" capability and have multiple locations involved, often find cycle counting difficult.

The important steps of a periodic physical inventory are described below:

Planning and Preparation

1. Determine method to be used
2. Write out the procedures in detail
3. Set schedule
4. Notify all concerned, including sales force, suppliers, customers
5. Determine labor power required
6. Assign responsibilities
7. Make physical preparations in warehouse
8. Determine needs for supplies and equipment
9. Train personnel
10. Ensure that all outstanding transaction records (orders, receiving records, credit memos, breakage reports, etc.) are processed

Conducting the Inventory

1. Count inventory: first, second, and third counts
2. Establish and maintain firm paperwork controls
3. Process counts against computer on-hands

4. Identify and correct large discrepancies
5. Update computer records
6. Obtain acceptance from auditors

Postinventory

1. Analyze and discuss problems encountered
2. Correct inventory procedures
3. Prepare and submit final report[19]

In recent years, barcoding technology has become a great boon to taking physical inventories and cycle counts. The use of bar code symbols and handheld scanning terminals has greatly increased accuracy and productivity in counting. Other high-tech aids to counting include electronic scales to count small items and radios or walkie-talkies to facilitate communications between counters and the counting managers or product experts.

Cycle Counting

Cycle counting has emerged as a potent tool for the inventory manager in maintaining and improving inventory accuracy. Cycle counting entails the systematic counting of each item carried in stock at least once per year at a planned interval or frequency, which is often based on velocity or ABC classification. Cycle counting is also used to correct known errors or to handle special situations. It is meant to be a system of both *measuring* and *controlling* how well the inventory control process is functioning. An important dimension is determining and repairing the *causes* for discrepancies, in addition to just finding and correcting inaccurate counts.

The procedures for establishing and conducting cycle counts are similar to those noted above for taking a periodic physical inventory, with the exception that, because it is an *ongoing* activity, not as much preparation is required.

An important planning step is determining the cycle length or interval time for each item carried in stock. Accuracy declines with time, and the degree of decline is a function of the number of transactions that occur for an item. Thus, the higher the integrity desired for an item, the more frequently it should be counted. Because of this, an item's ABC classification is often incorporated into setting a desired accuracy level. Early, APICS-recommended tolerances were 0.2% for A items, 1% for B items, and 5% for C items.[20]

Neeley has proposed the following mathematical framework for determining the cycle length of an item[21]:

$$RCL = (1 - ALD) \div (ALD \times P_v)$$

where:

RCL = required cycle length (in weeks)

ALD = accuracy level desired (e.g., 99%)

P_v = probability of a variance occurring in a given week

Thus, for a B item with 99% accuracy required, and experience showed a system integrity where 20 out of 10,000 items were usually in error, the following calculation would apply, meaning that the item should be counted on a five-week interval:

$$RCL = (1 - 0.99) \div [0.99 * (20 \div 10{,}000)] = 5.05 \text{ weeks}$$

Performance Measurement in Inventory Management

This section discusses measuring performance in inventory control (that is, calculating accuracy levels), as well as measuring overall performance in inventory management. Overall performance is measured both in terms of inventory service levels to customers as well as controlling inventory investment.

Inventory Control Performance

The degree to which accuracy in inventory records is maintained is the primary measure of inventory control performance. This is usually stated as an *accuracy level* in terms of the percent accuracy found in an audit or sampling program. It might also be expressed as an *error rate,* which would simply be 100% minus the accuracy level. A company with a 95% accuracy level would have a 5% error rate.

As noted above, companies engaged in an ongoing cycle count program have an automatic means to measure accuracy levels. The accuracy level is the percent of the total counts in a given period that were correct. If a company makes 10,000 counts in a year and 9,750 are correct, its accuracy level is 97.5%. Most accuracy reporting systems might also break down accuracy levels into ABC categories or other relevant affinity groupings, such as product categories.

For companies taking a periodic physical inventory only, the accuracy level becomes the number of SKUs counted that exactly match the computer count. If a physical inventory is taken only annually, this matchup will often be very low; even some of the best organizations achieve only a 50% accuracy level. Recognizing that small deviations over a long period of time are not significant, some companies calculate the accuracy level based on the physical count being within a tolerated deviation, which is often determined in "days of supply." Such a *tolerated accuracy level* might then be the percentage of items counted that was within the computer count, plus or minus a five-day supply.

Companies not doing cycle counts might augment accuracy measurement by implementing a sampling procedure for counting. Such companies also sometimes use surrogates for accuracy levels, such as recording found deviations in the form of *in stock omits* or *negative on-hands.*

Inventory Service Levels

Companies have adopted many ways to measure inventory system performance in regard to satisfying customers. Measures differ depending on the type of company or even the industry involved. Manufacturing companies measure service differently from service companies or merchandising companies like wholesalers or retailers. Different measures are also applicable to different types of inventory. Service levels for finished goods inventories are regarded differently from service levels for raw materials or work-in-process. Finally, service level measures incorporate time factors (e.g., percent of orders shipped on schedule), inventory availability conditions (e.g., a fill rate such as percent of lines shipped vs. total lines ordered), or a combination of both (e.g., percent of lines shipped on schedule).

A 1988 study of customer service by the Council of Logistics Management also found several different methods for viewing inventory capability.[22] The survey asked respondents to identify their primary order fill measure. The following results, shown in Table 16-5, were reported.

The Council of Logistics Management's customer service survey also ascertained that "core customers" of over 300 respondents received the following service levels (Table 16-6).

TABLE 16-5
Primary Order Fill Measures

Primary Order Fill Measure	Percent
Lines filled/Lines ordered	28.2
Cases shipped/Cases ordered	26.8
Dollars shipped/Dollars ordered	8.9
Promised delivery date	19.3
Invoices shipped complete/Total invoices	8.9
Other	7 9
Total	100.0

Source: Bernard J. La Londe, Martha C. Cooper, and Thomas G. Noordewier, *Customer Service: A Management Perspective* (Oak Brook, Ill.: Council of Logistics Management, 1988), p. 41.

As a further example of the many different types of measures available, the following is a listing by Fogarty, Blackstone, and Hoffman of various measures a manufacturing firm might use[23]:

Percentage Measures

- Orders shipped on schedule
- Line items shipped on schedule
- Total units shipped on schedule
- Dollar volume shipped on schedule
- Profit volume shipped on schedule
- Operating item days not out of stock
- Ordering periods without a stockout

Absolute Value Measures

- Order days out of stock
- Line item days out of stock
- Total item days out of stock
- Dollar volume days out of stock
- Idle time due to material/component shortages

TABLE 16-6
Perfomance Provided to Core Customers

Category	Measure
Actual fill rate	95.1%
Minimum acceptable fill rate	89.1%
Percent orders back-ordered	6.6%
Average back-order time	11.1 days
Maximum acceptable back-order time	16.7 days

Source: Bernard J. La Londe, Martha C. Cooper, and Thomas G. Noordewier, *Customer Service: A Management Perspective* (Oak Brook, Ill.: Council of Logistics Management, 1988), p. 41.

It is important to consider customers' needs in selecting service criteria to measure. Firms have sometimes selected standards only to learn later that they have no relevancy for their customers. For example, many companies measure inventory service levels on the basis of dollars shipped to dollars ordered because this is important internally in terms of profit performance. But many of these companies' customers view their performance on the basis of a line or case fill rate.

Inventory Investment Performance

As with service measures, there are many ways to view how well the company's inventory management system is performing from an investment viewpoint. These measures, too, can vary: what is "customary" may differ from industry to industry or by type of inventory.

The most common measures are aimed at assessing the productivity of the company's investment in inventory. Input, the inventory investment, is compared with output—usually sales, cost of sales, or gross profit. The following are often used.

Inventory Turnover Ratio (ITR)

Annual cost of goods sold (ACGS) is divided by average inventory (AvgInv). It is particularly important to use average inventory when seasonal businesses are considered.

$$ITR = ACGS \div AvgInv$$

Days Sales in Inventory (DSI)

Average inventory (AvgInv) is divided by an average day's sales, or annual sales (AnnSls) divided by 365.

$$DSI = AvgInv \div (AnnSls/365)$$

Net Inventory Turnover Ratio (NITR)

Annual cost of goods sold (ACGS) is divided by average net inventory. Net inventory is average inventory (AvgInv) less average accounts payable (AvgAP). This measure is important in merchandising businesses in which suppliers' dating or payment terms are significant.

$$NITR = ACGS \div (AvgInv - AvgAP)$$

Gross Margin Return on Investment (GMROI)

Annual gross margin (AGM) is divided by average inventory (AvgInv). This standard is frequently used in retail businesses.

$$GMROI = AGM \div AvgInv$$

Another dimension of investment performance that must be tracked deals with the quality of the investment, in particular the makeup of the inventory in regard to obsolescence. Inventory management is often charged with the responsibility of ensuring that valuation of individual items of inventory does not exceed current market value. *Markdown dollars* are often used as

TABLE 16-7
Sample Aging Schedule

Category	Last Purchased	Valuation (%)
Current	Within 6 months	100
X	6–12 months	75
XX	12–24 months	50
XXX	Over 24 months	0

the performance measure for obsolescence. Market values are often determined subjectively from estimates of value from an expert. However, some firms have implemented more objective approaches, like classifying all items into aging categories based on the last time an item was bought, sold, or used, and then subjecting these items to automatic devaluation. An aging schedule might be as illustrated in Table 16-7.

Benchmarking Inventory Performance

Suppose an inventory manager is interested in comparing the performance of the company with that of competitors or of similar companies. He is particularly interested in analyzing how well the firm's inventory is turning compared with that of others. He calculates the inventory turn ratio at 3.0 and then researches other companies in the industry. He discovers that all the other companies achieve turns from 1.5 to 2.5, and that the industry average is 2.2.

But what does this mean? Is he an instant hero? Should he rush the results of his research down the hall to the boss's office?

The answer is that maybe he does not know enough yet to be sure. Because inventory performance (as measured by a turn ratio) is affected by many noninventory factors, and because inventory is often used as a trade-off for other costs or for service, it is often difficult to compare one firm with another. Consider the following factors, any one of which might invalidate the manager's claim to industry greatness:

- The other companies may be producing more "value added" in their products. They may be producing components or subassemblies, where this firm is buying them. Presumably, then, their gross profit will be higher.
- This firm may be valuing inventory at average cost or FIFO, and the other companies at LIFO.
- The others may have secured quantity purchase arrangements with suppliers and are buying at better prices to offset the inventory investment.
- Similarly, the others may have secured dating arrangements with suppliers, so that they have accounts payable to offset inventory investment.
- This firm may be sourcing many components overseas at a favorable exchange rate.
- Competitors may be making products, key materials for which are in short supply. They may therefore be stockpiling to ensure good service.
- Competitors may have five to ten field warehouses for finished goods compared with this firm's two. Their order cycle time is two days; this firm's is five days.
- This firm's inventory service level is 90%. Theirs is 95%.

Benchmarking based on inventory management metrics, then, is extremely difficult. A "one-number" comparison between two firms can be misleading.

Notes

1. Edward A. Silver and Rein Peterson, *Decision Systems for Inventory Management and Production Planning* (New York: Wiley, 1985), p. 56.
2. Donald W. Fogarty, John H. Blackstone, Jr., and Thomas H. Hoffman, *Production and Inventory Management* (Cincinnati: South-Western, 1991), p. 318.
3. For a classic description of *kanban,* see Y. Sugimori, K. Kusinoki, F. Cho, and S. Uchikawa, "Toyota Production System and Kanban System," *International Journal of Production* 15, no. 6 (1977): 553–64.
4. Jin H. Im and Richard J. Schonberger, "The Pull of Kanban," *Production and Inventory Management Journal* 29, no. 4 (Fourth Quarter 1988): 54–57.
5. Peter Baily and Gerard Tavernier, *Stock Control Systems and Records* (Aldershot, England: Gower, 1984), pp. 38–52.
6. Andersen Consulting, *Logistics Software* (1991 ed.) (Oak Brook, Ill.: Council of Logistics Management, 1991). Also see annually updated editions.
7. Craig M. Gustin. *Trends in Logistics Information Systems* (Menlo Park, Cal.: SRI International, 1991), p. 3.
8. American Production and Inventory Control Society, *Dictionary,* 5th ed., Thomas F. Wallace, ed. (Falls Church, Va.: APICS, 1984).
9. Morris A. Cohen and Ricardo Ernst, "Multi-item Classification and Generic Inventory Stock Control Policies," *Production and Inventory Management Journal* 29, no. 3 (Third Quarter 1988): 6–8.
10. Evan C. Hu and James C. Sprague, "Designing an Effective Inventory Classification and Coding System," *Production and Inventory Management Journal* 28, no. 4 (Fourth Quarter 1987): 53–56.
11. C. John Langley, Jr., "Information-based Decision Making in Logistics Management," *International Journal of Physical Distribution and Materials Management* 15, no. 7.
12. A. T. Kearney, Patrick M. Byrne and William J. Markham, *Improving Quality and Productivity in the Logistics Process: Achieving Customer Service Breakthroughs* (Oak Brook, Ill.: Council of Logistics Management, 1991), pp. 123–41.
13. The Warehousing Research Center, *A Guide for Evaluating and Implementing a Warehouse Bar Code System* (Oak Brook, Ill.: Warehousing Education and Research Council, 1992), p. 1.
14. Intellogistics/Dialog, *Putting Expert Systems to Work in Logistics* (Oak Brook, Ill.: Council of Logistics Management, 1990), pp. 92–93.
15. Ibid., pp. 47–62.
16. Mary Kay Allen and James M. Masters, "The Application of Expert Systems Technology to the Operation of a Large-Scale Military Logistics Information System," *Journal of Business Logistics* 9, no. 2 (1988): 103–16.
17. Intellogistics/Dialog, *Putting Expert Systems to Work,* pp. 150–53.
18. Judith A. Swartley and James A. Hall, "Inventory Auditing: A Manufacturing Perspective," *Production and Inventory Management Journal* 29, no. 4 (Fourth Quarter 1988): 20–22.

19. Adapted from Joel Sutherland, "Physical Inventory and Cycle Count Systems," *The Distribution Handbook* (New York: Free Press, 1985), pp. 711–32.
20. Fogarty, et al., *Production and Inventory Management,* p. 320.
21. Parley S. Neeley, "A Framework for Cycle Counting," *Production and Inventory Management Journal* (Fourth Quarter 1983): 23–33.
22. Bernard J. La Londe, Martha C. Cooper, and Thomas G. Noordewier, *Customer Service: A Management Perspective* (Oak Brook, Ill.: Council of Logistics Management, 1988), p. 41.
23. Fogarty, et al., *Production and Inventory Management,* pp. 165–72.

CHAPTER 17

Distribution Resource Planning

Alan J. Stenger

Distribution resource planning (DRP) can be a powerful tool for improving distribution operations.[1] Although it is a relatively simple concept, to maximize its benefit, companies need to deal with both human and technical issues. The human issues include:

- Developing and training people to operate the computerized tools employed in the DRP process
- Breaking down the barriers to interfunctional coordination—particularly between marketing and distribution, and between distribution and production—to get those functions to use the DRP recommendations in their decision making
- Ensuring that the process becomes integrated in the regular business planning processes of the firm

The technical issues include:

- Gathering the necessary data and maintaining those data accurately, using database technology
- Acquiring (or developing) and implementing the data processing software needed to perform DRP
- Integrating the software with the other operating systems of the firm

Companies that successfully address these issues find that the DRP process can help them improve customer service while reducing overall finished goods inventories, cut transportation costs for replenishing distribution centers (DCs), improve the efficiency of operations at those DCs, and better link production plans with distribution plans for further efficiencies. For example, ServiStar Hardware, in a pilot study of DRP published in 1985, proved it could:

- Increase inventory fill rates at its Butler, Pennsylvania, distribution center from 90 to 95% while reducing inventories by 10%
- Save almost $1 million per year by consolidating freight and taking maximum advantage of vendor discounts
- Reduce administrative costs by placing fewer orders with suppliers
- Minimize warehouse overtime because "stock will come in as needed and on schedule, and costs for expediting will be slashed."[2]

While ServiStar is a distributor supplying its client hardware stores with thousands of items, manufacturers can realize similar benefits through DRP. In addition, manufacturers can gain additional improvements in manufacturing by using DRP output to drive the production planning and scheduling process.[3]

What Is DRP?

Firms use the DRP process to project when, and in what amount, individual stock-keeping units (SKUs) will need to be replenished for several weeks or months into the future. They then use this information in the following ways, among others:

- To coordinate the replenishment of SKUs coming from the same source (e.g., a company-owned or vendor's plant)
- To select transportation modes, carriers, and shipment sizes more cost-efficiently
- To schedule shipping and receiving labor
- To develop a master production schedule for each SKU

This replenishment planning is done in a way that provides the minimum amount of inventory required to meet demand and maintain safety stocks.

Developing this projection for each SKU requires the following data:

- *Forecasts of demand* (produced internally) and/or *demand schedules* (provided by customers) by time period. Generally the time period is a week, but this depends on the needs and capabilities of the organization implementing the process.
- *Current inventory level* of the SKU at that location. This is often referred to as the "balance on hand" (BOH).
- *Target safety stock* for the item.
- Recommended *replenishment quantity.*
- *Lead time for replenishment,* that is, the length of time it will take to receive a resupply shipment once it is scheduled.

Given this information, a firm can build replenishment projections as far into the future as the forecasts and/or demand schedules permit.

This chapter first discusses the process of developing the basic DRP "table." It then shows how managers and analysts can use these tables for the best use of distribution and production resources. Finally, it discusses the human issues involved in implementing DRP.

The Basic DRP Process

The basic DRP process consists of developing DRP tables for each SKU at each distribution location and then combining those tables in various ways to create the information by which we can improve the utilization of distribution and production resources.

The DRP Table

Table 17-1 shows a typical DRP table, prepared for an SKU at a distribution center. It consists of a variety of elements, each numbered and discussed below:

1. *Location* (distribution center) of this SKU.
2. *Stock-keeping unit (SKU)* or item represented in the table.

TABLE 17-1
A Typical DRP Table
1 *Columbus Distribution Center—Distribution Resource Planning*

9 WEEK	**Jan** **1**	**2**	**3**	**4**	**Feb** **5**	**6**	**7**	**8**	**Mar** **9**
	3 Source					**4** Carrier			
2 CHICKEN NOODLE:	**5** Current BOH			**6** Q =	**7** SS =	**8** LT =			
10 Forecast									
11 Sched. Receipt									
12 BOH-ending									
13 Planned Order									
14Actual Order									

3. *Source* of this item; that is, the plant, warehouse, or vendor that replenishes this item to the DC.
4. *Transportation carrier* selected by the traffic function to deliver replenishments to this DC from the source.
5. *Current inventory balance on hand* (BOH) for the item as we go into the planning period. This may need to be *projected* to the starting point if the planning process takes place days or weeks before the starting time of the table.
6. The recommended *replenishment quantity* (Q) for the SKU. This could range from one unit, to a pallet layer, to a unit load (pallet), to a full vehicle load. Sometimes this is given as a range, with a minimum and a maximum.
7. Target *safety stock* (SS) we wish to maintain for this SKU. This and the replenishment quantity are often computed using the techniques described in Chapter 15.
8. *Lead time* (LT) for replenishing the DC with this SKU, including processing time at the source and the transit time of the carrier to be used.
9. *Time increments,* often called the *time buckets,* for which we are developing the plan. For many companies, the logical time increment is one week, looking several dozen weeks into the future. Other companies may develop the plan by day for the first several weeks, by week after that for several months, then in monthly increments further into the future. How far to go into the future—that is, how long the *planning horizon* should be—depends on the business. Those with seasonal demand or supply often plan a full year ahead to cover the seasonal cycle, and then add the length of the logistics cycle to that. The logistics cycle is the time from when we first order raw materials for a unit of an item until that specific unit of the item arrives at the customer's point of use.
10. *Forecast* of demand, or a combination of a forecast and specific demand schedules supplied by major customers, for this item for each time period in the planning horizon.[4]
11. *Scheduled receipts,* the quantity and the period of arrival of those replenishment orders that have been placed with the supply point.
12. *Projected inventory* position, that is, ending balance on hand (BOH) at the end of each time increment, assuming the demand forecast materializes and all replenishments arrive on time
13. *Planned orders* proposed by the DRP process so as to meet projected demands and maintain safety stocks.

14. *Actual shipments.* Those replenishment quantities the decision maker specifically wants the source to ship during the time increment in question.

We will call elements 5 through 8 the *planning parameters* for the item. We want to choose the values of these elements so that we meet the forecast and maintain the needed level of product availability at the lowest combined cost for production, transportation, warehousing, and inventory.

Tables like this, developed for all SKUs at each DC, form the basis of the DRP process. By setting the right planning parameters and combining the planned and actual shipment rows, we can develop plans for using the distribution and production resources very productively, while providing the needed level of customer service.

Computing the Projections

The procedure for computing the planned shipments and projected inventory levels is quite straightforward. We take the *current inventory balance on hand* (element 5) and subtract from it the *forecast* for the first time period (element 10). If there is a *scheduled receipt* in this time period (element 11), we add that to the previous result. This gives the *projected inventory* at the end of period one (element 12), which is also the balance on hand at the start of period two.

For example, take the numbers shown in Table 17-2 for week 1:

Current Balance on Hand	(5)	4,314
Forecast	(10)	– 974
Subtotal		3,340
Scheduled Receipt	(11)	+ 0
Balance on Hand—ending	(12)	3,340

The balance on hand at the end of week 1 exceeds *the safety stock* (element 7), so we do not need to receive a replenishment in week 1 to maintain that safety stock. As we keep depleting the inventory by the forecast amount each week, we eventually do project inventories (the ending balance on hand) falling below the safety stock. When this situation occurs, we need to plan a receipt for that week (an amount equal to the *replenishment quantity*—element 6), and plan to ship it in the *lead time* number of periods (element 8) prior to the period of the need. This produces the *planned order* (element 13). In the example shown in Table 17-2, we project falling

TABLE 17-2
The DRP Calculations
Columbus Distribution Center—Distribution Resource Planning

WEEK	Jan 1	2	3	4	Feb 5	6	7	8	Mar 9
CHICKEN NOODLE: **5** Current BOH = 4,314 **6** Q = 3,800 **7** SS = 1,956 **8** LT = 1									
Forecast	**10** 974								
Sched. Receipt	**11** 0								
BOH-ending	**12** 3,340								
Planned Order	**13** 0								
Actual Order									

TABLE 17-3
Computing Planned and Actual Orders
Columbus Distribution Center—Distribution Resource Planning

WEEK	Jan 1	2	3	4	Feb 5	6	7	8	Mar 9
CHICKEN NOODLE:	Current BOH = 4,314		Q = 3,800		SS = 1,956	LT = 1			
Forecast	974	974	974	974	989	1,002	1,002	1,002	1,061
Sched. Receipt	0	0	3,800	0	0	0	3,800	0	0
BOH-ending	3,340	2,366	5,192	4,218	3,229	2,227	5,025	4,023	2,962
Planned Order	0	3,800	0	0	0	3,800	0	0	3,800
Actual Order									

below the safety stock in week 3. Because the lead time is one week, we need to plan an order for week 2. That order will arrive in week 3.[5]

We repeat the procedure for each period, always using the previous period's projected (ending) balance on hand as the starting point for the period. In this way we can project all the required replenishments for an item at a DC as far into the future as we have demand projections. Table 17-3 shows the completed DRP table. This table is for an SKU at the Columbus Distribution Center of a food manufacturer. Because of space limitations, we show only the first 9 weeks of the projection, but in fact the table in this case extends out for 52 weeks.

Combining Tables: The DRP Tree

The projection (plan) represented by any one table is of great value in its own right because it shows the inventory levels we need to maintain to meet demand and provide customers with the service needed (through the safety stock). It also indicates when replenishments—and their quantities—need to be scheduled to make the plan work. *But combining these tables in various ways leads to even greater advantage.*

It is important to use the tables to look at those SKUs at a distribution center that are supplied all from one source (e.g., a plant). In this way the distribution center can see all that it is receiving from that source for receipt planning. In addition, the traffic function can make the proper transportation arrangements. Another way of combining the tables is to look at all of them for an individual SKU supplied from a given source (i.e., look at all the DCs stocking that item). This provides the plant valuable information for scheduling production of that SKU. Figure 17-1 shows a DRP tree for an SKU, indicating all the tables for a set of distribution centers supplied by a plant. When we combine the requirements in this way, then the source has a complete projection of the needs for all SKUs and can use these data to develop production and shipping plans.

This combining process, done in various ways, gives the power to DRP. The next section describes the entire process in greater detail through several examples.

Using the DRP Tables to Improve Profitability

As we saw in the ServiStar case, using DRP can create improvements in service levels, inventories, transportation, and distribution center operations. Where the DRP data are fully commu-

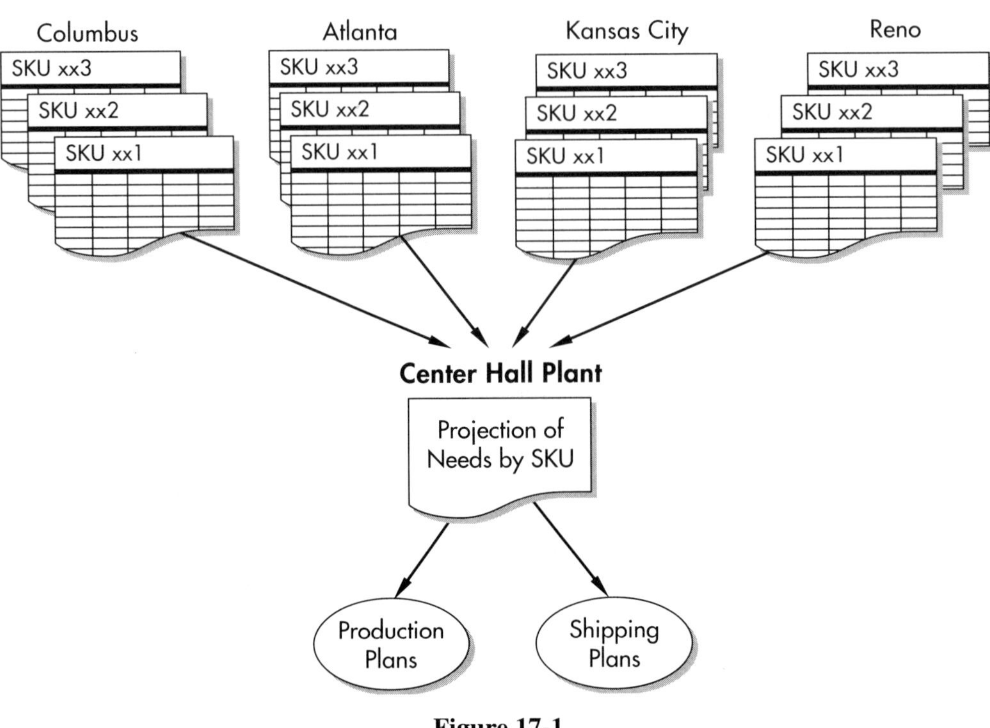

Figure 17-1
The Distribution Tree

nicated to the source—whether the source is our own plant or a vendor's location—then we can get savings in production and shipping efforts at the source as well. Those improvements can be leveraged by:

- Doing a better job of forecasting or by obtaining tables from our customers' own requirements planning processes[6]
- Fine-tuning the planning parameters—safety stocks, replenishment quantities, and lead times—in conjunction with our transportation decisions
- Rescheduling receipts at the DCs to better utilize warehouse labor
- Effecting transportation consolidations, and routing and scheduling improvements
- Rescheduling source shipments to better utilize loading labor
- Using the consolidated DRP shipping schedules to schedule production

Chapter 15 covers the concept of developing relationships with customers to improve demand estimates, and Chapter 14 deals with specific forecasting techniques. Chapter 15 also discusses the planning parameters—safety stocks, replenishment quantities, and lead times. This section of the chapter assumes that these data have already been appropriately developed, and we explore the use of the tables to achieve economies in resource utilization.

Receipt Scheduling at the Distribution Center

Table 17-4 shows the DRP tables for five SKUs stocked at the Columbus distribution center, all supplied by the Centre Hall plant. In each case the analyst has converted the *planned orders* into *actual orders*. This produces the lowest level of inventory for each item at the DC, while not violating rules for replenishment quantities or safety stocks. However, when we add up all the requirements, the order pattern varies substantially from week to week. For example we will be ordering 27,000 units in week 1 and no units in week 5. Because all the items have a one-period lead time, this means the receiving load will be erratic as well.

Smoothing out the receiving load to gain economies at the Columbus DC requires ordering some items earlier than the planned order date or violating the target replenishment quantity.[7] We may do some of both, although to what extent depends on the impact these initiatives might have on inventory carrying costs and/or on freight costs. Table 17-5 shows an example where the analyst has chosen to do both. In that case we cannot do much about the first week's orders (second week's receipts) because we must have this amount of product to maintain safety stocks and meet the forecasts. After that we have moved some orders earlier and increased the replenishment quantity in some cases. For example, note the order for beef noodle in week 5. Comparing the plan in Table 17-4 with this plan shows that we will ship this order a week early, and increase the amount somewhat.

The resulting receiving pattern shown at the bottom of Table 17-5 is not completely leveled, because we have tried to maintain the integrity of the replenishment quantities. However, this is superior to the receiving schedule shown in Table 17-3 in the sense that it is less erratic. On the other hand, we pay for this change with higher inventories at the distribution center. When we extend the tables out for an entire year, the average ending balance on hand for all products in Table 17-4 is about 34,000 units, while in Table 17-5 it is 39,300 units—a 16% increase.

Combining Orders for Transportation Savings

We can also use the DRP tables at a distribution center to plan shipment consolidations. Continuing with our same basic example as shown in Table 17-4, we note that the weekly quantities vary substantially and may not by themselves lead to efficient use of transportation vehicles. Assume that the carrier the firm plans to use for replenishments to the Columbus DC from the Centre Hall plant offers the following price structure:

Minimum No. of Units	to	Maximum No. of Units	Price Per Load
0		9,999	$600
10,000		18,999	700
19,000		41,999	800
42,000		58,000	900

Furthermore, several other economic factors apply to this situation:

Value of the product:	$0.95 per unit
Administrative ordering cost:	$15.00 per order
Inventory carrying cost:	$0.00457 per unit of ending inventory per week

One can experiment with different ordering strategies when these economics apply. For example, the ordering scenario defined in Table 17-4 (order exactly the minimum replenishment

TABLE 17-4
Combining SKUs for a Distribution Center
Columbus Distribution Center—Distribution Resource Planning

WEEK	**Jan** **1**	**2**	**3**	**4**	**Feb** **5**	**6**	**7**	**8**	**Mar** **9**
CHICKEN NOODLE:	**Current BOH = 3,235 Q = 5,700 SS = 2,935 LT = 1**								
Forecast	1,460	1,460	1,460	1,460	1,485	1,500	1,500	1,500	1,600
Sched. Receipt	0	5,700	0	0	5,700	0	0	5,700	0
BOH-ending	1,775	6,015	4,555	3,095	7,310	5,810	4,310	8,510	6,910
Planned Order	5,700	0	0	5,700	0	0	5,700	0	0
Actual Order	5,700			5,700			5,700		
BEEF NOODLE:	**Current BOH = 4,314 Q = 3,800 SS = 1,956 LT = 1**								
Forecast	974	974	974	974	989	1,002	1,002	1,002	1,061
Sched. Receipt	0	0	3,800	0	0	0	3,800	0	0
BOH-ending	3,340	2,366	5,192	4,218	3,229	2,227	5,025	4,023	2,962
Planned Order	0	3,800	0	0	0	3,800	0	0	3,800
Actual Order		3,800				3,800			3,800
VEGETABLE:	**Current BOH = 4,314 Q = 5,700 SS = 3,913 LT = 1**								
Forecast	1,948	1,948	1,948	1,948	1,980	2,003	2,003	2,003	2,123
Sched. Receipt	0	5,700	0	5,700	0	0	5,700	0	5,700
BOH-ending	2,366	6,118	4,170	7,922	5,942	3,939	7,636	5,633	9,210
Planned Order	5,700	0	5,700	0	0	5,700	0	5,700	0
Actual Order	5,700		5,700			5,700		5,700	
MUSHROOM:	**Current BOH = 7,190 Q = 7,100 SS = 4,891 LT = 1**								
Forecast	2,435	2,435	2,435	2,435	2,475	2,504	2,504	2,504	2,653
Sched. Receipt	0	7,100	0	7,100	0	0	7,100	0	0
BOH-ending	4,755	9,420	6,985	11,650	9,175	6,671	11,267	8,763	6,110
Planned Order	7,100	0	7,100	0	0	7,100	0	0	7,100
Actual Order	7,100		7,100			7,100			7,100
TOMATO:	**Current BOH = 3,235 Q = 8,500 SS = 8,500 LT = 1**								
Forecast	2,922	2,922	2,922	2,922	2,969	3,005	3,005	3,005	3,184
Sched. Receipt	0	8,500	8,500	0	8,500	0	0	8,500	0
BOH-ending	313	5,891	11,469	8,547	14,078	11,073	8,068	13,563	10,379
Planned Order	8,500	8,500	0	8,500	0	0	8,500	0	0
Actual Order	8,500	8,500		8,500			8,500		
TOTALS FOR ALL PRODUCTS									
To Be Received	0	27,000	12,300	12,800	14,200	0	16,600	14,200	5,700
Ordered	27,000	12,300	12,800	14,200	0	16,600	14,200	5,700	10,900

TABLE 17-5
Leveling DC Receiving
Columbus Distribution Center—Distribution Resource Planning

WEEK	Jan 1	2	3	4	Feb 5	6	7	8	Mar 9
CHICKEN NOODLE:	**Current BOH = 3,235 Q = 5,700 SS = 2,935 LT = 1**								
Forecast	1,460	1,460	1,460	1,460	1,485	1,500	1,500	1,500	1,600
Sched. Receipt	0	5,700	0	0	5,700	0	0	5,700	0
BOH-ending	1,775	6,015	4,555	3,095	7,310	5,810	4,310	8,510	6,910
Planned Order	5,700	0	0	5,700	0	0	5,700	0	0
Actual Order	5,700			5,700			5,700		
BEEF NOODLE:	**Current BOH = 4,314 Q = 3,800 SS = 1,956 LT = 1**								
Forecast	974	974	974	974	989	1,002	1,002	1,002	1,061
Sched. Receipt	0	0	3,800	0	0	4,200	0	0	3,800
BOH-ending	3,340	2,366	5,192	4,218	3,229	6,427	5,425	4,423	7,162
Planned Order	0	3,800	0	0	0	0	0	0	0
Actual Order		3,800			4,200			3,800	
VEGETABLE:	**Current BOH = 4,314 Q = 5,700 SS = 3,913 LT = 1**								
Forecast	1,948	1,948	1,948	1,948	1,980	2,003	2,003	2,003	2,123
Sched. Receipt	0	5,700	0	5,700	0	7,000	0	0	5,700
BOH-ending	2,366	6,118	4,170	7,922	5,942	10,939	8,936	6,933	10,510
Planned Order	5,700	0	5,700	0	0	0	0	0	0
Actual Order	5,700		5,700		7,000			5,700	
MUSHROOM:	**Current BOH = 7,190 Q = 7,100 SS = 4,891 LT = 1**								
Forecast	2,435	2,435	2,435	2,435	2,475	2,504	2,504	2,504	2,653
Sched. Receipt	0	7,100	0	7,100	0	0	12,000	0	0
BOH-ending	4,755	9,420	6,985	11,650	9,175	6,671	16,167	13,663	11,010
Planned Order	7,100	0	7,100	0	0	7,100	0	0	0
Actual Order	7,100		7,100			12,000			
TOMATO:	**Current BOH = 3,235 Q = 8,500 SS = 5,869 LT = 1**								
Forecast	2,922	2,922	2,922	2,922	2,969	3,005	3,005	3,005	3,184
Sched. Receipt	0	8,500	9,000	0	8,500	0	0	8,500	0
BOH-ending	313	5,891	11,969	9,047	14,578	11,573	8,568	14,063	10,879
Planned Order	8,500	8,500	0	0	0	0	8,500	0	0
Actual Order	8,500	9,000		8,500			8,500		8,500
TOTALS FOR ALL PRODUCTS									
To Be Received	0	27,000	12,800	12,800	14,200	11,200	12,000	14,200	9,500
Ordered	27,000	12,800	12,800	14,200	11,200	12,000	14,200	9,500	8,500

quantity at the latest possible moment) produces a total annual cost of $42,220, broken down as follows:

Freight	$33,400
Administrative ordering	750
Inventory carrying	8,070
Total Annual Cost	$42,220

Table 17-6 shows a scenario where we have chosen always to ship the maximum load possible, 58,000 units. In this case we arrived at the specific timing and quantities per order for each item using the following decision rules:

- A mixed order is launched in a given week whenever at least one of the jointly replenished items is projected to fall below its safety stock
- For each item, the amount ordered is sufficient so that the next required order for each item falls into the same week (and, of course, the total order equals 58,000 units).

This scenario produced the total costs shown below:

Freight	$9,000
Administrative ordering	150
Inventory carrying	10,946
Total Annual Cost	$20,096

Clearly the transportation savings of bigger shipments in this case far outweigh the cost of the additional inventory such a strategy produces. Of course, the product line obviously has a relatively low value per unit—in another situation, the inventory costs may dictate a completely opposite strategy, as might be the case if we were dealing with expensive pharmaceuticals or valuable electronic components.

Production Planning Using DRP Tables

DRP tables logically provide the input for production planning and scheduling decisions. The planned orders for an SKU, aggregated across all the DCs stocking the item, become the "gross requirements" that the plant must meet each week. The plant does this through a combination of inventory and additional production. It is this additional production that needs to be scheduled.

Table 17-7 shows the DRP tables for chicken noodle soup at the four distribution centers where it is stocked. Actual orders have already been planned by the distribution analyst out through week 9. The sums of these, by week, make up the first row—labeled gross requirements—of the plant table (shown below the four DC tables). Computing the quantity of material "required from production"—the second row—is simply a matter of making the same kinds of calculations we made in the DRP tables. In this case, however, the safety stock is set at zero, and there is no minimum production quantity (Q).[8] Judging from the current balance on hand and the gross requirements, we will not need to receive any new production until week 4, when 8,000 units will be required. Because there is a one-week production lead time, we will need to start this run the previous week (see line four, minimum production start). Subsequent runs will be for 17,000 and 3,800 units in weeks 6 and 7, respectively.

The production plan developed with this approach produces the minimum inventory but

TABLE 17-6
Combining Orders for Transportation Savings
Columbus Distribution Center—Distribution Resource Planning

WEEK	Jan 1	2	3	4	Feb 5	6	7	8	Mar 9
CHICKEN NOODLE:	**Current BOH = 3,235 Q = 5,700 SS = 2,935 LT = 1**								
Forecast	1,460	1,460	1,460	1,460	1,485	1,500	1,500	1,500	1,600
Sched. Receipt	0	9,200	0	0	0	0	8,000	0	0
BOH-ending	1,775	9,515	8,055	6,595	5,110	3,610	10,110	8,610	7,010
Planned Order	5,700	0	0	0	0	5,700	0	0	0
Actual Order	9,200					8,000			
BEEF NOODLE:	**Current BOH = 4,314 Q = 3,800 SS = 1,956 LT = 1**								
Forecast	974	974	974	974	989	1,002	1,002	1,002	1,061
Sched. Receipt	0	3,800	0	0	0	0	6,000	0	0
BOH-ending	3,340	6,166	5,192	4,218	3,229	2,227	7,225	6,223	5,162
Planned Order	0	0	0	0	0	3,800	0	0	0
Actual Order	3,800					6,000			
VEGETABLE:	**Current BOH = 4,314 Q = 5,700 SS = 3,913 LT = 1**								
Forecast	1,948	1,948	1,948	1,948	1,980	2,003	2,003	2,003	2,123
Sched. Receipt	0	11,500	0	0	0	0	12,000	0	0
BOH-ending	2,366	11,918	9,970	8,022	6,042	4,039	14,036	12,033	9,910
Planned Order	5,700	0	0	0	0	5,700	0	0	0
Actual Order	11,500					12,000			
MUSHROOM:	**Current BOH = 7,190 Q = 7,100 SS = 4,891 LT = 1**								
Forecast	2,435	2,435	2,435	2,435	2,475	2,504	2,504	2,504	2,653
Sched. Receipt	0	12,500	0	0	0	0	14,000	0	0
BOH-ending	4,755	14,820	12,385	9,950	7,475	4,971	16,467	13,963	11,310
Planned Order	7,100	0	0	0	0	7,100	0	0	0
Actual Order	12,500					14,000			
TOMATO:	**Current BOH = 3,235 Q = 8,500 SS = 5,869 LT = 1**								
Forecast	2,922	2,922	2,922	2,922	2,969	3,005	3,005	3,005	3,184
Sched. Receipt	0	21,000	0	0	0	0	18,000	0	0
BOH-ending	313	18,391	15,469	12,547	9,578	6,573	21,568	18,563	15,379
Planned Order	8,500	0	0	0	0	8,500	0	0	0
Actual Order	21,000					18,000			
TOTALS FOR ALL PRODUCTS									
To Be Received	0	58,000	0	0	0	0	58,000	0	0
Ordered	58,000	0	0	0	0	58,000	0	0	0

TABLE 17-7
Master Production Scheduling, I
Chicken Noodle Soup—Master Production Scheduling from DRP

WEEK	Jan. 1	2	3	4	Feb 5	6	7	8	Mar 9
COLUMBUS DC:	**Current BOH = 3,235**		**Q = 5,700**		**SS = 2,935**		**LT = 1**		
Forecast	1,460	1,460	1,460	1,460	1,485	1,500	1,500	1,500	1,600
Sched. Receipt	0	9,200	0	0	0	0	8,000	0	0
BOH-ending	1,775	9,515	8,055	6,595	5,110	3,610	10,110	8,610	7,010
Planned Order	5,700	0	0	0	0	5,700	0	0	0
Actual Order	9,200					8,000			
ATLANTA DC:	**Current BOH = 6,314**		**Q = 3,800**		**SS = 1,956**		**LT = 1**		
Forecast	974	974	974	974	989	1,002	1,002	1,002	1,061
Sched. Receipt	0	0	0	0	3,800	0	0	0	3,800
BOH-ending	5,340	4,366	3,392	2,418	5,229	4,227	3,225	2,223	4,962
Planned Order	0	0	0	3,800	0	0	0	3,800	0
Actual Order				3,800				3,800	
KANSAS CITY DC:	**Current BOH = 4,314**		**Q = 5,700**		**SS = 3,913**		**LT = 1**		
Forecast	1,948	1,948	1,948	1,948	1,980	2,003	2,003	2,003	2,123
Sched. Receipt	0	7,000	0	8,000	0	0	0	7,000	
BOH-ending	2,366	7,418	5,470	11,522	9,542	7,539	5,536	10,533	8,410
Planned Order	5,700	0	5,700	0	0	0	5,700	0	0
Actual Order	7,000		8,000				7,000		
RENO DC:	**Current BOH = 17,190**		**Q = 7,100**		**SS = 4,891**		**LT = 1**		
Forecast	2,435	2,435	2,435	2,435	2,475	2,504	2,504	2,504	2,653
Sched. Receipt	0	0	0	0	0	10,000	0	0	10,000
BOH-ending	14,755	12,320	9,885	7,450	4,975	12,471	9,967	7,463	14,810
Planned Order	0	0	0	7,100	0	0	7,100	0	0
Actual Order				10,000			10,000		
CENTRE HALL PLANT:	**Current BOH = 30,000**			**SS = 0**	**Production Lead Time= 1**				
Gross Requirements	16,200	0	8,000	13,800	0	8,000	17,000	3,800	0
Required from Production	0	0	0	8,000	0	8,000	17,000	3,800	0
Balance on Hand	13,800	13,800	5,800	0	0	0	0	0	0
Minimum Production Start	0	0	8,000	0	8,000	17,000	3,800	0	0
Master Production Schedule		8,000		8,000	17,000	3,800			

is very "lumpy." Obviously the planner may want to modify this. As before in developing a shipping or receiving schedule, the planner may do so as long as production is scheduled not later than needed to meet the matching gross requirement. Table 17-8 shows a new master production schedule that is extremely stable, indicating a constant production rate of 6,760 units per week. This schedule is simply an average of the gross requirements for weeks 1 through 12.[9]

TABLE 17-8
Master Production Scheduling, II
Chicken Noodle Soup—Master Production Scheduling from DRP

WEEK	Jan. 1	2	3	4	Feb 5	6	7	8	Mar 9
COLUMBUS DC:	**Balance on Hand = 3,235**			**Q = 5,700**		**SS = 2,935**		**LT = 1**	
Forecast	1,460	1,460	1,460	1,460	1,485	1,500	1,500	1,500	1,600
Sched. Receipt	0	9,200	0	0	0	0	8,000	0	0
Balance on Hand	1,775	9,515	8,055	6,595	5,110	3,610	10,110	8,610	7,010
Planned Order	5,700	0	0	0	0	5,700	0	0	0
Actual Order	9,200					8,000			
ATLANTA DC:	**Balance on Hand = 6,314**			**Q = 3,800**		**SS = 1,956**		**LT = 1**	
Forecast	974	974	974	974	989	1,002	1,002	1,002	1,061
Sched. Receipt	0	0	0	0	3,800	0	0	0	3,800
Balance on Hand	5,340	4,366	3,392	2,418	5,229	4,227	3,225	2,223	4,962
Planned Order	0	0	0	3,800	0	0	0	3,800	0
Actual Order				3,800				3,800	
KANSAS CITY DC:	**Balance on Hand = 4,314**			**Q = 5,700**		**SS = 3,913**		**LT = 1**	
Forecast	1,948	1,948	1,948	1,948	1,980	2,003	2,003	2,003	2,123
Sched. Receipt	0	7,000	0	8,000	0	0	0	7,000	0
Balance on Hand	2,366	7,418	5,470	11,522	9,542	7,539	5,536	10,533	8,410
Planned Order	5,700	0	5,700	0	0	0	5,700	0	0
Actual Order	7,000		8,000				7,000		
RENO DC:	**Balance on Hand = 17,190**			**Q = 7,100**		**SS = 4,891**		**LT = 2**	
Forecast	2,435	2,435	2,435	2,435	2,475	2,504	2,504	2,504	2,653
Sched. Receipt	0	0	0	0	0	10,000	0	0	10,000
Balance on Hand	14,755	12,320	9,885	7,450	4,975	12,471	9,967	7,463	14,810
Planned Order	0	0	0	7,100	0	0	7,100	0	0
Actual Order				10,000			10,000		
CENTRE HALL PLANT:	**Balance on Hand = 30,000**			**SS = 0**		**Production Lead Time = 1**			
Gross Requirements	16,200	0	8,000	13,800	0	8,000	17,000	3,800	0
Required from Production	0	6,760	6,760	6,760	6,760	6,760	6,760	6,760	6,760
Balance on Hand	13,800	20,560	19,320	12,280	19,040	17,800	7,560	10,520	17,280
Minimum Production Start	0	0	0	0	0	0	0	0	0
Master Production Schedule	6,760	6,760	6,760	6,760	6,760	6,760	6,760	6,760	6,760

As in the case of transportation planning in DRP, we can attach costs to the various possible master production schedules (MPS) and decide which one best meets the needs of the business. The appropriate MPS for an item, of course, will depend on the manufacturing technology used, the degree to which we can use the equipment for other items, the cost trade-offs between manufacturing and logistics, and so on. The next chapter discusses manufacturing issues in more detail.

The DRP Process

Once DRP is implemented, it should become a key operating process for the firm. The process goes like this:

- Each week all the DRP tables are produced for each SKU at each DC, as we have seen in the above exhibits (for example, see Table 17-4).
- The logistics analysts will decide which planned orders will become actual orders and "lock" those in. Orders considered locked-in will not normally be changed. The lock-in period must be for at least one week if we are planning weekly but can be for several weeks. The longer the lock-in period, of course, the less quickly we can respond to changing needs. Table 17-9 shows a scenario with only the first week scheduled.
- Presuming the plant finds these latest actual shipments acceptable, they will plan to make them. Thus we can expect the 5,700 units of chicken noodle soup ordered in week 1 in Table 17-9 to arrive in week 2. The same goes for the other planned shipments. The DRP process is now complete for week 1.
- Table 17-10 shows the DRP tables computed at the beginning of the next week. Notice here that the balances on hand for each of the items differ from those projected the previous week. This is not unexpected, because the projections are all based on *forecasts.* In the case of chicken noodle, the difference is enough to shift the next required order for the soup from week 4 in Table 17-9 to week 3 in Table 17-10.

This process continues week after week, with the tables always being adjusted for the most recent information concerning demand and availability. Clearly we can automate this process more than we have shown here. The key is to identify *exceptional conditions* so that the analysts will be notified when any of those conditions arise.

Conclusions

Obviously, DRP techniques can be very helpful in improving resource productivity, as well as in enhancing inventory availability while employing the least amount of inventory possible. This section has covered the use of DRP to schedule shipping and receiving labor, and make the best use of transportation resources. Furthermore, we have seen that DRP provides a key input—*demand requirements*—to the production planning process. There remains the key issue of implementing DRP and using it in the organization.

Implementing DRP

Implementing DRP requires potential users to deal with various issues. We will only outline those here, because space does not permit a detailed examination.

- Understanding the circumstances under which DRP will be of most value to the firm
- Reviewing alternative software packages and selecting the most appropriate
- Defining the planning parameters, and preparing and maintaining the necessary databases
- Defining the process and training the people who will use the system

The remainder of this chapter discusses the key points associated with these issues.

TABLE 17-9
The First Week of the DRP Process
Columbus Distribution Center—Distribution Resource Planning

WEEK	**Jan 1**	**2**	**3**	**4**	**Feb 5**	**6**	**7**	**8**	**Mar 9**
CHICKEN NOODLE:		**Balance on Hand = 3,235**			**Q = 5,700**		**SS = 2,935**	**LT = 1**	
Forecast	1,460	1,460	1,460	1,460	1,485	1,500	1,500	1,500	1,600
Sched. Receipt	0	5,700	0	0	0	0	0	0	0
Balance on Hand	1,775	6,015	4,555	3,095	1,610	110	(1,390)	(2,890)	(4,490)
Planned Order	5,700	0	0	5,700	5,700	5,700	5,700	5,700	5,700
Actual Order	5,700								
BEEF NOODLE:		**Balance on Hand = 4,314**			**Q = 3,800**		**SS = 1,956**	**LT = 1**	
Forecast	974	974	974	974	989	1,002	1,002	1,002	1,061
Sched. Receipt	0	0	0	0	0	0	0	0	0
Balance on Hand	3,340	2,366	1,392	418	(517)	(1,573)	(2,575)	(3,577)	(4,638)
Planned Order	0	3,800	3,800	3,800	3,800	3,800	3,800	3,800	3,800
Actual Order									
VEGETABLE:		**Balance on Hand = 4,314**			**Q = 5,700**		**SS = 3,913**	**LT = 1**	
Forecast	1,948	1,948	1,948	1,948	1,980	2,003	2,003	2,003	2,123
Sched. Receipt	0	5,700	0	0	0	0	0	0	0
Balance on Hand	2,366	6,118	4,170	2,222	242	(1,761)	(3,764)	(5,767)	(7,890)
Planned Order	5,700	0	5,700	5,700	5,700	5,700	5,700	5,700	5,700
Actual Order	5,700								
MUSHROOM:		**Balance on Hand = 7,190**			**Q = 7,100**		**SS = 4,891**	**LT = 1**	
Forecast	2,435	2,435	2,435	2,435	2,475	2,504	2,504	2,504	2,653
Sched. Receipt	0	7,100	0	0	0	0	0	0	0
Balance on Hand	4,755	9,420	6,985	4,550	2,075	(430)	(2,504)	(2,504)	(2,653)
Planned Order	7,100	0	7,100	7,100	7,100	7,100	7,100	7,100	7,100
Actual Order	7,100								
TOMATO:		**Balance on Hand = 3,235**			**Q = 8,500**		**SS = 5,869**	**LT = 1**	
Forecast	2,922	2,922	2,922	2,922	2,969	3,005	3,005	3,005	3,184
Sched. Receipt	0	8,500	0	0	0	0	0	0	0
Balance on Hand	313	5,891	2,969	47	(2,922)	(3,005)	(3,005)	(3,005)	(3,184)
Planned Order	8,500	8,500	8,500	8,500	8,500	8,500	8,500	8,500	8,500
Actual Order	8,500								
TOTALS FOR ALL PRODUCTS									
To Be Received	0	27,000	0	0	0	0	0	0	0
Ordered	27,000	0	0	0	0	0	0	0	0

TABLE 17-10
The Second Week of the DRP Process
Columbus Distribution Center—Distribution Resource Planning

WEEK	Jan 2	3	4	Feb 5	6	7	8	9	Mar 10
CHICKEN NOODLE:	**Balance on Hand = 1,560**				**Q = 5,700**	**SS = 2,935**	**LT = 1**		
Forecast	1,460	1,460	1,460	1,485	1,500	1,500	1,500	1,600	1,659
Sched. Receipt	5,700	0	0	0	0	0	0	0	0
Balance on Hand	5,800	4,340	2,880	1,395	(105)	(1,605)	(3,105)	(4,705)	(6,364)
Planned Order	0	5,700	5,700	5,700	5,700	5,700	5,700	5,700	5,700
Actual Order									
BEEF NOODLE:	**Balance on Hand = 3,400**				**Q = 3,800**	**SS = 1,956**	**LT = 1**		
Forecast	974	974	974	989	1,002	1,002	1,002	1,061	1,061
Sched. Receipt	0	3,800	0	0	0	0	0	0	0
Balance on Hand	2,426	5,252	4,278	3,289	2,287	1,285	283	(778)	(1,884)
Planned Order	3,800	0	0	0	3,800	3,800	3,800	3,800	3,800
Actual Order	3,800								
VEGETABLE:	**Balance on Hand = 2,015**				**Q = 5,700**	**SS = 3,913**	**LT = 1**		
Forecast	1,948	1,948	1,948	1,980	2,003	2,003	2,003	2,123	2,212
Sched. Receipt	5,700	5,700	0	0	0	0	0	0	0
Balance on Hand	5,767	9,519	7,571	5,591	3,588	1,585	(418)	(2,541)	(4,753)
Planned Order	5,700	0	0	5,700	5,700	5,700	5,700	5,700	5,700
Actual Order	5,700								
MUSHROOM:	**Balance on Hand = 4,155**				**Q = 7,100**	**SS = 4,891**	**LT = 1**		
Forecast	2,435	2,435	2,435	2,475	2,504	2,504	2,504	2,653	2,765
Sched. Receipt	7,100	0	0	0	0	0	0	0	0
Balance on Hand	8,820	6,385	3,950	1,475	(1,029)	(2,504)	(2,504)	(2,653)	(2,765)
Planned Order	0	7,100	7,100	7,100	7,100	7,100	7,100	7,100	7,100
Actual Order									
TOMATO:	**Balance on Hand = 752**				**Q = 8,500**	**SS = 5,869**	**LT = 1**		
Forecast	2,922	2,922	2,922	2,922	2,969	3,005	3,005	3,005	3,184
Sched. Receipt	8,500	8,500	0	0	0	0	0	0	0
Balance on Hand	0	5,578	2,656	(266)	(2,969)	(3,005)	(3,005)	(3,005)	(3,184)
Planned Order	8,500	8,500	8,500	8,500	8,500	8,500	8,500	8,500	8,500
Actual Order	8,500								
TOTALS FOR ALL PRODUCTS									
To Be Received	27,000	18,000	0	0	0	0	0	0	0
Ordered	27,000	0	0	0	0	0	0	0	0

When DRP Is of Most Value

Before implementing DRP, firms should recognize that such a process can be expensive, time-consuming, and cumbersome. Managers interested only in minimizing the inventory level of an item at a specific location will find that classical reorder point theory—properly implemented with statistical safety stocks and rationally computed replenishment quantities—will do the best job. On the other hand, managers concerned about the costs of supplying that inventory and/or managers responsible for multiple levels or echelons in a supply chain will find DRP to be a good way to reduce costs and achieve interechelon coordination.[10]

The savings brought about by managing across echelons can be found in inventories, transportation, shipping and receiving, and manufacturing. In a pioneering study of DRP, Stenger and Cavinato showed that a distributor with both wholesale and retail operations could achieve significant inventory reductions at the wholesale level using a DRP approach. The old approach of forecasting wholesale shipments to the retail level using the history of past shipments forced the firm to hold a certain amount of safety stock at the DCs. When the DRP tables linked up aggregate retail forecasts with the wholesale distribution centers, DC safety stock inventories could be reduced substantially. These savings ranged from 23% for a high-volume item with a nine-day replenishment lead time to 87% for a low-volume item with a 36-day lead time.[11] The DRP process obviously greatly reduces the uncertainty faced by upstream supply points.

With regard to transportation savings, we have already seen the benefits of coordinated replenishment and the maximization of vehicle utilization possible through DRP in the examples above.[12] The additional benefit of projecting future replenishment needs, when communicated to the transportation provider, allows that provider to better plan to meet those needs—creating further efficiencies. However, if the transportation provider is not sophisticated enough to use such information to advantage, then potential benefits will not be achieved.

DRP can lead to savings in receiving or shipping labor, again because projecting shipping/receiving schedules allows for better planning of the needed resources. Obviously, this will have the greatest impact in high-volume situations. In all cases, the planning information will be of value only if the firm has the ability to use this information effectively, and is disciplined enough to follow the plan.

One of the greatest potential beneficiaries of DRP data is the manufacturing activity. As we also have seen in the examples above, DRP calculates the demand that manufacturing really needs to meet. This is of most value where the manufacturing processes are flexible, allowing shifts between products. Then manufacturing can optimize its loads while not producing excess inventories. On the other hand, where manufacturing has very little flexibility, as is the case with highly dedicated equipment that produces one product at a constant rate, then DRP information will not be of such great value.

Selecting Software

Many vendors supply software capable of doing distribution requirements planning. Software is available for almost all computer platforms—mainframes, minicomputers, and personal computers. Table 17-11 shows the number of packages available by computer platform type in 1991 and 1992, as reported by Andersen Consulting. Although close examination shows that not all of these truly do DRP in the sense described here, it is obvious that the potential user has a great deal of choice.

TABLE 17-11
DRP Software Packages by Computer Type

Computer Type	1991	1992
Mainframe	32	28
Minicomputer	62	75
Personal computer	35	46

Source: Andersen Consulting, *Logistics Software,* 1991 ed. and 1992 ed. (Oakbrook, Ill.: Council of Logistics Management, 1991 and 1992).

Much has been written about the process of selecting software, so we merely highlight the following key issues here:

- *Scope*—number of distribution echelons (levels) handled, number of facilities per echelon, number of SKUs per facility, and so on
- *Features*—forecasting, statistical safety stock calculations, minimum and maximum order quantities per SKU and logical increments in between (e.g., pallet layers), transportation load building, and so on
- *Linkages to other systems*—easy to tie into current product master files, inventory status files, production planning, accounting, and other existing systems with which the DRP system needs to relate
- *Flexibility and ease of use*—can adapt to our firm's changing needs, is easy to use, and has readable screens and user-friendly interface
- *Vendor support*—vendor offers training and other assistance for users, and frequently updates the program

Obviously any package to be purchased should offer good value relative to its purchase price and future maintenance costs. Any good vendor should help a buyer test data on the proposed system in some way to ensure that the result will be an improvement over the old way of doing things.

Because selection of the appropriate software is a very important and long-lasting decision, the potential buyer should spend a good deal of time and effort evaluating the various packages available.

Planning Parameters and Data Required

DRP systems require accurate and timely data to operate effectively, and the planning parameters need to be set and maintained carefully. This cannot be overemphasized. Without such care, the DRP system becomes bureaucratic and unacceptable for decision making. The planning parameters include lead times, safety stocks, replenishment quantities, lock-in periods, and planning horizons. When lead times are padded, the result is too much inventory and a lack of flexibility. When safety stocks are set by simple rules of thumb, some SKUs will have too much inventory and others will have frequent stockouts. Long lock-in periods cut responsiveness. Planning horizons that are too long force a lot of excess computation, but those that are too short (not projecting out a full season) may not leave enough time to plan for key future events.[13]

Key data elements that must be accurate include current inventory status by SKU by location, open and in-transit replenishment orders, SKU characteristics (physical size, units per unit load, value, etc.), characteristics of the transportation option chosen for each replenishment lane, and others specific to the situation. If these data are not accurate, the plans generated by the DRP system will not be of much value.

People Issues

No matter how automated the system, people will have to evaluate and use the result. At times they may need to override those results to deal with unanticipated events. In addition, the DRP system will be integrating several logistical activities—warehousing, inventory planning, and transportation—with the manufacturing and marketing functions. This means new processes will be put in place and people will have new roles when DRP is implemented. Therefore, any firm planning to use DRP will have to redefine the processes associated with distribution and production planning, and train people to operate in this new environment. *These key issues must not be underestimated.* Successful implementors are those who put a high priority on careful planning and on training and retraining those involved.[14]

Conclusion

This chapter has given the reader a flavor of what distribution requirements planning (DRP) can do for a firm's distribution and manufacturing operations.

DRP is a relatively simple concept, but when the powerful tools of statistical forecasting, demand planning with key customers, statistically set safety stocks, joint transportation and inventory decision making, and master production scheduling are integrated by the DRP process, major improvements can result. Properly implemented and managed, DRP can lead to better customer service and lower total logistics and manufacturing costs.

Notes

1. Readers will find it helpful to have reviewed Chapter 15.
2. Anonymous, "DRP Improves Productivity, Profit, and Service Levels," *Modern Materials Handling* (July 1985): 63–65.
3. For further discussion of this, see Mary Lou Fox, "Logistics Planning: The Supply Chain As an Integrated Process," *P & IM Review* 11, no. 7 (July 1991): 12–15. For a manufacturing orientation, see Thomas E. Vollman, William L. Berry, and D. Clay Whybark, *Manufacturing Planning and Control Systems,* 3d ed. (Homewood, Ill.: Irwin, 1992). Readers seeking a more detailed treatment of distribution resource planning might find the following book helpful: Andre Martin, *Distribution Resource Planning,* 2d ed. (Essex Junction, Vt.: Oliver Wight, 1990).
4. See Chapter 15 for more discussion on this.
5. This rule creates some excess inventory. That is, when we will just barely dip into the safety stock at the end of the week and the replenishment arrives at the beginning of the week, we have more protection than expected. One way around this is to go to daily time buckets for the first month of the schedule. Another way is to identify such situations and make those shipments later in the week. This shows the disadvantage of planning with weekly or longer time buckets.

6. For an example of this in the grocery industry, see Joseph Bonney, "LogiCNet Signs Giant Food Chain," *American Shipper* (February 1993): 28–30.
7. We never plan shipments to arrive later than the need, for to do so would be planning to use safety stocks. The safety stocks are held to protect against unforeseen problems, so we do not want to *plan* to use them. The exception comes when we absolutely have no other means to obtain the needed material.
8. The appropriate rules for production planning obviously depends on the specific technology and practices of the process being addressed.
9. Gross requirements for weeks 10, 11, and 12 (not shown) are 0, 30,800, and 0, respectively.
10. For an example of another approach, see Morris Cohen et al., "Optimizer: IBM's Multi-Echelon Inventory System for Managing Service Logistics," *Interfaces* 20, no. 1 (January-February 1990): 65–82.
11. Alan J. Stenger and Joseph L. Cavinato, "Adapting MRP to the Outbound Side—Distribution Requirements Planning," *Production-Inventory Management* 20, no. 4 (4th Quarter 1979): 1–14.
12. Admittedly, even early inventory management software like IBM's classic IMPACT package could do coordinated replenishment. However, such software remained based on reorder points and did not project future replenishments.
13. For a detailed discussion of all these issues, see Edward A. Silver and Rein Peterson, *Decision Systems for Inventory Management and Production Planning,* 2d ed. (New York: Wiley, 1985), pp. 431–53.
14. For suggested procedures in this area, see Vollman, Berry, and Whybark, *Manufacturing Planning,* and Martin, *Distribution Resource Planning.*

CHAPTER 18

Sourcing and Supplier Management

Joseph L. Cavinato

Until recently, purchasing was traditionally regarded by many companies as a mundane, stand-alone staff function. Today, it has gained new respect as a strategically important activity. This new status owes much to the realization that sourcing of components and raw materials should be viewed as an important source of cost control and competitiveness.

The new attention given to purchasing began in the mid-1970s, when such firms as chemical manufacturers experienced serious commodity shortages. In the 1980s and 1990s, sourcing decisions continued to gain importance as automotive and high-technology manufacturing firms sought new sources of competitiveness through tighter management of the supply marketplace.[1]

This chapter presents an overview of the purchasing field as it is currently practiced and as it continues to evolve. The overall management of supplier relationships is changing as purchasing takes on new and different roles for sourcing, creating, and maintaining the flow of products and services into a firm. Several factors play a part in these developments.

Increasing Demands for Cost Control, Quality, and Innovation

Sometimes purchasing is a firm's most significant logistics and product flow activity. The average manufacturing firm spends 55 to 60% of its revenue on material purchases. Capital acquisitions and operations support activities increase that figure. Firms on the high end, such as basic chemical and food firms, spend 70 to 85% of revenues on materials. On the low end, procurement may represent only 15% of revenues for companies in such industries as computers and instruments; however, in these firms, the impact of not having the right technology or not developing good relationships with the best and most competitive suppliers can have significant impacts.

Underutilized and Unrecognized Purchasing Capabilities

Senior management is awakening to the need for strong supply-side functions but often needs greater knowledge of what these functions can or should be. No longer seen as a passive, reactive function, the focus today is increasingly on new roles, skills, organization, and value-added contributions—often under the leadership of visionary managers who realize the importance of sourcing decisions.

Decreasing Functional Isolation

Purchasing must be viewed holistically, integrating the rest of the firm, suppliers, and even customers. As inbound, work-in-process, and outbound inventories decrease, the purchasing and manufacturing functions are becoming increasingly visible to customers and suppliers. For service firms, such visibility has been the norm for many years. Supply chain orientations, outsourcing, and fast product idea-to-launch cycles require procurement to be integrated in both the planning and operational flows of the firm. As many firms are discovering, purchasing can play a major role in both corporate strategy and product strategy. Purchasing can also be a major factor in product development.

Changing Nature of Markets

Traditional buying methods, approaches, and organizations are being challenged. The rapid pace of technological change, the intensifying of global competitiveness, and the need for time to be integrated into decision processes all create new imperatives for change. Purchasing activities like three bids, price taking, hierarchical approval processes, and cumbersome paperwork are thus being reconsidered in light of today's supply needs. As more and more managers are discovering, suppliers no longer fit the traditional mold of homogeneous firms hungry for business.

Scope of Supply Management

The quiet but significant evolution of purchasing is reflected in expanded roles, responsibilities, activities, and expectations by others in the firm. These changes can be seen in purchasing tasks and objectives, purchasing process trends, and new orientations in acquisition management.

Purchasing Tasks and Objectives

Many distinct activities and approaches define the contributions of purchasing in a supply role.[2]

Optimum quality: Traditionally, the purchasing department acquired items according to specifications developed and demanded by others in the firm. Today, purchasing often plays a role in actually developing those specifications based on a broad knowledge of which suppliers can meet demands for high quality and excellent service.

Lowest possible total cost: In the past, this meant "lowest price." Transportation deregulation and the introduction of integrated supply chain management concepts have shifted that focus. Now, total cost within a firm and its supply chain, as well as within competing supply chains, is central to purchasing decisions.

Developing and maintaining reliable, competitive suppliers: Assured and plentiful supplies of raw materials can no longer be assumed. In high-technology as well as other businesses requiring distinct competitive advantages, new relationships with suppliers are necessary. Many industries have therefore shifted from transaction-oriented purchasing toward relationship-oriented purchasing.

Contributing to low inventories and smooth flow: Firms cannot tolerate large inventories to feed production and act as cushions between factories and customers. Likewise, forcing suppliers to build and hold large inventories at the convenience of the firm is not always sensible. Excessive inventory buffering is detrimental to the performance of both the firm and the overall channel. High channel inventories, regardless of where they are held, incur increased capital, actual, and opportunity costs.

Cooperating and integrating with other functions: Purchasing has traditionally played a passive role, responding to other departments' requests and arranging the associated deliveries. The cycle generally started with a requisition and ended with a receiving report and invoice approval. Today, design considerations, flow efficiency, and overall materials effectiveness call for purchasing to play a strong, integrative role. At Caterpillar, for example, this integration occurs through "commodity teams" that have interdisciplinary responsibility for product and service components.

Purchasing Process Trends

The purchasing field has experienced several recent trends brought about by either changes in its tasks and objectives or new and emerging technologies.

Information Systems Replacing Paperwork

Automated purchasing began in earnest in the 1980s with the growing capabilities of computers, electronic link technology, and reliance on fewer suppliers. In some firms this process has been confined to requisitioning, often including direct purchase orders and acknowledgment linkages with key suppliers. In other firms, information systems have been expanded to pass along great amounts of detailed information like barcoded vehicle reports and statistical process control (SPC) results of forthcoming deliveries.

R&D Shifts to Suppliers

Many firms have been increasing their reliance on suppliers to provide research and development (R&D). The development of new products and technologies would otherwise be performed internally and the results specified to suppliers after the fact in orders. Such a trend requires more involvement in supplier relationships.

Outsourcing to Third Parties

To achieve time, process, and cost advantages, companies are increasingly seeking outside firms to perform activities previously conducted in-house. Such outsourcing makes sense for firms that lack the necessary economies of scale, skills, or technology to perform certain functions quickly or efficiently. Additionally, many firms seek third-party providers not because they are incapable but because they can focus on their own core competencies. Purchasing often takes the lead in creating and managing these outsourcing relationships.

Transition from Purchase Orders to Relationships

The buying strength of an entire firm can be consolidated through national agreements or partnerships that go beyond a simple, low-priced transaction typified by purchase orders (POs). This new approach requires collaborative efforts in planning, forecasting, consolidating demand, and sharing information both within the firm and with the supplier. The relationship between a firm and its supplier must be capable of being modified as prices, costs, and other factors impact either firm's business. This is a dramatic change from the individual, adversarial purchasing processes of former years. Relationship-based purchasing requires new skills, decision-making approaches, and performance measures.

New Concepts of the Acquisition Process

These changes have all expanded the scope of supply management. In years past, the "what" (product or service), "how" (lot size), and "when" (delivery date) of a purchase were determined by production, engineering, logistics, and other users in the firm. Purchasing merely carried out the process by deciding on the "who" (which supplier).

In today's environment production, engineering, purchasing, and other functions often cross traditional corporate boundaries in deciding upon the what, how, when, and who in a team approach with long-term strategic impacts in mind. Purchasing is expanding to include many new responsibilities today. The traditional, narrow definition included obtaining raw materials and supplies that others in the firm requested from it. In this way, there was little value added other than performing a mechanical task of processing paperwork and communicating with suppliers.

Figure 18-1 shows evolving concepts of the field through three views of acquisition. Buying is the narrowly defined processing of requisitions, purchase orders, and follow-up through tracing and expediting. As the figure shows, this is a newer clerical activity that begins only after purchasing receives a requisition from others in the firm.

Key contributing activities included in this scope of purchasing include selection of suppliers, buying on price, and ensuring delivery at specified dates. If involvement begins before a requisition is received (with such activities as transportation, inventories, and creating relationships with suppliers), then the function is seen as "procurement." In the broadest sense, "supply management" includes value-added activities even before the product is designed and created. There

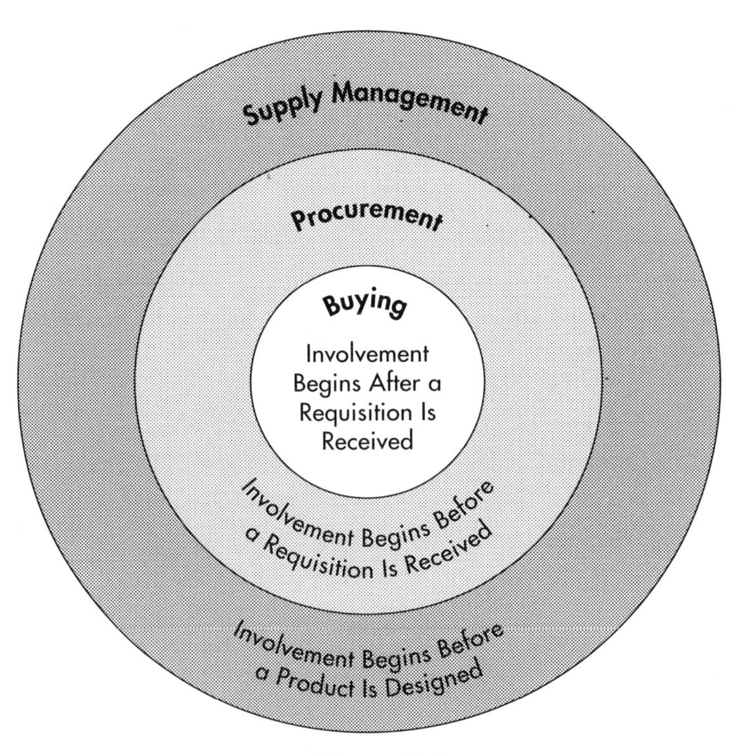

Figure 18-1
Three Views of Acquisition

are no boundaries to this scope of the field, because it includes anything that affects the firm's acquisition needs and processes. Some firms operating in such advanced ways expect purchasing to play a key role in working closely with suppliers as they try to develop new technologies. At this level, purchasing may also have profit-and-loss responsibility for managing product teams.

The Supply Process

The overall supply process is presented in Figure 18-2. This has traditionally been seen as focusing on the short term, but more recently it has been extended to longer-term macro approaches to supply management.

Short-Term Focus

Conventionally, the short-term focus on purchasing begins with a request from production or another user group in the firm ("need detection"), and it skips the make vs. buy decision to di-

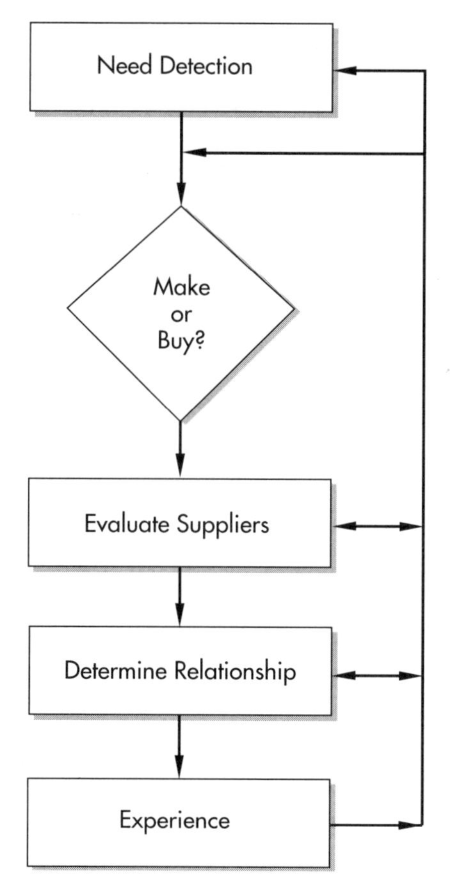

Figure 18-2
Macro Acquisition Process

rectly select previously evaluated suppliers with whom a buyer typically has long-term relationships. The selection is made either on a rotation basis or because a given supplier helped the buyer solve a past problem.

These "relationships" constitute little more than selection of a buying method that is often either an oral or written request-for-quotation (RFQ) process. The entire process is finished with a delivery. Little feedback exists except when quality or delivery is a problem, and then the complaints are handled in internal communications between production or other users and the purchasing department.

Long-Term Focus

The macro approach to purchasing involves a loop system beginning with the creation of a product or the alteration of an existing product and continuing through quality improvements and changes in supplier relationships.

Need detection focuses on defining the requirements for new or modified products or services. At this stage, the firm's own research and design functions play a major role, but the procurement department often contributes by working closely with suppliers.

The make vs. buy decision preceding the development of a new product or service typically involves three options: (1) producing completely in-house, (2) buying the completed items, or (3) outsourcing various functions, from purchasing through actual sales and marketing. Make vs. buy decisions involve costs, labor, quality, skills, capacity, supply availability and buying clout, timing, business risk, availability of capital, learning curves concerned with both costs and quality, and the desire or unwillingness to enter into that specific line of activity or business. In addition, financial factors play a role—whether to avoid or invest in personnel head count and in fixed plant and equipment. Similar factors affect outsourcing decisions, but a simple "buy or not buy" choice lacks the strategic implications of dealing with suppliers in a long-term business alliance.

Supplier evaluation can, of course, benefit from traditional research using directories, industrial registers, trade show contacts, opinions of colleagues and associates, magazine advertising, and other information-gathering methods. Factors that help reduce the number of choices in this sourcing step include buying locally or nationally, domestically or internationally, and directly from manufacturer or through distributors and third-party firms. In addition, it is important to evaluate the size of the buying firm compared with the size and capability of the selling firm, technological capability, quality performance, available transportation and logistics links, supplier ownership and owner's short- and long-term strategy for the business (a serious concern when the potential supplier is owned, for instance, by a financial leverage group), length of the relationship, and depth and balance of key management personnel.

The next step is to determine the relationship with the supplier. If it involves a joint development of technology, then a longer-term focused partnership would be useful. On the other hand, if it entails purchasing items that are widely available from many suppliers, then an arm's-length relationship is more appropriate.

A key element of this relationship is the actual buying method employed between the two firms. Types of methods are described below:

- *Request for bids (RFB):* A communication to determine whether a supplier is interested in an order and at what price. Its use is limited to situations where there are several suppliers, each has a common product that can easily be described and specified, and price is the key facet of the transaction. Disadvantages are that this method is less useful in designing a product, and it is difficult to apply where more than price is a deciding factor. Traditional purchasing departments still rely on this method exclusively.

- *Purchase orders:* The backbone of purchasing, this document is used for the largest number (but smallest overall dollar value) of transactions; it has the legal effect of an offer.
- *Purchase order drafts:* These are extensions of purchase orders that include a signed check. Upon shipment of a complete order, the supplier can detach and deposit the check. Used for many years by Kaiser Corp., these documents were useful for reducing the overhead cost of processing receiving documents, invoices, vouchers, and checks. These have been largely eliminated with the use of consolidated systems contracts and blanket agreements that provide for single billing.
- *Systems contracts and blanket agreements:* These terms loosely apply to relationships that have been set up with suppliers for consolidating volume, creating a relationship over a period of time and/or volume of goods, and for maintaining direct user-to-supplier links. The key advantages are consolidation, price, and simplification of ordering and payment. This buying method offers a useful starting point for implementing electronic data interchange (EDI).
- *Standing order:* A verbal or written communication that leads to a periodic delivery of a fixed or variable quantity of goods, this is becoming more common where suppliers are responsible for monitoring inventories inside their customers' firms and for replenishing without intervention of the buyer.
- *Consignment:* This is the placement of supplier goods inside the buyer firm. The payment for the goods occurs only after the buyer touches and uses the goods, or after the goods deteriorate or are lost or damaged. The buyer firm acts as a warehouser in a legal sense. The advantage to the buyer is instantaneous inventory availability and cash-flow benefit. The seller gains an advantage of the known quantity of sale but loses cash flow. Disputes often arise when the goods are not of adequate quality.

Still other aspects of a buy/sell relationship revolve around the documentation and information flows associated with both a purchase and relationship. The traditional documents used are as follows:

- Requisition or traveling requisition (user to purchasing)
- RFB (purchasing to prospective seller)
- Bid (seller to buyer)
- Purchase order (buyer to seller's order entry)
- Acknowledgment/confirmation (seller's order entry to buyer)
- Packing list (accompanies shipment)
- Inspection and receiving report (internal, dock, and inspection to buyer and others)
- Invoice (seller to buyer and /or accounting)
- Freight bill (carrier to traffic manager, buyer, and/or accounting)
- Bill of material (internal: user to buyer and materials)
- Shipping release (internal user direct to seller's order entry or internal production personnel)

Traditional systems involving all these documents are characterized by long administrative lead times and resulting inventory holdings. Electronic exchange of many of these documents goes far in reducing both lead times and inventories. These linkages often start internally with a requisition and extend to the purchase order or shipping release. Some firms use fax machines on the shop floor for users to order directly from suppliers' shop floors. Barcoding can go far in maintaining a clean, consistent bill of material and inventory count. This is useful in the receiving and inspection process. Invoicing and bill payment may still be late, mostly because a firm's treasury personnel hesitate to give up the benefits of float resulting from mailed checks. But this will no doubt come under examination in the near term as firms discover that processing invoices and writing checks averages between $25 and $60 per check.

The long-term, macro view of the acquisition process is taking on more importance today as companies place greater emphasis on quality in their corporate and product strategies. Shop floor experiences with deliveries (both logistics service and actual goods and services) are becoming measured and captured in forms that are useful as "report cards" in working with suppliers for immediate correction and future system improvements. The value of a statistical process control (SPC) approach is that below-standard performance can be measured and used in advance of actual shipment to halt the supply of more out-of-norm goods. In general, the procurement function is gaining greater capability to provide accurate, real-time input for identifying supply needs; choosing whether to make, buy, or outsource; evaluating suppliers; choosing the right buying method; and managing relationships with suppliers.

Contemporary Sourcing and Supplier Management

Changes in the purchasing field have brought new approaches to the objectives of quality, price, and assurance of supply. These are evolving toward proactive quality management, a shift away from price toward more comprehensive measures, and creating and managing the supply relationship.

Quality

In the past, "quality" was considered only at the design and blueprint phase and then in a post-production inspection. Today, supplier management often emphasizes strong statements of buyers' expectations of suppliers. Described below is one example of a supplier management program used by a consumer products firm.

Supplier Responsibilities

The firm's suppliers are expected to:

- Provide quality goods in a timely and reliable manner
- Utilize SPC or other control tools inside their operations, as well as require them of their suppliers
- Perform testing, gauging, and inspection with appropriate procedures to ensure control and consistency
- Verify equipment with documentation
- Consistently work toward zero defects and to verify these ongoing efforts

Supplier Categories

It is common for programs like these to classify suppliers according to certain standards. Each category attests to the attainment of consistent quality in some way, and each allows a different approach and relationship with the buyer firm. The categories may include those listed below:

Approved suppliers: Those currently dealt with and having a record of meeting certain minimal standards of acceptance

Qualified suppliers: Firms that produce goods satisfactorily and are qualified by the buyer firm's audit team. Typically the supplier has the capability to produce excellent goods and ship at a near perfect quality level, with few minor exceptions. Delivery and responsiveness are excellent. Other factors in this category include quality management (quality philosophy, technical competence, training, and reporting); test equipment calibration; manufacturing control; material status capability; and quality procurement. Also, such suppliers have caused no major quality problems during a three- or six-month period. A key facet of qualification is whether the supplier has the capability and willingness to use an on-line SPC system for goods delivered to the buyer firm.

Certified suppliers: All goods are shipped 100% fit for use each and every time. This is the level attained when all the previous criteria are successfully met. The suppliers in this category are usually given a special recognition award.

Programs like these thrust the procurement and supply personnel into line-management responsibilities. In the past, poor quality was "managed" by buyers over-requisitioning quantities and inspecting for good units; purchasing was scarcely even involved in this process. Today, procurement personnel often have prime responsibility for communicating and leading a quality program with suppliers.

Shifting Cost Paradigms

Time pressures, partnerships, and other trends are bringing traditional performance paradigms into question. Increasingly, the narrow report card measure of purchasing effectiveness, based on lowest price and price variance, is being challenged because it fails to meet a firm's strategic, long-term needs. Purchasing is increasingly being measured in terms of *total* cost, including scrap and production yields; long-term warranty costs; shipping and transportation terms; payment terms; rework and other costs associated with low quality; and external failure costs once the product is in the customer's hands.

New and more comprehensive measurements are emerging. The traditional focus on lowest price is changing as firms expand their understanding of overall costs. Transportation deregulation and a closer link between purchasing and traffic decisions have led some companies to emphasize lowest total cost. Still others are evolving toward a lowest total cost to the firm, which includes any and all cost, price, and rate factors that affect decisions of benefit to the entire firm.

Automobile alliances and supply "partnerships" of the 1980s have used another measure of lowest total cost up to the last firm in the chain, the one that sells to the final customer. This principle may be applied vertically throughout a supply chain in an effort to reduce costs along the entire flow of activities. The belief is that if the last firm gains the sale, then all firms in the channel can gain. When applied inside the supply chain, the principle holds that a firm in the middle can pass its cost savings downstream to other companies in the form of a lower price.

Another measure used in many firms with a strategic view of purchasing is "highest total value to the ultimate user." This focuses on product and service usefulness, cost-in-use, and the actual user, not the last buyer. A focus on the end user, according to this view, will lead to successful product development and sales and will drive quality, cost, and other key factors.

Contemporary approaches to measurement call for a broad view of costs transcending firm-to-firm boundaries. Such a global perspective is essential when setting up supply chain relationships and partnerships. Many cost management tactics being applied concern which firms have the (1) lowest labor cost, (2) best and most effective skills and process, (3) most capital, (4) lowest cost of capital, (5) highest tax rate, and (6) most depreciation and investment tax credits to take advantage of.[3] The presence of such factors, especially when dealing with firms across national borders, results in lower costs to the benefit of both firms in a competitive channel. This requires procurement and supply managers to have a broader understanding of "costs" and of contribution and value-added performance than in the past.

Creating and Managing the Supply Relationship

A spectrum of buyer/supplier relationships has evolved in the past two decades. Where purchasing was once confined to either passive or adversarial approaches, today an entire range of relationships is available in the acquisition process.[4] Figure 18-3 present this range of transactions and common titles.

Purchasing is passive and price-centered when goods are bought in commodity markets where quality is defined by outsiders and only the timing of a purchase can affect price. The traditional three-bid and price-driven approach to buying was common for nearly a century. However, as firms have increasingly sought more in a supply relationship—such as product modifications, delivery, and other specific needs—then a less price-driven and more cooperative type of relationship has begun to emerge.

Some of these relationships are typified by integrated supplier concepts applied by many firms. Here, the supplier provides many products and services according to long-standing agreements between its personnel and many different people inside the buying company. This integration cuts across such functions as production scheduling, logistics, and product modification. True partnerships exist when both firms seek to gain a benefit in the market at the expense of outsiders (rather than of each other). In this setting, a relationship is often created over a long term, usually around a critical product, technology, or service. This can extend to joint ventures as well.

Finally, the ultimate in close buyer/seller relationships is vertical integration, where the buy-

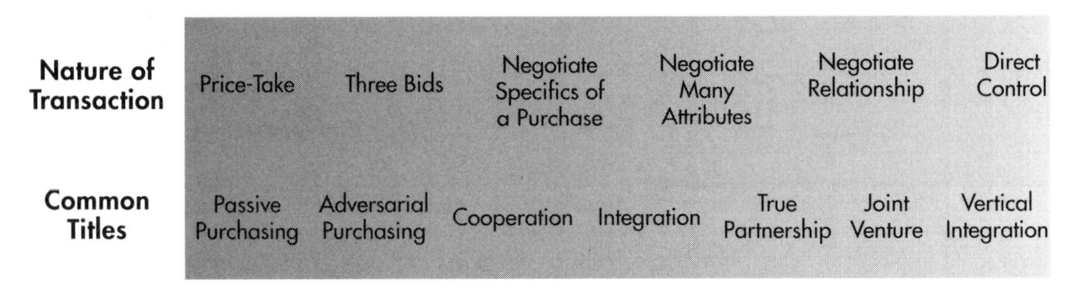

Figure 18-3
Spectrum of Buyer/Supplier Relationships

ing and selling firms are either the same or are owned by the same parent. This is not as common as it once was because many firms have sought to minimize labor power, assets, and investments.

Each of these relationships requires a different approach and different skills and relational attributes. Many successful joint ventures and partnerships are operated by teams of people from many different functions. Many of these, including outsourcing, require someone, whether in purchasing or another function, to act as a focal point in relationships between the buying firm and selling company.

In an outsourcing situation many activities and processes—such as those focusing on quality, engineering, production, design, costing, logistics, scheduling, and law—have to be coordinated. This requires external facilitation skills that are not typically found in traditional purchasing but are a necessary facet of today's supply management.

Effective Procurement Organizations

Procurement organizations traditionally have either been centralized or decentralized. In recent years other forms have evolved that pose special advantages.[5]

Centralized Procurement

Centralized procurement provides the firm with a single, collective sourcing and buying power. Typically such an approach involves a centralized logistics organization and operation. One advantage of such an organization is that the firm generally gains clout, an ability to coordinate the supply chain across the entire firm, and centralized intelligence regarding the supply market.

Decentralized Procurement

This organizational model calls for procurement to be located only at field sites. The personnel in these locations report directly to the general manager or line-of-business manager at these locations.

No centralized coordination or development of policies, other than what might be promulgated through financial or other operating policies of the firm, is present. Allied Corporation is one example of this model. It places all responsibility for procurement activities at the field locations, a policy that minimizes corporate overhead. Procurement suffers a disadvantage because it lacks managerial or operating strength to provide the group with the economies, synergism, and buying clout with suppliers and carriers that firms with centralized groups usually enjoy. In fact, research has revealed variations in pricing by suppliers and carriers to different divisions of many firms with decentralized procurement organizations. (Neither the divisions nor the overall firm had knowledge of such practices.)

One variation on the decentralized form consists of "procurement councils" based at field locations. A council consists of various local procurement personnel with similar product and service needs. They meet and coordinate a single source and acquisition as though they were a single group. Procurement and traffic councils tend to have mixed success. In some firms like Parker-Hannifin, the approach has succeeded when a senior manager is responsible for coordinating field locations that have an interest in a single product. This council then negotiates with and administers acquisitions from suppliers who "split-deliver" to Parker's various plants. Some decentralized firms utilize the same model when negotiating with carriers. In many firms, however, councils often disband because they lack leadership or senior management commitment.

Centralized Coordinator

In this approach, field procurement reports to a plant, division general manager at the local level, or strategic business unit managers but is assisted by a centralized coordinating group at corporate headquarters.

GE and United Technologies are two examples of firms using this model. GE has both a procurement and transportation group at a corporate headquarters level. The central group oversees issues of concern for the entire firm, and it seeks opportunities for the firm as a whole where individual plant site personnel might not see such a "big picture." The central groups often play a consulting role whereby they must liquidate their annual costs through sales of services to individual divisions and plants. The advantage of this model is that the firm gains the broader scope of the central group as well as the authority in dealing with suppliers and carriers, but it does not carry the complete overhead cost often found with fully centralized groups.

Area Planner

In this model, a central procurement group creates relationships with suppliers, but field production/logistics planners handle all the actual product flows. In some firms the function is called a "buyer-planner."

This system separates sourcing and vendor selection from processing the requisitions into orders for deliveries. Procurement handles the process of creating and monitoring vendor relationships. Production planners or logistics personnel handle the day-to-day orders for inbound movements, expediting, and follow-up. Transaction documentation generally follows the actual movements rather than preceding them to act as a stimulus for inbound deliveries.

This model is practiced at Kimberly-Clark and is being implemented at Lederle Labs at this writing. Procurement expertise is applied in vendor sourcing, analysis, negotiation, and selection, as well as ongoing monitoring of these raw materials acquisitions. Procurement monitors the relationship and the flow of materials on an after-the-fact basis. Procurement also steps in as the relationship manager if changes must be made in the contract or agreement, and it serves as the negotiator when this is needed.

Supply Manager

In this system, procurement (or a group that could be described as procurement) has materials management responsibility for nearly complete product lines of business. One firm in the generic pharmaceutical industry is experimenting with this approach, and a similar model is used at Galoob Toys. This method is also being applied for brand product procurement managers in wholesale, industrial distributor, and retail firms.

This approach places all supply, acquisition, materials, and production responsibilities onto one person. This manager oversees one or a few products, and his or her performance measurement is based on a contribution margin computed from sales price less costs accumulated up to the packaging end of the production line. This person has complete cost responsibility and authority along the entire chain, from suppliers to the firm's outbound delivery to the ultimate customer.

The supply manager can utilize the production facilities of the firm or use outside parties for all or part of the supply and production process. This model requires a very wide range of skills for those responsible for each product. It calls for a comprehensive knowledge of production scheduling, make vs. buy decisions, and inventory supply and cost factors. This is perhaps the broadest application and scope of what is considered as procurement or supply management: a single manager has responsibility for sourcing, materials, production, and often distribution activities as well.

Commodity Teams

This approach was originally found in construction, weapon systems, research and development, some industrial machinery, and many project-oriented settings, but it is now applied more broadly by some firms. Commodity teams adopt a full production orientation that is more expansive than a narrow sales view. They also avoid a single-function orientation. A company that has adopted this approach is Caterpillar, which has created commodity teams around critical success factors in the firm's products.

The value of the commodity-team approach lies in its comprehensive view of products, from start to finish. Instead of sequential and separate engineering, design, production engineering, procurement, materials, manufacturing, costing, distribution, and marketing input for a product, a team consisting of managers from all these areas works together on common goals. This group tends to consider the product and its success or competitive needs from the viewpoint of the customer and the customer's options. It also looks at the product from the perspective of total cost and total value.

Logistics Pipeline

The pressure for inventory velocity and near perfect customer service in the consumer products industry has led to a blended customer procurement/materials and seller distribution model involving both buying and selling firms. In this cooperative mode, logistics functions duplicated between the two firms and those that add no value are reduced and eliminated.

An illustrative case is the intertwined relationship between Procter and Gamble and Wal-Mart stores in the case of disposable diapers and other products. In this setting, the flow system from the Procter and Gamble factory to the Wal-Mart store shelf is made more efficient by eliminating the classic requisitioning, buying, order entry, and shipping processes of the two firms. The seller, Procter and Gamble, monitors the inventory of its products inside its customer's Wal-Mart stores. Responsibility for shipments, inventories, and replenishment are those of the seller.

This system offers several advantages for both parties. Several supply chain functions are eliminated or reduced; as a result, service is improved and costs for both firms are reduced. The distribution activities of one firm trigger the materials management activities of another. In a truly integrated supply chain, the buyer's procurement and seller's order entry processes can be combined. The seller's finished goods warehouse and buyer's inbound materials can also be managed as one. Transportation, handling, pricing, marking, and tagging can be more easily coordinated. Forecasting can be performed for the single "unit" instead of for two disparate organizations.

The seller gains competitive advantage in this arrangement because it can maintain a strong position inside the customer's organization. Further, the seller can usually monitor inventories of its products with closer attention and accuracy than the buying firm normally would. This greatly reduces surprise stockouts and demands for rush shipments. It also provides a competitive edge because the buying firm is less likely to switch to other brands with such a system in place. The buying firm gains the advantage of having the seller perform many of the physical and administrative processes of inventory monitoring, ordering, handling, fast throughput warehousing, and transportation.

In this system, the seller is performing many of the traditional materials and purchasing processes for the buyer. This approach offers opportunities for reducing some administrative effort and expenses of product flow between two cooperating firms.

Toward a Strategic Emphasis

Evolution of Procurement and Supply

To succeed consistently in today's marketplace, firms must synchronize purchasing and supply operations with the strategy of the firm and with variable external forces. No longer can purchasing provide merely "plain vanilla" services. For the enterprise to prosper, this critical function must transcend the methods and procedures of a decade ago. As firms adapt to ever-changing situations and move toward more proactive and strategic modes of operation, purchasing must also progress through various stages.[6]

Strategic management has been defined as "a system of corporate values, planning capabilities, or organizational responsibilities that couple strategic thinking with operational decision making at all levels and across all functional lines of authority in a corporation."[7]

In a study of 150 companies, authors Gluck, Kaufman, and Walleck determined that most companies follow a standard path in their evolution to strategic management. This path is segmented into four sequential phases: (1) basic financial planning, (2) forecast-based planning, (3) externally oriented planning, and (4) strategic management. A phase 2 orientation consists of forecasts and environmental monitoring to determine the type and size of "gap" to be bridged by the firm and organization in order to reach a desired short-term result. Phase 3 is externally oriented and typically consists of strategic business units (SBUs) that develop their own product planning. It does not facilitate corporatewide opportunities for synergies in such areas as research and development and purchasing. Concern over missed opportunities can push a firm into phase 4, strategic management. This is an effort to join strategic planning processes with operational decision making. Three factors impact a company's ability to accomplish this merger: (1) the planning framework, (2) the planning process, and (3) the corporate value system.

Research conducted at Pennsylvania State University into 142 procurement organizations in a wide range of industries uncovered purchasing operations with close parallels to the phases outlined by Gluck, Kaufman, and Walleck.[8] Table 18-1 presents facets of purchasing activities in terms of concept of the field, concept of strategy, expectations, management approaches, major activities, range of products, budgetary approach, management style, key personnel skills, and concerns.

In a phase 1 organization, the purchasing department is viewed as merely a buying service focused on lowest price. Out-of-pocket costs appear to be the major concern. The overall process is reactive and conformist in nature. A phase 2 purchasing organization, while still focused on cost minimization, will also seek cost-reduction and cost-avoidance opportunities. Quality becomes important, but most decisions are still reactive rather than proactive.

Phase 3 purchasing typically focuses on transportation, inventory, scheduling, outsourcing, and many other activities. The purpose of the group is to support a line of business, and a supply chain approach is often used. Strong planning and external activity skills are required here. In a phase 4 situation, the broad concept of supply management is applied. Little or no pur-

TABLE 18-1
Purchasing Emphases Throughout Range of Strategic Settings

Purchasing Attributes	**Stage I Basic Financial Planning**	**Stage II Forecast-Based Planning**	**Stage III Externally Oriented Planning**	**Stage IV Strategic Management**
Concept of the field	Buying	Purchasing	Procurement	Supply
Concept of "strategy"	Better price on next buy	Maintain favorable price/cost variances	Support line of business	Entrepreneurial team member
Expectation	Minimize costs	Cost minimization Cost avoidance Cost reduction Purchase for quantity	Contributions through value analysis, value engineering	Involved in product development and line of business management Line of business results
Management approach	Reactive	Reactive but plan for future	Fit department in with plans of rest of firm	Positive proactive
Major activities	Process requisitions into purchase orders and contracts	Management of the buying function Make process efficient	Fit buying cycle to the line of business product cycle	Manage commercial relationships for the firm Source for long term
Range of products	MRO items, office goods	Raw materials MRO items Office goods	Capital goods Raw materials MRO items Office goods Outsourcing management	Suggest source firms to purchase Suggest product changes in line with market opportunities and future constraints
Budgetary approach	Cost center	Cost center Planning for future	Supply chain management Shape future of department for 1 line of business or SBU	True supply management Partner in change
Management style	Clerical/reactive	Managerial forecasting	Managerial planning	Team member
Key personnel skills	Task-oriented	Some management	Managerial Strong interpersonal Strong analytical	Purchasing decisions are business decisions
Concerns	Conformance to norms, process problems	Basic managerial issues Concern with power regarding scope, back-door buying, head count, centralization, etc.	Supply chain management	Shape of function not important, results and output are the keys

chasing is actually done by people in the group but is instead the focal point of supply relationships among engineering, manufacturing, and other functions, both internally and within supplier firms.

Questions for the Future

This chapter has presented an overview of purchasing as it is evolving into supply management in today's progressive firms. No longer a static, reactive function, supply management has an opportunity to become a positive, proactive contributor to the firm's success. While purchasing approaches of the past still remain, companies will be wise to challenge the nature and management of the purchasing function in terms of several key questions:

- Is purchasing aligned with the firm's strategies, production development, and production logistics systems?
- Do purchasing personnel have the skills needed for these critical management functions?
- Is purchasing automation merely computerizing the manual processes used for the past 40 years?
- Is purchasing still focused only on buying at the lowest price, or does it look for total cost and value?
- Do top management and peer departments know the impact and significance of a quality purchasing decision?

Notes

1. This chapter is based on extensive research and field interviews by the author, including visits to over 270 firms on six continents in a broad range of industries.
2. Donald W. Dobler, David N. Burt, and Lamar Lee, Jr., *Purchasing and Materials Management* (New York: McGraw-Hill, 1990), chap. 1.
3. Joseph L. Cavinato, "Identifying Interfirm Total Cost Advantages for Supply Chain Competitiveness," *International Journal of Purchasing and Materials Management* 27, no. 4 : 10–15.
4. See, for example, Lisa M. Ellram, "Alternative Approaches to Purchasing Partnerships," paper presented at the *4th NAPM Educators' Research Symposium* held at Lehigh University (Temple, AZ: National Association of Purchasing Management, 1990).
5. Joseph L. Cavinato, "Evolving Procurement Organizations: Logistics Implications," *Journal of Business Logistics* 13, no. 1 (1991): 27–45.
6. See, for example, Michael E. Porter, *Competitive Advantage: Creating and Sustaining Superior Performance* (New York: Free Press, 1985).
7. Frederick W. Gluck, Stephen P. Kaufman, and Steven Walleck, "Strategic Management for Competitive Advantage," *Harvard Business Review,* No. 80404 (July-August 1980): 154–61.
8. Virginia T. Freeman and Joseph L. Cavinato, "Fitting Purchasing to the Strategic Firm: Frameworks, Processes, and Values," *Journal of Purchasing and Materials Management* 26, no. 1 (Winter 1990): 6–10.

CHAPTER 19

Production and Manufacturing Resource Planning in a Just-in-Time Environment

R. John Aalbregtse
Roy L. Harmon

Over the past decade, new techniques related to just-in-time (JIT) manufacturing have become widely accepted as ways to improve productivity.[1] JIT has expanded the productivity paradigm of many manufacturers beyond simply automating to improve productivity. In many cases, these techniques can provide low-cost solutions to competitiveness problems. As companies expanded their knowledge of JIT, they began to realize that process changes were required in their facilities and in their suppliers' facilities to implement small lot production and realize the true benefits of JIT. In many cases, product design changes were also required to enable many of the process changes that facilitate the movement to small lot production.

When applied to their fullest extent, JIT techniques encompass designing products for producibility, designing flexible production processes, and manufacturing to customer demand using small lot production. This chapter outlines the concepts used to achieve flexible production processes and small lot production. Although product design changes are generally beneficial in achieving the full benefits of JIT implementation, this chapter touches only briefly on that subject.

Implementation of JIT manufacturing generally requires relatively low investment and typically results in the following magnitude of performance improvement:

90%—Manufacturing lead-time reduction
90%—Work-in-process inventory reduction
90%—Lift-truck reduction
75%—Machine downtime reduction
75%—Defect reduction
50%—Plant floor space reduction
30–50%—Personnel productivity improvement

To achieve truly superior manufacturing performance, small lot production techniques need to be combined with effective product and process design. Studies have shown that improvements in product and process design can reduce product cost by as much as 40% through the elimination of nonvalue-adding processes and simplification or standardization of product components.[2]

In the past, product designers operated separately from the people who designed the production processes, and both groups worked separately from manufacturing. At each point in the development process, the designs were typically handed off to the next functional department with little communication or interaction. Today, many companies are implementing simultaneous engineering concepts that bring designers, suppliers, and manufacturing personnel together early in the development process. This promotes simpler designs and allows optimization of product cost while the designs are still on paper.

Products that are redesigned for improved producibility may still be manufactured in traditional facilities using existing equipment and infrastructure. Many of these facilities tend to be functionally organized, grouping common machines and process steps together to maximize machine utilization. Traditionally, the functional grouping of machines was believed to allow functional specialization of the workers required to set up, run, and maintain the machines. Over time, this has led to a proliferation of job classifications and increased scheduling complexity. The existing processes and equipment are generally not very flexible and may require a significant amount of time and labor to change over from one product to the next. In addition, the equipment required to produce components is usually located in many different areas within the plant, thus further reducing the flexibility and efficiency of the manufacturing processes because parts must be moved and stored in numerous areas of the plant before they are assembled. Flexible production processes are required to support small lot production and scheduling based on end-customer demand. This requires significant changes in the philosophy of how processes are designed to build in the desired flexibility.

The balance of this chapter focuses on JIT techniques related to small lot production. Broadly, these techniques fall into three categories. The first is *cellular manufacturing.* This technique groups products requiring similar processes and then designs a focused production area where the products can be manufactured from start to finish, with little intermediate storage or handling. The second is *quick changeovers.* One-touch changeovers are the ultimate goal where the change from one product to another can be accomplished with minimal downtime and a single touch by the operator. The third category is *pull scheduling.* Scheduling in a JIT environment is ideally accomplished by matching production to customer demand and producing only enough product to replenish what the customer has used or sold, rather than producing to a forecast of what the customer may require. To be effective, pull scheduling requires the product focus and process flexibility provided by cellular manufacturing and quick changeovers.

Cellular Layout to Support Small Lot Production

Ideally, customers would like to have their orders delivered shortly after placing them, because this helps improve flexibility to respond to their own customers. In reality, many factories require several weeks to produce an order. In addition, setup costs, incurred when a machine is changed from running one item to producing another, are high. As a result, production lot sizes must be relatively large. That means, for instance, when component requirements are produced in lot sizes of one month, a factory's flexibility for changing schedules is reduced.

The first step toward solving these problems is to rearrange the equipment used to machine and finish each family of manufactured items into a new layout called a "cell." Before rearrangement, the machines, processes, and workbenches used for each product family are typically located in widely separated areas of the factory, necessitating the moving of parts over great distances from one operation to another.

Cells can be arranged to permit operators to run multiple machines, especially when machine cycle times are long. In these cases, the number of machines operated by one person should increase dramatically. Savings can be even greater when simplification enables the elimination of operators through the use of low-cost, "put and place" automation.

In the past, there have been strong logical arguments in favor of functional process groupings, including those described below:

- Machines are quite complex, and each type requires significant time to master. Grouping machines of one type makes it possible to minimize the complexity of the jobs performed by specialists assigned only to this machine type.
- Some types of machines characteristically produce completed products and components. Because these so-called "one-operation-routing" machines do not need to be grouped with other machines, cells are not applicable.

Disadvantages of Functional Versus Cellular Organization

Properly designed, machine operations should be simple, primarily requiring the operator to load items to be machined and unload items when completed. There are several added costs and other disadvantages of functional versus cell organization, for example:

- Each machine requires a scheduled queue (backlog of work awaiting machining), leading to excessive work-in-process inventory and longer-than-necessary manufacturing lead time. Jobs usually travel from machine to machine in large containers, one production order or lot at a time. Subsequent steps are not carried out on the first piece in the lot until all prior operations have been completed for the last piece. Thus, although the labor performed on a single item may be seconds or minutes per piece, it may take days or weeks to process the lot through the factory.
- Different jobs that could use similar or identical setups can rarely be grouped to save setup time because of the complexity of scheduling parts with similar setups to arrive at a machine at the same time.
- Some machines do not fully use the worker's time while operations are in process.
- Each part travels several hundred feet, incurring materials handling costs that are much higher than necessary.
- Worker mobility and job satisfaction are limited by specialization.

In general, functional groupings of similar types of machines are rarely necessary; however, they continue to be applicable for one-operation–routing machines and for situations where there are virtually no families of items requiring operations on a common set of machines.

The Cell as the Fundamental Factory of the Future

In Figure 19-1, one of each type of machine required to completely process a group of parts has been grouped together in a U-form cell in the sequence in which operations are performed.

Parts machined in this cell flow continuously from one operation to the next, either one or a few at a time. Thus, the amount of time elapsed between the start of the first and last operations is approximately the same as the total machining and handling time for one piece. This differ-

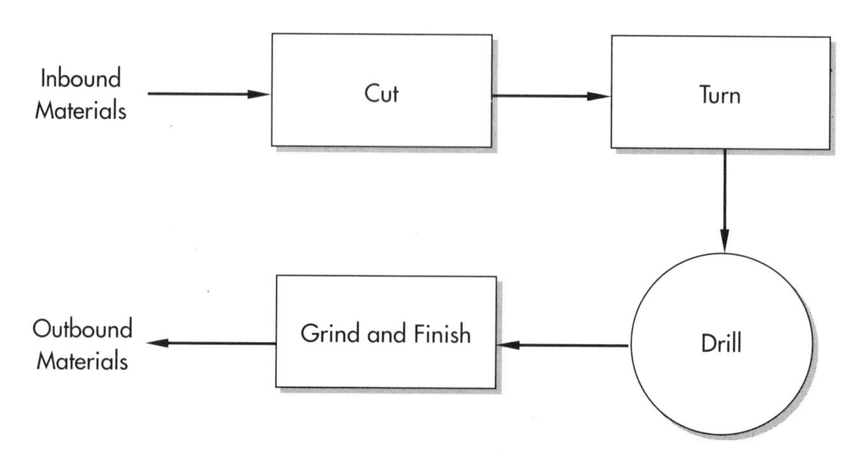

Figure 19-1
Example Cell Layout

ence—flowing production versus moving an entire lot from one operation to another—is the reason that production lead time is typically 90% lower in a cell than in a functionally organized factory.

With this organization, safety stocks of completed items and inbound queues of waiting jobs can be maintained at minimal levels. Thus, the inbound/outbound storage area of the cell is minimal. In the functional grouping of machines, there is usually one operator per machine. This results in high machine utilization but poor use of the operator's time because there is little productive work to do while the machine is cycling. In the cell grouping, the cell is most often manned with 50 to 70% fewer operators than machines. Moreover, the machines are located in close proximity to permit the operator to attend several at once with minimal wasted time and motion.

Some of the early efforts to create cells were unsuccessful because machine setup times were not reduced. As a result, larger production lots were forced through the cell, causing high inventories and longer lead times. A second reason for failure was inordinate machine downtime in the cell. When one machine broke down, all machines were stopped. For most successful cell operation, it is critical to decrease setup time and to reduce machine downtime.

In summary, some of the major benefits of the cell are:

- Large reductions in work-in-process lead time.
- Cross-training of workers to perform operations on multiple processes in the cell. This gives employees greater job satisfaction and enhances their skill base, making it easier to transfer them to other cells with similar processes.
- Cells can be run by a variable number of operators on different shifts. Thus, cell capacity has the flexibility to meet changing levels of requirements with appropriate levels of production.
- Inventory is reduced at least by the same proportion as work-in-process lead time. Because lead time is much shorter, just-in-case stock of completed items can also be drastically reduced.
- Setup times and costs are decreased by running items of similar setup needs in the same cell.
- The number of containers required and materials handling costs are substantially reduced.

Machine Utilization and Performance Standards

To comprehend machine capacity utilization in the cell, it is helpful to understand some basic facts about machine capacity, utilization, and load. It is also helpful to see the fallacy of certain myths about utilization and capacity:

- Cycle times, thus capacities of machines in a cell, can be balanced.
- Machine capacity in the factory can be fully utilized.
- Long-range machine load can be accurately or meaningfully forecast.

Why are these only myths? In many of the best factories around the world, machines are utilized at considerably less than 100%. Machine capacities of almost any factory are not and cannot be balanced in terms of every machine performing required operations for each part in the same amount of time. This is due to two basic facts: (1) different machines have different feeds and speeds, and (2) various part numbers require different processing times for each operation.

Long-range machine load cannot be forecast. Manufacturers worldwide have become increasingly aware of the impossibility of forecasting future demand. Because machine loads consist of varying loads for different products, it is even less possible to forecast future loads accurately. For this reason, most manufacturers either plan for excess capacity to meet peak demands or ration capacity to customers in periods of high demand.

These general observations hold true in most cases, but there are some rare exceptions. Some processes call for such large-scale investment in machines and equipment that profitability will require operating as close to 100% capacity as possible. Notable examples include paper, textiles, and plastic molding—in fact, most types of process manufacturing. These products require equipment that can be purchased from manufacturers who supply everyone in the same industry. Because everyone has, or can have, the same equipment, competition is usually fierce, and profit margins are extremely tight. Thus, the degree of equipment use can make the difference between profit and loss. The competitive conditions in other industries besides process manufacturing may also force companies to use equipment at near-full capacity. Industries specializing in such products as bearings, fasteners, and gaskets can be counted among the few examples. Again, such manufacturing requirements are not typical.

Many manufacturing executives, managers, and engineers spend more time than they should determining whether machines in a cell can be balanced and fully utilized. Some companies have rejected organization of machines into cells because they realize that it may result in very low individual machine utilization. However, it is typically erroneous to make such a decision before fully evaluating the following factors:

- The benefits of significantly reduced manufacturing lead time (and thus improved customer service, sales, and margins) through cell organization
- Whether or not real utilization in the cell is better or worse than in the existing factory
- Whatever demand exists or is likely to be developed for more capacity than the cell provides

The routine of developing detailed standards for every machine operation is deeply ingrained in management practice. These standards were originally developed for two purposes: (1) to spur increased productivity by providing a basis for paying incentives for production in excess of standard and evaluation of work performed versus standard, and (2) to provide a standard labor cost basis for pricing products and maintaining inventory accounts for work in process.

For motivating individuals and small groups to increase production, standard systems have produced desired results. When properly administered, they have been an effective foundation for cost and inventory accounting. These systems made sense when factories consisted of thousands of independent machine operators with no direct links to other operators or machines. In fact, when machining operations consist of large groups of independent machine operations, these systems *still* apply.

Standard systems have yielded significant benefits, but not without corresponding costs. For example, the administration of standard systems for pay, performance evaluation, standards development and maintenance, pricing, cost accounting, and inventory accounting adds a significant amount of nonvalue-added costs to manufacturing organizations. In addition, standard systems have not been well accepted by organized labor, but have been a frequent cause of poor labor relations, union grievances, and strikes. Over the years, numerous contract negotiations have focused on eliminating incentive standards. Furthermore, standards have usually been set below a reasonable pace for the average worker. This is evidenced by the fact that average production in factories covered by incentive systems is 25% higher than standard, while the pace of workers is still typically below the maximum achievable.

Superior manufacturing organizations utilizing focused subplants and cellular layouts have transformed the world of manufacturing. Worldwide, hundreds or thousands of individual operations have been replaced by far fewer "lines" of machines and/or groups of machines organized by product lines. Measuring the activities of each individual operation within a line is a waste of time because line output is limited by either the slowest worker or the one with the most amount of work to perform. If motivating incentives are to be implemented, they should be applied on a group, rather than individual, basis.

One-Touch Changeover

To support the alignment of machines into cells, flexibility is required to change over rapidly from one part to the next. When companies focus setup reduction attention on the same machine over a period of several years, they learn it is possible to reduce changeover time from double-digit to single-digit hours. Eventually, the single-digit hours can be reduced to double- or even single-digit minutes. A few companies have even achieved the ultimate objective: one-touch changeover, where the time required for changeover is near zero. No company can afford to stop work on setup reduction until it reaches this goal. The issue is not whether it is feasible, but rather what is necessary and how long it will take.

Although an unlimited number of techniques contribute to superior productivity, a few of these warrant special attention: (1) organizing small, focused subplants; (2) improving process flexibility and space utilization; and (3) reducing the time, costs, and complexity of setup or changeover. Of the three, setup reduction is the easiest, lowest-cost, and fastest type of improvement that most manufacturers can make.

Reduction of setup costs is important for three reasons:

- Production lot sizes are large when changeover cost is high; thus, inventory investment is high. When changeover cost is insignificant, it becomes possible to consider daily production of the customer requirements for each day, and to virtually eliminate inventory investment that results from large lot sizes.

- Fast, simpler changeover techniques eliminate the potential for mistakes in setting tools and fixtures. Thus, new changeover methods substantially reduce defects while eliminating the need for inspection.
- Fast changeover techniques can make additional machine capacity available. If machines are operating at or close to seven days a week, 24 hours a day, reducing changeover time may make it possible to delay purchasing new ones to gain additional capacity.

There are three types of setup operations—off-line, mainline, and unnecessary. Off-line setup operations can be performed before the machine is stopped to change over to production of the new part, for example, bringing the required raw materials, tools, and fixtures to the machine. Mainline setup operations are performed while the machine is stopped, after the last item is produced, but before production begins on a new item. Unnecessary operations include trial-and-error adjustment steps, travel time to obtain tools, and other waste-related activities.

Simply moving setup operations off-line does not justify changing lot sizes, because setup cost remains the same. There may be benefits associated with making more machine time available, however; these include cutting overtime costs and/or delaying the purchase of new machines.

Eliminating Trial and Error

Factory management often views the setup person as an artist. He or she is thought to be capable of adjusting machine settings and positioning tools without the benefit of predetermined calibration values and, indeed, without the aid of calibration scales or measurement devices. In virtually every setup, initial settings (usually brief) are followed by lengthy periods of trial-and-error runs of sample items, measurement of these parts, and additional adjustments of the settings.

As Figure 19-2 shows, the trial-and-error process usually produces defective items, which

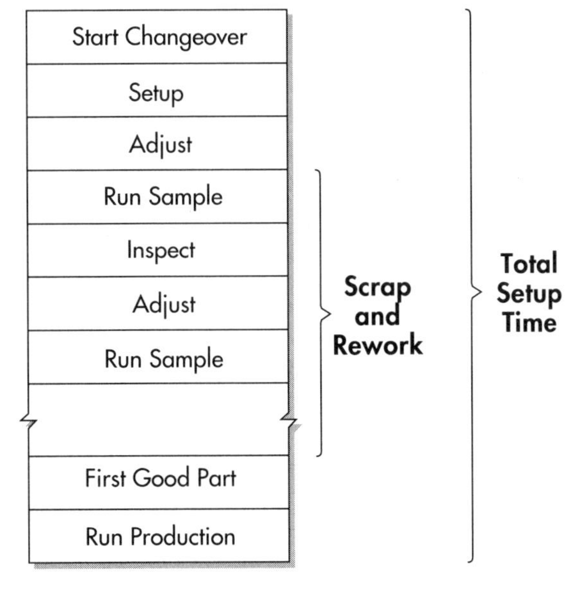

Figure 19-2
Trial-and-Error Setup

may need to be scrapped or reworked. Finally, the machinist determines that the parts meet the required specifications and produces an entire production lot. When the original measurements are wrong, all or part of the lot must be scrapped or reworked.

In Figure 19-2, note that setup time includes initial setup and subsequent trial-and-error cycles until the first acceptable part is produced. Many manufacturing personnel, when asked the length of setup time, routinely answer "two hours," yet it actually takes eight hours to produce the first satisfactory item. Their definition of setup time includes only the initial operation, not the trial-and-error adjustment cycles.

The objectives of every setup reduction effort should include eliminating trial and error. It is feasible to place machine setups and tool and fixture locations at the precise settings necessary to start production, all the while maintaining confidence that the first part produced will always be acceptable.

There is an infinite variety of ways to place machine and tooling settings at precise required positions. In many cases, calibrated scales, gauges, and meters are on the machine but are illegible because they are damaged or dirty. These devices have usually fallen into disuse or have never been used properly for reasons like the following:

- Setting specifications were never developed for each manufactured part, simply because no one took the time to document required settings.
- Because of machine variations, required settings are different for the same part produced on different machines. Thus, documentation of the settings for one machine would be helpful only when the part is produced on that particular machine. Because of the amount of work required, it would be impractical to develop and maintain data on separate settings for every machine.
- Because of play caused by wear and machine vibration, the components of a machine move, over time. As a result, machine measurement devices are often inaccurate.

Production and Resource Planning and Scheduling

After improving manufacturing flexibility and productivity through the implementation of manufacturing cells and quick changeovers, superior factories of the future need improved systems to drive production in all supplier operations in close synchronization with their customer demand. To do the best possible job, manufacturers must solve problems that have perpetually plagued them.

For example, radical swings of demands, which disrupt the entire production and distribution network, must be minimized. To do so is much easier after processes have been improved both within the factory and at suppliers. New, flexible processes reduce the pipeline lead time dramatically, making it much more feasible to increase the firmness of the schedule over the shortened lead time. When lead times in a network are reduced from one year to one month, it becomes practical to freeze either all or a major portion of remaining production lead time. Production planning systems, however, must not freeze the schedule. Exceptional swings of market demand always occur, and the superior manufacturer must be prepared to take exceptional action in response. Thus, the master schedule should be neither liquid nor frozen, but "slushy."

For two sound reasons, almost every repetitive manufacturer tries to produce to stock rather than to order. First, production lead times are too long to provide required levels of customer service. Second, major peaks and valleys in demand do not always equal the capacity for production.

To meet variations in anticipated demand, competing manufacturers could pursue the following alternative strategies: (1) produce to inventory in anticipation of peak demands, or (2) produce at peak levels when demand occurs. In most cases, the company with the plant, equipment, and management techniques necessary to produce at peak levels when the peaks occur is the superior manufacturer, in terms of minimizing product cost and meeting customer demands.

The concept of *production load leveling* has dominated most of the literature describing the ideal type of scheduling. Attempts at leveling production schedules have kept thousands of production planners busy worldwide. The primary reason behind a uniform level of production is clear and understandable: every change in capacity takes time and effort. To reduce capacity, employees must be transferred from one area to another, perhaps laid off, or assigned reduced workweeks. Equally disruptive is increasing capacity, which results in employee transfers, overtime, and hiring and training new employees. In general, even when changes in capacity are finally made, production cannot keep pace with need because of the time required to assimilate change. Additionally, managers are often reluctant to make changes simply because they require so much effort.

Companies that level schedules should examine the real costs of their policy. In the past, load leveling had a trade-off cost in inventory investment because of the difference between producing to inventory in anticipation of future demand peaks and incurring the costs of hiring and laying off personnel. There is no way to eliminate the costs of storing and financing load-leveling inventory, but the costs related to hiring and layoffs can be reduced and even eliminated by improving systems to support capacity planning and implementing changes in how work assignments are made, thus minimizing changes in the number of employees required. These improvements include the following:

- Permitting production volume to vary, within a practical limited range, without changing manpower. This means employees agree to work more slowly on some days and faster on others.
- Shifting employees from one cell to another and from one subplant to another, based on increases or decreases in demand. To minimize training and start-up production loss, manufacturers should design simpler jobs and encourage cross-training.
- Promoting sales in traditionally low-demand periods.
- Increasing overtime to meet peak periods of demand.

Superior manufacturers are those most likely to produce to the level of highest demand during the peak periods. In Figure 19-3, the demand pattern (solid line) is for sales of a product with strong seasonal demand, with peaks in April and November. The trend pattern (dotted line) shows the increased sales that can be expected in the long term, except during cyclical economic downturns.

However, there are some important points to keep in mind. Although the pattern of past demand is strong, the future forecast, for any discrete product, will be inaccurate. The further into the future the forecast, the greater the probable inaccuracy. Thus, leveling production to meet forecast demand is likely to result in producing more of some items than required and less of others. Furthermore, given a trend in demand, a completely level production schedule does not make sense. In Figure 19-3, high demand in the second year would require producing a substantial amount of inventory in the first year. The inventory investment required would usually be prohibitive. Companies must limit leveling to some short, practical planning period, because all item-level forecasts are inaccurate and almost all item demands trend either up or down.

An example of a short, practical load-leveling period would be a month or less. Leveling over

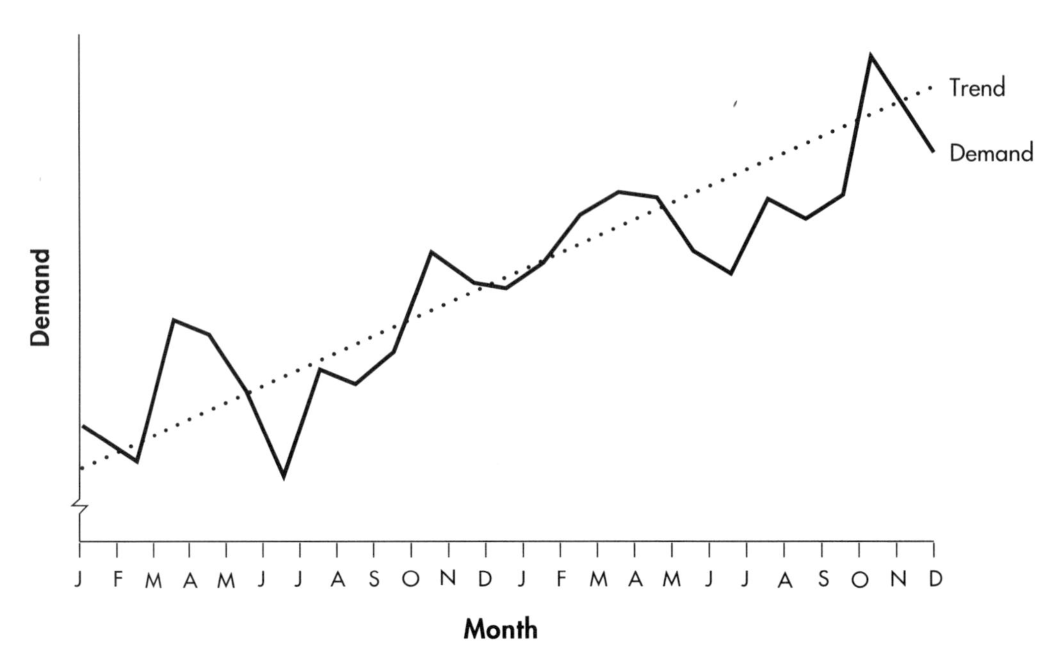

Figure 19-3
Trend/Seasonal Demand

a longer period, such as six months, usually carries penalties in terms of the inventory investment required. It is also likely that the leveled schedule cannot be maintained after two or three months because of a high probability that actual demand will differ substantially from initial forecasts.

In Figure 19-4, an example of leveling production over six months, it is not readily apparent that simply planning to produce at the average rate of demand (as indicated by the dotted lines) fails to meet peak needs in time to avoid shortages. The reason is that extra amounts produced in the first three months are less than peak demand in the last three. As a result, leveling cannot simply average production over the six-month schedule but may require producing more than the average both to level production and meet peak demands without experiencing shortages.

The frequency of peaks and valleys in production requirements is one of manufacturing management's worst problems. Most manufacturers compound their problems by producing unnecessarily large lot sizes. (Until it became clear that setup/changeover costs could be reduced, there were few alternatives to these production runs.) For most companies, running large lot sizes has meant a high level of finished goods, work-in-process, and purchased material inventories. In addition, shortages have continued to hinder meeting production schedules because some of the requirement peaks exceed normal production capacity. When production shortages are avoided, it is usually the result of either overtime work or excessively high inventory levels.

The effects of producing large lot sizes are illustrated in Figure 19-5. The end product X assembly schedule has been leveled at 10 units per day for the first 15 days of the month and 20 per day in the last. Presumably, this schedule would correspond with demand. It would be practical to meet this schedule by operating one shift through June 15, and two shifts thereafter.

Although the final assembly schedule has been leveled, converting subassembly Y to economic lot sizes results in requirements for only one of two days. The component Z of subassembly Y

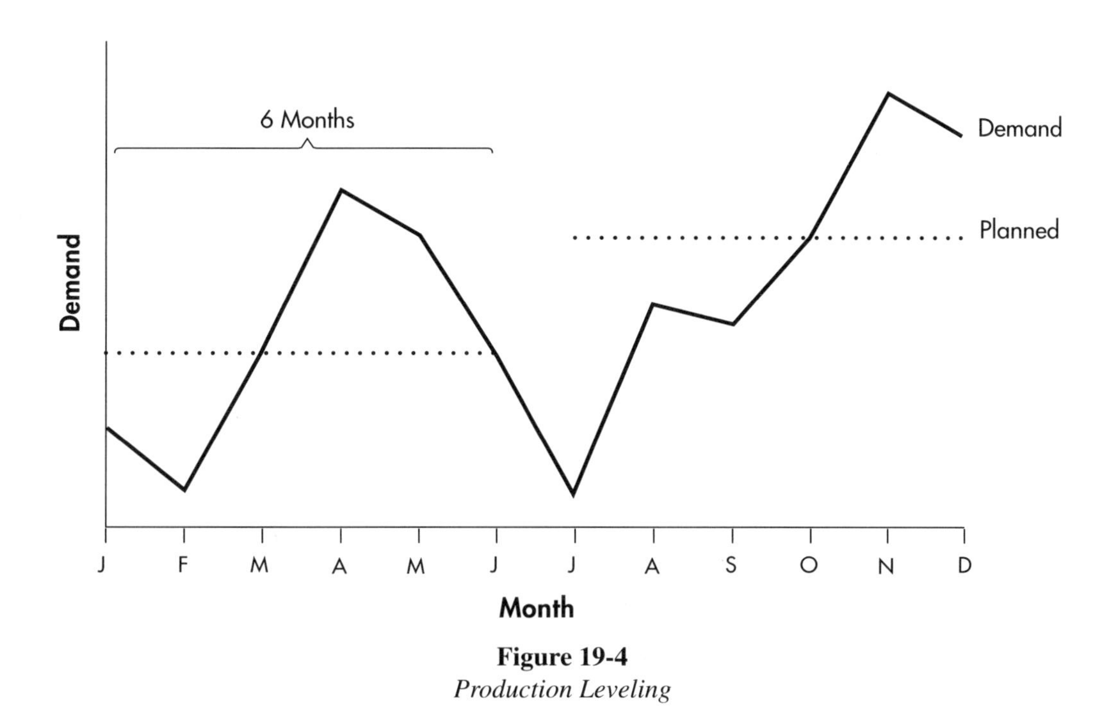

Figure 19-4
Production Leveling

has even more erratic requirements because it is lot-sized for production only one day out of four. The efforts of peak and valley lot sizing extend beyond producers to suppliers. Thus, factory production schedules that are really level will have benefits that impact the extended supply chain.

Leveling production over long periods is not practical and should be done over a shorter period. Uniform load, by half-month periods, is illustrated in Figure 19-6.

Leveling becomes possible when setup/changeover costs are reduced to the level that enables production of each item every day. The ultimate goal of most manufacturers should be to supply customer requirements from production, not from stock. This becomes feasible when total lead times are reduced, setup costs become minimal, and the range of available, flexible capacity is sufficient to meet all but the most unusual peak demands. Ideally, every manufacturer should strive to achieve a make-to-order environment.

Part Number	Description	June 13	14	15	16	17
X	End Product	10	10	10	20	20
Y	Subassembly		30		40	
Z	Component	70				80

Figure 19-5
Economic Lot Sizing

Part Number	Description	June 13	14	15	16	17
X	End Product	10	10	10	20	20
Y	Subassembly	10	10	20	20	20
Z	Component	10	20	20	20	20

Figure 19-6
Uniform Load

Production scheduling in a make-to-order environment can be accomplished by pull scheduling techniques. In Japan, as noted earlier, a card-based system called *kanban* links manufacturers to suppliers by signaling for replenishment only after a predetermined number of units has been consumed by the customer or by downstream producing operations. Similar systems are in use by superior manufacturers around the world. Although these systems operate in various ways, they generally involve two types of signals. The first signal is generated when the parts in a container are consumed and more are requested to be brought out to the producing operation. The second signal is generated when the demand for producing more of the required components has reached a predetermined level, thus signaling a changeover to begin production of the required components.

Depending on the volume and frequency of production requirements, a pull scheduling system can be operated in three different modes. For tight linkage in high-volume production environments with many different products, the system can be implemented electronically. High-volume production of a few different parts can be scheduled using a repetitive, two-card system. Low-volume or infrequent production scheduling can be accomplished with one-time production cards. One-time cards can be generated by material requirements planning (MRP) systems and are essentially a simplified production order.

Manufacturing Resource Planning

If an entire network of a factory and its suppliers convert to small lot production, their material requirements planning systems can be substantially simpler than those now needed in most factory/supplier networks. The key differences between current and superior systems are that:

- Production rate schedules (flow orders) are used in place of purchase and shop orders.
- Automatic flow order rescheduling eliminates manual review of suggested orders and order changes.
- Supplier schedules rather than orders are used to communicate requirements to factory subplants, to other company factories that supply components, and to vendors.
- Kanban support features are provided, including the ability to control an item by order (not by kanban), by kanban, or by one-time kanban.

The old-fashioned, conventional production order requires a separate authorization for each date on which an item is scheduled to be produced. If the item is scheduled for production once or many times per day, the number of orders required could be staggering. Instead of authorizing production orders separately for each day, master-scheduled items should be authorized for a daily rate of production for a specified period of time, like a month or week. This single-schedule authorization establishes a schedule for the next specified number of days and eliminates daily paperwork.

The uniform load depicted in Figure 19-6 illustrates a master-scheduled item with two different scheduled rates. It also shows how master-scheduled item requirements become the basis for lower-level needs, without distorting those requirements by planning different order quantities. This example best demonstrates how demands for the product should be converted to component requirements. In the conventional planning system, it is deemed necessary to review and approve every computer-suggested order manually—a very costly and time-consuming process. Additionally, suggested changes to previously released orders must also be reviewed to determine whether or not to modify the date and quantity manually if they do not coincide with requirements.

The reasons for manual review of computer calculations include:

- *Difficulty in locating paperwork.* Released orders have accompanying paperwork packets on the shop floor, and it would be necessary to find the shop packet to make a change. Usually, the number of orders released makes this impractical.
- *Impracticality of changing orders.* Even if orders in process could be located, it would not be practical to change their quantities, because they are produced in lots, one operation at a time. Thus, increasing an order from 100 to 150 pieces could require several operations on the 50 additional pieces until they catch up with the original 100. Conversely, cutting the quantity of an order already completed through several operations results in inventory of partially completed items.
- *Skepticism.* Some planners fear that the computer-calculated action may be inaccurate or not as current as the knowledge of the person performing the review.

In the superior factory, flow-order items are produced continuously, one part at a time, and not in lots. Moreover, the shop packet is eliminated. As a result, schedules of these items can be changed at any time without modifying anything more than the scheduled rate of production. If errors occur in the new focused factory, shop personnel are much better equipped to detect and correct them than the inventory analyst. The person on the floor sees actual components and materials. By contrast, the computer inventory analyst peers at abstract numbers on a display screen.

A diagram of both conventional and superior material requirements planning systems will further clarify the differences. The typical order flow of conventional systems is shown in Figure 19-7.

When the production planner updates master schedules at a computer terminal, the material requirements planning system then displays suggested actions to the inventory controller. The inventory controller, in turn, updates the indicated orders by changing, adding, or deleting them. Next, the system displays the updated actions to the buyer, who selects a vendor and/or changes, adds, or deletes orders. Finally, the computer system issues purchase orders, usually one per item requested, to be mailed to the suppliers. This process often takes a minimum of several days.

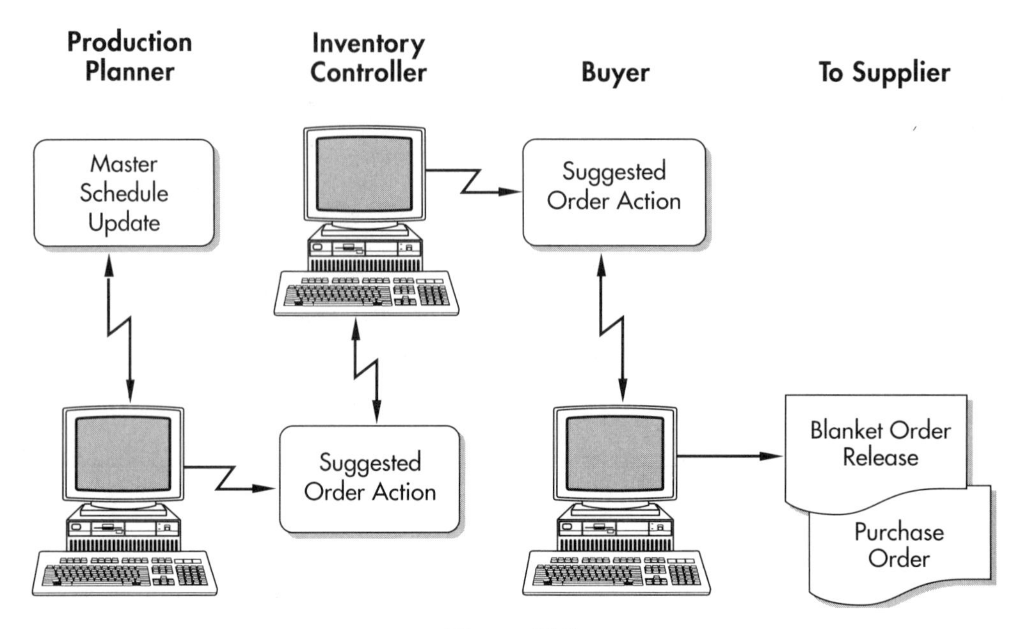

Figure 19-7
Typical Order Flow

In more modern schedule communication, depicted in Figure 19-8, the production planner also updates the master schedule.

Using rate-oriented scheduling in which both start and finish dates of the scheduling period and the rate of production are factored, the production planner needs substantially less work to maintain the schedule. Manual overrides of the computer system are eliminated. Schedules of manufactured and purchased components and materials required to support the master schedule are delivered directly to each supplier. In some cases, requirements are transferred from computer to computer via electronic data interchange (EDI); in others, by magnetic media; and in still others, by printed document.

In the diagram, the time elapsed between master schedule updates and availability of new schedules is only a few hours or perhaps a day. The supplier schedule, for one or more items, is detailed by day for short-term requirements, and by week and month for longer-term needs.

Multiplant Systems

Most assembled-product manufacturers rely on a network of supply sources. A basic converter of ore, chemicals, or other raw materials, for example, supplies cast, rolled, extruded, or ingot products to other manufacturers.

Thus, first-level (or uncut) products are converted by second-level suppliers into components. In turn, these components may be supplied to third-, fourth-, and fifth-level subassemblers and assemblers until, finally, one producer performs the final assembly operation. Some levels in the chain may be outside suppliers; others may be company-owned. Transmission of the latest requirements from the end product, through all levels of the supply network, to the

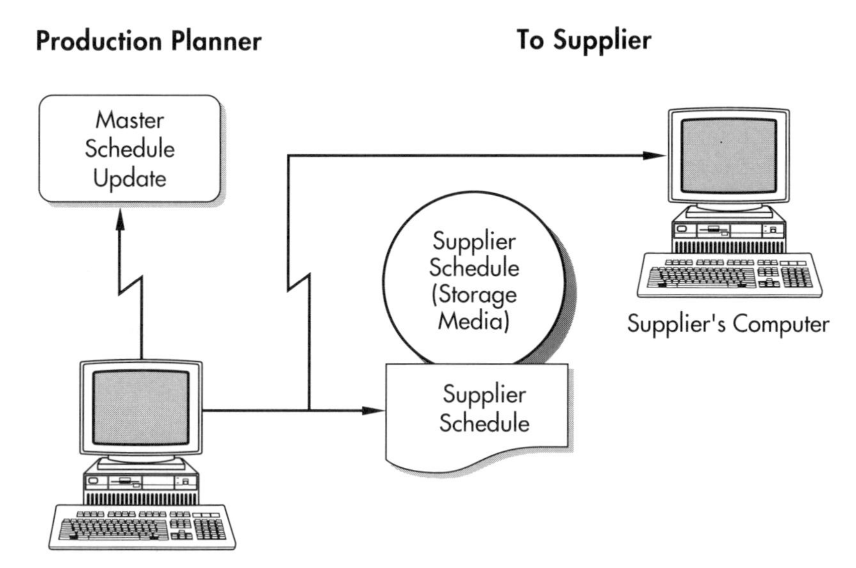

Figure 19-8
Modern Schedule Communication

first-level converter may take several weeks or even months. Consequently, it is that long before any action is taken to produce new or increased component requirements at any level in the chain of suppliers.

Such long delays in communication may cause two problems. First, the suppliers in the chain, working hard to meet the most recent schedule, often produce items no longer required or needed later than originally planned. This means they are not manufacturing other, more urgent components. Second, when the latest requirements become available, the pipeline is clogged with items in process that are no longer needed but usually continue to flow, delaying production of more urgent parts.

The ultimate solution to these problems is to turn the supply "chain" into a "pipeline." This can best be accomplished either by the design of a single system that simultaneously updates requirements at all levels of the chain or by linking all supplier systems in the chain, level by level, with rapid-response systems capable of receiving, processing, and passing current requirements to the next level in the chain. Such systems can reduce the time needed to pass requirements through the chain from weeks to a few days. When requirements are broadcast to the chain almost instantaneously, the chain can be transformed into a pipeline. Every supplier in the chain can simultaneously open its valves wider for some items and reduce the flow for others. Once this is achieved, lead time decreases drastically. When all valves in the pipeline are adjusted simultaneously, response to the latest requirements can be almost immediate.

In Japan, leading manufacturers like Yamaha, Toyota, and their major suppliers have been using multiplant computer systems for years to schedule all levels of the network simultaneously. They have learned to cut lead time through the network from months to days by taking all excess inventory out of the pipeline and using multiplant requirements systems. For example, the maximum lead time at Yamaha Motors has been reduced to 20 workdays. This is the total production time, from stocks of iron ore to shipping of motorcycles.

Summary

Several new techniques have entered the manufacturing arena over the past decade. These techniques have significant potential to reduce the overall length of—and delays through—the logistics pipeline as manufacturers are able to improve flexibility and respond to direct customer demand.

At the same time, the techniques provide the capability to reduce inventory levels, improve product quality, and increase customer service levels. Small lot production is at the heart of these changes, but the conversion to small lot production requires changes in many of the business processes and systems in use today. Building an understanding of the fundamental concepts behind these new techniques and how they should be applied at each level in the supply chain provides the key to achieving the full benefits of a just-in-time environment.

Notes

1. Portions of this chapter are excerpts from Roy L. Harmon, and Leroy D. Peterson, *Reinventing the Factory: Productivity Breakthroughs in Manufacturing Today* and *Reinventing the Factory II: Managing the World Class Factory* (New York: Free Press, 1990 and 1992, respectively).
2. Andersen Consulting studies of discrete manufacturers, 1988–1990.

CHAPTER 20

Packaging

Diana Twede

Packaging has a significant impact on the cost and productivity of logistical systems. Packing operations and the purchase and disposal of packaging materials are among the most obvious cost sources. However, because purchase and disposal costs are borne by firms on opposite ends of a distribution channel, and because the productivity effects permeate a logistical system, packaging-related costs are often overlooked and underestimated. Few firms manage packaging with a systematic approach.

Packaging affects the cost of every logistical activity. Transport and storage costs are directly related to the size and density of packages. Handling cost depends on unit loading techniques. Inventory control depends on the accuracy of manual or automatic identification systems. Customer service depends on the protection afforded to products as well as the cost to unpack and discard packing materials. And the packaging postponement/speculation decision affects the cost of the entire logistical system. For these reasons, an integrated approach to packaging can yield dramatic savings.

Packaging is generally categorized into two types: *consumer* and *logistical.* Consumer packaging (what consumers take home) is governed by sales and marketing concerns. Logistical packaging, on the other hand, is what facilitates product flow during manufacturing, shipping, handling, and storage. Logistical packaging includes shipping containers for consumer goods (which are almost always also in consumer packages), industrial packaging for production-related materials ranging from automobile parts to food ingredients, and institutional packages. There is also a packaging aspect to vehicle loading and unloading, as well as to intermodal containerization. Every factory and/or logistical operation receives and ships logistical packaging; most operations unpack, reconfigure, and repack products, as well as purchase and dispose of packaging materials.

This chapter provides a functional framework for diagnosing logistical packaging problems and identifying packaging opportunities. It is organized into the following four parts and ends with a list of references and sources of further information:

1. Logistical packaging functions and packaging performance measurement
2. Common and innovative logistical packaging forms
3. Typical packaging problems and recommended solutions
4. The general process for adopting innovative packaging

Packaging Functions

The functions of packaging are to provide *protection, utility,* and *communication.* In one sense, a package *is* its functions. Logistical packaging provides no great value of its own but adds value only as it functions in a logistical system.

Protection

The amount of protection that a package must provide depends on the characteristics of the product and conditions in the logistical system. The relationship can be conceptualized thus:

Product Characteristics + Logistical Hazards = Package Protection

The relevant *product characteristics* are those that can be damaged during distribution. Examples include the propensity of food to deteriorate because of improper temperature, oxygen, or moisture; the tendency for furniture to abrade during transit because of vehicle vibration; and the fragility of glass and electronic equipment, which easily breaks when dropped during handling.

The *hazards* of a logistical system depend on the types of transportation, storage, and handling used. For example, full truckload (TL) transportation generally causes less damage than less-than-truckload (LTL) transportation. In LTL, packages are handled repeatedly during transloading operations and have many more chances to be dropped or loaded beneath/beside damaging cargo. Railroad shipments often incur damage because of switching and coupling operations.

In general, protection from moisture and oxidation is accomplished by using barrier materials that keep water and water vapor, oxygen, and other destructive contaminants away from the product. Shelf life can be lengthened by the use of barrier materials and/or controlling the atmosphere inside food packages. Temperature protection requires insulated containers.

Impact protection can be provided by cushions for shock-sensitive products. Preventing impact from bursting a package wall requires improving the wall's tensile strength and puncture resistance. To prevent products from shifting during railroad switching and coupling impacts, loads are blocked and braced with wood to the boxcar floor. Vibration/abrasion protection often requires changing package surface or spring-mass characteristics. For stacking, compression strength may need to be added to package walls. One basic way to improve protection against impacts, vibration, and compression is to pack products tightly so there is no room to rattle and less reliance on box walls for stacking strength.

The relative protectiveness of alternative packaging systems can be evaluated and compared in laboratory and field tests. Standardized tests are available from several sources, such as the American Society for Testing and Materials, and can be used to develop more specialized tests to evaluate specific properties. For example, different methods to seal a multiwall paper bag can be compared in the laboratory by subjecting filled bags to impact tests. The best tests target the package's specific damage characteristics (e.g., do bag ends burst during side drops?) and provide a measure of the difference between alternative packages' performance (e.g., how much energy is required to burst?) rather than reporting on simple pass/fail criteria.

The more susceptible a product is to damage, and the more hazardous the logistical system's operations, the more packaging protection is required. It is important to note, however, that the amount of packaging protection is not directly related to the cost of packaging. In most cases, it is possible to improve protection *and* reduce packaging cost at the same time simply by choosing the most appropriate materials and methods. For example, the U.S. Food for Peace program has reduced the number of paper plies in multiwall bags *and* improved protection simply by changing the bag-sealing method.[1]

In many cases, it costs much less to reduce the hazards than to "improve" the packaging. Examples include:

- The use of refrigerated transportation and storage to protect fresh produce and minimize packaging insulation
- The use of storage racks in warehouses to reduce the need for compression strength in boxes and to improve cube utilization
- Good sanitation practices during distribution to reduce the need for packaging that prevents vermin infestation

In other cases, the lowest-cost solution is to design products to survive shipment.[2] Product design changes range from reducing fruit bruising through genetic modification to improving the impact resistance of an electronic product's circuit board fasteners. An impact-resistant electronic product requires little cushioning, minimizes cube in transit, generates little packaging waste and is more reliable in use than a fragile product.

Packaging must also protect people in the logistical system from injury and accidents. Packaging protects people from the contents of packages, such as hazardous materials. It can protect workers from injuries due to routine lifting and can prevent materials handling accidents.

Utility

The utility function of packaging relates to how packaging affects the productivity and efficiency of logistical operations. All logistical operations are affected by packaging utility, from truck loading and warehouse order picking productivity to transportation and storage cube utilization. Productivity is the ratio of real output to real input:

$$\text{Productivity} = \text{Number of Packages Output} \div \text{Logistics Input}$$

Logistical productivity is the ratio of the output of a logistical activity (like loading a truck) to the input (like required labor and forklift time). Most logistical productivity studies center around making the input work harder. But packaging unitization and size reduction initiatives easily increase the *output* of logistical activities.

Almost all logistical activity outputs are described in terms of number of packages. Some examples include number of cartons loaded per hour into a trailer, number of packages picked per hour at a distribution center, and cube utilization (number of packages that fit into a cubic foot of vehicle or warehouse).[3] For these reasons, palletization/unitization improves the productivity of most handling operations, and packing products in order quantities improves warehouse order picking operations. Unitization generally includes the pallets or slipsheets as a base and stretch film or between-package adhesive to hold the units together.

Cube utilization can be improved by reducing package size. Package size can be reduced by concentrating products (e.g., orange juice and fabric softener) or by eliminating air inside packages by shipping items unassembled, nested, and with minimal dunnage. In most cases, dunnage materials (like polystyrene foam "peanuts") can be minimized simply by reducing box size. IKEA, the Swedish retailer of unassembled furniture, emphasizes cube minimization to the point that it even ships pillows vacuum-packed. IKEA uses the cube minimization packaging strategy to compete successfully in the United States, even though it ships from Sweden.

Some experts believe that improving cube utilization offers packaging's greatest opportunity, and they predict that, in general, packaging cube can be reduced by 50%, doubling transportation efficiency.[4]

Cube minimization is most important for lightweight products (like assembled furniture), which "cube out" a transport vehicle far below its weight limit. On the other hand, heavy products (liquid in glass bottles) "weigh out" a transport vehicle before it is filled. Weight can be reduced by changing the product or the package. For example, substituting plastic bottles for glass significantly increases the number of bottles that can be transported in a trailer.

Communication

The function of communication is becoming more important for logistical packaging as logistical management information systems become more comprehensive. For all practical purposes, the package symbolizes the product throughout logistical channels. Correct identification of stock-keeping units (including name, brand, size, color, etc.), counting, special shipping instructions (e.g., "hazardous"), and address represent critical data. International shipments require the language of origin, destination, and intermediate stops, as well as international markings for handling instructions.

While modern barcoding highlights the communication function, even manually read packaging must be clearly legible to interface with logistical management information systems. Workers must be able to recognize a package quickly from its label. Inventory control, shipping and receiving, order picking, sorting, tracking—almost every logistical activity entails reading the package and recording/changing its status in an information system. Automatic identification technologies like barcoding and radio frequency identification allow a systems approach to managing logistical information where every input is standardized and errors are reduced.[5]

Performance Specifications for Packaging

The functions of packaging—protection, utility, and communication—are the basis for packaging performance specifications that outline what the package must do (for example, survive an impact). The specification of performance guides packaging changes that add value and reduce costs.

Many firms and government agencies have adopted packaging performance specifications. For example, the U.S. Department of Transportation has replaced hazardous materials packaging specifications with performance standards that do not specify material but do specify tests (e.g., impact, permeability, or compatibility tests) for specific product/package/hazard conditions. In another example, the U.S. Department of Agriculture (USDA) backs up its packaging material specifications for government food aid with performance specifications. If a supplier seeks USDA approval for a new package, tests are prescribed and the new package is judged for protection, utility, and communication acceptability.

Performance specifications encourage innovation, and innovation usually results in lower packaging costs. By adopting performance specifications, the USDA has saved millions of dollars per year over a more rigid system of materials specifications.[6] Materials specifications are necessary, of course, for routine packaging purchases, but adding a performance specification offers two benefits: (1) a firm that examines its current and expected levels of packaging performance will always uncover opportunities to cut packaging-related costs, and (2) suppliers invited to compete on a performance basis will always suggest lower-cost packaging solutions.[7]

Logistical Packaging Forms

Since the early 1900s, common carriers in the United States have undertaken to "regulate" the packages they transport. The American Association of Railroads and the American Trucking Association publish packaging material "requirements" in their freight classification books (National Classification Board of the American Trucking Association, and Uniform Classification Committee of the Western Railroad Association, the "Classifications"). Most of the requirements have been developed with the help of the Fiber Box Association (or its predecessors) and use more corrugated fiberboard material than is generally required for adequate performance.

The justification for these "cardboard rules" has been that carriers are financially responsible for in-transit damage. One of the carriers' common-law defenses is "an act of the shipper," including insufficient packaging. Carriers have tried to maintain that only the packages conforming to the Classifications standards are "sufficient."

These requirements have traditionally been a barrier to packaging innovation. The packaging materials specified have not changed much since the early 1900s, and every "new" type of proposed package is subject to a lengthy approval process. The existence of the cardboard rules caused many firms to make logistical packaging simply a purchasing responsibility, rather than an area for proactive management.[8]

But the barrier has fallen. Since 1980, carriers have exercised much less control over logistical packaging. After all, carriers are responsible only for in-transit damage, and the classification packages are not necessarily even the most protective.

The channel members who buy, own, and sell products have a much greater stake in preventing damage and controlling other packaging-related costs than do carriers. The underlying logic of integrated logistics management is this ability to control such systemwide costs. Furthermore, since transportation deregulation in 1980, less freight is subject to common carriers' packaging rules because much less freight pricing is governed by the Classifications and more contracts are negotiated. More freight is shipped by truckload, never handled by the carriers' workers, and therefore is not subject to much abuse in transit. Today, the Classifications' cardboard rules apply only to LTL common carrier freight. Even LTL carriers accept packaging outside the rules if it is certified as passing a series of performance tests established by the National Safe Transit Association.

This loosening of "rules" has triggered a new interest in logistical packaging. Shippers are questioning traditional packaging materials and forms and are experimenting with new, less costly packaging systems. For example, some appliance shippers have reduced the cost of their packaging by as much as 50% by replacing corrugated fiberboard with film-based (shrink- or stretch-wrap) packaging systems. Some furniture manufacturers have reduced their packaging purchase and disposal costs to almost nothing by utilizing "blanket wrap" (moving van) trucking service.

Most of the new packaging systems are simple variations of traditional packaging forms, using traditional materials in new and innovative ways. The common logistical packaging materials and forms include:

- Wood pallets, crates, blocking and bracing
- Corrugated fiberboard boxes, dividers, inserts and dunnage
- Solid fiberboard slipsheets and boxes
- Multiwall paper bags and drums
- Steel cans, pails, drums, and straps
- Steel racks and cages

- Fabric (burlap and woven plastic) bags and blankets
- Low-density plastic film shrink-wrap, stretch-wrap, bags, and barriers
- High-density plastic boxes, slipsheets, and pallets
- Plastic strapping
- Plastic foam cushioning and dunnage for fragile or irregular shapes

Descriptions, properties, performance parameters, and specifications of each of these materials is beyond the scope of this chapter.[9]

The balance of this part of the chapter explores, in more detail, six current trends in logistical packaging forms: film-based packaging, blanket wrapping, returnable containers, intermediate bulk containers, slipsheets, and pallet pools. Some of these trends are simply a new variation of an old concept. But they all have two things in common: (1) they are tailored to perform for specific products and logistical systems, and (2) they minimize packaging purchase and solid waste disposal costs.

Current Trends in Logistical Packaging

Film-Based Packaging

Film-based packaging uses flexible packaging to replace rigid (generally corrugated fiberboard) boxes. Although shrink- and stretch-film systems have long been used to stabilize unit loads, they are currently being used to form shipping cases for consumer packages like cans and bottles, furniture, appliances, and small vehicles. Most of these packages also involve rigid parts: cans are shrink-wrapped into a corrugated fiberboard tray, plastic bottle trays have corner support for stacking, filing cabinets have corrugated corner protection against nicks, and appliances have panel protection on two sides to facilitate clamp handling.

Flexible packaging offers several advantages over rigid packaging. Most film-based systems are much less expensive than corrugated boxes. They are automatic, which is an important advantage in industries like furniture manufacturing, where products have been manually boxed. There is also a standardization benefit: rather than keeping stocks of various-sized boxes to fit various-sized products, one roll of film fits all configurations. An added inventory benefit is the reduction of necessary storage space, since film rolls are much smaller than palletloads of empty boxes. Furthermore, less trash is generated when the product is unpacked. Film-based packages minimize weight and cube because the package is never much larger than its contents. Last, but for some shippers most important, is the benefit of reduced damage. Because the product is not concealed, neither is damage, and damaged products are not shipped farther. Workers handle freight more carefully when they see the product through a clear package. In most cases, the more fragile the package looks, the more carefully it is handled.

Film-based packaging is best for strong products that can bear a topload, because the package walls provide no compression strength for stacking. Most applicable products are square—a filing cabinet, an array of cans or bottles, a furnace—or round, like insulation rolls. For irregularly shaped products like chairs, finding a film-based solution is more difficult.

Blanket Wrapping

Blanket wrapping is the traditional form of packaging for household goods shipped by moving van. It is an ideal method for packaging irregularly shaped products like chairs because the uncartoned chairs can be nested. Product surfaces are protected by blankets and stacked; decking is erected with plywood and bars that lock into the trailer walls. Blanket wrapping can double the number of chairs shipped in a trailer, compared with packaging chairs in corrugated fiberboard boxes.

Commercial uncartoned transportation is a premium service offered primarily as a division of some household goods carriers. The carrier owns and manages the packaging system (clean blankets, strapping, plywood, and decking materials) and ensures that the shipper has enough. Trailers are loaded by trained workers directly accountable for preventing damage.

Blanket wrapping is best for large products that are relatively rugged and shipped in truckloads. Some examples include sofas, laboratory equipment, restaurant furnishings, store fixtures, and office furniture.

The benefits of uncartoned shipping are that there is no packaging to purchase, transportation cube is minimized, products are easier to unpack, and nothing is left to discard. Institutional furniture, which is often shipped in multiple-trailer load quantities to furnish a new building, is an ideal application. The disposal benefit is especially important when the building is in downtown Manhattan, for example, where the disposal cost for corrugated boxes is almost as high as their purchase price. Blanket wrapping increases some costs, adding a premium for transportation and the need for careful manual trailer loading and unloading.

Returnable Containers

Returnable containers have always been used for some products in some logistical systems. Automobile manufacturers have always used returnable racks for interplant shipment of auto body parts; chemical companies have always reused steel drums; and locally produced beverages have been sold in returnable bottles. There is a trend, however, to more returnable/reusable packaging for products like assembly parts, ingredients, and snack chips, and totes for transportation from wholesale warehouse to retail store and intraplant shipments.

The growing list of applications all have one thing in common: a short, vertical marketing system. A vertical marketing system (as contrasted to a free-flow marketing system) is one in which the primary participants both acknowledge and desire interdependence. Channel members are integrated by corporate ownership, contracts, or administration under the control of a single firm.[10]

A vertical marketing system is important because of the need to control container movement. All partners in a returnable system must cooperate to maximize container use, and an explicit relationship is required for coordination and control. Otherwise, containers are easily lost, misplaced, or forgotten in the back corners of warehouses. Alternatively, deposit systems may be necessary in free-flow marketing systems (groceries), where channel members are linked only by transactions. Deposit systems have been used for beverage bottles, pallets, and steel drums.

The shipment cycle should be short, in terms of time and space, to minimize the investment in the container "fleet" and to minimize return transportation costs. The size of the investment depends on the number of days in the cycle, volume per cycle, and the capacity and cost of each container.

The decision to invest in a returnable packaging system is a very different task from the decision to purchase expendable containers. One must consider the explicit relevant costs—purchase cost and return transport cost—versus the purchase and disposal cost of expendables. Intangible benefits like improved factory housekeeping, improved ergonomics, and decreased damage are often considered. There may be several unexpected costs, including sorting, tracking, reconditioning, and cleaning. Most financial analysis of returnable systems has been limited to "payback period" justification rather than net present value calculations, which would demonstrate the strategic benefits and profit potential of a returnable packaging system investment.

The automobile assembly industry has undertaken a massive conversion to returnable containers using various decision criteria. Some assembly plants have converted completely to returnables, especially where pallet disposal is prohibited. Other plants require strict cost justification for each converted stock-keeping unit. The investment can be enormous (it is estimated that General Motors's investment in returnable containers equals its assets in two factories).

Some automakers require that their suppliers purchase the containers. The materials vary; most are high-density plastic boxes or wire cages. Sometimes dunnage is returned, or it is discarded if the boxes are interchangeable. Sizes are modular, fractions of palletload size. Some containers nest or knock down; most are shipped back empty in truckload quantities. Many carriers offer a discount for return container transport. The Automobile Industry Action Group has developed an electronic data interchange standard for controlling the movement of containers. Initially, many parts suppliers resisted the change to returnables they were required to rebate the cost of the expendable package in their piece price), but the containers have now become so popular that third- and fourth-tier (subassembly) suppliers have adopted them.

Most reusable packages are steel or plastic, but some firms reuse corrugated fiberboard boxes. Many spare parts distribution centers, for example, reuse inbound bulk shippers for outbound picked orders. Frito-Lay salespeople deliver chips to stores, knock down the corrugated fiberboard boxes, and take them back to the bakery for reuse. Some pallet boxes are reused. There are also flexible reusable systems, including blanket wrapping and intermediate bulk containers like bulk bags.

Intermediate Bulk Containers

Intermediate bulk containers (IBC) are used for granular and liquid products shipped in intermediate quantities (smaller than tankcars and larger than bags or drums). Bulk bags and boxes are the most typical intermediate bulk containers. Bulk bags are made from woven plastic with a liner barrier and carry one to two tons. Bulk boxes (sometimes called "Gaylords") are usually pallet-size and lined with a plastic bag. Typical products are resin pellets, food ingredients, and adhesives. IBCs for wet products also require a rigid box or cage. Most components of IBCs are reused.

Slipsheets and Pallet Pools

Slipsheets and pallet pools have been developed to overcome traditional problems with disposable and exchange pallets. Although palletization has been packaging's greatest contributor to logistical productivity, it has also been a source of damage and high purchase and disposal costs.

Most pallets in the United States are either one-way disposables or standardized (40" × 48" Grocery Manufacturers Association standard) and exchanged. In exchange systems, consignees like food warehouses receive loads on pallets and return an equal number of used pallets to the truck driver; when the driver picks up the next load, the empty pallets are again exchanged, for full ones. Disposable pallets are generally much less sturdy than reusable ones but are still relatively expensive to purchase and discard. Disposable pallets may be made from wood (lighter weight than for reusable pallets), fiberboard, plastic, or composite materials.

Some disposable and exchange pallets fall apart and cause damage. Disposable pallets are sometimes not sturdy enough for even one trip. Exchange pallets break down (splinters and nails protrude) and become unsanitary the more times they are used. It is customary for a facility to exchange the "worst" pallets and keep the best ones, because there is no accountability for pallet integrity.

Pallet pools are third-party suppliers that lease high-quality sturdy pallets in good repair. They maintain stockpiles throughout the country. Such firms are common in parts of Europe and have recently entered the United States and Canada, targeting the grocery industry. They offer the promise of reduced damage, reduced disposal costs, and improved utilization of pallet resources. The growing popularity of pallet pools attests to the fact that it is hard to beat an old-fashioned wooden pallet for strength, protection, and utility (provided it is of sturdy construction and in good repair), despite decades of experiments with disposable and nonrepairable alternatives.

Effective palletization requires a good match of pallet and shipping container dimensions. Loads that overhang the pallet edges are often damaged because unsupported boxes tend to sag and tip.[11] Conversely, loads that do not fill the pallet to the edge are likely to shift in transit. Guides and computer programs are available to assist decisions regarding shipping container size and pallet pattern fit options, especially for the standard GMA pallet.[12]

Other unitization alternatives to pallets have been developed for specific applications and require special materials handling equipment:

- Clamp handling for lightweight, squeezable loads like tissue and breakfast cereal
- Slings for bags
- Toplift "Baseloid" box for appliances
- Slipsheets

A slipsheet is a solid sheet of fiberboard, corrugated board, or high-density plastic, upon which freight is unitized and stabilized with stretch wrap, glue, or tape. The sheet is handled by a special lift truck attachment that pulls the load onto a platform, as if onto a forklift's forks. To set the load into position (in a trailer or onto a pallet), the lift truck pushes the load off the platform with a large platen. Slip sheets cost little to purchase and discard and considerably reduce cube and weight in transit.

However, slip sheet and clamp handling have both been found to cause damage, and many shippers are reconsidering their use. Using them is a delicate task that requires a skilled worker's touch. Pushing or clamping a load requires that shipping containers and their contents directly bear the force of the materials handling equipment. When such equipment is carelessly used, poorly maintained, or out of adjustment, it tends to deform the products.

Film-based packaging, blanket wrapping, returnable containers, intermediate bulk containers, slip sheets, and pallet pools are part of a trend to tailor packaging to perform for specific products and logistical systems. They were developed to solve logistical packaging problems and to reduce packaging purchase and disposal costs. The next part of this chapter discusses some typical packaging problems and how to approach them.

Typical Logistical Packaging Problems

There are three types of logistical packaging problems: engineering problems, cost considerations, and logistical problems with packaging solutions.

Engineering Problems

Packaging professionals use engineering principles of materials science to develop new packages and solve protection problems. The most common materials properties that are scientifically determined are cushioning for fragile products, impact and vibration resistance of filled packages,[13] shelf life and permeability for oxygen- or moisture-sensitive products,[14] and compression strength for hard-to-stack products.[15] Packaging professionals also use some industrial engineering principles to configure packing operations and choose packaging machinery.

Management of logistical packaging, however, involves more than package engineering. Most packaging problem solving is not associated with developing new packages for new products. In fact, most "new" logistical packages are simply variations of packages used for similar products and require very little "engineering."

Costs

The second principal activity of a packaging professional is to reduce the cost of purchasing packaging materials and the cost of packing operations. Opportunities for substantial savings abound, especially for firms that have always purchased according to the Classification Commission standards and rely on their corrugated supplier to make packaging decisions.

The most common areas for cost reduction include light weighting, materials substitution, size reduction, automation of manual tasks, and standardization. Standardization reduces costs when there is a wide variety of product sizes and shapes and small volumes packed (for example, spare parts or artwork). Standardization can result in volume discounts and minimize inventory cost. But a standardized box is always too big for what is inside it and requires dunnage, compared with customized sizes that minimize materials, trash, and cube.

Innovative incremental packaging solutions that reduce cost and improve performance abound in the packaging supply industry. Manufacturers of packaging materials and equipment are sources of a great amount of free (if potentially biased) consulting advice, so it is wise to consult more than one. Potential suppliers can always suggest lower-cost packages, compared to the current supplier. Trade shows, such as the Pack Expo, WestPack, EastPack, and MacroPack, are staged to enable comparison shopping for materials and equipment. Industry catalogs, such as the *Packaging Machinery Manufacturers' Institute Directory,* packaging references in *The Bibliography of Logistics Management* (La Londe), and periodicals like *Packaging, Materials Handling Engineering,* and *Modern Materials Handling* and their annual buyers' guides, identify manufacturers of specific packaging systems components.

Logistical Problems and Opportunities

The third type of packaging challenge concerns logistical problems and opportunities with packaging solutions. Packaging can reduce the cost of every logistical activity: transport, storage, handling, inventory control, and customer service. Furthermore, changing the packaging postponement/speculation decision can dramatically reduce the cost of an entire logistical system. Integrated management of packaging and logistics is required if a firm expects to realize such opportunities.[16]

Ideas for innovative packaging solutions to logistical problems arise from many sources, including serendipity. Sometimes it simply takes a new perspective. Speaking with packaging consultants and packaging professionals from other firms and industries often yields good creative advice, once a problem has been identified. The topic can be approached in terms of several different challenges:

- Postponement and speculation
- Transportation, warehousing, and handling efficiency
- Logistical information management
- Workers' ergonomics and safety
- Customer service
- Damage
- Trash reduction
- Hazardous materials packaging
- Packaging for international logistics

POSTPONEMENT AND SPECULATION

Postponement and speculation are logistical concepts that question where and when to add value (time, place, and form utility) in distribution channels. The concepts derive from location theories that recommended processing "weight gaining" products near to consumption and "weight losing" products near to the source.[17] Bucklin formulated the principle of speculation to reduce cost: "Changes in form, and the movement of goods to forward inventories, should be made at the earliest possible time in the marketing flow in order to reduce the costs of the marketing system."[18]

But conversely, in a market of differentiated products, Alderson explained that the principle of time and form postponement reduces risk:

> The principle of postponement requires that changes in form and identity occur at the latest possible point in the marketing flow; and changes in inventory location occur at the latest possible point in time ... Postponement serves to reduce marketing risk. Every differentiation which makes a product more suitable for a specified segment of the market makes it less suitable for other segments.[19]

The inventory decision whether to reduce risk by postponement or to reduce cost with economies of scale is a traditional marketing trade-off.

Traditionally, also, the packaging point for bulk products has been postponed or speculated, according to product and market conditions.[20] For example, produce is canned in the autumn by contractors and stored in "bright" cans; labeling is postponed until food marketing companies buy and brand it at different times during the year. Labeling postponement minimizes the risk of inventory misforecasts and economizes on canning production during a busy season. On the other hand, processing and packaging of fruit concentrates like orange juice is an example of speculation. Such speculation results in low costs because weight is eliminated before shipping and homogeneous waste at the orchard is processed for animal food.

Postponement and speculation also apply to assembly and packaging of more sophisticated products in a global market with global sources. For example, some automobiles and electronic products are assembled in various locations around the world for local markets. When products are similar but differentiated for local markets, assembly and packaging postponement offers packaging opportunities for the inbound parts shipment (to minimize the high cost of worldwide transportation), as well as for customizing packaging for the local markets while minimizing differentiated inventory in the pipeline.

For example, one of the largest cost-savings initiatives (millions of dollars per year) in Hewlett-

Packard's history is a case of international packaging postponement. Two problems—high transport and inventory management costs—led Hewlett-Packard to consider a packaging solution.

The Transport Cost Problem: Packaged and cushioned electronic products occupy two to three times the amount of intermodal container space as the bare product; this results in a significant premium for transportation to Europe.

The Inventory Problem: Products for all European destinations were identical, except for the power adapter and language-specific carton and instructions. Products packed in the United States often needed to be unpacked and diverted once they arrived (a month later) in Europe. Furthermore, inventory was required to be labeled in every language.

The Solution: By postponing packaging—shipping products to Europe in "bulk packs," palletized and stretch-wrapped, with minimal interleaving between layers—transport and inventory costs were cut by more than half. Once there, products are packaged to order; differentiation and cushioning are postponed until the products are shipped LTL, as only then is the required language known and the risk of damage from dropping during handling increases.[21]

Transportation, Warehousing, and Handling

Transportation, warehousing, and handling problems are often solved by packaging. Storage and transport efficiency depend on cube utilization and the ability of the packaged goods to support the loads imposed on them. Order picking productivity depends on how easy the package is to find and recognize, whether items are packed in order picking quantities (e.g., dozens), and how easy it is to repack the heterogeneous order. Productivity throughout a logistical system depends on the compatibility of packages with both manual and mechanical handling systems.

Creativity is required to identify packaging opportunities that improve productivity. Some methods include benchmarking against other companies (in the same and other industries), surveys of customers and carriers, and audits by logistics and packaging professionals.

Testing alternative packages for their logistical efficiency is a simple matter of productivity measurement.[22] To compare two packaging systems for truck-loading productivity, time the loading and unloading of several trailers, and count the number of units. To compare packages for cube utilization, measure them, including their fit into trailer dimensions (trailer sizes vary; most are 48" long × 102" wide × 102" high). In productivity measurement, all relevant inputs should be considered, including package cost.

Logistical information management problems are often solved by improving packaging communication. Automatic identification (e.g., barcoding) can interface with information systems throughout a logistical system if symbology is standard. Such standardization generally requires an industrywide effort; examples include the grocery industry UPC code and the automobile industry's standards. Radio frequency (RF) tags are a new form of automatic identification that is reprogrammed as the product moves through logistical operations, and RF tags emit a signal that can be used to identify a package's location when called.

Workers' Ergonomics and Safety

Workers' ergonomics and safety problems may be alleviated by packaging solutions, especially because there are so many possibilities for injury while working with packages. Routine package handling causes chronic stress injuries, and materials handling accidents kill people.

Routine manual handling of packages has always been a widespread practice, but it is traditionally a source of many back injuries. To the question, "How heavy should manually handled packages be?" OSHA guidelines answer that it depends on how far and how often the lifting is done. For example, for "continuous high-frequency lifting, variable tasks" like manual receiving operations, weights below 17 pounds are acceptable and represent nominal risk, weights between 17 and 50 pounds are acceptable only with administrative or engineering controls, and packages weighing over 50 pounds are unacceptable.[23]

Accidents happen, and personal injury lawsuits involving packaging materials and methods are increasing. The liability exposure generally depends on whether the accident could have been foreseen and whether adequate packaging and training procedures were followed. For example, when a longshoreman is injured by a bag that slips from a stack, the fabric is accused of not complying with standards, the unit loading technique is examined (maybe it should have been stretch-wrapped), and the port practices are questioned. And when workers are injured from using a closure strap as a handle, the packaging firm must prove it warned workers: "This strap is not a handle." It is especially important for firms to evaluate packages involved in previous accidents to prevent future occurrences.

Customer Service

Packaging affects customer service because customers unpack the product. Customers also bear the cost of concealed damage, displaying or installing products, and trash disposal.

The cost of unpacking is seldom considered by the firm that packs products. But easy-opening features reduce customers' costs and reduce the damage that can occur when packages are difficult to open. For example, some food manufacturers have developed easy-open display-ready packages to improve grocery products' "direct profitability"—to reduce the possibility of box cutter damage, reduce shelving costs, and improve shelf-facing appearance.[24]

Damage

Damage is the symptom of a system out of adjustment. Damage results from product, handling, or packaging problems. Packaging is generally responsible for the quality maintained after the name goes on, although it should be the responsibility of logistics customer service quality control.

Packaging decisions regarding damage prevention are often made without sufficient information. For example, one area of package engineering research deals with quantifying impacts in distribution for test development. But objective measurement of forces ignores the reality of damage as specific to a product's characteristics and logistical system.

Accurate measurement of damage provides the most valuable information for directing attention to problems. For example, while a computer manufacturer's packaging staff was preoccupied with instrumenting handling impacts in an attempt to standardize tests, they overlooked customer complaints of specific types of damage (such as disk drive doors breaking off) that could be easily overcome with packages evaluated in tests that reproduce the specific damage.

However, typical reports of damage problems are nonspecific as to the amount, types, and causes. It is difficult to quantify costs for damage because they are scattered among firms in a logistical system.[25] Because carriers are responsible for the damage they cause, documented in-transit damage claims are the first place to look for damage trends.[26] Damage caused by wholesalers and retailers is more elusive, and the losses are rarely reported, tallied, and evaluated by manufacturers.

To reduce waste, improve customer service, and control packaging costs, some firms have developed systems to track and manage product quality during distribution.[27] Such logistics quality control systems resemble systems for managing product quality during manufacturing and include the following steps:

- Setting standards for critical defects
- Appraising conformance to standards
- Monitoring and collecting data (e.g., EDI tied to ordering system)
- Reporting and evaluating data (Pareto analysis)
- Corrective action (modify the package, product, or handling)[28]

Monitoring product quality during distribution is more complex than factory quality control because data must be collected from diverse sources. Firms in vertical marketing systems have the best chance to implement systemwide standards; once the product is sold, information is more difficult to obtain. Firms in nonvertical marketing systems may need to hire third-party contractors to survey damage; for example, a chain of grocery salvage centers collects and sells damage information to grocery manufacturers, standardizing stock-keeping unit data (via UPC code) and damage causes (such as "cut open").

Most damage information systems collect data only on returned goods, as it is difficult to get reports of marginal damage (which may routinely be repaired or salvaged). However, electronic data interchange of order entry and verification may provide a standard means for gathering distribution damage data.

Since a firm knows about its logistical damage, it can target initiatives that will do the most good. For example, Ethan Allen furniture company targets specific packages and products for improvement when damage quantity and/or costs are higher than normal.[29] Initiatives may include changing the product, changing the logistical hazards, or changing the package. Specific information about damage is particularly useful when developing package tests and alternative packages.

Trash Reduction

Trash reduction is another important customer service opportunity. Besides the environmental effects, disposal of logistical packaging costs money. Waste disposal costs are sharply increasing because communities have cut back on landfill availability. Some nations, such as Canada and Germany, have enacted legislation to reduce packaging waste.

Manufacturers with vertical marketing systems are likely to receive complaints of high trash cost directly, because customers' costs are explicitly dependent on the manufacturer. For example, powerful consignees like General Motors and Sears have issued waste minimization targets to their suppliers. In nonvertical systems (the grocery industry), there is more of a tendency for retailer trade groups (such as the Food Marketing Institute) to issue a "Solid Waste Policy Statement" to manufacturers.

Packaging solutions to waste problems include reducing, reusing, and recycling. Reduction of packaging also saves on packaging purchase costs. Packaging reuse generally adds some costs for sorting and return transportation. However, as the demand for recycling increases, its cost has been declining.

Recycling is a good disposal method for most logistical packaging waste, because it collects naturally in large homogeneous piles. Manufacturers, warehouses, and retailers discard large amounts of pallets, corrugated fiberboard, polyethylene film, plastic foam, and strapping. Recyclers appreciate such concentrated and relatively clean sources (compared with sorting and cleaning curbside and food service wastes). Likewise, purchasing packages made from recycled material encourages the growth of a recycled products market and infrastructure.[30]

HAZARDOUS MATERIALS

Hazardous materials packaging is regulated in the United States by the Department of Transportation and, internationally, by the United Nations. The reason for government regulation is that workers, the environment, transportation vehicles, and other freight must be protected from hazardous materials packages.

The recently revised hazardous materials packaging regulations are performance standards (drop tests, compatibility tests, etc.) specific to product/container combinations, and are published in the *Code of Federal Regulations.*[31] This revision, from traditional materials specifications, has caused a great deal of confusion regarding laboratory procedures and approvals, as well as whether traditional packages will pass the new tests. This is one packaging area with explicit rules that are unfortunately written in the obfuscatory language of government documents. The change to packaging performance standards is expected to increase innovation, decrease costs, and improve performance. Packaging suppliers generally know which packages are approved, but shippers are responsible for ensuring compliance.

INTERNATIONAL SHIPPING

International logistics is growing and so is the use of intermodal (generally 40-foot) containers. Containerization reduces some of the need for special "export packaging," because containerized packages are less likely to be exposed to shipboard moisture and are not handled at the port, compared with shipping "break bulk." A container is simply a larger package, facilitating handling and protecting from damage. Accordingly, when there are voids in containers, the loads must be blocked and braced, usually with wood, to prevent shifting during shipment or as the container is placed onto or removed from a flatbed railcar, trailer chassis, or ship.[32]

When shipments are not containerized, more protection is required. Traditional export packaging consists of crates, barrels, heavy-duty bags, and corrugated fiberboard boxes made with moisture-resistant components. As with all logistical packaging, the protection needs to be matched to product characteristics and logistical hazards. The hazards of international transportation range from flatbeds to bikecart. Materials handling devices range from hooks (used by longshoremen) to Europallets (standardized 1,200 mm × 800 mm). Even when products are shipped in containers, they will probably be handled in a break-bulk operation at an inland destination overseas and will require appropriate packaging performance.

International shipments might also suffer communication problems (languages, symbols), utility problems (incompatibility with overseas handling methods, trash disposal problems), and damage problems. The difficulty of communicating packaging problems among firms is compounded by the need to communicate among different languages and cultures. Generally, the problems require on-site investigations. As with most logistical packaging problems, the best way to find out more is to go and look. One of the best sources of information on export packaging, from a carrier's point of view, is the *Ports of the World* publication and video (published by the Insurance Company of North America).

Innovative Logistical Packaging

This chapter has approached logistical packaging from a nontraditional perspective to encourage innovative packaging solutions to logistical problems. Most traditional packaging forms date from the early 1900s and are the most costly packaging systems available. Innovation represents a dramatic potential for savings.

Packaging innovation is a process of problem identification, finding and testing potential solutions, deciding which action to take, and following through to implementation. It requires proactive management by a project champion (usually a packaging professional). It also requires a systems and team approach, because packaging affects so many other functions such as marketing, operations, plant and product engineering, logistics, accounting, and finance.[33]

Identification of packaging-related problems is the first step. Problems of cost, protection, utility, and communication may be identified by customers, salespeople, logistical managers, or packaging professionals. The priority of a problem depends on its perceived cost. Generally, it is difficult to determine the actual cost (and extent) of a packaging problem because packaging-related costs—like damage, handling productivity, and trash—are diverse and scattered throughout a logistical system.

The search for packaging solutions may be formal or informal, but the innovation process requires a potential solution before it can proceed. Sometimes problems languish for years before someone thinks of a good solution.

Ideas for potential solutions can come from suppliers, consultants, or colleagues and packaging professionals in other firms and industries. The primary U.S. professional packaging organization is The Institute of Packaging Professionals (IoPP).[34] IoPP has members in every industry and technical subcommittees on specific products and packaging forms, such as the Computer Packaging and Bag Committees. IoPP's membership directory contains references to packaging periodicals, information sources, related trade associations, solid waste agencies, and schools offering packaging education. Furthermore, many industries have their own packaging committees, such as the Automobile Industry Action Group and the Southern Furniture Manufacturers' Association.

Typically, a firm considering a change in packaging forms a team of people from affected departments: packaging, marketing, logistics, operations, quality control, materials handling, and engineering. Alternative packages are judged, subjectively or in lab tests, for their protection, utility, and communication performance, as well as for their systemwide cost implications. Next, the "best" solution packages are tested in the field (test shipments) and for market acceptance. The decision whether to adopt a new package is generally recommended by the team to upper management.

The early roll-out is a period of fine-tuning. Problems with the new package are discovered and corrected. Sustained implementation returns to a new level of business as usual—generally with substantial cost savings.

This chapter has shown that, beyond the purchase cost, packaging affects the cost of every logistical activity. Package size affects transportation cost; unitization methods affect order picking and handling costs; identification technique affects inventory control; and customer service depends on damage control and the cost of unpacking and discarding packaging. Firms that manage packaging from an integrated logistical rather than traditional purchasing perspective find many opportunities for improving profitability.

Notes

1. For further discussion, see Diana Twede, Bruce Harte, James W. Goff, and Steven P. Mitteff, "Breaking Bags: A Performance Specification Philosophy Based on Damage," *Journal of Packaging Technology* 4 (November/December 1990): 17–21.
2. Eiichi Maezawa, "Product Modification to Reduce Distribution Costs," *SPHE Journal* (Spring 1987): 21–22.
3. A. T. Kearney, Inc. *Measuring and Improving Productivity in Physical Distribution* (Oakbrook, Ill.: Council of Logistics Management, 1984).
4. James Goff, "Packaging-Distribution Relationships: A Look to the Future," *Logistical Packaging Innovation Proceedings* (Oakbrook, Ill.: Council of Logistics Management, 1991).
5. The periodical *Automatic I.D. News* is a good source of current information on this subject.
6. Twede, et al., "Breaking Bags."
7. Edmund A. Leonard, *Packaging Economics* (New York: Books for Industry, 1980).
8. Michael A. McGinnis, and Charles J. Hollon, "Packaging: Organization, Objectives, and Interactions," *Journal of Business Logistics* (1978): 45–62.
9. For more information regarding the traditional packaging forms, the reader is referred to the following references at the end of this chapter: Friedman and Kipnees's *Distribution Packaging* (1977), Bakker's *Encyclopedia of Packaging Technology* (1986), Paine's *Packaging User's Handbook* (1991), Hanlon's *Handbook of Package Engineering* (1971), Maltenfort's reference works on corrugated fiberboard shipping containers (1989 and 1990), and Plaskett's classic *Principles of [Wooden] Box and Crate Construction* (1930). The economics of traditional packaging forms is explored in Leonard's *Packaging Economics* (1980).
10. Louis P. Bucklin, "The Classification of Channel Structures," in *Vertical Marketing Systems,* ed. Louis P. Bucklin (Glenview, Ill.: Scott, Foresman, 1970), pp. 16–31, and "Postponement, Speculation, and the Structure of Distribution Channels," *Journal of Marketing Research* (February 1965): 26–31.
11. Food Marketing Institute, *Voluntary Industry Guidelines for Dry Grocery Shipping Containers* (Washington, D.C.: FMI, 1988).
12. Food Marketing Institute, *Pallet Patterns and Case Sizes for Dry Grocery Shipping Containers* (Washington, D.C.: FMI, 1988).
13. Richard K. Brandenburg and Julian June-Ling Lee, *Fundamentals of Packaging Dynamics* (Minneapolis: MTS Systems, 1985).
14. Wilmer A. Jenkins and James P. Harrington, *Packaging Foods with Plastics* (Lancaster, Pa.: Technomic, 1991).
15. George G. Maltenfort, *Performance and Evaluation of Shipping Containers* (Plainview, N.Y.: Jelmar, 1989).
16. For more information, see D. B. Carmody, *Packaging's Role in Physical Distribution* (New York: American Management Association, 1966); and James L. Heskett, Nicholas A.

Glaskowsky, Jr., and Robert M. Ivie, "Packaging," *Business Logistics* (New York: Ronald Press, 1973), pp. 572–602.

17. Alfred Weber, *Über den Standort der Industrien,* translated by C. J. Fredrich as *Alfred Weber's Theory of the Location of Industries* (Chicago: Univ. of Chicago Press, 1929).
18. Louis P. Bucklin, "Postponement, Speculation, and the Structure of Distribution Channels," *Journal of Marketing Research* (February 1965): 27.
19. Wroe Alderson, *Marketing Behavior and Executive Action* (Homewood, Ill.: Irwin, 1950), p. 424.
20. Walter Zinn, "Planning Physical Distribution with the Principle of Postponement," *Journal of Business Logistics* 9, no. 2 (1989): 117–35.
21. Kevin A. Howard, "Packaging Postponement Lowers Logistical Costs," *Logistical Packaging Innovation Proceedings* (Oakbrook, Ill.: Council of Logistics Management, 1991).
22. Kearney, *Measuring and Improving Productivity.*
23. American Industrial Hygiene Association, *Work Practices Guide for Manual Lifting* (Akron, Ohio: American Industrial Hygiene Association, 1987).
24. William Thompson, "Improving Customer Service 'Packages': Direct Product Profitability," *Logistical Packaging Innovation Proceedings* (Oakbrook, Ill.: Council of Logistics Management, 1991).
25. Joseph L. Cavinato, "Analysis of Loss and Damage in a Procurement Distribution System Using a Shrinkage Approach" (Ph.D. diss., Pennsylvania State University, 1975).
26. William Augello, *Freight Claims in Plain English* (Huntington, N.Y: Transportation Claims and Prevention Council, 1982); and Sue Smith, Alfred H. McKinlay, and William J. Augello, *Freight Claim Prevention in Plain English* (Huntington, N.Y.: Transportation Claims and Prevention Council, 1989).
27. Twede et al., "Breaking Bags."
28. Robert A. Novak, "Quality and Control in Logistics: A Process Model," *International Journal of Physical Distribution and Materials Management* (1989): 2–44.
29. Thomas J. Lowery, "Quality Control of Products During Distribution," *Logistical Packaging Innovation Proceedings* (Oakbrook, Ill.: Council of Logistics Management, 1991).
30. Susan E. M. Selke, *Packaging and the Environment: Alternatives, Trends and Solutions* (Lancaster, Pa.: Technomic, 1990).
31. *Code of Federal Regulations, Title 49* (Washington, D.C.: GPO, updated annually).
32. John Agnew and Jack Huntley, *Container Stowage: A Practical Approach* (Dover, England: Container Publications, 1972); Association of American Railroads, *Loading Methods for Closed Cars* (Chicago: AAR [multiyear publication]).
33. Diana Twede, "The Process of Distribution Packaging Innovation and its Relationship of Distribution Channel Structure" (Ph.D. diss., Michigan State University, 1988).
34. As this chapter was being prepared for publication, the IoPP could be reached by phone at (703) 318-8970.

References

A. T. Kearney, Inc. 1984. *Measuring and Improving Productivity in Physical Distribution.* Oakbrook, Ill.: Council of Logistics Management, 1984.

Agnew, John and Jack Huntley. *Container Stowage: A Practical Approach.* Dover, England: Container Publications, 1972.

Alderson, Wroe. *Marketing Behavior and Executive Action.* Homewood, Ill.: Irwin, 1950.

American Industrial Hygiene Association. *Work Practices Guide for Manual Lifting.* Akron, Ohio: American Industrial Hygiene Association, 1987.

American Society for Testing and Materials. *Annual Books of Standards.* Philadelphia: ASTM, revised annually.

Association of American Railroads. *Loading Methods for Closed Cars.* Chicago: AAR, Various years.

Augello, William. *Freight Claims in Plain English.* Huntington, N.Y.: Transportation Claims and Prevention Council, 1982.

Automatic I. D. News is published monthly. *Automatic Identification Reference Guide and Directory,* revised annually. Duluth, Minn.: Edgell Communications.

Bakker, Marilyn, ed. *The Wiley Encyclopedia of Packaging Technology.* New York: Wiley, 1986.

Brandenburg, Richard K. and Julian June-Ling Lee. *Fundamentals of Packaging Dynamics.* Minneapolis: MTS Systems, 1985.

Bucklin, Louis P. "Postponement, Speculation, and the Structure of Distribution Channels," *Journal of Marketing Research* (February 1965): 26–31.

Bucklin, Louis P. "The Classification of Channel Structures," in *Vertical Marketing Systems,* ed. Louis P. Bucklin. Glenview, Ill.: Scott, Foresman, 1970, pp. 16–31.

Carmody, D. B. *Packaging's Role in Physical Distribution.* New York: American Management Association, 1966.

Cavinato, Joseph L. "Analysis of Loss and Damage in a Procurement Distribution System Using a Shrinkage Approach." Ph.D. diss., Pennsylvania State University, 1975.

Ebeling, Charles W. *Integrated Packaging Systems for Transportation and Distribution.* New York: Marcel Dekker, 1990.

Goff, James. "Packaging-Distribution Relationships: A Look to the Future." *Logistical Packaging Innovation Proceedings.* Oakbrook, Ill.: Council of Logistics Management, 1991.

Food Marketing Institute. *Voluntary Industry Guidelines for Dry Grocery Shipping Containers.* Washington, D.C.: FMI, 1988a.

Food Marketing Institute. *Pallet Patterns and Case Sizes for Dry Grocery Shipping Containers.* Washington, D.C.: FMI, 1988b.

Friedman, Walter F. and Jerome J. Kipnees. *Distribution Packaging.* Huntington, NY.: Robert E. Krieger, 1977.

Hanlon, Joseph F. *Handbook of Package Engineering.* New York: McGraw-Hill, 1971.

Heskett, James L., Nicholas A. Glaskowsky, Jr., and Robert M. Ivie. "Packaging." *Business Logistics.* New York: Ronald Press, 1973, pp. 572–602.

Howard, Kevin A. "Packaging Postponement Lowers Logistical Costs." *Logistical Packaging Innovation Proceedings.* Oakbrook, Ill.: Council of Logistics Management, 1991.

Institute of Packaging Professionals. *Who's Who in Packaging.* Herndon, Va.: IoPP, phone: (703) 318-8970, revised annually.

Insurance Company of North America. *Ports of the World* movie and periodically updated monograph. Philadelphia: CIGNA.

Novak, Robert A. "Quality and Control in Logistics: A Process Model." *International Journal of Physical Distribution and Materials Management* (1989): 2–44.

Packaging magazine, published monthly. *Packaging Buyers Guide and Product Directory,* revised annually. Denver: Cahners.

Packaging Technology and Science. West Sussex, England: Wiley, published monthly.

Paine, Frank A., ed. *The Packaging User's Handbook.* Glasgow: Blackie, and in New York: AVI imprint of Van Nostrand Reinhold, 1991.

Plaskett, C.A. *Principles of Box and Crate Construction.* Technical Bulletin No. 171. Washington D.C.: United States Department of Agriculture, 1930.

Selke, Susan E. M. *Packaging and the Environment: Alternatives, Trends and Solutions.* Lancaster, Pa.: Technomic, 1990.

Smith, Sue, Alfred H. McKinlay, and William J. Augello. *Freight Claim Prevention in Plain English.* Huntington, N.Y.: Transportation Claims and Prevention Council, 1989.

Thompson, William. "Improving Customer Service 'Packages': Direct Product Profitability." *Logistical Packaging Innovation Proceedings.* Oakbrook, Ill.: Council of Logistics Management, 1991.

Transportation and Distribution. Cleveland: Penton, published monthly.

Twede, Diana. "The Process of Distribution Packaging Innovation and Its Relationship of Distribution Channel Structure." Ph.D. diss., Michigan State University, 1988.

Twede, Diana. "Distribution Damage Measurement, Analysis and Correction." *Packaging Technology and Science* 4 (1991): 305–10.

Twede, Diana, Bruce Harte, James W. Goff, and Steven P. Miteff. "Breaking Bags: A Performance Specification Philosophy Based on Damage." *Journal of Packaging Technology* 4 (November/December, 1990): 17–21.

Uniform Classification Committee of the Western Railroad Association. *Uniform Freight Classification.* Chicago: Uniform Classification Committee, revised annually.

Jenkins, Wilmer A. and James P. Harrington. *Packaging Foods with Plastics.* Lancaster, Pa.: Technomic, 1991.

Journal of Packaging Technology. Mahwah, JF: Technical Publications, published bimonthly.

La Londe, Bernard J. "Packaging" references in *Supplement to Bibliography on Logistics Management.* Oak Brook, Ill.: Council of Logistics Management, published annually.

Leonard, Edmund A. *Packaging Economics.* New York: Books for Industry, 1980.

Leonard, Edmund A. *Packaging Specifications, Purchasing and Quality Control.* New York: Marcel Dekker, 1987.

Lowery, Thomas J. "Quality Control of Products During Distribution." *Logistical Packaging Innovation Proceedings.* Oakbrook, Ill.: Council of Logistics Management, 1991.

Maezawa, Eiichi. "Product Modification to Reduce Distribution Costs;" *SPHE Journal* (Spring 1987): 21–22.

Maltenfort, George G. *Performance and Evaluation of Shipping Containers.* Plainview, N.Y.: Jelmar, 1989.

Maltenfort, George G., ed. *Corrugated Shipping Containers: An Engineering Approach.* Plainview, N.Y.: Jelmar, 1990.

Materials Handling Engineering, published monthly. *Materials Handling Engineering Reference Guide,* revised annually. Cleveland: Penton.

McGinnis, Michael A. and Charles J. Hollon. "Packaging: Organization, Objectives, and Interactions." *Journal of Business Logistics* (1978): 45–62.

Modern Materials Handling, published monthly. *Modern Materials Handling Casebook Reference Issue,* revised annually. Denver: Cahners.

National Classification Board of the American Trucking Association. *National Motor Freight Classification.* Washington, D.C.: National Classification Board, revised annually.

National Safe Transit Association. *Procedures for Pre-Shipment Testing.* Chicago: NSTA, 1990.

United States Government Printing Office. *Code of Federal Regulations, Title 49,* Parts 171–179, updated annually.

Weber, Alfred. *Über den Standort der Industrien,* translated by C. J. Fredrich as *Alfred Weber's Theory of the Location of Industries.* Chicago: University of Chicago, 1929.

Zinn, Walter. "Planning Physical Distribution with the Principle of Postponement," *Journal of Business Logistics* 9, no. (1989): 117–35.

SECTION V

Transportation Management

C. John Langley, Jr.

Innovation and creativity characterize the current and future state of the transportation industry in the 1990s. They represent notable and refreshing contrasts to the turbulent and traumatic changes faced by shippers and carriers in the preceding decade. Correspondingly, this section provides perspectives on several topics that are central to the types of changes that have been experienced, as well as those that lie ahead.

In Chapter 21, Michael R. Crum and Mary C. Holcomb provide an insightful outlook at, and evaluation of the transportation industry. In addition to analyzing changes in the motor carrier, railroad, and intermodal industries, they critique a number of relevant and effective transportation strategies. Among their concluding messages are thoughts regarding the challenges between modes of transportation, between carriers and shippers, and between carrier management and labor.

In Chapter 22, James M. Masters and Bernard J. La Londe offer an in-depth perspective on the role of new information technology in the practice of traffic management. Following a discussion of the forces facing the shipper's traffic function and a review of the new technology available in the traffic area, this chapter provides examples of how the new technologies are being used to improve the practice of traffic management. The emphasis of this chapter reinforces the role of information technology as a driver of logistical competence.

The integration of purchasing and transportation decision making is the focus of Chapter 23, in which Julie J. Gentry offers an insightful look at how these two key functions are coming together in the 1990s. Motivated significantly by the key changes in the logistics/transportation environment, an increasing effort exists today to integrate and strategically manage a coordinated, inbound transportation and purchasing function. This chapter reports the results of major research studies conducted to gain insight into these issues.

In Chapter 24, Hugh L. Randall provides a balanced outlook on the topic of contract logistics. Rather than suggesting that this key logistics/transportation strategy is for every firm, this chapter offers a perspective relating to the benefits and challenges that may be expected if this approach is pursued. The author concludes with a summary of what he feels are the key requirements for success in the area of contract logistics.

CHAPTER 21

Transportation Outlook and Evaluation

Michael R. Crum
Mary C. Holcomb

The rapid rate of change that occurred in the transportation industry in the 1980s was driven by technological, economic, social, demographic, and political factors. Although change has become a "constant" for the operating environment, the basic nature and role of transportation remains the same. Transportation is the largest component of logistics cost. In addition, transportation accounts for approximately 27% of total U.S. energy use and 63% of total petroleum use.[1] Thus, the management of transportation activities and functions is vital to efficient and effective service.

Prior to 1980 the transportation industry was noted for inefficient operations and mileage intensity.[2] Regulatory changes dramatically altered the marketplace in which transportation purchasing decisions are made. The traditional focus of moving products from point A to point B shifted to one of a strategic value-added process to be managed as part of the customer's logistics network. Transportation, as the vital link in this environment, will continue to evolve to meet the needs of shippers.

Overview of Economic Regulation and Deregulation

Federal economic regulation was imposed on the various transportation modes at different times, for different reasons, and with different results. Regulation of the railroad industry began in 1887 with the passage of the Interstate Commerce Act. Railroad regulation was primarily in response to the economic and social problems that stemmed from the monopoly power of many railroads. An independent federal agency, the Interstate Commerce Commission (ICC), was created to enforce the regulatory policies of Congress. The trucking industry was brought under the jurisdiction of the ICC in 1935 because of destructive competition in that industry. The severe national economic depression and the lack of entry barriers to the industry produced substantial excess capacity that manifested itself in below-cost rates, unreliable service, and high industry turnover. Airline regulation began in 1938, predominately to avoid such problems as had developed in the trucking industry. The primary goal of airline regulation was to promote the economic growth of safe air transportation. A separate agency, the Civil Aeronautics Board, was created to administer economic regulation.

The key principle underlying economic regulation was the concept of common carriage. The fundamental objective of common carriage is the provision of adequate, reasonably priced service to all transportation consumers on a nondiscriminatory basis. Toward this end, the regulatory agencies were given authority to control entry to and exit from the transportation markets, to regulate carrier prices and service offerings, and to regulate merger activity. Entry control was utilized to prevent excess competition and to permit cross-subsidization of traffic to facilitate common carrier service, while exit control was employed to protect shippers from loss of service. To prevent monopoly abuses and undesirable price discrimination, carriers were required to publish prices and obtain approval for price changes. Merger regulation was intended to prevent unwanted reductions in competition, and was utilized to combine financially weak carriers with strong carriers to prevent service abandonments and disruptions.

The common carriage objective of economic regulation was essentially attained, but the economic costs associated with regulation are high. Specific criticisms of regulation include:

- Existence of significant operating and pricing inefficiencies
- Lack of intramodal price competition
- Impediment of service and technology innovations
- Poor financial condition of the railroad system

Economic deregulation occurred because policymakers decided that the costs associated with regulation had surpassed the benefits and because conditions in the transportation industries had changed over time so much that the original reasons for regulating were no longer relevant. The various transport industries are still subject to some federal economic regulation, but the extent of regulation has been greatly reduced. Some regulatory reform from within the overseeing agencies generally preceded legislated deregulation for each mode. Deregulation legislation was enacted in the following years for the different modes:

1977—air freight
1978—air passenger
1980—trucking
1980—railroads

The principal freedoms bestowed on the transportation industries include:

- Greater latitude in pricing
- Ability to enter long-term contracts
- Greater freedom to enter and exit markets
- Less stringent regulation of mergers and consolidations

The most significant results of the new regulatory environment include reduced or slower increases in freight rates and passenger fares due to greater levels of competition in most markets, a substantial increase in the number of motor carriers (from approximately 17,000 to almost 37,000) and scheduled airlines (from fewer than 50 to almost 200), a much higher incidence of bankruptcy in the trucking and airline industries, more merger activity and industry concentration in all three modes, a much closer relationship between carrier costs and prices, and the general demise of the common carriage concept. It is generally agreed that, in the aggregate, shippers and the railroad industry have been the chief beneficiaries of deregulation, while organized labor and the trucking and airline industries have not fared as well. Of course, there have been winners and losers in each of the forementioned groups.

Changing Nature of the Motor Carrier Industry

Deregulation of the motor carrier industry has made an effective marketing program more important for the for-hire motor carrier. The market freedoms granted to carriers by deregulation, in conjunction with the widespread shipper adoption of just-in-time (JIT) inventory and production systems with demanding requirements for high-quality transportation service, has induced many shippers and carriers to establish closer, longer-term, more interdependent relationships. Characteristics of this emerging relationship, commonly referred to as "partnershipping," generally include reliance on a contractual rather than transactional relationship, closer integration of carrier and shipper operations, and greater mutual dependence arising from the distribution of freight among a smaller number of truck transport suppliers by individual shippers.

For other carriers and shippers, the deregulated environment has made carrier-shipper relationships less stable and the transportation purchase decision process more uncertain. The key changes in the structure and organization of the trucking industry include:

- Unprecedented growth in the number of ICC-regulated for-hire carriers
- Significantly increased level of industry concentration in the LTL sector
- Expanded range of services individual carriers may offer
- Greater role for transport organizers

With the advent of deregulation, the ICC greatly loosened its restrictive entry controls. Carriers must still be certificated or authorized by the ICC, which limits entry only to those carriers that are fit and able to provide service. From 1980 to 1986 the number of ICC-authorized motor carriers more than doubled, from 18,045 to 36,948.[3] The trucking industry comprises two basic segments: truckload (TL) carriers, who generally carry a full trailer's load of a single shipper's goods directly to the ship-to location, and less-than-truckload (LTL) carriers, who deliver smaller shipments, aggregating them to fill trailer capacity and using transshipment terminals in a network as intermediate transfer points. Most of the influx of new carriers occurred in the TL segment, which has no significant capital barriers to entry. A TL carrier can be as simple as an owner/operator with a single truck. LTL carriers are generally larger corporations with great investments in vehicles, trailers, transshipment terminals, and information processing systems. Indeed, the number of LTL carriers has decreased since deregulation as the number of bankruptcies and mergers in this segment has exceeded the number of new entrants.[4] Not surprisingly, the vast majority of new TL entrants are relatively small firms.

LTL carriers have increased their total market share through both internal expansions and mergers. Larger LTL firms offer their shippers many advantages over smaller ones, regardless of whether or not they have cost advantages. Greater geographic coverage permits the larger carrier to offer shippers a more inclusive service and to satisfy more of a shipper's transportation needs. This is especially important today as shippers prefer to deal with fewer carriers. These advantages are referred to as "marketing economies."[5]

Though industry concentration has increased significantly since deregulation, the important issue from a policy perspective is market concentration, which reflects the level of competition in individual transport markets. Industry concentration and market concentration may be related, but not necessarily closely. For example, one study of market structure found that while the number of LTL carriers decreased between 1979 and 1981, the geographic expansion by existing LTL carriers actually led to a greater number of competitors per route for 179 of the 248 major routes investigated.[6] The rate wars in the LTL sector, occurring during times of general prosperity, and the decrease in LTL rates and profit levels since 1980 also suggest substantial market competition in the highly concentrated LTL segment. A study of price competition and market structure in the trucking industry by the U.S. General Accounting Office failed to uncover any cases of predatory pricing by dominant carriers, and noted that the level of concentration in the trucking industry is no greater than in American manufacturing in general.[7]

Significant developments in the organization of trucking service have also resulted from deregulation. Specifically, the removal or reduction of commodity and geographic restrictions on individual for-hire carriers, permitting private carriers to haul the freight of other shippers (under certain conditions), and allowing long-term contracting for motor carrier service have resulted in an increased role for transport organizers and the emergence of shipper strategies that have produced fundamental changes in the purchasing and management of truck transportation service.

Prior to deregulation, transport organizers, known as motor freight brokers, played a significant role in truck transportation of exempt commodities but were rather an insignificant force in the regulated trucking sector. Exempt commodities are those for which truck transportation was not subject to government economic regulation. Motor freight brokers provide a matchmaking service, helping bring together trucking firms with available capacity and shippers requiring trucking service. The transaction costs for shippers and motor carriers involved in exempt commodities transportation were much greater than in the regulated sector because of the significantly larger number of exempt carriers and because freight rates were not regulated or published. Brokers were the catalyst in bringing trucker and shipper together, and played a key role in establishing the rate for the transportation service. Prior to deregulation there were more than 1,000 motor freight brokers of exempt commodities but fewer than 70 brokers of regulated commodities.[8]

The Motor Carrier Act of 1980, in addition to substantially deregulating trucking firms, greatly reduced the regulatory barriers to entering the motor freight broker industry. There are essentially no capital barriers to entry, because the ICC's bonding requirement, to ensure broker ability to meet financial obligations to shippers, can be met at a relatively low cost and a pure broker requires little in the way of equipment or facilities. At the same time, trucking deregulation stimulated the demand for broker service by both shippers and carriers. Shippers were suddenly faced with the task of choosing from among a much larger number of truck operators offering a wider array of rates and service levels. The market situation more closely resembled that of the exempt commodities' transport market before deregulation. Many traffic departments, particularly those of smaller shippers, found it too difficult or too costly to evaluate the multitude of rate/service offerings that had become available. In other words, shippers' transaction costs had increased.

Adding to the demand for brokers were private carriers who were now permitted to solicit freight from other shippers to fill their trailers or to generate backhaul loads. Most private carriers lacked both the staff and the expertise to take advantage of this new freedom. Similarly, the removal of commodity and geographical restrictions on the operating authority of for-hire carriers frequently expanded their market opportunities beyond the capacity of their sales forces. Brokers thus found their services in greater demand as shippers employed them to assist their traffic departments and carriers utilized them to supplement their marketing departments.

The result of this stimulated demand for brokers, and the relative ease of entry into this business has been an increase in the number of brokers from fewer than 70 in 1980 to approximately 6,000 in 1992. It has been estimated that brokers are currently involved in about 18% of all for-hire truck shipments, and that they generate between $10 billion and $20 billion in revenue per year.[9] The broker industry provides an important function in transportation markets by obtaining, assessing, and disseminating information that is more difficult and more costly to obtain since deregulation. Additionally, many brokers have expanded their service offerings beyond the traditional matchmaking function.

A 1984 survey revealed that brokers are often utilized to audit shippers' freight bills; to verify that carriers are properly certificated, licensed, and insured; to provide shipment tracing; to assist shippers with filing damage claims with carriers; to provide local pick-up and delivery of freight; and to provide goods storage and a variety of other transportation-related services.[10] The full-service transport organizer has become a significant component of the motor freight industry.

The adoption of JIT production and inventory systems, an emerging trend in the U.S. economy, has generally benefited the trucking industry. Firms employing JIT place a premium on dependable transportation service and often require smaller, more frequent shipments. JIT also necessitates quick response times and close coordination among manufacturer, supplier, and carrier. In response to the exacting demands of JIT and the opportunities provided by deregulation, shippers have adopted strategies designed to increase their control over truck transportation service. Specifically, shippers have reduced the number of carriers with whom they do business, increased their use of long-term contracts, promoted the advancement of electronic data interchange (EDI), and altered their private carriage operations.

Many shippers have greatly reduced the number of motor carriers they employ. For example, E. I. Du Pont de Nemours and Co., the large chemical company, has reduced the number of its motor carriers from 4,000 to 1,000 and plans to pare the number even further, perhaps to as few as 300.[11] Similarly, Union Carbide decreased the suppliers of trucking service for its chemical division from 125 in 1986 to just 5 by the end of 1987.[12] Economic regulation, because of the geographic and commodity restrictions placed on individual carriers, was not conducive to such a logistics strategy. Shippers with geographically dispersed facilities and several product lines were essentially required to utilize a number of different carriers. The advantages of concentrating freight volumes with fewer carriers are obvious. Shippers benefit from smaller transportation staffs, greater economic leverage over carriers, and services tailored to better meet their needs.

Perhaps the greatest benefit, given the significant rise in motor carrier bankruptcies, is the improved financial stability of the firm's carriers. Shippers generally desire a long-term relationship with dependable, high-quality carriers. Providing financial stability for a small core of trucking firms helps attain this goal.

There has been significant growth in contracting for trucking service. Contracting provides many benefits to both carriers and shippers, including better financial and operating performance for the carriers, carrier services tailored to shippers' logistical needs, direct relationship between freight rates assessed and the quality of service provided, and a generally better and closer relationship between the shipper and carrier. Additionally, long-term contracts minimize carriers' risks of investing in specialized equipment or facilities required to serve specific shippers, and guarantees shippers that such specialized service will be available. Carriers providing both general for-hire service (on demand and at tariff rates) and contract service will almost certainly give top priority to the needs of its contract shippers, because penalties for nonperformance are common features of motor carrier contracts. Thus, shippers under contract have greater influence over their carriers' behavior and often receive premium service.

The ultimate form of control over truck transportation service is shipper-provided transportation, or private carriage. Economic regulation prevented private carriers from providing truck service to other shippers. As a result, private carriers generally incurred higher rates of empty backhauls than the ICC-regulated for-hire carriers. In spite of this costly restriction, in 1980 private carriers transported an estimated 50% of the nation's intercity motor freight.[13]

Most shippers entered private carriage because of its inherent service advantages. However, shippers also entered private carriage for cost reasons. Regulated for-hire carriers employed higher-cost labor and cross-subsidized traffic. So those shippers paying the higher freight rates, thus subsidizing the carriers' unprofitable rate offerings, often turned to private carriage. The advent of deregulation provides conflicting incentives to firms engaged in private carriage. On the one hand, the freight rates of for-hire carriers have decreased significantly and the ability to negotiate long-term contracts enables a shipper to obtain dedicated, customized service. On the other hand, private carriers may potentially reduce their empty vehicle mileage by hauling for other shippers, subleasing idle equipment to for-hire carriers, or establishing for-hire motor carrier subsidiaries that can serve the parent company as well as other shippers. Before deregulation, empty backhauls for private carriers were estimated at about 25% of total vehicle miles, or about two-thirds greater than for-hire truckers. Today, empty backhauls are estimated at only 10% of total vehicle miles.[14]

Restructuring the Railroad Industry

The U.S. railroad industry was granted significant freedom from federal government economic regulation by the Staggers Rail Act of 1980. It was generally believed that economic regulation contributed to the declining role of rail freight transport because it often prevented the railroad industry from responding to changing economic conditions and the emergence of intermodal competition. Intermodal transportation involves delivering material by at least two transport methods, like rail and truck. The reduction of government regulation was intended to provide the railroads with the opportunity to better define their role in the national transportation system and to improve their financial situation.

The organizational and route structures of the railroad industry have changed dramatically since 1980 as a result of mergers among the largest carriers, rail line abandonments, and the divestiture of rail lines by the largest carriers to smaller corporations. The number of railroads in the United States has shrunk from 6,000 in the nineteenth century to just fewer than 500 today (including rail switching and terminal companies), primarily as a result of corporate mergers and consolidations.

Railroads have also benefited from the new regulatory attitude toward rail line abandonments and divestitures. The increased ability to shed profit-draining service has had a positive impact on the railroads' financial condition. From 1970 to 1979 an average of 1,977 miles of rail lines were abandoned each year, while the 1980 to 1987 average increased to 2,366 miles. An even more advantageous strategy for the Class I railroads is the divestiture of lines to smaller railroad corporations. Local and regional railroads can often provide service in low-density markets at a profit because they either utilize nonunion labor or are able to negotiate more favorable wage scales and work rules with the unions. Also, they frequently receive financial support from state and local governments and shippers, and they can increase traffic levels by tailoring service to the needs of shippers with whom they have a closer relationship than did the larger railroads.

The hypothesis that railroad rates were too high during the era of strict ICC economic regulation is supported by data on railroad price levels since 1980. While technological advancements, efficiency gains from route and organizational restructuring, and improved operating strategies have made railroads more cost-effective, railroads have also recognized the need to be more price- and quality-driven to offset service disadvantages vis-à-vis trucking. The level of competition among railroads has increased substantially since regulatory reform, resulting in increased pressure to reduce prices.

It has been estimated that up to 90% of railroad traffic is not presently subject to rate regulation because either it moves under contract between shipper and carrier or the railroad rate-to-variable-cost ratio is within the "zone of rate freedom" established by the Staggers Act. The Staggers Act established a zone of rate freedom within which the railroads have complete freedom of pricing. The zone is measured by the ratio of rate to variable cost, and the threshold for ICC rate regulation is 180%.

The railroad industry has wholeheartedly embraced contracting to improve customer service on an individualized basis and to improve operating performance. Since the passage of the Staggers Act, railroads and their customers have entered into more than 50,000 contracts—with more than 62% of all rail-hauled coal and 63% of rail-hauled grain now moving under contract.[15] Though rail rates established by negotiated contract are confidential, it is widely held that the vast majority of contracts provide rate reductions from published rates, and that contract rates are more closely linked to rail service performance.

Although the railroad industry's short-term performance has improved significantly during the 1980s, serious challenges remain for its long-term prospects. Tonnage originated by the railroads has not increased from volume levels attained in the early 1970s. The approximately 1.4 billion tons of freight originated in 1989 was 6.7% less than the 1.5 billion tons of freight originated in 1979.[16] The major commodity groups served by the industry do not provide a solid foundation on which to build future prospects. For instance, U.S. production of coal, the primary commodity hauled by the railroads (almost 40% of rail tonnage and more than 22% of rail revenue), has been hurt by declining exports as foreign competition and declining oil prices have taken their toll. Similarly, grain exports have also experienced substantial declines as a result of increased foreign production. The production of smaller and lighter automobiles has adversely affected rail tonnage in the automotive sector, not only for the finished product but also for component parts.

The effects of the railroads' new marketing/service orientation and technological innovations have not yet been fully realized. Decades of declining service are etched in the minds of the shipping community. Only significant and sustained improvements in service quality will convince shippers that rail transportation is a viable transport alternative in today's highly competitive, global economy.

Intermodal Transportation

Intermodal transportation involving railroads has increased significantly since deregulation and is the fastest-growing segment of both the railroad industry and transportation in general. Since its introduction in the 1950s, intermodal transportation has been viewed as having vast potential as a means for the railroads to arrest or reverse their declining market share of total domestic intercity freight transportation. The railroads have a significant line-haul cost advantage over trucking firms, particularly for long-distance movements, owing to lower labor and fuel costs per ton-mile. However, this potential has never been fully realized. At the end of World War II the railroads accounted for more than two-thirds of the total U.S. intercity freight ton miles. By 1986 the railroads' market share had declined to approximately 36%. The railroads' loss was the trucking and barge line industries' gain as the motor carrier industry's share of the total market increased from slightly more than 5% to about 25% over this same period, and the barge lines' share increased from approximately 3% to nearly 13%.

The redistribution of traffic among these modes of transportation can be attributed to the substantial increase in government investment in the highway system, particularly the limited-access interstate highway system and the inland river and canal system, along with the changing nature of the U.S. economy and patterns of domestic trade. The transition from basic industries to value-added products and service industries significantly benefited the trucking industry. Higher-valued goods incur larger inventory carrying costs per ton, resulting in shipper distribution strategies emphasizing smaller and more frequent shipments. Also, shippers are willing to pay a premium for better quality service (e.g., faster transit times, more dependable transit times, fewer incidents of damage), because freight rates represent a relatively small percentage of the delivered price of higher-valued goods.

Historically, truck transportation has provided better service than railroads with respect to dependability, damage performance, and transit time over a wide range of distances. The poor financial condition of much of the rail system during the era of economic regulation resulted in undermaintained track and rolling stock and, subsequently, poor service. Fragmented ownership of the rail system and the inability of railroads to provide door-to-door service for most shippers necessitate transfers of freight in-transit among carriers, which add to cost, transit time, and variability of transit time. Close coordination and cooperation among participating carriers is required if a shipper chooses to utilize intermodal transportation. Economic regulation did not foster coordination or cooperation. Restrictions on intermodal ownership, pricing policies that generally stifled technological development and innovation, and the natural propensity of motor carriers not to "short-haul" themselves inhibited the growth of intermodalism.

Intermodal freight movements by rail were completely deregulated by an ICC ruling in 1981. Additionally, barriers to intermodal ownership were greatly reduced after passage of the Staggers Act, and the wave of "end-to-end" vertical mergers among railroads has greatly improved the quality and reduced the cost of rail line–haul service. Railroads have taken advantage of these new freedoms and their improved financial situation to increase volume of intermodal traffic.

Although the growth of intermodal rail-truck transportation since deregulation has been impressive, some of it is the result of diversion of traffic from rail boxcars. Additionally, intermodal revenues equal only about 4% of the total revenue generated by ICC-regulated motor carriers, a figure that has not changed much over the years.[17] However, one transportation analyst estimates that approximately $30 billion of the $128.9 billion intercity truck market (which also includes motor carriers not regulated by the ICC) is susceptible to conversion into intermodal rail service.[18] Currently, trailer-on-flat-car (TOFC) and container-on-flat-car (COFC) collectively generate less than $3 billion annual revenue. The ability of the railroads to penetrate the intercity truck market will likely be enhanced by the developing shortage of long-haul truck drivers, which should in the long run result in higher truck labor costs and decreased truck capacity. Moreover, higher fuel prices resulting from increased truck fuel taxes and/or higher oil prices would work to the advantage of railroads.

The growth in COFC has exceeded that of TOFC, and many railroads are optimistic that high growth rates will continue in the movement of containerized import traffic arriving by ocean vessels. Over the last two decades, the preferred method of ocean shipping has switched from open-hold ships to cellular vessels that handle primarily the standardized 20-foot and 40-foot container "boxes." In 1969 there were 250,000 boxes in service. By 1985 that number had grown to 4,243,000. The world's containership fleet capacity expanded by 19.2% in 1982 and 22.3%

in 1983 and by a slightly lesser amount the following two years. The containerized share of U.S. liner trade grew from nothing to 70% of total ocean-borne volume over the period from 1963 to 1985.[19] The railroads are the chief land transport beneficiaries of this trend. For instance, more than 70% of container shipments between the United States and Asia are routed over American railroads for import and export via West Coast ports.[20] Continued growth in import/export traffic is, of course, contingent on the health of the world economy and the whims of politicians. The immediate future, however, looks bright for the railroads in this arena.

Carrier Strategies

One of the general trends in carrier management since the advent of deregulation has been the adoption of a stronger marketing orientation. In the past, railroads in particular were often accused of establishing operating practices for their own convenience and efficiency rather than in response to the needs of shippers. The railroads' aggressive pursuit of intermodal traffic exemplifies their new marketing orientation. The impressive growth in intermodal volumes has been attained despite many shippers' negative perception of intermodal service. A recent survey of 150 shippers indicates that, in general, most shippers view intermodal service as inferior to truck service on virtually all dimensions, but especially on the most important measures of door-to-door transit time and reliability or dependability.[21] Likelihood of damage and equipment dimension/size are two other areas of service where intermodal operates at a significant comparative disadvantage in the eyes of shippers. To overcome shipper concerns, railroads have adopted new technologies and operating strategies and have altered their relationships with their intermodal partners. Problems still remain, however, as the following discussions of intermodal strategies indicate.

Developments in Technology and Operating Strategies

Perhaps the most significant of the new technologies utilized by railroads is the double-stack rail car—a specially designed flatcar that permits the stacking of containers two high. Double-stack train operations, introduced in 1984, provide as much as 20 to 25% cost savings over conventional COFC equipment in high-volume corridors. Much of the containerized import traffic from Asia destined for inland U.S. points moves on railroad double-stack equipment. As of early 1988, approximately 76 weekly double-stack trains departed from the West Coast.[22]

The steamship companies that originate the import traffic are usually given the credit for the railroads' widespread adoption of the double-stack technology. Indeed, steamship lines often own or lease from outside suppliers the double-stack rail cars used to move cargo.[23] Railroads often provide dedicated service and move entire trains of double-stack cars for individual steamship lines in high-volume corridors. American President Lines, in particular, pioneered the use of double-stack trains and remains one of the largest users of dedicated double-stack trains. Sea-Land Service, another large steamship line, operates a giant intermodal terminal in Tacoma, Washington, and is the biggest single user of stack trains in the Northwest.[24]

The concept of dedicated trains that haul only intermodal equipment has also been adopted in the movement of TOFC. The advantage of these trains is that they do not need to go through rail yards, thus saving time and cost and improving transit time reliability. Dedicated, "run-through" trains have been successfully operated by the railroads in many large-volume, long-haul markets. One example is Union Pacific Railroad's double-stack service from the Ohio valley area to the West Coast. Union Pacific in conjunction with its subsidiary motor carrier, Overnite Transportation, has been able to provide consistent five-day door-to-door service in this market, a transit time very competitive with the long-haul motor carriers.[25]

While the development of new technologies and operating strategies has been a boon to the railroads, problems with technology compatibility among freight modes continues to plague intermodal service. One problem for TOFC service has been the changing dimensions of truck trailers over time. Initially, rail flatcars were designed to accommodate the standard 40-foot truck trailer. As truck trailers increased to 45 feet and, more recently, 48 feet as a result of changes in shippers' needs, the desire of motor carriers' to improve their operating efficiency (particularly in the LTL market), and federal and state policies governing vehicle length and weight, the fleet of rail flatcars has become less compatible and efficient. The railroads' ability to penetrate the long-haul truck markets via TOFC service has become impaired. The motor carrier industry is now pushing hard for the utilization of 53-foot equipment. To continue the growth in intermodal, railroads must invest in flatcars more suited to the new trailers, as well as replace their fleets of the old trailers.

Another compatibility problem facing TOFC service involves the way in which trailers are packed and loaded. Rail transportation of trailers inherently entails more jostling and thus damage to freight, than does over-the-road truck transportation, both in the line-haul movement and in the coupling of flatcars in the rail yards. Run-through trains avoid the rail yard operations, and the development of articulated cars has diminished the line-haul jostling. However, the likelihood of damage to freight remains a major concern of shippers contemplating intermodal service.

Although COFC service for import/export traffic is not generally confronted with these problems, as the containers shipped in international trade are standardized and usually packed tightly, containerization of domestic freight is not a common practice in the United States. Indeed, the railroads and steamship lines have the problem of empty backhauls of containers to the West Coast ports. Some analysts see COFC movements of domestic freight, perhaps on double-stack cars, as the next stage of rail intermodalism.[26] Such a development would shift some traffic away from TOFC and long-haul truck markets. Some shippers have already begun taking advantage of the reduced rates on empty containers returning to the West Coast, but large-scale conversion to containerized domestic freight is not considered likely in the immediate future.[27]

Continued growth in rail intermodal transportation depends on the railroads' ability and willingness to invest in new technology and equipment. Unfortunately for the railroads, the profitability of intermodal traffic has not yet been satisfactory by most measures. Earnings must increase to provide the necessary capital for replacement and expansion of equipment. If the railroads can continue to provide consistent, high-quality intermodal service, rates can be raised without seriously hurting demand. The future of intermodal transportation is also heavily contingent on good relationships and coordination among the various carriers participating in the movements. The following discussion examines two strategies for managing these relationships.

Managing Intermodal Partnerships

The relationship between the railroad and trucking industries has improved considerably over the last five to ten years, owing, in part, to the recognition that the growth of intermodalism will necessarily bring them into partnerships more often in the future. Evidence of this improved relationship is provided by one railroad chief executive officer who notes that the political warfare between the two industries over federal transportation policies has toned down considerably.[28] Of course, railroads and trucking firms remain fierce competitors in the marketplace, but there is increased awareness that they are also potential partners for much traffic.

Two distinct strategies for managing the relationship between intermodal partners are evident in today's transportation industry. One strategy is the creation of multimodal transportation companies, an option not available to carriers prior to deregulation. The second strategy involves programs for improving the coordination and cooperation among interlining carriers outside the sphere of multimodal ownership.

Prior to 1980 the ICC strictly regulated multimodal ownership on the grounds that multimodal companies could potentially engage in anticompetitive behavior such as predatory pricing to drive out independent operators. The few multimodal companies that existed were generally prevented from integrating their operations to provide intermodal service.[29] With the advent of deregulation, the ICC relaxed its restrictive intermodal merger policy, and there have been several intermodal mergers among large carriers in the last five years.

The CSX Railroad is probably the leading advocate of the "total transportation" concept and the synergies provided by multimodal ownership. In 1983 CSX, one of the five largest railroads in the country, purchased American Commercial Barge Lines, which was either the largest or second-largest barge line. CSX also formed a trucking company, Chessie Motor Express, and in 1987 acquired Sea-Land Service, a large steamship line. This latter acquisition was the nation's first merger between a railroad and a steamship company.

Other significant mergers include the 1985 acquisition of North American Van Lines, the nation's sixth-largest trucking firm at that time, by the Norfolk Southern, one of the five largest railroads in the country, and the 1987 acquisition of Overnite Transportation Co., the fifth-largest trucking firm overall and largest nonunion trucking company, by the Union Pacific, also one of the five largest railroads. In 1983 United States Lines, a large ocean carrier, received ICC authority to establish a nationwide trucking company to feed traffic to its shipping company. Air-truck ownerships include Consolidated Freightways, the third-largest trucking company; expansion into the air freight industry; and Tiger International, a multimodal company that operates Flying Tiger Line and a few motor carriers.

The formation of some of these multimodal companies was for investment rather than for providing integrated intermodal service. However, many of these companies have begun integrating the operations of their components as evidenced by the Union Pacific–Overnite example. The benefits of intermodal consolidations include the following:

- Duplicative expenses decline and economies of scope result from the horizontal nature of multimodal mergers.
- Improved and more cost-effective intermodal transportation service results from the improved economic and physical coordination inherent in an intermodal move controlled by one carrier.
- Improved pricing of intermodal services results from the ability to construct and price an entire intermodal move.
- Railroads now have increased capability to offer new marketing opportunities for shippers.[30]

Included in the aforementioned benefits are the usual arguments of the benefits of "one-stop shopping" such as reduced transaction costs. It is also argued that an integrated company would more likely route traffic to gain the maximum cost and service advantages from each mode under its control, given that it would maintain the traffic under any routing.

Future Directions

While it has been demonstrated that transportation has a causal effect on commerce, the reverse also holds true. Economic growth stimulates the demand for transportation. This basic nature of transportation necessitates that attention be given to strategic issues. Competitiveness in the 1990s will increase both domestically and globally. The consolidation of the European Economic Community is estimated to lead to billions of dollars in distribution savings.[31] This will be occurring during a time when many analysts believe that economic "softness" will continue.[32] To improve the U.S. competitive advantage, logistics costs, which have stabilized since 1985, must be reduced. Transportation is a viable means of achieving the needed reduction.

Three key areas characterized transportation improvements of the 1980s:

- Concentrated use of fewer carriers and suppliers
- Reduction of excess capacity
- Service quality improvements

As the opportunity for efficiencies in these areas lessens, the focus for cost savings will include state reregulation, technology, and equipment.

Reregulation. The potential for further efficiency improvements in transportation exists at the state level through uniformity of regulations. States to date have made little progress in developing standard and reciprocal systems to collect truck fuel taxes and registration fees. For example, under the International Fuel Tax Agreement, fuel purchases are reported only in the state where the truck is registered. Fuel taxes resulting from the purchases are apportioned to other states according to the mileage operated in the jurisdiction. Currently, this group comprises only 16 states, with several other states expressing an interest in joining.[33] Changes in registration for interstate operating authority would also improve the efficiency of the current process. The base-state approach, similar to the fuel tax plan, would simplify the process and introduce uniformity to truck registration across the states.

Technology. Technological innovations in trucking are expected to address such areas as engine and aerodynamic design, structural weight reduction, and intelligent vehicle systems. Quality of distribution services for railroads will be the most significant technological enhancement for the remainder of the twentieth century as advances in computers and communications make it possible to conduct business on a real-time basis.

Equipment. Equipment technology, which holds promise for intermodal service in both short-haul and long-haul markets and which avoids the technology incompatibility problems, is the so-called carless technology. The carless technology concept involves truck trailers with rail wheel assemblies either permanently affixed or detachable. One of its chief benefits is reduced handling at the rail terminals, which reduces transit time. Though this technology has been in existence for some time, it has not yet been widely adopted. Union Pacific's Rail-Rider provides service between Chicago and Dallas in which trailers ride directly on railroad wheel assemblies (i.e., no flatcars are used in the operation) to the destination rail terminal, at which point they are driven off the rail wheels and delivered, on rubber tires, directly to customers' loading docks. The Rail-Rider trains operate at 70 miles per hour and run on 26-hour schedules, five days a week.[34]

The evolving carrier/shipper relationship requires carriers to respond in new ways to the market environment. To move from an environment where transportation was perceived as an undifferentiated "commodity" to one offering a value-added service, it will be necessary to develop marketing strategies that proffer a wider range of both transportation and logistics services to shippers. The expanded role of transportation in the new environment will develop into mutually beneficial relationships for carriers and shippers.

Continuing Challenges

The changing transportation regulatory environment has provided many opportunities and challenges for carriers and shippers. Carriers have taken advantage of their new freedoms to alter their marketing and operating strategies. Shippers have implemented logistics strategies that were essentially not viable before deregulation. Innovations in transportation technology and service are occurring in quantum leaps rather than at the snail's pace of the prederegulation era.

Perhaps the greatest challenges posed by deregulation lie in the changing relationships among the modes of transportation, between carriers and shippers, and between carrier management and labor. The breakdown of the artificial barriers has greatly altered the relationships among modes. The barriers artificially separated modal ownership and operations and prevented any one firm from offering the full range of transportation and transportation-related services. Cooperation and coordination among the modes have improved and will continue to improve. Carriers and shippers are working together more closely than ever as a result of contracting for service, the advent of EDI, and the exacting requirements of logistics systems like JIT. The potential impact of this fundamental change in the shipper-carrier relationship on the organization of transportation industries has not yet been considered or addressed by transport policymakers or scholars. Finally, the unleashed competitive pressures of the marketplace have led to a serious deterioration in labor-management relations, and the unresolved issues in this area will continue to attract increasing attention from management, labor leaders, and government policymakers.

Notes

1. Stacy C. Davis and Patricia S. Hu, *Transportation Energy Data Book: Edition 11* (Oak Ridge, Tenn.: Oak Ridge National Laboratory, 1991).
2. Robert Delaney, "State of Logistics: Annual Report" (St. Louis: Cass Logistics, June 1991).
3. American Trucking Association, *American Trucking Trends. 1987* (Alexandria, Va.: American Trucking Association, 1988), p. 13.
4. James P. Rakowski, "Marketing Economies and the Results of Trucking Deregulation in the Less-Than-Truckload Sector," *Transportation Journal* 27, no. 3 (Spring 1988): 19.
5. Ibid., p. 13.
6. Denis A. Breen, "Market Structure and Competition in Trucking," Mimeo (Washington, D.C.: Bureau of Economics, Federal Trade Commission, September 1984), cited in Diane S. Owens, "Deregulation in the Trucking Industry: A Survey of the Literature," paper presented at the Annual Conference of the Transportation and Public Utilities Group of the American Economic Association, December 29, 1988, p. 15.

7. U.S. General Accounting Office, *Trucking Regulation: Price Competition and Market Structure in the Trucking Industry,* report to Congressional Requesters (Washington, D.C.: U.S. General Accounting Office, 1987), pp. 2–4.
8. Charles A. Taff, "A Study of Truck Brokers of Agricultural Commodities Exempt from Economic Regulation," *Transportation Journal* 18, no. 3 (Spring 1979): 5–6.
9. David M. Cawthorne, "Truck broker re-regulation: an issue whose time has gone," *Traffic World* (July 18, 1988): 18.
10. Michael R. Crum, "The Expanded Role of Motor Carrier Freight Brokers in the Wake of Regulatory Reform" *Transportation Journal* 24, no. 4 (Summer 1985): 5–15.
11. James Callari and James A. Cooke, "Deregulation Impact: The Shippers," *Traffic Management* (September 1987): 61.
12. Bruce Heydt, "Union Carbide: Looking for a Few Good Carriers," *Distribution* (January 1988): 41–42.
13. Standard & Poor's, "Railroads and Trucking: Basic Analysis," *Standard & Poor's Industry Surveys* 155, no. 14 (April 2, 1987): R36.
14. Ibid., p. R37.
15. Frank N. Wilner, *Railroads and the Marketplace* (Washington, D.C.: Association of American Railroads, 1987), p. 33.
16. Association of American Railroads, *Railroad Facts* (Washington, D.C.: 1991), p. 16.
17. "Picking Up On Intermodal's Promise," *Distribution* (June 1987): 14.
18. John G. Larkin, "Will High-Service Truckload Carriers Kill Intermodal Transportation?" *Private Carrier* (September 1987): 24.
19. "International Movements, Changing Rapidly, Offer Attractive Inbound Rates for Overseas Sourcing," *Inbound Traffic* (April 1985): 19.
20. Ibid., p. 20.
21. David L. Sparkman, "Rails Must Invest More for Intermodal to Thrive, Expo Told," *Transport Topics* (May 2,1988), p. 13. Study performed by Temple, Barker & Sloane, now part of Mercer Management Consulting.
22. Robert J. Bowman, "Ship lines, railroads, customers sorting out double-stack future," *Traffic World* (April 18, 1988): 44–48.
23. John Davies, "Double-Stack Growth Continues," *Journal of Commerce* (December 31, 1987): 4B.
24. Ibid.
25. "UP-Overnite Service Kicks In," *Distribution* (February 1988): 18.
26. See, for example, Robert J. Kursar, "Intermodal industry seen shaky, but on verge of breakthrough," *Traffic World* (May 2,1988): 10–11; and Bowman, "Ship lines," p. 44.
27. An excellent example of taking advantage of otherwise empty container backhauls is the development of the load and roll pallet, a device used to load lengths of metal products into sea containers, by Point Transportation, a Chicago-based firm involved in TOFC transportation of metal products.
28. "Rail Chief Explores Trends in Intermodalism: BN's Gaskins Sees New Era for Rail, Truck Partners," *Transport Topics* (March 24, 1986): 10–12.
29. For a review of the history of regulatory policy concerning intermodal mergers, see Michael R. Crum and Benjamin J. Allen, "U.S. Transportation Merger Policy: Evolution, Current Status, and Antitrust Considerations," *International Journal of Transport Economics* 13, no. 1 (February 1986): 57–69.

30. G. Paul Moates, "Transport Industry Concentration and Cross-Ownership—The Future of Intermodal Competition," *Eastern Transportation Law Seminar* (1984): 74–75.
31. Robert Delaney, "State of Logistics: Annual Report."
32. *Traffic World* (January 6, 1992): 24.
33. David M. Cawthome, "Focus on transport regulation shifts to the state level," *Traffic World* (March 11, 1991): 34–36.
34. Association of American Railroads, "New 'Rail-Rider' Service Operates Without Flatcars," *Rail News Update,* March 2,1988, p. 2.

CHAPTER 22

The Role of New Information Technology in the Practice of Traffic Management

James M. Masters
Bernard J. La Londe

Traffic management has always been an information-intensive undertaking. Planning, directing, and controlling the shipment of goods into and out of the firm in a timely and cost-effective way can be achieved only by mastering the information flow that must accompany the movement of the goods. Throughout the 1980s and early 1990s, many forces in the business environment combined to make the management of the traffic function more challenging than ever before. At the same time, new forms of information technology have become available that enable the contemporary traffic manager to meet the challenges presented by this new era and that enable the manager, in fact, to do a better job than ever before. This chapter outlines the challenges facing the traffic function, reviews new information technology now available in the traffic management area, and shows how this new technology is being used to improve traffic management.

For the purpose of this discussion, information technology is divided into three major categories: data processing hardware and software, and telecommunications. The combination of these technologies now available is transforming the way the traffic function is managed.

Data Processing Hardware. Data processing hardware encompasses the computers, central processing units (CPUs), direct access storage devices (DASDs), and so forth, that form the backbone of the modern information system. Throughout the 1980s and 1990s, these platforms have become more powerful and more economical with each passing month. The most spectacular growth has occurred in the area of the microcomputer, or personal computer (PC). The ready availability of these inexpensive and reliable machines has paved the way for significant changes in business practice throughout the American economy, and the traffic function is certainly no exception.

Software. Software programs are designed to store, retrieve, and manipulate data within the computer. Software might perform simple bookkeeping functions, or it might contain sophisticated problem-solving algorithms like those required for vehicle scheduling and dispatching. More powerful hardware platforms have allowed software developers to produce fast, flexible, graphics-oriented, user-friendly software tools to automate many aspects of the traffic management function. Software developers have now developed forms of artificial intelligence (AI) like expert systems (ES), which mimic the behavior of a human expert in the solution of a problem and have been applied to the traffic function for various tasks.

Telecommunications. Telecommunications technology automates the way that information is entered into a computer or passed from one computer to another. The most important examples of these capabilities from the traffic management perspective are barcoding and electronic data interchange (EDI). In barcoding, an item like a carton or a shipping container can be labeled with a bar code that can be optically scanned with simple hardware. The scanned data can be directly input to the computer, providing fast and accurate identification of property. In EDI, data are directly passed from one computer to another—often, from one firm to another. The data are passed electronically, in digital format, and in such a way that the receiving computer can process them directly. For example, a shipper might send a tracing inquiry to a carrier, a billing inquiry to a vendor, or an invoice to a customer. These transactions would be received via EDI and processed by the recipient's data system, then responses would be sent immediately via EDI to the shipper's data system, with no human intervention.

Forces of Change

The evolution of information technology is important for firms and managers to understand, as many have not yet experienced these changes. The current state of information technology in traffic management has been formed by several notable forces of change. These forces have increased the importance of information technology and require leading firms to apply it with greater sophistication.

Throughout the 1980s and early 1990s a number of significant events and trends in the general business environment provided new challenges and opportunities for traffic managers. In each case, these phenomena affected the way traffic managers used information to control the traffic function.

Transportation Deregulation

The economic deregulation of the transportation industry provided the shipper with new opportunities to negotiate freight rates and terms of service with a large number of carriers. This gave the astute shipper new ability to control cost and improve service through negotiating with carriers. On the other hand, deregulation also greatly increased the information complexity of the traffic environment. Carrier rates and routes, which had been very fixed and stable, were now completely fluid. Simple manual information systems that may have been adequate in a regulated environment were simply overwhelmed in a situation where rates and routes could change without notice. This provided a powerful incentive for firms to develop automated information systems of all types to cope with the dynamic changes occurring in the ground rules of traffic management.

Deregulation led to dramatic changes in the structure of the motor carrier industry. In the less-than-truckload (LTL) segment of the industry, the need to coordinate and control a large, capital-intensive network of terminals, transshipment operations, linehaul operations, and local pickup and delivery operations provided a significant barrier to new entrants in the field, and the number of firms in this segment has in fact decreased.[1] New information technology provided these large and efficient LTL carriers an important tool to better manage their own operations, reducing costs and improving service to shippers. To the extent that large and successful firms were able to employ these technologies, the development of these new ways of doing business reinforces concentration in the LTL segment.

However, deregulation led to an explosion in the number of new, small carriers offering to serve in the truckload (TL) segment of the industry. The number of interstate motor carriers, which had been about 15,000 from 1960 to 1975, grew to approximately 40,000 by 1987.[2] At the same time, the number of motor carriers that failed and left the marketplace also leaped. Carrier failures had averaged about 200 to 250 per year prior to deregulation. In 1987 alone, 1,548 motor carriers failed.[3] This constant churning of the carrier base led to a serious information problem for the shipper, who now needed a greatly improved information capability to stay abreast of the changes taking place. In some cases, third-party freight brokers helped to bring together shippers with freight and small TL carriers with equipment and drivers. Once again, the importance of information processing capability had increased.

Mergers and Acquisitions

The 1980s and early 1990s witnessed a wave of corporate mergers, leveraged buyouts, and acquisitions. The ownership of many firms changed hands three or four times over a ten-year period. In many cases these mergers made good corporate sense from a product line, marketing, and production point of view. However, the result was often a new firm that had, in effect, two traffic departments. Firms struggled with the issues involved in integrating the operation of the two departments, which typically operated in different ways with different carriers and used different information systems. The unified traffic department that eventually emerged usually had fewer employees than the two departments it replaced and typically had a more highly automated information system.

Downsizing

A third major factor that affected many corporate traffic operations was the general movement towards corporate downsizing. This was a deliberate effort on the part of many major corporations to reduce costs and improve their competitive position by reducing the number of employees, particularly in support positions like traffic. As a result, the average firm has reduced the number of employees, both clerical and managerial, in the traffic department at the same time that the information complexity of the traffic task increased, owing to the effects of deregulation and merger/acquisition forces. A general response to this challenge to do more with less was to automate information processing in the traffic function.

Innovations in Inventory Control

Throughout the 1980s and early 1990s many firms were radically revising their inventory control philosophy. The general goal was to reduce the total investment in inventory assets by replacing large, infrequent inventory replenishments with many frequent, small, tightly controlled inventory replenishments. In manufacturing environments, firms implemented materials requirements planning (MRP) systems to schedule the inbound flow of raw materials and components into the production facility. Firms implemented distribution resource planning (DRP) systems to coordinate the outbound flow of finished goods throughout the physical distribution channel. In each case, these systems allowed managers to substitute information for inventory, to reduce logistics costs, and to improve logistics system performance. These innovations also increased the burden on the traffic department. Because shipment sizes were smaller, more shipments (and more small shipments) were required. Because inventory safety stocks were reduced or eliminated, on-time delivery became even more important. Many production facilities moved toward just-in-time (JIT) inventory systems, where replenishment quantities were intended to support only a few hours' worth of production, and no safety stock at all was held. These systems placed the entire production process at risk of disruption if any delivery were late, and therefore they increased the information complexity and operational control problem of the traffic department. In the retail setting, many firms moved toward quick response (QR) inventory systems, which applied the JIT approach of many small, frequent replenishment shipments to the distribution of finished goods. All these types of inventory systems are feasible only in an automated inventory control environment. Their use has reduced inventory costs and improved customer service, and in many cases has improved the competitiveness and profitability of the firm. In many cases, these inventory innovations have also forced the traffic department to employ new forms of information technology to be able to support the inventory strategy.

Corporate Partnering

Many firms have also attempted to develop partnerships or alliances with their vendors, customers, and logistics service providers. The theory is that by entering into stable, long-term, "contractual" relationships based on trust, cooperation, and commitment, the firm can achieve better results than by employing the traditional, short-term, "transactional" relationships, with their focus on lowest-cost bid and the constant threat of withdrawal from the relationship. The application of this philosophy in traffic management has led many firms to greatly reduce the number of carriers with whom they do business and to greatly increase the volume and level of detail of the information they share with their carriers. This requirement to exchange large volumes of operating data on a very frequent, near real-time basis has impelled many firms to employ new forms of information technology throughout the traffic function.

Quality

The 1980s can be thought of as the decade in which many American firms rediscovered the importance of quality. Quality improvement efforts were first focused in the production area, but many firms quickly realized that the basic lessons of quality control and continuous improvement could and should be applied to all aspects of the firm's operation, including all logistics functions, as well as traffic management. Applying quality control techniques to the traffic process often involved collecting and analyzing detailed, transaction-level performance records. This sort of data analysis can be performed efficiently only in a large transportation system with a reasonably sophisticated automated information system; hence, the movement toward quality control was one more factor that increased the information complexity of the traffic activity and encouraged the adoption of new information technology to handle the information burden.

New Information Technology

A final factor that influenced the automation of the traffic function was simply the availability and proliferation of new hardware, software, and telecommunications technologies that have become available since 1980. These new technologies can be seen as the answer to the traffic manager's prayer. Technology provides a means to cope with the increasing information intensity and complexity of the traffic management task that has come about through the interplay of the forces of deregulation, merger, downsizing, inventory reduction, partnering, and quality. Many traffic departments have seized the initiative, embracing new information technology as a creative solution to their problem. In other firms, the traffic department has been more reactive. These firms have adopted new technology, particularly telecommunications innovations like barcoding and EDI, because their customer base or trading partners have begun to demand it.

Role of Information Technology

The use of computerized information processing in traffic management is not a new idea. Traffic management was, in fact, among the first applications of the computer in business, along with inventory control, payroll, and accounts receivable. In a study of the use of computers in distribution by *Fortune* 500 companies conducted in 1971, 75% reported using computer-based systems.[4] While 70% of these firms were using their computers for inventory control, 56% reported applications involving freight tonnage and cost analysis, and 46% were using these systems for shipment routing. In this era, however, data systems were largely administrative in nature. For example, computers were used for bill-of-lading preparation and carrier payment, but they were seldom used in a decision-making context or in any strategic sense. These systems were seen as a means to reduce costs and improve the accuracy and speed of routine transactions.

Many forward-thinking logistics executives have recognized the growing importance of information technology in the logistics arena. In 1987 the Council of Logistics Management (CLM) conducted a comprehensive study of logistics executives' opinions about future trends in logistics practice. The three most significant trends found in the study were as follows:

1. The rapid proliferation of data processing systems enables the distribution or logistics organization to handle and control information in ways that will change the traditional methods of servicing customers and supplying products.
2. Advances in computer technology will allow EDI to be pervasive by 1995. All phases of logistics will be involved, and communications technology will create opportunities for large savings.
3. The major difference between the logistics operating environment of 1995 and today will be the improvement in the timeliness and completeness of the exchange of information between channel members.[5]

By the early 1990s it was clear to most observers that the traffic function would be a major player in the ongoing evolution of logistics information systems. Another study published by the CLM in 1989 focused on the distinguishing characteristics that typified firms with superior levels of logistics competency, that is, firms that practiced leading-edge logistics. The study found a common thread among leading-edge practitioners compared with average firms:

- Leading-edge firms are more significant users of data processing technology and enjoy a higher quality of information system support than average firms.
- Leading-edge firms typically have more state-of-the-art computer applications and are planning more updates and expansions than average firms.
- Leading-edge firms are more involved in new technology like electronic data interchange and artificial intelligence than average firms.[6]

Levels of Implementation

New information technology is being adopted by shippers and carriers for many different reasons and for many different purposes. Some firms are merely reacting to customer demands, while others are taking a long-range, planning-oriented approach to information system redesign. A useful framework to think about the issues of information technology adoption has been proposed by David Jacoby, who suggests that information systems can be categorized as belonging to one of three levels of importance: the administrative level, the operational level, and the strategic level.[7]

Administrative-level Systems. Administrative systems take routine, repetitive tasks that had been done manually and automate them. Most of the first business applications of computers in the 1960s took this form, such as the automation of payroll, accounts receivable, and inventory accounting. The motivation here is usually to reduce costs by reducing payroll and to increase the accuracy and timeliness of the process. New technologies at this level in the transportation area include electronic billing, electronic rail car ordering, and so forth. Information innovation at this level should not be expected to fundamentally alter the cost structure of the firm or to affect its basic business strategy.

Operational-level Systems. At this level, more sophisticated information technology is used to help with the actual decision-making tasks involved in ongoing transportation operations. For example, Burlington Northern has developed a software package called ShipSmart that a customer can use to evaluate the cost, service, and inventory implications of various modal alternatives.[8] Other examples include TRUCKS and RoadShow, which are microcomputer-based software packages that a shipper can use to automate the scheduling and routing of a complex private fleet operation.[9] Information technology at this level can make a significant contribution toward reducing costs and improving customer service levels by improving the quality of day-to-day operational decision making.

Strategic-level Systems. In some cases, new information systems can be considered strategic in nature. Jacoby suggests the following criteria for a strategic information system:

- A strategic information system establishes the business, its primary competitive advantage, or a large proportion of its revenue.
- A strategic information system extends the product line by providing a new value-added service to clients, or becomes vital to the success of the firm by giving it a competitive advantage or a new revenue base.[10]

Examples of such strategic systems in the transportation industry include American Airlines' SABRE reservation system and the customer-oriented information systems developed by American President Lines. In the view of this firm's management, "We set ourselves apart from the competition by providing extensive and reliable information services."[11]

Automation of the Traffic Function

Many firms are developing administrative- and operational-level information systems to automate the traditional functions and processes in the traffic management area. For example, the 3M Corporation has developed an on-line integrated freight management system (FMS) to pro-

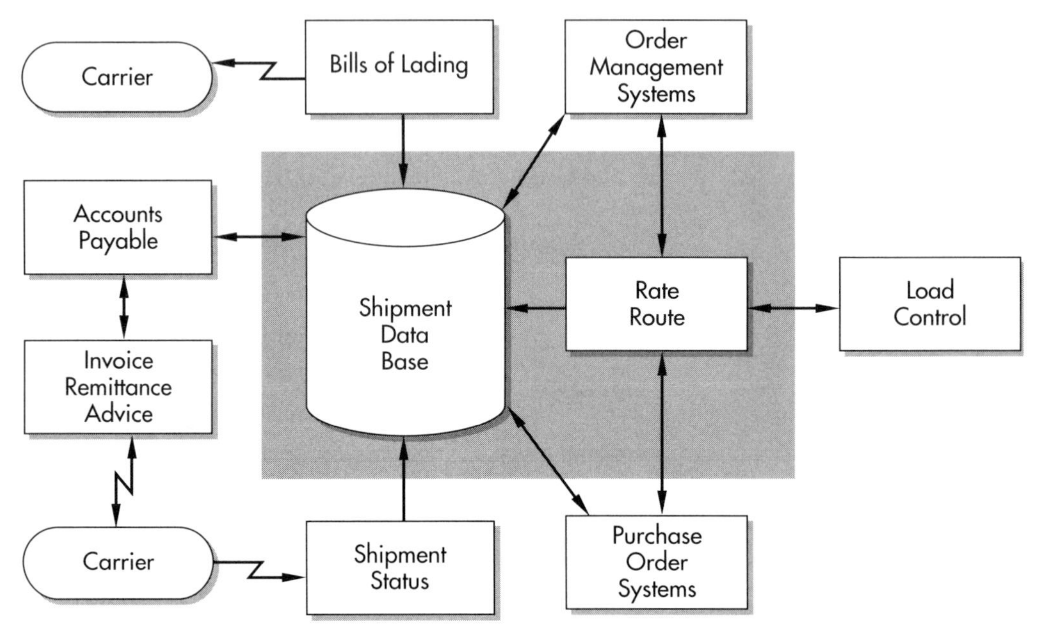

Figure 22-1
3M Freight Management System

vide shipment-related and customer service information, as well as decision support capability.[12] The FMS is designed to operate in an IBM mainframe environment to support traffic information needs for 3M in the areas of rating, routing, and pricing. The 3M traffic environment includes 170 shipping locations in the United States, over 50,000 products, and over 250,000 shipments per month. The FMS, which is designed to plan, track, and evaluate each shipment in the 3M system, is a large-scale system that was designed and implemented over a five-year time span. A schematic of the FMS is shown in Figure 22-1.

Commercial Software for Traffic Management

While some firms like 3M develop large-scale traffic information systems in-house through their corporate information systems departments, many other firms develop administrative- and operational-level traffic systems by purchasing off-the-shelf commercial software that has already been developed, debugged, and extensively field-tested by other users. By doing so, the traffic manager greatly reduces the cost, lead time, and considerable risks involved in developing a new system application from scratch. The trade-off, however, is that the manager is forced to live with the capabilities and limitations designed into the commercial software, and must determine how best to adapt the software to the firm's operation and vice versa.

In many cases the trade-off of limitations for simplicity is well worth making, in that hundreds of well-developed software packages are now available that offer a wide range of options to the traffic manager. In fact, so many software systems are now available that one of the biggest problems in an automation project is often the choice of the software package. Each year the CLM distributes a compendium of logistics software packages compiled by Andersen Consulting. Recent volumes of this book have been the size of a metropolitan telephone directory and have included descriptions of over one thousand logistics software systems and packages. In the Andersen survey, software developed for traffic management is grouped into three functional categories:

- *Transportation Analysis.* This software allows management to monitor costs and service by providing historical reporting of carrier performance, shipping modes, traffic lane utilization, premium freight usage, backhauls, and other analyses.
- *Traffic Routing and Scheduling.* This functional area provides features like the sequence and timing of vehicle stops, route determinations, shipping paperwork preparation, and vehicle availability.
- *Freight Rate Maintenance and Auditing.* These systems maintain a database of freight rates used to rate shipments and/or to perform freight bill auditing. It compares actual freight bills with charges computed using the lowest applicable rates in the database. It can then pay or authorize payment or report on exceptions.[13]

Growth in the Automation of Traffic Functions

The automation of information processing and decision-making processes in the traffic management function is a general trend occurring across the American business landscape. The movement toward increased information automation is highlighted in a comprehensive study of the traffic function conducted for the American Society of Transportation and Logistics (AST&L) in 1990.[14] The actual and forecasted automation trends for eight traffic activities are summarized in Table 22-1. If the automation percentages are combined across functions by weighting each function by time and effort expended, it can be estimated that the traffic function was 8% automated in 1980, was 26% automated by 1990, and will be 47% automated by 1995.

Trends in Information Technology Implementation

The 1992 CLM career patterns survey indicates significant trends in the implementation of JIT, barcoding, and EDI.[15] In each case, executives expect at least half of all traffic volume will fall

TABLE 22-1
Trends in Automation of the Traffic Management Function

		Percent Automated		
Traffic Activity	**Percent Time and Effort**	**1980**	**1990**	**1995**
Rate negotiation	22.8	4.7	19.0	32.0
Carrier selection	13.9	8.4	22.7	41.1
Private fleet*	13.7	5.4	17.4	33.0
Billing/auditing	9.8	17.1	46.4	75.7
Routing	9.1	13.9	38.3	62.8
Carrier assignment	9.0	12.1	29.6	56.1
Tracing/expediting	7.2	9.5	30.7	57.7
Claims	6.1	7.2	25.2	44.4

* 53% of the respondents reported that they operate a private fleet.

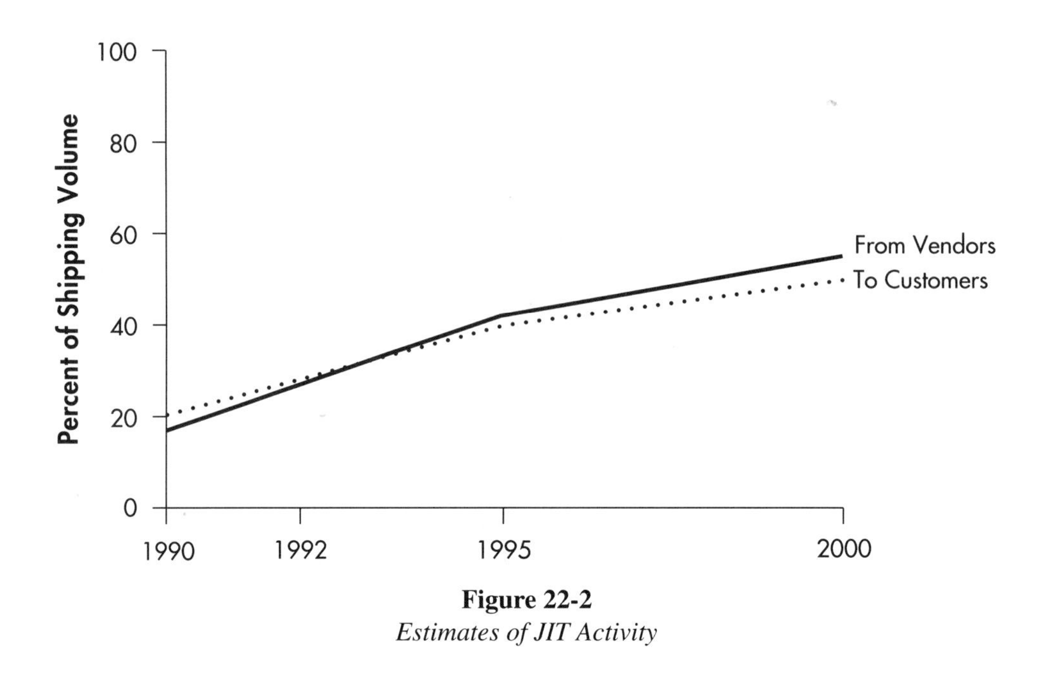

Figure 22-2
Estimates of JIT Activity

into one or more of these trends before the turn of the century. AI and ES systems are also being implemented to improve traffic management. Formerly the exclusive domain of university and research laboratories, these technologies are being brought to bear on traffic management. Although traffic management has traditionally been viewed as unglamorous, it requires great expertise, knowledge, and massive amounts of data in an increasingly complex marketplace with extraordinary volumes. These characteristics of traffic management present continual needs for increased efficiency and simplicity in everyday operations—benefits barcoding, EDI, AI, and ES technologies deliver.

Just-in-Time Inventory Control. As seen in Figure 22-2, logistics executives expect that in the near future roughly half of the typical firm's shipping volume, both inbound from vendors and outbound to customers, will move under some form of just-in-time control. These high levels of just-in-time activity provide a powerful stimulus to the traffic manager to build a modern information system that can provide detailed, real-time data necessary to operate and control a successful just-in-time system.

Barcoding. Bar codes provide the ability to quickly, accurately, and economically input large volumes of data into the traffic information system to guide, monitor, and control the movement of freight throughout the traffic system. As shown in Figure 22-3, adoption of barcoding technology is continuing to grow. By 1995 the typical executive expects to ship 60% of total product volume barcoded. Some individuals reported that their firms are planning on 100% barcoding of all shipments.

Electronic Data Interchange. This telecommunication technology allows the traffic manager to link the firm's internal traffic information system to those of its vendors, customers, and carriers. The potential gains from such linkages can be great, but the interorganizational aspects of this technology seem to be slowing the spread of EDI. As noted, executives at all levels recog-

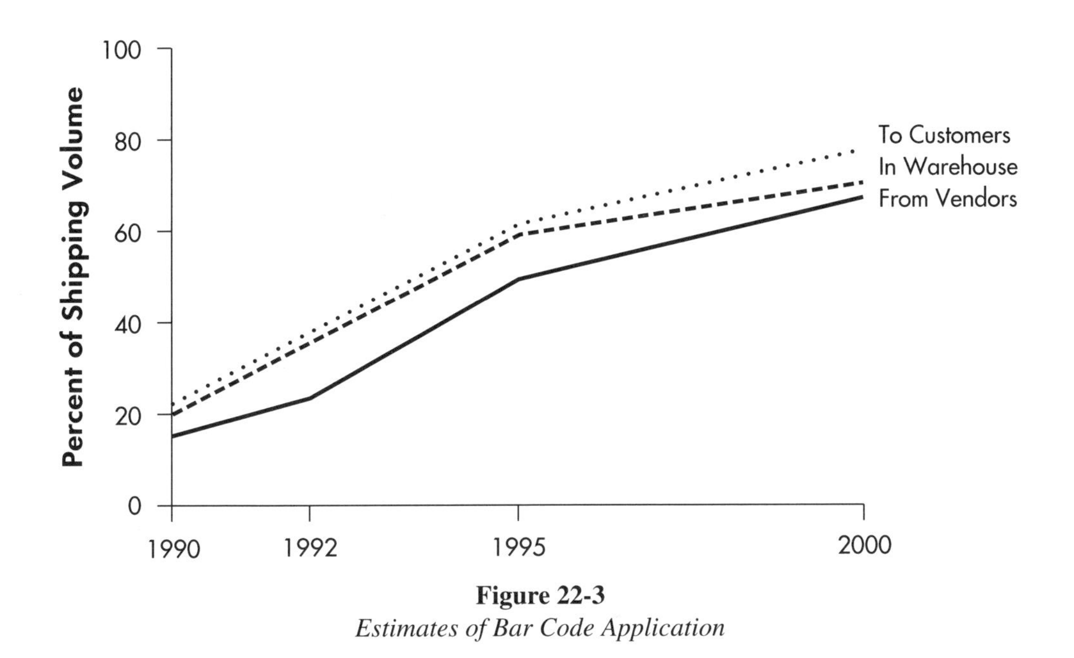

Figure 22-3
Estimates of Bar Code Application

nize the advantages and potential benefits of EDI, and they also project widespread acceptance and use of the technology. Figure 22-4 shows that logistics executives expect EDI usage to climb to the range of 50% to 60% of all transactions with vendors, customers, and carriers by the year 2000, with most of the growth occurring by 1995. These projections are consistent with other comparable forecasts; in the AST&L study, shippers projected rates of EDI usage for inbound and outbound traffic in the range of 40% to 45% by 1995.[16] However, actual growth achieved in the usage of EDI has been fairly slow and is in fact lagging behind previous estimates. In a comparable study of executive expectations conducted in 1988, EDI usage was projected to be from 44% to 52% by 1995, and the rate was expected to have climbed to 23% to 35% by 1990.[17] Thus the actual rates of EDI usage in the early 1990s have lagged behind what had been anticipated, and one might conclude that executives are again being overly optimistic.

Several factors have apparently delayed the rapid spread of EDI in traffic management. The lack of a universal standard for EDI transactions has complicated the implementation process for many firms. As a company tries to expand its EDI usage across its many vendors or customers or carriers, it often finds that it must deal with many different EDI formats and protocols. As a result, it is very easy to establish an initial level of EDI activity, but it becomes more difficult to expand the EDI linkage to all the firms with which the company does business. Third-party EDI networks have emerged as a response to this problem.

Many firms have entered into EDI implementation without an explicit understanding of its costs and benefits.[18] In most of these cases the motivation to begin EDI usage was not cost savings. Rather, EDI was viewed in a more strategic sense as a tool to provide competitive advantage.

Adoption of EDI for traffic management was studied from the point of view of the carrier in a 1990 study, which indicated that motor carrier EDI use was not extensive.[19] Carriers reported that they had replaced about 10% of their paper transactions in 1990 with EDI transactions and that they expected this number to grow to 23% by 1995. Carriers related that the principal limit to the growth of EDI was a lack of demand for the service from their shippers,

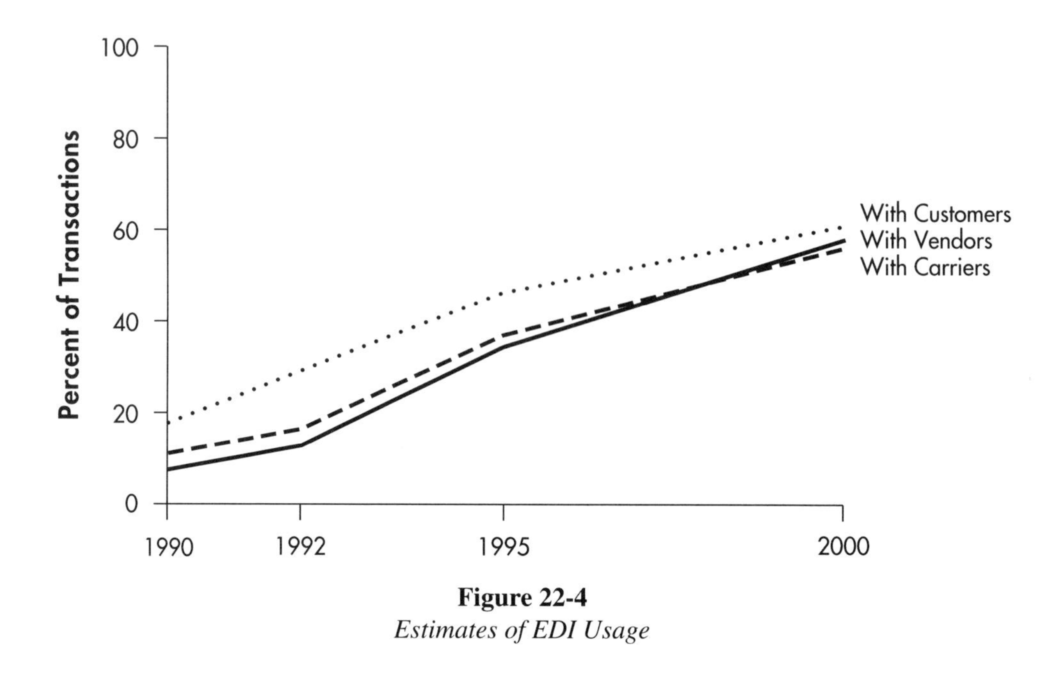

Figure 22-4
Estimates of EDI Usage

and they further suggested four important reasons why shippers have not been interested in EDI:

1. Lack of awareness of EDI benefits
2. Lack of customer training/education
3. High setup cost
4. Lack of uniform standards

The growth of EDI may not be occurring as fast as had been anticipated, but it is nevertheless occurring and will continue to do so. Successful integration of EDI linkages into traffic information systems remains an important goal for most firms in the 1990s.

Artificial Intelligence and Expert Systems. Another area of information technology that is beginning to influence traffic management practice is artificial intelligence (AI). AI can be generally thought of as the development of computers that perform functions that people perform. Although the more exotic forms of AI like intelligent robotics have not yet made an impact on traffic management, the AI discipline of expert systems (ES) is beginning to contribute to management practice. In an expert system, the knowledge, wisdom, and experience of a recognized human expert in a given area is captured by a "knowledge engineer"; then this knowledge and problem-solving capability are embedded in a computer program so that other workers, often novices, can perform the task at hand nearly as well as the expert. In this way the invaluable knowledge of key personnel can be shared throughout the firm. ES development software is now widely available, and useful systems can be constructed on microcomputer platforms. A study performed for the CLM demonstrates that several innovative firms are using ES in traffic organizations to reduce costs, raise productivity, and improve quality:

- Digital Equipment Corporation uses an expert system to route carriers. The system has reduced transportation costs by 10%.
- Burlington Northern uses an expert system to advise claims agents on how to process freight relief claims.
- Sea-Land Service uses an expert system to assist customer service representatives in the selection of preferred routings and schedules for ocean cargo.[20]

The application of ES to traffic management has only begun. Potential applications in this area are limited only by the imagination of the managers involved.

Increasing Importance of Information Technology

The AST&L study shows the relative importance of information technologies to the success of the traffic department (see Figure 22-5).[21] All information technologies were viewed as only moderately important during the 1980s, and all were projected to assume much larger roles during the 1990s. The microcomputer was thought to be the most important of all. This makes good sense, in that inexpensive, reliable, and powerful desktop machines used in traffic departments today have many different uses, from the relatively simple spreadsheet programs to assisting in rate analyses and negotiations to sophisticated graphics-oriented programs for performing route design and vehicle scheduling. It is also possible to establish an EDI program and design and to operate ES on microcomputers. This capability and flexibility allow the traffic organization to explore and test the possibilities of these technologies quickly and relatively inexpensively. It is

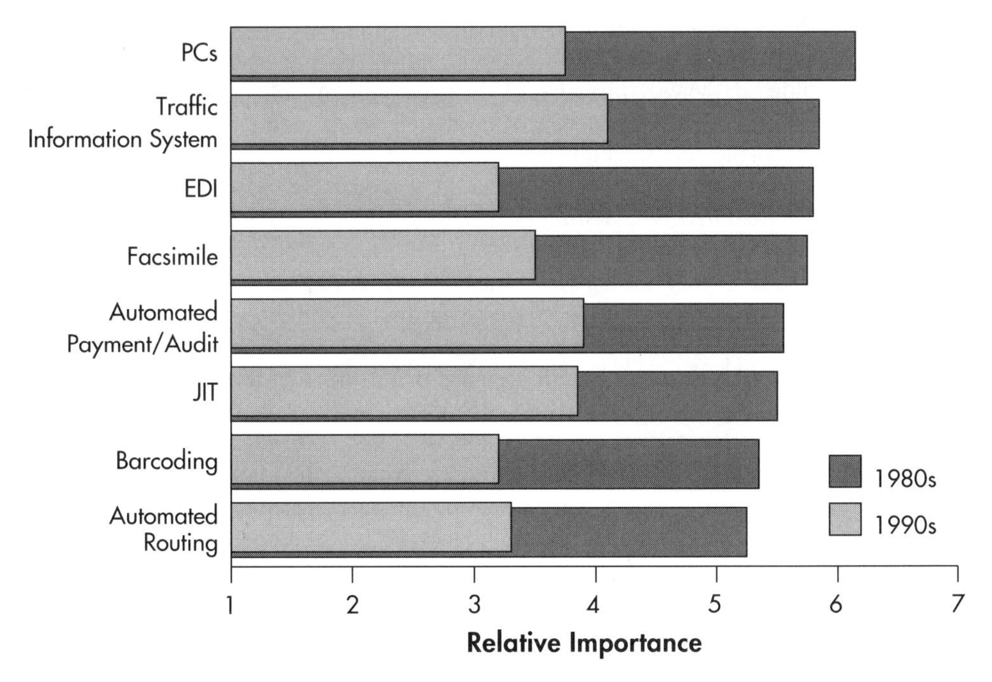

Figure 22-5
Relative Importance of New Technology in Traffic Management

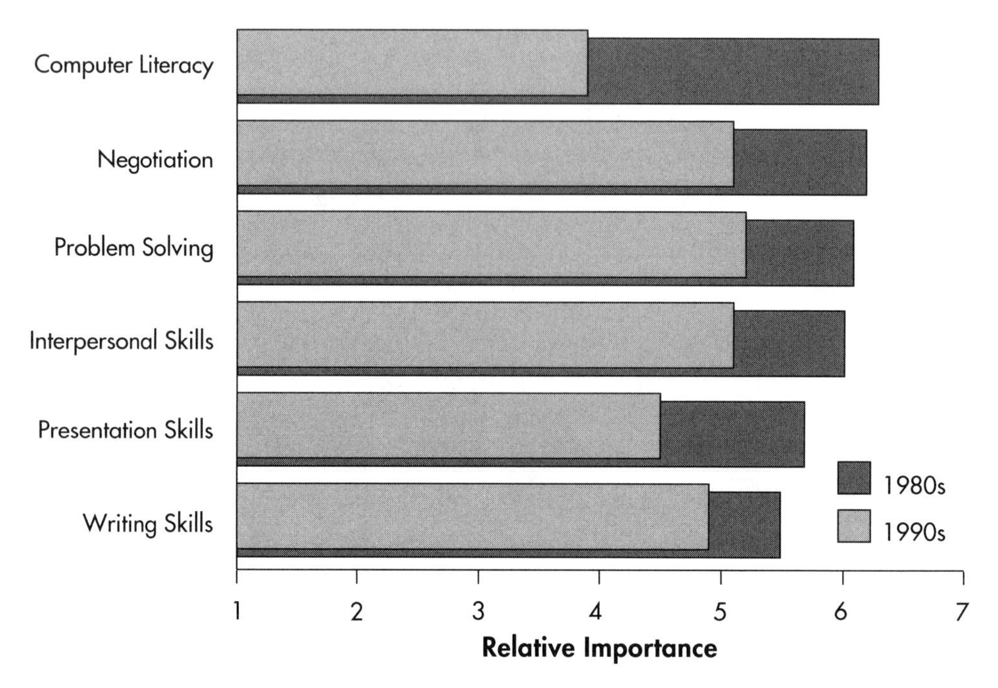

Figure 22-6
Relative Importance of Critical Personal Skills and Competencies

clear that the availability of microcomputers is the foundation for the ongoing growth in traffic information system development.

Changing technology in the workplace has also changed the mix of skills and expertise that successful managers must have. When asked to evaluate a set of management skills that traffic managers might need, the AST&L study respondents indicated that computer literacy, which had been relatively unimportant during the 1980s, had become the most important technical skill to be mastered in order to be successful in traffic management during the 1990s (see Figure 22-6).

As seen in Table 22-2, many important issues and trends are expected to influence the practice of traffic management during the 1990s. However, the most frequently mentioned factor was information technology.

We may gain some perspective on the importance of information technology by taking a broader look at the growing role of information technology in the economy as a whole. Some analysts and economists believe that the developed nations are in the midst of an ongoing transformation from an industrial to an information economy, and that this transformation will be as dramatic and profound as the shift from an agricultural to an industrial economy that preceded it. In fact, this transformation will be even more wrenching because it is likely to occur much more quickly. This does not mean that manufacturing will disappear—there will always be a manufacturing sector, just as there will always be an agricultural sector. It does mean, however, that there are likely to be fewer jobs in manufacturing, and that the growth in the economy will come in the information area. Just as the application of industrial technology to agricultural production reduced the labor input, improved productivity, and reduced costs, application of infor-

TABLE 22-2
Most Important Factors Influencing Traffic Management
"What do you think are the three most important factors that will shape the scope and role of the traffic function during the decade of the 1990s?"

Factor	**Number of Mentions Ranked by Level of Importance** 1st	2d	3d	**Total**	
Technology	44	36	29	109	18.8%
Innovative methods	28	37	31	96	16.6
International	27	15	12	54	9.3
Traffic organization	23	13	18	54	9.3
Carrier issues	9	22	18	49	8.4
Service/quality	18	16	9	43	7.4
Skills	7	14	12	33	5.7
Cost	8	12	10	30	5.2
Professional Issues	11	8	10	29	5.0
All other factors	21	30	32	83	14.3
Total	196	203	181	580	100.0%

mation technology in the manufacturing sector (and, for that matter, the agricultural sector) will improve productivity, lead to new jobs, and create wealth.

This transformation to an information economy can be thought of as the imbedding of information or intelligence in the products and service we create and sell. As Davis and Davidson put it:

> Today, information-based enhancements have become the main avenue to revitalize mature businesses and to transform them into new ones.... The more information you put into a product, or the more you are able to use a product to pull out information, the more you evolve beyond the original purpose into new ones. These new ones, which are based on information, may present even far greater opportunities than the original.[22]

Information enhancements may be incorporated in the product itself, such as the automobile. A 1990 model, even an inexpensive one, has an engine with computer-controlled electronic ignition and electronic fuel injection. This engine is more powerful, more fuel-efficient, less polluting, and vastly more maintenance-free than a comparable model produced in 1960, and the difference is due to the information processing ability. Information enhancements can also be incorporated into the distribution of the product by improving the availability, speed, reliability, and flexibility of the distribution system.

These new ways of doing business make the old ways obsolete. In an era of automated traffic information, operating with old information systems will be like trying to sell cars with carburetors—like it or not, you will be in the antique business. Worse than that, your customers will not be able to talk the same language with you. The challenge for the contemporary traffic manager is to build an information system that allows the firm to profit from the truly revolutionary transformations that are underway.

Notes

1. Nicholas A. Glaskowsky, Jr., *Effects of Deregulation on Motor Carriers,* 2d ed. (Eno Foundation for Transportation, 1990), pp. 5–9.
2. Ibid., p. 28.
3. Ibid., p. 8.
4. Jack W. Farrell, "Computerized distribution: Where it stands," *Traffic Management* (June 1971): 36–45.
5. James F. Robeson, "The Future of Business Logistics: A Delphi Study Predicting Future Trends in Business Logistics," *Journal of Business Logistics* 9, no 2, 1–14. Using a Delphi approach, a group of 76 senior executives established what they believed to be the 20 most significant issues and important trends that would affect logistics by the year 1995. Many trends were cited, but only the top three in terms of importance are presented here.
6. D. J. Bowersox, P. J. Daugherty, C. L. Droge, D. S. Rogers, and D. L. Wardlow, *Leading Edge Logistics Competitive Positioning for the 1990s* (Oak Brook, Ill.: Council of Logistics Management, 1989). The study team evaluated 695 corporations and identified 117 leading-edge firms.
7. David Jacoby, "Implementing Strategic Information Systems in the Transportation Industry," *Transportation Journal* 29, no. 3 (Spring 1990): 54–64.
8. "BN's ShipSmart Program Expanded," *Electronic Shipping News,* January 1989, p. 1.
9. Richard C. Haverly, et al., *Logistics Software—1992 Edition* (New York: Arthur Andersen & Co., 1992).
10. Jacoby, "Implementing Strategic Information Systems," pp. 54–64.
11. *APC Today,* Spring 1989, p. 3
12. Mark E. Grausnick, "Freight Management System." *Annual Conference Proceedings,* Council of Logistics Management, Vol. 2, 1988, pp. 357–71.
13. Haverly, et al., *Logistics Software,* p. 9. Also see the 1992 edition.
14. B. J. La Londe, J. M. Masters, A. B. Maltz, and L. R. Williams, *The Evolution, Status, and Future of the Corporate Transportation Function* (American Society of Transportation and Logistics, 1991). The survey covers 211 shipping organizations. Respondents were asked to assess the level of automation of eight basic traffic management processes in their firms in 1990, to compare these levels with the corresponding figures for 1980, and to project the planned level of automation for 1995.
15. B. J. La Londe, and J. M. Masters, "Career Patterns and Trends in Logistics," *Annual Conference Proceedings* (Oak Brook, Ill.: Council of Logistics Management, 1992). Transportation and logistics executives from 197 American firms participated in a survey in 1992 that sought to determine the rate at which new information technology was spreading throughout logistics organizations in manufacturing and merchandising firms. Executives were asked to report how much of their total business activity was, is, and will be conducted using just-in-time procedures, barcoding, and electronic data interchange. Respondents reported actual percentages of these activities for 1990 and 1992, and were asked to project their planned or anticipated levels of activity for 1995 and 2000.

16. La Londe, et al., *Evolution, Status, and Future of the Corporate Transportation Function,* p 73.
17. B. J. La Londe and J. M. Masters, "Logistics: Perspectives for the 1990s," *International Journal of Logistics Management* l, no. 1 (1990): 3.
18. Margaret A. Emmelhainz, "Strategic Issues of EDI Implementation," *Journal of Business Logistics* 9, no. 2 (1988): 57.
19. Deborah A. Johnson, Benjamin J Allen, and Michael R. Crum, "The State of EDI Usage in the Motor Carrier Industry," *Journal of Business Logistics* 13, no. 2 (1992): 43–68. A 1990 study of 78 motor carriers.
20. M. K. Allen, and O. K. Helferich, *Putting Expert Systems to Work in Logistics* (Oak Brook, Ill.: Council of Logistics Management, 1990), p. 66.
21. In the AST&L survey of shippers and carriers, executives were asked to rate the relative importance of information technologies to the success of the traffic department. Respondents rated the importance of each technology during the 1980s and estimated the impact each technology was expected to have through the 1990s. Importance was measured on a scale from 1 to 7, where:

    1 = unimportant
    3 = moderately important
    5 = very important
    7 = critically important—vital to success

22. S. M. Davis and W. H. Davidson, *2020 Vision* (New York: Simon & Schuster, 1991).

CHAPTER 23

Integration of Purchasing and Transportation Decision Making

Julie J. Gentry

In the last decade organizations increasingly emphasized the management of inbound freight and the movement of purchased goods and materials. A new area of transportation expertise has been developing to more effectively manage inbound freight movements and coordinate this function with other areas of the organization. Today there is also an increasing effort to integrate and strategically manage a coordinated inbound transportation and purchasing function. This chapter focuses on important new efforts to integrate these two functions.

Regulatory Reform

Purchasing and transportation had little reason to interface before a series of legislative events transformed the buying of transportation from a generic commodity purchase to a complex decision involving a myriad of price and service options. Prior to the regulatory reform that took place between 1977 and 1982, transportation decisions were generally outside the scope of purchasing because the transportation industry enjoyed antitrust immunity and rates were highly regulated.[1]

The heavily regulated transportation environment not only limited pricing competition, but severely restricted service differentiation as well. Little emphasis was placed on improving customer service because carriers were forbidden to independently increase rates to compensate for value-added services. In fact, many argue that rate increases were granted to mask operating inefficiencies rather than to fund service improvements. Thus, service improvement was not a high priority.

Regulation also minimized competition within certain traffic lanes, making service differentiation difficult for carriers within each mode. Given limited service differentiation and homogeneous intramodal rate structures, traditional inbound freight decisions primarily focused on mode choice. Evaluating modal options did not necessarily require the input of a purchasing professional.

Although the regulatory reform movement of the late 1970s and 1980s is commonly referred to as "deregulation," the legislative acts did not totally deregulate motor and rail transportation. Rather, regulatory control was loosened, with the underlying philosophy that increased competition and more emphasis on market forces were desirable and would result in more efficient carriers.[2]

Regulatory reform of the transportation industry changed the overall operating environment for all American businesses, at least indirectly. Both purchasing and transportation professionals suddenly faced an extremely volatile industry characterized by complex and interrelated decisions. The level of operating and service improvements attainable through integrating purchasing and inbound transportation was not fully appreciated in the early years of deregulation. Slowly, it became apparent that additional responsibilities would rest on both the purchasing and transportation functions.

Although trade literature has provided some case studies showing evidence of increased integration of the purchasing and inbound transportation management functions, empirical evidence to support the apparent trend has been deficient. However, a 1990 study by the Center for Advanced Purchasing Studies (CAPS) identified the degree of purchasing's involvement in transportation-related activities.[3]

FOB Freight Terms

Understanding freight terms is important for transportation decision making. In most transportation transactions there are three parties: the supplier of the goods (seller/shipper), the purchaser of the goods (buyer), and the carrier of the goods to move them from seller to buyer. Inbound motor transport costs are generally functions of the following factors:

Transportation cost variables:

- *Freight Classification:* Official Interstate Commerce Commission (ICC) broad product classification based on product type and value.
- *Distance:* Mileage from origin to destination within a "lane" of traffic.
- *Lane of Traffic:* The general description of the origin/destination locations. For example, the New York–Philadelphia lane may have a different cost per mile than the New York–Boston lane.
- *Weight:* The shipment weight is multiplied by the freight rate to yield the freight cost. However, there are generally economies of scale to be gained by shipping more material than less. So as shipment weight increases, rates generally decrease.
- *Cube:* The measurement of the material being shipped sometimes affects the cost. For example, very small but dense and thus heavy material may command a higher freight rate than lighter material of the same cube measurement, because it will cause a trailer to reach its maximum weight capacity more quickly than it reaches its cube capacity. Also, very light material may command a higher freight rate, as it will cause a trailer to "cube out" before it reaches its weight capacity.

These variables lead to:

- *Freight Rate:* Cost per hundred pounds of material shipped ($/cwt)
- *Freight Cost:* The final dollar amount charged on a freight bill; equal to freight rate multiplied by shipment weight.[4]

FOB is the abbreviation for "free on board" and primarily refers to when the ownership and title of goods pass from a supplier to a purchasing firm. In its most simplistic form, the term "FOB-origin" implies that the purchasing firm owns the goods in transit, handles any necessary claims, and eventually pays the freight bill. The term "FOB-destination" implies just the opposite, that the seller is responsible for freight charges and claims.[5] Some common FOB freight terms are summarized in Table 23-1.

TABLE 23-1
Common FOB Terms

	FOB Origin Collect	FOB Origin Prepaid (Absorbed)†	FOB Origin Prepaid (Invoiced)‡	FOB Destination Collect	FOB Destination Prepaid (Invoiced)‡
Title passes to buyer at...	origin	origin	origin	destination	destination
Freight charges					
Paid by...	buyer	seller	seller	buyer	buyer
*Borne by...	buyer	seller	buyer	buyer	seller
Carrier selected and controlled by...	buyer	seller	seller	buyer	seller
Ownership of goods in transit by...	buyer	buyer	buyer	seller	seller
Claims for loss, damage, and overcharge must be filed by...	buyer	buyer	buyer	seller	seller

* Of course, buyer ultimately bears the cost of freight, even if indirectly, through the price of the product.
† "Absorbed" means that knowledge of the actual cost of shipping is not available to the buyer. Rather, it is either built directly into the cost of the items being shipped and may be allocated on a per unit basis, or it is indirectly built into the item cost through a standard loading of item cost and recorded by the seller as some sort of general administrative or shipping expense.
‡ "Invoiced" means the buyer will see a shipping charge on the invoice for the product. This charge might be the actual cost; however, it could be inflated in several ways: (1) to reflect a reasonable loading for administrative purposes, (2) to reflect an unreasonable loading so that the shipping of goods becomes a profit generator for the seller, or (3) the "standard" ICC freight charge from standard full tariff freight tables, which is normally higher than the commonly discounted available market rates—again a profit generator.

Source: Mark Strickland and R. Edwin Howe, Andersen Consulting, proprietary internal report, adapted with permission.

For the CAPS study, the FOB-destination charges were defined simply as freight charges paid for by the supplier and included on the invoice, FOB-destination-prepaid-(invoiced), as seen on Table 23-1. The study investigated the extent to which firms were purchasing on a traditional "laid-down price" basis, with the cost of transportation included in the purchase price of the goods, versus buying on an FOB-origin-collect basis and thereby controlling the inbound freight transportation.

There has been a definite shift from purchasing the majority of goods on a traditional "laid-down price" basis to a full-control basis today. FOB-destination-prepaid-and-invoiced was the prominent practice before the 1980s, but now the majority of freight expenditures are made on an FOB-origin-collect basis (57% in 1989). Under traditional regulation, most carriers charged equal rates with little variation in service options, so it was convenient to have the supplier make the inbound transportation decisions. If the freight charges were included in the purchase price of the goods, the purchasing firm could monitor and evaluate the fair value of the freight charges, because rates were published, fairly standard, and relatively stable. However, deregulation brought about more flexible and aggressive transportation pricing and made it much easier for new carriers to enter the market. The heightened competition among carriers resulted in decreased freight rates and more volatile pricing, making it extremely difficult to monitor FOB-destination freight charges. Carriers began offering discounts to shippers that were well below the published tariff rate. These discounts are not necessarily passed on to a purchasing firm that purchases on an FOB-destination basis. A common practice is for the supplier (shipper) to pay a discounted freight rate while charging the purchasing firm the published tariff rate, thus turning the distribution function into a profit center.

Firms can benefit in many ways by purchasing on an FOB-origin basis. The same care and controls used for a firm's outbound distribution system can be used to monitor inbound shipments.[6] This gives the purchasing firm several advantages:

- Control and selection of carriers
- Negotiation of special commodity or discount rates with carriers
- Ability to select private carriage whenever the vendor's pickup can be offset with a loaded outbound movement
- Isolation and identification of freight as a cost separate from the piece price paid for the parts or materials.

Purchasing's Involvement in Transportation Activities

The purchasing department's involvement in transportation activities varies widely both among firms and among types of decisions. Table 23-2 shows the extent of involvement by the pool of firms in the CAPS study.

Deregulation has significantly changed the role of purchasing in transportation decision making. The importance of carrier choice, transportation pricing, and carrier rating was minimal before 1980, owing to the generic nature of transportation alternatives. These activities are now extremely critical to ensure that inbound carriers meet certain service and price objectives that reflect the goals of production and service strategies. Virtually thousands of different price/service options are available in today's deregulated transportation environment, and purchasing should be involved in making these decisions, as it is with any other product or service, regardless of which department ultimately controls the inbound freight.

Purchasing departments have developed systems and procedures to monitor vendors' price,

TABLE 23-2
Purchasing's Involvement in Transportation Decisions

Decision Type	Involved (%)	Not Involved (%)
Inbound management	90	10
Mode selection	88	12
Carrier selection	85	15
Transportation pricing	67	33
Carrier rating	54	46
Outbound management	49	51
Interplant management	47	53
Hazardous materials	42	58
Personnel travel	24	76
Household relocation	21	79

Source: Julie J. Gentry, *Purchasing's Involvement in Transportation Decision Making* (Tempe, Ariz.: Center for Advanced Purchasing Studies, 1991).

TABLE 23-3
Change in Purchasing Involvement, 1988–1990

Activity	Increased Involvement (%)	Decreased Involvement (%)	No Change in Involvement (%)
Hazardous materials	52	4	44
Inbound management	48	3	49
Transportation pricing	44	2	54
Personnel travel	44	4	52
Carrier selection	43	4	53
Carrier rating	37	3	60
Outbound management	36	7	57
Interplant management	36	6	58
Mode selection	34	3	63
Household relocation	32	11	57

Source: Julie J. Gentry, *Purchasing's Involvement in Transportation Decision Making* (Tempe, Ariz.: Center for Advanced Purchasing Studies, 1991).

quality, and contract adherence for materials and services. Thus, it is natural to integrate transportation into the purchasing process so it too can benefit from the existing expertise.

Purchasing professionals tend to be heavily involved in making general inbound transportation-related decisions, as well as choosing mode and determining price. These findings are not surprising because of the effect of modal choice on the overall inbound transportation strategy and the effect of transportation price on the total cost of goods. Conversely, purchasing professionals have little input in travel and relocation decisions.

There has been a substantial increase in purchasing's involvement in transportation-related activities. At least 30% of firms have increased involvement in ten major transportation management activities, while only an average of 5% have decreased similar involvement. Table 23-3 shows the degree of change in firms' purchasing departments' involvement in these transportation activities over a three-year period.

Hazardous materials movement has gained the most purchasing integration, with 52% of all CAPS survey respondents indicating increased involvement. Hazardous materials transportation is an extremely complex and increasingly risky and expensive business. The liabilities involved are extraordinary, packaging and labeling are crucial and rigidly regulated, and transportation costs are substantially more than those for nonhazardous materials. For example, nonhazardous materials shipped domestically by intermodal transportation cost approximately $1.00 to $1.50 per mile, but similar shipments of hazardous materials, which require special handling and insurance, usually cost more than $2.00 per mile.[7] The premium on freight costs for hazardous materials transport can be as much as 100%! Awareness of hazardous materials movement will continue to heighten, as regulations are constantly changing and growing more stringent. These escalations will require more input and coordination from the purchasing function to find satisfactory yet skilled and cost-effective vendors. Also, these regulations affect numerous other goods needed in a manufacturing organization, such as packaging materials, labels, transportation equipment, and storage and handling devices. Purchasers are frequently required to participate in their company's hazardous materials management programs, including the oversight of inbound and in-plant/interplant hazardous materials movement.[8]

Management has also become significantly more involved in inbound transportation over the last three years. Some of the reasons are:

- Greater emphasis on controlling/decreasing costs
- Implementation of a just-in-time manufacturing strategy
- Organizational changes and general downsizing of companies
- Greater emphasis on quality
- Increased use of contract and private carriers

In managing inbound freight, more flexible and aggressive pricing from carriers has allowed considerable cost savings to shippers and has increased opportunities to negotiate lower rates. Discounting among motor carriers has been rampant and has often exceeded what Congress expected from the Motor Carrier Act of 1980.[9] Although initial regulatory reform granted carriers the flexibility to decrease or increase prices within certain limits, the trend has been an overall decrease in freight rates. The effect of lower transportation rates on purchasing and inbound transportation is dependent on the individual organization, because only those companies that become more involved in inbound transportation can develop expertise in this area and benefit fully from reduced freight rates.

An increasing number of manufacturing firms are developing and implementing just-in-time (JIT) manufacturing strategies. Successful implementation of a JIT system requires an integrated effort among production, purchasing, and inbound transportation, to include linkages among purchasers, suppliers, and carriers. Inbound transportation must receive careful attention because the transportation of the inbound materials directly affects a manufacturer's ability to make product. Therefore, it is likely that a firm utilizing JIT will seek control of inbound transportation to ensure the continuity of supplies. Transportation-related activities affected by a JIT system include control of inbound shipments, size and frequency of shipments, lengths of haul, number of carriers used, modal and carrier selection, and vehicle utilization.[10]

Organizational restructuring and general downsizing are also reasons for changes in involvement in certain transportation-related activities. Recent overall business trends like mergers and consolidations, middle-management cuts, and restructuring have affected various functions of organizations. As long as these trends continue, an integrated effort for inbound transportation and purchasing strategy will be an effective competitive weapon by virtue of greater controls over service and costs. As the 1980s allowed purchasing professionals to take advantage of a deregulated transportation environment to lower costs, the 1990s will allow purchasing departments to marshal transportation functions for the benefit of the corporate strategy. Although only about 5% of National Association of Purchasing Management members have transportation-buying expertise, this number will likely grow to more than 20% by the end of the decade.[11]

The trend toward quality management has greatly changed the role of both the transportation and the purchasing professional. Much emphasis has been placed on the ability to source high-quality products, but service quality has become important too. It is now common to closely monitor inbound freight with respect to delivery times, loss and damage, and other service measures. Reliability of inbound transportation is critical, particularly in JIT operations. Choosing carriers and implementing continuous carrier rating systems are key to ensuring reliable, on-time, damage-free receipt of freight. Even where the purchasing organization does not control inbound freight, purchasing often monitors carrier utilization and performance. Inbound transportation can be evaluated just as purchased products are evaluated—by conformity to specifications. To implement transportation quality control, quantifiable service performance standards must be negotiated with carriers and suppliers and their performance must be tracked and documented. Carriers must perform to standards along such measures as delivery dates and times, elapsed transit time, damage, and cost. Suppliers must conform to the firm's shipping instructions, choosing the correct carriers, providing carriers with proper routing and billing information, and properly packaging shipments.

Many companies are benefiting from contractual arrangements with carriers for both inbound and outbound service. The number of contracts increased significantly over the last decade: railroads went from having 768 contracts at the end of 1981 to more than 12,000 by the end of 1983. Between 1980 and 1984, the number of motor carriers deriving over half their revenue from negotiated contract rates almost doubled.[12] Contracting allows shippers (or suppliers) to commit large portions of traffic to specific carriers. Contracting is a win-win situation because shippers receive a combination of improved rates and services, while carriers get the benefit of regular business.[13]

The ability to contract transportation has had several effects on the purchasing function. Organizations that choose to contract transportation services can use inbound freight in addition to outbound shipments to increase contracted volume and thus generate leverage to negotiate lower rates. Utilizing contracted carriers for inbound freight movements also requires additional transportation expertise and, in many instances, calls for changes in the designation of freight terms for purchased goods. Purchasing professionals have been forced to become knowledgeable about the carriers that must be used for certain commodities and routes to ensure that negotiated contract rates are utilized.[14] Also, purchasers have needed to renegotiate product and raw material supply contracts to reflect new transportation arrangements. These changes typically include specification of freight terms; approved carriers; and packaging, labeling, and shipping procedures. Special shipping procedures might include scheduling deliveries and sending information for "advanced receiving" to reduce receiving dock work and speed put-away.

The implementation of private carriage within a firm has substantial implications for an organization's overall purchasing strategy. Providing cost-effective private transportation service requires extensive coordination and communication among many departments within an organization.[15] Certainly, both the purchasing and transportation functions are crucial to an integrated effort. Purchasers of goods and materials must know when to utilize private transportation, and what liability exists for loss and damage. They must also know insurance and hazardous materials requirements and continually monitor the transportation regulatory environment.

Inbound transportation costs can be reduced by arranging pickups from suppliers and then coordinating both the inbound and outbound private fleet traffic. However, successful purchasing–private fleet programs require control and management by both purchasing and transportation professionals. Although the overall reduction in freight costs since deregulation has dissuaded many firms from the long-term commitments and heavy investments associated with private carriage, as rates begin to climb and the number of carriers continues to dwindle, more firms are likely to reconsider the long-term advantages of operating a private fleet. Although private fleets may not be viable for all firms, particularly low-volume shippers, those that do move toward private carriage to attain greater control and flexibility will place increased responsibility on the purchasing function.

Modal and Carrier Selection Decision Factors

Table 23-4 shows that required delivery date is the most influential factor when purchasers choose modes of transportation, twice that of the second most influential factor, cost of transport service.[16]

Inbound transportation is extremely time-sensitive, because the ability to meet required delivery dates takes precedence over cost of transport services. It has been traditionally thought that various modes are limited by their average delivery times: in general, air transport is the most expedient, followed by motor, then rail, and finally inland water and ocean transport. However, there has been a tremendous increase in the use of intermodal shipments during the late 1980s and early 1990s, which combines at least two modes in an effort to benefit from the inherent advantages of each.

The trend of increased intermodalism requires purchasing professionals to remain knowledgeable about all possible modal/intermodal options available for inbound transportation. This trend also requires that purchasers receive accurate and timely information on required delivery dates. This requirement demands assigning specific responsibility for determining required dates and lead times. If required delivery date is the primary determinant for choosing among modes, then ensuring that these dates are valid is a top priority.

Modal selection decisions are no longer single-faceted, standard decisions, so the purchasing professional must constantly monitor the options and cost/service trade-offs of each mode. It is vital to select the mode that best conforms to a firm's inbound objectives, without paying for too much premium transportation service.

Once the modal or intermodal choice has been made, the next task is selecting carriers. Table 23-5 illustrates the importance of influential decision variables for carrier choice according to the CAPS study.[17] On-time delivery, or reliability, is the most influential factor when purchasers choose among carriers, having more than twice the amount of most influential responses than the second-highest-ranked factor, rates. Only these two factors received "most influential" rankings; all others are clearly important but secondary considerations.

These results are consistent with those of previous studies, albeit other studies focus on out-

TABLE 23-4
Ranking of Influential Factors for Choosing Transportation Modes
(percent of total weighted points)

Decision Factor	Degree of Influence (%)
Required delivery date	37
Cost of transport service	17
Reliability and service quality	14
Shipment size	11
Transit time	10
Item type	7
Possibility of damage	2
Range of services	2

Source: Julie J. Gentry, *Purchasing's Involvement in Transportation Decision Making* (Tempe, Ariz.: Center for Advanced Purchasing Studies, 1991).

TABLE 23-5
Ranking of Influential Factors for Selecting Carriers
(percent of total weighted points)

Decision Factor	Degree of Influence (%)
On-time delivery	25
Rates	18
Geographic coverage	10
Transit time	10
Care in handling	6
Shipment tracing	6
Carrier financial condition	5
Other factors	20

Source: Julie J. Gentry, *Purchasing's Involvement in Transportation Decision Making* (Tempe, Ariz.: Center for Advanced Purchasing Studies, 1991).

bound carriers because of the nature of transportation purchasing prior to deregulation. The common conclusion is that shippers in the United States generally value service more than cost when selecting carriers. However, studies also indicate that shippers have increasingly emphasized cost since the 1980 deregulation, because price flexibility has become available. In short, shipper priorities have not changed significantly over the years.[18]

Organization for Transportation Decision Making

Responsibility for inbound transportation decisions is most often shared by purchasing and traffic/distribution. Figure 23-1 shows how firms describe their assignment of responsibility. For more than a quarter of firms, responsibility rests solely with the buyer in purchasing. In these cases, either transportation expertise is being developed in the purchasing function or buyers have responsibility but are passing inbound freight control to suppliers. In firms where the responsibility rests totally outside the purchasing function, responsibility is either passed on to suppliers or given to the transportation/traffic function completely. If suppliers make transportation decisions, firms may not fully benefit from deregulated market pricing. If the transportation/traffic department autonomously manages decisions, the firm may miss potential service advantages from integration of the purchasing and transportation functions.

In firms where the responsibility rests in the purchasing function but someone other than buyers makes the actual decisions, inbound transportation expertise has been developed and purchasing is being integrated with other key functional areas. In these cases, the people most often making decisions are the purchasing manager, traffic and/or transportation manager, materials manager, or freight analyst.

Fewer than 10% of firms place inbound transportation decisions with sales and marketing. These organizations generally market high-value products like pharmaceuticals or electronics, and the time to market is critical. In these cases, outbound and inbound transportation are more closely integrated. Another reason for close integration is to take advantage of empty backhauls on private equipment by coordinating inbound and outbound shipments.

Very few firms utilize transportation committees that include purchasing personnel for mak-

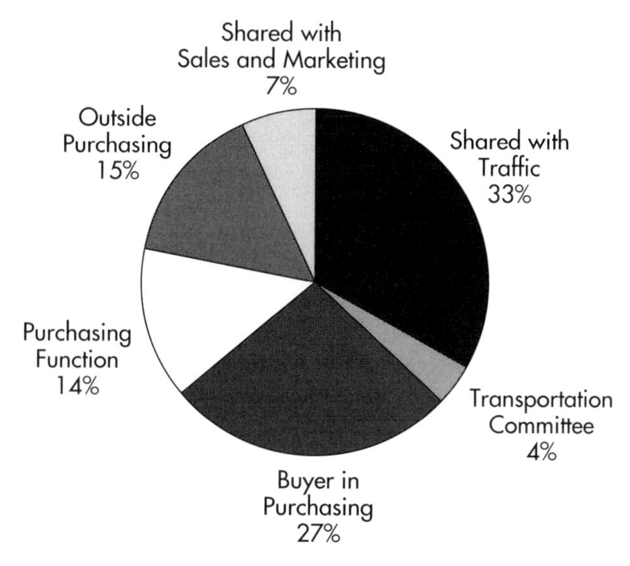

Figure 23-1

Responsibility for Inbound Transportation Decisions

Source: Julie J. Gentry, *Purchasing's Involvement in Transportation Decision Making* (Tempe, Ariz.: Center for Advanced Purchasing Studies, 1991).

ing inbound transportation decisions. However, this option is probably the most advantageous for effectively controlling inbound freight. This method of decision making will likely become much more popular in the future as more organizations begin to reap the benefits of integrating purchasing and transportation with other functional areas.

Larger firms tend to develop more specialized transportation departments, and smaller firms are more likely to pass the responsibility for inbound transportation to suppliers. However, it is also likely that smaller firms will develop more transportation expertise within the purchasing function, for a lower percentage of small firms make decisions outside the purchasing function and fewer decisions are shared with traffic and distribution. Figure 23-2 illustrates the breakdown of responsibility by firm size.[19]

Continued Integration

During the 1980s, the transportation and purchasing functions of organizations have progressed from virtually autonomous operating groups into a strategically managed and integrated director of the supply chain. Regulatory reform of the transportation industry opened opportunities for inbound freight savings, but an integrated effort between the purchasing and transportation functions is essential to exploit the full benefits of a new transportation environment.

The results of the CAPS study suggest that a definite trend of increasing involvement by purchasing professionals exists in all phases of transportation decision making. This trend has several implications. Not only will purchasing professionals need to gain transportation expertise but transportation professionals will also have to learn to appreciate the purchasing function. Purchasers will need to learn more about transportation and the various options and processes

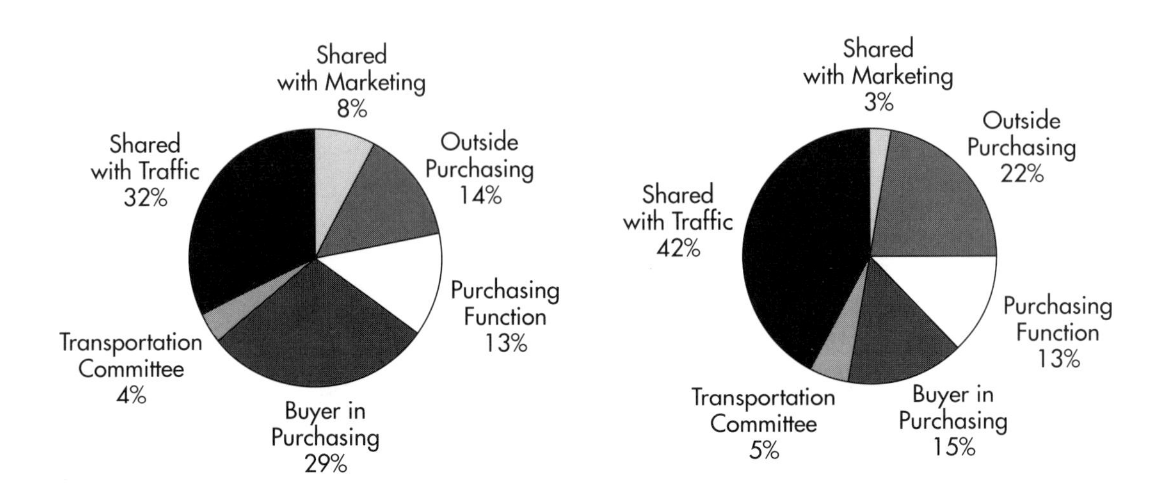

Figure 23-2

Responsibility for Inbound Transportation Decisions by Firm Size

Source: Julie J. Gentry, *Purchasing's Involvement in Transportation Decision Making* (Tempe, Ariz.: Center for Advanced Purchasing Studies, 1991).

available. Corporate traffic managers and carriers' sales and operations personnel will have to learn to think like purchasing professionals. Increased communication among vendors (shippers), inbound carriers, and purchasing firms is necessary to ensure that service standards are appropriate and agreed upon by all parties. Existing transportation departments must focus more attention on inbound transportation and educating their purchasing counterparts.

More integration of transportation and purchasing will be necessary in the future. Although the rate of change in transportation is likely to decelerate over the next decade, other driving forces will continue to reshape the transportation environment and pose new challenges and opportunities. These challenges and opportunities will call for further integration of the purchasing and transportation functions as logistics becomes a strategic issue rather than merely an operational task.

Notes

1. Peter J. Walters, "The Purchasing Interface with Transportation," *Journal of Purchasing and Materials Management* 24, no. 4 (1988): 21.
2. Martin T. Farris, "The Multiple Meanings and Goals of Deregulation: A Commentary," *Transportation Journal* 22, no. 2 (1981): 49.
3. Julie J. Gentry, *Purchasing's Involvement in Transportation Decision Making* (Tempe, Ariz.: Center for Advanced Purchasing Studies, 1991). The Center for Advanced Purchasing Studies (CAPS) is affiliated with Arizona State University and the National Association of Purchasing Management (NAPM). In 1990, a survey instrument was prepared and mailed to 3,100 purchasing professionals randomly chosen from the NAPM database. Of the 3,100 targeted participants, 678 usable responses from 29 different industries were returned, for a response rate of 22%. The results of the study are based on both manufacturing (67.1%)

and nonmanufacturing (32.9%) firms, with 56% of the responding organizations reporting 1989 revenues of over $50 million.

4. Mark Strickland, Andersen Consulting, proprietary internal report, adapted with permission. Copyright © 1991 by Andersen Consulting. All Rights Reserved.
5. Norman J. Stringfield, "Management Issues: Carrier Terms," *NAPM INSIGHTS,* November, 1990, p. 6.
6. Douglas M. Lambert and Jay U. Sterling, "Managing Inbound Transportation: A Case Study," *Journal of Purchasing and Materials Management* 20, no. 2 (1984): 27.
7. Donna Delia-Loyle, "Biting the Bullet on Safety," *Global Trade,* January 1991, p. 10.
8. Michael Yurconic, "Purchasing Becomes the Bridge to Right-to-Know," *NAPM INSIGHTS,* March 1991, p. 22.
9. Tommy F. Griffith, Norman E. Daniel, David L. Shrock, and Martin T. Farris, "Inbound Freight and Deregulation: A Management Opportunity," *Journal of Purchasing and Materials Management* 19, no. 3 (1983): 18.
10. Donald V. Harper and Karen S. Goodner, "Just-In-Time and Inbound Transportation," *Transportation Journal* 30, no. 2 (1990): 23.
11. Julie Murphree, "Inbound Transportation in 1990," *NAPM INSIGHTS,* January 1990, p. 6.
12. Lewis M. Schneider, "New Era in Transportation Strategy," *Harvard Business Review* 63, no. 2 (1985): 120–21.
13. Frederick J. Beier, "Transportation Contracts and the Experience Effect: A Framework for Future Research," *Journal of Business Logistics* 10, no. 2 (1989): 73.
14. Joseph L. Cavinato, "Transportation Contracts: Pointers and Pitfalls for Buyers," *Journal of Purchasing and Materials Management* 19, no. 1 (1984): 10.
15. Griffith et al., "Inbound Freight and Deregulation," p. 20.
16. In the CAPS study, respondents were asked to rank the three most important factors in making modal transportation choices. Each instance of a #1 rank was assigned 3 points, each instance of a #2 rank was assigned 2 points, and each instance of a #3 rank was assigned 1 point. The sum of weighted points is 2,998.
17. The total weighted ranking points for each factor in carrier selection decisions was computed in the same manner as the weighted ranking points for the modal selection decision. In the CAPS study, the respondents were asked to rank the top five factors in choosing between carriers, with each instance of a #l rank being assigned 5 ranking points, each instance of a #2 rank being assigned 4 ranking points, and so on down to a #5 rank being assigned 1 ranking point. The sum of weighted points is 7,135.
18. Michael A. McGinnis, "The Relative Importance of Cost and Service in Freight Transportation Choice: Before and after Deregulation," *Transportation Journal* 30, no. 1(1990): 17.
19. Large firms are defined as those with more than $500 million in annual sales. Small firms are those with $500 million or less.

CHAPTER 24

Contract Logistics

Is Outsourcing Right for You?

Hugh L. Randall

Logistics activities are expensive and capital-intensive. To move and store materials and distribute products requires a lot of space, a lot of equipment, a lot of people, and, increasingly, a lot of computer hardware and software. In today's climate of severely constrained resources, where enhanced asset productivity is often a prerequisite to survival, it is no wonder that managers are asking hard questions about their logistics functions:

- What, precisely, are we paying for each logistics activity?
- Do we really need direct control over our logistics assets?
- Can we afford to build a global logistics organization internally?
- Could we significantly cut our costs by contracting these activities out to a third party?

Cost, however, is only half the picture. The other half is service. The logistics channel forms one of the key business interfaces, linking a company with its suppliers at one end and its customers at the other. A breakdown along this channel, whether it be a miscommunication of an order, a shortage of a critical material or component, or a delayed or damaged delivery, can have devastating effects on customer and supplier relationships. As chains of supply and distribution become global and logistics in turn grows more complex, the opportunities for channel breakdowns only increase. Managers facing severe competition at ever-higher levels of quality must therefore factor another set of questions into the logistics equation:

- Can we maintain quality without direct control over our logistics functions?
- Is it prudent to forgo the development of internal expertise on international logistics?
- If we outsource our logistics functions, will we be trading short-term savings for a long-term loss of control over our customers?

Contract logistics—the outsourcing of logistics activities to third parties—represents a great opportunity in some circumstances but a significant risk in others. The uncertainty inherent in outsourcing is, in fact, one of the main reasons why so few contract logistics projects have actually been attempted in the United States. After all, it is always easier to stick with the status quo. Nevertheless, ignoring the potential of contract logistics is perhaps the riskiest course of all. Only through a clear-eyed, hardheaded analysis of the costs and benefits will a company be able to know whether logistics outsourcing is an attractive alternative to business as usual. This topic is also covered as a contemporary issue in Chapter 40.

What Is Contract Logistics?

Contract logistics is the use of an outside distribution company—a transportatio
house, or third-party freight manager—to perform all or part of a company's ma
ment or product distribution functions (Figure 24-1). The scope can be narrow, limited to the simple purchasing of traditional transportation or warehousing services, or broad, encompassing complex contracts for total supply chain management. It can be traditional, involving the outsourcing of services that exactly duplicate the work previously performed internally, or innovative, incorporating cutting-edge logistics management tools to improve the effectiveness of the logistics function.

In a typical contract logistics arrangement, the service provider integrates more than one function within the overall supply chain. For example, a consumer products company is using a North American contract logistics provider to manage an import supply channel. To manage this supply chain, the provider uses a comprehensive, item-level logistics information system that it developed over a number of years. A range of activities is provided:

- Consolidation of cargo from various locations in Asia
- Arrangement and management of full-load ocean and inland transportation to a Midwestern warehouse
- Deconsolidation and reconsolidation of products at the warehouse into store delivery consignments

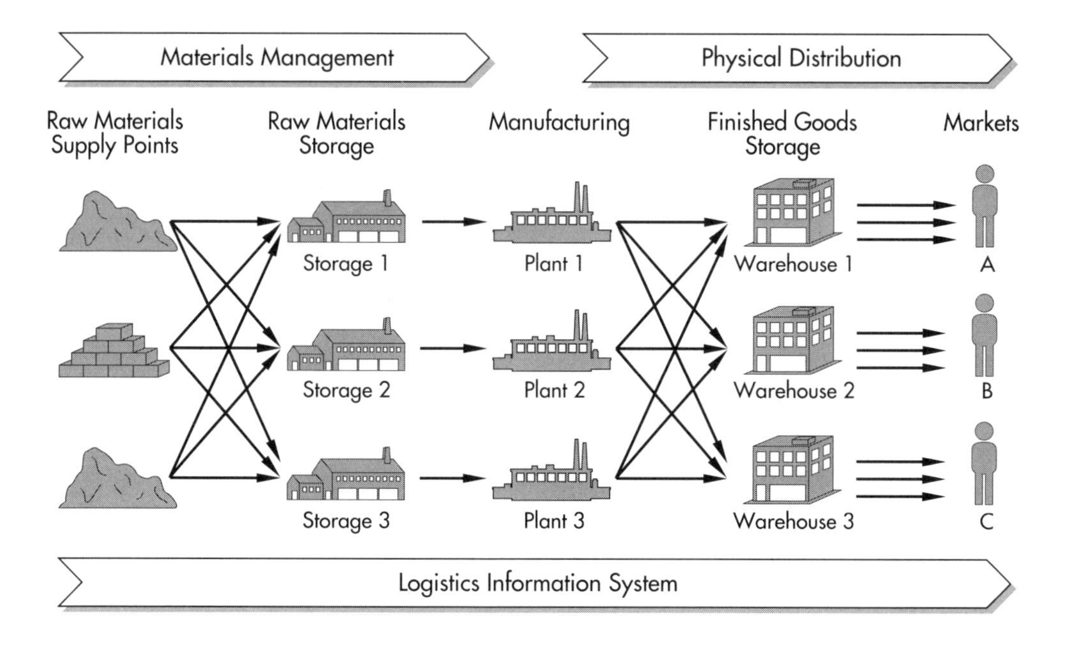

Figure 24-1
The Logistics Channel

- Arrangement and management of less-than-truckload (LTL) transportation to stores throughout the eastern United States

Contract logistics service providers usually supply physical and managerial infrastructure elements:

- trucks
- warehouses
- materials handling assets (although the provider may in turn have contracted for the use of such assets)
- labor and management services
- specialty services (in some cases) including:
  –inventory management
  –production preparation
  –strategic distribution planning
  –site acquisition
  –warehouse layout

As Table 24-1 shows, an array of value-added operational services can be included within contract logistics arrangements.

In the United States, most contract logistics activity has thus far involved high-service transportation and related materials handling activities. Customized Transportation, Inc. (CTI) has built a $125 million business providing such services, primarily to the North American auto industry. Ryder has been successful in providing dedicated contract carriage services, some of which involve materials handling, to a wide array of industries, garnering in the process annual revenues in excess of $280 million. Warehousing firms such as USCO, GATX Logistics, and Exel Logistics are gradually broadening their materials storage and handling activities to include distribution services. To date, however, these firms have generally not offered comprehensive supply chain management. Firms such as Caterpillar Logistics, Federal Express Business Logistics Services (BLS) subsidiary, and A.J. Fritz are now offering broader services, but relatively few full-service contract logistics projects have yet to be implemented domestically.

If contract logistics is still in its infancy in the United States, it is already in the adult stage in Europe. Companies like National Freight Corporation (NFC), Tibbetts and Britain, and Swift Transportation are successfully providing contract logistics services in the United Kingdom. In

TABLE 24-1
Value-added Services Included in Recent Contract Logistics

Inbound to Assembly	Finished Goods Distribution
Sequencing	Labeling
Subassembly	Packing
Modular assembly	Warehousing
Inspection	Consolidation
Deconsolidation	Kitting
Consolidation	Returned goods management
JIT flow management	

continental Europe, Frans Maas, a Dutch-based pan-European trucking company, has more than $100 million in annual contract logistics revenues. TNT, UPS Global International, and Kuhne and Nagel, a global Swiss-based freight forwarder, have also successfully implemented sizable European contract logistics projects.

A Range of Benefits

In today's highly competitive business environment, companies are always looking for a way to improve their operating effectiveness and achieve competitive advantage. A number of environmental factors have recently combined to make this search all the more pressing, particularly with regard to the logistics function:

- The worldwide economic slowdown has increased the pressure to reduce total costs and streamline organizations to maintain margins.
- The globalization of sourcing, manufacturing, and distribution is increasing the complexity and hence the costs of the logistics function.
- Competition has forced many companies to expand their product offerings, increase their responsiveness to customers, and shorten the life cycles of their products, adding still further complexity and cost to logistics.
- The resource constraints facing many companies mean that capital is often available only for critical activities like manufacturing and new product development. The capital required to renew logistics assets and enhance logistics information systems is often lacking.

When properly implemented, contract logistics can help management meet these challenges. The potential cost savings of outsourcing have been proven overseas, where many companies have succeeded in substantially reducing their logistics expenditures. For example, a multinational business products company has achieved dramatic improvements in efficiency by contracting with a European company for inbound materials management services (Table 24-2). It is not surprising that more and more corporations—in the United States as well as abroad—are carefully considering the cost-savings potential of contract logistics.

In addition, a contract logistics provider may enable a firm to realize transportation cost savings related to scale economies, more direct routings, and more door-to-door shipments, to name just a few advantages of using these specialists. Also, better planning and more supply chain predictability frequently result in a significant reduction in "emergency," premium-cost transportation services like air freight and truck charters.

TABLE 24-2
Project Payoff
European Inbound Material Management
(year 1 indexed to 100)

Year	Assembly Activity Level	Direct Head Count	Indirect Head Count	Inventories	Logistics Cost
1	100	100	100	100	100
7	280	123	48	27	53

The benefits of outsourcing are not limited to reducing logistics costs. Companies can also reap a number of other improvements in both service and efficiency:

- *Unified point of contact.* Dealing with a single provider with more services on a long-term basis is easier and more effective than working with a battery of third parties, as it enables shipper and supplier to get closer through the use of electronic data interchange (EDI), stationing supplier personnel in shipper organizations, and so forth.
- *Simpler, more reliable supply chain.* A single provider managing a supply chain can result in a more reliable, predictable flow of materials, reducing the need for in-channel safety stocks of inventory. Frequently, the speed with which material flows through the channel is also increased, further reducing inventory.
- *Increased customer responsiveness.* A predictable, reliable supply chain improves the quality of service provided to customers.
- *Access to innovative logistics management techniques and sophisticated channel management information systems.* Frequently, suppliers whose sole business focus is logistics management have developed techniques and systems that are more advanced than those individual companies are able to develop for themselves.
- *Expertise in unfamiliar geographic areas.* A third-party supplier may have distribution expertise in geographic territories that are new to a company.
- *Reduced investment requirements.* Utilizing assets supplied by others, such as trucks and warehouses, saves capital for critical needs like manufacturing and new product development.

Barriers to Implementation

Why, then, has the rate of implementation of contract logistics in North America been so slow? The reasons are complex, but they can be boiled down to five key barriers that exist in many companies.

Many functions are affected. Outsourcing supply chain management (integrated transportation/materials handling/inventory) is much more complicated than buying simple transportation or contract-carriage services. The functions affected by and thus involved in the decision include not only logistics but also manufacturing, sales and marketing, and even finance. As the number of functions increases, the decision-making process becomes more complicated. Also, because contract logistics is a relatively new concept, internal procedures have not been formalized in most companies to accommodate decisions on logistics outsourcing.

Functional buying behavior and reward structures may inhibit innovation. Implementation of a contract logistics opportunity may enable a company to reduce its transportation costs by realizing scale economies, simplified and improved routing, and other efficiencies. In many cases, however, the principal benefit is a reduction in *overall* logistics costs—not necessarily transportation costs. If the manager responsible for promoting a contract logistics opportunity is evaluated and rewarded solely by his ability to reduce transportation costs (and receives no credit for sponsoring a process that results in reduced overall logistics costs), the manager may be unwilling to undertake the difficult task of selling a contract logistics opportunity to the many different functions inside a corporation that need to buy in.

Inventory is "nobody's responsibility." For many companies, the principal benefit of a simpler, more reliable supply chain is reduced in-channel inventory. Although this benefit is real, in many organizations it is difficult to identify who is responsible for inventory levels and is thus the most interested in achieving inventory reduction. If the principal benefit is "nobody's responsibility," it may be difficult to find someone inside a corporation willing to sponsor the pursuit of a contract logistics opportunity.

Managers fear being locked in. Whereas a successfully implemented contract logistics project may enable a company to realize substantial benefits, it has a downside. Unlike the outsourcing of transportation services, which can be shifted relatively easily from one carrier to another, outsourcing distribution channel management responsibility means giving up some control over a complex process that may include inventory management, materials handling, and transportation. Changing suppliers becomes much more difficult. Because of their complexity, contract logistics relationships need to be long-term in nature, and many managers will be apprehensive about becoming overly dependent on one supplier.

Benchmarks are lacking. As discussed, securing approval for a contract logistics opportunity requires a reliable estimate of the financial benefit to be realized. However, it is difficult in some corporations to establish a benchmark of existing logistics costs for developing comparisons and, subsequently, for measuring the level of benefits from an implemented project. Furthermore, an incomplete record of existing costs may create the appearance that increased (rather than reduced) costs would result from a contract logistics project simply because previously unrecognized elements of total logistics costs are now taken into account.

Requirements for Success

In which companies will the benefits of outsourcing tend to be great enough to overcome the barriers? A company must evidence four major characteristics (Figure 24-2) that in combination make contract logistics viable.

Strong Need. A company's need for improved supply chain management is determined in part by the company's rate of change. Organizations undergoing rapid change as a result of acquisitions, divestitures, and changing markets and product lines often have the most to gain by establishing contract logistics partnerships. Similarly, companies facing significant capital and head count constraints or needing to implement significant logistics information system enhancements are more likely to benefit from contract logistics.

Tangible Value. Before they commit to contract logistics, companies want hard evidence that significant benefits will be realized. Determining the prospective benefits often requires a comprehensive feasibility study to benchmark existing practices, define opportunities for improvement, and quantify expected cost and service impacts. The study can be carried out by the company itself, by a prospective contract logistics supplier, or by outside consultants with the necessary expertise.

Supplier Credibility. Effective logistics management is critical to the successful performance of the manufacturing and sales functions within most corporations. Accordingly, a company

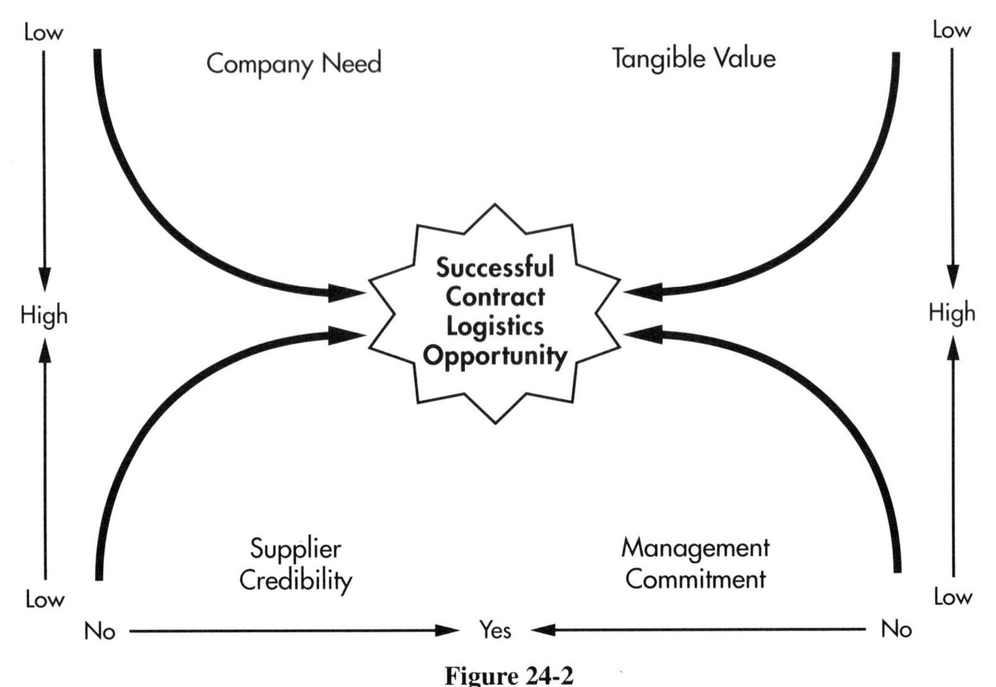

Figure 24-2
Four Requirements for Success

should not consider outsourcing a portion of this crucial activity unless it is confident of the credibility of the prospective supplier. For most companies, a supplier's credibility depends on:

- Experience in providing a broad range of transportation and distribution services
- A proven track record in implementing and operating contract logistics projects
- A comprehensive logistics information system and experienced logistics professionals
- Financial strength
- A multiyear commitment to the contract logistics business

Management Commitment. Translating a contract logistics opportunity into a successful and lasting relationship is a difficult task. For a contract logistics project to be implemented, management must be sufficiently committed to it to overcome the roadblocks that will undoubtedly emerge. Specifically, the complete commitment of someone willing to act as sponsor is usually required to guide a project from idea to reality. Although sponsors have generally been the heads of the traffic or logistics functions, in some instances they have been heads of finance or manufacturing. It all depends on who has the greatest stake in the initiative's success.

A contract logistics self-evaluation checklist, Figure 24-3, enables managers to get a quick fix on the prospects for contract logistics within their companies.

A Strategy for the Future

Today's business climate demands that managers take a new look at the way they manage every element of their business. Because logistics is central to a company's service quality as well as

Rate your company on these 25 criteria using a 1–5 point scale. Then add up the points. The key at the end will provide an indication of whether or not your company should pursue contract logistics opportunities.

I. Shipper Needs			
Acquisitions/divestitures within past 5 years	None	1 2 3 4 5	Multiple and significant
Expanding/contracting markets and products	Stable	1 2 3 4 5	Rapidly changing
Capital/headcount constraints	No impact	1 2 3 4 5	Significant and damaging
Customer/competitive requirements	Stable	1 2 3 4 5	Rapidly changing/ demanding
Logistics MIS enhancements	No problem	1 2 3 4 5	Urgent and important
II. Expected Benefits from Outsourcing			
Reduced transportation costs	No cost saving	1 2 3 4 5	Significant
Material handling and storage costs	No cost saving	1 2 3 4 5	Significant reduction
Inventory levels	No Impact	1 2 3 4 5	Significant reduction
Improved channel responsiveness	No impact	1 2 3 4 5	Significant
Improved channel control	None	1 2 3 4 5	Significant
III. Supplier Credibility			
Scope of services offered (geography/breadth)	Limited	1 2 3 4 5	Extensive meets all needs
Contract logistics experience/capability (MIS/people/projects implemented)	Limited	1 2 3 4 5	Experienced logistics orientation
Industry experience	None	1 2 3 4 5	Extensive
Proven ability to make things better (feasibility studies/service delivery)	Limited	1 2 3 4 5	Strong demonstrated capability
Supplier financial strength and commitment to contract logistics	Uncertain	1 2 3 4 5	Very strong
Competitive pricing	Noncompetitive	1 2 3 4 5	Very competitive
IV. Outsourcing Experience			
Contract trucking	None	1 2 3 4 5	Complete
Contract warehousing	None	1 2 3 4 5	Complete
Integrated contract trucking/warehousing	None	1 2 3 4 5	Extensive
Channel management outsourcing	None	1 2 3 4 5	Extensive
Performance-based contracting	None	1 2 3 4 5	Extensive

Figure 24-3
Logistics Self-Evaluation Checklist

Source: Mercer Management Consulting: TBS Transportation division (1993).

V. Management Commitment

Credible sponsor willing to convert opportunity to implemented reality	None	1 2 3 4 5	High level; very committed; very credible
Corporate culture for innovation and change	Change resistant	1 2 3 4 5	Change/ innovation regarded as essential
Reward/motivation systems	Highly inflexible; traditional	1 2 3 4 5	Responsive to multifunctional innovation
Ability to "benchmark" current costs against estimated and actual tuture costs	None	1 2 3 4 5	Well-established capability

Use this key to gauge your company's contract logistics potential.

Total Points	Evaluation of Results	Next Steps
Less than 50	Limited need/opportunity	None
50 to 90	Moderate need/opportunity	Feasibility study
More than 90	Significant need/opportunity	Feasibility study; evaluatge suppliers; request proposal(s); if positive, implement project

its cost structure, innovative approaches to logistics management like contract logistics are of particular importance. As companies become more familiar with the contract logistics alternative and as the capability and credibility of suppliers increases, the use of contract logistics in North America is certain to spread—as it has already in Europe. While contract logistics is not necessarily for everyone, it has the potential to provide large and lasting benefits in both cost reduction and service enhancement.

SECTION VI

Distribution Facilities Management

Thomas W. Speh

An effective distribution center has a major impact on the success of the organization's overall logistics mission. To maximize the opportunity to positively affect the logistics mission, the facility must be located at the optimal site, employ handling systems appropriate for the nature of the product, utilize proper handling equipment, and be supported by an effective information system. This section reviews these important aspects of facility management.

Gregory J. Owens and Robert Mann examine techniques for effectively designing the material's handling system in Chapter 25. The chapter explores management's role in designing the materials handling system to meet cost and service goals, while taking into account volume, product, and transaction requirements. The equipment to be used will need to match the underlying process involved in handling product. The chapter concludes with the specification and explanation of the steps involved in developing the system.

Once the concepts for designing the materials handling system are understood, Chapter 26, by Edward H. Frazelle and James M. Apple, Jr., attention turns to the materials handling technology to be employed in the facility. The entire range of materials handling equipment is described and then evaluated on the basis of its operating principles, applications, cost, advantages and drawbacks, and performance compared with other equipment alternatives. This chapter concludes with a discussion of the information linkages and systems required by the materials handling system.

Selection of the appropriate location for the warehouse is the focus of Chapter 27, by Thomas L. Freese. Site selection is presented as a three-step approach—macro-micro-specific site selection. The selection process begins with an analysis of the broad variables affecting the location of the facility and concludes with the determination of a specific site and an evaluation of whether to build or buy.

Chapter 28, by Morton T. Yoemans, examines warehousing information and how it is used. The chapter begins with an analysis of the types and sources of information used to manage the warehousing function. The focus then shifts to describing the manual and computerized approaches for collecting data and turning them into useful management information. The final section examines the analysis and use of data for staffing, inventory planning, and many other warehouse operations.

CHAPTER 25

Materials Handling System Design

Greg Owens
Robert Mann

A materials handling system is both the logical and physical manifestation of all the requirements, policies, and practices intended for a particular facility in the logistics pipeline. As such, it is much more than just a collection of equipment used for particular purposes within the operations. The key issue is *how* that equipment is used: the specific functions performed, the manner and sequence in which they are performed, the logic that manages and controls them, and the relationship among equipment, employees, and jobs.

It is perhaps helpful to think of each distribution facility as though it were a machine intended to take inputs in the form of product from suppliers and plants and—through a series of specific activities within the "machine"—convert these inputs into outputs tailored to the needs of the customer. Materials handling equipment can then be compared to the gears, levers, cams, and other components that such a machine might comprise.

Each of the machine's components might be useful in and of itself. Each could perhaps perform various functions. However, only the performance of the whole machine, as an integrated collection of processes, is important. A particular component may be perfectly designed, but if it fails to mesh with the other pieces, performance may suffer. If any piece is incorrectly chosen or designed, the machine will most likely perform below maximum potential.

A distribution center's information system can be viewed as the controls for the machine. It may enable the physical parts to function in a particular way. It may keep the process on track and communicate information from one activity to another so that all the processes work in harmony and toward the same goal. To achieve maximum performance, all pieces must work together; this is the essential meaning of the word *system.*

Anyone who has tried to process broken-case orders in a facility designed to handle a pallet-in/pallet-out process knows that an effective materials handling system must reflect the unique requirements of the operation. One size does *not* fit all!

The challenge is to recognize that requirements vary in many ways: by product, source, customer, and almost always over time. Such variations can create a dilemma: a design might be best for one set of requirements, but not for another, and too many compromises might be needed to fit all requirements into one process. At one extreme, in fact, a firm may want to implement "focused" operations dedicated to meeting a single set of requirements.

Balancing these needs is complicated further by the fact that some materials handling system options (particularly those taking advantage of the latest automated designs) incur significant initial costs. This may mean that a better overall solution can be found by force-fitting some requirements to a more generic system. Finding the right system design to meet all key requirements is both an art and a science. It requires knowledge of the options available, their range of applicability, the cost-benefit trade-offs, and what has (and has not) worked in similar situations for other companies.

This chapter offers logistics managers some practical guidance in designing their firms' materials handling systems. Key decision points are highlighted as well as the issues surrounding them, rules-of-thumb for the design process, and common solutions that have proven their effectiveness for real-world applications.

The Manager's Role in the Design Process

The design of a large-scale materials handling system can be a very complex process, requiring a thorough understanding of industrial and mechanical engineering principles. The process may require weeks or months for gathering background information and for developing and testing design options. Because of the range of skills and time required, many firms turn for assistance to the corporate engineering staff, suppliers of material handling equipment, or specialized consultants. However, regardless of the outside experts involved, a firm's own distribution operations manager must take overall responsibility for this important task.

Most managers face a complete redesign process only a few times in their careers. Typically, companies undertake a fundamental redesign of their distribution materials handling systems at about ten-year intervals. While a consultant or supplier who specializes in materials handling systems typically performs three or four such assignments every year, no one is in a better position to understand fully the business and technical requirements of a company's materials handling systems than the manager who must use them every day.

The manager's role is to ensure that the company's substantial investment in new materials handling systems will not only meet present and future business requirements but also deliver long-term competitive advantage through lower costs, better customer service, or both. To achieve that objective, the manager must:

- Understand common and advanced materials handling practices and equipment, at least within the particular industries
- Know where competitors have advantages, and identify leverage points to counter them
- Visualize and critically evaluate new ideas presented on paper
- Comprehend particular constraints that apply to the operations and ensure that they are met in the system
- Consider human resources and requirements to ensure that the materials handling system matches or exceeds them

General Considerations in Materials Handling System Design

The need for flexible response to customers' needs, changing products, and changing technology has led to less reliance on mechanical automation and more on intelligent understanding of the main role of such technology. A company would be unwise to invest in new materials handling technologies without careful consideration of the information systems needed to support or enhance them. Progress in information technology has, in fact, made it possible to eliminate equipment or greatly simplify operations.

Some technologies like barcoding and radio-frequency communications are becoming almost universal in their applicability. Others such as real-time transaction systems, imaging, and paperless operations are becoming more common as their costs and feasibility improve.

Most warehouse management systems (WMS) being installed today are based on local minicomputer platforms that allow easier integration of various technologies and materials handling components than a traditional mainframe. These systems are also increasingly based on a client-server environment that permits simpler integration of outside packages and may even permit a user to customize the system.

Although single-purpose, large-capacity, unit-load automatic storage and retrieval systems (AS/RS) were once widely embraced in materials handling applications, their inflexibility makes them less attractive today. (However, one way to ensure absolute accuracy is to use such a system to execute operations. In situations where errors absolutely cannot be tolerated, or where space constraints or labor costs are extreme, this type of automation may still offer advantages.) A more common approach today is the creative use of common equipment (conveyors, lift trucks, storage racks, etc.) to gain high performance and reasonably priced modification at a lower cost for fixed investment and ongoing operations. It generally seems best to start with fundamentals and to add more complex and costlier applications only where they offer significant cost savings or service advantages.

The Design Cycle

It is useful to view the materials handling design process as a cycle or set of cycles as shown in Figure 25-1.

There is an overall progression in the cycle, but certain considerations may be faced more than once. For example, physical product characteristics control many choices in the final design of a materials handling system. However, the physical characteristics of products are themselves controllable to an extent. In the first pass, a manager may assign a "cost" or "value" to having products in a particular form. He or she may then return to the beginning, asking, "Is it possible to have them in a different form? If so, at what cost?" With appropriate answers to these

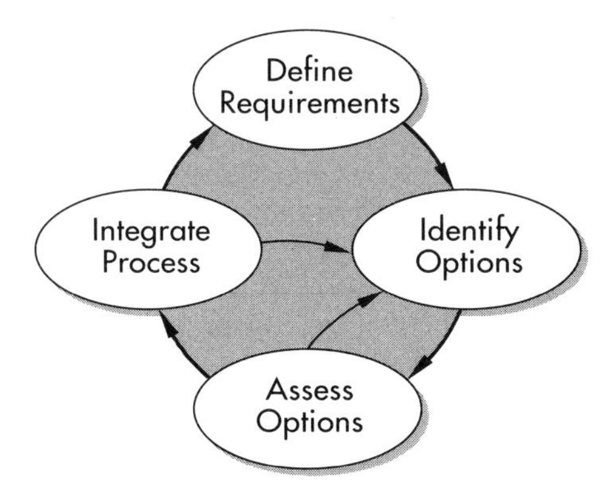

Figure 25-1
The Design Process

questions, an entirely different design may result. Experience can circumvent some of these steps, but only in certain instances.

Determining Business and Technical Requirements

Design of a materials handling system should fundamentally reflect the requirements it is expected to meet. By carefully stating those requirements, one is more likely to obtain a long-lasting and effective system. The challenge is to develop a requirements definition that provides a firm foundation for the system and its support of the business. Helping to establish that foundation is an important role for a manager involved in designing a new materials handling system.

Focus on the Future

It is not enough to design just for today's business. The resulting materials handling system would be not only incapable of handling future requirements but would also fail to provide long-term competitive advantage for the company.

Determining how far in the future is far enough may, of course, pose difficult challenges. How stable is the business? Are products changing rapidly? How long has the market existed? What external factors influence the logistics process? Are they changing?

For very stable, mature businesses, it may be possible to forecast requirements for a decade or more. However, for most business environments, it is neither practical nor desirable to look beyond about five years. Considering that major redesigns usually occur at ten-year intervals, a manager should realize that any new system will be expanded at least once before it is completely replaced.

System requirements typically fall into six categories:

1. Service
2. Product characteristics
3. Transaction characteristics
4. Volumes
5. Costs
6. Constraints

The goal is to define the expected performance of the system in objective, quantifiable terms. This definition in turn guides the development and selection of the design, and ultimately allows a manager to determine whether the design meets the needs of the company and its customers.

Service Requirements

Every statement of requirements should begin with a focus on the customer. Customers' expectations can be defined in terms of minimum performance standards, but finding economical ways to exceed those standards allows a company to gain competitive advantage. The four principal criteria used to define customer service are as follows:

1. Cycle times
2. Time fences
3. Accuracy and quality
4. Value-added services

Two sources of information are needed to address each of these criteria: (1) a thorough knowledge of existing service performance, and (2) a firm understanding of customers' expectations. The first of these should be available through routine internal performance monitoring. The second is developed through regular surveys of both customers and noncustomers. Together, these sources provide vital information to fill gaps in the materials handling system design.

Cycle time refers to the time it takes to complete each step in the entire logistics process, with particular focus on the time between receiving a customer's order and delivering it. The order processing cycle is a key element of customers' perception of service. The shorter—and more consistent—it is, the better.

The best-performing companies are capable of delivering an order to the customer in fewer than ten hours. However, this may not be economical for many companies; a more common "best" performance is between two and three days. Short cycle times compete directly with efficiency: the longer a cycle can be, the more opportunity there is for creativity in meeting customers' needs.

Time fences represent particular times of the day, or days of the week, before or after which certain events must happen. For example, a firm may allow orders to be taken up to 9:00 P.M. for delivery the next business day. Shift schedules are another form of time fence.

Time fences can be important in the materials handling system when they combine with cycle times to create a critical path. They may set limits on the type of acceptable technology or the amount of work-in-process inventory that can be allowed. For example, if the time between the arrival of the last order and the first required order departure is less than the normal order processing cycle time, some special process will be needed.

Both cycle times and time fences can often be self-imposed. When this is the case, creative alternatives can be developed that simplify the process. For example, traditional shifts may be modified to meet customers' expectations and logistical constraints.

Accuracy and *quality* have become the modern-day Holy Grail for most businesses. This is no less true in materials handling systems. Of the two characteristics, accuracy is the more controllable in the design of the system. Quality reflects policies and their implementation, embodied in aspects of the finished product (and the way in which it is delivered) beyond the simple fulfillment of an order as originally specified by a customer.

Short of automating the entire materials handling process (not a practical approach in most businesses), there will always be people involved and thus a potential for error. The goal should be to design the system to anticipate, isolate, and eliminate as many sources of error as possible.

To define an accuracy requirement, it is useful to think of the order *as the customer sees it.* Accuracy is often measured by suppliers in terms of percentage of order lines or units processed without error. While operationally this may appear to be a valid measurement, it may miss the point from the customer's perspective. To the customer, the only measurement that matters is the number of *orders* received without error (unless there is only one line per order, these numbers may differ widely). This means that businesses with larger numbers of lines (or units) per order must maintain higher accuracy levels to achieve the same level of customer satisfaction. In other words, a firm must determine what its customers *really* need and desire.

Value-added services can be a powerful differentiator. Barcoding, electronic data interchange, special unit loads, price marking, kitting, and similar services have been popular in the past and still are. They can tie a customer to a firm in ways that go beyond dollar-and-cents measurements of success. The variety of these extra services is almost endless, and knowing what should be offered takes a more detailed understanding of a customer's business. A firm should review the most onerous, costly tasks its customers perform and then imagine whether it could perform the same tasks cost-efficiently, perhaps in conjunction with another activity. If so, these services should be considered for inclusion in a redesigned materials handling operation. A company can determine the potential cost of the new service and weigh it against the potential competitive advantage it may offer.

Service requirements can be one of the most difficult areas to specify for a new materials handling system, particularly if they need to change from the current operations. They are difficult to quantify, and there are no "right" answers. Still, if approached with foresight and creativity, they provide a solid foundation for an outstanding materials handling design.

Volume Requirements

The most fundamental information needed for design of a materials handling system is an accurate estimate of the volumes of goods to be processed. This information is needed most critically for three activities—receipts, inventories, and shipments—because these common process flows in turn define most of the transaction volumes for particular activities in the system.

Information about these flows is typically viewed in two ways: the *absolute volumes* in some relevant unit of measure (eaches, cases, pallets, pounds), and the *volume fluctuation* over time Few companies have volumes that are even somewhat constant over time. Figure 25-2 illustrates

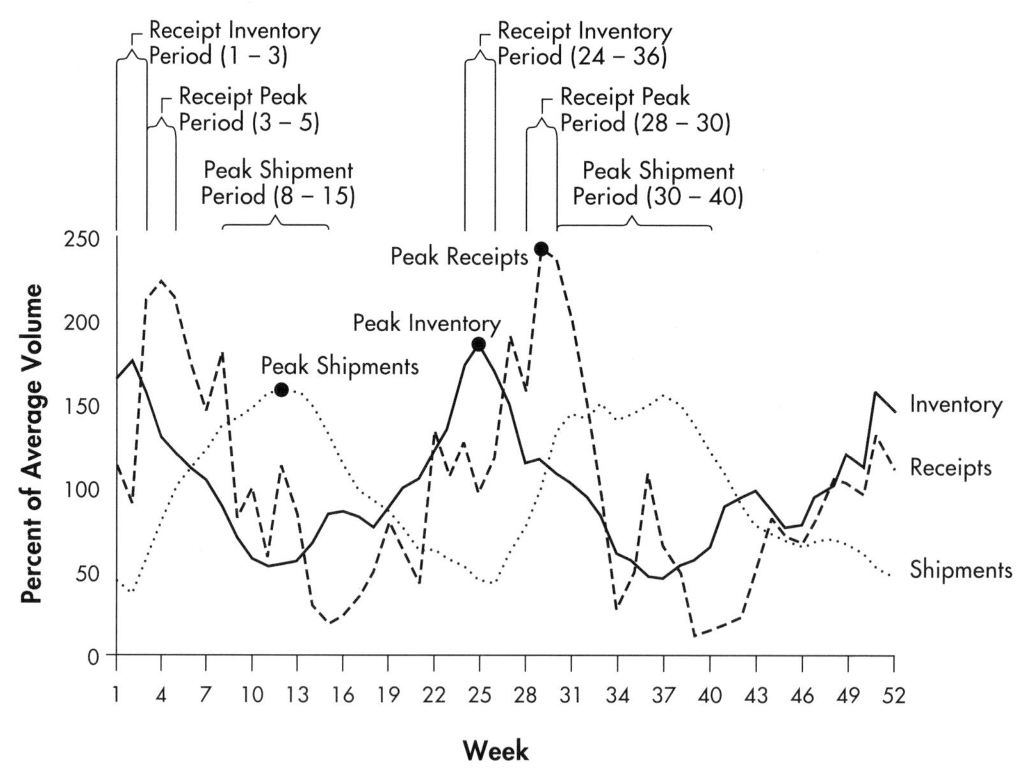

Figure 25-2
Typical Volume Variations

typical volume variations, expressed in terms of weekly values as a percentage of the overall average for each major flow.

Equipment for the materials handling system will ultimately impose some capacity constraint on the operation—a constraint that may be impossible or very costly to exceed, even momentarily. Trying to exceed the design capacity usually means increased work-in-progress inventory, *not* increased volume into or out of the operation. Cycle times and, ultimately, service will suffer. Excess inventory usually means inefficient storage methods or congestion in traffic spaces. Productivity will diminish.

None of these conditions is desirable for good customer service. To meet service requirements, the materials handling system must be capable of handling *all* anticipated volumes at a reasonable cost. The view in Figure 25-2 highlights factors that often are important to know for a particular operation.

All flows have peaks. Receipts are typically more volatile than either shipments or inventories and typically have higher peaks, requiring relatively more resources in the front end of the process, where receipt cycle times are critical to service.

Peaks are often out of sync with one another. This implies the potential to share resources between flows, allowing higher peak handling capacity with less investment. Peak activity periods are typically short. The shorter they are, the more challenging is the trade-off between increased investment for capacity and a temporary reduction in service capability. It is very tempting to avoid the added investment, and if the peak lasts only a short time, this may be the best choice. However, because peak shipping periods represent times of maximum customer need, they should be compromised only with care.

Figure 25-2 shows volumes at weekly intervals, a common measurement period. Unless required cycle times are a day or less, in-week peaks can usually be ignored, and weekly information is sufficient. However, the shorter the measurement interval, the larger the maximum peak is likely to be. This is one reason that higher service typically incurs higher costs (that is, because more investment in fixed capacity is needed). In these cases, the greater need should be reflected in greater frequency of information gathering.

Product Characteristics

The most fundamental information needed about the products to be handled is how many there are (that is, the number of stock-keeping units, or SKUs). While it may be relatively easy to determine the total number of SKUs in the inventory, it is usually more difficult to know how many are actively demanded at any given time. It is even more challenging to estimate accurately how the number of SKUs may change over several years. Nevertheless, a specific number is usually required to plan future storage requirements and to evaluate alternative picking methods.

Plans for specific new market segments must be considered in determining future SKU growth, because each new market usually generates a need or opportunity for new products. However, growth in existing markets may also imply additional products. A common assumption is that SKU growth for existing product lines will be related to unit volume growth for those lines. Historical trends can be used; if these are not available, the best approach is to use a growth *rate* for SKUs that is half the unit volume growth rate. This rule comes from the observation that existing markets are typically grown by a combination of expansion and deepening penetration with older products.

Consistent product classification categories should be used in developing a materials handling system. The value of such consistency is most evident when considering the various equipment available for moving and storing specific types of materials. Its value is less obvious but no less important in the overall process design. Product characteristics are perhaps the most natural dimensions for assigning categories. Because quantitative information is usually available only for the products handled now, the most common technique is to categorize them and to project the future course of each category.

There are four methods of product handling: bulk, unit load, cases, and selling units, listed in decreasing order of the potential for automation, and increasing order of complexity.

Product handling methods may change throughout the process. Products may be received in bulk and stored in silos. Siloed product may be packaged into cases and palletized into unit loads for storage. Cases may then be picked for customers and repalletized into mixed unit loads. The form of the product at each stage is fundamental to defining the materials handling method to be used.

Physical characteristics also play a part. Some specific variables that should be known about the handling types of each product include:

- Type of storage container
- Dimensions
- Weight or density
- Quantity ratios (for example, cases per pallet or units per case)
- Unit load stacking height (how high can pallets be stacked?)

If a company handles a small collection of products, it should be possible to determine this type of information for each individual product. However, as the number of products grows, the amount of information may become unwieldy, and the value of detailed knowledge of each product is reduced. It is usually more appropriate to create categories immediately and to treat the collections of products within each category as clones of one another. This greatly reduces the amount of information needed and simplifies analysis (details are compromised only slightly if enough categories are used). As the number of products grows to tens of thousands, a pragmatic approach dictates that data be collected only on samples of items.

Some products have special characteristics that force particular categories for the purpose of materials handling design. The law, if not common sense, generally requires special handling for hazardous regulated materials. This may simply entail special record keeping or may extend to complete segregation of all activities, as in the case of highly radioactive materials. Likewise, refrigerated products usually require temperature-segregated areas and, in extreme cases, special equipment. Many operations provide special handling for high-value products or those susceptible to shrinkage.

The last and most powerful means of defining categories of products is profiling. Pareto's Law, more commonly known as the 80-20 rule, has dramatic implications for the design of any materials handling system. It states that in any collection of items, a disproportionately large amount of attention will be given to a relatively small number of items. There is usually a continuous distribution of activity such as is that shown generically in Figure 25-3.

All the important volume and inventory requirements that can be associated with particular products can potentially benefit from profiling. This includes unit volumes, cubic foot volumes, and numbers of particular transactions. Profiles are useful when it is time to make preliminary judgments about storage and handling methods that deserve detailed attention.

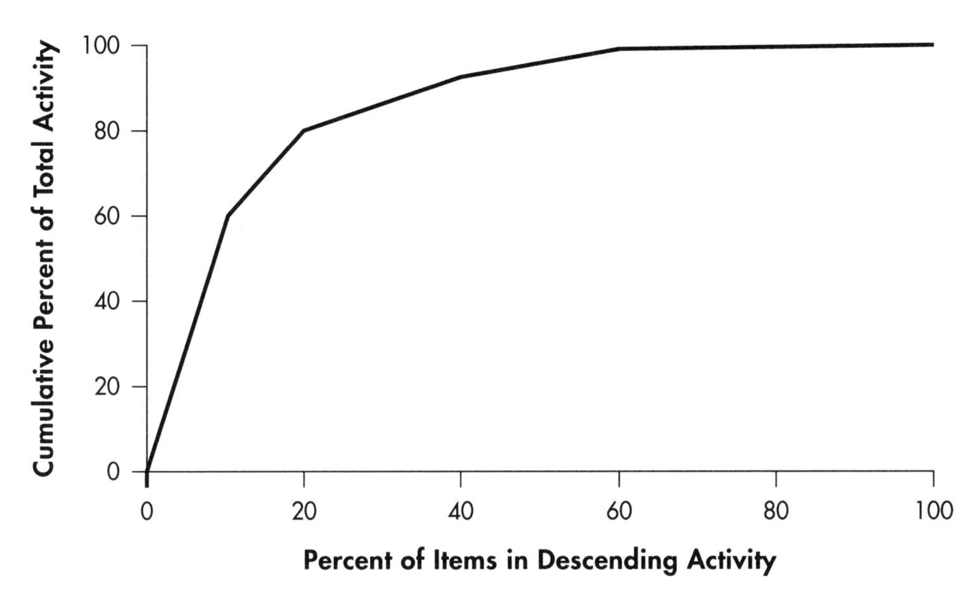

Figure 25-3
Typical Activity Profile

Transaction Characteristics

Volumes tell only part of the story for a materials handling system. In most cases, knowledge of the detailed characteristics of the receipts, orders, and other activities is critical for identifying meaningful options and for ensuring proper capacity levels. As with product characteristics, transactions should be profiled according to relevant measurements. Let's take the example of picking activities.

Regardless of the picking process used, fundamentally *shipments* are processed. A shipment may make up a portion of a customer order, a single order, or some set of orders. Yet all picking activities are directed to the goal of collecting all the shipment's components at one place and time. The specific characteristics of shipments that may be relevant in a particular business vary widely but generally include:

- Shipment method or mode
- Physical handling components, such as the number of full pallets, full cases, or individual pieces picked
- Complexity measures, such as the number of SKUs or frequency of special handling methods
- Physical size/weight measures

Each of these dimensions could be used to segment the shipments into groups that will ultimately lend themselves to consistent materials handling techniques. The segmentation should attempt to isolate categories of transactions that can be handled in a streamlined way. For example, shipments that represent a single SKU can often be handled separately in a much more productive fashion than multiple SKU shipments. Parcel shipments, by equating each package with an independent shipment, also may simplify the process. These examples illustrate the type of information that can be drawn from transaction profiles.

All transaction types that exist in a particular operation can be profiled in a similar way. Typical transactions that may be of interest in materials handling design include:

- Receiving
- Product packaging and preparation activities
- Intrafacility moves and replenishments
- Shipment packing
- Transport loading and unloading
- Returns and reverse flow processing
- Clerical activities, to the extent that they interact with the materials handling process

The specifics of the relevant information, profiling process, and conclusions to be drawn depend, of course, on the operation to be supported.

For the materials handling designer, it is unfortunate that few management reporting systems routinely monitor *all* the information potentially needed to complete a materials handling design. Actually getting such information may itself be a challenge requiring planning and creativity. Regardless of accessibility, and regardless of whether the information is known, it *will* become a part of the ultimate design. If it is not explicitly considered, it will be included implicitly and by assumption. That may be a good choice when a particularly inaccessible piece of information will have minimal impact. However, the maxim applies: no one has ever been killed by too much knowledge, but many have been killed by the lack of it.

The last two major categories of requirements limit feasible designs that are not necessarily technical and that may be imposed externally. In effect, they help further align the materials handling system with the business needs.

Cost Requirements

In businesses where logistics costs, particularly operations costs, are large relative to other costs, knowledge of the cost structure needed to be competitive is an important boundary. With comparable levels of optimization, service and costs trade off against each other. Thus, it may not be desirable to increase costs to gain higher service. This can be particularly true in commodity-product businesses where higher costs may either eliminate profits or force a high price that loses sales.

Even if there is cost flexibility, the relative amount of fixed costs compared with variable costs may be an issue. In the context of the materials handling system, fixed costs arise most often from investments in automation technologies. High fixed costs make costs much more sensitive to volume. If forecasts are susceptible to optimism, or there is the possibility for a downturn, high fixed costs increase risk. Likewise, special-purpose equipment suffers from the same effect. The volatility of the business should be recognized at the outset of the design process so that these risks can be properly balanced against benefits.

The last cost constraint that should be stated going into the design process is the required investment return criterion. Regardless of the financial analysis technique used, it is helpful to determine, early in the process, a clear hurdle for acceptable returns. This criterion can screen options that obviously fall short of expectations.

Despite the financial theory that says that discounted rate of return is the most appropriate criterion for weighing investment options, required investment returns are usually stated as "payback periods." This method is easy to use and simple to understand, and it eliminates the issue of the time phasing of benefits.

Process Constraints

Many potential factors, while not within the immediate scope of the materials handling system, may limit the allowable solutions in a design. Three examples of this type of constraint seem to occur more often than others: policies, regulatory requirements, and value of the products to be handled.

1. *Policies.* A company's management may establish or support particular policies that in effect limit solutions. For example, some companies require that all operations be made "handicapped-friendly," even though that may not be required under current regulations. Increasingly, companies require "green" operations that maximize the potential for ecologically sound activities like recycling. It is almost always more effective to plan for this type of policy at the very start of the design than to attempt a retrofit later.
2. *Regulatory requirements.* Regulatory requirements are factors that vary by industry and by degree. They may include rules regarding building design, fire safety, structural soundness, OSHA, and similar regulations that affect all businesses, or they may involve industry- or operation-specific regulations like those administered by the FDA and similar rule-making bodies. Whatever the particular regulation may be and regardless of its impact on either process design or equipment selection, such constraints *must* be recognized at the outset of design.
3. *Value of the products to be handled.* Certainly a process intended to handle diamonds will be different from one designed to handle steel plate. High-value items often require segregation, higher levels of access control, and more checks and balances in successive activities. Pilferable products may also fall into this category.

Identification of Options

It may be desirable to investigate and test all possible options for a company's logistics operating process and supporting materials handling system. After all, almost any process *can* be made to work in virtually any situation and, with appropriate modification, can meet almost any service requirement.

An exhaustive evaluation process may lead to novel approaches that defy conventional wisdom and provide particularly effective advantages. However, in any particular situation there are likely to be many more designs that do *not* work well than there are options with true potential for meeting the requirements at an acceptable cost. In short, the "brute force" approach will probably reach many dead ends and thus suffer from inefficiency.

A much more efficient process typically starts with common, basic principles of materials handling to identify a limited number of specific options for detailed analysis and selection. By using such principles and experience, the effort that would otherwise be wasted on an excessive number of impractical options can be better invested in finding a feasible and implementable solution. Balancing the trade-off between efficiency and exhaustive research requires "practical creativity" in identifying options.

General Principles of Evaluating Options

Seven general principles, shown in Table 25-1, distinguish successful solutions in many categories of business. They are not always in harmony; typically, they involve a balance of trade-offs. Nevertheless, they can provide a useful framework for defining sets of options that will ultimately yield good solutions.

When defining options, each choice should further one or more of these general principals. In cases where trade-offs are needed, it is likely the principle that promotes the lowest labor cost will dominate. This results from the fact that in most logistical operations the cost structure is largely labor-driven.

Process Design

If a materials handling process has already been well designed, a company may simply need a better equipment methodology for moving materials through it. This basic challenge can be met by using traditional engineering and economic decision processes. However, most companies recognize that there may be opportunities to restructure not only the equipment but the process itself. In doing so, a much more complex interaction is established where process and equipment must be considered simultaneously to find the best overall solution. Generally, "process" takes precedence because, except in very special cases, materials handling equipment already exists that can perform almost every conceivable function. Situations in which equipment must be the first priority are generally those where the products and services to be handled are so unusual or advanced that only a unique equipment design will meet the requirements (for example, exploration of outer space or implementation of new petrochemical technology).

There are two important guidelines for any process design: (1) do not automatically accept the status quo, because it will probably not provide long-term competitive advantage; (2) do not confine consideration only to within the "four walls" of the operation—look outside too.

One definition holds that the optimal design occurs when *each stage in the process is optimized with respect to all its inputs.* Whether one defines "optimal" to mean minimum cost, fastest service, or whatever is appropriate to the situation, the *inputs* to each stage are critical. This view of a process is the opposite of the conventional view—as a progression of activities from start to finish. Instead, it suggests working backward from the required output to the ultimate inputs needed to achieve it. Because inputs may ultimately come from outside the operation, this view reinforces the need to consider customizing inputs to fit the best process. Luckily, because the options available for the inputs at each stage are limited, the process remains manageable.

Information System Considerations

To this point we have concentrated on the physical aspects of materials handling systems and the associated processes. However, information flows are at least as important, if not more so, in some cases. It is a rare materials handling system design that does not also consider the information systems needed to support the process. Six attributes distinguish the information systems being put in place today, as summarized in Table 25-2.

Regardless of the specific features that apply to a particular information system, five important ideas ought to be reinforced in those that support materials handling systems:

TABLE 25-1
Principles for Evaluating Tradeoffs

Principle	Description	Rationale
Largest unit	Each movement of product should be done in the largest quantity possible at one time.	The larger the handling unit, the fewer moves there are, and thus the less labor required. Also, the equipment needed to handle larger units is typically less expensive per unit of capacity.
Shortest path	Products and activities should move through the shortest possible path.	Travel distances are a large factor for labor costs. In addition, costs for materials handling equipment such as conveyors are directly linked to distance.
Smallest space	The "territory" covered by any task should be as small as possible.	This is directly related to the previous principle. Also, smaller areas generally involve simpler operations that employees can better understand and perform.
Shortest time	The time needed for any activity or delay should be as short as possible.	Task duration is directly related to labor costs. Work-in-progress inventories and holding spaces are also related to holding time. Response time is a key measurement of customer service quality.
Minimum handlings	Products should be touched or handled as little as possible.	Labor and other resources are expended each time an item is manipulated. Each handling *must* add as much value, or incur as little cost, as possible.
Grouping and collection	Items and transactions that have similar characteristics should be handled together.	The larger the handling units, the higher the efficiency gained (and thus the lower the costs incurred). Also, by combining similar activities on multiple items, employees "shift gears" fewer times in a day.
Balanced line	Sequential activities must have matching capacities to minimize work-in-progress inventories and to achieve maximum overall throughput.	Any disparity in capacity between successive activities means that inventories build before the lower-capacity activity. Because throughput cannot exceed the limits of the lowest-capacity activity, higher capacity in other activities is wasted.

1. A significant amount of activity in traditional materials handling systems has been focused on transmitting information from one activity to another. When knowledge is captured solely on paper, it must first be absorbed by other workers before it can be used for decisions. Information systems should strive to capture a particular piece of information *once* and distribute it as needed.

TABLE 25-2
Attributes of Material Handling Information Systems

Information System Design Attribute	Visible "Feature"
"Real-time" orientation	• "Instant" availability
	• "Quick cycle" order batching
	• Detailed status tracking
Applied "intelligence"	• Real-world knowledge
	• Direction and confirmation
	• Detailed physical data
	• Detailed process structures
	• "Rule-based" logic
Integrated performance measures	• Transaction accountability
	• Key performance indicators
	• Measurement standards
	• Labor management
Auto ID technologies	• Industry bar code standards
	• Primary data acquisition tool
Radio-frequency communications	• Paper-reduced environment
	• Mobile communications
Flexible integration	• Integrated packages
	• Ad hoc processes
	• "Open" systems

2. The amount of information needed to make "optimum" decisions about logistical operations is much too great for most people to handle effectively at one time. Computers excel at solving complex, multifaceted problems, quickly and accurately.
3. Although there is certainly a need for initiative and human creativity in logistical operations, many complex decisions can be made using well-structured, repetitive processes. Computers can easily do things the same way each time and deliver consistent results. People find that difficult.
4. A materials handling system is by nature a fast-changing, dynamic environment. Computers are capable of keeping pace with the operations, while people can readily fall behind.
5. The costs of information systems technologies continue to fall rapidly. If a particular piece of hardware is only marginally economical today, plan for it anyway. You may not buy it now, but it will become affordable quickly.

Equipment Selection

Many of the options one might select for review are determined by the types of materials handling equipment that are generally available. Although it is certainly possible to create custom machinery to solve special problems (common in packaging operations), the high costs of such a solution make it less feasible in warehousing and general distribution. Generally one must choose from available commercial equipment offerings.

Paradoxically, it is both fortuitous and regrettable that fundamental changes in the nature of materials handling equipment have been rare in the last ten years. There have been technical refinements and cost improvements, to be sure, but excluding information handling, significant innovations are lacking. This is fortunate because it simplifies the process of learning about, and staying reasonably current with, materials handling equipment technology. It is regrettable because such lack of innovation limits a company's efforts to implement new, more creative solutions. The main difference today is that long-established equipment designs can often be used in new and more effective ways because of access to more information and more powerful decision support tools.

Categories of Equipment

A relatively brief review of the varieties of equipment and their applications is presented in Table 25-3. (See chapter 26, for an even more detailed survey of equipment and other technologies.)

Many other, more specialized types of equipment are available for particular needs. However, most common materials handling problems can be solved using the types listed here. Despite the fact that manufacturers generally list "stock" configurations in their catalogs, a company can usually order customized versions for a relatively small additional cost. In fact, equipment for most larger installations is typically made-to-order.

Sources for Information on Equipment

The easiest-to-find source of information on equipment applications is, of course, the company that makes it. Beyond simply providing stock literature on the equipment, the vendor can also, however, refer a prospective buyer to a more objective source—people who have used it before. (In fact, if a supplier seems reluctant to share installation references, one should be skeptical.) Most suppliers are eager to help match their products to a buyer's needs, but it is, of course, wise not to allow a vendor to "fit the problem to the solution."

To find the names of potential suppliers, handbooks and directories can be helpful. They are usually published annually by the several materials handling trade publications and provide product listings with company contacts.

Matching Equipment and the Process

There is a strong interrelationship between the process and the equipment that supports it. On the one hand, the process often dictates what types of items are to be handled. On the other, a particular piece of equipment may enable a company to use a particular process that otherwise would be impossible or impractical. For example, it might be advantageous to pick items without regard to the orders that own them. This might reduce the need to access a particular SKU and thus reduce picking labor. However, because items will then emerge from picking in an essentially random sequence relative to the orders that own them, some mechanism must be provided to *sort* the items for order accumulation. If volumes are large enough, there may be no economical way to do this without an efficient, high-speed sorter. Almost every task in the design of a materials handling system presents similar trade-offs.

TABLE 25-3
Overview of Available Materials Handling Equipment

Category	Description/Variations	Usage
Storage Racks		
Bin shelf/decked rack	Open frame and solid shelf, or with closed side walls. Metal or wood	High- and low-bay storage of loose, oddly shaped, or small quantities of packaged product.
Drawers	Closed, compartmentalized, usually metal construction	High-density storage of small products.
Selective	Steel structural member framework of uprights and horizontal beams.	Unit-load storage on pallets or slip sheets. With addition of wood or metal decking, becomes decked rack. In combination with normal lift trucks, allows storage up to two loads deep on each side of an aisle.
Drive-in/drive-thru	Deep storage by using cantilevered beams on selective-type uprights. Spacing between uprights allows entry of lift-trucks into storage rows.	High-density storage of unit loads. Unit-load size is rigidly constrained to fit. Usually used in a first-in,–first-out (FIFO) mode. Each "channel" (a section one load wide, the full height and depth) is usually allocated to one SKU.
Unit-load Flow	Arrays of small, inclined, roller conveyors that support unit loads in multiple levels at arbitrary depths.	Loads "flow" from the input side to the output side by gravity. Forces FIFO access. Each "lane" (one load wide and high, the full depth) is usually allocated to an SKU.
Case Flow	Similar to unit-load flow but for case-sized containers.	Similar to unit-load flow.
Cantilevered	Center-line uprights supporting horizontal "arms" either alone or with attached decking or other special devices .	Pipe, bar-stock, coiled metal storage with arm-only configuration. With decking, provides wide-span clear shelves without upright interference.
Push-back	Similar to unit-load flow, but loads are placed on stacked, individual load carriers and successively "pushed back" by the next load	Input and output on the same side. Forces last-in-first-out (LIFO) flow. Can be placed against a wall because only one aisle is needed
Mobile		Most racks are installed with fixed, permanent aisles for access. It is possible to configure most storage racks on movable carriers so that sections of rack may be moved aside to "create" an aisle where space is at a premium and/or frequency of access is very low.

TABLE 25-3 (continued)
Overview of Available Materials Handling Equipment

Category	Description/Variations	Usage
Rolling-stock and Lift Trucks		
Walkie	Low-lift unit-load handling trucks, maneuvered by means of a handle bar control. Usually electrical.	Truck unloading and short-distance unit-load relocation. Some picking operations.
Walkie/ride	Allows operator to mount the truck during operation. A two-load version is often called a transporter and is generally a high-speed device for long-distance horizontal travel. Usually electrical.	Longer-distance horizontal transport
High-lift Walkie	Similar to Walkie but with a taller, but still limited, lifting capacity. Usually electrical.	Close-quarters stacking, and rack access over limited distances.
Counterbalanced	High-lift truck with the load outboard of the wheel base. Usually with sit-down controls. Widest range of load capacities (very heavy at the upper end). Indoor and outdoor styles. Storage heights generally below 30 feet. Electrical or internal combustion engine.	Very stable within load limits. Useful on uneven surfaces, and from dock to truck. Often used for drive-in/drive-thru storage because of narrow front cross section. Typically requires 12-foot+ aisle.
Straddle/reach	High-lift truck with the load contained between front wheel "outriggers." Reach device allows loads to be extended beyond the outriggers. Usually with stand-up controls. Storage heights generally below 30 feet. Usually electrical.	Loads are limited by outriggers if reach device is not used. Smooth-floor operations, usually inside. Does not do well from dock to truck because of low ground clearance. Requires narrower 8-foot+ aisles.
Side loader	Very high lift with load generally at center of truck. Fork extension is side-to-side. Aisle-captive and free-roaming configurations. Extendable or fixed-extension masts. Multiload for AS/RS. Maximum heights are in excess of 100 feet. Can be very high speed in automated systems. Always electrical.	Unit-load handling. Like a walrus out of the sea when free-roaming version is out of the storage aisle. Aisle-captive configuration is used in manned crane/automated storage and retrieval systems (AS/RS). Aisle widths determined by load dimensions, generally very narrow. Manned operations at 45 feet or fewer have generally been assumed by more flexible turret trucks.
Turret	High-lift truck with a swivel-reach fork mechanism that allows forward and either-side load access. Overall chassis configuration may be similar to either a counterbalanced or stock-picker truck. Free-roaming. Man-up and man-down configurations. Storage heights up to about 45 feet. Universally electrical.	Unit-load handling. Only marginally useful outside the storage aisle. Aisle widths determined by load dimensions, generally very narrow. Man-up configurations can often double-duty as stock pickers.

TABLE 25-3 (continued)
Overview of Available Materials Handling Equipment

Category	Description/Variations	Usage
Automatic guided vehicles (AGVs)	Robotic devices that follow fixed or variable paths picking up and dropping load containers at fixed points. Most commonly guided by wire, chemical, or optical paths. Free-ranging on grid (FROG) vehicles use a calibrated "map." Both powered-unit carriers and train configurations are used. Some units can do limited stacking. Generally low speeds for safety.	For repetitive deliveries to well-defined points over longer distances than conveyor can economically service. For highly variable routing, again to well-defined points. Loads must be stable and have uniform base dimensions.
Conveyance		
Roller	Rollers directly support loads. Belt-driven, chain-driven, cable-driven and other drive types are possible. A wide variety of specialized components can accumulate, route, merge, or otherwise manipulate loads.	Most flexible package/unit-load conveyor. Very economical for fixed-path conveyance. Requires flat, smooth load bottoms.
Belt	Belt directly supports loads, further supported by a metal plate or rollers. With special controls provides accurate positioning, flow and speed control.	Often used for bulk materials. Conveys almost anything that can sit on the belt. Cannot be effectively used for accumulation.
Rail	Generally, an overhead pipe or track on which trolleys ride, carrying loads in various configurations. Trolleys can be very specialized to the load and functions surrounding the rail. Both powered and gravity versions are used. Generally one load per trolley. Trolleys can be switched, merged, and sorted automatically.	Usually configured in a closed loop, where trolleys originate from and return to the same points. Useful for positioning heavy work items because heights can be precisely matched. Provides convenient underneath clearance.
Tow chain (AKA: Tow-chain)	Similar to the concept of rail but with the track in the floor. Normally driven by a chain in the track that captures special carts at fixed intervals.	Usage may be similar to rail, but loads can be greater. Very difficult to position loads vertically.
Sortation	A wide variety of specialized conveyors is available, specifically designed for sortation, including simple divert, slat sorter, drop-frame, tilt-tray, etc.	Sorters are used whenever it is necessary to divert items or loads to several destinations very quickly. The type of sorter chosen depends on the sortation rate and load characteristics.

TABLE 25-3 (continued)
Overview of Available Materials Handling Equipment

Category	Description/Variations	Usage
Automated storage		
Unit load	A specialized form of selective rack, usually very tall (70 feet +), which is served by an automated side-loading crane (see side loader above). Sometimes configured as a rack-supported building. Cranes are usually captive, but system can be designed to exchange cranes between aisles.	Usually fed by either conveyor or AGVs. Used for very dense storage of relatively low-turning product in unit-load quantities.
Miniload	As the name suggests, similar to unit-load systems but generally handles smaller trays, or tote boxes with product in them.	Usually used for picking operations or for work-in-progress holding.
Carousel	A continuous loop of what are essentially independent bin shelving sections, which revolves past a single point.	Usually used for picking operations, or for holding work-in-progress.

Flexibility

Materials handling equipment may appear as an "asset" on the balance sheet, but components that do not effectively fill their intended role are anything but assets. As a general rule, materials handling equipment has essentially no resale value. This means that marginal investments in equipment, particularly in today's fast-changing business environment, pose large downside risks.

With a few notable exceptions, every piece of materials handling equipment has a particular function. Some functions may be generic, such as a lift truck moving a pallet from a receiving dock into storage. Others may be very specific, such as a towline that travels among three specific points. If storage must be relocated or even if the use of the racks changes in the future, the lift truck may still be able to fill the role. However, if a company needs to relocate the functions served by the towline, it will probably incur significant cost. (In some cases it may even be less expensive to simply abandon the original installation and start over.) Whenever special-purpose equipment such as a towline is being considered, it is wise to consider the cost and service impacts in light of changing future requirements. In a dynamic, unpredictable environment, generic solutions clearly offer much greater flexibility.

Ergonomic Considerations

With the increasing numbers of women in the workforce, along with the rapid rise in costs of insurance and worker's compensation, ergonomics has become an important consideration in materials handling design. Carefully designed ergonomics has always been important to achieving the ultimate in labor productivity. However, until recent years, it was often given little attention because of the time and expertise required to implement ergonomically correct applications. Today, good materials handling design aims, for example, at eliminating the need for employees to lift a load manually.

Evaluation of Options

One of the most important tools in developing the optimal materials handling design to support distribution operations is a financial economic analysis. This analysis is also commonly referred to as the cost justification or analysis of trade-offs among space, labor, and capital investment. These three elements must be carefully analyzed to determine the correct balance of automation that will reduce the square footage and/or labor requirements. It is most important when evaluating these economic measures that a company choose the right balance that will neither inhibit service by underautomating nor create an unreasonable cost burden by overautomating.

When developing the right mixture, it is important to evaluate the four key components that should be analyzed in developing the distribution center and the materials handling design. Those elements are highlighted in Figure 25-4.

In designing materials handling systems, it is first important to identify the correct methods and procedures that will most effectively support the company's strategic objectives and then apply the right mixture of physical support from materials handling equipment and information systems to meet the customer service requirements. This analysis should include detailed, comprehensive analyses incorporating the following cost breakdowns by alternatives. A complete and thorough analysis will incorporate all aspects of the following:

- Building square footage and associated costs
- Materials handling equipment investment
- Hardware and software investment
- Occupancy costs to operate the building
- Labor costs to operate the facility

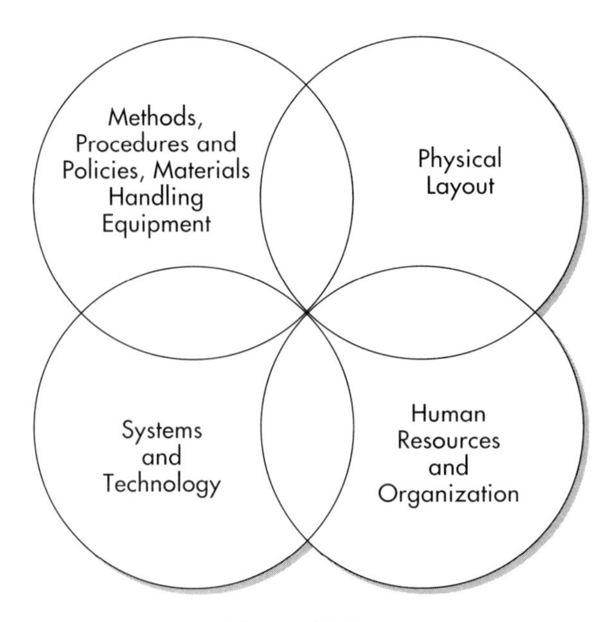

Figure 25-4
Four Key Components in Evaluating Materials Handling Design

- Management costs to manage the operations
- Total cost by alternative

By formally segmenting costs associated with each alternative and each subcomponent of the overall materials handling systems design, it is possible to identify different subcomponents within each alternative and to choose the right subcomponents to optimize the overall operation.

The primary objective is to provide the best customer service at the lowest level of fixed investment and operating cost. In determining the individual materials handling equipment that should be investigated, it is necessary to break down by subcomponent the qualitative and quantitative aspect of each alternative. This can be done by analyzing the overall cost of each materials handling component and determining the productivity of each of these subcomponents to develop the most cost-effective overall system.

Subcomponents should be evaluated by product characteristic and by product movement to help determine the right materials handling application and to identify the optimal productivity. These productivity goals or measurements should be maintained after implementation to benchmark the actual productivity and real savings produced by the new materials handling design.

Calculating Return on Investment

Crucial for gaining the approval of any management committee in materials handling system design is to provide a thorough economic analysis and justification that indicates a favorable return on investment. Return on investment (ROI) can be measured in several company-specific ways, depending on the firm's priorities.

Designing a new distribution center or a new materials handling system is a long-range, strategic decision aimed at supporting the company's essential mission in the marketplace, usually over a three- to five-year period. However, as the decisions turn more tactical and are involved in improving the cost structure of the distribution operations or increasing the service offering of the company, paybacks are typically expected to be in two years or less. Projects with ROIs beyond a two-year time frame usually take a backseat to those with faster and/or higher rates of return. In addition, an ROI analysis should be comprehensive and conservative so that when the results are tallied, the analysis will be proven to have been an achievable, credible goal.

Evaluating Qualitative Issues

One common mistake in materials handling design is to overlook or underestimate the importance of qualitative issues. Particularly in the 1990s, it has become increasingly important to differentiate a company through superior customer service as shown by faster response times and value-added activities. For example, retailers have focused on improving supply chain management and reducing the order cycle time from the vendor to the store shelf. As shown in Figure 25-5, such initiatives are aimed at creating a positive impact on all the critical trade-offs involved in logistics management:

For instance, consider the impacts of reducing the typical order cycle time (from vendor picking date to displaying the merchandise in stores) from 30 to 15 days. The retailer can keep less inventory on the shelves and more inventory in the pipeline, thus improving inventory turns (and profits) significantly. Such a move also has significant qualitative impacts, particularly with fashion merchandise. Cutting the time required to put fast-selling merchandise on the sales floor may spell the difference between gaining or losing customers. The faster throughput also increases

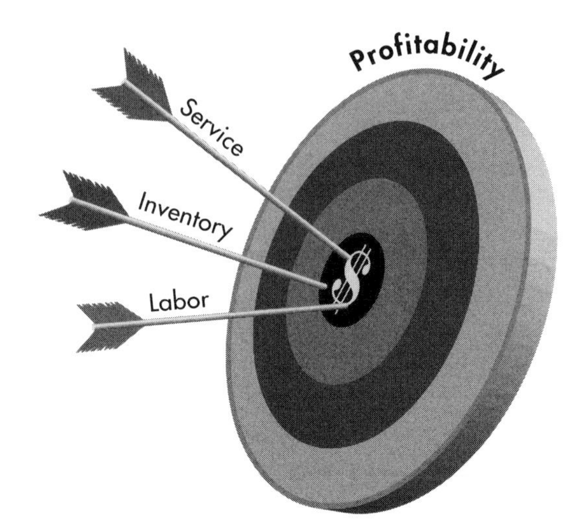

Figure 25-5
Qualitative Issues in Materials Handling Design

the sell-through of merchandise at the higher margins and thus cuts the markdowns the retailer must take. In addition, if the retailer must meet, say, a "net 100% after 30 days" requirement in its purchasing agreement with a vendor, the faster throughput gives the retailer 15 more days of sales time; in effect, this allows the retailer to gain a cost advantage similar to that of the wholesaler or manufacturer from whom the goods were purchased.

While such effects may be difficult to quantify, effective retailer managers have the business acumen to know their importance. They have come to understand the significant financial, service, and operating benefits of efficient distribution and materials handling systems.

Minimizing the Guesswork in Cost/Benefit Evaluations

Even after seeing detailed ROI calculations for a proposed materials handling design, many managers may still be skeptical or uneasy about moving ahead with the investment. They want more assurance.

One approach that can help set these concerns to rest is the use of a computerized simulation model. Today, this once arcane mathematician's tool has become an easy-to-use method for projecting the impact of a proposed materials handling system.

Two types of models are typically used, graphical simulation and spreadsheet simulation. A graphical simulation can be developed to consider options in the design of a distribution center, the materials handling system, and the information interfaces. This method will calculate and graphically display the advantages, productivity levels, capital investment cost, and service level trade-offs of each alternative being considered. A spreadsheet simulation, which is a more common modeling technique, does not graphically display the materials handling flow but does calculate the critical cost and service components. It can take into account, for instance, conveyor rates of speed, accumulation links, workstation productivity, and capital investment requirements. This form of simulation is based on traditional economic analysis and can produce an efficient, accurate forecast of the proposed design's impact.

Simulation is most suitable for expediting the "what if?" analysis required for a complex materials handling design calling for investments of several millions of dollars. This approach is particularly effective in analyzing piece-pick operations that require expensive materials handling equipment like A-frame sorters, automated storage and retrieval systems (AS/RS), and high-speed conveyor sortation. For less complex applications, simulation is usually not necessary and may, in fact, merely increase the cost of preliminary analysis.

System Procurement

A well-coordinated, multistep process is extremely important in developing a solution that will produce the desired results, on time and on budget.

Defining the Project Scope

Before actually inviting proposals from suitable vendors, a firm should carefully define several key parameters, including:

- Scope of the project
- Technical design
- Specialized equipment
- Systems integration
- Complexity of the installation

Preparing a Preliminary List of Vendors

A key step is to select the right vendor(s) to bid on the project. Projects with unique needs should start with the preparation of a list of potential vendors who offer the required experience, technical expertise, and stability needed in the project.

After selecting the vendors, the project team should meet in person with each vendor to discuss the bid and the scope of the work involved and to ensure a clear understanding of what is expected from the vendor. All vendors deserve equal access to the same information and an opportunity to survey the actual or planned facility where the new systems will be installed.

Potential vendors should be given adequate time to prepare a detailed response. Shortening the bidding process by rushing the vendors usually results in poor quality and service during and after the installation, as well as a tendency by them to overestimate expenses and fees. Such an approach is not conducive to building and maintaining a strong partnership between the company and its vendor. If it is imperative to fast-track the project, a firm should do this during the installation phase, when more construction or implementation crews can be brought on board.

Depending on the complexity of the project, a company may be wise to bid work out to various specialized vendors rather than to a single general contractor. For instance, in bidding the materials handling design of a complex flow-through distribution facility that also warehouses products, it would be desirable to obtain separate bids or specialized functions. This allows the company to receive better pricing on each equipment component, as well as the best equipment within each category. Components are typically grouped as follows:

- Conveyors
- Racks
- Mezzanines

- Materials handling vehicles
- Sortation systems
- Highly specialized technical equipment (e.g., AS/RS or AGVs)

Managing the Project

To achieve an integrated solution, it is often necessary to invest significant time in coordinating the work of several separate vendors. The most successful approach is to appoint a steering committee headed by a senior executive with experience in logistics, with assistance from outside specialists as needed. The combination of third-party expertise and internal project management helps ensure an unbiased approach to the selection of equipment and systems that will provide the best overall solution. The firm should also dedicate full-time resources for day-to-day management of the project to ensure good results.

Selecting the Winning Vendor(s)

Selecting the right vendor(s) for a materials handling design project should follow the same principles as those for any project requiring major capital investment. Each potential vendor's track record should be thoroughly checked, and references must be carefully researched. (It is important to probe as deeply and in as much detail as possible a vendor's results with previous customers.)

Obviously, equipment selection is the key in this process. Some vendors have a more desirable product on the market than others. However, other differentiating factors are also important, including:

- Project management skills (Were past projects done on time and on budget?)
- Amount of service required (Can the vendor supply detailed, verifiable statistics?)
- Proximity of service locations (Both time *and* distance should be considered.)
- Reputation of the vendor's company

If a highly automated system is designed to perform a large volume of operations that are invaluable to the company's logistics process each day, it is essential to ensure that the company is capable of solving equipment problems very quickly. As companies have grown larger, they have consolidated smaller facilities into much larger ones. In such situations, equipment failures are less tolerable because of significant cost and service impacts of downtime. Vendors have been forced to meet ever-growing demands for equipment reliability and maintenance or repair service, in both mechanical and computerized systems.

Other Evaluation Criteria

The above qualitative issues are extremely important in the vendor selection process; however, other quantitative factors should also be explored in selecting the winning vendors:

- Lead times
- Costs
- Used equipment
- Vendor project management experience

Lead Times

Each bid should be evaluated with the same ranking criteria in these categories. Equipment lead times are extremely important in the time cycle of the installation process. Depending on the sophistication of the equipment, the lead times will vary greatly. For instance, lead time on rack or gravity conveyors typically runs in the six- to eight-week range. However, lead times for more sophisticated equipment like turret trucks will more likely be around 26 weeks; for the most complex systems, such as A-frame sorters, lead times can often be up to one year.

Costs

As with automobiles, the costs of individual components of materials handling equipment, when purchased separately, greatly exceed the cost of the machinery taken as a whole. Thus, it is advisable to select a vendor that maintains inventories of spare parts that can be air-freighted, or a vendor that can repair the equipment in place on short notice. The company should, of course, keep a reasonable stock of parts that require routine replacement. For unusual or one-of-a-kind installations, spare parts may represent a significant investment.

Used Equipment

Many companies attempt to reduce the overall materials handling expense or investment by utilizing used components or used equipment. This can be desirable if the used components are in extremely good condition (those purchased from a company that has recently gone out of business and had very new equipment in its distribution facility) or have few moving parts (racks). Used rack and gravity conveyors are more likely to be a good investment than used high-speed sortation systems or automated picking systems.

As stated above, the overall cost of the project should be evaluated in terms of an acceptable pay-back period. In renovating an existing distribution facility, most companies expect to achieve a payback within two years. This allows for the investment of the materials handling equipment to provide a fairly quick return in labor, capital, or space utilization. However, to build and design a distribution facility to support the future business needs of the company by lowering the overall operating costs, it is generally accepted that the payback will occur within a five-year period. Effective distribution is regarded by most firms as essential for providing the service levels needed to help the company maintain and increase competitive advantage.

Vendor Project Management Experience

The project management skills of the vendor's staff are also an important factor. A company is wise to meet this staff *before* awarding a bid, to ensure that the necessary experience and expertise will be available.

Obviously, if the design is less complex and does not involve a large number of materials handling subcomponents, it may be easier, faster, and more cost-effective to choose a manufacturer's representative to install and manage the project. With minor materials handling subcomponents, the company will probably receive a more competitive quote because the vendor can utilize the same labor to install each of the materials handling components. However, the company should be aware that in choosing this approach, it is selecting a generalist who may lack the knowledge to ensure a smooth installation.

Using a Piloting Process

To minimize the risks that the new design will not achieve the company's goals for cost-efficiency and competitive advantage through improved customer service, a piloting approach may be effective. Prototyping is often done by a vendor in its own demonstration facilities. Reliable equipment vendors utilize the prospective customer's own products for the pilot. This helps demonstrate that the proposed solutions will not only work but also produce the desired levels of productivity and service.

The demonstration should thoroughly cover such key objectives as ergonomics, return on investment, and flexibility. It should also provide an opportunity to evaluate the unique interfaces between the equipment and the company's own staff. For example, in certain parts of the United States, the average workforce is shorter than in other parts of the country. Because of demographic facts like these, ergonomic workstation prototypes may need to be shorter or smaller to enable workers to be as productive as possible.

Equipment Specifications

Another important task is to develop clearly stated equipment specifications for inclusion in the request for proposal (RFP). Detailed specifications leave no room for misinterpretation or confusion by bidders as to what is to be provided, how it is to be installed, how it is to interact with other materials handling equipment or computer systems, and who has overall responsibility for the installation. Government regulations like OSHA rules, building codes, and fire safety rules should also be taken into account. Each of these components should be an integral part of the specification package and should be provided uniformly to all vendors so that each has an equal opportunity to prepare a fair and reasonably priced quotation.

Implementation Schedule

Installation and equipment start-up can be the simplest or the most difficult of all the phases, depending on the planning and project management dedicated to the project. Implementation should be based on a realistic and comprehensive schedule. Each project step, task by task, should be detailed in the implementation phase so that every individual involved, whether within the company or a vendor organization, knows precisely what is expected.

Frequent coordination meetings (daily or weekly, depending on the tasks involved) help ensure clear communications. Such meetings are particularly important for retrofits, compared with new facility designs; when installing new equipment in existing operations, the company must ensure ongoing service to customers without interruption. The retrofit design is usually performed in carefully phased segments. In such cases, the distribution facility manager must play a critical role.

System Start-up and Testing

After each component has been installed, the company then conducts the necessary testing and certification to ensure conformity to specifications and to desired business results, usually in stages. For a high-speed sortation system, for example, the test should be performed over many days and should be for no fewer than four to six hours at a time to ensure that results are not sporadic but consistent.

After testing is completed, a detailed "punch list" should be given to the vendors for any modifications that need to be made before formal system acceptance. This list should detail all modifications, whether major or minor. The vendor will then complete these modifications and the equipment will be tested again on an extended period before final acceptance.

Employee Training

After the equipment and systems have been planned, designed, and installed, the company needs to focus on employee and manager training. To ensure that the equipment achieves the full benefits expected, each manager, supervisor, and operator needs to be fully versed in all necessary details regarding operation, maintenance, and monitoring of the new system. Realistic productivity targets need to be clearly stated to ensure that no over- or understaffing occurs. Employees should be coached on their new roles and given the time and training needed to perform well. Some training is usually in formal group sessions, but much of it is performed one-on-one in the distribution center.

After this last phase has been completed, the company is ready to carry out the day-to-day operation of the new system.

Conclusion

A materials handling system is both the logical and physical manifestation of all the requirements, policies, and practices intended for a particular facility in the logistics pipeline. It is also a clear reflection of the understanding and care the designers used in its creation.

Care and diligence come from using a methodical approach: developing creative options, evaluating them, procuring them, and having them put into place. Yet, these activities are not the most important for the manager responsible for guiding the design process. The logistics manager's responsibility is to provide the understanding and the forward view that will be the seed for a well-conceived, long-lasting design, one that will create service or cost advantages within the company, translating into higher sales or profits. Having that guidance is what makes the difference in creating truly outstanding solutions for logistics materials handling systems.

CHAPTER 26

Materials Handling Technologies

Edward H. Frazelle
James M. Apple, Jr.

According to the Material Handling Institute, the market for materials handling systems—the hardware and software used to move, store, control, contain, and unitize materials in factories and warehouses—exceeds $50 billion annually. Much of the growth in size and variety of the market is fueled by major changes in the requirements of warehouse and distribution operations. For example, new initiatives in warehouse and distribution operations include reduced order cycle times, reduced inventory levels, reduced order sizes, SKU proliferation, increased accuracy of standards, and improved safety conditions. As a result, materials handling manufacturers have rapidly introduced a variety of systems for fast, accurate handling of small load sizes. These product introductions make the materials handling marketplace difficult to document completely. Nonetheless, this chapter overviews the major types of materials handling systems currently in use in warehousing and distribution operations.

The description follows the decomposition of a pallet load in a typical warehouse or distribution center, moving from pallet storage/retrieval systems to case picking systems to broken case picking systems to sorting systems. The chapter concludes with a description of the systems used to integrate the flow of materials and information in a warehouse or distribution center, material transport systems, and automatic identification and communication systems.

For each equipment type, the description includes its operating principle, its typical applications, its cost, and its advantages and disadvantages compared with other system types.

Pallet Storage/Retrieval Systems

Pallet Storage Systems

Block Stacking

Block stacking refers to unit loads stacked on top of each other and stored on the floor in storage lanes (blocks) two to ten loads deep. Depending on the weight and stability of the loads, the stacks may range from two loads high to a height determined by acceptable safe limits or by the building clear height. Block stacking is particularly effective when there are multiple pallets per SKU and when inventory is turned in large increments (i.e., several loads of the same SKU are received or withdrawn at one time).

A phenomenon referred to as "honeycombing" occurs with block stacking as loads are removed from a storage lane. Because only one SKU can be effectively stored in a lane, empty pallet spaces are created that cannot be utilized effectively until an entire lane is emptied. Therefore, to maintain high utilization of the available storage positions, the lane depth (number of loads stored from the aisle) must be carefully determined. Because no investment in racks is required, block stacking is easy to implement and allows flexibility with floor space.

PALLET STACKING FRAMES

Pallet stacking frames (or "racks") are portable and enable the user to stack materials, usually in pallet-sized loads, on top of one another, thus increasing mobility and making more efficient use of floor space. Portable racks can be either frames attached to standard wooden pallets or self-contained steel units made up of decks and posts. When not in use, the racks can be disassembled and stored in a minimum of space.

SINGLE-DEEP SELECTIVE PALLET RACKS

A simple construction of metal uprights and cross-members, a selective pallet rack provides access to each stored load. Unlike block stacking, when a pallet space is created by the removal of a load, it is immediately available. Loads do not need to be stackable and may be of varying heights and widths. When load depth is highly variable, it may be necessary to provide load supports or decking.

Selective pallet racks might be considered as the benchmark storage mode, against which

Figure 26-1
Typical Pallet Stacking Frame Storage System

Figure 26-2
Typical Single-Deep Pallet Rack Configuration

other systems may be compared for advantages and disadvantages. Most storage systems benefit from the use of at least some selective pallet racks for SKUs whose storage requirement is fewer than six pallet loads.

Double-Deep Racks

Double-deep racks are merely selective pallet racks that are two pallet positions deep. The advantage of the double-deep feature is that fewer aisles are needed, which results in a more efficient use of floor space. In most cases a 50% aisle space savings is achieved versus selective pallet racks. Double-deep racks are used where the storage requirement for an SKU is six pallets or greater and when product is received and picked frequently in multiples of two pallets. Because pallets are stored two deep, a double-reach forklift is required for storage or retrieval.

Drive-in Racks

Drive-in racks extend the reduction of space begun with double-deep pallet racks. Drive-in racks typically provide for storage lanes from five to ten loads deep. They allow a lift truck to drive in to the rack several pallet positions and store or retrieve a pallet. This is possible because the rack consists of upright columns that have horizontal rails to support pallets at a height above that of the lift truck. This construction permits a second or even third level of pallet storage, with each level being supported independently of the other. A drawback of drive-in racks is the reduction of lift truck travel speed needed for safe navigation within the confines of the rack construction.

Figure 26-3
Typical Double-Deep Pallet Rack;
Double-Deep Reach Truck for Retrieval

DRIVE-THROUGH RACKS

A drive-through rack is merely a drive-in rack accessible from both sides. It is for staging loads in a flow-through fashion where a pallet is loaded at one end and retrieved at the other. The same considerations for drive-in racks apply to drive-through racks.

PALLET FLOW RACKS

Functionally, pallet-flow racks are used like drive-through racks, but loads are conveyed on pallet wheels or roller conveyors from one end of a storage lane to the other. As a load is removed from the front of a storage lane, the next load advances to the pick face. The main purpose of the pallet-flow rack is to provide high throughput pallet picking and good space utilization. Hence, it is used for those items with high pallet throughput and rapid turnover of inventory.

PUSH-BACK RACKS

With a rail-guided carrier provided for each pallet load, push-back racks provide last-in/first-out deep-lane storage. As a load is placed into storage, its weight and the force of the putaway vehicle push the other loads in the lane back into the lane to create room for the additional load.

Figure 26-4
Typical Pallet-Flow Rack System

As a load is removed from the front of a storage lane, the weight of the remaining load automatically advances remaining loads to the rack face.

Mobile Racks

Mobile racks are essentially single-deep selective pallet racks on wheels or tracks that permit an entire row of racks to move away from adjacent rack rows. The underlying principle is that aisles are justified only when they are being used; the rest of the time they occupy valuable space. Access to a particular storage row is achieved by moving the adjacent row and creating an aisle in front of the desired row. Mobile racks are useful when space is scarce and inventory turnover is low.

Cantilever Racks

The load-bearing arms of a cantilever rack are supported at one end, as the name implies. The racks consist of a row of single upright columns, spaced several feet apart, with arms extending from one or both sides of the uprights to form supports for storage. The advantage of cantilever racks is that they provide long, unobstructed storage shelves with no uprights to restrict the use of horizontal space. The arms can be covered with decking of wood or metal or can be used without decking. They are applicable for long items such as sofas, rugs, rod, bar, pipe, and sheets of metal or wood.

Figure 26-5
Push-Back Rack

Pallet Storage Systems Summary

Table 26-1 grades each pallet storage/retrieval system in relative terms along several measures.

Pallet Retrieval Systems

Walkie Stackers

A walkie stacker allows a pallet to be lifted, stacked, and transported short distances. The operator steers from a walking position behind the vehicle. In a situation where there are low throughput, short travel distances, and low vertical storage height and a low-cost solution is desired, the walkie stacker may be appropriate.

Counterbalanced Lift Trucks

Counterbalanced lift trucks may be gas- or battery-powered. Besides forks, other attachments may be used to lift unique load configurations on a vertical mast. The height limitation is generally around 25 feet. A counterbalanced truck may not be used to store double deep. Counterbalanced trucks are available with operating capacities up to 100,000 pounds.

Just as the selective pallet rack is the benchmark pallet storage mode, the counterbalanced

Figure 26-6
Cantilever Rack

truck may be considered the benchmark storage/retrieval vehicle. When it is desirable to use the same vehicle for loading and unloading trucks and storing and retrieving loads, the counterbalanced truck is the logical choice. For use in block stacking, drive-in, and drive-through racks and pallet stacking frames, the operating aisles normally provided are suitable for counterbalanced trucks. Because counterbalanced trucks must turn within a storage aisle to retrieve a pallet load, the aisle width required to operate is wider than required for some other lift truck alternatives.

The relatively low cost and flexibility of counterbalanced trucks are their main advantages.

Straddle Trucks

A straddle truck is most often used in warehouses where aisle space is scarce and/or excessively expensive. The principle is to provide load and vehicle stability using outriggers instead of counterbalanced weight, thereby reducing the aisle width requirement. To access loads in storage, the outriggers are driven into the rack, allowing the forks to come flush with the pallet face. Hence, it is necessary to support the floor-level load on rack beams.

Straddle-Reach Trucks

The straddle-reach truck was developed from the conventional straddle truck by shortening the outriggers on the straddle truck and providing a "reach" capability. In so doing, the outriggers do not have to be driven under the floor-level load to allow access to the storage positions. Hence,

TABLE 26-1
Performance of Pallet Storage/Retrieval Systems
grade school scores: A to F

Measure	Floor Storage	Stacking Frames	Single-deep	Double-deep	Drive-in Rack	Drive-through	Flow Rack	Push-back	Mobile Rack	Canti-lever
Cost per position	n/a	$50	$40	$50	$65	$65	$200	$150	$250	
Potential storage density	A	B	D	C	B	B	B	B	A	B
Load access	F	F	A	C	B	B	B	A	F	A
Throughput capacity	B	D	B	C	C	C	A	C	F	C
Inventory and location control	F	F	A	C	D	D	C	C	D	B
FIFO maintenance	F	F	A	C	D	D	A	C	C	A
Ability to house variable load sizes	A	D	C	C	D	D	F	C	C	B
Ease of installation	A	A	C	C	C	C	F	C	F	B

no rack beam is required at the floor level; this conserves rack cost and vertical storage requirements.

Two basic straddle-reach truck designs are available: mast and fork. The mast-reach design consists of a set of tracks along the outriggers that support the mast. The fork-reach design consists of a pantograph or scissors mounted on the mast.

The double-deep–reach truck, a variation of the fork-reach design, allows the forks to be extended to a depth that permits loads to be stored two deep.

Turret Trucks

Turret trucks, swingmasts, and shuttle trucks are members of the modern family of designs that do not require the vehicle to make a turn within the aisle to store or retrieve a pallet. Rather, the load is lifted either by forks that swing on the mast, a mast that swings from the vehicle, or a shuttle fork mechanism.

Generally, these types of trucks provide access to load positions at heights up to 40 feet, which provides the opportunity to increase storage density where floor space is limited. They can also run in aisles 5 or 6 feet wide, further increasing storage density.

Narrow-aisle side-reach trucks generally have good maneuverability outside the aisle, and some of the designs with telescoping masts may be driven into a shipping trailer.

Since narrow-aisle side-reach trucks do not turn in the aisle, the vehicles may be wire-guided or the aisles may be rail-guided, allowing for greater speed and safety in the aisles and reducing the chances of damage to the vehicles and/or racks.

Figure 26-7
Typical Walkie Stacker–Reach Type

SIDE-LOADING TRUCKS

The side-loading vehicle loads and unloads from one side, thus eliminating the need to turn in the aisle to access storage positions. There are two basic side-loader designs. Either the entire mast moves on a set of tracks transversely across the vehicle, or the forks project from a fixed mast on a pantograph.

Figure 26-8
Typical Counterbalance Lift Truck

Aisle width requirements are less than for straddle trucks and reach trucks. A typical aisle would be 6.5 feet wide, rail- or wire-guided. Side-loaders can generally access loads up to 30 feet high.

The side-loader truck must enter the correct end of the aisle to access a particular location, which adds an additional burden to routing the truck.

A variety of load types can be handled using a side-loader. The vehicle's configuration particularly lends itself to storing long loads in cantilever racks.

Very-Narrow-Aisle (VNA) or Hybrid Storage/Retrieval (S/R) Vehicles

The VNA or hybrid S/R vehicle is similar to the turret truck, except that the operator's cab is lifted with the load. The VNA vehicle evolved from the S/R machine used in automated storage/retrieval systems. Unlike the S/R machine, the VNA S/R truck is not captive to an aisle but may leave one aisle and enter another. Presently available models are somewhat clumsy outside the aisle, but they operate within the aisle at a high throughput rate.

VNA vehicles operate in aisle widths ranging from 5 to 7 feet, allow rack storage up to 60 feet high in a rack-supported building, and may include an enclosed operator's cab that may be heated and/or air-conditioned.

Sophisticated VNA vehicles are able to travel horizontally and vertically simultaneously to a load position. The lack of flexibility, the high capital commitment, and the high-dimensional tolerance in the rack are the disadvantages of VNA systems.

Figure 26-9
Typical Reach Truck

Automated Storage/Retrieval Systems (AS/RS)

An AS/RS for pallets is commonly referred to as a unit-load AS/RS. It is defined by the AS/RS product section of the Material Handling Institute as a storage system that uses fixed-path storage and retrieval (S/R) machines running on one or more rails between fixed arrays of storage racks.

A unit-load AS/RS usually handles loads in excess of 1,000 pounds and is used for raw material, work in process, and finished goods. The number of systems installed in the United States is in the hundreds, and installations are commonplace in all major industries.

Figure 26-10
Typical Sideloading Truck

In a typical AS/RS operation, the S/R machine picks up a load at the front of the system, transports it to an empty location, deposits it in the empty location, and returns empty to the input/output (I/O) point. This is called a single command (SC) operation. Single commands accomplish either a storage or a retrieval between successive visits to the I/O point. A more efficient operation is a dual command (DC) operation. In DC operation, the S/R machine picks up a load at the I/O point, travels loaded to an empty location (typically the closest empty location to the I/O point), deposits the load, travels empty to the location of the desired retrieval, picks up the load,

Figure 26-11
AS/RS Front-End

travels loaded to the I/O point, and deposits the load. The key idea is that in a DC, two operations—a storage and a retrieval—are accomplished between successive visits to the I/O point.

A unique feature of S/R machine operation is diagonal travel. Consequently, the time to travel to any destination in the rack is the maximum of the horizontal and vertical travel times required to reach the destination from the origin. Horizontal travel speeds are on the order of 500 feet per minute; vertical, 120 feet per minute.

The typical unit load AS/RS configuration, if there is such a thing, would include unit loads stored one deep (i.e., single deep), in long, narrow aisles, each of which contains an S/R machine. The one I/O point would be located at the lowest level of storage and at one end of this system.

More often than not, however, one of the parameters defining the system is atypical. The possible variations include the depth of storage, the number of S/R machines assigned to an aisle, and the number and location of I/O points. These variations are described in more detail below.

When the variety of loads stored in the system is relatively low, throughput requirements are moderate to high, and the number of loads to be stored is high, it is often beneficial to store loads more than one deep in the rack. Alternative configurations include:

- Double-deep storage with single-load-width aisles. Loads of the same SKU are typically stored in the same location. A modified S/R machine is capable of reaching into the rack for the second load.
- Double-deep storage with double-load-width aisles. The S/R machine carries two loads at a time and inserts them simultaneously into the double-deep cubicle.
- Deep-lane storage with single-load-width aisles. An S/R machine dedicated to storing stores material in the lanes on either side of the aisle. The lanes may hold up to 10 loads

each. On the output side, a dedicated retrieval machine removes material from the racks. The racks may be dynamic, having gravity or powered conveyor lanes.
- Rack entry module (REM) systems in which a REM moves into the rack system and places/receives loads onto/from special rails in the rack.

Another variation of the typical configuration is the use of transfer cars to transport S/R machines between aisles. Transfer cars are used when the storage requirement is high relative to the throughput requirement. In such a case, the throughput requirement does not justify the purchase of an S/R machine for each aisle, yet the number of aisles of storage must be sufficient to accommodate the storage requirement.

A third system variation is the number and location of I/O points. Throughput requirements or facility design constraints may mandate multiple I/O points at locations other than the lower left-hand corner of the rack. Multiple I/O points might be used to separate inbound and outbound loads and/or to provide additional throughput capacity. Alternative I/O locations are at the end of the rack (some AS/RSs are built underground) and the middle of the rack.

Pallet Retrieval Systems Summary

Table 26-2 provides comparative specification data for several pallet retrieval systems. These data are approximations for use in relative comparisons.

Case Picking Systems

Pick-to-Pallet Systems

Pallet Jack or Pallet Truck Picking

Order pickers pull pallet jacks or drive pallet trucks along the floor, picking cases to pallets on the vehicles. Order pickers typically pick one order at a time, and because they do not have to pick above positions on the floor or the first or second level of pallet rack, productivity can range from 100 to 250 cases per hour. Productivity may be enhanced by picking more than one order at a time. This batch picking practice is sometimes facilitated with a double pallet jack, capable of handling two pallets at a time. Nonpowered pallet jacks cost around $1,000. Powered pallet trucks cost around $10,000.

TABLE 26-2
Pallet Retrieval Systems Specifications

Factor	**Counter-balance**	**Straddle**	**Straddle Reach**	**Side-loader**	**Turret**	**Hybrid**	**AS/RS**
Vehicle cost	$30,000	$35,000	$40,000	$75,000	$95,000	$125,000	$200,000
Lift-height capacity	22′	21′	30′	30′	40′	50′	75′
Aisle width	10–12′	7–9′	6–8′	5–7′	5–7′	5′	4.5′
Weight capacity (lbs., 000)	2–10	2–6	2–5	2–10	3–4	2–4	2–5
Lift speed	80 fpm	60 fpm	50 fpm	50 fpm	75 fpm	60 fpm	100 fpm
Travel speed	550 fpm	470 fpm	490 fpm	440 fpm	490 fpm	490 fpm	500 fpm

Note: fpm = feet per minute.

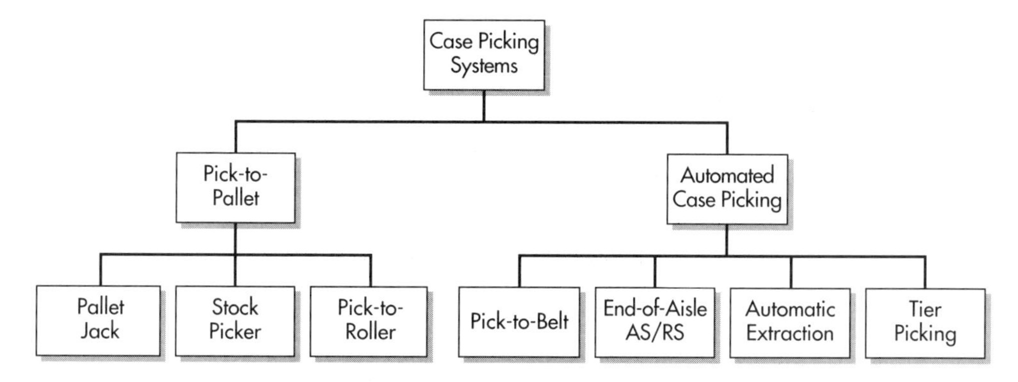

Figure 26-12
Case Picking System Classifications

Stock or Order Picker Trucks

Stock pickers, sometimes referred to as order picker or cherry picker trucks, allow the order picker to travel to pick locations well above floor level. In so doing, picking productivity is reduced to between 50 and 100 cases per hour. Productivity can be enhanced by minimizing vertical travel through popularity-based storage and/or intelligent pick tour construction. Typical order picker trucks cost approximately $30,000.

Figure 26-13
Case Picking with a Pallet Truck

Figure 26-14
Case Picking with a Tow Truck

Pick-to-Roller Conveyor

Empty pallets are inducted onto a pallet roller conveyor at the beginning of a case picking line. Pallets pass by order pickers stationed at zones along the pick line. With this method, the travel time for the order picker is nearly eliminated. In addition, the pickers are essentially palletizing and establishing order integrity as they pick. The productivity of these operations ranges from 175 to 350 cases per hour. The initial system cost is about $1,000 per linear foot of pallet roller conveyor.

Automated Case Picking

Pick-to-Belt

In pick-to-belt (or wave-picking) systems, order pickers are assigned to small zones along a case picking line. The case picking line typically comprises pallet floor positions, single-deep selective pallet racks, or pallet-flow lanes. A powered belt or roller conveyor runs along each location on the picking face.

During a pick wave, typically ranging from 20 to 60 minutes, an order picker walks down the locations in his or her zone, picking cases from locations on the pick line directly to the belt or roller conveyor. Because travel distances are limited and order pickers have no knowledge of order composition, productivity can range from 250 to 400 cases per hour. Because order pickers have no knowledge of order composition, order integrity must be established downstream from the picking operation. This is typically accomplished with one of the many mechanized sorting systems described below.

Figure 26-15
Case Picking with a Stock Picker Truck

End-of-Aisle AS/RS

End-of-aisle picking systems typically comprise a unit-load AS/RS for pallet storage and retrieval and a conveyor delivery system to transport pallets to remote case-picking stations. Order pickers are stationary and located at remote picking locations serviced by a pallet roller conveyor. As pallets are presented to the order pickers, the order pickers remove the correct number of cases and return the pallets to the AS/RS for storage. The principle advantage of the end-of-aisle system is the excellent floor space utilization provided by the high-rise AS/RS and the elimination of travel for the order pickers. Picking rates range from 200 to 300 cases per hour. The system cost includes the AS/RS cost ($250,000 to $400,000 per S/R machine) and the pallet conveyor cost ($1,000 per foot).

Automatic Extraction

Automated case extracting systems comprise case flow racks for case storage and an automated storage/retrieval machine for case putaway and retrieval. The automated storage/retrieval machines run on guide rails in the floor and ceiling and are equipped with telescoping conveyors for case handling to/from the putaway/pick face. While one machine puts cases into the back of the case flow rack, another retrieves cases from the front of the flow rack. Each machine operates at a rate of approximately 500 to 800 cases per hour and costs between $150,000 and $200,000.

Figure 26-16
Case-Pick-to-Belt

Tier Picking

When the typical number of cases ordered for an item is at least a pallet layer, case picking productivity can be enhanced by electing layer or tier quantities from the pallet as opposed to individual cases. One method for tier picking is to transport pallets to a device that clamps the top tier on the pallet and singularly places the cases along a takeaway conveyor. This device is sometimes referred to as a depalletizer. The depalletizer works at rates between 1,000 and 1,500 cases per hour and costs around $150,000. For cost comparisons, the cost of the system must also include the pallet conveyor for feeding the depalletizer and transporting pallets back to storage.

Pick-to-Pallet and Automated Case Picking Summary

Table 26-3 compares the approximate volumes and investments for several case picking systems.

Broken Case Picking Systems

The major difference between part-to-picker systems and picker-to-part systems is the answer to the question, "Does the picker have to travel to the pick location, or does the pick location travel to the picker?" If the pick location travels to the picker, the system is termed a "part-to-picker system."

Picker-to-Part Systems

In picker-to-part systems, the order picker either walks or rides a vehicle to the pick location. The four major equipment groups under the heading of picker-to-part or in-the-aisle systems are

TABLE 26-3
Comparison of Case Picking Systems:
Volume and Investment

System Type	Picking Rates (cases/hour)	Initial Cost
Pallet jack	100–250	$1–$10k/vehicle
Stock picker	50–100	$30k/vehicle
Pick-to-roller	125–250	$1k/ft.
Pick-to-belt	250–400	$200/ft. + $2K/divert
End-of-aisle AS/RS	200–300	$300–$450k/aisle
Auto extract	500–800	$175k/m/c + $125/lane
Tier picking	1,000–1,500	$150k/m/c

bin shelving, modular storage drawers in cabinets, gravity flow racks, and man-aboard AS/RS. The key distinguishing feature of the first three systems from the fourth is the mode of travel of the order picker. In the first three systems, the order picker typically walks to the pick location and uses a cart to accumulate, sort, and/or pack orders (i.e., cart picking) or picks to a tote pan transported with a roller or belt conveyor. In the man-aboard AS/RS alternative, the picker rides aboard a storage/retrieval (S/R) machine to the pick location.

Picker-to-Part Systems Storage

BIN-SHELVING

Bin-shelving systems are the oldest and still the most popular (in terms of dollar sales volume and number of systems in use) equipment alternative in use for small parts order picking. Their low initial cost ($100 to $150 per unit), easy reconfigurability, easy installation, and low maintenance requirements are at the heart of this popularity.

It is important to recall that the lowest-initial-cost alternative may not be the most cost-effective alternative or the alternative that meets the prioritized needs of the warehouse. With bin-shelving systems, savings in initial cost and maintenance may be offset by inflated space and labor requirements.

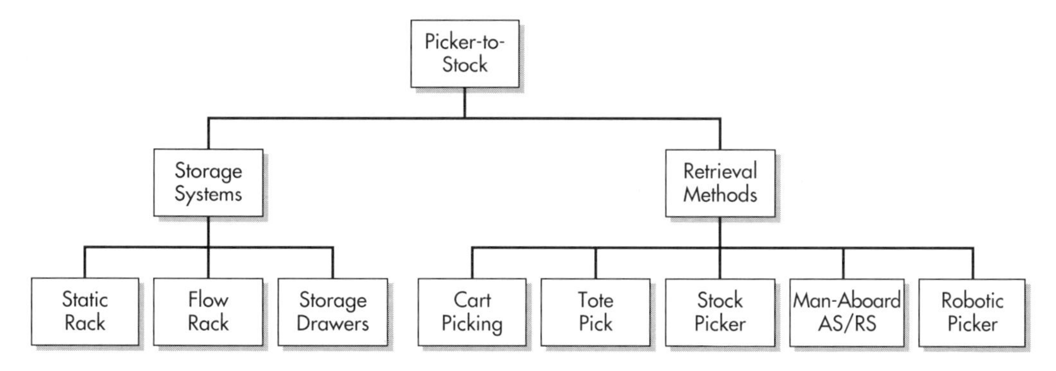

Figure 26-17
Broken Case Picker-to-Stock Storage and Retrieval System Classifications

Figure 26-18
Typical Bin-Shelving System

Space is frequently underutilized in bin-shelving systems, because the full inside dimensions of each unit are rarely usable. Also, because people are extracting the items, the height of the shelving units is limited by the reaching height of a human being. As a result, the available building cube may also be underutilized.

The consequences of low-space utilization are twofold. First, low-space utilization means that a large amount of square footage is required to store products. The more expensive it is to own and maintain the space, the more expensive low space utilization becomes. Second, the greater the square footage, the greater the area that must be traveled by the order pickers, and thus, the greater the labor requirement and cost.

Two additional disadvantages of bin shelving are supervisory problems, and security and item protection problems. Supervisory problems arise because it is difficult to supervise people through a maze of bin-shelving units. Security and item protection problems arise because bin shelving is one of a class of open systems (i.e., the items are exposed to and accessible from the picking aisles).

As with all the system types, these disadvantages must be evaluated and compared with the advantages of low initial cost and low maintenance requirements to make an appropriate system selection.

Modular Storage Drawers in Cabinets

Such drawers are called modular because each storage cabinet houses modular storage drawers subdivided into modular storage compartments. Drawer heights range from 3 to 24 inches, and each drawer may hold up to 400 pounds of material. The storage cabinets can be thought of as shelving units that house storage drawers.

The primary advantage of storage drawers/cabinets over bin shelving is the large number of SKUs that can be stored and presented to the order picker in a small area. According to cabinet and drawer suppliers, one drawer can hold from 1 to 100 SKUs (depending on the size, shape, and inventory levels of the items), and a typical storage cabinet can store the equivalent of 2 to 4 shelving units of material. This dense storage stems primarily from the ability to create item housing configurations within a drawer that very closely match the cubic storage requirements of each SKU. Also, because the drawers are pulled out into the aisle for picking, space does not have to be provided above each SKU to provide room for the order picker's hand and forearm. This reach space must be provided in bin-shelving storage; otherwise, items deep in the unit could not be reached.

Several benefits accrue from the high-density storage characteristic of storage drawer systems. First and obviously, the more material that can be packed into a smaller area, the smaller the space requirement. Hence, space costs are reduced. When the value of space is truly at a premium, as on a battleship, an airplane, or the manufacturing floor, the reduction in space requirements alone can be enough to justify storage drawers and cabinets. A second benefit resulting from a reduction in square footage requirements is a subsequent reduction in the travel time, and hence labor requirements, for order picking.

Additional benefits achieved by storage drawers include improved picking accuracy and protection for the items from the environment. Picking accuracy is improved over that in shelving

Figure 26-19
Typical Modular Storage Drawer System

units because the order picker's sight lines to the items are improved and the quantity of light falling on the items to be extracted is increased. With bin shelving, the physical extraction of items may occur anywhere from floor level to 7 feet off the ground, with the order picker having to reach into the shelving unit itself to achieve the pick. With storage drawers, the drawer is pulled out into the picking aisle for item extraction. The order picker looks down onto the contents of the drawer, which are illuminated by the light source for the picking aisle. (The fact that the order picker must look down on the drawer means that storage cabinets must be fewer than 5 feet high.) Item security and protection are achieved because drawers can be closed and locked when items are not being extracted from them.

As one would expect, these benefits are not free. Storage cabinets equipped with drawers range in price from $1,000 to $1,500 per unit. Price is primarily a function of the number of drawers and the amount of sheet metal in the cabinet.

Gravity Flow Racks

The gravity flow rack, or just "flow rack," is another popular picker-to-part equipment alternative. Flow racks are typically used for active items stored in cartons of fairly uniform size and shape. The cartons are placed in the back of the rack from the replenishment aisle and advance or roll toward the pick face as cartons are depleted from the front. This back-to-front movement ensures first-in, first-out (FIFO) turnover of the material.

Essentially, a section of flow rack is a bin-shelving unit turned perpendicular to the picking aisle with rollers placed on the shelves. The deeper the sections, the greater the portion of warehouse space that will be devoted to storage as opposed to aisle space. Further gains in space efficiency can be achieved by using the cubic space over the flow rack for full pallet storage.

Flow racks range in price from $3 to $10 per carton stored, depending on the length and weight capacity of the racks. As is the case with bin shelving, flow racks have very low maintenance requirements and are available in a wide variety of standard section and lane sizes from a number of suppliers.

The fact that just one carton of each line item is located on the pick face means that a large number of SKUs are presented to the picker over a small area. Hence, walking and therefore labor requirements can be reduced with an efficient layout.

Mezzanines

Bin shelving, modular storage cabinets, flow racks, and even carousels can be placed on a mezzanine. The obvious advantage of using a mezzanine is that nearly twice as much material can be stored inexpensively ($10 to $20 per square foot) in the original square footage. The major design issues for a mezzanine are the selection of the proper grade of mezzanine for the loading that will be experienced, the design of the materials handling system to service the upper levels of the mezzanine, and the utilization of the available clear height. At least 14 feet of clear height should be available for a mezzanine to be considered.

Mobile Storage

Bin shelving, modular storage cabinets, and flow racks can all be "mobilized." The most popular method of mobilization is the train-track method. Parallel tracks are cut into the floor, and

Figure 26-20
Typical Gravity Flow Rack System

wheels are placed on the bottom of the storage equipment to create "mobilized" equipment. The space savings accrue from the fact that only one aisle is needed between all the rows of storage equipment. The aisle is created by separating two adjacent rows of equipment. As a result, the aisle "floats" in the configuration between adjacent rows of equipment.

The storage equipment is moved by simply sliding the equipment along the tracks, by turning a crank located at the end of each storage row, or by invoking electric motors that may provide the motive power.

Figure 26-21
Two-Level Mezzanine-Picking Operation

The disadvantage to this approach is the increased time required to access the items. Every time an item must be accessed, the corresponding storage aisle must be created.

Picker-to-Part Retrieval Systems

Cart Picking

A variety of picking carts is available to facilitate the accumulation, sortation, and/or packing of orders as an order picker makes a picking tour. The carts are designed to allow an order picker to pick multiple orders on a picking tour, thus dramatically improving productivity as opposed to strict, single-order picking for small orders. The most conventional vehicles provide dividers for order sortation, a place to hold paperwork and marking instruments, and a step ladder for

Figure 26-22
Cart Picking

picking at levels slightly above reaching height. Additional levels of sophistication and cost bring powered carts, light-aided sortation, on-board computer terminals, and on-board weighing.

TOTE PICKING

Tote picking systems use conveyors to transport tote pans to successive picking zones for order completion. The tote pans establish order integrity and merchandise accumulation and containment. An order picker may walk one or more totes through a single picking zone, partially completing several orders at a time. Or an order picker may walk one or more totes through all picking zones, thus completing one or more orders on each pass through the picking zones.

MAN-ABOARD AS/RS

The man-aboard AS/RS, as the name implies, is an automated storage and retrieval system in which the picker rides aboard a storage/retrieval machine to the pick locations. The storage locations may be provided by stacked bin shelving units, stacked storage cabinets, and/or pallet racks. The storage/retrieval machine may be aisle-captive or free roaming.

Typically, the picker leaves from the front of the system at floor level and visits enough storage locations to fill one or more orders, depending on order size. Sortation can take place on board if enough containers are provided on the storage/retrieval machine.

The man-aboard AS/RS offers significant square footage and order picking time reductions over the previously described picker-to-part systems. Square footage reductions are available because storage heights are no longer limited by the reach height of the order picker. Shelves or storage cabinets can be stacked as high as floor loading, weight capacity, throughput requirements, and/or ceiling heights will permit. Order pick times are reduced because the motive power for traveling is provided automatically, hence freeing the order picker for productive work while traveling and because search time is reduced because the picker is automatically delivered to the correct pick location.

As one might expect, these reductions in square footage and pick times come with a price tag. Man-aboard automated storage and retrieval systems are far and away the most expensive picker-to-part equipment alternative. Aisle-captive storage/retrieval machines reaching heights up to 40 feet cost around $100,000.

Robotic Retrieval Systems

In rare instances, robotic retrieval systems are applied. Each robotic picking vehicle is equipped with a small carousel to permit order sortation, accumulation, and containment. The carousel travels up and down a mast on the robot as the robot traverses the picking aisle(s). A storage drawer is pulled from a storage location onto the picking vehicle.

Part-to-Picker Systems

In part-to-picker systems, the travel time component of total order picking time is shifted from the picker to a device for bringing locations to the picker. Also, the search time component of total order picking time is significantly reduced, because the correct pick location is automatically presented to the order picker. For well-designed systems, the result is a large increase in the pick rate capacity of the order picking system. In poorly designed systems, potential improvements can be quickly eroded if the picker is required to wait for the device to present the parts.

The two most popular classes of part-to-picker systems are carousels and the miniload automated storage and retrieval system (AS/RS). A third, less popular class is the automatic item picker. Each class is described below.

Carousels

Carousels, as the name implies, are mechanical devices that house and rotate items for order picking. Three classes of carousels are currently available for order picking applications: horizontal, vertical, and independently rotating racks.

Horizontal Carousels. A horizontal carousel is a linked series of rotating bins of adjustable shelves driven on the top or on the bottom by a drive motor unit. Rotation takes place about an axis perpendicular to the floor at about 80 feet per minute.

Items are extracted from the carousel by order pickers who occupy fixed positions in front of the carousel(s). The order pickers may also be responsible for controlling the rotation of the carousel. Manual control is achieved via a keypad that tells the carousel the bin location to rotate forward, and a foot pedal releases the carousel to rotate. The carousels may also be computer-controlled, in which case the sequence of pick locations is stored in the computer and brought forward automatically.

A management option with carousel systems is the assignment of order pickers to carousels. If an order picker is assigned to one carousel unit, he or she must wait for the carousel to rotate to the correct location between picks. Order pickers assigned to two or more carousels may pick

Figure 26-23
Man-Aboard Order Picking

from one carousel while the other is rotating to the next pick location. Remember, the objective of part-to-picker systems is to keep the picker picking. Humans are excellent extractors of items; the flexibility of limbs and muscles provides this capability. We are not efficient searchers, walkers, or waiters.

Horizontal carousels vary in length from 15 feet to 100 feet, and in height from 6 feet to 25 feet. The length and height of the units are dictated by the pick rate requirements and building

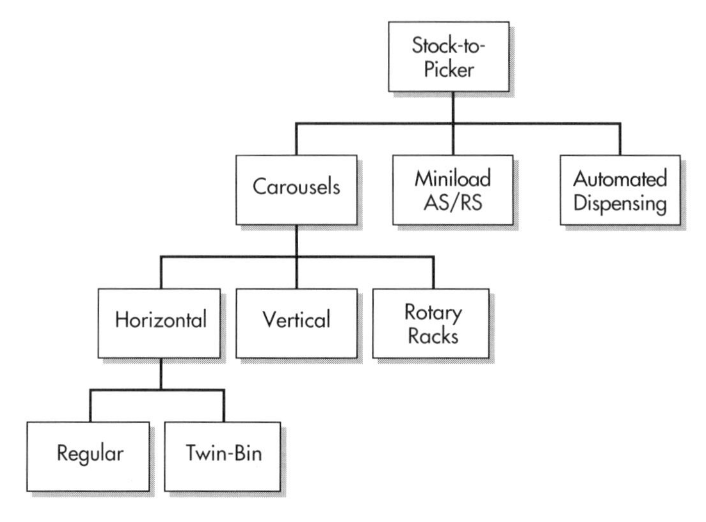

Figure 26-24
Broken Case Part-to-Picker System Classifications

restrictions. The longer the carousel, the more time required, on average, to rotate the carousel to the desired location. Also, the taller the carousel, the more time required to access the items. Heights over 6 feet require ladders or robot arms on vertical masts to access items.

In addition to providing a high pick rate capacity, horizontal carousels make good use of available storage space. Very little space is required between adjacent carousels, and the only lost space is between parallel sections of bins on the same carousel unit.

One important disadvantage of horizontal carousels is that the shelves and bins are open. Consequently, item security and protection can be a problem.

The price of a carousel unit starts at $5,000 and increases with the number of bins and the weight capacity.

Vertical Carousels. A vertical carousel is a horizontal carousel turned on its end and enclosed in sheet metal. As with horizontal carousels, an order picker operates one or more carousels. The carousels are indexed either automatically via computer control or manually by the order picker working a keypad on the carousel's work surface.

Vertical carousels range in height from 8 feet to 35 feet. Heights (as lengths were for horizontal carousels) are dictated by throughput requirements and building restrictions. The taller the system, the longer it takes, on average, to rotate the desired bin location to the pick station.

Order pick times for vertical carousels are theoretically less than those for horizontal carousels. The decrease results from the items always being presented at the order picker's waist level. This eliminates the stooping and reaching that goes on with horizontal carousels, further reduces search time, and promotes more accurate picking. (Some of the gains in item extract time are negated by the slower rotation speed of the vertical carousel. Recall that the direction of rotation is against gravity.)

Additional benefits provided by the vertical carousel include excellent item protection and security. In the vertical carousel, only one shelf of items is exposed at one time, and the entire contents of the carousel can be locked up.

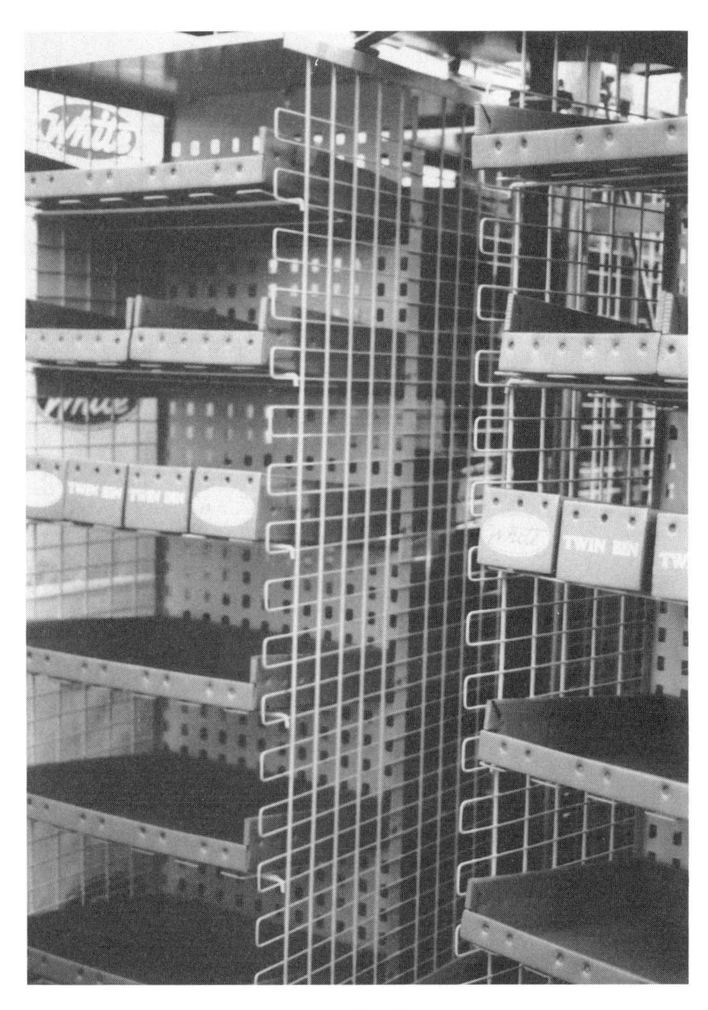

Figure 26-25
Twin-bin Horizontal Carousel System

The price of a vertical carousel begins at $10,000 and increases with the number of shelves and the weight capacity. The additional cost of vertical over horizontal carousels is attributed to the sheet metal enclosure and the extra power required to rotate against the force of gravity.

Independent Rotating Rack Carousels. Independent rotating rack carousels are like multiple one-level horizontal carousels stacked on top of one another. As the name implies, each level rotates independently. As a result, several pick locations are ready to be accessed by the order picker at all times and the order picker can pick continuously.

Clearly, for each level to operate independently, it must have its own power and communication link. These requirements force the price of independent rotating rack carousels well beyond that of vertical or horizontal carousels. (Specific price estimate information is scarce and unreliable because there are relatively few system installations of this type.)

Figure 26-26
Vertical Carousel Picking Operation

Miniload Automated Storage and Retrieval Systems

In the miniload automated storage and retrieval system, a storage/retrieval (S/R) machine travels horizontally and vertically simultaneously in a storage aisle, transporting storage containers to and from an order picking station at one end of the system. The order picking station typically has two pick positions. As the order picker is picking from the container in the left pick position, the S/R machine is taking the container from the right pick position back to its location in the rack and returning with the next container. The result is that the order picker ping-pongs between the left and right pick positions.

The sequence of containers to be processed is determined manually by the order picker keying in the desired line item numbers or rack locations on a keypad, or the sequence is generated and processed automatically by computer control.

Miniloads vary in height from 8 feet to 50 feet and in length from 40 feet to 200 feet. As in the case of carousels, the height and length of the system are dictated by the throughput requirements and building restrictions. The longer and taller the system, the longer the time to access the containers. However, the longer and taller the system, the fewer the aisles and S/R machines that will have to be purchased. At between $150,000 and $300,000 per aisle, the determination of the correct system length, height, and number of aisles to meet the pick rate, storage, and economic return requirements for the warehouse becomes critical.

The transaction rate capacity of the miniload is governed by the ability of the S/R machine (which travels approximately 500 feet per minute horizontally and 120 feet per minute vertically) to continuously present the order picker with unprocessed storage containers. This ability, coupled with the benefits of presenting the containers to the picker at waist height in a well-lit area, can produce impressive pick rates.

Square footage requirements are reduced for the miniload because of the ability to store material up to 50 feet high, the ability to size and shape the storage containers and the subdivisions of those containers to closely match the storage volume requirements of each SKU, and an aisle width determined solely by the width of the storage containers.

The disadvantages of the miniload system are probably already apparent. As the most sophisticated of the system alternatives described thus far, the miniload carries the highest price tag of any of the order picking system alternatives. Another result of its sophistication is the significant engineering and design effort accompanying each system. The consequence of this effort is a delivery time ranging from 4 months to 18 months. Finally, greater sophistication leads to greater maintenance requirements. It is only through a disciplined maintenance program that miniload suppliers are able to advertise uptime percentages of between 97% and 99.5%.

Automatic Item Pickers

Automatic item pickers act much as do vending machines for small items of uniform size and shape. Each item is allocated a vertical dispenser ranging from 2 inches to 6 inches wide and from 3 feet to 5 feet tall. (The width of each dispenser is easily adjusted to accommodate variable product sizes.) The dispensing mechanism kicks the unit of product at the bottom of the dispenser out onto a conveyor running between two rows of dispensers configured as an A-frame over a belt conveyor. A tiny vacuum conveyor or small finger on a chain conveyor dispenses the items or carton. A single dispenser can dispense at a rate of up to 6 units per second. Automatic item pickers are popular in industries with high throughput for small items of uniform size and shape: cosmetics, wholesale drugs, compact discs, videos, publications, and polybagged garments.

Virtual order zones begin at one end of the conveyor and pass by each dispenser. A virtual order zone is the length of conveyor belt that has been temporarily allocated by the order picking system to receive all the various items for a single order so that these items are grouped together at the end of the conveyor line, avoiding sortation, for quick packing. If an item is required in the order zone, it is dispensed onto the conveyor. Merchandise accumulated at the end of the conveyor into a tote pan is an example.

Replenishment is performed manually from the back of the system. This operation significantly cuts into the savings in picking labor requirements associated with pick rates on the order of 1,500 picks per hour per pick head.

Picker-to-Part Retrieval Systems Summary

Table 26-4 compares the relative capabilities of several picking methods.

Sorting Systems

Sorting systems congregate material (e.g., cases, items, totes, garments) with a similar characteristic (e.g., destination, customer, store) by correctly identifying like merchandise and transporting it to the same location. The components of a sorting system include transport systems,

Figure 26-27
Automated Item Picking System

divert mechanisms, induction systems, identification and communication systems, and accumulation media.

Transport Systems

Conveyor systems are by far the most common mechanism for transporting merchandise through a series of diverters. Belts, rollers, and carriers on chain conveyors are used. The application of each type of conveyor will become clear in the description of alternative divert mechanisms.

Divert Mechanisms

The wide variety of divert mechanisms available for mechanized sortation is evidence of the variety of throughput, size, and weight requirements that can be satisfied with alternative sorting systems. The divert mechanisms are comprised of four major sorter types: surface, pop-up, tilting, and carriers.

SURFACE SORTERS

Surface sorters are distinguished from other types of sorting mechanisms because the material to be sorted is diverted along the surface of the belt or roller conveyor. There are four types of surface sorters.

TABLE 26-4
Comparison of Picking Methods

Factor	Pick-to-cart	Pick-to-tote	Man-aboard Vehicle	Horizontal Carousel	Vertical Carousel	Miniload AS/RS	Automatic Picker	Batch Picking
Pick rate (lines/hr)	25–125	100–350	25–250	50–250	50–350	25–100	500–1,000	300–500
Storage cost* ($/ft^3)	$5–15† $3–5‡	$5–15† $9–15‡	$5–15† $25–30•	$20–35	$40–70	$30–40	n/a	$5–15† $3–5‡
Picking accuracy	Medium	Medium	Medium	Medium	High	High	High	Medium
Maintenance requirements	Low	Medium	High	Medium	Medium	High	High	High
Human factors	Below average	Below average	Average	Above average	Excellent	Excellent	Excellent	Below average
Item security	Low	Low	Low	Medium	High	High	High	Low
Reconfigurability	High	Medium	Low	Low	Low	Low	Low	Low

Notes: This table is intended as a guide only; data are compiled from historical observations and survey results. Pick rates depend on the layout, equipment and control system enhancements, stock location assignment strategies, and other variables. Cost estimates are for equipment hardware only.

* Assumes 100% space utilization.

† Shelving.

‡ Flow racks.

• Modular drawers.

Source: Distribution Design Institute (DDI).

Deflectors. Deflectors consist of stationary or movable arms that deflect product flow across a belt or roller conveyor to the desired location. They are necessarily in position before the item to be sorted reaches the discharge point. Stationary arms remain fixed and are a barrier to items coming in contact with them. The stationary arm deflector deflects all items in the same direction. Movable arm or pivoted paddle deflectors are impacted by the item to be sorted in the same manner as the stationary arm deflector. However, the element of motion has been added. With the movable arm deflector (i.e., the paddle), items are selectively diverted. Pivoted deflectors may be equipped with a belt conveyor flush with the surface of the deflector (a power face) to speed or control the divert. Paddle deflecting systems are sometimes referred to as steel belt sorters because at one time steel belts were used to reduce the friction encountered in diverting products across the conveyor. Deflectors can support medium throughput (1,200 to 2,000 cartons per hour) for up to 75-pound loads.

Push Diverters. Push diverters are similar to deflectors in that they do not contact the conveying surface but sweep across to push the product off the opposite side. Push diverters are mounted beside (air- or electric-powered) or above the conveying surface (paddle pushers) and can move items faster and with greater control than a deflector. Overhead push diverters are capable of moving products to either side of the conveying surface, whereas side-mounted diverters move conveyed items in one direction only (to the side opposite that on which they are mounted). Push diverters have a capacity of 3,600 cases per hour for loads up to 100 pounds.

Rake Pullers. The rake puller sorter is best applied when the items are heavy and durable. Rake puller tines fit into slots between powered or nonpowered roller conveyors. Upon com-

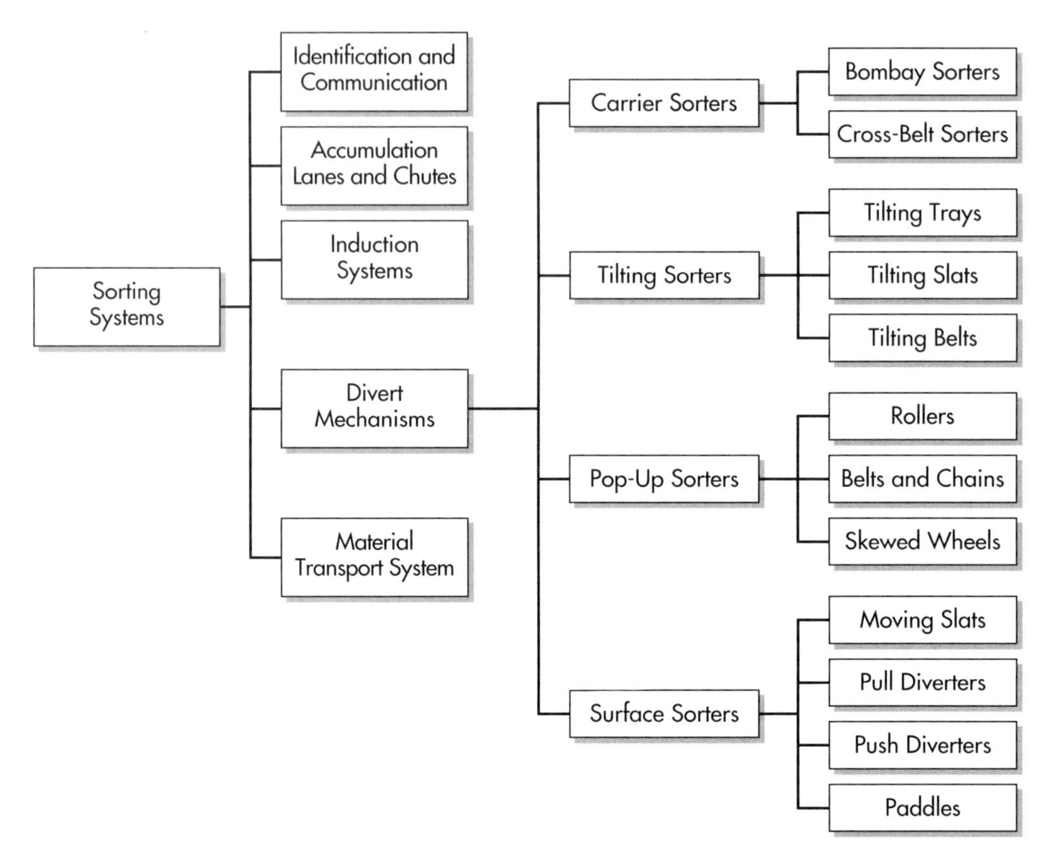

Figure 26-28
Sorting System Classifications

mand, a positioning stop device and the tines pop up from beneath the roller conveyor surface to stop the carton. The tines pull the carton across the conveyor and then drop below the roller surface for a noninterference return to the starting position. During the return stroke, the next carton can be moving into position.

Moving Slat Sorters. The moving slat sorter is differentiated from other surface sorters by the diversion that takes place in-line along the roller conveyor.

Pop-up Sorters

Pop-up sorters have a wheel, belt, chain, or roller that pops up at the divert point to deflect products to the proper sortation lane.

Pop-up Skewed Wheels. Pop-up skewed wheels can sort flat-bottomed items. The skewed wheel device pops up between the rollers of a powered roller conveyor or between belt conveyor segments and directs sorted items onto a powered takeaway lane. Rates of between 5,000 and 6,000 cases per hour can be achieved.

Figure 26-29
Deflector Diverter on Roller Conveyor

Pop-up Belts and Chains. Pop-up belt and chain sort devices are similar to pop-up skewed wheels in that they rise from between the rollers of a powered roller conveyor to alter product flow. Belt and chain sortation devices are capable of handling heavier items than wheeled devices can.

Pop-up Rollers. Pop-up rollers rise up between the chains or rollers of a chain or roller conveyor to alter the flow of product. They provide a relatively inexpensive means for sorting heavy loads, at rates of 1,000 to 1,200 cases per hour.

Tilting Sorters

Tilting sorters are distinguished from other sorters because the conveyor belt or slats that support the load and individual carriers are not distinguished along the conveyor.

Tilting Slat Sorters. Products in a tilting slat sorter occupy the number of slats required to contain their length. The sort is executed by tilting the occupied slats. Hence, tilting slat sorters are best applied when a wide variety of product lengths are handled. The tilting slat is capable of tilting in either direction. Slats may be arranged in a continuous over-and-under configuration.

Figure 26-30
Deflector Diverter on Belt Conveyor

CARRIER SORTERS

Carrier sorters are distinguished from other sorters by the fact that each individual item is transported on and diverted by a dedicated carrier. Carrier sorters include tilt-tray sorters, cross-belt sorters, and bombay sorters (the last is not discussed in detail).

Tilt-tray Sorters. Continuous chains of tilting trays are used to sort a wide variety of lightweight merchandise. The trays may be fed manually or by one of the many available induction devices. Tilt-tray systems can sort to either side of the sorter. Tilt-tray sorters do not discriminate for the shape of the product being sorted. Bags, boxes, envelopes, documents, and software can all be accommodated. The tilt-tray sorter is not appropriate for long items. The capacity of the tilt-tray sorter, in pieces or sorts per hour, is expressed as the ratio of the sorter speed to the pitch or length of an individual tray. Rates of 10,000 to 15,000 items per hour can be achieved.

Cross-belt Sorters. Cross-belt sorters are so named because each item rests on a carrier equipped with a separate powered section of belt conveyor that operates orthogonally to the direction of material transport. Hence, the sorting capacity is enhanced and the width of the accumulating chutes can be reduced.

Figure 26-31
Push Diverter

Divert Mechanisms Summary

Table 26-5 provides relative comparisons of several sorting systems.

Induction Methods

Pushoff Induction

The simplest induction is a gravity roller conveyor section placed next to the sorter. An operator codes each article as it passes this section and then pushes the article onto the moving sorting conveyor. This type of induction is suitable for surface, pop-up, and tilting sorters.

Hand Induction

When distribution systems are used for lightweight articles, the coding operator simply places each article onto the sorter with one hand while entering the sort code on the keyboard with the other. A beam of light, moving synchronously with the sorter conveyor, indicates the correct spot for the article to be placed. This type of induction is typical for tilt-tray sorting systems.

Figure 26-32
Typical Moving Slat Sorter

Over-the-End Induction

In some situations it is possible to induct articles "on the fly." A belt conveyor carries articles past a coding operator (at a speed at which the operator can recognize the code) and then conveys them directly onto the sorter. Throughput can be increased by adding a second coding operator; the two operators code alternate items as they pass by.

Automated Induction

Automated induction systems accept, orient, and deposit items on sorters without losing proper orientation. The physical induction is typically executed with a belt conveyor operating at a 45-degree angle to the direction of the sorter.

Identification and Communication Systems

The fundamental control requirement in mechanical sorting is the ability to identify a product, its destination, and its place on the sorter. Product identification may be done manually, with induction operators reading labels related to product codes and types. The identification may be automated with bar code or optical character recognition labels applied to or integrated into the product packaging. The product identification is then communicated by hand with keyboard data entry, by mouth with voice input, or automated with bar code scanners or vision systems.

Figure 26-33
Pop-up Chain Conveyor

Accumulation Lanes and Chutes

The last major component in a sorting system is the mechanism used to accumulate merchandise at a discharge point. Depending on the weight and dimensions of the items and the number of divert points, the range of options for lanes and chutes is vast. For surface and pop-up sorters, accumulation lanes usually comprise some type of wheel or roller conveyor ranging from a simple gravity flow rack or skate wheel conveyor to a heavy-duty pallet roller conveyor. For tilting and carrier sorters, an even greater array of chute designs is available. Chutes are widely variable in configuration (e.g., single lane, double lane, drop door) and material (e.g., metal, wood, or cloth).

Figure 26-34
Pop-up Roller Conveyor

Materials Transport Systems

Conveyors

Conveyors are used when material is to be moved frequently between specific points; they move material over a fixed path. Hence, there must be a sufficient amount of movement to justify dedicating the equipment to the handling task. Depending on the materials to be handled and the move to be performed, a variety of conveyors can be used.

Conveyors can be categorized in several ways. For example, the type of product being handled (bulk or unit) and the location of the conveyor (overhead or floor) have served as bases for classification. Interestingly, such classification systems are not mutually exclusive. Specifically, a belt conveyor can be used for bulk and unit materials and can be located overhead or on the floor.

Bulk materials, such as soybeans, grain, dry chemicals, and sawdust, might be conveyed with chute, belt, pneumatic, screw, bucket, or vibrating conveyors. Unit materials—such as castings, machined parts, and materials placed in tote boxes, on pallets, and in cartons—might be conveyed with chute, belt, roller, wheel, slat, vibrating, pneumatic, trolley, or tow conveyors. Material can be transported on belt, roller, wheel, slat, vibrating, screw, pneumatic, and row conveyors mounted either overhead or at floor level.

Figure 26-35
Tilt-Tray Sorter

Flat Belt Conveyors

A flat belt conveyor is normally used for transporting light- and medium-weight loads between operations, departments, levels, and buildings. It is especially useful when an incline or decline is part of the conveyor path. Because of the friction between the belt and the load, the belt con-

TABLE 26-5
Sorting Systems: Summary Comparison

Factor	Manual	Push Divert	Pull Divert	Slat	Pop-up Wheels	Pop-up Rollers	Tilt-tray
Maximum sorts per minute	15–25	30–35	30–40	50–150	65–150	15–20	65–300
Load range (lbs.)	1–75	1–75	10–100	1–200	3–300	10–200	1–300
Minimum distance between spurs	Touching	5′–7′	2′–3′	4′–5′	4′–5′	Almost touching	1′
Diverter impact on load	Gentle	Medium	Medium to rough	Gentle	Gentle	Gentle	Medium to rough
Initial cost	Lowest	Medium	High	High	High	Low to medium	High
Maintenance cost	Lowest	Low	Medium	Medium to high	Medium	Low	Medium to high

Figure 26-36
Flat Belt Conveyor

veyor provides considerable control over the orientation and placement of the load; however, friction also prevents smooth accumulation, merging, and sorting on the belt. The belt is generally supported by either rollers or a slider bed. If small and irregularly shaped items are being handled, then the slider bed would be used; otherwise, the roller support is usually the more economical. A typical roller-supported flat belt conveyor costs between $50 and $100 per linear foot.

Roller Conveyors

The roller conveyor, a very popular type of materials handling conveyor, may be powered or nonpowered. The nonpowered version is referred to as a gravity conveyor, as motion is achieved by inclining the roller section. Powered (or live) roller conveyors are generally either belt- or chain-driven. However, one manufacturer has employed a revolving driveshaft to power the rollers; rollers are connected individually to the driveshaft by an elastomeric belt. The roller conveyor is well suited for accumulating loads and merging/sorting operations. Because of the roller surface, the materials being transported must have a rigid riding surface. A gravity roller conveyor costs between $15 and $30 per foot for light-duty applications and between $40 and $80 per foot for heavy-duty applications. A powered roller conveyor costs between $100 and $225 per linear foot.

Figure 26-37
Powered Roller Conveyor

Wheel Conveyors

The wheel, or skate-wheel, conveyor is similar to the roller conveyor in design and function; a series of skate wheels is mounted on a shaft. Wheel spacing depends on the load being transported. Although wheel conveyors are generally more economical than the roller conveyor, they are limited to light-duty applications. A skate-wheel conveyor costs between $10 and $15 per foot.

Trolley Conveyors

The trolley conveyor consists of a series of trolleys supported from or within an overhead track. They are generally equally spaced in a closed-loop path and are suspended from a chain. Specially designed carriers can be used to carry multiple units of product. They have been used extensively in processing, assembly, packaging, and storage operations. A trolley conveyor costs between $75 and $200 per foot.

Tow Conveyors

The tow, or towline, conveyor provides power to wheeled carriers like trucks, dollies, or carts that move along the floor. Essentially, the tow conveyor provides power for fixed-path travel of carriers that have variable path capability. The towline can be located overhead, flush with the

Figure 26-38
Skate-Wheel Conveyor

floor, or in the floor. Towline systems often include selector-pin or pusher-dog arrangements to allow automatic switching between power lines or onto an unpowered spur line for accumulation. Tow conveyors are generally used when long distances and considerable movement are involved. Towline conveyors cost between $80 and $120 per foot.

Industrial Vehicles

Nonpowered Vehicles

The two most popular nonpowered industrial vehicles for use in materials transport are pallet jacks and walkie stackers. A typical pallet jack costs between $500 and $1,000. Walkie stackers were described above.

Powered Vehicles

The powered vehicles used for materials transport in warehousing have all been described in previous sections and include pallet trucks, counterbalanced lift trucks, and tow trucks.

Automated Guided Vehicles

An automated guided vehicle (AGV) is essentially a driverless industrial vehicle. It is a steerable, wheeled vehicle driven by electric motors using storage batteries, and it follows a prede-

Figure 26-39
Trolley Conveyor

fined path along an aisle. AGVs may be designed to operate as a tractor pulling one or more carts, or they may be unit-load carriers.

The path followed by an AGV may be a simple loop or a complex network with many designated load/unload stations along the path. The vehicle incorporates a path-following system, typically electromagnetic, although some optical systems are in use.

With an electromagnetic path-following system, a guide wire that carries a radio frequency (RF) signal is buried in the floor. The vehicle employs two antennae so that the guide wire can be bracketed. Changes in the strength of the received signal are used to determine the control signals for the steering motors so that the guide wire is followed accurately. When it is necessary for the vehicle to switch from one guide wire to another (e.g., at an intersection), two different frequencies can be used, with the vehicle being instructed to switch from one frequency to the other. Obviously, a significant level of both analog and digital electronic technology is incorporated into the vehicle itself. In addition, the vehicle routing and dispatching system may employ not only programmable controllers but also minicomputers or even mainframes.

The electromagnetic path-following system may also support communication between a host control computer and the individual vehicles. In systems with a number of vehicles, the host computer may be responsible for both the routing and dispatching of the vehicles and collision avoidance. A common method for collision avoidance is zone blocking, in which the path is partitioned into zones and a vehicle is never allowed to enter a zone already occupied by another vehicle. This type of collision avoidance involves a high degree of active, host computer–directed control.

Optical path-following systems use an emitted light source and track the reflection from a

Figure 26-40
In-floor Towline Conveyor

special chemical stripe painted on the floor. In a similar fashion, codes can be painted on the floor to indicate to the vehicle that it should stop for a load/unload station. Simple implementations require all actions of the vehicle to be preprogrammed (for example, stop and look for a load, stop and unload, or proceed to the next station). The vehicles typically are not under the control of a host computer and must therefore employ some method for collision avoidance other than zone blocking. Proximity sensors on the vehicles permit several of them to share a loop without colliding.

The state of the art in AGVs is advancing rapidly. "Smart" vehicles can now navigate short distances without an electromagnetic or optical path. Similarly, vehicles are being equipped with sufficient on-board computing capability to manage some of the routing control and dispatching functions. Current developments in the field are leading to path-free, or "autonomous," vehicles that do not require a fixed path and are capable of "intelligent" behavior. Much of the

Figure 26-41
Overhead Towline Conveyor

work currently underway in the AGV field is driven by the availability of small, powerful, but relatively inexpensive microcomputers.

Automated guided vehicle types in use in warehousing include unit-load carriers, tow vehicles, and storage/retrieval vehicles. Unit-load carriers range in price from $35,000 to $65,000, depending on their weight capacity. Fork truck AGVs range in price from $60,000 to $90,000. The approximate cost of guide path ranges from $20 to $60 per linear foot.

Automatic Identification and Communication Systems

Automatic Identification and Recognition

Automated status control of material requires that the real-time awareness of the location, amount, origin, destination, and schedule of material be achieved automatically. This objective is in fact the function of automatic identification technologies—technologies that permit real-time, nearly flawless data collection. Examples of automatic identification technologies at work include the following:

- A vision system to read bar code labels and identify the proper destination for a carton traveling on a sortation conveyor
- A laser scanner to relay the inventory levels of a small-parts warehouse to a computer via radio frequency

Figure 26-42
Unit-load AGV with Powered Roller Table

- A voice recognition system to identify parts received at the receiving dock
- A radio frequency or surface acoustical wave (SAW) tag used to permanently identify a tote pan
- A card with a magnetic stripe that travels with a unit load to identify it through the distribution channels

Bar Code Systems

Bar Codes. A bar code consists of a number of printed bars and intervening spaces. The structure of unique bar/space patterns represents various alphanumeric characters. The same pattern may represent different alphanumeric characters in different codes. Table 26-6 provides a summary of paperless warehousing schemes. Primary codes or symbologies for which standards have been developed include:

Figure 26-43
Towing AGV

- *Code 39:* An alphanumeric code adopted by a wide number of industry and government organizations for both individual product identification and shipping package or container identification.
- *Interleaved 2 of 5 Code:* A compact, numeric-only code still used in a number of applications where encoding is not required.
- *Codebar:* One of the earlier symbols developed, it permits encoding of the numeric-character set, 6 unique control characters, and four unique stop/start characters that can be used to distinguish different item classifications. It is primarily used in nongrocery retail point-of-sale applications, blood banks, and libraries.
- *Code 93:* Accommodating all 128 ASCII characters plus 43 alphanumeric characters and 4 control characters, Code 93 offers the highest alphanumeric data density of the 6 standard symbologies. In addition to allowing for positive switching between ASCII and alphanumeric, the code uses 2 check characters to ensure data integrity.
- *Code 128:* Provides the architecture for high-density encoding of the full 128-character ASCII set, variable length fields, and elaborate character-by-character and full symbol integrity checking. Provides the highest numeric-only data density. Adopted in 1989 by the Uniform Code Council (U.S.) and the International Article Number Association (EAN) for shipping container identification.
- *UPC/EAN:* The numeric-only symbols developed for grocery supermarket point-of-sale applications and now widely used in a variety of other retailing environments. Fixed-length code suitable for unique manufacturer and item identification only.

Figure 26-44
Storage and Retrieval AGV

- *Stacked Symbologies:* Although a consensus standard has not yet emerged, the health and electronics industries have initiated programs to evaluate the feasibility of using Code 16K or Code 49, two microsymbologies that offer significant potential for small-item encoding. Packing data in from 2 to 16 stacked rows, Code 16K accommodates the full 128-character ASCII set and permits the encoding of up to 77 characters in an area of less than

TABLE 26-6
Paperless Warehousing

	UPC	**39**	**2 of 5**	**128**	**Codabar**	**11**	**49**
Year Developed	1973	1974	1972	1981	1972	1977	1987
Character set	Numeric	Alpha-numeric	Numeric	Alpha-numeric	Numeric	Numeric	Alpha-numeric
Form	Continuous	Discrete	Continuous	Continuous	Discrete	Discrete	Continuous
Number of characters	10	43/128	10	103/128	16	11	128
Density: Units per character	7	13–16	7–9	11	12	8–10	—
Density: Characters per inch	13.7	9.4	17.8	9.1	10	15	294/sq.in.
Application areas	Retail, auto supply	DoD	Industrial	Varied	Blood banks, libraries	Telecom	Varied
Data security	Moderate	High	High	High	High	High	—

Figure 26-45
Light Pen, Contact Bar Code Reader with Handheld RF Terminal

.5 square inches. Comparable in terms of data density, Code 49 also handles the full ASCII character set. It encodes data in from 2 to 8 rows and has a capacity of up to 49 alphanumeric characters per symbol.

Bar Code Readers. Bar codes are read by both contact and noncontact scanners. Contact scanners can be portable or stationary and use a wand or a light pen. The wand or pen is manually passed across the bar code. The scanner emits either white or infrared light from the wand or pen tip and reads the light pattern reflected from the bar code. This information is stored in solid-state memory for subsequent transmission to a computer. More sophisticated (and expensive) hand-held units include fixed- and moving-beam scanners employing light-emitting diodes (LEDs), low-power helium-neon lasers, or the latest development, laser diodes. These devices can scan bar code labels from distances up to six feet.

Contact readers are excellent substitutes for keyboard or manual data entry. Alphanumeric

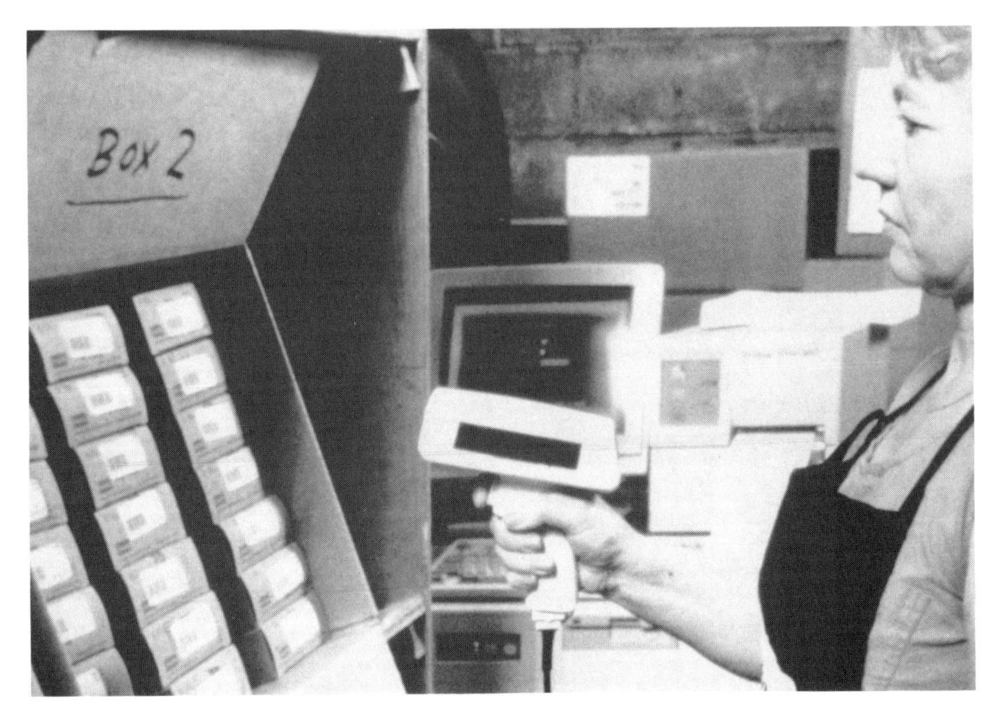

Figure 26-46
Typical Handheld Laser Scanner

information is processed at a rate of up to 50 inches per minute, and the error rate for a basic scanner connected to its decode is 1 in 1,000,000 reads. Light-pen or wand scanners with decoder and interface cost around $2,500.

Noncontact readers are usually stationary and include fixed-beam scanners, moving-beam scanners, and charged couple device (CCD) scanners. These scanners employ fixed-beam, moving-beam, video camera, or raster scanning technology to take from one to several hundred looks at the code as it passes. Most bar code scanners read codes bidirectionally by virtue of sophisticated decoding electronics that distinguish the unique start/stop codes peculiar to each symbology and decipher them accordingly. Further, the majority of scanner suppliers now provide equipment with an autodiscrimination feature that permits recognition, reading, and verification of multiple symbol formats with no internal or external adjustments. Finally, at least two suppliers have introduced omnidirectional scanners for industrial applications capable of reading a code at high speed throughout a large field of view, regardless of its orientation.

Fixed-beam readers use a stationary light source to scan a bar code. They depend on the motion of the object to be scanned to move past the beam. Fixed-beam readers rely on consistent, accurate code placement on the moving object.

Moving-beam scanners employ a moving light source to search for codes on moving objects. Because the beam of light is moving, code placement on the object is not critical. In fact, some scanners read codes accurately on items moving at a speed of 1,000 feet per minute.

CCD scanners have only recently been used to read bar codes. A CCD scanner is more like a camera than a bar code scanner. Changing camera lenses and focal lengths allows scanners to

Figure 26-47
Overhead, Stationary Bar Code Scanner

read various bar codes at various distances. As is true of any camera system, the quality of the picture (the accuracy of the read) depends on the available light. When installed correctly, the CCD scanner is 99% accurate. It costs around $4,000, including decoder.

Table 26-7 provides a summary of bar code reading equipment.

Optical Character Recognition Systems

Optical character recognition (OCR) systems read alphanumeric data so that humans as well as computers can interpret the information. The OCR label is read with a handheld scanner, much as a bar code is read. OCR systems operate at slower read rates than bar code systems and are

TABLE 26-7
Bar Code Readers

	Light Pen	Handheld Laser Scanner	Fixed Beam Stationary Scanner	Omnidirectional Scanner
Range	Contact	60″	60″	100″
Depth of field	Contact	24″	40″	30″–40″
Scan rate	Manual	32–100/sec.	200–3,450/sec.	1,440–2,400/sec.
Resolution	0.0040–0.0075 in.	0.0040–0.0075 in.	0.004–0.040 in.	0.004–0.040 in.
Price	$100–$1,000	$1,300–$2,500	$1,000–$10,000	$15,000–$40,000

priced about the same. OCR systems are attractive when both human- and machine-readable capabilities are required.

Until recently, the commercial applications of optical character recognition have been confined to document reading and limited use for merchandise tag reading at the retail point of sale. Without tight control of character printing and the reading environment, OCR's performance has not met the criteria established by other automatic identification techniques. A single printing anomaly, such as an ink spot or void, can easily obscure or transpose an OCR character—rendering the label unreadable or liable to misreading. On the other hand, where encoding space is at a premium and the environment is relatively contaminant-free, OCR may be a viable alternative.

Radio Frequency Tags

Both radio frequency (RF) and surface acoustical wave (SAW) techniques encode data on a chip that is encased in a tag. When a tag is within range of a special antenna, the chip is decoded by a tag reader. RF tags can be programmable or permanently coded, and can be read from up to 30 feet away. SAW tags are permanently coded and can be read only within a 6-foot range.

RF and SAW tags are typically used for permanent identification of a container, where advantage can be taken of the tag's durability. RV and SAW technologies are also attractive in harsh environments where printed codes may deteriorate and become illegible.

A tag reader costs around $10,000. Nonprogrammable tags range from $8 to $50; programmable tags, from $50 to $150.

Magnetic Stripes

Magnetic stripes can store large quantities of information in a small space. The stripe is readable through dirt or grease, and the data contained in the stripe can be changed. The stripe must be read by contact, thus eliminating high-speed sortation applications. Magnetic stripe systems are generally more expensive than bar code systems.

Vision Systems

Vision system cameras take pictures of objects and codes and send the pictures to a computer for interpretation. Vision systems read at moderate speeds with excellent accuracy, at least for limited environments. Obviously, these systems do not require contact with the object or code. However, the accuracy of a read is strictly dependent on the quality of light. Vision systems are becoming less costly but are still relatively expensive.

Automatic, Paperless Communication Systems

Radio Frequency Data Communication

Again, although not technically a member of the automatic identification systems family, handheld and lift-truck-mounted radio data terminals (RDTs) are rapidly emerging as reliable tools for both inventory and vehicle/driver management. RDTs incorporate a multicharacter display, full keyboard, and special function keys. They communicate and receive messages on a prescribed frequency via strategically located antennae and a host computer interface unit. Beyond the basic thrust toward tighter control of inventory, improved resource utilization is most often cited in justification of these devices. Further, the increasing availability of software packages

Figure 26-48
Typical Track-Mounted RF Terminal

that permit RDT linkage to existing plant or warehouse control systems greatly simplify their implementation. The majority of RDTs installed in the plant environment use handheld wands or scanners for data entry, product identification, and location verification. This marriage of technologies provides higher levels of speed, accuracy, and productivity than could be achieved by either technique alone. In 1989, initial installations of RDTs and voice data entry devices provided equally promising results.

Light- and Computer-Aided Order Picking

The objectives of light- or computer-aided order picking (CAOP) are to reduce search time, extract time, and documentation time portions of total order picking time and to improve picking accuracy. Search time is reduced when a computer automatically illuminates a light at the pick location(s) from which the next pick(s) are to be made. Extract time is reduced by displaying the quantity to pick on a display at the pick location. Documentation time is reduced by allowing the order picker to push a button at the pick location to inform the computer that the pick has been completed. The result is accurate order picking at a rate of up to 600 picks per labor hour.

CAOP systems of this type are available for bin-shelving, flow rack, and carousel systems and cost around $100 per storage location.

Systems of this type are also available for use with the miniload AS/RS. These systems provide a computer display over each pick station. On the display is a picture of the configuration of the storage container in that pick station. The compartment in the container from which extracting is to be done is illuminated, and the quantity to select is displayed on the computer screen.

The basic solution approach of CAOP systems is to take the thinking out of order picking. Consequently, an unusual human factor challenge is introduced: the job becomes too easy, hence boring and even degrading to many people.

Voice Input/Output

Voice recognition (VR) is a computer-based system that translates spoken words into computer data without special codes. VR systems are attractive when an operator's hands and eyes must be free for productive operations. Though VR systems are in their infancy, some systems recognize up to 1,000 words and are 99.5% accurate. VR systems are still relatively expensive and must be dedicated to one operator at a time.

Bibliography

"A Guide for Evaluating and Implementing a Warehouse Bar Code System." Warehousing Education and Research Council, Oak Brook, Ill., 1992.

Apple, James M. *Material Handling System Design.* New York: Ronald Press, 1972.

Frazelle, E. H. *Material Handling Systems and Terminology.* Atlanta: Lionhart, 1992.

———, "Small Parts Order Picking: Equipment and Strategy," Material Handling Research Center Technical Report Number 01-88-01, Georgia Institute of Technology, Atlanta, Georgia.

Frazelle, E. H. and L. F. McGinnis. "Automated Material Handling," in *The Encyclopedia of Microcomputers,* ed. A. Kent and J. G. Williams. New York: Marcel Dekker, 1988.

Hale, C. A. and M. N. Harrell. "Lift Truck Storage." SysteCon Technical Presentation, SysteCon, A Division of Coopers & Lybrand, Atlanta, Georgia.

Hill, J. M. "Automatic Identification Perspective 1992." Proceedings of the Material Handling Short Course, Georgia Institute of Technology, Atlanta, Georgia, March 1992.

Horrey, R. J. "Sortation Systems: From Push to High-Speed Fully Automated Applications." 1983 International Conference on Automation in Warehousing Proceedings, Institute of Industrial Engineers, Atlanta, Georgia, pp. 77–83.

Jenkins, Creed H. *Modern Warehouse Management.* New York: McGraw-Hill, 1968.

Kulwiec, R. "Material Handling Equipment Guide." *Plant Engineering* (August 21, 1980: 88–99.

Material Handling Engineering, 1984 Casebook Directory. Boston: Cahners, 1984.

Materials Handling Handbook, ed. Raymond A. Kulwiec. New York: Wiley, 1985.

Muther, Richard. *Systematic Layout Planning.* Boston: CBI, 1973.

Suzuki, J. "Guide to the Installation of Automated Sorters." 1990 International Conference on Automation in Warehousing Proceedings, Institute of Industrial Engineers, Atlanta, Georgia.

Tompkins, J. A. and J. A. White. *Facilities Planning*. New York: Wiley, 1984.
Warehouse Modernization and Layout Planning Guide. U.S. Naval Supply Systems Command Publication 529, U.S. Naval Supply Systems Command, Richmond, Virginia, 1988.

For More Information

Automated materials handling encompasses a wide and growing range of equipment, computer, and communication technology. This chapter has touched briefly on the most common equipment types. For additional and up-to-date information, the interested reader is directed to two relevant periodicals:

Material Handling Engineering
Penton/IPC, Inc.
1111 Chester Avenue
Cleveland, OH 44114

Modern Materials Handling
Cahners Publishing Co.
275 Washington Street
Newton, MA 02158

The major trade association for manufacturers of materials handling equipment and materials handling systems integrators is:

The Material Handling Institute, Inc.
8720 Red Oak Boulevard
Suite 201
Charlotte, NC 28210

The Material Handling Institute sponsors several trade shows and education programs related to materials handling. In addition, the institute publishes a number of excellent booklets, videotapes, and slide sets on materials handling.

The major academic research center for material handling is:

The Material Handling Research Center
813 Ferst Drive
Georgia Institute of Technology
Atlanta, GA 30332-0206

In addition to conducting research on materials handling problems in manufacturing and warehousing, the Material Handling Research Center sponsors two annual week-long education programs focused on materials handling.

The major professional society representing users of materials handling equipment is:

The Materials Handling and Management Society
8720 Red Oak Boulevard
Suite 204
Charlotte, NC 2821

CHAPTER 27

Site Selection

Thomas L. Freese

Site selection is one of the most challenging assignments ever faced by a logistics manager. To the inexperienced, it may appear to be a simple task—just a matter of real estate prices and availability. In reality, the job is much more complex. Selecting a site for new distribution facilities has a major impact on logistics costs and operational efficiency, and even on a company's overall marketplace success. It also involves a web of related but difficult decisions.

Fortunately, a solid understanding of how to get and use the right information for decision making can make the task much easier and more efficient. Contrary to the old saying that there are only three important factors in real estate decisions ("location, location, and location"), intelligent selection of distribution sites involves many other factors. They can be classified into three categories: macroanalysis, microanalysis, and specific site selection, as shown in Figure 27-1.

What is the "right" location? How many and what type of facilities are needed? What size and what function should they perform? All these strategic questions must be answered before considering any real estate discussions. In each of the major decision areas, numerous issues must be examined. This chapter addresses each analysis issue in detail in Table 27-1.

The site selection process requires the solution of three location problems in a particular order:

1. *Macroanalysis.* Macroanalysis defines the number of facilities and determines in what parts of the country they should be located.
2. *Microanalysis.* Microanalysis defines a geographic area in which to locate the facility (within a metropolitan area, and/or more specifically, within a section of that metropolitan area).
3. *Specific site selection.* Specific site selection identifies a particular site or property for locating the facility. Consideration must also be given to the company's requirements regarding the time frame in which a facility is needed, available capital, and the detailed issues involved in constructing or modifying a facility and property. Hence, "construction site considerations" is the second half of selecting a specific site.

This chapter, as is the decision-making process itself, is divided into sections corresponding to these three steps. Each section outlines the specific objectives and process, and documents the approach with a hypothetical example for demonstrating the intended results. The location selection process begins at the highest strategic (macro) level and works down to the tactical level, where a specific real estate parcel is chosen. A running case study emerging throughout the chapter is developed as the last section to highlight the specific site selection issues.

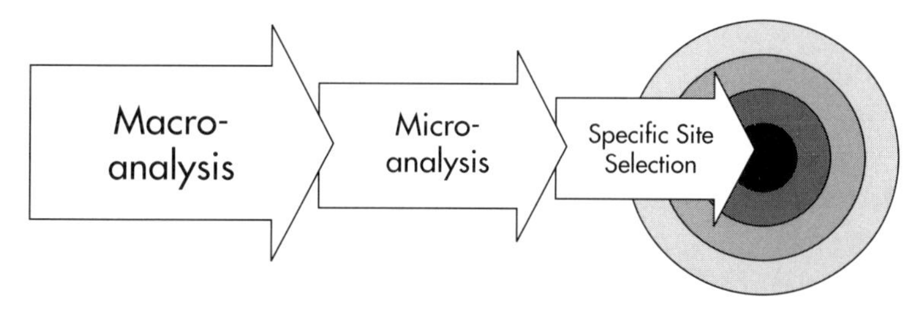

Figure 27-1
Site Selection Components

Macroanalysis

Macroanalysis begins with a definition of an organization's overall distribution network requirements—the big picture. The objective is to identify the optimal number of potential locations and, at a strategic level, show where they should be located. At this early stage, the chosen location is only broadly defined—for instance, the southeastern United States. Macroanalysis focuses mainly on a high-level evaluation of the economics of various strategies that may be relevant to a company's now and future distribution needs.

This section examines the ever-changing distribution trends, various modeling approaches with which to conduct a macroanalysis, the underlying economic equations of all such analysis, and the basic pitfalls and requirements of any such analysis. The macroanalysis approach is shown in Figure 27-2.

Twenty years ago, many manufacturers had stocking locations in almost all major markets because transportation economics dictated such an approach. Deregulation of the transportation industry in the 1980s drastically altered those transportation economics and led to a new approach to location strategies.

In addition to deregulation, an important factor has been the dramatic reduction in the cost

TABLE 27-1
Analysis Issues

		3) Specific Site Selection	
1) Macroanalysis	**2) Microanalysis**	**Location Considerations**	**Construction Site Considerations**
Service requirements	Socioeconomic area	Labor pool	Zoning
Transportation economics	Government services	Utilities	Zoning appeals process
Materials handling	Transportation	Neighbors	Construction permits
Fixed costs	Highway congestion	Support services	Code requirements
Inventory costs	Proximity to air, rail, and ports	Transportation	Exceptions and appeals process
Number of facilities	Availability of labor	Taxation	Environmental impact
Location of facilities	Unemployment rate	Fire codes	Topographical maps
	Land values	Union activity	Building site restrictions
	Competitive climate		Incentives

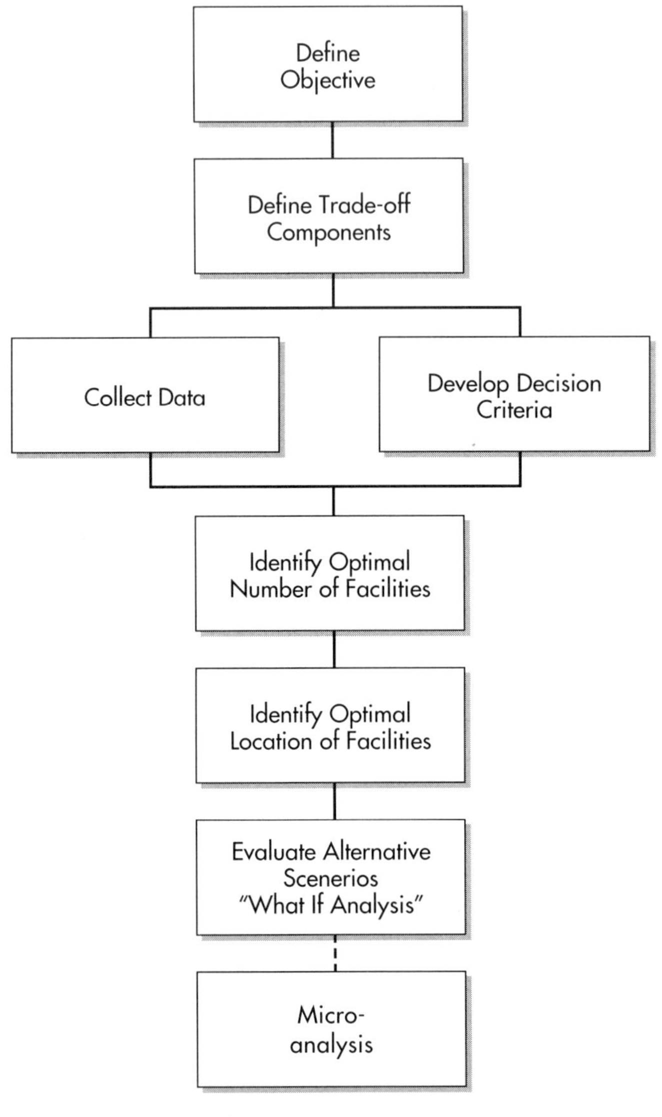

Figure 27-2
Macroanalysis Approach

of information and its transmittal. As a result, inventories—and the number of locations where they are stored—have been significantly reduced. These radical changes in logistics strategy and tactics have resulted in networks of three to six regional distribution centers to serve the entire country. A logistics manager's challenge is reducing 20 or 30 locations to 4 or 5 and still offering just-in-time delivery, effectively meeting regional and international competition, and at the same time ensuring that those 4 or 5 locations are, in fact, the best.

Computer models are increasingly being used to analyze and evaluate alternatives. Such alternatives may be numerous and complex. Examples include:

- A single distribution point used as a mixing location *versus* shipping individual products directly from their point of manufacture.
- Regional mixing of distribution points, adjacent to or combined with each manufacturing location, *versus* numerous centralized locations, one for each market being served.

Although a variety of approaches is available for modeling alternatives, there are three major types:

- Mathematical optimization models
- Network simulation models
- Computer spreadsheet models

Models are briefly discussed here and in greater detail in Chapter 7. All three techniques yield a lowest-cost solution based on the application of the individual cost components of inbound freight, outbound freight, materials handling labor, space, fixed overhead, and inventory carrying costs. The three methods differ in their approach to structuring the problem and solving it.

Mathematical optimization is the most sophisticated approach because it addresses each alternative location as a mathematical formula and solves for a specific value, identifying the alternative with the lowest total cost as the optimal solution.

Network simulation is actually an outgrowth of the mathematical simulation in that it utilizes the formula concept. However, rather than solving each alternative location as a distinct formula, network simulation typically solves simultaneously for a hypothetical network of locations. This network is an alternative configuration costed as if it were actually serving the organization's need for lowest total network cost.

The third approach uses computerized spreadsheets for structuring and solving any form of the potential macroanalysis. The spreadsheet approach is a tool rather than a formula per se. With the rapidly expanding capabilities of personal computers and inexpensive application software, this approach is beginning to replace the more complicated earlier technology.

Experience in applying the modeling techniques has shown that increasing the complexity of the model does not necessarily improve the decision provided by the modeling exercise. It is generally more important to define truly implementable alternatives and to collect accurate, comprehensive data to be used by a model.

Regardless of the method used, the purpose of network modeling is to find the best balance of critical trade-offs among inbound freight, outbound freight, materials handling labor, space, fixed overhead, and inventory carrying costs. From this analysis, it is possible to identify the lowest overall cost.

Regardless of the degree of sophistication used in modeling, its purpose is to help identify a distribution site that offers the *lowest total costs.* Many variables can be considered: lessen the freight-out or LTL (less-than-truckload) transportation costs by placing the goods closer to the market place; lessen the inbound truckload transportation cost by locating the goods closer to the point of manufacture; reduce the materials handling labor by reducing the number of times the product is transferred from one location to another; reduce or increase the cost equation of space based on the amount of space and physical location; and, finally, influence the equation's outcome by considering the amount of inventory required to satisfy safety stock requirements (calculated using inventory carrying costs based on the number of locations and the total inventory deployed).

In theory and in some actual instances, the network modeling exercise can be done with pencil and paper. If the problem is simple enough, the solution can be just as accurate as one pro-

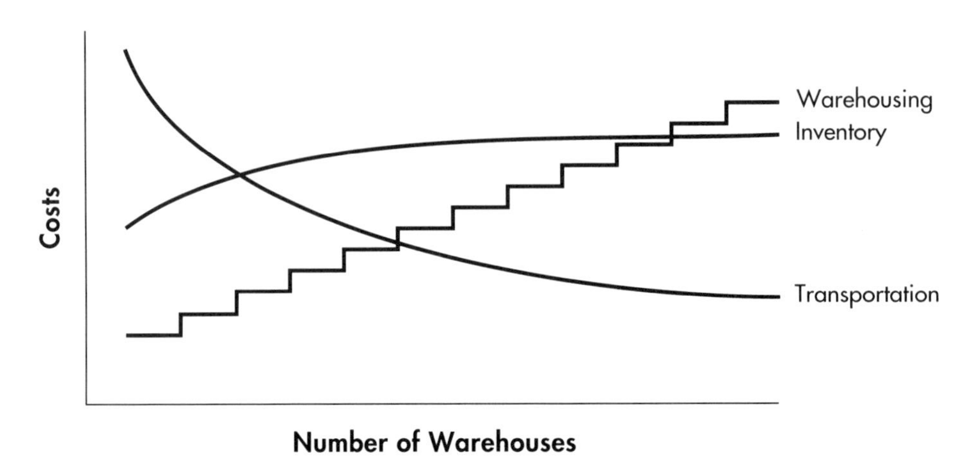

Figure 27-3
Cost-balancing Equation

duced by any of the computerized methods. Accuracy of the data used and consideration of *all* viable alternatives still remain the most important considerations. Each modeling method presents advantages and disadvantages, as discussed below.

Computer Spreadsheet Models

A spreadsheet network model depicts each alternative by way of an equation. Various columns in the spreadsheet contain the key data: demand, transportation rate, distances, inventory, percentage inventory carrying cost, and so on. The spreadsheet software provides calculations to compare alternatives. For example, it may focus on a three-facility network. Alternative 1 might be a facility in the Northeast, one in the Midwest, and one on the West Coast. Alternative 2 might be a facility in the Northeast, one in the Southeast, and one in the mountain states.

The spreadsheet method permits these two alternatives to be compared by analyzing the various volumes in terms of transportation rates, inventory carrying costs, materials handling costs, and so on, to arrive at a total cost for each of the alternative network configurations. The spreadsheet allows quick change, recalculation, and comparison for any data elements.

A basic spreadsheet variable cost analysis is shown in Table 27-2.

The three potential alternative locations are compared as follows:

TABLE 27-2
Spreadsheet Analysis of Facilities

Facility Alternative	Distribution Markets						Total Cost
	Atlanta	Miami	Washington	Chicago	Denver	Los Angeles	
Atlanta	10,000	15,000	15,000	25,000	40,000	35,000	140,000
Chicago	30,000	35,000	30,000	9,000	25,000	24,000	154,000
Los Angeles	50,000	55,000	55,000	28,000	15,000	7,000	210,000

TABLE 27-3
Total Cost Analysis

	Inbound Freight	Outbound Freight	Warehousing Costs	Facility Costs	Total Costs
Atlanta	10,000	140,000	75,000	100,000	326,000
Chicago	45,000	154,000	94,000	124,000	417,000
Los Angeles	75,000	210,000	70,000	90,000	445,000

- Projecting the volume to be shipped to each market and then extending that by the transportation rate from the alternative location to the market, resulting in an outbound cost of transportation by market.
- Totaling these outbound freight costs with total inbound freight costs to each alternative location, annual warehouse operating costs, and facility lease costs, as in Table 27-3.
- The estimated annual costs are totaled and then compared.
- Recommendation: select Atlanta as the national distribution facility because of its projected annual cost, which is approximately 25% less than the other options. Atlanta's low cost results from a combination of its proximity to the manufacturing plant and position relative to the markets.

The primary constraint on spreadsheet-based models is the size of the problem; it must be small enough to be effectively input and solved. Low-cost spreadsheet models can be developed with up to 1,000 origin/destination pairs (for example, 100 markets and 10 shipping points). Larger problems may be better addressed using customized modeling languages.

Network Simulation Models

A model can simulate a defined network of origin and destination points by taking a given demand at the market level and sourcing it from a point of manufacture through a set of alternative distribution points. This is accomplished by using preestablished transportation rates, materials handling rates, and inventory carrying cost rates. These rates are applied by extending the individual shipments from the distribution point to the market against the LTL freight rate, then adding that to the cost of truckload freight to resupply the distribution point from the point of manufacture. Added to that are the per unit materials handling cost, the facility fixed cost, and the per unit inventory carrying cost (in terms of the total number of units of inventory deployed). The sum total of this then becomes the cost of this alternative simulation.

This result can then be compared with other simulated alternatives to find the least-cost solution. A strong advantage is that the simulation model permits what-if analysis in which alternative configurations can be easily and quickly changed. Locations can be added or deleted, and then new simulations prepared.

Mathematical Optimization Modeling

As the name implies, an optimization model allows the computer to determine facility locations mathematically from a theoretically infinite number of locations. The primary constraints on optimization models are computer storage capacity and run time. Most optimization models limit the number of potential alternatives in which the model may optimize, resulting in limitations similar to those for simulation models.

Logistics Modeling Data Requirement Summary

The most limiting factors in any modeling are the availability, collectibility, and format of data to drive the model. All distribution network modeling requires the same basic data elements:

- *Product demand data.* Ideally, one year's sales history broken down by product category, market, shipping plant, and shipment weight category. Demand data should reflect both units and points shipped.
- *Freight rates.* Rates are needed for each origin/destination/weight category to be modeled. Published common carrier rates can be used and then discounted to reflect expected actual rates.
- *Facility costs.* Facility costs per square foot for each location to be evaluated.
- *Labor content.* Handling and shipping labor costs in terms of number of wages (workers × hourly rate) plus benefits per pound and/or unit shipped.
- *Labor costs.* Labor costs for each location evaluated.
- *Capacities.* Storage and shipping capacities for all existing facilities. Production capacities for existing plants.
- *Customer service requirements.* Required delivery times from point of shipment.

Computer modeling is obviously a valuable tool in the macroanalysis process. However, the results of any modeling exercise are only as reliable as the data that was inputted, and the conclusions drawn are only as valid as the assumptions made in the modeling process.

All too often, computer models yield nothing more than a perpetuation of an inefficient and inadequate service network. A full macroanalysis and strategic study must consider alternatives other than present arrangements. If present distribution is through a series of centers where product is provided to local markets, one should consider other distribution alternatives like manufacturer-direct shipments, cross-docking, delivery direct to customers, plant-to-store door delivery, third-party warehouses to distribute goods, premium transportation substituting for numerous distribution points, and consignment inventories at the customer's location.

Microanalysis

Microanalysis identifies a particular sector, district, or area located in the geographic region identified in the macroanalysis. Taking the high-level results from the macroanalysis, the microanalysis focuses on issues other than transportation economics and identifies the sector of a metropolitan area that is best suited to become the site of a company's actual facility.

Once the number of warehouse locations is decided and the general geographic area is determined, attention shifts to microanalysis, in which less hard data are available. Some economic considerations still hinge on transportation economics from one location to another, although most are driven by other considerations. The macroanalysis has already shown that the market is best served from a general geographic area; fine-tuning the location from one sector of a metropolitan area to another will result in minimal transportation economics impact. In many cases the transportation rates remain constant throughout a metropolitan area and/or an entire geographic region.

Microanalysis thus focuses more on an analysis of population demographics, union activity, taxes, space costs, availability of new industrial sites and/or existing locations, labor requirements and availability, proximity of transportation services, local and interstate highway access, rail service, proximity to air service, congestion, availability of support services, local utility service, zoning, and the general fit of the company's business within the area.

A thorough microanalysis begins with a broad appraisal of a given geographic area. First, one must identify the potential major metropolitan divisions within that area. Attention then turns to general background information, which reveals how industry and business have developed within the area and how it should be analyzed in terms of sectors, zones, or districts.

Useful sources of information include the local or regional chamber of commerce; industrial real estate brokers; and local, state, and federal development groups. Interviews and on-site inspections of the area are also needed. The information obtained from this research will be used to identify which sector is best suited as a potential location for the prospective distribution facility. The evaluation then takes into account a variety of important factors:

- Availability of sites/existing locations
- Labor availability
- Proximity to transportation terminals
- Rail service
- Proximity to airports and seaports
- Highway access
- Congestion
- Local utilities
- Availability of support services
- Zoning
- Taxes
- Location within region
- Potential as a distribution hub
- Competitive climate
- Types of commerce within the area

The process is highlighted in Figure 27-4.

The microanalysis should be conducted as objectively as possible and be based on a clearly defined set of facility requirements. The criteria should be given a specific numeric value, based on their importance to the site-selection process.

Sample Microanalysis

The following example highlights the key components of microanalysis.

The microanalysis for a 150,000-square-foot grocery manufacturer's northern Georgia facility includes three general steps:

1. Overview of the metropolitan area and identification of districts, divisions, or (in this case) quadrants
2. Comparative information on each quadrant

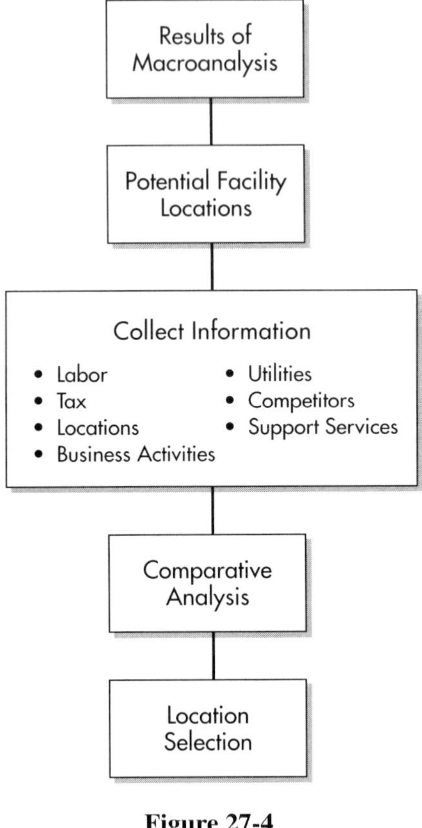

Figure 27-4
Microanalysis Approach

3. Analysis and development of the recommended quadrant in which to conduct the specific site selection

Overview of Atlanta, Georgia

Metropolitan Atlanta serves as the Southeast's center for commerce, transportation, communications, and finance. With a population of 2.4 million, it is the thirteenth-largest metropolitan area in the United States. Unrestricted geographically, this region now includes 18 counties in a total area of 5,134 square miles, which is linked by I-285, a 63-mile outer-belt highway. Since its founding in 1837, the city has been a crossroads and distribution hub. Today it is a national business center from which over 400 of the *Fortune* 500 industrial firms in the United States conduct business.

Atlanta's position in the Southeast is highlighted in Figure 27-5. From its location at the intersections of I-20, I-75, and I-85, Atlanta is an excellent distribution point from which to serve Alabama, Florida, Georgia, Kentucky, Mississippi, North and South Carolina, and Tennessee. Overnight delivery service is available within a 400-mile radius, serving such major metropolitan markets as Nashville, Knoxville, Frankfort, Louisville, Greensboro, Charlotte, Raleigh, Columbia, Charleston, Savannah, Jacksonville, Tallahassee, Mobile, Jackson, Montgomery,

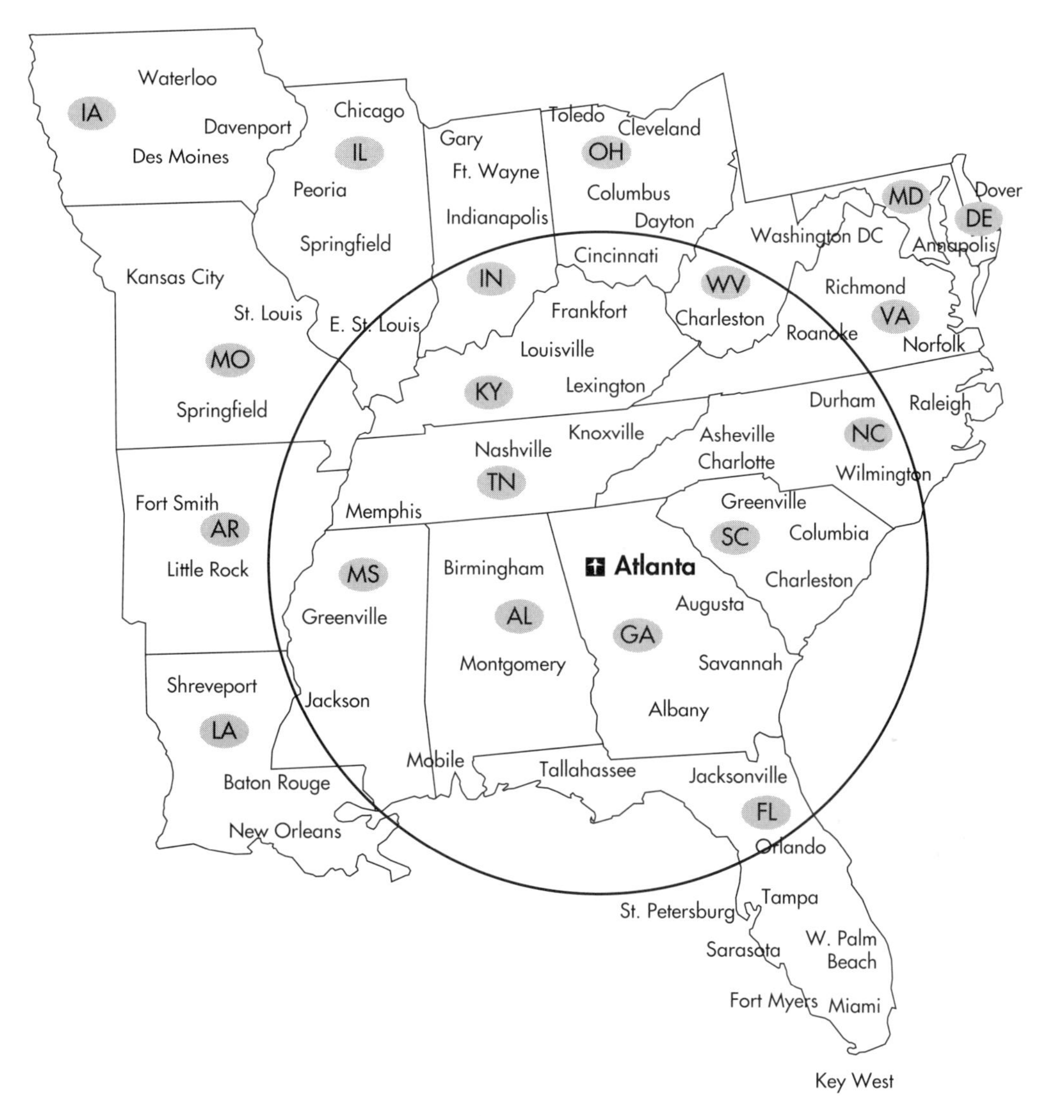

Figure 27-5
Atlanta's Position in the Southeast

Birmingham, Chattanooga, and Memphis. Second-day service is readily available to serve the balance of the markets in Florida and the secondary markets throughout the Southeast.

The metropolitan area is easily subdivided into four quadrants: north/south is divided by I-20; east/west is divided by a line through the city center parallel to I-75 extending north to Route 400. These quadrants are shown in Figure 27-6 and described in more detail.

Northeast. The Northeast quadrant, centered in Gwinnett County, is the fastest-growing county in the United States and consists mainly of upper- to middle-class suburban homes and

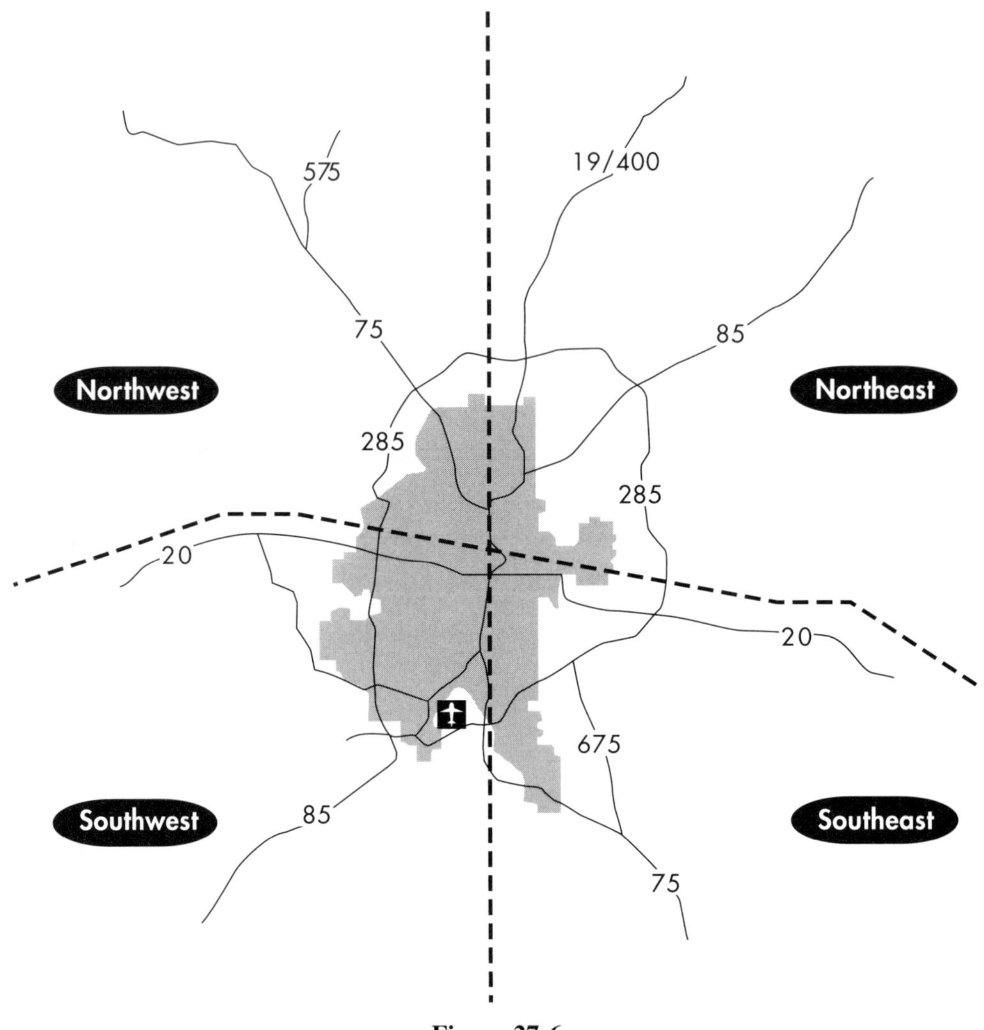

Figure 27-6
The Four Quadrants of Atlanta

white-collar business complexes. This area's rapid growth has outstripped the growth of services, creating significant traffic congestion and long lead times in obtaining basic services in the area.

Southeast. The Southeast quadrant—the least-developed and historically least desirable area of metropolitan Atlanta—has become a principal common carrier truck terminal area because of low land costs and available blue-collar labor. Growth of this area will be spurred by development of a major foreign trade zone directly across from Hartsfield Cargo Terminal, completion of I-675 connecting I-285 and I-75 near Stockbridge, and speculative development of Atlanta International Industrial Park near the 1-675 and 1-285 intersection.

Northwest. The Northwest quadrant, primarily Cobb County, has a large suburban population. The area, as shown in Figure 27-6, is dominated by I-75 and rail-hub activity. Commercial development here has been in light industrial business parks, showrooms, and light distribution facilities. The Northwest offers a good availability of blue-collar workers, with Marietta providing a mixture of blue- and white-collar labor.

Southwest. The Southwest quadrant is experiencing a strong development boom. This growth is a result of available low-priced land near the center city, growth of Hartsfield International Airport, and the development of Camp Creek Parkway, connecting I-85 at the airport with I-285 and 1-20 near Austell. The population in the Southwest has traditionally been blue-collar. Fulton Industrial Park, which was the first major distribution area in metropolitan Atlanta, is now experiencing rapid growth and new development. With this growth and new development, the Southwest offers an abundant supply of new and second-generation distribution space. This availability of space holds real estate prices down and permits a number of public warehouse operations.

Warehousing Space in Atlanta

By working with local industrial real estate representatives, reviewing industrial real estate listings, and evaluating the buildings that meet basic requirements for its application, a basis for the following summary of warehouse space within this metropolitan market has been developed.

Atlanta warehouse construction places minimal emphasis on insulation, dock seals, and dock shelters. Most older, second-generation buildings tend to be of masonry. New facilities still use brick, given the availability of Georgia clay, low labor rates, and minimal installation requirements. The majority of Atlanta warehouse space is single-story, modern, truck-served (minimal rail-served), flat roof, and fewer than 250,000 square feet.

At the time of this analysis, Atlanta has a surplus of available bulk warehouse space and as such is a buyer's market. In the 100,000- to 200,00-square-foot range, there are presently more than 20 available buildings. Additionally, the area's three principal developers are continually adding to the inventory of speculative bulk warehouse space. Most of the available "large" bulk warehouse space is south of I-20 and principally in the Southwest quadrant. However, requirements could be met by any of the major developers in all four quadrants.

Atlanta's warehouse space is dominated by developments of leasable space of three developers—M. D. Hodges, a local Atlanta developer; LaSalle Partners, a Chicago-based group; and Tramell Crow, a national developer. All three maintain an inventory of land for development as well as speculative warehouse space for lease.

On a quadrant-by-quadrant basis, typical space availability in the 100,000- to 200,000-square-foot range is shown in Table 27-4.

According to the "Industrial Marketing Report" published by Rubloff Business Properties Group, an Atlanta-based commercial real estate broker, at the time of this analysis rental rates for bulk warehouse space in the four quadrants range from $2.25 to $4.50 per square foot, as shown in Table 27-5.

The on-site survey of available properties in the 100,000- to 200,000-square-foot range found 19 buildings currently available or under construction that would fit basic needs. Six of these facilities are located in the Southwest; five are in the Northwest; and the Southeast and Northeast quadrants each have four, as shown in Figure 27-7.

In comparison with leasing, the cost of construction approximates $17.00/square foot for the

TABLE 27-4
Space Availability

Quadrant	New Bulk Space	Second-generation Space	Multiple-tenant Adaptable Space
Southwest	High	High	High
Southeast	Moderate	Low	High
Northwest	Low	Low	Low
Northeast	Minimal	Low	Low

shell building, plus tenant improvements, office furnishings, and site preparation. With land, a typical 200,000-square-foot facility in the Southwestern quadrant would cost approximately $22.00/square foot, while the same building in the Northeast quadrant would cost $25.00 to $30.00/square foot.

Given the amount of available space and the current buyer's market, there is no advantage to building the company's own grocery products bulk warehouse in this market at this time.

Tax Considerations

Georgia utilizes an ad valorem property tax as the primary source of revenue for all governmental units. This tax is assessed on all real property, including inventories. However, "Freeport Local Option" permits taxing jurisdictions to exclude most inventories from this tax. Clayton, Cobb, and Fulton Counties make up most of the Southeast, Southwest, and Northwest quadrants, respectively. These counties exclude most inventories from their tax base, as noted below.

The ad valorem tax is based on the value of real and personal property, including inventory, which is subject to the tax. By law, property is valued or "assessed" at 40% of its fair market value. The Freeport local option amendment allows exemption from that tax under three conditions:

Class I—Manufacturer's raw materials and goods in the process of being manufactured or produced
Class II—Finished goods held by the original manufacturer
Class III—Finished goods held by distributors and wholesalers that are destined for shipment out of Georgia

TABLE 27-5
Atlanta Warehouse Rental Rates

Quadrant	Bulk Warehousing Rental Rates (per square foot)	Office/Warehousing Rental Rates (per square foot)
Northeast	$2.75–$4.50	$4.50–$7.00
Northwest	$2.65–$4.25	$4.25–$7.00
Southeast	$2.50–$4.25	$3.00–$4.75
Southwest	$2.25–$4.50	$2.75–$5.00

Source: Rubloff Business Properties Group, "Industrial Marketing Report."

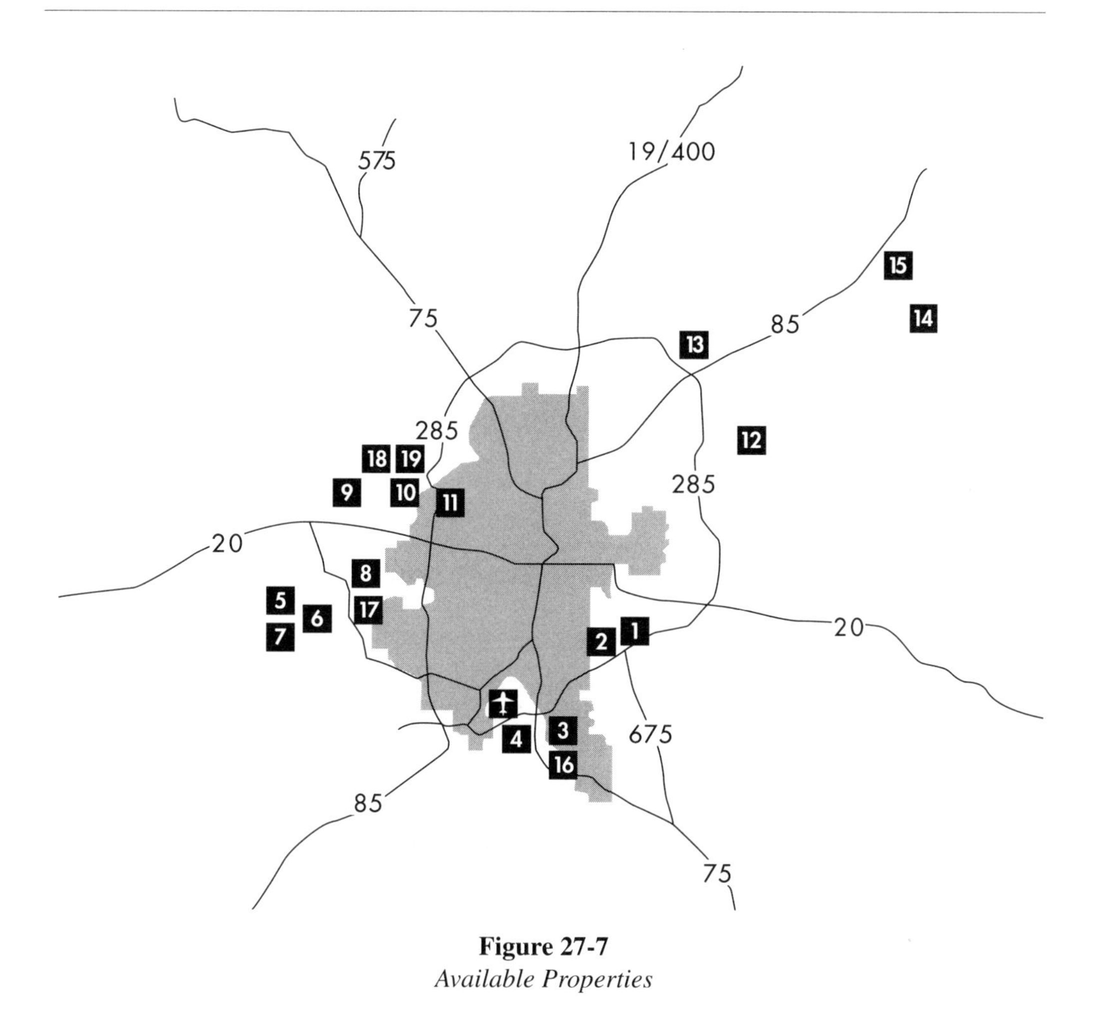

Figure 27-7
Available Properties

Exemptions in effect in metropolitan Atlanta as of date of the analysis are shown in Table 27-6.

Owing to the "Freeport Local Option" and current tax rates in the areas considered, the actual impact of the ad valorem tax should not be a decisive factor in selecting the company's new facility, because the tax impact is relatively equal for all areas being considered.

Local Labor Conditions

Atlanta is predominantly a nonunion area. The State of Georgia is a right-to-work state and, as such, even those facilities that are union-organized are open shop (union membership is voluntary).

General warehouse labor ranges from $8.00 to $14.00/hour, plus fringe benefits of 20 to 40%. While the cost of warehouse labor does not vary greatly from one quadrant to another, the availability and quality of workforce does. Blue-collar labor is abundant south of I-20 in the metropolitan area but very scarce in the Northeast quadrant because of high housing costs and demand for service labor. The Northwest quadrant has more available blue-collar labor than the Northeast, but not as much as the two southern quadrants.

TABLE 27-6
Tax Exemptions

Jurisdiction	Class I	Class II	Class III
Fulton County	100	100	100
City of Atlanta	20	20	20
DeKalb County	80	80	100
Cobb County	100	100	100
City of Marietta	80	80	80
Clayton County	100	100	100
Gwinnett County	80	80	80
Douglas County	100	100	100

Recommendations

As illustrated in Table 27-7, an Atlanta distribution center should be located in the Southwest quadrant's Fulton Industrial Park area because of the following factors: presence of the majority of customer locations and competitors' distribution points, availability of public warehouse operators and blue-collar labor, lower land and warehouse lease costs, less traffic congestion, and more available large warehouse space.

Once the macro- and microanalyses are complete, the specific site selection can be conducted. The macroanalysis has ensured that (1) locations within this section have the basic labor pool required; (2) rail, highway, and air transportation are accessible; and (3) basic services are available.

The analysis now begins to focus on the specific location within the sector. Attention is concentrated on highway access; land values; land availability; real estate taxation; environmental concerns; local governmental boundaries; local taxation; local covenants, restrictions, attitudes, and philosophies; utility services; public transportation; local labor availability; ground water and site preparation requirements; existing facility availability; the fit of the business into the community; and individual land assessments and covenants.

TABLE 27-7
Quadrant Comparisons

Criteria	Southwest	Southeast	Northwest	Northeast
Warehouse space availability	1	2	3	4
Warehousing costs	1	2	3	4
Labor availability	1	1	3	4
Congestion	1	1	3	3
Concentration of customers (Grocery)	1	2	3	4
Concentration of customers (Food service)	1	2	3	4
Concentration of competitors	1	1	4	4
Concentration of public warehouses	1	1	4	4
Quadrant Ranking	1	2	3	4

Scale: 1 = Very Attractive; 4 = Not Attractive

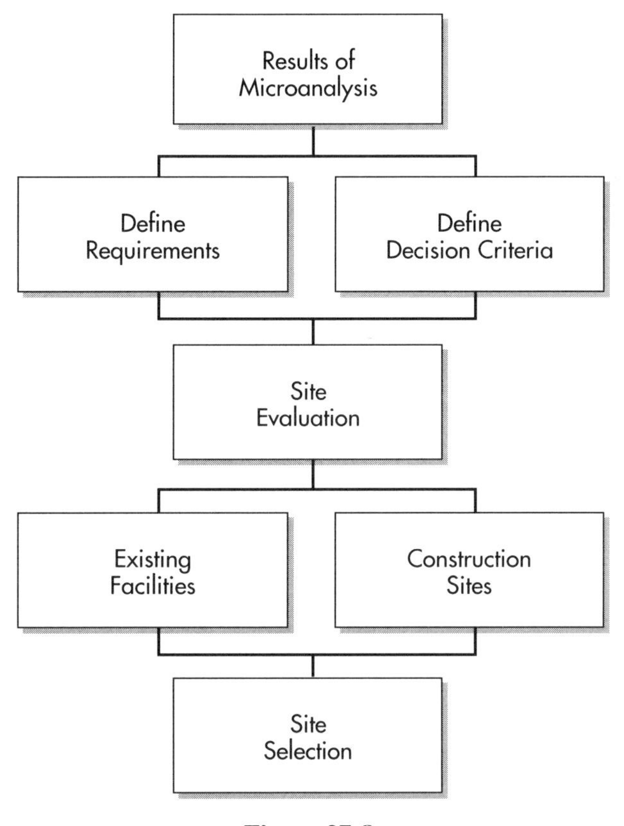

Figure 27-8
Location Selection Approach

Although similar in general categories to the microanalysis, specific site selection goes into much greater detail. The location selection approach is shown in Figure 27-8. In the microanalysis, the acceptance of averages and general conditions is reasonable. In the specific site selection process, specifics by location are mandatory. Details as to building characteristics, tax rates, port services, governmental restrictions, and labor pool availability must be collected and analyzed.

The specific site selection approach is a multistep process:

1. Define the microanalysis and the organization's specific facility need.
2. Define the building requirements with details regarding ceiling height and other specifications.
3. Define the decision criteria in terms of an objective evaluation.
4. Conduct on-site facility evaluations of existing and/or proposed construction sites detailing the data collected from each site.
5. Utilize the decision criteria to evaluate the site data, analyze their advantages and disadvantages by location, and recommend a specific site.

Detailed site selection is a very time-consuming and detail-oriented process. Selection of the wrong location will be conspicuously evident for a long time. Unfortunately, the specific site selection process is one in which most logistics managers have little experience.

How, then, is the task successfully accomplished? By taking a detailed methodical approach, allowing the necessary time to execute the search, and seeking advice from outside experts. Some sources of advice are the local chamber of commerce, the local utility companies, industrial real estate brokers, and consultants. Each source has its own advantages and disadvantages.

Utilities and chambers of commerce will provide only that information that is advantageous to the areas they serve. If there is an ideal site outside their service territory, they are not likely to provide such information. Additionally, their information tends to be positively biased and must be objectively reviewed before acceptance.

Industrial real estate brokers are generally the best source of actual location selection information. However, because their compensation is based on sales or lease agreements, they are inclined to promote properties that financially benefit them.

Consultants, if independent and not financially or otherwise obligated to any other entity, can be very helpful. They tend to be unbiased and experienced in the site selection process, and can add experience and expertise from other companies and other industries. The drawback is, of course, their fees.

Up to this point, no reference has been made to the difference between a site selection search to build a warehouse distribution center facility or one that would seek to select an existing facility to be adapted to meet the company's needs. In actual practice, there is no meaningful difference between the two searches. Only after a location has been selected does one need to apply selection criteria that distinguish between developing a new building versus adapting an existing facility.

Warehouse/Distribution Center Requirements and Decision Criteria

The analysis begins with defining needs and specific requirements to be satisfied by the facility. In this case, the requirements include, but are not limited to, the following:

- Building specifications like square footage, and ceiling height and shape
- Office requirements such as square footage and configuration
- Dock doors, receiving, shipping, and floor level
- Heating, ventilating, and air-conditioning (HVAC) office and warehouse to include temperature and humidity control
- Workforce size and special requirements
- Functional use of the specific facility
- Sales and marketing requirements like appearance and location of local sales office
- Number of trailers to be staged and/or stored in the yard and/or at permanent dock assignments
- Number of operating shifts per day and operating days per week
- Daily receipts and shipments measured by number of trucks and rail switchings per day
- Waste disposal and storage requirements
- Utility requirements for electric, natural gas, communication lines, and water
- Floor load requirements
- Special storage requirements and/or considerations (e.g., high-density sprinkler systems)

- Union considerations like strict avoidance of unions or presence of specific "locals"
- Other specific needs, requirements, and/or desirables

Decision Criteria

Specific decision criteria should be established before the evaluation process commences. They should take the requirements from above and define each with detailed specifications such as "Ceiling height required is 24 feet clear". Assigning numeric values to each requirement allows an objective evaluation of the variable alternatives that will form the basis for a final recommendation and ultimate site selection. This process gives structure to the evaluation and decision processes, but unfortunately, it does not simplify the detailed review and analysis of all potential alternatives. For evaluating ceiling heights, rankings might be as follows:

- *27 foot clear* would represent the ideal and be assigned a numeric value of 10
- *24 foot clear* would meet the requirements and be assigned a numeric value of 8
- *21 foot clear* would be acceptable but less desirable and as such would be assigned a numeric value of 6
- *18 foot clear* would be the minimal acceptable height (though requiring additional square footage) and would be assigned a numeric value of only 4
- *16, 14, and 12 foot clear* heights would not be acceptable and as such receive no numeric value

Details of Specific Location Selection—Common Elements

Regardless of whether a company plans to occupy an existing facility or to construct a new one, the following elements must be evaluated:

- *Labor pool.* Distribution requires a pool of semiskilled and unskilled labor. Any potential site must be evaluated in light of the potential labor pool from which it will draw. The main factor to consider is the amount of competition, both now and in the foreseeable future, for similar class labor within the surrounding area. If the immediate residential area does not support the labor pool a company requires, one should consider the possibility of other residential communities providing the labor pool and then evaluate the distance from each and the ease of commuting.
- *Utilities and communications.* Obviously, all locations must have access to utilities and communications services. Important concerns include (1) the potential limitations of the utilities, (2) long lead times for utility hookup, (3) intermittent service interruptions, and (4) potential development within the area that could severely constrain available resources. Certain communication tie-ins are more dependable than others and provide a full range of services, while others have limited availability of dedicated lines. Electric utilities, for example, may be limited as to phased service or the ability to provide immediate tie-in to high-amperage requirements. Similarly, availability of large quantities of water for potential processing and/or potential fire protection by means of high-density sprinkler systems should be examined. Availability of water mains, sizes, and pressures could require potential on-site reservoirs or booster pumps with significant cost implications.
- *Surrounding neighbors and tenants.* A survey of each potential site should be made to evaluate surrounding commercial neighbors and surrounding tenants. The general neighborhood should also be examined to determine its principal use. For example, predominantly residential use of the area may eventually limit facility expansion. (This analysis also supplements research

into availability of labor and support services.) The absence of similar facilities in the area may be a negative. Similarly, a dominance of like facilities in the area could show either the presence of desirable location factors or a high demand for services and labor that may lead to undesirable competition and congestion in the future.

- *Local support services.* The availability of local support services should be evaluated for potential sites. Such services include waste disposal, liquid propane gas (LPG), materials handling equipment maintenance, computer equipment service, fire protection, and sanitation. The absence of these services may require a company to incur higher costs for self-sufficiency or downtime.
- *Transportation pick up services.* Transportation pickup services include local cartage, parcel deliveries, proximity to parts and air freight terminals, and LTL carrier pickups; competition for such services should be investigated.
- *Local taxes.* Taxes include corporate, local, regional, and personal; property assessments; inventory taxes; fees; licenses; and ad valorem taxes. Many of these taxes, not necessarily reflected in a real estate appraisal, could add significant costs to the operating budget. Local personal or regional personal income taxes may require higher wage rates to offset such taxes.
- *Fire codes and protection.* Fire codes and fire marshals' interpretation of codes may vary in different jurisdictions. These variations may result in significant impacts on insurance and risk costs for alternative sites, and on operational and capital expenditure requirements to prepare the facility for specific use. The site should also be considered in light of local fire protection provided (for example, volunteer fire departments, full-time professional fire departments, cooperative agreements with adjoining municipalities, and distance to nearest firehouse).
- *Union activity.* Regardless of the company's view on union activities, all potential alternative locations should be evaluated in light of existing labor union activity. Some companies will look for extremes in union avoidance, while others seek specific union alliances. Few companies, however, are eager to move into a location known for militant union activity, constant work interruptions, excessive grievance filing, and the like.

Construction Site Considerations

To build a new facility or seek existing space depends upon several variables, including (1) the availability of existing facilities, (2) make vs. buy financial analysis, (3) availability of sufficient lead times to construct and occupy a facility, and (4) customization requirement for a facility to support a particular usage.

In general, existing properties should be evaluated even if there is an inclination to build to suit because availability of an existing property at a lower cost may influence the decision and/or provide strong negotiating points. The location selection process should go forward on both the construction as well as the existing facility evaluation and not be limited to one or the other. This is generally the most prudent approach unless there is an overriding reason that would eliminate one of the two alternatives, such as inadequate lead time to permit construction and/or a prior corporate mandate to construct all buildings.

Construction site evaluations should be conducted in a three-step approach:

1. An inventory of potential sites for construction
2. Familiarization with local building practices and site preparation procedures
3. Specific site evaluations

Evaluation of Potential Sites for Construction

A listing of all potential construction sites that meet minimum requirements should be assembled. These include all locations that offer sufficient acreage to support the size of facility required, and/or that could reasonably be expected to have sufficient zoning to support the type of construction desired, and are within the area of supporting services. While potential sites are being identified, the prevailing construction practices, costs, and local peculiarities should be examined.

Managers responsible for site selection in an unfamiliar area often are led to believe that conditions already familiar to them are the same throughout the United States. Unfortunately, this is not true. Some areas require much more land preparation (for example, soil compaction, deeper pilings, or more complex drainage). Some areas are subject to heavy rains, flooding, or severe freeze-and-thaw cycles, all of which can have significant impact on floor construction and site preparation times and costs. Similarly, some regions have different requirements for roofs because of weather considerations (e.g., snow accumulations, high winds, etc.). These points, as well as local construction practices and costs, should be understood. Different construction methods may be more or less desirable in different geographic areas because of their costs, availability, and local building codes.

With these points identified, examination of potential construction sites can begin. The list that follows, although brief, is in addition to all the previous considerations that are common to both construction and existing facilities:

- *Zoning and zoning appeal process.* The zoning for the construction of the desired building (heights, total square footage, construction materials, aesthetic design, number of employees, and building use) may or may not exist on the particular sites being examined. If it exists and meets all needs, it is a major advantage. If the desired zoning is not available, it is important to understand how much time and expense will be needed to obtain necessary permits, appeals, and exceptions.
- *Construction permits, code requirements, exceptions, and appeal process.* As with zoning, each site should be evaluated in terms of a particular municipality's building codes.
- *Building site restrictions.* Specific sites, industrial development areas, industrial parks, and local ordinances may impose a variety of building site restrictions. Some of the common restrictions include building setbacks, percentage of the total land that can be developed, the percentage of the property that must remain as "green space," and possibly, highway appearance considerations like minimal landscaping requirements and landscaping blinds to cover parking areas, utility boxes, and meters.
- *Environmental impact.* Most sites require an environmental impact study. A company should identify the cost of such a study, the length of time required to conduct it, and the likelihood that it will reveal environmental impacts that could pose significant delays or cost consequences. Whether or not an environmental impact study is required for a particular site, today's movement toward greater environmental concerns may well affect the construction of new facilities. All facilities should be researched to determine the precontamination responsibility for both known and unknown cleanup requirements. As with natural resource rights and ownership, future contamination liabilities should be considered for all evaluated sites. Such possibilities should be evaluated to determine a company's potential long-term liabilities.
- *Topographical maps.* Each potential location should have a topographical map, which should be examined to help identify potential site preparation costs, potential ground water con-

siderations, and impacts of floodplains at various incremental levels (20-year, 50-year, and 100-year flood scenarios).

- *Incentives.* Many areas seeking development may offer certain incentive financing like revenue bonds, tax abatement, or employee training credits. These should be identified and analyzed as to whether they are site-specific or area-specific and whether the requirements to obtain them would make them worthwhile for a company to pursue.

Existing Facility Considerations

All available facilities that meet minimum requirements in terms of square footage, land use, and other noncorrectable physical characteristics should be listed. A second list should be prepared of like properties in the same geographic area that have been recently sold or leased. While these two lists are being compiled, it is necessary to become familiar with local construction costs and practices, as well as maintenance considerations related to local climate and wind conditions. Chicago-area buildings, for example, tend to use internal truck docks; in California, open loading and receiving docks are common because of the dry climate. Local peculiarities should be understood before examining existing potential facilities.

A list of available facilities should include a description of the following physical characteristics:

- total square footage
- type of construction
- additions
- number of dock doors
- space on site for expansion
- sprinkler systems
- ceiling height
- date of construction
- square footage of office space
- paved yard area
- presence or availability of rail connections
- building occupancy and use zoning

Armed with this information, a manager can begin the actual site search. The search requires a physical examination of each potential property as well as some secondary research to evaluate the following items:

- *Sprinkler systems.* Type, construction, maintenance, and condition.
- *Safety requirements.* Fire walls, fire curtains, shear walls (how well they meet existing requirements, and impacts on the facility's operations).
- *Situation of building on property.* The direction the building faces should be considered in regard to prevailing winds, potential temperature effect, and glaring sun on office or amount of sunlight available to skylights.
- *Building appearance.* The aesthetic value of the building should be considered as a potential marketing tool as well as highway visibility for potential promotional advantage.

- *Previous tenants and building history.* Historical information may be invaluable to help identify building characteristics both advantageous and detrimental. This information may also be valuable in helping the company evaluate building maintenance and wear.
- *Building's original construction design and intended use.* This also can be helpful in identifying building characteristics, construction specifications, advantages, and potential disadvantages of the building.
- *Expansion capabilities.* Determine whether the building is part of a larger complex that would allow growth into adjoining areas of the same building; identify adjoining buildings within the same industrial park and/or land for potential expansion.
- *Building modification requirements.* A listing should be kept of required building modifications. This may include such items as covering existing indoor railroad sidings to expand usable square footage, addition of dock doors and seals, installation of dock levelers, installation of people-doors, revamping and/or installation of sprinkler systems, construction of an aerosol room, conversion of an explosion-proof truck bay to an aerosol room, conversion of production space to storage space and/or office space.
- *Building maintenance.* An evaluation of building maintenance should be made to help identify the condition of the building as well as looming maintenance expenditures.
- *Physical examinations.* Walls, floors, roofs, and paved areas, as well as other physical features, should be examined as follows:

  Walls should be examined for structural integrity. Visual inspection should be made to determine if moisture is seeping through the walls, if apparent cracks allow light to be visible through the walls, if there is separation of mortar or insulation joints, if rust is seeping through the walls, and if there are potential entryways for rodents and insects.

  Floors should be walked and examined for cracks that might indicate the ground underneath collapsing, being hollowed out by inadequate drainage, and/or heaving as a result of the freeze/thaw cycles (may also be an example of inconsistent floor thickness and/or symptomatic of other potential problems); the floor should also be examined for irregularities like lack of levelness, which may interfere with materials handling equipment and systems to be installed (e.g., wire-guided systems, high-level narrow-aisle equipment, AS/RS systems, etc.).

  Roofs should be physically examined for low spots that hold water, apparent deterioration, lack of gravel (on flat roofs), open seams, and the presence or absence of maintenance. Roofs vary greatly in style, design, and installation and also represent the single largest potential maintenance cost and one of the most common maintenance problems.

  Paved areas should be examined for potholes, cracking, separation, and collapse. The edge of the paved areas should be inspected to evaluate adequate drainage and potential surface depths. Yard drainage should be checked to ensure it is adequate and in working order.
- *Insulation.* Facilities should be examined for insulation to determine potential impact on heating and cooling costs, as well as potential impact on products being stored and handled.
- *Docks, doors, and dock levelers.* The facility should be examined as to the number of dock doors and the natural material flow from receiving to shipping docks. Consideration should be given to spacing between docks, the existence of floor-level docks for access of maintenance vehicles, use of fork lifts; number and location of people-doors adjacent to docks; presence, type, and condition of in-floor dock levelers; and dock seals and dock locks.

- *Lighting.* Light fixtures in the warehouse should be inspected to determine if they are mercury or sodium vapor, or fluorescent or incandescent, and to ensure that there is a minimum of 20 to 30 foot-candles in the intended aisle ways.
- *Skylights.* Given the particular geographic location, skylights may be quite advantageous to improve the amount of natural light coming into the building, reduce potential artificial light costs, as well as generally improve the workplace environment. The absence or presence of skylights should be examined as well as the type, condition, and maintenance.
- *HVAC.* Heating, ventilating, and air-conditioning systems should be examined for age, maintenance, and efficiency.
- *Office space.* Existing office space should be examined for its ability to meet requirements. Expansion or contraction of the amount of office space should be considered, as well as potential alternative uses for excess office space, ability to disconnect HVAC to unused office space (i.e., for converting it to storage, production, or assembly space). Office space should also be evaluated in terms of the renovation needed to bring it to the required standard.
- *Trailer parking.* Depending on operational requirements for staging of loaded and unloaded trailers, the availability of trailer parking on site should be evaluated. If the site contains sufficient space to hold the number of trailers, does the trailer parking space offer sufficient security? Furthermore, is there going to be a penalty for having to retrieve and spot trailers because of the proximity of the space to the dock doors?
- *Sanitation.* Evaluation should be made of each facility as to the level of sanitation maintained by previous occupants and the building's ability to meet company sanitation requirements.

Case Study

The following is an example of a specific site selection process for a 150,000-square-foot grocery manufacturer's northern Georgia distribution facility. In this specific site selection we go through the three basic steps:

1. Define selection criteria
2. Identify advantages and disadvantages of each potential facility
3. Analyze the facilities and recommend the best choice

Criteria

For this specific site selection the Southwest quadrant of Atlanta has been selected as a result of the previous microanalysis. A 150,000-square-foot grocery distribution facility with 24-foot clear ceiling height that meets food grade sanitation requirements is being sought. The facility is intended to operate as a coordinated satellite of the current manufacturing operation and to be used to supplement the manufacturing warehouse's overrun storage requirements. The facility will also be utilized as a truck and trailer staging site for store delivery vehicles, and as such it should accommodate 100 trucks.

Available Facilities

In conjunction with local industrial real estate brokers, a listing of five facilities has been identified that appear to meet the basic requirements. All are in the Southwest quadrant and are currently available for lease. These facilities, in the order in which they will be examined, are as follows:

1. Norcross Parkway
2. Camp Creek Parkway
3. Cascade Road
4. Ben Hill Road
5. Decatur Street

After the secondary information has been assembled, individual properties are inspected. The advantages and disadvantages of each are then presented. What follows is a summary of them for each property, along with some potential negotiating points for each property.

Norcross Parkway

Norcross Parkway facility is some distance outside of Atlanta and beyond the Southwest quadrant. The facility is a former manufacturing plant that has been vacant for some time. Its lease rate of $3.40 per square foot is very low.

Positive Points

- Very low lease rate
- Space available for future expansion
- Adequate trailer parking

Negative Points

- 70 miles from the manufacturing plant
- Designed as a manufacturing facility—not configured for distribution
- Not a food-grade facility
- Insufficient docks—poor layout for dock expansion
- Apparent roof problems, damp interior
- Low ceiling height—18 foot clear

Camp Creek Parkway

The Camp Creek Parkway facility is a former food service facility in which warehousing and distribution of food products, prepreparation, and food assembly were carried out. The facility has been very well maintained and its layout is quite flexible. Although the entire facility is large enough to meet the criteria, the warehouse portion itself is only 100,000 square feet; the remaining 50,000 square feet are made up of office, food preparation, and assembly areas.

Positive Points

- Excellent condition
- Food-grade facility
- Available space to expand trailer parking
- Direct access to interstate system

Negative Points

- Too Small—100,000 square feet with 50,000-square-foot office service area
- 50 miles from the manufacturing plant

Negotiating Points

- Insufficient dock doors
- Insufficient current trailer parking

Cascade Road

The Cascade Road facility is at the intersection of two interstates. It sits on a large property with significant expansion opportunities. The facility was originally designed for heavy manufacturing and is not configured well to serve as a distribution center. It has extremely high ceiling height, with bays of 30-feet and 45-feet clear height.

Positive Points

- Excellent highway access to interstate system and outer belt
- Additional space available for future expansion
- Adequate trailer parking

Negative Points

- 45 miles to manufacturing plant
- Manufacturing facility—not configured for distribution
- Extremely high ceiling height, with bays 30 and 35 feet high

Negotiating Points

- Insufficient dock doors, poor lighting, poor heating

Ben Hill Road

The Ben Hill Road facility is currently under construction but approximately 75% complete. The facility is very eye-appealing, with excellent road access and visibility. The building easily meets all the construction and building specification requirements and offers extremely good flexibility because it is still under construction; the office spaces have not yet been designated, the dock doors have not yet been installed, and the landlord is willing to alter these to the desired specifications.

Positive Points

- New building still under construction
- Can specify lighting, heating, dock doors, office space, and mezzanine requirements
- Adequate space and excellent configuration
- Attractive lease rate—landlord *wants* a tenant
- Very flexible building

Negative Points

- 20 miles to the manufacturing plant

Negotiating Points

- Trailer parking is unconfirmed
- Expansion is feasible in adjacent building

Decatur Street

The Decatur Street facility is less than one mile away from the current manufacturing plant. The facility is a former food distribution center with an abundance of trailer parking and dock doors.

Positive Points

- Less than one mile from the manufacturing plant
- Adequate space
- Adequate dock doors
- Four acres of trailer parking (170 trailers)
- Opportunity to share the manufacturing plant's trailer pool and staging
- Available adjacent office space
- Food grade facility

Negative Points

- Long, narrow building limits materials handling layout

Negotiating Points

- Aging building
  –Excessive floor settling
  –Docks in disrepair
- Poor overall maintenance
- Inside rail and truck docks waste interior space

Analysis and Recommendations

After the on-site evaluations of the potential facilities, an analysis matrix has been assembled evaluating all five against the seven decision criteria on a scale with 1 being the highest mark and 4 the lowest. The matrix is presented in Table 27-8.

Recommendation

Of the available buildings, the Decatur Street is the best suited for the current needs. It is the only facility that meets all the evaluation criteria.

The Norcross, Camp Creek, and Cascade Road buildings do not fit the criteria for functionality and proximity to the current manufacturing plant. The Ben Hill Road facility currently under construction is by far the best building with respect to functionality and flexibility, but its attractiveness is diminished by the uncertainty of the availability of trailer parking, the somewhat limited support services, and distance from the manufacturing plant.

TABLE 27–8
Facility Comparison

	Decatur Street		Ben Hill Road		Cascade Road		Camp Creek		Norcross Parkway	
Functionality and Flexibility	Good (warehouse)	2	Excellent (new bldg.)	1	Poor (mfg. bldg.)	4	Fair (small bldg.)	3	Poor (mfg. bldg.)	4
150,000 sq. ft. and 24 ft. clear	Yes	1	Yes	1	Yes (30–35 ft.)	1	100,000 sq. ft.	4	18 ft. clear	3
Proximity to mfg. plant	Excellent (.5 miles)	1	Fair (20 miles)	3	Poor (45 mile)	4	Poor (50 miles)	4	Poor (70 miles)	4
Availability of support services	Excellent	1	Good	2	Good	2	Good	2	Poor	4
Food grade	Yes	1	Yes	1	Yes	1	Yes	1	No	4
Cost	Fair ($4.50 ft.)	3	Good ($4.00 ft.)	2	Poor ($5.00 ft.)	4	Good ($4.00 ft.)	2	Excellent ($3.40 ft.)	1
Truck parking	Excellent	1	Fair (unconfirmed)	3	Good	2	Poor	4	Good	2
Total Score		10		13		18		20		22

Scale: Excellent = 1 Good = 2 Fair = 3 Poor = 4

The Decatur Street building, on the other hand, provides excellent opportunities for coordination of management and operations with the manufacturing plant, exceeds all the functionality and flexibility requirements, and has excellent availability of support services and trailer parking.

Facility Selection

Norcross, Camp Creek, and Cascade Road buildings do not fit the criteria for functionality or proximity to current manufacturing plant. The newly constructed building on Ben Hill Road is by far the best building with respect to functionality and flexibility. However, the Decatur Street building provides excellent opportunities for coordination of management and operations with the manufacturing plant, and it adequately meets the functionality and flexibility criteria, despite somewhat higher quoted leased costs, and is thus the site selected.

Summary

Site selection is a top-down analysis of macro, micro, and specific site issues. The traditional real estate wisdom that stresses location, location, and location understates the detailed analysis required to conduct a truly useful site selection.

The recommended three-step approach—macroanalysis to define the geographic region, microanalysis to identify a sector of that area, and the specific site selection itself—ensures a thorough analysis of all issues that impact the efficiency, flexibility, and marketplace effectiveness of a company's distribution facilities.

Bibliography

Akerman, Kenneth B. *Practical Handbook of Warehousing.* Washington, D.C.: Traffic Service Corp., 1983.

Bowersox, Donald J. *Logistical Management.* New York: Macmillan, 1978.

Coopersmith, Jeffrey A. *Designing Your Next Fulfillment Warehouse.*

The Distribution Handbook. ed. in chief James F. Robeson. New York: Free Press, 1985.

Gold, Steven. "A New Approach to Site Selection," *Distribution* (December 1991).

Heskett, James L. *Business Logistics.* New York: Ronald Press, 1973.

Industrial Engineering Handbook. ed. in chief H. B. Maynard. New York: McGraw-Hill, 1971.

Jenkins, Creed H. *Modern Warehouse Management.* New York: McGraw-Hill, 1968.

Morse, Leon W. *Practical Handbook of Industrial Traffic Management.* Washington, D.C.: Traffic Service Corp., 1987.

CHAPTER 28

Using Warehouse Information

Morton T. Yeomans

An experienced warehouse manager once said, "The more you know about your warehouse, the better you can operate it." This manager understood the essence of sound warehouse management and was able to provide excellent service through his warehouses as a result. By understanding operations and sharing that information with employees, the manager improved warehouse operating procedures, reduced errors, maintained a good relationship with staff, and provided a reasonable cost level.

This chapter deals with warehouse information and its value in operating the facility. It reviews the reasons for collecting operating data, how to gather them, and what to do with them once they have been accumulated.

The Importance of Information

The use of information is not limited to daily operations but can be effectively applied to many important activities, including the following:

- *Planning future changes.* For example, data collected for incoming order volumes by period during the day can be compiled to assist in scheduling staggered work hours.
- *Measuring and evaluating results.* After adding part-time workers to the staff, information can be gathered to indicate whether the additional staff have been able to smooth out peaks in the workload.
- *Monitoring operations on a continuing basis.* Statistics concerning incoming and outgoing volumes can ensure that order processing is meeting customer service needs on a regular basis.

This chapter indicates the various methods that can be used to identify and collect data, shows how data can be portrayed usefully, and discusses some of the interpretations that can be made and the changes that can result from application of the accumulated information.

Sources of Information

There is a wealth of information available in every warehouse. Because it is not readily at hand, managers are unable to tap the power of the information to help understand the processes involved in their warehouses. Too often, the available measurement is the "noise level" generated by unhappy customers or the sales force. The absence of noise (complaints) is often interpreted to mean that everything is fine. In fact, it may mean the opposite, because customers and sales force have grown tired of complaining. The only real test of service is provided by an information system that measures activity and service level on a continuing basis.

Most companies have data available from the information services department that assists in understanding and monitoring warehouse functions. The essential data that should be identified and collected deal with the following:

- Number of products (stock-keeping units [SKUs])
- Amount of inventory of each product
- Volume processed (orders, lines, pallets, cases, units, etc.)
- Cycle times (order processing, returns, and error correction)
- Staffing (management, hourly, and part-timers)

Other data that may not be collected but useful in managing an operation fall into these categories:

- Damage rates
- Storage fill rates
- Warehouse errors

To fully utilize operating data (statistics about the daily operation, such as numbers of orders, quantities stored, hours worked), additional information is needed. This support information concerns the basic factors of the warehouse and explains them in sufficient detail to be used effectively in monitoring and assessment. These factors include the following:

- *Product descriptions as to dimensions, weight, cube, and type of storage required.* Often referred to as the "item master files," these contain pertinent data about the products processed in the warehouse.
- *Processing standards by function.* These usually include information like units per hour, pallets put away per hour, and items picked per carton.
- *Storage fill rates and storage density factors.* This information relates to the number of pieces, units, or pallets that can or should be stored in a particular area. It can also include the height, width, and length of lanes and storage bays. This information can be used to determine the effectiveness of the storage activity.
- *Priority stocking assignments for products.* This can be specific bin numbers, bay areas, or shelf locations. The primary use is for directing put-away and picking activities.
- *Product velocity movement data.* This relates to the quantity of each item that has been shipped during the past 12 months as a percentage of the total volume processed during that period.

Manual Collection of Data

The starting point for data gathering for most warehouses is the number of orders processed, the lines per order, and the quantity of items per order. This basic information is usually available from the data processing department as a by-product of the order processing runs. However, if the information is not available, a daily count of orders received is the initial step in collecting data. Understanding the number of orders received daily, weekly, and monthly is a critical task.

TABLE 28-1
Order Volume Analysis

Period (week #)	Customer Orders	Intercompany Orders
1	1,875	300
2	1,500	150
3	2,250	300
4	2,625	150
5	1,500	150
6	2,250	300
7	2,625	300
8	3,000	150
9	1,875	300
10	2,250	150
11	2,250	150
12	2,625	150
13	3,000	150
Total	29,625	2,700
Avg./week	2,279	208
Avg./day	456	42

The volume processed—both inbound and outbound—and the companion service level requirements are the key to staffing levels, shift scheduling, and the achievement of customer service targets. A manual record can be maintained to establish a base. This record should be maintained until a pattern is established, and then it should be checked periodically.

If no data have been accumulated, some historical data should be available to provide the base for a manual collection. The types of orders, the service requirements for each type, and the volume by category over a period of time should be identified.

Table 28-1 illustrates a format that might be used to portray order volume data.

Table 28-1 shows that the collection of basic data can provide operating tools. For instance, it indicates that volume of customer orders increases during the last two weeks of the month. This is somewhat offset by lower volumes in intracompany shipments. The total impact will depend on the volumes involved in each type of order. The short service requirement for customer orders (same-day processing) places them in a higher processing priority, while the longer service requirement (same-week processing) for intracompany orders allows that category to be used as a filler in workload planning.

The next bits of information that can be identified and used are the number of lines per order and the units per line. Accumulating these data, on the same basis as the number of orders, enables management to determine required staffing levels to meet desired service levels (see Table 28-2). Staffing levels can be estimated by assigning processing volumes per labor hour to each type of order and dividing the volume by the amount processed by each worker in one hour. Historical information is a good basis for calculation. For example, if the volume processed in one labor hour is 75 orders, the number of people required in week 1 for customer orders is 5 per day plus 2 for intercompany orders, as shown in Table 28-2.

TABLE 28-2
Order Volume Analysis and Staffing Requirements

	Customer Orders				Intercompany Orders			
Period (week #)	**Total Orders Per Week**	**Total Lines/ Week**	**Average Lines/Day**	**No. of Staff Required**	**Total Orders/ Week**	**Total Lines/ Week**	**Average Lines/Day**	**No. of Staff Required**
1	1,875	15,000	3,000	5	300	6,000	1,200	2
2	1,500	12,000	2,400	4	150	3,000	600	1
3	2,250	18,000	3,600	6	300	6,000	1,200	2
4	2,625	21,000	4,200	7	150	3,000	600	1
5	1,500	12,000	2,400	4	150	3,000	600	1
6	2,250	18,000	3,600	6	300	6,000	1,200	2
7	2,625	21,000	4,200	7	300	6,000	1,200	2
8	3,000	24,000	4,800	8	150	3,000	600	1
9	1,875	15,000	3,000	5	300	6,000	1,200	2
10	2,250	18,000	3,600	6	150	3,000	600	1
11	2,250	18,000	3,600	6	150	3,000	600	1
12	2,625	21,000	4,200	7	150	3,000	600	1
13	3,000	24,000	4,800	8	150	3,000	600	1
Total	29,625	237,000			2,700	54,000		
Summary:								
Avg. orders/week		2,279				208		
Avg. lines/order		8				20		
Lines/labor hour		75				75		

3,000 lines per day ÷ by 75 lines per hour ÷ 8 hours = 5 employees for customer orders
1,200 lines per day ÷ by 75 lines per hour ÷ 8 hours = 2 employees for intracompany orders

The number of employees required to process orders varies by the volume. When the number required is compared with the number of available employees, the shortfall or excess will become apparent. Table 28-3 illustrates how to do this calculation.

The same type of calculations can be made for other functions in the warehouse, such as receiving and put-away. Support functions like janitorial services can be calculated in a similar manner. When added together, these data can project the level of staffing required to operate a facility and can also monitor tracking and adjust staff levels as volumes change.

Table 28-4 demonstrates how the total employee requirement can be compiled to identify the number of employees needed to process all the functions in the warehouse operation.

Data Collection by Computers

With the proliferation of computers, there is opportunity to take advantage of the wealth of data collected by most computer systems. Whether the system is a package that has been installed and modified or a custom system designed specifically for a company, it undoubtedly contains data that can be useful to warehouse management.

While many systems providing data to the warehouse management team were designed for

TABLE 28-3
Staffing Analysis:
Staff Required to Process Orders

Period	Customer Orders	Intercompany Orders	Total	Staff Available	Difference
Week 1	5	2	7	6	−1
Week 2	4	1	5	6	1
Week 3	6	2	8	6	−2
Week 4	7	1	8	6	−2
Week 5	4	1	5	6	−1
Week 6	6	2	8	6	−2
Week 7	7	2	9	6	−3
Week 8	8	1	9	6	−3
Week 9	5	2	7	6	−1
Week 10	6	1	7	6	−1
Week 11	6	1	7	6	−1
Week 12	7	1	8	6	−2
Week 13	8	1	9	6	−3

other functions, such as accounts receivable or inventory control, they do accumulate useful data for operating the warehouse. Most systems track all transactions and generally categorize data into the groups shown in Table 28-5.

By identifying desired data and extracting them from the system, a warehouse management team can learn a great deal about the operation and modify it considerably to improve performance and quality.

Many computer systems have a built-in report generator module, or an add-on package can be obtained to design and generate reports from data contained in the computer system.

Useful data categories fall into these groupings:

- Customer service levels
- Product availability—fill rates
- Processing times/productivity
- Accuracy

TABLE 28-4
Daily Volume Plan

Activity	Staff Hours Required	Employees Required
Order processing	56	7
Receiving	32	4
Put-Away	16	2
Returns/adjustments	8	1
Total staff		14

TABLE 28-5
Data Useful for Warehouse Management

Data Group	Data Detail
Personnel	Hours, wage rates, etc.
Product	Volumes processed, units, cases, etc.
Storage	Total spaces, filled slots, etc.
Processing	Number of orders, lines, units
Adjustments	Returns, error adjustments, inventory adjustments

By extracting data from computer files in these categories, management can build a base reference to assess performance and monitor changes as they are made.

Analysis and Use of Data

The first and foremost concern of all warehouse operations is to provide high levels of customer service. The specific level and measure of service varies from company to company, but customer service is generally focused on delivering to customers the products they order on time, in good condition, and on a regular basis.

An assessment of the level of customer service is often provided from the noise level (or lack of it) from customers and/or the sales force. However, firms are well advised to develop a systematic approach for gathering information about customer and sales force perceptions of service.

Toward this end, it is a good practice to visit customers and talk to them about the service provided and the problems they experience. If on-site visits are not possible, telephone calls can assist in gathering a great deal of information.

However, it is more important to measure the company's performance and to make adjustments to eliminate errors and to improve service levels. This can be done by measuring key factors in each area of concern. Information collection can be done by telephone survey, personal visits to customers, or a questionnaire with a return envelope mailed to customers.

Questions to be asked of customers and the sales force include some or all of the following:

- Are the service levels satisfactory?
- Do shipments contain the right products and correct quantities?
- Are shipments delivered on time and in good condition?
- Are invoices delivered with the shipment or shortly thereafter?
- What other problems or concerns are associated with the service provided by the company?

Management should be sure to review all customer and sales force complaints and requests and respond as quickly as possible. Much customer confidence can be gained by acknowledging problems and either resolving them rapidly or providing a logical explanation.

Error-Free Performance

An area of high concern is processing quality, that is, the processing of product and orders in a manner that delivers the right product to the right customer, and at the right time.

Product and order processing can be monitored by carefully checking each step and designing reports that provide the incidence of error and the steps required to correct those errors. The intent should be to catch errors before they cause the customer problems. Warehouse procedures should be designed to make it easy for personnel to process product and orders, and to make it difficult to make mistakes.

If the firm does not have basic procedures for ensuring error-free operations, it will be difficult to measure and improve its operations. Where procedures do not exist, they should be prepared as quickly as possible and used to train employees in the best practice for each function. This then becomes the basis for monitoring performance and improving customer service.

In any event, order processing deals with human beings, and humans make mistakes. Computer systems should be in place to identify errors and track corrections. Depending on the program and equipment involved, the company will be able to record a variety of errors and receive summary reports. Listed below are most of the primary activities in the warehouse and the types of error reports needed for each:

Receiving and Put-Away Errors

- Receipt of incorrect product
  –This kind of error can be caught by reading the bar code label of the product and the computer identification of incorrect human data entry.
  –Wrong quantity can be entered, caught, and brought to the attention of warehouse per sonnel.
  –Some errors are caught only by cycle count or at physical inventory time.
- Put-away or replenishment in wrong bin or storage location
  –These errors can be caught at the time of put-away and recording of storage location.
  –After-the-fact reports can be issued and can be identified with warehouse personnel if desired.
  –If batch terminals or radio frequency terminals are used, the system will tell the operator at the time the error is made. The correct placement can be made, and the system will record the occurrence.
  –Often these errors are caught at the picking step when an alert warehouse worker notices the wrong product in the bin.

Order Picking and Replenishment Errors

- Wrong item picked
- Incorrect quantity pulled
- Consolidation of orders in error

Packing and Shipping Errors

- Lack of proper dunnage
- Wrong carton
- No packing list
- Incorrect address

The checking function is an important activity in most companies that do not have computer-assisted processing. In performing the verification, the checker should catch all errors made in picking and packing. However, checker efficiency catches only 90 to 95% of the errors. The remaining errors, which go undetected, leave the warehouse, causing problems for customers.

It is important that the checking function catch as many errors as possible. It is an added task for the checker to record all identified errors. But it is an excellent tool to use in reducing errors, so it should be encouraged. It may be possible to design a simple record sheet to be filled out by the checker that lists the error, the pick list number, and the warehouse worker. The supervisor can then work with the warehouse staff to determine the cause of errors and reduce them through training.

Identification and correction of errors as they occur provide the basis for changing procedures and practices to ensure error-free performance. As errors are detected, they should be brought to the attention of the appropriate warehouse worker, and corrective training should be provided. With proper training and coaching, error-free processing can dramatically increase customer service levels.

Staff Planning

One of the more difficult tasks of the warehouse manager is to maintain the size of warehouse staff to provide a consistent level of customer service. Very few warehouses have a steady volume. Many facilities have wide swings in the number of receipts processed as well as the number and type of orders shipped.

These volume variations may occur within the week or the month and occasionally by the season. Some operations have heavy inbound shipments on Mondays and Tuesdays and are very light for the rest of the week. Order processing may complement that by being heavy in the latter part of the week. But most often, the volume problem is compounded by orders being heavy on Mondays as well.

It is essential that the warehouse management team have a good idea of how the volume fluctuates in order to plan appropriate staffing levels. First, the basic pattern should be established: daily, weekly, or monthly. Then the number of employees can be determined for each level of volume.

When the basic workload has been determined, the permanent staff can be set. Variations in volume below and above the basic level can be dealt with in a variety of ways. Permanent part-time employees are becoming a viable addition to permanent full-time staffs. In addition, trained pools of temporary or casual workers are proving useful in handling widely fluctuating volumes.

The number of employees required to maintain a constant level of customer service can vary considerably. Figure 28-1 illustrates this variation. Inbound volume varies by work period. Outbound volume varies also, but not to the same degree and in different periods. The end result is that the average staffing level rarely meets volume demands.

With this type of data on hand, the warehouse management team can make provisions for additional work to fill in low-volume periods and additional staff for excess-volume periods.

Product Information

Data concerning products and inventory are usually available but often are not used in the daily operation of warehouses. This information is contained in the computer data files under such categories as "item masters" or "product descriptions" and is used by the purchasing, accounting, and inventory planning departments. Access to these files is readily available, and they can provide meaningful information to the warehouse management team.

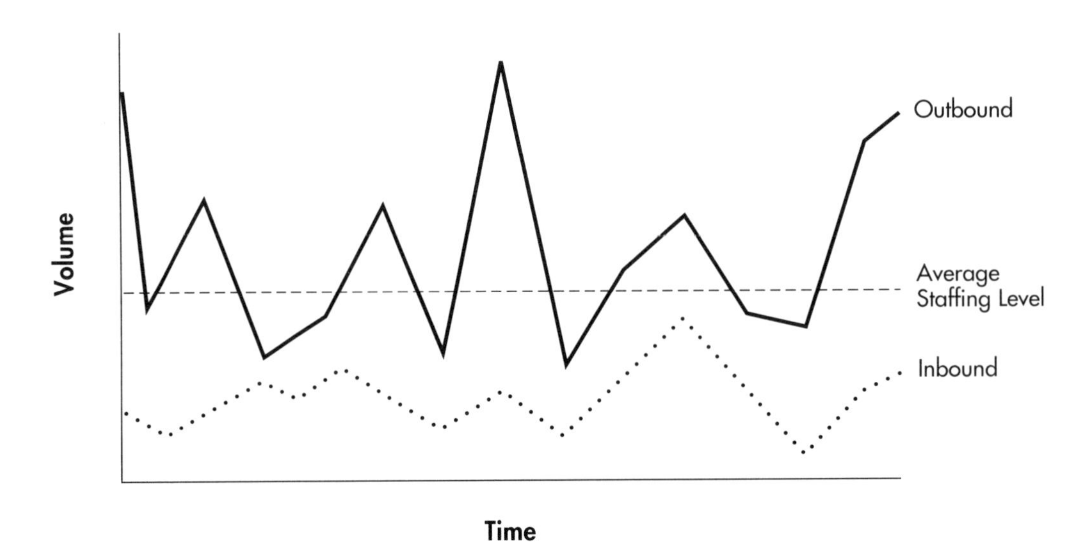

Figure 28-1
Staffing Requirements

When designing or reworking the warehouse layout, it is helpful to know the dimensions of each product. Not only the size of the shipping unit, but the size, weight, and cube of the cartons and pallets is of use as conditions change and the layout is revised. Carton size is used to determine the size of primary picking areas, backup or reserve storage, and staging areas.

Shipping unit, carton and pallet weights will be used to size pallet and flow racks and select fork lift equipment. Cubic dimensions will be of value when storage areas are laid out and truckloads are calculated.

Inventory Information

The amount of money invested in inventory is usually the second-largest expenditure for most companies. The large volumes of inventory on hand and warehouse throughput create an opportunity for each facility to increase service level and reduce costs by more efficient processing.

To achieve these objectives, it is important to understand the inventory stored in each warehouse. The information to do this is usually stored in the company computer and often is already available in a variety of forms. The inventory planning and control department will probably have calculated an "ABC" stratification/categorization analysis to determine the fast and slow movers. The finance or accounting department will have information from the annual physical inventory that indicates turnover rates and volumes of slow-moving or discontinued product.

There are several ways to analyze these data and use them to improve warehouse operations. One effective method used by a number of companies is to prepare a product velocity profile.

The product velocity profile is determined by obtaining data from the most recent 12-month period. This ensures that all seasonal cycles have been covered and that volume variations by product by month are included. The data should be arranged in decreasing order of volume; the fastest-moving items should be first, and the listing should proceed through the slowest movers to the nonmovers.

Table 28-6 shows the format used by some companies to collect and report these basic data.

TABLE 28-6
Product Velocity Profile Data Listing

Product Number	Description	Cumulative Number of SKUs	Cumulative Percent of Total SKUs	Cumulative No. of Units Shipped	Cumulative Percent of Total Shipped
XXXX	Widget 2″	1	0.0	80,600	2.8
XXXX	Widget 10″	10	0.1	503,060	17.7
XXXX	Whatsit 12″	88	1.0	1,298,860	45.7
XXXX	Widget 34″	438	5.0	2,000,870	70.4
XXXX	Whatsit 18″	2,189	25.0	2,628,984	92.5
XXXX	Widget 24″	4,378	50.0	2,799,513	98.5
XXXX	Widget 130″	8,756	100.0	2,842,145	100.0
Totals		8,756		2,842,145	

Note that the fastest movers are listed first. The form provides the volume processed by item during the 12-month study period and calculates the individual unit volume as a percent of the total volume shipped.

In these calculations, the basic shipping unit is probably the best denominator. However, the same basic results can be obtained by using sales dollars, pallets, cartons, cases, or other units common to the business. The intent is to identify the products that are handled the most and the least in normal warehouse operations.

The calculations in Table 28-6 also show the number of SKUs and the cumulative percent of the total number of SKUs.

From this information, a product velocity profile can be calculated and portrayed, as illustrated in Figure 28-2. This chart clearly indicates that a very small number of items provides the largest part of the volume processed. In many companies, the slowest 50% of SKUs accounts for less than 5% of the volume processed.

Table 28-6 shows the data from which this chart is derived. The first-time analysis of these data is often startling to warehouse management. They know that there are fast movers and slow movers, but they do not realize how extreme some of these variations are.

The data in Table 28-6 is from a real company situation and indicates the following:

- One item accounts for 2.8% of the total volume.
- Ten items, or 1/10th of 1% of the total SKUs, account for 17.7% of the volume.
- Eighty-eight items, or 1% of the total SKUs, account for 45.7% of the volume.
- Four hundred thirty-eight items, or 5% of the SKUs, account for 70% of the volume.
- Twenty-five percent of the SKUs account for 92.5% of the volume.
- Fifty percent of the SKUs account for 98.5% of the volume.

This also illustrates the point made earlier, that the slowest 50% of the SKUs account for only a small volume. In this instance, the slowest 50% accounts for 1.5% of the total volume.

Further analysis of the data from the computer files relates to the amount of inventory on hand. Table 28-7 shows the amount of stock on hand for each of the SKU categories by velocity movement. The fastest-moving item has 6% of the inventory on hand, while the slowest-moving 50% of the SKUs have 13.8% of inventory on hand.

The conclusions that can be drawn from this kind of analysis provide information for in-

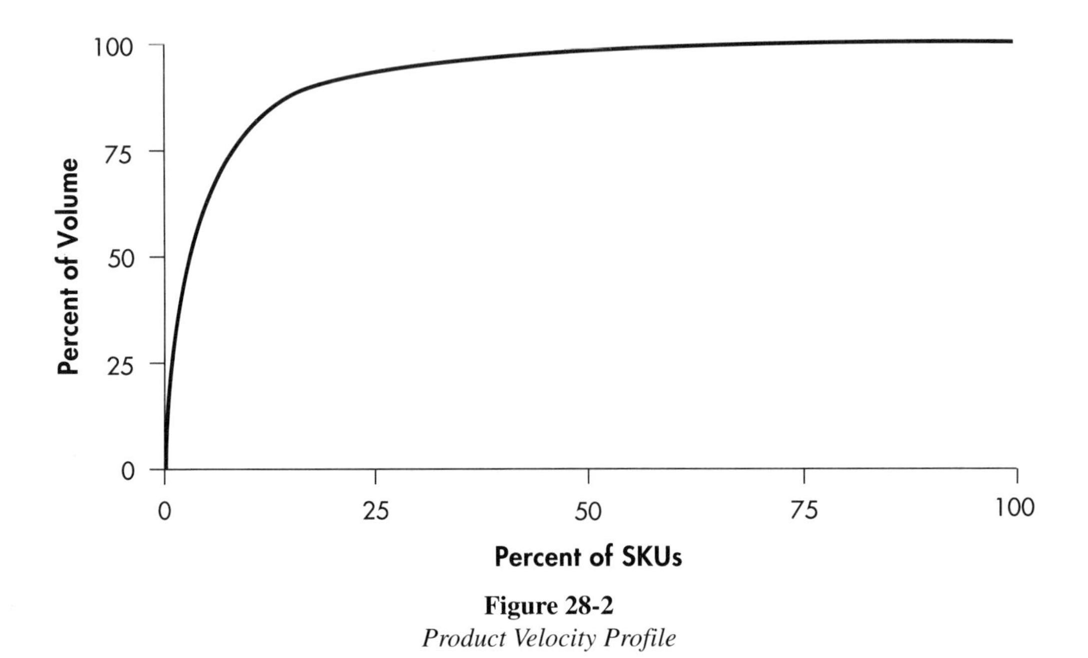

Figure 28-2
Product Velocity Profile

creasing the productivity of the operation. For example, because 25% of the SKUs account for 92.5% of the volume, these items should be stored near the shipping dock to facilitate picking, thus improving the efficiency of that function.

Some of the common applications of a product velocity analysis are shown below:

- Warehouse Layout
  - –Primary picking locations for fast movers should be located in the warehouse so that put-away from receiving and picking for shipment can be done most efficiently.
  - –Primary picking locations for slow movers should be located out of the main flow to avoid conflict with processing of fast and medium movers.
  - –Reserve inventory for fast movers should be located in close proximity to primary picking areas.

TABLE 28-7
Product Velocity Profile Data:
Shipments and Inventory

SKUs			Inventory	
No. of SKUs	Cumulative Percent of Total SKUs	Cumulative Percent of Shipments	Amount ($)	Cumulative Percent of Total Inventory
1	0	2.8	3,262,287	6.0
88	1	45.7	11,581,120	21.3
2,189	25	92.5	37,788,162	69.5
4,378	50	98.5	47,194,424	86.8
8,765	100	100.0	54,371,456	100.0

–Nonmovers and discontinued items should be removed from the warehouse if space is tight or removed to remote areas to minimize interference with processing of items that do move.
–For bulk-stored items, this information can be used to determine the proper number and size of storage slots, keys, or bays.

- Order Processing
  –Picking locations should be coordinated with order processing to provide ease of access to the items that move the fastest.
  –Sequencing of items through the warehouse in logical bin order can increase productivity.
  –Batching of slow movers can reduce travel time through the warehouse.
  –Replenishment scheduling will vary for fast and slow movers.
  –Loading of fast movers can be combined with batch picking of slow movers.
- Space Utilization
  –Different storage methods such as bulk versus rack may apply to movers of different velocities.
  –Removal of slow movers, nonmovers, and discontinued items provides room for other items and functions.
  –Selective stocking of items by movement can be an effective tool in the design of a warehouse distribution network.

Attentiveness to Information

In warehouse operations, there is only one way to constantly improve performance: to collect data concerning the various functions performed and to use that information to adjust to more effective methods.

Constant attention to the flow of material, the productivity of the operators, and especially the satisfaction of customers will enable the warehouse manager to assess overall performance and determine service levels. By doing this on a routine basis, the manager will be able to identify changes as they begin to occur and, if they are detrimental, eliminate them before they become a major problem.

In today's changing environment, with emphasis on cost reduction and customer service in equal degree, it is important that the warehouse management team stay in touch with customer requirements. The sales force provides daily information on the demands they face. Direct contact with customers will confirm new requirements and provide the opportunity to change before the competition does. In this way, the warehouse manager can be an effective member of the total team and assist in increasing business through satisfied customers.

SECTION VII

International Logistics Management

David L. Anderson

Section Editor

It's the new world order. Countries are banding together into regional trading blocs, redefining the concept of global competition, and creating new opportunities to sell products on a worldwide basis. Innovations in transportation and streamlined regulations are accelerating product flows. The Madonna CD released this Friday in Los Angeles is available by next Friday in Tokyo, Moscow, and Cairo.

The message is becoming clear—we are on the verge of a global trade revolution. Are we truly on the way to developing a global economy, or will international logistics managers see "more of the same" (e.g., nontariff barriers, inefficient modal hands-offs, complex paperwork) in the 1990s? No longer may companies focus entirely on their home markets or in selected worldwide markets. Global competitors, using scale production economies, superior logistics, and detailed, real-time consumer preference data, will negate brand and location advantages. Survival will depend increasingly on the flexibility and responsiveness of a company's products and global logistics network. Will your company be a global winner in the 1990s? The role of logistics is crucial, if not paramount, to its success.

The two chapters in this section explore how changing patterns of global trade will alter logistics management over the coming decade. Today's international logistics experts must acquire significantly broader skills than their predecessors. In Chapter 30, by Dennis Colard and David L. Anderson, and in Chapter 31, by William W. Goldsborough and David L. Anderson, the authors provide readers with a keen understanding of rapidly changing market opportunities, because their companies' products must be integrated with the ability to get to worldwide consumers cheaply and rapidly. Second, instead of overcoming customs/regulatory obstacles on a transaction-by-transaction basis, the manager must have mechanisms in place to assure "no problem" border passage for a variety of products, shipment sizes, and movement timing. Finally, international logistics managers must know "where their products are" on a continuous basis and be able to alter product configuration or destination at a moment's notice to meet changing consumer demands.

The reader is also directed to a recent, in-depth study, *Reconfiguring European Logistics Systems* (Council of Logistics Management, Oak Brook, IL., 1993) that uses case studies to determine how companies are adapting to the changing political and economic environments in Europe.

CHAPTER 29

The International Logistics Environment

David L. Anderson
Dennis Colard

The 1990s will be remembered as the decade of the global competitor. By the year 2000, companies will spend over $2 trillion moving goods across the globe.[1] With product life cycles declining and with growing pressure to increase sales and profits, companies are seeking new, worldwide markets on an unprecedented scale. In an effort to hold off competitors, leading-edge producers are in effect shrinking the globe through just-in-time manufacturing and quick-response delivery systems to satisfy emerging consumer needs.

Several innovative business strategies are driving global logistics:

- *Rapid product introduction:* bringing new products to market in record time across numerous regions
- *Focused market needs:* customized design, packaging, and service offerings to meet varying consumer requirements
- *Quick-response delivery:* distributing sufficient product quantities to meet consumer demand as it occurs
- *Expanded services:* linking innovative, value-added services (like product kitting or 24-hour customer hotlines) to product offerings
- *Innovative channels:* using minimal-echelon, store (or consumer)-direct delivery systems to reach customers rapidly at lower cost

World-class logistics strategies are necessary to support these ambitious global marketing and sales initiatives. Moving a wide variety of products around the globe—24 hours a day, 365 days a year—requires operations very different from those that serve national markets alone. In particular, close partnerships with carriers, tightly linked information systems, flexible service and response capabilities, and customer-driven operations are hallmarks of truly successful global competitors.

In addition, global competitors must be sensitive to wide differences in culture, regulations, and business customs to avoid costly—and even market-threatening—mistakes. The rapid shift to simplifying international commerce among trading blocs and nations not only creates an opportunity for greater global competition but also adds significant complexity because of fast-changing regulations. Success today is defined across many dimensions and attributes—not only "fastest and least-cost" distribution but also innovative, proactive logistics that can respond effectively to both customers and competitors.

Our view of the international logistics environment begins with a detailed examination of how economic, business, and logistics conditions are changing within the three major global trading regions—Europe, the Far East, and North and South America.

Major global economic and governmental changes will drive business and logistics strategy revisions in the 1990s. The European Community's progress toward a single market and other European nations' trade agreements, coupled with the breakdown of the Soviet Union into independent nations, will create the world's largest market by the end of the decade. In the Far East, growing consumer demand from Australia to China, as well as a shift in manufacturing operations toward less-developed areas, will result in long supply chains and other logistics challenges for businesses. The North American free trade agreements (among the United States, Canada, and Mexico), as well as the growing movement to create a unified South American market, will result in a third bloc of countries with freer mutual trade but possibly greater barriers to outsiders.

Next, we examine five global success stories—companies that have developed sophisticated and innovative approaches to meeting customer service needs in diverse markets around the world. The worldwide business and logistics strategies of Benetton, Canon, Xerox, Sony, and Hewlett-Packard are described in detail.

Finally, key success strategies for designing and implementing global logistics systems in the 1990s are discussed and illustrated with additional case studies.

Europe: Creating the World's Largest Market

Two important developments make Europe today a large and important market—the drive for a unified market, and the fall of communism in the East bloc. The movement toward a united Europe began soon after World War II with the creation of the European Coal and Steel Community in 1951. In the past 30 years, despite overwhelming complexities, much progress has been made in removing the protectionist barriers that prevented individual countries—and Europe as a whole—from competing more effectively in international business.

Europe 1992

The European market is immense and growing. Although member countries of the European Community number only 12 at this writing (Belgium, Denmark, France, Germany, Greece, Ireland, Italy, Luxembourg, the Netherlands, Portugal, Spain, and the United Kingdom), that figure could grow to 25 and include 450 million people, with over $7 trillion in spending power, by the year 2000. Such a market would dwarf that of the United States and Japan in terms of people, capital, resources, and territory.

Europe in the 1990s consists of the European Community (EC), those subscribing to the European Free Trade Agreement (EFTA: Austria, Finland, Iceland, Norway, Liechtenstein, Sweden, and Switzerland), the associated members of the European Community, and the countries of central and eastern Europe.

At this historical crossroads, those who do business in Europe will face new challenges, risks, and opportunities, especially in the planning and management of logistics operations.

Central and Eastern Europe

Dominated for over 30 years following World War II by the Soviet Union, central and eastern Europe promise to be an important new growth market. Major corporations already do significant business in both EFTA and EC countries. (For instance, Volkswagen recently acquired the Czechoslovak automaker Skoda and plans to upgrade its facilities and product quality to develop it into a major European brand.) Removing the final barriers will likely improve the efficiency of these operations. Central Europe will also offer new markets and rich potential for new businesses. Central and, to a lesser degree, eastern Europe consume minuscule amounts of Western goods today. By combining the markets of EFTA, the European Community, and central Europe, all three entities may enjoy greater growth.

Many large U.S. and Japanese firms consider central Europe one of the world's most promising growth markets in the 1990s. (For instance, apparel manufacturer Levi Strauss & Company recently announced plans to develop an integrated, stand-alone vendor-to-customer manufacturing, distribution, and retail delivery system for Poland.) Some analysts project a rate of growth for the area close to that of West Germany after World War II, or about 8% per annum. Other observers expect even faster growth, contending that the seven core central European countries will see a 170% rise in gross domestic product over the next 15 years.

Countering this optimism is the fear that a severe tightening of credit will reduce companies' abilities to expand. In addition, widespread food and consumer goods shortages in the former Soviet Union may force millions of refugees westward to seek relief from already weakened governments and economies in this region. Either scenario would dramatically impact Germany, the largest and wealthiest member of the EC. The EC has already felt the effects of a downturn resulting from higher taxes and tighter credit policy brought on by Germany's need to finance reunification with the former East Germany.

The Centre for Economic Policy Research estimates that central Europe will need $200 billion per year for the next ten years in the form of Western loans to bring their economies up to par. Offsetting this massive need is the possibility that tax surpluses in the faster-growing central and eastern European economies may be available to help finance the recovery.

Much of central Europe's success will depend on the export of products to the EC and EFTA. Before 1990, central Europe's exports to the EC represented only 2% of the community's imports. In 1990, the EC granted liberalized trade packages and lowered duties on shoes, television sets, and chemicals, while removing quotas from many manufactured goods.

The abortive coup in the USSR, having stirred fears of economic instability, drove the EC to develop an accelerated plan for free trade. In ten years, all products traded between central Europe and the EC will be without tariffs, duties, or quotas. The limits on steel were dropped in 1992; tariffs on these products are scheduled to end in 1995. Restraints on textiles will end in 1997. On farm produce, the EC will drop tariffs 60% in three years, and quotas 50% in five years. Central Europe, which is already the lowest-cost producer of agricultural goods for eastern Europe, will likely compete effectively against EC farmers (who, outside of the Japanese, are the highest-subsidized and least-efficient in the world). Farm products, which are central Europe's chief exports, should see a significant boost. So, too, should the logistical systems that must be implemented to meet the demands of this growing market.

Member Countries of the New Europe

The European Community (EC). The EC consists of a 12-member community comprising Belgium, Britain, Denmark, France, Germany, Greece, Ireland, Italy, Luxembourg, the Netherlands, Portugal, and Spain, with a combined population of 325 million consumers.

The European Free Trade Agreement (EFTA). Countries belonging to EFTA include Austria, Finland, Iceland, Norway, Liechtenstein, Sweden, and Switzerland—32 million of the world's most affluent consumers. Currently, these member countries do almost 60% of their trading with the EC. A recently concluded agreement with the EC calls for elimination of trade barriers between EFTA and EC members beginning in 1993. EFTA members (like EC members) have no tariff barriers among themselves. Austria and Sweden have petitioned the EC for full membership, and their applications are pending. Both expect to be admitted by 1995.

Countries Seeking Status as Associate EC Members. The Czech Republic, Hungary, and Poland have all agreed to open their markets to the EC over a ten-year period, beginning in 1993. All have expressed a strong desire to join the community after they open their markets. The EC is publicly discussing a plan to admit these countries around the year 2000.

Countries Having Trade Agreements with the EC. Albania, Bulgaria, Romania, and Yugoslavia have signed trading agreements with the EC bloc. While they hope for eventual induction into the EC, analysts suggest it may be decades before that occurs. In January 1992, Bulgaria and Romania began talks regarding the end of all trade barriers with the EC.

The EC Governing Bodies

The European Parliament, which meets in either Luxembourg or Strasbourg, France, originally consisted of 198 representatives nominated by the parliaments of the member states. In 1979 a system of direct election by the voters of the member countries was adopted; the number of representatives was also increased, reaching 518 with the accession of Spain and Portugal in 1986. The parliament is a general deliberative body and supervises the executive organs. It has the power to dismiss the commission on a motion of censure approved by a two-thirds majority. Reforms enacted in 1985 allow the parliament and the commission jointly to overrule the Council of Ministers.

The Court of Justice, with one judge from each member country, adjudicates disputes arising out of the application of the treaties and community legislation. It is also located in Luxembourg. The European Council is composed of the heads of government of the member states. It meets for informal discussion three times a year.

The mere adoption of a proposal by the commission, or its implementation by one or more EC states, does not necessarily make it a law for all EC members. For non-Europeans and even for many Europeans, the evolution of an EC proposal from a "directive" into a law applicable to all member countries may be difficult to comprehend. Although progress toward the full political and economic integration of Europe (the single market) has been dramatic, it would have been unrealistic to expect that the "new Europe" would be completely free of internal frontiers as of January 1, 1993. Integration is a process, not an event.

European Trade Practices: Barriers and Constraints

One study estimates that the removal of trade barriers throughout Europe will lead to a rise in economic output ranging from 2.5 to 6.5%; another analysis concludes that this figure could be five times greater. In any event, the projected growth will have a major impact on demands for logistics services and infrastructure.[2]

Although such growth projections imply a future Europe that could dominate international trade, the reality of doing business in Europe today still involves many restrictions and constraints that particularly impact the work of logistics managers.

Logistics Challenges in a Changing European Marketplace

In addition to rapid changes in the macroeconomic relationships within Europe and between European countries and their trading partners around the world, the emergence of new logistics management concepts and advanced technology—especially in the fields of information and communications—will greatly influence the way individual companies manage and control their supply chain operations through the end of this century.

Opportunities for Greater Efficiency and Asset Utilization. EC-wide standards for products will alleviate the need for local manufacturing and storage, previously necessary to satisfy nationally specified quality and design restrictions. Movement of products among member states is improving but will not be completely free until detailed voluntary product standards have been developed by the European standards institutions, a process expected to take several more years. Removal or easing of local content and production restrictions will also improve the ability of manufacturers to centralize production and stockholding. Opportunities for international sourcing will also increase. Progress is already evident in such well-known companies as Gillette, whose operations are described in detail in the final section of this chapter.

Both the removal of local content and production restrictions and EC-wide product standards will facilitate the development of pan-European products in industries where such strategies are viable. A product design sold throughout Europe, with possible variations only in packaging and labeling, is well suited for application of *postponement strategies.* In a typical postponement strategy the final manufacturing steps (configuration to local preference, labeling, packaging, etc.) are postponed until product is needed to fill a customer order. Product is then finished to order and delivered. Postponement strategies improve asset utilization by allowing a company to hold products of a single design in a central point, delaying the final assembly to meet individual customers' specifications until the last possible moment.

In the longer term, the implementation of economic and monetary union will improve companies' abilities to link pan-European or regional manufacturing and warehousing operations with local sales operations by removing the burden of managing order processing systems with a myriad of local currencies and fluctuating exchange rates.

Pan-European versus Nationally Based Logistics Strategies. Many observers agree that the hope for a more smoothly integrated EC economy is unlikely to be realized without the implementation of more streamlined distribution and transportation links. The efficient movement of raw materials and finished goods across national borders obviously requires more than mere easing of trade restrictions.

Almost every company expecting to operate profitably in the EC must consider nothing less than complete "Europeanization" of its business strategy and supply chain operations. At the same time, however, many individual firms would benefit greatly from an improved, nationally based strategy rather than a totally new Europe-wide marketing/distribution strategy grafted onto its existing business. The deciding factor appears to be not the theory behind an economically unified Europe but the actual needs and wishes of European customers—in other words, *customer-driven logistics.*

Achieving competitive advantage requires companies to deliver the right products and customer service cost-effectively. In Europe, this means achieving the benefits of large-scale operations while focusing on the unique service needs of each class of customers, whether local, regional, national, or international. One example of a company succeeding at customer-driven logistics is consumer products manufacturer Unilever, which has taken advantage of the increasingly unified European market by standardizing, for example, soap product formulations and packaging to reduce manufacturing and marketing complexity of its product lines.

The European marketplace is changing today and will continue to change rapidly during the remainder of the 1990s. Change will affect different companies and industries in different ways. For example, some transport companies will expand to satisfy manufacturing customers' needs for Europe-wide distribution. Some manufacturers, however, may find their customers remaining regionally or nationally based, buying a mix of national and European brands.

An objective assessment of the market and of customer trends is essential for understanding the customer service target and providing a sound base on which to develop and implement a company's European strategy. Revamped manufacturing and distribution structures can produce substantial efficiencies that improve customer service and reduce costs. Many companies in Europe, however, are hampered by their history of national orientation. Often, national manufacturing units produce a full product range, delivered through complex national warehousing and delivery systems. This is an inefficient way of serving a unified European market.

Implementing revamped management structures, systems, and supply chain operations will depend on a mix of political skills, information technology expertise, and logistics and marketing know-how. It will require an understanding of the delicate balance among powerful competing forces—nationally oriented management structures versus international corporate efficiencies, and local and regional logistics decision making versus systemwide economies of scale. It is likely that only those companies successfully managing these complex trade-offs will survive and prosper in the new Europe.

Far East: New Markets and New Exporters

The Far East region is one of the largest and fastest-growing regions in the world. Although Japan remains the dominant economic power in the Far East, boasting a 1991 GNP of $3.4 trillion, several countries formerly known as the "Tiger" countries—Hong Kong, Singapore, South Korea, and Taiwan—have experienced the highest growth rates in the region. The combined GNP for the Tigers totaled $486 billion in 1991. South Korea is the largest of these, with a 1991 GNP totaling $273 billion, compared with $175 billion for Taiwan. As indicated in Figure 29-1, Hong Kong grew the most in 1991.

Several other countries are also experiencing rapid growth in the Far East region, including Malaysia, Thailand, the Philippines, Indonesia, and China.

While these existing and emerging economies represent the fastest-growing countries in the Far East, Japan's slightly lower 1991 GNP growth rate of 4.5% continues to outpace the growth

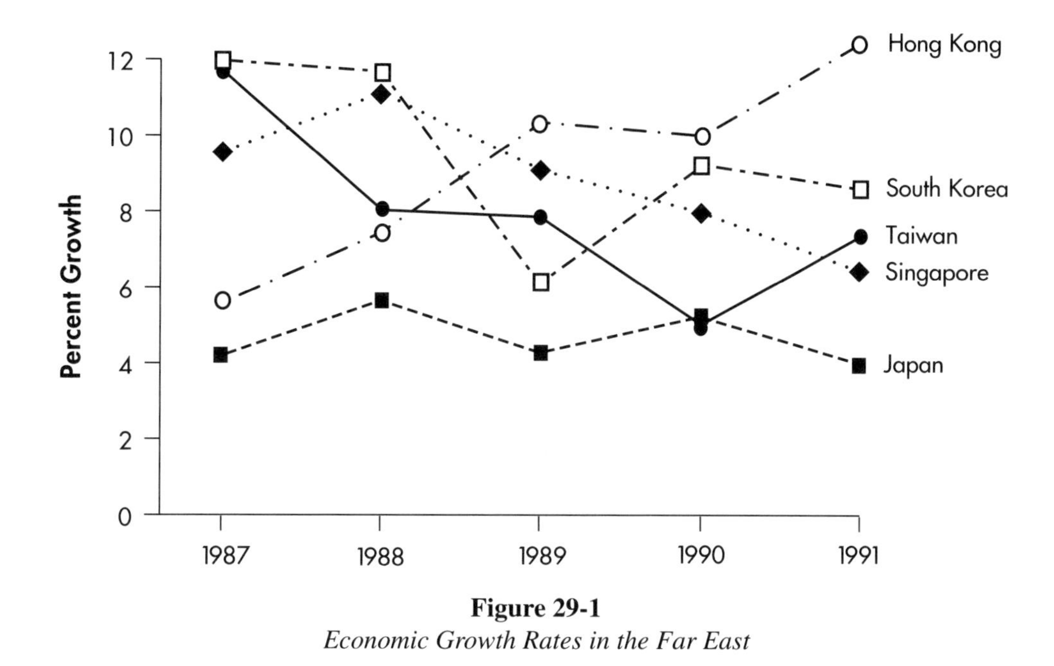

Figure 29-1
Economic Growth Rates in the Far East

of U.S. and European markets, which grew at approximately 1% and 4%, respectively. Japan ranks third in population compared with Europe and the United States, but Japanese consumers have more disposable income per capita than those in the U.S.

Competing in Japan

Many foreign companies have long done business in Japan because they know this affluent market offers significant opportunity for growth in revenues and profits. For example, in 1989 IBM employed 26,000 people and earned $9.2 billion in revenues in Japan. That same year, the Japanese operations of American Express produced $800 million in sales.

Outsiders can best compete against the Japanese corporation (*kaisha*) by operating inside the country. However, successfully penetrating the Japanese market requires not only high-quality products but also excellent service to customers. It also calls for patience and flexibility in dealing with various trade barriers and logistics complexities.

Examples of companies that have learned how to adapt and compete in the Japanese market include Hewlett-Packard, IBM, BMW, and Xerox. The operations of two companies—Coca-Cola and McDonald's—are described below.

Coca-Cola Japan: "Overnight Success in 30 Years"

A Long History of Innovation. The brown soda eventually known as Coca-Cola was created in 1886 by Georgia pharmacist Dr. John S. Pemberton. In the century that followed, it became the leading soft drink in the world, with over 419 million servings consumed daily in over 160 countries. By the early 1900s, the drink had already been introduced to Japan. Coca-Cola is even mentioned in poet Kotaro Takamura's *Dotei* (A Journey, 1914). However, in those early years, the drink was an expensive imported delicacy.

Even after World War II, when a Coca-Cola bottling plant was set up in Japan, the supply was limited to the allied occupation forces. Not until 1957, with the formation of Nippon Inryo Kogyo, the predecessor of Coca-Cola Japan, did the drink become available to the Japanese general public. In 1958, Nippon Inryo Kogyo changed its name to Coca-Cola (Japan) Co., Ltd., and two years later it began producing the Coca-Cola concentrate. Only three years later, the company had established Coca-Cola bottlers in 17 regions nationwide and was marketing the product nationwide.

A Modern Success Story. Some 30 years after its inception, Coca-Cola Japan's annual income reached the level of 40.5 billion yen (1988), ranking 99th in sales among all Japanese companies. (Among foreign-affiliated firms in Japan, the company is first by a wide margin.) Coca-Cola products enjoy a 35% market share for all soft drinks in Japan, and a staggering 60% market share among carbonated drinks. In 1972, Coca-Cola Japan became the first foreign-affiliated firm to join the Federation of Economic Organizations; the next year, it joined the Japan Federation of Employers Association—two actions that indicated the company's effort to be identified as a "Japanese" company.

High-quality Products. A cola drink is a simple product, but that simplicity requires stringent quality control to ensure product consistency among all bottlers. Exacting quality standards must also be followed by bottle and can manufacturers. Coca-Cola's Japanese bottling equipment and systems are among the fastest and most efficient in the world. Coca-Cola's growth has also spurred the development of the Japanese vending machine industry.

Aggressive Marketing and Distribution. Coca-Cola's unique production and marketing system was also completely new in Japan. It is founded on strong partnerships among Coca-Cola Japan, the 17 bottlers, and over 600 suppliers nationwide. The bottlers are responsible for procuring all equipment and materials other than the cola concentrate, and for the production and sales of the products. Coca-Cola Japan, besides supplying the concentrate, gives the bottlers technical advice, marketing assistance, and help in developing new sales channels. The 600 plus suppliers provide raw materials, vending machines, coolers, and route trucks.

The 17 bottlers distribute product in their own regions through the route sales method. The shareholders of the bottling companies include leading Japanese corporations like Mitsui and Co. Ltd., Mitsubishi Corp., and Kirin Brewery Co. Ltd. The direct route sales method, which requires that bottlers develop their own sales bases, was so different from the traditional wholesale-oriented Japanese distribution system that it was initially resisted by retailers whose wholesalers disliked being bypassed. Cash sales, another Coca-Cola policy, were also rare in Japan at the time. However, Coca-Cola Japan management opted not to "Japanize" its operations. With the immense worldwide resources of Coca-Cola to rely on, the bottlers' front-line salespeople gradually succeeded in securing sales bases. Each Coca-Cola salesperson plays multiple roles—driving delivery trucks, developing new customers, marketing products, retrieving bottles, and collecting payments.

Solid Market Position. No other firm has introduced a completely new drink to the Japanese public with such success. Its secret is summed up in these words from a company spokesperson: "The quality of the product, aggressive sales, and the fact that the Japanese corporations in partnership with the bottlers were all first-rate companies are all key factors. There is really no shortcut to success in the Japanese market. What our management always stresses is a combination of cultural understanding and patience. It took us 30 years to get to where we are today."

McDonald's Co. (Japan): Adapting a Global Product to the Local Market

The Power in a "Household Word." When the first McDonald's opened in the Soviet Union in January 1990, Muscovites formed a waiting line one kilometer long, bearing witness to *perestroika* and newly unleashed consumer power. Including the Moscow store, the McDonald's Corporation has more than 11,000 restaurants in 53 countries, with 1989 sales of $17.3 billion. The U.S. chain dominates its industry worldwide.

Selling Big Macs in Japan. Next in sales to the U.S. operations is McDonald's Co. (Japan) Ltd. McDonald's Japan was established in May 1971 as a fifty-fifty joint venture by McDonald's Corporation and Fujita Shoten. McDonald's worldwide business policy—"local management over local stores"—was also adopted in Japan. The parnership, beginning with only five stores, grew by 1982 to 347 outlets with annual sales of 70.3 billion yen. McDonald's Japan soon dominated the "food away from home" industry. By 1989, the company had increased its chain stores to 706, with annual sales of 162.7 billion yen.

Catering to Japanese Preferences. The first McDonald's in Japan was a shop on the first floor of Ginza Mitsukoshi, a leading department store—a location very different from the popular drive-in's in the United States. McDonald's executives concluded that Japan at that point had not reached the automobile age so evident in the United States: "According to our research, most customers just drop in a hamburger shop as they happen to pass by. To attract a large number, a good location is essential." The Ginza McDonald's attracted young people seeking the latest fashions. And in fact, such consumers living outside Tokyo came to Ginza just to eat at McDonald's.

In 1977, the first drive-in McDonald's in Japan appeared; today, two thirds of the new branch shops follow that design. Before the advent of McDonald's Co. Japan, there was no concept of "fast food." There were almost no restaurants as clean as McDonald's, nor did there exist a chain serving staple meals at reasonable prices. "We are very proud of the fact that we developed a new restaurant concept that Japan never had before," says the company spokesperson. The new style is now widely accepted by many Japanese, no doubt because of the firm's dedication to qualities demanded by such consumers—"Good Quality, Service, and Cleanliness."

Wherever in the world one travels, Big Macs have a consistent taste. (In fact, the product is so universal that the British journal *Economist* compares general consumer prices around the world using the Big Mac Index.) However, McDonald's amazing success in Japan with a thoroughly American product sold in an American style would have probably been impossible without the company's efforts to meet the unique demands of that market.

Logistics Challenges in Japan

Japan's distribution system is complicated for various reasons. Probably the most important is that multiple layers of large, powerful wholesalers virtually dictate product choices and delivery methods for an immense network of small retailers. Additionally, the highly restrictive Large-Scale Retail Store Law (LSRL), which permits existing small neighborhood retailers to block the establishment of competing "hyperstores," has effectively prevented any company, Japanese or foreign, from using such distribution channels.

In 1988, Japan had more than 436,000 wholesale distributors, compared with 376,000 in the United States. On a per capita basis, Japanese wholesalers outnumber their foreign counterparts by a factor of two. An even more telling statistic is the total of 1.6 million retailers (3.7 for every wholesaler), most of which are small "mom and pop" stores. This multitiered distribution system not only results in higher logistics costs per sales unit but its complexity also hinders the introduction of foreign products to Japanese consumers.

Barriers to Entering the Japanese Market

Many tariffs and quotas limit the import of goods to Japan. As of 1988, Japan had a total of 18 such barriers, including 17 for agricultural products and 1 for minerals. Except for France, with a total of 46 trade barriers, Japan has more than twice as many as any other industrialized country.

Perhaps the biggest obstacle to foreign competition in Japan is the large number of nontariff barriers. Examples include requirements for retesting drugs already approved by U.S. Federal Drug Administration, individually inspecting every component of foreign-manufactured motor vehicles, complex safety rules, and weight regulations on U.S. plywood. The Large-Scale Retail Store Law, mentioned previously, is another example of a powerful, nontariff trade restriction.

At the same time, however, the Japanese protect their own manufacturers by allowing generous tax rebates and accelerated depreciation rules for domestic industries.

In an effort to avoid trade wars with countries whose own industries increasingly protest what they regard as the Asian giant's unfair import restrictions, Japan is beginning to lower some trade barriers. Japanese consumers' demand for low-cost American products has also spurred this move. Since 1981, several major policy changes have been enacted to improve Japanese market opportunities for foreign countries.

Included in these changes were amendments to the Japanese Large-Scale Retail Store Law, which limited to 18 months the adjustment period during which new large stores must buy out small stores around them; required disclosure of deliberations on adjustments along with establishment of stores; allowed unrestricted establishment or addition of up to 100 square meters of floor space for imported goods; and waived notification of store closings before 7 P.M. and waived notification of store holidays of 44 days or more.

It has been recognized that one factor maintaining high prices for imported goods is the exclusive right to sale held by many importing agents. To lower this barrier, amendments are also being considered to the Anti-Monopoly Law. However, because Japan already has antitrust laws that it chooses not to enforce, it is reasonable to assume that changes in the antimonopoly law will also remain unenforced.

Opportunities for New Markets and Exports

Japan is currently America's second-largest export market and has recently been purchasing more American products. In 1990, U.S. exports to Japan totaled $264 billion. Future growth can be expected in such categories as agriculture, tobacco products, iron and steel, automobiles, wine and liquor, high-tech semiconductors, telecommunications, and retailing.

The Japanese marketplace has already been successfully penetrated by a few U.S. companies, including Toys "R" Us and Virgin Records in the retailing industry, and Motorola, Hewlett-Packard, and Intel in certain high-technology business and consumer product segments.

Growing Japanese Awareness of Logistics

In a 1991 survey of the current logistics situation in Japan conducted for the Society of Logistics Engineers in Tokyo, 120 respondents reported increasing interest in the role of logistics in maintaining their companies' global competitiveness.

The top three expected benefits from improved logistics management were (1) reduction in life cycle costs, (2) better control over distribution channels, and (3) competitive advantage over other companies. Improved customer service and higher profits—key goals for most U.S. logistics managers—were ranked fifth and sixth out of the 12 benefits evaluated.

Respondents also expressed concern that physical distribution costs were too high (73% of respondents); 54% believed that more computerization was necessary for logistics operations; 48% sought more efficient transportation options; and 42% of those surveyed believed that logistics staff should be better trained. Nearly 50% of the respondents indicated that their logistics operations were insufficient to meet emerging global marketing and competitive challenges in the 1990s.

Logistics Options: Third-Party versus Owned

Any company interested in entering the Japanese market must choose whether to rely on its own distribution approach or to work with third-party Japanese service providers. The four most common approaches are joint ventures, distribution agreements, licensing, and subsidiaries.

Joint Ventures. Joint ventures offer the advantage of low start-up cost and good opportunity for initial success, but they incur the risk of eventual failure because of dependence on potentially unreliable Japanese distributors or partners. Such arrangements generally offer a useful means of quickly gaining market exposure, good relations with customers, and "Japanese" identity for a company.

Examples of successful joint ventures include a piggyback approach used between Coca-Cola and Blue Diamond Almonds, Federal Express and a small Japanese trucking company, Merck and Ranyu Pharmaceuticals, Sun Microsystems and Toshiba, Fuji-Xerox and Fujitsu, and Texas Instruments and Hitachi.

The Ajinomoto/General Foods joint venture is worth describing in some detail. This agreement leveraged Anjinomoto's prestige and recognition among Japanese consumers to penetrate the market successfully.

General Foods, then the world's largest manufacturer of consumer food products, established a wholly owned subsidiary in Japan in 1954. In 1973 it merged in Japan with the Ajinomoto Co., Inc., and since then has done business as Ajinomoto General Foods, Incorporated (AGF). It manufactures and sells instant and roasted coffee as its core products. The instant coffee brands Maxim and Blendy are firmly entrenched in the Japanese market, holding a 20% to 30% market share.

At the beginning, General Foods experienced problems stemming to some degree from its American-style emphasis on quarterly and annual results. It was not until the company joined Ajinomoto and became AGF that sales expanded significantly. In Japan, the Ajinomoto brand had achieved much greater penetration with the consumer than did the General Foods name. By piggybacking on the Anjinomoto name and by using Ajinomoto sales and distribution channels, General Foods sales dramatically increased throughout Japan.

With Ajinomoto's investment participation, management reflected a successful blend of American and Japanese styles. For example, until the merger, the American top-down approach to corporate decision making was dominant. This was later replaced by the bottom-up, consensus-seeking approach (*ringi*) favored by Japanese management. Although it is dramatically slower than that favored in the United States, it offers the significant benefit of smooth teamwork and mutual goals based on the principle that every manager should participate in defining the company's mission.

Moreover, even though the venture is a corporation with foreign affiliation, the employees are all Japanese. In the premerger days, almost all the executives, from the company president on down, were Americans. Because almost none of them spoke Japanese, it was difficult to promote the mutual understanding essential for successful penetration into Japanese distribution channels. In addition, the Japanese believe it is mere common sense to include a special salary allowance for employees with families—an idea that is regarded as discriminatory by American and European managers. The joint venture did not, however, scrap all American management approaches. For example, it retained the U.S. company's emphasis on market testing of new products and respected the value of those tests to better sales planning.

In general, AGF's success appears to have been based on a wise blend of Japanese and American decision-making styles. Its dominant position in the retail coffee market also owes much to its emphasis on product quality in a country where consumers demand nothing less than the best products that fit their unique preferences. Maxim, for example, is sold in both Japan and the United States, but its flavor is subtly different in the two countries. When an official from General Foods U.S. headquarters visited Japan and praised the local Maxim, as "the most delicious coffee in the world," the Japanese regarded this not as mere flattery but as a high compliment.

The Japanese are also particular about safety, packaging, labeling, and after-sales service. If a consumer complains about inferior merchandise, AGF has a special office to deal with such problems.

Shoji Matsura, an associate manager, joined the company in 1965, when it was still wholly owned by General Foods. As a person who has experienced both pre- and postmerger organizations, he notes that "the Japanese market and Japanese management are by no means perfect, but if you are going to do business in Japan, I would like you to learn at least the Japanese way of doing things first. Problems will not be solved just by debating difference in cultures and systems."

Instant coffees directly imported from the United States are now being sold in Japanese grocery stores. Although inexpensive and enjoying favorable sales, these new rivals may face future challenges. "For the Japanese consumer," says Matsura, "price alone will not give a product currency. After all, product quality, safety, and after-sales service must be properly taken care of. Even if these competing products have good sales now, they won't continue for long unless they can meet these criteria."

Distribution Agreements. Distribution agreements are another option for companies planning to enter the Japanese market. Two types of trading companies are used to establish such agreements—the *sogo sosha,* a large, general trading company, and the *semmon shosha,* a specialty trading company.

This arrangement offers the advantages of immediate market access, minimal start-up costs, a name known to consumers, and solid cash flow. Its drawbacks include unfamiliarity with the importer's products, a relatively small number of channels and partnerships, limited direct contact with customers, need for special attention, difficulty in obtaining market feedback, and limited technical support.

Licensing Agreements. Licensing agreements are viewed as the least risky and most effective method for quickly entering the Japanese market. While they offer excellent immediate cash flow and future residual revenues, they may also allow competitors to exploit the foreign company's technology with impunity. And because they create no local presence for research and development, marketing, or manufacturing, they cannot establish a strong or long-lasting identity.

Rather than establishing a full presence in Japan, RCA entered a licensing agreement several years ago and now receives $50 million a year for color television technology. However, the Japanese quickly improved upon RCA's technology and soon became a world leader in the color TV market.

Subsidiaries. A subsidiary organization is a do-it-yourself approach that offers direct exposure to the Japanese market. Setting up a subsidiary may require a company to make significant investments in its own distribution network to deal with trading, shipping, and logistics. Although many companies can benefit from using other strategies, only a direct subsidiary can offer solid, long-term market presence and revenues.

A subsidiary offers the advantages of close customer relationships, market responsiveness, a clear assessment of future needs and opportunities, and a unified strategy for serving customers. It also allows a foreign company to leverage economies of scale through corporate globalization, and to aim for world-class status. Most important, it gains significant cost advantages (estimated at 45% in Japan) through elimination of multiple layers of traders, wholesalers, and other middlemen. Its disadvantages include high start-up costs, significant time for building customer relationships, labor hiring challenges, and the lack of off-load capability in down cycles.

Benetton, Toys 'R' Us, and Virgin Records are examples of companies that have successfully penetrated the Japanese market through their own subsidiary networks.

The Americas: Integrating the Free Trade Agreements

U.S./Canada Free Trade Agreement

This agreement, effective January 1, 1989, established a new trading relationship between Canada and the United States that focused on phasing out tariffs by 1998, lifting import quotas, harmonizing technical standards, and opening borders for investment. Its eight separate chapters deal with (1) customs duty, (2) rules of origin, (3) certificates of origin, (4) national treatment of goods, (5) technical standards, (6) government procurement, (7) temporary entry for business persons, and (8) investment.

The consensus of those favoring the agreement is that it will allow the building of plants on either side of the Canada-U.S. border to realize maximum efficiencies. They also believe that benefits will accrue from the availability of single-source manufacturing facilities. Understandably, the proponents also look favorably on the opening up of a total U.S.-Canada market of 275 million people, most of whom share a common language and cultural heritage.

Opponents of the agreement fear it will lead to Canada's loss of a distinct identity and to plant closings and layoffs. In general, they believe that only the largest corporations will benefit from this new trading relationship.

It is clear that domestic Canadian issues impact the true effect of the Free Trade Agreement (FTA). Canada's higher taxes, government monetary policies, and higher interest rates are key factors. In addition, Canadian workers are generally perceived as high-cost compared with the U.S. workforce. The separatist movement in Quebec may also influence the agreement, especially as it calls for bilingual (French and English) consumer product labels, user manuals, and other communications.

In transportation, which is not subject to rules of the FTA, important factors are Canada's relatively high fuel costs, trade barriers among Canadian provinces, and the lack of a national transportation policy.

Although the agreement does not specifically address transportation issues, it seems apparent that it will have an impact on them. Among effects already evident are the shift from east-west to north-south movement of goods, the continued acquisition of Canadian International Operating Permits by U.S. carriers, consolidated manufacturing and transportation organizations, ongoing cabotage controversies, and integration with Canadian efforts at reregulating the transportation industry.

At the beginning of 1988, Canada reregulated the industry with the passage of the National Transportation Act. While it allowed volume rebates, confidential contracts, and negotiations over price and service, it eliminated entry restrictions, truck tariff bureaus, and rail collective rate-making actions. It also provided captive shipper relief.

Today, transportation strategies are evolving and driving change in the marketplace. Air Canada, for example, extends its reach into the United States through its trucking operations. Motor carrier triangulation networks, package coordination by shippers, and the prearrival review system (PARS) are all reducing costs and improving service for shippers and carriers.

U.S./Mexico Free Trade Agreement

Many events over the last 30 years have played a role in the initiation of free trade negotiations between the United States and Mexico. The establishment of Maquiladora legislation and facilities in the 1960s allowed U.S. companies to use Mexican facilities and labor in a zone 26 kilometers wide on the Mexican side of the border with the United States. It established duty only on value-added activities and reduced manufacturing and assembly costs for U.S. manufacturers.

From 1982 to 1990, employment of Mexican workers by U.S. companies climbed from 120,000 to 450,000. The number of U.S.-owned plants established in Mexico during that period rose from around 500 to almost 2,000. In value-added manufacturing/assembly activities, there was a similar dramatic increase, from less than $1 billion in 1982 to around $4 billion in 1990.

Throughout the 1980s, several important developments inhibited the growth of economic relations and cooperation between these two North American neighbors, including the collapse of Mexican oil prices, increased burden for debt service, depreciation of the peso, rising inflation, the flight of capital out of Mexico, and large public-sector expenditures.

In 1986, Mexico joined the General Agreement on Tariffs and Trade (GATT). This resulted in the removal of protectionist layers in the Mexican economy, the elimination of license requirements on most imports, and the removal of quotas on most products. It also led to the reduction of tariffs below GATT maximums, the initiation of private ownership of state-owned companies, and the welcoming of foreign investment. During this period, the countries holding the largest share of investment in Mexican facilities included the United States (63%), United Kingdom (6.7%), West Germany (6.3%), and Japan (5.1%).

From 1982 to 1990, under the leadership of two presidents—Carlos Salinas de Gortari and Miguel de la Madrid—the Mexican economy became more progressive. The budget deficit was reversed, many government industries were privatized, and import license costs were reduced. Mexico also reduced maximum tariffs, opened its economy to more foreign ownership, and made dramatic improvements in its overall economic health.

In June 1991, the U.S. Congress approved negotiations for a free trade agreement. The final agreement was approved by Congress in 1993. The key issue in Mexico impacting complete approval of the agreement is low wages (in 1989, the average hourly wage and benefits amounted to $1.63 for a Mexican worker, compared with $14.32 for the U.S. counterpart). Other concerns are severe environmental pollution, a decaying highway and bridge infrastructure, and severe transportation inadequacies. U.S. opponents of such an agreement include, as one might expect, organized labor, environmentalists, U.S. steel producers, and American textile manufacturers.

Transportation is excluded from the free trade agreement negotiations. The Mexican constitution, in fact, protects this industry and has closed the 26-kilometer commercial border zone to all U.S. carriers. The United States, at the same time, has refused to grant operating authority to Mexican carriers for a ten-year period. Thus, shippers sending goods in either direction across the border must use relatively inefficient and costly interlining operations. Mexican trucking companies are still adjusting to the Mexican deregulation of the transportation industry implemented in 1989.

Today, transportation strategies are evolving, and much change can be expected throughout the 1990s. Among key developments that have already happened is a partnership between the U.S. carrier Southern Pacific Railroad and the National Railways of Mexico. Union Pacific Railroad has also sold advanced transportation software to this Mexican carrier, and other companies have explored joint ventures, including the Roadway Bodegas y Consolidación, C.H. Robinson, and J.B. Hunt/Hunt de Mexico.

North American Trilateral Free Trade Agreement

Commerce among all three North American countries will be influenced by the movement toward a trilateral free trade agreement. In 1990, the combined population of the three countries was 362 million; combined gross national product, $6.1 trillion; and total trade, $225 billion, divided as follows—U.S./Canada, $171 billion; U.S./Mexico, $52 billion; and Canada/Mexico, $2.3 billion.

The economic statistics showing the greatest contrast among the three trading partners are those concerned with average hourly wage and gross national product, as shown in Table 29-1.

The first step toward a trilateral agreement was taken in early 1991, when Canada joined the United States and Mexico for negotiations. In the middle of that year, the three countries opened formal talks in Toronto, Canada, and later met in Zacatecas, Mexico, to negotiate details of the agreement.

The general goal was to establish a North American Free Trade Agreement to phase out all economic barriers among the three partners within ten years of enactment.

U.S./Canada/Mexico Transportation Concerns

A survey conducted in August 1991 probed transportation issues important to both shippers and carriers. Respondents included logistics executives representing 258 shippers (247 from the United States and 11 from Canada), and 28 carriers (27 from the United States and 1 from Canada).

TABLE 29-1
Comparison of North American Economic Data

	United States	**Canada**	**Mexico**
Population (millions)	250	26	86
GNP ($US)	$5.5 trillion	$463 billion	$225 billion
Average hourly wage ($US)	$14.31	$14.72	$2.32

In answer to the question of whether free trade is in the "best interests" of the three North American trading partners, the overwhelming majority of respondents agreed. However, only about 30% indicated that they "fully understand" the free trade agreement with Canada and free trade negotiations with Mexico.

Almost 30% of shippers surveyed indicated that their companies or divisions have already implemented single-source manufacturing in one of the three countries to sole-source supply North America. Another 22% indicated that their companies were "considering" such a move. While only 5% of shippers surveyed noted that their companies had closed manufacturing facilities as a result of free trade, 33% indicated that their companies "could close" manufacturing facilities in the future. A growing interest in the impact of free trade agreements was evident in the fact that 33% of these shippers' firms have formed a task force to research free trade developments. When asked whether their companies had Maquiladora operations in Mexico, 17% replied yes. Of those operating private fleets, only 5% had such operations in Mexico, compared with 53% in the United States and 18% in Canada.

In response to a request for rating the progressiveness of U.S.-based transportation modes at implementing change and introducing service for free trade and intercountry transportation, the shippers gave their highest approval to air freight providers (51% of the shippers described these carriers as "effective" or "very effective"). Motor carriers received a similar rating, but lower ratings were given to rail (only 20% of the shippers described it as "effective" or "very effective") and ocean modes (26% rated waterborne transportation in the top two categories).

Among the key concerns voiced by carriers surveyed in the study was the inadequate infrastructure of roads and bridges in Canada and Mexico, which was seen as a major obstacle to rapid development of free trade. This group also expressed ongoing worries over what it perceived as costly delays caused by complex and inconsistent government regulations, particularly in vehicle standards, driver hours, operating permits, and taxes.

An Emerging Latin American Common Market: The Mercosur

The four nations of Argentina, Brazil, Paraguay, and Uruguay—representing a combined market of 190 million people, with $427 billion total gross regional product and Latin America's biggest industrial base—have formed the Mercosur, a new and potentially significant international trading bloc. While the region's external trade has traditionally focused on Europe and the United States, its intrabloc trade has already risen rapidly (between 1987 and 1991, it increased from $2.2 billion to $4.9 billion). Under a treaty signed in Asunción, Paraguay, in March 1991, the four nations agreed to cut duties every six months, aiming to eliminate all tariff barriers by the end of 1994.

Already, several major multinational companies have begun to take advantage of the new free trade conditions presented by the Mercosur. Eastman Kodak is building a new distribution center near São Paulo, Brazil, from which it plans to distribute internationally sourced products to customers in the region. In 1992, the Ford-Volkswagen Autolatina joint venture opened a $230 million factory in Cordoba, Argentina, to supply transmissions for cars built by its plants in the region. Monsanto has formed a joint venture with Argentina's PASA Petroquímica to manufacture plastics in both companies' plants.

Although it is too early to predict the full impact of this new development in free trade, the Mercosur—combined with the U.S. government's Enterprise Initiative for the Americas—clearly points toward a vast new continental trade area that can play an important role in the changing global economy, especially in the Western Hemisphere. The logistics impacts of such developments will certainly be significant.

Case Study: U.S.-Mexican Operations

To understand both the risks and opportunities of North American free trade developments, it is useful to focus on the logistics operations of a company already doing business in all three countries.

One such firm is a large U.S. manufacturer of garage door openers. Until the 1980s, the company's manufacturing operations were entirely based in the United States. Today, its plants are only in Mexico and Canada. It supplies U.S. customers exclusively from Mexico, and supplies European customers from its Canadian facilities.

Among the difficulties experienced by this manufacturer in establishing Mexico-based operations have been shipping delays at the U.S.-Mexico border, recruiting and retaining qualified hourly and salaried workers, language differences, quality assurance, lengthened supply lines, and devaluation of the Mexican peso.

The company has attempted to solve these problems by developing a three-pronged strategy to take advantage of the move toward free trade:

- Increasing the local content of its products
- Implementing a vertical manufacturing integration program
- Instituting a transportation consolidation program

Increasing Local Content of Products. The growth of industries in the Maquiladora corridor, the development of new companies in the interior of Mexico, and the overall turnaround of the Mexican economy have vastly improved the quality of components and finished goods manufacturing in Mexico. This manufacturer, like others, is increasing the local content—in both components and raw materials—of products assembled in its Maquiladora operation.

Increasing local content offers major benefits in reducing manufacturing lead times. Compared with previous operations in which raw materials were purchased in Asia or the United States, manufacturers can lower their lead times from weeks to days. Increasing local content also supports the establishment of JIT operations, which can dramatically improve a firm's competitive advantage.

Vertical Manufacturing Integration Program. Vertical manufacturing concepts are being developed to gain more control over the entire manufacturing process, as well as lower the total cost of producing goods. This manufacturer has moved backward into the manufacturing process to self-produce wiring harnesses, chains, transmitters, and other components of its garage door products. As a result, all major components can now be produced in the same facility at considerably lower net cost.

Transportation Consolidation Program. The garage door manufacturer has also implemented a transportation consolidation program to ease delays at the Mexico-U.S. border. In addition to decreasing transit times, it has also significantly reduced less-than-truckload (LTL) transportation costs.

In the past, inbound vendor shipments of components and raw materials from the United States were shipped directly via a large number of LTL carriers. Delays at the border were compounded by the need to interline shipments from U.S. to Mexican carriers. Today, LTL consolidation points are established at the company's Arizona, Arkansas, and Illinois finished products distribution centers. Vendors are instructed to ship via LTL to one of these consolidation points, and truckload carriers are then hired to move full loads across the Mexican border directly into the Maquiladora plant.

Logistics Success Stories

Leading-edge global companies are using varied but integrated business and logistics strategies to manufacture and sell products in the increasingly liberalized world markets.

The following case studies of Benetton, Canon, Xerox, Sony, and Hewlett-Packard present a cross section of successful strategies for entering foreign markets. Clearly, while companies evaluating entry into such markets must develop a unique set of business and logistics strategies, they can gain valuable insights from the examples of those international business pioneers that began their initiatives before the era of more liberalized trade. In general, the companies profiled here have developed highly refined operations that capitalize on deregulation to expand their overseas presence and profits.

Benetton: Europe to the United States and Japan

A History of Innovation and Rapid Growth. At its founding in 1964, Benetton was a small family enterprise in Treviso, Italy. It focused on producing woolen sweaters by hand from proprietary designs. Four years later, the company pioneered a technique for softening wool without shrinking it—an innovative methodology that put Benetton ten years ahead of others in its industry. In 1970 the company sold its first retail franchise, and nine years later it acquired obsolete hosiery machines and converted them into unique wool-knitting machines, thus increasing the equipment's value 100 times. These machines were later replaced with the first computerized controlled knitting machines in the industry. By 1975, Benetton had 200 stores across Italy, both company-owned and franchised.

Its first export sales—$1.5 million on total sales of $78 million—occurred in 1975. By 1982, aggressive expansion throughout Europe boosted its sales to $311 million. By early 1983 Benetton had 32 stores operating in the United States. In 1985, the company expanded to Japan with its first outlet. (Today, 33% of its 6,100 stores are located there.) In 1986, Benetton opened its first eastern European store. Five years later, the company opened its first store in the former Soviet Union, bringing to 82 the number of countries in which the company has a presence. Sales that year reached the 2 trillion lire mark.

Potent Blend of Aggressive Merchandising and High Technology. Benetton Group S.p.A.'s growth into a $1.2 billion multinational corporation is due in part to its successful use of information systems and communications technology. The company's information systems effort is controlled at its central headquarters in Ponzano Veneto, Italy. A team of 100 works with an annual budget of $12.8 million to control key operations like its international EDI network. The network is at the core of Benetton's ordering cycle, which is initiated by agents who use the network to bridge the gap between the Benetton Group's need for information and its franchisees' desire for autonomy. The network facilitates worldwide information exchange between the Italy-based company and its retail outlets.

A Model of World-Class Logistics. Benetton owes much of its success to its early and effective commitment to the principles and practices of world-class logistics. The sportswear manufacturer distributes 50 million pieces of clothing worldwide through a highly efficient quick-response linkage among manufacturing, warehousing, sales, and the retailers it serves.

When, for example, a popular style of winter-weight slacks is about to sell out early in the fall, a Benetton retailer reorders the product through direct links with Benetton's mainframe computer in Italy. The order is downloaded to an automated machine that makes the slacks in the necessary range of sizes and colors. Workers pack the order in a barcoded carton addressed to the retail store, and then send the box to Benetton's single warehouse—an automated $30 million facility shipping 230,000 pieces of clothing a day to over 6,000 stores in more than 80 countries. Including manufacturing time, Benetton can ship a new order in only four weeks. It also benefits from its policy of requiring firm orders for all goods before they are produced; the company does not accept returned goods from its retailers.

As a world leader in the retailing industry, Benetton represents the vanguard of what some observers call "supply chain management"—a level of operational performance that will increasingly become the norm rather than the exception.

Canon: Japan to the United States and Europe

Long-Range Planning for Market Dominance. Today a well-known manufacturer of copiers, laser printers, calculators, and scores of other consumer and business electronic products, Canon dominates its markets worldwide. Beginning in 1937, this powerful Japanese company has successfully pursued a strategy that emphasizes long-term planning, major investment in research and development, and aggressive marketing and pricing.

Between 1968 and 1983, Canon introduced 22 separate models of products in an effort to flood the market and gain market share. Today, Canon and Xerox—the only two manufacturers whose products span the entire spectrum of electronic office and consumer lines—are locked in a market share battle in every segment throughout the world. Canon is also a joint venture partner with Apple Computer in Japan, and expects this relationship to yield valuable knowledge that will help Canon eventually produce its own brand of computers.

From Imitator to Innovator. To achieve this success, Canon has used reverse engineering—a method of imitating and producing competitors' products at low cost, and then aggressively marketing similar products at below-market prices.

However, to evolve from a company that imitates others' designs to one that creates original products, Canon has invested heavily in research and development, and has made substantial investments in advertising to establish a strong market presence. Maintaining a single-minded focus on market share, often at the expense of short-term profits, Canon sees its strategy in terms of 15- to 20-year development efforts.

Logistics Secondary to R&D and Marketing. As a result of its focus on high-quality products at the lowest possible price, Canon's customers have been willing to tolerate its average materials management and logistics performance. Canon compensates for its distribution systems by creating and marketing products that are in such high demand for their quality and innovation that millions of customers are willing to forgive slower deliveries. The firm prefers to use the least expensive logistics network alternatives, often not the most effective in providing customer-driven service. Its logistics information systems are fragmented—only a few of Canon's plants worldwide use any barcoding systems, and each manufacturing, marketing, and R&D facility operates with a separate system. None of them can easily access the central system at Canon's corporate headquarters.

In the United States, Canon uses one LTL hauler and one truckload hauler for delivery to dealers and direct accounts. In each sales region, Canon uses one large central warehouse for all the goods it manufactures. For the United States and Canada, all Canon products are shipped to a single warehouse in the Los Angeles area. Goods produced by different divisions are all shipped here and distributed from these central sites. All European Canon goods are shipped to Amsterdam. The system is identical worldwide for Canon. Thus, Canon believes it has an economy of scale that few other firms can match.

Canon uses some local suppliers for products built outside Japan. In its California plant, 30% of the product is locally sourced; in Virginia, that figure drops to below 20%. In the German plant, local sourcing rises to 40% of the products manufactured. In many cases, suppliers are members of the Fuyo *keiretsu,* the powerful Japanese trading cartel to which Canon belongs. Canon prefers to work with *keiretsu* members first, then other Japanese firms, and then local firms.

Canon relies on Japanese information systems for virtually all operations abroad. Furthermore, the firm believes that its computer and network systems should all be developed internally. This attitude probably stems from the firm's belief in its research and development strengths. Thus, the company uses Japanese software systems developed primarily in-house for all materials management, inventory, sales forecasting, transportation, and logistical services. These systems are not, however, networked into a single integrated design.

Unlike Benetton, which has viewed exceptional supply chain management as a key to its manufacturing and retailing success, Canon epitomizes a firm that to date has maintained its rapid growth through relentless competition in the arena of price and quality.

Xerox: United States to Europe

Until the 1970s, Xerox represented one of the biggest success stories in the modern era of U.S. business. As a pioneer in the development and marketing of dry-process document copiers, the company reached the $1 billion sales revenue mark faster than any previous company in history. It went on to become a leader in many other high-technology business products as well.

New Competition. As its initial patents began to expire in the early 1970s, Xerox saw its competitors quickly joining the battle for customers in the lucrative photocopier market. In 1973, the company was found in violation of U.S. and U.K. antitrust regulations. As a result, it was forced to divest 49% of its interest in its European firm, Rank Xerox, and to license its patents and technologies to competitors. The company also suffered other blows over the next few years—between 1971 and 1983, Xerox's share of the copier market fell from 96% to an estimated 35%. In Europe, it was forced to split the market with Japanese competitors, notably Canon.

In response to these pressures, throughout the 1980s Xerox trimmed its workforce, implemented new quality-control programs, increased research and development spending to meet challenges from Asian and European competitors, and diversified by acquiring financial services companies. In the logistics arena, it began to institute integrated decision support systems and to develop more efficient standardized procedures for inventory management and field service logistics. The firm placed considerable faith in benchmarking, a structured approach to managing change through competitive research, managerial consensus, and interdisciplinary teamwork. It also introduced its Global Account Strategy, a program aimed at allowing its representatives to speak with a single voice to customers throughout the world. By 1991, these and other major improvement efforts began to yield significant rebounds in market share and financial performance.

Embracing Its Own Technology. The company's increasingly successful response to a rapidly changing global marketplace owes much to its innovative use of information systems. As a provider of high-technology products to customers, Xerox has generally learned how to avoid the shoemaker's children syndrome, which leads some companies to excel in the marketplace yet fail internally. Nowhere is this more evident than in its development and implementation of advanced logistics operations and systems, especially in its U.S. and European markets.

European Logistics. In Europe, Xerox meets its customers' needs for new products, supplies, and maintenance through a central distribution center in Venray, Holland. (Interestingly, the company's sophisticated logistics modeling analysis has located the theoretically best site for its European logistics operations only 20 miles from this existing facility.) Including older machines, Xerox estimates it must maintain a 100,000-item catalog to meet customer support requirements. The company uses air transport for priority shipments. To meet the needs of Europe 1992, Xerox has entered into long-term strategic alliances with surface carriers that transport copiers and replacement parts. These contracts include provisions for a common tracking system for inventory management. As of this writing, Xerox estimates that 80% of all repairs and parts deliveries can be performed within one day, 98% by the second day, and 100% by the third day. The company's goal is to improve its performance to 98% within one day.

Its European logistics systems are seen as a model for those in the United States and, eventually, in all its markets around the globe. The company aims to establish a new manufacturing plant near its Venray distribution center. Its benchmarking approach focuses on qualitative measurements of logistics and overall corporate performance, including responsiveness to customers, profitability, and return on assets. Plans call for establishing a build-to-order/direct delivery system for manufacturing and transportation, and linking this electronically with Xerox management, suppliers, shippers, and customers. Currently, the company estimates that its progress toward this goal has reduced its inventory as a percent of revenue from 25% to 14%.

As a large and complex multinational firm, Xerox has shown the value of combining integrated logistics, advanced information technology, and customer-responsive management to prosper in a fast-changing global marketplace. The company appears well positioned to meet the challenges of Europe 1992 and beyond.

Sony: Japan to United States and Europe, and United States to Asia

Producer of some of the world's best-known and most respected brands in consumer electronics products, Sony began as the Tokyo Telecommunications Engineering Company (TTK) in a burned-out department store in post–World War II Japan. From these humble origins it has grown into a $26 billion (1991 world revenues) global giant, dominating many of the markets it serves. Such innovative devices as the pocket transistor radio, the battery-powered TV, the Walkman portable cassette tape player, the Betamax videocassette recorder, the Trinitron TV, the video camcorder, compact disc player, and digital-audio cassette tape recorder—though not in all cases actually pioneered by Sony—were first made widely available as high-quality products by this innovative company.

Today, the company continues to be a leader in the consumer electronics field as it capitalizes on (and sometimes even creates) a demand for increasingly user-friendly, portable products like the Data Discman, the Palmtop electronic notebook, and compact disc–based games and reference tools.

A Unique Management Style. Unlike many Japanese and foreign rivals that stress a follow-the-leader approach in product design and marketing, Sony believes in encouraging innovation, creativity, and originality. Sony cofounder Masaru Ibuka describes Sony's success in these terms: "We must concentrate on clear-headed, original ways to turn ideas into products."

To achieve this aim, Sony has always encouraged engineers and other employees at all levels to contribute new ideas. The slavish adherence to consensus-based management that sometimes slows the introduction of innovative products at other Japanese and foreign firms is anathema at Sony. As Sony chairman Akio Morita puts it, "Our basic concept has always been to challenge the customary way of doing things. We encourage our staff constantly to look for new convenience, new methods, or new benefits in existing or not yet invented products for our customers. It is impossible to succeed at this approach unless people are given freedom to make mistakes and explore new ways of doing things."

In this respect, Sony's style is considerably more Western than that of most Asian competitors. For instance, while its guarantee of lifetime employment and its compensation policies resemble those of other Japanese firms, it encourages employees to make the best use of good ideas wherever they can be found, whether in Japan or elsewhere. Staff are given the freedom and responsibility to move among different jobs within the company. Sony thus minimizes the "not invented here" syndrome, which is the bane of many rigidly structured companies.

Emphasis on Research & Development, Training, and Marketing. Sony's initial successes have come from its innovative product base, but such innovation would have been impossible without significant spending on R&D, product promotion, excellent logistics, and after-sales service. The firm's R&D costs have averaged 6% of sales for the past 25 years, and it also invests heavily in training its sales and service staff. Another factor in Sony's success is the cross-training of employees and the high level of education it provides for every employee. Perhaps most significant in Sony's historically high return has been its reinvestment of profits. Short-term gains and high dividends have little place in the company's investment philosophy. Instead, it requires its workers to own a larger share of the company than do most competitors, and it rewards them for productivity and creativity, not just production output.

Captive Logistics Operations. Early in the firm's history, Sony relied on the distribution capabilities of other established firms for exports. As its foreign sales grew, however, the company realized it would need to develop its own sales, marketing, and distribution capabilities in each region around the world so that its service to customers matched the quality of its innovative products.

Sony had to train its own logistics staff and build its own systems. The firm believes that this emphasis on the internal role of sales and distribution, coupled with its policy of cross-training employees, has allowed it to prosper. When all staff—especially product engineers—are given sales and distribution roles, they gain a firsthand appreciation of customers' actual needs and preferences. When they return to their roles of product designers, they thus have a much better grasp of what it takes to move a new idea from the design stage to the manufacture and distribution of a commercially successful product.

Sony has developed full-service captive logistics operations in the United States, Japan, and Singapore. In the United States, Sony's Logistics Services Company (LSC) functions as an in-house third-party contractor that charges individual divisions on the basis of actual services used. Its database (which includes calculations for import services, throughput, storage, freight, and export services) gives product marketing and sales groups accurate, timely information on logistics costs. The LSC also provides analytical support to help users reduce costs, and to justify its ongoing existence to corporate management.

This has become increasingly important because of the growing complexity of Sony's supply chain. Although the firm once focused on distributing products imported into the United States from Sony's Asian production facilities, today that simple one-way trade pattern no longer dominates. Certain difficult-to-ship products like large-screen projection TV sets, which quickly cube out a container, are now being made locally.

As do Honda and other Asian companies, Sony also ships U.S.-made products back to Asian customers. The result is a truly globalized logistics operation that calls for sophisticated management of critical cost/service trade-offs. To achieve that objective, LSC provides sales staff with charts that show at a glance what it costs to move a product from node to node. It has also developed an interface with the U.S. Customs Service's Automated Commercial System and a new import-export management system. Like "real" third-party contractors, it surveys customers to identify improvement opportunities. The LSC has also taken a proactive role in developing environmentally friendly logistics operations by focusing on returnable pallets, reduced energy consumption, and recyclable packaging materials (see Chapters 30 and 41).

In short, Sony's LSC tries to bring the same professionalism to its operations that one would expect of any competent third-party provider that must compete aggressively on the basis of consistently strong performance (see Chapters 24 and 40).

Hewlett-Packard: United States to Europe and Japan

As a multinational company, Hewlett-Packard (H-P) designs, manufactures, and markets computers, computer peripherals, analytical instruments, test and measurement instruments, medical instruments, and components for other manufacturers. The company receives over half its revenues from outside the United States.

H-P has prospered in part by consistently adhering to its founders' goal of autonomous entrepreneurial management centered around product lines. Since its founding in 1937, H-P has tried to avoid monolithic bureaucratic structures that impede innovation and decision making. H-P pursues this objective by emphasizing rapid, creative response to customers' needs.

Long-Range Planning, Economy of Scale, and Technological Leadership. H-P sets objectives and evaluates performance over longer time periods than many of its competitors. The company consistently puts long-term customer satisfaction and loyalty ahead of quarterly profits. It also uses its experience and scale as a barrier to competitors. In calculators and minicomputers, for example, H-P's large scale and diversification allow cost sharing and savings that many smaller rivals cannot match. Despite its size and international scope, however, the company has tried to retain the flexibility needed to exploit technological advances that often elude large, bureaucratic companies.

Despite efforts to avoid bureaucratic complexity, H-P's rapid growth forced it to restructure in 1990. It returned to the small-team approach it had used successfully in building its RISC computers and LaserJet printers. The firm reduced its workforce, streamlined management, and reorganized its worldwide sales force into separate groups, each of which answers directly to the product group it represents.

Key Role of Logistics in a Service-Oriented Company. Given the priority it places on rapid, innovative responses to customer needs, H-P naturally emphasizes excellent logistics performance. Five years ago the company established an enterprisewide initiative to shorten the time-to-market cycle. The company implemented programs to tightly link R&D and manufacturing and has been successful in significantly reducing the "concept-to-delivery" time. H-P's logistics organizations have played a key role in this program.

One of H-P's strategic initiatives for the 1990s is to improve the effectiveness and efficiency of the order fulfillment process. Delivering and installing products and solutions to meet or exceed customers' expectations is the priority, but objectives have also been set to dramatically reduce the cost of taking and processing the order and transporting the products to the customer. H-P expects to achieve its ambitious goal—a tenfold reduction in order and delivery defects—by the end of 1997, and the company's logistics professionals are once again in the mainstream.

Global Logistics Success Strategies

Global competitors in the 1990s must integrate business and logistics strategies to satisfy consumer needs and meet competitive threats at the same time. (See Section 2.) Many different logistics strategies can be used to ensure sustainable competitive advantage, as seen in the preceding company profiles. Despite the wide variety of approaches to moving product and information worldwide, four common characteristics define successful global logistics strategies:

Customer-Driven Logistics. Many logistics systems are often least-common-denominator operations, striving to achieve an industry average rather than seeking to meet specific customer needs or provide world-class service. Successful global corporations constantly research changing customer service needs in key markets and adapt their operations to meet them. For example, manufacturers of the Japanese luxury cars Lexus and Infiniti focus on providing same-day repairs for 99% of all customers by centrally managing parts stocking and replenishment policies at their dealerships.

Integrated Logistics Management. Most logistics operations are still managed on a functional basis, with "product handoffs" among manufacturing, distribution, and the customer often resulting in backfield fumbles or dropped passes. World-class companies have evolved to manage a set of customer-driven "processes" (ordering, product shipment, post-sale administration, etc.) to ensure satisfaction across the entire range of customer/company interactions. For example, Dell Computer has highly trained engineers as initial order takers, helping customers design the right personal computer for their needs. Units are custom-assembled and shipped within one or two days directly to the customer. A 24-hour hotline is also run by trained engineers to provide after-sale assistance, ensuring ongoing customer satisfaction.

Responsive Distribution Channels. Many companies still operate multiechelon, time-consuming methods of delivering product to consumers. Often, product must flow through a maze of manufacturer, distributor, and retailer warehouses before finding its way to the retail store. Besides extending the time it takes the product to reach the consumer, excessive "fingerprinting" (moving the product from dock to shelf to dock in each warehouse) adds substantial costs to the final delivered price. Innovative global companies are seeking to eliminate unnecessary middlemen and additional in-channel storage and handling costs on product moves. For example, Wal-Mart, a leading U.S. mass merchant, is encouraging manufacturers to go "retail-direct" to its stores, eliminating plant and distributor warehousing and replenishing shelves on a just-in-time basis for many common, "everyday low price" products.

Logistics Outsourcing. Most North American companies practice do-it-yourself logistics. Because our marketplace is one of the largest in the world (and was relatively safe from foreign competitors until the 1970s), this strategy once worked well. Corporations knew how best to move product around the United States, and regulations kept carriers and warehousing companies from offering broad logistics management services. However, the globalization of the 1980s has shattered two myths—that we can continue to develop our own logistics systems, and that third parties cannot provide full-service logistics management on a global basis. For example, Benetton, the highly successful Italian specialty apparel manufacturer and retailer highlighted earlier in this chapter, supplies products to 6,000 stores in 80 countries via a third-party logistics partnership with Avandero Shipping, which included advanced in-channel product tracking and shipment redirection capabilities.

Recent research has confirmed that companies providing high levels of customer satisfaction have higher sales and profitability than competitors. For example, a recent article in the *Harvard Business Review* (September 1990) indicated a high correlation between customer satisfaction and customer loyalty, with increasing loyalty having a dramatic positive impact on profits. Research among major North American companies has shown that a 5% improvement in customer satisfaction yields profit increases of 25% to 85%. Given such results, it is understandable that global corporations are investing in innovative logistics and customer service operations to guarantee customer satisfaction.

Logistics Outsourcing

Many believe that outsourcing international logistics operations makes the most sense for companies entering new global markets in the 1990s. Setting up complex delivery systems in countries where management has little knowledge of local customs or regulations incurs not only high costs but also significant business risks. For that reason, many corporations are turning to third-party providers for their global logistics management.

What form will the successful third-party outsourcing venture take in the 1990s? Third-party providers will manage global purchasing and product delivery channels, providing full-service shipment management among divisions, countries, and channel partners. Inbound materials management will be handled by the third party via releases from suppliers using existing open-to-buy contracts. Material delivery to plants will include customs clearance, quota management, and trade finances, including duty drawback arrangements. Duty drawbacks allow exporters to reclaim a portion of duties paid on imported raw materials used in the manufacture of products being exported (see Chapter 30). Third parties will also assist in channel development across global markets, including the selection and control of distributors, direct delivery services, and related options. Finally, third parties will maintain account delivery and service profiles of key customers in global markets, ensuring high-quality delivery operations and continuous improvements in service offerings.

Although this may sound far-fetched, leading third-party logistics providers are in fact already performing similar services for global companies today. INTRAL, a third-party international logistics management company, provides global shipment management services to connect Gillette International's far-flung operations.

Gillette and INTRAL: A Win/Win Logistics Partnership

INTRAL is a relatively new provider of international logistics management services, having been founded in 1987. INTRAL's major client is the Gillette Company, although it also performs logistics management for several smaller companies. INTRAL was founded by former Gillette logistics executives who realized that profit-driven logistics management could yield significant cost and service benefits for global corporations.

INTRAL's mission is to provide a full-service global logistics management team to support its clients' strategic business objectives. INTRAL replaces internal logistics managers with specialists who focus on developing creative, more efficient ways of moving product on a global basis. Although INTRAL focuses on managing day-to-day shipments among client facilities and customers, it constantly evaluates shipment routing, carrier performance, and customer needs to ensure high levels of performance.

INTRAL serves as the logistics partner between its clients and their suppliers or customers. Clients rely on INTRAL to provide all logistics-related services to meet production schedules or customer delivery requirements, often among facilities on different continents. INTRAL controls the global logistics process, using a technique it calls "supply loop management." Each customer has a dedicated INTRAL "logistics manager" responsible for controlling shipments from source to destination. The INTRAL manager arranges for all transportation, customs clearance, local delivery, and related services. As a final step, the INTRAL manager monitors the performance of each provider at every step in the process to ensure compliance with client needs and to evaluate improvement opportunities.

As a globally focused consumer products company, Gillette seeks competitive advantage in the development, manufacture, and sale of high-quality personal care products. Gillette competes in three large worldwide businesses—health and beauty aids, stationery products, and small electric appliances. In 1990 the company's net sales were $4.3 billion and operating profit was $773 million. Sales and profit have grown at an average rate of 13% and 16% per year since 1985.

Products are sold and distributed through wholesalers, retailers, and agents in over 200 countries and territories around the world. Gillette is truly an international company, with headquarters in Boston. In 1985 Gillette's sales were $2.4 billion—43% in the United States and 57% in international markets. From 1985 to 1990, Gillette's international markets have grown at a faster rate, and last year represented 67% of the company's total sales.

Gillette International, a subsidiary, produces and sells traditional razors and shaving blades, personal care products, and stationery products in some 185 countries around the world. This huge market represents 88% of the company's employees and produces 22% of its operating profit. The subsidiary operates 27 factories, varying from large, state-of-the-art facilities in Brazil to miniplants in China. Gillette International has sales units around the world in such countries as Peru, Ecuador, Japan, and Korea.

Traditionally, Gillette International handled its overseas logistics operations with an in-house staff. This department was closed early in 1987; later that year, Gillette International began doing business with INTRAL.

INTRAL's function is to manage and administer the procurement and flow of direct and indirect materials from sources in the United States and export these materials to Gillette units and customers around the world. In 1990, INTRAL made 2,700 separate shipments on behalf of Gillette International to a variety of customers. The value of these shipments exceeded $140 million and incurred more than $4 million in transportation costs. Gillette does business in some remote areas of the world; the total transportation budget is divided about evenly between surface and air modes.

Most consumers may think of Gillette's business as just shaving products, but its product line is actually much more complex. The company has more than 7,300 active SKUs; more than half of these are repair parts for the machines designed and built by Gillette's technical staff. The balance represent raw materials and semifinished and finished goods. INTRAL procures these materials, primarily from the five Gillette manufacturing units within the United States. To ensure speed and efficiency, Gillette is in the process of expanding this role and putting INTRAL in direct contact with its vendors.

In terms of customers, INTRAL manages shipments to some 55 Gillette units around the world and approximately ten third parties. INTRAL is not a middleman and never takes ownership of goods. Its service is managing the flow of goods from a Gillette unit—for instance, Gillette Argentina or Gillette Brazil. The firm provides raw materials, holds them, packages them if necessary, consolidates shipments, and moves them around the world. INTRAL also assists in the importation of some raw materials and shipments into the United States.

INTRAL collects Gillette's export statistics and reports to the U.S. Department of Commerce on Gillette's behalf. It prepares documentation and reports to senior Gillette management and customers, and ensures compliance with government regulations, both within and outside the United States. INTRAL's experienced, knowledgeable managers also help Gillette reduce freight costs, delivery times, and overall complexity in its international logistics operations.

In 1990, international shipments increased 32% compared with 1986, the last complete year in which Gillette handled its logistics in-house. In terms of communications, administration, and on-time shipments, Gillette believes it has significantly improved since that time. In absolute dollar terms (adjusted for inflation and based on actual 1986 in-house department costs), Gillette's 1990 logistics costs with INTRAL were lower, despite the 32% increase in shipment tonnage.

In summary, Gillette's move to third-party logistics has been successful. The company has been able to focus on its core competencies in product development and marketing, while relying on INTRAL for logistics expertise. The win/win partnership benefits not only Gillette and INTRAL but also Gillette's customers.

The Gillette/INTRAL example highlights a progressive approach to international logistics management that can provide significant competitive and operational advantages to other global companies.

Notes

1. Andersen Consulting estimate, 1992.
2. Andersen Consulting research, 1992.

673

CHAPTER 30

,port/Export Management

William W. Goldsborough
David L. Anderson

At one time, personnel responsible for the import/export function within a typical North American company could perform their duties with only minimal training. In exports, the position was often part-time, filled by marketing or manufacturing staff who also had other duties. The importance given to the job reflected the overall status of international business within the firm.

When a company viewed the export market as a place to unload mature product lines, extensive training in international distribution planning and procedures was not needed. The attitude toward import shipments was not much different. When the principal reason retailers or manufacturers sourced offshore was to supplement low-end product lines or to replenish supplies of raw materials, managing the process required little specialized skill.

Today, all that has changed. To be competitive, companies must understand all facets of global sourcing and marketing. They depend on imports to feed time-sensitive production lines and to supply consumers with a wide range of merchandise. Exports are essential to expand sales, enter new markets, and supply components to factories and assembly plants around the world. For these reasons, today's international logistics manager must be a well-trained, full-time professional experienced in managing complex international logistics decisions.

Figure 30-1 shows that U.S. dependence on global sources and markets has grown significantly over the past 20 years.

Just as important, however, is the increase in world foreign direct investment (FDI), which reached $1 trillion in 1990, up 19 times over its 1960 level. The United States has kept pace with this trend, increasing its foreign investment nearly 30% annually since 1990.

From a logistics point of view, this is significant because foreign investment inevitably requires flows of materials, products, design patterns, information, and financial transactions among plants, divisions, and distribution facilities located abroad. These flows, though not reported in U.S. government trade flow data, are substantial and growing. Corporate logistics personnel will need to develop new skills and methods for managing these interfacility, offshore activities.

Senior management recognizes that competitiveness depends on improving internal management processes, including international logistics. Logistics managers will be severely tested as they manage such worldwide supply chains. Furthermore, they will be expected to control global logistics costs, estimated at 10% to 30% of sales today, depending on the industry.

To improve processes, logistics managers must develop cost-effective, customer-focuse

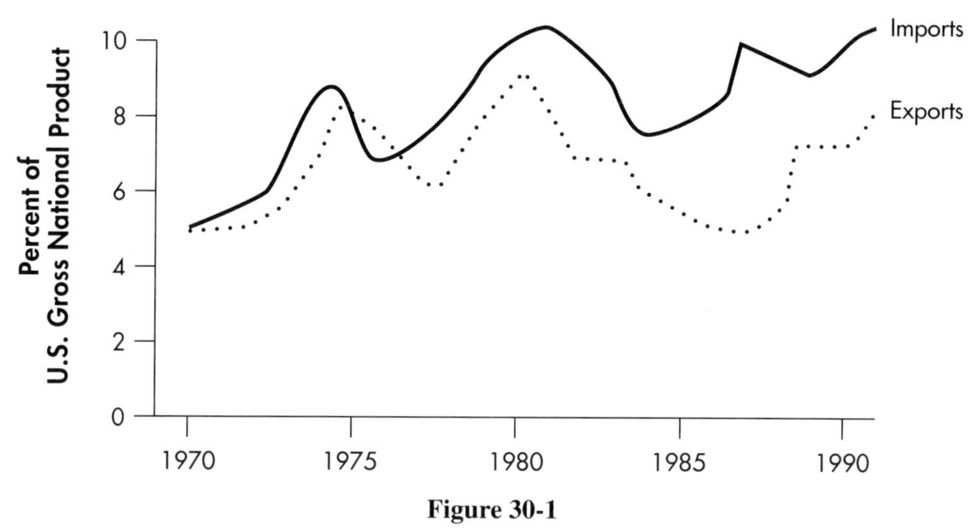

Figure 30-1
Imports and Exports as a Percent of U.S. Gross National Product

Source: U.S. Department of Commerce.

import/export programs. They must identify the critical success factors involved in managing a program for their companies' product and competitive strategies. This involves establishing customer service requirements, productivity goals, asset utilization requirements, and vendor assessment programs. Logistics managers will be expected to manage an import/export program that supports and complements overall company strategy.

Four General Principles. In general, successful international logistics strategies should be guided by four broad principles:

1. *Logistics planning should be integrated into the company's strategic planning process.* For example, DuPont, the $40 billion chemical giant, has recently implemented "total supply chain management" programs throughout its 30 major businesses operating in about 100 countries. The programs' purpose is to focus more on markets and customers, including just-in-time delivery of chemicals and inputs to their product processes. To achieve these objectives, logistics personnel have been added to each business unit to assist in planning activities ranging from site location to customer delivery programs.
2. *Logistics departments need to be guided by a clear vision and must measure output regularly.* Baxter Healthcare Corporation, the $8 billion multinational company, is accomplishing this through its unique arrangement with Trammel Crow, the real estate management firm. In the late 1980s Baxter set out to rationalize its logistics operations. Its goal was to increase the total space available to handle materials and products from 6.5 million square feet to 9 million square feet. Moreover, Baxter wanted to decrease the number of cities in which it had a facility from 50 to 40, and reduce the total number of facilities from 91 to 49. Baxter entered into a seven-year contract aimed at producing $15 million in savings. All relevant logistics cost and service parameters are measured, ac-

cording to Jerry Arthur, Baxter's vice president of distribution staff operations. The system tracks labor hour savings, land cost savings, rental savings, revenue, and tax incentives. A formal steering committee comprised of members from both organizations meets quarterly to monitor performance and suggest improvements.

3. *Import/export management should try to ensure integrated management of all elements of the logistics supply chain, from origin to destination.* This is especially important as major structural and regulatory changes are under way across the globe. Deregulation in transport, both in the United States and increasingly in Europe, Mexico, Japan, and other areas, permits negotiation of creative "door-to-door" service and price packages with carriers. This allows shippers to design and manage their supply channels so that delivery can be tailored to customer specifications at a reasonable cost.
4. *Opportunities to integrate domestic and international operations should be pursued to leverage total company volumes with globally oriented carriers.* This usually requires change in organizational thinking, but major opportunities exist for companies that can move in this direction. A good starting point is to make a list comparing domestic with international logistics activity. Table 30-1 presents a framework that can help managers think about where synergies exist for their particular organizations.

Basic Elements of Managing International Logistics

If a market exists abroad for a company's products or if viable offshore sourcing alternatives are available, logistics planning can begin. The first step is to ensure that government regulations permit the flow of imports and exports between specified countries, and that reliable transport carriers and adequate port and road facilities are available. If a basic trading infrastructure is in place, the company can begin to focus on managing the key elements of the international supply channels.

The intercontinental line haul segment of an import/export shipment is by far the most important component. The typical transit time for an ocean shipment between Japan and the U.S. West Coast is about ten days. Assuming approximately three days for merchandise to move from a Japanese supplier to on-board-vessel status in Japan, two days for vessel unloading and U.S. customs clearance, and two days for delivery to the U.S. buyer, the transport line haul represents 58% of total elapsed transit time.

In air freight, although the ratio of line haul time to total elapsed cycle time is lower than in sea freight, line haul still represents a significant portion of the move. For these reasons, logistics managers must select modes and carriers according to the specific goals and objectives of their logistics strategy and cost structures.

Sea Freight

Ocean carriers can generally be divided into two categories: bulk and container.

Bulk Carriers

These carriers make up about 75% of the world's fleet. They tend to carry cargo with a low dollar-per-ton ratio whose speed of delivery is not a primary consideration. Two main types of

TABLE 30-1
Comparison of Domestic and International Logistics

	Domestic	International
Cost	About 10.5% of U.S. GNP today	Estimated at 16% of world GNP today. Total global expenditure expected to reach $2 trillion by year 2000
Transport mode	Mainly truck and rail	Mainly ocean and air, with significant intermodal activity
Inventories	Lower levels, reflecting short-order lead-time requirements and improved transport capabilities	Higher levels, reflecting longer lead times and greater demand and transit uncertainty
Agents	Modest usage, mostly in rail	Heavy reliance on forwarders, consolidators, and customs brokers
Financial risk	Minimal	High, owing to differences in currencies, inflation levels, and little recourse for default
Cargo risk	Minimal	High, owing to longer and more difficult transit, frequent cargo handling, and varying levels of infrastructure development
Government agencies	Primarily for hazardous materials, weight, safety laws, and some tariff requirements	Many agencies involved (e.g., customs, commerce, agriculture, transportation)
Administration	Minimal documentation involved (e.g., purchase order, B/L, invoice)	Significant paperwork. The U.S. Department of Commerce estimates that paperwork cost for an average shipment is $250.
Communication	Voice, paper-based systems adequate, with growing usage of electronic data interchange	Voice and paper costly and often ineffective. Movement toward electronic interchange but variations in standards hinder widespread usage.
Cultural differences	Relative homogeneity requires little product modification.	Cultural differences require significant market and product adaptation.

cargo are transported: dry and liquid bulk. Crude oil is the main cargo handled by liquid carriers. Dry bulk carriers' cargoes consist mainly of iron ore, steel, grain, and logs.

Bulk carriers are often owned by foreign companies, and voyage management is handled by port agents. Rates are usually quoted on a per ton basis (e.g., $80 per ton of shipped cargo) and vary according to supply and demand of available shipping tonnage. Because competition among carriers is intense, negotiation is usually worthwhile. (All quotations should be confirmed in writing.)

Identifying carriers is easy. Private publishing companies print shipping schedules for container carriers and some bulk ships. Because bulk carriers do not maintain the same rigorous schedules as container carriers, the shipper should check with the port agent to confirm arrival and departure dates. A typical bulk carrier that follows a schedule will call a major port (e.g., New York, Tokyo, or Rotterdam) every six or eight weeks.

Risk of cargo damage, pilferage, or transit delay is greater when shipping on a bulk carrier than when shipping on container vessels, because the ship may be old (20% of the U.S. fleet has 30 plus years service) and therefore less able to withstand harsh weather on the high seas. Pilferage can occur because bulk-shipped merchandise is exposed to considerable handling by agents, shipping crews, dock workers, customs officials, and warehouse workers. Transit time may be very uncertain because ship owners try to maintain full ship utilization to minimize costs. For this reason, management will sometimes delay sailings or call on unscheduled ports to take on extra cargo.

Bulk ships can be chartered, either exclusively or as partial charters. Charters can be for a specific period of time or for a single prescribed trip. Prices are quoted daily on a charter vessel market. Shippers can buy a whole package from the ship's owners/managers, which includes loading and unloading of cargo at origin and destination, respectively.

Container Carriers

Although container carriers make up only 25% of the world's seagoing fleet, they transport about 80% of cargo as measured by value. Merchandise that is time-sensitive because of demand or value, or is sensitive to such external elements as weather or excess handling, moves via container ship today. For this reason, virtually all retail merchandise, industrial parts and assemblies, transport equipment and parts, office equipment, computers, and many other products move by container vessel or air freight.

Container ships offer three key advantages over conventional bulk carriers—speed, reliability, and predictability. Liner carriers publish schedules of port and inland destination arrivals and departures. At one time variance from these schedules was common, but that has changed. In today's just-in-time environment, shippers will not tolerate a carrier that does not meet schedules. Moreover, carrier management tries to avoid delays because of the high costs incurred when the vessel is berthed in port.

Daily fixed and variable costs, including port fees, can run as high as $20,000 for a container vessel. The bigger the vessel, the more expensive it is to operate. The mega vessels common today can carry up to 4,500 TEUs (twenty-foot equivalent unit, a standard 20-foot container unit). Because a ship with a capacity of 4,500 TEUs—approximately three football fields (275 meters) long—may take several days to load and unload, ship owners place a high value on efficient port operations with state-of-the-art equipment, 24-hour labor crews, and modern intermodal transfer facilities. Their goal is to discharge and load cargo as quickly as possible, then set sail for the next port of call.

Container carriers can be divided into two principal categories: conference and nonconference. A *conference vessel* belongs to a consortium of carriers that serve specified trade routes. For example, the Asia North American Eastbound Rate Agreement (ANERA) comprises carriers that carry cargo from Asia to North America. The Far Eastern Freight Conference (FEFC) is a liner consortium covering eastbound and westbound cargo moving between Asia and Europe. In each of these examples, members are granted the right to meet in closed forum and establish service standards and tariff schedules for carrying and handling cargo. Historically the rationale for granting conference members antitrust immunity was to guarantee them a reasonable return on their invested capital, and to provide the shipping public with consistent, high-quality service. Membership in the consortium is open to any carrier that meets minimum qualifications in terms of capitalization, vessel tonnage, and similar criteria and agrees to abide by decisions of the conference members.

Nonconference carriers are those that choose not to be bound by the rules and common rates of conference members. Thus, they are free to change rates and enter or leave markets at will. At one time there was a substantial difference in both quality of service and rate structures between the two carrier groups. The shipper/importer who chose to "ship conference" would receive dependable, fast cargo delivery but at a premium over the less reliable nonconference rival. Differences between conference and nonconference carriers still exist, but they have narrowed considerably because of competition and regulatory modification.

Competition. Excess vessel tonnage, coupled with a general decline in the last several years in world GNP growth relative to the first half of the 1980s, has helped keep ocean container rates low. Moreover, many of the nonconference carriers today can offer very high-quality service. Carriers like Evergreen Shipping (a Taiwanese-owned company) provides service comparable in many respects to conference carriers at a tariff rate that may be 10% to 15% less than conference rates.

Regulatory Modification. The U.S. Shipping Act of 1984 was landmark legislation that introduced significant elements of competition into the previously anticompetitive rule- and rate-making environment of the conferences. Now shippers can legally negotiate long-term time/volume contracts with members at reduced rates. Under specific circumstances, carriers wanting to negotiate rates and service packages directly with shippers may do so, irrespective of the wishes of other conference members. Smaller shippers now have legal means available for pooling their cargoes and negotiating volume contracts with carriers and conferences.

Air Freight

By tonnage, approximately 2% of international merchandise moves via air freight. Measured by value, however, about 30% of U.S. merchandise trade is shipped by air. Moreover, international air freight has been growing at double-digit rates in recent years and is projected to average about 15% growth through the end of the century. Greater reliance on international air freight is a reflection of several factors:

- Industrial restructuring has reshaped American industry. A service-intensive economy tends to ship smaller cargoes more frequently. These smaller shipments narrow the price gap between unitized rail/truck freight and air freight.
- Globalization has led to extensive intracompany shipping patterns in which such time-sensitive cargoes as blueprints, design patterns, computer media, and critical replacement parts move rapidly around the world.
- There is a general desire to be market-responsive without accumulating large inventories.
- Shippers today, with a better understanding of logistics cost/service trade-offs, are more willing to pay premium freight rates to lower total delivered cost (including transport, inventory holding, etc.).

- Air carriers, finding that carrying cargo can be profitable, have improved their service. Moreover, improved service from integrated carriers has pressured conventional carriers to respond.
- Costs have dropped as a result of more efficient aircraft, lower fuel prices, and greater competition.

The obvious reason to ship by air is to minimize transit time. For certain products there is usually little choice. Perishable items like fruits, fresh meats, and cut flowers usually cannot withstand a long sea journey. The same is true for certain pharmaceutical products with a very short shelf life. For these items, shippers pay transport rates that may be as high as two to three dollars per pound. For most products, however, the shipper chooses air freight to meet tight production schedules or to satisfy shifting market demand in distant locations without stockpiling excessive, expensive, and soon-obsolete inventories.

In choosing air freight, a shipper has several alternatives: charter vs. commercial; integrated vs. freighters or combination aircraft; and forwarders vs. direct.

CHARTER VS. COMMERCIAL

Because of extremely high cost, only the largest shippers can afford to charter an entire aircraft for shipping merchandise. The payload of a chartered Boeing 747, for example, is about 100 kilotons and may cost $250,000 or more for a one-way intercontinental flight. Because of excess capacity today, aircraft may be available on fairly short notice during off-peak seasons. The growth in offshore sourcing is making the auto industry increasingly dependent on foreign producers for major subassemblies and components. At the same time, manufacturers are maintaining lean inventories to adhere to just-in-time manufacturing policies. To stay on schedule, such companies sometimes enter the charter market.

The fashion apparel industry also charters aircraft, especially in the peak demand periods of spring and fall. Because commercial space is often at a premium during these periods, such high-volume apparel companies as The Limited will arrange for charters well in advance to ensure that the product is available to the consumer, and that government-mandated quotas have not closed before merchandise arrives in the United States.

ALL-CARGO, COMBINATION, AND INTEGRATED CARRIERS

In choosing to ship by commercial aircraft, shippers today can select among pure cargo companies, companies that carry a combination of passengers and cargo, and integrated companies that carry only cargo but also provide forwarding and other value-added services.

Since Flying Tiger Lines, the airline that dominated the all-cargo industry in the 35 years following World War II, became part of the Federal Express integrated air fleet, there are only two all-cargo airlines of any consequence serving the U.S. market. These are Martin Air and Cargolux, both European-based carriers. Between them, these companies operate about 12 flights per week out of key U.S. markets. Payloads are mostly high-value merchandise destined for markets in Europe and Asia. (Cargolux recently added a flight to key Latin American markets.)

All major international airlines carry a combination of passengers and cargo and serve all important markets of the world. For most major trade lanes, shippers have a choice of many carriers, who compete intensely for cargo. Although cargo managers at airlines often complain that management is guided principally by a desire to maximize passenger revenues, potential profits from air freight are getting more attention.

The pricing of cargo space is an interesting aspect of air freight, particularly in the case of combination carriers. Although published tariffs exist, as flight time approaches and excess capacity remains, airlines often negotiate rates with the major international freight forwarders and, increasingly, with shippers themselves.

There are two principal reasons for excess cargo capacity: (1) much cargo tends to be seasonal (e.g., preceding the Christmas merchandising season), while passenger traffic is less so; and (2) 65% of all cargo goes to 35 major world industrial centers, resulting in considerable excess cargo capacity in other lanes that still must serve passenger traffic. For these reasons, as long as variable costs and a portion of fixed costs are covered, airlines may offer steep discounts to fill the aircraft.

Within the last half decade, integrated carriers have become a major competitive force. Led by Federal Express and United Parcel Service in the United States and TNT in Europe, these carriers handle regular commercial heavy freight on a shipper's-door-to-receiver's-door basis. Besides airborne transportation, such carriers also provide documentation, surface transport at both origin and destination, information tracking, and other value-added services. Especially on some heavy-volume routes, the integrated carriers even handle booking, routing, and documentation—tasks traditionally performed by freight forwarders. For this reason many international forwarders, as well as combination (or "combi") airlines, have declared open warfare on integrated carriers.

Because an average international air freight shipment is airborne only about 20% of total elapsed door-to-door transit time, one can understand that appeal offered by integrated carriers. If they can efficiently manage all the links (line haul and secondary carriers) and nodes (consolidators, warehouses, customs, ports, etc.) that make up an international shipment, they make a shipper's job much simpler.

Intermodal Shipping

Intermodalism is a major feature of international shipping today. Spawned by transport deregulation in the United States but made possible by technological advances in equipment interchangeability and information processing, containerized shipments can be smoothly transferred from mode to mode as they travel through the global pipeline. Today, containers can be unloaded from oceangoing vessels directly to double-stack rail cars where rail sidings exist at container ports. Ocean carriers maintain huge pools of containers at inland points scattered around the country, to be loaded by exporters for truck or rail delivery to a seaport.

A more recent development is combined sea/air transport. These intermodal shipments, which combine the speed of air freight with the lower cost of sea freight, may appeal to shippers because of tariff oddities. For example, the air tariff for shipping electronic parts from Japan to Europe is nearly twice what it is for shipping eastbound to the United States. Unwilling to tolerate the all-air freight cost to Europe or the slowness of an all-sea transit via the Suez Canal, Japanese shippers transport goods by sea to the U.S. West Coast, then by air directly to various European destinations. Both Cargolux and Martin Air exist primarily to provide this sea/air transportation service.

Cost/Service Trade-Offs

Except for the international exporter or importer who is constrained entirely by minimum cost or maximum speed considerations, the shipper that takes control of the international transportation channel enjoys an abundance of price and service offerings from carriers. And the number of alternatives is even greater if transport offerings available from third-party agents are included. (The role of third parties is discussed later in this chapter.)

When negotiating with carriers, shippers should have a clear understanding of their cost and service objectives. They should also understand the economics that drive carrier operations. Before approaching carriers for service packages, they must first answer some important questions: Is the user more concerned about maximizing speed or minimizing risk? Is reliability of service (arrival at port or interior location when promised) more important, or can the shipper accept the risk that merchandise may be a day or two late, in return for substantial cost savings? How much extra transit cost can be tolerated for substantial reduction in inventory levels?

A further consideration involves cargo control. How valuable to the shipper is the "one-stop shipping" intermodal serviced now commonly offered by carriers to points around the world? Can better pricing or even service be obtained by "unbundling" the package and contracting for each logistics element separately?

All these trade-offs should be considered today in careful consultation with prospective carriers. And once a program with a transport company or companies is agreed upon, careful monitoring of actual carrier performance is important to ensure that the carrier is providing high-quality customer service and meeting its obligations.

Consolidation Services

For reasons outlined above in the discussion of air freight, the average size of an international shipment has shrunk. Shipping smaller orders more frequently drives up line haul transport cost and increases the risk of damage because of additional handling. This problem is particularly acute when shipping internationally because of long distances and the myriad intermediaries involved, whether for imported or exported shipments. For this reason, many shippers rely on outside vendors for consolidation and distribution services.

For many years, the apparel industry has depended on consolidators for shipments from the Far East to the United States. In Hong Kong, for example, consolidators perform several functions. At any one time, they might receive copies of purchase orders placed on as many as five to ten garment suppliers in Hong Kong and southern China. They then book full container space on an ocean carrier and monitor the production status of orders with vendors. Merchandise would be delivered to an off-dock consolidation facility, where it would be received, verified for completeness, inspected for damage, and loaded into a 20- or 40-foot container, often sequenced for efficient unloading at the U.S. discharge port. Other value-added services could be performed as well, including garment tagging, pressing, and packaging. The consolidation charges may be as high as \$200–\$300 per container, but this cost is usually offset by the lower full-container per unit transport cost, as compared with the less-than-containerload (LCL) per unit cost.

Consolidators may be affiliated with, or owned by, an international freight-forwarding company. The forwarding company will buy full container space from ocean carriers, often at a discount, and ship in its own name. When functioning in this capacity, the forwarder is called a nonvessel-operating common carrier (NVOCC). The NVOCC makes its profits by soliciting LCL freight from multiple shippers (unlike the previous example of a single shipper with multiple vendors), consolidating these shipments in a single container, and issuing its own NVOCC bills of lading to shippers. Gross profit is the difference between its payout to carriers and its billout to shippers.

Consolidators also handle exports from North America. Construction companies like Bechtel and petroleum companies like Chevron rely heavily on consolidators to pack and ship to offshore job sites. But NVOCC-type consolidators are less common in U.S. export trades, mainly because of the trade configuration of U.S. exports—heavy reliance on air freight; the large number of full-container, single-source shipments; high volume of agricultural and natural resources shipped; and fewer general-merchandise retail shipments.

Distribution Services

Increasingly, importers and exporters are using distribution service companies to reduce distribution cycle time and costs. At one time, it was standard operating procedure for an importer to clear U.S. customs and automatically bring merchandise into a company-owned or -operated facility for receiving, inventorying, and customer distribution. Double handling and transport costs would result as freight was taken from port of entry to a distribution center, and then reshipped to regional warehouses or to customers.

For imports, time pressures are driving some companies to distribute merchandise directly from port of entry. Often these so-called drop shipments are handled by the U.S. agent of the foreign freight forwarder or the U.S. customs broker, who may serve as the agent of the foreign forwarder. The agent is in a good position to handle this business because he or she may have received advanced information from the forwarder that will expedite customs clearance and permit rapid receipt, logging, and domestic inbound shipping preparation (for example, arranging in advance for proper transport equipment). Prospective users of distribution agents should take extra care, however, in making sure the agent is truly capable of performing in this capacity. Facilities should be large, inventory management and information systems adequate, and a commitment to first-rate domestic distribution clearly evident.

Within the last few years, American exporters have shown an interest in using outside service companies for distribution services in customer locations. This tendency has grown rapidly in Europe within the last few years but is also spreading to Asia. With the coming integration of a single European market for goods and services, many U.S. firms (especially those with limited foreign operations) are shipping merchandise to central European logistics centers and then redistributing from there into pan-European or regional distribution channels. In Asia this same kind of practice is emerging in Singapore. This free trade island nation, which promotes itself as a commercial entrepot, solicits traders from the United States, Europe, Japan, and Australia to redistribute product to regional customers from Singapore-based distribution facilities.

Government Regulations

Every country establishes import/export regulations to protect and promote its vital interests, including national security; the health, safety, and welfare of its citizens; and the protection of its industries from foreign competition.

U.S. Exports

Except in the most bureaucratic sense, most products exported from the United States require no "license." Most shipments require only a statement on the export declaration that the item is being shipped under the general licensing procedures of the Department of Commerce.

A few products—primarily those in short supply, strategic in nature, or incorporating special types of high technology—do require a validated license formally issued by the Department of

Commerce's Office of Export Administration, or by the Department of State in the case of war materials. Traditionally most of the regulations governing the licensing procedure involve exporting to selected countries considered hostile to U.S. interests. In some instances, all trade is prohibited (as with Cuba), or sanctions are imposed because of international hostilities (as during the 1990–91 Persian Gulf war against Iraq). In other cases, only the export of selected items like military technology is prohibited.

The Coordinating Committee on Multilateral Export Controls (COCOM) is a voluntary group made up of Japan and all NATO members (except Spain and Iceland) that was formed to keep high-technology products from being diverted to countries in the former Soviet bloc. The Department of Commerce's Department of Export Control is an enforcement arm that has monitored shipments to prevent diversion to these restricted countries.

Recent economic and political developments in eastern Europe, however, have challenged the rationale for restricting the export of technology-intensive products. Some goods like personal computers, whose export to eastern Europe poses no threat to U.S. national security, have been dropped from the COCOM list. Currently, the entire list is under review by all member governments following the end of the Cold War. (In fact, one has to wonder at this writing how long the COCOM organization will continue to exist as an official multilateral agency.)

U.S. Imports

A major purpose of import regulations is to ensure that imported products meet the same health and safety standards as products made in the United States. The U.S. Department of Transportation, for example, publishes regulations governing the importation of motor vehicles. Vehicles must meet not only minimum safety standards but also stringent emission control standards imposed by both the federal and state governments. The importation of fresh and processed agricultural products must meet strict controls imposed by the Department of Agriculture and the Food and Drug Administration.

Regulations also exist to inform American purchasers of a product's origin. These regulations inform potential buyers of possible quality variation and provide a clear choice for consumers among either foreign or domestic products. All foreign-made products must be clearly and indelibly identified by country of origin.

Import regulations may vary depending on country of origin. Products imported from the industrially developed countries that are signatories of the General Agreement on Tariffs and Trade (GATT) are dutiable at the same tariff rate. Because of multiple rounds of tariff negotiations held among GATT members over the last 40 years, tariff rates on most items have been reduced substantially. An average duty today is only about 5% of the commercial value of the imported product.

Products imported from the industrially emerging bloc of GATT countries receive preferential treatment on tariffs (customs duty is waived), provided that most of the product was made locally. These countries are subject to the General System of Preferences (GSP); a certificate issued by the origin country and signed by a government official must be present when entry paperwork is submitted to U.S. Customs.

Goods imported from the former Communist bloc countries are penalized with tariffs that may be two or three times higher than those applied to GATT-member industrially developed countries. Many of these countries, however, have applied for GATT membership and, in some instances, their products are assessed the same duty rate as other GATT members. Russia, for example, was recently granted Most-Favored-Nation status by the U.S. Congress.

Some imported items are governed by regulations that grow out of single-purpose multilateral conventions. For instance, the United States is a signatory to the International Ivory Convention, which prohibits the importation of ivory from any country that has not ratified the accord. Country-of-origin certification must accompany each shipment.

Many regulations have been established to regulate the flow of selected categories of products from a single country or bloc of countries. These regulations normally originate in actions taken by domestic interest groups seeking government protection from imported foreign products. For instance, the U.S. textile industry has attempted to stem the flow of foreign-made textile products. As a result of its political activity, duty rates are high (10% to 30% of product valuation), and origin country quotas have been established. Although quotas technically violate the free trade principles of GATT, an attempt is made on the part of the developed importing countries like the United States and EC members to give the quotas legitimacy through multilateral signed conventions. Thus the Multi-Fiber Arrangement is an agreement among 54 nations that annually regulates by category the quantity of textile products that can flow between any two countries.

There is an increasing tendency for bilateral trade pacts to govern trade flows between nations. Two examples involve automobiles and semiconductors imported into the United States from Japan. In each agreement, the U.S. government has pressured the Japanese to establish "voluntary" limits on the dollar value of automobiles and semiconductors that will be exported to the United States.

Information Sources

Any prospective importer or exporter who enters into an international commercial contract without first understanding all regulations governing the transaction does so at considerable risk. Stories abound about frustrated importers losing sales because products were either illegally imported or delayed because they were subjected to expensive, time-consuming procedures to comply with government regulations. Exporters, of course, can experience the same frustrations. Exporters must be aware not only of export country regulations but the foreign importing country regulations as well. For example, there are no U.S. regulations prohibiting the export of Washington State cherries to Japan. But it is illegal to import them to Japan before July 5. Cherries imported before that date sit in port, losing freshness (and thus monetary value) by the hour.

Numerous sources provide country-specific information about regulations governing the import or export of specific products. For rules, commodity classifications, and licensing requirements for U.S. exports, the U.S. government publishes the *Statistical Classification of Domestic and Foreign Commodities Exported from the U.S.* For regulations governing the import of American-made products into foreign countries, the shipper can consult the *International Trade Reporter,* published by the Bureau of National Affairs. However, to understand the specific regulations, duties, and tax rates for a given product, the exporter should consult individual country publications or consult with importers and customs authorities in the targeted country.

The U.S. Customs Bureau provides more or less the same information for imports. In addition, all products of potential importation are given a tariff classification available in the *Annotated Tariff Classification* publication of the U.S. Customs Bureau.

For imports into the United States, customs brokers are always a good source of information. It is also advisable to consult with U.S. customs officials at local ports of entry; customs officials at the national level in Washington are also cooperative and well informed. Moreover, a shipper should never hesitate to contact competitors, whether for imports or exports. Most of them are willing to share their knowledge about their experiences in dealing with the regulations of specific countries, governing specific product lines. They can also help make informed judgments about what the business future may portend for a particular country.

Documentation

International trade is very document-intensive. It has been estimated, for example, that the actual cost of documenting a typical single international shipment exceeds $250. Government and commercial documents are required for both import and export transactions.

Exports: Government Requirements

For a routine export shipment, the only required U.S. government document is the export declaration, whose purpose is to describe the exported merchandise. It resembles an international bill of lading. Products are identified according to standard commodity code numbers known as the schedule B classification. Products are licensed for export under a blanket general licensing provision of the Department of Commerce (DOC); either the carrier's or the shipper's forwarder is responsible for periodically sending this information to the DOC. This document is also used as the statistical source for the DOC's compilation of published trade data.

As mentioned above, some products in scarce supply, or intended for consignees in specific areas of the world, do require a separate license for shipping. This DOC or Department of State "validated" license must be applied for in advance of the shipment and must be included in the document set presented to the carrier at time of shipment.

For a few products, inspection certificates may be required by government agencies. Before shipping fresh produce abroad, for example, the Department of Agriculture (DOA) requires a phytosanitary certificate issued by a DOA official in the state from which the commodity originates.

The country of destination, especially if it is among the industrial developing nations, may require specific documents before shipments are allowed entry. The primary purpose of these requirements is either to preserve scarce foreign exchange or to protect local industries from competition. A consular invoice in the language of the foreign country is a requirement for shipping to a few countries. Some also require a certificate of origin, commonly issued in the United States by the local chamber of commerce and given a visa by the consul.

Exports: Commercial Documents

To satisfy foreign customs officials and legal obligations among shipper, importer, and vendors, several commercial documents are generally required:

- *Commercial invoice* indicating product description, pieces, unit value and extended (total) value. It should also show shipper and consignee and be signed by an authorized representative of the shipper.

- *Packing list* indicating carton numbers, markings, and content. (Most countries permit the invoice to serve as a packing list if carton markings are noted on it.)
- *Bill of lading* (*B/L;* also known as a *waybill* for air shipments). The bill of lading serves a dual purpose: (1) contract of carriage between the shipper and carrier and (2) evidence of title. Bills of lading are issued by carriers, completed by the shipper for the agent, and returned to the carrier. Ocean B/Ls can be either negotiable or nonnegotiable. When payment is received through letter of credit or documentary draft instruments, B/Ls must be negotiable, allowing for a bank or authorized representative to endorse it over to the consignee after payment or signature. Almost all air freight shipments move under *straight* or *nonnegotiable bills of lading.*
- *Collection documents.* If a letter of credit or a bank draft is employed to collect payment for the shipment, the entire packet of documents is routed through banking channels or an authorized representative of the consignee. The documents are accompanied by a letter of instruction to the bank indicating collection and disbursement procedures.
- *Insurance certificate.* Unlike domestic carriers, ocean carriers are not liable for loss or damage of merchandise unless negligence can be proven. Air carriers do provide blanket coverage, but the extent of their liability is limited to $9.00 per pound of freight. Therefore, exporters are wise to obtain standard cargo insurance whenever shipping under cost/insurance/freight (CIF) or even cost-and-freight (CNF) terms. Different levels of coverage can be obtained, including basic perils of the sea, broad perils of theft, pilferage, and damage, or all-risk covering any damage from any external cause. Separate war risk coverage can also be secured.

Imports

The U.S. government's Bureau of Customs and selected federal and state agencies responsible for certain categories of products require several documents before a shipment is released to the importer. The commercial documents that generally accompany an import are similar in kind to those for exporting:

- *Commercial invoice, packing list* (unless contained in the commercial invoice) and *transport bill of lading.*
- *U.S. Customs entry documents.* Using values taken from the commercial invoice, officials assign individual items an import tariff classification obtained from the *Annotated Tariff Classification* of U.S. Customs, and submitted to customs by the importer or the agent. About 50% of these entries are now submitted electronically by brokers under the bureau's automatic broker interface (ABI) program. Under this program about 80% of merchandise is released, without physical examination, within two hours. The other 20% must be given an intense physical examination before release.
- *Entry summary.* Once cargo is released, the importer has ten working days to file this document, which formally classifies the import into its many tariff classifications, and requires a deposit of estimated duties at that time.
- *Customs bond.* Required for every shipment valued in excess of $1,000, this bond protects the government's revenue if there are liquidated damages assessed against the cargo after it is released to the importer. Liquidated damages may be assessed for many reasons. Most common are revaluation of merchandise or improper tariff classifications resulting

in undercollected duties. Bonds are easily obtained from surety companies. A blanket bond, permitting unlimited shipments during the course of a year, would normally cost about $300 to $500.

- *Special documents.* To comply with specific requirements of customs and other federal agencies, the following documents may be required: (1) *quota declarations* for products like garments, shoes, steel, and automobiles shipped under trade quotas; (2) *textile country-of origin declarations;* (3) *FCC Form 740* for consumer electrical products; (4) *Fish and Wildlife Form 3-177* for endangered species; (5) *Food and Drug forms* for radiation and for products that come in contact with food or beverages; and (6) *environmental protection forms* for pesticides and pollution control. In addition, importers of goods from the newly emerging counties (NECs), eligible for duty-free status under the General System of Preferences of the United Nations Conference on Trade and Development (UNCTAD), must present a document attesting to the percentage of the product that was manufactured in that country. All these documents must be presented at the time of entry, unless bond is posted.

Duty Drawback

The duty drawback provision was initially authorized by the first tariff act of the United States in 1789. Its purpose was then—and is still today—to help exporters compete in foreign markets. Several types of drawback are authorized under section 1313, Title 19, United States Code. Because sections A and B contain the key provisions that benefit a broad range of exporters, only these are discussed here.

Section A incorporates the basic elements of the drawback law. An exporter of a product manufactured in the United States using imported materials may recover any duty paid on the imported components, less 1%, which is retained by customs to defray costs.

Section B allows an exporter to recover duty paid on materials in a like or substituted product that is of U.S. origin. Section B addresses the concerns of the exporter who uses both domestic and imported products that are identical. As long as proper records are kept that indicate original amounts imported and the contents in the exported product, drawback can be claimed even though domestic product was substituted for imported product. This provision obviates the need for the exporter to maintain separate record-keeping systems for imported and domestic products.

Both provisions permit exporters who have purchased product from a domestically based importer to recover duties even though they never directly paid duties. The rationale for this provision is that the exporters in effect paid these fees when they satisfied the vendor's invoice. A drawback claimant must establish that the articles on which drawback is being claimed were exported within five years after original importation.

International Communications

Today, successful import/export management is impossible without controlling the flow of goods and materials across thousands of miles, multiple time zones, and diverse business cultures. Managing this activity becomes more difficult by the day, as more product lines are outsourced and more sales are sought in export markets.

The logistics manager, however, receives little sympathy from senior managers or customers, who demand that full product lines be delivered faster, more reliably, and less expensively. To achieve these goals, the international logistics manager must coordinate numerous internal and external links and nodes in the supply network to make sure materials flow smoothly betw operations and customers, as shown in Figure 30-2.

The logistics process, therefore, begins early in the delivery cycle when the customer first places an order, and ends only when the customer is satisfied with the delivery of that product and then pays for it.

Many companies now recognize that the key to making the process work in a far-flung global enterprise is information linkages. They understand that achieving high levels of performance requires close coordination among internal functional departments and between the company and outside vendors. Order processing, manufacturing, inventory control, and distribution departments must integrate their processes *internally,* and these processes must in turn be coordinated *externally* with those of carriers, agents, and port authorities. The common objective for every player in the supply pipeline is to provide cost-effective service to customers. Information about specific customer requirements allows each player to perform as effectively and efficiently as possible.

When this pipeline information is nonexistent, late, or of poor quality, costly delays in the physical flow of materials and product are inevitable—manufacturing produces the wrong product, styles, or color; inventory control is understocked in raw materials; transportation fails to book carrier space early enough; customer service does not obtain visas for quota merchandise.

High-technology manufacturer Texas Instruments (TI), recognizing that a significant competitive edge could be established by linking operations and vendors in the United States, Canada, Japan, Europe, and the Far East, is continuing the development of its global information network. Over 150 company facilities are linked by 41 IBM mainframes, 1,746 distributed processors, and 27,273 personal workstations. Today, when an order from any worldwide location is received in TI's semiconductor division, it is automatically routed through order entry, inventory control, purchasing, production, and distribution to prepare for customer delivery. Through large-scale databases, all channel members—including some outside logistics service suppliers—have immediate access to important information they need to expedite product through the supply pipeline.

However, a company need not be as big as Texas Instruments to improve its logistics information capabilities. The key is understanding the important role played by information in making a company competitive, and then making prudent investments where and when appropriate. A logistics information hierarchy that has moved beyond a paper-based mail and telex capability might develop through the following stages:

1. *Fax.* Available throughout the world, this paper-based telecommunications technology permits free-form, immediate, person-to-person transmission of key logistics information. Among other things, purchase orders can be received from customers, order acknowledgments transmitted by suppliers, instructions sent to distribution facilities, bookings made to carriers, and cargo status inquiries made to international agents. Today, importers and exporters of all sizes depend heavily on fax technology to manage international logistics processes.
2. *Electronic messaging.* These E-mail systems unite widely separated business operations and selected outside service providers through an electronic web of public and private telecommunications linkages. Such major telecommunication companies as GE Information Services (GEISCO), AT&T, and BT Tymnet provide satellite-linked network services that permit companies, large and small, to transmit in real time, or store for later retrieval, electronic messages among as many or as few facilities and vendors as they desire.
3. *Electronic Data Interchange (EDI)—proprietary or industry-specific software formats.* These systems require little or no human intervention in transmitting formatted informa-

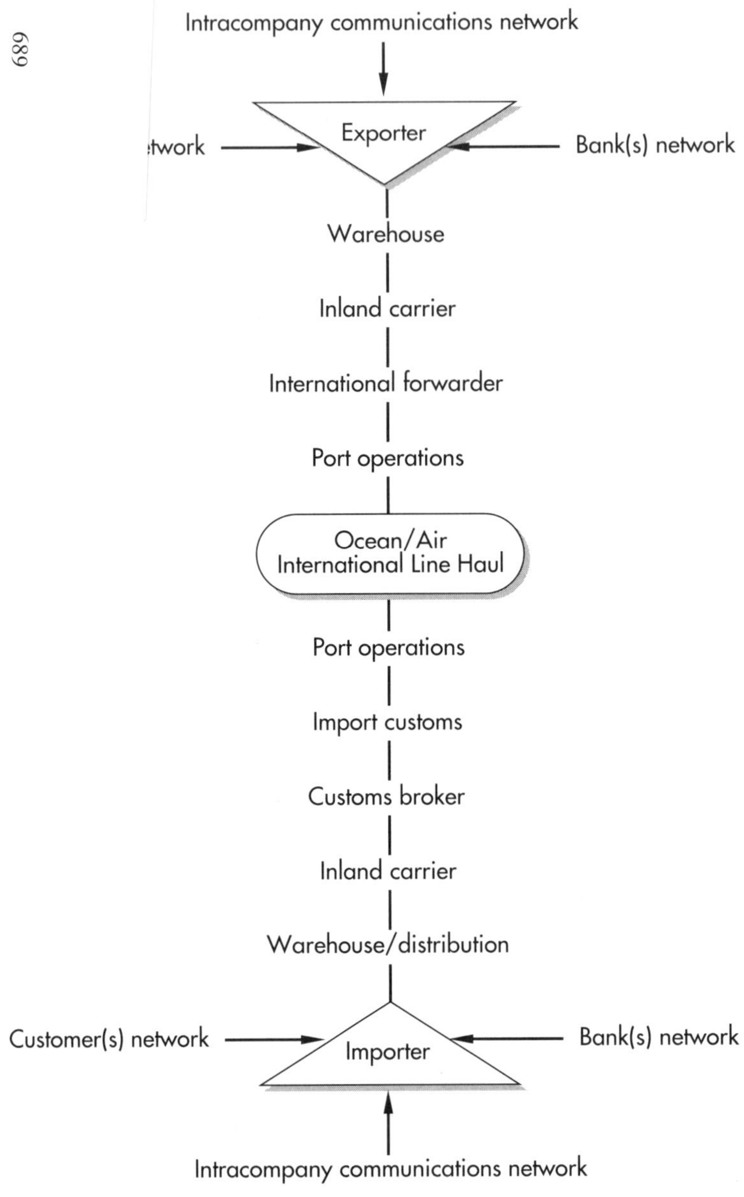

Figure 30-2
The International Supply Pipeline

tion between computers. Data elements for purchase orders, acknowledgments, bills of material, invoices, booking notices, bills of lading, customs documents, and other transactions flow automatically between internal and external company computers around the world. Large companies like General Motors and IBM have developed powerful EDI systems, inducing key product and service suppliers to accept their proprietary company or industry standards to remain part of their preferred supplier network. Widespread availability of software allows such service providers as carriers and customs authorities to link into these systems inexpensively today. Some providers like U.S. Customs have even become the channel drivers for interconnectivity by developing their proprietary system. The U.S. Customs Automated Commercial System, for example, permits brokers and certain large importers to file entries, obtain cargo releases, receive liquidation notices, and exchange a variety of trade-related information automatically.

4. *EDI—broad-based standard formats.* Until all parties in the supply pipeline can automatically send and receive information in real or near real time, full integration of supply chain nodes and links will be lacking. And as long as channel members adopt proprietary or industry-specific computer and communication standards, the full potential of broad-based integration will go unrealized. These broad-based standards have now been developed and officially adopted by the EDIFACT working group within the United Nations. Companies across a wide spectrum of industries, including carriers, brokers, forwarders, financial institutions, and insurance companies, are or soon will be using these standards. Government agencies are gradually accepting and phasing in these standards as well.

Ultimately, perhaps within the next decade, large and small international traders will be able to tap into an integrated logistics information channel that spans the world. This will enable them to make proactive decisions that can optimize trade-offs in their import/export channels.

The Changing Logistics Organization

The growing importance of logistics within companies today is driving them to address the way logistics activities are organized and managed. Leading-edge companies are reorganizing their logistics departments, giving them more responsibility and including them in both short- and long-term company strategic planning. For many companies, this increased responsibility has been coupled with the centralization of such logistics functions as inventory control, materials management, transportation, and warehousing, under a single logistics director or even vice president. This has provided focus and control that allows companies to leverage their logistics strengths across multiple business units.

For firms already dependent on either imports or exports as major sources of supply or markets, or for those whose shares of either are growing, responsibility for managing related logistics activities should be combined with domestic activity under one department head. This is sometimes difficult because firms are often divided into domestic and international divisions or even companies. Because of this, functional activities are often duplicated, resulting in significant diseconomies of scale. Furthermore, opportunities to combine international and domestic volumes in negotiating with carriers or third-party providers are lost.

The steady march toward globalization, however, is compelling firms to address these organizational issues. Increasingly, their structures reflect global strategies, markets, and sources of supply.

The apparel industry, for example, has grown steadily dependent on foreign vendors and manufacturing for supplying worldwide markets. Levi Strauss has historically been two organizations, Levi Strauss and Levi Strauss International. Each organization has had its own sources of supply, marketing channels, and physical distribution groups. Today, the parent company is reevaluating this division in the interests of gaining the benefits of logistics synergies by combining domestic and international responsibility—joint transport contracts with intermodal carriers, shared information systems, improved leverage with suppliers serving both domestic and international divisions, and more efficient policies and procedures.

High-technology companies in the computer, networking, and microchip industries are also reexamining their logistics organizations. More and more this is resulting in the creation of worldwide structures that do not distinguish between international and domestic logistics. Driving this reassessment are complex international sourcing patterns for raw materials, a growing dependency on export sales (some of the major computer and microchip companies derive over half their revenues from international sales), and a need to control product and service at deep levels in the supply channels.

These companies seek to increase sales by offering their customers a competitive landed price from factory to receiving dock, delivered according to precise schedules. Successful management of this *total* supply chain requires no less than controlling the movement of materials, products, and information from scattered worldwide shipping locations and plants, through one or more layers of distribution centers, on to carriers, through customs, and finally to the customer. In between, of course, are complex layers of middlemen and regulations that must be managed.

Under pressure to provide virtually error-free customer service as well as excellent value in product design, quality and price, high-technology industries that have heretofore downplayed the importance of integrated global logistics management are moving rapidly toward focused, central organizations.

International logistics, however, is sometimes caught in a dilemma by these trends. Today's push for centralized decision making—for example, coordinated customer policies, integrated information systems, comprehensive accountability, and a general blurring of the lines between domestic and international business—occurs side by side with decentralizing trends. These include the need to meet specific customer requirements—to determine, for instance, how, where, and when product should be delivered, which local truckers should be used, how to comply with local or national customs, and how to hire, train, and retain qualified staff.

The successful companies will likely be those that can gain the best of both worlds. They must balance two competing but equally important demands—one for a central organization that sets and executes broad policies regarding strategy, systems planning, and economies of scale and scope, and another for providing highly competitive service to local customers whose needs may vary markedly from one nation, region, or culture to another. In a sense, therefore, successful logistics managers in global companies must have the wisdom to distinguish between overmanaging and undermanaging.

Third-Party Logistics

Many U.S. companies today are shifting significant portions of their internal logistics and distribution activity to outside service providers. This tendency goes beyond merely using commercial transportation and warehousing services in place of company-owned distribution assets.

Unlike traditional, transaction-based buyer/seller relationships, successful third-party arrangements require a significant commitment and trust from both parties to achieve mutually agreed-upon goals extending over long periods of time. Agreements often can be viewed as "business partnerships" where both parties gain by agreeing to meet specific productivity goals like a percentage of on-time deliveries, high order fulfillment ratios, increased productivity levels, and acceptable levels of return on corporate assets.

In nearly all these relationships, the provider—whether a traditional transport carrier or a public warehouse—must be prepared to offer value-added services to its clients if it expects to function as a full-service company. Accordingly, carriers are discovering that they must develop product distribution and information management skills that only a few years ago they would not have considered part of their service portfolio. Similarly, warehousing companies that want to pursue true third-party logistics partnerships must develop new competencies in such areas as information management, transportation, and even in-store product display management.

Two converging developments are driving emerging third-party relationships. The first is the desire on the part of shippers to concentrate on what they do best: designing, making, and selling products. (Few manufacturers and retailers regard logistics management as their core competency.) The second development is that logistics service providers are gaining a greater desire and ability to offer (and, more important, *deliver*) bona fide third-party value to the clients. The successful efforts of Roadway Logistics Services, Menlo Logistics, Skyway Freight Systems, and Exel Distribution Services, among many others who have made this commitment, attest to this. (Also see Chapter 29 for a discussion of INTRAL.)

International Outsourcing

Within the last few years, the primary focus of third-party activity has been the domestic market because it represents a more immediate and manageable market for many firms and therefore becomes their first priority. Moreover, because their roots are in the United States, many of the largest, most asset-intensive providers have been aggressively promoting domestic outsourcing business.

However, rapid development of international logistics outsourcing can be expected through the second half of the 1990s for four reasons, as follows:

1. A rapid descent down the learning curve is occurring as the domestic providers gain experience in handling U.S.-based business. Users are also becoming more accustomed to working with third-party companies.
2. Domestic providers already handle occasional international transactions and are thus gaining valuable experience in this arena.
3. Firms of all sizes are becoming increasingly dependent on foreign sourcing and markets. In rationalizing sources of supply and channels of distribution, firms will view the entire world as a logistics playing field. To minimize overhead and reduce risk, they will depend on third parties for a myriad of value-added services in distant geographical areas. These will include not only such traditional services as forwarding, transport, and warehousing but also sourcing activities like product purchasing, inventory replenishment, financing, quota management, light assembly, and decision support. Nontraditional distribution activities could also include various functions necessary to move product to end users, such as product preparation, channel management, and product installation and maintenance.
4. Some international agents and carriers are developing information and management systems to enable themselves to manage a complete pipeline of services from origin to destination.

Although an international pipeline is more difficult to manage than a domestic pipeline, advances in information and transport technology are providing the tools for this. For example, AMR (parent company of American Airlines) and CSX (one of the largest intermodal railroad companies in the United States) have formed Encompass, a joint-venture company offering worldwide shipment tracking and management through sophisticated, turnkey software and innovative messaging technologies.

The Fritz Companies, a U.S.-based customs broker and freight forwarder, provides a broad base of services for Sears, Roebuck & Company. In addition to performing standard customs brokerage for all Sears products imported from the Far East, Fritz negotiates and manages contracts with eastbound carriers out of Hong Kong and Singapore, books cargo, consolidates merchandise into container loads, manages cargo to Sears distribution facilities in the United States, and provides information regarding cargo disposition as cargo moves through the pipeline.

Regardless of the focus, if third-party relationships are to work, shippers must feel that providers are accountable for achieving specified results—for instance, decreased order cycle times, on-time performance, and improved cargo status. In the domestic arena, third parties are increasingly willing to commit, often in contractual form, to achieving these results. If performance falls short, some third parties have agreed to compensate the shipper according to established penalty clauses.

International logistics service providers are naturally reluctant to make such commitments because of the greater difficulty of controlling the many variables involved in a typical international shipment (as highlighted in Table 30-1). However, with the continuous improvement in information and intermodal systems, the growth of integrated carriers, and demands of performance-hungry users, a few of the larger, better-managed global third parties will increasingly agree to performance clauses with selected shippers. At first, the scope of these agreements will be limited, covering specific lane segments for specific product lines. Over time, it is reasonable to expect that these agreements will cover broad geographical areas, product lines, and transport modes, as well as multiple value-added services.

Managing International Logistics into the Twenty-First Century

The 1990s and beyond will be a period of intense business globalization. To compete, many companies will expand their potential sources of supply and distribution channels. The former Soviet bloc countries, as well as regions in Asia, Africa, and North and South America, will be increasingly considered as points of supply or distribution to customers.

Using Logistics for Competitive Advantage

These expanded options will have a profound impact on the way logistics is managed within firms of all sizes. Large, multinational companies will find ways to use their logistics systems to leverage their position in the marketplace. Accordingly, they will make strategic investments in systems, professional staff, and facilities to improve their logistics capabilities.

Small and medium-sized companies that today are only marginally engaged in the global marketplace will be compelled by competition to broaden the scope of their businesses. In doing so they will discover that effective management of international materials and products requires an in-depth understanding of the global pipeline. Effective management will depend on having more than a manager with part-time responsibility for the import/export department. It will require instead a commitment to developing a focused, integrated logistics management capability.

Challenges for International Logistics Managers

Change will be the one "constant" for logistics managers through the rest of the decade and beyond. Important dimensions of such change can already be identified:

• *Static logistics management will give way to dynamic logistics management.* Senior management will insist on continuous productivity improvements in the way materials and product flow through the pipeline. Logistics managers will need to develop the capability to measure, manage, and control on-time deliveries, order fill rates, order picking productivity, inventory carrying costs, and transportation unit costs.

• *Distinctions between international and domestic logistics activity will blur.* Management will increasingly recognize opportunities to leverage total company product volumes, expansion of third parties or carriers into international markets, and global or large regional planning strategies adopted by internationally oriented firms. Logistics personnel will need to be equally at ease in managing domestic and international logistics activity. Significant personnel cross-training can be expected.

• *Information will continue to replace brick-and-mortar facilities and inventory assets.* Companies will reduce the number of physical control points—such as regional warehouses that serve as safety stock buffer points—in favor of control provided through a combination of carriers, third parties, and integrated information systems. Further, marketing and other functional areas within the supply channel will have to become comfortable with just-in-time inventories constantly flowing through the pipeline.

• *Computers will grow even more important.* Decisions regarding facility location; merchandise routing; carrier, port and vendor selection; optimum shipment size; and customer service strategy will be managed with the help of information technology rather than "rules of thumb." This trend will be driven partly by advances in decision-support capabilities, and partly by the necessity to cope with the almost overwhelming variety of alternatives facing global managers.

• *Logistics managers will take on new responsibilities.* Customers want added value in their product purchases today, and providing this is often the duty of logistics personnel. Retailers, for example, in attempting to reduce product replenishment cycle times and thus reduce inventory safety stocks, are asking suppliers to provide services they once performed themselves. To be accommodating, garment manufacturers are attaching product identity tags to each apparel item so that retailers can move products directly to store shelves upon receipt at store receiving docks. In addition, to the extent that third parties are asked to handle remote offshore activities like component purchasing, minor assembly, and product distribution, company logistics staff will be responsible for managing their performance.

Innovative Logistics Management Structures

New structures will emerge to manage worldwide logistics responsibilities. A common feature of global companies will be cross-functional management teams whose job is to transcend (or even remove) the functional "turf" barriers that hinder operational efficiency. They will look closely, for example, at the impact that launching a new product will have on all functional areas of the firm, from purchasing to manufacturing and distribution. Logistics will play an important role on these cross-functional, often globally focused teams.

The growing reliance on third parties will result in management organizations made up of personnel from both user and provider. These may be working groups that "cross-pollinate" by placing personnel in each other's organizations for brief or even lengthy tours of duty. This will strengthen the bond between these companies, providing momentum to a growing international third-party trend. Such a development is common in Japan today.

Companies will be willing to experiment with innovative international logistics partnerships. In addition to third-party relationships that could be structured along joint-venture lines, companies will enter into various close relationships with competitors, customers, suppliers, and even government agencies like port authorities in an attempt to source and distribute products more efficiently around the globe. (This trend is already well underway. According to one recent report analyzing U.S. international alliances between 1983 and 1988, improving logistics capabilities was cited as the principal reason for forming the partnership in 130 of 729 cases.)

Finally, in an attempt to increase productivity, companies will experiment with turning their logistics cost centers into profit centers by selling their services to outside firms. This has the potential for lowering cost, improving asset productivity, increasing efficiency, and using logistics for strategic market advantage. It will also offer professional logistics managers an opportunity to prove they have the entrepreneurial skill and mind-set needed to help themselves and their companies succeed.

SECTION VIII

Logistics Information Systems

Donald J. Bowersox

One of the oldest elements of business operations is logistics. No commercial activity is possible without logistical support. Despite its fundamental and historical foundations, the field of logistics is undergoing dramatic change. Many observers feel that logistical management is experiencing a renaissance—more change has occurred during the past decade than during all decades combined since the Industrial Revolution. Information technology is at the core of this change. The availability of timely, accurate, and inexpensive information is opening the door for unprecedented quality and productivity improvements in the logistics process. Armed with expanded information capabilities, managers are reengineering traditional processes to better meet customer and operating requirements. The four chapters that constitute perspectives on logistics information systems view varied impacts of information technology on logistics best practice.

In Chapter 31 David J. Closs provides an overview that positions information in logistics. This lead chapter provides a framework scoping the varied ways that information impacts logistical planning and operational control. Closs focuses on methodology of logistics information system design. The scope of his chapter highlights the comprehensive nature of planning information requirements. The applications required to manage a transaction-intense process like logistics and the resulting architectural complexity are developed. In Chapter 32 Thomas K. Fox provides a design approach for logistics information systems including guiding principles and considerations specific to integrated logistics systems. In combination, Chapter 31 and Chapter 32 establish the foundation for developing a comprehensive logistical information plan.

In Chapter 33 Margaret Ann Emmelhainz extends the information paradigm beyond the internal operation of a single enterprise. Her treatment of electronic data interchange (EDI) provides a foundation for establishing paperless communications between trading partners and with service companies. Chapter 34, by Patricia J. Daugherty, positions the use of electronic capability in a strategic context. Her treatment of electronic linkage demonstrates the need to share information to maximize alliance effectiveness. Information sophistication and the willingness to share strategic plans is the key element in leveraging through alliances.

In total, these four chapters offer a wide range of insights into varied ways that information technology is stimulating logistical process reengineering. They should remind us that the logistical renaissance has just begun.

CHAPTER 31

Positioning Information In Logistics

David J. Closs

Research clearly indicates that leading-edge firms use information technology to increase their competitiveness and develop sustained competitive advantage.[1] Technology applications range from electronic data interchange (EDI) to enhanced order management and transportation control systems. They often include process automation such as barcoding and radio frequency (RF). While individual technologies typically generate substantial payback, the systems concept suggests that the high-yield breakthrough potential is in developing integrated systems capable of providing information to manage the overall supply chain process. To attain supply chain integration, it is necessary to understand the information requirements of all participants and design systems that facilitate cooperation.

Logistics information systems combine hardware and software to manage, control, and measure logistics activities. These activities occur within specific firms as well as across the overall supply chain. Hardware includes computers, input and output devices, communication channels, ancillary technology like bar code and radio frequency devices, and storage media. Software includes system and application programs used for logistics activities. The focus of this chapter is application software. Logistics itself includes the activities required to plan, execute, and measure the movement of product from the raw material suppliers through the firm and ultimately to the final consumer.[2]

This chapter has two objectives. First, a classification of information technology application areas in logistics today and in the foreseeable future is developed. The classification construct groups software uses into coordination and operations. Second, this chapter develops logistics application characteristics, reviews typical problems, and discusses solutions firms are using to overcome problems. The directional assessment is based on leading-edge firms' plans to improve technological competency.

Classification of Logistics Information Application

Logistics information systems include two flows that incorporate coordinating and operational activities, respectively. Figure 31-1 illustrates the key activities within each plane. Coordinating activities include scheduling and requirements planning throughout the firm. Typical activities are the development of strategic, capacity, logistics, manufacturing, and procurement plans.

Operational activities are the information procedures that initiate and track receipts, inventory assignment, and shipment of replenishment and customer orders. Replenishment orders control finished goods inventory movement between distribution facilities. Customer orders initiate inventory movements between distribution points and customer facilities. A typical replenishment or customer order requires a series of operational activities initiated by order receipt. For

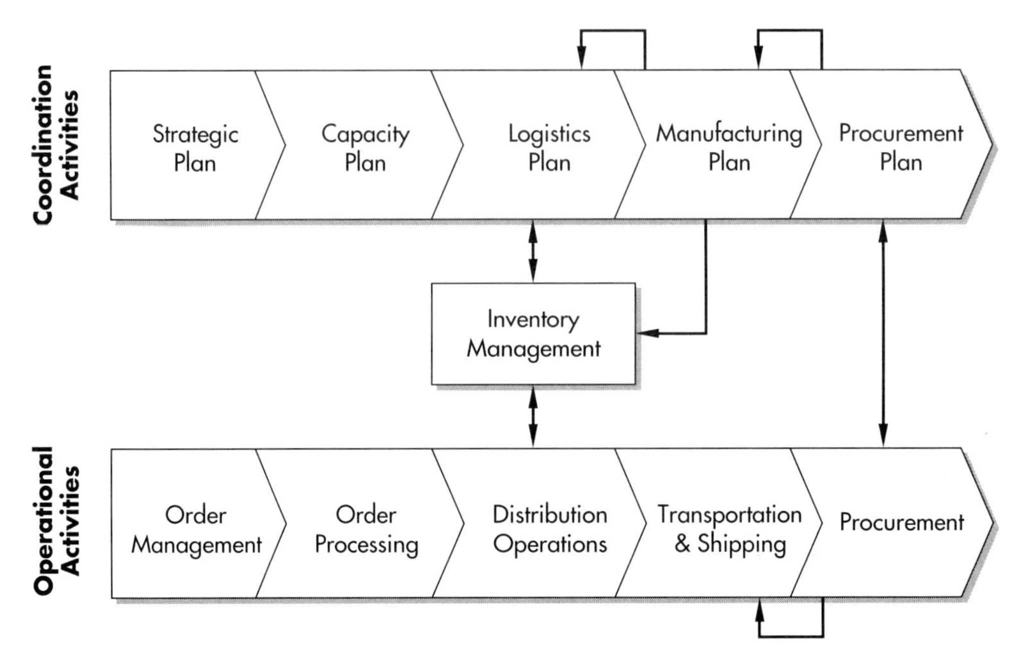

Figure 31-1
Logistics Information Flow

a single replenishment or customer order cycle, typical activities include order receipt, modification, processing/inventory allocation, picking, and shipment. The procurement order cycle is another activity of the operational plane.

Specific coordinating and operational applications are discussed to develop additional perspectives on trends in logistics system information applications.

Coordination Flow

The coordination flow represents the backbone of overall information architecture for firms that primarily manufacture or distribute products. Logistics applications coordinate core activities that guide firm resource allocation and performance from procurement to finished product delivery. Logistics applications control primary value-added activities necessary for firm stability and profitability.

The shaded components in Figure 31-2 illustrate logistics coordination flow. Corresponding with the activities identified above, coordination flow actions are as follows: (1) strategic planning, (2) capacity planning, (3) logistics planning, (4) manufacturing planning, and (5) procurement planning. As Figure 31-2 illustrates, inventory management directly interfaces with both operational and coordinating information flows. Inventory management is an integral part of both flows. Each coordinating activity is discussed below.

The primary information drivers for manufacturing and distribution firms are strategic plans that seek to achieve marketing and financial goals. The marketing considerations include target markets, products, marketing mix plans, and the role of logistics value-added services.

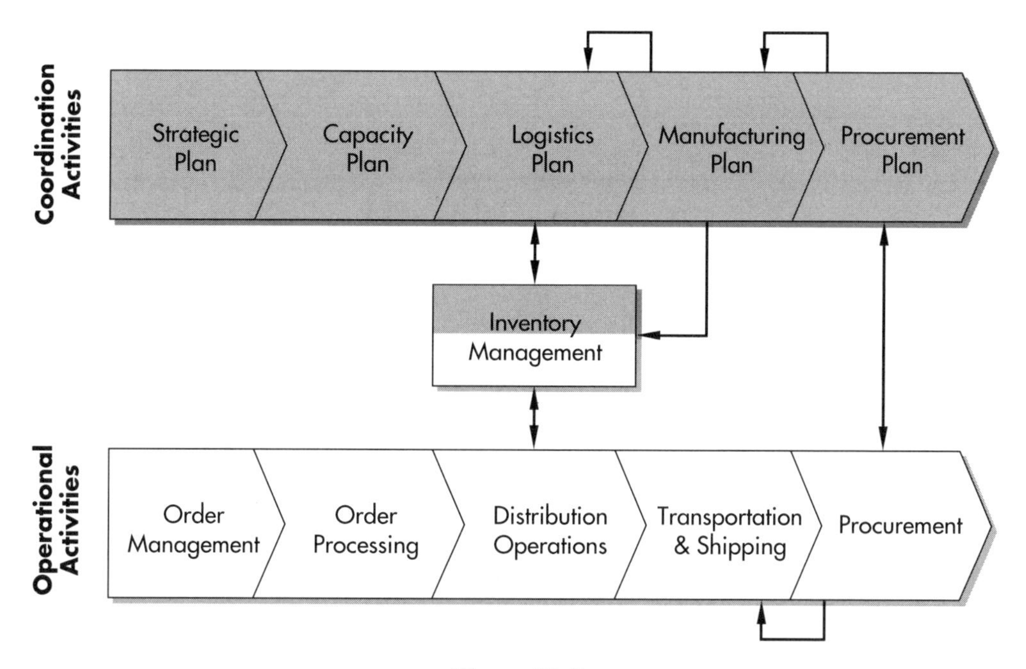

Figure 31-2
Coordination Flow

These considerations define the nature and location of customers, the breadth of products and services, and planned performance levels. Marketing goals are the customer service policies and objectives that establish logistics activity and performance targets. Typical logistics performance targets include case fill rate, line fill rate, order-cycle-time objectives, and order-cycle-time consistency. Financial considerations include capital, operating cost, and human resource requirements. The financial aspects of the strategic plan serve as funding constraints for receivables, inventory, facilities, and equipment. The primary strategic planning deliverable is the annual or quarterly aggregate activity level such as shipments, dollar volume, or total cases.

Capacity, logistics, manufacturing, and procurement plans all are generated from the strategic plan. The capacity plan concerns internal and external manufacturing capacity. Based on the strategic plan, the capacity plan identifies and resolves barriers or bottlenecks within the materials management system. The capacity plan considers aggregate production or throughput limitations such as annual or monthly capacities. The barrier or bottleneck resolutions may take the form of product and location speculation or postponement. Speculation reduces bottlenecks by anticipating production and capacity needs and scheduling the limited resources prior to the actual product need. Postponement delays production or shipment of product until specific requirements are known and capacity can be allocated. It is often necessary to offer customer incentives like discounts or allowances when a postponement strategy is followed. Other ways to formally impact capacity planning include asset acquisition and alliance partnerships such as contract manufacturing or facility leasing. The capacity plan focuses the firm's strategic plan in a time-phased dimension that considers facility, financial resource, and human resource constraints. The primary capacity planning output is monthly or weekly requirements that specify dollar or unit volume by product group or market region.

A comprehensive logistics plan specifies facility, equipment, labor, and inventory requirements. Using inputs from forecasts, customer orders, and inventory status, the logistics plan coordinates cross-functional performance by quantifying future requirements and developing inventory requirements. Product forecasts are based on sales and marketing input and past experience. Customer orders include orders in process, future releases, and contract commitments. Promotional orders are particularly important when planning customer requests, because they often represent a large percentage of the total volume and have a major influence on capacity requirements. Inventory status is product available to ship.

The logistics plan is primary to inventory management, which, in turn, is the interface between coordination and operations. As such, some inventory management characteristics are discussed within each information flow. Inventory management schedules replenishment and transfers between manufacturing and distribution facilities. The logistics plan may be developed from reactive or planning logic or a combination on the two.[3] Reactive logic uses customer requirements to initiate finished goods inventory replenishment. Reorder point logic (ROP) is an example of the reactive mode. Planning logic, on the other hand, initiates replenishment based on forecast. Distribution resource planning (DRP) is an example of logistics planning logic. Planning logic orients inventory management more closely to the coordinating plan, while reactive logic shifts inventory management closer to the operational plane. The primary deliverable of the logistics plan is a statement of time-phased inventory requirements.

The logistics plan is also a key input to manufacturing planning, which includes both the master production schedule (MPS) and the manufacturing requirements plan (MRP). MPS defines weekly or daily production and machine schedules. Given MPS input, MRP time-phases raw material and component requirements to support the designated manufacturing plan. The manufacturing plan schedules resources and attempts to resolve day-to-day capacity bottlenecks, such as raw material or daily capacity limitations within the materials management system. The manufacturing plan deliverable is the day-to-day production schedule and material requirements.

The procurement plan schedules raw material release, shipment, and receipt. The procurement plan uses the capacity plan to drive overall decisions concerning range of acceptable suppliers, degree of material speculation, and desirability of long-term contracts. The procurement plan uses MRP to drive short-term vendor releases. The procurement plan deliverables are important to both long- and short-term purchasing requirements.

While each planning activity can, and in the past frequently has, operated independently, the potential for inconsistency can create operating inefficiencies and excessive inventories. Failure to fully appraise the impact of strategic plans can result in uncoordinated manufacturing and logistics inventories. Similarly, failure to consider procurement, manufacturing, or logistics capacity can create facility and processing inefficiencies. Such failure to coordinate can lead to otherwise unnecessary safety stocks to buffer independent performance.

Operational Flow

The second information flow involves the logistics operational modules required to receive, process, and ship customer and purchase orders. The shaded boxes in Figure 31-3 illustrate major logistics operating modules and their interrelationship. The modules are as follows: (1) order management, (2) order processing, (3) distribution operations, (4) inventory management, (5) transportation and shipping, and (6) procurement. As the primary interface between the co-

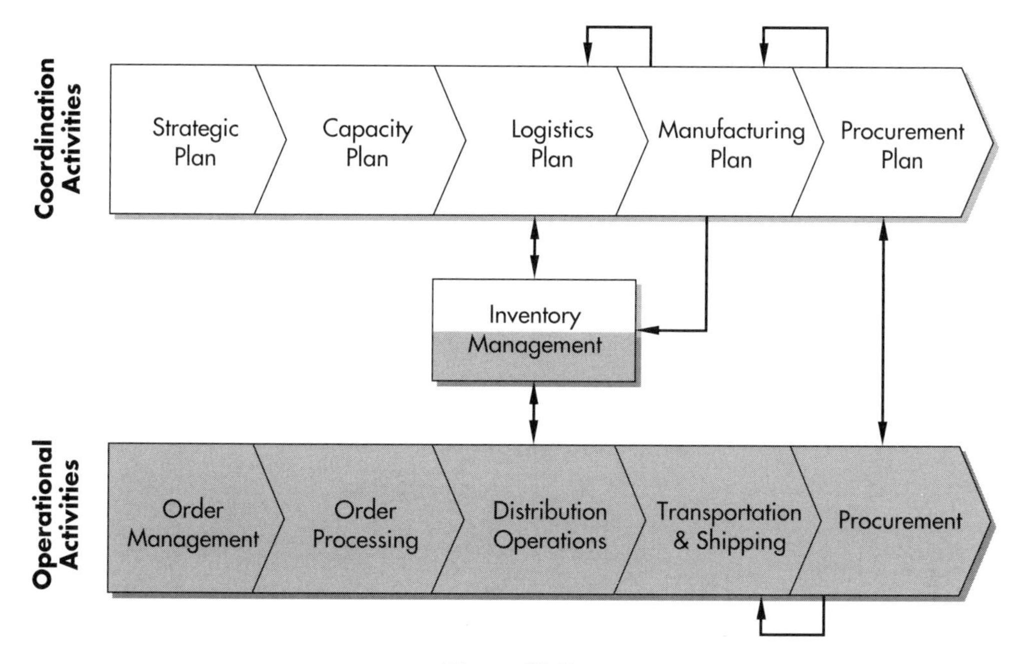

Figure 31-3
Operational Flow

ordinating and operational flows, inventory management is fundamental to both. Each module is briefly described below.

Order Management

The order management module is the customer entry point. Its primary purpose is to facilitate entry and maintenance of customer orders using a variety of technologies like phone, mail, fax, or EDI. Typically the orders are edited for appropriate values and then entered for processing. Table 31-1 lists order management functions.

Order Processing

The order processing module allocates and assigns inventory to open orders. Allocation may take place on a real-time basis as the orders are received or in batch mode. The typical order processing module assigns existing inventory or capacity. In advanced applications, however, the module works interactively with sales or customer service to generate an order solution that both satisfies customer requirements and remains within the firm's resource limitations. Table 31-2 lists typical order processing functions.

Distribution Operations

The distribution operations module includes warehouse activity transactions like materials movement and storage, product receipt, and order picking. This module controls all activities performed within a logistics facility, using a combination of real-time and batch components.

TABLE 31-1
Order Management Functions

1. Blanket order entry
2. Credit checking
3. Electronic order entry
4. Inventory availability check
5. Manual order entry
6. Service measurement
7. Order acknowledgment
8. Order editing
9. Order modification
10. Order pricing
11. Order status inquiry
12. Price and discount extensions
13. Promotion checking
14. Reassignment of order source
15. Returns processing

Throughout industry there is a strong trend toward real-time operations to reduce overall processing cycle times. Technologies like barcoding, radio frequency, and computerized handling equipment are capable of reducing elapsed time between decision and action. Table 31-3 lists typical distribution operations functions.

Inventory Management

As the primary interface between the coordinating and operational planes, inventory management directly uses inventory requirements developed in the coordinating plane to initiate and control replenishment throughout the logistics network. Figure 31-3 illustrates these transactions as the partially shaded inventory management module. The module typically uses a combination of human and automated decision processes. Table 31-4 lists common inventory management functions.

TABLE 31-2
Order Processing Functions

1. Create back order
2. Generate invoice
3. Generate picking documents
4. Reserve inventory
5. Process back order
6. Reassign order source
7. Release reserved inventory
8. Release blanket order
9. Verify shipment

TABLE 31-3
Distribution Operations Functions

1. Assignment of storage locations
2. Cycle counting
3. Inventory control
4. Labor scheduling
5. Lot control
6. Performance measurement
7. Picking replenishment
8. Receiving
9. Stock storage and retrieval
10. Tracking of storage locations

Transportation and Shipping

The transportation and shipping module consolidates orders for shipment and produces supporting documentation. This module increasingly incorporates shipment schedule communication to customers and may facilitate invoicing using EDI. The transportation and shipping module typically uses a combination of manual and technology-assisted information to build cost- and service-effective shipments. This module may also select and route carriers. Table 31-5 lists transportation and shipping functions.

Procurement

The procurement module manages purchase order preparation and modification, releases purchase orders to vendors, tracks performance, and measures overall compliance. Increasing procurement modules are electronically linked to suppliers. Table 31-6 lists procurement functions.

TABLE 31-4
Inventory Management Functions

1. Forecast analysis and modeling
2. Forecast data maintenance
3. Forecast data updates
4. Forecast parameter selection
5. Forecast technique selection
6. Inventory parameter calculation
7. Inventory simulation
8. Inventory requirement plan
9. Promotion data integration
10. Replenishment order build
11. Replenishment order release
12. Replenishment order schedule
13. Service objective establishment

TABLE 31-5
Transportation and Shipping Functions

1. Carrier selection
2. Carrier scheduling
3. Dispatching
4. Document preparation
5. Freight payment
6. Performance measurement
7. Shipment consolidation and routing
8. Shipment rating
9. Shipment scheduling
10. Shipment tracing and expedition
11. Vehicle loading

The preceding discussion provided an overview of logistics coordinating and operational information flows. There are three conclusions that suggest changes for future systems.

1. *There typically has been minimal information exchange between the two information flows.* In most situations, there are planning data and operating data. Rarely are the data the same for planning and operations. If the firm is using operating information to develop plans, there is usually a substantial delay before the data are adequately formatted and available for use. The result is often inconsistency between coordination and operations.
2. *Coordinating activities are generally not integrated into operational modules.* This is true even when such coordination would be desirable. For example, the order management module typically assigns an order to a predefined shipping location based on a prescribed policy. If the predefined source does not have adequate inventory, the typical action is a back order or stockout. An application with integrated coordination and operations might have the capability to assign the order to an alternate shipping facility with available inventory *and* be able to adjust all coordinating plans to reflect the change.
3. *Both coordinating and operational flows are linear.* This suggests a sequence in which the activities of one module must be completed before initiating the next. While the sequence

TABLE 31-6
Procurement Functions

1. Match-and-pay
2. Open order review
3. Purchase order entry
4. Purchase order maintenance
5. Purchase order receipt
6. Purchase order status
7. Quote request
8. Requirements communication
9. Schedule receipt appointment
10. Supplier history

discussed for both the coordinating and operational flows follows a logical relationship, there are situations where a more simultaneous or flexible flow is desirable. For example, when planning vehicle loads in the transportation and shipping module, it may be desirable to have the flexibility to return to order processing to add or delete products to efficiently size final shipments.

Although these and other limitations have traditionally been acceptable as result of policies, hardware, and/or software constraints, such practices are now viewed as inflexible and inefficient. Current hardware and software offer the technology to create flexibility. Achievement of logistics flexibility typically requires policy change and process reengineering.

Using Information to Manage Logistics

Integrated supply chain management is characterized as the interdependent performance of planning, execution, and monitoring activities. In the past, these activities were typically performed at different times, often by different individuals and sometimes in different forms. Today's competitive pressures require that coordinating and operational activities be integrated and remain timely.

Increased performance requires quicker decisions covering more complex alternatives. Information technology offers one way to satisfy these requirements. Logistics information applications, problems, and directions are discussed in this section. The discussion is focused on the primary concerns related to planning, execution, and performance monitoring.

Observations are drawn from in-depth interviews completed with 50 managers and executives in 6 consumer products firms during 1992. The interviews focused on the activities presented in Figure 31-1. Each manager was asked three questions:

1. What characteristics make logistics applications different from other firm information system applications?
2. What are the major problems with current logistics applications?
3. What actions are being taken to advance logistics applications and overcome the problems?

The responses come from a limited number of nonrandom interviews. However, the interviews clearly indicated common perceptions and problems.

Application Characteristics

The interviews indicated four characteristics of logistics applications that differentiate them from other information system applications. Logistics applications:

1. are data-intensive
2. have multiple flows
3. place significant demands on the application/user interface
4. have high levels of sequential processing

The explicit perception was that these characteristics make logistics systems more difficult to design, implement, and manage than other applications. Each characteristic is briefly discussed below.

- *Data-intensive.* Logistics applications are very data-intensive because they must include information from all dimensions of customer, product, facility, and logistics activity. For each dimension, logistics application contain historical, current, and planned values. For example, for each combination of customers, products, and facilities, logistics applications must maintain past orders (historical), current orders (current), and forecasts (planned). In addition to the order and forecast volumes, logistics must also maintain the historical, current, and planned costs for completing each logistics activity. The sheer number of combinations results in very data-intensive applications.
- *Multiple flows.* Logistics applications have substantial interaction between coordinating and operating flows. While other applications like accounting have coordinating and operating flows as well, dynamic interaction is not as critical because there are defined closing times at which information is exchanged and updated. Logistic applications, on the other hand, require dynamic interchange between coordinating and operating information flows. As future orders are entered into the application via the order management module, order information must be incorporated into the logistics, manufacturing, and procurement plans. This exchange of information cannot occur at a single point in time but must be continuous because the system is dynamic. Significant information exchange is necessary to achieve integrated coordination plans and operational activities.
- *Application/user interface.* Some aspects of logistics applications like order entry are structured. However, there are many more that depend on user selection from a range of alternatives. Examples include product substitution, promotional pricing, replenishment planning, and assignment of shipping locations. In some applications, users are guided through selection. Such on-line direction is not common in today's logistics applications. Further development of on-line decision aids is particularly important when one considers the experience and training of individuals who interface logistics and applications. Logistics application users frequently are young, inexperienced, and not well trained, and also change jobs often. This user profile, along with increasingly complex alternatives, places significant demands on the user interface and on-line decision aids.
- *Sequential process.* Logistics activities involve a high level of sequential processing for operational applications. In most logistics applications, there is a prescribed sequence for completing operational module procedures. The transactions initiating this processing are often initiated manually. For example, orders are entered and changed using a transaction. Then inventory is assigned to orders from individual or batch transactions. Completed orders are finally picked, shipped, and released as the last step in the sequential process. Inventory replenishment requests are processed similarly. The transactions are usually very structured in terms of initiator, receiver, data requirements, and processing sequence. An example of the difficulty imposed by structured sequential processing is illustrated by the relationship between order entry and credit checking. If the order is changed following credit checking, it may be necessary to route the order back to credit a second time. Many logistics applications have difficulty with rerouting because it is counter to the standard sequence. Transactions in most logistics applications still model the sequence and structure of the paper flow transactions that existed prior to computerization. The paper procedures required very sequential processing and allowed limited paper routing flexibility.

Although these three characteristics are not unique, the managers interviewed indicated that these characteristics magnified the logistics application problems. The following section identifies and illustrates the specific problems.

Application Problems

From the general characteristics discussed above and other factors that are not as generic, the management interviews identified seven key problem areas for logistics applications: (1) integration, (2) decision support, (3) flexibility, (4) exception processing, (5) process measurement, (6) process feedback, and (7) process knowledge.

1. *Integration.* The first and most common problem cited in the interviews is poor data and functional integration. The data integration aspect concerns the lack of commonality and consistency of data between coordination and operations. For example, many logistics applications do not share future order data (order maintenance module) and forecasts (logistics plan). A second example cited is the data inconsistencies between the product database that supports coordination and operation. The interviews cited situations where order maintenance uses one list of products while planning has a different product master file. This results in customers' ordering products that manufacturers no longer produce. The functional integration aspect is more interesting. Many interviews cited cases where the separate application modules performed well individually but not as an integrated package. Examples cited included logistics and manufacturing planning, which are typically very sophisticated individually. However, data inconsistency or time delays between the two planning applications often occur even though they should be contiguous processes. The result is failure to integrate. The same lack of integration occurs in the operations between the order processing and transportation and shipping modules. Specifically, while filling the order, the order processing module does not always build loads that fit within the transportation vehicle constraints. This occurs when the order is too large for the transportation vehicle.

2. *Decision support.* The second problem cited is the failure to evaluate or analyze alternate coordinating and operational decisions. Logistics application users are frequently so driven for volume throughput that they do not take the time to evaluate alternative solutions. Examples cited include logistics plans, manufacturing plans, order management, and transportation and shipping decisions. A specific order management example is failure to consider alternate sources, delivery modes, or delivery schedules. In many situations, the order is accepted as requested by the customer even though it may be impossible to meet the customer's requirements. Adequate decision support could assist the customer service representative in developing a mutually agreeable plan for order fulfillment.

3. *Flexibility.* The third problem identified is a lack of flexibility in current logistics applications. The two aspects of inflexibility mentioned are process sequence and information. Inflexible process sequence concerns the inability of most applications to deviate from the standard sequence. The requirement that credit checking be completed before inventory allocation is an example of process sequence inflexibility. Lack of information flexibility refers to the inability to maintain or retrieve specialized information on standard application data structures. An example frequently cited is the difference between military and regular orders. Military orders are typically larger and require different information than civilian orders. However, many logistics applications do not have the capability to accept or maintain the additional data. As a result, it is necessary to augment the process with manual or awkward solutions.

4. *Exception processing.* The fourth problem cited is the lack of exception processing. Even though there are large numbers of accounts, products, orders, and shipments, many logistics applications do not have adequate exception processing capabilities. For example, many applications still require inventory clerks or planners to review a long list of products to identify items requiring replenishment. The review process takes time that could be used to better advantage.

There is increasing use of exception processing, but logistics planning, inventory management, and transportation and shipping were cited as weak exception processing areas.

5. *Process measurement.* The fifth problem cited is the lack of total process measurements. Current logistics measurements and management rewards focus on individual functional or activity excellence rather than total process excellence. For example, logistics applications are designed to record order fill rates and inventory levels. Management and staff are then rewarded according to their ability to meet specific objectives while maintaining minimum inventory levels. Applications report and often reward speed and consistency of internal order cycle time but do not consider that order consolidation could result in even lower total cost and in some situations even better service. Internal measures do not typically consider total customer satisfaction, which is the ultimate logistics mission. The total customer satisfaction measures include total process time, ability to meet agreed delivery schedule, and providing timely order information as well as order fulfillment.

6. *Process feedback.* The sixth problem cited, which is related to the previous one, is inadequate process feedback. Current logistics application performance measurement, when it is provided, is not timely enough to modify decisions or processes. For example, while order fulfillment is measured on each order, many logistics applications don't report it until the end of an operating period, such as a week or a month. This is usually too late to highlight a problem or take corrective action. However, the managers interviewed feel that there is substantial room for improvement in most logistics applications.

7. *Process knowledge.* The final problem commonly cited is a lack of knowledge about the integrated logistics application. User and management training has focused on the individual modules, with little consideration for dynamics between modules. The problems generally cited include a lack of knowledge of integrated system impacts, performance measures that don't consider total system impact, and inadequate training in alternative analyses. As a result, there is strong motivation to stay with traditional procedures. An example frequently cited is the failure of order management personnel to understand the impact of their decisions on inventory management and logistics planning. A second example is the inventory planning positions, which typically have high turnover but can significantly impact firm assets through inventory and purchase decisions. This problem exists because the individual applications were typically developed as an end-to-end process while very few individuals have a total process perspective. This was acceptable in the past because safety stock inventory was available to absorb deficiencies. However, reduced inventory levels have taken out the buffers; therefore, order management has a more direct impact on inventory management and logistics planning. Management and staff have not been educated about the increasing dynamics between the coordinating and operational planes and among modules within the planes. This results in decisions that cause significant problems for processes that are "upstream" or "downstream" within the coordinating or operational plane.

The problems cited above are neither trivial nor simple to solve. In many cases, they are related to the structure of the logistics applications, which have evolved over time and require substantial investment. Until recently, the typical application was not replaced or substantially upgraded for a number of years. In addition, existing processes are well entrenched within the organization structure and procedures. Substantive solutions for these typical problems will require significant change in the logistics process and applications. Although some of the interviewed firms have undertaken the necessary reengineering process, others have not.

Directions

The management interviews identified six initiatives that the firms have used to overcome these basic problems: (1) boundary spanning, (2) education and training, (3) measurement perspective, (4) information substitution, (5) decision integration, and (6) process reengineering. Some of the initiatives are relatively easy and can be implemented in stages. Others, however, require a substantial up-front investment prior to implementation.

Initiatives

1. *Boundary spanning.* The first initiative is the boundary-spanning activities that address the integration problem between coordinating and operational activities and between firms. Logistics application boundary-spanning activities include the integration and sharing of common information across activity and firm boundaries. The sharing may be through common data or via EDI transfers. Examples of boundary spanning include the sharing of forecast or requirement data within the firm and with suppliers and customers. Other examples common today include EDI transmittal of orders, invoices, and shipment data.

EDI boundary spanning is relatively easy to initiate and can be done incrementally by integrating additional activities, customers, and suppliers. Even though interviewed firms had substantial EDI activity in place, the managers indicated significant additional opportunities. The opportunities most frequently cited were internal to the firm rather than between other members of the supply chain.

2. *Education and training.* The second initiative focuses on the knowledge problem. The management interviews suggested that past logistics applications have allowed approximately 5% of the development budget for application training. The training focused primarily on application use, with emphasis on keyboard skills. This developed clerical and management users who could efficiently enter the data but who had little understanding of the overall impact. The management interviews indicated that current and future development budgets are allowing 20% of the project cost for education and training. The majority of the increase is to support education of all users on the integrated impact of their actions. A specific example is the education of order management personnel on how their actions influence logistics planning. The logistics and manufacturing planners are also educated about the realities of daily order management activities. The additional training in other activities offers much better understanding of the dynamics and results in improved decisions by the line personnel.

3. *Measurement perspective.* The third initiative focuses on metrics and measurement. As firms change from a total process perspective to a commitment to customer satisfaction, key metrics must be viewed overall. Although the problem is obvious, implementation requires significant changes in procedures and technology applications. As new applications are being implemented, the managers indicated that broader performance measures are being included. In addition to standard fill-rate performance measures, the broader metrics include meeting delivery appointments, invoice discrepancies, damaged merchandise, and total cycle time. While technology advances will continue to make the measurement information more timely and integrated, management objectives and rewards must be tied to these metrics as well.

4. *Information substitution.* The fourth initiative is to educate employees and customers so they will understand that information is a viable substitute for maintaining finished inventories. Examples of such applications include product substitution, delivery date confirmation, and forecast exchange. In these situations, firms typically maintain inventories to buffer the uncertainties

associated with product availability, delivery uncertainty, and forecast uncertainty. Although many firms currently use these initiatives, they are not yet applied universally. The primary constraints are lack of logistics applications that can provide reliable data and are capable of supporting the required flexibility, and the discomfort in exchanging sensitive data, such as forecasts, between firms. The data reliability issue is addressed through the data and process integration initiatives discussed earlier. The discomfort is being addressed through alliances with key accounts where the exchange, though painful, has resulted in positive benefits for both parties. The interviewed firms are taking these incremental steps with both their logistics applications and the key accounts.

5. *Decision integration.* The fifth initiative incorporates additional planning and decision tools into the operational applications. Current operational activities do not effectively evaluate alternatives as customer or replenishment orders are processed. Past logistics applications processed the orders with parameters and guidelines that were established using generic assumptions, and thus they may not reflect the current situation. The interviews pointed to examples where service representatives can identify and evaluate alternate service strategies when special customer requests in terms of timing, contents, or delivery requirements are received. To complete this analysis and evaluation, decision analysis tools must be integrated into the operational information system.

6. *Process reengineering.* The final and most comprehensive initiative calls for reengineering the entire process, including both the coordinating and operational information and activity flows. Reengineering obviously requires substantial commitment for both executive and operations management. The reengineering process includes a redefinition of objectives, responsibilities, and tasks instead of traditional training. The objective must include the concept of customer-focused marketing, where the goal is to offer customer satisfaction. The responsibilities must include flexibility to respond to customer needs, along with the accountability and motivation to initiate actions profitable for the firm. The tasks must include consideration of alternative solutions for satisfying the customer, such as alternate sources, products, or delivery times. Although this reengineering requires substantial effort and resources, the majority of the firms interviewed were in the process of significant reengineering. The involved managers indicated that the process was painful and time-consuming, but they also acknowledged that reengineering is necessary to make a quantum leap in competitiveness.

Conclusion

Logistics applications will continue to expand significantly throughout the rest of the 1990s. Information is one resource whose price continues to decline while its capabilities are increasing. This increased role suggests three responses by logistics management.

1. *Logistics systems will expand both up and down the supply chain to achieve integration.* Customer and replenishment orders are communicated via EDI today, and this process will be further enhanced as requirement changes, schedules, invoices, and payments are instantly communicated between supply chain partners. This application extension suggests increased standardization and interface compatibility, as well as increased willingness to share information on a "win-win" basis.

2. *As logistics applications become more complex and decision making is further delegated, there is need for additional education and training.* The research strongly indicates that user education and training is a weakness in current applications environments. Although the applica-

tions and decisions are more complex, owing to time compression and the number of alternatives, training and particularly education have not increased commensurately.

3. *Existing logistics applications must be extensively reviewed or reengineered to shift from a functional to a process focus.* Current systems are designed around the traditional logistics activities of order entry, order processing, distribution operations, inventory, transportation, and procurement. As suggested above, newer designs focus on the process of fulfilling customer requirements. The process-oriented systems require dramatically new architecture, as evidenced by the inability of the interviewed firms to identify "off-the-shelf" software approaches to meet customer order management requirements. While the firms cited a preference for "purchased" applications, only one firm was able to identify an off-the-shelf operational system capable of meeting its requirements. The reengineering often must start with a "blank page" and evaluate the processes that the firm currently uses to satisfy customers. The existing application should be a starting point for the reengineering process, not a template for design.

Information technology offers one way to achieve improved logistics performance at a reduced cost, but substantial investments in hardware, software, reengineered solutions, education, and training are required. Before such an investment, management must understand key customer response and measurement requirements, modify measurement and performance systems, evaluate and redefine current processes, and train and educate the operating-level decision makers.

Notes

1. Donald J. Bowersox, Patricia J. Daugherty, Cornelia L. Dröge, Dale S. Rogers, and Daniel L. Wardlow, *Leading Edge Logistics: Competitive Positioning for the 1990's* (Oak Brook, Il.: Council of Logistics Management, 1989).
2. The Council of Logistics Management (Oak Brook, Il.) has recently revised its definition to read: "Logistics is the process of planning, implementing, and controlling the efficient, effective flow and storage of goods, services, and related information from point of consumption for the purpose of conforming to customer requirements."
3. Donald J. Bowersox, David J. Closs, and Omar K. Helferich, *Logistical Management* (New York: Macmillan, 1986).

CHAPTER 32

Logistics Information Systems Design

Thomas Fox

Logistics can be characterized as a transaction-oriented and information-intense business function.[1] Orders must be entered, processed, and tracked; inventory must be received, put away, picked, and shipped; transportation must be arranged and paperwork generated; and performance must be measured. To effectively manage these activities, integrated transaction-based systems must be in place to accurately collect data and quickly communicate information. To gain competitive advantage, however, companies must be willing to experiment with specialized technologies and take advantage of automated tools to increase both efficiency and the precision with which decisions are made. Examples of technologies used by companies with leading-edge logistics operations include electronic data interchange (EDI) and point of sale (POS). These technologies dramatically improve communications with business partners (i.e., suppliers and customers) and enable companies to identify and respond to business needs real time.

Automated tools are also available to improve the decision-making process in many areas of logistics. Tools used to enhance efficiency in the transportation area, for example, provide companies with the ability to route and schedule vehicles dynamically, depending on delivery requirements and cost factors. These companies enjoy higher customer service levels and lower transportation costs than the competition. Clearly, information technology is critical to logistics performance. Companies that realize there is a competitive advantage to be gained through practical applications of technology will be the ones to excel in the 1990s.

The effectiveness with which systems are conceptualized, designed, and implemented can mean the difference between leading the competition or simply remaining on par with it. This chapter discusses a systems design process to assure success. Before outlining this design process, it is useful to review the major forces of business change today and their impact on systems. The design approach is then reviewed and a discussion of guiding principles that can shape the design process follows. The chapter concludes with some thoughts regarding the design considerations specific to integrated logistics systems.

Forces of Business Change and Their Systems Impact

Many would say that business today is going through unprecedented change. Traditional business approaches are being challenged, and often dismantled and replaced by new and very different approaches. Obsolete business processes are being reengineered to support the total business strategy using the guiding principles discussed later in the chapter. Even casual observers of the business community recognize the impact of both foreign competition and the changes that just-in-time approaches have had on traditional manufacturing and distribution principles. Companies that are competitors are also forming joint ventures. New products and extensions of existing lines are aimed at new niches created by changing demographics and emerging geographic markets. The forces at work in today's business environment are many, but four major forces specifically affect a logistics system design: marketplace, regulatory, technology, and globalization.

Marketplace

The marketplace in almost every industry is becoming intensely competitive. Cost pressures are escalating as margin protection and financial performance, particularly in the short term, dominate management thinking. Simultaneously, customers are becoming more discriminating, demanding more service from suppliers, establishing higher standards of performance, and creating preferred relationships with suppliers that can meet their higher expectations. Suppliers, in turn, are striving to achieve differentiation by delivery techniques, information and communication capabilities, and policies and procedures that are often tailored to the unique needs of individual customers. Additionally, speed is now becoming a critical dimension of competition—speed in getting new products to market, speed in moving merchandise that is in great demand, speed in responding to customer emergencies and unique requests, and speed in making timely communications. These marketplace forces—less cost, more service, more speed—directly impact the logistics function, for it is logistics that is directly challenged by, and responsible for, all three marketplace forces.

Regulatory

Regulatory changes can be relatively minimal, such as additional reporting requirements. They can also be significant, such as the deregulation of transportation in the 1980s, which resulted in dramatic changes in carrier strategies and shipper-carrier relationships. Regardless of their impact, new legislation and regulation represent a force and a business requirement that must be met.

Technology

Advances in technology are occurring at faster rates than ever before. Capitalizing on new technology can often provide a powerful marketplace advantage. For example, consider what electronic data interchange (EDI) and barcoding have made possible by gathering point-of-sale information, communicating transaction information, and tracking and more precisely controlling the flow of materials. Businesses are now experimenting with leading-edge technologies like remote telemetry, satellite tracking, radio frequency communications, and client-server architectures, to name just a few. The pace and nature of technology development is a major force in the business world today. The use of technology is a significant business challenge; keeping pace with it and applying new technologies appropriately requires a combination of objectivity, prudence, vision, and a willingness to experiment.

Globalization

The marketing, financial, and operational reach of companies is becoming global. As supply lines become longer and more complex, the risk and penalty for service breakdown and failure escalates dramatically. Yet this risk must be managed without losing responsiveness and speed. This challenge must be shouldered by logistics professionals to establish reliable, long-distance operating capabilities supported by information systems and technologies that provide control and allow timely decision making. Globalization is pressuring companies to perform at much higher levels of competency.

Systems Impact

These marketplace, regulatory, technology, and globalization forces are causing companies to respond along many dimensions. Integrating functions within a business as well as integrating business partners in the supply and marketing channel is often fundamental to achieving higher levels of service at lower cost. Structuring organizations, developing corporate cultures, and building information systems are done to maintain maximum flexibility in responding to new business demands that have not yet been envisioned or even contemplated. Clearly, companies are looking toward technology to provide the control and communications to manage their global reach with precision. Thus, the logistics system's challenge is to support the needs for business integration, maximum flexibility, practical applications of technology, and control and communication. How these needs can be accommodated in the design process is discussed in the next section.

Design Approach

The use of an approach or methodology is critical to the success of any logistics system project. A methodology provides guidance and direction, from setting objectives in a business reengineering initiative to implementing a system solution. It will suggest the activities to be performed and the deliverables to be developed. The benefit of using a methodology can be substantial, and the cost of not using one is significant. An example of such a methodology is METHOD/1, developed by Andersen Consulting for extensive use with many of their custom and packaged system development efforts.[2]

A methodology by itself does not guarantee success for a logistics system project. Expertise is essential in functional, technical, and managerial areas. A methodology enables project resources to work productively on the right tasks at the right time. It provides a road map to deliver a solution on budget and on schedule.

System Development Life Cycle

The forces of business change lead to constant review and improvement of logistics processes and systems. Multiple stages are required to plan, design, and build the best solution. A common breakdown is illustrated in Figure 32-1.

Value-driven reengineering and information and *technology planning* are the front-end stages of a system development effort. The objectives include reengineering key business processes and establishing a strategy, architecture, and overall plan for information system development. These efforts are fundamental to current system development and set the stage for addressing future business needs.

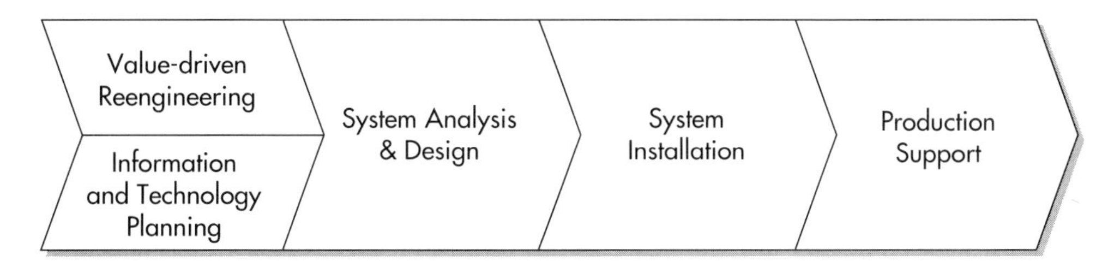

Figure 32-1
System Development Life Cycle

System analysis and design activities address the development of an application design that supports the strategic objectives of the organization and add value to the business processes being addressed. In this phase, the current system is evaluated and alternative solutions for problem areas are identified and documented.

The *system installation* phase finalizes the system design and includes activities to build, test, and integrate the application with the business process.

Production support is where the "live" application is supported and enhanced to meet changing business needs. Although all stages are critical to developing and maintaining the best solution, we focus on the system analysis and design phase of work in more detail.

System Analysis and Design

A system design can be performed in many ways. One of the most common methods, custom system analysis and design, calls for a thorough, formal exercise to develop functional and technical designs and detailed implementation plans. Each segment in this method creates an output (deliverable) that advances the project toward the solution of the system development problem and provides the input to the following segment in a critical pathlike sequence.

Other methods include modeling/prototyping and packaged systems. Selecting the appropriate approach depends on the issues surrounding the project, including the extent of change from the current process, breadth and depth of function, complexity of the application, amount of risk involved, and system reliability, flexibility, and cost. Table 32-1 shows important application attributes and the fit of each of the above-noted methodologies.

Many organizations are trying to dramatically reduce the time frame for designing and implementing new processes and systems while lowering the system development cost. Packaged systems offer lower development costs and a shorter development time frame. They are best suited, however, for environments in which they meet the majority of the critical business needs of an organization. The remaining critical business needs would be addressed through modifications or enhancements to the software. For logistics applications, the Council of Logistics Management publishes a software selection guide to aid logistics practitioners in the package selection process.[3]

The emphasis in this section is on the custom system analysis and design phase, because it applies to most logistics system development challenges. The approach is quite similar to the analysis and design approach of a custom system. Noticeable differences for a packaged system approach are a reduced design time frame, a software selection effort, some customization of the package, and third-party involvement in the testing of the system.

TABLE 32-1
Methodology Fit to Application Attributes

Application Attributes	Custom System Analysis and Design	Modeling/ Prototyping	Packaged Systems
Much change	M	H	L
Broad functionality	H	M	M
Complex application	H	M	M
High risk	M	M	M
High reliability	H	L	H
Great flexibility	H	H	M
Superior performance	H	L	M
Low cost	M	H	H

(H = high degree of fit; M = medium degree of fit; L = low degree of fit)

Custom System Analysis and Design Methodology

The custom system analysis and design methodology involves the segments of work outlined in Figure 32-2.

The methodology consists of core and ancillary components. The core components (grouped in shaded phases in Figure 32-2) address the analysis and design tasks of the business process. The surrounding components are necessary to manage and deliver a cost-effective solution.

The following discussion emphasizes the core components, with a brief discussion of the surrounding components. Next, the deliverables developed in a custom system analysis and design effort are discussed. Finally, a case example is cited to illustrate the methodology and its associated deliverables. The core components of the methodology include the following:

100—Project organization. This first core segment of work contains the activities necessary to set and manage project scope and objectives and to develop the detail work plans (work breakdown structures) and work programs (resource loading or scheduling). Individuals who have the required skills to complete the tasks are assembled into a project team.

200—Quality requirements. This segment of work describes how well the intended system needs to perform its functions. This includes characteristics like system performance, reliability, usability, and flexibility while meeting given cost-benefit criteria on schedule. Quality requirements ultimately determine the design of the system; it is to satisfy the quality requirements that design options are weighed against one another. The deliverables are a set of documents describing each of the specific quality requirements.

300—Functional requirements. This segment includes identifying, decomposing, and documenting the business processes. It assumes that the functions will be performed in the same manner as they are performed today or as prescribed by a reengineering initiative. Major deliverables are documents describing the flow of data through the organization and how they will be processed. The functional requirements specify what the system will do and is composed of an event model, a data model, and a process model. Techniques to gather this information consist of one-on-one interviewing and group requirements definition sessions (e.g., joint application requirements (JAR) session and joint application design (JAD) sessions).

400—Application architecture design. Documents resulting from this segment specify how the functional requirements will be implemented using a specific class of technology in a given architecture. Architecting a system suggests "layers" of potentially different software and hard-

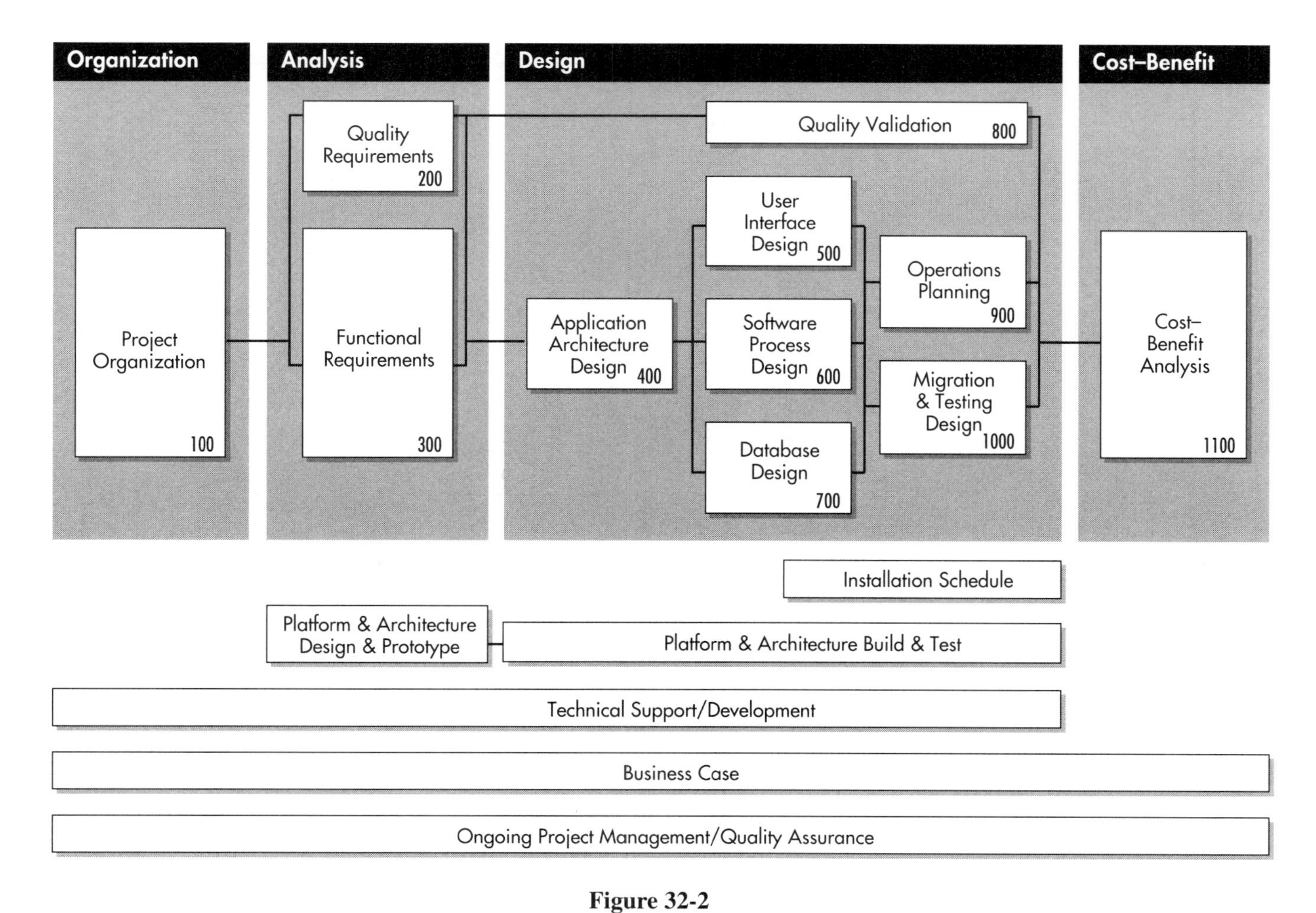

Figure 32-2
Custom System Analysis and Design

ware to allow for quicker and easier development and for easier maintenance. The scope of the architecture design will include the hardware platform, communications approach, and the software structures to be used in the application.

500—User interface design. The effort in this segment consists of designing the screens/windows and reports (layouts and descriptions) to support the functional requirements of the business processes. A dialogue or screen flow is also specified, as is a reporting delivery approach. Design standards and the consideration of human factors (i.e., ergonomics) help ensure consistency and ease of use.

600—Software process design. This segment contains the overall application flow and program/module descriptions. Each program in the system is described in terms of its processing functions and the data structures it uses. When required, system interfaces are described, and batch programs are organized into job streams.

700—Database design. The deliverables of this segment include a logical and a physical database design. The logical design consists of developing a data model that describes the applications or business view of the data. This includes file/table and element relationships and descriptions. The physical design consists of developing a data model based on the physical characteristics of the database management system (DBMS). These might include where the data physically reside and descriptions of indexes.

800—Quality validation. This segment consists of the activities to review the quality requirements and the application design to determine whether or not certain requirements can be met despite technical constraints (e.g., cost-effectiveness of long retention of large volumes of data). Quality requirements that cannot be fully met are addressed, and changes are discussed. Some changes may result in major rework to the design to ensure a minimum quality standard.

900—Operations planning. In this segment a preliminary plan for operating the system is established to include the necessary hardware and personnel resources and procedures for the day-to-day operation of the system (e.g., backup and recovery, timetables of operation).

100—Migrations and testing design. A migration plan and a test plan are developed in this segment. Often there are complexities in migrating from an old system to a new one. High-level plans are established during the design phase to identify a going-in position for migration to the new logistics system. Additionally, early views of the testing approach are developed during the design phase. Both efforts help to estimate the resource requirements for the installation phase of development.

1100—Cost-benefit analysis. In past years, the cost-benefit analysis was a fairly routine task conducted near the conclusion of the system design phase. The purpose was to quantify the costs to develop and maintain the system and weigh them against the anticipated benefits from implementing the system. Assuming the benefits outweighed the costs over a certain payback period (typically two to five years), the system project was approved to move forward for implementation. This process was routine because logistics system projects typically replaced specific business functions being performed either manually or by an outdated computer system. The costs and benefits of transaction-based systems were generally straightforward to quantify. For example, if a new order entry system was being designed, the cost to develop it could be calculated by estimating the workday effort to program, test, and implement it. The estimated workdays were multiplied by an average cost per workday to find the estimated development cost. The ongoing operational costs could be calculated by estimating (over the course of the payback period) hardware costs, computer usage, and operations and system maintenance costs. The expected benefits of transaction systems were typically based on cost reductions as a result of reduced labor to process, track, and file paperwork (in this example, orders).

For the most part, traditional cost-benefit analysis was simply a formality, because any opportunity to automate routine, manual tasks would result in a cost reduction. More recently, the cost-benefit analysis has taken on new dimensions. *Revenue enhancement* and *revenue protection* are strategic perspectives of logistics system technology with long-term implications that outweigh operational cost considerations.

- *Revenue enhancement.* In addition to transaction-based systems, forward-thinking organizations are beginning to use information technology for competitive advantage in the marketplace. These "mission-critical" systems are typically more sophisticated and expensive to build and cannot be justified on cost savings alone. As a matter of fact, the airline that developed the concept of frequent-flyer mileage awards probably added an entire department just to manage this program. Clearly, this system is justified based on revenue enhancement rather than cost reduction. Revenue enhancement justification is less tangible to quantify and is typically included as part of a larger business case sponsored by the organization's marketing function. These business cases usually include different revenue scenarios (best and worst case) based on market analysis of the new product or service. In these types of business cases, it is usually critical to introduce the new product or service before the competition in order to gain the biggest advantage. In these situations, senior management often enlists the services of an outside systems integrator to help manage the risk of timely system delivery.
- *Revenue protection.* An even more elusive cost-benefit analysis resulted from an outgrowth of companies using technology to gain a competitive advantage. That is the need to keep up with the competition. Using the frequent-flyer system as an example, it quickly became essential for other carriers to offer (and automate) similar bonus programs. In such cases, the justification for the business case was not revenue enhancement but revenue protection. This type of justification is even less tangible to quantify because the business case needs to anticipate the market reaction to the competition as well as to the organization's response to match the competition. More often than not, these catch-up system projects are sold to senior management as a "matter of survival," with very subjective cost justification.

The Ancillary components of custom system analysis and design methodology include the following:

Installation schedule. The installation effort is estimated and scheduled. Enough work has been performed to this point to develop a detailed plan (work breakdown structure) and schedule for the build, test, and migrate stage of the application. The work breakdown structure is developed to a low enough level of detail (fewer than 15–20 days of work per unit of work; 5–10 days on average) so that it becomes possible to control the work effort.

Platform and architecture design and prototype. This segment of work is performed when there is enough uncertainty about the feasibility or the consensus to justify more detailed investigations. For example, most users have not used graphical user interfaces (GUI). Consequently, to obtain consensus on the usability requirement goal, it is necessary to demonstrate the GUI.

Platform and architecture build and test. The selected platform and architecture are developed and tested as preparation for the installation phase.

Technical support/development. The project team will require tools to develop and maintain the design documentation and deliverables. Activities in this segment are performed to develop, implement, and maintain the design tools. This segment also includes activities to provide technical support for the project team.

Business case. The business case activities continue through the system analysis and design

TABLE 32-2
Key Deliverables

Phase	Core Work Segments	Key Deliverables
Organization	100—Project organization	Work plan
Analysis	200—Quality requirements	Performance, security, and control requirements
Analysis	300—Functional requirements	Function chart
Design	400—Application architecture design	Technical architecture overview
Design	500—User interface design	Screen/window and report specifications
Design	600—Software process design	Concept diagram, data flow diagrams
Design	700—Database design	Logical data model, physical data model
Design	800—Quality validation	Performance, security, and control approach
Design	900—Operations planning	Operating approach and resource requirements
Design	1000—Migration testing and design	Migration and testing plan
Cost-benefit	1100—Cost-benefit analysis	Cost-benefit summary

phase to verify the benefits to be gained from the project. More information about the costs and benefits to be incurred are uncovered during the design activities, and the value of continuing with the development of the system is confirmed.

Ongoing project management/quality assurance. Project management activities are performed to track and report progress, and monitor and manage issues and risks as the project proceeds. Communication is supported by team status meetings and meetings with upper management (e.g., project steering committee). Quality assurance reviews are periodically performed by an independent authority to ensure that the approach and deliverables of the project are being managed properly and do not involve major risks.

Custom system analysis and design deliverables. A number of deliverables are developed in the custom system analysis and design effort. Many of them are described in detail in *Foundations of Business Systems.*[4] The discussion below describes key deliverables produced in each core segment, as identified in Table 32-2.

Work plans. The work plan, produced in the project organization segment, is a schedule for system development that includes the steps to be performed and the required time frame for each step. Personnel requirements can also be included.

Analysis phase. Performance, security, and control requirements are produced in the quality requirements segment. They identify any constraints that should be imposed on the system or its users and ensure integrity of the system. The function chart is produced in the functional requirements segment and identifies the business processes to be supported by the new system.

Design phase. The technical architecture overview is produced in the application architecture design, defines how user performance and functional requirements are met by the system, and lists the components and how they work together. The screen/window and report specifications are produced in the user interface design segment and depict the exact screen/window report layouts with accompanying detailed descriptions. The concept and data flow diagrams are produced in the software process design segment. The data flow diagram describes the required movement of data through the system to support the business function. The concept diagram represents all data used in the business in the form of an integrated logical data model, described in database design. The logical and physical data models are produced in the database design segment. The logical data model includes the definition of all data elements, records, data relationships, and access paths in the business. The physical data model identifies the data repositories required to perform a processing function and provides the necessary information for program design and development of the logical data model. The performance, security, and control approach is identified in the quality validation segment and outlines the procedures for monitoring and reporting system performance. It also sets forth the design that all new programs and data must support for security and integrity requirements. The operating approach and resource requirements are produced in the operations planning segment. It defines hardware resource requirements and identifies personnel resource requirements by using volume and timing estimates of business events. The migration and testing plan is produced in the migration testing and design segment. It identifies testing and migration processes related to controls, procedures, data collection, and any programming needed to test and migrate the system.

The cost-benefit phase. The cost-benefit summary is produced in the cost-benefit analysis segment. It documents the costs, savings, competitive benefits, and other issues that result from implementation of the system. Deliverables will evolve over the course of the project. As new information or ideas become available, updates to previously completed deliverables may be required.

Case Study

The most effective way to understand how to use a design methodology is to obtain hands-on experience as a part of a project. For purposes of this handbook, a case study of an actual, completed logistics system design project is included for reference. This case study illustrates some of the events and deliverables associated with logistics system design project.

An industrial products distributor was interested in lowering its operating costs through improving the efficiency of its logistics operation. Specifically, the company believed it could reduce operating costs by being more proactive in meeting customers' demands. Consequently, the company initiated a project with two main objectives:

1. To reengineer the logistics processes to provide proactive customer service
2. To develop a new logistics system that would enable proactive customer inventory management

Functional Requirements. The functional requirements contain a description of business functions for order entry, trip planning, delivery management, and billing. The deliverables include a detailed listing of all functions and a description of what must occur in each. An example of a function chart is shown in Figure 32-3. A detailed description of what must occur in each function would normally accompany this chart.

Quality Requirements. The following requirements were considered when designing the logistics system:

- Three- to five-second response time on average; eight seconds for complex transactions
- File capacities to hold data for 90 days
- Security processing to allow for controlled access to the system based on the level of the user (e.g., planner, manager, system administrator)
- Controls to ensure the accurate and timely feed of financial data

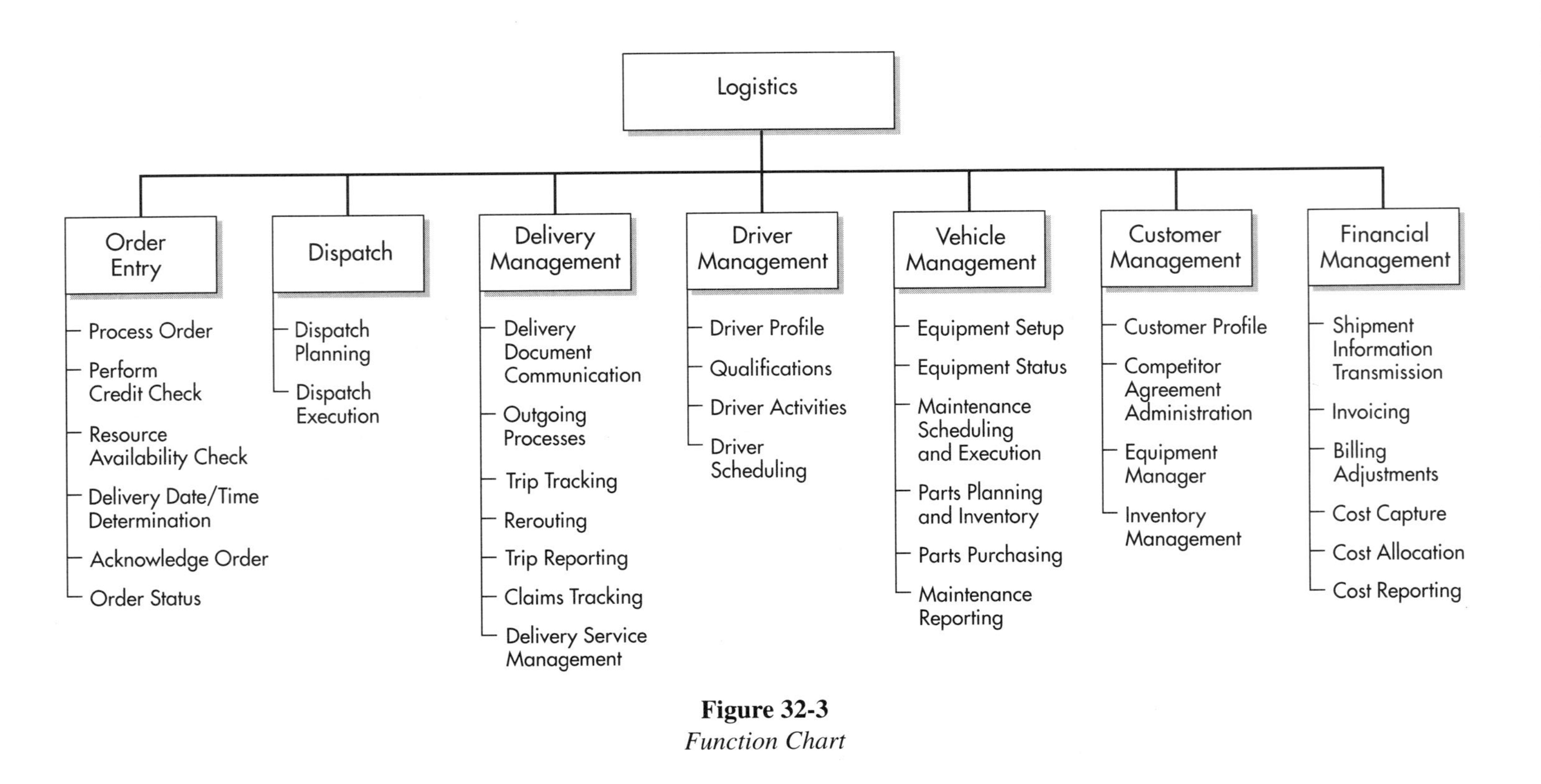

Figure 32-3
Function Chart

Application Architecture Design. To meet these requirements and ensure a user-friendly computer interface, an application architecture was designed utilizing workstations with a "windowing" environment for graphical presentation of data connected to a mainframe, where the business logic and the database resided. This is known as client-server architecture. To provide better customer and driver management, specialized technologies like remote telemetry units and on-board computers were integrated into the application.

User Interface Design. The user interface design was driven by the application architecture design, which specified a windowing/graphical user interface (GUI) delivery of information. The user interface design consisted of the layout of the specific screens/windows and reports to support the functions specified in the functional requirements. The screens/windows consisted of *list, detail,* and *prompt* designs with a standard approach for pull-down menus and *widgets* (radio buttons, scroll bars, etc.). Reports were designed to support management reporting needs.

Software Process Design. A system flow diagram, shown in Figure 32-4, was developed to illustrate the relationships of the major business functions and data repositories. The diagram was used in the early segments of the system installation phase, where a detailed design of the functions was performed.

Database Design. A database design was developed to support the logistics application as well as other users of logistics data. The deliverable for this portion of the design was a logical and physical data model and a listing of the data elements and their attributes. The data model consisted of over 180 entities (files).

Operations Planning. This component of the design was a high-level operating plan that described the resources required to convert and operate the new system. It also specified backup and recovery methods.

Migration and Testing Design. The migration plan from the old system to the new system was developed in this segment and specified that a phased implementation would be appropriate. Additionally, the testing plan was developed and specified the particular cycles of testing (three weekdays, two months, and one annual cycle of business activity) and the key types of data to be prepared for testing. Resources and the schedule for migration and testing were also developed.

Implementation Planning. Based on functional requirements, quality requirements, and preliminary application design, a schedule of the system installation division of work was generated. This schedule consisted of all the major segments of work and the detailed tasks for each segment, the approximate due dates, and the approximate resources required to accomplish the tasks. The system installation schedule is shown in Figure 32-5.

Guiding Principles

Historically, information systems have been developed in response to specific business problems. The result has been business systems that have tended to be function-specific, with information not shared effectively across departmental boundaries. Companies now realize that an integrated information systems approach provides more benefit to the business as a whole. The concept of

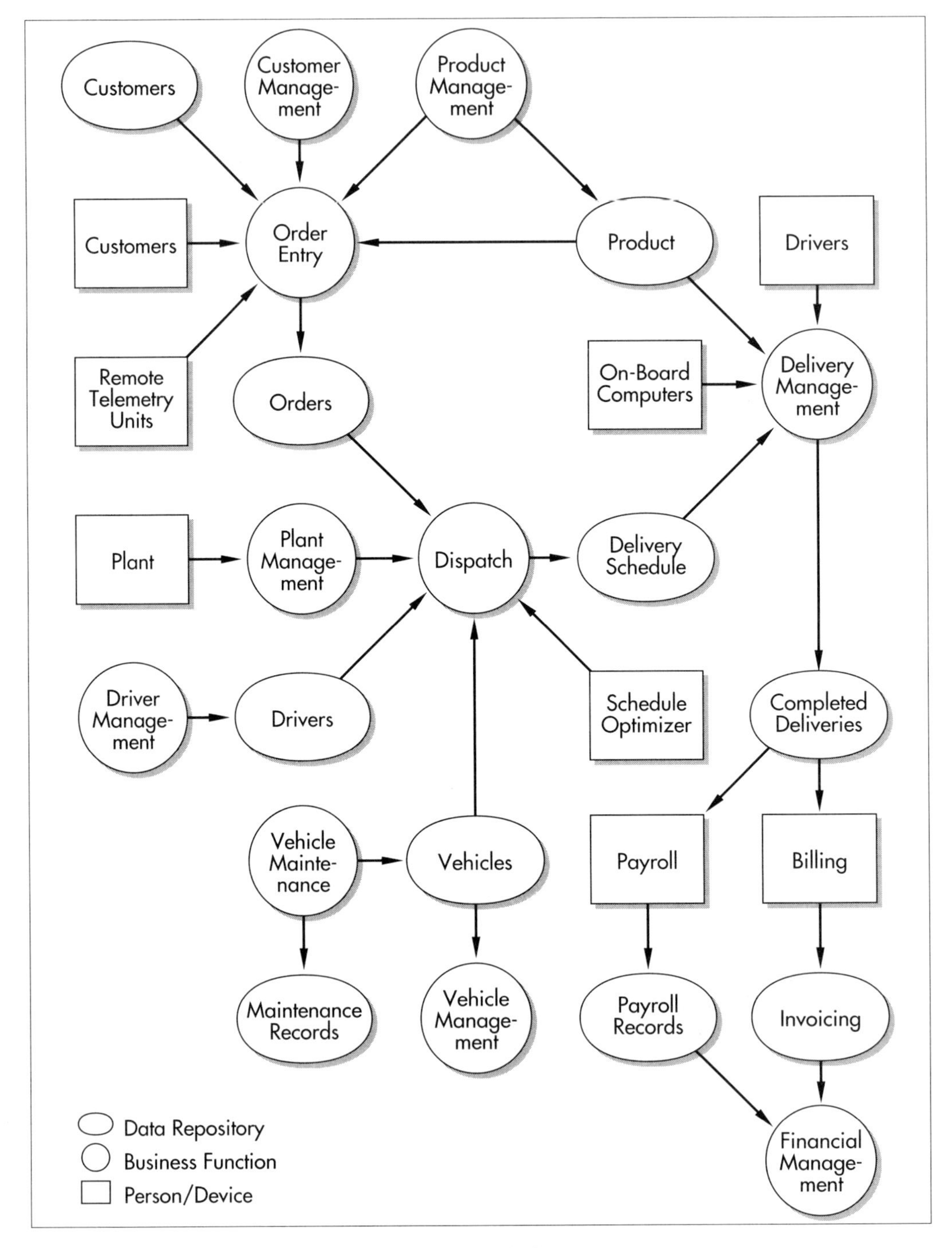

Figure 32-4
System Flow Diagram

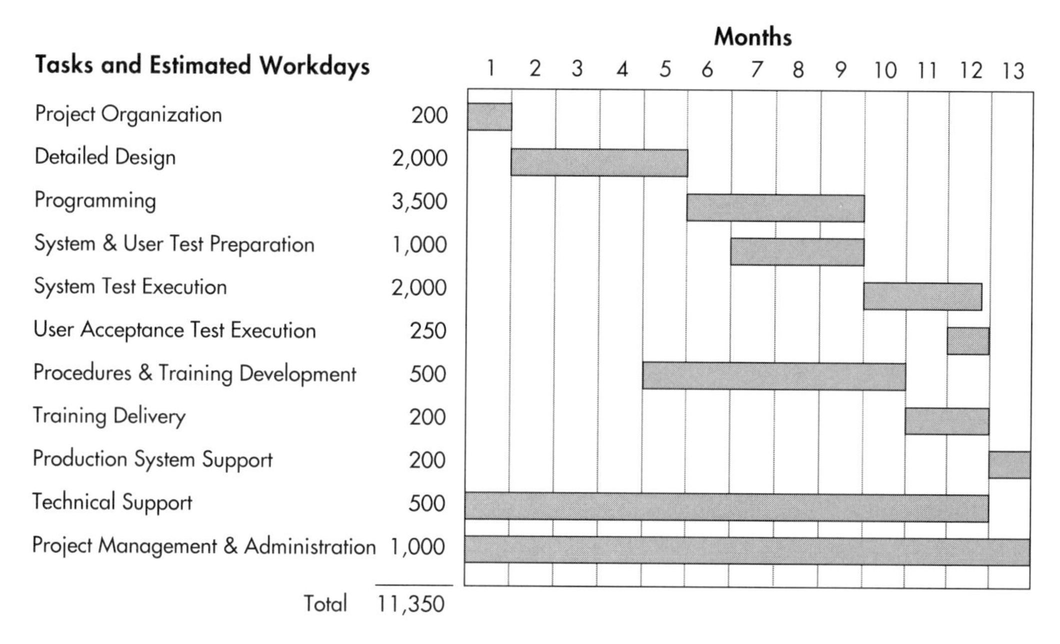

Figure 32-5
System Installation Schedule

building and managing information systems across the entire business is called *business systems integration.* This is an especially important concept for logistics systems, because logistics is inherently an integrating function—integrating activities and managing trade-offs within a company as well as providing linkage with customers and suppliers to achieve channel integration.

The four major components of business systems integration are depicted in Figure 32-6.

Strategy

To move from point solutions toward total business solutions, it is important to drive systems development from the company strategy rather than functional business issues. A well-defined business and technology strategy sets the direction for system building. The purpose of system development is to enhance an organization's ability to meet its strategic business objectives.

A sound business strategy defines the key performance goals for an organization, then a business system is designed to help achieve and monitor those goals. For example, in an organization utilizing a large warehousing network, the management of inventory is both critical and complex. A business system must provide visibility, coordination, deployment, and the controls to minimize investment while achieving target service levels.

Business Process Reengineering

Today many companies are revisiting their business processes to remain competitive or to leapfrog competition. "Bold, innovative changes were the precursors of past successes and will continue to be the hallmark of future giants."[5] *Business process reengineering* is one of the many

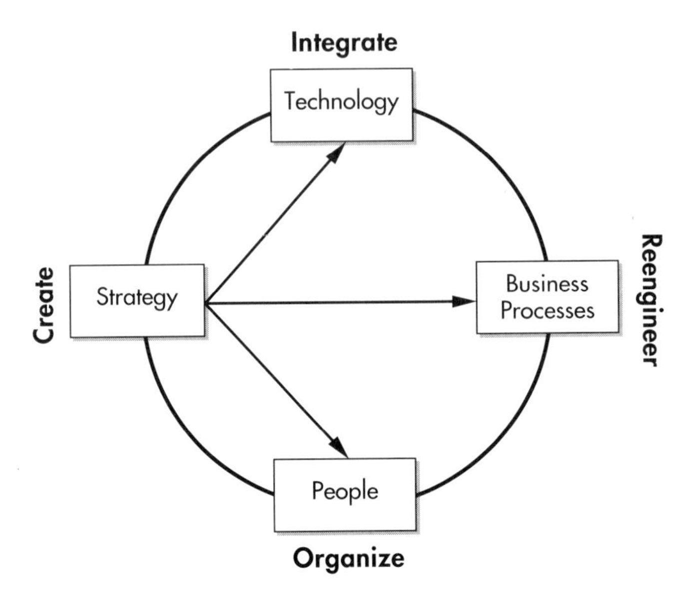

Figure 32-6
Business Systems Integration

terms used today to describe the process of reinventing the way a business operates. As an organization makes these changes, the business system must change or develop to support the "new" business. Business process reengineering realigns and changes the operations of a business to achieve a quantum increase in the value it delivers. More simply stated, business reengineering is a way of thinking of how best to create and deliver the products or services that customers value. Companies often find themselves operating in today's markets with business processes supporting strategies and visions of a business environment that has long since disappeared. There were times in the recent past when long-distance communications were difficult, traditional mail service was the norm, transportation was costly, machines were expensive, and labor was abundant. That is not the world of the 1990s.

When a business uses old processes to meet new business conditions, it may fail to meet its key objectives. Successful businesses have adapted to new conditions. One example of this type of business change in logistics is the trend toward developing long-term relationships with suppliers. This relationship is typified by long-term purchase contracts, quality guarantees by the supplier, and JIT delivery of goods packaged for use on the production floor. Traditional purchasing systems do not properly handle this new supplier-customer relationship. They are built on strategies of buying from the vendor with the lowest price, quality inspection by the customer at the dock, and large lots of goods in bulk packaging received when economically advantageous.[6]

Value-driven Reengineering Approach

Automating "what exists" is generally not acceptable; reengineering is integral to system development. Processes must be reconsidered before support systems can be designed.

Value-driven reengineering occurs in four phases: (1) developing a *vision,* (2) creating a *master plan,* (3) preparing the *design,* and (4) performing the *implementation.*

The first two phases—vision and master plan—occur early in the system development life cycle.

Vision. Reengineering must be directed by an organization's business strategy. This strategy sets the framework for achieving the organization's long-term goals and establishing the direction and priorities for reengineering. The strategy is the basis for developing an "overall vision" of what the company wants to achieve and an "operational vision" stating practical objectives across all dimensions of operations—people, processes, technology, and infrastructure (facilities, equipment, financial resources, intangible assets, etc.).

Master Plan. When the operational vision has been stated, the next phase of work is to develop the reengineering master plan. Here the project team is organized, current operations are profiled, and the reengineering solution models are adopted. The solution models provide the basis for estimating the effort, impact, and benefits of the reengineering process for the organization. The reengineering master plan is typically developed in conjunction with the information planning effort, which introduces technology to the reengineering solution. Completion of the master planning phase should result in senior management approval of the solution model, as well as its expected benefits, costs, and impact on the organization.

Design. The next phase in the reengineering process is to design the blueprints for the solution. This phase is performed hand in hand with the systems design phase, as many of the tasks performed are the same. The existing processes are inventoried and analyzed, the new business flow is generated, and the supporting technology is designed. Implementation issues and barriers are documented and raised for resolution. Meanwhile, the systems design team is analyzing new information flows, prototyping the new computer system, and drafting the new system procedures. The final task of the solution design phase (and the systems design phase) is to develop plans for implementing the solution.

Implement. In the final phase of work, the solution as well as the system is integrated into the organization's business process. From the design created in the previous phase, the solution is developed, then tested in a simulated business environment. After a successful test, the solution can be applied to the live business environment. A carefully planned and executed implementation is crucial to the organization's confidence in, and acceptance of, the business reengineering solution.

Reengineering Benefits

A question with regard to business reengineering is what benefits should be expected from it. Or, for that matter, why are we subjecting our organization to potential turmoil? The answer can be summed up in one word—*results*—concrete, tangible, meaningful results. Business reengineering raises tenfold improvement potential; that is, one should not think in terms of 10% improvement but tenfold (10X) improvement! Organizations that undertake business reengineering initiatives should strive to achieve these improvements in such areas as product time to market, customer responsiveness, operating costs, and administrative costs. Reengineering efforts should also strive to maximize the organization's available resources (e.g., human, financial, technical, etc.). These are the results that world-class organizations will need to achieve to be competitive in a rapidly changing global economy. In the 1990s, the way to get tenfold improvement is not to automate existing processes but to reinvent them.

Justification for Reengineering

The cost-benefit analysis of a business reengineering project is far more complicated than that of a business systems project alone. The anticipated benefits analysis must take into account cost reduction benefits (resulting from the elimination of nonvalue-added tasks), revenue-enhancing benefits (resulting from the ability to offer improved information-based services), and intangible benefits (resulting from the ability to be more responsive to rapidly changing market demands). The investment to initiate a business reengineering project is also more difficult to quantify. It goes beyond the cost to develop and operate the systems. It must consider the impact on the organization both internally and externally. It must also consider the risk of undertaking a poorly planned project. For these reasons, the cost-benefit analysis for a reengineering project is an essential task to be performed during the planning rather than waiting until the design phase. It must be validated at the end of the design phase, however, to ensure that the cost and benefit assumptions still hold true. In addition, techniques for measuring expected benefits must be included as part of the reengineering vision phase. This ensures that senior management has clear expectations of the project before it moves forward. The driving force that makes reengineering worthy of the investment is that, if planned, supported, and executed properly, 10X results are obtainable.

Technology to Support Reengineering

Technology is an enabler for business integration. Whereas business process reengineering is a catalyst for change, technology is a tool to support and enhance the impact of the change. Too often, technology is used because "it's the thing to do." Instead, technology should meet a defined business need for which the cost-benefit analysis is satisfactory. For example, satellite tracking of delivery vehicles may be too expensive for just-in-case scenarios, but it may be cost-effective if in-transit diversion of vehicles is required to meet strategic customer service levels.

Two basic types of technology are integrated into systems designs: computer and enabling. Computer technology involves the hardware and software necessary to plan, transact, and manage a business. An example of computer technology is the client-server architecture, which distributes the processing load of various software applications among multiple networked hardware platforms, providing increased computing power with increased flexibility. Enabling technology is specialized technology that mainly supports the business at a transaction level. Examples of enabling technologies are electronic data interchange (EDI), remote telemetry unit (RTU) devices, and point-of-scale (POS) devices. Most of these devices make the gathering or exchange of business transaction information easier and more timely. When they are not used, the information is either gathered manually and keyed into a computer system or not gathered at all. These devices can also be used for competitive advantage. For example, RTUs can gather customer inventory information. When the customer reaches a reorder point, product can be delivered without a phone call. This technology assists with improving customer service at lower cost, thereby creating a barrier against competitors.

Organizational Impact of Reengineering

New systems. New technology. New business processes. New organizations. New markets. New products . . . the list goes on and on. In the 1990s change will be continuous. The winning organizations will successfully manage change rather than being managed by it. Managing change throughout all levels of the organization reinforces the corporate vision, inspires team spirit, enables information to be shared throughout the organization for better decision making, and creates a sense of ownership for future change. Change management requires vision, commitment, communication, and leadership. Its success is essential to achieve the tenfold improvement results of business reengineering.

Involvement of the system's users in the systems design process is the key to success. They must be given the authority and responsibility to make the system as good as possible. Involving users early in the design process and throughout its implementation helps ensure that the system will be accepted by the people who will work with it daily and that it will be "owned" by a user community committed to improving it throughout its life cycle. Many system implementation failures occur because the system does not meet user needs or falls into disuse owing to lack of "ownership."

When introducing technology (change) to an organization, the workforce needs to be well prepared with the right business processes, structure, and skills to achieve the full benefit of the technology. To assimilate technology into the workplace, it is necessary to analyze the unique impacts on different user groups. This analysis should be conducted early in the information systems design phase, and its results should drive the design of the change management programs for each user group.

The impact analysis forms the basis for designing and developing the communications and training delivery vehicles required to prepare the organization for change. The most important element in change management is an early start. Preliminary organization impact assessments should begin during the information planning phase of systems development. The design and development of the training materials should coincide with the design and development of the information system and/or the reengineering solution. Because of the specialized nature of change management and the potential risks for an unprepared organization, many organizations turn to an outside consultant who specializes in providing technology change management services for assistance. After all, a dynamic organization is only as flexible as its people.

Achieving Business Integration

The integration of strategy, business processes, technology, and people to achieve competitive advantage is a challenge, but the payoff can be great. Business that have achieved systems integration have been able to carve out leadership positions in industry. Of the four components of systems integration, the reengineering of business processes is perhaps the most important to achieving competitive advantage. Reengineering not only allows companies to better integrate systems but it streamlines the business processes that provide significant benefit even without systems.

Strategy should be the starting point for business integration. All design decisions must be based on achieving the objectives set out in the business plan. Before a design is started, business process reengineering should be seriously considered and applied where benefits can be obtained. Similarly, technology should be considered where costs and benefits meet business objectives. Finally, users must drive the integration process and own the resulting systems. Business integration is not a state to be achieved at one point in time but a process of continuous improvement based on the changing business environment.

Logistics Systems Design Considerations

There are six categories of design considerations for a logistics system. While the other parts of this chapter provide information on how to design a logistics system, this part highlights some of the details that should be considered in the design.

1. Materials pipeline segment
2. Degree of materials pipeline integration
3. Industry
4. Application sophistication
5. Productivity tools and techniques
6. Administrative

Materials Pipeline Segment

The materials pipeline in Figure 32-7 represents the movement of materials through procurement, production, and distribution. Each segment of the pipeline represents a distinct function impacting the flow of materials.

Depending on the business, a logistics systems design addresses one or more of these pipeline segments. Design considerations, with corresponding systems design implications for each of the segments, are as follows:

Procurement

- Supplier lead-time length and variability:
  –Electronic data interchange (EDI) for immediate communications with suppliers
  –Supplier performance reporting
- Preferred supplier relationships
  –Maintain automated contracts for preferred suppliers
  –For replenishment, automatic sourcing of product is from the supplier with the most favorable contract terms
- Dynamic sourcing decisions

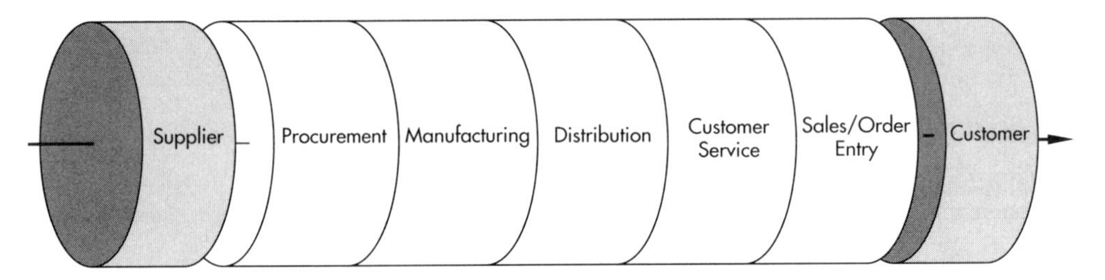

Figure 32-7
Materials Pipeline

–Connection to co-packer, contractor, or supplier scheduling/ordering systems (e.g., via EDI)

- Product quality assurance
  –Quality inspection capabilities (e.g., reserve product for inspection, track product quality status)

Manufacturing

- Work-in-process inventory
  –Manufacturing requirements planning (MRP) capabilities to facilitate master scheduling
- Finished goods inventory
  –Integrate MRP with market intelligence applications
- Quality control
  –Statistical process control principles
  –Quality control reporting

Distribution

- Distribution network flexibility
  –Capability to consolidate or transfer historical and product data related to opening or closing warehouses, such as order history or customer/ship-from-location assignment (that is, assigning the stocking location that serves a customer)
- Product demand variability
  –Sophisticated statistical forecasting capabilities
  –Ability to distinguish planned from unplanned demand
  –Ability to integrate with customer forecasting system
- Inventory management
  –Replenishment and forecasting algorithms differentiated by product demand and value
- Transportation
  –Dynamic routing and scheduling capabilities

Customer Service

- Stockouts
  –Use a reasonable target customer service level (e.g., number of stockouts divided by total number of orders) to balance customer service with inventory costs. For example, a 100% target service level will cause inventory costs to skyrocket.
  –Ability to differentiate target service level by customer and criticality of the product to the customer (e.g., the cost of a stockout)
  –Ability to switch to substitute products
- Customer order status
  –Customer order tracking capabilities

Sales/Order Entry

- Capturing sales
  –Point-of-sale (POS) capability to capture sales data immediately and report them back to the distribution center automatically
  –Ability to check product availability at time of order

–Ability to integrate sales data with forecasting function
- Customer validation
  –Customer credit checking functionality
- Order flexibility
  –Potential need to handle several order types (e.g., drop-ship orders, blanket orders, retail orders)

Degree of Materials Pipeline Integration

The degree of pipeline integration denotes the extent to which the business spans multiple segments of the materials pipeline. Whether the business falls into one or more than one segment of the pipeline, the overall pipeline perspective should be maintained when designing a logistics system. Businesses should approach a logistics systems design with the aim of tearing down walls between functions, not building them up.

Given the desire for greater integration across the materials pipeline, the following are the more critical systems design considerations:

- *System connectivity.* Selection of hardware and software that can be easily linked is vital. This may be achieved through third-party EDI networks or standard transaction formats (e.g., UCS, WINS).
- *Standardized application interface format.* For those applications that do not have industry standard transaction formats, a consistent transaction format and interface method permits the application to remain stable, even though interfaced systems may change.
- *Consistent application user interface.* As users are asked to adapt an overall pipeline perspective, consistent "look and feel" across functions will facilitate user acceptance.
- *Context-specific help capability.* Given the increased span of responsibility experienced in a pipeline environment, most users must master multiple systems. This process is aided by implementing context-specific and/or field-level help functions.
- *Availability of a training database.* As with the situation above, users may need extensive access to a training database before receiving certification on the entire logistics pipeline system.

Industry

Each industry has unique requirements beyond the basic logistics capabilities. For example, a logistics system in the pharmaceutical industry needs to address lot control, controlled substance reporting, and expiration date monitoring; cube weight calculations and transportation cost minimization are important design considerations for the construction industry. An example in a production environment is found in the discrete manufacturing industry, where most of the products are made-to-order and customized specifications must be transferable to and from the customer's engineering department via electronic CAD/CAM links. For food industry systems, expiration dates for raw materials and finished goods should be sensitive to different storage requirements and perishability constraints, depending on the production facility and warehouse.

Application Sophistication

When designing a logistics system application, the physical constraints of the business must be considered, then matched with an appropriate level of application sophistication. For example, a distribution requirements planning (DRP) package design and implementation will yield little benefit in an environment with a single manufacturing and distribution location. A simple spreadsheet or basic replenishment algorithm may suffice.

Productivity Tools and Techniques

Several productivity tools and techniques are available to organize and improve systems design, development, and installation. Three of the more useful tools and techniques are CASE tools, designware, and structured, essential systems analysis.

- *CASE Tools.* CASE (Computer-Aided Systems Engineering) tools clearly provide benefit to a design effort when properly understood and used. There are many varieties of CASE tools, but they generally provide facilities to aid with activities like screen/window and report design, database design, process design, and the like. A single design repository is the most valuable approach because it provides the project team with a single, centralized location of the application design. Information is easily shared, and the design is captured and maintained in one location.
- *Designware.* A popular use today is designware as a starting point for a system design. Many organizations have completed application designs available to other companies. This option is generally considered for application designs specific to an industry and a functional domain.
- *Structured systems analysis/essential systems analysis.* Although a structured approach to system design is recommended, some of the activities can be eliminated by performing only the essential analysis in the early stages of the design. By avoiding much of the detailed documentation, the design can be developed in a much shorter time. For example, if the designers are experienced and familiar with the business process, much of the work to document the current system is unnecessary. Likewise, the custodial elements of the design (system administration, security, and controls) can be left to a later time in the design, allowing the team to focus its effort on the primary business process.

Administrative

Scope management. A key to success for any logistics project is to aggressively define and manage its scope. This means developing a clear and unambiguous description of the functions to be addressed and the processes to be automated. Once defined, all changes are discussed in terms of the impact on delivery, system quality, and so forth. As the project moves through the system development life cycle, changes in scope can have a dramatic effect on the design and delivery of the system.

Project team organization and staffing. The most creative systems result from collaborative efforts of users and information services personnel; a unique solution requires deep knowledge of both the business problem and the capabilities of technology. A team that consists of full-time user and information systems personnel reporting to a single project manager typically has the skills and commitment to deliver a quality solution on time. At least 15% to 20% of the project team should be users.

Conclusion

A logistics information systems design and implementation can provide significant benefits to an enterprise, provided that the design supports the business and logistics strategy, incorporates process and procedural changes identified through business process reengineering, and includes industry-specific and pipeline integration design considerations. A proven design approach like the one described in this chapter can ensure a successful logistics systems design effort.

To differentiate themselves from the competition, companies must be willing to experiment with leading-edge technologies and use productivity tools to empower employees. Taking advantage of new technologies and tools improves an organization's overall performance, enhances its decision-making capabilities, and creates a distinct competitive advantage in the marketplace. Finally, recognizing the forces of business change—and capitalizing on them in the logistics system design—places the organization in a position of strength and leadership for the 1990s.

Notes

1. Acknowledgments are due to the following Andersen Consulting personnel for their assistance in preparing this chapter: Mike Ballanco, Warren Dodge, Chris Draper, Jeff Hamilton, Paul Lomas, and Mike O'Neill. All figures and charts in this chapter are property of Arthur Andersen & Co., S.C.
2. Method/1 (Chicago: Andersen Consulting, Arthur Andersen & Co, S.C., 1989), n. p.
3. *Logistics Software* (Stamford, Conn.: Andersen Consulting, Arthur Andersen & Co, S.C. for the Council of Logistics Management, 1993), n. p.
4. Per O. Flaatten, Donald J. McCubbrey, P. Declan O'Riordan, and Keith Burgess, *Foundations of Business Systems* (Philadelphia: Dryden, 1989), n. p.
5. Roy L. Harmon, *Reinventing the Factory II* (New York: Free Press, 1992), p. 1.
6. For an in-depth discussion of the new supplier-customer relationship, see ibid., pp. 107–11.

CHAPTER 33

Electronic Data Interchange in Logistics

Margaret A. Emmelhainz

The use of information is becoming increasingly important in logistics. One critical component of logistics information systems is electronic data interchange (EDI). EDI has become quite common in logistics operations, and some estimate that by 1995 over 80% of orders will be transmitted via EDI.[1]

This chapter presents an overview of EDI, beginning with an introduction that explains the definition of and the concepts behind EDI. The components of an EDI system (standards, software, and third-party networks) are introduced and discussed. Various ways of configuring an EDI system are evaluated. An implementation approach to EDI is suggested, and typical problems in implementation are highlighted with recommended solutions. Costs and benefits of doing EDI are presented. Finally, case studies of EDI used in logistics operations are presented as guidelines for further use.

Electronic Data Interchange Defined

What Is EDI?

Electronic data interchange is the organization-to-organization, computer-to-computer exchange of business data in a structured, machine-processable format. The purpose of EDI is to eliminate duplicate data entry and to improve the speed and accuracy of the information flow by linking computer applications between companies. This can best be illustrated by the example of a buyer and seller who exchange purchase order and invoice information.

PAPER-BASED SYSTEMS

Figure 33-1 shows both the traditional paper-based system of exchanging information and an EDI-based system. In the former, a purchase order is generated, sometimes manually, but often by a computerized purchasing system, and is printed. The paper purchase order is then transmitted in some form (e.g., mail, fax, field sales representative) to the seller, who in most cases enters nearly all the information into a computerized order entry system. This reentry of data is

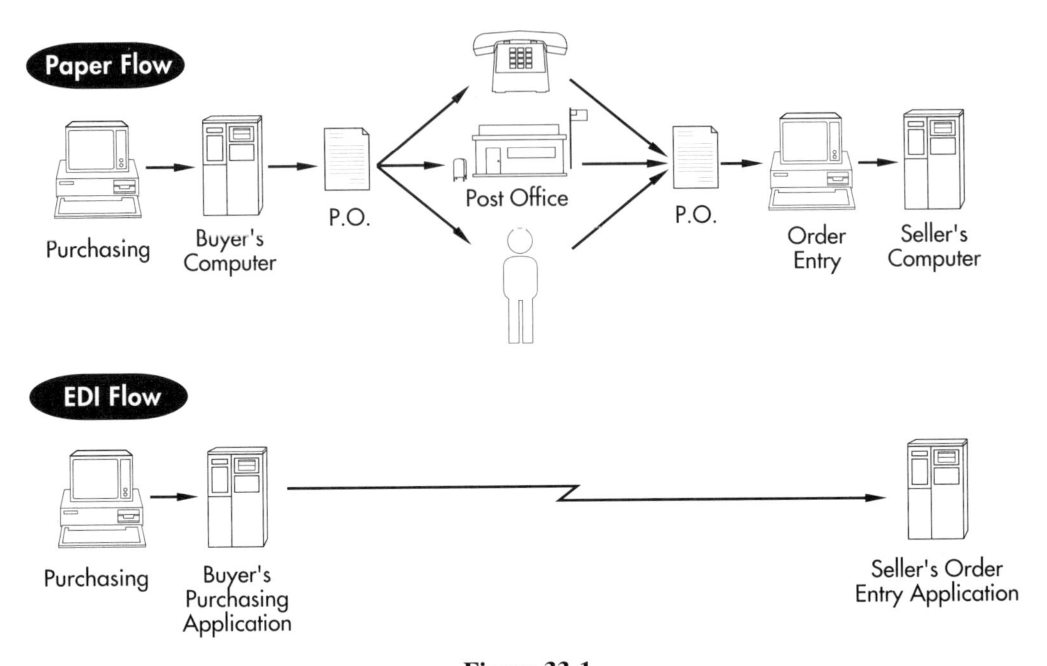

Figure 33-1
Comparison of Paper and EDI Flows

fairly common in business. As a matter of fact, it is generally accepted that 70% of one company's computerized business data output becomes another company's business data input.

A paper-based system has a number of inherent problems that impact logistics productivity. First, it has built-in delays. There is the time necessary to physically transmit information between trading partners and the time to reenter the data. Also inherent in a paper-based system is data inaccuracy. Because of the repeated data entry of the same information, the chance of errors is high. Repeatedly entering the same data at various points in the information flow significantly increases the number of data entry steps involved, thereby increasing the opportunities for error. Because manual data entry in the paper-based system is performed repeatedly throughout the information flow, the system is very labor-intensive. Finally, a paper-based manual system is also uncertain. Owing to variable mailing and processing delays, a sender of information is often unsure whether and when information is received. An EDI system removes these inherent problems by eliminating the need to reenter data.

Electronically-Based Systems

With an EDI-based system, a purchase order is generated based on a computerized purchasing system, but instead of then being printed out, the purchase order information is electronically entered into the seller's order entry system. Once received by the seller, the information flows into processing without additional human interpretation or coding. The result of this process is an improvement in data accuracy and a decrease in information transmittal, processing time, and potential delays.

What EDI Is Not

The key component of EDI is the computer-to-computer link and the elimination of the need for human interpretation of data. This makes EDI very different from other forms of electronic communications like E-mail or facsimile transmission, both of which are person-to-person exchanges that take place through a computer. When a facsimile or an E-mail message is received, it must be interpreted by a person and the data entered into a computer for further processing. Although both these methods achieve quick transmission time, neither eliminate the need for data reentry.

Components of EDI

EDI is not a technically complex system. Rather, it is the integration of three basic components into a network of information flow. The three basic components include standards, software, and a communication medium.

EDI Standards

As defined earlier, EDI is the organization-to-organization, computer-to-computer transmission of business data in a structured, machine-processable format. This format is obtained through the use of standards. EDI standards are rules and guidelines that establish a basic syntax for formatting information electronically. Just as the English language has an agreed-upon set of words (vocabulary) and an agreed-upon set of rules for arranging those words (grammar and syntax), so does EDI.

Standards are critical to the operation of EDI. In a paper-based world, a human operator receives and interprets information before it is entered for computer processing. For example, an order entry clerk understands that 6/30/95 is the same as June 30, 1995. However, in the EDI world, the information is sent computer-to-computer, without human reinterpretation. Therefore, there must be no ambiguity in the context or the structure of the words. For the computer to "read and understand" a message, it must know the format exactly in which the information is presented and exactly what the information means. EDI standards provide the required structure.

Types of Standards

There are two basic types of EDI standards: proprietary and generic. Proprietary standards are guidelines for electronic communications that are unique to one company and its trading partners. In the mid-1960s, many large companies established computerized formats for information transfer and expected all suppliers to follow such guidelines. However, because the "standards" varied from company to company, suppliers had to be able to handle a number of different format guidelines.

Generic standards are used by companies on an industrywide, nationwide, or international basis. Generic standards were first conceptualized by the transportation industry in the late 1960s. At that time, a group of transportation executives formed the Transportation Data Coordinating Committee (TDCC), for developing industrywide standards for the transportation industry. A number of other industries followed this development pattern as they began to establish their industry-specific standards. For instance, the warehouse industry developed guidelines called Warehouse Industry Network Standards (WINS), and the grocery industry developed a set of guidelines called Uniform Communication Standards (UCS).

In addition to the industry-specific development of standards, the 1970s saw the emergence of cross-industry standards. The American National Standards Institute (ANSI) chartered an Accredited Standards Committee (ASC) to develop EDI standards. This committee became identified as the ANSI ASC X12. The committee has developed guidelines for electronic communication and the processing of business data across industry lines. The committee, composed of volunteers from industry who are actual users of the standards, is an example of a situation in which the standards were developed by those who desired to use them. Today the X12 standard is the most commonly used standard in North America. Although industry standards remain, in 1990 an effort was made to render the industry standards completely compatible with ANSI X12. As a result, the industry standards and the X12 standard use and arrange the same "words" and follow identical syntax.

What the X12 Standard Establishes

Specifically, the X12 standard establishes information arrangement for electronic transmission. As illustrated in Figure 33-2, in the language of ANSI X12, a *document* is a *transaction set.* A *line* of information, arranged in a set way, is a *data segment;* and a *unit* of information is a *data element.*

Nearly two hundred documents have been formatted into transaction sets. Each document or transaction set is assigned a unique identifier. The identifying number indicates the origination of the transaction set: TDCC-based, UCS-based, X12-based, and so on. For instance, numbers 100–400 indicate TDCC origination, 800–869 indicate X12-developed, and 870–899 indicate UCS-developed.

The X12 standard establishes information structuring for electronic communication. The standard establishes:

- What documents can be transmitted electronically
- What information is required on each document (e.g., what is the minimum amount of information that must be included on a bill of lading?)
- The sequencing of the information (e.g., which comes first, the freight bill number or the date?)
- The format for writing the information (e.g., dates are always written in a YYMMDD format)
- The meaning of information (e.g., the standard specifies that, as a unit of measure, "CA" means "case")

Although a detailed description of how information is translated or mapped into the X12 standard is beyond the scope of this chapter, Table 33-1 shows the relationship between a paper purchase order and identical information formatted for EDI communication.

International Standard

One additional standard of importance to logistics managers is UN/EDIFACT, the international standard for EDI. UN/EDIFACT stands for United Nations/EDI For Administration, Commerce, and Transport. This standard, which is being developed under the auspices of the United Nations and the International Standards Organization, is an attempt to establish a cross-national

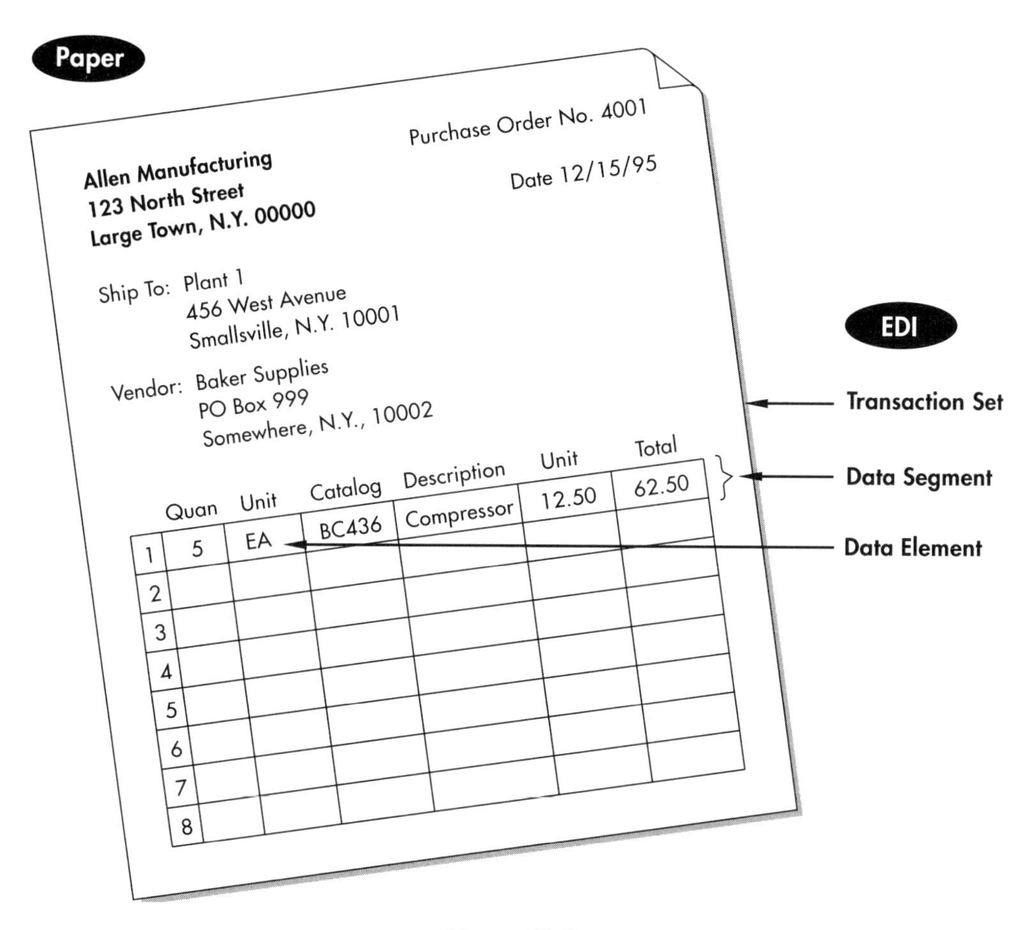

Figure 33-2

The Language of ANSI

Source: Adapted from Margaret A. Emmelhainz, *Electronic Data Interchange: A Total Management Guide* (New York: Van Nostrand Reinhold, 1990), p. 66. Used with permission.

EDI standard. The current UN/EDIFACT standard is not identical to the X12 standard, but there are similarities. Both standards use the same dictionary and a similar syntax. It is expected that the X12 standard eventually will be a completely compatible subset of the UN/EDIFACT standard.

Today the UN/EDIFACT standard is in use primarily in Europe and is expected to be the standard of choice in that part of the world. A number of U.S. government organizations, including Customs, are currently using the UN/EDIFACT standard for trade with European partners.

EDI Software

Standards offer a common language for electronic communication. However, because few companies have arranged and structured their internal data in a standard format, a mechanism is

TABLE 33-1
ANSI X12 Purchase Order

Paper Purchase Order	X12 EDI Document
Start of transaction P.O. No. 4001 Date:12/15/95	ST•850•0001 N/L BEG•00•NE•4001••951215 N/L
Buyer: Allen Manufacturing 123 North Street Large Town, NY 00000	N1•BT•Allen Manufacturing N/L N3•123 North Street N/L N4•Large Town•NY•00000 N/L
Vendor: Baker Supplies P.O. Box 999 Somewhere, NY 00002	N1•VN•Baker Supplies N/L N3•PO Box 999 N/L N4•Somewhere•NY•00002 N/L
Ship to: Plant 1 456 West Ave. Smallsville, NY 00001	N1•ST•Plant 1 N/L N3•456 West Ave. N/L N4•Smallsville•NY•00001 N/L
5 EA BC436 Compressors @$12.50 each	P01•1•5•EA•12.50••BC436•PD•Compressor N/L
Number of line items = 1 End of transaction	CTT•1 N/L SE•14•0001 N/L

Note: N/L indicates a new line character.

Source: Adapted from Margaret A. Emmelhainz, *Electronic Data Interchange: A Total Management Guide* (New York: Van Nostrand Reinhold, 1990), p. 73. Used with permission.

needed to translate information from company into standard format. That mechanism is EDI translator software, which performs three basic functions, as shown in Figure 33-3.

Software Functions

In creating outgoing EDI, the first necessary function is extraction of data from an application database. For instance, in the development of a purchase order, basic information must be abstracted from vendor files, product files, and the like. This function is called *data conversion* or *data extraction*. Data are pulled from the company's database and usually placed in a *"flat file"*—a data file with predetermined positions for the data. Data extraction usually requires some in-house programming, because each company's application database is unique. Once the data are in a flat file, the next step is to format them into the appropriate standard. For instance, a date from the flat file is arranged in a YYMMDD format and placed in the correct data segment for the specific transaction set being generated. This step is referred to as *formatting* or *transaction generation*. Software is commercially available to perform this step. Finally, once a transaction set has been generated, it must be communicated to a trading partner. Again, this is performed by commercially available software.

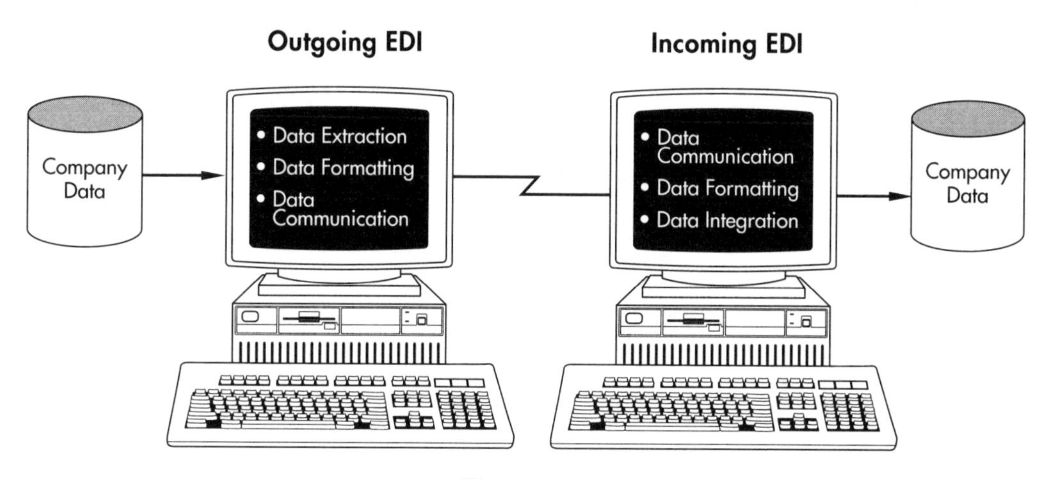

Figure 33-3
EDI Software Functions

Software Availability

For inbound EDI, similar functions are performed but in the reverse order. Most companies involved in EDI purchase formatting and communications software. Numerous vendors offer software packages covering nearly all computer platforms, from personal computers (PCs) to mainframes. Such EDI software is available for as little as $1,000, with most mainframe packages beginning at about $30,000. The checklist in Table 33-2 suggests factors that should be considered in the purchase of commercially available translation software.

Third-party Networks

Standards provide the language and structure of EDI, and software translates data into the proper standard. The final component of EDI is a communication medium. The electronic transmission of information can be completed in many different ways. For instance, exchange of magnetic

TABLE 33-2
EDI Software Checklist

- If PC-based, is the software user-friendly?
- Is the software compatible with the computer platform?
- Does the software support all necessary standards?
- Does the software allow for audit reports and control reports?
- Is the software vendor experienced in the industry?
- Is a vendor hotline available for quick help on problems?
- How often is the software updated to reflect changes in standards?
- What are the acquisition and maintenance costs?
- Is the software expandable in the future?
- Is the software compatible with current application systems?
- Does the software provide special features like password control, encryption, and authentication?

tapes or PC diskettes containing bank account information qualifies as EDI if the information is in a standard format and capable of being processed upon receipt. In common usage, however, EDI involves the electronic transmission of data through a computer-to-computer dial-up arrangement. Dial-up can occur directly or through a third-party network.

Direct Links

Through direct dial-up linkage, data are transmitted from origin to destination computers. For instance, a carrier directly dials into a shipper's computer and transmits a freight bill. For direct linkage to occur, the communications protocols used by the two computers must be compatible. For example, data transmission speed must be the same as receipt speed. A direct linkage is the most appropriate when:

- A limited number of trading partners are involved.
- A large volume of data is exchanged.
- Communications equipment and software are compatible.
- Neither party has a capacity problem in terms of ability to receive information (e.g., phone lines are open and accessible when data are sent).

Linkages Through a VAN

Many EDI users prefer to send information through a third-party network or value-added network (VAN). As shown in Figure 33-4, the function a VAN performs is somewhat similar to that of the postal service in transmitting of paper documents. When using a VAN, a shipper sends an

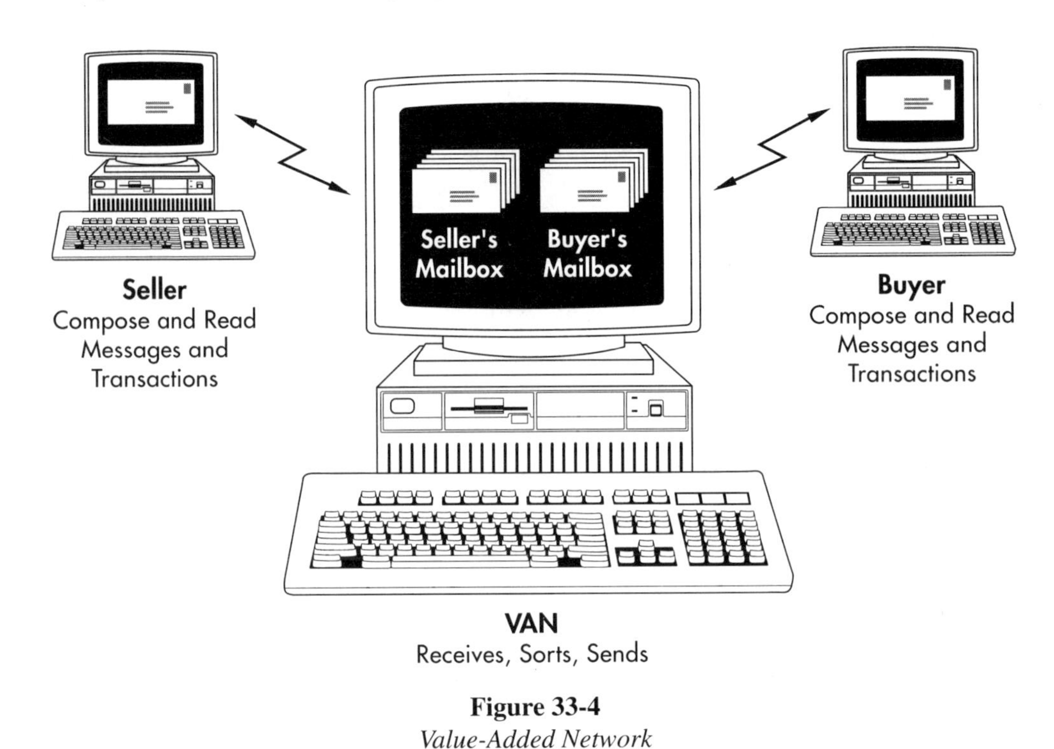

Figure 33-4
Value-Added Network

electronic message to the VAN, which sorts messages by receiver and stores them in a designated mailbox. The receiver can have all messages delivered by the VAN at a set time or may call in to the VAN to receive mail. With a VAN, there is no direct link between companies exchanging data. The direct links are between participating parties and the VAN.

Additional VAN Services

In addition to mailbox services, third-party networks provide additional value-added services. Many third-party networks offer the following services:

- In-net translation
- Paper conversion services
- Dial-out services
- Encryption and authentication
- Training and setting up of trading partners
- Control reports and audit logs

In-net translation involves translation from company-specific to standard format. Some but not all VANs allow a company to transmit data in a flat file. The VAN provides translation to standard format and then communicates to the trading partner. In other words, the VAN, in lieu of the sender of a message, provides the translation software. Although this value-added service offers the benefit of "outsourcing" EDI software implementation and maintenance, over the long term it is likely to be more costly and burdensome than doing the translation in-house and sending a standard EDI message to the VAN for communication.

Another service offered by some VANs is paper conversion. Conversion systems are a way to communicate with trading partners who are not EDI-capable. For instance, if a shipper is sending bills of lading to a group of carriers that are not all EDI-capable, the VAN converts the electronic bills of lading to paper for delivery via facsimile or mail to those without EDI capabilities. Using this service, a shipper can generate all documents electronically, despite the fact that some carriers are not EDI-capable.

Dial-out services offered by a VAN are a method of data retrieval. A number of large organizations make data on their in-house systems available to trading partners. However, to obtain those data, the trading partner must dial into the company's database at a designated time. A VAN can perform this dial-out activity, retrieve the information, and place it in the mailbox for later delivery or pickup. In this way, a company can participate in a retrieval arrangement without performing its own dial-out.

Encryption and authentication are additional features offered by VANs. Encryption is a method of coding data to ensure secrecy as the data move between trading partners. Authentication is a method of verifying the identification of the sender of the information and of ensuring that the data were not changed during transmission. These security measures are appropriate when transmitted data are sensitive or proprietary. VANs can also provide audit and control reports detailing what activity took place at what time. For instance, most VANs maintain logs that record what was received and when it was forwarded or picked up.

One final service provided by VANs is implementation assistance and training. Third-party networks often work with a company's potential trading partners to help them become EDI-ready. Such assistance can be a valuable service when a company plans to initiate EDI with a large number of trading partners at the same time.

Availability of VANs

A large number of third-party networks are currently available. Factors to consider in selecting a specific VAN are shown in Table 33-3.

EDI Hardware

Computer hardware is necessary for an EDI system. However, no unique EDI hardware is required. In establishing an EDI system, nearly any type of computer platform can be used. As mentioned previously, software is available for all sizes of computers. In establishing an EDI system, a variety of hardware and software configurations can be used.

At one extreme, the EDI system can be totally PC-based. In this arrangement, for outgoing EDI, data are entered on a PC. Residing on the PC is translation and communication software that maps the entered data to a standard and transmits the EDI message. For incoming EDI, the PC receives a standard message and prints it out for manual use or entry into a computerized system. The major advantage of a PC system is that it is cheap and relatively easy to install. It can be up and running in a few days. A PC arrangement is a good way to initiate EDI, to conduct pilot tests, or to respond quickly to mandates by a major customer that the company be able to participate in EDI transmission. The major disadvantage of PC-based systems is that duplicate data entry is typically not eliminated. In essence, EDI in this configuration replaces mail or facsimile systems but does not link application systems.

At the other extreme, EDI can be totally mainframe-based. In this configuration data extraction, formatting, and communication to the VAN or trading partner are completed on the origin mainframe. Mainframe configuration is fast and offers high capacity. It has the advantage of potentially integrating EDI into application software. While such integration typically requires significant development, a mainframe configuration has the potential to develop seamless conversion from transaction processing to EDI.

A third arrangement is to use PCs as front-end processors to a mainframe. Under this arrangement, data are extracted from databases on the mainframe and then downloaded to the PC. The translation and communication software reside on the PC. This arrangement has the potential of mainframe integration of EDI with application software while using low-cost translation software.

A final configuration is a special-purpose minicomputer that acts as a front end to a main-

TABLE 33-3
Value-Added Network Checklist

- Do most of my potential trading partners have accounts with this VAN?
- Does the VAN provide training and installation for trading partners?
- Does the VAN interconnect with other VANS? If so, at what cost?
- Does the VAN have adequate security procedures?
- Does the VAN have the capability to handle all the communications protocols that I or my trading partners use?
- Does the VAN offer local technical assistance?
- Does the VAN do compliance checking to ensure that messages placed in my mailbox are technically correct and not "junk EDI"?
- Does the VAN have data recovery procedures in case of a failure?

frame. A number of vendors offer specialized front-end processors to perform data extraction, formatting, and conversion.

EDI Implementation

As discussed earlier, EDI is not technically complex, but it can be difficult to implement. EDI modifies the way work is typically performed within an organization. Before implementation, processes and procedures must be modified. Although all EDI implementations are different, a general guideline of required steps is detailed in Figure 33-5.

Determine Strategy

The first step in the process is to develop an overall EDI strategy. This involves identifying why EDI is desired and how comprehensive the application should be. For example, if the reason for implementing EDI is simply to respond to a customer's directive to receive electronic purchase orders, a PC-based system may be adequate. On the other hand, if the reason for implementing EDI is to integrate EDI into application software to improve customer service, then a more comprehensive application may be appropriate. Therefore, the first step is to specify the drivers behind the decision to implement EDI.

Gain Senior Management Support

The second step in the implementation process is to obtain senior management support. The most successful EDI implementations, in terms of extensive use, at high transaction volumes, across functional areas, have been in those companies where strong senior management encouragement and support existed from the outset. EDI activity cuts across traditional organizational boundaries when fully integrated with application systems, and such installations may have a relatively long payback period (two to three years). Therefore, senior management support is essential to stimulate the interdepartmental cooperation needed to see EDI through to completion and success.

Establish a Project Team

The third step is the establishment of a project team. Because EDI cuts across traditional organization boundaries, it is important to establish cross-functional teams to develop strategy and implementation plans. Of particular importance are system users and those whose work procedures will be affected by the installations. For example, if bills of lading are transmitted by EDI, accounts receivable needs to be involved because it is responsible for reconciling freight bills.

All functional areas impacted by the EDI application, such as transportation, purchasing, marketing, and accounting; staff areas such as legal and audit; and technical support such as management information systems and data processing must be involved. In other words, all users who will be affected by an EDI application must be involved in the implementation process from the beginning.

Perform EDI Audit

The fourth step is to perform an EDI audit. This requires reviewing and fully understanding the paper system. This procedure ensures that users fully understand the scope of EDI functions.

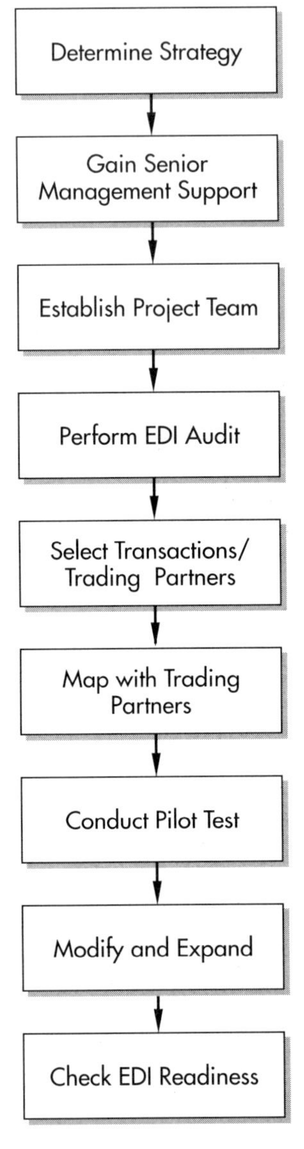

Figure 33-5
EDI Implementation Steps

The flow of all existing information—paper, verbal, and electronic—must be tracked and analyzed. An EDI audit should answer the questions posed in Table 33-4.

Once the basic information flow is understood, the audit processes can be examined to identify potential changes prior to implementing EDI. For example, is it really necessary that eight different copies of the purchase order be kept internally? While some companies implement EDI without performing such an audit, they risk inadvertently eliminating essential information or, conversely, incorporating redundant paper duplication in a faster, but still wasteful, system. The

TABLE 33-4
Questions in an EDI Audit

What are the types and volumes of information exchanged?
How is the information initiated? In what form, and by whom?
What is the internal flow of the information?
Who currently receives copies, for instance, of bills of lading?
How long are documents stored, where, and by whom?
What reports are produced and what documentation are they based on?
Who initiates the reports, and who uses them?
What specific data is required by application programs?
For instance, to issue a check, what specific information does accounts payable require?

EDI audit offers an opportunity to streamline the business flow of information. A major part of an EDI audit can be a cost-benefit justification for implementing EDI. However, recent research indicates that fewer than 25% of firms prepare a formal cost-benefit justification.[2]

Select Transactions/Trading Partners

After the audit, the next step is to select EDI transactions to be exchanged. Although the strategy may plan across-the-board implementation, most users begin EDI with just one or two transactions. There are three considerations for selecting the transactions to incorporate in the EDI application.

- *Requests from major trading partners.* One of the driving forces behind EDI implementation is customer request or demand. In this situation, the customer often determines which EDI transactions are required.
- *Expected payoff in terms of paper and manual labor reduction.* The EDI audit should indicate key transactions that are the highest in terms of paper volume and manual activity (such as reconciliation). Most companies initiate EDI with paper- and labor-intensive activities.
- *Use by others in the industry.* Another factor to consider is whether the transaction is being exchanged by others in the industry. Selecting a transaction in widespread use throughout the industry increases the likelihood of finding EDI trading partners.

In addition to selecting EDI transactions, specific trading partners must be identified. Assuming that the firm has not been mandated to implement EDI and is free to select trading partners, three guidelines that should be considered:

- *Is the trading partner doing EDI with someone else?* If possible, it is best to begin with a company that has experience with EDI for easier implementation.
- *Does the trading partner account for a large percentage of transaction volume?* Applying the 80-20 rule to trading partners is a way to increase the payoff from EDI. Most companies identify the top 10 to 20 trading partners that account for a large percentage of transactions and focus their EDI efforts on that group.
- *Is there a good relationship with the trading partner?* Implementing EDI with a trading partner requires close cooperation and coordination. This is achieved more easily if there is a strong relationship between the parties.

Map with Trading Partners

Once a willing trading partner has been identified, the next step is to "map." Mapping consists of reaching agreement on how to perform EDI. It is the process of matching trading partner requirements with EDI standards. The trading partners should discuss data required for their application systems and how to configure these data in standard formats. EDI standards establish guidelines on structuring data but do not help trading partners determine what should be exchanged. For instance, the standards provide product code identification. However, it is up to the trading partners to establish what type of code to use (buyer's, vendor's, industry's, etc.). Trading partners must agree on all optional elements and segments of the standards to be used.

Often as a result of mapping, a trading partner agreement is signed. This agreement specifies documents to be exchanged and may address selected legal issues related to implementation. Because an EDI transaction does not contain the typical paper document signature, trading partner agreements specify that this contract signature is relevant for all EDI transactions.

Conduct Pilot Test

The typical next step is to conduct a pilot test. The usual first stage of a pilot test is the transmission of "dummy" transactions. The dummy transactions are designed to test the technical operation of the system. Following the dummy test, a parallel test is run in which the same data are sent through traditional paper channels as well as through the EDI system. This permits comparison of the two systems to test functional aspects of the EDI system. Following parallel operations, the paper flow is discontinued and EDI is run "live."

Modify and Expand Usage

The pilot test often identifies areas where additional mapping is required between trading partners, where internal information flows need to be modified, or where additional EDI implementation could be useful. In expanding an EDI implementation, the best approach is normally incremental. In other words, expansion is accomplished either by exchanging current transaction sets with new trading partners or by exchanging new transaction sets with existing trading partners. Most firms have found that simultaneously adding both new trading partners and new transaction sets significantly increases implementation complexity.

Check EDI Readiness

The checklist in Table 33-5 provides a guideline for launching an EDI implementation. It can be used as a final check to determine whether a company has covered all bases and is ready to start EDI.

Barriers to Implementing EDI

Even when all the steps outlined in Figure 33-5 are followed, companies may face implementation problems. Whereas EDI is not technically complex, it can be complex to manage. The implementation of EDI cuts across traditional organizational boundaries, and therefore its implementation often faces organizational resistance. The following list summarizes some common barriers to EDI implementation and suggests an approach for resolution.

TABLE 33-5
EDI Readiness Checklist

Have company personnel and trading partners been trained in EDI?
Is top management supportive of the EDI effort?
Has a decision been made on e standards to support?
Has a VAN been selected?
Have the documents to be exchanged been determined?
Has mapping between trading partners taken place?
Will EDI be integrated with applications? If so, have necessary software modifications been made? Has a schedule for pilot testing and full implementation been established?
Has an EDI contact point been established and passed on to trading partners?
Have the contacts with the VAN and with trading partners been established?

- *Noncomputerized trading partners.* As firms expand their EDI usage, many find that potential trading partners do not have a computerized system or the necessary computer skills to implement EDI. In this case, providing a PC with software, and some training, is a way to implement EDI. Many firms have found that the cost of providing assistance is more than offset by the benefits of implementing EDI with suppliers and customers.
- *EDI is implemented in one functional area but impacts another.* It is very common for the most significant impact of a purchasing implementation of EDI to be in the accounting area. The answer to this is to have senior management support and cross-functional training for EDI. Top management support helps overcome departmental concerns.
- *EDI moves documents faster, which will mean a loss of cash float.* A common resistance to EDI is a concern over earlier payment as a result of faster movement and processing of invoices and payment. Although EDI can result in faster payment, it is not required. Furthermore, if payment is made faster, new terms can be negotiated to offset the faster payment.
- *An EDI document has no signature.* There has long been concern over the legality of EDI documents, because they are not "signed" in the conventional sense. EDI trading partner agreements can handle this problem. The American Bar Association has developed a model trading partner agreement that addresses such issues.

Costs of EDI

While the majority of firms no longer perform a cost-benefit justification before implementing EDI, costs to implement and fully integrate an EDI effort with a firm's application system are not insignificant. In general, costs can be classified into four categories: (1) software and hardware, (2) communication, (3) training and outside support, and (4) personnel.

Software and Hardware Costs

Software and hardware costs for EDI vary significantly, depending on the approach taken. When EDI is fully integrated with application systems, associated software cost will be high. Normally, some modification or in-house development will be needed for each affected application system. This requires MIS support and time. Furthermore, the translation software for mainframe applications normally exceeds $30,000. If a PC-based system is used, translation software is relatively inexpensive, with many packages costing under $1,000. Regardless of the approach taken, hardware costs are not likely to be significant. EDI can be run on nearly any computer platform, so additional hardware purchases are usually not required.

Communication Costs

There is a cost involved in the actual transmission of an electronic message between trading partners. If a third-party network is used, a onetime start-up cost may also be required. Most third-party networks charge by the message or the character, subject to a monthly minimum. Most EDI users have found network charges to be a small percentage of total EDI costs.

Training Costs

Training is one EDI cost that is often hard to estimate. EDI implementation requires training of both internal personnel and trading partners. Lost work time to participate in training, as well as the actual cost of the training, can be significant. Many companies use outside consultants or EDI service vendors to conduct training.

Personnel Costs

The final cost of EDI is for involved personnel. If a company appoints an EDI task force headed by a full-time coordinator, a significant amount of time is usually spent in planning, project management, and implementation. Personnel costs are difficult to track because they are reallocations of existing resources. Personnel can account for a significant portion of total EDI implementation costs.

A similar type of cost is for personnel time devoted to EDI. If a company appoints an EDI task force headed up by a full-time EDI coordinator, a significant amount of time is usually spent in planning for, discussing, and implementing EDI. These costs are sometimes difficult to track because they are not out-of-pocket expenses, yet they can account for a significant portion of total EDI implementation costs. Although EDI costs can be high, in nearly all cases they are offset by benefits.

Benefits of EDI

The benefits gained from EDI can be significant. Most firms obtain benefits in one or more of the following areas: (1) improved responsiveness to customers, (2) improved channel relationships, (3) increased internal productivity, (4) increased ability to compete internationally, and (5) decreased operational costs.

Improved Responsiveness to Customers

According to recent studies, a key element in the ability to respond quickly to customer requests is accurate and timely information. The 1988 Council of Logistics Management and The Ohio State University study on customer service concluded that information is a key ingredient in a firm's ability to provide excellent customer service.[3]

EDI provides accurate and timely information required for high levels of customer service and customer responsiveness. Moreover, many companies are finding that they are being "requested" or mandated by major customers or suppliers to implement EDI. In other words, implementing EDI is a clear-cut way of responding to customer requirements.

Improved Channel Relationships

The concept of supply chain management has become increasingly popular in recent years. EDI provides a way of improving and strengthening supply chain relationships. The majority of EDI users feel that its implementation has strengthened relationships within the channel.[4] The cooperation and coordination required to implement EDI leads to a stronger bond between trading partners. Linkages created by EDI are also seen as a strong level of commitment between trading partners. Another impact of EDI on supply chain relations is its ability to reduce the number of vendors. As a result, EDI implementation typically results in a supply chain with fewer, but stronger, relationships.

Increased Internal Productivity

While EDI is typically seen as a way of improving communications and relationships with customers and suppliers, its implementation often leads to a significant improvement in internal operations. One reason is the EDI audit performed before implementation, during which existing paper-based processes are examined. This review often identifies ways to improve the existing processes. For instance, many firms find unnecessary duplication when reviewing paper flows between departments. The use of EDI is also seen by many firms as necessary for the implementation of other management techniques. For instance, the auto industry has repeatedly stated that full implementation of JIT is not possible without EDI.

EDI can also enhance personnel productivity. Because it eliminates or significantly reduces data entry and processing, human resources can be freed for other work. For instance, one major food wholesaler found that before implementing EDI, salespeople viewed their job as primarily administrative and paper-intensive. Furthermore, in meeting with buyers, the salespeople normally spent approximately 12 of every 15 minutes discussing administrative issues or completing forms. After EDI implementation, the salespeople found they no longer spent time discussing administrative items and had more time for selling.[5]

Increased Ability to Compete Internationally

Business in general, and logistics operations particularly, are increasingly becoming global in nature. EDI helps firms compete internationally in two ways. (1) EDI can speed the design and production process, allowing firms to market new products more quickly, and (2) EDI can reduce the cost and time involved in international documentation. In industries like automobiles and electronics, manufacturers and suppliers are using EDI to exchange drawings and CAD/CAM data, in addition to transaction documents. This exchange has allowed companies to more closely integrate engineering, procurement, and production, thus reducing time to market and improving international competitiveness. EDI is also critical in international trade owing to the volume and complexity of international documentation.

Decreased Operational Costs

Although most firms implement EDI to provide improved customer service, the operational costs of business may be reduced, too. EDI has been shown to reduce costs associated with (1) document processing, (2) personnel, (3) inventory, and (4) error consequences. Paper processing costs are directly associated with the volume of documents. With EDI, there is no paper document to produce, reproduce, distribute, store, or control. Impact research has shown a 10:1 ratio between the processing costs of each "transaction" in EDI versus the processing cost of each paper document.[6]

EDI can result in significant cost savings in areas requiring reconciliation. In accounts payable, firms without EDI typically perform manual reconciliation of purchase orders/bills of lading with invoices/freight bills. With EDI, such reconciliation can be completed electronically. One major shipper reduced staff dedicated to freight bill reconciliation and processing by 17%.[7]

EDI can also significantly reduce inventory. Traditionally, safety stock is held to compensate for variability in demand as well as for the length and variability of the order cycle. EDI addresses these factors. With EDI, both the length of the order cycle and its variability are reduced. In addition, whereas EDI cannot change demand patterns, it can change the impact of demand uncertainty by quickly providing accurate information. For instance, in the retail industry, EDI combined with point-of-sale scanning can result in manufacturers' receiving nearly real-time information on store-level unit sales. As a result, demand can be better serviced.

The use of EDI can significantly cut the cost associated with errors. Because EDI reduces or eliminates duplication in entry, the number of errors is reduced. Such error reduction can generate significant savings. For example, if a clerk enters an order for 10 items when in fact 100 items were intended, the cost to correct the error can be high. Additional paperwork, premium freight, and perhaps a discount to placate an unhappy customer could be required. EDI greatly reduces the chance of such errors.

Examples of EDI in Logistics

EDI is used in logistics for two primary reasons: (1) to improve customer service, and (2) to improve logistics efficiency. The majority of users have implemented EDI in response to a customer request or to have access to better and more timely information. EDI has also greatly improved logistics operations.

The second major reason for promoting EDI is improvement in logistics operations. Discussed below are selected examples of how various firms have used EDI to improve logistical operations.

Transportation

EDI originated in transportation because of the large volume of documentation regularly exchanged between shippers and carriers. Today EDI is becoming the accepted way of conducting business. Industry leaders report that a critical mass of EDI capability has been reached among carriers, allowing for regular EDI use by shippers.[8]

Procter and Gamble currently uses EDI for processing freight bills with over 75% of carriers, which involves over 65% of all related documents. The resulting reduction in processing time and errors produces significant savings for both Procter and Gamble and the carriers.[9]

Materials Management

In materials management, organizations are using EDI to enhance materials requirements planning (MRP) and JIT systems. An example is The Woodbridge Group, which supplies car seats to major auto manufacturers. The company has EDI linkages with its suppliers as well as with the auto manufacturers. Manufacturers provide their production schedules to Woodbridge, which integrates them into its MRP system, which then generates component purchase orders, which are in turn transmitted to suppliers. In this way, Woodbridge is able to satisfy the JIT requirements of the auto manufacturers.[10]

Another example of EDI productivity enhancement is in contract maintenance, repair, and operations (MRO) replenishment. One manufacturer reports use of a computerized MRO system that permits users to log MRO requirements on a daily basis. At the beginning of each day, the logged requirements are reviewed and authorized requirements are transmitted to suppliers. As a result, suppliers can replenish requirements within eight hours, substantially reducing MRO inventory levels.[11]

Purchasing

One of the most common EDI uses is for purchase order processing. Typical firms using EDI in purchasing have experienced reduced processing time, improved accuracy, and increased human resource productivity, as well as improved supplier relations. In a number of industries, electronic entry of the purchase order has become the norm rather than the exception. In the grocery wholesale industry, for example, over 75% of orders are now transmitted electronically.

Inventory

As indicated at several earlier points, EDI can favorably impact the critical area of inventory requirements. Firms in all industries have experienced inventory reductions without adversely impacting customer service. The automotive, grocery, pharmaceutical, and chemical industries have all realized significant inventory reductions throughout the supply chain from implementing EDI.

Distribution

Some firms have achieved not only a reduction in inventory but also simultaneous customer service improvements. In retailing, EDI—combined with product coding and point-of-sale scanning—has created a strategic initiative called *quick response* (*QR*). Using QR, manufacturers bar code products. When the products are sold at the retail level, the bar code is scanned and inventory stock status is updated. When inventory drops to a predetermined level, a replenishment order is generated and transmitted via EDI to the manufacturer. As an example of the effectiveness of this program, Levi Strauss, in combination with JC Penney, has been able to reduce inventory over 24% while improving customer service over 20%.[12]

The use of electronic data interchange is now a common way of conducting business. Its adoption has impacted all areas of logistics. Although EDI is still the exception rather than the rule across a broad range of industries, the situation is rapidly changing. Particularly in labor- and paper-intensive areas like order processing, freight bill reconciliation, and shipment tracing, EDI applications can be projected to grow dramatically. EDI will increasingly become the operational norm among well-managed logistics organizations.

Notes

1. 1992 study by The Ohio State University and the Council of Logistics Management. Martha Cooper, C. Daniel E. Innis, and Peter R. Dickson, *Strategic Planning for Logistics* (Oak Brook, Ill.: Council of Logistics Management, 1992), p. C59.
2. The EDI Groups, Ltd., "Respondent Report for the State of U.S. EDI," 1990.
3. Bernard J. La Londe, Martha C. Cooper, and Thomas G. Noordewier, *Customer Service: A Management Perspective* (Oak Brook, Ill.: Council of Logistics Management, 1988).
4. Margaret A. Emmelhainz, "The Impact of Electronic Data Interchange on the Purchasing Process" (Columbus: Ohio State University, 1986), p. 126.
5. George Klima, former Director of Accounting Systems, Super Valu Stores, personal interviews, October 1988.
6. Margaret A. Emmelhainz, *Electronic Data Interchange: A Total Management Guide* (New York: Van Nostrand Reinhold, 1988), pp. 29–30.
7. Walter Weart, "Procter & Gamble's War on Paper," *Distribution* (May 1988), pp. 88–89.
8. Lisa H. Harrington, "EDI: Up and Running at Last," *Traffic Management* (August 1988): 655.
9. Weart, "Procter & Gamble's War on Paper."
10. Ibid.
11. "Maintenance and Purchasing Can and Do Work Together," *Maintenance Technology* (September 1988): p. 40.
12. Susan Reda, "Decoding UPC and EDI," *Apparel Merchandising* (August 1988): 51–53.

CHAPTER 34

Strategic Information Linkage

Patricia J. Daugherty

Competitive challenges and changing customer service requirements are driving the use of information linkage between trading partners. Leading firms are increasingly using information capabilities to gain faster response time, higher-quality response, and closer relationships with trading partners. To be fully effective, such information-based capabilities need to go beyond basic EDI. This chapter outlines the nature of strategic information linkage between supply chain partners.

Changing Buyer-Seller Relationships

Business practices that position trading partners against each other in a classic adversarial win/lose stance are losing attractiveness. In today's most successful business arrangements, adversarial positioning has been replaced with a philosophy of winning through cooperation. Longer-term perspectives focusing on joint commitment to gain mutual advantage are becoming more commonplace. These cooperative relationships are often called *strategic alliances.*

Strategic alliances emphasize achieving, maintaining, and enhancing a supply chain's competitive advantage.[1] The goals of such strategic relationships are "to leverage critical capabilities, increase the flow of innovation, and improve flexibility in responding to market and technological changes."[2] Before covering strategic alliances in greater depth, we provide a brief discussion of supply chain management as a useful starting point.

Supply Chain Management

Supply chain management and partnership or alliance-type arrangements have achieved considerable attention recently as "a means of simultaneously meeting the firm's customer service objectives while minimizing inventory throughout the supply chain."[3] Supply chain management is an integrative philosophy for managing the total flow of a distribution channel from supplier to the product user.[4] Supply chain management extends the focus of internal firm process integration to a channelwide focus. By integrating operations with partners like suppliers, customers, and third-party service providers, overall channel efficiency can be improved. Such coordinated effort allows the supply chain partners to be more responsive to the needs and wants of end customers.

Supply chain management centers on leveraging multiple firms' resources into an integrated, customer-directed effort. Implementation is not easy. Leveraging resources across firms requires focused and nontraditional approaches by participating firms. Because many paradigms are challenged, executive-level commitment is required. Key executives must set the tone for their organization and develop specific performance goals to guide day-to-day operations. Employees must accept "ownership" of the new business arrangement and demonstrate strong commitment to achieving supply chain success.

For a firm to be fully effective in a supply chain, internal logistics operations need to be highly integrated. This means that a firm must be highly effective and efficient to span boundaries with customers, vendors, and/or third-party service suppliers. Commitments are only as good as a firm's capability to perform. To become effective, supply chain participant firms must be willing to share information. For example, Wal-Mart's private satellite communication system allows the company to send point-of-sale data directly to its 4,000 vendors daily.[5] Thus, Wal-Mart suppliers have a clear vision of what is selling at retail. Information sharing is at the heart of supply chain management.

The potential of supply chain management is best captured by illustration. Retailing giant J. C. Penney, Inc. has implemented a system to distribute direct imports that allows the company to get merchandise from suppliers to stores and catalog customers—rapidly and at the lowest total cost.[6] The quick response (QR) program for handling imports is dependent on close coordination between JC Penney and trading partners. An exchange of information among buyers, stores, distribution staff, transportation providers, and suppliers supports the system.

JC Penney operates a "pull" system. The company does not force-distribute to its 1,314 stores. Instead, stores retain total accountability for sales, inventory, and profitability. Close communication between the company's buyers and the stores provides trend information before a typical selling season. To assign specific responsibility, individual stores are empowered to prepare sales forecasts and assign orders. Given this planning input, buyers coordinate with JC Penney's distribution personnel to ensure product availability and positioning for quick response.

JC Penney's distribution department facilitates the actual supply chain performance. For example, prepacking of product is arranged so that individual stores receive the desired size and color variety while retaining case lot distribution. The JC Penney distribution department also establishes supplier shipping dates, programs desired transit time, and arranges offshore consolidation. To control product flow, JC Penney has developed an internal control and tracking system, referred to as the Import Reporting System (IRS). From information received from consolidators' advance shipment notices, IRS monitors the direct import supply pipeline by providing information including date of shipment, estimated port arrival time, and customs clearance.

Once merchandise has been received Stateside, it either enters the domestic distribution system (PEPS, Penney's Expedited Package System) or is shipped directly to stores via motor carriers or package distribution services. Store manager input is critical to finalizing service requirements.

JC Penney's system effectiveness depends on communication among various internal divisions and with suppliers. Information technology plays a critical enabling role in integrating supply chains. Suppliers, working with JC Penney, jointly achieve desired customer service performance.

JC Penney's commitment to cooperative relationships with trading partners and expanded use of information technology is not limited to import operations. Domestic operations also rely heavily on information linkages. In total, EDI linkages are active with over 1,300 trading partners.

A New Mind-set

Achieving the level of cooperation and information sharing necessary for successful supply chain management is not easy. Coordination and working closely as partners is not the traditional way of working with suppliers. Managers have traditionally protected proprietary information. Therefore, a new mind-set must be developed to operate effectively in an environment based on extensive interfirm dialogue and information exchange.

To facilitate supply chain partnerships, potential partners should be fully aware of the unique set of issues involved. Potential partners must also have full knowledge of the traditional supply process used and the methods that have proven most effective, and an assessment of the resources of the individual trading partners.

The challenge in supply chain management is to develop an integrative philosophy that can manage across the distribution channel. Firms committed to a supply chain management philosophy realize they cannot conduct business as usual, nor can they go it alone. Recognizing the synergistic value of cooperation, supply chain–oriented firms place a high priority on developing strategic alliances. The following sections provide information on strategic alliances and speculate as to why interest in alliances has increased in recent years.

Alliance Arrangements

An *alliance* is a cooperative relationship between two or more independent organizations. The alliance is an agreement to work together to achieve specific, predefined objectives. The guiding principle is that parties to an alliance arrangement should each specialize in performing individual tasks related to core competencies, thereby eliminating as much duplication as practical. In general, alliances provide an opportunity "to achieve long-term stability through sharing resources and skills."[7] Developing successful alliance relationships is not easy. Alliances typically extend over a considerable time, involve procedures to share benefits and risks, are the product of extensive planning, include extensive information exchange, and are operationalized by cross-firm operating controls.[8] By their very nature, alliances are complex and typically require significant modifications in standard business practices.

Types of Business Alliances

Alliances can be structured in a variety of ways. Four distinct types related to logistics have been identified.[9] They include:

1. *Between product marketer and service firm.* A common alliance design involves coordination between service providers and one or more customers. Integrated service arrangements among product marketers, transportation carriers, and warehouse firms fit this format.
2. *Between service firms.* This type of alliance promotes greater efficiencies by linking resources of service providers. The service firms involved may jointly provide an integrated service to a product marketer.
3. *Between vertically aligned product marketers.* Product marketers working together represent a common alliance format. Two or more firms engaged in product marketing join together to achieve improved efficiency. Inventory ownership is usually transferred between the alliance partners in some form of JIT or QR arrangement.
4. *Between horizontally aligned product marketers.* This final type of alliance involves two or more independent firms selling to the same customer base and represents one of the most complex alliance formats. Service providers like transportation carriers frequently participate in this alliance format.

The strategic alliance between Ryder Distribution Resources and General Motors' Saturn Corp. typifies the product marketer/service firm partnering. Ryder was chosen to handle all of Saturn's inbound logistics for the new plant. Ryder edged out competing carriers because it shared the Saturn philosophy of pursuing "quality through partnerships." Because of Saturn's just-in-time operations, service assurances were critical. Performance standards were built into the initial agreement, as well as provisions for contingency or backup services. The alliance has been extremely successful and continues to be strong. Ryder has since entered into an alliance with Toyota.

Much of the growth in intermodal transportation in recent years can be attributed to alliances between transportation service firms. Major trucking companies, including J.B. Hunt Transport, Inc., and Schneider National, Inc., have entered into alliances with railroads to offer reliable service at competitive rates. Industry experts believe that "Intermodal service has finally hurdled the primary barrier of competition versus cooperation."[10] Under the cooperative arrangements, trucks are used for pickup and delivery and the railroad performs point-to-point line-haul service.

Wal-Mart's "largely invisible logistics technique known as cross-docking" depends on close relationships with vertically aligned marketers (i.e., trading partners).[11] For example, Wal-Mart has developed an alliance with Procter and Gamble. With cross-docking, products delivered to a Wal-Mart warehouse are selected, repacked, and transported to stores, usually without ever sitting in inventory. Interlocking support systems have been developed, and cooperation between Wal-Mart and Procter and Gamble has become routine. Wal-Mart's alliances with partners have resulted in efficiencies like costs lower than the industry average. Suppliers also gain. The systems allow faster payment. The average "days payable" (time between receipt of an invoice from a supplier and the date it is paid) for Wal-Mart is 29 days, compared with 45 at Kmart.

The corporate alliance formed by Abbott Laboratories and 3M is an example of an alliance between horizontally aligned product marketers that has received considerable publicity. Others who participate in the corporate alliance are Standard Register Company (business forms), IBM Corporation (computer network services), Kimberly-Clark Corporation Professional Health Care Division (nonwoven disposal products), and C.R. Bard Urological Division. The alliance's objective is to more effectively compete against Johnson and Johnson Hospital and Baxter Healthcare than any of the members could do if operating alone.

Rationale for Alliances

Although alliances take different formats, they all require significant commitment of time and resources. The rationale for working out such arrangements is to increase effectiveness and reduce cost. These goals materialize in the form of at least five types of improvement:

1. Cost reduction through specialization
2. Joint synergy/shared creativity
3. Increased information to support planning
4. Customer service enhancements
5. Reduced or shared risks

Cost Reduction Through Specialization

Alliances are typically structured to facilitate core strength focusing. Each member should attempt to focus on what it does best—what it can do most efficiently and most economically.

Such specialization is grounded in the theory of scale economies. An individual firm should be positioned to enjoy increasing returns on select activities and avoid diminishing returns on others. This means trying to perform activities that are cost-effective internally while relying on others to perform those offering limited or no cost reduction potential. Therefore, firms should concentrate on performing activities with potential for increasing return on investment. Functions with diminishing returns are more efficiently performed by an alliance partner. One important criterion in forming alliances is to seek prospective partners with the ability to provide high levels of expertise at a lower cost than could be achieved internally.

Joint Synergy and Shared Creativity

Entering into an alliance arrangement allows more resources, more talent, and more time to be focused on business solutions. One benefit of synergistic arrangements is that alliance partners are jointly able to accomplish more by working together than by going it alone. Alliance partners should be selected because of their complementarity. In such situations, the alliances offer the potential for gaining access to new skills, new technologies, new markets, and/or innovative approaches to conducting business.

Increased Information to Support Planning

Parties to an alliance typically agree to share information not normally divulged to customers or suppliers. Each party in an alliance should develop a far better understanding of the other's business. Combined planning becomes more relevant because of the expanded understanding realized from information sharing.

Customer Service Enhancements

Escalating customer requests for higher quality and consistent service have forced many firms to develop improved logistics competency. The key to satisfying a customer is to work together to create innovative solutions and service approaches that increase competitiveness. The alliance offers an effective arrangement to gain service footholds.

Reduced or Shared Risks

Alliance arrangements are particularly attractive because of the potential for reducing risk. For example, cooperative relationships can help firms reduce costs associated with research and development and/or launching new products. Through cooperation, it may be possible to reduce total elapsed time from new product conceptualization to commercialization. Pooling knowledge and talent of alliance members allocates more resources toward the goal, thereby increasing the probability of success.

Critical Success Factors

As discussed previously, alliance arrangements can be structured in a number of ways. However, successful alliances seem to share a number of common attributes. Some critical success factors include the following:

- Selective matching
- Information sharing
- Role specification
- Ground rules
- Exit provisions[12]

Selective Matching

Alliances require partners to work closely together. This necessitates a blending of corporate values and cultures if the relationship is to survive and prosper. Selection of alliance partners sharing common beliefs and values makes this much easier to accomplish. In the alliance between Saturn and Ryder mentioned above, when Saturn began the search for a transportation partner, compatibility was key. Saturn sought a carrier firm with similar values, one that was willing to "absorb" Saturn's own philosophy.

Information Sharing

Exchange of strategic and tactical information is critical to alliance success. This involves divulging proprietary information and represents a dramatic change from standard business practices of hoarding information. However, sharing of vital information like sales data, demand forecasts, inventory availability, and long-term plans allows firms to make decisions in a timely manner and be more responsive to customer needs. Most alliances utilize electronic linkages to facilitate ready access to information for their partners.

Role Specification

New working relationships present opportunities for confusion and duplicated efforts. Precise role specifications made at the outset help avoid this. Precise definition of responsibility and accountability make cooperative alliance operations run more smoothly and save time.

Ground Rules

Ground rules should be developed to guide day-to-day alliance operations. An alliance represents a new, interfirm business entity. New joint guidelines incorporating and modifying each party's previous policies must be developed. Guidelines set performance expectations and can help to avoid or resolve conflict. Developing basic ground rules establishes routine procedures and, thus, frees management time that can be devoted to longer-term planning and handling nonroutine or unexpected events. Ground rules often extend to performance standards specifying rewards and penalties based on mandated service levels.

Exit Provisions

Not all alliance partners live happily ever after. Consideration should be given to the possible dissolution of an alliance. Along with operating guidelines and policies, procedures should be developed for terminating the arrangement. Exit provisions should include buy-sell arrangements specifying who has either the right or the obligation to purchase equipment and facilities or to assume lease obligations.

Success Ingredients

The above items provide an overview of the requisite planning and areas to be considered during alliance development. It is imperative that potential alliance partners take a long-term perspective and thoroughly evaluate or investigate options. The list presented in Table 34-1, developed by Schneider National, Inc., provides a guide for developing successful alliances.

Common Reasons for Failure

Alliances offer the potential for significant benefits; however, there is also significant risk of failure. Alliances dramatically alter standard business practices. Therefore, they must be properly positioned if they are to succeed. Some of the most common pitfalls and reasons why alliances fail include the following:

- Lack of senior management support
- Lack of trust
- Fuzzy goals
- Uneven commitment
- Loss of control

Lack of Senior Management Support

Alliances must have "the shoulder" of management behind them, committed to making them succeed. One of the biggest obstacles to alliance success is a general resistance to change. People naturally mistrust the unknown and, too frequently, fear change. Therefore, management must do a good job of selling the concept of alliance partnering. In addition to the support of key managers at all levels, sufficient resources must be allocated to alliances. Funding is especially important in the area of communication and information.

TABLE 34-1
Basic Ingredients for a Successful Logistics Alliance

1. Thorough assessment of participant strengths
2. Consistency of values
3. Clear understanding of objectives
4. Agreement on measurement standards
5. Long-term focus
6. Commitment of multiple levels
7. Working relationship at interface level
8. Limited number of relationships
9. Elimination of quid pro quo mentality
10. Negotiated prices—not bid and subject to change

Source: Adapted from Donald J. Bowersox, Patricia J. Daugherty, Cornelia Dröge, Richard Germain, and Dale S. Rogers, *Logistical Excellence: It's Not Business as Usual* (Bedford, Mass.: Digital Press, 1992).

Lack of Trust

Trading partners must stop viewing information as proprietary and consider it a shared resource. Alliance participation requires trading partners to work closely together and develop an atmosphere of trust. Unless there is a free exchange of ideas and relevant information, the partnership is unlikely to work.

Fuzzy Goals

Careful preplanning and formalized statement of operating guidelines can help an alliance to succeed. This includes specification of roles, long-term goals, and performance objectives. If clear-cut goals are not developed, the chances for alliance success are greatly reduced. Vague objectives such as "increasing sales" or "improving service levels" are of no value. In addition to clear-cut goals, performance measures should be specified up front and a plan developed to routinely monitor performance in key areas. Some alliance partners accomplish this through annual or semi-annual service surveys. Thus, problems can be identified and communications are enhanced.

Uneven Commitment

Alliance participants are unlikely to be equal. Almost certainly one of the partners will have more at stake than the other(s) and therefore is likely to be more committed to alliance success. Levels of commitment are frequently related to power differentials. The alliance partner with more power is likely to be less committed to the relationship and, in some instances, may try to leverage the power advantage. This can subvert the basic premise of alliance building—the existence of a foundation of trust and commitment by all involved parties.

Loss of Control

Alliance partners reveal proprietary information and, to a degree, relinquish a certain amount of control over their own operations. Partners cannot act autonomously; decisions must be made jointly and operations closely coordinated. Many alliance participants do not feel comfortable with such an arrangement. If the alliance is to continue, the benefits gained through cooperation must more than make up for the lost autonomy.

Information Support for Advanced Alliance Relationships

Alliances for the most part have been formed to reduce costs, minimize or reduce risks, or gain access to skills not available internally. A select few alliances have been formed for a different purpose—to achieve competitive advantage. The intent of alliance designers is to pool resources to position alliance participants to achieve competitive advantage. Information support is especially critical in what are often referred to as *strategic alliances.*[13]

Strategic alliances are typically supported by advanced electronic data interchange (EDI) applications. EDI allows the linking of independent firms and promotes close working relationships. Fully exploited EDI capabilities enable efficient supply chain management and facilitate both internal and external integration. For an alliance to be truly strategic, the trading partners must cooperate to the extent that the boundaries between the firms almost disappear or become transparent. EDI provides the electronic link to make the necessary coordination and exchange of information possible. However, more than EDI is required for strategic linkage.

EDI Linkage Versus Strategic Linkage

EDI provides the basis for establishing strategic linkages, but its technical aspects alone are not sufficient to achieve strategic linkage. Rather, EDI should be viewed as necessary for, but not sufficient to guarantee, strategic linkage.

Intercompany computer-to-computer exchange of information typically results in increased speed, improved accuracy, and reduced cost. Typical indirect benefits include shorter and more dependable order cycles; decreased labor, freight, and materials costs; improved cash flow; reduced inventory; and improvements in overall business efficiency as a result of the availability of complete, timely, and accurate information.

The benefits of EDI can be substantial, but significant benefits are possible beyond basic EDI. EDI firms can establish electronic linkage as the nucleus of a strategic alliance.

Electronic Linkage

Alliance arrangements that qualify as strategic build upon electronic linkage to share information. The attributes of electronic linkage are information access, connectivity, and formalization.[14] Each is discussed briefly and a model is presented to illustrate interaction of the three attributes.

Strategic linkage cannot be achieved without freedom of *information access*. Linkage partners must commit to sharing key information on demand. The information access aspect of strategic linkage means that firms routinely share a wide range of database elements.

Connectivity refers to the level or capability of interactivity. Installation of sophisticated communications systems does not automatically guarantee high levels of connectivity. Access must be responsive to partners' needs. Such responsiveness is achieved by direct connectivity that allows access as needed. Information must be capable of being configured to meet specific needs, and it must be readily available. Connectivity involves speed and precision. Thus, the emphasis is on ease of information transfer rather than the technical aspects of electronic linkage.

Formalization, or the creation of interfirm rules and procedures, is critical for a strategic alliance. The parties involved must develop a joint interorganizational culture and working environment. Establishment of rules and procedures provides guidelines for the alliance and direct assignment of responsibilities.

Achieving Strategic Linkage: An Integrated Model

The simultaneous interaction of information access, connectivity, and formalization provides the key to distinguishing between strategic linkage arrangements and other cooperative ventures. The existence of a high level of the three attributes and their interaction provide the bases for gaining competitive advantage. The three-dimensional model presented in Figure 34-1 illustrates interaction of the three key attributes.

Figure 34-1 illustrates that the levels of the three attributes can vary. Individual alliance arrangements may place different emphasis on specific attributes. Depending on the level of

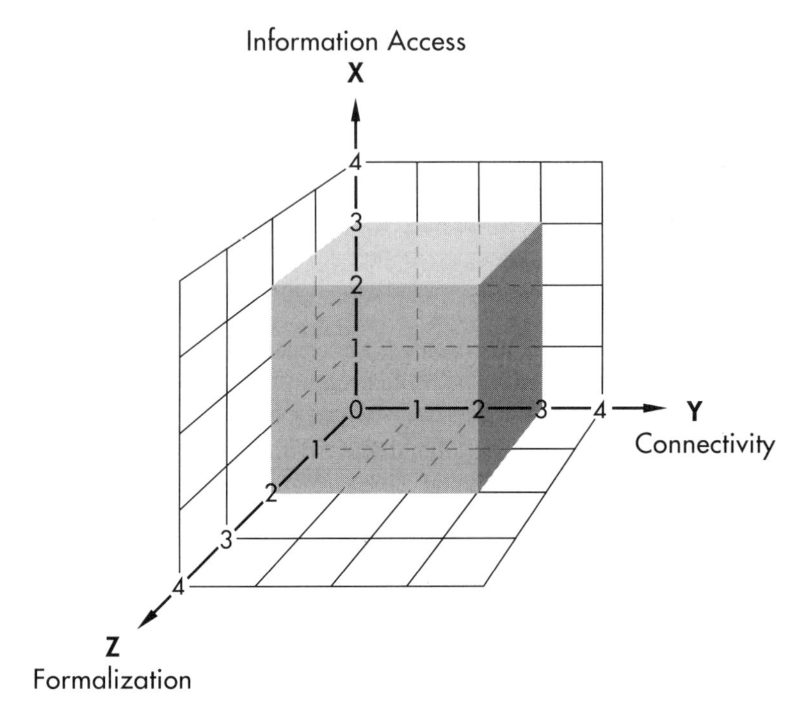

Figure 34-1
Relationship of Key Alliance Attributes

Source: Adapted from Donald J. Bowersox et al., *Logistical Excellence: It's Not Business as Usual* (Bedford, Mass.: Digital Press, 1992).

each attribute, a different size of package or box would be depicted. For example, a "box" that is the full size of the model would indicate that the alliance partners have extensively developed capabilities in all three areas—information access, connectivity, and formalization.

During formation, alliances may initially work to develop information access but remain relatively unsophisticated with respect to connectivity and formalization. In this case, the integrated model would be presented as a tall box that was relatively narrow in width and depth. The trading partners would have routine access to a wide variety of database elements without restriction. Such capability should work to enhance decision-making speed and quality.

Another linkage arrangement might initially emphasize connectivity to a greater extent than the other two attributes. The focus would be on responsiveness to partners' information requirements. In this instance, the model would be depicted by a wide box, somewhat flat and not very deep. The preceding discussion makes clear that a broad range of paths is available when developing linkage arrangements. However, to function as a strategic linkage, all three attributes must be fully present. The interaction and resultant synergy are critical to the strategic alliance. Focusing on only one or two of the elements does not create competitive advantage. Although the minimum or threshold level of each attribute required to enable a strategic alliance is unclear, examination of business arrangements among alliance firms that have achieved competitive advantage reveals high and balanced commitment to the three attributes.

Alliance Relationship Development

Achieving strategic relationships does not happen instantaneously. It is a process that evolves over time. The commitment between alliance partners must be strong and long-term. The key is to increase interactivity between the participants. In advanced alliances, direct-linked information systems would operate in a real-time environment. There would be instant access to a wide range of information. Without question, partners in a strategic alliance would jointly seek to reduce any barriers that restricted exchange of strategic information.

Examination of strategic alliances suggests a general development pattern. The initial stage between trading partners is likely to center around basic EDI. The focus is on exchanging routine business documents. Elementary information access capabilities are developed to satisfy EDI requirements.

As the linkage arrangement develops, information access capabilities are expanded beyond basic business documents. For example, a supplier might desire access to inventory data to create replenishment orders automatically. To become operational, immediate access to information is critical. Alliance partners could access information as needed, instead of requesting information and then waiting for a response.

Increasing the level of connectivity facilitates information access. As information is required and access is authorized, connectivity makes alliances work. Immediate access to order status gives partners the capability to make changes based on up-to-date information. The highly responsive environment helps to improve decision making and is especially important to support quick response systems. Considering the extreme emphasis on speed and reducing cycle time, connectivity is a key dimension of alliances.

The above illustration highlights the importance of information access and connectivity. When trading partners introduce jointly agreed upon operating rules, the alliance moves toward becoming truly strategic. Formalization is the foundation for interorganizational coordination and joint planning. Because rules and procedures are developed to guide day-to-day operations, there is more time to handle nonroutine situations and to develop flexible responses.

When all three attributes reach high levels of development, partners begin to function as a single unit or as an integrated supply chain. Electronic interaction and communication become routine. The ultimate result is that the strategic alliance gains competitive advantage for its participants. In a recent article in the *Journal of Commerce,* ten firms including Wal-Mart, Dayton Hudson Corporation, Melville Corporation, and The Price Company were singled out as new retail winners. These companies have demonstrated years of commitment to developing information capabilities and, more recently, to quick response systems.[15] Now they are reaping rewards because of the commitment: sales of products backed by quick response systems increased 15% in 1991.

Risks Associated with Strategic Alliances

Naturally, strategic alliances also involve risk. A degree of risk is associated with disclosing sensitive proprietary information. Alliance arrangements tend to create dependency that can be detrimental if a partner fails to fulfill obligations and to perform to predefined standards.

Alliance partners are rarely, if ever, equal in terms of relative power and resources. If extreme differences exist, problems may develop. If one of the alliance partners dominates the relationship, a tendency may exist to take advantage of the arrangement. Smaller organizations have the potential for greater loss if the alliance fails. Therefore, they are vulnerable to manipulation by stronger partners.

Alliance participants commit significant time and resources to the relationship. Frequently this means they cannot take advantage of new opportunities. Therefore, it is imperative that parties carefully evaluate the potential risks and benefits before entering into an alliance. Rewards must be sufficient to compensate for reduced autonomy and the constraints that accompany alliance involvement.

Strategic alliances are paradoxical. One of the most attractive benefits associated with strategic alliances is also a major weakness—being locked into the relationship. Active participation in an alliance means focusing resources and efforts to ensure the achievement of mutual gain. It also means that partners must accept a great deal of risk and diminished autonomy. Many alliance opportunities are passed up because of this fear of losing self-determination. In some instances, loss of autonomy is believed to be more important than the potential benefits associated with cooperative strategic alliances.

Conclusion

Strategic alliances realized through the development of strategic linkages offer significant potential. The pooling of resources creates the opportunity to jointly accomplish objectives and performance goals that could not be achieved if operating in isolation. Alliance partners should be carefully selected to provide complementary skills and/or resources that allow efficiency improvements that could not have been achieved otherwise.

Although there is strong interest in creating closer buyer-seller relationships and alliances, few examples of strategic linkage arrangements currently exist in North America. The preceding discussion has focused on how firms can achieve linkages that provide the basis for strategic alliances and gaining competitive advantage. Three attributes are essential to strategic alliances—information access, connectivity, and formalization. Trading partners are advised to develop expertise in those three areas and to be open to considering new approaches to doing business. A new mind-set is needed; yesterday's strategies won't be good enough.

The achievement of gaining advantage through strategic linkage with trading partners is a moving target. Customers' needs change, and in response, "standard" business practices must be revamped. The optimal level of each of the three essential ingredients of a strategic alliance needs to be reconsidered as technological innovations and improvements increase the opportunities available to trading partners.

Notes

1. Godfrey Devlin and Mark Bleackley, "Strategic Alliances—Guidelines for Success," *Long-Range Planning* 21, no. 5 (1988): 18–23.
2. Stanley J. Modic, "Strategic Alliances," *Industry Week* 237, no. 7 (October 3, 1988): 46–52.
3. Lisa M. Ellram and Martha C. Cooper, "Supply Chain Management, Partnerships, and the Shipper-Third Party Relationship," *International Journal of Logistics Management* 1, no. 2 (1990): 1–10.

4. Graham C. Steven, "Integrating the Supply Chain," *International Journal of Physical Distribution and Materials Management* 8, no. 8 (1989): 3–8; and John B. Houlihan, "International Supply Chains: A New Approach," *Management Decision* 26, no. 3 (1988): 13–19.
5. George Stalk, Philip Evans, and Lawrence E. Shulman, "Competing on Capabilities: The New Rules of Corporate Strategy," *Harvard Business Review* 70, no. 2 (March-April 1992): 57–69.
6. Joseph Bonney, "Penney's System for Imports," *American Shipper* 33, no. 11 (1991): 51–53.
7. For an expanded discussion, readers are referred to chap. 7 of Donald J. Bowersox, Patricia J. Daugherty, Cornelia Dröge, Richard Germain, and Dale S. Rogers, *Logistical Excellence: It's Not Business as Usual* (Bedford, Mass.: Digital Press, 1992).
8. John Gardner and Martha C. Cooper, "Elements of Strategic Partnership," *Partnerships: A Natural Evolution in Logistics,* Proceedings of the 1988 Logistics Resource Forum, 1988, pp. 15–32.
9. Donald J. Bowersox, "The Strategic Benefits of Logistics Alliances," *Harvard Business Review* 68, no. 4 (July-August 1990): 36–45.
10. David L. Sparkman, "Intermodalism Growing, Gaining Shippers' Confidence," *Transport Topics* no. 2953 (March 9, 1992): 12, 14.
11. Stalk et al., "Competing on Capabilities."
12. Donald J. Bowersox, "Logistical Partnerships," *Partnerships: A Natural Evolution in Logistics,* Proceedings of the 1988 Logistics Resource Forum, 1988, pp. 1–14.
13. Barrie G. James, "Alliance: The New Strategic Focus," *Long-Range Planning* 18, no. 3 (1985): 76–81; and Devlin and Bleackley, "Strategic Alliances."
14. Donald J. Bowersox, Patricia J. Daugherty, and Maurice P. Lundrigan, "Logistics Strategy and Structure: Strategic Linkage," Proceedings of the Annual Conference of the Council of Logistics Management, Vol. 1, 1990, 53–63.
15. Tony Seideman, "Quick Response Makes Switch from Esoteric to Essential Equipment," The *Journal of Commerce* (January 27, 1992).

SECTION IX

Logistics Organizations and Human Resources Management

Jonathan L. S. Byrnes

The focus of logistics has shifted in a subtle but crucial way. Both executives and educators speak increasingly of "logistics management" rather than simply "logistics" when they describe their most important issues achievements. Because logistics is rooted in product flow, and product flow crosses both functional department and company boundaries, the insightful management of organizational relations and human resources has become the key ingredient for success.

In Chapter 35, Donald J. Bowersox, David J. Frayer, and Judith M. Schmitz of Michigan State University present an overview of organizing for effective logistics management. The authors describe the evolution of logistics organizational forms within the context of company development. They conclude by thoughtfully exploring the characteristics of emerging logistics organizations for tomorrow's companies.

In Chapter 36, William W. Allport of Leaseway Transportation discusses labor relations in the 1990s. The author notes that there has never been a better opportunity to obtain commitment and productivity from employees. He covers the topics of communication and collective bargaining in rich detail. He also provides valuable information on new legislation covering sexual harassment, employment-at-will, disability regulations, civil rights, and worker adjustment and retraining.

In Chapter 37, Jonathan L. S. Byrnes and Roy D. Shapiro of M.I.T. and Harvard, respectively, cover focused human resources management as the key to logistics effectiveness. The authors note that effective logistics executives must shift from managing assets and direct reports to achieving results by influencing the actions of others. By harnessing the power of human resources management, managers can effect sweeping programs of change, within their companies and in other companies as well. The authors discuss effective policies in compensation and performance measurement, recruitment and selection, career development, and promotion and termination. They also discuss a new, integrative approach to career development involving knowledge and work experience outside a company's boundaries.

In Chapter 38, Frederick Hewitt of Xerox develops a systematic approach for proactive change management in logistics. The author notes that managing continuous and sometimes dramatic change will be essential for logistics executives, and that effective managers must be change agents as well as visionaries. Hewitt carefully discusses the components of proactive change management, including creating and sharing a vision, and techniques for implementing change. He argues that continuous improvement is a requirement for business success, and that the ability to proactively manage change will be the differentiating characteristic of the best enterprises.

CHAPTER 35

Organizing for Effective Logistics Management

Donald J. Bowersox
David J. Frayer
Judith M. Schmitz

An effective and efficient logistics organization is a vital part of a firm's strategic management process. As attention focuses on achieving high levels of customer service, satisfaction, and success, the performance of logistics management becomes increasingly critical. The ability of managers to visualize the entire supply chain, from source of supply to final consumer, is a complex task that requires creative logistical performance and solutions. In this dynamic environment, a primary consideration for senior managers is, "How should a firm be organized to best achieve effective and efficient logistics management?"

This chapter discusses organization development including:

- *Fragmented management*—the practice of traditional management
- *Organizational evolution*—the transition from functional to integrated management over the past four decades
- *The extended enterprise*—the extension of management in the future (organizations will be capable of facilitating integration across the entire supply chain)

Fragmented Management

Logistics organizations developed to help managers achieve control over individual logistics functions like transportation, warehousing, inventory management, and purchasing. The functional command and control organization encouraged fragmented management, because each operational area was managed to perform independently within budget. In addition to organization structure, fragmented logistics management grew as a result of general accounting practice and the sheer size of transportation expenditures relative to other, less clearly identifiable logistics costs. To fully understand the context from which logistics integration emerged, it is important to understand the practices that impeded integration.

Separate Activities Imbedded Within Strong Functions

Traditionally, key components of logistics like transportation and inventory management were directed and organized as subsets of larger functions, such as marketing, manufacturing, or finance. Under a command and control structure, this typically meant that logistics managers were responsible for isolated activities. For example, transportation managers were responsible for selecting modes, choosing carriers, and negotiating prices without regard for inventory accountability. These managers controlled and managed transportation and were typically located at a plant or warehouse. While these managers most often had dotted line accountability to a corporate staff officer, they reported directly to a local manager. Similarly, inventory management was isolated often as part of operations at a plant level or part of marketing within a sales district. Thus, inventory investment facilitated manufacturing efficiency or was used to provide customer service. Under such an isolated arrangement, logistics activities were managed as cost centers. The primary goal was to hold expenditures to a minimum. When managing key logistical components in such a fragmented manner, it was difficult to envision, let alone capture, systemwide functional trade-offs. Trade-off opportunities between individual logistics activities were difficult to quantify. As a result, the overall enterprise operated at efficiency levels lower than necessary despite the fact that each of the key logistical components was being performed at lowest possible cost.

Such fragmented practice was exacerbated by generally accepted accounting principles. Total logistics costs were difficult to identify because individual expenditures were grouped in natural categories like heat, light, interest, and salaries. Expenditures were typically combined into departmental statements that had no direct application to the actual process that consumed the resource. Total logistics costs related to warehousing, inventory management, and order processing could not be identified. Thus it was nearly impossible to identify the total cost of a specific order, let alone its profitability. Furthermore, there was a tendency, particularly in the case of freight, to abandon accrual concepts for time-of-payment accounting. This practice could result in costs incurred in one time period being reported with revenues from another period. Overall continuity was lost when freight bills, for example, were expensed when paid with no regard for when the associated orders were booked as revenue. Fragmented command and control organization structures, combined with traditional accounting methods, made it extremely difficult to identify logistics expenditures, pinpoint overall logistics responsibility, or perform trade-off analyses.

High Transportation Visibility

The idea that overall logistics should be managed on an integrated basis was to a degree inhibited by the relative size of transportation expenditures, which have traditionally been the largest single component of logistics costs. Today, transportation expenditures alone account for 50% of total logistics expenditures, even though transportation as a percent of total logistics cost has declined substantially since 1980.[1] The ratio and visibility of transportation expenditures relative to other logistics costs stimulated a high degree of managerial attention. Freight bills have been monitored, tracked, and audited by firms for decades. The ease with which some transportation costs, like freight bills, can be identified, coupled with the sheer size of such expenditures, resulted in many firms' limiting cost reduction and containment to this one operating area.

In a transportation-dominated environment, the potential benefits of total cost logistics were difficult to capture. Trade-offs among transportation, inventory, order processing, and other related logistics costs were difficult to quantify. Even when such trade-offs were identified, it was difficult to buck the trend of cost reduction and to spend more on transportation in an effort to capture trade-offs that reduce total cost. A strong functional orientation, focused on reducing transportation cost, typically resulted in failure to effectively manage overall logistics.

Forces of Change

Realization that opportunities existed to minimize the total cost of logistics created initial interest in integration. Starting in the late 1950s, crystallization of integrated logistics resulted from at least four major developments:

1. total cost analysis
2. systems methodology
3. concern for improved customer service
4. increased attention to marketing channel arrangements[2]

A 1956 study of air freight economics by Lewis, Culliton, and Steele provided a perspective for viewing logistics decisions on an integrated basis.[3] In an effort to illustrate economic justification for high-cost air transport, the authors introduced total cost analysis. Though total cost awareness had existed in manufacturing for decades, its application in a logistics context was truly innovative. Total cost measurement, coupled with the application of systems methodology for integrated analysis, made logistics functional integration a realistic goal.

The growth and development of the marketing concept, pioneered by General Electric in the 1950s, created increased concern for customer service. Firms began to consider the potential of consistent logistics performance as a means to satisfy customers. This increased attention to customer-focused marketing developed into the quality mandate of the 1980s. To be a truly quality-oriented firm means that all work must be focused on achieving customer satisfaction. The strategic application of logistical competency provides one additional way to achieve customer satisfaction.

The drive toward integration seldom stops with the efforts of a single firm. Rather than considering logistics responsibilities as beginning and ending within the efforts and boundaries of one firm, an interorganizational or channel perspective emerged. Functional duplication throughout the channel can be a serious barrier to increased efficiency. The early work of Alderson and Forrester helped emphasize the importance of positioning the channel as the relevant competitive unit.[4] This channel perspective grew into the extended enterprise discussed in greater detail later in this chapter.

In the 1990s, increased attention to integrated logistics management continues to be fueled by five drivers:

1. *Logistics strategy.* A broad group of senior managers have become aware that logistics can be positioned and managed to create competitive advantage.
2. *Integrative philosophy.* Failure to develop an integrative philosophy of logistics management creates a deficiency that can be serious in today's highly competitive environment.
3. *Process control.* Logistical process control offers a way to benefit from trade-offs that occur throughout the supply chain. The ideal accomplishment is a movement/storage system that spans and integrates the total supply chain and provides significant cost reduction through trade-offs and enhanced synergistic potential for all who participate.

4. *Channel management.* Integration of logistical operations in a channel can reduce cost by eliminating duplication and reducing some of the risk associated with anticipatory distribution.
5. *Business complexity.* The complexity of business in the 1990s requires innovative logistical solutions that are attainable only through integrated effort.

Organizational Evolution

Organizational evolution accompanied the realization that integration could be beneficial. Firms seeking to achieve more integrated logistics have been observed to pass through some clearly definable configurations. Initially, most logistics efforts were functionally driven, which resulted in adoption of time-tested command and control organization structures. The current thrust in integration emphasizes process management and seeks the development of linkages in work flow as contrasted to functional grouping. This focus on integrated process management is resulting in new organization structures and working relationships centered around facilitating best practice. The evolution can be traced from functional grouping to process-oriented organizations.

Functional Grouping

Initial research on organization evolution indicated that management was concentrating on functional grouping as the best way to manage logistics. Research suggested three evolutionary levels of development for achieving logistics functional integration.[5]

Complete fragmentation. The starting point was complete fragmentation, in which logistics activities were dispersed over command and control structures and reported to traditional organizations like marketing, manufacturing, or finance. So-called integration at this level depended on cooperation between managers who were responsible for related functions.

Functional organization. The next level of organization development occurred when two or more major logistics functions were organizationally combined to form the nucleus of a materials management or physical distribution group. The perception was that integration would be facilitated when logistics-oriented groups were structured independently from marketing, manufacturing, or finance in the command and control organization hierarchy.

Functional integration. The third and highest level of integrated development was envisioned to occur when materials management and physical distribution organizations were combined to create a group responsible for overall logistics.

All three levels of structural development focused on the organizational grouping of logistics-related functions. At the initial level, whatever integration resulted was limited to cooperation. At the later two levels, functions were assigned to a specific group viewed as part of the formal command and control structure. The basic assumption was that close proximity and reporting to a single executive would facilitate integrated performance.

One of the early research efforts sought to track the order in which specific functions migrated into a specialized logistics organization. Under the so-called stages paradigm, firms were classified as stage I through stage III according to the sequence through which functions were grouped into a formal logistics organization.[6] Another research stream studied organization change by observing career patterns of logistics executives.[7] Both research efforts, although independent, confirmed a trend toward increased functional grouping. For example, an increasing number of logistics executives were observed as heading a logistics or distribution department.

However, while the trends identified by organizational research tended to confirm that logistics functions were being grouped together, no evidence supported the hypothesis that organizational functional grouping could or did result in performance integration. In fact, such organizations tended to conform to traditional command and control paradigms.

Over time, the line of research concerning career positioning concluded that the organization development pattern of logistics appeared to be focusing more on process integration. Process integration occurs when management attention moves from pure functional excellence to concerns related to cross-functional linking of work effort to attain specific operational or strategic goals. The trend toward process integration was supported by data confirming a shift from pure staff or advisory positions to more general involvement in line activities or a combination of line and staff activities managed from a centralized logistics perspective. Line positioning in which the centralized organization was directly involved in day-to-day management of overall logistics constituted a major paradigm shift. As process integration awareness and interest emerged, it became clear that researching functional organization grouping and migration was not the best way to understand the dynamics of logistics management.

Process Orientation

A pilot study conducted in 1987 hypothesized that leading-edge logistics organizations would move to a variety of different structures focused around best practice in an effort to achieve broader involvement in quality initiatives and to develop process decision making.[8] The exploratory research confirmed that leading-edge logistics organizations were gaining responsibility over a wider span of control for both traditional and supplemental logistics functions. Functional grouping was being viewed by managers as less important than in the past. Managers were becoming increasingly concerned with driving logistical performance to support specific missions. The pilot study reconfirmed the early conclusions of career-tracking research. The trend confirmed a shift from management and grouping of functions toward best-practice process management.

As contrasted with managing logistics functions, leading-edge firms focus on processes that manage the interfaces between internal and external groups. Tasks and interrelationships are best viewed as being connected by a vertical structure of order cycles that form a logistics operating arena. By focusing on order cycle arrangements, all tasks from purchasing, through engineering design and manufacturing, to finished goods distribution can be planned and coordinated as an integrated process that cuts across traditional command and control functions. As a result, logistics serves as a main process to support the strategic mission of the enterprise.

Process management requires rethinking traditional organization. Organizations must be configured to facilitate process integration. Such reconfiguration, in contrast to traditional command and control organization structures, might more closely resemble a hospital where a team of specialists combine talents to complete a surgical process.[9] The shift from a functional emphasis is one force reducing the need for middle managers who have traditionally served as gatekeepers for command and control organizations. Thus, the hierarchical organization structure that supported functional management was observed as moving toward a flatter, process-oriented structure. "Process reengineering" is a term commonly used to denote the reconfiguration of both operations and command and control structures to parallel the activities (processes) the firm performs.

Many feel that the ultimate implementation of cross-functional process teams will require complete disintegration of traditional command and control organizations.[10] Disintegration is viewed as occurring at three levels:

1. among consumers
2. across product life cycles
3. within organization structures

Evidence suggests that consumer behavior is changing and has been radically transformed. Consumers have access to more information and a greater choice of products because of market globalization. As a result, they are becoming less brand-loyal. They are able to demand more value-added services and sophisticated options. As firms examine new ways to service these more demanding consumers and attempt to redefine marketing mix strategies, logistics offers one way to gain competitive advantage.

Moreover, product life cycles are accelerating and disintegrating. The result is less time to recover research and development investment. Life cycle reduction demands faster time to market for new products and services and places a premium on supporting marketing, manufacturing, and logistics operations. The prevailing belief is that the flexibility required to deal with this faster competitive pace is inhibited by command and control organization. Process management, by concentrating on order cycle dynamics, seeks to reduce waste and duplication, thereby decreasing time to market and increasing system flexibility.

Disintegration is also occurring as hierarchical organization structures become flatter for reasons other than consumers, product life cycles, and organization structures. As firms seek to reduce head count, functions traditionally performed internally are being outsourced. Furthermore, managers' responsibilities have broadened beyond traditional functional borders as they seek to integrate within the process mandate. For example, logistics is becoming responsible for activities outside the traditional functional borders of materials management and physical distribution operations.[11]

The command and control organization sought to manage interdependencies between functional areas by structuring firms into departments, product lines, and divisions. Process management seeks to use information to coordinate such interdependencies. Process integration requires a unique set of tools. Technology like EDI is one tool that enables information interdependencies between functions to exist and facilitates process management. Activity-based costing (ABC) is an accounting tool that attempts to eliminate the shortcomings of traditional accounting methods discussed previously. ABC seeks to group expenditures so the appropriate cost is charged to the activity or process that consumed the resource. As such, it provides the accountability framework required for process management.

The concept of fifth-generation management, which seeks organizational interdependencies and leverage through teaming arrangements, was constructed by Savage.[12] From Savage's perspective, interdependencies can be managed only through information networks that have access to common, process-oriented databases. Fifth-generation teams are driven by a unified strategic vision by utilizing and sharing accumulated knowledge and by access to information throughout the network system.

One of the benefits of managing interdependencies is increased operational flexibility. Flexibility is the essence of logistics leadership; it permits firms to achieve extraordinary service over and above that of competitors by performing a variety of value-added functions.[13] The firm that effectively manages process interdependencies finds it easy to deviate from routine operating procedures when opportunities to gain greater customer impact present themselves. Surprisingly enough, logistics flexibility is achieved via formalization. When a firm formalizes policies, procedures, and rules, duplication of effort is minimized and work becomes value-adding.[14] This formalization may be as simple as documenting how the current environment operates or teaching and continuously reminding employees of the policies, procedures, and rules. Furthermore, formalization may occur as a by-product of reengineering. Focusing on value and reducing waste promotes flexibility and allows managers to seek and exploit new opportunities for competitive advantage.

While varying on specifics, most experts agree that the traditional command and control structures driven by functional control mechanisms have outlived their usefulness. They simply are not the best way to operate in an information-based competitive environment. The exact structure of the dominant organization form in the future remains to be seen, but management experts identify a broad range of challenges that must be addressed in making the conversion:

1. Teams must be empowered and given the necessary authority to make decisions. For teams to be empowered, they need training, new tools, and a shift in cultural norms.
2. As the need for middle management is reduced or eliminated, retraining middle management for new roles in the organizational structure is difficult.
3. Turf battles must be controlled so that ownership of information is eliminated and information is shared freely among team members.
4. A unified vision must be created so that self-interest is shifted to team and company interest.
5. Norms, values, and politics must be adapted to promote team-building skills.
6. New rewards, recognition, and career opportunities need to be developed that promote teamwork and motivate networking.
7. Developing and recruiting capable top management is more difficult.
8. As managers and team members' role complexity increases, high levels of training are required.
9. The shift from command and control to integrated structures is ultimately a management process, not an information systems design process. As such, it requires time, flexibility to change, and leadership.
10. Creating an effective information infrastructure is a serious challenge.[15]

The Extended Enterprise

The availability of inexpensive information technology has propelled logistics organizations beyond the challenges of internal process integration. In today's environment, firms are seeking and achieving logistics process integration across the entire supply chain. This emerging view that logistical arrangements can serve as the unifying force for the distribution channel provides significant opportunities for firms positioned to take advantage. Ford, and later General Motors, envisioned channelwide synergism as attainable only by vertical ownership. In today's business climate, the style of monolithic ownership sought by Henry Ford is not practical because of the immense cost of labor and capital, as well as the potential loss of flexibility. The alternative to ownership is partnership. Information technology is the key to extending the enterprise beyond existing boundaries to include vertical partnerships.

The following discusses the extended enterprise through examination of time-based strategies, boundary spanning, and partnerships. Each of these concepts has a direct impact on logistical organization structures of the future.

Time-based Strategies

The rapid deployment of sophisticated information technology has facilitated implementation of time-based competitive strategies.[16] These strategies focus on elimination of waste and duplication of effort while reducing inventory in manufacturing and distribution systems.[17] Selected industries including automotive, retail, and software are using time-based strategies to create competitive advantage.

Just-in-time (JIT) and quick response (QR) are two interorganizational arrangements that position inventory and information technology to maximize asset utilization. JIT relies on zero defects, elimination of nonvalue-added activities, and real-time information exchange. JIT directs inventory to be available precisely as needed in the channel. Inventory velocity benefits the participating enterprises in at least two ways. First, production is initiated by customer order. Postponing production until order receipt eliminates manufacturing in anticipation of sales and removes much of the obsolescence risk. Second, the order cycle duration under JIT is reduced to the minimum by eliminating defects and nonvalue-added work. This reduction in order cycle time improves customer service and creates a difficult-to-duplicate competitive advantage. The result is direct benefit for all involved.

Toyota's car assembly in Japan illustrates the far-reaching benefits obtainable from JIT. Japanese dealers utilize on-line computers to communicate orders directly to the assembly plant when customers order. Upon an order going "in system," the entire production process is initiated and coordinated down to the individual component part level. By using JIT, Toyota is able to deliver a finished car, built to customer specification, within a week to ten days.[18] Such quick delivery is one reason Toyota's market share in Japan recently hit an all-time high; customers receive their personalized end product sooner than previously thought possible and significantly faster than from any competitor. Furthermore, JIT procedures reduce waste, which results in significantly high profits for Toyota.

QR, popularized in the retail industry by companies like Target Stores, Kmart, Wal-Mart, JC Penney, and Levi Strauss, is a different form of information-based system that is revolutionizing deployment of finished inventory. Similar to JIT, QR is based on sequencing retail delivery of merchandise to more closely match consumer buying patterns.[19] By utilizing real-time information exchange, retailers can coordinate working arrangements with suppliers and facilitate overall supply chain performance.

Logistics information service companies like DEC and EDS are developing information reservoirs or warehouse-type databases to further facilitate real-time interorganizational communications. These concepts use a combination of EDI, protocols, and customized standards to extract critical data elements from transaction processing systems for sharing among supply chain partners. These data are maintained in a configuration that facilitates and disseminates information to supply chain participants on demand. Such shared databases permit information, structured in generic formats, to be rapidly shared between organizations. The availability of shared information facilitates boundary spanning.

Boundary Spanning

Although the notion of boundary spanning in channels of distribution is not new, recent technological advances have rendered it practical because of improved control resulting from information networking. The primary concern with outsourcing has always centered around maintaining adequate control. Through information networking, firms are able to instantaneously share critical operating information like manufacturing schedules, material availability, and customer orders. Such information permits process integration without the cumbersome organizational structure previously required to ensure adequate control and accountability.

Boundary spanning is key to managing the process from source of supply to the point of final consumption. The goal of achieving seamless logistics can become reality through a commitment among firms to work together. A single firm, no matter how important, cannot illicit sufficient process control to pull off seamless logistics without working closely with both suppliers and customers. As cooperation becomes more critical to the success of the channel, partnerships evolve as a practical way to coordinate overall supply chain performance.

Partnerships

Adversarial relationships within the distribution channel have lost favor as a way to effectively manage the process. Enlightened self-interest dictates that firms explore the potential of cooperation through partnerships with key suppliers or customers. Such relationships encourage specialization within the channel, which ensures maximum performance toward achieving overall process goals. Firms like Schneider National, Roadway Logistics Systems, United Parcel Service Inventory Express, and Menlo Distribution frequently tailor unique logistics solutions designed to link organizations along the supply chain. Most often, sophisticated information technology applications are the key to such arrangements.

Partnerships are predicted to increase during the decade ahead.[20] The objectives behind many such arrangements are to lower logistics-related costs and to streamline overall operations. Partnerships provide competitive advantages by allowing members to specialize and develop specific areas of expertise.

Japan's *keiretsu* system utilizes vertically and horizontally aligned networks for firms with interlocking ownership as a way to promote cooperation and combine forces for fierce competition outside the partnership.[21] European firms achieve similar coordination by financial institutions having overlapping ownership of cooperating firms. Domestic firms in the United States are rapidly developing similar strategies through joint research under the provisions of cooperative research and development legislation.[22] For example, the Big Three domestic automakers and the federal government have aligned to work jointly on new battery technology for use in electric cars. Firms in the United States are also creating strategic partnerships aimed at increasing joint operating efficiencies. The idea is that firms can combine to provide more than just good customer service. Together, concerned firms are seeking key customer success. The idea is simple—if customers are successful, all firms involved in the supporting supply chain will prosper.

Wal-Mart is often cited as a firm whose commitment to managing the entire supply chain has propelled it to the forefront of modern retailing. Some observers feel the key to Wal-Mart's success has been its ability to combine a highly efficient internal distribution network with carefully selected channel partnerships. While Wal-Mart provides one possible operationalization of process integration throughout the supply chain, its particular formula for success is not the only one.

Firms can engage in vertical arrangements between marketers, such as DuPont, Milliken, Leslie Fay, and Dillard Department Stores, which seek to coordinate channel activities from source of supply to point of consumption. Horizontal arrangements between marketers, such as IBM and Apple Computer, link firms at the same level in the channel. Partnerships between product marketers and service suppliers and also between two or more service suppliers offer unique opportunities for establishing competitive advantage via process integration throughout the supply chain. The recent growth in intermodal transportation provides evidence of the impact that partnerships between transportation suppliers can have on industry distribution practice.

However, a number of barriers prevent full establishment of supply chain integration. In many ways, these are the same barriers confronted when firms sought internal logistics integration. The persistence of traditional command and control organization structures hinders effective management of supply chain by emphasizing function rather than process integration. Ownership of inventory within the channel presents a second challenge to achieving supply chain integration. The desire to shift ownership of inventory toward customers or suppliers without considering channelwide impact creates destructive conflict. Such practice can damage relationships necessary to ensure efficient and effective supply chain operation. A third barrier involves knowledge transfer between firms. Knowledge, or best-practice, transfer is difficult because it requires sophisticated control mechanisms and a high degree of trust between partners. Many firms continue to operate under the assumption that all corporate information is proprietary. Some firms find it difficult to share strategic information with channel partners, which tends to hinder process integration within the channel. Finally, the widely acknowledged failure to develop adequate financial information across the channel prevents true network integration. This is evidenced by a lack of channel-based performance measurement systems. Although such systems are expensive to develop and require sophisticated information technology, firms like Wal-Mart, Kmart, and Target have invested in the capability to link information and financial support for the benefit of the entire supply chain. The potential for achieving strategic advantage through cooperative leveraging appears limitless. As awareness of process integration increases, the difficulty of overcoming these barriers to supply chain management should be substantially reduced.

Emerging Logistics Organizations

As companies head into the twenty-first century, it is becoming increasingly clear that logistical performance will remain a critical success factor. What is not clear is which logistics organizational blueprint will fully satisfy the dual requirements for internal process integration and external enterprise extension. As exacting logistics performance becomes increasingly critical, firms will seek more efficient and effective ways to organize and manage customer service. This will require creation of entirely different organization solutions that extend well beyond the internal operations of a firm.

It is equally clear that logistics management will continue to be impacted by new technologies, information networking capabilities, and the ability of executives to manage interdependencies throughout the trading channel. It is likely that formal logistics organization structures will become increasingly seamless as all units of the overall organization become sensitive to logistics performance.[23] It is also likely that formal command and control structures will give way to teams linked by information networks. Independent of what organizational structures emerge in the future, it is imperative that firms develop soundly designed logistics operations capable of handling the countless daily details that make up the complex task of satisfying customers. The logistics system of the future will require the capacity to surge and capture new opportunities. It is the development of a ready and waiting reserve capacity to do the extraordinary that translates logistical competency into competitive advantage. As managers apply their creativeness to determine how best to organize, the answers will be customized to individual circumstances. It is doubtful that textbooks of the future will be able to diagram what constitutes an "ideal" logistics organization structure.

Notes

1. Robert V. Delaney, "State of Logistics Annual Report: End the Stalemate and Improve Our World Competitiveness," presentation given at the National Press Club, Washington, D.C., on June 7, 1991.
2. See Donald J. Bowersox, David J. Closs, and Omar K. Helferich, *Logistical Management,* 3d ed. (New York: Macmillan, 1986).
3. Howard T. Lewis, James W. Culliton, and Jack D. Steele, *The Role of Air Freight in Physical Distribution* (Boston: Division of Research, Graduate School of Business Administration, Harvard University, 1956).
4. Wroe Alderson, *Marketing Behavior and Executive Action* (Homewood, Ill.: Irwin, 1957); Jay W. Forrester, "Industrial Dynamics," *Harvard Business Review* 36, no. 4 (1958): 37–66; and Jay W. Forrester, *Industrial Dynamics* (Cambridge, Mass.: MIT Press, 1961).
5. See Donald J. Bowersox, David J. Closs, and Omar K. Helferich, (1986), *Logistical Management,* 3d ed. (New York: Macmillan, 1986); A. T. Kearney (1981), "Organizing Physical Distribution to Improve Bottom Line Results," *Proceedings of the Council of Logistics Management,* 1981, pp. 1–14; A. T. Kearney, "Measuring and Improving Productivity in Physical Distribution," *Proceedings of the Council of Logistics Management,* Vols. 1 and 2, 1984.
6. Bowersox et al., *Logistical Management.*
7. Bernard J. La Londe, (1991), "The 1991 OSU Survey of Career Patterns in Logistics," *Proceedings of the Council of Logistics Management,* Vol. 1, 1991, pp. 43–64.
8. Donald J. Bowersox and Patricia J. Daugherty, "Emerging Patterns of Logistics Organizations," *Journal of Business Logistics* 8, no. 1 (1987): 46–60; Donald J. Bowersox, Patricia J. Daugherty, Dale S. Rogers, and Daniel L. Wardlow, "Integrated Logistics: A Competitive Weapon/A Study of Organization and Strategy Practices," *Proceedings of the Council of Logistics Management,* Vol. 1, pp. 1–14.
9. Peter F. Drucker (1988), "The Coming of the New Organization," *Harvard Business Review* 88, no. 1 (1988): 45–53.
10. Christopher Meyer and David Power, "Enterprise Disintegration: The Storm Before the Calm," *Commentary* (Lexington, Mass.: Temple, Barker and Sloane, 1989).
11. Donald J. Bowersox, Patricia J. Daugherty, Cornelia L. Dröge, Dale S. Rogers, and Daniel L. Wardlow, *Leading Edge Logistics: Competitive Positioning for the 1990s* (Oak Brook, Ill.: Council of Logistics Management, 1989).
12. Charles M. Savage, *5th Generation Management: Integrating Enterprises Through Human Networking* (Bedford, Mass.: Digital Press, 1990).
13. Bowersox et al., *Leading Edge Logistics;* Bowersox, Donald J., Patricia J. Daugherty, Cornelia L. Dröge, Richard N. Germain, and Dale S. Rogers, *Logistical Excellence: It's Not Business As Usual* (Bedford, Mass.: Digital Press, 1992).
14. See Chapter 35, Patricia J. Daugherty (1992), "Strategic Information Linkage."
15. For further discussion see Drucker, "The Coming of the New Organization," pp. 45–53; Savage, *5th Generation Management;* Meyer and Power, "Enterprise Disintegration"; and John F. Rockart and James E. Short, "IT in the 1990s: Managing Organizational Interdependence," *Sloan Management Review* (Winter 1989): 7–17.

16. Donald J. Bowersox, "The Strategic Benefits of Logistics Alliances," *Harvard Business Review* 68, no. 4 (1990): 36–45.
17. Richard J. Schonberger and Adel I. El-Ansary, "Just-in-Time Purchasing Can Improve Quality," *Journal of Purchasing and Materials Management* (Spring 1984): 1–7.
18. Alex Taylor III, "Why Toyota Keeps Getting Better & Better & Better," *Fortune* 122, no. 13 (November 19, 1990): 66–79.
19. "EDI and QR: A Lot More Than Alphabet Soup," *Chain Store Age Executive,* January 1988, pp. 89–90.
20. Brian Bremmer, "The Age of Consolidation," *Business Week,* October 14, 1991, pp. 86–94.
21. "Learning from Japan," *Business Week,* January 27, 1992, pp. 52–60.
22. For further elaboration, see the National Cooperative Research and Development Act of 1984.
23. Bowersox et al., *Logistical Excellence.*

CHAPTER 36

Labor Relations in the 1990s

William W. Allport

The practice of labor relations has greatly improved in the last two decades. With the improvements, the specialty of labor law has evolved into a highly complex area of practice. Unfortunately, the increased complexity does not auger well for businesspeople. Many businesspeople have thrown up their hands in despair over the growing quagmire of judicial and governmental regulation. However, consider the following points before writing off labor relations:

- Without a committed and motivated workforce, goals for operations, productivity, and streamlining are nothing more than lofty dreams.
- Motivating and securing commitment from a workforce, a union workforce in particular, is not impossible.
- In fact, with increasing economic and competitive pressures, there has never been a better opportunity to obtain commitment and productivity from employees than today.

A great deal has changed since the zenith of organized labor, witnessed in the 1950s and 1960s. During those decades, organized labor became accustomed to receiving annual cost-of-living adjustments in addition to productivity increases. Benefits including comprehensive health insurance; welfare and pension programs; dental, orthodontics, and optical packages; prepaid legal services; wage guarantees; and liberal vacation and holiday packages typified the American industrial worker's compensation package. However, all this largesse rested on a ballooning economy that eventually burst.

It is no secret that the labor heyday of 20 years ago ascended to its peak and has fallen. A new and highly competitive, cutthroat economy has emerged. Not only must a business be concerned with meeting domestic competition; it must also devise strategies to compete in the international marketplace. The emergence of a world economy has been disastrous for many industries. For example, the U.S. trucking industry has felt the brunt of international competition combined with deregulation. Customers now demand subterranean freight rates so they can compete with offshore manufacturers. The problem of slim margins has been exacerbated by newly permitted price wars and the exposure of inefficient operations and policies. As a result, many trucking companies failed, causing the elimination of many jobs.

In most companies the cost of labor accounts for 65% to 75% of revenue. With that amount of expenditure, devising and implementing a cost-effective labor strategy is crucial to success in the 1990s and beyond. Therefore, when devising a business plan the management of labor becomes one of the most significant factors.

This chapter examines various methods that can be utilized to attain the goal of productivity, commitment, and labor relations security. The major labor relations topics covered are:

- *Communication.* A way to ensure that employees understand the issues facing their employer and provide them with opportunities to help the employer for mutual benefit.
- *Collective bargaining.* A guide to negotiating union contracts, bargaining associations, and self-reliant grievance procedures.
- *New legislation.* A review of important, recent labor legislation and possible corporate responses to avoid legal adversity.

Communication

The most important factor in achieving motivation is communication. If a management team expects to be successful in motivating its employees, it must establish an effective communication program. Generally, people want their employer to succeed; nobody enjoys being part of a losing effort. If workers are included in the process they will support it; if not, they will be neutral at best and disruptive at worst.

There is little difference between motivating a union or a nonunion workforce. However, because from a legal perspective union workforces require more careful handling than their nonunion counterparts, this chapter focuses on techniques for unionized companies. Managers at nonunion companies will find the ideas equally helpful, but implementation guidelines need not be as rigid.

An effective communication program ensures that employees are actively supporting the firm's goals. An employee's reason for supporting the organization is to ensure that he or she personally benefits in terms of monetary income, psychological income, and job security. The only way to secure this commitment is to actively seek and listen to employees' ideas. If employees believe they are contributing to the process, they will adopt and support the program. Therefore, the program must focus on the individual employee and be solicitous. To establish an effective communication program, consider the following points:

One-way Communication. Effective communication does not occur in bulletins, memos, letters from the CEO, videotapes, and company newsletters. These are necessary efforts and should be continued, but at best they are a one-way street. The author of the letters, bulletins, and other materials is telling the employees what he or she wants them to hear. The employee is a passive participant and has not been involved in the communication process. In fact, relying only on these one-way communication materials falsely assumes that employees actually read them. The most important part of communicating, from a management standpoint, is to listen: "If you're doing most of the talking, you're not listening." If managers are not listening, employees will not feel they are involved in the process. Thus, the program must actively involve the employee.

Subject Matter. The program must be sufficiently interesting and vital to capture employees' interest. One of the most difficult tasks in establishing a communication program is to initially select topics that are interesting to employees. As the program progresses, employees themselves will provide plenty of topics.

Continued Commitment. Employees must perceive the program as a continuing effort. It will fail if employees believe the effort is only a bargaining ploy to secure concessions. Many companies have instituted so-called communication programs immediately before a collective bargaining agreement is due to expire. Employees become conditioned to seeing the boss, typically in shirtsleeves, walking around the plant or standing on the dock shaking hands. Such executives give every appearance of being concerned with employees. They talk to them about their concerns and assure them they will take their suggestions to heart. Most employees who experience the precontract management vote blitz accept it for what it is—politicking rather than communicating. Although most employees enjoy shaking the hand of their "big boss," the actual effect of the effort is probably nil. Therefore, employees must appreciate that the program has been devised to become a regular and permanent part of their work environment. It will not stop after the contract has been ratified.

Management Mind-set. Finally, the mind-set of management must be changed from expecting miracles in 30 days to assuming a much more mature, relaxed, and self-confident approach to labor relations. Most American business is focused on solving every problem immediately. The labor factor is usually treated in this short-term manner. "Let's get the contract we need and move on to other problems." We have all heard such a statement and may have even said it ourselves. Labor is not a "problem" that lends itself to pressurized decision making. Labor is people and people want management patience. They want management to listen to them. If management relaxes, it will be successful.

American business has expended great effort defining corporate missions, delineating supporting strategies, and implementing commensurate programs. This money may be wasted, as the mission of every company is fundamentally identical: to maximize profits for shareholders by producing and/or selling competitively priced services and/or products.

The means to achieving that end, the strategy or mission, is to field a motivated and committed workforce. Most business strategies either completely ignore employee motivation or deal with employees as an overpaid unit of production. The strategy employed to deal with this "line item" has been simply to continually reduce expenditures on income and benefits. This deconstructionist philosophy spawns a vicious cycle. First, the workforce becomes unmotivated and uncommitted upon observing expenditure and head count reductions. Then, productivity declines, which leads to higher per unit costs and subsequent lost sales. Finally, these new financial pressures are addressed with further workforce expenditure reductions—instigating a new cycle!

Alex Warren, the senior American executive of Toyota USA, offered sage advice in a speech: "American workers can compete with the Japanese, if we let them!"[1] Letting employees compete is the challenge of every American management team in the 1990s and beyond. Employees must no longer be thought of as a factor of production but a cornerstone necessary to achieve the corporate mission.

Many companies believe it is necessary to perform an attitude survey before implementing a communication program, but this may be a waste of time and money. With the exception of a few fringe discrepancies, the results of an attitude survey rarely vary; predictably, they are as follows:

- The boss could be a better communicator.
- Senior managers could be better communicators.
- Employees do not believe they have effective voices in the management of the company.
- Employees are concerned about job security.
- Employees believe they are left in the dark.
- Younger employees believe they are underpaid.
- Older employees believe benefits should be improved—especially health care and retirement.

Attitude surveys can have adverse effects on employees. An employee who engages in this process may be worse off than one who does not. Hopes for change are heightened by the process, for an employee is able to officially and safely criticize management, the boss, co-workers, and a host of subjects. This blowing off steam can be therapeutic. The difficulty comes later, when employees believe that changes will take place in response to their individual critiques. Rarely, however, does the ensuing management development program match employee expectations. Most employees are left with a feeling that management wasted a substantial amount of money. The following simple seven-point communication program will increase productivity and ensure smooth operations:

1. Establish a focal point.
2. Provide an incentive.
3. Review progress.
4. Demonstrate commitment.
5. Keep it simple.
6. Compose the team.
7. Select seed topics.

Establish a Focal Point. The terminal manager, warehouse supervisor, or senior-level official responsible for the work location in question is charged with the responsibility of "quarterbacking" the program and ensuring its success. This person is the focal point of the communication program on a local level. He or she must deliver the corporate messages in a personalized manner and, more important, receive employees' personalized responses and ensure that the company truly acknowledges and considers them.

Provide an Incentive. The quarterback, or local program leader, should be offered cash inducements through an incentive program to ensure that the communication program receives top priority.

Review Progress. The local program leader's efforts to implement the program should be regularly reviewed by direct superiors and executive management. The local program leader quickly becomes aware that superiors are not solely interested in bottom-line financial performance—they are equally interested in how he or she manages and motivates the workforce.

Demonstrate Commitment. The board of directors, CEO, executives, and senior managers must pay more than lip service to the program. The program must receive primary managerial focus and commitment. Each level of management should participate. The communication breakdown in American industry is not simply between white-collar and blue-collar employees; it is generally absent at all levels of management. Most white-collar managers are as uninformed as their blue-collar brethren.

The presence of the various functional managers at communication meetings shows employees that they are important enough to warrant these individual managers' time and introduces them to those responsible for the functions—no longer are the functions faceless entities. The amorphous "sales and marketing" department now becomes "Sue Blair, whom we met last week. I've got her phone number and am going to call her today with an idea I have." Employees begin to appreciate why certain departments are present in the corporate structure, and they have a deeper awareness of what it takes to run a corporation. Employee involvement does not just happen—the pump must be primed.

Also, the presence of the functional manager in the discussion group provides employees with immediate answers to their questions and a forum for their ideas. Managers should be present throughout the meeting and should never permit themselves to be called away, no matter how important the interruption. Leaving a meeting is a clear signal to the participants that the meeting is not important. This is devastating to the communication program. The role of the functional manager is to introduce the topic and the presenter and then facilitate the discussion. During the first few meetings he or she may have to prepare planted questions to stimulate discussion. However, experience has indicated that planted questions are rarely necessary.

Keep It Simple. The program should have a simple goal, simple preparation, and a simple format. The goal is to inform the employees and become informed about their concerns and ideas. An employee can never be overinformed; there is a direct correlation between the amount of operational information employees receive and their productivity. The program is effective and inexpensive and involves nothing more than regularly reporting the status of corporate activities and providing employees a forum to discuss these activities.

Preparation should be straightforward: choose a topic, choose managers with expertise to present and moderate, schedule the meeting, and meet. Do not waste resources studying what type of communication program should be used. Also, do not waste resources training managers how to communicate; their skills will develop and improve as the program progresses. Send invitations to employees' home addresses. The invitation should state the discussion topic with a brief outline ("Our Competition" or another subject sure to invoke interest), the time, and place. Indicate that attendance is voluntary, but that this is the commencement of a permanent, continuous program and the most important aspect is employee participation. If the firm is financially strong, hold the meeting off-site and pay for everything—including overtime wages. If not affordable, then meetings immediately before work, after work, or luncheon-style can be effective. Whether or not the meeting is on company time, refreshments should be served.

The format should consist of a brief but factually rich background presentation to introduce the topic, provide relevant historical and/or technical insight, and describe the company's current status and plans regarding the topic. Then, the most important part of the meeting is the question-and-answer period, which should be allotted the majority of the time. Questions should be answered directly and honestly. If an answer is not known, the facilitator should promise to have an answer as soon as possible. Be sure to follow up and answer the questions. Each program should be a combined effort between the managers primarily responsible for the discussion topic and the work group supervisor. Ensure that appropriate representation from sales, marketing, finance, legal, and other departments are present to help with the presentation and handle specific questions that arise. Use visual aids in all forms. Employees enjoy watching slide shows, video tapes, and other "pitch" devices the sales staff use to introduce customers to the company's products and services. Promotional brochures tend to capture employee interest.

Before closing each meeting, poll participants for topics they would like to discuss in subsequent meetings. Do not be put off by mundane suggestions such as "how about softer toilet paper." No topic introduced by employees should be ignored, because they may be critical to employees and their attitude toward the firm. Such suggestions also inspire more probing topics: Who does the purchasing? What type of budget constraints are present? What are our priorities in purchasing? Why do we use the suppliers we do? How can we save money in purchasing? Do we have our priorities straight? How can employees help the company save money by conserving supplies? Conservation of resources is another program topic generated from a question about toilet paper!

Compose the Team. A team representing several areas of management should initially develop topics of interest to employees. Do not yield to the temptation of automatically entrusting this responsibility to the human resources (HR) department. It sounds like an HR job—but it is not. HR may be a part of the process, but the people responsible for devising and implementing the program should be line management, as they know the hot spots of the operation. Representatives from sales, marketing, operations, and finance should make up the preliminary team formulating the initial discussion topics. At or after the first meeting, operations employees should volunteer as members. Every committee member should have an equal vote with respect to selecting topics and managing the meetings:

Select Seed Topics. Some topics seem to appeal to employees in every industry and thus make good starting subjects. After the first few meetings have taken place, solicit employee suggestions as to what topics would interest them. Play to the audience. Each of these topics can provide substantial interest and material for several meetings.

- *Competitors.* Employees are generally very interested in learning about the other players in their industry. With whom do we compete? Who manages our competitors? How do they take business from us? Where has this happened? What can each of us do to ensure it does not happen again? How are they financed? Where are they located? What are their strengths? What are their weaknesses? What is our projection for their future effectiveness? What do we do about their attempts to steal our customers? How can we best compete against them? The sales and local management teams are natural choices for presenting the material and moderating the discussion.
- *Marketing.* Employees are equally fascinated by the techniques utilized by their employers to compete for business. They want to learn their corporation's plans and strategies that will be utilized to fight the competition. They want to know where new business opportunities are located and what prices are needed to successfully bid on work. They want to know how many jobs might be added and how long new business is expected to last. More important, they want to know how they can help secure new business. Frequently, employees offer business leads on their own. They may see a new business opening up or hear of potential leads and offer this information to the sales staff. Indeed, it is helpful to have a sales staff for whom every employee in the company generates leads. The information employees gather is truly impressive. Many companies offer incentive compensation payments to employees who supply leads that ultimately produce sales.
- *Customers.* The continued existence of most companies is directly dependent on the economic well-being of its customer base. Employees should be made aware of this fact, for in a very real sense, job security is directly related to:
  –economic health of the corporation's major customers
  –strength of relationships between the firm and its customers
  Once employees appreciate that their job security is a direct function of the customer's economic health, they tend to view customer service from a personal perspective. Employees gain a new awareness as to how their courteousness and professionalism with customers will benefit their own job security. Thus, each employee becomes genuinely interested in learning about the customer's economic health. How strong (or weak) are the customers? Relative to competition, how does the company perform in servicing cus-

tomers? The employees are a tremendous source of information in determining how to better serve the customer. The communications program should include a projection of where customers are headed:
–the future plans they have (or do not have) for the company
–how the company and employees can better serve customers
–service errors that irritate customers
–how customers are capitalized
–the identity of customers' competitors (a topic of great interest)
–how customers compete and survive
–forecasts for each customer's economic future
Including customer representatives in the program enhances success. Employees appreciate receiving the "inside story" directly from the customer, and customers similarly appreciate being involved in the process (and most are favorably impressed by the adoption of such a program).

- *Finance.* Employees are extremely interested in the financial structure of the business:
  –sources of revenue
  –nature and identity of expenses
  –economic health relative to competition and industry standards
  –financing of new operations
  –percentage of revenue dollars earmarked for wages and fringes
  –debt structure and its burdens
  –ways in which finances can be improved
  –prospects for short- and long-term survival
  Employees can understand very sophisticated financial discussions if the explanations are given in everyday language using everyday examples. Avoid jargon and buzzwords. Preview the presentation using "average" employees to determine if the topics are discussed understandably. There is nothing worse than presenting material that is not understood by the audience. Supply charts and handouts to each employee—the more hard copy the better.
- *Law.* Employees are interested in the legal issues the business faces, including significant current lawsuits, the impact of increased governmental regulation, and efforts to protest unduly burdensome regulations. Employees like to be briefed on new laws such as the Civil Rights Act of 1991 and the Americans with Disabilities Act (ADA). They also appreciate legal advice on estate planning, wills, and other personal matters that can be offered by management using existing resources.
- *Other.* Also of interest are deregulation, labor relations, employee benefits, day care for infants, strategic planning, and cost cutting methods. Holding companies can spend several weeks discussing sister subsidiaries; employees are always interested in learning about the other facets of their company.

This program does not necessarily advocate quality circles or group incentive schemes. Rather, it merely suggests that regularly scheduled employee discussions will result in an informed workforce with a sense of belonging and commitment. The communication program runs hand in hand with the collective bargaining process. If organized employees come to the bargaining table with an appreciative, sympathetic understanding of the company, the probability of securing a cost-effective contract is greatly increased. With a committed workforce that has empathy for economic reality, the problems faced in the 1990s will be more easily solved.

Collective Bargaining

Years ago, representatives of management and the union would begin meeting only several weeks before the expiration of their collective bargaining agreement. The first meeting would involve an exchange of written proposals followed by a few weeks of banter. As the midnight hour approached, marathon bargaining would occur. Management would plead poverty, the union would threaten a strike, and ultimately a contract would be agreed upon. The collective bargaining process occurred very quickly.

Today, bargaining the old-fashioned way could be disastrous. A standoff between the might of management and the corresponding power of labor could be detrimental to the continued existence of a company and therefore fatal to the continued employment of the bargaining unit members. Contemporary economic, social, and regulatory pressures do not allow speedy resolutions. For example, deregulation of the trucking industry resulted in new competition entering the marketplace that the unions have been unwilling or unable to organize. As a result, any type of work stoppage is an incentive for the inconvenienced shipper to seek alternative modes of transportation. In a regulated industry, competitors charge very similar prices; but in deregulated or nonregulated industry, low-cost nonunion competitors are very attractive alternatives.

Companies are less able to weather strikes because customers may seek alternate supply sources and even cancel contracts or partnerships in favor of signing with more dependable nonunion providers. Costly settlements will result in increased costs, necessitating increased prices, further discouraging customers. The result of lost business and higher prices is frequently the failure of the company and, of course, the loss of jobs for its employees. Even when such situations do not precipitate complete failure, the reduction of business frequently still leads to job reduction.

Can employees count on their union to be sensitive to their predicament? Sadly, the answer is probably not. By demanding exorbitant wage rates and benefits in highly competitive market situations and/or during extremely unfavorable economic periods, unions actually work to the detriment of members. Members lose jobs when their employer is shunned by customers because of excessive prices required to cover increased labor expenditures. Thus, even though union agents may initially look like heroes to bargaining unit members when they negotiate a substantial wage increase, the euphoria may quickly pass when the company falters and employees lose jobs. What good is a whopping wage increase on the unemployment line?

Politics cause both the insensitivity and the dilemma. Although most union agents understand the inherent contradiction of their approach, they nevertheless continue to press unrealistic demands. The reason for this intransigence is that union agents (also known as business agents) are political, for they must be elected to stay in office. Business agents believe, perhaps for good historical reasons, that to be elected they must continually present a tough, nonconciliatory posture to the electorate. They perceive that by agreeing to wage freezes, wage reductions, benefit curtailments, contributory health and welfare programs, and the like, they are buying a one-way ticket back to the production line. Even though agents may understand that their hard-line approach may eventually put the company out of business, they nevertheless maintain a nonconciliatory posture lest they suffer the consequences of being voted out of office.

Therefore, the collective bargaining process has become complex. Most unions have taken an Armageddon bargaining stance that must be toppled. By implementing an effective communication program, a firm can avoid a no-win situation.

Because union agents believe they must present a nonconcessionary and tough posture to their electorate, the key to success is the electorate—your employees. The primary goal of the communication program is to educate the electorate so that it will require its union representative to negotiate a realistic contract. Employees do not want to lose their jobs and most will agree to a concessionary contract if they believe the concessions are temporary and their employer is genuinely in financial or competitive distress.

If a union agent is faced with a group of employees who have categorically indicated that they want him to negotiate a contract that contains certain economic features to ensure the continued existence of the company, the agent will be hard-pressed to ignore their wishes. Such an effort takes time. The old process, which relegated collective bargaining to the final few weeks of the contract, will never permit sufficient time to establish and implement a successful communication program, which needs at least two years to build a sympathetic workforce.

A New Approach to Bargaining

Preparation for bargaining the next agreement should begin literally the day the current agreement being bargained is ratified and signed. Additionally, the collective bargaining process should not be relegated to the labor relations staff. Although that staff will act as the catalyst, virtually every member of the management team should be involved. These long-term and team philosophies characterize the new approach to bargaining, which has eight easy steps:

1. Set bargaining goals.
2. Compose the bargaining committee.
3. Develop bargaining strategies.
4. Implement a communication program.
5. Establish an operations review committee.
6. Ensure uniform application of sacrifices.
7. Void unfair labor practices.
8. Recognize union politics.

Set Bargaining Goals. Immediately determine the firm's bargaining goals. As quickly as possible after agreeing to a new contract, project the firm's bargaining needs for the next contract. The U.S. Bureau of Labor Statistics supplies enough projections to make even the most ardent number cruncher blush; avail the firm of these services. Review cost-of-living-adjustment (COLA) projections and wage earner projections. A good horizon is about ten years; that is, three years (normally) for the duration of the current contract, plus three years for the next, plus three or four more years for good measure. Generally, near-term projections (one to three years) are fairly accurate and indicate where the economy might be during the next contract negotiation. With those figures, approximate the necessary expenditure increases to satisfy the union's expected demands. Rest assured that the union agent's demands will be similar to the approximation, as he or she is likely to use the same projections. Then, determine if these increases are affordable and/or acceptable. If unaffordable or unacceptable, then commence work immediately on convincing employees that such demands will be detrimental to them. Document the expected demands versus the desired package. The bargaining goal is twofold. First, educate employees to inform their business agent that they want the firm's package. Second, achieve ratification and signing of the firm's package as the contract by presenting reasonable and compelling arguments in favor of it.

Compose the Bargaining Committee. After setting goals, identify the firm's bargaining committee. It should not consist solely of the people who will physically bargain the next contract but should comprise a financial representative, several operations people, the chief bargaining spokesperson, and labor counsel. This committee will make all bargaining decisions.

Develop Bargaining Strategies. The next step is identification of the bargaining strategy and establishment of implementation guidelines. One difficult facet in agreeing on a package is avoidance of needless conservativeness. The package should permit the company to improve its financial and market positions. At thc same time, it should be fair to employees. The economic health and profitability of both parties must be considered. The benchmark for a good contract is an agreement that appeals to no more than 51% of employees, thereby ensuring ratification. Do not waste time establishing bargaining goals that employees will never accept.

The bargaining goals should be aggressive, because the reality of bargaining is that the parties will engage in a genuine give-and-take process. Thus, allow room to give (and take). Do not present the final offer at the first bargaining session. However, do inform employees of the concepts and justifications behind the fundamental components of the firm's desired package.

Establishing the bargaining team, bargaining goals, and bargaining strategy should take no longer than two months. For a three-year contract, that leaves 34 months before the next contract vote to talk with employees and inform them of the firm's bargaining needs.

Implement a Communications Program. After identifying bargaining needs in terms of monetary and nonmonetary items, determine how to present these needs positively to the workforce. Consider two or three discussion topics relating to customers' delicate financial conditions, the strength of the competition, and the overall state of the economy and its impact on the firm's marketplace. Spend four or five months considering these subjects with employees and spend several more months in brainstorming solutions. Employees, in most instances, will suggest concessions that nearly match those of the bargaining goals. People prefer self-determination and are averse to mandates. Thus, the communications program should give sufficient knowledge that, if accepted, will result in employees' concluding for themselves, individually, that their prosperity and the firm's prosperity are inseparable.

When the communications program is firmly established, begin face-to-face discussions of the projected package with employees. Newsletters and other distributed materials are fine supplements and reinforcements, but nothing can replace direct meetings for effectiveness.

The purpose of the meetings is to educate and inform employees as to the realities of the marketplace and competition. For instance, if a customer is experiencing fierce competition and is engaged in cost-cutting measures, then it is self-evident that the firm, too, will have to curtail and/or reduce expenditures. This is especially true if the firm's own competition is able to undercut prices because of cost savings realized by employing a nonunion workforce. Answer any and all employee questions. Provide hard copy of all facts and figures, as printed copy of crucial information aids in comprehension and endures as a clear reminder.

Once the financial picture has been explained, ask employees to think about containing labor expenditures. Management is normally wage-cut oriented, for it is the easiest solution to overpriced labor. However, there are a number of components to the union financial package. By entrusting employees with the responsibility of suggesting ideas, management may be surprised by employee proposals. If employees are convinced that reductions are necessary, they will generally accept them if the parameters are self-determined.

Most employees favor a multifaceted reduction of their total package rather than a singularly focused reduction of wages. Therefore, do not be surprised if employees suggest a reduction package that not only reduces wages (slightly) but also reduces sick days, vacations, and health and welfare benefits (or requires partial contributions) and eliminates costly work rules and/or past practices. By spreading the reduction over as many benefit areas as possible, the total impact of the reduction seems less than straight wage reductions.

Employees appreciate being masters of their destiny. However, one feature that seems to be sacred is pension contributions. For example, in the trucking industry, employees tend to refuse to consider reduced or a partially contributory pension plans.

One caution: *This program needs a lot of time to work.* It cannot be compressed into a three- or four-month time frame. It takes years of talking and listening. They key is full disclosure of all relevant operational information to employees.

Establish an Operations Review Committee. Establish a permanent operations review committee with an equal number of management and employee representatives—both union and nonunion. Schedule meetings at least quarterly. The committee should review operations to ensure that the business is functioning cost efficiently.

The review process is crucial when operating in a concessionary mode. People who have given up wages and benefits are naturally interested in how the company is faring after the reduction and want to be involved in directing operations. Meetings should commence with a knowledgeable manager presenting an overview—what is good, what is bad, what business has been gained, what business has been lost, and the status of competitors, customers, and suppliers. Committee members should discuss the issues, raise new concerns, and resolve operating and cost problems. Suggestions from all members of the committee should be solicited and acted upon. A comprehensive, timely report with the overview, resolutions, and other important issues should be issued to all employees. Also, consider a monthly financial report prepared in everyday language. As soon as the company has some indication when the financial situation will return to normal and concessionary measures will end, employees should be notified. If no indications are available, that too should be stated. People who are well informed are far more likely to support a concessionary strategy.

Ensure Uniform Application of Sacrifices. An important aspect in obtaining concessions is management's commitment that *all* employees share the same sacrifices as the union employees. The term "all employees" includes the CEO as well as the least skilled position in the company. Management compensation increases and management criticism of the union during wage reductions or freezes are counterproductive. If a management team unilaterally accepts a total compensation reduction for themselves *before* asking employees to share concessionary measures, then it is far more likely that employees will agree to similar reductions. Quite simply, what's good for the goose is good for the gander.

Avoid Unfair Labor Practices. The employee communications program should not result in the union's filing an unfair labor practice charge. The National Labor Relations Act provides that an employer may bargain only with the duly appointed representative, that is, the union representatives. Therefore, it is crucial not to bargain directly with employees during communication meetings. A major purpose of the communication meeting is to *inform* employees of essential matters for the operation of the business. Equally important is to foster a discussion in which employees are free to ask questions and express ideas. Many companies invite business agents and other union representatives to these meetings. Union representatives are a very real part of the process and, if they attend the meetings, they too benefit from the information shared.

Recognize Union Politics. A communications program is not a thinly veiled management ploy. Actually, good communications greatly aid the union. Sufficient information showing that a certain wage settlement is necessary will, in turn, be indicated to the union agent by employees who want to accept a realistic, mutually beneficial package. When the union agent hears from the majority of members that a certain package is what they want, there is no longer any need for the representative to maintain an intransigent bargaining position.

However, the key to bargaining in the 1990s is to recognize that, at best, the union will be a passive player in selling concessionary needs to employees. Unions, for political reasons, cannot be counted on to support and/or actively campaign for concessionary contracts that may be necessary to preserve the business. Therefore, with this knowledge the firm must not only calculate and establish bargaining goals immediately after the most recent collective bargaining agreement is signed but it must also establish a strategy to ensure that the next contract will be accepted without a work stoppage. Do not waste time trying to convince union leaders of the firm's bargaining needs. Union leaders will demand increases if a clear mandate to the contrary is not ordered by employees. It is management's job to ensure that employees receive sufficient information so that they appreciate the need for concessions before the commencement of bargaining.

Multiemployer Bargaining Associations

Frequently, employers band together into bargaining associations. Like their employees who have joined unions with many members, these firms believe there is strength in numbers. Furthermore, like their organized employees, these firms believe a united industry has more clout at the bargaining table. Bargaining associations perform several important functions:

- Provide members with industry information.
- Monitor similar contractual settlements.
- Perform grievance resolution.
- Research legal issues in labor.
- Lobby legislative bodies.
- Provide industrywide benefit plans.

However, bargaining associations have become irrelevant in most industries. Bargaining associations flourished in times of economic prosperity, domestically confined markets, and heavily regulated industry. The usual reason for joining such an association was fear of being whipsawed into contract settlements less favorable than the association's. Firms believed, perhaps rightly, that "the lone sheep gets eaten first." Because of the high proportion of total expenditures dedicated to labor, combined with a more dynamic economy, global markets, and industry-based deregulation, bargaining a cost-effective collective agreement is perhaps one of the most important undertakings facing a business. If the contract is not cost-effective, then the enterprise will not be able to market a competitively priced product.

As long as there is a national focus on bargaining for an industry, individual association members will be unable to obtain contracts unique and favorable to their specific operations, markets, or particular problems. When industries were regulated, national bargaining associations made sense. However, since deregulation each association member is interested in pricing his or her operation competitively to meet new, open-market competition. New competitors in the market are rarely members of a bargaining association. Sometimes a generic contract may be in a firm's best interest, but often it is not—especially when facing stiff competition from nonsignatories.

A Self-directed Grievance Procedure

The only way to avoid extraordinary and unnecessary competitive limitations is to assume complete responsibility for the firm's collective bargaining function. Once self-control is achieved a firm can then decide if a multiemployer bargaining association provides advantages. Withdrawing from an association frightens companies that have traditionally relied on associations to handle collective bargaining and grievance resolution responsibilities, but no company can afford to blindly entrust these responsibilities to an outsider.

Withdrawing from a multiemployer bargaining association requires a self-directed grievance procedure. Although required in union situations, the due process theories can also be adopted and modified by nonunion companies that seek to ensure employee satisfaction and elude unionization. A simple, three-level, escalating procedure can resolve grievances:

- *Level 1—Attempt local resolution.* When a grievance is initially filed, the grievant, his or her steward, and the immediate supervisor should collectively attempt to resolve the matter. This meeting should take place during working hours, in a private meeting room, with plenty of advance notice given to both parties. The parties to this meeting should discuss the grievance with a genuine intent of resolving it at this level.
- *Level 2—Attempt advanced resolution.* If the grievance is not resolved at the first level, a second meeting should take place between the grievant, his business agent, the immediate supervisor and next-level supervisor to adjust the grievance. This meeting should be similar to the first level meeting. Once again, grievances should be resolved at the lowest level possible.
- *Level 3—Accept arbitration.* If the grievance is not resolved at the second level, a neutral arbitrator should be selected by the parties from a list supplied by the Federal Mediation and Conciliation Service or the American Arbitration Association.

The parties should agree to exclude lawyers from the grievance process. Certainly either party can consult legal counsel during this process, but the presence of counsel at the hearing generally results in unnecessary expenditures.

The fee charged by the arbitrator, which usually involves one day of hearing and two days to consider the argument and write an opinion, is generally shared equally by the parties. Some rules provide for the losing party to pay the entire fee. The latter practice has a very positive effect on reducing the number of dubious grievances filed. It also encourages grievance resolution at lower stages.

One way to save money is to require the arbitrator to render a decision orally on the day of the hearing. The only exception would be a case involving a discharge. Rendering decisions through the mail avoids physical confrontation at the hearing and ensures clarity of the ruling.

Some companies attempt to resolve many grievances at one time by scheduling three or four arbitration hearings per year. A neutral arbitrator is selected to serve as a permanent arbitrator for a year or two. This arbitrator hears as many cases as are pending on a given day and is paid a daily fee for services. However, a single arbitrator is best for each case. There is a regressive effect that single-case arbitration has on the number of grievances that are automatically deadlocked at lower levels. If an arbitrator must be selected to hear each individual grievance that is not resolved, two things occur. First, the number of spurious grievances will be reduced because the company and the union will not want to pay to have them heard and dismissed. Second, the parties will have the incentive to honestly attempt resolution at lower levels. Also, the threat of the cost of an arbitrator will provide the parties an effective incentive to resolve grievances immediately.

New Legislation

During the last few years, several important pieces of legislation have been enacted by various regulatory and legislative agencies. Some of the issues and laws that will be regularly encountered during the 1990s are:

- Sexual harassment
- Employment-at-will
- The Americans with Disabilities Act
- The Civil Rights Act of 1991
- The Worker Adjustment and Retraining Notification Act

This discussion is not exhaustive but highlights legislation that may be new to managers or otherwise warrants review. Along with each issue or law, possible responses are suggested that may help firms avoid legal adversity.

Sexual Harassment

Perhaps one of the most controversial areas of labor employment law is that of sexual harassment. Sexual harassment is a specific type of sex discrimination prohibited by Title VII of the Civil Rights Act of 1964. Many state civil rights acts have also prohibited sexual harassment. Not all conduct of a sexual nature constitutes sexual harassment. Although we generally tend to think of harassers as being male and the victims female, the gender roles are quite often reversed. Prohibited conduct can also occur between individuals of the same sex. There are essentially two types of sexual harassment: quid pro quo and environmental.

Quid Pro Quo Sexual Harassment

Quid pro quo is a Latin phrase that basically means "one thing for another." Quid pro quo sexual harassment is defined as "unwelcome sexual conduct to which an employee's submission or rejection will be used as a basis for an employment decision". Quid pro quo sexual harassment generally arises in a relationship between a supervisor and a subordinate. Usually the employee complains that he or she was denied a tangible job benefit or entitlement because he or she refused sexual advances. Employees generally complain of lost wages or discharges because they refused to consent to unwelcome sexual advances. Similarly, positive inducements by a supervisor for sexual favors, such as offering extra overtime work or extra pay and promotions for granting sexual favors, is classified as quid pro quo sexual harassment and is similarly prohibited.

Victims of sexual harassment do not always have to be the direct object of the sexual demands or harassment of a supervisor. For example, a male worker denied a promotion may claim sexual harassment because a female employee has submitted to her supervisor's sexual demands. He has been sexually harassed because his supervisor denied him a promotion on the basis of a sexual relationship with another employee.

Environmental Sexual Harassment

Environmental harassment is defined as "unwelcomed sexual conduct which unreasonably interferes with an individual's job performance or creates an intimidating, hostile or offensive work environment." Environmental sexual harassment differs from quid pro quo sexual harassment in that the latter involves a superior using beneficial or detrimental sexual coercion, whereas the former involves an employer permitting a work atmosphere to exist that is hostile to members of either gender.

To constitute environmental sexual harassment, the conduct in question must be "hostile" and "unwelcomed." "Hostile" conduct is usually perceived by the person claiming that discrimination has occurred. Thus, conduct that may not be considered hostile by men may well be found by a court to be hostile to women. Most courts believe that conduct is "unwelcomed" if the employee in question did not solicit the conduct either directly or indirectly. Thus, by "playing along" with purportedly hostile conduct, an employee may unwittingly diminish the strength of his or her complaint later (or even unwittingly waive the right to complain). Most courts believe that a failure to complain about the conduct is generally an indication that the conduct was welcomed.

Discouraging Sexual Harassment

As the decade unfolds, employers will likely confront an ever-increasing number of sexual harassment claims. To minimize the risk of being charged with sexual harassment, the following actions are advisable:

- *Definition and education.* First, define sexual harassment for employees. Let them know what is permitted and prohibited conduct. Next, conduct an educational training seminar for all employees to inform them of the parameters of sexual harassment. This topic is a natural for your communications program. The legal department or personnel professional can make a very effective presentation on the subject of sexual harassment.
- *Written policy.* Prepare a written policy that such conduct is prohibited. List specific examples of conduct that will not be tolerated by the company.
- *Complaint procedure.* Establish a procedure wherein complaints protesting sexual harassment can be directed to a specific company official for immediate investigation and resolution. The names of individuals within the company to whom these complaints can be addressed should be listed in the policy. Employees should not be required to make these complaints to their immediate supervisor because frequently that person is the offending party.
- *Penalties.* Penalties for violations of the policy should be clearly stated. Any form of sexual harassment that can be proven should result in immediate discharge or reassignment, depending on the circumstances.

Most employers can greatly minimize the possibility of being the subject of a sexual harassment claim by implementing a policy and regularly discussing it with employees. It is important to prepare and present sexual harassment seminars on at least a yearly basis so that new employees also receive this information and veteran employees are reminded. By proper education and strict enforcement, exposure under the sexual harassment laws can be minimized.

Employment-at-will

Approximately ten years ago, the more progressive states, California and Massachusetts, began eroding what was then known as the "employment-at-will" doctrine, which states that if an employment arrangement makes no provision for the duration of employment, such a relationship is not a contract of employment but is in fact terminable at the will of either party. Thus, until recently an employer could discharge a nonunion employee at any time for any reason (or no reason at all). This was thought to be an inherent right of management. The employment-at-will doctrine was universally applicable to all nonunion employees throughout the United States until the erosion began. Since then, virtually every state has in one way or another followed California and Massachusetts.

DEFENDING TERMINATIONS

Employment-at-will lawsuits are proliferating. Many state courts are now ruling that an employer may actually or impliedly create an employment contract by virtue of written or oral statements. If such an implied employment contract can be inferred from the facts of a particular relationship, then an employer may terminate the employee only if "just cause" is present. Those that have dealt in the union context are quite familiar with just cause, for in virtually every collective bargaining agreement in the United States an employee may be discharged only for just cause. "Just cause" essentially means that the employee knowingly committed an act prohibited by the employer. The concept of "industrial due process" has arisen around the just cause concept. Thus, to successfully discharge an employee, the employer must show that "cause" for the discharge existed. The employer can sustain this burden by proving that:

1. A rule existed in the workplace.
2. The employee in question was aware of the rule.
3. The employee was warned in writing on a prior occasion relative to violating the rule.
4. The employee was suspended on a prior occasion relative to violating the rule.
5. The employee was discharged for violating the rule once again.

Industrial due process consists of the progressive disciplinary steps contained in those five steps. It is obviously very difficult to establish just cause. Additionally, if an employer fails to establish the existence of just cause, the employee in question will be returned to work with full back pay and benefits. Certain courts have also begun entertaining requests for emotional suffering in addition to the usual back pay awards.

Essentially what the courts have done is require employers to treat their nonunion employees in the same fashion as they treat union employees with respect to discharge cases. Prior to taking disciplinary action, it is wise to review a discharge with an individual experienced in the employment-at-will requirements in the firm's state. Awards can easily exceed the cost of such reviews.

The law of implied contract of employment varies on a state-by-state basis. Many states are extremely liberal in finding the existence of implied employment contracts. Other states remain quite conservative. Essentially, the court will find the existence of a contract of employment where an employer has made statements, either oral or in writing, that would lead a reasonable person to believe that he or she is being employed for a specific time period. Statements in employment handbooks and other employee benefit brochures to the effect that "you will have a job with us as long as you abide by the rules contained in this employee handbook" or "you can be assured of lifetime employment so long as you do a good job" have been held to constitute an implied contract of employment.

CLARIFYING EMPLOYMENT AGREEMENTS

It is advisable to prepare a written disclaimer that each employee should sign. The disclaimer should state in no uncertain terms that the relationship between the parties shall be one of "at-will employment." Furthermore, the existence of any type of actual or implied employment agreement should be denied by both parties. It is also important that the disclaimer states that only the CEO of the company may vary the terms of the disclaimer, by written agreement. If such a disclaimer is not present in all personnel files, the risk of defending an implied contract of employment lawsuit increases. Avoid such an eventuality at all costs; juries are generally claimant-oriented.

The requirements of a disclaimer vary on a state-by-state basis and thus one is not presented here. Firms without such disclaimers should seek counsel to prepare them immediately. At the very least, firms should include the disclaimer in employment applications of all new hires.

The Americans with Disabilities Act

The Americans with Disabilities Act (ADA) was passed in 1990. The ADA essentially prohibits discrimination in all aspects of employment against a person who may have a "disability." Previous legislation concerning persons with disabilities generally extended only to private business that had substantial federal government contracts. As of July 26, 1992, the ADA applies to all employers with 25 or more employees, employment agencies, labor organizations, and joint labor-management committees. Employers with 15 or more employees are covered as of July 26, 1994.

Title 1 of the ADA prohibits discrimination in employment against a qualified individual with a "physical or mental impairment that substantially limits one or more of the major life activities," or "a record of such impairment," or "being regarded as having such an impairment." The Equal Employment Opportunity Commission (EEOC) has attempted to simplify this definition by stating that a physical or mental impairment is "any physiological disorder, or condition, cosmetic disfigurement, or anatomical loss affecting one or more of the following body systems: neurological, musculoskeletal, special sense organs, respiratory (including speech organs), cardiovascular, reproductive, digestive, genitourinary, or any mental or physiological disorders such as mental retardation, or organic brain syndrome, emotional and mental illness, and specific learning disabilities." The definition of impairment is intended to include AIDS-related diseases.

To qualify as having a covered physical impairment, an individual must show that the impairment "substantially limits one or more of the major life activities." A life activity includes "caring for oneself, performing manual tasks, walking, seeing, hearing, speaking, breathing, learning, and working." One of these functions must be "substantially limited" by the impairment for the ADA to apply. Temporary ailments like broken limbs, colds, and similar items are not considered disabilities. Additionally, specifically excluded from the definitions of covered disabilities are homosexuality, bisexuality, transvestitism, exhibitionism, gender identity disorders not resulting from physical impairments, other sexual behavior disorders, compulsive gambling, kleptomania, pyromania, and illegal use of drugs.

To be covered by the ADA, an individual with a disability must be qualified to perform the "essential functions" of the work in question. The ADA states that a prospective employee is qualified to perform a job's essential function if that person possesses the necessary skill, experience, education, and other job-related characteristics, even though the person may require some "reasonable accommodations." If a disabled individual can show that he or she is qualified, then the burden shifts to the employer to "reasonably accommodate" the prospective employee's disability. The ADA requires the employer to make reasonable accommodations for the known physical or mental limitations of an otherwise qualified individual with a disability who is an applicant or employee, unless such employer can demonstrate that the accommodation would impose an "undue hardship" on the operation of the business.

Because the ADA is relatively new, there has not been a substantial number of cases to define what constitutes a reasonable accommodation. The ADA and EEOC define "reasonable accommodation" to include the following actions:

> making existing facilities, including work areas accessible; job restructuring; part-time or modified work schedules; reassignment to a vacant position; modifications of equipment or devices; adjustment of job qualification examinations, training materials, or policy; provision of leaders, interpreters, or other personal assistance; permitting employees with disability to use their own accommodations, such as guide dogs; and permitting occasional unpaid leave.

It is the responsibility of the employee claiming a disability to inform the prospective or existing employer that an accommodation is needed. Once that notification has been given, the burden then shifts to the employer to discuss the situation with the employee and discern exact needs. An employer is not required to make an accommodation that will result in an "undue hardship being vested on his business entity." In assessing whether a specific accommodation will result in an "undue hardship," the following factors are generally considered:

- The nature and net cost to the employer of the required accommodation.
- The financial resources of the covered entity, the number of its employees, and the number, type, and location of its facility.
- The financial resources of the facility involved in providing the accommodation, the number of persons employed at such facility, and the effect on resources.
- The type of operations of the covered entity, including the composition, structure, and functions of its workforce.
- The impact of the accommodation on the operation of the facility, including the impact on and ability of other employees to perform the duties and the impact on the facility's ability to conduct business.

The ADA is a new and potentially complex piece of legislation. Firms will be dealing with this law for many years. If facing an employment decision concerning a handicapped employee or prospective employee, contact legal counsel immediately to ensure compliance with the act. Additionally, review with legal counsel the specifics of the firm's operations to determine what steps should be taken to conform with the requirements of the law.

The Civil Rights Act of 1991

On November 21, 1991, President Bush signed the Civil Rights Act of 1991 into law. The act is significant in that it does not substantially broaden the coverage of the Civil Rights Act of 1866 and 1964 so much as it makes recovery under those laws much easier for the claimant. Prior to the enactment of the Civil Rights Act of 1991, the Supreme Court of the United States had issued very restrictive interpretations of the Civil Rights Acts of 1866 and 1964. Several public interest groups lobbied Congress to pass legislation that would essentially override the decisions rendered by the Court. Congress ultimately passed the Civil Rights Act of 1991 to redress the wrongs that it believed were committed by the Court.

The Civil Rights Act of 1991 is a technical act that was drawn specifically to reverse the impact of adverse decisions. Two changes brought about by the act involve technical legal proof requirements that eliminate certain employer defenses to an employment discrimination claim. Other parts of the act expand employee rights to sue for employment discrimination. One new section of the law permits persons employed in the transportation industry to bring suits that challenge seniority systems. Previously, employees could challenge a seniority system only at the time it was adopted. Now, suits challenging such systems can be brought either when the system is adopted or when it adversely affects the individual claimant. Finally, the Civil Rights Act of 1991 has expanded the range of damages available for many types of race discrimination and employment, hiring, firing, promotion, harassment, and other suits.

The bottom-line importance of the Civil Rights Act of 1991 is that it makes recovery against an employer much easier and substantially broadens the range of damages available to an individual employee. EEOC cases are no longer assessed monetarily only on the basis of actual lost wages and benefits. The previously precluded pain and suffering damages, as well as punitive damages in certain instances of intentional discrimination, are now available and all are potentially very costly. (The 1991 act has jokingly been retitled the "Full Employment for Lawyers Act.") If faced with a potential EEOC claim, review the facts with qualified counsel before making decisions.

Worker Adjustment and Retraining Notification Act

The Worker Adjustment and Retraining Notification Act (WARNA) was enacted to provide employees with at least 60 days advance notice of plant closings or mass layoffs. An employer, in addition to providing employees with advance notice, must also provide the union and the appropriate local and state government agencies with similar notifications of closings and layoffs.

WARNA is essentially a law of definitions. A plant closing is defined as a "permanent or temporary shutdown of a single site of employment or a shutdown of one or more units at a single site of employment resulting in an employment loss for at least 50 full-time employees during any 30-day period." The same notification requirement is prescribed for "mass layoffs," defined as an employment loss for "at least 500 full-time employees or 50 full-time employees who constitute at least 33% of the full-time workforce." The term "employment loss" is defined as "a reduction in hours of at least 50% for a period of more than six months."

WARNA notices are not complex and essentially supply the affected employees and the state and local agencies who can help them find work with essential information pertaining to the shutdown or layoff. The notices contain the identity of the employer, the address of the affected operation, the date of the closing or layoff, the anticipated length of the layoff, the identity of the job functions of the affected employees, and the name and address of a company official who can be reached for additional information.

The penalties for noncompliance with WARNA can be substantial. Each individual not given appropriate notice must be provided normal pay for each day notice was not given. Thus, if employees are given only five days' notice of a shutdown, each is entitled to receive 55 days of pay.

One exception to the notice requirement relates to "unforeseen business circumstances." This extremely narrow exception provides an employer with relief from the 60-day notice requirement if the closing or layoff is caused by "business circumstances that were not reasonably foreseeable as of the time the notice would have been required." For example, if a trucking company is canceled by a key customer and only seven days' notice of cancellation is given by the customer, the trucking company, upon receipt of such notice, should immediately give the appropriate parties notification of necessary shutdowns or layoffs. Assuming that the company had no idea before the seven-day notice that a shutdown was imminent, the company will probably be excused from the dire consequences of a 53-day back pay and benefit judgment.

Prognosis for the 1990s

Greater government regulation of the employer-employee relationship is likely in the 1990s. Government regulation appears to have achieved the permanence of death and taxes! It is safe to assume that the employment-at-will concept of nonunion employment will continue to erode until, by the turn of the century, nonunion employees will enjoy the same protections respecting discharge as their union counterparts. The union employee's protection from arbitrary discharge will be found in the "just cause" termination process of collective bargaining agreements. The nonunion employee's "just cause" protection will be judicially and/or legislatively created.

Mature American business will face a serious dilemma until unions are able to either organize their low-cost, nonunion competition on a worldwide basis or find some structure that allows them to offer more competitive rates while still adequately serving, attracting, and retaining members. However, unions will likely continue to be extremely reluctant in grant concessions, and the result will erode market share for unionized employers owing to nonunion competition. Such a development will require American industry, perhaps more so than at any other time in history, to ensure that employees are educated and knowledgeable about operations and that they contribute thoughts and ideas. Those companies that meet this challenge will be successful; those that do not will fail.

Note

1. Alex M. Warren, Jr., executive for Toyota USA, in a speech given at Cleveland, Ohio's City Club.

CHAPTER 37

Focused Human Resources Management

Key to Logistics Effectiveness

Jonathan L. S. Byrnes
Roy D. Shapiro

Logistics is a functional area capable of sweeping, innovative results, yet it has traditionally experienced difficulty delivering. Logistics authorities long have proclaimed the coordinative power of the logistics function as one that can most easily integrate the product flow–related functions of marketing, manufacturing, and supply procurement to achieve quantum gains in customer service and profitability. However, many companies' actual experiences often reflect the story of a logistics executive who developed an insightful vision and motivated his or her logistics managers into action but then ran into the polite yet pervasive unwillingness of lower-level managers to change. This resistance comes both from within the company and from its suppliers and customers.

Consider the following comments by executives in a recent study of intercompany operations and logistics innovation:

- The vice president of logistics of a *Fortune* 100 company stated, "Sometimes I feel that our manufacturing group has better relations with its suppliers than we do with our manufacturing group."
- The vice president of a semiautonomous supply division of a major company observed, "I can't get our customer divisions to change their plans, even if it will save the company millions of dollars."
- The president of a large apparel manufacturing company noted, "Our customers' buyers will not spend more than two minutes of a sixty-minute conversation on inventory turns and return on investment because they are so focused on short-term deals. They want a Chinese menu, with service from column A and price from column B."
- The director of materials management at a large consumer goods company said, "In trying to coordinate logistics operations with our key customers, we have seen an unholy alliance develop between our salespeople and our customers' buyers in resisting change. Both are afraid that otherwise they will lose control and status."
- The director for logistics of a large computer company observed, "Most of my time is spent in internal selling."[1]

These individuals articulated a common frustration of logistics professionals: responsibility without authority. They needed to obtain coordinated action from numerous managers with different concerns, objectives, and perspectives, over whom they had no formal authority.

The executives understood both the great promise of logistics and the great difficulties in implementation. But some of them were able to move beyond the ever-present inertial resistance to implement sweeping, effective programs. In later conversations, they made the following, revealing statements:

- "Our salespeople and account managers resist our efforts to coordinate with our customers. Their incentive compensation gets in the way. Our top managers see the big picture, but they insist on product loading to meet Wall Street's quarter-end goals."
- "The big issue is how to get people to take a strategic, rather than a tactical, view—how to make a strategic decision that tactically may not look right to a buyer or a salesperson. The stumbling blocks are compensation and promotion."
- "Our company is not run on a cash basis. Our officers prefer increased business to inventory savings, even if ROE drops. We need better internal controls and measures."
- "You can explain the vision, they [counterpart managers] can see the vision, but then they do what they are paid to do."
- "The big issue is taking down internal barriers to improve customer-supplier relations within the company. Planning and performance measurement must change radically for business processes to change."

Many of these managers did not turn from this task. Rather they identified the underlying behavioral drivers that were causing resistance, and developed powerful new measures to rechannel them to accomplish their programs. They understood that both the sources of resistance and the key points of management leverage are rooted in people. Thus we turn our attention to human resources management (HRM) with the discussion of the following topics:

- Fundamentals of human resources
- Focused human resources management
- The new strategic imperative
- Ensuring effectiveness
- The new logistics management

Fundamentals of Human Resources

Human resources management policies—compensation and performance measurement, recruitment and career development, and promotion and termination—play a major role in determining the behavior and capabilities of the employees in a company. These policies enable a company's management to:

- Define and communicate the company's goals
- Motivate and focus employees to accomplish the goals
- Obtain and develop the human capabilities necessary to move the business forward

Compensation and performance measurement are crucial both in defining and communicating management's goals, and in motivating behavior that enables the company to achieve those goals. Many companies focus inordinately on the technical issues of constructing their compensation programs but overlook the need to precisely define their goals. This problem may stem from the difficulty of achieving strategic clarity. It leads to a situation in which different departments within a company have implicit objectives that either are too vague or embody conflicting local goals. In this circumstance, individual functions work at cross-purposes and stubbornly resist change; the performance measurement system usually reflects and reinforces these problems.

Recruitment and selection policies at all levels largely determine the portfolio of human resource capabilities available to a company over time. Because individuals can be very capable in some areas but weak in others, it is crucial that management understand what areas are essential both now and in the future. This is not as easy as it sounds. For example, a company that faces an increasing need for interdepartmental or intercompany coordination will need individuals who not only are technically competent but also have flexibility and good interpersonal skills. These personality characteristics often cannot be taught.

Career development encompasses not only job progression but also knowledge building and training. Traditionally, early career development programs have focused on teaching technical functional skills, and later career programs have sought to impart more general management capabilities. Some companies blend this focus with multiyear job rotations that enable individual managers to gain knowledge and experience in a variety of functional areas.

This traditional approach to career development can cause problems in two respects. First, traditional programs are internally focused and fail to develop managers with a full understanding of customer and supplier companies, to say nothing of best practices in other industries. Second, because the implicit objective of these programs is the development of general capabilities and knowledge, they often are too unfocused to further specific business objectives.

Managers must break sharply with tradition and see that career development not only must cross functional lines but also company boundaries. Cross-company career development requires more than knowledge; it requires well-structured direct work experience in other companies for a select number of key company managers.

Promotion policies have importance beyond simply reinforcing goal definition and motivation. Through promotions, management communicates its goals and seriousness of intent. This occurs in two ways. First, promotion itself is a strong incentive as well as an obvious signal to the whole organization. Second, promotion moves capable individuals, whose actions are consistent with corporate goals, into positions of increased responsibility. This amplifies their effects on the company.

Termination may send an even stronger and more obvious signal to the whole company. At one time or another, most companies must terminate employees in response to inadequate performance or unfavorable business conditions. But it is unusual for a company to have sufficient goal clarity and resolve to terminate fairly an otherwise competent employee who consistently acts in conflict with the company's objectives. All too often in such cases, the real problem is that top management has failed to communicate its goals clearly in training, or (more commonly) the company's performance measures or incentives conflict with the goals. This difficulty allows widespread counterproductive behavior to continue uncorrected, and this quiet but pervasive resistance is a key impediment to coordinated strategic progress.

Focused Human Resources Management

While poorly constructed behavior drivers imbedded in human resources (HR) policies can act as a sea anchor on coordinated product flow initiatives, well-constructed policies have the potential to focus and energize cross-functional and cross-company programs. The problem that the logistics professional faces is that managing companywide HR policies to effect *coordinated* change is often outside his or her management scope. This removes the greatest point of leverage in accomplishing cross-functional integration for those who have such responsibility without commensurate authority. Moreover, it is extremely difficult to tailor coordinated HR policies that span functional departments; many logistics professionals lack knowledge and experience in this complex area.

In cases where logistics professionals have the scope and ability to affect companywide HR policies to accomplish their programs, the results are striking. For example, Xerox's Central Logistics and Asset Management group (CLAM) reduced inventories and related assets by nearly a billion dollars by coordinating the product flow through its channel of supply and distribution (see Chapter 38).

The head of CLAM reports directly to the company's top corporate officers and is responsible for setting the company's basic operating strategy in selected, strategically important areas like supply chain integration. Often, these activities require the suboptimization of one business unit, if considered in isolation, to achieve corporate goals. For example, to decrease finished goods inventories, the manufacturing group must hold more work-in-process (WIP) inventories and finish to demand.

The vice president in charge of CLAM sets the joint operating direction in cooperation with the business units, and has the ability to influence directly resource allocation, compensation, and performance measurement. By harnessing the power of HRM, this organization creates great leverage to accomplish companywide change.

If logistics professionals are to be consistently effective, they must have:

- *Integrative vision*—the vision to craft integrative, cross-functional, and cross-company programs that enable product to flow rapidly and responsively through the company and the channel.
- *Human resources ability*—the ability to harness the power of HR policies to ensure that the programs are implemented effectively throughout the company.

The economic power of cross-functional coordination is becoming widely recognized, and the first capability is now increasingly in evidence in our profession. Unfortunately, however, the second is all too uncommon. This is a root cause of the classic logistics dilemma, and it is preventing many companies from achieving their objectives. Because efficient, responsive product flow is essential to strategic success in most companies, focused HRM must become a core element in the logistics professional's portfolio.

The New Strategic Imperative

The new strategic imperative is the coordination of product flow, also known as supply chain management. Product flow always has been important to companies, but now it has become clearly essential to strategic success in most industries. Problems with product flow coordination, both within companies and *among* the companies in a channel, have been widely recognized as one of the greatest deficiencies of U.S. companies relative to their global competitors, notably the Japanese. Numerous U.S. companies have lost considerable market share and, concomitantly, profitability, for this reason. Logistics effectiveness is increasingly recognized to be a key success factor in many industries, and this requires both vision and carefully tailored HR policies—including, significantly, a new form of career development.

A profound change transforming a variety of industries is requiring fundamental changes in the way that managers operate their businesses. In the future, it will be harder for a company to succeed alone. Effective managers must integrate product flow not only among the functional units within a company but also among tightly coordinated networks of companies in a channel. This presents complex new challenges to the logistics professional.

Critical to the success of this new form of competition are coordinative mechanisms that we call "intercompany (or interorganizational) operating ties" (IOTs). These mechanisms create huge savings and new competitive advantage by redefining the traditional boundaries of companies and fundamentally changing the way product flows, both within a company and from one company to another, through supply and distribution channels.

The common trait of IOTs is that channel members work together to ensure smooth, efficient, and reliable product flow. In each case, tight integration is needed across the functional departments of the companies involved, and new forms of coordinative behavior must be identified and developed. IOTs introduce a further management complexity because one channel member, by mutual agreement, may take over activities or decision-making authority that previously had been the prerogative of the other. However, the benefits outweigh the difficulties (which subside as time passes and relationships strengthen). A few examples illustrate IOTs:

- *Baxter Healthcare.* Baxter pioneered a "stockless" system in which it effectively manages hospital supply ordering and replenishment—in contrast to traditional uncoordinated buying by its hospital customers—by distributing a wide variety of hospital supplies (including those purchased from its competitors) directly to hospital wards; this largely replaces the traditional internal hospital materials management function.
- *Bose.* Bose developed an innovative "JIT II" concept, in which supplier representatives are situated in a Bose facility; among other unusual prerogatives, these individuals have full authority for scheduling shipments from their own plants.
- *PPG.* Companies increasingly are taking advantage of key suppliers' knowledge of products and technology by asking that the suppliers actually operate part of the buyer's production process, rather than simply purchasing parts and materials on an arm's-length basis. For example, PPG manages painting operations in certain General Motors factories.
- *Polaroid.* Continuous product replenishment has begun to revolutionize many retail industries, including apparel, groceries, and office products. Suppliers have responded. For example, Polaroid receives daily sales figures from several large customers and effectively "pushes in" stock, without receiving orders.

Our research found that the companies who streamlined their product flow through both interfunctional coordination and intercompany operating ties generated extraordinary gains. These included operating cost reductions often exceeding 30%, as well as significant gains in sales, improved supply continuity, and quicker response to changes in customer needs. The largest gains were produced early through process coordination, but they required that managers develop fundamentally new ways of managing their businesses.

There are persistent reasons why the huge benefits of coordinated product flow have remained untapped for so long, and most of these are rooted in narrow, long-standing turf-protecting behavior—often reinforced by HR policies that have outlived their usefulness. These reasons are:

- *Traditional boundary views.* Many functional managers have maintained a traditional view of their operational boundaries—especially the decisions that are "rightfully" theirs to make—and this has both obscured and then constrained the new paradigm. This perspective has been reinforced by inward-looking compensation and performance reporting systems that act as organizational blinders.
- *Lack of resources and expertise.* Many executives lack the channelwide data, knowledge, and new methods of analysis necessary to see the vast magnitude of the problems and opportunities. General purpose corporate development programs fail to provide this focused expertise.
- *Traditional functional barriers.* Traditional barriers between the functional departments of many companies hamper necessary internal coordination. For example, customer relations often is allocated to marketing and supplier relations to purchasing. Structural change can entail heated turf battles.
- *Short-term focus.* A pervasive executive focus on short-term earnings, which leads to chronic quarter-end "product loading" sales tactics and "hockey-stick" financial performance, has bred subtle concern among some managers because artificially "managing" quarterly results is not possible in the context of coordinated, responsive product flow. Similarly, the forward buying associated with trade deals is threatened, creating a perceived threat to both salespeople and buyers.

But today, even more powerful forces are breaking down these barriers, forcing managers to respond. The huge gains achieved by a few innovators are becoming widely known, and these innovators are serving as role models. More powerful telecommunications-intensive information systems, shorter product cycles, customer cost pressure, the need to differentiate products further, and demands from "mega-retailers" are driving change.

The strategic imperative for coordinated product flow is accelerating rapidly in many industries, requiring decisive and effective logistics initiatives, both within companies and across channels of supply and distribution. In retail channels, there is a snowball effect: retailers are focusing suppliers to match one another, and proactive suppliers are vying to offer innovative intercompany arrangements as "value-added services" to their customers. In industrial sectors, the huge gains and implementation complexity of IOTs are causing companies to greatly narrow their supplier and distributor bases. Already in some industries, as one executive put it, "The rule is adapt or get engineered out."

The emerging strategic imperative for product flow coordination creates a clear set of issues for top management. Both of the following actions are necessary to strategic success, and neither alone is sufficient:

1. The top executives of a company must recognize that coordinated product flow is essential to the company's strategic success.
2. Then, top executives must invest enough authority in the logistics executive to enable him or her to directly influence companywide HR policies to effect coordinated change.

Ensuring Effectiveness

Effective HRM for coordinated product flow requires both clear operating goals and savvy construction of myriad HR policies. This is a very complex process because coordinating product flow usually requires quantum changes in a company's business processes involving all functional departments. These operational changes must be supported by complementary changes in the company's HR policies. Without these parallel processes and HR policy changes, the company will not be able to accomplish its goals.

An Illustrative Case

The case of one company in our study illustrates both the pervasive operational changes needed for product flow coordination and the key role of focused HRM in driving these changes. The case is all that much more powerful in showing that even relatively simple changes in product flow patterns require surprisingly deep changes in company processes, and complex alterations in companywide HR policies.

ESC, Ltd. is the disguised name of a leading European industrial supply company. In order to look at the company's business in a new way, the company's CEO instructed the vice president of operations to review the company's product flow through the whole channel, including suppliers and customers.

The vice president found that virtually all high-volume products were consumed steadily by the end users. Yet these same products were characterized by a surprisingly erratic order pattern. This forced the company to carry high inventory as well as excess capacity, and often to interrupt manufacturing schedules to accommodate unexpected peaks. (See Figure 37-1, graphs A-C). The company's suppliers were similarly affected.

Further analysis showed that these order fluctuations were caused primarily by a few large customers that dominated the order patterns and thus were causing most of the problem. (See Figure 37-1, graph D). These erratic orders were costly for the customers as well.

The solution seemed startlingly simple: synchronize the channel so that, for the few large customers who accounted for most of the fluctuations, product would flow smoothly and steadily from the beginning to the end of the channel. The company proceeded to develop a "standing order" arrangement with these few large customers, to provide steady weekly deliveries of their high-volume products. Delivery quantities were reset in periodic meetings of supplier and customer operations managers, with contingency plans so that customers could order increased quantities if an unexpected need arose.

This steadied the channel product flow and allowed the vice president to reduce inventories and reorganize the manufacturing process. (See Figure 37-1, graphs E-H.) The operating costs of the channel fell by over 35%. Inventory levels were cut in half, the company was spared a multimillion-dollar capital program, and stockouts dropped substantially. Logistics-related labor costs per unit of product decreased greatly, owing to a more stable workload at the warehouses, increased flow-through transshipments, and newly standardized work practices.

The company became able to ship more frequently and pack in a standard format that was very easy for customers to receive and put away, significantly reducing their costs and inventory levels. Because product delivery patterns now were predictable, the company was able to more easily stabilize its manufacturing schedules. The new stability also allowed the company to issue firm, long-range forecasts to its suppliers, with commitments to purchase the materials

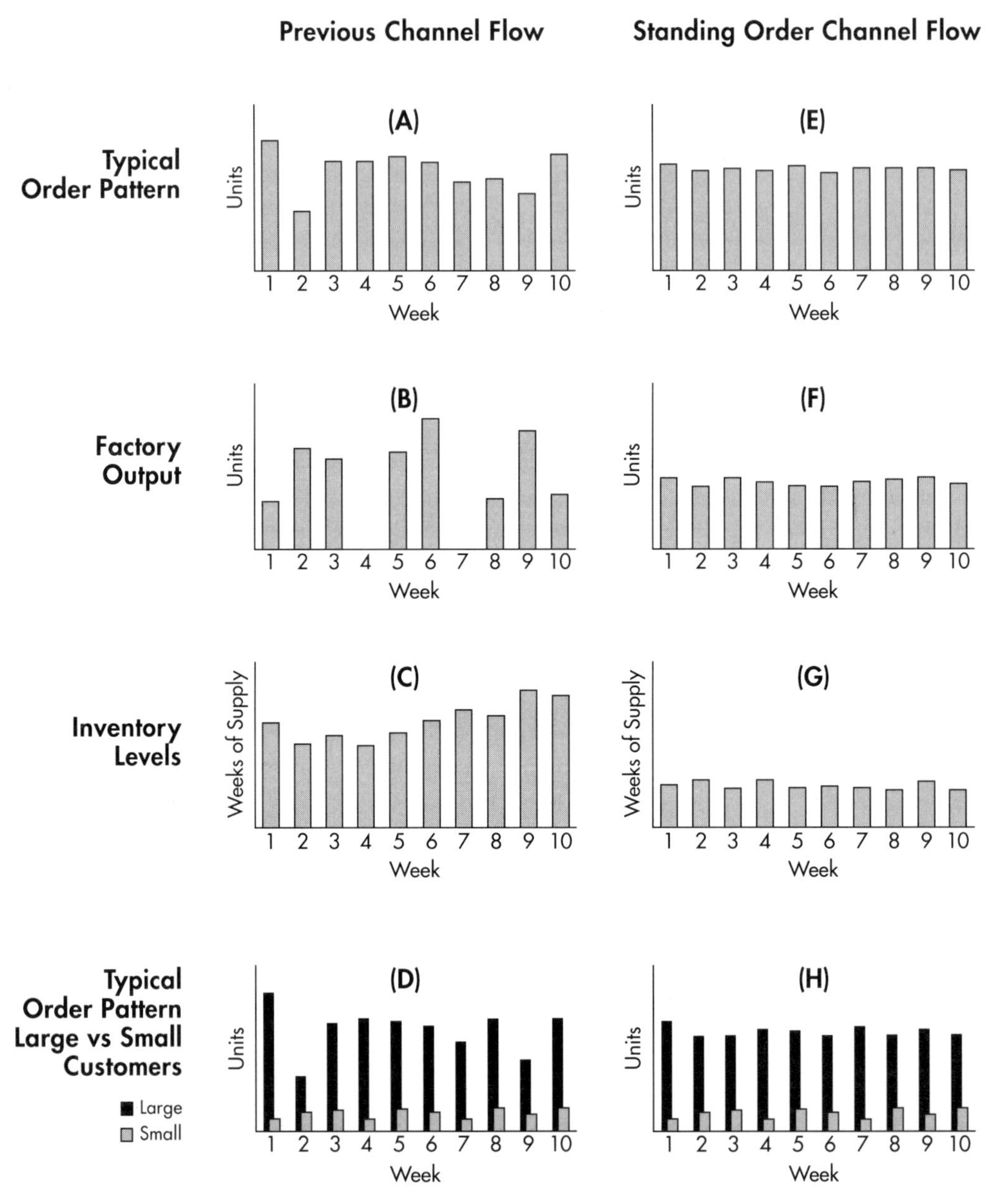

Figure 37-1
Channel Dynamics of a Typical Product

on a "take or pay" basis, in return for significantly lower prices and supply certainty. Everyone in the channel gained substantially.

The company found that its sales process changed in unexpected and favorable ways as well. The efficiency of the new system freed the sales reps from the need to respond to customer service complaints—often exacerbated by wild fluctuations in product flow patterns—which had taken a substantial amount of their time. The reps began to focus much more on the other aspects of the sales process, such as end-user selling. In newly created periodic operational review meetings between the company's regional operations managers and the customers' purchasing and operations managers, new relationships and trust developed. The combination of the increased sales focus on more productive selling and the enhanced efficiency of product flow led several large customers to broaden their purchases of the company's product line.

The process of implementing the standing order system required surprisingly broad changes in the company. Over half of it was affected: regional operations managers began to meet periodically with key customers to review service and adjust standing order levels; regional warehouses were reconfigured and downsized; materials managers began to track products beyond the company's boundaries; the procurement organization worked to develop long-range purchase commitments for its suppliers in return for price reductions and supplier guarantees of priority service and contingency backups; and manufacturing schedules and accompanying new procedures drew new efficiencies from the new, more stable demand pattern. Underlying these were pervasive changes in HR policies, not only in ESC's functional departments but also across the functional departments of the customers and suppliers.

Major changes were needed in compensation and performance measurement throughout the company. First, compensation and performance measurement had to change to reflect that several departments had incurred greater costs to achieve even larger gains elsewhere. Second, both compensation and performance measures had to shift to align them with longer-run objectives. For example, under the new system, short-term product loading to meet quarterly sales quotas and short-term purchase loading to take advantage of purchase deals were forbidden.

Recruitment and career development had to change to give the company new knowledge essential to intercompany product flow coordination. For example, the company's managers had to learn to map and redirect the product flow both within the company and through the functional departments of the other companies in the supply and distribution channel.

New management skills were required because the new system entailed much more interpersonal coordination. For example, the inventory control managers formerly had worked in relative isolation. In the new system, however, they had to be in constant communication both with the regional operations managers and with the plants and suppliers. The old system, with its large inventory buffers, allowed these managers to work in a relatively stable environment, but under the new system they had to monitor carefully for unexpected but allowed changes in standing order quantities, unexpectedly large orders from smaller customers, and problems in the plants and supply chain. In fact, the standing order system provided a guideline that allowed large inventory reductions, but it required surprisingly tight day-to-day pipeline management. As another example, each salesperson formerly had a high degree of autonomy, but in the new system, he or she had to work as a coequal team partner with the regional operations manager.

Appropriate promotion and termination policies were essential to reinforce the new system and to move capable individuals into key positions. The new system required "broad-gauge" managers comfortable working in a rapidly changing, highly interpersonal team environment. The withdrawal of traditional inventory buffers required these individuals to seek out and remedy problems before they became impediments, not only within their respective functional departments but also in other functional departments, and in the customer and supplier companies as well. This required a broad understanding and a willingness to compromise.

Despite the company's substantial investment in training and development, a number of otherwise capable individuals could not adapt to the new environment. Some managers simply could not learn to be effective, and others wisely understood that they did not enjoy the new mode of work. Over time, a number of the company's affected managers either resigned or were terminated. The magnitude of change was as great in the customer and supplier companies.

In light of the broad nature of these changes, it is not surprising that a major competitor had failed because it approached a similar arrangement purely as a new marketing program. Customer alienation and operating cost overruns, stemming from the attempt to provide a "new" service with an "old" system, forced the company to abandon the initiative. The competitor had not understood that coordinated product flow requires pervasive, fundamental changes both in a company's functional operations and in its underlying people policies. Our study showed that this is the single most important success factor in large-scale logistics innovation.

Essential Top Management Role

Because the potential gains from product flow coordination are so large, and because the required changes are so sweeping, top management must be directly involved on an ongoing basis. This is the bedrock precondition for success. Top management must drive the program in several concrete ways.

The general management of a company must publicly confirm both the strategic imperative of rapid, responsive product flow and the wisdom of the proposed operational changes. Top management must communicate explicitly that cooperative behavior is necessary to gain the new benefits, that the executive responsible for logistics has the authority to focus and tailor the company's HR policies to accomplish this goal, and that uncooperative behavior will not be tolerated. The top executives of a company must take a personal stake in the program's success.

"Top-to-top" contact is crucial in developing effective intercompany operating partnerships. A company's top executives must show their counterparts in the partner company that it is essential for both companies to alter and focus their HR policies to drive the cooperative arrangement at the grass roots level. In IOTs, it is not sufficient for only one partner to change. There must be an explicit agreement at the onset of the relationship. In our study, we found that the failure to specify and gain this agreement was the root cause of many problems in otherwise promising partnerships.

Top management involvement is necessary to invest the logistics executive with the authority to go beyond persuasion and to enable him or her to influence key HR policies to implement sweeping, innovative programs. Because product flow crosses through all functional departments, coordination requires broad changes in the behavioral drivers throughout a company. Logistics cannot be an independent, isolated function. Rather, it must provide an integrated vision and have the ability and savvy to work through the other departments to effect change. Logistics executives must identify new points of leverage and become expert in using them to deliver results. HR policies provide these new points of leverage.

Compensation and Performance Measurement

Coordinated product flow imposes a complex set of requirements upon a company's compensation and performance measurement system. Because all of a company's functional departments must coordinate to streamline product flow, the logistics executive must start with a precise understanding of the role that each department's managers must perform, both within their own function and jointly with counterparts from other functions. This detailed clarity is the essential first step in designing an effective compensation and performance measurement system.

Responsive and efficient product flow requires that an executive focus the company's functional managers not simply on the performance of individual functions or activities but instead on the larger companywide and channelwide benefits. Manufacturing may have to carry higher levels of WIP inventories to minimize finished goods inventories; inventory control may need more personnel, or more likely, new information technology resources to track product flow; and procurement may have to guarantee larger volumes to fewer suppliers to ensure unimpeded raw materials availability. In each instance, the functional compensation and performance measurement systems must be adjusted to reflect the new expectations, generally by altering the variance standards.

In addition, effective companies often supplement their systems with more global measures that reflect coordinated performance across departments. For example, one very successful company compensates its managers throughout the business on three measures: customer satisfaction, return on assets, and market share. Several effective companies in our study used special bonuses to share a portion of the measurable gains from improved product flow with the managers involved to motivate and direct the necessary changes.

Resistance from sales and purchasing departments is one of the most commonly cited difficulties that arises in coordinating product flow. The classic sales problem is that many sales compensation systems drive salespeople toward counterproductive product loading to meet monthly or quarterly sales quotas. This induces a customer's purchasing department to wait for quarter-end price reductions and then make large purchases. For example, in an actual case in one company studied, a salesman who had not met his quota called a major customer in late December and persuaded him to order ten (unneeded) truckloads of product before the year's end, arguing that he would get them for free because of the volume discount structure. This general problem suggests that long-run customer penetration and profitability gains must form a new basis for compensation and performance measurement, and that the elimination of trade dealing often is a necessary adjunct.

In most cases where more than one company is involved in coordinating product flow through a channel using IOTs, coordinated changes will be required in both companies' compensation and performance measurement systems. Often, this involves an intercompany redistribution of benefits. For example, companies that hold large WIP inventories and finish to demand in order to lower overall channel inventories and increase responsiveness will find that their manufacturing and inventory costs rise, even while their customers' inventory levels and costs decline by a far greater amount. In these cases, a compensating price adjustment is needed, and the new benefits specifically must flow through the supplier company's variance-based performance measurement system to offset the planned cost increase. This removes a subtle, but major, impediment to change.

Intercompany price adjustments and performance measurement offsets are complex to devise. But when the benefits are properly distributed through the compensation and performance measurement systems of all of the companies involved, the functional managers in both the customer and supplier companies have a compelling incentive to ensure that the relationship continues. Skillfully crafting this key behavioral driver is essential to logistics effectiveness.

Recruitment and Career Development

Recruitment and career development policies largely determine the human resource capabilities that either creatively move a company forward or constrain its progress. Coordinating product flow, both within a company and through the companies in a channel, presents a fundamentally new set of management tasks in most companies. Long-run success requires both a critical mass of flexibile, broad-visioned managers and a new and different career path management process.

Ironically, recruitment policies must respond to a company's upcoming needs, but its existing portfolio of managers generally reflects past needs. In times of relative stability, this is not a problem. But instituting coordinated product flow requires quantum change in all of the company's activities. Many existing managers may have trouble adapting, and some new managers may need to be recruited early on to ensure that the company has a critical mass of experience and skills.

The day-to-day business of management changes dramatically in the context of coordinated product flow. Managers must assume a much broader perspective that spans not only the detailed operations of a particular department but also the whole company, as well as the other companies in the channel. Change is more rapid, and managers must be more responsive in the absence of the traditional inventory buffers.

Teamwork and coordination are essential, and this requires managers with strong interpersonal skills. For example, one large consumer products company has reformed its major account team to include managers from four departments: sales/marketing, distribution/operations, finance, and information systems. These teams are partially resident in the major customers' facilities, and their prime responsibility is coordinating intercompany product flow, not only at the customer-supplier interface but also deep within both companies' operations. This new coordinative management approach will become increasingly common. Recruitment policies at all levels and in all functional departments must directly address this new need.

Career development also must change dramatically, and logistics is central to the change. No longer will a large, centralized logistics department be sufficient, or in many cases even appropriate. Rather, a logistics executive must develop a concrete vision of interorganizational product flow and take specific measures to ensure that flexible, hands-on logistics capabilities permeate the company's functional departments. The new role of the logistics executive must be to ensure that the new vision and capabilities are fully developed throughout the company and are reflected broadly in the company's actions.

Because product flow responds to changing markets, managing it is an organic, constantly changing task. Logistics executives cannot "call in the plays from the sidelines," just as they cannot, by themselves, manage product flow. Logistics effectiveness, therefore, must stem form the flexibility and the capabilities of the managers in all of the company's functional departments. A new, sharply focused form of career development is essential to meet this new need.

The first principles of an effective integrative career development program are that it cannot be limited to logistics managers, and it cannot be confined to the activities that take place within the "four walls" of the company. The prime function of the program must be to quickly and effectively build into every functional department the logistics-related skills necessary for coordinated product flow. Key managers in every functional department must gain the essential knowledge and abilities, and they must be seeded rapidly throughout the organization. Such a focused career development program has five elements:

1. *Structured knowledge.* Managers must be given structured knowledge of the product flow process throughout the company and the channel. This knowledge should span the whole channel from point of supply to point of ultimate consumption. It should include quantitative information on actual product flow over time, and qualitative information on the behavior and role of the different functional organizations in all the companies involved as they affect product flow. These managers also must gain working familiarity with the new tools used to analyze the dynamics and costs of product flow.
2. *Direct experience.* This program must give each manager a portfolio of direct work experience that encompasses all the functional areas that control product flow in a company. Unlike a classic work rotation program with multiyear stints in a variety of functional po-

sitions, however, a focused program should provide in-depth expertise in one department, and brief but concentrated work experience, often as part of a multifunctional team, in other functional areas on tasks specifically related to managing product flow. This has two objectives: developing widespread understanding of the factors affecting product flow, and nurturing the interpersonal relationships necessary for close, cross-departmental teamwork.

3. *External experience.* The third element provides the most striking break from traditional career development programs. Because multiple companies must coordinate closely throughout a company's supply and distribution channel, a select number of the company's key managers should be given *direct, focused work experience* outside company boundaries—in representative customer and supplier companies. This will give these managers the knowledge, relationships, and understanding needed to bring the companies of a channel into operational convergence. The experiences of several successful companies in our study suggest that managers from one company working in other companies in the channel discover fundamentally new ways of structuring both companies' operations. Cross-channel training programs require an attitude of openness and cooperation that was rare in the past but now is mandatory to achieve the huge new gains that come from effective intercompany operating ties. Incidentally, it is not sufficient simply to hire managers who have had experience while employed elsewhere. Although varied backgrounds are undoubtedly beneficial, managers' experience must be gained with the perspective and mindset of the home firm for truly integrative and cooperative ideas to flourish.
4. *Best practices and benchmarking.* Managers must be systematically exposed to best practices and benchmarks of particularly effective product flow coordination practices in other industries. This will show them a range of fundamentally different logistics paradigms. In fact, because industries and companies differ, the best approach for a particular company will be a unique combination of observed systems.
5. *Human resources knowledge.* The final element in an effective career development program is a working knowledge of how to tailor and align the HR policies of the functions throughout a company to achieve coordinated product flow. This knowledge will provide immediate benefits as the managers who are seeded into the functional areas will be able to identify subtle barriers to coordination rooted in inappropriate HR policies. In the longer run, as these managers rise in the organization, they will be able to develop new HR policies to achieve sweeping, cooperative results, even where they have responsibility without authority.

Promotion and Termination

Top management must send a simple, clear message through its promotion and termination policies: cooperative, constructive behavior is expected and will be rewarded, and uncooperative behavior will not be tolerated. The new standard must be applied first and foremost to the top management group; otherwise, the rest of the organization will respond with skepticism and cynicism.

Even if all of a company's managers intend to comply, the difficulties of working in a rapidly changing environment that requires tight interpersonal coordination will create performance and job satisfaction problems for some managers. This should be expected, as it is the unfortunate but natural by-product of quantum change.

A company's top executives have to be very sensitive to newly created matches and mismatches between individual managers and evolving positions. They must identify the managers who can succeed and rapidly move these individuals into positions of increased responsibility. They must carefully locate the managers who are having trouble performing in the new environment, and use the career development process supplemented by intensive coaching to try to teach these struggling managers the new skills they will need. And when other measures fail, top management must use termination to end the quiet, grass-roots resistance that so often is fatal in interdepartmental product flow initiatives.

The New Logistics Management

A new set of strategic imperatives is transforming corporate logistics management. The focus of logistics executives must shift from managing assets and direct reports to creating a new vision of coordinated product flow, and implementing it by influencing the actions of others. Logistics professionals must learn to harness the power of human resources management to effect sweeping programs of change, not only in their own companies but in other companies in their supply and distribution channels as well.

Farsighted top managers will see the huge strategic and financial gains of coordinated product flow and will give their logistics executives new avenues of influence commensurate with their crucial responsibility. Perceptive logistics executives will realize that crafting companywide HR policies is much more difficult than it might seem, and they will focus on acquiring this proficiency.

Ultimately, the vision and savvy with which logistics professionals tailor companywide HR policies that drive coordinated product flow will go far to determine both their own effectiveness and their companies' long-run success.

Note

1. Study by Jonathan L.S. Byrnes and Roy D. Shapiro involving over 120 executives in more than 40 major companies.

CHAPTER 38

Proactive Change Management in Logistics

Frederick Hewitt

Much has been written about the accelerating pace of change that characterizes today's business environment. Peter Drucker's works on *The Changing World of the Executive* and *Managing in Turbulent Times,* although written a decade ago, and Tom Peters's more recent classic, "Thriving on Chaos," are worth rereading as we edge toward the last years of the twentieth century. The overall messages from these and similar studies are as applicable to logistics professionals as to any other managers, perhaps more so. As a natural "linking" or integrating function, logistics is influenced both directly by the changing economic and social environment in which all companies operate today and indirectly by changes in related functions, such as manufacturing's move to focused factories or marketing's search for total customer satisfaction. Logistics functions cannot stand still. The only choice is between being reactive or proactive toward change.

Because it is an integrating function, logistics has the potential to lead companywide change. However, leadership is in itself a new experience for most logistics professionals. The function has traditionally been regarded as ancillary to either manufacturing or marketing or both, a necessary but nonstrategic element of most companies' activities. Logistics managers need to consciously prepare themselves for an active role in change management. Some of today's logistics managers will thrive on the challenge, others will feel uncomfortable but will adjust, and many, perhaps the majority, will find the role of change agent unacceptable and will eventually leave the profession. Similarly, anyone entering the profession today should do so in the knowledge that managing continuous and sometimes dramatic change will be their normal task. This is very different from the role played by preceding generations of distribution managers, who were often the epitome of stability, reliability, continuity, and longevity within their enterprises.

Although there is clearly no single recipe for success in change management, there are certainly a number of prerequisites without which success is virtually impossible. First among these is the creation of a vision of the way things should be. Perhaps some change agents have stumbled upon success by accident, but most successful and lasting change comes from continually knowing where you need to be compared with where you are today, and plotting a course, not necessarily a direct one, to get there. A second prerequisite is sharing the vision, or in other words, building alliances and partnerships with real buy-in that enables the changes to be made. It is almost impossible to overestimate the human capacity for stubbornness and resistance to imposed change and to underestimate the enthusiasm and ingenuity generated by ownership of an idea. Permanent change comes only with the transfer of ownership of the changes from the change agents to the practitioners. Third, early success is critical and therefore implementation of change must be monitored continuously and demonstrably linked to specific results. Fundamental change takes time to implement and even more time to become embedded in an enterprise, hence the need for reinforcement based on demonstrable and tangible results. In the case of most enterprises the desired results will be improved profits and a healthier balance sheet.

Creating a Vision

A logistics vision statement elucidates the potential contribution of logistics to the success of the overall enterprise. This vision is best defined in terms of process and functionality such as actions performed, rather than organizational constructs like positioning within the hierarchy. The vision should concentrate on how the key business processes within the enterprise will change, not who will do what. A vision statement that can be construed as an internal power play by one function is doomed to failure, and it is worth the effort to strenuously avoid the possibility of such an interpretation. One way of doing this is to ensure that the vision statement is outward looking and customer focused. The reason for doing any logistics process is to provide quality materials in the right quantity to the right point in the supply chain at the right time. In this respect, if positioned correctly, logistics may have the advantage of being perceived as a positive, supportive, and nonthreatening function. Figure 38-1 illustrates these points in relation to a conventional manufacturer with a direct sales operation.

It is a wise and rare management team that initiates change before it is required, and even these rare occasions are usually reactions to perceived future threats from outside. Recognition of the need to change is almost always stimulated by factors external to an enterprise and adverse to its well-being. It is logical, therefore, that the creation of a vision of a "desired state" should begin by examining these threats. In this context, the logistics vision should define the way in which the improved logistics processes will combat these threats and ultimately provide a strategic advantage to the enterprise. The process elements listed in Figure 38-1 resulted from a substantial analysis of end customer requirements and competitive offerings in the office products business.

Benchmarking, both against competitors and with like-minded, noncompetitive organizations is a useful aid in vision formulation. It is also an antidote to skepticism. There is no quicker way to gain agreement to process improvements than to examine the proposed process already in operation elsewhere. At the very least, the debate moves from "it cannot be done" to "it won't work here." If the benchmarking encompasses both process and results analysis, and demonstrably better results are achieved from the proposed alternative process, even this second level of human reaction can usually be turned to an analysis of "how can we make it work here?" To this end, a good vision statement should also include hard, trackable metrics, with some form of assessment against a timeline to achieve world-class performance. Figure 38-2 illustrates a possible format.

Overall, therefore, a vision statement should include both a view of the way processes will operate and an assessment of the expected business results. It should be outward looking, addressing customer requirements and confronting competitive threats. In today's vision of logistics it should not be constrained by traditional functional barriers but should address the full supply chain from suppliers through the enterprise to end customers. It should be seen to be constructive and credible. In short, it should form the reference point to be used by a corporatewide "vision community" that will buy into it and then be capable of translating it into implementable performance improvement projects on behalf of the total enterprise.

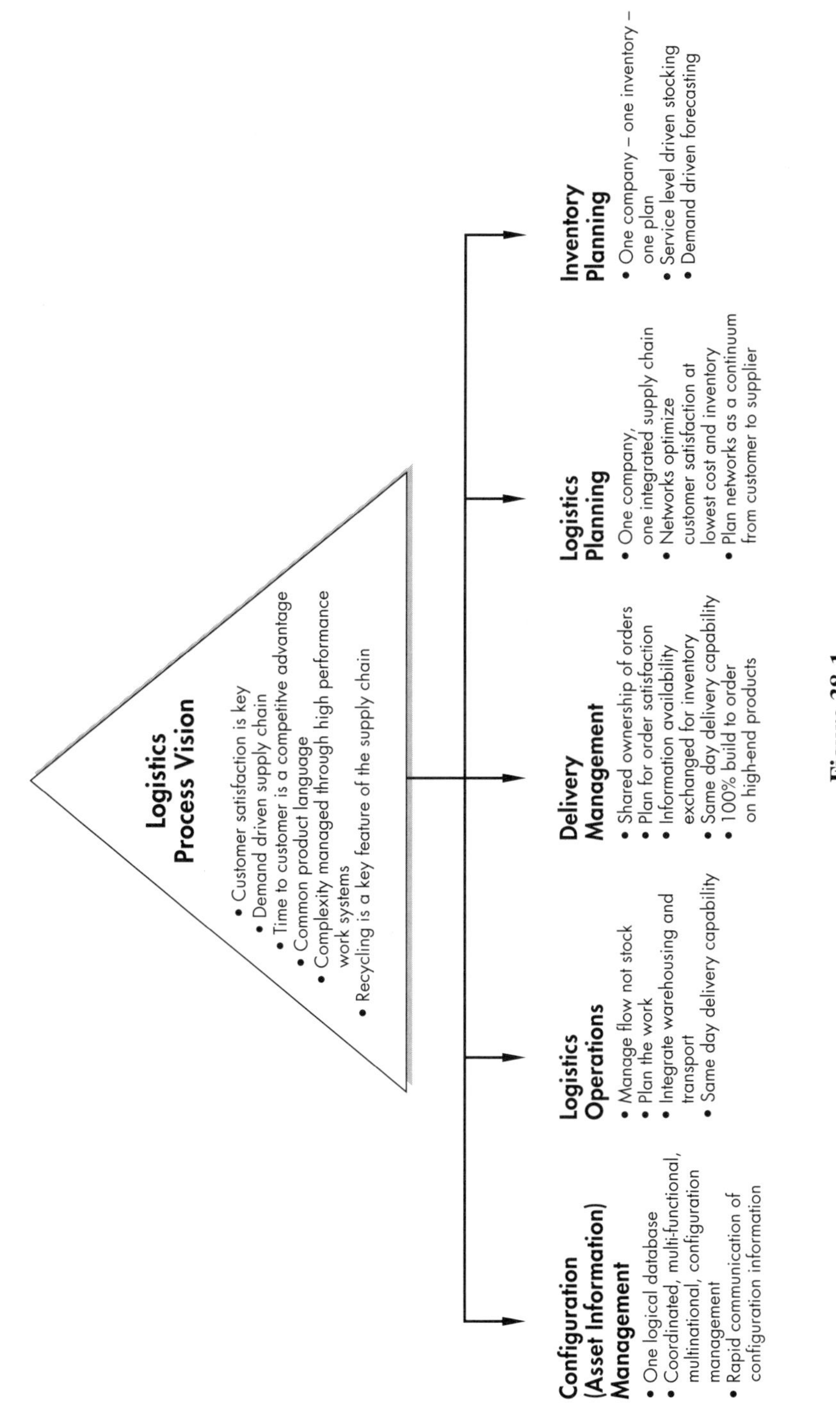

Figure 38-1
Logistics Process Vision

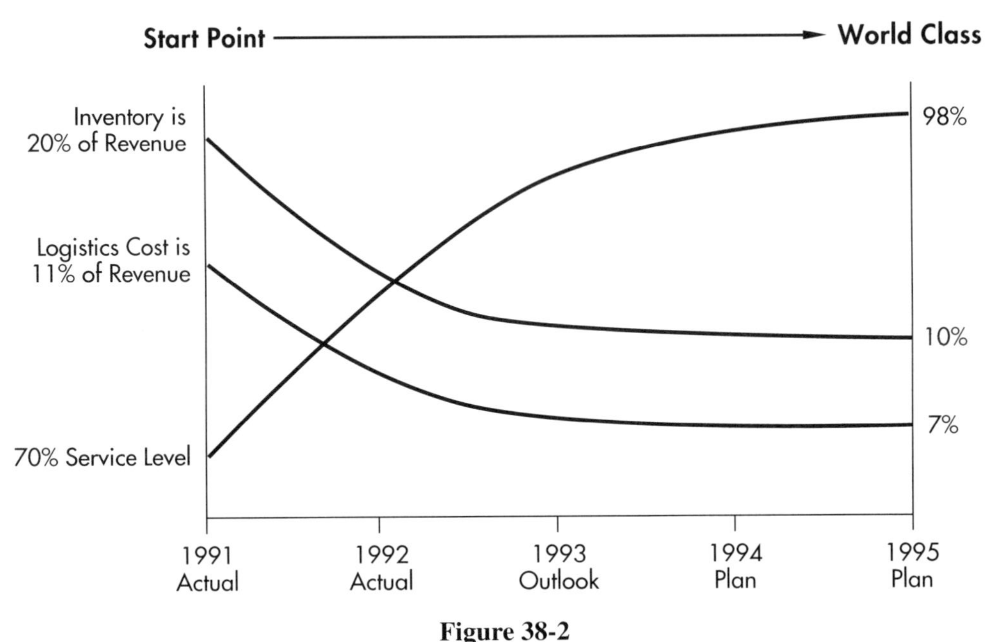

Figure 38-2
Logistics Performance Vision

Sharing the Vision

Change is disruptive and will be resisted. Senior management support is therefore essential if proactive change is to be successful. To be relevant enough to merit attention from senior executives, however, the company's logistics change agenda must fit comfortably within these executives' view of the evolving mission of the overall enterprise. The logistics vision should be positioned as a part of the full set of change initiatives at play within the total enterprise.

The good news for logistics managers is that initiatives that are currently at the forefront of most senior executives' minds tend naturally to highlight the potentially strategic role of logistics within most corporations. As major corporations search for the effectiveness breakthrough that will differentiate them from their competitors in the 1990s, certain key imperatives are beginning to emerge:

- Customer focus
- Quality as a way of life
- Flexible responsive business processes

These all heighten the awareness of the importance of world-class logistics processes. Described properly, a logistics vision that sheds the old "trucks and warehouses" image and positions logistics as one of the few key business processes capable of simultaneously improving customer satisfaction, profits, and asset performance will therefore get a good reception in most of today's boardrooms. The late 1980s was the age of customer satisfaction and total quality, and the 1990s are likely to be the age of simplification, flexibility, and total cycle time optimization. Within this context, a vision of logistics as integrator—linking the company to its suppliers and its customers and operating cross-functionally to the benefit of suppliers, customers,

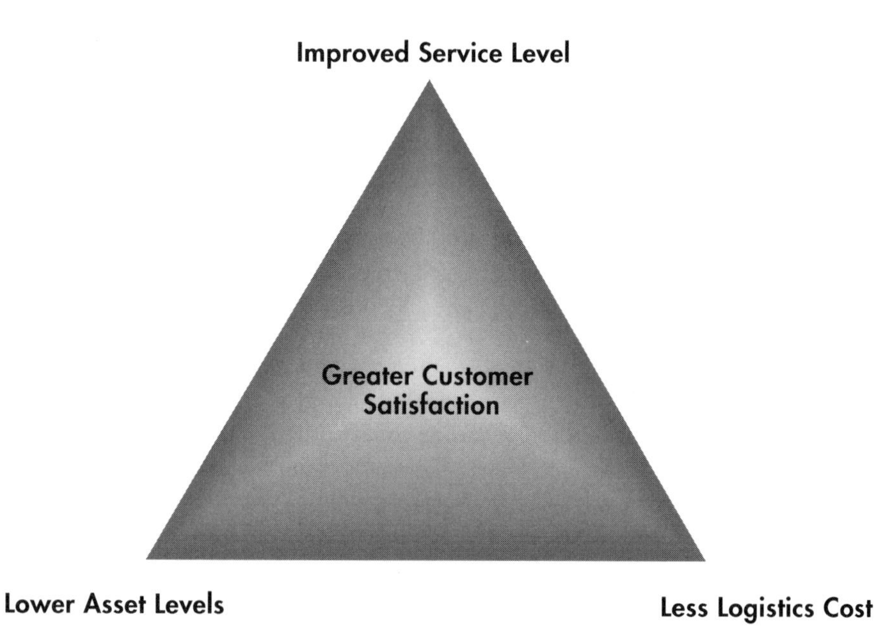

Figure 38-3
Logistics Impacts

and shareholders—is an appealing concept. Provided that the link between the logistics vision and the corporate goals can be made explicit, senior management support will usually be gained without much difficulty. Figure 38-3 has proved effective in communicating this linkage.

The old paradigm of trade-off between service level and cost must be replaced by a new paradigm in which service levels, costs, and asset utilization are all improved through simpler, speedier logistics business processes. Which group of corporate officers will not support changes that simultaneously achieve several corporate objectives?

Middle management forms perhaps the most difficult and yet most crucial group of people who need to be brought into the vision-sharing community. After all, they will be responsible for implementing and then managing the new processes. For many years the Western business model has depended on functional specialization within a hierarchical structure. We have been taught that, below the CEO level, specialization is necessary before excellence can be achieved. Although this may be true to a certain extent, there is also a large body of evidence that overspecialization has become the norm, particularly at middle-management levels. Functional structures have led to dysfunctionality within most enterprises. Other than at the corporate officer level we train, reward, and recognize people for optimizing their own function, not the overall effectiveness of the business. Conflicts between "stubborn" and "inflexible" manufacturing types, "conservative" and "unimaginative" finance types, and "wild" and "unreliable" sales types is the stereotypical view of most Western companies. For the logistics professional who wishes to proactively lead change rather than to react to it, it is essential that all these disparate functional specialists share and support the logistics change agenda that affects all their daily lives.

Getting true buy-in to this is perhaps the single most difficult aspect of logistics change management.

A number of devices are usually required to gain buy-in. The change requirements may be positioned within an overall corporate initiative such as a total quality program or a company-wide business process reengineering effort, which looks cross-functionally at all the key processes through which the enterprise achieves its business goals. This is particularly useful if the umbrella program carries specific change management training within it. It is natural to feel uneasy about change but not to block all change. It may also be advisable to create a multifunctional process change steering group to take ownership of change management where the required changes cross functional boundaries. For example, in one major corporation senior corporate officers have been formally assigned cross-functional business process sponsorship roles in addition to their functional responsibility. The vice president of logistics is also the business process sponsor for inventory management across the entire corporation and the chairperson of a multifunctional group chartered to reengineer and simplify the total inventory pipeline from suppliers to customers. Figure 38-4 depicts a possible functional/business process matrix.

Participation is key to buy-in, and middle managers must understand their roles in terms of the matrix. The objective is to establish ownership of the vision by the people who will be affected by the changes and will be expected to supervise their implementation. Procurement, manufacturing, sales, and service must all regard the logistics process as their process, meeting their requirements. Although logistics personnel may, and probably should, lead many of the process reengineering teams, any agenda seen as merely aggrandizing the role of the logistics department will surely fail.

At more operational levels within the supply chain, the primary concern of most employees is that they understand what is required, are empowered to meet those requirements, and are recognized for doing so. A fundamental business process change redistributes the knowledge base and authority load within the corporation. Because modern technology is enabling the dispersal of authority outward and downward within organizations, it is not usually threatening to front-line staff. The usual result is job enrichment and greater diversity within one job. The general rule is that if it is good for the customer, it will be readily accepted by operational staff, provided that the changes are explained, performance criteria are adjusted, and enabling training and work support systems are made available.

Techniques For Implementing Change

Adoption of ownership of the improved business process by the total enterprise is the objective of change management. This comes only after another series of mind-set changes have taken place. Figure 38-5 shows some of the rungs to climb.

Few if any of us go to work with the objective of being grossly ineffective or of purposely spending our time undertaking unnecessary activities. In fact, most of the minor process changes successfully implemented in companies result from employees' own creative initiatives and their natural wish to become more productive. On the other hand, few employees are in a position to see the full picture of what is happening along the total supply chain, and most employees are therefore understandably ignorant of the potential benefits of radical process simplification. Indeed, the initial awareness of such an alternative way of doing business usually triggers a defensive reflex in the form of either covert or open resistance. This is a natural human reaction. Any radical change in the status quo may be read as "I have been wasting my time all these years!" and also carries the threat "And now you don't need me anymore!" In any change man-

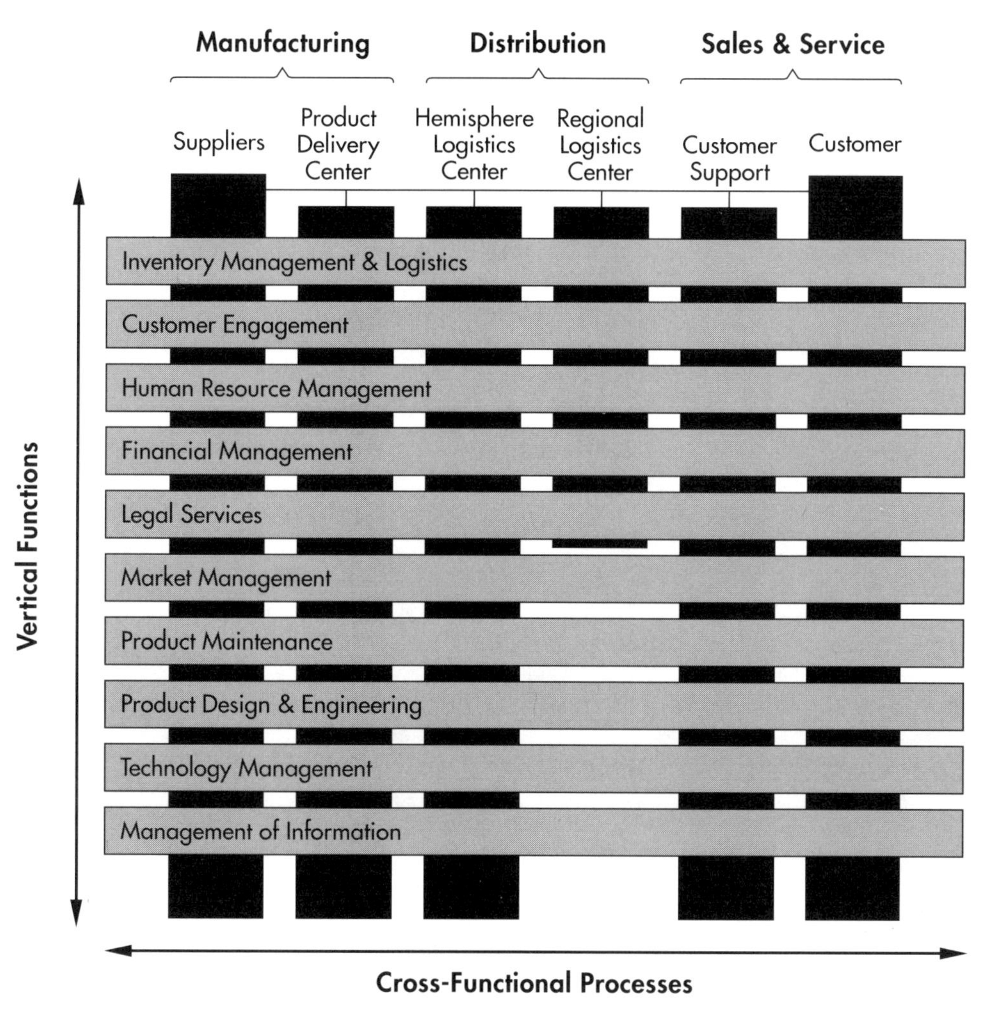

Figure 38-4
Functions vs. Processes

agement exercise, conversion is undoubtedly the most critical phase. Allowing time for self-reorientation is critical to the future adoption process. Unless the key individuals who will implement and operate the new process become converts and active participants, the chances of true adoption of the ideas and therefore of the changes being permanent are minimal.

During the implementation phase each change project should be periodically assessed for its position on the "adoption ladder." It is also probable that subelements of the change agenda will be adopted with differing speed, and a good implementation plan should allow for this. Overall the message is that in implementing change, the human, or "cultural," aspects are at least as important as the technical changes to be made in the individual processes, and they should be given careful attention.

As to the more technical aspects of change implementation, Table 38-1 takes one process element from Figure 38-1, and by comparing the current state with the desired state of this process

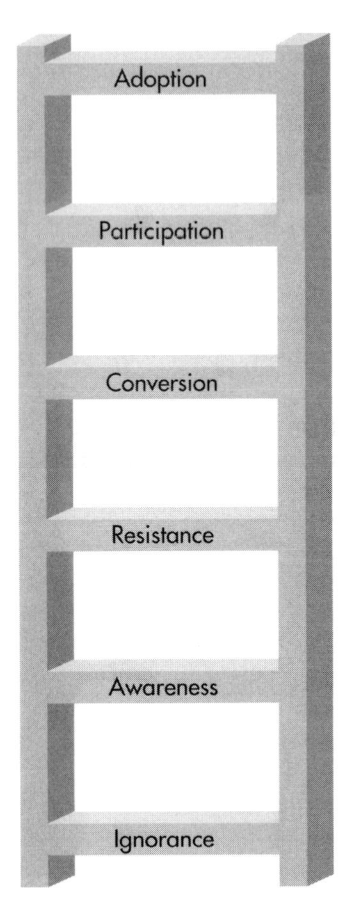

Figure 38-5
Reactions to Change–Adoption Ladder

identifies the changes required to attain desired state status. In Figure 38-6 and Table 38-2 this approach has been applied through the supply chain to identify, prioritize, and finally assign responsibility for individual projects or subelements of the overall proactive change plan. Although the projects will differ from one enterprise to another, this actual example indicates the likely range of improvement opportunities that this approach may identify.

With this magnitude of change it is clear that some kind of formalized project management process will be required, both for the individual projects and for their interaction as an overall change agenda. It is possible that one of the many readily available software-driven project control packages will already be in use in the organization, perhaps in the information management department, in which case it can be adopted fairly quickly. Familiarity with the use of these packages is fast becoming a requirement for effective management in any area. The interactive nature of the changes frequently means that the multifunctional policy formulation groups and subgroups created at the visioning stage will continue to function in the implementation stage, this time as steering committees. These groups are also valuable for reinforcing the change requirements and counterbalancing the traditional change rejection antibodies that exist in any organization. The actual change agency group may become implementation team leaders, using

TABLE 38-1
Change Analysis:
Delivery Management Process

Current Process	Changes Required	Desired State
• Sales, Administration, Distribution cannot identify what components are necessary to satisfy an order • Customer orders are split by asset type –manual linkages • We are often surprised when activities don't occur –reactive problem resolution • Customer doesn't know the status of his order –delivery to customer's required date not tracked	• Construct an integrated Customer Order Satisfaction process which covers assets and activities –explode the order into assets and establish activity work plans –develop order routing rules –supply chain performance monitoring to track lead times	• Shared ownership of orders –central focus on each order's fulfillment • Plan for Order Satisfaction –order tracking (assets and activities) permits proactive problem resolution • Information availability exchanged for Inventory –orders routed to right place (manufacturing, logistics, supplier) • Same day delivery capability • 100% build to order on high-end products

the output of the project management package to plot progress and report back to the steering committees.

It is important to integrate the change management infrastructure into the overall decision-making and investment prioritization process of the enterprise. In a company that has a formal business planning process and an annual operating plan or budget-setting process, the likelihood of obtaining and retaining the resources required to pursue the change agenda will be greatly enhanced if the agenda forms an integral part of the normal investment review process. This integration should include a feedback or progress reporting loop that continually ties implementation progress to improved business results. Figure 38-7 illustrates a possible approach.

One final technique that is useful in implementing change links the human/cultural aspects, the technical requirements for change, and the need for demonstrable business results. This is the matter of reward, recognition, and compensation. Traditionally functional managers have been rewarded for the achievement of functional results. At the same time project managers have been rewarded for on-time completion of projects. But what should happen in a situation where the same executive is both a functional line manager and a cross-functional business process change agent? What seems clear is that if he or she is still remunerated solely on the basis of performance in the line job, a strong message has been sent concerning the relative importance of the two roles. To bring the two roles more into balance, the logistics business process sponsor in a major corporation has been given the authority to establish joint bonus schemes for the key individuals in sales, manufacturing, and distribution, who together form the company's supply chain. Rewards are tied to total company business results in such a way that significant incremental remuneration is available, but only if the company's asset turns, service levels, and revenues all show significant year-over-year improvement. Either all participants receive the bonuses or none does. The implied message is very strong. The results in terms of cross-

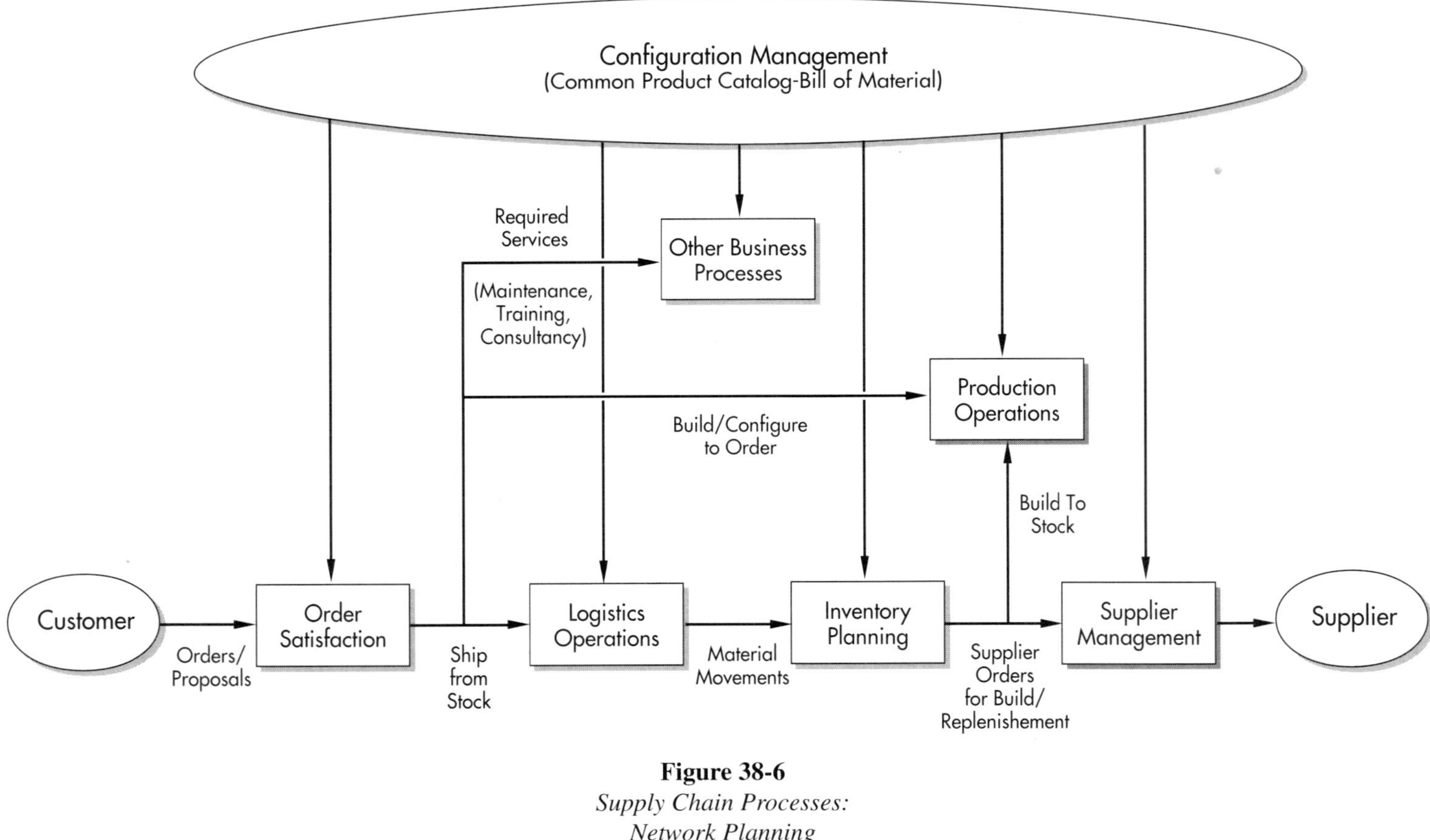

Figure 38-6
Supply Chain Processes:
Network Planning

TABLE 38-2
Proactive Change Plan:
Infrastructure Activities

Plan Year	Customer Interface	Order Satisfaction	Logistics Operations	Inventory Planning	Production Operations	Supplier Management
1995	• network planning		• kit control process	• identification and selling of excess products/spares	• manufacturing just in time	
1996	• congruent goals • electronic data interchange	• next day delivery • centralized ordering	• bar coding for new build and remanufactured products • centralized stock	• revised planning process • revised forecasting processes		• electronic data interchange capability with suppliers and interplant
1997	• configuration rules	• full systems order process		• simple spares planning interface • revised manufacturing resource planning	• integration site • extended asset recycle	
1998	• full configuration process	• customer order linked to order satisfaction	• automated central warehouse for Western hemisphere	• real time inventory information available	• extended process for integration	
1999		• shared order book capability		• integrated supply/demand planning		

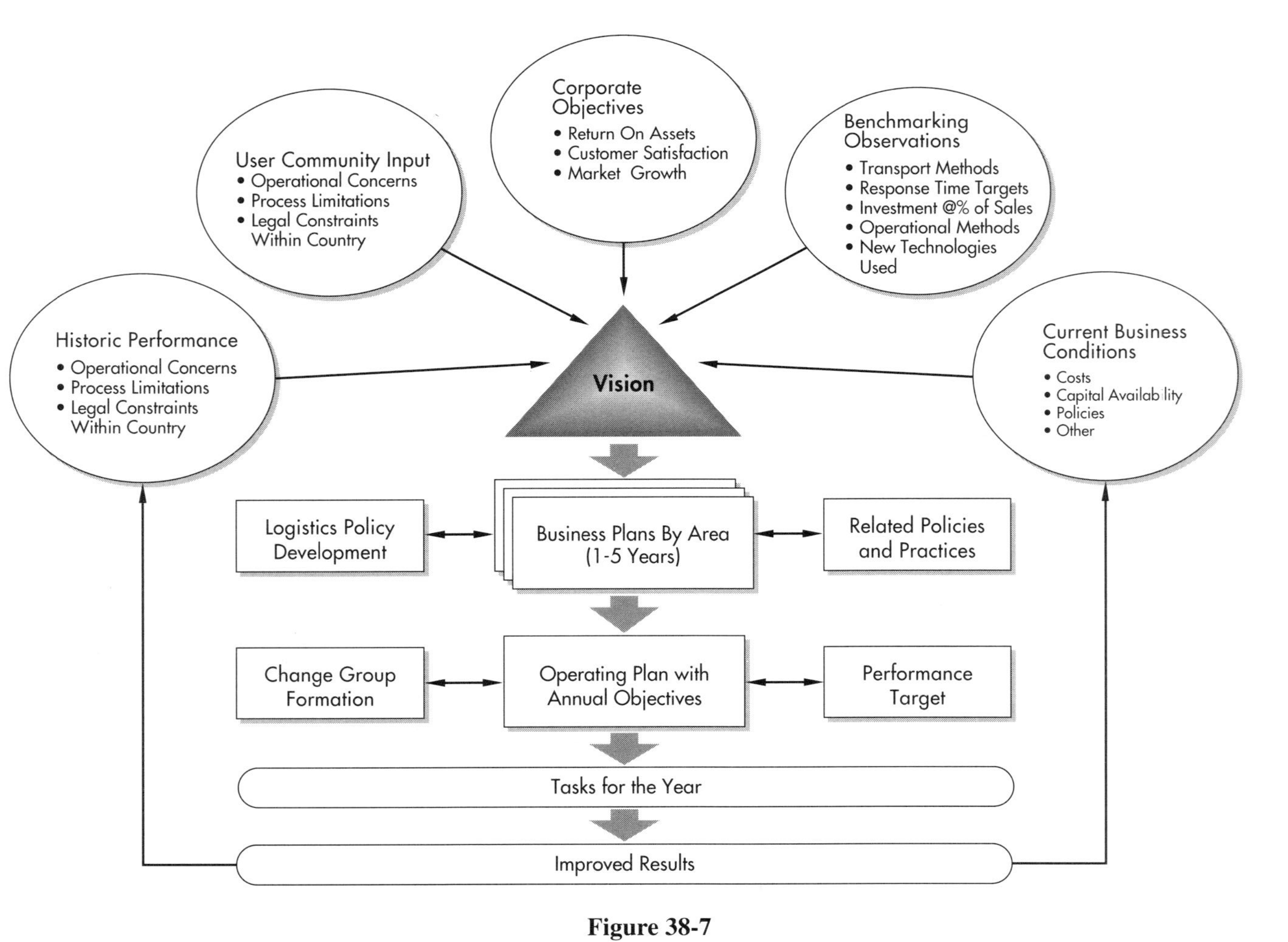

Figure 38-7
Integrated Planning

functional collaboration have been dramatic. The company's bottom-line results have improved significantly, and nobody doubts senior management's commitment to drive cross-functional proactive process changes. In the final analysis everyone in the supply chain wants to do what is right for the customer and the shareholder, so why not reward them jointly for doing it?

Continuous Change Management

Barriers and inertia have always been anathema to logistics professionals. Trade barriers and national boundaries are the most obvious examples, but functional barriers within corporations have been no less powerful enemies of logistics optimization initiatives. But we now find ourselves in an age when barriers are coming down and change is accelerating. Just as trade barriers are being reduced because of economic necessity and national boundaries are redrawn to reflect new political realities, so functional barriers are also disappearing because of technological changes. New, more flexible ways of organizing corporations are beginning to emerge, with the emphasis on simplicity and speed of action. These are the so-called lean and mean enterprises, focused organizations that consistently meet their customers' requirements with a variety of high-quality products. These will be the winners in the late 1990s.

Within this context, logistics professionals, if they are to merit that description, will also have to be flexible and versatile, recognizing the need for continual change fueled by continuous improvement in business results. Resistance to change will be professional suicide. Even acceptance of and reaction to change will not be sufficient for success. The ability to proactively manage change will be the differentiating characteristic of the best enterprises. The leaders of these companies will require a breadth of vision, a level of technical competence and a proficiency in interactive skills and human resource management greater than that traditionally required by a single-function manager.

SECTION X

Contemporary Issues in Logistics

R. William Gardner

This section focuses considerable attention on the late 1990s and the early 2000s. Chapter 39, by R. William Gardner and C. Lee Johnson, deals with material concerning third-party logistics, a development receiving considerable attention as this is written, which draws heavily on research by Delaney and La Londe and identifies the more significant performers and directions of the industry. The chapter is intended to be a summary of the options and trends in third-party logistics in vogue as this handbook goes to press.

Chapter 40, by James R. Stock and Ivy Penman, identifies some of the initial efforts to improve performance in an area of serious concern, the environment. With authors from the United States and the United Kingdom, we have responsible authorities who are keenly aware of current activity. In Chapter 41, by James L. Heskett and Carl D. Evans, reference is made to the landmark study done on service for the Council of Logistics Management, and a summary of some of those findings is available. One of the most important arenas of logistics calling for effort during the late 1990s and early 2000s will be the recognition of the logistics issues associated with all service businesses.

Finally, in Chapter 42, by John A. White and T. Ron Gable, the authors anticipate the results of the impact of current trends and efforts in the materials handling equipment area and even more broadly in some overall technology issues.

The overall effort of the authors of this section is one of documenting current trends, identifying areas of opportunity, and awakening the reader to the many possibilities for improvement of practices that yield significant cost savings and margin improvement opportunity as corporations face the challenges of "right-sizing" their business enterprises.

CHAPTER 39

Third-party Logistics

R. William Gardner
C. Lee Johnson

Third-party logistics has recently gained popularity as a broad-based contemporary issue. However, outsourcing logistics functions was the original way people stored or moved products. Public warehouses, railroads, and commercial trucking, along with the U.S. mail, the telegraph, and the telephone have been around longer than the industrial revolution in the United States. However, recent demands of market forces are causing considerable attention to be focused on logistics functions and revitalizing interest in outsourcing them. The need to efficiently and economically adjust logistics support to meet rapidly changing market demands is growing significantly. Logistics is playing a role it has never played before, with a size dimension not previously contemplated. In light of this, outsourcing to third parties has become a strategic issue demanding greater attention in corporate boardrooms.

The term *third-party logistics* first became widely used in the mid- to late 1980s as a descriptor for the outsourcing (subcontracting) of elements of the logistics process. A 1988 customer service survey for the Council of Logistics Management first made reference to "the third-party providers," and in the follow-on study published in 1989, the term received considerable attention as a result of new insights into the customer service function.[1] The term has also been used to describe "strategic alliances with service providers," and "logistics service providers" in particular.[2] *Contract logistics* is also used to refer to the outsourcing of logistics functions.[3]

The principal focus of all these terms—third-party logistics, strategic alliances with service suppliers, and partnerships—was to bring increased attention to the growing role of service providers in the logistics arena. A broadened perspective includes not only those functions of warehousing, transportation, freight payment, and EDI information exchange, but also order fulfillment, automatic reordering, carrier selection, packaging and labeling, product assembly, and customs processing. Firms are increasingly turning to contract suppliers to provide not only the aforementioned services but a host of additional functions as well.

Third parties are currently providing over 20% of the principal logistics functions (transportation, warehousing, materials management, and associated administration like freight payment), as opposed to less than 10% in 1982.[4] Considerable impetus for the move to subcontracting has resulted from deregulation of the motor freight industry, the increased sophistication of many of the warehouse/transportation suppliers, and the significant progress made by users and providers toward readily exchanging key logistics and market information. Growth of the personal computer and the explosion in electronic data interchange have facilitated the ease with which simple outsourcing arrangements can be accomplished.

Areas receiving increased attention are those associated with more exclusive relationships between user and provider: to wit, strategic alliances, exclusive use arrangements, and true logistics partnerships. These relationships, which demand much greater information disclosure on the part of both parties, press the limits of normal business relationships and require behavior changes from a "transaction-based" business arrangement to a more integrated, longer-range "partnership." The obvious benefits to both sides of this type of business relationship are system reliability, improved customer service, and more efficient cost performance. Leaving the adversarial baggage of the more traditional "transaction" relationship is as difficult for a user as it is for a third-party supplier.

Industry continues to expand its use of third parties in the logistics area, and there is a general expectation that the 1990s will bring increased use, new relationships, and new ways to utilize this growing phenomenon to improve channels of distribution to meet customer service requirements.[5]

Providers of Third-party Services

As manufacturers focus increasingly on their basic business, they tend to look for those providers of contract services (third-party logistics providers) who are identified with particular niche interests. A host of different providers, stemming from different businesses, are in the third-party field. Traditional backgrounds for those companies coming to the forefront are public warehousing, common carrier transportation, property brokerage and freight forwarding, and banking (which comes from the need for expedited payment plans).

The largest current suppliers of contract logistics services with roots in the warehouse industry include:

- Exel Logistics, a subsidiary of NFC
- GATX Logistics, a subsidiary of GATX Corporation
- Dry Storage Company

Each of these companies offers integrated logistics services, including some form of transportation, extensive warehousing, EDI information processing, and many other value-added services. Each has a strong presence in the U.S. market and achieved 1992 revenues in excess of $200 million. Exel Logistics, based in the United Kingdom, offers services not only in the United States but also in Canada, Mexico, and continental Europe. Several consolidations and the rapid growth of the industry have combined to create a growing list of companies in this service arena.

Transportation carriers providing services in third-party logistics who have been active in developing contract relationships and strategic alliances include:

- Leaseway Transportation
- Schneider National
- Menlo Logistics (Consolidated Freightways)
- Federal Express Corporation
- TNT Contract Logistics, and many other established firms

The above list is by no means exhaustive but gives prominent suppliers. In 1991 Menlo Logistics announced a $100 million third-party contract with Sears Logistics Services, which was the largest contract of public record in recent years. The transportation industry is undergoing considerable change, which is adding to the innovative arrangements.

One of the early providers of third-party services and a continually creative and supportive third-party innovator is Cass Logistics, Inc. Services are primarily oriented toward freight payment plans and software systems, as Cass Logistics is a subsidiary of a holding company primarily involved in banking.

Some manufacturers have sought to become third-party logistics service providers as a way to utilize surplus space and capacity. None has yet made significant market headway but each continues to grow and provide services to a limited number of clients. Examples include:

- Caterpillar (Caterpillar Logistics)
- W.R. Grace (W.R. Grace Distribution)

Property brokers and freight forwarders who have entered the business on a broad scale include:

- Kuehne and Nagel
- C.H. Robinson Company

Along with the successful current providers, there are some entrants who stayed only briefly in third-party logistics. Union Pacific Corporation had a logistics operation, UP Logistics, in place for several years. Union Pacific finally terminated operations in 1991, having determined that a broader range of services beyond those transportation organizations within their established infrastructure was not practical. Itel entered the business with the purchase of the Leaseway Distribution organization and several other operations, only to give up the effort and dispose of the acquisitions, also in 1991.

There have been other "starts" that have died for lack of encouragement or sufficient market. Frequently, the intended entrants underestimate the magnitude and complexity of the logistics job or feel that "rounding out their offering" will not be difficult when they start with a portion of the base. There is little question that the increasing complexities of logistics solutions require specialists. This increasing complexity is further grounds for the utilization of competent third-party suppliers rather than continuing development of in-house capabilities that ultimately lack the economies of scale associated with specialization.

Users of Third-party Services

The largest group of users of third-party services has typically been manufacturers of products sold in grocery stores like household cleaning products, paper supplies, and toiletries, as well as food products. Chemical manufacturers have also been prolific users of third-party services.

A 1989 study of leading-edge logistics firms concluded that "leading edge firms have a greater tendency to manage logistics as a value-added process, reflect a stronger commitment to achieving and maintaining customer satisfaction, and place a premium on flexibility, particularly in regard to accommodating special or non-routine requests." The study further pointed out that although these leading-edge firms do many things differently, they converge on some points to form a common profile:

First, leading edge organizations seek to use logistical competency to gain and maintain competitive superiority.

Second, excellent companies seek to add value to the products and services they market, supporting this goal by operating a cost-effective logistics system.

> And, *last,* leading edge firms leverage their assets by forming strategic alliances with service suppliers. These alliances help the firms achieve preferred-supplier status with key customers.[6]

The study supports the fact that those companies primarily concerned about exploiting their market opportunities through customer satisfaction move aggressively to work with specialists and third-party suppliers to insure the ultimate competence in meeting customer demands.

Many of the leading-edge firms have chosen to either identify single-source suppliers for particular disciplines within logistics or, at the very least, move to limited sourcing. In this way, administration of the process is simplified and economies of scale become possible by concentrating the available business on a limited number of resources. Logistics alliances are, by nature, "win-win" endeavors creating greater efficiencies for the system as a whole.[7]

The prominent management author Peter Drucker says that the organization of the future will be a "knowledge-based . . . and information-based organization."[8] With the increasing emphasis on downsizing (right-sizing) leading to outsourcing of many labor-intensive functions, third-party logistics activities will increasingly grow. Drucker's hypothesis lends further support to the trend.

Future Directions

Integration of functions and the development of process management will guide many organizations to decisions about internal and external sourcing. Company philosophies influence many decisions of this nature. For example, if distribution is truly a part of marketing, the control of distribution activities may be integrated into marketing, while the physical functions may be outsourced. A broader organizational concept, such as product management, may require many of the logistics functions to remain internal. These internal functions could include order entry, inventory control, and forecasting, while the firm looks outside for transportation, warehousing, and communications.

The future direction of logistics, as well as third-party logistics, will be determined by market requirements. A global market and its development will affect the timetable and manner in which logistics proceeds. Global marketing requirements will demand expansion and increased speed. Sellers will want to be closer to their customers. For example, many retailers are already moving to a replacement mode and a faster cash cycle. This will force much of the supply chain further back in the channel, with the manufacturers and wholesalers or their surrogates taking on more inventory responsibility. The retailer, instead of building more distribution centers, will better utilize existing ones and depend on more direct shipments to stores from suppliers. Replenishment needs and "pipeline inventory" will be a major part of forecasting, with quick response required.

Political considerations will play an important role in determining the pace and nature of logistics. Early development may be regional or even hemispheric. The European Community, starting out with 12 countries, will likely expand. Events in eastern Europe and Russia have opened up opportunities never thought possible a short time ago. The North American Free Trade Agreement (United States, Canada, and Mexico) will lead to faster expansion of logistics than previously considered possible. The transfer of power over Hong Kong from the United Kingdom to China is already having a significant impact on Asia, and may have more of an effect than many expect. Asia is opening up quickly. Although regional development will not overshadow globalization, it may have a stretching effect as companies strain to remain logistically competitive. This strain will drive many companies to third parties. Smaller firms will not have the technology or financing to meet requirements internally. Larger firms will be expanding at such a pace that they will have neither the time nor the expertise to develop everything they need. Those that want to stay in the game at higher levels will have to contract out!

Meanwhile, those already in the outsourcing business will be expanding and improving their own productivity. This will make them more predictable suppliers and of greater service to their customers. Much of the groundwork being laid by the forward-thinking third-party suppliers will pay off in the long run. This is not a fad but a strategy with significant long-term rewards. Those contractors who have well-developed customer relations and can become a part of the customer marketing effort will be winners. Being in a position to grow with customers and contribute to their success will be the formula for profitability in the future for those in third-party logistics.

Notes

1. Bernard J. La Londe, Martha C. Cooper, and Thomas G. Noordewier, *Customer Service: A Management Perspective* (Oak Brook, Ill.: Council of Logistics Management, 1988); and their follow-on study, *Customer Service: A Management Perspective* (Oak Brook, Ill.: Council of Logistics Management, 1989).
2. Donald J. Bowersox, Patricia J. Daugherty, Cornelia L. Droge, Dale S. Rogers, and Daniel S. Wardlow, *Leading Edge Logistics: Competitive Positioning for the 1990's* (Oak Brook, Ill.: Council of Logistics Management, 1989).
3. See Chapter 24.
4. Robert V. Delaney, Third Annual "State of Logistics Report," National Press Club, Washington D.C., June 15, 1992.
5. Ibid.
6. Bowersox, et al., *Leading Edge Logistics.*
7. Donald J. Bowersox, "The Strategic Benefits of Logistics Alliances," *Harvard Business Review* (July-August 1990): 36–45.
8. Peter F. Drucker, "The Coming of the New Organization," *Harvard Business Review* (January-February 1988): 45–64.

Bibliography

Anderson, David L. "Contract Logistics." *American Shipper* (February 1988): 42–47.

Copacino, William C. "Service Key to Third-Party Success." *Traffic Management* (December 1991): 59.

Delaney, Robert V. "Warehousing: Entering the 21st Century." WERC Annual Conference, Atlanta, Georgia, June 1, 1992.

Ellram, Lisa M. and Martha C. Cooper. "Supply Chain Management, Partnerships, and the Shipper-Third Party Relationship." *International Journal of Logistics Management* 1, no. 2 (1990): 1–10.

Knee, Richard. "Outsourcing Might Not Be the Best." *American Shipper* (June 1992): 10–13.

La Londe, Bernard J. *Supplement to Bibliography on Logistics and Physical Distribution Management.* Council of Logistics Management, 1981 through 1992.

Maltz, Arnold Bennett. "Outsourcing the Corporate Logistics Function: Economic and Strategic Considerations." Ph.D. diss., The Ohio State University, 1992.

Sheffi, Yosef. "Third Party Logistics: Present and Future Prospects." *Journal of Business Logistics* 11, no. 2: 21–39.

CHAPTER 40

Environmental Issues in Logistics

Ivy Penman
James R. Stock

"Green marketing," global warming, recycling, waste disposal, energy conservation, pollution, and other environmental issues have become significant agenda items during the 1990s for individuals, businesses, and governments. The issues impact all facets of society, both domestically and internationally.

An abundance of statistics has been published in the popular, trade, and academic presses that has highlighted the issues and the scope of the problems and opportunities associated with environmentalism. For example, the following items have appeared:

- 70% of businesses in the United Kingdom do little or no monitoring of their environmental impact.[1]
- 56% of U.K. firms had no environmental policy.[2]
- Over 30% of the municipal solid waste stream in the United States is made up of packaging materials.[3]
- 70% of the 14,000 landfills that existed in 1978 in the United States closed by 1988. More than one-half of all those remaining are projected to reach capacity by 1995.[4]

Environmental awareness has become an emotional, political, and financial issue that has impacted logistics and the supply chain in many areas, including purchasing and procurement, transportation, and warehousing. The various approaches that can be taken by logistics in response to environmental issues include source reduction/conservation (use less), recycling (reuse what we do use), substitution (use environmentally friendly materials), and disposal (dispose of what we cannot use).[5]

The flow model in Figure 40-1 encompasses many of the issues and responses relating to environmental materials management. The model begins with the use of virgin (often referred to as "primary") or secondary materials in processing and manufacturing. Products are produced and sold to consumer or industrial markets. After consumption by customers, they are disposed of in some fashion. Some items become mixed waste, that is, they are not separated into various components. Others are separated or segregated by source material.

The majority of mixed wastes end up in landfills or are incinerated. Hazardous wastes are disposed of in approved sites or destroyed. Items that can be economically recycled are reprocessed into secondary materials. These reprocessed materials are used as inputs in processing and manufacturing, and so the materials flow continues.

In addition to the materials flows, by-products or conditions created by manufacturing and

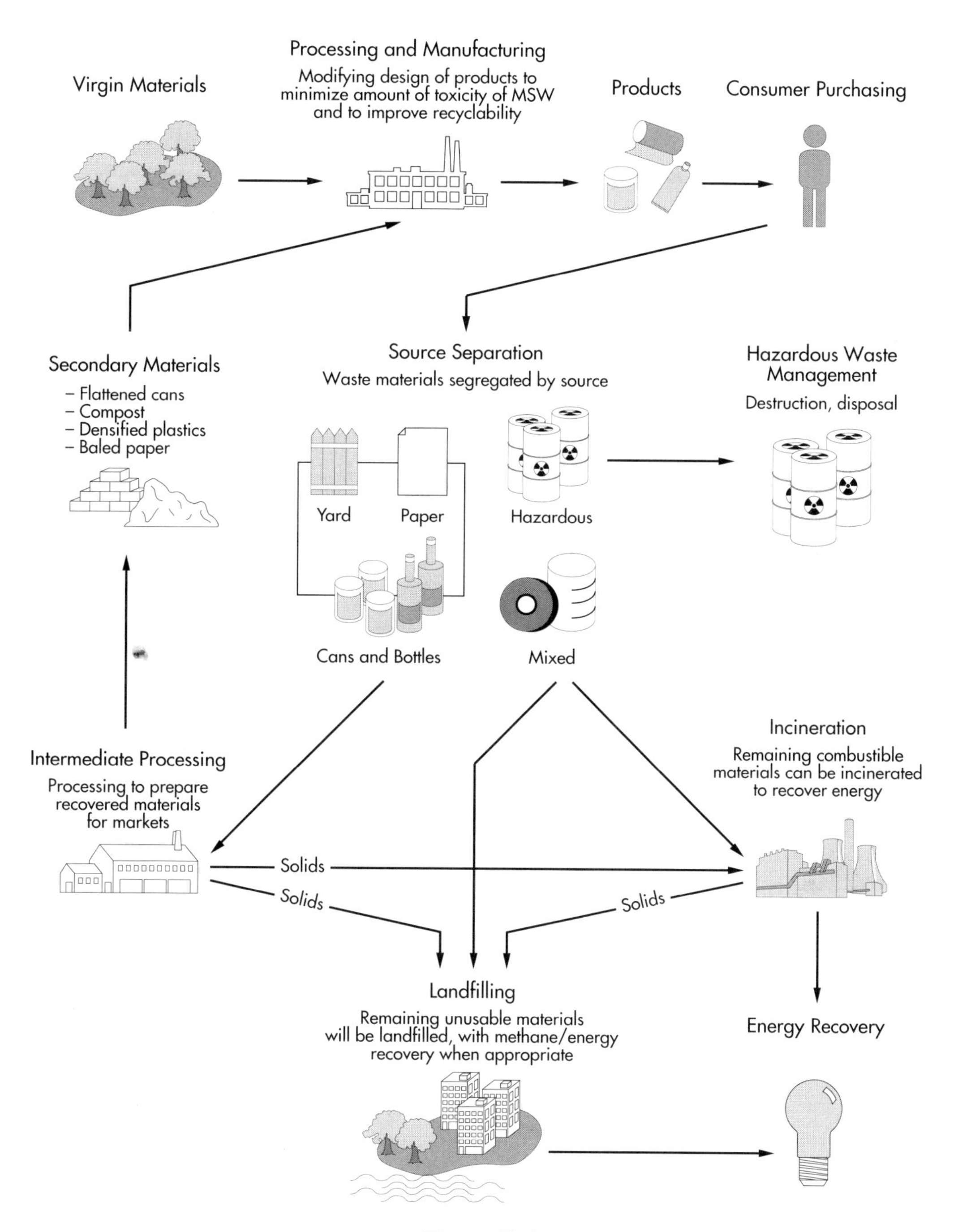

Figure 40-1
Waste Prevention and Materials Management

Source: *A Guide to Solid Waste Disposal Options*, brochure published by the Georgia Power Company, Atlanta, Ga., 1990, p. 38.

logistics activities have environmental effects. Examples include global warming, pollution, depletion of the ozone layer, and traffic congestion. These issues, as well as the materials flows relating to logistics, are discussed in the remainder of this chapter. Discussion of the environmental issues of logistics specifically address:

- Purchasing and procurement
- Physical distribution (including transportation and warehousing)
- Waste materials (hazardous and nonhazardous)
- Recycling

Some conclusions are presented with a brief examination of the future directions and implications of the environmental movement (referred to as "green marketing").

Purchasing and Procurement

The purchasing of environmentally friendly raw materials, components, and packaging is an important responsibility of materials procurement.[6] Acquisition of "unfriendly" materials that are difficult to dispose of or recycle is not an optimal environmental strategy, although at times it may be the most economical.

Virgin materials often cost less than secondary materials. From an economic perspective, companies can be at a financial disadvantage if they purchase secondary materials. Studies have shown that firms will not use recycled materials unless they are priced at least 25% below virgin materials.[7]

Other issues also impact the purchasing of secondary materials rather than virgin materials. Many individuals and companies perceive that recycled or secondary materials are inferior. Additionally, industry inertia makes it easier to maintain the "status quo," that is, to continue to make no changes in processes or systems and continue to utilize virgin materials. Some production processes may have to be changed when secondary materials are used in manufacturing. Prices charged to customers may have to be increased to cover the costs of recycling, and many firms are fearful of being placed at a competitive disadvantage.

A number of environmental options exist for manufacturers, wholesalers, retailers, and logistics service providers that engage in purchasing and procurement. For example, suppliers with which the organization already does business can often provide recycled, substitute, and other environmentally friendly materials to replace virgin materials that are being purchased.

Waste exchange organizations can also be used by companies. In the United States, the National Association for the Exchange of Industrial Resources (NAEIR), Southeast Waste Exchange (SEWE), and other similar groups provide information and materials to firms wishing to increase their use of secondary materials.[8]

Source reduction activities in purchasing and procurement can have positive environmental impacts as a result of one or more of the following efforts:

- Providing employee training that educates people on the benefits and specific activities associated with source separation, reuse, and other source reduction activities
- Purchasing materials on a just-in-time (JIT) basis so as to minimize the potential of spoilage or obsolescence
- Requiring vendors to minimize unnecessary packaging and to utilize recycled and recyclable materials, and to use returnable packages whenever possible

- Requiring vendors to provide cost and availability information regarding virgin and recycled materials that are being procured

With respect to substitution actions, firms can substitute lightweight materials like recyclable plastics for heavier materials like glass and metal. This will result in positive impacts on transportation, warehousing, and inventory costs, in addition to potential environmental benefits.

Disposal of materials is also important for purchasing and procurement. Although the major concern of firms is the inbound movement of goods, consideration must be given to how materials that enter the firm will eventually leave it. Therefore, a life-cycle approach to purchasing and procurement is optimal.[9]

Physical Distribution

Within logistics, physical distribution is concerned with the distribution of finished goods to intermediate and final customers. Physical distribution activities include many components, with transportation and warehousing being particularly important with respect to the environment. Each can impact the environment in both positive and negative ways.

It is possible for a distribution company to adopt a socially responsible attitude to the environment. Exel Logistics, a U.K. based contract distribution company, spent more than a year researching and identifying the key environmental issues before launching a comprehensive environmental policy. Also, The Institute of Logistics and Distribution Management recently published a handbook to guide its U.K. members through environmental pitfalls and possible solutions, while U.K. companies like TDG, a trucking and warehousing firm, and TNT have launched environmental policies.

The cornerstone of any environmental policy for a distribution operation will be centered around vehicles. Key areas that can be successfully tackled include fuel reduction, noise and emissions, and congestion. Providing that customer service objectives can be met, the option of rail transport should always be considered. Intermodal transport options should also be evaluated. As technology improves and the range of bimodal options increases, this alternative should become increasingly attractive. This will be the case in Europe as the Channel Tunnel (the "Chunnel") links Great Britain with the rest of the European market.

Transportation equipment utilized in the five basic modes—air, motor, pipeline, rail, water—is not environmentally friendly. This is particularly true for trucking. As trucking activity increased in the 1980s, partially owing to deregulation, market expansion, and a larger number of companies implementing JIT programs, the negative environmental impact of trucks also increased. In Europe, where rail freight is less common than in the United States, goods moving by truck increased 33% during the 1980s. At the same time, rail, with its more environmentally friendly image, saw freight traffic reduced by 12%.[10]

The distribution industry in the developed industrialized economies is a victim of success. Although consumers are delighted to have an ever-increasing choice of goods, the downside of a commensurate increase in transport activity is not so welcome.

Although road transport vehicles contribute to environmental harm, automobiles, by their sheer numbers, cause far more damage than trucks. In the United Kingdom, heavy trucks (over 3.5 tons) represent approximately half a million out of a total vehicle pool of 25 million, and account for only 7% of miles traveled.

Warehousing, although less emotive, still intrudes upon the environment. For example, refrigerated warehouses can use chlorofluorocarbons (CFCs), which deplete the ozone layer. Additionally, the packaging used in the storage and transport of products creates waste, which must then be disposed of, recycled, or reused.

As firms become more involved in recycling and other environmental responses, warehouses will have to reevaluate several operational aspects. Facilities will have to be redesigned and/or reconfigured to handle recycling and waste management in receiving areas. Decisions such as locating recycling and reprocessing equipment and the selection of the appropriate materials handling equipment must to be made.

Warehousing plays a key role in a number of reverse logistics issues relating to source reduction, recycling, substitution, and disposal. "Reverse logistics" refers to the role of logistics in source reduction, recycling, substitution, reuse of materials, disposal (including hazardous and nonhazardous materials), and product recalls. Within that context, relevant warehousing issues include facility location, layout and design decisions, use of materials handling equipment, and salvage and scrap disposal techniques and procedures.

In environmental terms, what are the key issues? Are trucks more environmentally harmful than cars? Are CFCs in temperature-controlled warehousing and vehicles damaging and to what degree? These and other issues like them are important.

Global Warming

Possibly the biggest single threat to the environment is global warming. In this century, average world temperatures have risen. Carbon dioxide (CO_2) emissions, together with methane, nitrous oxide, and ozone, have been classified as "greenhouse gases"; that is, they remain in the lower atmosphere, retaining heat produced by the sun. CO_2 is the most significant greenhouse gas, and road transport is currently responsible for 18% of the U.K. emissions of it.[11] It has been estimated that if all further CO_2 emissions were stopped, the earth would already be committed to temperature rises of between 0.5° C and 1.5° C. The resulting long-term effects of the sea level rising and the shifting of existing climatic zones may be devastating. To combat global warming, air pollution must be reduced.

Air Pollution

Road transport is a significant contributor to air pollution. In 1988, road transport was responsible for a significant proportion of pollutants in the United Kingdom, shown in Table 40-1.[12]

Toxic CO is produced when fuel is burned inefficiently. UK. output of CO has risen by 10%

TABLE 40-1
Road Transport's Contribution to U.K. Pollution in 1988

Pollutant	Portion of U.K. Total (%)
Carbon monoxide (CO)	85
Oxides of nitrogen (NO_x)	45
Smoke	34
Volatile organics	30
Sulfur dioxide (SO_2)	1

Source: *Transport Statistics of Great Britain, Digest of Environmental Protection and Water Statistics.*

in the last ten years, in the main owing to a 20% increase in road transport.[13] Automobiles are the largest producers of CO in the United Kingdom, although reductions should occur as a result of catalytic converters becoming mandatory on new cars from the end of 1992.[14]

Road transport is now the largest U.K. producer of NO_x, a major cause of acid rain. Gasoline and diesel engines contributed 23% and 22%, respectively, of all 1988 U.K. output of nitrogen oxides.[15] The United Nations has imposed a target to contain 1994 levels to those present in 1978, with further reductions thereafter.

With respect to smoke, road transport produces 34% of all suspended particulate matter in the United Kingdom. This causes respiratory ailments and is possibly carcinogenic. The road transport industry has increased its proportion of total smoke production as the Clean Air Act has brought about a decline in emissions from traditional "smokestack" industries. Similarly, 30% of volatile organic compounds, such as benzene, are produced by road transport. However, like CO and smoke, benzene will be reduced as a result of 1993 legislation.[16]

Sulfur dioxide (SO_2) is released during the burning of sulfur-containing fuels like coal and oil. Prolonged exposure can cause respiratory problems. Road transport is a low contributor to SO_2 pollution in the United Kingdom, and projected decreases in the sulfur content of diesel fuel will further improve the situation.

Although road transport is a major cause of air pollution, the majority of pollutants arise from automobiles. Legislation on emissions, already in place for the first half of the 1990s, will considerably reduce this problem. Vehicle manufacturers, petrochemical producers, and others who are developing products like fuel additives and particulate traps are working hard to reduce pollution from diesel engines.

Fuel additives appear to be beneficial in reducing fuel consumption and emissions. Some claim to reduce particulates by 50%.[17] For example, several companies utilize various fuel additives in their fleets of vehicles. Particulate traps are not yet economically viable for commercial operation, and it is hoped that engine and fuel technological improvements will make their use unnecessary.

Responsible logistics operators should ensure that all automobiles in use throughout the company utilize unleaded fuels and have catalytic converters. Such requirements are placed on all new automobiles manufactured in the United Kingdom, the United States, and many other industrialized countries.

Engine manufacturers and fuel suppliers are endeavoring to reduce emissions. Reducing sulfur content and increasing the cetane value of diesel fuel could reduce harmful emissions by 50%.[18] New 1996 European Community standards on vehicle emissions will tighten these considerably and bring Europe in line with the stricter standards presently in effect in California and other locations in the United States.[19]

Noise Pollution

The noise caused by trucks has already received considerable attention by vehicle and tire manufacturers, and improvements in technology have recently been made by most vehicle manufacturers. Many more developments are underway.

Air brake silencers significantly contribute to noise reduction. Quietness concerns vehicle manufacturers and should also be an important criterion in the equipment-purchasing decision. Vehicle refrigeration units create unwelcome and often unnecessary noise. Operators should provide plug-in power points at depots and warehouses to minimize this intrusion.

Depletion of the Ozone Layer

The ozone layer, 15 to 50 kilometers above the earth's surface, forms a protective shield, preventing penetration of the sun's harmful ultraviolet rays. Only relatively recently have the ozone-depleting properties of CFCs become known. For every CFC molecule that is prevented from entering the atmosphere, 100,000 molecules of the ozone layer are saved.[20] Because CFCs are the most common vehicle refrigerants, the distribution industry is a potentially harmful contributor of CFCs. With the increased demand for refrigerated foods, coupled with new legislation relating to their temperature control during transit, refrigerated vehicles will continue to play a vital role in food distribution.

However, the role of the distribution industry in contributing to ozone depletion must be put into perspective. CFCs are harmful only when released into the atmosphere. Therefore, measures taken in the short term should concentrate on release prevention. Safe disposal of refrigerated vehicles on decommissioning, together with leak-proof systems, can minimize the adverse impact of CFCs. Long-term measures should concentrate on substitution of CFCs with more environmentally friendly alternatives. Less harmful CFCs and alternatives with reduced ozone-depleting potential are being developed for vehicle refrigerant use; for example, R22 instead of R11 and R12 in the United Kingdom. In Europe, Imperial Chemical Industries (ICI) is developing such alternatives. The distribution industry is only one user of CFCs. Aerosols for cleaning should be banned, and fire extinguishers and other dispensing devices should use only ozone-friendly propellants. Common CFC applications other than distribution include:

- propellants in aerosols
- coolants in air conditioning (the United States being a major user)
- refrigerants (especially in domestic refrigerators)
- blown foam production
- manufacture of silicone chips
- solvent production

Depletion of Resources

Fossil fuels are finite. Practical commercial alternatives to petroleum have not yet been developed. As a major user of petroleum, the distribution industry has been depleting this nonrenewable resource. However, technological advances will almost certainly produce viable alternatives to fossil fuel in the long term. For example, some firms have begun to use multifuel vehicles, that is, power units that run on a variety of fossil and synthetic fuels. The United Parcel Service utilizes such vehicles for local pickups and deliveries.

There are a number of ways in which significant progress can be made in reducing fuel consumption. By paying attention to the highest standards of maintenance, engines can be tuned to give optimum fuel economy. Driver training can alert drivers to the benefits of fuel-efficient driving practices and refresher courses can help maintain heightened awareness. Disciplinary procedures for speeding can be enforced, and strict fuel monitoring can also help identify areas for improvement.

As examples, speed limiters are now mandatory on new heavy goods vehicles in the United Kingdom. Aerodynamic kits for trucks can now show up to 20% fuel savings and are extremely cost-effective on high-mileage, long-distance routes.

Fuel efficiency should be a top priority when purchasing new vehicles. Manufacturers are making very good progress in this area, and it is not unusual to find up to 20% fuel savings with the most fuel-efficient new designs. It is also important not to over-specify a vehicle for a particular transport operation—a common fault in the industry. Tractor units are currently available with more than 500 brake-horse-power (BHP), whereas 350 BHP is sufficient for existing U.K. weight limits. For firms purchasing used equipment, fuel efficiency factors should be considered.

Days Distribution Services, a contract warehousing firm in the United States, developed the Environmentally Awarehouse.[21] The facility attempted to maximize environmental efficiencies. One aspect of operations where significant results were achieved was in lift truck utilization. The company used nonpolluting electric lift trucks, which cost approximately 15% more than conventional forklifts. However, they neither burned fuel nor created waste oil. Maintenance was minimal. Overall, operating costs for electric lift trucks were approximately 50% of those for conventional equipment. While electric lift trucks may be less polluting, they require batteries and recharging for power. The recharging electricity is generated by utility companies that, of course, create pollution. Therefore, the overall efficiency of electric lift trucks, when one includes all aspects of electricity generation, is not as great as typically assumed. However, one unit of energy generated by a centralized utility is generally less expensive and less polluting than an equivalent unit generated on site. So battery-powered vehicles and machinery are preferable to those driven by engines.

Congestion

In major metropolitan areas like Los Angeles, Amsterdam, London, Tokyo, and Rome, highway congestion is a significant problem. Some cities have considered banning automobile and truck traffic during certain hours of the day.[22] Closely related to congestion is vehicle emissions. In addition to delays in transit times, vehicle emissions must necessarily increase as trucks "sit" in traffic jams or travel at very slow speeds on public highways. In the United Kingdom, it is estimated that congestion has cost industry £15 billion.[23]

However, it is important to recognize the limited impact of commercial vehicles on congestion. As previously stated, automobiles cause most of the transport pollution. Likewise, they contribute most to highway congestion. Although the number of U.K. trucks is forecast to increase by 17 to 31% by the end of the century, a potential reduction of 9,000 vehicles could be achieved by the introduction of 44 ton weight limits.[24]

In Japan, the congestion problem is much more significant. Not only are there more automobiles (in terms of density) causing congestion, the significant use of just-in-time (JIT) deliveries results in a large number of trucks being on highways during peak traffic hours. In combination with automobiles, this creates significant traffic flows and congestion.

Trucks can help alleviate congestion by installing in-cab communications devices. In the United States, Schneider Transport, a national truckload carrier, utilizes such equipment. The devices can make drivers aware of accidents ahead and other potential delays. Information technology can also assist vehicle utilization by means of optimal routing and scheduling.

With cabotage restrictions being progressively eliminated in Europe, "empty miles" are becoming less problematic for road transporters. In 1992, empty miles accounted for over 30% of the total mileage driven by a typical truck.[25] However, backhaul opportunities should be continuously sought.

Harmonization of transport standards, allowing the United Kingdom to operate the 44 ton vehicles that are already used in other European countries, will help reduce congestion and pollution, while increasing fuel efficiency. This will also improve the economic efficiency of the transport industry. Larger vehicles coupled with reduced restrictions that eliminate empty miles will provide both transportation and warehousing with efficiencies. Several U.K. retailers are now able to more efficiently utilize their vehicle fleets, minimizing empty miles through increased backhauls.

Congestion also leads to highway wear and tear. Air suspension, although an additional cost, can help reduce highway destruction. In Europe, forthcoming legislation will allow vehicles with air suspensions to operate at greater gross weights (again reducing congestion).[26]

Warehouse designers should determine the proper number and location of truck bays that will result in the least amount of congestion and minimize vehicle loading/unloading time.

Waste

Disposal of old vehicles and vehicle by-products is also a problem. Incineration of old tires causes air pollution. Improper disposal of oil and batteries can result in contaminated groundwater. A number of recycling efforts exist in many countries to handle items such as used oil, tires, and batteries to minimize contamination.

For example, in Germany, BMW has introduced a recycling facility on its Bavarian production line and Volkswagen is increasing the recycled content of new cars from 70% to 80% by partnershipping with recycling companies.[27] Other similar initiatives from vehicle manufacturers can aid in the waste disposal problem. Additionally, at least 80% of all lead acid batteries used in transportation and materials handling equipment are now recycled.[28]

Trucks are used to transport nonrecyclable items to incinerators or landfills. Hazardous wastes are much more difficult to transport, and such movements are regulated in most parts of the world.[29] Effective January 1, 1991, hazardous materials moving to, through, or from a United Nations member country had to be packaged, labeled, and certified as meeting UN packaging standards. Those requirements have impacted all parties involved in the handling, storage, and transport of hazardous materials.[30] In the United States, the Environmental Protection Agency (EPA) requires that a one-page shipping manifest accompany hazardous materials shipments, and all parties in the process must acknowledge their involvement.[31]

Vehicle washes should recycle water and use biodegradable cleaning chemicals. In general, maintenance activities should be scrutinized for wastefulness.

Potential environmental solutions for warehouse waste reduction include:

- Use of returnable and/or recyclable containers and pallets
- Determination of the best methods for locating and handling recyclables and disposables within the warehouse
- Use of methods to control inventory levels and thereby minimize waste (e.g., stock rotation and using the oldest purchased materials first, FIFO)
- Determination whether outdated stock can be returned to suppliers for regeneration.

Physical Distribution Initiatives

Most would agree that the environmental problems discussed (global warming, air pollution, noise pollution, depletion of the ozone layer, depletion of resources, congestion, and waste) are significant and deserve attention. Of course, logistics organizations are focused on day-to-day

TABLE 40-2
Sample Logistics Initiatives to
Meet Environmental Objectives

Logistics Initiative	Environmental Objective
Install air brake silencers on vehicles.	Reduce noise pollution.
Install plug-in power for vehicle refrigeration at depots and warehouses.	Reduce noise pollution and resource depletion.
Install or inspect existing catalytic converters on automobiles.	Reduce air pollution.
If using diesel fuel, only use low-sulfur, high-cetane variants.	Reduce air pollution.
Use emission-reducing fuel additives.	Reduce air pollution.
Inspect refrigeration and cooling systems for leaks.	Reduce air pollution.
Use substitutes for CFCs (or at least alternative lower-impact CFCs).	Reduce depletion of ozone layer.
Properly decommission refrigeration units and properly dispose of unwanted CFCs.	Reduce depletion of ozone layer.
Heighten vehicle maintenance standards for better engine turning.	Reduce depletion of resources.
Purchase only fuel-efficient vehicles.	Reduce depletion of resources.
Do not overspecify vehicles.	Reduce depletion of resources.
Use electric forklift trucks.	Reduce depletion of resources.
Use in-vehicle communications to avoid traffic.	Reduce congestion.
Use routing and scheduling systems.	Reduce congestion and air pollution.
Utilize backhaul capacity.	Reduce congestion and air pollution.
Move materials in the largest loads practicable.	Reduce congestion and air pollution.
Use air suspension vehicles.	Reduce congestion.
Find and use recycling programs or services for oil, tires, batteries, packaging materials, and scrapped vehicles and other metal.	Reduce waste.
Use returnable containers and pallets.	Reduce waste.
Use waste and obsolescence-minimizing materials management techniques.	Reduce waste.
Regenerate outdated stock.	Reduce waste.

business activities and are thus unlikely to battle broad environmental problems if presented as such. Rather, logistics managers must translate broad environmental objectives into specific, tangible logistics initiatives.

Companies can become environmentally responsible before being forced to do so by government regulators. Beating regulators has several advantages, including improved public relations and the opportunity to reduce regulatory compliance costs by instituting initiatives with forethought rather than with frenzy under the threat of penalties.

Table 40-2 summarizes the initiatives presented in the previous discussions. Although this is not a comprehensive list of initiatives, it provides an example of how environmental objectives can be formed into logistics initiatives.

Waste Materials

The logistics of handling, storing, and disposing of waste is enormous. All sectors of the economy create some type of waste. In the United States, often referred to as the "throwaway society," over 160 million tons of garbage are produced each year.[32] Waste materials include both hazardous and nonhazardous items. Each category of waste has its own individual set of problems, opportunities, and solutions.

Each country in Europe has its own regulations and legislation relating to waste. In April 1992, the Environmental Protection Act became effective in the United Kingdom. The act stated that carriers of waste had to be certified or licensed, and had to produce a certificate on collection. The producer remains responsible for the waste and is liable for prosecution if the disposal contractor fails to dispose of it correctly. By placing the onus on the producer of the waste, this makes a firm's choice of disposal contractor critical.

Similar legislation exists in the United States in the form of the Resource Conservation and Recovery Act (RCRA) and amendments, referred to as the Hazardous Solid Waste Amendments (HSWA). The act and amendments give the EPA authority over three major waste management areas:

- Controlling hazardous wastes from generation until ultimate disposal ("womb-to-tomb" tracking)
- Control of solid (primarily nonhazardous) waste, such as household waste
- Regulation of toxic substances and petroleum products stored in undergound tanks[33]

Logistical issues relating to hazardous waste disposal are the most politically sensitive. Table 40-3 shows the results from national polls indicating the top environmental concerns to citizens of the United States.[34] It is noteworthy that the most often mentioned concerns are waste-related.

One of the most appropriate responses to environmental waste is to include consideration of it in a firm's accounting system. Accounting systems need to include the costs of materials disposal:

TABLE 40-3
U.S. Citizen's Environmental Concerns

Issue	Portion of Population Concerned (%)
Actively used hazardous waste sites	67
Abandoned hazardous waste sites	65
Water pollution from industrial waste	63
Worker exposure to toxic chemicals	63
Accidental oil spills	60
Destruction of the ozone layer	60
Radiation from nuclear power plant accidents	60
Industrial accidents releasing pollutants	58
Radiation from radioactive wastes	58
Outdoor air pollution from factories	56

Source: *The Nation's Hazardous Waste Management Program at a Crossroads,* EPA/530-SW-90-069 (Washington, D.C.: Environmental Protection Agency, July 1990), p. 6.

As waste streams are assessed for reduction potential, develop accounting systems that calculate the true cost of disposal and recognize benefits of waste reduction. This means going beyond handling, transportation, treatment and disposal costs. Lost revenue of materials that could have been sold as recyclables should be included in accounting systems, as well as the value of wasted input material.[35]

A number of corporate, industry, and government efforts have attempted to minimize or eliminate waste materials. For example, the European Recovery and Recycling Association has identified a number of key questions that must be addressed by logistics executives and corporate managers if waste reduction strategies are to be successful:

- Can a waste be reused within the process or a nearby process? Or does the waste have market value through a waste exchange?
- Should raw materials be purchased in smaller quantities?
- Can some of the toxic materials in the process be eliminated?
- What production technology would yield the same or better product with less waste?
- How can production scrap be reused by the firm or someone else?
- Is it necessary to remove so much semifinished product from production for quality sampling?
- Is the product designed for easy repair and/or recycling?
- Would better inventory practices, such as clearly marking all stocked items, maintaining segregation of unlike materials, using returnable containers and thoroughly emptying all containers, reduce waste?
- Are potential revenues from discarded materials lost because of unnecessary mixing or contamination? What housekeeping practices are necessary to prevent these losses?[36]

In sum, companies should attempt to minimize the creation of waste materials. Source reduction (use less) techniques that utilize lesser amounts of materials that create waste are the optimal solution. When waste is created, especially that which cannot be reused or recycled, it must be properly disposed of using acceptable handling, transportation, and storage techniques and procedures.

Recycling

Customers are placing more emphasis on environmental issues in their purchasing decisions. For example, approximately two-thirds of U.S. consumers have indicated that package recyclability affected their decision to purchase various products.[37] A Gallup survey conducted for the American Paper Institute found that 70% of consumers would be very likely or fairly likely to purchase products packaged in recycled paper.[38] With the green marketing revolution, recycling has become an important issue to customers, businesses, and governments.

Considerable attention has been focused on the German environment during the early 1990s. A key trigger factor was the unification of East and West Germany. West Germany found that it had inherited one of the most polluted landscapes in Europe, the former East Germany. To illustrate, West Germany had previously sent wastes, including toxic wastes, to East Germany for disposal. After unification, it was discovered that the wastes sent to East Germany had been left to accumulate rather than having undergone proper disposal. As a result, reunified Germany faces a massive cleanup which is being addressed in three-stages:

1. From December 1991, manufacturers and retailers are responsible for the disposal or recycling of all packaging used for transporting goods.
2. From April 1992, traders and retailers are obliged to accept the return of all "unnecessary" packaging, including plastic, paper, and cardboard, that was used for advertising.
3. From January 1993, traders and retailers are responsible for all containers used to hold drinks, washing powders, cleaning liquids, paints, and pastes, including such items as toothpaste tubes. To encourage the return of the containers, the products will carry a 50-pfennig deposit.[39]

Other countries have also embraced recycling. Italy established recycling targets for 1993 of 50% for glass and metal drink containers, and 40% plastic containers.[40]

Companies create significant amounts of waste that can be recycled. Examples include cardboard boxes, pallets, other types of boxes, shrink-wrap, and miscellaneous transportation and storage materials. Estimates are that more than 90% of all manufactured products move in a corrugated box at some point in the logistics process.[41]

Most companies in the manufacturing, retailing, and logistics service industries conduct some type of recycling effort. The Honda of America Manufacturing facility located in Marysville, Ohio, developed a recycling program that saved the company $214,000 in a six-month period by avoiding landfill costs and generating income from the sales of recyclable materials.[42] The Burlington Northern Railroad developed and implemented a recycling program in 25 states. In two years, Burlington Northern recycled 2.2 million pounds of paper and baled 1.7 million pounds of corrugated cardboard. At the same time, waste hauling fees were reduced by 50%.[43]

In Germany, more than 400 major companies such as Coca-Cola, Pepsi-Cola, Wilkinson Sword, Nestlé, Unilever, and Schweppes have formed a joint company—Duales System Deutschland (DSD)—for recycling household cast-off packaging.[44] Expectations are that DSD will help reduce the amount of household rubbish by 25 to 30% within four years.

The success of DSD in achieving its goal will depend on the public's willingness to cooperate. DSD street containers for glass and paper have been added to existing local authority containers—one for every 500 inhabitants in urban areas and for every 200 in rural areas. Each household has been provided with a large, bright yellow trash can to take all recyclable materials not suitable for street containers. Existing household trash containers will include only food-related kitchen waste.

DSD requires an initial investment of £2.4 billion, which will be recouped from an average two-pfennig surcharge on each consumer item purchased. The products that are recyclable display a green dot to notify consumers. Producers are charged 1 to 20 pfennigs for the right to include the green dot on their products. Companies that have not joined DSD will eventually be required to make alternative arrangements for recycling with individual retailers—a costly exercise.

In Germany, Tengelmann, a major grocery retailer, and Scholler, a packaging company, have cooperated to reduce transit packaging waste. They have developed a modular propylene packaging system called RPS that protects groceries in transit and has a life of ten years. Tests show this packaging is comparable in cost to conventional outer cartons. As the cost of waste disposal rises, RPS will become increasingly cost-effective. Because the modular construction can be broken down into stackable units, the packaging system takes 70% less volume than cardboard outers. It is proposed that a third-party service company will rent the containers.

Globally, recycling has become big business, with most major corporations involved to some degree. Recycling can provide both environmental and economic benefits. The obvious benefits to the environment are the use of more secondary materials rather than virgin or primary materials, and the preservation of natural environments and habitats. For business, some benefits include financial gains from selling scrap materials for reprocessing and creating a positive corporate image with customers and other groups.

The uses for recycled materials are increasing and creating extensive global markets. As one writer noted:

> Once materials are recycled, they are utilized for a variety of purposes. For example, corrugated cardboard packaging is reprocessed into cardboard for reuse as packaging. Glass can be cleaned, crushed, and melted to make new bottles. Aluminum is recycled and reprocessed into a variety of aluminum products. Plastics can be recycled and made into fiberfill, tape for carton strapping, and plastic foam used in composting.[45]

Other examples of recycling efforts relating to logistics are the following:

- Each year, more than two billion Kellogg Company packages display the "made from recycled paper" symbol.
- 98% of the dry goods produced by General Mills, Inc., are packaged in recycled paperboard.
- Colgate-Palmolive Company's powdered laundry detergent is packaged in recycled paperboard and is shipped in boxes using recycled materials.
- Grocery industry goals and standards to recycle stretch wrap, corrugated boxes, postconsumer plastic grocery bags, and shipping pallets are being formulated.[46]

In summary, logistics can play a vital role in recycling. In combination with source reduction, recycling can significantly reduce the use of landfills and incineration wastes, and thus have a large environmental impact.

Environmental Implications for Business

Within the logistics function, road transport represents the biggest environmental threat. Using nonrenewable natural resources, contributing to air and noise pollution, trucks are environmentally unfriendly. Any steps to reduce transport activity will help minimize negative impact. In particular, noxious emissions must be reduced, but in the long term more environmentally friendly vehicles are required.

Companies throughout the world have recognized the importance of environmentalism and the role of logistics in structuring a corporate response to environmental issues like recycling, waste disposal, pollution, and many others. Reverse logistics, the term often used to represent the role of logistics in environmentalism, is gaining acceptance by firms.[47]

Within logistics, transportation is an important activity in the recycling and disposal aspects of reverse logistics. The "products" transported include recyclable materials, scrap, hazardous wastes, and reprocessed materials. Therefore, transport issues like routing and scheduling of vehicles, mode and carrier selection, use of private versus public transportation, driver and equipment safety issues, and aspects of the traffic management function are relevant to reverse logistics. For example, transport accounts for over 25% of recycling costs that occur before reprocessing activities.[48]

Warehousing does not create emissions to any significant degree compared with transportation, but it plays a vital role in reverse logistics. Issues like facility location, warehouse layout and design, use of materials handling equipment, and salvage and scrap storage are important concerns. The following case study involving United Stationers in the United States illustrates how site selection decisions can be impacted by environmental issues:

> "[A]fter purchasing land in New Jersey for a massive DC [Distribution Center], the state's E.P.A. did soil tests which uncovered extensive toxic contamination. Luckily, United Stationers' attorney had inserted a clause in the purchase contract which protected the company from liability for cleanup costs . . . $1.5 million . . . But the E.P.A. still wouldn't allow United Stationers to build on the land."[49]

Other issues involving warehousing, as well as transportation, are the use of pallets and recyclable containers. Warehousing stores products on pallets or in containers. Transportation moves those products, perhaps on the same pallets or in the same containers. Therefore, the proper selection, use, and disposal of pallets and containers are considerations in transportation and warehouse management.

In addition to transportation and warehousing, all elements of the logistics process are important participants in responding to environmental issues. Environmentalism has become another component in the firm's cost-service trade-off analysis. In the same way that cost and service issues are considered when making logistics and marketing decisions, environmental issues must be examined as well.

Although there may be obstacles or impediments—perceptual, technical, operational, and regulatory—to implementing reverse logistics strategies, they are not insurmountable. Maintaining focus and persistence will result in successful strategies and programs. Organizations "environmentally evolve." Firms begin by complying with environmental regulations and laws. They typically develop partial, then complete, recycling programs, which are followed by significant changes in products and packaging. Gradually, firms fully integrate environmentalism into their corporate cultures until it becomes a way of life.[50]

A Future Perspective

Effective corporate responses to environmental issues require comprehensive solutions and approaches to difficult problems. As noted in *Packaging for the Environment,*

> The emerging "green" corporation of tomorrow accepts the environmental imperative and willingly assumes the mantle of environmental leadership . . . It favors voluntary product and process redesign, as well as the avoidance of pollution and waste. In short, it takes the long-term view and addresses environmental issues by attacking their root causes.[51]

Ultimately, environmentalism becomes part of a firm's way of doing business, and all members of the company recognize their role in responding to environmental issues. The direction is clear. Firms must be involved in reverse logistics in proactive, rather than reactive, ways. To be successful in the 1990s and beyond, a firm must be "green"! Firms can respond in a number of ways in the future.

> First, logistics executives must anticipate future environmental regulatory changes and be an active participant in shaping . . . legislation.
>
> Second, logistics executives should become knowledgeable about the green marketing

revolution and how it can impact the components of the logistics process. There will certainly be some cost and service implications of green marketing.

Third, purchasing and procurement should be made aware of the company's priority in acquiring secondary raw materials rather than virgin materials. Formal policies and procedures need to be established that evaluate the relevant factors associated with secondary and virgin materials. Additional vendors and suppliers may have to be added to approved purchasing lists. Purchasing personnel need to buy into the notion that buying recycled materials is good business.

Fourth, logistics executives must plan their firm's reverse logistics system so that the strategies of source reduction, recycling, substitution and disposal can be implemented as efficiently and effectively as possible.

Finally, some management individual must be assigned reverse logistics and/or environmental responsibility. In most successful organizations, the person in charge of environmental affairs is located at a middle or upper level management position. The person must have sufficient authority and responsibility to get the job done.[52]

Environmental issues will not go away! In fact, they will become much more important to individuals, corporations, industries, and governments. A socially responsible attitude to the environment can tip the balance in relationships with customers, end users, employees, suppliers, and governments. A socially responsible attitude can even help win business. It makes good sense for firms to respond efficiently and effectively to environmental concerns and problems.

Notes

1. National Materials Handling Centre, United Kingdom; also see Perry A. Trunick, "Take Action on the Environment," *Transportation and Distribution* 33, no. 5 (May 1992): 60
2. National Materials Handling Centre, United Kingdom.
3. E. Joseph Stilwell, R. Claire Canty, Peter W. Kopf, and Anthony M. Montrone, *Packaging for the Environment: A Partnership for Progress* (New York: AMACOM, 1991), p. 2.
4. *Solid Waste Disposal Overview* (Washington, D.C.: National Solid Wastes Management Association, 1991), p. 2.
5. See *Decision-Makers Guide to Solid Waste Management*, EPA/530-SW-89-072 (Washington, D.C.: Environmental Protection Agency, November 1989).
6. Portions of this section are adapted from James R. Stock, *Reverse Logistics* (Oak Brook, Il.: Council of Logistics Management, 1992), pp. 25–27.
7. Resource Integration Systems, Ltd., *Market Study for Recyclable Plastics*, February 1987, p. vii.
8. Julie Murphree, "Revisiting Investment Recovery," *NAPM Insights* (March 1991): 24–25.
9. For a discussion of how life-cycle analysis can be applied to environmental issues, see Robert G. Hunt, Jere D. Sellers, and William E. Franklin, "Resource and Environmental Profile Analysis: A Life Cycle Environmental Assessment of Products and Procedures," *Environmental Impact Assessment Review* (Spring 1992): 1.
10. *Transport Statistics of Great Britain.*
11. White Paper entitled "This Common Inheritance," published by HMSO, 1991.
12. *Transport Statistics of Great Britain, Digest of Environmental Protection and Water Statistics.*

13. Ibid.
14. "The Route Ahead," report published by the World Wildlife Fund for Nature.
15. *Digest of Environmental Protection and Water Statistics.*
16. EC Legislation, ECE R49 88/77/EEC, Phase II.
17. Literature published by High Speed Lubricants, Ltd., 1991.
18. Volvo, Environment and Development, RSP 62990.12.91.
19. EC Legislation, ECE R49 88/77/EEC, Phase II.
20. Earthworks Group, *50 Simple Things Your Business Can Do to Save the Earth* (Earthworks Press, 1989).
21. E. J. Muller, "The Greening of Logistics," *Distribution* 90, no. 1 (January 1991): 30.
22. *Financial Times.*
23. Confederation of British Industry (U.K.), 1990.
24. Freight Transport Association (U.K.).
25. Ibid.
26. EC Directive 8513.
27. British Broadcasting Company, June 1992.
28. *Solid Waste Management in Florida*, 1990 Annual Report, Florida Department of Environmental Regulation, March 1991, p. 61.
29. See Jay Gordon, "The Environmental Nitty Gritty," *Distribution* 91, no. 5 (May 1992): 36–44.
30. William Craze, "New Rules for Hazardous-Materials Packaging," *Army Logistician* (May-June 1991): 9.
31. *Solving the Hazardous Waste Problem,* EPA/530-SW-86-037 (Washington, D.C.: Environmental Protection Agency, November 1986), p. 10.
32. *Recycling Works! State and Local Solutions to Solid Waste Management Problems*, EPA/530-SW-89-014 (Washington, D.C.: Environmental Protection Agency, January 1989), p. 3.
33. *The Nation's Hazardous Waste Management Program at a Crossroads*, EPA/530-SW-90-069 (Washington, D.C.: Environmental Protection Agency, July 1990), p. 6.
34. Ibid., p. 5.
35. Resource Recycling Systems, Inc., *Waste Reduction—Getting Started*, Publication # 8902A (Lansing, Mich.: Office of Waste Reduction Services, December 1989), p. 2.
36. European Recovery and Recycling Association, *ERRA Principles of Action: A Comprehensive Household Recovery and Recycling System* (Brussels, Belgium: February 1, 1991), p. 11.
37. *Packaging* (July 1990): 8–10.
38. "Public Attitudes Toward Recycled Paper Packaging," The Gallup Organization Inc. for the American Paper Institute, January 20, 1989.
39. *Guardian*, February 22, 1992.
40. Frances Cairncross, "How Europe's Companies Reposition to Recycle," *Harvard Business Review* 70, no. 2 (March-April 1992): 38.
41. Daniel Goldberg, "Cost Avoidance Makes Recycling Pay," *Transportation and Distribution* 30, no. 10 (October 1989): 52.
42. Ibid.
43. Example provided by the Burlington Northern Railroad, December 1991.
44. Cairncross, "How Europe's Companies Reposition to Recycle," p. 36.
45. Stock, *Reverse Logistics*, p. 17.
46. Grocery Manufacturers of America, *Our Fair Share*, undated.

47. See Stock, *Reverse Logistics*, pp. 28–30.
48. *The Blueprint for Plastics Recycling* (Washington, D.C.: Council for Solid Waste Solutions, 1991).
49. Muller, "The Greening of Logistics," p. 27.
50. Stilwell et al., *Packaging for the Environment*, p. 7.
51. Ibid., p. 164.
52. Stock, *Reverse Logistics*, pp. 51–52.

CHAPTER 41

Logistics in the Service Industries

James L. Heskett
Carl D. Evans

Service activities make up nearly 80% of economic activity in the United States and comparable percentages in other developed economies. This figure will not decline as the world becomes more affluent, sated with the products necessary to meet its basic needs, and more deeply concerned with such things as keeping the products functioning, the quality of life, and personal fulfillment.

We are told daily and in many ways that the quality of service in many parts of the world is poor. Whether this is a product of rising expectations and the greater accessibility of services to larger numbers of people (as in airline services) or whether it represents an absolute measure of service quality is not clear. We are told also that productivity increases in the service sector, at least in the faulty ways we measure them, lag far behind those in manufacturing.

The primary objectives of any service organization must be to deliver good value and foster customer retention and referral. The delivery of good value involves providing excellent quality in relation to the total cost to the customer of acquiring the service.[1] High productivity contributes to service value, but it must be measured both in terms of work performed and results achieved. (This is the crux of most complaints about how service productivity is measured—firms tend to focus on procedures rather than results.)

Nevertheless, if opportunities equivalent to those in manufacturing exist for the rationalization of logistics activities in the service sector, the potential cost benefits may be substantial. One study estimates that the value of economic activity associated with the service industries is $2.9 trillion. It goes on to suggest that "if logistics improvements in service industries match the improvements experienced in goods industries over the last ten years [about 10 percent] then the savings potential is $200 billion!"[2] Although the difficulties of differentiating manufacturing from service activities may raise questions about the figures, significant opportunities exist in the service sector from the systematic application of thinking that has led to improvements in manufacturing logistics in recent years.

The topic of this chapter is confined to logistics in services, regardless of the mix of manufacturing and service activities associated with an industry or business. Hence, service logistics includes after-sale service associated with most manufacturing.

Why Examine Logistics in the Service Industries?

To date, nearly all the logistics profession's attention has been focused on supply chain logistics.[3] That is, people associate logistics with "the traditional process associated with the acquisition and distribution of goods."[4] The meaning of logistics should be broadened to include *service response logistics,* "the process of coordinating nonmaterial activities necessary to the fulfillment of service in a cost and customer effective way."[5] Of particular importance is establishing networks to satisfy customer needs.

Any discussion of logistics in services presents particular challenges, primarily because service logistics activities are much less homogeneous in their basic nature than manufacturing logistics activities. Think, for instance, of the basic differences between the logistics of a high-technology consumer information service delivered electronically and that of a house-cleaning service with a high human input delivered on the customer's premises and often in the customer's presence. Or what about the differences between services delivered to customers and those such as self-service and self-delivery in which the customer participates to a much greater degree? There are even vast differences between the logistics of retail banking, requiring emphasis on location and transaction processing, and those of investment banking, requiring emphasis on the network of personal relationships so necessary for completing successful deals at the right price and the right time.

Clearly, no generalizations will serve us in this chapter. Therefore, it is important to understand at the outset that all generalizations in this chapter are generally invalid—except this one.

The concepts of service logistics are inherently difficult to grasp, for they focus on the supply of products that do not physically exist. So the easiest way to understand the logistics of service industries is by examination of their differences as distinct from their manufacturing counterparts. The most important of these differences involve the following.

Focus on People. Service logistics emphasizes people as opposed to product. In particular, customers at various times can be regarded not only as customers, but also as service providers and even as inventory. Many times, all of the above apply.

Importance of Location. Location is much more important for many services than for manufacturing, especially for services created at the point of sale. Retailers tell us that the three most important factors in retail success are location, location, and location. They are suggesting that the marketing impact of location in many services is much greater than in the logistics of most manufacturing enterprises.

Challenge of Urban Locations. There is a relatively high incidence of urban locations for services. Because just-in-time and other supply chain logistics strategies are carried out in such locations, serious potential traffic congestion and environmental problems can be created.

Management of Demand. For many services, the inventory management problem takes on a very different character relative to most manufacturing logistics. Because many services cannot be inventoried, the problem becomes one of demand-supply management and capacity planning. It is ironic that at the time many manufacturing enterprises are developing flexible manufacturing and logistics systems to produce a greater proportion of goods to order rather than to stock, service firms are seeking ways to inventory services by various means.

Industries associated with after-sale service in which parts, people, and equipment all have to be brought together at the same time and place find that characteristics of inventory management problems are similar to those of manufacturing logistics.

Nature of Information. The nature of information is critical. In particular, experiential databases are at the very core of some of the most successful service firms, as well as effective after-sale service management in manufacturing.

Role of Networks. There is a somewhat different role of networks and network planning and management in many services. These networks comprise physical facilities, as in transportation services; information, as in computing and communication services; and relationships, as in investment banking. In particular, the latter are key success factors in many services, particularly professional services.

At the same time, the similarities in the development of both manufacturing and service industry logistics should not be overlooked. Some of the exciting trends that are similar include the increasing attention to time-based and fast-response systems, the increasing reliance on computing and communication, and the creative development of experiential databases to aid in anticipating demand for both goods and services.

People vs. Product

Service logistics excellence requires an understanding of people, particularly customers. Because customers take on varied roles in service purchasing and providing processes, the management of service logistics requires an understanding of human behavior unprecedented in manufacturing.

The Customer as Customer

Many services, such as retailing, communication, transportation, medical, and others, are performed at the point of sale and at the point of contact with customers. Jan Carlzon has labeled these points of contact "moments of truth."[6] This requires either that the service be brought to the customer, as in many communication services, or that the customer be brought to the service.

Services are being brought to customers to an increasing degree. We see it in medical services, for example, as outpatient clinics, neighborhood treatment centers, and in-home care services are developing rapidly.

Computing and communication capabilities, brought into the home, have allowed many users to alter their working styles and locations. Stanley Davis's concept of "future perfect," the inexorable trend toward being able to supply anything, anywhere, and at any time is at work, with many services taking the lead over manufacturing.[7] This requires an understanding of customers' willingness to adapt to new technologies and even new living and working patterns.

At the same time, many services still rely for their success on customers' coming to the point of sale (and manufacture). Thus, what we call the "service inventory location" decision becomes critical. McDonald's must know how far consumers are willing to drive for a Big Mac, a question that produces different answers depending on the amount of competition, the driving habits of people in different parts of the market, and other factors.

Customers as Service Providers

Many service businesses have built their operating strategies around the idea of customers as service providers. Merely by transporting themselves to the point of service delivery, customers become a critical part of the logistics of service. But today we ask customers to do much more than this. We ask them to serve themselves in food and other retailing establishments, to input information accurately in information services, and to actually perform services themselves in do-it-yourself service businesses like discount furniture retailing, in which customers are given the option of transporting and even assembling their purchases. In fact, some companies have found that the involvement of customers in the delivery of services is an effective way of building customer loyalty.

Customers as Inventory

In many services, the unit of demand is the customer. And customers can be inventoried. For example, in a restaurant customers are regularly inventoried in a holding area often known as a bar. In fact, any service employing or requiring queuing or lines is inventorying customers. This practice heightens the importance of queue management for these services.

Unlike the queuing of product in manufacturing processes, however, human beings are much less cooperative and docile than manufactured product. They have minds, feelings, and very definite opinions of acceptable lengths of time they are willing to be inventoried. As a result, queue management in the service establishment requires a study of human behavior. For example, airlines have discovered that under most circumstances, five minutes is the maximum acceptable time that passengers are willing to be inventoried in a ticket counter line. Of course, the time might be much shorter near plane departure time. But this information is critical to the planning of capacity and the delivery of good service.

Fortunately, humans can be entertained and otherwise diverted from the task of waiting (being inventoried). The service logistics strategy of the Disney organization, for example, concentrates on entertaining visitors to its theme parks who actually spend most of their time waiting in lines but who enjoy performances by roving Disney characters or other diversions while doing so.

The Disney organization has for years maintained a group of operations specialists who concentrate not only on designing facilities to ease guest flow but also to "engineer" waiting facilities so that guests often cannot see the entire group of customers being inventoried for a particular attraction.[8] The potential dissatisfaction from this practice is lessened by Disney's extensive efforts to keep guests informed about the estimated lengths of their waits at various points in the line.

Location, Location, Location

The logistics of location is one of the most critical elements in the marketing of many services depending for their success on proximity to customers. Retail services ranging from department store to fast-food retailing have developed sophisticated techniques for analyzing trade patterns as well as the willingness of consumers to travel varying distances and cross natural or artificial barriers to travel.

Furthermore, in a multisite service like fast food, care must be taken to evaluate the degree to which one location can cannibalize, or detract from, sales at other locations. When such retail units are franchised, a misstep in this decision can lead to litigation.

Services taken to customers are more likely to face many of the same decisions required in locating plants and distribution centers in manufacturing logistics. But even here, the location decision is complicated by acceptable response times and the supply and location of service technicians, as well as the location of parts and equipment inventories. Such decisions, characteristic of much after-sale service activity in manufacturing, have received relatively less attention than the more traditional manufacturing logistics problems.

The Urban Location Challenge

Given the importance of accessibility to potential customers, as we have noted, certain service industries require urban or at least densely populated suburban locations for their success. By the same token, the high cost of such locations creates added incentives to minimize the amount of inventory held on site. As a result, industries like consumer retailing have long practiced a form of just-in-time inventory replenishment, a strategy exacerbated by the high value of certain types of retail products such as pharmaceuticals. Daily or even more frequent deliveries are the rule in such services.

The problem, of course, is that such frequent deliveries have to be achieved in a setting of dense population and traffic, often in vehicles incapable of making enough stops during a work shift to fully utilize carrying capacity. The result is extra urban congestion and pollution. An extreme example of this is Tokyo, where Japan's Ministry of Industry Trade and Information (MITI) has stepped in to study ways of reducing congestion from just-in-time delivery strategies that have frequently brought Tokyo's traffic to a stop and rendered the city's retailing activities even less productive than they already are.

Managing Demand and Supply

The management of supply lies at the heart of manufacturing logistics. In services, particularly where peaks in demands are especially severe, it is often impossible to inventory supply and very costly to meet all demands for service. Success often depends on the ability to manage demand as well as supply. This can be achieved both through marketing efforts and the inventorying of demand.

Marketing and Demarketing

Marketing efforts may be employed to shift demands for service from peak to slack periods. They may include pricing, such as the peak load pricing increases employed by power companies to reduce peak load demand, or off-season price reductions by airlines.

The service offering itself may be altered to accommodate customers with varying needs and tastes at various points in time. Hotels, for example, experiencing slack demand on weekends may design weekend packages to attract families or couples. Ski resorts are developing summer attractions like water slides which utilize the same assets but increase capacity utilization during out-of-ski-season periods.

Advertising and other communications are used to attract customers to nonpeak usage. In particular, power utilities have become increasingly creative in their information programs to educate power users in the effective use of their services. Where this involves discouraging customers to lower their long-run demands (in the case of power utilities, to preclude the need to build expensive new facilities), this practice has come to be known as "demarketing."

Even "distribution" strategies can be employed in the management of service demand. Thus, one benefit of the clustering of hotels in a given metropolitan area is that overflow demand for one hotel can often be accommodated at an alternative facility operated by the same company.

Inventorying Demand

Special attention in many services is given to two important ways of inventorying demand: queue management and reservation systems. We have already mentioned ways in which Disney expertly manages guests at its theme parks by making waiting time less onerous. In fact, the largely quantitative science of queuing theory has been greatly expanded in practical application to include a large component of psychology. As Maister has pointed out, the conditions under which people wait play a large part in determining the acceptability of the wait. Thus, he concludes, among other things, that people waiting alone perceive time passing more slowly than people waiting in a crowd or those whose attention is diverted away from the fact that they are waiting. The more valuable the service, the longer people are willing to wait. The longer people wait without being acknowledged by the "system," the longer waits seem (a phenomenon that explains why airline personnel in well-managed operations "work the back of the line" to make people at the end feel their problems are being addressed sooner than they are.)[9]

Reservation systems provide less painful means to the customer of inventorying demand. And they are most necessary where the capacity to supply a service has an absolute maximum, as in services operated with fixed seating capacity, for example. Such systems have become vital to companies offering several levels of service, expressed in terms of time, location, or other features, each commanding a different price.

Managing Service Supply

Two basic strategies for managing supply—the "chase demand" and "level-capacity" strategies—have been identified by Sasser.[10] The former may be most appropriate where peaks and valleys in demand are great and the costs of providing service are largely variable. For example, the daily "shape-up" of longshoremen on the waterfront provided the opportunity for terminal companies to pursue "chase demand" service strategies before unions organized workers and obtained assurances of more steady working conditions.

Organizations electing "level-demand" strategies must decide on the level of demand to satisfy. In such cases, more traditional inventory management, taking into account both the costs of meeting demand and the costs of the failure to meet it, is brought into play. In addition, of course, the costs of alternative means of inventorying supply and meeting demand must also be considered:

- Maximizing efficiency during periods of peak demand
- Using part-time employees and rental equipment
- Cross-training employees
- Sharing capacity
- Calling on employees to deliver superhuman effort

Work can be organized to perform nonessential jobs during slack periods and only the most essential tasks actually associated with the delivery of a service during periods of peak demand. Thus, housekeeping duties or maintenance activities often are performed on the least busy shift.

Personnel and equipment can be purchased from contractors. This has been an outstanding accomplishment of many organizations in downsizing by eliminating entire departments in which the amount of standby capacity has become very great. It accounts for the shift of many service activities from manufacturing firms that previously performed them themselves to outside contractors.

Employees can be trained to perform two or more jobs. Some of the most effective recent labor-management bargaining has resulted in greater flexibility in the assignment of employees. This has also resulted in more training and broader job classifications for service workers. For example, Southwest Airlines has achieved the lowest labor costs in the airline industry through the cross-training and job shifting, where necessary, of employees.

Capacity sharing is yet another way of inventorying supplies of services. Of course, it is a large part of what third-party service providers like freight carriers and public warehousing organizations sell. Increasingly, however, manufacturing and service firms alike are directly exploring the possibility of sharing capacity with companies engaged in compatible activities requiring some of the same kinds of capacity.

Capacity sharing is a major competitive weapon at firms like CompuServe, the diversified information services firm. Operating both a large computing facility and extensive network services (both intra- and intercompany), CompuServe prices its services to encourage business use during working hours and consumer use at night and on weekends.

As we have seen, most services are highly people-dependent. And the capacity of the human being is hard to measure, particularly during short periods of time. This perhaps explains why particularly professional services rely on superhuman effort to meet peaks in demand. Public accountants at tax time, medical professionals during emergencies, and investment bankers facing immediate deadlines all know that superhuman effort is a common method of meeting peaks; it is made possible by slack periods of demand that enable people to prepare physically and psychologically for demand peaks or to recover from them.

Heavy Use of Experiential Information

Experiential, or historical, data have long been used for inventory control purposes. Increasingly, they are being used to anticipate and even prevent demand for certain types of services.

The development of the experiential database is time-consuming but often very worthwhile. For example, it enables technicians at General Electric's Medical Systems division to anticipate maintenance needs and potential problems with the company's CAT scanners located throughout the world and become proactive in preventing problems from occurring. It enables American Express's Card division to approve rapidly card-associated purchases that fall within a pattern of past usage, described either in terms of size of purchase or purchase location. And it enables Schlumberger to sell the experience it has obtained in helping drillers find oil at a majority of the world's oil wells, experience that includes the carefully collected and organized information about the geological structure of every major oil field in the world.

By combining reservation systems with methods of collecting demand history and reserving the supply of service on the basis of forecasts of likely demand, a few firms have created so-called yield management programs to obtain the greatest total revenue from available service capacity. Airlines, for example, have elevated yield management to a science built around the experiential database. A yield management system is based on the recognition that the same service may have different value for different customers. Thus, the business traveler values a seat at several times that for a pleasure traveler on no particular schedule. From historical information, seats can then be held longer in the yield management system for business travelers typically making their plans much closer to the time of departure. Through yield management, airlines achieve higher per-seat-mile revenues than their competitors, making yield management an important competitive weapon.

In fact, yield management has been cited as playing a role in hastening certain airline bankruptcies. "Field management" is the process of matching seats with those people willing to pay the most for them. It requires collecting and processing data sufficient to give airline managers a required level of confidence that seats held close to flight time (not sold in advance at low prices to economy-seeking travelers) will be purchased for full price by those business travelers unable to plan their travel far in advance. It is perhaps the most sophisticated form of inventory management for either products or services today in an industry in which the difference between large profits and loss may be whether an airline is able to sell 15% or 25% of its seats at full fare.

People Express, which did not have such a system, fell prey to competitors who used their yield management programs to selectively cut fares on certain seats to capture economy-minded People Express customers while holding fares on other seats for full-fare paying customers.

Donald Burr, CEO of People Express at the time, commented that competitors "were able to harness that [yield management] technology to set their prices at or lower than People Express on a point-specific basis . . . They were able to compete with low cost procedures in a very specific way without trashing their yields."[11] Clearly, a failure to combine superior technology with superior information management in part accounted for People Express's demise.

The Centrality of Networks

Whether described in terms of physical facilities, information, or relationships, networks and their management are central to the success of many service enterprises.

The hub-and-spoke network used with such great success for years by UPS was given greater visibility more recently by Federal Express as it elevated the concept to a national level. This provided the model for many airline organizations applying the concept to human freight. But it is also the underlying concept for the distribution warehouse that serves as a mixing point for products made at several specialized manufacturing plants.

Networking is becoming a common term too in the collection, communication, and particularly sharing of information. It is at the heart of the fastest-growing form of transportation—wire. It has provided business opportunities for new "carriers," like CompuServe, as well as the more traditional competitors, like AT&T. The communications and information network makes possible electronic data interchange, which is becoming more critical in the efficient inventory and distribution of tangible goods.

A heavy reliance on networks comprising business relationships distinguishes many services. This is certainly true of all brokers, whether the service being brokered is investment banking or automobile leasing. Networks, or relationships, are about all that investment bankers have to sell. And even firms like PHH corporation, which leases fleets of autos and trucks as well as providing a range of services associated with the relocation of employees, defines its very distinctive expertise in terms of its ability to create and manage relationships.

Implications for Future Research

Differences between the logistics of manufacturing and services raise a number of questions about past and future emphases on our efforts to understand good management practice and improve upon it. They start with the very definition of good service.

Quality of service is defined by the most widely used quantitative techniques in terms of five generic dimensions: reliability, responsiveness, assurance, empathy, and tangible evidence (provided to the service purchaser). And yet in considering the logistics of good service, we know that proximity to customers is critical to the success of many services. This suggests the need to broaden our definition of service quality to at least include accessibility of the service to the buyer. And it raises the question of whether we adequately recognize the importance of customer inputs to the service delivery effort. Although this phenomenon is clearly understood by retailers like Levitz furniture stores, which reward customers for carrying out logistics activities such as the transport of their own purchases, it is often overlooked in logistics research.

With the exception of La Londe and a few other researchers, we have left urban logistics to traffic engineers. And yet the future of many city center–oriented services and in a broader sense the cities themselves is at risk if we do not concentrate on ways not only to make them more pleasant places to live and work but also better places to do business, in part through more efficient logistics services in such congested areas.

Experiential databases provide the backbone for many services. And yet our understanding of them is minimal. For one thing, the database, even though it may be the most valuable of assets, often carries no value on a company's balance sheet. It accumulates value over time. But is such value cumulative or even geometrically increasing in its nature? And under what circumstances? Can any of what we have learned from extensive research about networks and their characteristics be applied to examinations of experiential databases?

As Barry and Coyle have suggested, questions raised by the logistics of services call for a redefinition of logistics itself.[12] They have provided a useful starting point for rethinking such a definition.

Implications for Logistics Management

Over the past several decades, logistics has evolved and matured in the manufacturing sector of the economy. It has received notoriety, and depending upon the company or industry, has gained increased stature in the organization. These advances have produced a body of knowledge with its own jargon and, even more important, a large segment of management engaged in "generally accepted logistics procedures."

For many manufacturing logistics practitioners, the concepts associated with service response logistics will appear as different as those used to describe the other functional areas of their own organization. A major challenge facing the profession is the development of a bridge that will enable the transfer of concepts, technologies, and management concepts from traditional supply chain logistics to service response logistics, and vice versa.

In the research conducted by Barry and Coyle, four industries (hospitals, telephone compa-

TABLE 41-1
Service Response Equivalents to
Supply Chain Activities

Supply Chain Activity	**Service Response Activity**
Sales forecasting	Service request forecasting
Sourcing/purchasing	Partnership development, staff hiring, data acquisition
Production planning	Staff and equipment scheduling, distribution channel selection, capacity planning
Inbound transportation	Data collection, customer (e.g., patient) pickup, repair part pickup
Inventory management	Capacity management, database management, customer record management, personnel training
Warehousing	Data/information storage, retrieval, and management
Customer service	Quality measurement and management, expediting, billing
Order processing	Interfacing, assessing need, negotiation, and committing to the customer, monitoring delivery process
Distribution systems	Network layout, network planning, systems planning, channel planning
Field warehousing	Data/information storage, retrieval, and management
Distribution control	Network control, communications control
Intracompany transportation	Personnel/customer movement, data/information movement
Distribution administration	Network administration
Outbound transportation	Customer reporting, service engineering routing, and scheduling to customer transportation sites

Source: *Logistics in Service Industries* (Oak Brook, Ill.: Council of Logistics Management, 1991), pp. 12–13.

nies, retail banking, and high-tech field service) were analyzed to determine the applications to services of logistics management concepts broadly practiced in the manufacturing sector. One of the most important elements of that research was the development of a table suggesting equivalent terminology for supply chain and service response logistics (Table 41-1).

Our discussion suggests that the logistics of services cannot be as neatly packaged organizationally as even the logistics function in a manufacturing firm, which has been debated in print for at least the last 30 years. One function or manager will not be responsible for computing, communications, location, the development of networks and experiential databases, and the management of the demand and supply patterns for a particular service.

The diffuse nature of logistics in service organizations may lead us to overlook opportunities in practice for establishing competitive superiority. It suggests the need to broaden our areas of interest and training to enable managers to prepare themselves for the demands of retailing, communications, or financial service firms with which they may be associated. And it implies that the skills required to manage logistical challenges in service organizations will continue to be found in a number of ways and places outside the traditional boundaries of manufacturing-oriented logistics organizations.

It suggests the need to think of logistics not as an organizational function or a set of activities but as a way of thinking about and solving problems faced in business, whether the business is manufacturing or service-producing. This mind-set will encourage us both to focus on new issues and to broaden our outlook as researchers, educators, and managers.

Notes

1. James L. Heskett, W. Earl Sasser, Jr., and Christopher W. L. Hart, *Service Breakthroughs* (New York: Free Press, 1990), pp. 5–10.
2. Jack Barry and John J. Coyle, "Logistics in the Service Industries: A Summary of Findings," in *Annual Conference Proceedings, Council of Logistics Management,* September 29–October 2, 1991, p. 207.
3. This section draws heavily on work by Jack Barry and John J. Coyle for a Council of Logistics Management–commissioned study on logistics in the service industries. The study was performed by Arthur D. Little.
4. Ibid.
5. Ibid.
6. Jan Carlzon, *Moments of Truth* (Cambridge, Mass.: Ballinger, 1987).
7. Stanley M. Davis, *Future Perfect* (Reading, Mass.: Addison-Wesley, 1987).
8. Richard Saltus, "Lines Lines Lines Lines Lines . . . The Experts Are Trying to Ease the Wait," *Boston Globe*, October 5, 1992, pp. 39, 42.
9. David A. Maister, "The Psychology of Waiting Lines," in John A. Czepiel, Michael R. Soloman, and Carol F. Surprenant, eds., *The Service Encounter* (Lexington, Mass.: D.C. Heath, 1985), pp. 113–23.
10. W. Earl Sasser, "Match Supply and Demand in Service Industries," *Harvard Business Review* (November-December 1971): 74–80.
11. Daniel F. Cuff, "Builder of People Express Links Failure to Technology," *New York Times*, October 31, 1988, p. D-A.
12. Barry and Coyle.

CHAPTER 42

Logistics Technology in the Twenty-first Century

T. Ron Gable
John A. White

Judging from the degree of change that has been experienced in logistics during the past decade, we can expect significant changes to continue to occur during the balance of the decade and well into the next century.[1] To take advantage of those changes, we must understand the driving forces for them. The primary "driver for change" in logistics technology will be profitability, which will be strongly influenced by global competition, human resources, environmental impact, and critical technologies. This chapter examines the technologies expected to be critical to the competitive delivery of logistics services in the twenty-first century.

Global Competition

Firms compete in many ways, including product function and features, price, quality, timeliness, and customer service. Logistics plays a major role in providing timely and competitive service to customers; it is also the largest component of cost for many firms. Furthermore, the quality of the delivered product is critically dependent on the quality of the logistics service. As firms reduce the time required to go from product design to delivery to customers, product function and features will provide only a short-term competitive advantage. Hence, corporate executives will place greater emphasis on logistics providing a competitive advantage during the coming decade.[2]

It is clear that increasing emphasis will be given to time-based competition and quick-response systems; increased attention to customer-supplier partnerships will result in error-free, rapid responses to market demands.[3] Shifting expectations for overnight delivery, for example, will dramatically impact the design of the logistics system.

An example of a new paradigm that will emerge in creating strategic linkages among suppliers, customers, and customers' customers is provided by Milliken and Company. It formed "three-way partnerships" involving Milliken, garment manufacturers, and retailers. In one such partnership, Milliken obtained information daily on individual sales that occurred in the retail stores. Rather than wait for garment manufacturers' fabric orders based on forecasts, Milliken determined fabric needs based on retailers' sales and produced orders on a quick-response basis. The results were extremely positive for all three parties.

Why did Milliken decide to focus on its customer's customer? It was a matter of survival!

Imports were destroying the domestic garment industry. Milliken could achieve its goals by depending on an export strategy. However, history showed that garment manufacturers depended on domestic suppliers of fabric. Milliken's long-term interests required a healthy domestic garment industry and Milliken realized it needed to do all it could to help its customers remain profitable.[4]

JIT II, the purchasing and transportation program developed by Bose, is another example of the new paradigm in vendor-customer partnerships. The responsibility for purchasing critical components for Bose's products was given to suppliers. Although this might sound like letting a fox manage the chicken coop, Bose found that the quality of the components increased, their cost decreased, and it received parts in a more timely fashion than before. Its partnership with a transportation firm resulted in on-time delivery increasing substantially with the carrier. Bose and its suppliers strongly support the partnership arrangement they created.[5]

In addition to the creation of partnerships among suppliers and customers, it is expected that "designer logistics" will become standard. "Designer logistics" means a logistics system specifically designed to meet the needs of an individual customer. The "customer is king" attitude is expected to continue and increase to the point that private labeling is likely to become a dominant force in retailing. The impact on the logistics system of individualized attention to customers will be significant.

As an example, if a firm must insert special promotional literature in each package for a particular customer, then should the firm store generic product in bulk, so that packaging and literature insertion occur at the same time? If a knit shirt is sold to multiple customers each of whom requires a special label, when should the label be sewn in the shirt? Should inventories of unlabeled shirts be maintained as well as labeled shirts, or should labeling, packaging, and literature insertion occur in a continuous flow process? If a continuous flow process is used, should those steps be performed at the manufacturing plant or the distribution center? If a postponement strategy is used, why is there a need for the distribution center? These questions illustrate the impact of customer service on the design of the logistics system.

The move toward common markets and the need for firms to have a significant "presence" in markets within which they compete will impact decisions concerning the location of research and development, manufacturing, assembly, and logistics "hubs." Because of the role of logistics in a firm's competitive position, location decisions will weigh more heavily the contribution of logistics to market share and profitability.

Human Resources

What will the logistics workforce look like in the twenty-first century? What will be its demographic makeup? What will be the education level? What will be the strength and dexterity of the logistics worker?

Even though technology will have a significant impact on the delivery of logistics services, the dependence on well-educated individuals to create, improve, operate, and manage technology will play a greater role in the twenty-first century than it did in the twentieth century. Owing to the prospect of increased demand for an anticipated shrinking pool of qualified personnel, logistics firms will have to rely more heavily on technology and make continuing investments in training and developing the personnel currently employed.

Computerized logistics workstations will play a significant role in the next century. It is evident that coupling very sophisticated optimization packages with significantly improved computing speed will allow expert systems to be placed in the hands of logistics personnel at affordable prices.[6] However, such systems will continue to rely on trained personnel.

In addition to "intelligence" issues, human resources will have a significant impact on logistics practice because of an aging workforce. Additionally, governmental regulations and humane practice will restrict the weight an individual will be permitted to lift. The design of beverage containers, for example, will be affected because of the limitations on how much weight a delivery person or stocking clerk is allowed to lift in restocking shelves in a supermarket.

Ergonomic considerations will play a greater role in the design of warehousing and materials handling systems, including loading and unloading of transport carriers. As a result, it is expected that technology will be developed for movement of small loads, those between 25 and 50 pounds, for use at workstations, on receiving and shipping docks, and in trailers and railcars.

Environmental Impact

The impact of logistics on the environment is significant.[7] For this reason, it is anticipated that environmental controls will dramatically impact logistics practices in the next century. The energy required for transportation, coupled with stringent emission controls, may result in significantly changed methods for inner-city deliveries. Pooling of small-parcel deliveries might be mandated. Underground delivery of merchandise might become a necessity; as a result, mass transit systems heretofore used almost exclusively to transport people may assume a greater role in materials transport.

The Japanese Technology Evaluation Center (JTEC) of the National Science Foundation (NSF) sponsored a comparison of materials handling technology in the United States and Japan. The study noted Japan's investment in tunneling with the expectation that much of the logistics activity would be performed underground in Japan and other highly congested areas of the world.[8]

Not only will the transportation dimension of logistics be impacted by environmental concerns but also the design and packaging of products will be affected. The use of environmentally benign materials for products and packaging/packing materials will increase. Recycling of products and materials will result in as much attention being given to reverse flow as forward flow in logistics systems. Returnable containers and goods will pose new challenges to logistics system designers. Fast-food chains, grocery stores, shoe manufacturers, electronics assemblers, automobile manufacturers—all will be affected significantly by the drive to ensure that logistics is an environmentally neutral function.

Critical Technologies

The technologies critical to the delivery of logistics services include modeling, transportation, communications, and materials handling.

Modeling Technologies

Significant advances in computing power, database generation, automatic matrix generation, and optimization codes have made it possible to expect network design and vehicle routing and dispatching decisions to be made quickly and optimally in the twenty-first century. Logistics workstations have been developed to facilitate human decision makers interacting with very powerful computers. In the future, massively parallel processors will be available to support routine logistics decisions. The only excuse for not taking advantage of the modeling technology will be "I don't know how." The popular excuses "I can't afford it" and "It doesn't apply to my problem" will be eliminated.

Massive databases are being developed, including not only geographic information systems (GIS) but also economic data. The U.S. government, as well as private firms, are making sizable investments in the development of databases that will be of enormous value to logisticians. Freight rates for all modes and materials categories and point-to-point distances, exact to individual residences, are available to logisticians who must make decisions quickly, accurately, and repeatedly.

Because of the extraordinary speed with which combinations can be evaluated, enumeration and quasi-enumeration approaches will displace heuristics in many logistics applications. Exact solutions will be obtained from optimization codes for problems heretofore unresolvable. For example, researchers at Georgia Tech have worked with a number of firms and agencies to solve large-scale optimization problems. In one case, a fleet assignment problem for Delta Air Lines involved 41,325 constraints and 62,088 decision variables, and the computer run time required to solve the problem was only 43 minutes.[9]

Large network optimization problems can also be solved by IBM PC–class microcomputers. For example, problems with 8,000 nodes and over 100,000 arcs have been solved on an IBM PC/AT.[10] A generalized network optimization (GNO) system was developed for use on an IBM 4341 minicomputer to solve large-scale military logistics problems involving up to 3 million arcs; the code was rewritten in the C language to create the microcomputer version. In addition to vehicle routing and scheduling decisions, significant advances have occurred in the development of warehouse design models and facility location models.[11]

Transportation Technologies

Transportation modes include air, sea, and land, with the latter including rail, over-the-road motor carriers, and pipelines (which are excluded from this discussion). It is anticipated that speed and delivered capacities will increase among all options; furthermore, it is expected that environmental considerations will result in changes in engine design and power sources for a number of transportation technologies.

The greatest potential change in transportation technology will be the intelligent vehicle highway system (IVHS). Considerable attention is already being given to IVHS in Europe and Japan. The technologies being pursued include new materials and design strategies for highways, intelligent controls along the highway as well as in the vehicle, and sophisticated communications technologies to allow real-time control and dispatching of vehicles at high speeds.

Although it is premature to provide specifics regarding the impact on logistics, it is anticipated that designated highways, corridors, or lanes will be used to speed the movement of carriers. Moreover, as the IVHS becomes more widely accepted, payloads of delivery vehicles will be increased significantly via tandem loading and larger trailers.

The NSF JTEC study of materials handling technology noted the progress being made in Japan in the development of high-speed rail and water transport. Through the use of superconductivity and magnetic levitation (MagLev), significant advances are being made.[12] The developments in high-speed water transport are expected to make sea transport more competitive, as well as generate increased use of river and canal transport.

In the United States, the intermodal movement, primarily using trucks for short-haul moves and rail for long-haul moves, is expected to grow. Furthermore, strategic linkages among trucking firms and rail firms are expected to increase. A few mega-firms will evolve and provide a full range of transportation services.

Communication Technologies

Telecommunications, electronic data interchange (EDI), automatic identification, and radio data communication are among the technologies that will impact logistics in the next century. Telecommunications will play an increasingly important role in ensuring the visibility of inventory and carriers throughout the supply chain. Real-time tracking and dispatching, for example, will require affordable and reliable telecommunications when carriers are distributed over large geographic areas.[13]

Automatic Identification

Automatic identification technology has grown rapidly over the past two decades and is expected to experience increased usage over the coming decade. A $3.6 billion industry in 1990, it is expected to exceed $20 billion by the turn of the century. Although speed, reliability, and cost have improved significantly for all members of the automatic identification product family, for the foreseeable future it is expected that *bar codes* will continue to be the dominant automatic identification technology.[14]

While UPC/EAN continues to be the dominant code on finished products, changes are occurring in the popularity of industrial codes. Whereas Code 39 and Interleaved 2 of 5 have been adopted as standards for many groups, Code 128 is growing in popularity. Additionally, high-density codes, called "stacked symbologies," have been developed to facilitate the storage of information in less space. Two examples of high-density codes are Code 49 and Code 16K. High-density codes pack many times more information in the same amount of space as conventional codes. Or, more important, high-density codes provide the same information in dramatically fewer amounts space.

In addition to requiring two-dimensional scanning due to stacking of symbology, high-density codes are expected to be developed utilizing machine vision technology to achieve fast and accurate identification without having to identify the object itself. The primary impediments to *machine vision* as an automatic identification technology have been speed and cost. Structured symbologies (including the use of colors) is reducing the number of pixel combinations required to identify objects. This allows application of less sophisticated variants of machine vision, increasing speed and lowering cost. One approach being evaluated involves the use of a 2-D dot matrix encoding technique.

The use of machine vision for automatic identification is being accelerated not only by the development of structured codes but also by the use of small, solid-state charge-couple-device (CCD) cameras having better resolution than their predecessors. Although high-density codes might not have a significant impact on logistics systems outside manufacturing, it is expected that they will gain market share in the electronics, automotive, and food and beverage industries in product identification and tracking applications.

Radio frequency (RF) and *surface acoustical wave* (SAW) tags are used to identify products, containers, carriers, and other items. In logistics, RF tags have been applied the most in identifying, tracking, and controlling access of railcars, sea containers, trucks, buses, and automobiles. Because of their cost, RF tags have not proven to be competitive with barcoding and tend to be applied where line-of-sight and/or environmental conditions precluded other means of automatic identification.

Even though increased use of bar codes, machine vision, RF, and SAW in logistics is anticipated, this is not the situation for all members of the automatic identification family. For example, it is not expected that optical character recognition (OCR) and magnetic stripe identification will gain "market share" in logistics during the coming decade.

Although not technically a member of the automatic identification technology product family, *voice recognition systems* facilitate the identification of product and data entry process and hence deserve brief mention. Voice recognition systems have not been used extensively in materials handling or warehousing. However, because of their use in appliances, toys and games, and security systems, they have improved in reliability, user friendliness, and cost. For this reason, it is anticipated that they will become more significant in data entry. Depending on the discipline applied to labeling packages and cartons from suppliers, the receiving function is a potential area for application of voice recognition systems, owing to the tremendous variety of labels encountered and their frequently poor legibility. If labels can be read only by the human eye, then voice recognition is an ideal means of entering data into computer systems without having to generate a bar code label or manually key in data at a terminal.

Whereas decisions concerning automatic identification technologies were made in the past as either-or decisions, it is expected that the future generation of automatic identification systems will consist of integrated technologies. For example, rather than using exclusively bar codes or magnetic stripes, a system may involve a combination of bar code, machine vision, RF, and voice recognition with interfaced communication and data transfer.

Managers should be aware that a high degree of synergism exists between EDI and barcodes. Namely, EDI and barcodes have produced increased use of each other. The ability to communicate accurately, rapidly, and economically across the supply chain will depend on broadscale application of automatic identification. Simply stated, humans cannot perform data entry as quickly or as accurately as automatic systems. For EDI to be viable, it must have accurate data entry.[15]

Radio Data Communication

Handheld and lift truck radio data terminals (RDTs) have become very important in warehousing and materials handling. With handheld wands and portable laser scanners, bar code data are entered into the RDT and communicated to the warehouse or materials handling control computer. Via RDTs, conventional warehouse and materials handling operations are able to maintain real-time linkages with their host computers and thus achieve timely and accurate data entry, tracking, status, location verification, and dispatching of personnel and equipment. These operational changes have dramatically improved productivity and database quality.

Although RDTs have traditionally had their greatest impact on inventory control, the on-line mobile feature, coupled with increasingly sophisticated software and enlarged storage capacity, will play a significant role in providing RF links in local area networks linked to larger RF networks controlling the supply chain. RDTs are not limited to in-plant or in-warehouse applications.

Material Handling Technologies

To facilitate a consideration of materials handling technology in the twenty-first century,[16] consider the five generations of materials handling that have evolved to date:

1. Manual
2. Mechanized
3. Automated
4. Integrated
5. Intelligent

The fifth generation, intelligent materials handling, will play a greater role in future logistics systems. Intelligent materials handling systems are expected to have the greatest impact on design and practice over the next several years.

Materials handling includes moving, storing, protecting, and controlling materials. A broader definition is providing the right amount of the right material at the right place, at the right time, in the right sequence, in the right condition, in the right orientation, and at the right cost by using the right methods.[17] This portion of the chapter considers each of the five materials handling generations and concludes with consideration of the NSF JTEC results.[18]

First-Generation—Manual

The first materials handling generation involves moving, storing, protecting, and controlling material *manually.* Although it has existed since the first order (an apple) was picked, first-generation materials handling occurs to some degree in contemporary installations. A high percentage of human activity in logistics is involved in performing first-generation materials handling.

Although many argue that we live in the "automation age" and most materials handling publications, courses, and conferences focus primarily on later-generation solutions, first-generation materials handling is more the rule than the exception. Also, first-generation solutions continue to be *the correct solutions* for many materials handling requirements.

The use of manual pushcarts and dollies to facilitate materials movement, the use of bin shelving and modular storage drawers for materials storage, and the use of cards, forms, and kanbans to achieve materials control are examples of first-generation materials handling. First-generation materials handling occurs at and between workstations. Also, it is common to find significant levels of manual materials handling even when a high degree of mechanization and/or automation occurs, such as a person lifting a tote box of material from a conveyor or placing a tote box in a miniload AS/RS pan.

First-generation materials handling systems regained their respectability during the late 1980s and early 1990s because of the success of just-in-time (JIT). JIT advocates were highly critical of all but first-generation materials handling solutions. They argued that "human cart pushers" were more flexible than other materials handling technologies, and the resulting face-to-face contact stimulated communication and reduced "process-to-process problems."

Because first-generation materials handling systems are the "economic choice" in many situations, why is so little attention paid to designing them? Often, workstations are poorly designed, both in terms of ergonomics and materials handling. Excessive reaching results from poorly positioned materials and improper workplace dimensions; inefficient movement between workstations occurs owing to poorly designed layouts; accidents occur because of excessive lifting; and other basic materials handling principles are often ignored when designing first-generation systems.

Experience suggests that the solution most often overlooked in terms of its potential economic benefits is the first generation. When first-generation systems are feasible, if the system design received as much attention as later-generation systems, it probably would be difficult to justify some elements of later-generation systems. Products designed for automatic assembly, for example, often can be assembled manually at far less expense. Similarly, in designing materials handling systems, first-generation solutions often emerge as the winner.

The number of materials handling–related accidents denotes the lack of attention given to designing first-generation materials handling systems. Materials handling activities are the major source of industrial accidents. Many such accidents are lower-back injuries due to manual lifting. If adequate attention were given to the design of first-generation systems, all such accidents could be eliminated. For example, using properly designed containers; using ball transfer tables; and standardizing the height for workplaces, AGV beds, and conveyors would eliminate lifting heavy loads.

Manual movement of material is a serious issue. Many governments, especially in Europe, have significantly reduced the maximum allowable weight an individual may lift. As a result, smaller containers are being used and loads greater than 25 to 35 pounds are being eliminated from first-generation systems. According to one U.S. engineer, "We must design containers to be either so small that it would be impossible to overload them or so large that no person would attempt to lift them manually—anything in between will result in lost time accidents." More attention must be paid to manual materials handling, and greater emphasis must be given to designing materials handling systems in which humans are integral components.[19]

Second-Generation—Mechanized

Second-generation materials handling includes conveyors, industrial trucks, industrial manipulators, monorails, cranes, and hoists to move material; the storage of material in racks, shelving, carousels, and storage racks using human-controlled storage and retrieval equipment; the protection of material by unitizing it with straps, stretch-wrap, and shrink-wrap, as well as applying foam-in-place, inner packing, and dunnage; and the use of limit switches, solenoids, mechanical stops, and mechanical "dogs" to control equipment.

Although mechanized handling predates the Egyptians' use of gourds, rope, and a wheel to pump water, it was not until the late 1800s that considerable impetus was given to using mechanized handling methods. Second-generation systems continued to represent the state-of-the-art until automated solutions emerged after World War II.

In one of the earliest books on materials handling, Hunt claimed that two principles govern the economical handling of materials: *perform only the handling operations that are absolutely necessary, and perform these operations in the way that secures the lowest cost.* He noted:

> The solving of handling problems is secured not only by the use of mechanical devices, but also by the attitude of mind of the designer. A proper mental attitude toward the work is a prerequisite to success. If the manager is convinced that the problem is worth solving from the manufacturing standpoint, and thoroughly believes that simplicity of mechanism and method are not only essential, but are the direct evidence of a wise solution, he will reject the various plans contemplated and refuse to consider his work accomplished until he has an absolutely simple plan with which to do the work.[20]

Despite claims by some JIT zealots who have fallen in love with first-generation solutions and believe they are *the* materials handling solution, mechanized handling is still the economical method of moving, storing, protecting, and controlling materials with certain requirements. As noted, manual handling is *the correct solution* for many applications. However, first-generation handling does not always dominate later-generations, especially second-generation handling.

Mechanized handling extends a human's capacity in terms of speed, precision, and repeatability of movement; weight lifted and carried; extent of reach; and endurance. Although some claim that manual handling is more flexible than later-generation solutions, if one defines flexibility in terms of the ability to accommodate variable requirements for speed, precision, repeatability, weight, height, and endurance, then it is clear that first-generation solutions are not always more flexible than second-generation solutions.

Another claimed benefit of manual handling is the person-to-person communication between successive operations. If that is the primary reason for choosing a first-generation solution, then one must question the choice, given today's "communication age." Many highly effective communication options are available in addition to face-to-face contacts.

Having briefly considered the positive aspects of second-generation handling methods, we must note the downside of mechanized handling: capital investment, maintenance costs, and technological obsolescence. Preventive maintenance programs and planned replacement programs are essential to second-generation solutions continuing to be the *long-run economic choice.*

The choice between first- and second-generation handling involves trade-offs between capital investments and operating expenses. In an environment where handling requirements change radically, capital investments are difficult to justify. Also, when second-generation equipment is in place, it is often difficult to justify replacing equipment "that still works" with equipment having improved performance characteristics.

In general, materials handling is undercapitalized in U.S. industry; greater attention is paid to maintaining and upgrading materials handling equipment in Europe and Japan than in the United States. The if-it-ain't-broke-don't-fix-it philosophy is certainly not benefiting the United States. Instead, firms should consider adopting the approach of one particularly progressive firm: management requires that continued use of all equipment older than five years be rigorously justified.[21]

THIRD-GENERATION—AUTOMATED

Third-generation materials handling—automated materials handling—is not new! Many logistics managers appear to believe that the third-generation appeared on the materials handling scene during the past decade. In fact, the earliest patents for automated guided vehicles, automatic palletizers, automated storage and retrieval machines, automatic identification, robots, and automatic sortation systems were issued in the 1950s and 1960s—over 30 years ago! During the 1970s and 1980s, automatic controls were added to monorails, lift trucks, carousels, towlines, flow racks, cranes, and other handling equipment.

Initially, the demand from the user community was for increased hardware sophistication. As a result, sophisticated hardware controls were developed. However, owing to the rapid development of computer technology during the 1970s and 1980s, the demand soon shifted to increased sophistication in the methods used to control materials and other manufacturing and distribution operations. Unfortunately, the demand for sophistication outpaced the ability to deliver the required software. As a result, a number of horror stories emerged in which systems were delayed for years and cost overruns exceeded original quotations. The need for simplicity of design learned by the first and second generations was relearned by the third generation.

Hunt's advice concerning the use of purchased versus homemade equipment is applicable today in terms of materials handling hardware and software:

> It must be constantly borne in mind that manufacturing plants are built and operated to produce their own products. They are not jobbing shops to do engineering work and conduct experiments in handling apparatus. Therefore, purchase your apparatus; don t make it. To make it takes time and machines that should be devoted to the manufacture of your product. Of course there are cases in which novel apparatus is required which cannot be purchased, but they are comparatively few. And the greatest care should be exercised when deciding this point, as it will frequently be found that the special device is dictated by a misapprehension of the actual needs, or a lack of application of standard devices that can be used with slight modification.[22]

Too many firms insist that a supplier provide customized software or write their own software, rather than purchasing standard, off-the-shelf packages "that can be used with slight modification."

If only one of the four dimensions of materials handling (moving, storing, protecting, and controlling material) is to be automated, then automating the controlling dimension is advisable. Examples of third-generation computer control being provided in conjunction with first- or second-generation movement, storage, or protection include linking lift trucks and the computer via radio terminals, using computer prompts in flow racks for manual order picking, placing computer terminals on manual pushcarts in order picking, and the use of automatic identification equipment in an otherwise first- or second-generation system.

Note that "control" includes both hardware or machine control and management or systems control. Although some prefer to distinguish between the hardware control technology required to control a storage/retrieval machine and management control technology required to control a warehouse, the two are actually attempting to do the same thing: obtain a desired response from a given set of inputs. The difference, of course, in machine and management controls is that machines are easier to "control" than people.

A promising development in control systems for warehouses is object-oriented programming. Too often, a disconnect occurs between the design of a warehouse system and the control system that is produced. A major reason for this is the handoff of responsibility from the warehouse system designer and the control system designer. With object-oriented programming, one should be able to produce the control system directly from the warehouse system design.

Given the rapid improvements in communications technology and the competitive pressures to gain market share in information, control systems will surely play a greater role in logistics systems in the coming decade than in any past decade. It has been said that the person or organization that controls information controls the world. This has certainly proven to be true in the world of logistics. However, for the control system to deliver maximum advantage, it must move beyond third-generation thinking and embrace fourth- and fifth-generation thinking.

Fourth-Generation—Integrated

During the late 1970s and early 1980s, as automation was applied in more and more areas within manufacturing and distribution, it became apparent that the resulting "islands of automation" needed to be integrated. Soon after, the concept of integrated systems was being heralded as the "ultimate solution."

From a review of magazines and conference brochures, one could conclude that the decades from the late 1800s through the 1950s were the era of mechanized handling; the decades of the 1960s and 1970s were the automated handling era; and the decades of the 1980s and 1990s were the integrated handling era. However, even though the emphasis during the latter decades has been on integrated systems, few "true" integrated systems have been installed. Instead, piecemeal, incremental approaches have been used. The resulting systems tended to be interfaced, not integrated.

The promised synergistic benefit of systems integration was that "the whole would be greater than the sum of its parts." However, incremental justification procedures failed to capture fully the benefits of integration. As a result, it was difficult to justify systemwide integration.

What are the implications of the current status of integrated systems for the twenty-first century? First, it is obvious that the fourth generation has not fully matured. Second, if systemwide integration is to occur, individual components will need to "lose their identities"; instead of separate control systems for distribution and manufacturing, a single control system should exist in an integrated system. Third, a firm might not want to have integrated systems; interfaced systems might be exactly what the firm needs *at this point in time.* Fourth, not only have firms failed to integrate materials handling hardware and software, they have also not integrated the materials handling function across the manufacturing and distribution organization.

In essence, an integrated system should be viewed as a single machine rather than a collection of machines. In a more limited context, this occurs in the design of multispindle, multifunctional machine tools, where the movement, storage, protection, and control of tooling and work pieces is an *integral* part of the machine. Similar combinations of functions occurred in developing automatic packaging and automatic palletizing machines.

The single machine concept provides a useful goal for those who strive for integrated systems. In a vast number of instances, the bottlenecks to achieving a single machine version of a warehouse are logistics, not technological, bottlenecks. The primary problems to be overcome appear to be those associated with moving, storing, protecting, and controlling materials, containers, supplies, and scrap. The solution to these problems depends critically on eliminating unexpected variation in the system.

Based on the National Bureau of Standards' terminology, the resulting integrated system might be a "virtual machine," not a single, physical machine. The virtual machine would behave like, but not necessarily resemble, a single machine. Within the virtual machine, first-, second-, and third-generation materials handling technologies would be used. Hence, fourth-generation solutions might involve integrating (or interfacing) people, equipment, and control systems.[23]

Fifth-Generation—Intelligent

The fifth-generation—intelligent handling—is only in an embryonic state compared with previous generations. It is important to distinguish between artificial (or machine) intelligence and natural (or human) intelligence. In the case of materials handling, both play important roles.

Although artificial intelligence (AI) and its associated expert systems have not had the expected impact on logistics practice and design, recent signs of progress suggest that the fifth generation will play a prominent role in the twenty-first century. Expert systems are being used by automated guided vehicles and "smart" monorails in making on-line routing and dispatching decisions. In receiving and shipping, expert systems are being sought to direct a robot in palletizing or depalletizing mixed loads, unloading or loading delivery trucks, and assigning storage locations to mixed loads. To assist the designer, expert systems have been developed to configure AGV guide paths and buffers and to configure and select storage technologies for unit loads and small parts.

However, for AI to have the maximum payoff, it must be based on a firm foundation of natural intelligence. Because the quality of its performance will be no better than the quality of its input, it is important for natural intelligence to precede artificial intelligence; an expert is needed if an expert system is to be developed. More attention must be given to educating upper and middle management concerning the role of materials handling in integrated systems.

An important dimension of intelligent materials handling is the development of increased understanding concerning best practice in designing, implementing, and operating materials handling systems. The maturation of the field, coupled with intense professional development programs, has resulted in the availability of a large number of very capable material handling professionals.

Above all, in designing fifth-generation logistics systems, it is important to learn the lessons from the past. Hunt's advocacy of "simplicity of mechanism and method" and admonition to "avoid as you would the plague, hampering your imagination or 'falling in love' with your own scheme" will be as applicable in 2020 as it was in 1920!

JTEC Study

The NSF JTEC study of materials handling technology found that much greater emphasis was given to third-generation materials handling in Japan than in the United States.[24] The study team evaluated the current status of materials handling technology in Japan, as well as the trends for the technologies. Furthermore, they considered both technology development and technology application.

In assessing the current status of *development,* it was concluded that Japan was ahead of the United States in miniload AS/RS, small automated electrified monorails (AEMs), sorting transfer vehicles (STVs), rotary racks, intelligent pick carts, light-aided picking, clean room systems, dock management, and implementation time and smooth start-up of automation installations. They felt that the United States was in the lead in conveyor sortation and carousel *development.* Finally, they felt that the United States and Japan were at about the same level in the *development* of unit load AS/RS, AGVs, unit load AEM, and transport conveyor.

In assessing the current status of *application*, it was concluded that Japan led in AS/RS, AGV, AEM, STV, intelligent pick cart, light-aided picking, RF for operator control, dock management, and implementation time and smooth start-up. The study team concluded that the United States led in the *application* of conveyor sortation, carousels, clean room systems, RF for machine control, warehouse management systems, automatic identification, and EDI. They felt that the status of *application* of transport conveyor, depalletizing for case pick, and rotary rack was equal between the two countries.

Although the current status is important, of greater interest is the priority attention being given to materials handling technology in Japan versus the United States. In assessing the trends, it was concluded that the Japanese materials handling industry is gaining ground in comparison with that of the United States in the *development* of unit load and miniload AS/RS, AEMs, transport conveyors, STVs, rotary racks, intelligent pick carts, light-aided picking, clean room systems, and dock management. It was also concluded that Japanese industry is gaining ground in the *application* of AS/RS, AGV, AEM, STV, intelligent pick carts, light-aided picking, RF for operator control, and dock management.

The only technologies in which the Japanese materials handling industry was losing ground to the United States were conveyor sortation and carousel conveyor *development* and carousel conveyor, automatic identification, and EDI *application.*

The Japanese materials handling industry has virtually captured the clean room materials handling market and is making substantial inroads on other applications within the electronics industry. Japanese materials handling suppliers have also demonstrated the viability of modular design of hardware and software products. Moreover, they have successfully developed and marketed standardized automated products of high quality and relatively low cost, whereas in the United States each automated solution tends to be tailored to the specific application.

Materials handling systems sales grew at an annual compound rate of 20% in Japan over the past decade. In the United States, over the same period the growth was less than 6%. In 1990, nearly 3,000 storage/retrieval machines were in operation in Japan, whereas fewer than 300 were in operation in the United States. Free-standing AS/RS was preferred to rack-supported AS/RS in Japan. Also, in Japan it was far more common to have AS/RS installations with only one or two aisles than in the United States.

Finally, the JTEC study concluded that a significant difference existed in the relative weight given to level of automation, information/control system, information/process integration, and customer service in Japan and in the United States. In particular, the ordering just given is a priority ordering in Japan, whereas almost a reverse ordering applies in the United States. Hundreds of Japanese logistics professionals were asked to rank the factors they used in evaluating warehouses. The highest priority was given to automation in Japan, while customer service was given the highest priority in the United States. To put the result into perspective, supplier-customer partnerships were already well established in Japan, with some partnerships extending over several generations. Because of land cost, an aging workforce, capital availability, low interest rates, and long-term perspectives, automation was both more highly valued and more easily justified in Japan than in the United States.

Not only is it important to know how materials handling in the United States compares with that in Japan, it is also important to know how materials handling in your facility compares with that in other facilities here and abroad. Competitive benchmarking provides valuable information concerning the application of logistics technology.[25]

Notes

1. John A. White, "Warehousing in a Changing World," *Proceedings of the 5th International Conference on Automation in Warehousing*, John A. White, ed., Atlanta, December 1983, pp. 3–6; John A. White, "Warehousing in the New Age," *Proceedings of the 7th International Conference on Automation in Warehousing*, John A. White, ed., San Francisco, October 1986, pp. 31–38.
2. John A. White, "World-Class Warehousing: The Competitive Edge," *Proceedings of the 8th International Conference on Automation in Warehousing* and *Proceedings of the 5th International Conference on Automated Guided Vehicle Systems,* Taruo Takahashi, ed., Tokyo, October 1987, pp. 37–59; John A. White, "Warehousing in the New Age," *Proceedings of the 7th International Conference on Automation in Warehousing,* John A. White, ed., San Francisco, October 1986, pp. 31–38; John A. White, "World-Class Warehousing: The Competitive Edge," *Proceedings of the 8th International Conference on Automation in Warehousing* and *Proceedings of the 5th International Conference on Automated Guided Vehicle Systems,* Taruo Takahashi, ed., Tokyo, October 1987, pp. 37–59.; John A. White, "The Evolution of Materials Handling in Warehousing," *Automation in Warehousing: Proceedings of the 9th International Conference,* and *Automated Guided Vehicle Systems: Proceedings of the 6th International Conference,* Ludo F. Gelders and Robert H. Hollier, eds., Brussels,

October 1988, pp. 33–47; and John A. White, "Dimensions of World-Class Warehousing," *Proceedings of the Annual Conference of the Council of Logistics Management,* Vol. 1, St. Louis, October 1989, pp. 215–27.
3. See Chapter 9.
4. John A. White, "Customer-Supplier Partnerships," *Modern Materials Handling* 47, no. 9 (August 1992).
5. John A. White, "Let Foxes Run Chicken Coops!," *Modern Materials Handling* 46, no. 14 (December 1991): 27.
6. See Chapter 7.
7. See Chapter 40.
8. *Workshop on Materials Handling Technology in Japan,* Edward H. Frazelle and Richard E. Ward, cochairs (Washington, D.C.: Japanese Technology Evaluation Center, National Science Foundation, May 21, 1992).
9. Roy E. Marsten, private communication, June 1992. Other examples include a refinery scheduling problem for UNOCAL that consisted of 18,401 constraints and 33,905 variables; it required 24 minutes of computer run time to solve. A personnel assignment problem for the U.S. Army consisted of 24,962 constraints and 42,838 decision variables; it required 116 minutes to obtain an optimum solution. A distribution planning problem for Ford Motor Company consisted of 43,387 constraints and 106,908 variables; it required only 7 minutes to obtain an optimum solution. These linear programming problems were solved using OB1 Code on an IBM RS6000 Model 540/550 computer.
10. William G. Nulty and Michael A. Trick, "GNO/PC Generalized Network Optimization System," *Operations Research Letters* 7, no. 2 (April 1988): 101–2.
11. For further information, see Richard L. Francis, Leon F. McGinnis, Jr., and John A. White, *Facility Layout and Location: An Analytical Approach*, 2d ed. (Englewood Cliffs, N.J.: Prentice-Hall, 1992); John A. White and Michael A. Mullens, "Management Support Systems for Warehousing," *Proceedings of the Annual Conference of the National Council of Physical Distribution Management*, Dallas, September 1984, pp. 557–70; John A. White and Ira W. Pence, Jr., eds., *Progress in Materials Handling and Logistics*, Vol. 1 (New York: Springer-Verlag, 1989); and John A. White, Ira W. Pence, Jr., Robert J. Graves, Leon F. McGinnis, Jr., Michael R. Wilhelm, and Richard E. Ward, eds., *Progress in Materials Handling and Logistics*, Vol. 2 (New York: Springer-Verlag, 1991).
12. *Workshop on Materials Handling Technology in Japan.*
13. See Section 8 for information technology discussions, especially Chapter 33. Also see Chapters 25 and 26 for discussions of automatic identification and radio frequency technologies.
14. John M. Hill, "Automatic Identification Perspective 1992," *Proceedings of the Material Handling Short Course*, Georgia Institute of Technology, Atlanta, Ga, March 1992.
15. Ibid.
16. See Chapters 25 and 26 for discussions of materials handling systems design and a review of materials handling equipment.
17. James A. Tompkins and John A. White, *Facilities Planning* (New York: Wiley, 1984).
18. *Workshop on Materials Handling Technology in Japan.*
19. White, "The Evolution of Materials Handling in Warehousing," and *Automated Guided Vehicle Systems: Proceedings of the 6th International Conference.*
20. William F. Hunt, *Handling Material in Factories*, (New York: Industrial Extension Institute, 1920), p. 11.

21. White, "The Evolution of Materials Handling in Warehousing," and *Automated Guided Vehicle Systems: Proceedings of the 6th International Conference.*
22. Hunt, *Handling Material in Factories*, pp. 24–25.
23. White, "The Evolution of Materials Handling in Warehousing," and *Automated Guided Vehicle Systems: Proceedings of the 6th International Conference.*
24. *Workshop on Materials Handling Technology in Japan.*
25. See Chapter 13 and Karen A. Auguston, "Compare Yourself to the Best . . . and Worst!" *Modern Materials Handling* 47, no. 6 (May 1992): 48–51.

APPENDIX A

Publications and Other Sources of Information

Richard Shreve
Director, Cargo Services
AIR TRANSPORT ASSOCIATION
OF AMERICA
1301 Pennsylvania Avenue NW
Washington, DC 20004-1707
(202) 626-4128

Dennis Jorgenson
Chief Operating Officer
AMERICAN MARKETING ASSOCIATION
250 S. Wacker Drive
Chicago, IL 60606-5819
(312) 648-0536

Harvey Brelin
President & COO
AMERICAN PRODUCTIVITY &
QUALITY CENTER
123 N. Post Oak Lane
Houston, TX 77024-7797
(713) 681-4020

David Howard
Editor
AMERICAN SHIPPER
PO Box 4728
Jacksonville, FL 32201
(904) 355-2601
FAX (904) 791-8836

Paul Hyman
Director, Cargo Services
AIR CARGO
6209 Lakeview Dr.
Falls Church, VA 22041

Tricia Neff
Executive Vice President
AMERICAN SOCIETY OF
TRANSPORTATION & LOGISTICS
216 East Church St.
Lock Haven, PA 17745
(717) 748-8515

Michael Jenkins
President & CEO
AMERICAN WAREHOUSE ASSOCIATION
1300 W. Higgins Road, Suite 111
Park Ridge, IL 60068
(708) 292-1891

Victoria Fagouri
Associate Editor
AIR CARGO WORLD
6151 Powers Ferry Road NW
Atlanta, GA 30339-2941
(404) 955-2500
FAX (404) 955-0400

Glenn Cella
AMERICAN INSTITUTE
FOR SHIPPERS ASSOCIATION
PO Box 33457
Washington, DC 20033
(202) 628-0933

Donald Ledwig
Executive Director
AMERICAN PRODUCTION & INVENTORY
CONTROL SOCIETY (APICS)
500 West Annandale Road
Falls Church, VA 22046
(703) 237-8344

Laura A. Masapollo
Publisher
AMERICAN PUBLIC
WAREHOUSE REGISTER
PO Box 750
Sicklerville, NJ 08081
(609) 728-9745

Joseph Bonney
Managing Editor
AMERICAN SHIPPER
5 World Trade Center Suite 9259
New York, NY 10048
(212) 269-9198

Thomas J. Donohue
President & C.E.O.
AMERICAN TRUCKING ASSOCIATION
2200 Mill Road
Alexandria, VA 22314
(703) 838-1700

Richard Green
Editor-in-Chief
APICS-THE PERFORMANCE ADVANTAGE
2555 Cumberland Parkway #299
Atlanta, GA 30339
(404) 435-2849
FAX (404) 432-6969

Terry R. Speights
Editor
ARMY LOGISTICIAN
US Army Logistics Management College
A Avenue, Building 12301
Fort Lee, VA 23801-6044
(804) 734-6400

E. Dale Jones
Executive Director
ASSOCIATION OF TRANSPORTATION
PRACTITIONERS
19564 Clubhouse Road
Gaithersburg, MD 20879
(301) 670-6733

Lea Tonkin
Managing Editor
ASSOCIATION FOR MANUFACTURING/
TARGET NEWSLETTER
8909 S. Robin Hill
Woodstock, IL 60098
(815) 338-9036

Lincoln Millstein
Business Editor
BOSTON GLOBE
135 Morrisey Road
Boston, MA 02107
(617) 929-2000

Manfred Schaar
BUNDESVEREININGUNG LOGISTIK E.V.
Contrsarpe 45
28795 Bremen 7
GERMANY
(427) 335-680
FAX (427) 320-369

Christopher Power
Staff Editor
BUSINESS WEEK
1221 Avenue of the Americas
New York, NY 10020
(212) 512-3105

Charles C. Whitchurch
Managing Director
ASSOCIATION FOR
MANUFACTURING EXCELLENCE
380 West Palatine Road #7
Wheeling, IL 60090
(708) 520-3282

Sergi I. Golubez
Secretary for Foreign Contacts
ASSOCIATION OF SIBERIAN &
FAR EAST CITIES
630093 Novosibiersk
U1 Revolutsii, 4
FEDERATION OF RUSSIA
(383) 237-950
FAX (383) 232-439

Mark David
Editor-in-Chief
AUTOMATIC I.D. NEWS
7500 Old Oak Boulevard
Cleveland, OH 44130
(216) 243-8100

Peter Goldman
Managing Editor
BOARDROOM REPORTS
330 West 42nd Street
New York, NY 10036
(212) 613-5250

Bill Castle
Business Editor
BOSTON HERALD AMERICAN
1 Harold Square
Boston, MA 02106
(617) 426-3000

Ann Arellano
Managing Editor
BUSINESS MARKETING
740 Rush Street
Chicago, IL 60611
(312) 649-5417

Thomas Dulaney
Editor
C.S. REPORT, INC.
PO Box 696
Uwchland, PA 19480
(215) 458-6410
FAX (215) 458-6415

David Long
Executive Director
CANADIAN ASSOCIATION OF
LOGISTICS MANAGEMENT
610 Alden Road, Suite 201
Markham, Ontario
CANADA, L3R 9Z1
(416) 513-7300
FAX (416) 513-0624

Patricia Cancilla
Editor
CARGO EXPRESS
310 DuPont Street
Toronto, Ontario
CANADA, M5R 1V9
(416) 968-7252
FAX (416) 968-2377

Alfonso M. Fernandez
Tecnico Director
CENTRO ESPAÑOL DE LOGISTICA
Paseo de La Castellana, 114-4a
Madrid
SPAIN 28046
(341) 411-6753
FAX (341) 564-0910

Lisa Holton
Financial Editor
CHICAGO SUN-TIMES
401 North Wabash Avenue
Chicago, IL 60611
(312) 321-3000

J. P. Donlon
Editor
CHIEF EXECUTIVE
233 Park Avenue South
New York, NY 10003
(212) 979-4810
FAX (212) 979-7431

Bob Parija
Associate Manager of Transportation Policy
CHAMBER OF COMMERCE, THE US
1615 H Street NW
Washington, DC 20062-2000
(202) 463-5528
FAX (202) 887-3445

Patsy Mackle
Operations Coordinator
CANADIAN INDUSTRIAL TRANSIT
LEAGUE
1090 Don Mills Road, Suite 602
Don Mills, Ontario
CANADA M3C 3R6
(416) 447-7766

Bonnie Joews
Editor
CANADIAN TRANSPORTATION/LOGISTICS
1450 Don Mills Road
Don Mills, Ontario
CANADA, M3B 2X7
(416) 445-6641

T. Sokolava
Executive Manager
CENTER FOR COMMERCIAL
INFORMATION; MARIA ASSOCIATION
LTD.

24 Butyrski Val Moscow
FEDERATION OF RUSSIA, 125047
(095) 258-1237

Business Editor
CHICAGO TRIBUNE
435 North Michigan Avenue
Chicago, IL 60611
(312) 222-3503

Hu Junming
Secretary General
CHINESE SOCIETY OF LOGISTICS MANAGEMENT
25 North Street Yuetan
Beijing
CHINA 100834
(861) 839-1388
FAX (861) 839-2774

Charles M. Naylor
Executive Director
CLAIMS PREVENTION COUNCIL
PO Box 301
Oak Forest, IL 60452
(708) 535-2772
FAX (708) 535-2773

Richard Ward
Vice President, Operations
COLLEGE-IND COUNCIL ON MATERIAL HANDLING
8720 Red Oak Boulevard #201
Charlotte, NC 28217
(704) 522-8644

Herb Schild
Editor
INTERMODAL CONTAINER NEWS
6151 Powers Ferry Road NW
Atlanta, GA 30339-2941
(404) 955-2500

Mary B. Klinkenbergh
Manager, Professional Development
COUNCIL OF CONSULTING ORGANIZATIONS
521 Fifth Avenue
New York, NY 10175
(212) 697-9693
FAX (212) 949-6571

Adam Lashinsky
Associate Editor
CRAIN'S CHICAGO BUSINESS
740 North Rush Street
Chicago, IL 60611
(312) 649-5354

Bob Hurd
Liaison
DATA INTERCHANGE STANDARDS ASSOCIATION
1800 Diagonal Road, Suite 355
Alexandria, VA 22314
(703) 548-7005
FAX (703) 548-5738

Dee A. Walker
Executive Director
DELTA NU ALPHA
530 Church Street, Suite 300
Nashville, TN 37219
(615) 251-0933
FAX (615) 254-7047

Parry Desmond
Executive Editor
COMMERCIAL CARRIER JOURNAL
Chilton Way
Radnor, PA 19089
(215) 964-4529
FAX (215) 964-4512

Raul Arellano
Executive Director
CONSEJO MEXICANO DE ADMN. EN LOG.
Dr. Santos Sepulveda 130-3Piso
Monterrey, N.L.
MEXICO, C.P. 64710

Jane Boyes
Editorial Director
CONTAINERIZATION INTERNATIONAL
72 Broadwick Street
London
ENGLAND, W1V 2BP
(71) 439-5602
FAX (71) 439-5299

George A. Gecowets
Executive Vice President
COUNCIL OF LOGISTICS MANAGEMENT

2803 Butterfield Road #380
Oak Brook, IL 60521-1156
(708) 574-0985
FAX (708) 574-0989

Arthur Brown
Metropolitan Editor
DAILY NEWS
220 East 42nd Street
New York, NY 10017
(212) 210-2100

Joseph G. Mattingly
Editor
DEFENSE TRANSPORTATION JOURNAL
University of Maryland
College of Business and Management
College Park, MD 20742
(301) 405-2289
FAX (301) 314-9157

Thomas A. Foster
Editorial Director
DISTRIBUTION
One Chilton Way
Radnor, PA 19089
(215) 964-4379
FAX (215) 964-4381

Peter Rowlands
Editor
DISTRIBUTION BUSINESS
Quadrant House
250 Kennington Lane
London
ENGLAND, SE11 5RD
(071) 587-1691
FAX (071) 587-0607

Mike Witter
Associate Publisher
EDI EXECUTIVE
1639 Desford Court
Marietta, GA 30064
(404) 428-9919

Gregory B. Harter
President
ELECTRONIC DATA INTERCHANGE ASSOCIATION
225 Reinekers Lane #550
Alexandria, VA 22314
(703) 838-8042
FAX (703) 838-8038

Roland A. Ouellette
President
ENO TRANSPORTATION FOUNDATION, INC.
44211 Slatestone Court
Lansdowne, VA 22075
(703) 729-7200
FAX (703) 729-7219

Patricia E. Steele
VP & Associate Editor
EXPORT TODAY
733 15th Street NW #1100
Washington, DC 20005
(702) 737-1060

James W. Michaels
Editor
FORBES
60 Fifth Avenue
New York, NY 10011
(212) 620-2200

Anita Rosepka
Editor
DISTRIBUTION CENTER MANAGEMENT
215 Park Avenue South
New York, NY 10003
(212) 228-0246
FAX (212) 228-0376

John Zyskowski
Editor
EDI NEWS
7811 Montrose Road
Potomac, MD 20854
(301) 340-2100

Hans E. Van Goor
Honorary Secretary
ELA, EUROPEAN LOGISTICS ASSOCIATION
PO Box 26g
5680 A9 Best
NETHERLANDS

Susan Hash
Managing Editor

EXECUTIVE REPORT ON
CUSTOMER SATISFACTION
215 Park Ave. South, #1301
New York, NY 10003
(212) 228-0246

D. Lewis Smith
Publisher/Editor
FLORIDA CARGO NEWS
8107 NW 33rd Street
Miami, FL 33122
(305) 591-9475
FAX (305) 591-9575

Marta Dorion
Story Development Editor
FORTUNE
Time Life Building
Rockefeller Center
New York, NY 10020
(212) 522-1212

Daniel Seligman
Associate Managing Editor
FORTUNE
Time Life Building
Rockefeller Center
New York, NY 10020
(212) 522-1212

Joerg Breker
Executive Director
GERMAN SOCIETY OF LOGISTICS
Heinrich-Hertz-Strasse 4
Dortmund
GERMANY 44227

Richard Mulville
Publisher
GROCERY DISTRIBUTION
455 S. Frontage Rd. #116
Burr Ridge, IL 60521
(708) 986-8767
FAX (708) 986-0206

Alan M. Webber
Managing Editor
HARVARD BUSINESS REVIEW
Soldiers Field
Boston, MA 02163
(617) 495-6191

Felecia Stratton
Editor
INBOUND LOGISTICS
Five Penn Plaza
New York, NY 10001
(212) 629-1560

Kim Blass
INDUSTRIAL ENGINEERING
25 Technology Park
Norcross, GA 30092
(404) 449-0461
FAX (404) 263-8532

Carla Rapoport
Associate Editor
FORTUNE INTERNATIONAL
153 New Bond St.
Time Life Building
London
ENGLAND W1Y 0AA

Gregoire Laurent
President
FRENCH ASSOCIATION FOR
LOGISTICS (ASLOG)
119 rue Cardinet
Paris
FRANCE 75017

John M. Gray
Vice President, Education and Industry Affairs
GROCERY MANUFACTURERS OF
AMERICA
1010 Wisconsin Avenue NW #800
Washington, DC 20007
(202) 337-9400
FAX (202) 337-4508

John A. McQuaid
President
INTERMODAL ASSOCIATION
OF NORTH AMERICA
6410 Kenilworth Ave. S–108
Riverdale, MD 20737-1202
(301) 864-4160

James E. Stover
President
HEALTH INDUSTRY DISTRIBUTORS
ASSOCIATION

225 Reinekers Lane #650
Alexandria, VA 22314-2875
(703) 549-4432

George Gendron
Editor-in-Chief
INC.
38 Commercial Wharf
Boston, MA 02110
(617) 248-8000

Brian Moskal
Associate Editor
INDUSTRY WEEK
Two Prudential Plaza #2525
Chicago, IL 60601
(312) 861-0880

R. Cullis
Assistant Research Officer
INSTITUTE OF GROCERY DISTRIBUTION
Letchmore Heath
Watford, Herts
ENGLAND WD2 8DQ
(092) 385-7141
FAX (092) 385-2531

Ian C. Canadine
Chief Executive
INSTITUTE OF LOGISTICS
Douglas House\Queens Square
Corby, Northants
ENGLAND NN17 1PL
(536) 205-500

William C. Pflaum
Executive Director
INSTITUTE OF PACKAGING PROFESSIONALS
481 Carlisle Drive
Herndon, VA 22070-4823
(703) 318-8970
FAX (703) 318-0310

Kurt C. Hoffman
Editor
INTERMODAL REPORTER
600 Marcia Lane
Rockville, MD 20851
(301) 762-8250

Erik Ipsen
Editor
INTERNATIONAL HERALD TRIBUNE
63 Long Acre
London
ENGLAND WC2E 9JH

Gregory Balestrero
Executive Director
INSTITUTE OF INDUSTRIAL ENGINEERS
25 Technology Park/Atlanta
Norcross, GA 30092
(404) 449-0461
FAX (404) 263-8532

Greg Miles
Senior Editor
INTERNATIONAL BUSINESS
500 Mamaroneck Avenue, #314
Harrison, NY 10528
(914) 381-7700

Madalyn B. Duerr
Executive Director
INTERNATIONAL CUSTOMER SERVICE ASSOCIATION
401 N. Michigan Avenue
Chicago, IL 60611-4267
(312) 321-6800
FAX (312) 321-6869

Morrison Cain
VP Legal and Public Affairs
INTERNATIONAL MASS RETAIL ASSOCIATION
1901 Pennsylvania Avenue NW
Washington, DC 20006
(202) 861-0774
FAX (202) 785-8265

J. William Hudson
President
INTERNATIONAL ASSOCIATION OF REFRIGERATED WAREHOUSES
7315 Wisconsin Avenue #1200N
Bethesda, MD 20814
(301) 652-5674
FAX (301) 652-7269

James R. Stock
Editor

INTERNATIONAL JOURNAL OF
PHYSICAL DISTRIBUTION &
LOGISTICS MANAGEMENT
University of South Florida
Dept. of Marketing
Tampa, FL 33620-5500
(813) 974-4201
FAX (813) 974-3030

Joseph L. Mazel
Editor
INVENTORY REDUCTION REPORT
29 West 35th Street, 5th Floor
New York, NY 10001-2200
(212) 244-0360

Minoru Oikawa
Director
JAPAN MANAGEMENT ASSOCIATION
JMA Building 3-1-22, Shiba Pk
Toyko
JAPAN 105

Ellis Murphy
Executive Director
INTERNATIONAL SAFE TRANSIT
ASSOCIATION
43 East Ohio St. #914
Chicago, IL 60611-7291
(312) 645-0083

Jae-won Park
Management Consultancy Department
KOREA PRODUCTIVITY CENTER
C.P.O. BOX 834
Seoul
KOREA

Kerry Hammond
Chairman
LOGISTICS MANAGEMENT
ASSOCIATION OF AUSTRALIA
Management House/PO Box 112
St. Kilda Victoria
AUSTRALIA 3182
(613) 534-8181
FAX (613) 534-5050

Robert K. Windsor
President
INTERNATIONAL TRADE
FACILITATION COUNCIL
1800 Diagonal Road, Suite 220
Alexandria, VA 22314
(703) 519-0661
FAX (703) 519-0664

Karen Thuermer
Editor
INTERNATIONAL TRADE ADVISOR
PO Box 1024
Berwyn, PA 19312
(215) 254-8810

Kunio Kakuta
Executive Vice President
JAPAN INSTITUTE OF
LOGISTICS SYSTEMS
Shuwa Dai-2, Shiba Pk. Building
Shiba Daimon, Minato-Ku
Toyko
JAPAN 105

Pat Chandler
Editor/Publisher
JET CARGO NEWS
PO Box 92052 #398
Houston, TX 77292-0952
(713) 681-4760
FAX (713) 682-3871

John J. Coyle
Editor
JOURNAL OF BUSINESS LOGISTICS
Pennslyvania State University
509 Business Admn. Bldg. 1
University Park, PA 16802
(814) 865-1866
FAX (814) 863-7067

Gregory S. Johnson
Reporter
JOURNAL OF COMMERCE (NY)
2 World Trade Center
New York, NY 10048-0662
(212) 837-7120

Larry Smith
President
LOGISTICS MANAGEMENT ASSOCIATION
OF AUSTRALIA LTD. NSW
PO Box 943
Auburn, NSW

AUSTRALIA 2144
(02) 502-2336
FAX (02) 502-3240

Michael G. Grace
Executive Secretary
LOGISTICS MANAGEMENT ASSOCIATION
OF NEW ZEALAND
PO Box 553
Manurewa
NEW ZEALAND
(649) 267-9075

Georgina Hatch
Editor
LOGISTICS NEWS–SOUTH AFRICA
49A 7th Ave./Pktown North 2193
PO Box 966
Parklands 2121
SOUTH AFRICA

Mary-Pat Volino
Assistant Director
MARITIME ASSOCIATION OF
THE PORT OF NY/NJ
17 Battery Place #1006
New York, NY 10004
(212) 425-5740

Bernard Knill
Editor
MATERIAL HANDLING ENGINEERING
1100 Superior Avenue
Cleveland, OH 44114
(216) 696-7000
FAX (216) 696-7658

A. L. Leffler
CEO
MATERIAL HANDLING INSTITUTE
8720 Red Oak Boulevard #201
Charlotte, NC 28217
(704) 522-8644
FAX (704) 522-7826

Dena Brooker
Assistant Editor
MATERIALS MANAGEMENT &
DISTRIBUTION
777 Bay Street
Toronto, Ontario
CANADA M5W 1A7
(416) 596-5710

Lisa Woodie
Editor
MHI NEWS
8720 Red Oak Boulevard #201
Charlotte, NC 28217-3992
(704) 522-8644
FAX (704) 522-7826

Nick Allen
Editor
LOGISTICS EUROPE
Castle Chambers/85 High Street
Berkhamsted Hertfordshire
ENGLAND HP4 2DF
(442) 878-787

Tom Feare
News Editor
MODERN MATERIALS HANDLING
275 Washington Street
Newton, MA 02158
(617) 558-4548

Stephen McClelland
Editor
LOGISTICS WORLD/IFS PUBLICATIONS
35-39 High Street
Kempston Bedford
ENGLAND MK42 7BT
(023) 485-3605

Gregg Cebrzynski
Managing Editor
MARKETING NEWS
250 South Wacker Drive #200
Chicago, IL 60606
(312) 993-9517

Tony S. Coletti
Executive Vice President
MATERIAL HANDLING EQUIPMENT
DISTRIBUTORS ASSOCIATION
201 Route 45
Vernon Hills, IL 60061
(708) 680-3500
FAX (708) 362-6989

Martin Coleman
Editor

MATERIALS HANDLING & DISTRIBUTION
POB 606
Rozelle, NSW2039
AUSTRALIA
(02) 956-9445
FAX (02) 956-6090

Laura Souhrada
Editor
MATERIALS MANAGEMENT IN
HEALTH CARE
737 N. Michigan Ave., 7th Floor
Chicago, IL 60611
(312) 440-6800
FAX (312) 951-8491

Charles Wilson
Editor
MODERN BULK TRANSPORTER
4200 South Shepard #200
Houston, TX 77098
(713) 523-8124

Jane Sanders
Executive Director
LOGISTICS COUNCIL ATA
2200 Mill Road
Alexandria, VA 22314
(202) 838-1915

Edward Emmett
President
NATIONAL INDUSTRIAL
TRANSPORTATION LEAGUE
1700 N. Moore St. #1900
Arlington, VA 22209-1904
(703) 524-5011
FAX (703) 524-5017

Ronald J. Streck
President and CEO
NATIONAL WHOLESALE DRUGGISTS'
ASSOCIATION
1821 Michael Faraday Dr.
Reston, VA 22090

Donna F. Behme
Executive Director
NATIONAL ASSOCIATION OF FREIGHT
TRANSPORTATION CONSULTANTS
PO Box 21418
Albuquerque, NM 87154-1418
(505) 299-0615

Joseph Cutrona
Executive Director
NATIONAL SMALL SHIPMENTS
TRAFFIC CONFERENCE
1750 Pennsylvania Ave. NW #111
Washington, DC 20006
(202) 393-5505

Dennis Madsen
Director, Distribution Services
NATIONAL AMERICAN WHOLESALE
GROCERS ASSOCIATION
201 Park Washington Court
Falls Church, VA 22046
(703) 532-9400
FAX (703) 538-4673

F. Hal Van Diver
Executive Director
MATERIALS HANDLING &
MANAGEMENT SOCIETY
8720 Red Oak Blvd. #224
Charlotte, NC 28217
(704) 525-4667

Erik S. McMahon
Editor
PACIFIC SHIPPER
562 Mission Street #601
San Francisco, CA 94105-2919
(415) 546-3946
FAX (415) 546-3962

Thomas K. Zaucha
President & CEO
NATIONAL GROCERS
ASSOCIATION
1825 Samuel Morse Dr.
Reston, VA 22090
(703) 437-5300

Gene S. Bergoffen
Executive Vice President
NATIONAL PRIVATE TRUCK COUNCIL
66 Canal Center Plaza, Fl. 6
Alexandria, VA 22314
(703) 683-1300
FAX (703) 683-1217

Roger Thompson
Senior Editor
NATION'S BUSINESS
1615 H Street NW
Washington, DC 20062
(202) 463-5650

R. Jerry Baker
Executive Vice President
NATIONAL ASSOCIATION OF
PURCHASING MANAGEMENT, INC.
PO Box 22160
Tempe, AZ 85285-2160
(602) 752-6276
FAX (602) 752-7890

Kenneth E. Miller
Managing Director
OFFICE FURNITURE DISTRIBUTORS
ASSOCIATION, INC.
PO Box 326
Petersham, MA 01366-0326
(508) 724-3267

Greg Erickson
Editor
PACKAGING
PO Box 5080
Des Plaines, IL 60017-5080
(708) 635-8800

Peter Bradley
Transportation Editor
PURCHASING MAGAZINE
Cahners Building
275 Washington Street
Newton, MA 02158
(617) 558-4359
FAX (617) 558-4327

Gus Welty
Editor
RAILWAY AGE
175 W. Jackson Blvd./A1927
Chicago, IL 60604
(312) 427-2729

Shawn Williams
REGULAR COMMON CARRIER
CONFERENCE
5205 Leesburg Pike #1110
Falls Church, VA 22041
(703) 824-8775

Robert Bowman
Correspondent
SHIPPING AND TRADE NEWS
38 Seal Rock Drive
San Francisco, CA 94121
(415) 752-4884
FAX (415) 387-1105

Norman Michaud
Executive Director
SOCIETY OF LOGISTICS ENGINEERS
8100 Professional Pl. #211
New Carrollton, MD 20785
(301) 459-8446
FAX (301) 459-1522

Blanca E. Adornos
Business Services Division
NATIONAL RETAIL FEDERATION
701 Pennsylvania Ave. NW
Washington, DC 20004
(202) 783-7971

David Lighthall
Publisher
STAGING AREA
PO Box 500
South Orleans, MA 02662
(508) 255-9099
FAX (508) 255-9879

Leslie Hansen Harps
President
Leslie Harps & Company
4120 Military Road NW
Washington, DC 20015
(202) 363-5822

Leslie Stroh
Publisher
THE EXPORTER MAGAZINE
34 West 37th Street
New York, NY 10018
(212) 563-2772

Charles Wilson
Editorial Director

REFRIGERATED TRANSPORTER
4200 S. Shepherd #200
Houston, TX 77098
(713) 523-8124
FAX (713) 523-8384

Dee Reif-Taylor
Executive Director
SALES & MARKETING COUNCIL-ATA
2200 Mill Road
Alexandria, VA 22314
(703) 838-1926
FAX (703) 836-6070

Lt. Gen. E. Honor
President
NATIONAL DEFENSE TRANSPORTATION ASSOCIATION
50 S. Pickett Street #220
Alexandria, VA 22304-3008
(703) 571-5011

Frank Quinn
Editor
TRAFFIC MANAGEMENT
275 Washington Street
Cahners Publishing
Newton, MA 02158–1630
(617) 964-3030
FAX (617) 558-4327

Jean V. Murphy
Editor
TRAFFIC WORLD
National Press Building #741
Washington, DC 20045
(202) 383-6145
FAX (202) 737-3349

William J. Augello
Executive Director/General Counsel
TRANSPORTATION CLAIMS & PREVENTION COUNCIL
120 Main Street
Huntington, NY 11743
(516) 549-8984
FAX (516) 549-8962

Oliver B. Patton
Editor
TRANSPORT TOPICS
2200 Mill Road
Alexandria, VA 22314
(703) 838-1781

David N. Luttenberger
Editor
PACKAGING TECHNOLOGY & ENGINEERING
401 North Broad Street
Philadelphia, PA 19108
(215) 238-5356

Dennis Grim
Executive Producer
TRANSPORTATION DIGEST
575 Tollgate Rd. #B
Elgin, IL 60123-9321
(708) 741-0018
FAX (708) 741-0180

Richard Guggolz
Administrator
TRANSPORTATION RESEARCH FORUM
1730 North Lynn Street #502
Arlington, VA 22209
(703) 525-1191
FAX (703) 276-8196

C. G. Vermelis
Executive Director
VERENIGING LOGISTIEK MANAGEMENT
Neuhuyskade 40/PO Box 90730
2596 XL Den Haag
NETHERLANDS
(070) 318-0268
FAX (070) 324-9263

Kenneth B. Ackerman
Publisher and Editor
WAREHOUSING FORUM
1328 Dublin Road
Columbus, OH 43215-1059
(614) 488-3165
FAX (614) 488-9243

Annette E. Petrick
Executive Director
TRANSPORTATION BROKERS CONFERENCE OF AMERICA
5845 Richmond Highway, Suite 750

Alexandria, VA 22303
(703) 329-1894
FAX (703) 329-1898

P.J.M. Bluyssen
Editor-in-Chief
TRANSPORT EN OPSLAG
Postbus 4
7000 BA Doetinchem
NETHERLANDS

M. J. Baker
National Secretary
SOUTH AFRICA INSTITUTE
OF MATERIAL HANDLING
PO Box 3656
Rivona
SOUTH AFRICA 2128
(11) 883-0339

Perry Trunick
Editor
TRANSPORTATION & DISTRIBUTION
1100 Superior Avenue
Cleveland, OH 44114
(216) 696-7000
FAX (216) 696-4135

John C. Spychalski
Editor
TRANSPORTATION JOURNAL
509 Business Admn. Bldg.
University Park, PA 16802-3005
(814) 865-2872
FAX (814) 863-7067

Thomas B. Deen
Executive Director
TRANSPORATION RESEARCH BOARD
2101 Constitution Ave. NW
Washington, DC 20418
(202) 334-2934

Richard L. Lesher
President
US CHAMBER OF COMMERCE
1615 H Street NW
Washington, DC 20062
(202) 659-6000

Nicolas Bray
Correspondent
THE WALL STREET JOURNAL EUROPE
76 Shoe Lane, 11th Floor/Intl Pr. Ctr.
London
ENGLAND EC4 A3JB

Daniel Machalaba
Transportation Editor
WALL STREET JOURNAL
200 Liberty Street
New York, NY 10281
(212) 416-2000

Thomas E. Sharpe
Executive Director
WAREHOUSING EDUCATION &
RESEARCH COUNCIL
1100 Jorie Boulevard #170
Oak Brook, IL 60521
(708) 990-0001
FAX (708) 990-0256

Ann Hagen
Editor
WORLD WIDE SHIPPING
77 Moehring Drive
Blauvet, NY 10913-2093
(914) 359-1934
FAX (914) 359-1938

Guenther Pawellek
Editor
ZEITSCHRIFT FUER LOGISTIK
Postfach 90 14 03
D-2100 Hamburg 90
GERMANY
(023) 747-4328

APPENDIX B

Trade and Professional Organizations of Interest to Logistics Management Personnel

This material provides the name and address of the chief elected and chief operating officers of several associations that have direct or tangential interests in logistics management. It outlines the objectives of each organization, shows the current level of dues, and lists the approximate number of members.

Air Transport Association of America
American Marketing Association
American Production & Inventory Control Society
American Productivity & Quality Center
American Society of Transportation & Logistics, Inc.
American Trucking Associations, Inc.
American Warehouse Association
Association for Quality and Participation
Association of American Railroads
Association of Professional Material Handling Consultants
Association of Transportation Practitioners
Canadian Association of Logistics Management
Canadian Association of Warehousing and Distribution Services
Canadian Industrial Transportation League
Centro Español De Logistica
Council of Consulting Organizations, Inc.
Council of Logistics Management
Delta Nu Alpha
Deutsche Gesellschaft fur Logistik e.v. (German Society of Logistics)
The Electronic Data Interchange Association
Eno Transportation Foundation, Inc.
European Logistics Association
French Association for Logistics
Grocery Manufacturers of America, Inc.
Health and Personal Care Distribution Conference, Inc.
Institute of Industrial Engineers
Institute of Logistics & Distribution Management
Institute of Management Accountants
Institute of Management Consultants, Inc.
Institute of Materials Handling, Transport, Packaging, and Storage Systems
The Institute of Materials Management
Institute of Packaging Professionals
Intermodal Association of North America
International Association of Refrigerated Warehouses
International Customer Service Association
International Mass Retailing Association
International Society for Inventory Research
The International Trade Facilitation Council
Japanese Council of Logistics Management
Korea Productivity Center
Logistics Management Association of Australia
Material Handling Equipment Distributors Association
Material Handling Institute, Inc.
Materials Handling & Management Society
National American Wholesale Grocers' Association
National Association of Freight Transportation Consultants
National Association of Manufacturers

Source: This appendix was compiled by the Council of Logistics Management and is reprinted with permission (Council of Logistics Management, Oak Brook, ILL., © 1993, All Rights Reserved).

National Association of Purchasing Management, Inc.
National Defense Transportation Association
National Grocers Association
National Industrial Transportation League
National Perishable Transportation Association
National Private Truck Council
National/International Safe Transit Association
National Small Shipments Traffic Conference
National Society of Professional Engineers
National Wholesale Druggists' Association
Norsk Innkjops-og Material Administrasjonsforbund (NIMA)(Norwegian Association of Purchasing and Materials Management)
Office Furniture Distribution Association, Inc.
Society of Logistics Engineers
Swedish Materials Administration Forum
Transportation Brokers Conference of America
Transportation Claims & Prevention Council, Inc.
Transportation Research Board
Transportation Research Forum
United States Chamber of Commerce
United States China Business Council
VDI—Gesellschaft Foerdertechnik Materialfluss Logistik
Vereniging Logistiek Management
Warehousing Education & Research Council
Western Traffic Conference

Air Transport Association of America
Type: A trade association in which airlines hold membership.
Number of Members: 21
Dues: Corporate dues are on a sliding scale based on revenue ton miles. Membership is open to any US air carrier authorized to conduct passenger and/or cargo air transport service under a certificate issued pursuant to Section 604 of the Federal Aviation Act of 1958 that operates a minimum of 20 million revenue ton-miles annually and operated at or above such minimum level during the twelve months immediately preceding the date of membership application.
Purpose/Objective: The Air Transport Association of America is the trade and service organization of the largest airlines of the United States.
Chief Elected Officer:
James E. Landry
President
Air Transport Association of America
1301 Pennsylvania Avenue NW
Washington, DC 20004
(202) 626-4000
Chief Operating Officer:
Same as above

American Marketing Association (AMA)
Type: A professional organization in which individuals hold membership.
Number of Members:
30,000 professional members
28,000 collegiate members
Dues: $145 per person per year.
Purpose/Objective: The American Marketing Association is an international professional society of individual members with an interest in the study, teaching, or practice of marketing. AMA's principal roles are to urge and assist the professional development of members and to advance the science and practice of the marketing discipline.
Chief Elected Officer:
Joseph Barry Mason
Dean
College of Business Administration
PO Box 870233
Tuscaloosa, AL 35401
(205) 348-8932
Chief Operating Officer:
Dennis Jorgenson
Chief Operating Officer
American Marketing Association
250 S. Wacker Drive
Chicago, IL 60606
(312) 648-0536
FAX (312) 993-7542
Remarks: Membership is based on an interest in the ethical practice of marketing.

American Production & Inventory Control Society (APICS)
Type: A professional organization in which membership is extended on both an individual and corporate basis.
Number of Members: 70,000
Dues: $60 per person per year, plus chapter dues.
Purpose/Objective: APICS' primary objectives are to develop professional efficiency in resource management through study, research, and application of scientific methods; to disseminate general and technical information on improved techniques and new developments; and to further develop the

professional body of knowledge and through the organized resources of the profession, thereby advance the general welfare of the industrial economy.
Chief Elected Officer:
Michael D. Sheahan
President
M. Sheahan & Associates
PO Box 785
Oswego, IL 60543
(708) 554-3982
Chief Operating Officer:
Donald E. Ledwig
Executive Director
American Production & Inventory Control Society
500 West Annandale Road
Falls Church, VA 22046
(703) 237-8344

American Productivity & Quality Center (APQC)
Type: An organization in which membership is extended on both an individual and a corporate basis.
Number of Members:
400 corporate members
300 individual members
Dues: Corporate dues are on a sliding scale based on various categories in which fees are tied to levels of benefits. Individual membership is $150 per person per year.
Purpose/Objective: The purpose of APQC is to increase productivity and quality through an approach that emphasizes total quality management. APQC has expertise in measurement, innovative pay systems, and employee involvement and has done action research in white collar, professional, and administrative areas. APQC issues a variety of publications, and offers public seminars, conference information, and consulting services.
Chief Elected Officer:
C. Jackson Grayson, Jr.
Chairman of the Board
American Productivity & Quality Center
123 North Post Oak Lane
Houston, TX 77024
(713) 681-4020
Chief Operating Officer:
Harvey Brelin
President
American Productivity & Quality Center
123 North Post Oak Lane
Houston, TX 77024
(713) 681-4020

American Society of Transportation & Logistics, Inc. (AST&L)
Type: A professional organization in which individuals hold membership.
Number of Members: 1,800
Dues: Certified $ 75
Founder $ 60
Sustaining $130
Educator $ 75
Associate $ 55/$70
Affiliate $ 55
Purpose/Objective: To establish, promote, and maintain high standards of knowledge and professional training; to formulate a code of ethics for the profession; to advance the professional interest of members of the organization; to serve as a source of information and guidance for the fields of traffic, transportation, logistics, and physical distribution management; and to serve the industry as a whole by fostering professional accomplishments.
Chief Elected Officer:
Donald W. Veidt (President)
Managing Director, Forest Products
Southern Pacific Lines
5 Center Pointe Drive, Suite 550
Lake Oswego, OR 97035
(503) 624-2439
Chief Administrative Officer:
Tricia Neff
Executive Vice President
American Society of Transportation and Logistics
216 East Church Street
Lock Haven, PA 17745
(717) 748-8515
FAX (717) 748-9118
Remarks: Offers a five part certification examination and correspondence courses on topical subjects, publishes quarterly journals and newsletters, and holds regional educational workshops and an annual meeting.

American Trucking Associations, Inc. (ATA)
Type: A trade organization representing the interests of the trucking industry.
Number of Members: 4,000
Dues: Dues for motor carriers are assessed on the

basics of revenue. Private carrier dues are based on fleet size and supplier dues are based on revenues generated from the trucking industry.
Purpose/Objective: ATA is the national trade assocation of the trucking industry. ATA has 51 affiliated trucking associations (all states and DC), as well as 10 affiliated conferences. The mission of the American Trucking Associations, Inc., (ATA) is to serve the united interests of the trucking industry; enhance the trucking industry's image, efficiency, productivity, and competitiveness; promote highway safety and environmental responsibility; provide educational programs; and work for a healthy business environment.
Chief Elected Officer:
Thomas J. Donohue
President and CEO
American Trucking Associations, Inc.
2200 Mill Road
Alexandria, VA 22314
(703) 838-1700

American Warehouse Association
Type: A trade association in which corporations hold membership.
Number of Members: 500
Dues: Corporate dues are on a sliding scale based on square footage.
Purpose/Objective: To promote the general interests of persons, firms, and corporations engaged in the public merchandise warehousing industry, and to promote a high standard of business ethics therein; to collect and disseminate statistical and other information pertinent to the business of its members; to conduct research into ways and means of improving efficiency in the conduct of the business of its members; to advise its members of national legislation and regulations affecting them; and in general, to engage in all activities for the benefit of its members.
Chief Elected Officer:
Steve Tigner (Chairman)
President
Parkside Warehouse, Inc.
5960 Falcon Road
Rockford, IL 61109
(815) 397-9614
Chief Operating Officer:
Michael Jenkins
President and CEO
American Warehouse Association
1300 West Higgens Road, Suite 111
Park Ridge, IL 60068
(708) 292-1891
FAX (708) 292-1896

Association of American Railroads
Type: A trade association of railroad companies.
Number of Members: 70
Dues: Dues are assessed on the basis of revenues.
Purpose/Objective: The Association of American Railroads serves two major purposes for its members. It provides industry support on matters that require cooperative handling to better enable the railroad to operate as a national system in the areas of operation, maintenance, safety, research, economics, finance, accounting, data systems, and public information. It also provides leadership for the industry, working with committees made up of representatives of member railroads on matters affecting the progress of the industry as a whole.
Chief Elected Officer:
Edwin L. Harper
President & CEO
Association of American Railroads
50 F Street NW
Washington DC 20001
(202) 639-2403
FAX (202) 639-2868
Chief Operating Officer:
David B. Barefoot
Chief Financial & Administrative Officer
Association of American Railroads
50 F Street NW
Washington, DC 20001
(202) 639-2400
FAX (202) 639-2868
Remarks: Members account for 79% of rail mileage and haul approximately 93% of the nation's rail traffic. They employ 91% of the nation's rail workers.

Association for Quality and Participation (AQP)
Type: An organization in which membership is extended on both an individual and a company basis.

Number of Members: 10,000 members, 81 chapters
Dues: Individual membership is $95 per person per year. Group discounts are $85 per person for five or more people from one organization. Membership is open to any individual or organization that is interested in quality through participation.
Purpose/Objective: AQP is a nonprofit professional association dedicated to serving all phases of quality improvement and participation. The AQP promotes these concepts through training programs, national and regional conferences, resource materials, publications, and the support of local chapters.
Chief Elected Officer:
Mitch Manning (President)
Section Head,
Operative Technical Training
Burroughs Wellcome Company
PO Box 1887
Greenville, NC 27835
(919) 830-2810
Chief Operating Officer:
Cathy E. Kramer
Executive Vice President
Association for Quality and Participation
801-B West Eighth Street, Suite 501
Cincinnati, OH 45203
(513) 381-1959

Association of Professional Material Handling Consultants (APMHC)
Type: A professional organization in which individuals hold membership.
Number of Members: 45
Dues: $150 per person per year.
Purpose/Objective: APMHC promotes and coordinates the exchange of ideas and information among members; encourages the improvement of analysis, synthesis, installation, and training; advances the profession through the development of standards of performance; and aids and assists other groups in promoting material handling generally and the consulting profession specifically.
Chief Elected Officer:
Robert Footlik
President
APMHC
8720 Red Oak Boulevard
Charlotte, NC 28217
(704) 529-1725
Chief Operating Officer:
F. Hal Van Diver
Executive Director
Association of Professional
Material Handling Consultants
8720 Red Oak Boulevard
Charlotte, NC 28217
(704) 529-1725

Association of Transportation Practitioners
Type: A professional organization in which individuals hold membership.
Number of Members: 1,600
Dues: $95 per person per year. For members who have been active for at least ten years and are retired from active duties and professional services, dues are $45 per year. $25 for full time students.
Purpose/Objective: To promote the proper administration of the Revised Interstate Commerce Act, related acts, and other laws regulating transportation; to uphold the honor of practice before the Interstate Commerce Commission and other agencies regulating transportation; to cooperate in fostering educational opportunities; to maintain high standards of professional conduct; and to encourage cordial discourse among its members.
Chief Elected Officer:
Steven A. Brigance (President)
Assistant to CEO
Burlington
Northern Railroad Co.
1550 Continental Plaza
777 Main St.
Ft. Worth, TX 76102
(817) 878-1534
Chief Operating Officer:
E. Dale Jones
Executive Director
Association of Transportation Practitioners
1725 K Street NW, Suite 301
Washington, DC 20006-1401
(202) 466-2080

Canadian Association of Logistics Management (CALM)
Type: A professional organization in which individuals hold membership.

Number of Members: 550
Dues: $220 per person per year.
Purpose/Objective: The Canadian Association of Logistics Management is a nonprofit organization of business professionals interested in improving their logistics and/or distribution management skills. It works in cooperation with the private sector and various organizations to further the understanding and development of the logistics concept. It does this through a continuing program of format activities, research, and informal discussion designed to develop the theory and understanding of the logistics process; promote the art and science of managing logistics systems; and foster professional dialogue and development within the profession.
Chief Elected Officer:
Paul Inglis (President)
Vice President
A.T. Kearney, Inc.
20 Queen St. West, #2314
Toronto, Ontario MSH 3R3
(416) 977-6886
Chief Operating Officer:
David Long
Executive Director
Canadian Association of Logistics Management
610 Alden Road, Suite 201
Markham, Ontario L3R 9Z1
(416) 513-7300
FAX (416) 513-0624

Canadian Association of Warehousing and Distribution Services (CAWDS)
Type: A trade association in which corporations hold membership.
Number of Members: 60
Dues: Corporate dues are on a sliding scale based on gross annual revenue.
Purpose/Objective: To encourage, promote, and further the use of public warehousing and distribution services among potential and existing users. To establish and enforce adherence to appropriate industry operating standards. To provide an information, statistical, and communications resource for the membership at large. To provide a forum for members to meet, study, and discuss problems and opportunities of common interest, and to encourage a spirit of cooperation in the implementation of solutions and the pursuit of those opportunities. To make representations to governments at all levels and their regulatory agencies for the benefit of the industry, its members, and their clients. To provide a vehicle for industry-related educational services.
Chief Elected Officer:
C.R. Beck (President)
KN Distribution
100 Alfred Kuehne Blvd.
Brampton, Ontario L6T 4K4
(905) 791-6661
Chief Operating Officer:
David I. Kentish
Executive Director
Canadian Association of Warehousing and Distribution Services
1272 McClure Court
Oshawa, Ontario L1H 8H2
(905) 436-8801

Canadian Industrial Transportation League (CITL)
Type: A trade association in which corporations hold membership.
Number of Members: 420 member companies represented by approximately 1,000 member representatives.
Dues: Dues are on a sliding scale based on number of employees
Purpose/Objective: To develop a thorough understanding of the transportation and distribution requirements of industry; and to promote, conserve, and protect commercial transportation interests.
Chief Elected Officer:
Andrew Kampf (Chairman)
Traffic Manager
Joseph E. Seagram & Sons, Ltd.
1430 Peel Street
Montral, Quebec H3A 159
(514) 849-5271
Chief Operating Officer:
Maria Rehner
President
Canadian Industrial Transportation League
1090 Don Mills Road
Don Mills, Ontario M3C 3R6
(416) 447-7766
Remarks: Canadian counterpart to the National Industrial Transportation League.

Centro Español De Logistica (CEL)
Type: A professional organization in which mem-

bership is extended on both an individual and a corporate basis.
Number of Members:
300 corporate members
130 individual members
Dues: $450 per company per year, and $120 per person per year.
Purpose/Objective: CEL is a nonprofit organization of companies, academics, and others interested in the logistics field. By offering training courses, journeys, roundtables, visits, and publications, it seeks to improve the standard of individual and corporate skills in the area of logistics management.
Chief Elected Officer:
Carlos Knapp Boetticher (President)
Logistics Enterprice S.L.
Ronda Avutarda;
11 Parque Conde De Orgaz
Madrid, Spain 28043
(34) 1 300 35 31
FAX (34) 1 300 11 03
Chief Operating Officer:
Paloma Marcitllach Aranda
Director
CEL-Centro Español De Logistica
Paseo De La Castellana, 114-2a 4o
Madrid, Spain 28046
(34) 1 411 67 53
FAX (34) 1 564 09 10

Council of Consulting Organizations, Inc.
Type: An umbrella organization with two divisions: ACME, representing management consulting firms, and IMC representing individual consultants.
Number of Members:
50 firms
2,200 individuals
Dues: ACME corporate dues are on a sliding scale based on annual revenues. IMC dues are $120 for a regular membership and $300 for a certified member.
Purpose/Objective: To contribute to the development and better understanding of the art and science, practice, and role of management consulting. To conduct research for the development and improvement of the practice of management, and disseminate the results of such research in the public interest.
Chief Operating Officer:
Edward D. Hendricks
President
Council of Consulting Organizations, Inc.
521 Fifth Avenue
New York, NY 10175
(212) 455-8221
FAX (212) 949-6571

Council of Logistics Management (CLM)
Type: A professional organization in which individuals hold membership.
Number of Members: 9,000
Dues: $175 per person per year.
Purpose/Objective: The mission of the Council of Logistics Management is to provide:

- Leadership in defining and understanding the logistics process.
- A forum for the exchange of ideas among logistics professionals.
- Research that contributes to enhanced customer value and supply chain performance.
- Awareness of career opportunities for logistics management.

This is an open organization which offers individual membership to persons in all industries, types of businesses, and job functions involved in the logistics process. The Council of Logistics Management operates on a nonprofit, self-supporting basis, with emphasis on quality and in a cooperative manner with other organizations and institutions.
Chief Elected Officer:
Gary J. Sease (President)
Senior Vice President
Operations Services
American National Can Company
8770 West Bryn Mawr Ave.
Chicago, IL 60631
(312) 399-8484
Chief Operating Officer:
George A. Gecowets
Executive Vice President
Council of Logistics Management
2803 Butterfield Road, Suite 380
Oak Brook, IL 60521-1156
(708) 574-0985
FAX (708) 574-0989
Remarks: As with any professional organization, membership in the Council of Logistics Management is on an individual basis. The membership belongs to the individual and not to his or her company.

It is not transferable. The Council of Logistics Management, as an organization, is not aligned with shippers, carriers, warehouse operators, material handling equipment manufacturers, consultants, or any other similar industrial grouping. Because its members have widespread and varying interests within the logistics industry, the Council will not get involved in legislative or similar matters in which industrial segments have contrary interests.

Delta Nu Alpha
Type: A professional organization in which individuals hold membership.
Number of Members: 5,000
Dues: $50 to $100 per person. Must have enrolled in or completed one year of traffic, transportation, or related education, or possess practical experience in transportation or a related field. In addition, regions and chapters have nominal dues added.
Purpose/Objective: To be a service organization providing educational opportunities to those having a professional interest in transportation, logistics, and related fields. To serve as a sustaining resource for future needs of the industry.
Chief Elected Officer:
J. Wesley McKnit (President)
The Latter Day Saints
50 East North Temple
Salt Lake City, UT 84150
(801) 240-2491
Chief Operating Officer:
Dee Ann Walker
Executive Director
Delta Nu Alpha
530 Church Street, Suite 300
Nashville, TN 37219
(615) 251-0933
FAX (615) 254-7047
Remarks: Membership is open to anyone who is interested in transportation. Members are able to meet with others in their profession or related professions. Delta Nu Alpha was designed to provide the novice as well as the executive with a forum in which to learn more about his or her chosen profession.

Deutsche Gesellschaft fur Logistik e.v. (German Society of Logistics)
Type: An organization in which membership is extended on both an individual and/or corporate basis.
Number of Members:
250 corporate
800 individual
Dues: 120 Deutsche marks (DM) per person per year (approximately $73 US). Corporate dues are on a sliding scale based on number of employees.
Purpose/Objective: The purpose of the organization is the promotion of scientific and practical research and development in the field of logistics, with particular consideration of industry, commerce and services, and educational programming.
Chief Elected Officer:
Wolfgang Zwillich (Chairman of the Board)
Member of Board
Siemens AG
Werner-von-Siemens-Strasse 50
Erlangen, Germany 91052
Chief Operating Officer:
Joerg Breker
Executive Director
Deutsche Gesellschaft fur Logistik e.v.
Heinrich-Hertz-Strabe 4
44227 Dortmund, Germany
(231) 754 43-220
FAX (231) 7 54 43-222

The Electronic Data Interchange Association (EDIA)
Type: A trade association in which corporations hold memberships.
Number of Members: 425
Dues: This information is confidential.
Purpose/Objective: To promote electronic data interchange as the method of business transactions both in industry and government.
Chief Elected Officer:
Henry W. Meetze
Chairman
Railinc Corporation
50 F Street NW
Washington, DC 20001
(202) 639-5501
Chief Operating Officer:
Gregory B. Harter
President
The Electronic Data Interchange Association

225 Reinekers Lane
Alexandria, VA 22314
(703) 838-8042
FAX (703) 838-8038

Eno Transportation Foundation, Inc.
Type: Private Operating Foundation endowed in 1921 by William Phelps Eno (not a grant or charitable organization).
Number of Members: N/A
Dues: N/A
Purpose/Objective: To undertake and promote research in all areas of transportation, to inform the public on transportation matters, and to encourage and support professional training in transportation.
Chief Elected Officer:
John L. Sweeney
Chairman
Eno Transportation Foundation, Inc.
44211 Slatestone Court
Landsdowne, VA 22075
(703) 729-7200
Chief Operating Officer:
Roland A. Ouellette
President
Eno Transportation Foundation, Inc.
44211 Slatestone Court
Landsdowne, VA 22075
(703) 729-7200

European Logistics Association (ELA)
Type: An umbrella organization of European logistics associations.
Number of Members: 35
Dues: 2,000 Swiss francs
Purpose/Objective: The mission of ELA is: to link the professional bodies in Europe into a functioning organization to service both industry and trade in Europe; to define the European logistics terminology on a multilingual basis to ensure ease and correctness of communication from country to country; to develop a "European" body of knowledge using information not only from within Europe but also by tracking new developments in other parts of the world and to act as a focal point for logistics research in conjunction with academics, industry, and government; and to formulate a European Education Certification Program in order to have uniform standards within the European community.
Chief Elected Officer:
H. J. Bendel (President)
Director
Linde Lansing AG
Alte Duebendorferstrasse
Dietlikon CH 8305
Switzerland
(41) 1 833 10 25
Chief Operating Officer:
Honorary H.E. van Goor
Secretary
European Logistics Association
Rue Archimede 5, 6th Fl.
B-1040
Brussels, Belgium
(32) 2 230 0211

French Association for Logistics (ASLOG)
Type: An organization in which membership is extended on both an individual and a corporate basis.
Dues: 1900 French francs (FFR) per person per year (approximately $425 US). 3800 FFR (approximately $845 US) for corporations.
Number of Members:
650 individuals
80 corporate
Purpose/Objective: To promote logistics in companies through such activities as meetings, symposia, and special studies.
Chief Elected Officer:
Gregoire Laurent
President
ASLOG
119, rue Cardinet
75017 Paris, France
(33) 1 40 53 85 59

Grocery Manufacturers of America, Inc. (GMA)
Type: A trade association in which corporations hold membership.
Number of Members: 140 corporate members.
Dues: Sliding scale based on sales.
Purpose/Objective: The Grocery Manufacturers of America, Inc. is a trade association of the leading manufacturers and processors of food and nonfood

products sold in retail grocery outlets throughout the United States. GMA's objective is to solve for member companies those problems for which GMA group action is more effective than action by member companies working individually or through other associations.
Chief Elected Officer:
William D. Smithburg (Chairman)
President & CEO
Quaker Oats Company
321 North Clark Street
Chicago, IL 60610
(312) 222-7525
Chief Operating Officer:
C. Manly Molpus
President & CEO
Grocery Manufacturers of America, Inc.
1010 Wisconsin Avenue NW, Suite 900
Washington, DC 20007
(202) 337-9400
FAX (202) 337-4508
Remarks: The staff member responsible for distribution related programs is Patrick Kiernan, Vice President, Industry Relations, Grocery Manufacturers of America.

Health and Personal Care Distribution Conference, Inc. (H&PCDC)
Type: An industrial transportation trade association.
Number of Members: 70
Dues: Varies with company sales.
Purpose/Objective: H&PCDC addresses concerns common to the shippers of drugs, medicines, toilet preparations, and health and personal care products. It represents their views in Washington and before state and federal agencies and courts. It provides seminars and educational speakers at its meetings.
Chief Elected Officer:
Charles T. Bennett (President)
Manager, Distribution Services
Rhone-Poulenc Rorer
PO Box 1200
Collegeville, PA 19426
(215) 454-8929
Chief Operating Officer:
William Moran
Executive Director
The Health and Personal Care
Distribution Conference, Inc.
1090 12 Street
Vero Beach, FL 32960
(407) 778-7782

Institute of Industrial Engineers (IIE)
Type: A professional organization in which individuals hold membership.
Number of Members: 35,000
Dues: $75 per person per year.
Purpose/Objective: The purpose of IIE is to advance the general welfare of mankind through the resources and creative abilities of the industrial engineering profession and to encourage and assist education and research in the art and science of industrial engineering.
Chief Elected Officer:
Leland T. Blank
Institute of Industrial Engineers
25 Technology Park Atlanta
Norcross, GA 30092
(404) 449-0460
FAX (404) 263-8532
Chief Operating Officer:
Gregory Balestrero
Executive Director
Institute of Industrial Engineers
25 Technology Park Atlanta
Norcross, GA 30092
(404) 449-0461
FAX (404) 263-8532

Institute of Logistics
Type: A professional organization which is supported by contributors from corporations and individual membership.
Number of Members: 11,000
Dues: $86 per person per year; $312 for corporate membership.
Purpose/Objective: To promote the art and science of logistics and physical distribution management. To provide services to members, including library, information services, regional activities, career advice, and educational facilities.
Chief Elected Officer:
J. Boatman
Chairman
NFT Distribution Ltd., Azalea Close
Clover Nook Ind. Estate, Somercoats

Alfreton, Derbys
England DESS 4QX
Chief Operating Officer:
Ian C. Canadine
Director General
Institute of Logistics
Douglas House, Queens Square
Corby, Northants
England NN17 1PL
(0536) 205500

Institute of Management Consultants, Inc. (IMC)
Type: A professional organization in which individuals hold membership.
Number of Members: 2,300
Dues: certified members $300 per year; members $120 per year
Purpose/Objective: Professional certification (the "CMC") is pursued to assure the public that members possess the ethical standards, the professional competence, and the independence required for membership, and are, therefore, qualified to practice.
Chief Elected Officer:
Pamela Yardis (Chairman)
Chestnut Hill Consulting Group, Inc.
PO Box 15755
Stamford, CT 06901
(203) 968-1888
Chief Operating Officer:
Wendy Benz
Executive Director
Institute of Management Consultants
521 Fifth Avenue, 35th Fl.
New York, NY 10175
(212) 697-9693

Institute of Materials Handling, Transport, Packaging, and Storage Systems (IMADOS)
Type: A scientific research and self-supporting professional organization which solves problems related to logistics and physical distribution, automatic control systems for material and technical supply handling, transportation, packaging, and storage.
Number of Members: 40
Dues: This information is confidential.
Purpose/Objective:

- research and development of project-engineered activities for technical and building equipment for the workplace in the spheres of production and physical distribution
- research and development of special machines, devices, and equipment for materials handling, transportation, storage, and packaging engineering
- technical standardization
- information service systems for Czechoslovakia and foreign countries
- publishing of professional monthly periodical *Material Handling, Storage, and Packaging* (in Czech and Slovak languages), with summaries in English, German, and Russian
- regular, professional training, conferences, and symposia for experts in the spheres of materials management, storage, packaging, and logistics systems
- high-tech commercial, technical, and marketing services both for capital investors and producers
- delivery of most effective handling and storage systems in the shortest terms
- improved product quality for reasonable prices and terms

Chief Elected Officer:
Karel Rehak
Director
IMADOS, a.s.
Konevova 141
Praha 3 130 83
Czech Republic
Chief Operating Officer: Same as above
Remarks: In early 1989, SYMAS (Systems of Materials Handling and Storage) was founded. SYMAS is an association of 22 prominent Czechoslovakian development, projection, and production enterprises, engaged in solving problems related to materials handling and storage.

Institute of Packaging Professionals (IoPP)
Type: A professional organization in which individuals and/or corporations hold membership.

Number of Members:
7,500 individual
100 corporate
Dues: Individual member—$90 per year
Corporate member—$850 per year for level 1; $1,250 per year for level 2
Junior Member—$45.00 per year.
Level 1 is for companies with gross annual sales under $50,000 and includes four individual memberships. Level 2 is for companies with gross annual sales over $50,000 and includes six individual memberships.
Purpose/Objective: IoPP's purpose is the professional development of packaging and handling professionals. The Institute of Packaging Professionals is an individual, professional membership organization of those who apply packaging design, engineering, production, and distribution principles and technologies and of those who manage these technologies and related production processes.
Chief Elected Officer:
Ed Church (Chairman)
President
Lansmont, Inc.
6539 Westland Way, #25
Lansing, MI 48917
Chief Operating Officer:
William C. Pflaum
Executive Director
Institute of Packaging Professionals
481 Carlisle Drive
Herndon, VA 22070
(703) 318-8970
FAX (703) 318-0310

Intermodal Association of North America
Type: A trade association in which individuals and corporations hold membership.
Number of Members: 500
Dues: Dues are on a sliding scale based on intermodal revenues/expenses (whichever is greater).
Purpose/Objective: The purpose of this organization is to promote and encourage intermodal transportation, cooperation between the modes, and standard practices and procedures.
Chief Elected Officer:
Donald G. McInnes (Chairman)
Vice President-Intermodal
Atchison, Topeka & Santa Fe Railway Co.
1700 E. Golf Road
Schaumburg, IL 60173-5860
(708) 995-2680
FAX (708) 995-2929
Chief Operating Officer:
John A. McQuaid
President
Intermodal Association of North America
6410 Kenilworth Avenue, Suite 108
Riverdale, MD 20737-1202
(301) 864-4160
FAX (301) 864-4163

International Association of Refrigerated Warehouses
Type: A trade association in which corporations hold memberships.
Number of Members: 500
Dues: Dues are based on the company's gross refrigerated space.
Purpose/Objective: To advance the interests and welfare of the refrigerated warehousing business; elevate and improve industry standards; and promote better understanding of its functions within the food distribution industry and among the general public.
Chief Operating Officer:
J. William Hudson
President
International Association of
Refrigerated Warehouses
7315 Wisconsin Avenue, Suite 1200N
Bethesda, MD 20814
(301) 652-5674
FAX (301) 652-7269

International Customer Service Association (ICSA)
Type: A professional organization in which individuals in management positions hold membership.
Number of Members: 3,200
Dues: $195 for the first year, $145 for renewal. Members of ICSA are management professionals and ICSA programs focus on customer service management and related aspects.
Purpose/Objective: ICSA is an organization dedicated to developing the theory and understanding of the total quality service process, advancing the art and science of managing that process, and en-

couraging professional dialogue in the achievement of customer satisfaction.
Chief Elected Officer:
Beverly Grace (President)
Customer Service Senior Supervisor
Exxon Chemical Company
13501 Katy Freeway L2-468
Houston, TX 77079
Chief Operating Officer:
Madalyn B. Duerr
Executive Director
International Customer Service Association
401 N. Michigan Avenue
Chicago, IL 60611-4267
(312) 321-6800
FAX (312) 321-6869
Remarks: ICSA actively engages in the professional development of customer service management; sound customer service practices; open discussion and debate of customer service issues; and investigation of emerging technologies and their application to customer service.

International Mass Retailing Association (IMRA)
Type: A full-service trade association.
Number of Members:
125 retail company members
500 associate members
Dues: For retail members, based on annual sales.
Purpose/Objective: IMRA represents the nation's discount and variety general merchandise retail industry. IMRA's memberships include companies that operate more than 40,000 discount, variety, dollar, junior department, family center off-price, factory outlet, catalog showroom, and other general merchandise stores. Members range widely in size and include many of the nation's largest retail chains.
Chief Elected Officer:
Warren White
Executive Vice President & General Manager
Clover
801 Market Street
Philadelphia, PA 19107
(215) 629-7700
Chief Operating Officer:
Robert J. Verdisco
President
International Mass Retailing Institute
1901 Pennslyvania Avenue, NW
Washington, DC 20006
(202) 861-0774
Remarks: The IMRA maintains contact with the entire retail community through its lobbying efforts and state legislative reporting service. In addition, the IMRA offers a professional development conference in the areas of physical distribution, advertising/merchandising, finance and information systems, public relations, loss prevention, store planning, and design.

International Society for Inventory Research
Type: An organization in which membership is extended on both an individual and corporate basis.
Number of Members:
300 individuals
45 corporate
Dues: $35 annually for individual members, $175 annually for corporate members.
Purpose/Objective: The Society, which is a professional, nonprofit organization, provides those engaged in inventory research with an opportunity to exchange views and experiences on an international and interdisciplinary basis. The Society's mission is to provide an appropriate and comprehensive framework for the dissemination of research results attained in the member's country and to take initiative in the development of research and higher education.
Chief Elected Officer:
Michael C. Lovell
Professor of Economics
Wesleyan University
Middletown, CT 06459
(203) 347-9411
Chief Operating Officer:
Attila Chikan
First Vice President and Secretary General
International Society for Inventory Research
Veres Palne u. 36
Budapest, Hungary H-1053
(36-1) 117-2959

NCITD-The International Trade Facilitation Council (NCITD)
Type: A trade association in which corporations hold memberships.

Number of Members: 200 corporations
Dues: Corporate dues are on a sliding scale based on the corporation's needs.
Purpose/Objective: NCITD is a nonprofit, industry-financed membership organization dedicated to simplifying and improving international trade documentation and procedures, including information exchange by either paper or electronic methods. Working through individuals and companies, members and nonmembers, United States and overseas governmental departments and agencies, and duly constituted national and international committees and organizations, NCITD serves as coordinator and as a central source of information, reference, and solutions to problems on international trade information exchange and procedures.
Chief Elected Officer:
Robert Shellman (Chairman)
Manager, Ocean Transportation
Union Carbide Corporation
39 Old Ridgebury Road
Danbury, CT 06817-0001
Chief Operating Officer:
Robert K. Windsor
President
NCITD-The International
Trade Facilitation Council
1800 Diagonal Road, Suite 220
Alexandria, VA 22314
(709) 519-0661
FAX (709) 519-0664

Japanese Council of Logistics Management (JILS)
Type: An organization in which membership is extended on both an individual and a corporate basis.
Number of Members:
780 corporate members
130 individual members
Dues: The dues are $270 per individual per year; $1,100 per corporation per year.
Purpose/Objective: To contribute to the development of the national economy and to develop activities relating to the modernization of physical distribution. To promote physical distribution systems in the commercial field. To conduct seminars, workshops, and conferences, and to sponsor overseas tours that are of interest to physical distribution management personnel.
Chief Elected Officer:
Hiroshi Saito (Chairman)
President
Nippon Steel Corporation
c/o JILS Shuwa No. 2 Shiba Park Bldg.
2-12-7, Shiba Daimon Minato-ku
Tokyo, 105 Japan

Korea Productivity Center (KPC)
Type: An organization in which corporations hold membership. KPC was established as a special corporate body in accordance with the Industrial Development Law in 1986.
Number of Members:715 corporate members.
Dues: 560,000 Korean Won (approximately $800 US).
Purpose/Objective: The major objectives of the Korea Productivity Center are to:

- stimulate interest in productivity and to promote productivity consciousness
- to render consultancy services to industries to increase their managerial and operational efficiency
- to train industrial personnel to improve their productivity
- to collect and disseminate information relating to productivity improvement
- to act as the integrated focal point of all organizations engaged in productivity improvement drives.

Chief Elected Officer:
Moon Hi Whoa (Chairman)
Korea Productivity Center
CPO Box 834
Seoul, Korea 110-052
(02) 739-5868
Chief Operating Officer:
Park Worl Saeng
Executive Director
Korea Productivity Center
CPO Box 834
Seoul, Korea, 110-052
(02) 739-5868

Logistics Management Association of Australia (LMA)
Type: A professional organization in which individuals hold membership.
Number of Members: 400
Dues: $100 per person per year.
Purpose/Objective: The LMA is an association representing the interests of those involved in logistics. This includes warehousing, distribution, purchasing, marketing, sales, customer service, and materials managers. The aim to increase the professionals of members is achieved by acting as the representative body for managers engaged in logistics functions; providing opportunities for interaction and sharing of experiences with other professionals; conducting monthly meetings to discuss topics and issues of interest; and providing opportunities for learning through participation in seminars, site visits, and tertiary courses.
Chief Elected Officer:
Kerry Hammond (President)
Consultant
172 Nicholson Street
Fitzroy, Victoria 3065
Austrailia
(61) 3-416-2677
FAX (61) 3-416-2742
Chief Operating Officer:
Kevin James Duck
Executive Officer
Logistics Management Association of Australia
PO Box 943
Auburn NSW Australia 2144
(02) 502-2336
FAX (02) 502-3240

Material Handling Equipment Distributors Association
Type: A trade association in which corporations hold membership.
Number of Members: 760
Dues: Corporate dues are on a sliding scale based on gross sales and commission for distributors. Flat fee for allied/associate members.
Purpose/Objective: To educate distributor members in the methods and practices necessary for them to become the most efficient medium through which materials handling equipment manufacturers distribute their products. To educate manufacturers and suppliers on the value of distributors in the distribution of material handling products. To enhance the professional image of the distributor handlers of the marketplace and to endeavor in every way to make the material handling industry better tomorrow than it is today.
Chief Elected Officer:
William J. Witcroft (President)
President
The Babush Corporation
9400 N. Fountain Blvd.
Menomonee Falls, WI 53052
(414) 255-5300
FAX (414) 255-1808
Chief Operating Officer:
Tony S. Coletti
Executive Vice President
Material Handling Equipment Distributors Association
201 Route 45
Vernon Hills, IL 60061
(708) 680-3500
FAX (708) 362-6989

The Material Handling Institute, Inc. (MHI)
Type: A trade association in which corporations hold membership.
Number of Members: 650
Dues: Depends on affiliation.
Purpose/Objective: MHI has two divisions; the MHI itself and the Material Handling Industry of America (MHIA). Since 1945, MHI has provided industry information and discourse. MHIA provides an industry voice and sponsors trade events.
Chief Operating Officer:
A.L. Leffler
CEO
The Material Handling Institute, Inc.
8720 Red Oak Boulevard, Suite 201
Charlotte, NC 28217
(704) 522-8644
FAX (704) 522-7826

Materials Handling & Management Society (formerly the International Material Management Society)
Type: A professional organization in which individuals hold membership.

Number of Members: 1,500
Dues: $125 per person per year. Members must be directly involved in the field of material handling or material management in their occupation.
Purpose/Objective: The Materials Handling & Management Society is a professional society dedicated to enhancing the professional stature of its members and their fields on all levels through promoting public recognition of material handling and material management as vital professional business activities, and providing members with activities and information which facilitate acquiring increased knowledge and skills in the areas of material handling and material management.
Chief Elected Officer:
James L. Dean (President)
Business Manager, Voice Paging
AT&T
PO Box 650345
Dallas, TX 75265
(214) 308-2500
Chief Operating Officer:
F. Hal Vandiver
Executive Director
Materials Handling & Management Society
8720 Red Oak Boulevard, Suite 224
Charlotte, NC 28217
(704) 525-4677
FAX (704) 522-7826

The National American Wholesale Grocers' Association (NAWGA)
Type: A trade association in which corporations hold membership.
Number of Members: 308
Dues: Corporate dues are on a sliding scale based on company wholesale sales volume.
Purpose/Objective: The purpose of The National American Wholesale Grocers' Association and its foodservice division is to improve the efficiency and increase the profitability of the wholesale grocery and foodservice distribution industry by:

- providing training and education in operations, management skills, and ways to improve productivity; and
- effectively representing members' interests in Washington, DC. Success in our mission will benefit the consuming public as well as our membership.

Chief Elected Officer:
Boyd Lee George (Chairman of the Board)
Vice Chairman of the Board/Chairman
Merchants Distributors, Inc.
120 Fourth Street SW
Hickory, NC 28602
(704) 323-4100
FAX (704) 323-4435
Chief Operating Officer:
John R. Block
President
National American Wholesale
Grocers Association (NAWGA)
201 Park Washington Court
Falls Church, VA 22046
(703) 532-9400
FAX (703) 538-4673

The National Association of Freight Transportation Consultants
Type: A professional organization in which individuals or companies hold membership.
Number of Members: 80-100
Dues: $150 minimum to $350 maximum.
Purpose/Objective: Nonprofit association of consultants in freight transportation who perform all phases of such services for shipper clients, and in some cases motor carriers and other clients.
Chief Elected Officer:
Glenn Choffin
President
National Association of Freight
Transportation Consultants
PO Box 21418
Albuquerque, NM 87154-1418
(505) 275-2390
Chief Operating Officer:
Donna F. Behme
Executive Director
National Association of Freight
Transportation Consultants
PO Box 21418
Albuquerque, NM 87154-1418
(505) 275-2390
Remarks: Two annual meetings per year are held in different locations throughout the United States.

The National Association of Manufacturers (NAM)
Type: A trade association in which corporations hold membership.
Number of Members: 12,500
Dues: Corporate dues are on a sliding scale based on company net worth.
Purpose/Objective: To promote America's economic health and productivity, particularly in the manufacturing sector.
Chief Elected Officer:
Robert Cizik (Chairman)
Chairman of the Board and CEO
Cooper Industries, Inc.
PO Box 4446
Houston, TX 77210
(713) 739-5401
Chief Operating Officer:
Jerry J. Jasinowski
President
National Association of Manufacturers
1331 Pennsylvania Avenue Suite 1500N
Washington, DC 20004-1703
(202) 637-3000

The National Association of Purchasing Management, Inc. (NAPM)
Type: An educational organization in which individuals hold membership.
Number of Members: 36,000
Dues: Dues vary, depending on which affiliate one belongs to.
Purpose/Objective: The National Association of Purchasing Management is committed to providing national and international leadership on purchasing and materials management. Through its 170 affiliated associations and over 36,000 members, the association provides opportunities for purchasing and materials management practitioners to expand their professional skill and knowledge, and works to foster a better understanding of purchasing and materials management concepts.
Chief Elected Officer:
John P. McSherry, C.P.M.
Director of Purchasing
Pfizer, Inc.
235 East 42nd St.
New York, NY 10017
(212) 573-2121
Chief Operating Officer:
R. Jerry Baker
Executive Vice President
National Association of Purchasing Management
PO Box 22160
Tempe, AZ 85285-2160
(602) 752-6276
FAX (602) 752-7890

The National Defense Transportation Association (NDTA)
Type: A nonprofit educational association.
Number of Members:
8,200 individual
140 corporations
Dues: Individual—$35 per year
Under age 35—$25 year
Student—$10 per year
Corporate—$1,100 per year
Purpose/Objective: The National Defense Transportation Association is an educational, nonprofit, worldwide organization which combines the transportation industry's manpower and skills with the expertise of those in government and the military to achieve the mutual objectives of a strong and responsive transportation capability. NDTA membership represents the transportation operators, users, mode carriers, manufacturers, traffic managers, and related industries, and military and government interests.
Chief Elected Officer:
Jeff Crowe
Chairman of the Board
Landstar System, Inc.
1000 Bridgeport Ave.
Shelton, CT 06484
(203) 925-2900
Chief Operating Officer:
Lt. Gen. Edward Honor, USA (Ret.)
President
National Defense Transportation Association
50 S. Pickett Street, Suite 220
Alexandria, VA 22304-3008
(703) 751-5011

National Grocers Association (NGA)
Type: A trade association in which corporations hold membership.

Number of Members: 2,500
Dues: Corporate dues are on a sliding scale and range from $200 to $22,000.
Purpose/Objective: To advance the common interests and enhance the mutual understandings and relationships of independently operated retailers, retailer-owned/cooperatives and voluntary wholesale distributors engaged primarily in the sale and distribution of food and related products so as to better serve the customer.
Chief Operating Officer:
Thomas K. Zaucha
Executive Vice President
National Grocers Association
1825 Samuel Morse Drive
Reston, VA 22090
(703) 437-5300
FAX (703) 437-7768

The National Industrial Transportation League (NITL)
Type: A transportation trade association.
Number of Members: 1,300
Dues: Corporate dues are on a sliding scale based on a company's gross sales.
Purpose/Objective: The League's purposes are: to promote adequate national and international transportation; to interchange ideas and information concerning traffic and transportation matters as permitted by law; to cooperate with the regulatory agencies, both federal and state, the DOT, and other transportation companies; and to develop a thorough understanding of legislation that will be helpful to commerce.
Chief Elected Officer:
Roger W. Wigen (Chairman)
3M
Bldg. 225-5N-07
St. Paul, MN 55144
(612) 736-0310
Chief Operating Officer:
Edward M. Emmett
President
National Industrial Transportation League
1700 N. Moore Street, Suite 1900
Arlington, VA 22209-1904
(703) 524-5011
FAX (703) 524-5017

National Perishable Transportation Association
Type: A trade association in which shippers, motor carriers, warehouses, and receivers involved in the manufacture, distribution, and sale of perishable products hold membership. Also, those teaching transportation courses may hold membership. Membership belongs to the organization. Each organization may appoint up to two management level members.
Number of Members: 135
Dues: $150 annually.
Purpose/Objective: To provide a forum where shippers, carriers, and receivers can meet to discuss the problems inherent to the distribution of perishable commodities. Legal counsel attends all meetings to preclude antitrust violations.
Chief Elected Officer:
Leonard K. Sackson (President)
Executive Vice President
Wilson Refrigerated Express
PO Box 6946
Rochester, MN 55903
(507) 282-6715
Chief Operating Officer:
William Towle (Executive Director)
PO Box 3021
Oak Park, IL 60301
(708) 524-1020
Remarks: Membership is limited to senior transportation representatives.

The National Private Truck Council (NPTC)
Number of Members: 1,300
Dues: Corporate dues range from $300 to $1,450.

- Regular member: any business enterprise engaged in the operation of one or more trucks (either as an owner or lessee) in furtherance of any primary commercial enterprise.
- Associate member: any business that is transportation related and which serves the private trucking industry.

Purpose/Objective: The purpose of the National Private Truck Council is to represent the interests of the private trucking industry before legislative, administrative, regulatory, or judicial branches of government; to collect and disseminate information concerning matters of interest to private fleet operators; to provide fleets; and to foster and promote greater public understanding and appreciation of the private trucking industry. In addition, NPTC publishes a monthly management journal, *The Private Carrier,* and the monthly newsletters, *The Private Line* and *Safety & Complience News.*

Chief Operating Officer:
Gene S. Bergoffen
Executive Vice President
National Private Truck Council
66 Canal Center Plaza, Suite 600
Alexandria, VA 22314
(703) 683-1300
FAX (703) 683-1217

Remarks: NPTC has a new affiliate, the Private Fleet Management Institute (PFMI). PFMI is a nonprofit affiliate established to give a clear focus to education and research activities, and allow corporations, foundations, and government agencies to sponsor industry studies and research projects. The Certified Private Fleet Manager Program (a program administered by PFMI) was established to validate and recognize the professionalism and knowledge of those in the field of private fleet management. It is a new designation awarded by NPTC and administered by the PFMI. Certification is awarded on the basis of professional experience of passage and a two part exam.

The National Small Shipments Traffic Conference (NASSTRAC)

Type: An organization in which membership is extended on both an individual and a corporate basis.

Number of Members: 550

Dues: Corporate dues are on a sliding scale based on gross domestic sales.

Purpose/Objective: The purpose of NASSTRAC is to:

- assist members in identifying new and innovative ways to save money on LTL distribution of goods;
- provide an educational program for professional development of executives;
- provide a vehicle for professional interchanges and an introduction to experienced LTL distribution officials who can provide guidance as needed;
- keep members up-to-date on development in LTL distribution techniques and on regulatory and rate matters;
- provide legal representation for appropriate litigation and basic legal guidance;
- provide a platform for professional interchange with carriers.

Chief Elected Officer:
Charles A. Gerardi
Director of Distribution/Logistics
Schneider North America
Square D Company
1100 Burlington Pike
Florence, KY 41042

Chief Operating Officer:
Joseph F.H. Cutrona
Executive Director
National Small Shipments Traffic Conference
1750 Pennslyvania Avenue NW Suite 1111
Washington, DC 20006
(202) 393-5505

The National Society of Professional Engineers (NSPE)

Type: A professional organization composed of individuals registered under the law of any state or territory in the US or Canada, or graduates of a recognized engineering program.

Number of Members: 78,000

Dues: National dues $77. Individuals' dues include local chapter, state society, and national society—total ranging from approximately $85 to $252.

Purpose/Objective: NSPE is dedicated to the protection and promotion of the profession of engineering as a social and economic influence vital to the affairs of society and the United States. It has actively promoted effective stage registration laws for professional engineers to safeguard the public.

Chief Elected Officer:
T. Dudley Hixson (President)
Meyer, Meyer, LaCroix, & Hixon
PO Box 5444
Alexandria, LA 71307
(318) 448-0888

Chief Operating Officer:
Donald G. Weinert, P.E.
Executive Director
The National Society of Professional Engineers

1420 King Street
Alexandria, VA 22314
(703) 684-2800
FAX (703) 836-4875

The National Wholesale Druggists' Association (NWDA)
Type: A trade association in which corporations hold membership.
Number of Members: 68 wholesalers; 350 associate suppliers, 40 international. Wholesalers must be full service drug wholesalers in business for at least five consecutive years, and suppliers must be engaged in a health-care related industry and in business for at least five consecutive years.
Dues: Graduated on the basis of annual sales volume.
Purpose/Objective: The NWDA is a national trade association of full-service drug wholesalers. More than 300 manufacturers of pharmaceuticals, nonprescription drugs, and health and beauty aids are associate members. NWDA was founded in Indianapolis, Indiana in 1876. Its primary purposes are to strengthen relations between wholesalers' suppliers and customers; to serve as a forum for major industry issues; to research and communicate information on new business systems, logistics technologies, and management practices for drug wholesalers; and to represent the industry on legislative and regulatory matters.
Chief Elected Officer:
John F. McNamara
Chairman and CEO
Alco Health Services Corp.
PO Box 959
Valley Forge, PA 19482
(215) 296-4480
Chief Operating Officer:
Ronald J. Streck
President and CEO
National Wholesale Druggists' Association
PO Box 2219
Reston, VA 22090
Remarks: Maintains ten standing committees; sponsors an annual meeting and marketing and productivity/technology conferences; and publishes an annual membership directory, operating survey, bimonthly newsletter, and various monthly bulletins and newsletters.

Norsk Innkjopsog Material Administrasjonsforbund (NIMA) (Norwegion Association of Purchasing and Materials Management)
Type: A professional organization in which individuals hold membership.
Number of Members: 1,800
Dues: $75 per person per year.
Purpose/Objective: To raise the professional standard of members, and others engaged in the profession. NIMA has for many years and in many ways tried to get attention from the official school authorities to get purchasing and logistics on the time table.
Chief Operating Officer:
Karl-Erik Bastiansen
Director General
Norsk Innkjops og Material
Trondheimsveien 80
N-0565 Oslo
Norway
(4722) 37 97 10
FAX (4722) 38 53 23
Remarks: Special efforts have been made to qualify Norwegian purchasers on the international market. In this respect NIMA obtained financial aid from Naeringsdepartementet (the department for commerce and industry) and Naeringslivets Hovedorganisasjon (the organization for employers within Norwegian business life).

North American Logistics Association
Type: A trade association in which corporations hold membership.
Dues: Dues are on a sliding scale based on number of employees and gross sales.
Purpose/Objective: The North American Logistics Association is a newly-created trade association which is being developed in order to market the various disciplines of outsourced logistics as an industry. The mission of the North American Logistics Association is to promote the awareness and use of outsourced logistics by educating and motivating key corporate decision makers who have logistics needs. The North American Logistics Association will focus public, political, and corporate attention on outsourced logistics so that it is recognized as an industry of immense importance.
Chief Operating Officer:
Michael Jenkins

President and CEO
North American Logistics Association
1300 West Higgins Road, Suite 111
Park Ridge, IL 60068
(708) 292-1891
FAX (708) 292-1896

Office Furniture Distribution Association, Inc. (OFDA)
Type: A trade and professional organization in which office furniture manufacturers hold membership.
Number of Members: 40
Dues: Corporate dues are a sliding scale based on annual sales volume.
Purpose/Objective: OFDA is a nonprofit office furniture shippers' association whose object, as stated in our constitution, is to promote the common interests of its members as to transportation and distribution management development through educational articles, seminars, programs, and presentations of views to regulatory agencies concerning these common interests. These common interests include rules, regulations, ratings, rates, and packing requirements of carriers as they relate to the transportation of office furniture.
Chief Elected Officer:
Russell Matthews (Chairman)
Corporate Traffic Director
LA-Z-BOY Chair Company
1284 N. Telegraph Road
Monroe, MI 48161
(313) 241-3822
Chief Operating Officer:
Kenneth E. Miller
Managing Director
Office Furniture Distribution Association, Inc.
PO Box 326
Petersham, MA 01366-0326
(508) 724-3267
Remarks: OFDA now allows associate members to join who are carriers for or suppliers to the office furniture industry.

Society of Logistics Engineers (SOLE)
Type: A professional organization in which individuals and corporations hold membership.
Number of Members:
7,500 individual
20 corporate
Dues: $75 per person. Corporate dues are on a sliding scale based on the number of employees.
Purpose/Objective: The Society of Logistics Engineers is a nonprofit, international organization devoted to scientific, educational, and literary endeavors to enhance the art and science of logistics technology, education, and management.
Chief Elected Officer:
Michael J. Monahan
Manager of ILS Test Operations
Northrop Corp., B-2 Div.
3520 E. Ave. M
Palmdale, CA 93550
(805) 272-8500
Chief Operating Officer:
Norman P. Michaud
Executive Director
8100 Professional Place, Suite 211
New Carrollton, MD 20785
(301) 459-8446
FAX (301) 459-1522
Remarks: Membership is open to corporations and all individuals working, studying, or having an interest in the career fields of logistics technology, management, education, product support, and physical distribution.

Swedish Materials Administration Forum (SMAF)
Type: A professional organization in which individuals hold membership.
Number of Members: Approximately 450
Dues: $100 per person per year. Companies or other types of organizations active within the field of logistics can be accepted as supporting members; dues quotes not available at this time.
Purpose/Objective: The main objectives of SMAF are:

- To establish a bridge and unite common interests of different functions in the field of materials administration within a company and the society in general.
- To stimulate activities within the materials administration field and emphasize high quality work.

- To stimulate research and other similar activities within the materials administration area.
- To support education and training of materials administration staff by presenting courses of our own and arranging seminars and conferences in order to inform about trends and current developments in materials administration.
- To develop and support an integrated overall view of the concept of materials and administration.
- To present for the press and other groups of interest a wide picture of the development within the materials administration field and to stress the importance of materials administration in the total economy of the society.
- To stimulate and support activities related to contacts with international organizations dealing with materials administration, logistics, and materials handling.

Chief Elected Officer:
Annica Sundberg
Operating Manager
Swedish Materials Administration Forum
Box 608 S-131 21
Nacka
Sweden
46 (8) 7181280
FAX 46 (8) 7180025
Chief Operating Officer:
Goran Lundborg
President
Swedish Materials Administration Forum
Box 608 S-131 21
Nacka
Sweden
46 (8) 7181280
FAX 46 (8) 7180025

Transportation Brokers Conference of America (TBCA)
Type: A professional and trade association in which corporations hold membership.
Number of Members: 1,000 corporations.
Dues: $350/$450 year. Must be a licensed (ICC) broker. Must have a surety bond and sign the code of ethics. There are also associate memberships available and no requirements needed to join. This category would represent anyone who may be interested in the transportation industry.
Purpose/Objective: The TCBA is the professional association for licensed general commodity freight brokers in the US. Created in 1978, the TBCA is a nonprofit corporation whose sole purpose is to serve the needs and represent the interests of professional brokers. The TBCA seeks to promote professionalism in the brokerage industry; maintain high ethical standards; provide continuing education opportunities; represent brokers' interests to the ICC and other government agencies; and promote the benefits of professional brokerage to the public and other segments of the transportation industry.
Chief Operating Officer:
Annette E. Petrick
Executive Director
Transportation Brokers Conference of America (TBCA)
5845 Richmond Hwy, Suite 750
Alexandria, VA 22303
(703) 329-1894

Transportation Claims & Prevention Council, Inc. (formerly Shippers National Freight Claim Council, Inc.)
Type: A trade association in which corporations hold membership.
Number of Members: 650
Dues: $345 regular membership
$295 multiple subscribers
$295 associate members
Purpose/Objective: Transportation Claims & Prevention Council, Inc. is an educational institution developing the latest teaching tools and techniques on carrier liability and claims administration through seminars and publications. The objective is to develop a greater degree of professionalism in claims management.
Chief Elected Officer:
Mildred Dockery
Sunkist Growers
PO Box 7888
Van Nuys, CA 91409
(818) 379-7293
Chief Operating Officer:
William J. Augello
Executive Director/General Counsel
Transportation Claims & Prevention Council, Inc.

120 Main Street
Huntington, NY 11743
(516) 549-8984
FAX (516) 549-8962

Transportation Research Board (TRB)
Type: An organization in which membership is extended on both an individual and/or corporate basis.
Number of Members:
Individuals—2,200
Corporations—200
Committee Members—4,000
Dues: Committee membership size is limited. Nominations require individual expertise in the subject matter of a committee and approval by committee chairperson and TRB Executive Director. Individual and organizational membership; payment of required fee.
Purpose/Objective: To advance knowledge concerning the nature and performance of transportation systems by stimulating research and disseminating the information derived therefrom.
Chief Operating Officer:
Thomas B. Deen
Executive Director
Transportation Director
Transportation Research Board
2101 Constitution Avenue, NW
Washington, DC 20418
(202) 334-2959
FAX (202) 334-2003

Transportation Research Forum
Type: A professional organization in which individuals hold membership.
Number of Members: 700
Dues: $60 per person.
Purpose/Objective: The purpose of the Transportation Research Forum is to provide an impartial meeting ground for carriers, shippers, government officials, consultants, university researchers, suppliers, and others seeking an exchange of information and ideas related to both passengers and freight transportation.
Chief Operating Officer:
William M. Drohan,
Executive Director
Transportation Research Forum
1730 N. Lynn Street, Suite 502
Arlington, VA 22209
(703) 525-1191
Remarks: There are 13 regional chapters in the US. Another six chapters are related to special interests in transportation and do not have a geographical focus. These concentrate on transportation matters in their respective fields.

Uniform Code Council, Inc.
Type: A trade association in which corporations hold membership.
Number of Members: 120,000
Dues: Dues are on a sliding scale based on revenues.
Purpose/Objective: The mission of the Uniform Code Council is to take a global leadership role in establishing and promoting multi-industry standards and services that support product identification and electronic data interchange. The goal is to enhance the transaction process and enable distribution channels to operate more efficiently and effectively while contributing added value to customers.
Chief Operating Officer:
Harold P. Juckett
Executive Vice President and CAO
Uniform Code Council, Inc.
8163 Old Yankee Road, Suite J
Dayton, OH 45458
(513) 435-3870
FAX (513) 435-4749

US Chamber of Commerce
Type: A business federation comprised of corporations and small businesses, associations, and chambers of commerce.
Number of Members:
215,000 companies
3,000 chambers of commerce
1,200 associations
80 American Chambers of Commerce abroad
Dues: Dues schedule available upon request.
Purpose/Objective: To advance human progress through a better economic, political, and social system based on individual freedom, incentive, opportunity, and responsibility.
Chief Operating Officer:
Richard L. Lesher
President

US Chamber of Commerce
1615 H Street NW
Washington, DC 20062
(202) 659-6000
FAX (202) 463-5836

United States China Business Council
Type: A trade association in which corporations hold membership
Number of Members: 200
Dues: Dues are on a sliding scale based on annual gross sales.
Purpose/Objective: The United States China Business Council is the focal point for China trade and investment in the United States. American companies look to the Council for representation in developing and continuing their trade and investment relations with the People's Republic of China.
Chief Elected Officer:
Jonathan Schofield (Chairman of the Board)
President
United Technologies International
Chief Operating Officer:
Donald M. Anderson
President
The United States China Business Council
1818 N Street NW, Suite 500
Washington, DC 20036
(202) 429-0340

VDI-Gesellschaft Foerdertechnik Materialfluss Logistik (VDI-FML), a division of Verein Deutscher Ingenierure (VDI)
Type: An organization in which membership is extended on an individual and/or corporate basis.
Number of Members: 4,000 members
Dues: $125 per year in US funds.
Purpose/Objective: The purpose of this organization is to promote science and development in the fields of material flow, transportation, and logistics; to exchange experience among members and with external experts; to cooperate with industry, commerce, and educational institutions; and to set and publish technical rules and standards.
Chief Elected Officer:
Helmut Schulte
Miglied des Vorstandes der agiplan A G
Postfash 100151
45401 Mulheim
Germany
Chief Operating Officer:
Kurt Redeker
Executive Secretary
VDI-FMI; VDI-Gesellschaft Foerdertechnik Materialfluss and Logistik
Postfach 10 11 39
4002 Düsseldorf
Germany
(0211) 6214-437

Vereniging Logistiek Management (formerly NEVEM)
Type: An organization in which membership is extended on both an individual and a corporate basis.
Number of Members: 1,500
Dues: Dues are $70 per person year. Corporate dues are on a sliding scale based on the number of employees.
Purpose/Objective: The purpose of Vereniging Logistiek Management is to promote the knowledge and dissemination of information about integral goods flow control. There is a wide variety of education programs and a certification system which is under government supervision.
Chief Elected Officer:
N. J. Visser
President
Vereniging Logistiek Management
Chief Operating Officer:
C. G. Vermelis
Executive Director
Vereniging Logistiek Management
Neuhuyskade 40/POB 90730
2509 LS Den Hague
Netherlands
(070) 318 02 68
FAX (070) 324 92 63

Warehousing Education and Research Council (WERC)
Type: A professional organization in which individuals hold membership.
Number of Members: 3,100
Dues: $185 per year

Purpose/Objective: WERC's purpose is to provide education and to conduct research concerning the warehousing process; and to refine the art and science of managing warehouses. WERC will foster professionalism in warehouse management. It will operate exclusively without profit and in cooperation with other organizations and institutions.

Chief Operating Officer:
Thomas E. Sharpe
Executive Director
Warehousing Education & Research Council
1100 Jorie Boulevard, Suite 170
Oak Brook, IL 60521
(708) 990-0001
FAX (708) 990-0256

Women in Packaging

Type: A professional organization in which membership is extended on both an individual and a corporate basis.

Number of Members: 131 individual, 203 corporate

Dues: $50–$75 per person per year. Corporate dues are on a sliding scale based on dollar sales or purchases.

Purpose/Objective: Women in Packaging, Inc. is an international, nonprofit professional organization established in January 1993. The group was formed to provide a forum for networking and education for the personal and professional development of women; to promote and encourage the growth and success of women in the packaging industry; to promote diversity across all levels in the industry; to educate the packaging industry about the contributions and potential of qualified women in packaging and help to eliminate misconceptions, stereotypes, and discrimination against women in the profession.

Chief Elected Officer:
JoAnn R. Hines
Executive Director
Women in Packaging
4290 Bells Ferry Road, Suite 106-17
Kennesaw, GA 30144-1300
(404) 924-3563
FAX (404) 924-3563

ABOUT THE CONTRIBUTORS

R. John Aalbregtse is an Associate Partner in Andersen Consulting's Strategic Services practice specializing in manufacturing strategy and productivity improvement. He holds a B.S. in Engineering and received an M.B.A. from the University of Michigan. Mr. Aalbregtse has consulted with numerous *Fortune* 500 manufacturing companies and has conducted assessments of plant productivity in the United States, Europe, and Japan. His experience spans numerous industries including automotive, chemicals, appliances, glass, food processing, and heavy equipment.

William W. Allport is Vice President–Chief Labor Counsel of Leaseway Transportation Corp. Prior to joining Leaseway, he was employed as an attorney with the law firm of Baker & Hostetler in Cleveland, Ohio, where he specialized in employee relation matters. He received his Juris Doctor from Case Western University in 1969. He served as editor of the *CWRU Law Review* while in law school. Mr. Allport performed his undergraduate work at Gettysburg College. Mr. Allport is licensed to practice law in the states of Ohio and New York.

David L. Anderson is a Partner in Andersen Consulting's Strategic Services Logistics practice and is based in its San Francisco office. He specializes in logistics and supply chain strategy, customer services, logistics information systems, and operations outsourcing. Dr. Anderson has lectured frequently on logistics management at many public forums as well as at leading universities including the Massachusetts Institute of Technology, Northwestern, and Ohio State. He is a member of the Institute of Physical Distribution Management, the Council of Logistics Management, and the Canadian Association of Logistics Management. He is currently serving on the National Science Foundation Committee on Surface Freight Transport Regulation and has published numerous articles on global logistics trends, outsourcing, and operations management. He is a member of the Board of Directors of the San Francisco Roundtable of the CLM. Dr. Anderson holds a Ph.D. from Boston College in Economics and Transportation and a B.A. from the University of Connecticut in Economics.

James M. Apple, Jr., is a Senior Advisor at Vanderlande Industries, a Director of the Distribution Design Institute, and a founder of SysteCon. He has directed over 100 warehouse operations improvement and design projects in the United States, Europe, and Canada. His contributions to the improvement of distribution practices have been recognized in his receipt of the prestigious Reed-Apple Award for lifelong contributions to the advancement of the materials handling profession and the Institute of Industrial Engineers' Facilities Planning and Design Award. He is the author of numerous articles and books on warehousing and logistics operations and is a popular speaker on seminar and conference programs. He holds bachelor's and master's degrees in industrial and systems engineering from the Georgia Institute of Technology.

Donald J. Bowersox is The John H. McConnell Chaired University Professor of Business Administration in The Eli Broad Graduate School of Management at Michigan State University. He has served in various management capacities including Vice President and General Manager of the E.F. McDonald Company. He has been a consultant or speaker for more than 200 *Fortune* 500 corporations and has written more than 100 articles on marketing, transportation, and logistics. He is author or coauthor of numerous books including *Strategic Marketing Channel Management, Logistical Excellence: It's Not Business As Usual, Leading Edge Logistics: Competitive Positioning for the 1990's,* and *Logistical Management.* He was a founder and the second president of the Council of Logistics Management.

Jonathan L. S. Byrnes is President of Jonathan Byrnes & Co. and Senior Lecturer at M.I.T. His firm is a highly focused consulting company specializing in (1) strategic customer-supplier relations, (2) operating partnerships, and (3) corporate logistics management. His M.I.T. responsibilities include teaching the graduate course Case Studies in Logistics Management, as well as supervising research and teaching in executive programs. Dr. Byrnes has an M.B.A. (Smith Prize) from Columbia and a D.B.A. from Harvard Business School, where he specialized in Logistics and Strategy. He has written over 50 books, articles, cases, and notes, and has consulted with senior executives in leading companies.

Robert C. Camp is Manager, Benchmarking Competency, Quality Office for Xerox Corporation's US Customer Operations (USCO). He has a B.S. in Civil Engineering from Cornell University and an M.B.A. from Cornell University's Johnson School of Management. He also earned a Ph.D. in Logistics and Operations Research from Penn State University. Dr. Camp was responsible for creating the benchmarking program for Xerox Corporation's Logistics & Distribution organization. He has also written *Benchmarking: The Search for Industry Best Practices That Lead to Superior Performance* as a reference guide on the process for employees and customers. Dr. Camp, as the Xerox representative, helped establish the International Benchmarking Clearinghouse, a service of the American Productivity and Quality Center in Houston. For the past nine years he has been on the Executive Committee of the Council of Logistics Management and has served as its president. From 1972 until 1985 Dr. Camp was an adjunct professor, Marketing Logistics, at the Rochester Institute of Technology.

Joseph L. Cavinato is an Associate Professor of Business Logistics at The Pennsylvania State University. He received B.S. and M.B.A. degrees from American University and a Ph.D. from Penn State University. In 1974 he won the Council of Logistics Management A. T. Kearney Doctoral Dissertation Award. He has written over 100 articles and cases in logistics, transportation, purchasing, and materials management. He is editor of the "Logistics Tools" column of *Distribution Magazine* and is on the editorial review boards of the *International Journal of Physical Distribution and Logistics Management* as well as the *International Journal of Purchasing and Materials Management.* He is the author of the following books: *Purchasing and Materials Management: Integrative Strategies, Finance for Transportation-Distribution Managers,* and *Transportation-Logistics Dictionary.* He is coauthor of the texts *Transportation* and *Traffic Management.*

Paul T. Chapman is an Associate Partner in Andersen Consulting's Strategic Services Logistics practice and is based in its Boston office. He received his B.A. degree from the University of North Carolina at Chapel Hill (Phi Beta Kappa) and M.A. and Ph.D. degrees from the Massachusetts Institute of Technology, where he was a Hertz Fellow in the Applied Physical Sciences. Dr. Chapman specializes in the application of the decision and computer sciences to planning and scheduling problems in corporate operations. He focuses on the design and construction of innovative software for managing a variety of supply chain issues—including logistics network design, tactical planning, distribution requirements planning, deployment, and production scheduling.

Martin Christopher is Professor of Marketing and Logistics Systems at Cranfield School of Management, where he is head of the Marketing and Logistics Faculty and Chairman of the Cranfield Centre for Logistics and Transportation. In addition, he is Deputy Director of the School of Management responsible for Executive Development Program. Professor Christopher has worked for major international companies in North America, Europe, the Far East, and Australia and is a nonexecutive director of a number of companies. He has written numerous books and articles, is on the editorial advisory board of a number of professional journals, and is coeditor of the *International Journal, of Logistics Management.* His recent books have focused on relationship marketing, customer service, and logistics strategy. He has held appointments as Visiting Professor at the University of British Columbia, Canada; the University of New South Wales, Australia; and the University of South Florida. He is a Fellow of the Chartered Institute of Marketing and of the Institute of Logistics Management. In 1987 he was awarded the Sir Robert Lawrence medal of the Institute of Logistics and Distribution Management for his contribution to the development of logistics education in Great Britain.

David J. Closs is Professor of Marketing and Logistics in The Eli Broad Graduate School of Management at Michigan State University. He received a Bachelor's degree in Mathematics and Master's and Doctoral degrees in Marketing and Logistics from Michigan State University. Dr. Closs was Manager of System Development of Systems Research, Inc., and President of Dialog Systems, Inc. He has served as a consultant to a number of industry and government organizations and regularly speaks at executive seminars. He has coauthored *Logistics Management* and has authored numerous articles for both scholarly and professional journals. He is the systems editor of the *Journal of Business Logistics* and on the editorial review board of the *International Journal of Physical Distribution and Logistics Management.*

Dennis Colard is Vice President of Logistics for Read-Rite Corporation. He was formerly Corporate Logistics Manager of Hewlett-Packard Company, with the company from 1968 to 1993. At Hewlett-Packard, he served in many logistics-related positions, including buyer, materials manager, manufacturing manager, and logistics manager. His international experience with H-P includes positions as materials manager in Grenoble, France, from 1978 to 1981 and manufacturing manager in Aguadilla, Puerto Rico. In 1993 he joined Read-Rite. He holds a B.S. from the University of Northern Colorado.

Martha C. Cooper is Associate Professor of Marketing and Logistics at The Ohio State University. She received a B.S. in Math/Computer Science and a Master's degree in Industrial Administration from Purdue University. Her doctorate is from Ohio State. She has been on the marketing faculties of two other universities. Dr. Cooper has coauthored three books: *Customer Service: A Management Perspective, Partnerships in Providing Customer Service: A Third-Party Perspective,* and *Strategic Planning for Logistics,* and published in several leading logistics, marketing, and statistical journals. She has been active in several organizations, especially CLM, where she was president of the Columbus Roundtable for 1988–89 and was the Finance Chair for the 1992 annual conference. She has taught in continuing education programs and professional programs in the United States, Poland, Hungary, and Czechoslovakia.

William C. Copacino is the Managing Partner of Andersen Consulting's Strategic Services practice in the Northeast. He formerly served as the head of Andersen Consulting's Worldwide Logistics practice. He had directed over 200 strategic and operational assessments of logistics and supply chain management activities for leading companies around the world. He is the coauthor of *Modern Logistics Management,* published by John Wiley and Sons (1985). He writes a monthly column on "Logistics Strategy" for *Traffic Management* magazine. He has also served on the editorial review boards of the *Journal of Business Logistics* and the *International Journal of Logistics Management,* and he serves on the Executive Committee of the Council of Logistics Management. He holds a B.S. in Industrial Engineering from Cornell University and an M.B.A. from the Harvard Business School.

Michael R. Crum is Associate Professor of Transportation and Logistics in the College of Business at Iowa State University. He received his B.S., M.B.A., and D.B.A. degrees from Indiana University. Dr. Crum is a coauthor of two books in the area of transportation and the author or coauthor of numerous articles that have been published in both scholarly and professional journals. He was a Fulbright Scholar in transportation economics at the Central School of Planning and Statistics in Warsaw, Poland, during the 1988–89 academic year. He is the editor of the *Journal of Transportation Management.*

Patricia J. Daugherty is Assistant Professor of Marketing and Distribution in the Terry College of Business at The University of Georgia. She received her Ph.D. from Michigan State University in 1988 and was the A. T. Kearney Post Doctoral Fellowat Michigan State, 1988–89. She is coauthor of *Leading Edge Logistics: Competitive Positioning for the 1990's* and *Logistical Excellence: It's Not Business As Usual,* and has published in a number of academic journals including *International Journal of Logistics Management, International Journal of Physical Distribution and Logistics Management, Journal of Business Logistics* and *The Logistics and Transportation Review.*

Adel I. El-Ansary is the Eminent Scholar and first chairholder of the Paper and Plastics Education and Research (PAPER) Foundation Endowed Research Chair in Wholesaling at the College of Business Administration of the University of North Florida. In addition to his duties as Research Professor, he serves as Director of the Center for Research and Education in Wholesaling. Prior to joining the faculty at the University of North Florida in 1990, he served as Professor and Chairman of Business Administration at George Washington University. His publications include research monographs and articles in leading journals. He coauthored three books, the latest of which is *Marketing Channels* (with Louis W. Stern), currently in its fourth edition, published by Prentice-Hall.

Margaret Ann Emmelhainz is an Associate Professor of Marketing and Logistics at the University of Dayton. She holds a Master of Science degree in Logistics Management from the Air Force Institute of Technology and a Doctoral degree in Logistics from The Ohio State University. Dr. Emmelhainz is a Certified Professional Logistician and a Certified Professional Contracts Manager. She has been active in the EDI field for over eight years and she regularly conducts EDI research and training. She is the author of the internationally distributed book *EDI: A Total Management Guide,* which is in its second edition and has been translated into both Japanese and French.

Carl D. Evans is Group Director Logistics and Transportation for Keebler Company, a leading manufacturer of snack food products. After receiving his Bachelor's degree from the University of Texas at Austin, Mr. Evans has spent his entire career in the distribution of food products. He has frequently been a guest speaker at local universities and professional meetings discussing a variety of logistics topics. In addition, he has served on the Executive Distribution Committees of the Grocery Manufacturers of America and the National Council of Farmer Cooperatives. As a member of the Council of Logistics Management's Executive Committee, he chaired the project that produced the Logistics in Service Industries research.

Thomas K. Fox is a Partner with Andersen Consulting's New York Metro Office. Mr. Fox has been with Andersen since 1974, working primarily with consumer and industrial products companies. He has assisted many companies in logistics and customer service business challenges through the use of advanced technologies. He has been the US Northeast Region Director for Transportation since 1991. He received a B.S. in Industrial Management from Purdue University.

David J. Frayer is a doctoral candidate studying marketing, logistics, and international business in The Eli Broad Graduate School of Management at Michigan State University. He is coauthor of *Logistics Technology International,* and his case studies appear in *Strategic Marketing Channel Management* (McGraw-Hill) and *Logistical Management,* 4th Ed. (McGraw-Hill). He received his B.A. and M.B.A. in Marketing from Michigan State University.

Edward H. Frazelle is Director of The Logistics Institute at Georgia Tech, where he is also a member of the faculty of the School of Industrial and Systems Engineering. His experience in private industry includes logistics consulting, management, and engineering positions with The Progress Group, the Distribution Design Institute, Coopers and Lybrand, and General Motors. He has lectured in the United States, Japan, and Canada and is the author of *Material Handling Systems and Terminology* (Lionhart, 1992) and coauthor of *Facilities Planning* (Wiley, 1993). Dr. Frazelle is a recipient of the Council of Logistics Management's Doctoral Research Grant and is a past president of the International Material Management Society. He is a doctoral graduate in industrial and systems engineering from Georgia Tech and a valedictorian graduate in industrial engineering from North Carolina State University.

Thomas L. Freese is Principal of Freese and Associates, Inc., a management and logistics consulting firm in Chagrin Falls, Ohio. Mr. Freese received his B.S. in Business Administration, and an M.B.A. with a concentration in business logistics from The Ohio State University. He is experienced in customer service evaluations, information systems, distribution operations and organizations, site selections, warehouse design and layout, materials handling equipment specifications, public and contract warehouse operations and development of inventory, purchasing, transportation, warehousing and logistics strategies. Before establishing Freese & Associates, Inc., he served as Manager of Physical Distribution for Parker-Hannifin Corporation, Director of Distribution for Brush Wellman, Inc., and in line and staff distribution positions for Unocal. He is past president of the Northwestern Ohio WERC chapter and an active member of CLM, International Customer Service Association, and WERC. He has contributed articles to the *Journal of Business Logistics, Traffic Management, Food Business,* and *Distribution Center Management.*

T. Ron Gable is a Partner with SysteCon, a Division of Coopers and Lybrand based in Atlanta. Prior to that he was a Principal with A. T. Kearney. He has concentrated in the logistics field for almost 20 years, primarily consulting to large consumer products companies grappling with internal and external supply chain issues. He has been active in CLM, IIE, and the Georgia Tech Logistics Institute in various capacities.

R. William Gardner is president of Distribution Properties, Inc., a property management and investment firm based in Columbus, Ohio. Until April 1992, Mr. Gardner served as Chief Executive Officer of Exel Logistics, North America. Prior to that he was Chairman and Chief Executive Officer of Distribution Centers, Inc., until its acquisition by NFC PLC to become a part of Exel Logistics in September 1989. A registered professional engineer, he received a B.S. in Industrial Engineering and an M.B.A. from The Ohio State University. He has been active in CLM, WERC, IIE, and AWA in educational roles, serving on the executive committee of CLM and as president of WERC. In addition, he has authored several articles in the field of distribution and warehousing and coauthored one of the early books on the subject.

Julie J. Gentry is on the faculty of the Department of Marketing and Transportation at the University of Arkansas. She received her doctorate in Purchasing and Logistics Management at Arizona State University and her Bachelor's and Master's degrees from the University of Tennessee. Dr. Gentry recently served as a Research Associate at the Center for Advanced Purchasing Studies (CAPS), where she authored a major research report entitled *Purchasing's Role in Transportation Decision Making,* published by CAPS and the National Association of Purchasing Management. She has published in the *International Journal of Logistics Management* and the *International Journal of Purchasing and Materials Management.* She has industry experience in logistics at Phillips Petroleum Company, Ryder Truck Rental, and Phoenix Transit Systems.

William W. Goldsborough is a Principal in William Goldsborough and Associates, a management consulting firm that specializes in logistics and trade management issues. He has more than 18 years of experience in international logistics management, including 3 years at SRI International, where he was program manager in SRI's Global Logistics Program. In addition, Dr. Goldsborough has held positions as Vice President of Consulting Services at the Harper Group, a global forwarding and logistics management company, and Manager of International Distribution for Crown Zellerbach Corporation. He was an instructor on the faculty at Colorado State University and continues to teach as an adjunct professor in the San Francisco Bay Area M.B.A. programs. He holds an M.B.A. and a Ph.D. in Political Economy from the University of Nebraska, Lincoln. He has published several articles on global logistics management and is an authority on managing the process of logistics outsourcing.

William L. (Skip) Grenoble is Administrative Director and Research Associate for the Center for Logistics Research at Penn State University. Mr. Grenoble obtained a Bachelor's degree from Princeton University and an M.B.A. from the Columbia University Graduate School of Business. Before joining the logistics team at Penn State, he worked extensively in the field of wholesale distribution with McKesson Corporation and Weyerhaeuser. He is the coauthor of articles published in several logistics journals and was principal researcher and coauthor of a major study, *Logistics in Service Industries,* published by the Council of Logistics Management.

Roy L. Harmon is the author of the widely acclaimed "Reinventing" series of books: (1) *Reinventing the Factory: Productivity Breakthroughs in Manufacturing Today,* (2) *Reinventing the Factory II; Managing the World Class Factory,* and (3) *Reinventing the Warehouse: World Class Distribution Logistics* (Free Press). Now an independent consultant, he founded Andersen Consulting's factory productivity practice, growing it from a one-person operation to one employing more than 2,000 consultants on six continents. He currently provides his personal services exclusively to Andersen Consulting and its clients. Mr. Harmon gained factory productivity renown as a result of working in Japan in the 1970s, with Yamaha and its customer, Toyota. He was the first consultant to export "Japanese" techniques to the Western world, and lists dozens of *Fortune* 500 companies as his clients. In the process, he helped them to develop the visions that drive their programs of continuous product and process improvement. His first U.S. client, Harley-Davison, is now world renowned for its Just-in-Time achievements. In a career spanning 35 years, he has worked in both industry and consulting.

James L. Heskett is UPS Foundation Professor of Business Logistics at the Graduate School of Business Administration, Harvard University. He completed his Ph.D. at the Graduate School of Business, Stanford University, and has been a member of the faculty of The Ohio State University. He is a member of the Board of Directors of Cardinal Distribution, Inc., the Equitable of Iowa Companies, Anchor Glass Container Corporation, and First Security Services Corporation. He is a member of the North American Advisory Board on Swissair, Inc.; the Advisory Board of IPADE, a Mexican business school; the Advisory Board of INCAE, a Central American business school; and has served as a consultant to companies in North America, Latin America, and Europe. Professor Heskett is a member of the editorial boards of the *Journal of Business Logistics* and the *International Journal of Service Industry Management.* He was the 1974 recipient of the CLM John Drury Sheahan Award and the 1992 Marketing Educator of the Year Award of Sales and Marketing Executives International. Among his publications are books including coauthorship of *Corporate Culture and Performance* (Free Press, 1992); coauthorship of *Service Breakthrough: Changing the Rules of the Game* (Free Press, 1990); coauthorship of *The Service Management Course* (Free Press, 1991); *Managing in the Service Economy* (Harvard Business School Press, 1986); coauthorship of *Logistics Strategy: Cases and Concepts* (West, 1985); *Marketing* (Macmillan, 1976); coauthorship of *Business Logistics, Revised Edition* (Ronald Press, 1974); and numerous articles in such publications as the *Harvard Business Review, Journal of Marketing, Sloan Management Review, California Management Review* and others. He has been a member of the faculty of the Harvard Business School since 1965.

Frederick Hewitt is head of the business school at Aston University in Birmingham, England. He had previously been Vice President of Logistics and Asset Management for Xerox Corporation, operating out of dual offices in Rochester, New York, and Marlow, England. He received his B.S., Ph.D., and C.Ed. degrees from Bristol University, England. Dr. Hewitt has taught in universities in the United Kingdom and Canada and has also acted as a public-sector consultant in both countries. Throughout his career he has maintained close ties with a number of educational institutions and professional organizations. He has published a number of papers in the areas of total quality management, business process reengineering, and supply chain management; and his work at Xerox has been featured in case studies at Harvard, MIT, and the University of Tennessee. In October 1993 he returned to the United Kingdom to take up his current position.

Mary C. Holcomb is Assistant Professor of Transportation and Logistics at Iowa State University. She received her B.S., M.B.A., and Ph.D. degrees from the University of Tennessee. Her studies at the doctoral level included a concentration in the areas of logistics and transportation and a secondary field in civil engineering. Her professional career involved 18 years at the Oak Ridge National Laboratory in transportation research for the U.S. Department of Energy and

U.S. Department of Transportation. Dr. Holcomb's industry experience involvement with Burlington Northern Railroad, Procter and Gamble, and General Motors. She is the author of numerous articles and technical reports concerning logistics.

R. Edwin Howe is President of Eto, a clothing manufacturer, and maintains an association with Andersen Consulting's Strategic Services Logistics practice, where he was previously employed. He has participated in strategic and operational projects involving marketing and a broad range of logistics issues in the telecommunications, home entertainment, and retail industries. Mr. Howe has served as the marketing director for a start-up venture in high-end consumer electronics and is a founder and honorary director of The Miami University Student Federal Credit Union. He is a member of CLM and holds a B.S. in Finance from Miami University (Ohio).

C. Lee Johnson is president of Limited Distribution Services, a subsidiary of The Limited, Inc. He is responsible for the engineering and construction of new facilities, as well as shipping and transportation for the corporation, which serves over 4,200 specialty stores. Prior to joining Limited Distribution Services, Mr. Johnson was Senior Vice President of Operations for Beatrice US Foods and Vice President for the US Distribution Division of Warner-Lambert Company. During the spring of 1983, he headed a delegation of American businesspeople, consultants, and academicians who visited the People's Republic of China under the auspices of People-To-People International. He holds a B.S. degree in Marketing from the University of Illinois. He was named one of *Traffic Management* magazine's Annual Professional Achievement Award recipients in 1980. He is a member of the Council of Logistics Management and has held several offices in that organization, as well as serving on the Executive Committee. Presently, he is a member of the Business Advisory Council at Miami University. He is also a member of the Board of Directors of the Port Authority in Columbus, Ohio, a member of the Board of the Columbus Chamber of Commerce, serving on the Executive Committee, and serves as Chairman of the Inland Port Commission.

Douglas M. Lambert is the Prime F. Osborn III Eminent Scholar Chair in Transportation, Professor of Marketing and Logistics, and Director of The International Center for Competitive Excellence at the University of North Florida, Jacksonville. Dr. Lambert has served as a faculty member for over 250 executive development programs in North and South America, Europe, Asia, and Australia. He is the author of *The Development of an Inventory Costing Methodology* (1976), *The Distribution Channels Decision* (1978), *The Product Abandonment Decision* (1985), and coauthor of *Management in Marketing Channels* (1980), and *Strategic Logistics Management* (1993). His publications include more than 100 articles and conference proceedings. In 1986 he received the CLM Distinguished Service Award for his contributions to logistics management. He holds an honors B.A. and M.B.A. from the University of Western Ontario and a Ph.D. from The Ohio State University. Dr. Lambert is Coeditor of *The International Journal of Logistics Management.*

Bernard J. La Londe, who has his Ph.D. from Michigan State University, has taught at the University of Colorado, Michigan State University, and currently as Raymond E. Mason Professor of Transportation and Logistics at The Ohio State University. He has authored or coauthored a number of books and monographs and is a frequent contributor of articles to professional journals and the trade press. Dr. La Londe has been active as a consultant on logistics issues and as a lecturer in executive development programs for a wide range of companies. He has lectured on various aspects of logistics in Europe, Australia, and Japan. He serves on the Editorial Review Board of the *International Journal of Logistics Management* and served as founding editor of the *Journal of Business Logistics* from 1978 to 1989. In the public sector, he has served as a consultant to the U.S. Department of Transportation, U.S. Postal Service, Department of Defense, and the State of Ohio. He has been awarded the Eccles Medal by the Society of Logistics Engineers for his outstanding contribution to logistics education, the CLM Distinguished Service Award for significant contributions in distribution research, and the honorary Harry E. Salzberg Medallion for teaching and research contributions to distribution and transportation from Syracuse University.

C. John Langley, Jr., is The John H (Red) Dove Distinguished Professor of Logistics and Transportation at the University of Tennessee. He received his B.S. (Mathematics), M.B.A. (Finance), and Ph.D. (Business Logistics) degrees from Penn State University. Dr. Langley is a coauthor of two texts: *The Management of Business Logistics* and *Traffic Management: Planning, Operations and Control.* Additionally, he has published widely in professional journals such as *Journal of Business Logistics* and the *International Journal of Physical Distribution and Logistics Management.* He participates in executive development programs at several universities and is the author of over 80 logistics-relation publications. He served on the Executive Committee of the Council of Logistics Management from 1984 to 1992 and as president of the CLM from 1990 to 1991. He has worked for Raytheon Company in the capacity of Associate Engineer and has served as a consultant to numerous corporations. He has recently traveled to Japan, China, Europe, the Middle East, and Africa on logistics-related visits. In 1989 he was honored as the Outstanding Alumnus of the Penn State Business Logistics program.

Robert Mann is a Senior Manager in Andersen Consulting's Strategic Services Logistics practice and is based in the Atlanta office. He specializes in logistics strategy, distribution operations design, implementation, and performance management across a wide variety of industries. Mr. Mann has particular experience in addressing broad logistics issues for direct marketers, department stores, and specialty retailers. Prior to joining Andersen Consulting, he was a Principal with Kurt Salmon Associates' Distribution Services Group. He has also been employed by Hoechst Fibers Industries. Mr. Mann is a member of the CLM. He is also a frequent contributor to *Catalog Age* magazine and a frequent speaker for the Direct Marketing Association (DMA). He holds a B.Ch.E. from Georgia Institute of Technology and an M.B.A. from the University of North Carolina–Chapel Hill.

James M. Masters is a member of the faculty of The Ohio State University and conducts research in the areas of the organization of the logistics function, the implementation of logistics information systems, and the application of quantitative techniques to logistics decision making. His professional background includes 20 years of service as a logistics officer in the United States Air Force.

Kevin A. O'Laughlin is a Partner in Andersen Consulting's Strategic Services Logistics practice and is based in its Boston office. His client work has involved designing responsive forecasting systems and inventory reduction programs, improving customer service and warehouse productivity, and developing integrated logistics information systems. He has worked with several firms in Europe to address international logistics issues related to economic integration, and has helped firms in the Far East to develop export distribution strategies. Mr. O'Laughlin was elected to Phi Beta Kappa and Sigma Xi and holds memberships in the CLM, the Operations Research Society of America (ORSA), and The Institute of Management Science (TIMS). He is past president of the Boston Chapter of TIMS. He holds a B.A. from Boston College and an M.S. from Stanford University.

Gregory J. Owens is a Partner in Andersen Consulting's Strategic Services Logistics practice and is based in its Atlanta office. Mr. Owens focuses primarily on distribution operations. His areas of expertise include distribution network analysis, facility planning, detailed design, operations management, and productivity enhancement through standards and incentives. Prior to joining Andersen Consulting, he was an Executive Vice President with the Garr Consulting Group. He is a member of the Materials Management Society (MMS), the CLM, and the National Retail Federation (NRF). In addition, he has lectured at several professional conferences and written numerous articles for *Retail Systems Alert, Chain Store Age Executive,* and *Modern Materials Handling.* He holds a B.S. degree in Industrial Engineering from Georgia Institute of Technology.

Ivy Penman is Head of Marketing Planning for NFC plc. With an M.A. from St. Andrews University in Philosophy and Psychology and an M.B.A. from the School of Management, Ms. Penman has extensive experience in strategic planning, marketing, and management consulting with the BOC Group, A. T. Kearney, and NFC. She is developing an international expansion strategy for Exel Logistics, currently in the United States, the United Kingdom, France, Germany, Benelux, and Spain. She worked closely with a team of senior managers in Exel Logistics to develop a comprehensive environmental policy, launched in June 1991, which has won four major awards.

Terrance L. Pohlen is Assistant Professor at the Air Force Institute of Technology, Wright Patterson AFB in Ohio. Major Pohlen holds a Ph.D. in Business Logistics from The Ohio State University. His research interests include inventory management, logistics planning, and the implementation of logistics information systems, particularly in the area of activity-based costing. Major Pohlen has over 13 years of logistics experience in the United States Air Force.

Hugh L. Randall, Vice President in charge of the Transportation Group at Mercer Management Consulting, is an authority on international transportation and contract logistics. During his career Mr. Randall has held line and staff management positions in various modes of transportation and in logistics, and has worked as a management consultant specializing in international transportation and logistics. Before joining Mercer, he was Senior Vice President and Managing Director of CSX/Sea-Land Logistics in Alexandria, Virginia, Managing Director of Frans Maas/Sea-Land Logistics of Dusseldorf, Germany, and Vice President of Booz, Allen and Hamilton, Inc. As Executive Vice President of Ryder/PIE Nationwide, Mr. Randall was responsible for that trucking company's financial, planning, and administrative functions. He was also General Manager of the Atlantic Region and assistant Vice President–Operations for Consolidated Rail Corporation (Conrail). He received a B.A. in Accounting and Administration from Antioch College and an M.B.A. from the Harvard Graduate School of Business Administration.

James F. Robeson is Dean (retired), The Richard T. Farmer School of Business Administration, Miami University. He also served as a faculty member and administrator at The Ohio State University. He has served as a consultant to a number of companies on a wide variety of management, marketing, and distribution problems. He currently serves on four corporate boards of directors. The author or coauthor of more than 50 books, monographs, and articles, he served as Editor-in-chief of *The Distribution Handbook* (Free Press, 1985). He is a founding member and past president of the Warehousing Education and Research Council, a past president of The Ohio

Distribution Roundtable, and has served as a member of the executive committee of the CLM and as annual program chairman. In 1987 he was named Marketing Educator of the Year by Sales and Marketing Executives International. Dr. Robeson holds a bachelor's and master's degree from the University of Cincinnati and a Ph.D. from Penn State University.

Allen D. Rose is Director, Operations Development, in the Corporate Office of Operations Technology and Development of Johnson and Johnson. His area of focus includes operations strategy development and the integration of operations capabilities with customer-focused business strategy. A former commissioned officer in the United States Navy, Mr. Rose joined Johnson and Johnson in 1970 from a sales management position with the NCR Corporation. Within Johnson and Johnson he has held both line and staff management positions in manufacturing, logistics, industrial engineering, and strategic business planning, and has extensive consulting experience with a broad range of companies in both the United States and around the world. He is a senior member of the Society of Mechanical Engineers and the Institute of Industrial Engineers, a member of the CLM, a founding member of the Boston University Manufacturing Executives Forum, and a member of the New Jersey Institute of Technology Industrial Advisory Board. He serves on the board of directors of several organizations dedicated to manufacturing and logistics research and is a frequent speaker at professional association functions and guest lecturer at leading U.S. and international business schools. He holds a B.S. from the Illinois Institute of Technology.

Donald B. Rosenfield is a Senior Lecturer in Operations Management at the MIT Sloan School of Management and is Director of the Leaders for Manufacturing Fellows Program (a dual degree master's program run by the School of Management and the School of Engineering in partnership with 13 leading U.S. corporations). He has served at MIT since 1980 as Lecturer, Senior Lecturer, and Visiting Associate Professor. He has also served on the faculties of Harvard Business School, the State University of New York, Boston University, and on the staff of Arthur D. Little, Inc. Dr. Rosenfield has an S.B. in Mathematics, S.M. in Operations Research, and an E.E. degree from MIT and a Ph.D. in Operations Research from Stanford University. He has written over 20 articles in such journals as *Harvard Business Review, Operations Research Management Science, Sloan Management Review, Journal of Business Logistics,* and *Journal of Economic Theory.* He is the coauthor of *Modern Logistics Management* (Wiley, 1985).

Judith M. Schmitz is a doctoral candidate studying marketing and logistics in The Eli Broad Graduate School of Management at Michigan State University. She has published as a coauthor in the *Journal of Business Research,* and her case studies appear in *Logistical Management,* 4th ed. (McGraw-Hill). She received her B.S. in Management Systems from G.M.I. Engineering and Management Institute.

Roy D. Shapiro is the Jesse Philips Professor of Manufacturing at the Harvard University Graduate School of Business Administration. He received an S.B. in Mathematics, an M.S. in Operations Research, and an E.E. in Electrical Engineering from MIT, and a Ph.D. in Operations Research from Stanford University. Professor Shapiro's primary research and teaching interests are in the areas of production and operations management, logistics, and supplier management. He is the author of textbooks in optimization models and service strategy, and of casebooks in both operations research and logistics strategy. He has written numerous case studies, and articles that have appeared in *Harvard Business Review, Management Science, Journal of Economic*

Theory, Interfaces, and others. He has been a consultant to many leading American firms as well as companies in the United Kingdom, Finland, France, Italy, Brazil, and Japan.

Thomas W. Speh is the Joseph C. Seibert Professor of Marketing and Chair of the Marketing Department at Miami University (Ohio). In addition, he is the Director of the Warehousing Research Center, which engages in research to enhance the effectiveness of warehousing management. Dr. Speh is coauthor of *Business Marketing Management,* 4th ed., and *An Approach for Determining Warehousing Costs,* a PC-based model for calculating total warehousing costs. He has published widely in a number of logistics and marketing journals and regularly consults for many leading companies. He is a past president of the Warehousing Education and Research Council and has been active in various capacities with the CLM.

Alan J. Stenger is Associate Professor of Business Logistics in the Mary Jean and Frank P. Smeal College of Business Administration, Penn State University. Dr. Stenger has engaged in a wide range of research and educational and consulting activities both in the United States and abroad. At Penn State he is graduate adviser for the Department of Business Logistics, has supervised numerous Ph.D. theses and master's papers, and teaches graduate and senior-level courses in logistics. As Faculty Director of the Program for Logistics Executives, he is responsible for its content and faculty leaders. He is also Associate Director of Research in the Center for Logistics Research. He has published in a variety of academic and professional journals focusing on the logistics field and has engaged in a host of consulting and educational activities with leading firms in the United States. He is a member of the Editorial Review Board of the *International Journal of Logistics Management* and *Logistics Information Management.* From 1964 through 1969 he served in a variety of logistics positions with the Dow Chemical Company. He received his Ph.D. from the University of Minnesota and his M.B.A. and B.S. degree from the University of Michigan.

Jay U. Sterling is Associate Professor of Marketing at the University of Alabama's College of Commerce and Business Administration. Dr. Sterling has over 35 years of hands-on experience in corporate management. He received his B.A. from DePauw University and a Ph.D. from Michigan State University. He is also a Certified Public Accountant. Dr. Sterling was Director of Distribution for the Limited Stores, Inc., and Director of Physical Distribution for Heil-Quaker Corporation, and held a number of accounting and logistics-related positions at Whirlpool Corporation. He has been actively involved in all areas of logistics management, and has performed major funded research projects for numerous corporations. He is author or coauthor of articles in such journals as the *Journal of Business Logistics, Journal of Purchasing and Materials Management, International Journal of Physical Distribution and Materials Management, Production and Inventory Management Review,* and *Marketing Management.* He is an active member of the CLM and the American Marketing Marketing Association.

Louis W. Stern is the John D. Gray Distinguished Professor of Marketing at Northwestern University's J.L. Kellogg Graduate School of Management. He received an A.B. from Harvard College, an M.B.A. from the Wharton Graduate Division of the University of Pennsylvania, and a Ph.D. in Marketing from Northwestern. He has published numerous articles and books, among which is *Marketing Channels* (with Adel I. El-Ansary), now in its fourth edition. In 1986 he was given the American Marketing Association's Paul D. Converse Award for "outstanding contribution to theory and science in marketing."

James R. Stock is a Professor of Marketing and Logistics at the College of Business Administration, University of South Florida, Tampa. Dr. Stock held previous faculty appointments at Michigan State University, the University of Oklahoma, and the University of Notre Dame. From 1986 to 1988 he held the position of Distinguished Visiting Professor of Logistics Management at the School of Systems and Logistics, Air Force Institute of Technology, Wright-Patterson Air Force Base. He is the author or coauthor of over 70 publications including books, monographs, articles, and proceedings papers. He is coauthor of *Strategic Logistics Management* (Irwin, 1993) and author of *Reverse Logistics* (Council of Logistics Management, 1992). He currently serves as Editor of the *International Journal of Physical Distribution and Logistics Management* and Managing Editor of the *Logistics Spectrum.* He received the Armitage Medal (1988) from the Society of Logistics Engineers in recognition of his scholarly contributions to the discipline of logistics. He holds B.S. and M.B.A. degrees from the University of Miami (Florida) and a Ph.D. from The Ohio State University.

Diana Twede is an Assistant Professor in the School of Packaging at Michigan State University, where she has served in a research and teaching position for 15 years. Her expertise is in the economics and performance of packaging in marketing and logistics systems, and she has participated in many government- and industry-sponsored studies. She leads a long-term project sponsored by the federal government to provide technical packaging assistance to U.S. food aid programs. Her dissertation, "The Process of Logistical Packaging Innovation," was the 1986 winner of the Council of Logistics Management Doctoral Dissertation Award.

John A. White is the Eugene C. Gwaltney Professor, Regents' Professor, and Dean of Engineering at Georgia Tech. As a member of the National Academy of Engineering, he is past chairman of the American Association of Engineering Societies and past president of the Institute of Industrial Engineers. Dr. White has authored, coauthored, or edited numerous books, handbooks, chapters, and papers on the subjects of logistics, warehousing, material handling, facilities planning, and continuous quality improvement. A member of the CLM, IIE, and WERC, he speaks frequently on the same subjects of national and international conferences. His industrial engineering degrees were earned at the University of Arkansas, Virginia Tech, and The Ohio State University. He has served as consultant to a wide range of organizations, including AT&T, CAPS Logistics, Coca-Cola, Coopers and Lybrand, DuPont, Federal Reserve Bank, Ford, IBM, L.L. Bean, U.S. Navy, Westinghouse, and Xerox.

Morton T. Yeomans is Principal of the Yeomans Company, a logistics consultancy. With over 30 years in senior management positions with several *Fortune* 500 companies, he has managed all facets of the discipline including customer service, warehousing, transportation, inventory planning and control, purchasing, and manufacturing. More recently, Mr. Yeomans has been actively designing modern warehouse systems and distribution facility networks. Companies now using or installing systems designed by him include a nationally known shoe company, a major uniform rental company, a national computer and office supply company, and the largest appliance parts manufacturer and distributor in the country. During his 30 years of management experience, he worked for Johnson and Johnson, E.R. Squibb, Fisher Scientific, and Litton. A former president and member of the Executive Committee of the CLM, he continues as a contributing member. He is also active in the Warehousing Education and Research Council (WERC). He is an active lecturer.

Index